LeBlonds'
1-2-3 for Windows
Handbook

LeBlonds' 1-2-3 for Windows Handbook

The LeBlond Group

Geoffrey T. LeBlond
Laura D. Mann
William B. LeBlond
Charles J. LeBlond

BANTAM BOOKS
TORONTO · NEW YORK · LONDON · SYDNEY · AUCKLAND

LeBlonds' 1-2-3 for Windows Handbook
A Bantam Book / February 1992

All rights reserved.
Copyright © 1992 by The LeBlond Group
Cover design © 1992 by Bantam Books, Inc.
Interior design by Nancy Sugihara
Produced by Micro Text Productions, Inc.
Composed by Context Publishing Services, Sausalito, CA

ISBN 0-553-35439-6

Published simultaneously in the United States and Canada

Bantam Books are published by Bantam Books, a division of Bantam Doubleday Dell
Publishing Group, Inc. Its trademark, consisting of the words "Bantam Books" and the
portrayal of a rooster, is Registered in U.S. Patent and Trademark Office and in other countries.
Marca Registrada, Bantam Books, Inc., 666 Fifth Avenue, New York, New York 10103.

PRINTED IN THE UNITED STATES OF AMERICA

0   9   8   7   6   5   4   3   2   1

Preface

I first saw 1-2-3 in 1983 when I was an M.B.A student in search of a summer job. Que Corporation, then a fledgling publishing company, was looking for a writer with some PC experience (a rare commodity at the time) to help coauthor a book about this new, yet scarcely known spreadsheet program.

Previous to that summer, Doug Cobb, an editor at Que (now the president of the Cobb Group, a Louisville-based publisher of software newsletters), happened to have an office in the same building as Lotus Development Corporation in Cambridge, Massachusetts. Since Doug had gotten an early copy of 1-2-3 and had been working with it for several months, he knew his way around the program, and was able to show me several of the tricks and techniques that would soon become the *lingua franca* of the business world.

The program Doug and I were looking at was an early test copy, but it was clear that it was something quite special. The ease with which you could enter complex formulas and instantly get results made the financial modeling programs I was using look archaic. And although I had seen VisiCalc running on an Apple computer, 1-2-3's speed on an IBM PC, and its intuitiveness, put it in a league all its own. We knew we were onto something.

During that summer, Doug and I wrote *Using 1-2-3* for Que, which became an instant bestseller. In a few short years, it sold well over a million copies as 1-2-3's sales skyrocketed, and it became the stuff of industry lore.

Ever since that summer I have been working with 1-2-3 in one way or another. I have written several books about it and started a software company to develop add-in software for it. In the past three years alone, our company—The LeBlond Group—has written books on 1-2-3 Releases 2.2 and 3, as well as 1-2-3/G.

WHY WE WROTE THIS BOOK

We at the LeBlond Group wrote this book because of our ongoing interest in 1-2-3 and our extensive experience with Windows. As veteran 1-2-3 users, we wanted 1-2-3 for Windows to retain the familiar feel and keystrokes from previous releases. At the same time, we wanted it to incorporate many of the powerful features that are native to the Windows environment.

We weren't disappointed. In fact, if you're an experienced 1-2-3 user, you'll find that it *is really easy* to get started with 1-2-3 for Windows. Likewise, if you're an experienced Windows user, you'll also feel right at home.

ABOUT THIS BOOK

This book is designed to be the most comprehensive guide to 1-2-3 for Windows available. If you're a new user, you'll find all you need in the early chapters to get going quickly. If you're an intermediate or advanced 1-2-3 user, you'll find many tips and techniques that are specially tailored to help further your knowledge and make the most of 1-2-3 for Windows.

In *LeBlonds' 1-2-3 for Windows Handbook*, we've made a special effort to pick up where the documentation leaves off. For example, we've included extensive sections on copying and moving data, managing windows, and creating macros. And these are just a few of the areas where we've filled in the gaps.

WHAT'S COVERED IN THIS BOOK

This book is organized into 17 chapters and 2 appendices that cover the full range of 1-2-3 for Windows.

Chapter 1, "1-2-3 for Windows Basics," discusses many of the most prominent features of 1-2-3 for Windows. By reading this chapter, you'll have the understanding you need to use the worksheet portion of the program.

Chapter 2, "Working with Data," describes how you can enter, edit, name, and search for data in 1-2-3 for Windows. This chapter will familiarize you with all the different ways to manipulate data using 1-2-3 for Windows new graphical interface.

Chapter 3, "Managing Windows," describes how to control the display of multiple files and worksheets within the 1-2-3 work area. For example, you learn how to split windows horizontally or vertically and how to freeze portions of a worksheet on the screen to keep them always in view.

Chapter 4, "Managing Files," covers all of 1-2-3's File commands. For example, you'll learn how to use File Open to open multiple files in 1-2-3's work area and File Extract To to extract part of an active worksheet file and save it to a file on disk.

Chapter 5, "Formatting Worksheets," describes how to improve the appearance and layout of your worksheets. You'll learn how to format cells, insert and delete columns and rows, and protect worksheets.

Chapter 6, "Fonts and Styles," shows you how to take advantage of 1-2-3's styles—for example, shading and borders. It also describes how to use fonts for creating presentation-quality output.

Chapter 7, "Cutting and Pasting Data," discusses the commands you use to edit your worksheets in 1-2-3 for Windows. Topics include how to use the Edit Cut, Copy, and Paste commands to interact with the Windows Clipboard and how to use the Edit Clear Special command to erase the contents, formats, and style settings from cells.

Chapter 8, "Printing," examines all the topics related to printing in 1-2-3 for Windows. For example, you'll learn how to send output to a printer or file and how to combine worksheets and graphs on the same printed page.

Chapter 9, "Functions," is a reference chapter on all the @functions available in 1-2-3 for Windows. Functions are organized by category for easy reference.

Chapter 10, "Graphs," describes a full range of topics related to 1-2-3's graphics capability. You'll learn all about 1-2-3's basic graph types as well as how to enhance graphs to suit your needs.

Chapter 11, "Database Management," describes how to create a database in 1-2-3 and how to use the Data commands to organize and query it. Other topics include how to sort a database and how to search a database for information.

Chapter 12, "Advanced Data Analysis," focuses on 1-2-3 for Windows' commands for data analysis—Data Fill, Frequency, Regression, Matrix, and What-if Table. For example, you'll learn how to use the Data Regression command to analyze trends or relationships through linear regression, and how to use the Data Matrix command to manipulate matrices to determine the unique solution to a set of constraints.

Chapter 13, "Advanced Sensitivity Analysis," describes how to use the Backsolver and Solver, 1-2-3 for Windows' most sophisticated sensitivity analysis tools. Look to this chapter for the most practical discussion you'll find anywhere on two of the most powerful features of 1-2-3.

Chapter 14, "Creating Macros," describes how to use 1-2-3 for Windows' macro facility and includes many useful examples to increase your understanding. It also describes how to use the Transcript window to replay keystrokes and save them as macros.

Chapter 15, "The Macro Programming Language," is a reference to 1-2-3 for Windows macro programming commands. You'll learn how to use these commands to create sophisticated macro programs of your own design.

Chapter 16, "Networking," explains how to take advantage of 1-2-3's built-in networking features. For example, you'll learn how to use 1-2-3's file reservation system to manage files in shared directories on a network as well as how to seal your files to protect sensitive areas and settings.

Chapter 17, "Sharing Data," covers a broad range of topics related to sharing data between 1-2-3 and other programs. For example, you'll learn how to use Dynamic Data Exchange (DDE) to create a live link between a 1-2-3 for Windows worksheet and Word for Windows document.

Appendix A, "Customizing 1-2-3 for Windows," tells you how you can modify 1-2-3 for Windows to suit the way you work. The main emphasis of the appendix is on creating and modifying 1-2-3's SmartIcons.

Appendix B, "The Adobe Type Manager," describes how to take full advantage of this unique program in providing fonts to 1-2-3 for Windows. For example, you'll learn how to install the program and how to modify its settings to better suit your own circumstances.

CONCLUSION

1-2-3 for Windows brings the power and familiarity of 1-2-3 to the Windows graphical environment. At the same time, it has many more features than any of its predecessors.

In this book we've endeavored to give you the real substance behind 1-2-3 for Windows. We've also taken special care to describe all its new features and how it takes advantage of the Windows environment.

We believe we've written the most comprehensive and useful book available on 1-2-3 for Windows, and we hope our enthusiasm for the program passes on to you.

Geoff LeBlond

Acknowledgments

To Nikhil Mirchandani, Cliff Fischbach, and Suzanne Mann for their help with the graph chapter.

To Rob Weinstein for his insight on LaserMaster printers.

To Alan Rose for going the extra mile to make sure that the figures looked great.

And to Ron Petrusha for his unique appreciation of 1-2-3 for Windows and his unparalleled editing.

Contents

xi

3   Managing Windows   115

4   Managing Files   137

9 Functions

10 Graphs   445

12 Advanced Data Analysis

13 Advanced Sensitivity Analysis

1

1-2-3 for Windows Basics

1-2-3 for Windows is the Microsoft Windows version of the highly popular Lotus 1-2-3 spreadsheet program for DOS. Although other spreadsheets are available for Windows, 1-2-3 for Windows is the only one that offers such complete compatibility with earlier versions of 1-2-3.

As a Windows application, 1-2-3 for Windows bears many trademarks of that environment, such as WYSIWYG (what you see is what you get) display, windowing, mouse support, dialog boxes, pulldown menus, and presentation-quality output. In addition, 1-2-3 adds some new features to the Windows interface, like SmartIcons and the 1-2-3 Classic menu, that give it a special look all its own.

This chapter teaches you the basics of 1-2-3 for Windows. You will learn how to navigate in worksheets using the mouse and keyboard as well as how to use menus, accelerators, and many other features of 1-2-3's graphical interface. Along the way you'll learn several new terms associated with 1-2-3 for Windows. When you've completed this chapter, you'll have all the basic tools you need to perform worksheet-related tasks in 1-2-3.

NEW FEATURES OF 1-2-3 FOR WINDOWS

As you would expect, 1-2-3 for Windows has many new features that are by-products of Windows' graphical user interface (GUI), such as mouse and Clipboard support, as well as the ability to change fonts and colors. It also has many enhancements to 1-2-3's familiar capabilities. These include the following features that will be covered in the first two chapters of this book:

- 3-D worksheets: Like 1-2-3 Release 3.1, every 1-2-3 for Windows worksheet file can contain up to 256 worksheets. (Although a new file contains only a single worksheet, you can add additional worksheets to the file by inserting them.)

- New range features: You can specify 3-D ranges that span multiple worksheets. You can also use undefined range names that you later assign coordinates to.

- GUI selection order: You can preselect a range and then apply a command or action to it. This lets you apply multiple formatting and style commands to a single pre-selected range.

- 1-2-3 Classic Menu: If you are familiar with 1-2-3, you'll find working with 1-2-3 for Windows quite comfortable because you can resort to the keystrokes you already know. When you press the / (slash) key in 1-2-3 for Windows, the 1-2-3 Classic menu appears in a window. There you'll find the standard 1-2-3 Release 3.1 menu at your beck and call.

- Help: 1-2-3 for Windows uses the standard Windows help engine (WINHELP.EXE) to bring you the most comprehensive help system in any release of 1-2-3. In fact, Lotus has gone so far as to place most of the documentation for @functions and macros in the help system.

1-2-3 FOR WINDOWS TERMINOLOGY

Many of the terms used in 1-2-3 for Windows are common to all Windows applications. However, Lotus has assigned some unique names to certain areas of the 1-2-3 window.

When you start 1-2-3, a window like the one in Figure 1-1 appears. There are six main parts to the 1-2-3 window: the title bar, the menu bar, the control panel, the SmartIcon palette, the work area, and the status line. The sections that follow describe these areas in more detail.

The Title Bar

1-2-3's *title bar* shows its program and window name. (This is the same name that appears in the Task List when you press CTRL+ESC.) Like most Windows applications, 1-2-3 also includes a control menu box and maximize and minimize buttons.

The Menu Bar

The *menu bar* contains the main menu for the currently active window. Because a worksheet is active in Figure 1-1, the worksheet menu is displayed. You'll see a different menu if a graph window is active, and yet a third menu if a Transcript window is active.

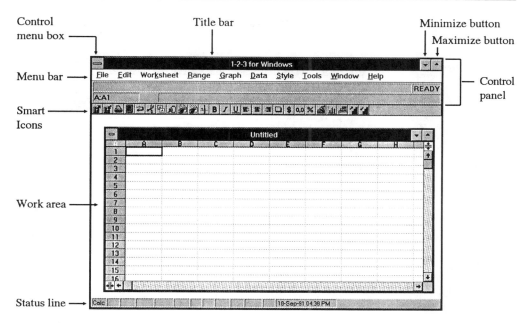

Control
menu box

Title bar

Minimize button
Maximize button

Menu bar

Control
panel

Smart
Icons

Work area

Status line

Figure 1-1 Elements of the 1-2-3 window

Note: Selecting menu items is covered later in this chapter under "Menus."

In 1-2-3 for Windows, you can also access the 1-2-3 Classic menu, which is the menu used in 1-2-3 Release 3.1. The Classic menu isn't visible through the standard Windows menu bar, but is placed in a separate window. See "The 1-2-3 Classic Menu" later in this chapter.

The Control Panel

The *control panel* is composed of the following four lines:

- Title bar
- Menu bar
- Format line
- Edit line

The first two you are already familiar with. As you can see in Figure 1-2, the *format line* displays nonglobal format and style settings that are assigned to a cell. For example, cell C2 has been assigned a Currency 2 decimal places numeric format (C2), a TimesRmn 10-point font (TimesNewRomanPS10), a column width of 11 ([W11]), a drop shadow (Shadow), and an outline around the entire cell (LRTB).

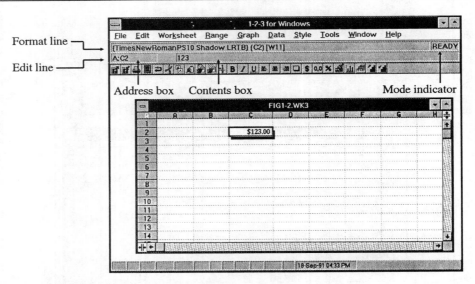

Figure 1-2 The edit and format lines

Note: Formatting is discussed in Chapter 5 and styles are discussed in Chapter 6.

The format line also includes the *mode indicator*, which provides information about the state that 1-2-3 is in (see "Mode Indicators" later). In Figure 1-2, 1-2-3 for Windows is in READY mode.

The *edit line* (also called the *input line*) is used for entering and editing data in worksheets. When a worksheet window is active, as in Figure 1-2, the input line shows the current cell address in the *address box* on the left. The contents of the cell appear in the *contents box* on the right. In the example, cell A:C2 contains the value 123.

The SmartIcon Palette

1-2-3 for Windows includes *SmartIcons*—shortcuts for commonly used commands and macros. 1-2-3 automatically provides the default icon palette you can see in Figure 1-2 below the edit line. To use a SmartIcon, you simply click on it.

You can customize the SmartIcons included in the icon palette, as well as the position of the icon palette in the work area. SmartIcons are discussed throughout the book; see Appendix A to learn how to customize the icon palette.

The Work Area

In 1-2-3 for Windows, your work is displayed in the work area. The *work area* is the entire area of 1-2-3's window below the control panel. You can place worksheets, graphs, or the Transcript window in the work area and arrange them as you please. The work area is also where 1-2-3 for Windows displays dialog boxes and the SmartIcon palette.

Status Line

The *status line* at the bottom of the screen displays the current date and time. It may also display one or more status indicators—for example, CALC in Figure 1-1. See "Status Indicators" later for more.

TYPES OF WINDOWS IN 1-2-3

The windows that appear within the work area can be any of the following:

- A worksheet window where you can enter and display data. Whenever you start 1-2-3 for Windows, a worksheet window appears on the screen.

- A graph window that contains a graph—usually created from data in a worksheet window. Graphs are discussed in Chapter 10.

- A Transcript window records every keystroke you make in 1-2-3 for Windows and lets you replay those keystrokes directly or place them in a macro. See Chapter 14, "Creating Macros."

WINDOW BASICS

1-2-3 uses the Multiple Document Interface (MDI) standard to allow you to work with multiple child windows (in this case, spreadsheet and graph windows) within a single application. This is the same interface that File Manager uses to show the contents of multiple directories and Program Manager uses to show multiple group windows.

When you look at a worksheet or graph in 1-2-3, you are viewing it through a *child window*. By placing child windows in the work area, you can view several different worksheets or graphs at once. For example, you might view a graph in one child window and a worksheet in another, or you can view two worksheets in two different child windows. You can have up to 16 child windows open at once in 1-2-3.

Figure 1-3 shows the elements of a worksheet window. Four of these elements are common to all child windows.

- Control menu box: When you click on this box or press ALT and – (minus), 1-2-3 displays the window's *control menu*. You can use this menu to control the size and placement of a child window in the work area.

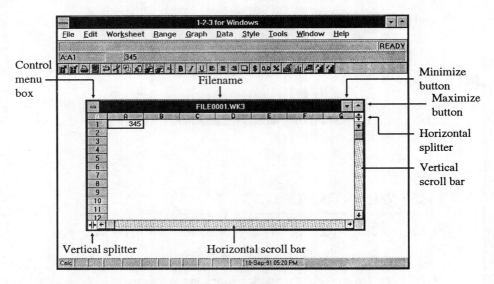

Figure 1-3 The elements of a worksheet window

- File or Window name: This area of the window title bar shows the current worksheet filename and, in the case of graphs, the current graph name. When the Transcript window is active, "Transcript" appears in this space.

- Minimize button: When you click on this button, the window is reduced to an icon. (You can achieve the same effect by selecting Minimize from the window control menu.) If, after minimizing the window, you want to restore it to its previous size, double-click on the window's icon.

- Maximize button: Click on this box to expand the window to occupy the entire work area and, afterward, to restore the window to its previous size. (Select Maximize from the window control menu to achieve the same effect.) When you maximize a window in the work area, 1-2-3 displays the control menu box for the window in the menu bar.

▼ *Tip:*   The easiest way to close a child window with the mouse in 1-2-3 is to double-click on its control menu box. You can also close 1-2-3 (or any other Windows application) by double-clicking on its control menu box.

THE WORKSHEET

When you first start 1-2-3, a worksheet window appears within the work area—this is quite natural because the worksheet is what you will use most often in 1-2-3 to do your work. Figure 1-3 shows the elements of a worksheet window.

The worksheet is divided into columns labeled with letters across the top, and rows labeled with numbers down the side. Like a sheet of graph paper, the intersection of the columns and rows form a series of small boxes known as *cells*. Each cell starts out empty and is filled when you enter data in it.

The point at which a column and a row meet defines the location of a cell. The combination of the column letter and row number is the *cell address*, such as A9 or CA11. The column letter is always specified first, followed by the row number. You are always located at some cell address called the *current cell address*. The current cell address matches the location of the *cell pointer*, a blue outline surrounding the current cell.

The worksheet area that appears within a window is actually a view onto a much larger worksheet space. In fact, a 1-2-3 worksheet has 256 columns and 8192 rows. (The lower rightmost cell in a worksheet is IV8192.) The worksheet area that appears on your screen is limited by the size of the window. You can expand and contract the size of the window, but you can still see only a small portion of the worksheet at any one time. Later on you'll learn how to shift the contents of the window to view different parts of the worksheet.

Another aspect of a cell address is its worksheet letter. When you first start 1-2-3 for Windows, only a single worksheet appears—worksheet A. As you'll learn later, you can actually have up to 256 worksheets in a file—worksheets A through IV.

CELL INFORMATION

In the control panel you can see information about the location and contents of the current cell and its settings. As mentioned, the edit line (the third line of 1-2-3's window) shows the current cell address in the address box on the left of the line. In Figure 1-3, for example, the current cell address is A:A1. Notice that this matches the location of the cell pointer, and that the address appears as a worksheet letter followed by a colon, a column letter, and row number.

The contents box appears on the right side of the edit line and serves as a window where you can enter and edit information that is ultimately added to the worksheet. In Figure 1-3, the contents of cell A:A1 is the number 345. Had the cell contained a label entry (text), such as Sales, the entry would be preceded by a *label prefix*, for example, 'Sales. You'll learn more about label prefixes in Chapter 2.

INDICATORS

1-2-3 has two types of indicators, status and mode indicators. Mode indicators appear on the right-hand side of the format line. Status indicators, on the other hand, appear on the status line at the foot of 1-2-3's window.

Mode Indicators

Mode indicators provide information about what 1-2-3 for Windows is doing. When 1-2-3 is idle—waiting for input—the mode indicator shows READY. When something is going on, the mode indicator changes from READY to some other single keyword indicating an activity or condition. Table 1-1 shows the different mode keywords and what each means.

TABLE 1-1 Mode Indicators

EDIT	You pressed EDIT (F2) to edit a cell entry; you made an error entering a formula; or you are entering text in a text box.
ERROR	Something is wrong and 1-2-3 is displaying an error message. Select OK to clear the error and continue. Press HELP (F1) to see help information.
FILES	The 1-2-3 Classic window is active and 1-2-3 is displaying a list of filenames.
FIND	You selected Data Query Find to find database records matching certain criteria, and 1-2-3 has located such a record. This indicator also appears when you press QUERY (F7) to repeat the latest Data Query Find command.
LABEL	You are entering a label (text).
MENU	You activated the menu bar by clicking on it or pressing ALT or MENU (F10). This indicator also appears when a dialog box is active and the dotted box is in a list box or on a check box, option button, or command button.
POINT	You are specifying a range while working in a dialog box or entering a formula. This indicator also appears when you preselect a range prior to selecting a command.
READY	1-2-3 is waiting for input.
VALUE	You are entering a value (a number or formula).
WAIT	1-2-3 is busy—it is either completing a command or recalculating.

Status Indicators

Status indicators are linked to a key that you press to put the system in a particular state, such as END. They can also warn about a condition that may need your attention, such as CALC or CIRC. Table 1-2 describes 1-2-3's various status indicators and the activity that is associated with each of them.

Table 1-2 Status Indicators

CALC	The worksheet needs recalculating; press CALC (F9). This indicator may also appear when 1-2-3 is performing background recalculation.
CAPS	You pressed CAPS LOCK and capitalization is on.
CIRC	1-2-3 has detected a circular reference (a formula that refers to itself). Select Help About 1-2-3 to see a cell involved in the circular reference.
CMD	1-2-3 is running a macro.
END	You pressed END, and 1-2-3 is waiting for the next key; press a pointer-movement key (Table 1-7) or press END again to cancel.
FILE	You pressed CTRL+END, and 1-2-3 is waiting for the next key; press another key to move between files (see Table 3-1 in Chapter 3).
GROUP	The current file is in GROUP mode.
MEM	1-2-3 has detected that available memory is less then 32K.
NUM	The NUM LOCK key is on.
RO	You are using 1-2-3 on a network, and the current file has read-only status—you can change the worksheet file, but you can't save it under the current name. To get the file's reservation so that you can save it using the current filename, use File Administration Network Reserve Get. (RO is the only status indicator that does not appear in the status line—it appears in the worksheet window's title bar, to the right of the filename.)
SCROLL	You pressed SCROLL LOCK. If you use any of the pointer-movement keys, 1-2-3 will scroll the entire window in the direction of the key.
SST	A macro is running in single-step mode and has paused for input.
STEP	You pressed STEP (ALT+F2) to execute a macro one step at a time (single-step mode).
ZOOM	After using Window Split to split a worksheet into two panes or three contiguous worksheets, you pressed ZOOM (ALT+F6) to have the current pane or worksheet expand to fill the entire window.

FUNCTION AND ACCELERATOR KEYS

Function keys and *accelerator keys* are assigned to common tasks you want 1-2-3 for Windows to perform. Many are simply shortcuts to menu commands, while others perform tasks you can't perform in any other way. In 1-2-3, you can use F1 through F10 alone, or in conjunction with CTRL or ALT. These are the names assigned to the different combinations:

Key	Alone	CTRL	ALT
F1	HELP		COMPOSE
F2	EDIT		STEP
F3	NAME		RUN
F4	ABS	CLOSE WINDOW	CLOSE 1-2-3
F5	GOTO		
F6	PANE	NEXT WINDOW	ZOOM
F7	QUERY		ADD-IN 1
F8	TABLE		ADD-IN 2
F9	CALC		ADD-IN 3
F10	MENU		ADD-IN MENU

Table 1-3 shows the different activities assigned to 1-2-3's function and accelerator keys. Note that some keys work only in a particular mode, or work differently depending on the mode. For those keys, the table also shows the mode in parentheses. Each of these keys is explained fully in the appropriate chapters of this book.

GETTING HELP

As mentioned, you can access 1-2-3's help at almost any time. To get *context-sensitive help*, use any of the following methods:

- Press HELP (F1).
- Click on the Help button when it is available in a message box. (This is particularly convenient for getting information about error messages.)
- To see an index of @functions, type @ and press HELP (F1).
- To get help with a particular @function, type @ followed by the name of the function and ((left parenthesis)—for example, **@AVG(**—and then press HELP (F1). 1-2-3 will display help on the function you typed.
- To see an index of macro commands, type { and press HELP (F1).
- To get help with a particular macro command, type { followed by the name of the command—for example, **{MENUBRANCH**—and then press HELP (F1).

Still another way to get help is to select an item from the Help menu shown in Figure 1-4. Table 1-4 describes the function of the Help menu options.

TABLE 1-3 Function and Accelerator Keys

Key	Name	Description
F1	HELP	Displays 1-2-3's help.
F2	EDIT	Switches to EDIT mode to let you edit a cell entry (READY, POINT, LABEL, or VALUE mode).
F3	NAME	Displays a list of named ranges from which to choose (POINT mode). If you type + – / ^ (or * and then press NAME, 1-2-3 displays a list of range names in the worksheet (VALUE mode); if you type @ and then press NAME, 1-2-3 displays a list of available @functions from which to choose.
F4	ABS	Toggles a cell or range address from relative, to absolute, to mixed (POINT, EDIT, or VALUE mode). Anchors the cell pointer so that you can select a range (READY mode); see Chapter 2.
F5	GOTO	Allows you to reposition the cell pointer at a given cell address, the upper-left corner cell of a named range, another worksheet in the same file, or another open file (READY mode).
F6	PANE	Moves between two windows you have set up with Window Split Horizontal, Vertical, or Perspective (READY mode).
F7	QUERY	Repeats the last Data Query command (READY mode).
F8	TABLE	Repeats the last Data Table command (READY mode).
F9	CALC	Recalculates all formulas in the worksheet, except formulas that reference files on disk (READY mode); converts a formula to its current value (VALUE and EDIT modes).
F10	MENU	Activates the menu.
ALT+F1	COMPOSE	Lets you enter characters you cannot type from the keyboard.
ALT+F2	STEP	Toggles STEP mode on and off; STEP mode lets you run a macro a single step at a time.
ALT+F3	RUN	Displays a list of range names from which you can select a macro to run (same as Tools Macro Run).

(continued)

TABLE 1-3 Function and Accelerator Keys *(continued)*

Key	*Name*	*Description*
ALT+F4	CLOSE 1-2-3	Ends 1-2-3.
ALT+F6	ZOOM	Expands the current vertical or horizontal pane or perspective worksheet to fill the entire window. (Press a second time to have the pane or worksheet revert to its original size.)
ALT+F7, ALT+F8, ALT+F9	Add-ins	Activates attached add-ins.
ALT+F10	Add-in menu	Displays the Add-in menu in a 1-2-3 Classic window.
ALT+ – (minus)	Window control menu	Displays the window control menu for the current window.
ALT+ BACKSPACE	Undo	Reverses the last change you made.
ALT+ SPACEBAR	1-2-3 control menu	Displays the 1-2-3 control menu.
CTRL+F4	Close window	Closes the active child window.
CTRL+F6	Activate window	Activates the next open child window.
CTRL+INS	Copy	Copies data to the Clipboard.
DEL	Clear	Deletes the current selection permanently.
SHIFT+DEL	Cut	Moves data to the Clipboard.
SHIFT+INS	Paste	Moves data from the Clipboard to the location of the cell pointer (you can also paste to graphs and text boxes).

Like most Windows applications, 1-2-3 uses the standard Windows help program, WINHELP.EXE, to display its help (see Figure 1-5). If you've used help in other Windows programs, you already know how to interact with 1-2-3's help. If you're not familiar with the Windows help program, here are some pointers:

• *Cross-references*—items that you can get further help on—appear in green and are underlined. To select a cross-reference with the mouse, simply click on it. With the keyboard, press TAB to highlight a word or group of words and press ENTER.

• You can use one of the five help buttons to locate a help topic. Table 1-5 describes the help buttons.

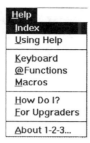

Figure 1-4 The Help menu

- You can use WINHELP's menu commands to set bookmarks, add your own annotations, copy help text to the Clipboard, and so on. Table 1-6 summarizes these commands.

You can eliminate the Help window from the screen just as you would any other Windows application. Here are the most common ways:

- Press ALT+F4.
- Double-click on the window control box.
- Select File Exit.

TABLE 1-4 1-2-3's Help Menu Options

Option	*Displays*
Index	An index of 1-2-3's help topics.
Using Help	How to use 1-2-3's help.
Keyboard	Information about 1-2-3's function, accelerator, and navigation keys.
@Functions	A description of an @function and shows 1-2-3's @function categories.
Macros	Gives a basic description of a macro and 1-2-3's macro command categories.
How Do I?	The alphabet allowing you to select a 1-2-3 help topic using its first letter.
For Upgraders	A description of the 1-2-3 Classic menu and lets you access help for each command in 1-2-3 Release 3.1.
About 1-2-3	When a CIRC indicator appears in the status line, the cell address of a cell involved in a circular reference.

Figure 1-5 A sample help window

TABLE 1-5 Help Buttons

Button	Displays
Index	1-2-3's help index.
Back	The last topic you viewed.
Browse <<	The previous topic in a group of related topics, until you reach the first topic in the group. Then the button is dimmed.
Browse >>	The next topic in a group of related topics, until you reach the last topic in the group. Then the button is dimmed.
Search	All of 1-2-3's help keywords; pick one to go to a particular help topic.

TABLE 1-6 Help Window Command Options

Option	Lets you
File	Load help files from other Windows applications, print help topics, and exit help.
Edit	Copy help text to the Clipboard and attach an annotation to a help topic.
Bookmark	Assign a bookmark to a help reference, which you can later jump to using the Bookmark menu.
Help	Switch to Windows help. To switch back to 1-2-3's help, select the Index button.

MOVING WITHIN A WORKSHEET

Before you can enter data into the cells that make up the worksheet area, you must move the cell pointer to the cell where the information belongs. When you first start 1-2-3 for Windows, the cell pointer is sitting in cell A:A1. To make an entry in another cell, you must move the cell pointer there. 1-2-3 offers a variety of ways to navigate within a worksheet window using the mouse or the keyboard. As you work with 1-2-3, you are likely to use a combination of the two to navigate in a worksheet window.

Moving with the Mouse

Because 1-2-3 takes full advantage of Windows' graphical user interface, navigating with the mouse is especially easy. The sections that follow describe basic mouse movements.

Moving to a Cell within the Window

When a cell appears within the current worksheet window, the easiest way to move to that cell in 1-2-3 is to click on it. 1-2-3 immediately shifts the cell pointer to that cell, and you can enter or edit information there.

Scrolling with the Mouse

Because a worksheet contains 256 columns by 8192 rows, a worksheet window can't possibly display all the cells at once. To view other areas of the worksheet, you must scroll the window. *Scrolling* involves using the vertical and horizontal scroll bars that border the worksheet window, as shown in Figure 1-6.

You can scroll in any of the following ways with the mouse:

- To scroll up or down a row at a time, click on the top or bottom arrow in the vertical scroll bar. You can scroll continuously by pointing to the top or bottom arrow and holding down the mouse button. Figure 1-7 shows how the window in Figure 1-6 appears after you scroll down a row.

- To scroll left or right a column at a time, click on the right or left arrow in the horizontal scroll bar. You can scroll continuously by pointing to the left or right arrow and holding down the mouse button.

- To scroll up or down a windowful of rows, click above or below the scroll box in the vertical scroll bar.

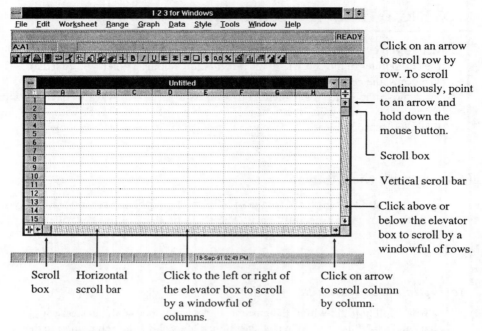

Figure 1-6 The function of 1-2-3's scroll bars

- To scroll left or right a windowful of columns, click to the left or right of the scroll box in the horizontal scroll bar.

- To scroll to the *home position*—cell A1—drag the scroll box in the vertical scroll bar all the way to the top and in the horizontal scroll bar all the way to the left.

Note: When you scroll using the mouse, the cell pointer always remains in view. For example, when you scroll down a row in Figure 1-6, the cell pointer shifts to cell A:A2, as shown in Figure 1-7.

Moving with the Keyboard

Because of its character-based heritage, 1-2-3 has many powerful keys for navigating in the worksheet. Table 1-7 lists those keys and how each works.

The Arrow Keys

The arrow keys move the cell pointer a single cell at a time. For example, with the cell pointer located in cell A:A1, as in Figure 1-6, if you press ↓, the cell pointer moves to

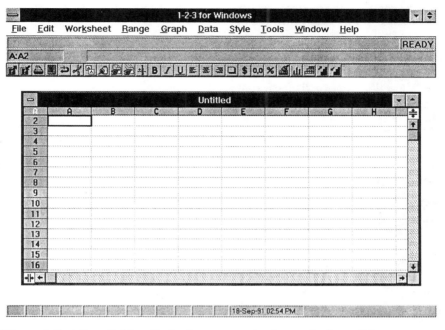

Figure 1-7 After clicking the bottom arrow in the vertical scroll bar

cell A:A2. If you then press →, the cell pointer shifts to cell A:B2. Pressing ↑ shifts the cell pointer to cell A:B1. Finally, pressing ← returns the cell pointer to cell A:A1.

Moving the Window Around the Worksheet

As mentioned, when you press an arrow key to navigate in the worksheet, 1-2-3 moves the cell pointer to an adjacent cell, but it may or may not scroll the window. Only when you move beyond the edge of the window does 1-2-3 scroll the window contents so that it always keeps the cell pointer in view.

The way that 1-2-3 scrolls the screen when you move beyond the edge of the window depends on many factors, including the size of the window and the number of columns and rows. For example, suppose 1-2-3 contains the worksheet window in Figure 1-6 with the cell pointer in cell A:A1, and you press → until the cell pointer resides in cell A:H1. If you press → an additional time to move beyond the edge of the window, 1-2-3 will update the screen to bring all of column I into view and moves the cell pointer to cell I1 (column A no longer appears on the screen). Now suppose you press ↓ to move the cell pointer to cell I15, and then press ↓ one more time to move beyond the edge of the window. 1-2-3 scrolls the screen so that it appears as in Figure 1-8.

TABLE 1-7   Keyboard Navigation

Key	Moves the cell pointer
←	Left one column.
→	Right one column.
↑	Up one row.
↓	Down one row.
CTRL+← or SHIFT+TAB	Left one windowful of columns.
CTRL+→ or TAB	Right one windowful of columns.
HOME	To cell A1 in the current worksheet.
END	When followed by an arrow key, in the direction of the arrow.
END HOME	To the lower right corner of the active area in the current worksheet.
PGDN	Down one windowful of rows.
PGUP	Up one windowful of rows.
CTRL+PGUP	To the next worksheet.
CTRL+PGDN	To the previous worksheet.
CTRL+HOME	To cell A:A1 from any worksheet in the file.
END CTRL+HOME	To the last cell containing data in the last worksheet.
END CTRL+PGUP	Forward through worksheets to the intersection of a blank and a nonblank cell.
END CTRL+PGDN	Backward through worksheets to the intersection of a blank and a nonblank cell.

Moving the Cell Pointer a Windowful at a Time

1-2-3 has four keys for moving the cell pointer around the worksheet a windowful at a time: PGUP, PGDN, CTRL+→ (or TAB), and CTRL+← (or SHIFT+TAB). These keys are convenient for moving around a worksheet in large steps.

The PGUP and PGDN keys let you move the cell pointer up and down a windowful of rows at a time. Suppose you have the worksheet window in Figure 1-6, which shows just over 15 full rows, and the cell pointer is located in cell A:A1. If you press PGDN, 1-2-3 will shift the cell pointer down 15 rows and display cell A:A16 in the upper-left corner. If you press PGDN a second time, 1-2-3 will shift the cell pointer down to cell

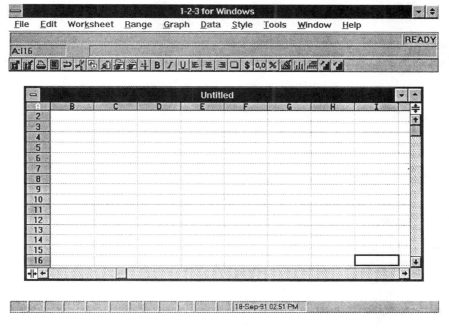

Figure 1-8   After moving beyond the edge of the window

A:A31. If you then press PGUP, 1-2-3 will shift the cell pointer back up to cell A:A16. Press it a second time, and 1-2-3 returns the cell pointer to cell A:A1.

To move horizontally a windowful of columns at a time, you use the CTRL+→ and CTRL+← commands. (Pressing TAB is identical to pressing CTRL+→, and pressing SHIFT+TAB is identical to pressing CTRL+←.) For example, starting with the worksheet window in Figure 1-6, if you press CTRL+→, 1-2-3 will shift the cell pointer eight columns to the right and display cell A:I1 in the upper-left corner. If you then press CTRL+←, 1-2-3 will shift the cell pointer eight columns to the left, returning the cell pointer to cell A:A1.

The END Key

The END key lets you move the cell pointer to the end of a range of cells. When you press END, 1-2-3 waits until you press an arrow key before moving the cell pointer in the direction of the arrow. 1-2-3 then places the cell pointer at the next filled cell (a cell that contains data or a label prefix) that is followed or preceded by a blank cell. If 1-2-3 doesn't encounter a filled cell, it will place the cell pointer at the worksheet boundary.

For example, suppose you have the worksheet in Figure 1-9, and you press END →. 1-2-3 moves the cell pointer to cell C2 (the last nonblank cell in the direction of the arrow).

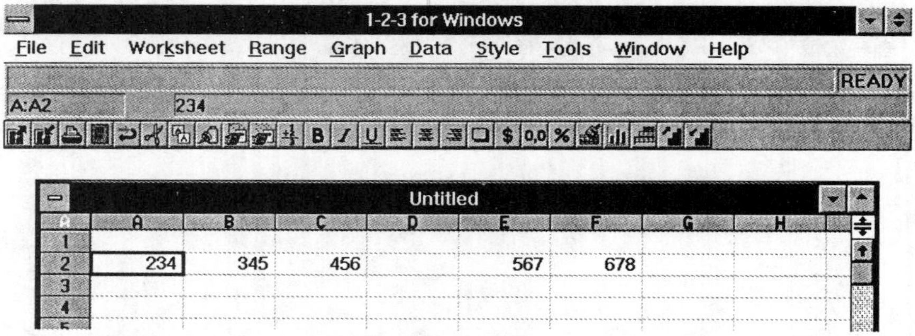

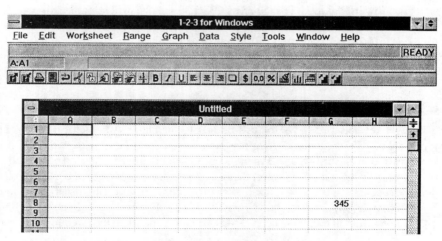

Figure 1-9 The effect of the END key

If you press END → again, 1-2-3 will move the cell pointer to cell E2 (the first nonblank cell in the direction of the arrow). Press END → a third time, and 1-2-3 moves the cell pointer to cell F2 (the last nonblank cell). Press END → the fourth time, and 1-2-3 moves the cell pointer to IV2 (the worksheet boundary).

The HOME Key

Pressing HOME moves the cell pointer to cell A1 in the current worksheet. Cell A1 is known as the *home position* in a worksheet.

Pressing HOME can be quite convenient when it's your intent to move to the home position. It isn't uncommon, however, to press HOME inadvertently while moving around the worksheet.

Unfortunately, there is no convenient key combination to return the cell pointer to its previous position after accidentally pressing HOME. You'll probably have to use PGDN,

Figure 1-10 A worksheet with a single entry in cell G8

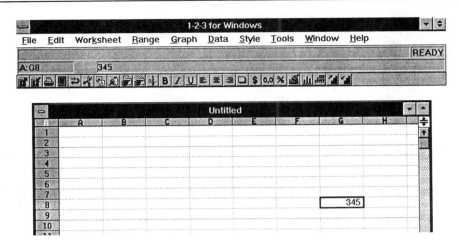

Figure 1-11 The effect of END HOME

CTRL+→, and other key combinations or mouse movements to return the cell pointer to its previous position. You can also select GOTO (F5), type the appropriate cell address, and press ENTER.

The END HOME Combination

The END HOME key combination moves the cell pointer to the lower-right corner of the active area in the current worksheet. The *active area* is a rectangular block that encompasses every entry in the worksheet, including formatted cells that are blank.

For example, suppose you have the worksheet in Figure 1-10 with only a single entry in cell G8. If you press END HOME, 1-2-3 will move the cell pointer to cell G8, which represents the lower-right corner of the active area, as shown in Figure 1-11.

The SCROLL LOCK Key

By pressing the SCROLL LOCK key, you can use the keyboard to scroll a worksheet window in the same way you use the mouse to scroll the window. Suppose you have the worksheet in Figure 1-6, and you press SCROLL LOCK followed by ↓. 1-2-3 shifts the screen so that it appears as shown in Figure 1-7. Note that this is exactly the same as using the mouse to click on the bottom arrow in the vertical scroll bar.

MENUS

As you know, whenever you start 1-2-3 for Windows, the menu bar appears on the second line of the control panel. It is through this menu bar that you can generate graphs, print data, save files, and perform many other powerful operations for which 1-2-3 for Windows is known.

If you're an experienced Windows user, you'll soon discover that 1-2-3's menu bar works in the same fashion as other Windows applications. What is unique is the 1-2-3 Classic menu, because it provides backward compatibility with previous releases of 1-2-3.

Accessing Menus

To access 1-2-3's main menu with the mouse, simply click on any command in the menu bar. The command will then appear highlighted and its pulldown menu displayed; the first item in the pulldown menu also appears highlighted. In addition, 1-2-3 displays a capsule description of the highlighted item on the first line of the control panel. After you've accessed the menu, you can then select an item from within the menu by clicking on it as well.

For example, Figure 1-12 shows the menu you'll see when you choose Edit from the main menu. Note that the first menu choice, Undo, is highlighted, and the description, "Reverse the effect of the last undoable command or action," is displayed in the first line of the control panel.

▼ *Tip:*   When using the mouse to access 1-2-3's menus, one of the easiest ways to see all the available menu choices and their associated capsule descriptions is to drag the menu pointer from one menu item to the next (keep the left mouse button depressed as you move the mouse). When you reach the item you want, release the button to select it. If you want to bail out of the menu without selecting a command, simply release the mouse button outside the menu area or choose another command.

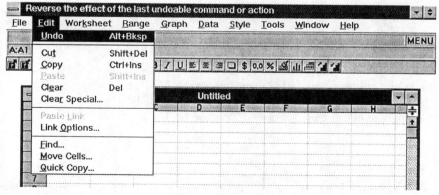

Figure 1-12 The Edit menu

To access 1-2-3's menu bar with the keyboard, press ALT or F10 (MENU), then choose a menu item by typing its underlined letter. (When a letter is underlined, it is known as a *mnemonic*.) For instance, press ALT and then type **E** to access the Edit menu shown in Figure 1-12. To leave the main menu and return to the worksheet, press ESC or CTRL+BREAK.

Once a pulldown menu appears, you can select an item within it by pressing that item's mnemonic. To choose the Move Cells command in the Edit menu, for instance, type **M**. To leave the pulldown menu and return to the worksheet, keep pressing ESC or press CTRL+BREAK.

▼ *Tip:*   You can also use SmartIcons as shortcuts for many commands; , for instance, is a shortcut for the Edit Undo command. SmartIcons are discussed throughout this book. To customize your icon palette, see Appendix A.

Menu Conventions

1-2-3 uses the standard conventions for Windows menus. If you're new to Windows, they are:

* *Grayed text* means that a command can't be chosen at the moment. For example, when you access the Edit menu, you can see in Figure 1-12 that the Paste command is gray. This is because there is nothing in the Clipboard, so the command is not operative.

* An *Arrow* (▼) indicates that a command has related items available in a cascade menu.

* *Ellipses* (. . .) after a menu item means that the command will produce a dialog box that will prompt you for information.

* An *underlined letter (or mnemonic)* appears for each item in a menu. By typing the underlined letter, you can select the command (see the previous section).

* *Accelerator keys* shown to the right of a command are an easy way to access the command. For example, you can see in Figure 1-12 that pressing ALT+BACKSPACE is a shortcut for Edit Undo.

* *Horizontal lines* separate related commands in a menu.

The 1-2-3 Classic Menu

If there is one feature that sets 1-2-3 for Windows apart from any other Windows spreadsheet, it is the 1-2-3 Classic menu. This is the same menu that appears in 1-2-3 Release 3.1.

To access the 1-2-3 Classic menu, you press the slash (/) key. Figure 1-13 shows the window that appears.

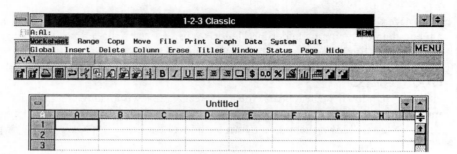

Figure 1-13 The 1-2-3 Classic window

Here are some unique features of the 1-2-3 Classic menu:

- Many 1-2-3 Classic menu commands are direct equivalents of 1-2-3 for Windows commands. Others are completely distinct and separate. For example, if you create a graph with the 1-2-3 Classic /Graph command, you can't access it through the Graph command in the menu bar unless you name the graph. Even then, any changes you make to the graph using the main menu won't be recognized when you access the graph through the Classic menu, and any changes you make to a graph using the Classic menu won't automatically be recognized when you access the graph through the main menu. (See Chapter 10.)

- Some menu items no longer work, even though they are still included in the Classic menu. For example, the /Worksheet Status command no longer works; the new equivalent is Help About 1-2-3, accessed through the main menu.

- Some 1-2-3 Classic commands are easier to use than their Windows' equivalents. For example, the Classic menu's /Copy command is much easier to use than Edit Quick Copy.

- You can't use the mouse to bring up or select from the 1-2-3 Classic menu.

Canceling a Menu Command

Suppose you have selected a command and then decide that you don't want to use the command after all. You can cancel the command with the mouse in any of the following ways:

- Click anywhere outside the menu, and 1-2-3 will return you to the worksheet. Clicking on a blank area of the 1-2-3 work area is best, so that you don't inadvertently select something else in the window.

- Click on another command to select it instead; this technique won't work when 1-2-3 is displaying a dialog box, however.

- When a dialog box is active, select Cancel.

To cancel a command with the keyboard, press ESC or CTRL+BREAK. You can use either one from within any 1-2-3 command, and even from within a dialog box.

DIALOG BOXES

In previous releases, 1-2-3 relied on a multilevel menu system to present all of its commands. In 1-2-3 for Windows, however, the menu system is only one level deep, with all additional commands and options provided by dialog boxes.

1-2-3's dialog boxes operate the same as in other Windows applications. So if you're an experienced Windows user, you'll find little new in this section. You should know, however, that specifying a range or cell in a dialog box is unique in 1-2-3 for Windows.

Types of Controls

A dialog box contains *controls*, which are areas where you make selections or enter information; there are different kinds of controls, depending on what kind of information is needed. Figures 1-14 and 1-15 show some sample dialog boxes and the different controls you'll encounter in 1-2-3. Here's a description of the different control types:

- A *text box* is an area in which you type information. Editing the contents of a text box is similar to editing a cell entry; see Chapter 2.

- A *list box* contains the names of available choices—for example, the names of files and directories on the disk.

- A *drop-down list box* is similar to a standard list box except that its list is hidden until you request it. You can open (and close) a drop-down list box by clicking on the downward-pointing arrow at the right of its selection field. (Use ALT+↓ to open a drop-down list box with the keyboard and ALT+↑ to close it.)

- The *title bar* shows the name of the command you used to activate the dialog box. To move the dialog box, grab the title bar and drag it to a new location.

- *Command buttons* generally carry out or cancel commands when they are chosen; these buttons have labels—OK and Cancel, for example—to indicate what the buttons do.

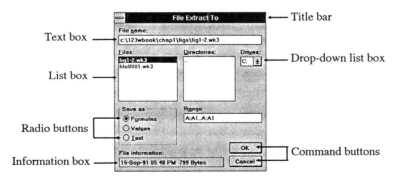

Figure 1-14 The File Extract To dialog box

Check boxes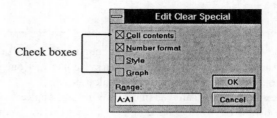

Figure 1-15 The Edit Clear Special dialog box

- *Radio buttons* are circular and let you select options for a particular command. In a group of radio buttons, only one button at a time can be selected, since they represent a set of mutually exclusive choices.

- *Check boxes* are square and let you turn an option on or off. An X appears in the box when you turn an item on. In a group of options with check boxes, several options can be selected at the same time. When 1-2-3 cannot determine the current state of a selection, it displays the check box as filled.

- *Information boxes* usually display information about a file, including its size, date of creation, and time of creation.

▼ *Tip:* 1-2-3 for Windows dialog boxes are slightly unusual in that you can't switch away from them to another application using ALT+ESC or ALT+TAB. You can switch away by pressing CTRL+ESC to activate the Task List.

Dialog Box Conventions

1-2-3 uses the standard conventions for Windows dialog boxes to indicate what options and items you can choose and how you can choose them. Again, if you're new to Windows, here's a description of each:

- An *underlined letter* in an item indicates that you can press ALT in combination with that letter to select the item. In Figure 1-15 for instance, you can type ALT+C to select the Cell contents option.

- A *dotted box* indicates the currently selected item. You can press TAB to cycle forward and SHIFT+TAB to cycle backward through the available options and, in the process, move the dotted box from one option to the next.

- *Grayed commands or options* are inactive, which means that you can't currently use them.

- A *highlight* in a list box indicates that it is the currently selected item. To choose the highlighted item in a list box and leave the dialog box in the process, double-click on the item in the list box, or press ENTER.

Changing the Selection in a Range Text Box

Many commands display a dialog box that contains a text box entitled "Range" or a similar name. This text box indicates the cells in the worksheet to which the command will be applied. Initially, a Range text box will display the location of the cell pointer before you selected the command. In Figure 1-15, for example, because the cell pointer is located in cell A:A1 when the Edit Clear Special command is chosen, the Range text box displays A:A1.

> ▼ *Tip:*   You can preselect a cell or range before you choose a command so that
> 1-2-3 for Windows automatically displays this selection in the Range
> text box for you. See Chapter 2.

To change the selection in a Range text box, you must activate the text box. As you have learned, you can activate a text box at any time by clicking on it, by pressing TAB to move to it, or by pressing ALT in combination with its underlined letter (usually ALT+A for the Range text box).

Once the Range text box is activated, you can change the current selection by typing a new selection, for example A:B6. As you start typing, 1-2-3 clears the Range text box to make room for your new entry. You can also return to the worksheet by pressing F6 and pointing to a new cell or range (see Chapter 2).

MULTIPLE WORKSHEETS

When you first start 1-2-3 for Windows, only a single worksheet appears in the window, just as in Figure 1-16. This is called worksheet A. Because the cell pointer is located in worksheet A, it is also called the *current worksheet.*

In Release 2 and earlier releases, a file and a worksheet were the same. That is, each file contained one worksheet like the one in Figure 1-16, composed of 256 columns and 8192 rows. In 1-2-3 for Windows and 1-2-3 Release 3, however, a single worksheet file can contain up to 256 worksheets named A through IV. Think of these worksheets as individual sheets of paper stacked one behind the other in your computer's memory. Each worksheet is the same size, 256 columns by 8192 rows.

Some of the advantages of using multiple-worksheet files include:

- Rather than having to shoehorn everything into one large worksheet, you can easily divide your work into smaller, more natural segments and place them in different worksheets. For example, you can place a spreadsheet in one worksheet, a database in another, and macros in a third, all in the same worksheet file. Or place 1991 data in worksheet A, 1992 data in worksheet B, 1993 data in worksheet C, and so on.

- It can be easier to consolidate information. For instance, you can place the budget for each department in a separate worksheet, then use formulas to link them to a single

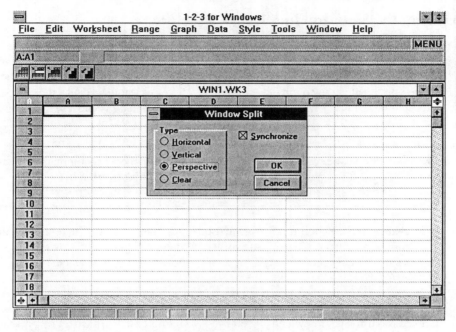

Figure 1-16 A 2-D view of a single worksheet

master worksheet in the same file, worksheet A perhaps. When you make a change to one of the departmental worksheets, you can easily see the effect on the master worksheet. (An alternative would be to place each departmental budget in a separate worksheet file, and then use link formulas to link them all to a single master worksheet file. See Chapter 17.)

- Data in one worksheet is protected from other worksheets. That is, you can change one worksheet at any time without moving, reformatting, or accidentally erasing data in other worksheets in the file. The exception is when you work in Group mode, a topic discussed later in this chapter.

- You can use Group mode to simultaneously assign formats—numeric formatting and column widths, for example—and Styles—fonts, shading, and outlines, for instance—to the same cells in multiple worksheets. You can even use Group mode to insert and delete the same rows or columns in multiple worksheets.

Cell Addressing in a Multiple Worksheet File

Because a file can have multiple worksheets, a cell in 1-2-3 for Windows is described by its worksheet letter followed by a colon, the column letter, and the row number. For example, the cell address B:C6 refers to the second worksheet, third column, and sixth row, while the cell address C:C6 refers to the same cell in worksheet C. This method of cell referencing is called *full cell addressing*.

You don't have to use a full cell address when you reference a cell that is in the current worksheet; instead you can use *abbreviated cell addressing,* where you reference only the column and row—for example, A7. You'll learn more about this in Chapter 2.

Creating a 3-D Perspective of a Worksheet File

You can use Perspective mode to create a three-dimensional view of a worksheet file. In a file with a single worksheet like Figure 1-16, for instance, select the Window Split command and then turn on Perspective, as shown. When you press ENTER or choose OK, the worksheet will look like Figure 1-17.

> ▼ *Tip:*   While in Perspective mode, maximizing the worksheet window will give you the largest view of each worksheet.

As you can see, Perspective mode *always* allocates space to three worksheets—this can't be changed. So for a file with multiple worksheets, you can view up to three worksheets at once. (You can see this by looking ahead to Figure 1-18.) Because the file in Figure 1-17 currently contains just one worksheet, 1-2-3 displays the outline of two worksheets in the space that would be allocated to the other worksheets.

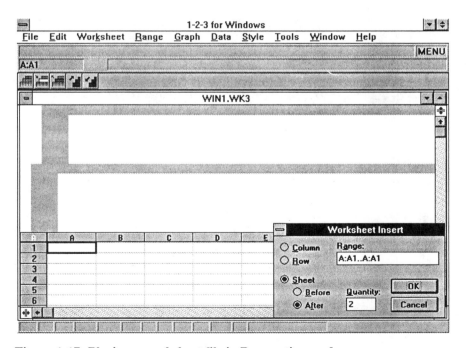

Figure 1-17 Placing a worksheet file in Perspective mode

▼ *Tip:*   The ⊞ icon turns Perspective mode on and off. Select this icon once, and 1-2-3 for Windows puts the worksheet file in Perspective mode. Choose it again, and 1-2-3 clears Perspective mode and only displays the current worksheet.

If a worksheet contains only three files (look ahead to Figure 1-18), then Perspective mode doesn't change when you move between worksheets. That is, if you move to worksheet C, worksheet C is still the last worksheet displayed. When a file contains four or more worksheets, however, 1-2-3 for Windows usually makes the current worksheet the first worksheet displayed. For instance, if a worksheet contains worksheets A through E, and you move to worksheet C, Perspective mode will show worksheet C first, then worksheet D, and worksheet E in the back. Moving between worksheets is discussed later in this section.

▼ *Tip:*   To display noncontiguous worksheets in Perspective mode, hide the worksheets you don't want to see (see Chapter 5). For example, imagine a file that contains worksheets A through E. If you hide worksheets B and D, Perspective mode will display worksheets A, C, and E.

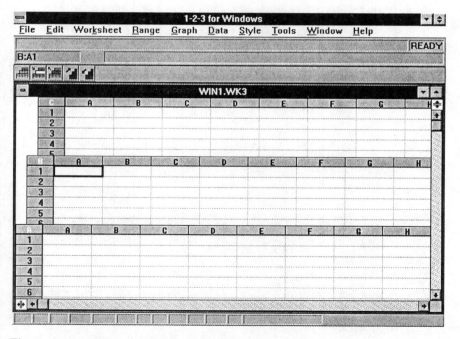

Figure 1-18 Adding worksheets to a file

To return to a single-worksheet (2-D) display, use the Windows Split command and turn on the Clear option. 1-2-3 for Windows will then display only the worksheet in which the cell pointer is positioned.

Inserting Worksheets

Note: You don't have to be in Perspective mode to insert worksheets into a file.

You can add as many as 255 additional worksheets to a file. For instance, to add two more worksheets to Figure 1-17, first position the cell pointer in the worksheet you want to insert worksheets before or after. In Figure 1-17, the cell pointer is located in cell A:A2. Select the Worksheet Insert command and specify the settings shown in Figure 1-17—turn on Sheets, accept the After option, then enter **2** in the Range text box. When you press ENTER or select OK, you can see in Figure 1-18 that 1-2-3 for Windows adds two more worksheets, called worksheets B and C, behind worksheet A. In addition, the cell pointer is now located in the same cell, A1, but in worksheet B.

▼ *Tip:*   Each time you select 📇 , 1-2-3 for Windows adds a new worksheet be-hind the worksheet the cell pointer is located in.

If you had turned on the Before option in the Worksheet Insert dialog box, 1-2-3 for Windows would have added two worksheets before worksheet A. Then the existing worksheet A would become worksheet C.

How Inserted Worksheets Affect Formulas

When you insert a worksheet between existing worksheets, 1-2-3 for Windows automatically adjusts any affected formulas. For example, imagine a file contains two worksheets, A and B. Cell A1 in worksheet A contains the formula +B:A1, referring to cell A1 in worksheet B. Cell B1 in worksheet A contains the formula @SUM(A:A2..B:A2), which sums the contents in cells A:A2 and B:A2.

Note: Ranges, formulas, and using ranges in formulas are discussed in Chapter 2.

If you insert a worksheet after worksheet A, 1-2-3 inserts the blank worksheet B, and changes the existing worksheet B to worksheet C. The formula in cell A1 of worksheet A is automatically converted to +C:A1. But the formula in cell B1 of worksheet A is converted to @SUM(A:A2..C:A2) so that it now sums the contents of cells A:A2, B:A2, and C:A2.

MOVING BETWEEN WORKSHEETS

In 1-2-3 for Windows, you can use the mouse, keyboard, and even SmartIcons to move between worksheets in a file. Actually, you'll probably find using the mouse to move between worksheets the least efficient method. One reason is that the file must be in Perspective mode for you to do so. (See "Creating a 3-D Perspective of a Worksheet File," earlier.) Only then can you move between worksheets by selecting a cell in the worksheet you want to move to.

> ▼ *Tip:*   When you scroll the screen using the Horizontal or Vertical scroll bars, 1-2-3 for Windows synchronizes the scrolling in all worksheets in the window. For example, if you click on the bottom arrow in the Vertical scroll bar, 1-2-3 scrolls all the worksheets down one row. To scroll worksheets independently of each other, see Chapter 3.

In fact, you'll most likely find using the keyboard or SmartIcons the easiest way to go in many instances. One reason is that even if you're not in Perspective mode, you can still use the key sequences and SmartIcons discussed in the following sections.

Moving to Cell A:A1

Regardless of which worksheet the cell pointer is located in, pressing CTRL+HOME returns you to cell A:A1. If the cell pointer is located in cell C:E4 of Figure 1-18, for instance, pressing CTRL+HOME will move the cell pointer to cell A1 in worksheet A.

Moving to the Last Active Cell in the Worksheet File

When you press END followed by CTRL+HOME, 1-2-3 for Windows takes you to the last cell in the last worksheet that contains data. To see this, look at Figure 1-19, which contains historical employee data. Actually, two other blank worksheets have also been inserted in this file—worksheets D and E. (You can see them by looking ahead to Figure 1-20.) Notice that the cell pointer is located in cell A:E3. If you press END, then CTRL+HOME, 1-2-3 for Windows will move the cell pointer to cell C:D5. That's because C:D5 is the last cell in the worksheet file that contains data.

Moving to Another Worksheet

Each time you press CTRL+PGUP, 1-2-3 for Windows moves the cell pointer forward one worksheet (from A to B, for instance). By contrast, each time you press CTRL+PGDN, 1-2-3 moves the cell backward one worksheet (from C to B, perhaps). When you do so, 1-2-3 for Windows remembers the cell pointer's previous position in each worksheet.

For instance, notice that the cell pointer is located in cell A:E3 in Figure 1-19. Press CTRL+PGUP once, and the cell pointer moves to B:E3; press CTRL+PGUP again and the cell pointer comes to rest in C:E3.

> ▼ *Tip:*   and produce the same result as CTRL+PGUP and CTRL+PGDN.

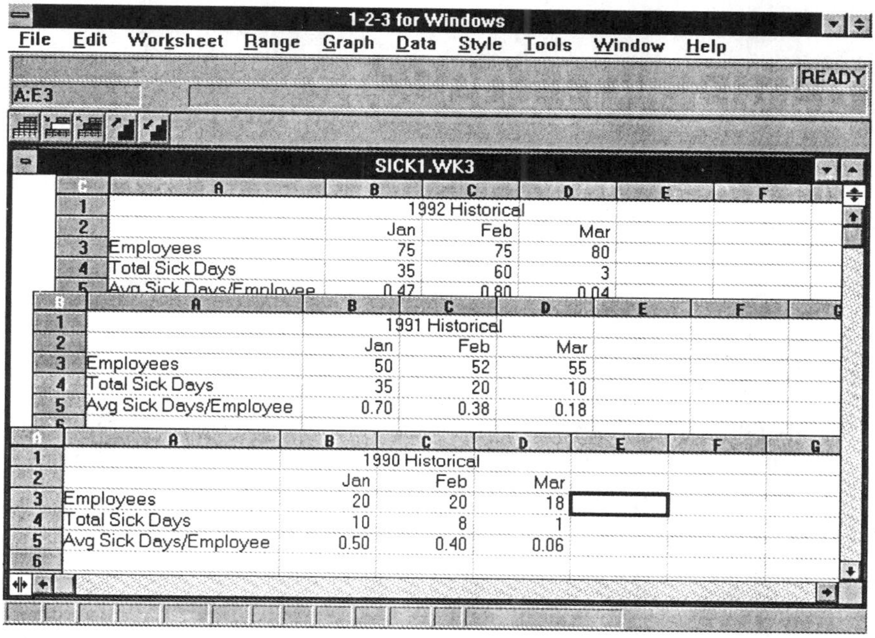

Figure 1-19 A portion of a worksheet containing five worksheets A through E

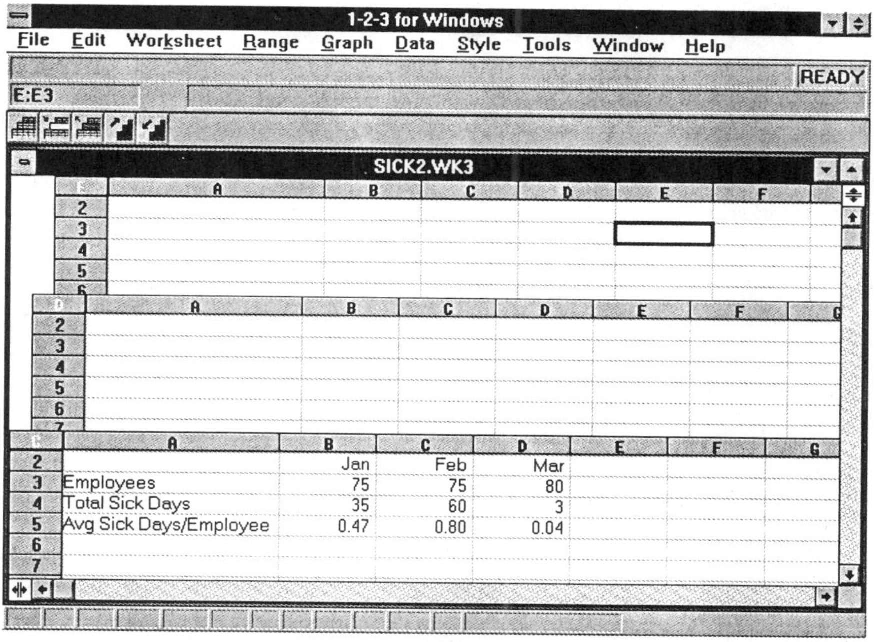

Figure 1-20 Pressing END CTRL+PGUP

When you move between worksheets, 1-2-3 may display different worksheets. (See "Creating a 3-D Perspective of a Worksheet File.") Figure 1-19 actually includes two more blank worksheets, D and E. Thus, when you move to worksheet B, it becomes the front worksheet, with worksheets C and D displayed behind it. Likewise, when you move to worksheet C, worksheets C, D, and E are displayed.

Moving to the Last or First Filled Cell in a File

1-2-3 for Windows has two additional key sequences—END CTRL+PGUP and END CTRL+PGDN—that you can use to move backwards and forwards through 3-D space. The concept is essentially the same as when you press END followed by one of the arrow keys in 2-D space. These key sequences will produce different results, depending on the beginning location of the cell pointer as well as the contents of the file.

To see this, let's return to Figure 1-19. Imagine that the cell pointer is located in cell A:B2, which contains the label "Jan." You can see that cells B2 in worksheets B and C also contain data. If you press END then CTRL+PGUP, 1-2-3 for Windows will move back through 3-D space to the last filled cell, C:B2. If you now press END followed by CTRL+PGDN, 1-2-3 for Windows will move forward through 3-D space to the last filled cell, and again returns you to cell A:B2.

Notice that the cell pointer in Figure 1-19 is actually located in cell A:E3, which is an empty cell. Moreover, cells E3 in worksheets B, C, D, and E are all empty. (Remember, Figure 1-19 also contains two empty worksheets not displayed, worksheets D and E.) If you press END CTRL+PGUP, you can see in Figure 1-20 that 1-2-3 moves the cell pointer back through 3-D space to the last empty cell—cell E:E3. Likewise, press END CTRL+PGUP, and you'll return to A:E3.

Deleting Worksheets

The procedure used to delete worksheets in a file is very similar to inserting worksheets. For example, to delete worksheet B in Figure 1-21, position the cell pointer in any cell in that worksheet, like cell B:A2. Next, select the Worksheet Delete command, and you'll see that B:A2..B:A2 is already displayed in the Range text box. When you turn on Sheet and then press ENTER or select OK, you'll get the result in Figure 1-22.

> ▼ *Tip:* Each time you select 🔲 , 1-2-3 for Windows deletes the worksheet the cell pointer is located in. The cell pointer then moves to the same cell in the preceding worksheet.

1-2-3 for Windows not only deletes worksheet B and all data in this worksheet, but moves up any existing worksheets. That is, if you compare Figures 1-21 and 1-22, you'll see that worksheet C has become worksheet B, and worksheet D has become worksheet C. In addition, 1-2-3 moves the cell pointer to the same cell, A2, but in worksheet A.

Note: When you delete a worksheet, any formulas that refer to data in this worksheet will return ERR. Immediately pressing ALT+BACKSPACE (Undo) will restore a deleted worksheet.

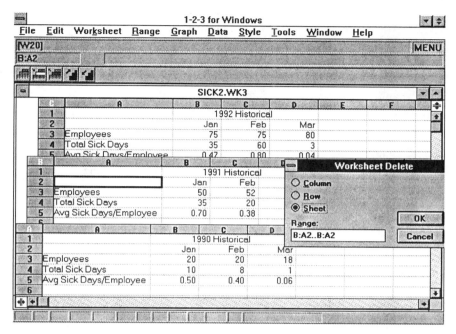

Figure 1-21   Deleting worksheet B

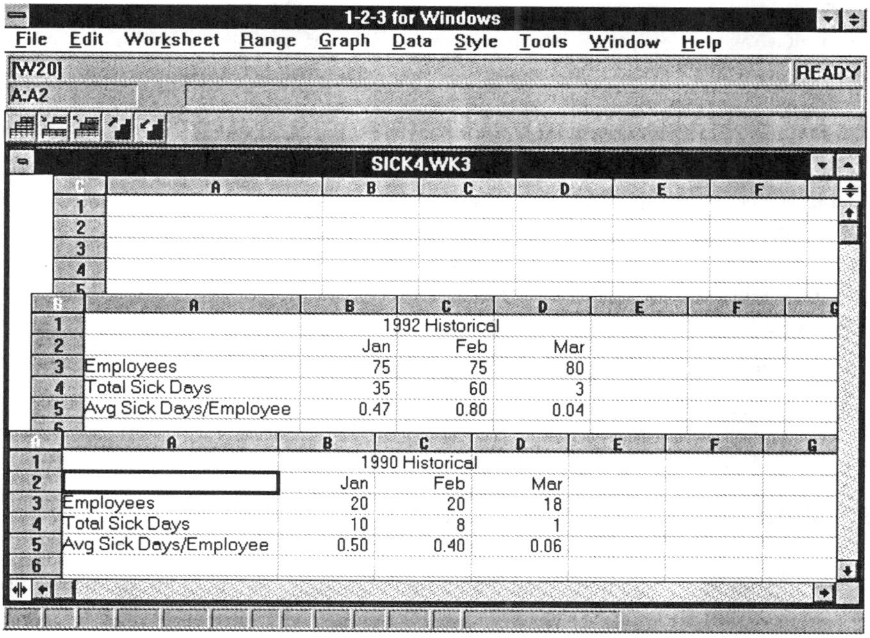

Figure 1-22   The result of deleting worksheet B

TABLE 1-8 Commands that Work in Group Mode

Worksheet Commands	Range Commands	Style Commands
Global Settings	Format	Font
Hide	Protect	Alignment
Unhide	Unprotect	Border
Insert Column or Row		Color
Delete Column or Row		Shading
Column Width		
Row Height		
Page Break		
Titles		

GROUP MODE

Group mode allows you to simultaneously assign formats and styles, or to insert and delete columns and rows in all the existing worksheets in a file. Table 1-8 shows the commands that work in Group mode.

To turn on Group mode, select the Worksheet Global Settings command and then turn on the Group mode option. When you press ENTER or select OK, 1-2-3 for Windows will display the GROUP indicator in the status line, just as in Figure 1-23A.

Figure 1-23A shows how Group mode works. Here, the cell pointer is located in cell B2 of worksheet A. Next, the Style Font command is selected and the Bold option is turned on. (Fonts are discussed in Chapter 6.) Notice that only the selected cell, A:B2, is displayed in the Range text box. When you press ENTER or select OK, you'll get the results in Figure 1-23B. Because Group mode is on, 1-2-3 for Windows assigns a bold style to cell B2 in worksheets A, B, and C. So in Group mode, 1-2-3 actually evaluates a 2-D selection like A:B2 as the 3-D range A:B2..C:B2. (Ranges are discussed in Chapter 2.)

Note: To turn off Group mode, choose the Worksheet Global Settings command and turn off Group mode.

INSERTING COLUMNS AND ROWS

Frequently, after you've entered data in a worksheet, you'll need to make room for additional data. Although you can move data to make room (see Chapter 7), in many instances inserting columns or rows is more efficient.

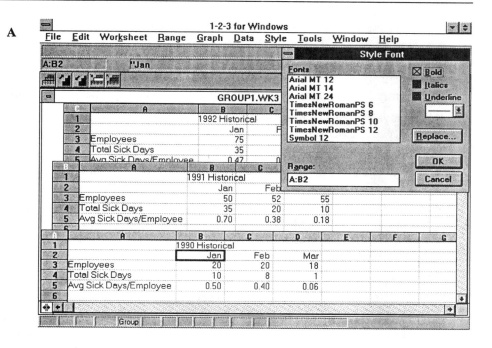

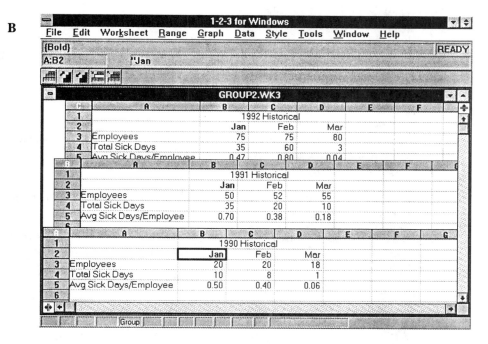

Figure 1-23 Using Group mode to assign a bold font to cell B2 in all worksheets

When you insert rows and columns, you should keep in mind the following:

- In a 1-2-3 database, inserting a row may create a blank record, while inserting a column can create a blank field. (See Chapter 11.)

- Inserting a row or column may create a blank space in a print range. (See Chapter 8.)

- If you've used cell addresses rather than range names in macros, you'll have to update the macros. Moreover, inserting a blank row in the middle of a macro may cause the macro to end prematurely. (See Chapter 14.)

- You can't insert rows or columns in a worksheet when it is globally protected. (See Chapter 5.)

- Inserted columns and rows are formatted using the Worksheet Global Settings defaults (usually, a column width of 9, left label alignment, and a General numeric format), the default font set by the Style Font command, and the default row height determined by this font. (See Chapters 5 and 6.)

Inserting Columns in One Worksheet

The worksheet in Figure 1-24A contains third and fourth quarter sales data in columns B and C, which is totaled in column D. Suppose that you now want to include the sales from the first and second quarters in this worksheet to the left of column B. Here's the easiest way to insert two columns:

1.   Move the cell pointer to any cell in the column immediately to the left of where you want the columns inserted. Since you want to insert columns to the left of column B, move to any cell in column B, such as cell B3.

2.   Preselect a range that indicates the number of columns you want to insert. Since you want to insert two columns, preselect cells B3 and C3. To do this using the mouse, select cell B3 and then drag the pointer so that B3 and C3 are outlined. To select these cells using the keyboard, press F4 to anchor cell B2, press → so that B3 and C3 are outlined and A:B3..A:C3 is displayed in the contents box, and then press ENTER to confirm.

Note: Preselecting ranges and specifying them after choosing a command are discussed in Chapter 2.

3.   Select the Worksheet Insert command. You'll see the dialog box in Figure 1-24A. Make sure that Column is turned on and A:B3..A:C3 is displayed in the Range text box.

4.   Press ENTER or select OK to confirm these settings and complete the command.

Figure 1-24B shows how 1-2-3 for Windows inserts two empty columns to the left of column B. In the process, column B in Figure 1-24A now becomes column D in Figure 1-24B, column C becomes column E, and so on. In addition, inserted column B and C

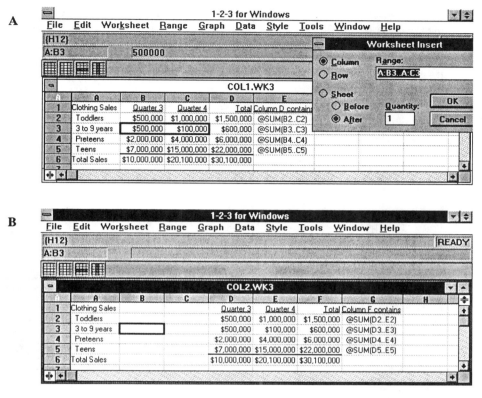

Figure 1-24 Inserting two columns to the right of column A

use the Worksheet Global Settings defaults for column width, label alignment, numeric format, and so on; you may want to assign new formats to them (see Chapters 5 and 6).

▼ *Tip:*   The 🖽 icon inserts the number of columns indicated in a preselected range. If you preselect the range B3..C3 in Figure 1-24A, for instance, then select this icon, 1-2-3 for Windows will insert two columns to the left of column B, just as in Figure 1-24B. To customize your icon palette, see Appendix A.

Inserting Rows

You insert rows much in the same way you insert columns. For example, consider Figure 1-25A, which depicts the same worksheet as Figure 1-24A. To insert two rows above row 2, first move the cell pointer to any cell in row 2, cell B2 perhaps. Next, preselect a range indicating the number of rows you want to insert. So to insert two rows, preselect the range B2..B3.

Now when you choose the Worksheet Insert command, the range A:B2..A:B3 will already be entered for you in the Range text box, just as in Figure 1-25A. Simply turn on Row, and then press ENTER or select OK. As Figure 1-25B shows, 1-2-3 for Windows inserts two rows above the old row 2, which now becomes row 4. Because the inserted rows 2 and 3 use the Worksheet Global Settings defaults for column width, label alignment, and numeric format, as well as the default font assigned to the worksheet, you may want to assign other formats and styles to them (see Chapters 5 and 6).

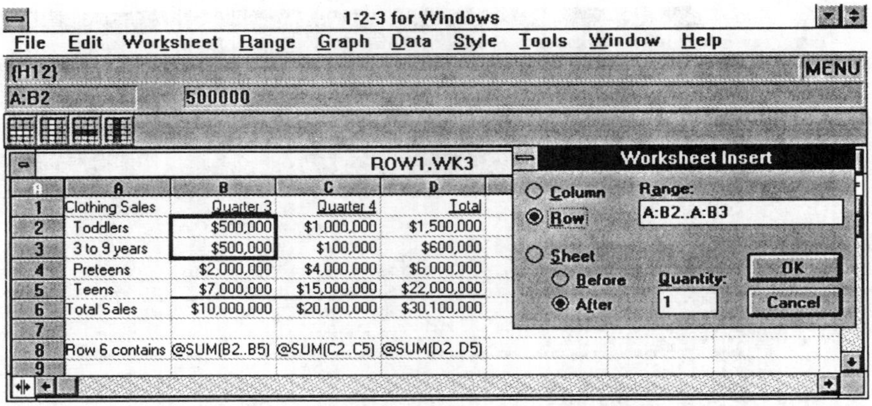

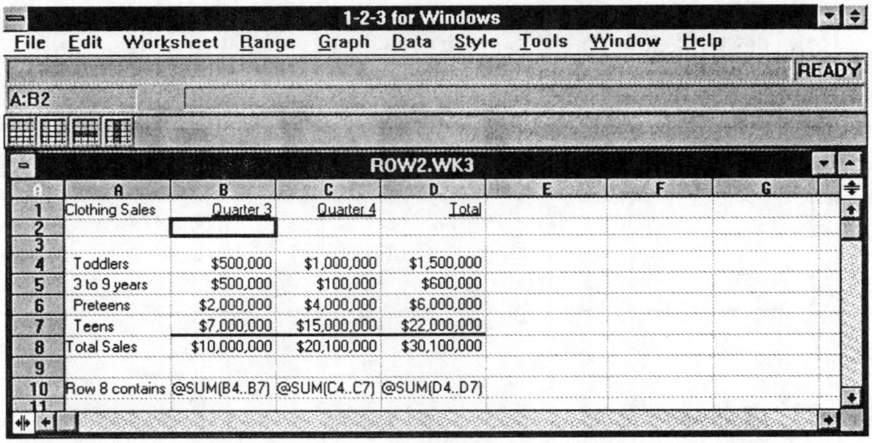

Figure 1-25 Inserting two rows above row 2

> ▼ *Tip:*   The ▦ icon inserts the number of rows indicated in a preselected range.
> If you preselect the range B2..B3 in Figure 1-25A, for example, and then
> select this icon, 1-2-3 for Windows will insert two rows above row 2,
> just as in Figure 1-25B. To customize your icon palette, see Appendix A.

Inserting Columns and Rows in Multiple Worksheets

When you want to insert the same columns or rows in multiple existing worksheets, the easiest way to do so is to use Group mode. For example, this is the easiest way to simultaneously insert a column to the left of column E in worksheets A, B, and C of Figure 1-26A:

1. Choose the Worksheet Global Settings command and turn on Group mode. When you press ENTER or select OK, you'll see the GROUP mode indicator in the status line as in Figure 1-26A.

2. Preselect a range indicating the number of columns you want to insert. Because you want to insert one column to the left of column E, use either the mouse or the keyboard to move to any cell in column E, such as E2 in worksheet A. (Because Group mode is on, you only need to select this cell in one worksheet.)

3. Choose the Worksheet Insert Column and you'll see the dialog box in Figure 1-26A. Make sure that Column is turned on and A:E2..A:E2 is displayed in the Range text box. Press ENTER or select OK to confirm these settings and complete the command.

You can see the results in Figure 1-26B. Although you only selected cell E2 in worksheet A, Group mode tells 1-2-3 for Windows to insert the same column in all existing worksheets. So 1-2-3 inserts a blank column E in worksheets A, B, and C, and the old column E becomes column F.

How Inserted Columns and Rows Affect Formulas

As you probably know, a range is a rectangular block of continuous cells which is defined by the two cell addresses representing its upper-left and lower-right corners. For example, the range reference A1..B2 represents cells A1, A2, B1, and B2. (Ranges and using ranges in formulas are discussed in Chapter 2.)

When you insert columns and/or rows in the middle of a range reference, 1-2-3 for Windows automatically expands the range reference to include the inserted rows or columns. On the other hand, if the inserted rows or columns aren't in the middle of a range reference, the range reference isn't expanded. In both cases, 1-2-3 for Windows adjusts a formula range reference to account for its new location in the worksheet after the columns or rows are inserted.

A

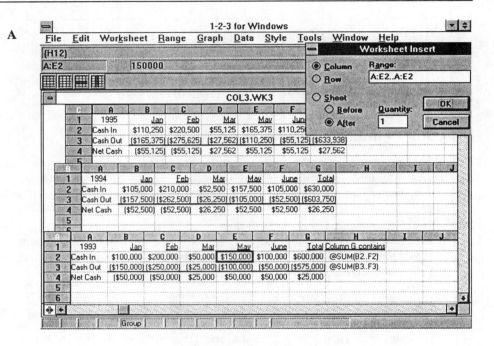

B

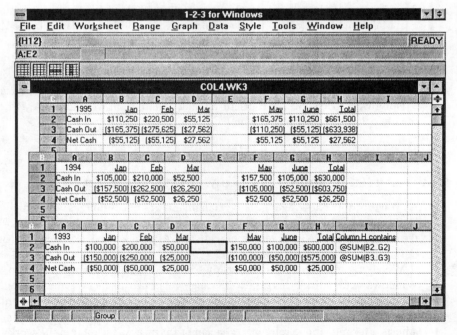

Figure 1-26 Using Group mode to insert the same column in multiple worksheets

To see this, compare Figures 1-24A and 1-24B. In Figure 1-24A, the total $1,500,000 Toddler sales in cell D2 is calculated using the formula @SUM(B2..C2). Because two columns are inserted to the left of column B in Figure 1-24B, column B becomes column D, column C becomes column E, and column D becomes column F. So 1-2-3 for Windows adjusts this formula to @SUM(D2..E2). Note however, that the inserted columns aren't incorporated into this range reference. If you enter a value in cell B2 of Figure 1-24B, this value won't be included in the Total Toddler Sales computed in cell F2.

1-2-3 for Windows does adjust the range references in formulas when the inserted rows or columns are in the middle of a referenced range. In cell A:G2 of Figure 1-26A, for example, 1993 Total Cash In of $600,000 is originally calculated as @SUM(B2..F2). Because a column is inserted in the middle of this range reference in Figure 1-26B, the inserted column (column E) is incorporated into this range reference. If you enter a value in cell A:E2 of Figure 1-26B, for instance, the formula in cell A:H2, @SUM(B2..G2), will use this value in the Total Cash In computation.

Note: 1-2-3 for Windows adjusts range names in the same manner. (See Chapter 2.)

DELETING COLUMNS AND ROWS

The way you delete columns or rows is very similar to the way you insert them. For example, suppose Figure 1-27A contains your historical personal financial statement. Unluckily, the IRS has disallowed your SEP (Self-Employed Pension) Plan. To delete this asset altogether from the worksheet, you decide to delete row 5. Simply preselect any cell in row 5, such as cell F5. When you choose the Worksheet Delete command, A:F5..A:F5 is already displayed for you in the Range text box. Now turn on Row, then press ENTER or select OK. As Figure 1-27B shows, 1-2-3 for Windows deletes row 5, including the data in this row. It also moves the other rows up; for example, row 6 becomes row 5, row 7 becomes row 6, and so on.

> ▼ *Tip:*   ⊞ deletes the rows, and ⊞ deletes the columns in a preselected range. To customize your icon palette, see Appendix A.

You can also use Group mode to simultaneously delete the same rows or columns in all existing worksheets in a file. For example, imagine that Figure 1-27A actually contains three worksheets, A, B, and C. If Group mode is on (see "Group Mode," earlier), and you preselect cell A:F5, choose the Worksheet Delete command, and then turn on Row, 1-2-3 for Windows will delete row 5 in worksheets A, B, and C.

> ▼ *Tip:*   Immediately pressing ALT+BACKSPACE (Undo) will restore deleted rows or columns, the data in these rows or columns, and the formulas referencing this data. Undo is discussed later in this chapter.

When you delete rows and columns, you should keep in mind that:

- You can't delete rows or columns in a worksheet when it is globally protected. (See Chapter 5.)

- Deleting a row that contains a macro can seriously affect the operation of the macro. (See Chapter 14.)

- When deleting columns or rows will cause the loss of valuable data or affect macros, rearrange a worksheet by moving data. (See Chapter 7.)

How Deleted Columns and Rows Affect Formulas

Regardless of whether deleted columns or rows are in the middle of or define a referenced range, 1-2-3 for Windows automatically adjusts the range reference for you. You can see this by comparing the formula that computes 1992 Total Assets in Figures 1-27A and B. In cell F6 of Figure 1-27A, Total Assets is calculated using the formula @SUM(F2..F5). After row 5 is deleted in Figure 1-27B, this formula is adjusted to @SUM(F2..F4). So, even though you deleted cell F5, the lower-right cell that originally defined this range reference, 1-2-3 for Windows automatically adjusted this formula. (Ranges, and using ranges in formulas are discussed in Chapter 2.)

Note: In earlier releases, a deleted column or row that contained a cell defining a formula range reference caused the formula to return ERR. That is, if you deleted row 5 in Figure 1-27A, the formula @SUM(F2..F5) would have become @SUM(ERR) and would have returned ERR.

JUMPING TO CELLS

To speed up navigation, 1-2-3 for Windows provides the GOTO (F5) key that lets you jump to a specific cell within a worksheet file. You can also use it to move between open worksheet files (See Chapter 3).

When you press GOTO (F5) or select the Range Go To command, 1-2-3 for Windows presents the dialog box in Figure 1-28A, and displays the address of the current selection in the Range box. As you can see, the current selection is A:A1. To jump to a specific cell or named range, you can type any of the following in the Range(s) text box and press ENTER:

- An *abbreviated cell address, such as J32*: 1-2-3 for Windows takes you directly to cell J32 in the current (same) worksheet, as shown in Figure 1-28B. Notice that when you use GOTO and the cell isn't in view, 1-2-3 places the cell in the upper-left corner of the window and locates the cell pointer in that cell. When the cell is already in view, 1-2-3 places the cell pointer in the cell without shifting the window contents.

- A *full cell address, such as D:A10*: 1-2-3 for Windows takes you directly to worksheet D, cell A10, of the current file.

- A *range name*: 1-2-3 takes you to the top left cell in the range. You can also select from among the range names that appear in the list box. (Naming ranges is discussed in Chapter 2.)

> ▼ *Tip:*   You can also select ▣ to access the Range Go To dialog box in Figure 1-28A. See Appendix A to customize your icon palette.

A

	A	B	C	D	E	F	
1		1988	1989	1990	1991	1992	Cell in column F contains
2	Cash	$5,000	$5,000	$25,000	$40,000	$20,000	
3	Securities	$100,000	$50,000	$60,000	$65,000	$80,000	
4	House	$250,000	$275,000	$325,000	$350,000	$280,000	
5	SEP Plan	$30,000	$30,000	$50,000	$60,000	$70,000	
6	Total Assets	$385,000	$360,000	$460,000	$515,000	$450,000	@SUM(F2..F5)
7							
8	Credit Cards	$2,000	$7,000	$4,000	$8,000	$14,000	
9	Taxes	$10,000	$0	$2,000	$3,000	$3,000	
10	Student Loans	$25,000	$22,000	$18,000	$13,000	$8,000	
11	Mortgage	$200,000	$198,000	$194,000	$188,000	$180,000	
12	Total Liabilities	$237,000	$227,000	$218,000	$212,000	$205,000	@SUM(F8..F11)
13							
14	Net Worth	$148,000	$133,000	$242,000	$303,000	$245,000	+F6-F12

Worksheet Delete: ○ Column ◉ Row ○ Sheet   Range: A:F5..A:F5   [OK] [Cancel]

{H11}   A:F5   70000   DELETE1.WK3

B

	A	B	C	D	E	F	G	H	I	J	
1		1988	1989	1990	1991	1992	Cell in column F contains				
2	Cash	$5,000	$5,000	$25,000	$40,000	$20,000					
3	Securities	$100,000	$50,000	$60,000	$65,000	$80,000					
4	House	$250,000	$275,000	$325,000	$350,000	$280,000					
5	Total Assets	$355,000	$330,000	$410,000	$455,000	$380,000	@SUM(F2..F4)				
6											
7	Credit Cards	$2,000	$7,000	$4,000	$8,000	$14,000					
8	Taxes	$10,000	$0	$2,000	$3,000	$3,000					
9	Student Loans	$25,000	$22,000	$18,000	$13,000	$8,000					
10	Mortgage	$200,000	$198,000	$194,000	$188,000	$180,000					
11	Total Liabilities	$237,000	$227,000	$218,000	$212,000	$205,000	@SUM(F7..F10)				
12											
13	Net Worth	$118,000	$103,000	$192,000	$243,000	$175,000	+F5-F11				
14											

{H11 T}   A:F5   @SUM(F2..F4)   READY   DELETE2.WK3

File Edit Worksheet Range Graph Data Style Tools Window Help

Figure 1-27 Deleting row 5

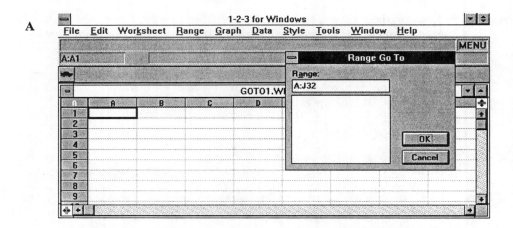

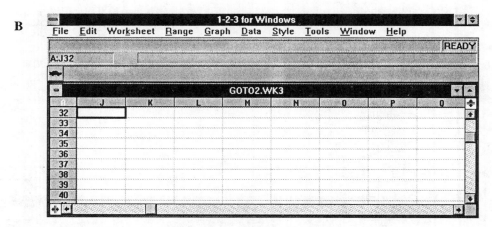

Figure 1-28   Using F5 (GOTO) to move to cell J32

USING UNDO

1-2-3 for Windows has an undo feature that allows you to reverse the effect of the last command or action that either changed worksheet data or worksheet settings. For example, here are just some of the actions Undo can reverse or restore:

- Data you've overwritten or deleted during a copy, move, or delete operation, including any formulas that referred to this data.
- Deleted columns or rows, including the data in these columns or rows, and any formulas that referred to this data.

- The worksheet's previous status after you've run a macro, regardless of the number of changes the macro made.

- The File Close command, even if you chose No and didn't save the file. 1-2-3 for Windows will restore the latest version.

- A worksheet deleted using the Classic menu's /Worksheet Erase command.

Turning Undo On

When you first start 1-2-3 for Windows, Undo is off unless you chose to turn it on when you installed 1-2-3. If you didn't turn Undo on during installation, you can turn it on using the Tools User Setup Enable Edit Undo command. To save the Undo setting for all future 1-2-3 sessions, select Update in the Tools User Setup dialog box.

▼ *Tip:*   Turn Undo off to reclaim additional memory for your work.

Activating Undo

Once Undo is turned on, access it by selecting the Edit Undo command or by pressing ALT+BACKSPACE—the shortcut for the Edit Undo command. This applies to all cell entries, commands, and changes to settings. When Undo is enabled, 1-2-3 creates an undo history—a temporary backup copy of all data and settings affected by the latest activity. You can then use it to reverse the last activity that changed data or settings in the worksheet.

▼ *Tip:*   ⏎ is also a shortcut for the Edit Undo command.

For example, suppose you place a formula in a cell and then press ALT+BACKSPACE. 1-2-3 for Windows removes the formula from the cell and returns the worksheet to the way it was before you entered the formula.

Another instance might be if you use the Worksheet Delete command to delete rows 8 through 11 in Figure 1-29A. You can see the result in Figure 1-29B. Since the formulas in row 8 (originally row 12 in Figure 1-29A) used to refer to the data in the deleted rows, they now return ERR. The formulas in row 10 also return ERR because they refer to row 8. If you immediately select Edit Undo or press ALT+BACKSPACE, Figure 1-29C shows how 1-2-3 for Windows restores rows 8 through 12, the data in these rows, and the formulas that referred to these rows (see "Deleting Rows and Columns," earlier).

Note: If you try to select Undo while a dialog box is open, 1-2-3 for Windows beeps and disregards your action. If, after completing your work in the dialog box, you select Undo, 1-2-3 for Windows reverses all the settings you made in the dialog box.

Undo is not a toggle key. In other words, if you change your mind about what you just undid, you cannot select Undo again to reverse the effect.

A

1-2-3 for Wind...

File   Edit   Worksheet   Range   Graph   Data   St...

{H11}   MENU

A:B8   2000

Worksheet Delete

○ Column
● Row
○ Sheet

Range:
A:B8..A:B11

OK   Cancel

UNDO1.WK...

	A	B	C	D	E	F
1		1988	1989	1990	1991	1992 Cell in column F contains
2	Cash	$5,000	$5,000	$25,000	$40,000	$20,000
3	Securities	$100,000	$50,000	$60,000	$65,000	$80,000
4	House	$250,000	$275,000	$325,000	$350,000	$280,000
5	SEP Plan	$30,000	$30,000	$50,000	$60,000	$70,000
6	Total Assets	$385,000	$360,000	$460,000	$515,000	$450,000 @SUM(F2..F5)
7						
8	Credit Cards	$2,000	$7,000	$4,000	$8,000	$14,000
9	Taxes	$10,000	$0	$2,000	$3,000	$3,000
10	Student Loans	$25,000	$22,000	$18,000	$13,000	$8,000
11	Mortgage	$200,000	$198,000	$194,000	$188,000	$180,000
12	Total Liabilities	$237,000	$227,000	$218,000	$212,000	$205,000 @SUM(F8-F11)
13						
14	Net Worth	$148,000	$133,000	$242,000	$303,000	$245,000 +F6-F12
15						

B

1-2-3 for Windows

File   Edit   Worksheet   Range   Graph   Data   Style   Tools   Window   Help

{H11 T}   READY

A:B8   @SUM(ERR)

UNDO2.WK3

	A	B	C	D	E	F	G	H	I	J
1		1988	1989	1990	1991	1992	Cell in column F contains			
2	Cash	$5,000	$5,000	$25,000	$40,000	$20,000				
3	Securities	$100,000	$50,000	$60,000	$65,000	$80,000				
4	House	$250,000	$275,000	$325,000	$350,000	$280,000				
5	SEP Plan	$30,000	$30,000	$50,000	$60,000	$70,000				
6	Total Assets	$385,000	$360,000	$460,000	$515,000	$450,000	@SUM(F2..F5)			
7										
8	Total Liabilities	ERR	ERR	ERR	ERR	ERR	@SUM(ERR)			
9										
10	Net Worth	ERR	ERR	ERR	ERR	ERR	+F6-F8			
11										

Figure 1-29   Using Undo to restore deleted rows

You may get some unwelcome results if you use Undo after an activity that *doesn't* change worksheet data or settings in the worksheet. For example, imagine that you use Worksheet Delete to delete rows 8 through 12 in Figure 1-29A. Next you press F5 (GOTO) to move to cell F10. If you now press ALT+BACKSPACE, Undo will the reverse the Worksheet Delete operation because pressing F5 (GOTO) didn't change worksheet data or worksheet settings.

C

```
─ Reverse the effect of the last undoable command or action        ▼ ≑
 File  Edit  Worksheet  Range  Graph  Data  Style  Tools  Window  Help
[H11]  Undo            Alt+Bksp                                    MENU
A:B8   Cut             Shift+Del
       Copy            Ctrl+Ins
       Paste           Shift+Ins
       Clear           Del
       Clear Special...
       Paste Link                  UNDO3.WK3                        ▼ ▲
       Link Options...       D       E        F        G       H    I   J
  1                        1990     1991     1992  Cell in column F contains
  2                      $25,000  $40,000  $20,000
  3                      $60,000  $65,000  $80,000
       Find...
  4                      325,000 $350,000 $280,000
  5    Move Cells...     $50,000  $60,000  $70,000
  6    Quick Copy...    460,000 $515,000 $450,000  @SUM(F2..F5)
  7
  8  Credit Cards     $2,000   $7,000   $4,000   $8,000  $14,000
  9  Taxes           $10,000       $0   $2,000   $3,000   $3,000
 10  Student Loans   $25,000  $22,000  $18,000  $13,000   $8,000
 11  Mortgage       $200,000 $198,000 $194,000 $188,000 $180,000
 12  Total Liabilities $237,000 $227,000 $218,000 $212,000 $205,000  @SUM(F8..F11)
 13
 14  Net Worth      $148,000 $133,000 $242,000 $303,000 $245,000  +F6-F12
```

Figure 1-29 Using Undo to restore deleted rows *(continued)*

Likewise, the action Undo reverses when you press ESC or CTRL+BREAK to escape a macro or command will also depend on whether the command or macro changed worksheet data or settings. If the macro or command did change the worksheet, then Undo will reverse these changes. If the worksheet wasn't affected by the command or macro, then Undo will reverse the last command that did change worksheet data or settings.

Note: The Translate utility can be used to recover lost data or restore the worksheet after you've completed more than one action or command. In effect, you can use the Translate utility as a multilevel Undo. In the current release of 1-2-3 for Windows, however, you'll find that the Translate utility isn't always reliable. See Chapter 14.

Actions that 1-2-3 Cannot Undo

Although Undo in 1-2-3 for Windows is significantly more powerful than in any previous version of 1-2-3, there are still certain commands and actions that it cannot undo. These are:

- Navigation actions. For example, if you move the cell pointer or scroll the screen, 1-2-3 can't undo the action. This includes mouse movements.

- Selection of cells, ranges, or worksheets.

- Recalculating the worksheet by pressing CALC (F9) when recalculation is set to manual (see Chapter 2), or using File Administration Update Links (see Chapter 17).

- GOTO (F5) or Range Go To.

- PANE (F6).

- A change to the SmartIcon palette.

- Data stored in the Clipboard during an Edit command (see Chapter 7) and subsequently removed. For example, if you undo the Edit Cut command, the data moved to the Clipboard is restored to the worksheet. However, any data previously in the Clipboard isn't restored.

- File Print and File Printer Setup commands.

- Graph menu commands.

- Changes to files on disk. For example, if you attempt to undo a File Save command, the overwritten file saved on disk is not restored.

- New default settings of any command for which you can select Update. For instance, if you select the Window Display Options command, choose a new Cell contents color, select Update, and then select OK to return to the worksheet, Undo won't restore the previous Window Display Options default settings.

- Minimizing or maximizing a worksheet.

- Tools Macro Debug and Show Transcript commands.

- All commands that affect external files but don't affect the active worksheet file. These include, for example, the Data External Options commands and the File Administration Network Reserve command.

Note: If you open a second file, use Window Display Options to tile or cascade the two open files, and then press ALT+BACKSPACE, 1-2-3 for Windows will close the file you just opened. Undo doesn't reverse either Window Display Options Tile or Cascade. (See Chapter 3.)

SAVING AND RETRIEVING FILES

When you have completed your work in the current worksheet file, you must decide whether you want to save the file for future use. Because 1-2-3 for Windows doesn't automatically save the worksheet file for you, your changes are lost if you should close the worksheet window or quit 1-2-3 without saving them. This is a blessing when a worksheet file is a total loss and you never want to see the likes of it again. It's a disaster, though, if you inadvertently lose some important work.

As you've undoubtedly noticed, when you first start 1-2-3, it automatically assigns the name "Untitled" to the first worksheet window and displays the name in the title bar. If you then create a new file with the File New command, 1-2-3 assigns it the name FILE0001.WK3. The next new file is assigned the name FILE0002.WK3, and so on.

To save a file using its existing name, use the File Save command. 1-2-3 immediately writes the file to disk.

Figure 1-30 The File Save As dialog box

Note: When you save the contents of the "Untitled" window to disk, 1-2-3 automatically assigns it the next available default file name—for example, FILE0003.WK3.

Because 1-2-3's automatic filenames aren't very descriptive, you'll probably want to change them as you save your work. To change a filename while saving, select the File Save As command. 1-2-3 displays a dialog box like the one in Figure 1-30. You can then enter your own more descriptive filename in the File name text box and select OK.

To use the file again, select the File Open command to load the file into memory. Chapter 3, "Managing Windows," describes how to work with multiple files in memory, and Chapter 4, "Managing Files," discusses all the File commands in detail.

Closing a Window

Suppose you've completed work on a worksheet file, and you now want to close its window. The available methods are:

- Press CTRL+F4.

- Double-click on the window control menu box in the upper-left corner of the window.

- Choose Close from the window control menu.

- Choose File Close from the menu bar.

Whichever method you use, if you've made any changes to the file and haven't yet saved them, 1-2-3 displays the message box in Figure 1-31. Select Yes if you want to save the file before closing; 1-2-3 displays the File Save As dialog box shown in Figure 1-30. Select No if you want to close the window without saving the file. Finally, select Cancel if you want to cancel the command and return to READY mode.

Although closing a worksheet window clears its associated file from memory, it does not remove the file from disk. For that, you'll need to use Windows File Manager or the 1-2-3 Classic /File Erase command. (See Chapter 4.)

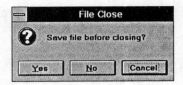

Figure 1-31 The File Close message box

Note: You can restore a window you've closed by immediately pressing ALT+BACKSPACE to trigger undo.

SWITCHING TO ANOTHER WINDOWS APPLICATION

Rather than quit 1-2-3 for Windows altogether, you may simply want to leave 1-2-3 running but move to another Windows application. Here are the ways to switch away from 1-2-3:

- Press ALT+ESC to access the next application.
- Press CTRL+ESC to access the Task List.
- Select Switch To from 1-2-3's window control menu to access the Task List.

Because these are the standard methods for all Windows applications, you can also use them to return to 1-2-3.

 Tip: Many experienced Windows users prefer to use ALT+TAB to switch between applications. Unfortunately, 1-2-3 for Windows occasionally has
trouble recognizing ALT+TAB if you press the sequence too quickly.
You'll have better luck with ALT+TAB if you press the sequence firmly.

QUITTING 1-2-3 FOR WINDOWS

To quit 1-2-3 for Windows and close all open windows, select File Exit. When you select this command, 1-2-3 presents the message box in Figure 1-32. Selecting Cancel returns you to 1-2-3. If you select Yes, 1-2-3 checks to see if you have made any changes to the files in memory and saves them if necessary. If you want to leave 1-2-3 without saving any files, select No. Be aware, however, that if you select No, all the changes in any unsaved files will be lost, and you will not get a chance to reconsider.

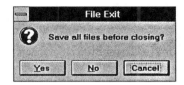

Figure 1-32 The File Exit message box

Here are some other ways to quit 1-2-3 for Windows:

- Press ALT+F4.
- Double-click on 1-2-3's window control menu box.
- Select Close from 1-2-3's window control menu.

2

Working with Data

The ways in which you enter, edit, select, name, and search data in 1-2-3 for Windows have been considerably updated from previous releases. In fact, experienced 1-2-3 users will find that there are new, more efficient ways to perform many of these basic tasks. As just one example, preselecting a range before you invoke a command is usually the most efficient way to specify a range.

1-2-3 for Windows also includes methods you can use to handle data in multiple worksheets and to take advantage of the mouse. For example, when you assign formatting and styles, you'll find that Group mode allows you to simultaneously select the same range in multiple worksheets. And in many cases, using the mouse is now the easiest way to select a 2-D range.

ENTERING DATA

1-2-3 for Windows classifies entries as either values or labels. Values are number and formula entries, while labels are text entries. 1-2-3 determines the type of cell entry you are making by the first character you type. If the first character you type is a number, 1-2-3 assumes you're entering a number; if the first character is a letter or blank cell, it assumes you're entering a label. 1-2-3 changes the mode indicator to VALUE or LABEL to show the type of entry you are making.

For example, suppose you want to enter the value 123 in cell A1. First position the cell pointer in A1, then type **123**. As you can see in Figure 2-1A, 123 appears in the contents box and the VALUE indicator is displayed in the upper-right corner. When you press

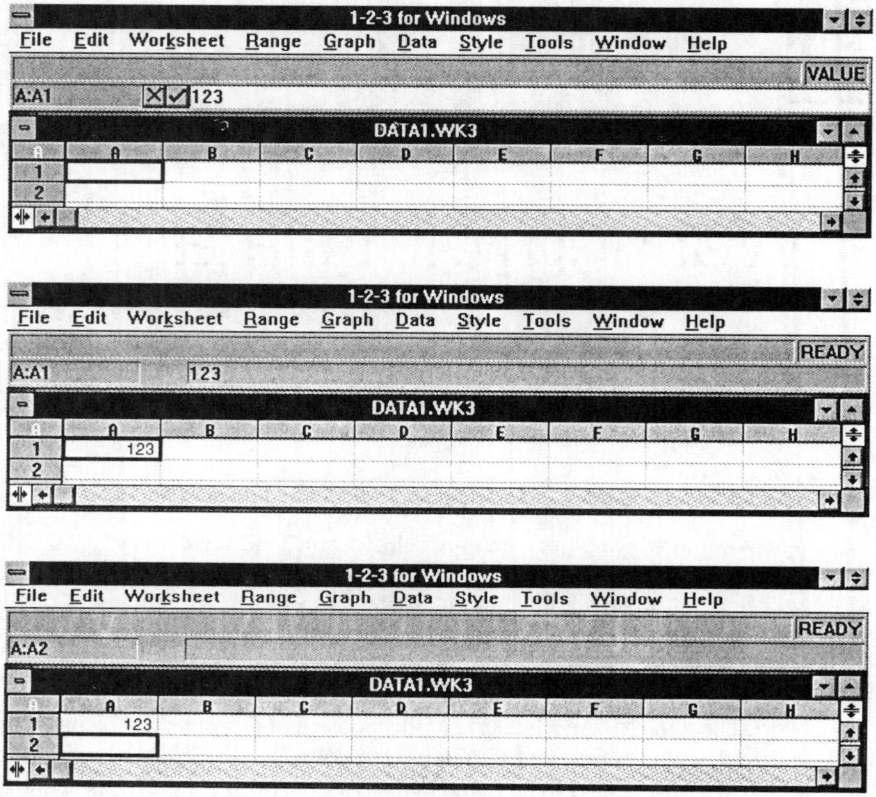

Figure 2-1 Entering Data

ENTER, you can see in Figure 2-1B that 1-2-3 for Windows places this entry in cell A1 and returns to READY mode.

Note: Sometimes you'll need to enter a number, such as the zip code 08540, as a label rather than a value. See "Values," later in this chapter for the reasons this is necessary.

Confirming an Entry

Confirming an entry transfers it from the input line to the current cell. There are different ways to confirm an entry after you've finished typing it, depending on where you want the cell pointer to end up afterward.

For example, pressing ENTER will place the entry in the current cell and leave the cell pointer in this cell, just as in Figure 2-1B. So will clicking on the Confirm (✔) button 1-2-3 displays in the input line (see Figure 2-1A) whenever you begin to type an entry.

You can also confirm an entry and move the cell pointer to another location all in one step. For example, suppose you want to enter a column of numbers, moving downward as you go. Figure 2-1C shows what happens when you type **123** in cell A1 and then press ↓—1-2-3 enters 123 in A1, then moves the cell pointer to B1. Actually, any of the movement keys will confirm a cell entry and move the cell pointer accordingly, including ↓, ↑, →, ←, PGUP, PGDN, HOME, END, CTRL+PGUP, and CTRL+PGDN.

Note: If you make a mistake when entering data in a cell, such as trying to enter 123W (which combines a numeric value with a label) as a value, 1-2-3 won't let you confirm the entry. Instead, 1-2-3 for Windows puts you in EDIT mode. In this case, it then places the cursor at the end of the entry. Making changes in EDIT mode is discussed in detail under "Editing Cell Entries" later in this chapter.

Changing Cell Entries Before Confirming Them

Suppose you start to make a cell entry and then decide that you want to change it before confirming it. You can:

- Cancel the entire entry and return to the worksheet in READY mode by pressing ESC or selecting the Cancel (X) button in the input line (see Figure 2-1A).

- Delete the character to the left of the cursor by pressing BACKSPACE.

- Delete part of the entry by using the mouse to highlight the text to be deleted, then pressing DEL. (You can also press SHIFT+← repeatedly to highlight everything to the left of the cursor, and Shift+→ to highlight everything to the right.)

- Access EDIT mode by pressing F2 (see "Editing Cell Entries," later).

- Insert data within the entry by using the mouse to click on this point.

Labels

A *label* is a text entry no longer than 512 characters. In Figure 2-2A for example, the label "Sales—Year Ending 1993" is being entered in cell A1.

When you begin a cell entry with a letter or a blank space, 1-2-3 for Windows assumes you are entering a label. Because this entry begins with "S", the LABEL indicator is displayed in the upper-right corner of Figure 2-2A. When you press ENTER, 1-2-3 places this entry in cell A1 and returns to READY mode. Notice in the contents box of Figure 2-2B that 1-2-3 automatically includes ', a left label prefix, at the front of this entry.

Label Prefixes and Alignment

All labels begin with a *label prefix*, which determines how text is aligned in a cell. When you begin a cell entry with a letter or a blank space, as in Figure 2-2A, 1-2-3 assumes

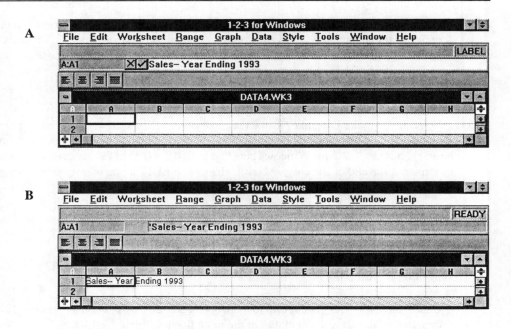

Figure 2-2   Entering a label

you're entering a label and automatically supplies the default label prefix, typically ' for left alignment. (To change the label prefix 1-2-3 for Windows uses, see "Changing the Label Alignment for an Entire Worksheet," later.)

1-2-3 for Windows, however, provides other label prefixes shown in Table 2-1 to align text. Figure 2-3 shows how each of these label prefixes affect the label Gross Profit. (To check the label prefix of a label, move the cell pointer to that cell and look at the special character that precedes the text in the contents box.)

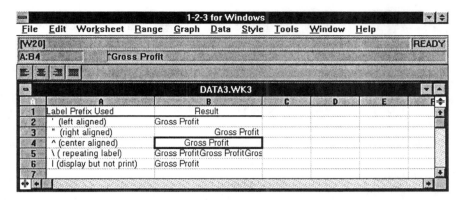

Figure 2-3   Label prefixes and their affect on alignment

Entering one of the label prefixes in Table 2-1 at the beginning of an entry tells 1-2-3 that you are entering a label as well as the alignment you want to use. For instance, entering ^**Sales** in a cell tells 1-2-3 to center align this label. In fact, you must enter a label prefix first when you begin a text entry with a number or a numeric symbol (see "Values" later). Otherwise, 1-2-3 assumes you've made an error and won't allow you to confirm the entry.

For example, suppose you type **12/90 Sales** in cell A1 and press ENTER. Because you started the entry with a number, 1-2-3 assumes you're trying to enter a value. Instead of letting you confirm the entry, 1-2-3 changes to EDIT mode. To fix this entry, press HOME (or click just before the "1") to move to the start of the entry (see "Editing Cell Entries" later). Next, insert a label prefix like ' in front of the first character. When you press ENTER, 1-2-3 stores this entry as **'12/90 Sales** in the contents box and displays the left-aligned label **12/90 Sales**.

TABLE 2-1   Label Prefixes

Character Description

'	Aligns a label with the left edge of a cell (default).
"	Aligns a label with the right edge of a cell.
^	Centers a label in a cell.
\	Repeats characters in a label to fill the entire cell.
|	Displays a label on screen but doesn't print it.

> ▼ **Tip:** You can also use the Range Format Label command (see Chapter 5) to prespecify that an entry will be a label. Then you don't have to include a label prefix when you type the entry.

Some other instances in which you'll have to enter a label prefix are telephone numbers, social security numbers, and street addresses. For example, to enter the social security number "272-45-7865" in the current cell, type a label prefix (') before entering the numbers. Otherwise, 1-2-3 assumes that you're entering a numeric formula and will return a negative number in the cell.

> ▼ **Tip:** After you've entered a label in a cell, you can change its alignment using the ▣ , ▣ , ▣ , and ▣ icons shown in Figure 2-3. These are short-cuts for the Style Alignment command discussed in Chapter 6.

Changing the Label Alignment for an Entire Worksheet

1-2-3 for Windows assigns a left label alignment setting to every cell in a new worksheet. Although you can't change this for all future sessions, you can change it for a specific worksheet using the Worksheet Global Settings Align Labels command. To change the default label prefix from ' (left alignment) to " (right alignment), for example, turn on the Right option. Chapter 5 discusses how to change the default label alignment and other global defaults in more detail.

Long Labels

When a label is a *long label*, it is longer than the width of a column and extends into the next column to the right. For example, "Sales—Year Ending 1993" in cell A1 of Figure 2-2C is a long label because it extends into cell B1.

When you enter data into the cell immediately to the right of a long label, any text that extends into that cell disappears from view. For example, cell A3 of Figure 2-2C also contains "Sales—Year Ending 1993", but 1-2-3 cuts it off because of the entry "200000" in cell B3. If you examine the contents box, however, you'll see that cell A3 still contains the entire entry. To display the entire label you can expand the width of column A (see Chapter 5) or change the font the label is displayed in (see Chapter 6).

Repeating Characters

The \ label prefix followed by a label repeats the characters in the label as many times as will fit in a cell. You can see this in Figure 2-3, where the entry \Gross Profit causes Gross Profit to be repeated across the entire width of cell B5. If you increase the width of column B, Gross Profit would automatically be repeated across this new column width.

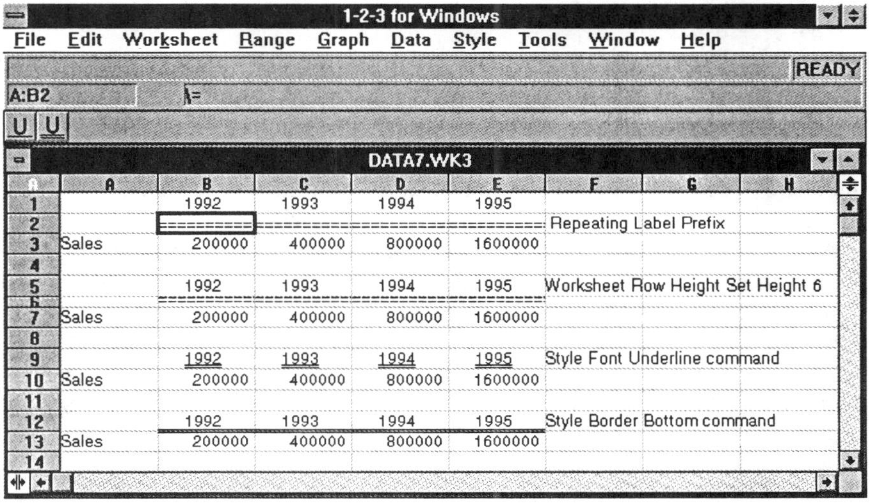

Figure 2-4 Using the \ label prefix to fill a cell

Traditionally, one of the most common uses for repeating characters has been to underline cells and create dividers between cells. In Figure 2-4, for example, \= forces 1-2-3 to fill cell B2 with equal signs. (* or \- creates a similar effect). Cell B6 contains the same entry; however, the height of row 6 has been decreased to fit this label (see Chapter 5).

▼ *Tip:* Figure 2-4 also shows ways to underline an entry in 1-2-3 for Windows without using an extra row. In row 9, for example, the Style Font Underline command is used to underline only the text in a cell. (In fact, the U and U icons shown in Figure 2-4 are shortcuts for this command.) In row 12, the Style Border Bottom command creates a border along the bottom edge of each cell. Chapter 6 discusses these Style options.

Values

A *value* is a number or formula that begins with one of the numbers 0 through 9 or with one of the numeric symbols + - (. @ # $. When you begin an entry with a number or one of the numeric symbols, the mode indicator changes to VALUE. (An entire section later in this chapter, "Entering Formulas," is devoted to numeric formulas.)

Note: 1-2-3 always right aligns numeric values.

Numbers

You can enter any number as long as it is between 1^{-99} and 9.99^{99}. 1-2-3 also allows you to enter a number in scientific notation (1.23E09 or 10E-06, for example) as a percentage (like 24%), as long as the % follows the number, or even as a fraction (like 3/25). Because 1-2-3 always assumes the number you are entering is positive, you must enter a negative number by preceding it with -, a minus sign (from the numeric keypad) or a hyphen. However, a number *cannot* include spaces, or 1-2-3 will disallow the entry.

Although you can include commas or dollar signs when entering numbers, 1-2-3 will discard them unless you use the Range Format Automatic command beforehand (see Chapter 5) to set 1-2-3 for automatic formatting.

If you enter values followed by alphabetic characters or spaces, such as "1993 Sales", 1-2-3 won't let you confirm the entry because it thinks you are trying to enter a value but made an entry error. To make such an entry, you must enter it as a label. See "Labels" earlier in this chapter.

Values and Formatting

The *numeric format* determines how a value is displayed in the worksheet. 1-2-3 for Windows assigns a General numeric format to every cell in a new worksheet. Although you can't change this for all future sessions, you can change it for a specific worksheet using the Worksheet Global Settings Format command discussed in Chapter 5.

You can also change the format for a particular cell either before or after you enter data in it. For example, to format a cell to show a dollar sign, commas between thousands, and two decimal places, you use the Range Format Currency 2 command (see Chapter 5).

▼ *Tip:*   For a preselected range or cell, the icon assigns a Currency 2 decimal places numeric format; the [0.0] icon a , Comma 0 decimal places numeric format, and the [%] icon a Percent 2 decimal places numeric format. These icons are shown in Figure 2-5. (Icons are discussed in Chapter 1 and formatting is discussed in Chapter 5.)

Long Values

When a value is a long value, it is too wide to fit within its column and is displayed as asterisks. 1-2-3 for Windows treats a long value differently, however, depending on the numeric format of the cell. Here are the precise rules that 1-2-3 follows for a long value:

- For a General (the default) numeric format, 1-2-3 displays the rounded integer portion of the entry if it can't fit the decimal portion in the cell. When even the integer portion

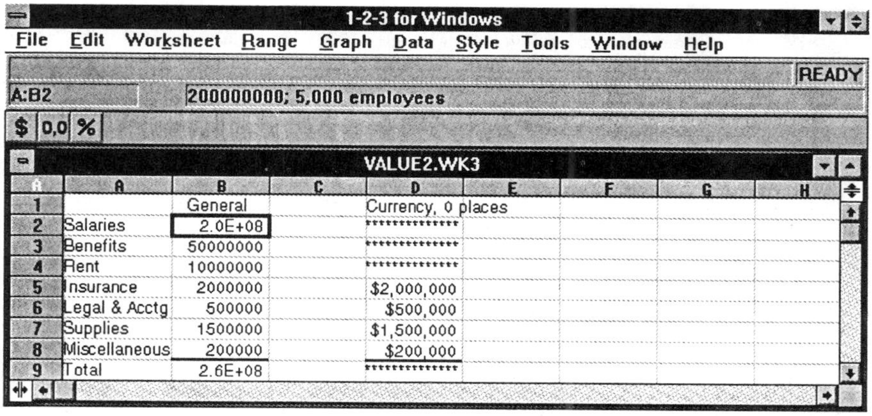

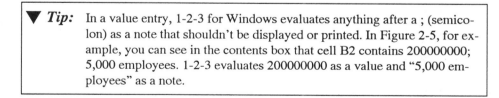

Figure 2-5 Long value displayed as asterisks

is too wide for the column, 1-2-3 first tries to display the number in scientific notation just as in cell B2 of Figure 2-5; if the column width is still too small, 1-2-3 displays asterisks instead.

- For a numeric format other than General, 1-2-3 displays asterisks, as shown by the Currency 0 places format in column D of Figure 2-5.

To see the entire long value, you must widen the column or change the font the value is displayed in. Yet another alternative is to change the numeric format of the cell. A , Comma 0 decimal places format, for example, requires less space than a Currency 2 decimal places format. (Chapter 5 discusses numeric formats and changing column widths. Fonts are discussed in Chapter 6.)

▼ *Tip:*   In a value entry, 1-2-3 for Windows evaluates anything after a ; (semicolon) as a note that shouldn't be displayed or printed. In Figure 2-5, for example, you can see in the contents box that cell B2 contains 200000000; 5,000 employees. 1-2-3 evaluates 200000000 as a value and "5,000 employees" as a note.

Dates

1-2-3 has a special numbering system for handling dates. Each date from January 1, 1900 to December 31, 2099 has been assigned a sequential number, starting with 1 and ending

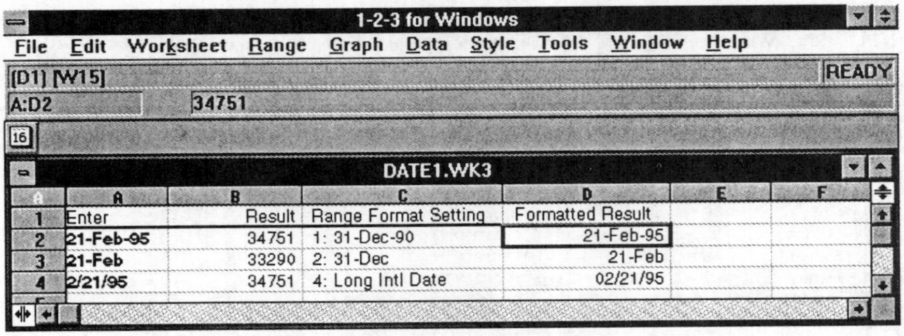

```
 ⊖                          1-2-3 for Windows                        ▾ ▴
  File   Edit   Worksheet   Range   Graph   Data   Style   Tools   Window   Help
 [D1] [W15]                                                          READY
 A:D2                34751
 16
 ⊖                          DATE1.WK3                                ▾ ▴
         A           B            C                   D           E        F      ⬍
  1  Enter              Result   Range Format Setting  Formatted Result           ▲
  2  21-Feb-95          34751   1: 31-Dec-90           21-Feb-95
  3  21-Feb             33290   2: 31-Dec                21-Feb
  4  2/21/95            34751   4: Long Intl Date        02/21/95                 ⬇
```

Figure 2-6   Entering a date directly into a cell

with 73050. These numbers are called *date numbers*. For example, the date number for January 31, 1993 is 34000.

> *Note:* Dates are discussed in Chapter 9; formatting dates is discussed in Chapter 5.

Although you can enter the date number representing a date, it's much easier just to type a date directly into a cell using one of the three date formats shown in Figure 2-6. For example, if you type **21-Feb-95** in a cell, 1-2-3 automatically converts it to the date-number 34751 shown in cell B2. You still have to use Range Format, however, to display the date rather than the date number. For instance, if you choose Range Format 1: 31-Dec-90, you can see in cell D2 that 1-2-3 displays this date number as 21-Feb-95. If you look at the contents box, however, you'll see that cell D2 still contains the date number 34751.

If you type **21-Feb**, however, you can see in cell B3 that 1-2-3 for Windows returns a different date number, 33290. That's because 1-2-3 takes the current year—1991—from Windows. If you formatted this date number to show the year, it would be displayed as 21-Feb-91.

You can't, however, enter a date directly into a cell using the D3 (3: Dec-90) and D5 (5: Short Intl Date) formats. If you try entering Feb-95, for instance, 1-2-3- enters it as the label 'Feb-95. If you enter 2/21, on the other hand, 1-2-3 thinks it's a fraction and returns .0952381.

> *Note:* To return today's date, see Chapter 9.

You can also use the @DATE(*year,month,day*) function (see Chapter 9) to enter a date. For example, @DATE(95,2,21) also returns the date number 34751 for February 21, 1995. You still need to format this date number using one of the Range Format command's date formats discussed in Chapter 5.

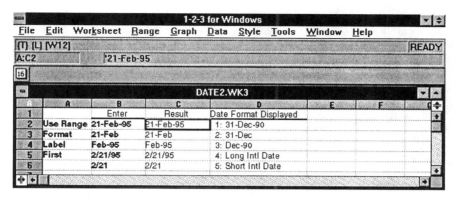

Figure 2-7 Entering a date as a label

▼ *Tip:*   You can use the Range Format Label command to type a date directly into a cell and have it displayed as a label. Figure 2-7 shows how to do this for any of the five date formats you can use. For example, if you position the cell pointer in a cell, select Range Format Label and press ENTER, then type **21-Feb-95**, you can see the result in cell C2. The date 21-Feb-95 is displayed. If you look at the input line, you'll see that 1-2-3 doesn't store this date as a date number. Instead, 1-2-3 adds the default label prefix and stores this date as the label '21-Feb-95. The drawback to this method is that you can't use the result in date calculations.

Times

1-2-3 also uses a sequential numbering system for times. Each time from midnight to 11:59.59 PM has been assigned a decimal number from .000000 to .999999. These are known as *time numbers*.

Note: Times are further discussed in Chapter 9; formatting times is discussed in Chapter 5.

Although you can enter a time number to represent a time, it's actually much easier just to type a time directly into a cell using one of the four time formats shown in Figure 2-8. If you type **2:30:00 PM** in a cell, for example, 1-2-3 for Windows automatically converts it to the time number 0.6041667 shown in cell B2. You can then use Range Format to display this time number as a time. If you select Range Format 6: 11:59:59 AM, for example, you can see in cell D2 that 1-2-3 displays 2:30:00 PM; however, this cell still contains the time number 0.6041667.

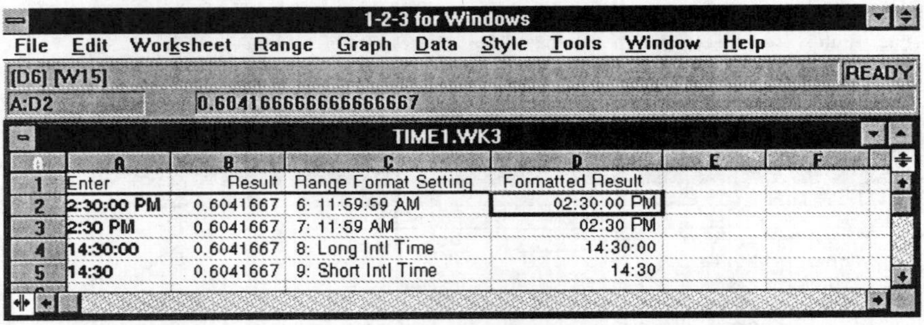

Figure 2-8 Entering a time directly into a cell

Note: You can see in Figure 2-8 that the Long and Short Intl Time formats use a military clock. That is, 2:30 PM must be entered as 14:30.

You can also use the @TIME(*hours,minutes,seconds*) function (see Chapter 9) to enter a time. For example, @TIME(14,30,00) also returns the time number 0.60416667. (Notice that @TIME uses a military clock.) To make the time recognizable, however, you'll need to use the Range Format command discussed in Chapter 5.

▼ *Tip:*   Like dates, you can use Range Format Label to type a time directly into a cell and have it displayed and stored as a label. Once again, however, you won't be able to use the result in time calculations.

Figure 2-9 shows how to do this for any of the four time formats. For example, if you position the cell pointer in a cell, select Range Format Label and press ENTER, then type **2:30:00 PM**, you'll get the result in C2. Not only is the time 2:30:00 PM displayed, but it's stored as the label '2:30:00 PM, not as a time number.

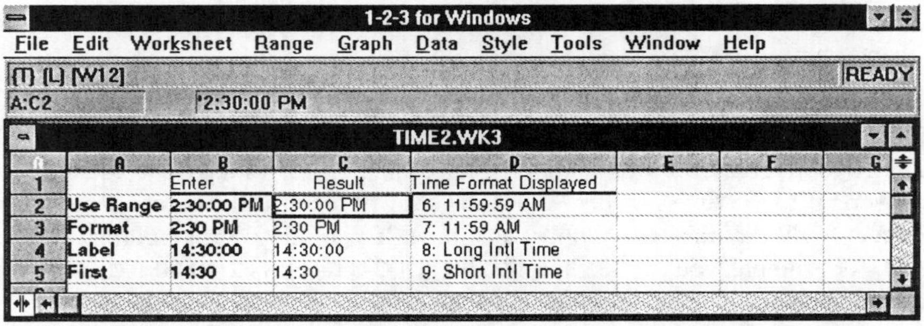

Figure 2-9 Entering a time as a label

Combined Date/Time Entries

Dates and times are actually part of the same sequential numbering system. To see how this works, place the @NOW function in a cell to return the combined date and time number for the current date and time. For example, enter **@NOW** in a cell at 7:20 PM on August 12, 1991, and 1-2-3 returns the combined date/time number 33462.805556. The integer portion, 33462, is the date; and the decimal portion, .805556, is the time.

You can format this date/time number to display either the date or time. If you format the cell containing this number with the Range Format 4: Long Intl Date command, for example, 1-2-3 will use the integer portion of the value and display 8/12/91, the current date. On the other hand, use Range Format 7: 11:59 AM, and 1-2-3 will use the decimal portion of the value and display the current time, 7:20 PM.

Note: The result returned by @NOW is updated every time the worksheet is recalculated. See Chapter 9 for further discussion.

ENTERING FORMULAS

Formulas provide 1-2-3 for Windows with much of its underlying power. Basically, a *formula* is an entry that performs a calculation such as addition, subtraction, multiplication, or division. In 1-2-3, however, you can also use string formulas to perform label manipulation and analysis. And by using logical formulas or @functions, you can perform powerful and complex data manipulation.

In 1-2-3 for Windows, a simple formula is like the algebraic ones you are used to: 100+65-15*(2000/12), for example. A formula can be up to 512 characters long and uses values and operators to compute a result. A formula in 1-2-3, however, must start with a number or one of these characters: + - (.) @ # $. Otherwise, 1-2-3 will think you're entering a label. In fact, using + at the beginning of a formula is a way to tell 1-2-3 that you're entering a formula that doesn't begin with a number or one of these characters.

1-2-3 for Windows also provides the special characters shown in Table 2-2 that you'll want to use when you enter a formula. These symbols represent mathematical operators, such as >, or special instructions to 1-2-3 in regard to formulas. For example, & (ampersand) tells 1-2-3 to *concatenate*—join together—two strings. Many of these symbols are used in the following sections.

Numeric Formulas

Numeric formulas perform calculations on numbers and return a number. You're probably familiar with numeric formulas that perform simple arithmetic calculations like

TABLE 2-2 Formula Symbols

Symbol	Description
+	Positive number or addition in a numeric formula
–	Negative value or subtraction in a numeric formula
*	Multiplication in a formula
/	Division in a formula
^	Exponentiation
@	String following this symbol is an @function name
.	Decimal point
(	Precedes @function argument or changes order of preference
)	Closes @function argument or changes order of preference
#	Starts or ends a complex logical operator (#AND#, for instance)
>	Greater than logical operator
<	Less than logical operator
=	Equal to logical operator
< >	Not equal to logical operator
&	Concatenates two strings
$	Freezes a worksheet, row, or column component in an absolute or mixed address ($A:$A$4, for example)

division or multiplication. In 1-2-3 for Windows, however, you can also use numeric formulas to easily perform more complicated calculations, such as determining the internal rate of return of a series of unequal cash flows or calculating the standard deviation of a sample population.

The simplest numeric formula adds values together. For example, try moving the cell pointer to cell C1, typing **28+60+31**, and pressing ENTER to confirm the entry. This formula will appear in the contents box, while the result 1-2-3 calculates, 119, will be displayed in cell C1.

Although 1-2-3 for Windows accepts a formula that includes a blank space between a mathematical operator and a value, it deletes these spaces when you press ENTER. Remember that if you start a formula with a blank cell, 1-2-3 evaluates it as a label instead.

Other mathematical operators typically used in simple numeric formulas are – (minus) for subtraction, * (asterisk) for multiplication, / (slash) for division, and ^ (caret) for exponentiation. Try using them in the formulas shown in Figure 2-10.

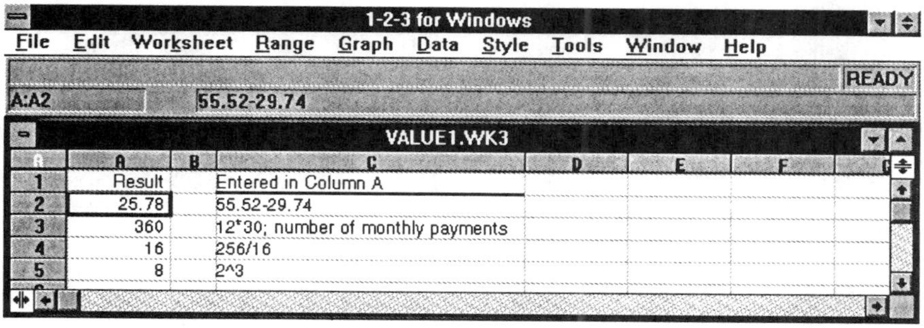

Figure 2-10 Examples of simple numeric formulas

▼ *Tip:* In a formula entry, 1-2-3 for Windows evaluates anything after ; (semicolon) as a note that shouldn't be displayed or printed. In Figure 2-10, for example, cell A3 contains "12*30; number of monthly payments." 1-2-3 evaluates everything before the semicolon as a formula and returns the result 360. It evaluates everything after the semicolon, "number of monthly payments," as a note.

Using Cell References

To really begin using the power of formulas in 1-2-3 for Windows, you'll want to include cell references in your numeric formulas. When you include a cell reference, the formula uses the contents of the cell in calculations. More important, when the contents of the referenced cell change, 1-2-3 uses the new value in the formula and displays the new result. This allows you to play *what-if* or scenario analysis.

For example, try entering **10** in cell A1, **20** in cell B1, and the formula **100+A1+B1** in cell C1. When you press ENTER to confirm this formula, 1-2-3 will display in cell C1 the result this formula returns: 130. This formula is still displayed in the contents box, however. If you now enter **20** in cell A1, 1-2-3 immediately updates the formula in C1 and returns 140. So using cell references in this formula creates a dynamic situation in which the value of cell C1 depends on the values in cells A1 and B1.

Note: If you begin a formula with a cell reference, you must precede the cell reference with a numeric operator, typically + - (. or $. For example, 1-2-3 evaluates +D1*B2 as a formula, but D1*B2 as the label 'D1*B2.

When 1-2-3 for Windows Uses Abbreviated Cell References

1-2-3 for Windows treats cell references differently, depending on where the cell is located in relation to the formula. You can see this in Figure 2-11, which shows a simple sales/growth model being created. Because the sales from one month to the next depend

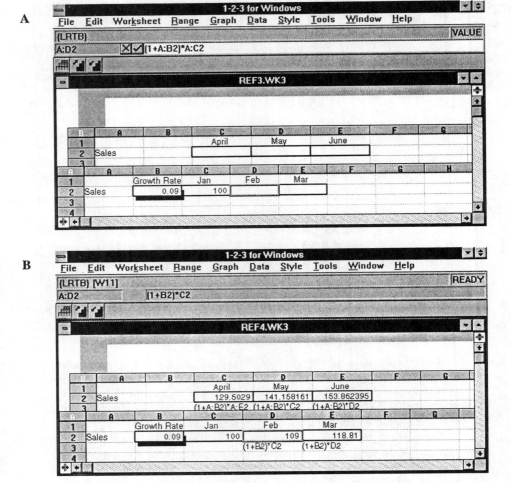

Figure 2-11 Using cell references to create a sales growth model

on a growth factor, the sales in each month will be calculated using a formula that refers to the growth rate, .09, in cell A:B2. The first month's sales in January are entered as the value 100 in cell A:C2.

To create a formula that calculates February sales as (1+growth rate)*January sales, enter **(1+A:B2)*A:C2** in cell A:D2. When you press ENTER to confirm this entry, you can see in Figure 2-11B that this formula returns 109. If you examine the contents box of Figure 2-11B, however, you'll also see that 1-2-3 adjusts this formula to (1+B2)*C2, which only contains abbreviated cell addresses. 1-2-3 does this because the referenced cells B2 and C2 and the formula location D2 all reside in the same worksheet, worksheet

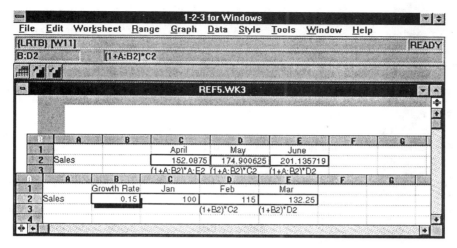

Figure 2-12   The effect of changing the value in cell A:B2

A. So to calculate March sales as a function of February sales and the growth rate, just enter the formula **(1+B2)*D2** in cell A:E2.

When a cell and a formula that refer to this cell reside in different worksheets, however, you must include the worksheet component in the cell reference. In cell B:C2 of Figure 2-11B, for example, enter the formula **(1+A:B2)*A:E2** to calculate April sales as a function of the growth rate in A:B2 and March sales in A:E2. If you don't include the worksheet components in this formula, 1-2-3 will reference cells B2 and E2 in worksheet B, not worksheet A.

When you enter **(1+A:B2)*B:C2** in cell B:D2 to calculate May sales, however, 1-2-3 for Windows adjusts this formula to (1+A:B2)*C2. In this case, 1-2-3 retains only the worksheet component for the cell reference A:B2; it adjusts the reference to April sales to C2 because this cell resides in the same worksheet as the formula. (You can see this by looking ahead to the contents box of Figure 2-12.) Likewise, when you enter **(1+A:B2)*B:D2** in cell B:E2, 1-2-3 adjusts this formula, which calculates June sales as (1+A:B2)*D2.

Once you've entered these formulas, you can examine the effect that changing the growth rate will have on sales. If you enter a new growth rate in cell A:B2, .15 perhaps, Figure 2-12 shows how 1-2-3 for Windows immediately updates all the sales values, because they are computed using formulas that refer to A:B2.

Pointing to Cell References

Instead of typing in a cell address in a formula, you can *point* to the cell after entering a mathematical operator (see Table 2-2) and have 1-2-3 for Windows automatically include the cell address in the formula. Not only is pointing easier, but it can also prevent errors in your formulas.

Using the mouse is the easiest way to point to cell addresses while creating a formula. For example, suppose you want to create the formula (1+B2)*C2 shown in cell A:D2 of Figure 2-11B by pointing. To do this:

1.   Place the cell pointer in A:D2 and type **(1**.
2.   Add the cell address A:B2 to the formula by typing **+**. Then select cell A:B2. The cell pointer returns to cell A:D2, and 1-2-3 appends that cell address to the end of the formula in the form of a range. As you can see in the contents box of Figure 2-13A, the formula now reads (1+A:B2..A:B2. Type **)** to close this portion of the formula.
3.   Add the cell address A:C2 to the formula by typing ***** and then selecting cell A:C2. 1-2-3 for Windows once again moves the cell pointer back to cell A:D2, where the formula now reads (1+A:B2..A:B2)* A:C2..A:C2 in the contents box. Press ENTER to complete the formula.

You can see in the contents box of Figure 2-11B the result, (1+B2..B2)*C2..C2. So when the mouse is used to point to a cell reference in a formula, such as B2, 1-2-3 treats it as the single-cell range B2..B2. The 109 result returned, however, is the same as for the formula (1+B2)*C2 in Figure 2-11. (See "Using Cell References," above, for the reasons 1-2-3 for Windows deletes the worksheet components in this formula.)

Creating the same formula using the keyboard takes a bit more work. First, move the cell pointer to A:D2 and enter **(1**. Next, add the cell address A:B2 to the formula by

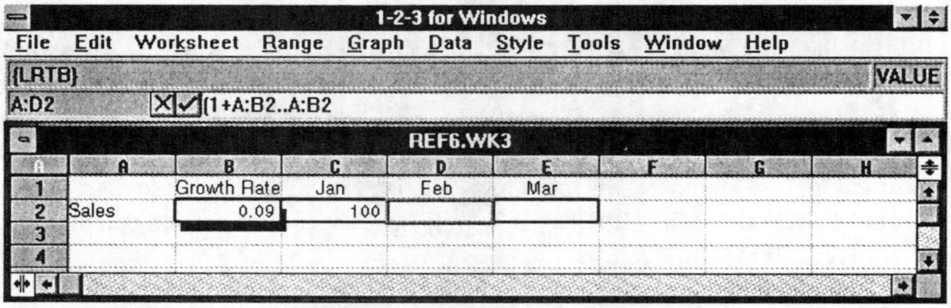

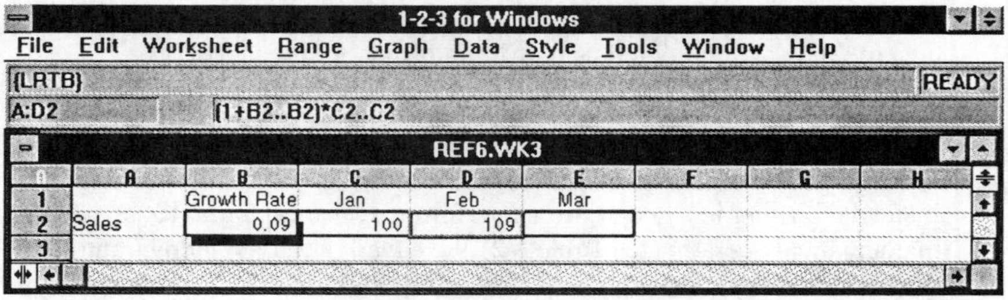

Figure 2-13 Using the mouse to point to a cell address used in a formula

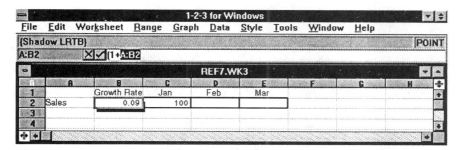

Figure 2-14 Using the keyboard to point to a cell address used in a formula

typing **+** then pressing the ← key twice to move the cell pointer to cell A:B2. (As you move the cell pointer in the worksheet, the cell address in the contents box follows your movement from A:D2 to A:C2 to A:B2.) You can see in Figure 2-14 how 1-2-3 adds this address, A:B2, to the end of the formula in the contents box so that it reads (1+A:B2. Now type **)** to accept A:B2 as part of the formula. 1-2-3 immediately moves the cell pointer back to cell A:D2 (the original cell), and the formula now reads (1+A:B2).

To add the cell address A:C2 to the formula, type *****, then press ← to move the cell pointer to A:C2. 1-2-3 for Windows appends this address to the end of the formula so that it now reads (1+A:B2)*A:C2 in the contents box. Press ENTER to complete the formula and move the cell pointer back to cell A:D2. You can see the result, (1+B2)*C2, in the contents box of Figure 2-11B.

Note: For more information on selecting cell addresses, see "Selecting Cells and Ranges" later.

Absolute and Relative References

There are three types of cell addresses in 1-2-3 formulas: relative, absolute, and mixed. The type of reference you use affects how 1-2-3 for Windows adjusts cell references when you copy or move a formula to another cell.

Note: In previous releases of 1-2-3, how cell addresses were affected by copy and move operations was quite straightforward. In 1-2-3 for Windows, however, the command you use to copy or move a formula can also affect how cell references are adjusted. Chapter 7 discusses this in detail.

So far in this book, only *relative* references like +A5 or +C:D5 have been used. When a relative cell address like +B:A5 is copied to another location, 1-2-3 adjusts the references relative to the worksheet, column, and row location of the destination cell. To see this, imagine that cell C2 contains the formula +A1. When this formula is copied from cell C2 to cell D3, the result is +B2. Because cell D3 is one column to the right and one row down from cell C2, 1-2-3 adjusts the column component of the formula by one column (from A to B), and the row component by one row (from 1 to 2).

With an *absolute* cell reference 1-2-3 doesn't change the references when it is copied to a new location. For instance, the absolute reference in the formula +$B:$A$5 will remain the same when you copy it to cell A:P20 or Z:C100. In 1-2-3 for Windows, placing an $ symbol before a worksheet, column, or row component "freezes" that portion of the reference. So to freeze all components in +B:A5 and create an absolute address, a $ is placed in front of the worksheet component B:, the column component A, and the row component 5.

A *mixed* cell reference is a combination of relative and absolute references. Examples of mixed cell references are $B:$A5, $B:A$5, and B:A$5. That is, the worksheet, column, or row components that are "frozen"—preceded by a $—don't change when the formula is copied to a new location. Any relative components, however, do change to reflect the new location.

> ▼ *Tip:*   You can also use ABS(F4) to create an absolute, mixed, or relative address. See "Copying Formulas" in Chapter 7.

String Formulas

A *string* formula, which returns a string (text), can be used to manipulate labels. For instance, you can employ the *concatenation* operator & (ampersand) to create a string formula that concatenates, or strings together, two labels. To see this, imagine that cell C1 contains the label "Strategic Partners, Inc." and cell C2 the label "Cash Flow." If you enter **+C1&" "&C2** in cell C3, this string formula returns the label "Strategic Partners, Inc. Cash Flow."

> *Note:*   You can't use the & symbol to concatenate a string and number. To do this, see Chapter 9.

When you enter a string formula that begins with a double quotation mark, make sure to precede the formula with a + symbol. For example, the formula +"Preventive"&" Maintenance" is an acceptable formula. But "Preventive"&"Maintenance" is not, because the first character, ", tells 1-2-3 to evaluate everything following it as a right-aligned label.

> ▼ *Tip:*   You can also use string functions, discussed in Chapter 9, to manipulate labels. For example, the @UPPER function converts all the characters in a string to uppercase.

Logical Formulas

A *logical formula* tests a condition. If the condition is true, a logical formula returns 1 (true); if the condition is false, it returns 0 (false). A *condition* uses one of the logical operators in Table 2-3 to compare values, labels, formulas, or cells containing any of these. Some of the most common uses of logical formulas are to perform logical tests in @IF functions (see Chapter 9) and to create criteria for querying a database (see Chapter 11).

TABLE 2-3 Logical Operators

Simple Logical Operator	Operation
=	Equal to
>	Greater than
<	Less than
>=	Greater than or equal to
<=	Less than or equal to
< >	Not equal to

Complex Logical Operator	Operation
#AND#	Both condition 1 and condition 2 are true
#OR#	Either condition 1 or condition 2 is true
#NOT#	Condition 1 is *not* true

For example, if you place the formula +B2>=1000 in a cell, 1-2-3 returns 1 (true) when the value in cell B2 is greater than or equal to 1,000. If the value is less than 1,000, this logical formula returns 0 (false).

Functions

Another type of 1-2-3 formula is the @function. An *@function* is a built-in formula that performs some type of calculation and returns a value or a string. (Chapter 9 is solely devoted to explaining each @function.) For example, Figure 2-15 shows how you can use @SUM(B2..B8) in cell A:B9 to total the expenses in column B. Using @SUM is much more efficient than its equivalent formula, +B2+B3+B4+B5+B6+B7+B8.

Error Values

Occasionally you'll enter a formula that will yield ERR rather than a label or value. Although there are many reasons why this might occur, here are some of the more common ones:

- A value is being divided by zero, which usually happens when a cell address refers to 0, a label, or a blank cell. If cell B2 is blank for example, the formula +B1/B2 in cell B3 will return ERR.

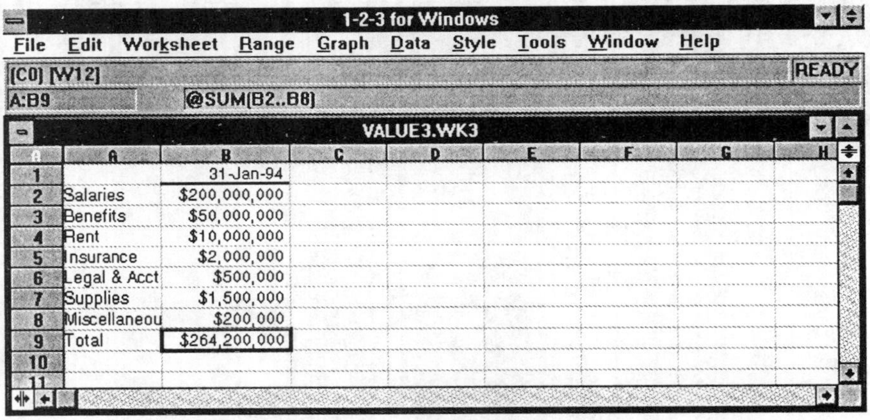

Figure 2-15   Using the @SUM function to sum expenses

- A cell reference used in a formula was deleted when a row, column, or worksheet was deleted. If you use the Worksheet Delete Column command to delete column B, for example, the formula +A2+B2+C2 in cell D2 will return ERR.

- A cell reference used in a formula was written over during a copy or move operation. See Chapter 7 for a complete discussion.

Order of Precedence

As you know, operators like +, &, or > perform mathematical, string, or logical operations in formulas. Because you can have any number of operators in a formula, 1-2-3 for Windows uses an *order of precedence* to determine the sequence in which it should evaluate operators.

For each operator, 1-2-3 for Windows automatically assigns the order of precedence shown in Table 2-4. Because the ^ (exponentiation) operator has an order of precedence of 1, it is always evaluated first; #AND#, #OR#, and & are always evaluated last because they all have an order of precedence of 7. Operators with the same precedence number are evaluated from left to right. For example, because * and / both have an order of precedence of 3, 1-2-3 evaluates the formula 5*2/4 by first multiplying 5 by 2, which returns 10, then dividing 10 by 4 to return 2.5.

The order of precedence rule can substantially affect the result returned by a formula. For example, let's look at how 1-2-3 evaluates the formula 3+5*.2. Because * (multiplication) has a higher order of precedence than + (addition), 1-2-3 first multiplies 5*.2 and returns .1. Then 1-2-3 adds 3 to .1 to return 3.1.

You can override 1-2-3's order of precedence by using parentheses. So any operation enclosed in parentheses is always evaluated first. For example, 1-2-3 evaluates (3+5)*.2 by first adding 3 and 5 to return 8. It then multiplies 8 by .2 to return 1.6.

TABLE 2-4 Order of Precedence

Order	Operator	Operation
1	^	Exponentiation
2	-	Negative
2	+	Positive
3	*	Multiplication
3	/	Division
4	+	Addition
4	–	Subtraction
5	=	Equal to test
5	<>	Not equal to test
5	<	Less than test
5	>	Greater than test
5	<=	Less than or equal to test
5	>=	Greater than or equal to test
6	#NOT#	Logical NOT test
7	#AND#	Logical AND test
7	#OR#	Logical OR test
7	&	String concatenation

RECALCULATION

When you enter a formula in a worksheet that refers to other cells, 1-2-3 automatically updates the formula when you change any entries that the formula refers to, or you change the formula itself. This updating is known as *recalculation.*

Note: Recalculation doesn't affect link formulas. To update link formulas between open files or files on disk, you must use the File Administration Update Links command discussed in Chapters 4 and 17.

In releases prior to Releases 2.2 and 3, the entire worksheet was recalculated each time you made an entry. This process of recalculating the worksheet became a time-consuming problem when a large worksheet contained many complex formulas. While 1-2-3 was busy recalculating the worksheet, you couldn't use your computer because it used *foreground recalculation.*

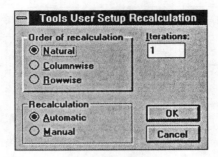

Figure 2-16 The default Recalculation settings

The 1-2-3 Classic equivalent is the /Worksheet Global Recalc command. However, the 1-2-3 Classic command, /Worksheet Status, which previously provided information about recalculation, no longer works.

Like other recent versions of 1-2-3, 1-2-3 for Windows gets around these problems by using minimal and background recalculation. With *minimal recalculation*, you can add or edit a cell in 1-2-3, and only the cells that are affected by the entry are recalculated. 1-2-3 also recalculates in the *background* while you continue to do your work; it performs the recalculation between your keystrokes. You can view and edit your worksheets, for instance, or even minimize 1-2-3 to work on another Windows application.

You can override how 1-2-3 for Windows recalculates a worksheet using the Tools User Setup Recalculation command. The default settings shown in Figure 2-16—Natural and Automatic turned on—cause 1-2-3 to recalculate the way it does. You can change these settings and make recalculation occur only when you initiate it manually. In addition, you can control the order in which 1-2-3 recalculates cells.

Note: All open worksheet files automatically use the same Recalculation settings, which are those from the last file opened. Any changes you make to the Recalculation settings in one open file are automatically reflected in the Recalculation settings in all other open files.

Controlling When Recalculation Takes Place

As in previous releases of 1-2-3, you can specify that recalculation take place either automatically or manually. The default, Automatic, causes 1-2-3 for Windows to use minimal and background recalculation to update the worksheet file whenever you make an entry in a cell that affects an entry in another cell.

You'll usually want to switch to Manual recalculation in a large worksheet with many complex formulas that take a lot of time to recalculate. When you have finished entering or updating data, you can press CALC (F9) to have 1-2-3 recalculate the worksheet all

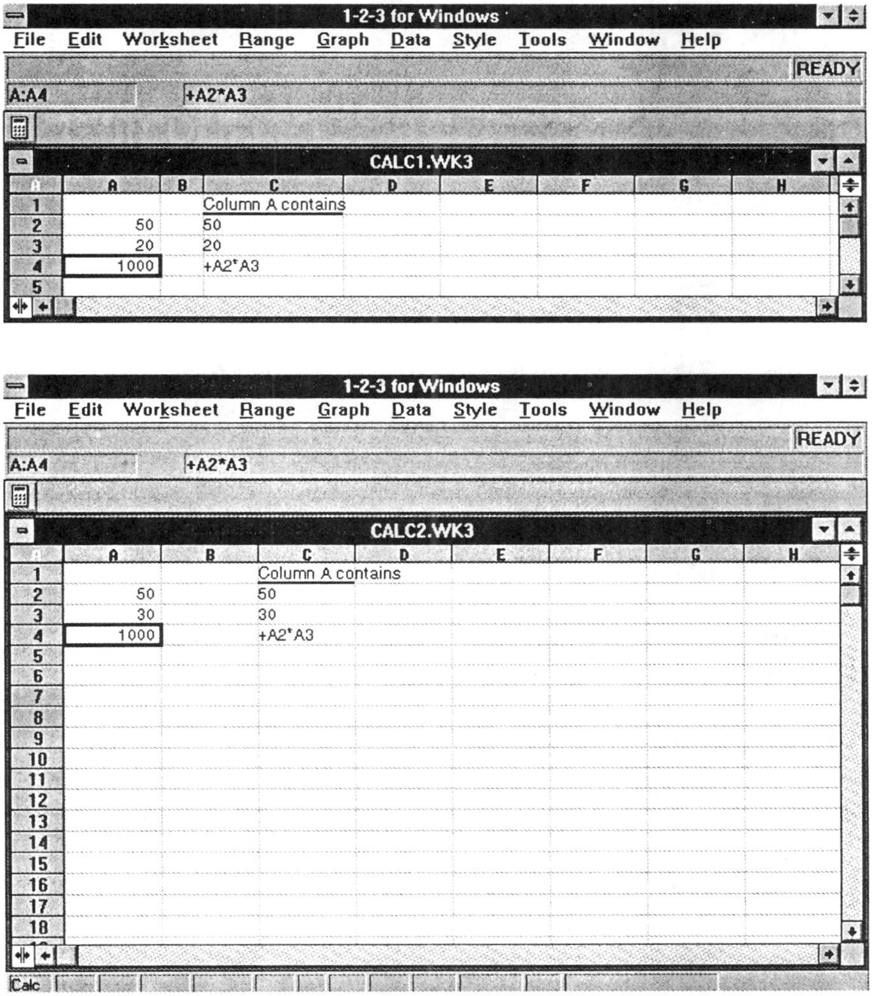

Figure 2-17 Using manual recalculation

at once. Manual uses foreground recalculation, so you can't perform other functions until 1-2-3 for Windows finishes recalculating.

Figure 2-17 illustrates how manual recalculation works. In Figure 2-17A, cell A2 contains 50, cell A3, 20, and cell A4, the formula +A2*A3. When this formula is entered, 1-2-3 returns 1000.

In Figure 2-17B, Tools User Setup Recalculation is first used to turn on Manual recalculation. Then 30 is entered in cell A3. Notice that the formula in cell A4 still displays its original value, 1000, even though it should return 1500. Because 1-2-3 doesn't automatically recalculate the worksheet, a CALC indicator appears in the lower-left

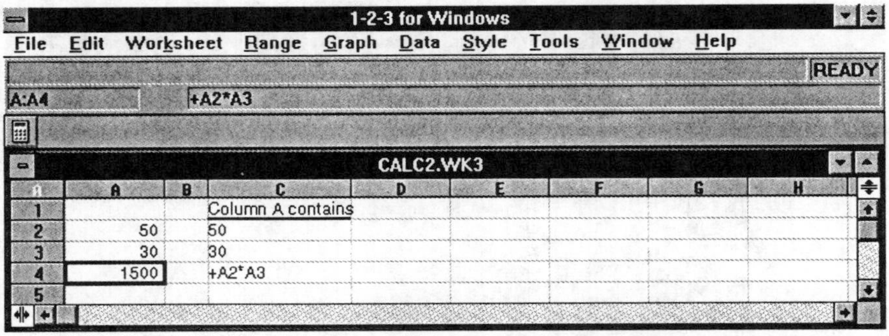

Figure 2-17 Using manual recalculation *(continued)*

corner. This indicator means that 1-2-3 has detected a change in the worksheet file and that you should press CALC (F9) to recalculate the worksheet.

Figure 2-17C shows what happens when you press CALC (F9) to recalculate the worksheet. The formula in cell A4 is recalculated and now returns 1500. In addition, the CALC indicator disappears.

▼ *Tip:*   The 🖩 icon shown in Figure 2-17 also recalculates the worksheet.

Order of Recalculation

As you can see in Figure 2-16, 1-2-3 for Windows provides three different ways to control the order of recalculation: Natural, Columnwise, and Rowwise. By default, 1-2-3 uses a Natural order of recalculation. In this method, 1-2-3 for Windows begins with the most fundamental formulas in the worksheet—those that must be recalculated first before any other formulas that depend on them can be recalculated. Then, 1-2-3 recalculates the next most fundamental formulas, and so on until all the formulas in the worksheet have been recalculated.

To get a better understanding of how Natural recalculation works, let's examine Figure 2-18A. Notice that the formula in cell A4, +A2+A5, depends on cell A5. In addition, the formula in cell A3, +A2+A4, indirectly depends on cell A5 through the reference to cell A4.

Consider how 1-2-3 recalculates the worksheet when you enter 300 in cell A5. 1-2-3 for Windows begins by recalculating the formula in cell A4 first, even though it isn't the first formula in the worksheet. Then it recalculates the formula in cell A3, which depends on the result of the formula in A4. You can see in Figure 2-18B that the formulas are automatically updated.

1-2-3 for Windows will calculate this worksheet differently, however, if you change to columnwise or rowwise recalculation. With columnwise and rowwise recalculation,

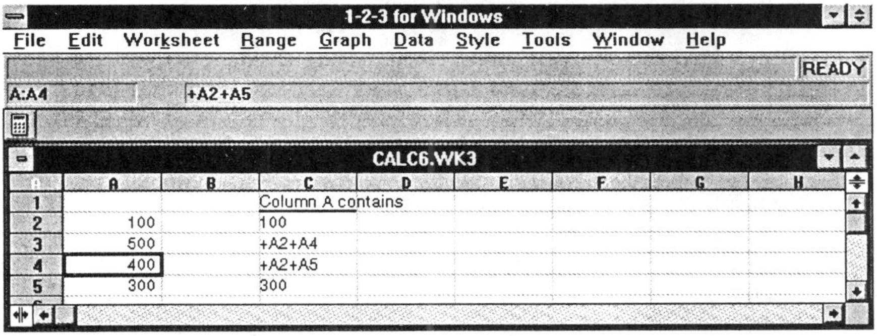

Figure 2-18 Using a Natural order of recalculation

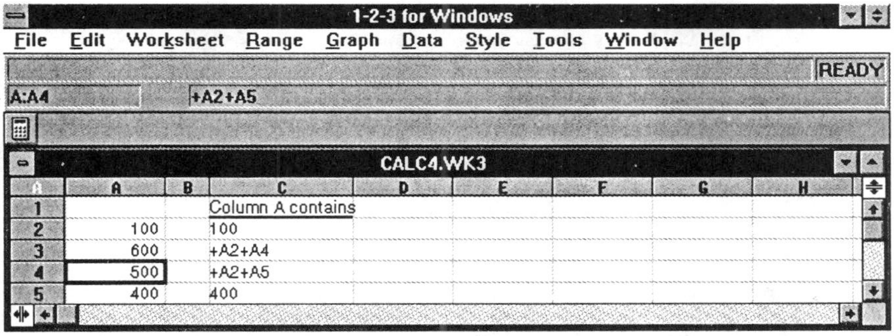

1-2-3 doesn't evaluate the formulas in the worksheet. Rather, it always recalculates a worksheet file in the same way. For example, if you turn on Columnwise recalculation, 1-2-3 always begins recalculating at cell A:A1, then works its way down column A cell by cell until it reaches the last filled cell in column A. It then moves to column B and works its way down that column, and so on. When it finishes recalculating worksheet A, it moves to worksheet B, then to worksheet C, and so on until it has recalculated all the worksheets in the file. Then 1-2-3 moves to the next open file and repeats this process.

Rowwise recalculation is similar to columnwise recalculation. The only difference is that 1-2-3 recalculates in a rowwise fashion; that is, across row 1 of worksheet A, then row 2, and so on.

In most instances, the results are the same regardless of whether 1-2-3 uses natural, columnwise, or rowwise recalculation. When a worksheet has a forward reference, however, columnwise and rowwise recalculation can yield incorrect results while natural recalculation does not.

A *forward reference* occurs when a formula refers to another cell that is lower in the worksheet. This happens in Figure 2-18, because the formula in cell A3, +A2+A4, includes a forward reference to cell A4. Likewise, the formula in cell A4, +A2+A5

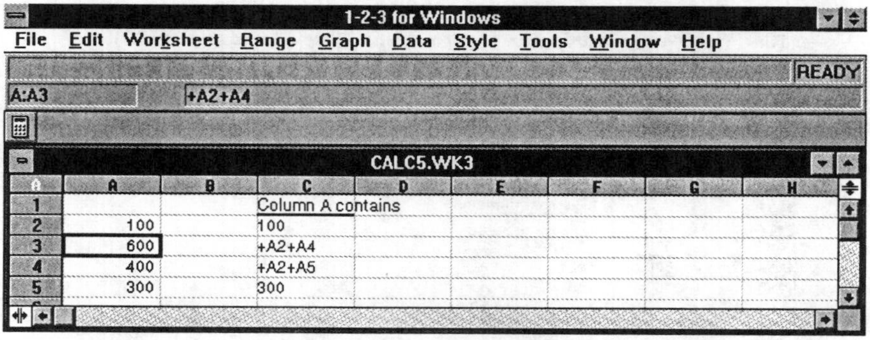

Figure 2-19 Using a columnwise order of recalculation

contains a forward reference to cell A5. (A reference to a cell in a later worksheet is also a forward reference. For example, the formula +B:A1 in cell A:A1 is a forward reference.)

Figure 2-19 shows what happens when 300 is entered in cell A5 and columnwise recalculation is specified. Because 1-2-3 calculates the result in A3 before it calculates the result in A4, the formula in A3,+A4+A5, still returns 600. By looking at cells A2 and A4, however, you can see that it should return 500.

Even when a worksheet contains a forward reference and columnwise or rowwise recalculation is specified, you can usually get 1-2-3 for Windows to reflect the proper results for all formulas by pressing CALC (F9) twice. (Occasionally, you may need to press CALC more than twice.)

An alternative is to use the Tools User Setup Recalculation command and set Iterations to 2 or greater. (You can specify up to 50 iterations.) For a columnwise or rowwise order of recalculation, the Iterations option specifies how many times 1-2-3 for Windows recalculates the formulas in a worksheet and any other open files. For a natural order of recalculation, 1-2-3 only uses the Iterations setting when a circular reference exists in the worksheet.

Circular References

A *circular reference* occurs when you place a formula in a cell whose value depends on that same cell. Although a circular reference is usually caused by an entry error, sometimes it can be intentional.

The simplest form of circular reference occurs when a formula refers to itself. In Figure 2-20, for example, cell A3 contains 200 while cell A2 contains the formula A2+A3, which refers to itself. Notice that 1-2-3 displays a CIRC indicator in the lower-left corner, indicating a circular reference exists in the worksheet.

Unfortunately, 1-2-3 for Windows is incapable of resolving many circular references; the simple circular reference in Figure 2-20 is one example. On the other hand, there are some circular references that 1-2-3 can resolve, provided you increase the iteration count (see "Resolving Intentional Circular References," later).

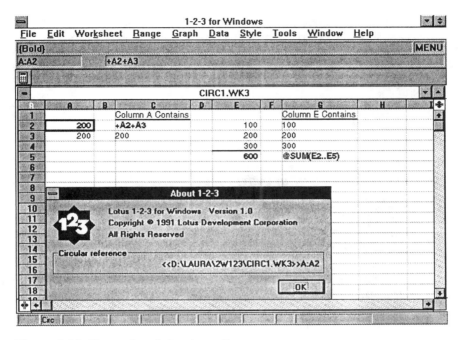

Figure 2-20 Examples of circular references

Eliminating Mistaken Circular References

The 1-2-3 Classic command, /Worksheet Status, no longer provides information about circular references. When you need to eliminate a circular reference from your worksheet file, you'll find the Help option, About 1-2-3, to be of considerable assistance. For example, if you select the Help command followed by About 1-2-3, 1-2-3 for Windows exhibits the dialog box shown in Figure 2-20.

This dialog box indicates the first circular reference in the active worksheet—in this case, cell A:A2 of the file CIRC1. Actually, this worksheet file contains another circular reference—the function @SUM(E2..E5) refers to the cell it resides in, cell E5. However, the About 1-2-3 dialog box won't tell you about cell E5 until you resolve the circular reference in A2.

To do this, select OK to return to the worksheet. Then fix the formula in A2; enter +A3+A4, for instance. 1-2-3 will still display the CIRC indicator because cell E5 also contains a circular reference. If you select About 1-2-3 from the Help menu again, 1-2-3 for Windows will indicate that cell A:E5 contains a circular reference. You can continue to use Help in this way to eliminate all circular references in a worksheet.

In some instances, it can be quite difficult to correct a circular reference, even when you know one of the problem cells. You'll find it especially difficult when several formulas are involved, some of whose references are not involved in the circle. What's more, the cell indicated in the About 1-2-3 dialog box may not be the cell causing the problem. (The next section shows such a situation.)

In fact, correcting a circular reference can easily become a wild-goose chase. About all you can do is try to chase down each cell that is involved in the circular reference chain. For example, you should first try to find all those cells that reference the cell identified as a circular reference. If this doesn't work, try examining all the cells that indirectly reference this cell.

▼ *Tip:*   The Edit Find command can help you locate circular references. See "Searching and Replacing Data" at the end of this chapter.

Resolving Intentional Circular References

Occasionally you'll intentionally enter a circular reference that you want 1-2-3 to resolve. For example, Figure 2-21 computes both state and federal taxes. However, state taxes are calculated as 3% of federal taxable income. In cell C9, this is represented by the formula 0.03*D14, or $922. Furthermore, state taxes are deductible for federal tax purposes on Schedule A, and are reflected in the Total Schedule A amount, computed as @SUM(C6..C12) in cell D13. This causes an intentional circular reference—you need to calculate state taxes in order to calculate federal taxable income, yet state taxes are based on federal taxable income. In Figure 2-21, the CIRC indicator reflects this circular reference.

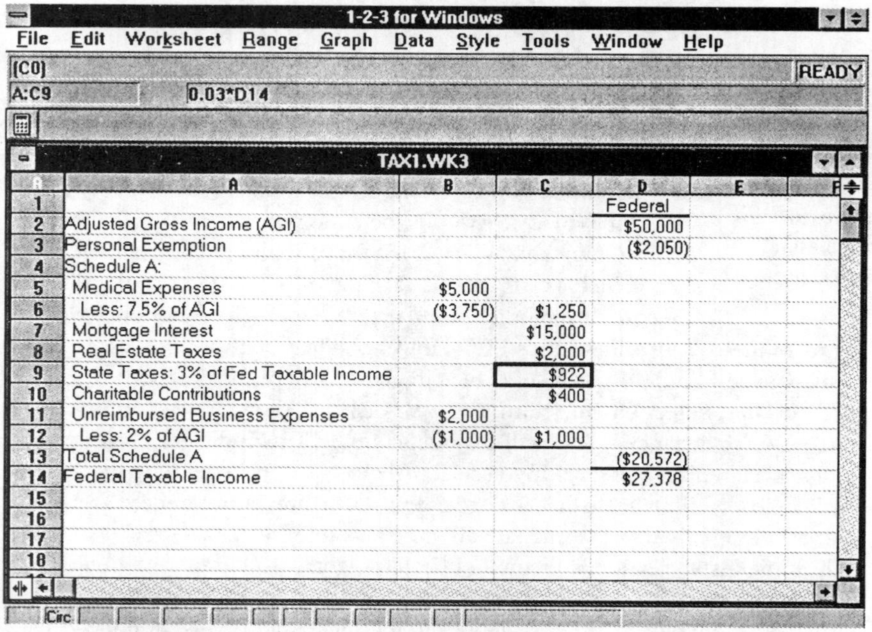

Figure 2-21   An intentional circular reference

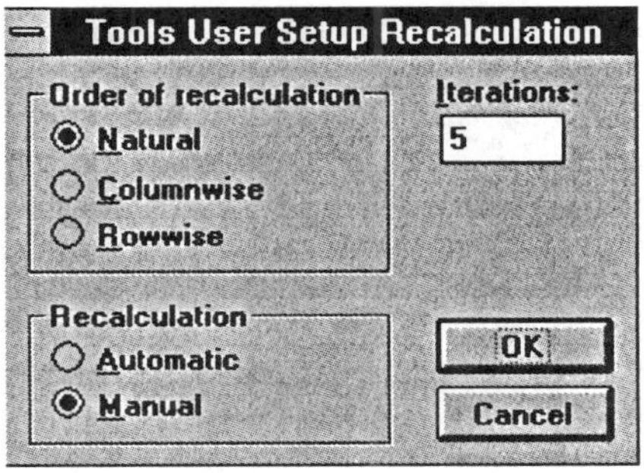

Figure 2-22 Specifying five iterations

To compute the correct tax due, you must force 1-2-3 for Windows to recalculate the worksheet file more than once. To do this, select Tools User Setup Recalculation, and specify more than one Iteration. In Figure 2-22, for example, 5 Iterations are specified. The number of Iterations corresponds to the number of passes 1-2-3 will make on the worksheet file before it completes recalculation.

Figure 2-23 shows what happens when you return to the worksheet and press CALC (F9). After five iterations, 1-2-3 returns $824 in cell C9. With each iteration, 1-2-3 comes closer to resolving the circular reference. In fact, this is how 1-2-3 recalculates the worksheet after each iteration:

Iteration number	State Taxes (Cell C9)	Total Schedule A (Cell D13)	Federal Taxable Income (Cell D14)
1	821.347	-20471.347	27378.228
2	824.360	-20474.360	27478.653
3	824.269	-20474.269	27475.640
4	824.272	-20474.272	27475.731
5	824.272	-20474.272	27475.728

You should always press CALC (F9) again to make sure that 1-2-3 has converged on the correct values. In this case, pressing CALC (F9) again causes 1-2-3 to recalculate the worksheet five more times. Because it returns the same values as in Figure 2-23, you know that 1-2-3 performed enough passes. The CIRC indicator will still be displayed, though.

	A	B	C	D	E	F
1				Federal		
2	Adjusted Gross Income (AGI)			$50,000		
3	Personal Exemption			($2,050)		
4	Schedule A:					
5	Medical Expenses	$5,000				
6	Less: 7.5% of AGI	($3,750)	$1,250			
7	Mortgage Interest		$15,000			
8	Real Estate Taxes		$2,000			
9	State Taxes: 3% of Fed Taxable Income		$824			
10	Charitable Contributions		$400			
11	Unreimbursed Business Expenses	$2,000				
12	Less: 2% of AGI	($1,000)	$1,000			
13	Total Schedule A			($20,474)		
14	Federal Taxable Income			$27,476		
15						
16						
17						
18						

Cell reference: [C0] A:C9 0.03*D14 READY
Window: TAX1.WK3

Figure 2-23   Figure 2-21 after five iterations

Note: Help's About 1-2-3 is inconsistent, and doesn't always indicate the cell causing the circular reference. Although the dialog box in Figure 2-24 does indicate cell C9, in some instances it indicates cell D14 instead, which contains the Federal Taxable Income formula @SUM(D2..D13), and indirectly depends on cell C9. The cell 1-2-3 for Windows identifies in the About 1-2-3 dialog box seems to depend somewhat on the last formula you entered or edited.

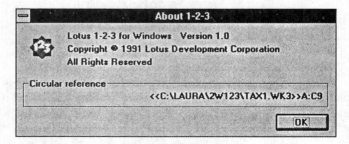

Figure 2-24   The cell causing the circular reference

EDITING CELL ENTRIES

Once you've entered a label, value, or formula in a cell, you can easily modify it using EDIT mode. For example, imagine cell A1 contains the misspelled label **Marketing Porposal**. To use the keyboard to modify this label, move the cell pointer to A1 and press EDIT (F2). 1-2-3 enters EDIT mode and places the cursor at the end of 'Marketing Porposal in the contents box. To make a change, use the keys in Table 2-5.

Note: While entering data in a cell for the first time, you can enter EDIT mode by pressing EDIT (F2).

To correct the spelling, for instance, press CTRL+← once to move to the "P", then → once to locate the cursor under the first *o*. Press DEL to remove the *o*. The contents box now reads 'Marketing Prposal. Next, press →, then type **o**. The entry now appears as 'Marketing Proposal. Press ENTER to confirm the entry.

TABLE 2-5 Edit Mode Keys

Key	*Action*
←	Moves the cursor left one character.
→	Moves the cursor right one character.
END	Moves the cursor to the end of the entry.
HOME	Moves the cursor to the beginning of the entry.
CTRL+→ or TAB	For a label, moves the cursor to the beginning of the previous word. For a value or formula, moves to the beginning of the previous value or cell reference.
CTRL+← or SHIFT+TAB	For a label, moves the cursor to the end of the next word. For a value or formula, moves to the end of the next value or cell reference.
DEL	Deletes the character to the right of the cursor. In READY mode, deletes everything in a cell, including Style settings.
SHIFT+←	Highlights the character to the left. Keep pressing ← to continue to highlight characters.
SHIFT+→	Highlights the character to the right. Keep pressing → to continue to highlight characters.
BACKSPACE	Deletes the character to the left of the cursor or the highlighted characters.
ESC	Erases the entry from the contents box so you can type a new entry and press ENTER to confirm it. Pressing ESC again, however, restores the original entry, quits EDIT mode, and returns you to the worksheet.

You can also edit this label using the mouse. To do this, select cell A1, then move the mouse pointer to the contents box and click on the location where you want to make the change—just before the first *o*. 1-2-3 enters EDIT mode and places the cursor just before the *o*. Press DEL to remove the *o* then press → to move the insertion point one character to the right. Type *o* and the entry now appears as 'Marketing Proposal. To confirm your changes and place the edited entry in the current cell, either press ENTER or select the Confirm (✔) icon in the input line.

> ▼ *Tip:*   Double-clicking on a cell selects it, places you in EDIT mode, and lo-cates the cursor at the end of the entry in the contents box.

On the other hand, to erase this entire entry while in EDIT mode and begin again, press ESC. You can then type a new entry from scratch and confirm it. However, pressing ESC a second time cancels all the changes you made while in EDIT mode, restores the original entry, and returns you to the worksheet in READY mode.

While you are editing a value or formula, you can enter POINT mode. For example, suppose you are in EDIT mode and the formula 50+20 is displayed in the contents box. Type an operator like +, and 1-2-3 changes to VALUE mode. When you use the mouse or any of the cursor-movement keys to point to a selection in the worksheet, 1-2-3 enters POINT mode (see "Pointing," above).

> ▼ *Tip:*   To convert a formula to its displayed value, press CALC (F9) while in EDIT mode. For example, imagine you move the cell pointer to cell A4, which contains @SUM(A1..A3) and displays 50, then press EDIT (F2) to enter EDIT mode. Press CALC (F9), and 1-2-3 converts the contents of A4 to 50. Press ENTER to confirm the entry and place it in the work-sheet.

Deleting Part of an Entry

You can also use the keyboard or the mouse to delete just part of an entry. Imagine that cell A1 contains the label '1991 Expenses. To delete only the year 1991 from this label using the mouse, double-click on cell A1 to select this cell and enter EDIT mode. In the contents box, highlight "1991 ", then press DEL or BACKSPACE. The label will now read 'Expenses. Press ENTER or select the Confirm (✔) icon to confirm this entry and return to the worksheet.

To do this using the keyboard, position the cell selector in cell A1, then press EDIT (F2) to enter EDIT mode. The cursor will be located at the end of the entry. Press HOME to move the cursor to the beginning of the entry, then → to move to the first "1". Press and hold down SHIFT, then press → five times to highlight "1991 ". Press BACKSPACE or DEL to delete the highlighted characters, then press ENTER to confirm the edited label and return to the worksheet.

Note: To delete the contents of a cell, use the 1-2-3 Classic /Range Erase command. To erase everything in a cell, except Style settings, press DEL (see Chapter 7).

RANGES

A *range* is a rectangular block of contiguous cells, as small as a single cell or as large as the entire worksheet file. A range is defined by two cell addresses representing the upper-left and lower-right corners. In Figure 2-25, for example, the *two-dimensional* (2-D) range B:B1..B:B4 encompasses cells B:B1, B:B2, B:B3, and B:B4. And the cell C:B4 is considered the single-cell range C:B4..C:B4.

Similarly, the range A:F2..C:H5 represents a three-dimensional (3-D) range. A *three-dimensional* range consists of the same contiguous cells in multiple worksheets. For example, A:F2..C:H5 consists of the 2-D range F2..H5 in worksheets A, B, and C.

Note: A range can't encompass multiple worksheet files. Instead, specify multiple ranges. To select a range in another open file, see Chapter 4.

A range is an efficient way to specify data in commands or in formulas. In fact, many 1-2-3 for Windows commands and @functions act on a range. For example, if you select the Edit Move Cells command, 1-2-3 asks you to supply a range to move from and a range to move to. Similarly, you'll usually use the @SUM function to sum a range of values. You can select a range:

- In READY mode, before you choose a command.
- In POINT mode, during a command.
- In POINT mode, while entering a formula.

Each of these selection methods is discussed in detail in the following sections.

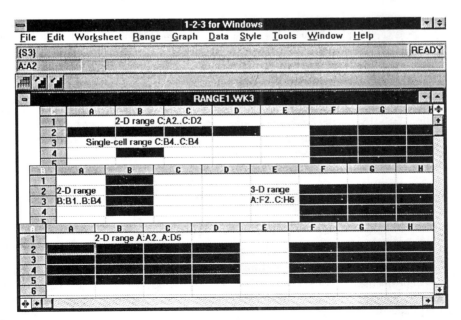

Figure 2-25 Example ranges

Preselecting a 2-D Range

You can also pre-select a range before you choose a command from the 1-2-3 Classic menu.

By preselecting a range before you select a command, the range remains selected even after the command is completed (unless of course the command eliminates the selection; for example, /Worksheet Erase eliminates the selection because it erases the entire worksheet). The main advantage of preselecting a range is that you can use several commands on the same data without having to select the same range for each command. For example, you might want to preselect a range, then use the Range Format command to assign numeric formatting and the Style Font command to assign a font.

Using the mouse or the keyboard to preselect a 2-D range before invoking a command is really a matter of personal preference. You'll want to employ different methods using the keyboard, however, depending on whether the range is empty or is filled (contains values and labels).

Preselecting an Empty 2-D Range

You can use either the mouse or keyboard to preselect an empty 2-D range, B2..D5 in Figure 2-26, for example. Using the mouse, select the upper-left corner cell, cell B2. This is called the *anchor cell*. Begin to drag the mouse to the diagonally opposite corner—cell C5—which is called the *free cell*. As you do so, 1-2-3 will show the range currently outlined in the contents box. Continue to drag the pointer until A:B2..A:C5 is outlined and displayed in the contents box as in Figure 2-26A. When you release the mouse button, you can see in Figure 2-26B that A:B2..A:C5 stays selected in the worksheet.

Note: If the diagonally opposite corner cell of the range doesn't appear within the current worksheet window, move the mouse pointer to the edge of the window in the direction of the desired cell, and 1-2-3 will scroll the contents of the window in that direction.

You can now select any command that requires a range, and 1-2-3 will automatically apply the command to your selection. For example, Figure 2-26B shows how A:B2..A:D5 is automatically displayed in the Range text box when you select the Range Format command. If you don't immediately select a command, 1-2-3 for Windows cancels a preselected range whenever you move the cell pointer to a cell other than the anchor cell, or you select another range.

To select this empty 2-D range using the keyboard, follow these steps:

1. Move the cell pointer to cell B2.
2. Press F4 to anchor the cell pointer in B2, which is now the anchor cell. The contents box will display this as the single-cell range A:B2..A:B2.
3. Press → twice then ↓ three times. This moves the free cell (the cell diagonally opposite the cell pointer) to cell D5. The range A:B2..A:D5 will now be outlined and displayed in the contents box, just as in Figure 2-26A. Press ENTER to confirm this range.

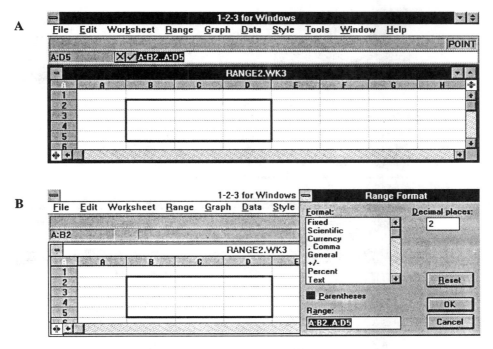

Figure 2-26 Using the mouse to preselect an empty 2-D range

Note: The icons you can use to move around a worksheet don't work when you are selecting a range.

Selecting a Filled 2-D Range

When a range is filled with values and labels, you can use shortcuts to preselect this range. For example, the 2-D range B2..C5 in Figure 2-27 is filled with values and labels. To preselect this range, first, move the cell pointer to B2, the upper-left cell. Then press F4 to anchor the cell pointer in this cell.

Next, press END then →. Because this range is filled with values, 1-2-3 automatically moves to the last contiguous cell that contains an entry, cell D2. Figure 2-27A shows how A:B2..A:D2 is outlined and displayed in the contents box.

Now press END then ↓, and 1-2-3 automatically moves to the last contiguous cell in column D that contains an entry, cell D5. Figure 2-27B shows how A:B2..A:D5 is now outlined and displayed in the contents box. Press ENTER to complete this selection.

Note: Using the mouse, you preselect a filled range in the same way as an empty range. See the previous section.

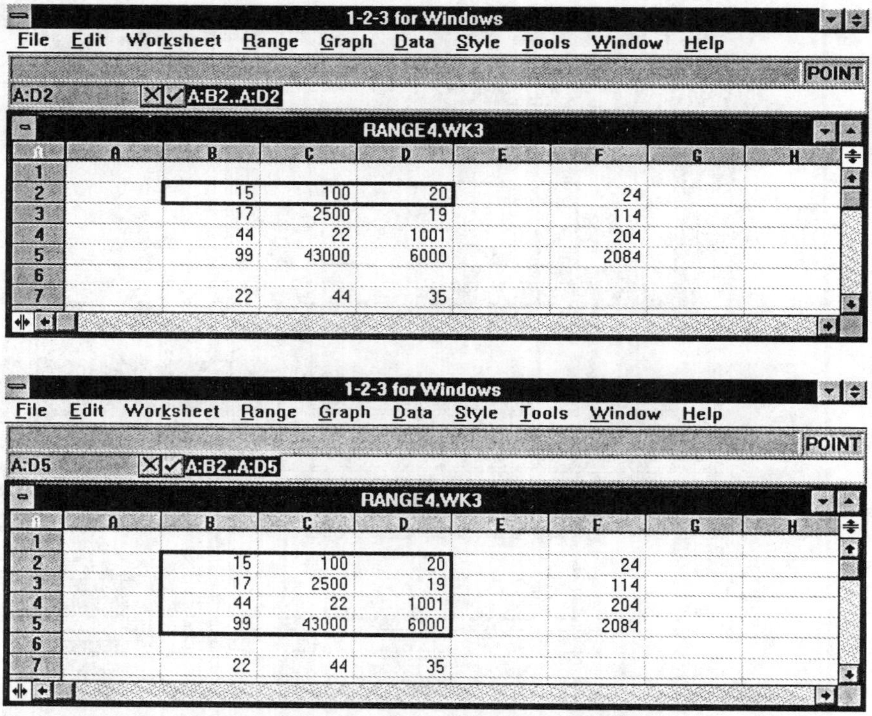

Figure 2-27 Using the keyboard to preselect a filled 2-D range

Preselecting a 3-D Range

You can't preselect a 3-D range using the mouse. On the other hand, preselecting a three-dimensional (3-D) range using the keyboard really isn't very different from pre-selecting a 2-D range. For example, to preselect the 3-D range A:A1..C:D4 in Figure 2-28, follow these steps:

Note: Remember from Chapter 1 that you use the Worksheet Insert Sheet command to add worksheets to a file, and the Window Split command (or the 🔳 icon) to place the worksheet file in Perspective mode.

1. Move the cell pointer to the upper-left cell of the range, A:A1.

2. Press F4 to anchor the cell pointer in cell A:A1.

3. Move to the diagonally opposite corner of the range within worksheet A, cell A:D4. Press END, then →, END again, and then ↓ to locate the cell pointer at cell A:D4. You can see in Figure 2-28A how A:A1..A:D4 is displayed in the contents box and outlined in the worksheet.

4. Press CTRL+PGUP twice to highlight the same range in worksheets B and C. Figure 2-28B shows how the entire range A:A1..C:D4 is displayed in the contents box and outlined in the worksheet.

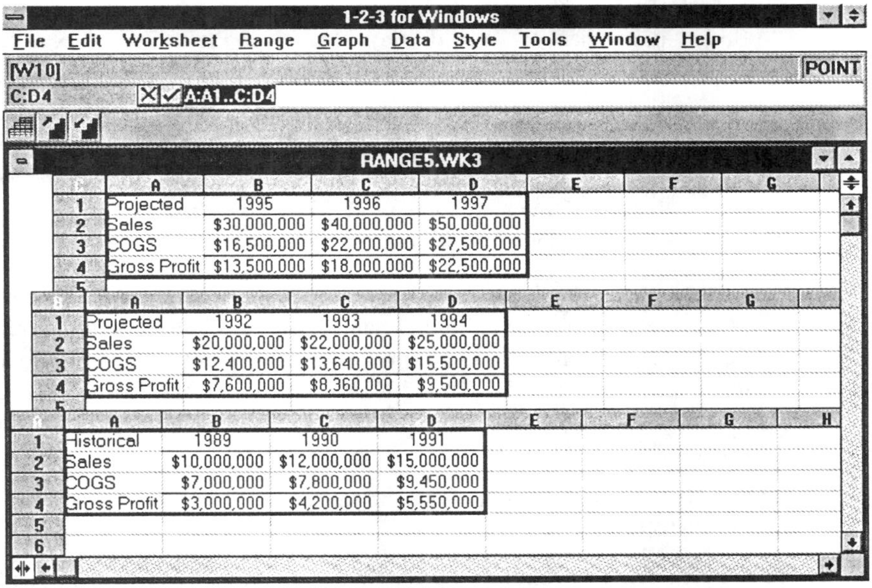

Figure 2-28 Using the keyboard to preselect a 3-D range

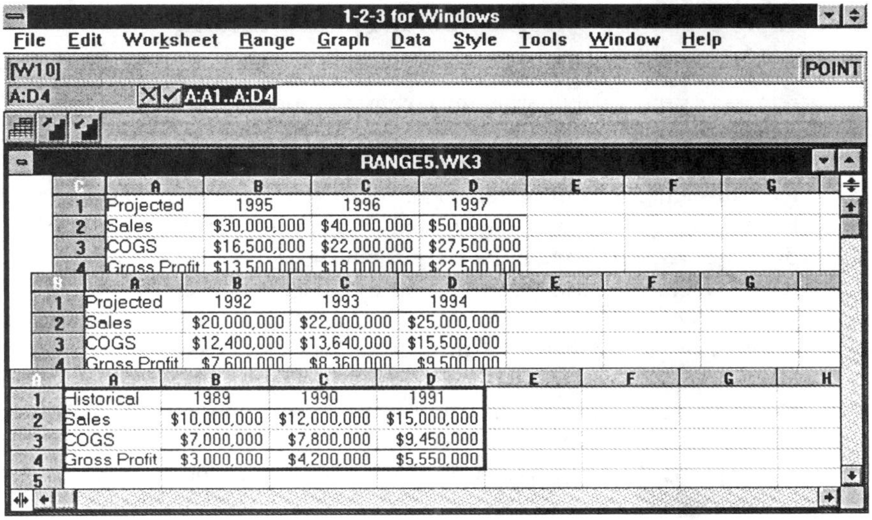

Note: You can't use the 🔲 and 🔲 icons to select a 3-D range.

5.   Press ENTER to confirm this selection.

▼ *Tip:*   You can also preselect a 3-D range using Group mode. See "Using Group Mode to Specify a 3-D Range," later.

Selecting a Range After Choosing a Command

You can also select a range after you choose a command. When you do so, the range remains selected only during the command; afterwards, the cell pointer returns to the location it was in before you invoked the command. As you become familiar with 1-2-3 for Windows, you'll probably agree that pointing to a range during a command is the least appealing and efficient method. While you're trying to point to a range, the dialog box constantly seems in the way, even though you can move it. If that doesn't faze you, the way 1-2-3 for Windows slowly zooms in and out between the worksheet and the dialog box (especially when you point with the mouse) certainly will.

The way you select a range during a command is similar to the way you preselect a range. You can see this in Figure 2-29A. The cell pointer is located in cell A1, and the Style Alignment command (see Chapter 7) has been selected. To specify a center label alignment in the range A1..E1, turn on the Center option in the dialog box, then press TAB twice to move to the Range text box.

To specify the range A1..E1 by pointing, follow this procedure:

1. Press F6 to return to the spreadsheet. As you can see in Figure 2-29B, 1-2-3 changes to POINT mode. The cell pointer is located in cell A1, its position before you selected Style Alignment. 1-2-3 also displays this cell in the contents box as the single-cell range A:A1..A:A1. The cell pointer is unanchored, however.

    Note: Some commands, like Range Format, automatically anchor the cell pointer when you return to the worksheet during a command. Likewise, when you choose a command from the 1-2-3 Classic menu, the cell pointer is anchored in the current cell. If you need to, press ESC to unanchor the cell. Then move the cell pointer to the upper-right corner of the range you want to select before you anchor it by pressing . (period).

2. Use the mouse or keyboard to outline the range A1..E1. For example, pressing . (period) to anchor the cell pointer in cell A1. END, then → will outline this filled range. The contents box in Figure 2-29B shows how 1-2-3 for Windows displays this range as A:A1..A:E1. Press ENTER to confirm this selection. 1-2-3 returns you to the dialog box, where the range A:A1..A:E1 is now displayed in the Range text box just like in Figure 2-29C.

    Note: To cancel a selected range and return to the dialog box, press ESC twice. To change a selection, press ESC to cancel the current selection, then start over again.

3. To complete this command, press ENTER or select OK. You can see the results in Figure 2-29D.

> ▼ *Tip:*   Some commands, like File Print, accept multiple ranges when they are separated by a ; (semicolon). For example, to specify A1..A:D20;A:A50..A:D70 from the File Print Range text box, press F6 to return to the worksheet, select A:A1..A:D20, then press ENTER. When 1-2-3 returns you to the dialog box, type ;, press F6 again to return to the worksheet, select A:A50..A:D70, and then press ENTER to confirm and return to the dialog box.

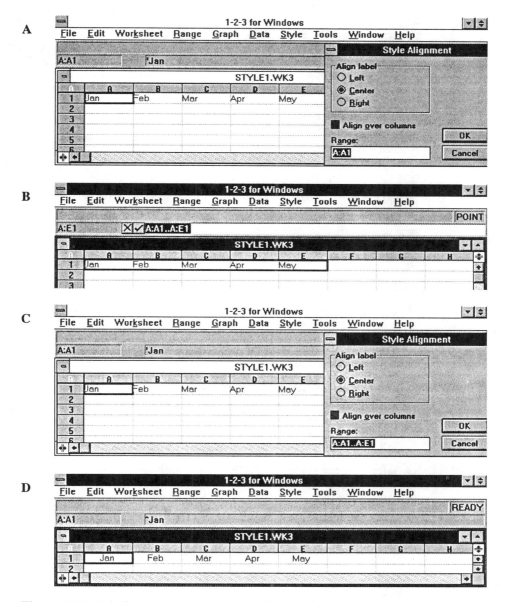

Figure 2-29 Pointing to a range after selecting a command

Using Group Mode to Select a 3-D Range

When you are going to use commands that format or add styles to a range, you can also use Group mode (see Chapter 1) to select a 3-D range before or during a command. To see this, let's examine the 3-D worksheet in Figure 2-30A.

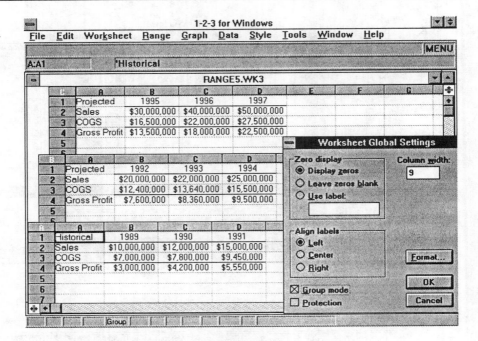

Figure 2-30 Using Group mode to select a 3-D range

Imagine that you want to center the labels in column A of worksheets A, B, and C. First, select the Worksheet Global Settings command. In the dialog box shown in Figure 2-30A, turn on Group mode and select OK to confirm. 1-2-3 for Windows displays the Group indicator at the bottom of the worksheet, indicating that Group mode is on.

Next, you can either preselect the range or specify it after you choose the Style Alignment command. For example, Figure 2-30B shows what happens when you select Style Alignment, turn on the Center option, move to the Range text box, press F6 to return to the worksheet, select the *2-D* range A:A1..A:A4, and press ENTER to confirm. Notice that just this 2-D range appears selected in the worksheet and in the Range text box. 1-2-3 for Windows actually evaluates it as the 3-D range A:A1..C:A4, however. When you press ENTER or select OK, you can see in Figure 2-30C that 1-2-3 centers the labels in column A of worksheets A, B, and C.

Selecting a Range during a Formula

You can also point to a range while you are entering a formula. For instance, here's how you would create the formula @AVG(C2..C4) in cell C5 of Figure 2-31:

1. Move the cell pointer to cell C5. Then enter **@AVG(**. As you can see in Figure 2-31A, 1-2-3 enters VALUE mode.

B

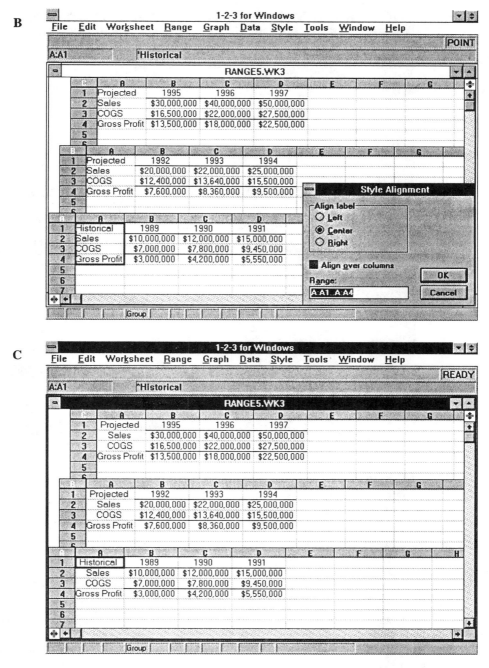

C

Figure 2-30   Using Group mode to select a 3-D range *(continued)*

A

1-2-3 for Windows

File   Edit   Worksheet   Range   Graph   Data   Style   Tools   Window   Help

[F0]   VALUE

A:C5   X✓@AVG(

FORM1.WK3

	A	B	C	D	E	F	G	H
1			Sales					
2	Jan		200000					
3	Feb		400000					
4	Mar		350000					
5								
6								

B

1-2-3 for Windows

File   Edit   Worksheet   Range   Graph   Data   Style   Tools   Window   Help

{B} [F0]   POINT

A:C4   X✓@AVG(A:C2..A:C4)

FORM1.WK3

	A	B	C	D	E	F	G	H
1			Sales					
2	Jan		200000					
3	Feb		400000					
4	Mar		350000					
5								
6								

C

1-2-3 for Windows

File   Edit   Worksheet   Range   Graph   Data   Style   Tools   Window   Help

[F0]   READY

A:C5   @AVG(C2..C4)

FORM1.WK3

	A	B	C	D	E	F	G	H
1			Sales					
2	Jan		200000					
3	Feb		400000					
4	Mar		350000					
5			316667					
6								

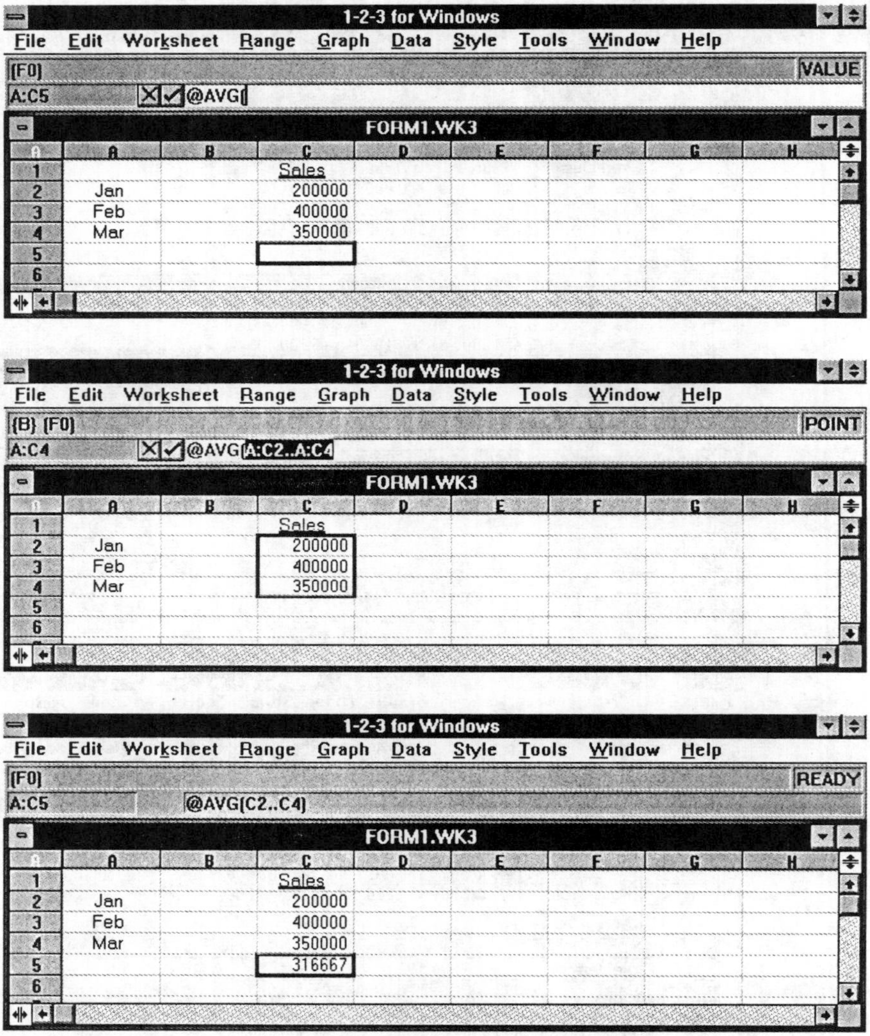

Figure 2-31 Pointing to a range while creating a formula

2. Move the cell pointer to cell C2 by pressing ↑ three times. 1-2-3/W enters POINT mode.

3. Select the range C2..C4 using the mouse or keyboard. For example, press . (period) to anchor the cell pointer in C2. The formula will now read @AVG(C2..C2 in the contents box. Then press ↓ three times to outline this filled range. Figure 2-31B shows that the formula now reads @AVG(A:C2..A:C4.

4. Press ENTER to confirm this range. 1-2-3 automatically adds the closing parentheses to create @AVG(C2..C4), returns to READY mode, and displays 316667 in cell C5

of Figure 2-31C. (For the reasons why 1-2-3 eliminates the worksheet components of the cell references, see "When 1-2-3 for Windows Uses Abbreviated Cell References," earlier.)

▼ **Tip:**   If you later insert or delete columns, rows, and/or worksheets that are included in a formula range, 1-2-3 automatically adjusts the formula range reference. If you delete row 2 in Figure 2-31C, for instance, 1-2-3 adjusts the formula @AVG(C2..C4) to @AVG(C2..C3) because row 3 becomes row 2, and row 4 becomes row 3 (see Chapter 1).

NAMING RANGES

Thus far, all ranges have been defined as cell addresses, such as A:A1..A:B3. You can assign a name to a range, however, and then use the range name in commands and formulas. The biggest advantage of using range names is that they are much easier to remember than cell addresses.

Release 2.2 users will find a new feature: undefined range names. Because an undefined range name has no defined cell coordinates, you can create formulas using undefined names, and then supply the coordinates later.

Note: The 1-2-3 Classic menu includes the /Range Name Note command, which isn't accessible through the 1-2-3 for Windows menu. This command allows you to add or delete notes to range names.

Creating a Named Range

Suppose that you want to assign a name to the range B2..B4 in Figure 2-32A. To do so, preselect this range ("Ranges," above, explains why this is the easiest way), then choose the Range Name Create command. You'll see the dialog box shown in Figure 2-32A, which displays A:B2..A:B4 in the Range name text box. (If this is the first time you're assigning a range name in the worksheet file, you won't see any names in the list box.)

While you are deciding on a range name, keep in mind the following rules:

- Range names can be up to 15 characters long. If you try to enter a longer name, 1-2-3 truncates the name.

- Capitalization doesn't matter; for instance, 1-2-3 evaluates "legal", "LEGAL", and "LEgal" as the same range name.

- You can include spaces, periods, underscores, or any other LMCS character (see Chapter 9) in a range name. It's wise to avoid + – * / & > < @ # { and ?, which may cause you (and 1-2-3) to confuse a range name with actual formulas. Similarly, don't start a range name with ! (exclamation point).

- Don't use a number as the first character of a range name—1-2-3 won't let you use that range name in a formula.

- Don't assign a name that resembles a cell address, row number, or column letter. For example, 1-2-3 won't evaluate Q1, 1990, or BT entered in a formula as a valid range name.

- Don't use @Function names (such as @AVG) and macro key names (such as GOTO) for range names (see Chapters 9 and 14).

- You can enter a range name as an absolute address by preceding it with $. (See "Copying Formulas" in Chapter 7.)

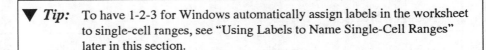

▼ *Tip:*   To have 1-2-3 for Windows automatically assign labels in the worksheet to single-cell ranges, see "Using Labels to Name Single-Cell Ranges" later in this section.

After you type a name, **JAN** for example, press ENTER or select OK to complete the command. (Select Create to continue to create range names.) The next time you select Range Name Create, you'll see JAN as a defined range name in the list box, just as in Figure 2-32B. Figure 2-32B also shows other range names created in this worksheet.

If a newly created range name defines a multicell range, 1-2-3 immediately substitutes the range name into all existing formulas using this range. By comparing cell B5 in Figures 2-32A and B, for example, you'll see that 1-2-3 for Windows converts @SUM(B2..B4) to @SUM(JAN). For a single-cell named range no substitution takes place.

Using a Range Name

Once you've named a range, you can use that name in place of cell addresses when you enter formulas and when you respond to commands. In Figure 2-32B for example, entering the formula @SUM(JAN) in a worksheet is now equivalent to entering @SUM(B2..B4). Likewise, you can use a name that defines a single-cell range anywhere you would use a cell address, as in +C5*GOODS/4 or +COGS/AVG_PRICE, for example. If you use a range name that defines a multiple-cell range in a formula where 1-2-3 expects a single-cell range, however, the formula will evaluate to ERR.

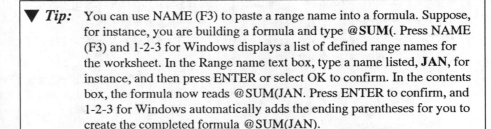

▼ *Tip:*   You can use NAME (F3) to paste a range name into a formula. Suppose, for instance, you are building a formula and type **@SUM(**. Press NAME (F3) and 1-2-3 for Windows displays a list of defined range names for the worksheet. In the Range name text box, type a name listed, **JAN**, for instance, and then press ENTER or select OK to confirm. In the contents box, the formula now reads @SUM(JAN. Press ENTER to confirm, and 1-2-3 for Windows automatically adds the ending parentheses for you to create the completed formula @SUM(JAN).

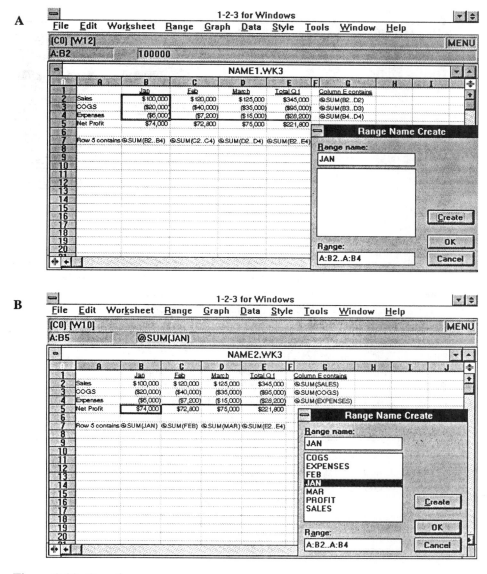

Figure 2-32 Creating a range name

When you move the contents of a named range using /Move or Edit Move Cells, 1-2-3 automatically adjusts the range name to conform to this new location. For example, if you move the data in B2..B4 of Figure 2-32B to I2..I4, 1-2-3 reassigns the JAN range name to I2..I4. (The exception is when you use Edit Cut and Paste. See Chapter 7.)

Similarly, if you delete the row or column that contains the upper-left or lower-right corner cell of a named range, 1-2-3 for Windows also adjusts the cell coordinates assigned

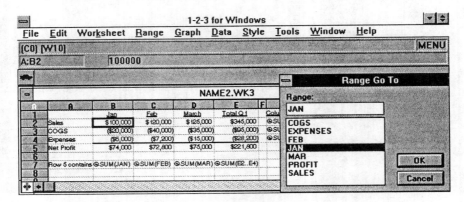

Figure 2-33 Using GOTO to move to a defined range

to a range name. Delete row 2 in Figure 2-32B, for instance, and 1-2-3 adjusts the cell coordinates assigned to JAN from B2..B4 to B2..B3. Delete the contents of cell B2, however, and the cell coordinates of JAN aren't affected.

It's a different matter if you move data into the upper-left or lower-right corner cell of a named range. When you do, 1-2-3 for Windows invalidates the range name, and any formulas that reference the named range will return ERR. If you move data from a cell into cell B2 of Figure 2-32B, for instance, cell B5 will still contain @SUM(JAN), but it would return ERR because the range name JAN will be undefined (see "Using Undefined Range Names," later). If you select Range Name Create, JAN will no longer be displayed in the list box. Neither will SALES, originally assigned to B2..D2, so @SUM(SALES) in cell E2 will also return ERR.

> ▼ *Tip:*   When you use GOTO to jump to a location in a worksheet file, 1-2-3 will display a list of defined range names you can choose from. Press GOTO (F5), or select the Range Go To command or the ⬛ icon, and 1-2-3 displays the Range Go To dialog box shown in Figure 2-33. Select JAN from the list, for instance, and you can see that 1-2-3 moves the cell pointer to the first cell in JAN, cell B2.

Inserting a Range Name Table into a Worksheet

You can use the Range Name command to place a list in the worksheet containing all current range names in alphabetical order, followed by the cell coordinates each name is assigned to. (Undefined range names, discussed later in this section, don't appear in the table.) You'll find a Range Name Table especially helpful for troubleshooting, or when you're having trouble remembering what cell coordinates you've assigned to range names.

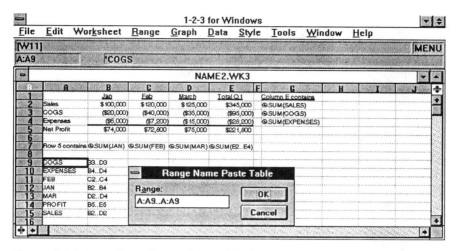

Figure 2-34 Creating a Range Name Table

Note: Be sure to a choose a starting location that has enough empty cells below it and an empty column adjacent to it to accommodate the table. Otherwise, 1-2-3 for Windows will write over any existing data when it creates the table. Remember, however, that pressing ALT+BACKSPACE will activate Undo and reverse the effect of the Range Name Paste Table command.

For example, to create a Range Name Table for the range names shown in Figure 2-32B, preselect the upper-left corner cell where you want the table to begin—cell A9, for instance. Then select the Range Name Paste Table command. You'll see the dialog box shown in Figure 2-34, which displays A:A9..A:A9 in the Range text box . When you select OK or press ENTER, 1-2-3 creates the two-column table that appears in A9..B15. Thus, the name COGS has been assigned to the range B3..D3.

Using Labels to Name Single-Cell Ranges

For a single-cell range, you can use the Range Name Labels command to assign a label in an adjoining cell as its range name. For example, you can use the labels in column A of Figure 2-35 as range names for the adjoining cells in column B. To do this, first preselect the *labels* you want to use as range names—A2..A11. Next, select the Range Name Label Create command.

You'll see the dialog box shown in Figure 2-35A, with the preselected range A:A2..A:A11 displayed in the Range text box. The Right, Left, Up, and Down options allow you to specify where the cells you want to name are located in relation to the labels. In Figure 2-35A, for example, the values to be named are in column B, just to the right of the labels in column A. So the default, Right, is the correct selection.

A

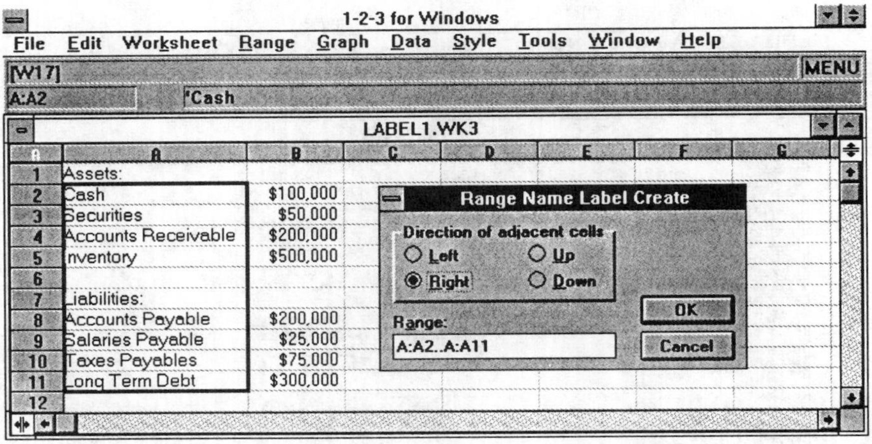

```
1-2-3 for Windows
 File   Edit   Worksheet   Range   Graph   Data   Style   Tools   Window   Help
[W17]                                                                        MENU
A:A2              'Cash
```

	LABEL1.WK3						
	A	B	C	D	E	F	G
1	Assets:						
2	Cash	$100,000					
3	Securities	$50,000					
4	Accounts Receivable	$200,000					
5	Inventory	$500,000					
6							
7	Liabilities:						
8	Accounts Payable	$200,000					
9	Salaries Payable	$25,000					
10	Taxes Payables	$75,000					
11	Long Term Debt	$300,000					
12							

Range Name Label Create

Direction of adjacent cells
○ Left   ○ Up
◉ Right   ○ Down

Range:
A:A2..A:A11

[OK]   [Cancel]

B

```
1-2-3 for Windows
 File   Edit   Worksheet   Range   Graph   Data   Style   Tools   Window   Help
{Helvetica8} [W13]                                                           NT
A:D2              'ACCOUNTS PAYABL
```

Range Name Paste Table

Range:
A:D2..A:D2

[OK]   [Cancel]

	LABEL2.WK3			
	A	B	C	D
1	Assets:			
2	Cash	$100,000		ACCOUNTS PAYABL B8..B8
3	Securities	$50,000		ACCOUNTS RECEIV B4..B4
4	Accounts Receivable	$200,000		CASH B2..B2
5	Inventory	$500,000		INVENTORY B5..B5
6				LIABILITIES: B7..B7
7	Liabilities:			LONG TERM DEBT B11..B11
8	Accounts Payable	$200,000		SALARIES PAYABL B9..B9
9	Salaries Payable	$25,000		SECURITIES B3..B3
10	Taxes Payables	$75,000		TAXES PAYABLES B10..B10
11	Long Term Debt	$300,000		
12				

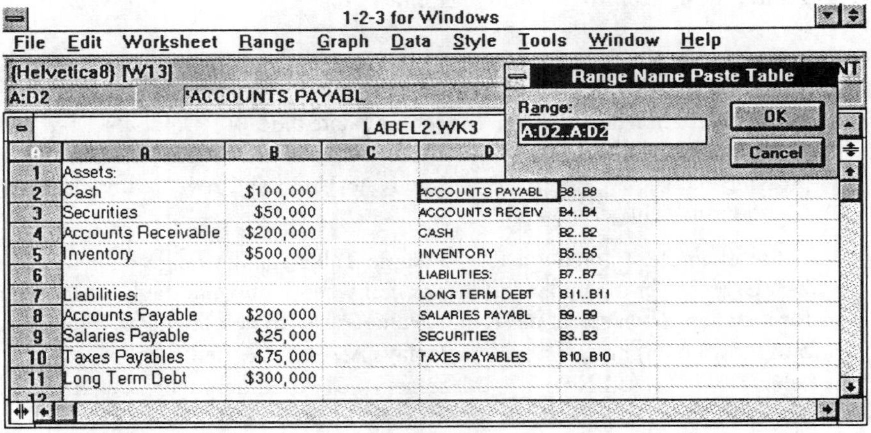

Figure 2-35   Using labels to name single-cell ranges

Note: The cells you want to name *must* be adjacent to the corresponding labels. If the values in Figure 2-35 were located in column C, not column B, 1-2-3 for Windows would still assign the labels in column A to the corresponding blank cells in column B.

When you press ENTER or select OK, 1-2-3 for Windows creates single-cell range names using the labels in column A. To see this, the Range Name Paste Table command has been used in Figure 2-35B to create a Range Name Table beginning in cell D2. As you can see, 1-2-3 assigns the range name ACCOUNTS PAYABL to the single-cell range B8..B8, ACCOUNTS RECEIV to B4..B4, and so on. So 1-2-3 automatically truncates range names that would exceed the 15-character limit. You should also notice that 1-2-3 assigns the range name LIABILITIES: to the blank cell B11.

Because these range names are assigned to single-cell ranges, 1-2-3 doesn't substitute them into any existing formulas. If cell C2 contained the formula +B2/2, for example, 1-2-3 wouldn't convert it to +CASH/2.

Using Undefined Range Names

An *undefined range name* has no defined cell coordinates. If you enter a formula with an undefined range name in it, 1-2-3 for Windows lets you complete the formula, but the formula evaluates to ERR until you define the range name using the Range Name Create command. You can't specify an undefined range name during a command.

The advantage of using undefined range names is that you can create formulas but supply the cell coordinates later. Without having to stop and define each range name before using it, you can be much more fluid in developing your worksheets.

The disadvantage to using undefined range names is that there's no easy way to keep track of them. Undefined range names don't appear in any of the Range Name list boxes, nor are they included in a table created using the Range Name Table command.

To create an undefined range name, simply use it in a formula. For example, you can enter the formula +TOTAL_SALES/12, even though TOTAL_SALES hasn't been defined. This formula evaluates to ERR, though, until you use the Range Name Create command to assign a cell address to TOTAL_SALES.

You can also change a defined range name to an undefined range name by breaking the link between the name and its cell coordinates. For example, imagine you want to make the defined range name JAN, assigned to B2..B4 in Figure 2-32B, an undefined range name. To do this, select the Range Name Delete command. You'll see a dialog box listing all the defined names in the current worksheet file. (Figure 2-36 shows the Range Name Delete dialog box.) Select JAN from the list box, then select Undefine. Press ENTER or select OK to confirm.

Because JAN is now an undefined range name, 1-2-3 for Windows unlinks the range name from its previously assigned cell coordinates, B2..B4. So any formulas, like @SUM(JAN) in cell B5 of Figure 2-32B, still refer to JAN but return ERR.

Changing a Named Range

You also use the Range Name Create command to change the cell coordinates assigned to an existing range name. To see this, let's return to Figure 2-32B, where the range name JAN has been assigned to B2..B4. Suppose, however, that you want this name assigned to I2..I4.

The easiest way is to first preselect the new cell coordinates, I2..I4. Then select the Range Name Create command. The preselected range A:I2..A:I4 will be displayed in the Range text box at the bottom of the dialog box. In the Range name text box, type **JAN**.

(You don't want to choose JAN from the list box, because 1-2-3 will change the Range text box to show that JAN is currently assigned to, A:B2..A:B4.) When you press ENTER or select OK, 1-2-3 assigns JAN to these new coordinates. Any formulas that refer to JAN, like @SUM(JAN) in cell B5, will automatically refer to this new range.

Note: To change the name a range is assigned to, first use Range Name Delete to delete the old range name. Then use the Range Name Create command and assign the range to the new name.

Deleting a Range Name

Deleting a range name is simple. For example, to delete the defined range name JAN in Figure 2-32B, select the Range Name Delete command. From the list of range names displayed, select JAN. (You can see this dialog box by looking ahead to Figure 2-36.) When you press ENTER, select OK, or choose Delete (to continue to delete range names), 1-2-3 for Windows deletes JAN as a defined range name.

In any formula in the worksheet that used this range name, 1-2-3 substitutes the cell coordinates in place of the deleted range name. Because JAN was assigned to B2..B4 in our example, 1-2-3 for Windows would change @SUM(JAN) in cell B5 of Figure 2-32B to @SUM(B2..B4).

Deleting All Range Names

The 1-2-3 Classic equivalent is /Range Name Reset. Once in a while, you may want to remove all the named ranges in the current worksheet file and start over with a clean slate. The Range Name Delete command's Delete All option wipes out all the named ranges in the current worksheet file. Named ranges in other open files are unaffected, even if they're referenced in the active file. (The next section discusses linking files with range names.)

Caution: The Delete All option doesn't ask for confirmation. Once you select it, the range names in the current worksheet file are gone. They're not irretrievably lost if you immediately press ALT+BACKSPACE to activate Undo and reverse the effect of Range Name Delete Delete All.

If you begin with Figure 2-32B, for example, and then select Range Name Delete Delete All, 1-2-3 for Windows deletes all the assigned range names. In addition, 1-2-3 substitutes the corresponding cell coordinates in all the formulas in Figure 2-32B that contain range names. In effect, the worksheet reverts back to Figure 2-32A. For example, @SUM(SALES) in cell E2 of Figure 2-32B reverts to @SUM(B2..D2), as in Figure 2-32A.

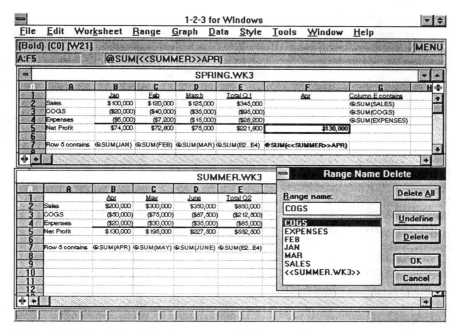

Figure 2-36 Referencing a range name in another file

Referencing Range Names in Other Worksheet Files

In a worksheet, you can reference range names in other worksheet files. Figure 2-36 shows an example of how to do this. For the most part, the file SPRING.WK3 contains the same information as Figure 2-32B. The file SUMMER.WK3 contains similar financial information, except for the months of April, May, and June. In fact, in SUMMER.WK3, the range name APR has been assigned to B2..B4, MAY to C2..C4, and JUNE to D2..D4.

Note: Chapter 3 discusses opening multiple files; Chapters 4 and 17 discuss file linking.

In cell F5 of SPRING.WK3, the formula @SUM(<<SUMMER>>APR) refers to the range APR in SUMMER.WK3. Notice that this formula returns 130,000, the same as the formula @SUM(APR) in cell B5 of SUMMER.WK3. This formula creates *file linking*; when the values in the range APR of SUMMER.WK3 change, so will the resulting value in cell F5 of SPRING.WK3.

From the active file, SPRING.WK3, you can even undefine (or delete) a range name defined in SUMMER.WK3, APR for instance. When you select Range Name Delete, you'll see the dialog box in Figure 2-36. Select <<SUMMER.WK3>>, then choose APR from the new list displayed. Choose Undefine and then press ENTER or select OK to confirm. (Remember that any formulas that refer to the undefined range name APR now evaluate to ERR.) The Delete All option, however, only deletes the range names in the active file, SPRING.WK3; it doesn't affect range names created in other open files, even if they're referenced, as <<SUMMER>>APR is, in the active file.

▼ *Tip:*   When more than one worksheet file is open, as in Figure 2-36, you can access the range names in all open files when you use NAME (F3) to create a formula. In Figure 2-36, for example, you can create the formula in cell F5 of SPRING.WK3 by first entering @SUM(. Then press NAME (F3), and you'll see <<SUMMER.WK3>> at the bottom of the Name list box. Select <<SUMMER.WK3>>, and you'll see a list of its named ranges: APR, MAY, and JUNE. Select APR, press ENTER to confirm, and the formula will read @SUM(<<SUMMER>>APR in the contents box. Press ENTER again, and 1-2-3 completes the formula as @SUM(<<SUMMER>>APR) by supplying the ending parentheses.

When you use GOTO (F5) or the 🔲 icon, you can also access range names from other open files in the same way. If you press GOTO (F5) in this example, you'd also see <<SUMMER.WK3>> in the Range Go To dialog box. Choose this selection, then choose APR from the list of SUMMER.WK3 range names listed. Press ENTER or select OK, and 1-2-3 will move the cell pointer to the first cell in APR, or cell B2 in the SUMMER.WK3 file.

SEARCHING AND REPLACING DATA

The 1-2-3 Classic equivalent is /Range Search.   In 1-2-3 for Windows, you'll want to use the Edit Find command to search a range for a character or a label. Or use this command to search for a text string within formulas such as a cell reference or a range name. You can even supply a replacement that 1-2-3 substitutes whenever it finds this string.

Although 1-2-3 for Window's Edit Find command is more powerful than in previous releases of 1-2-3, it's still incapable of performing some standard search tasks. For example, Edit Find can't find a value, such as 100, when it is alone in a cell. Neither can Edit Find locate formula results—that is, a value or label that is the result of a formula. So it can't find the value 100 when it's the result of the formula @SUM(A1..A2), although 1-2-3 for Windows can find the value 100 in the formula 100*20, or in the string "100 bananas." And finally, Edit Find won't search hidden columns or worksheets unless you redisplay them first.

Searching for a String

Imagine that you've previously entered the data in Figure 2-37. This worksheet contains formulas that reference the defined range name TOTAL. (See "Range Names," earlier.) Suppose that you want to search this range and check whether you have used TOTAL in the right formulas.

Rather than searching the worksheet yourself, you can have the Edit Find command do this for you. First, select Edit Find, and you'll see the dialog box shown in Figure 2-37.

▼ *Tip:* The 🖹 icon shown in Figure 2-37 is a shortcut for Edit Find.

In the Search for text box, enter the string you want to find. The string can be either text or numbers, but it can't exceed 512 characters. In this case, enter **TOTAL** or **total**. (Edit Find doesn't distinguish between cases.) Then accept the Action Find mode.

Next, choose the type of search you want to perform:

* **Formulas** searches only cells containing formulas.

* **Labels** searches only cells containing labels.

* **Both,** the default, searches cells containing labels and formulas.

Note: Edit Find never searches a cell that contains only a value.

In this case, choose Formulas. Otherwise, 1-2-3 for Windows will also "find" the Total labels in cells A2 and E1. Next, enter the range you want to search, **A1..E6** in the Range text box. Select Find Next to begin the search.

Note: If you preselect the range to be searched, A1..A6 in this example, 1-2-3 won't physically move the cell pointer to the cells where it locates TOTAL. 1-2-3 for Windows, however, will still display in the contents box the contents of each cell it moves to.

In A1..A6, 1-2-3 begins to look for the string TOTAL, but only in cells that contain formulas. As you can see in Figure 2-37B, it finds the first occurrence in cell E5. Notice that 1-2-3 moves the cell pointer to E5, so you see the formula +TOTAL-E4-E6 in the contents box.

To continue the search, select Find Next again. Each time 1-2-3 finds an occurrence of TOTAL, it moves the cell pointer to that cell. You have to choose Find Next each time to continue the search. (Select Cancel at any time to abort the search.)

When 1-2-3 for Windows doesn't find another occurrence of the search string, you'll see the "No more matching strings" error message shown in Figure 2-37C. Press ESC or ENTER, or select OK to clear this message and return to the worksheet. 1-2-3 leaves the cell pointer in the last cell it found TOTAL in, cell E5.

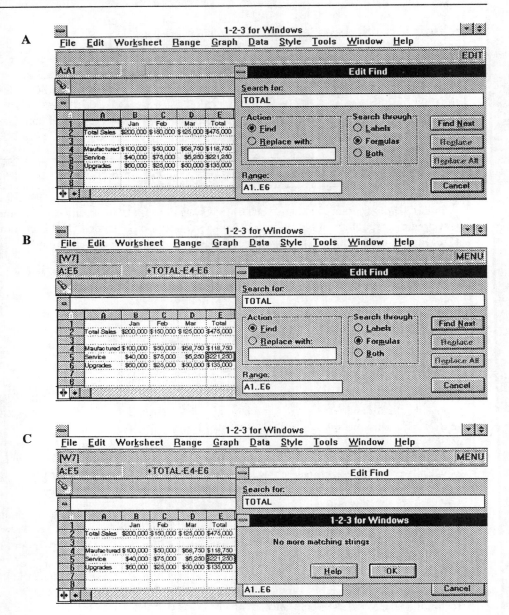

Figure 2-37 Using Edit Find to search for a string

Replacing a String

To replace a specified string in a range, 1-2-3 for Windows uses almost the same method as it does for finding a string. To see this, let's examine Figure 2-38. This worksheet contains the same information as Figure 2-37, except all the values in column E are calculated using the @SUM function, as explained in column F. For example, the $475,000 Total Sales in cell E2 is computed as @SUM(B2..D2). This is explained in cell F2 by the *label* '@SUM(B2..D2).

Note: The @SUM and @AVG functions are discussed in Chapter 9.

Now suppose that you want column E to contain average values instead, which can be computed using the @AVG function. You can use Edit Find to change not only the formulas in column E, but the labels in column F.

Note: If you use Edit Find to replace all or part of a formula, be sure to check the results of the command. 1-2-3 doesn't warn you when replacing a formula results in ERR.

First, select Edit Find. In the dialog box displayed, enter the settings shown in Figure 2-38A. Type the string you want to search for, **@SUM,** in the Search for text box. Then turn on the Action Replace with mode. In the text box activated, enter the string that will be substituted, **@AVG.** Then enter the range to be searched, **A1..F6,** in the Range text box. Accept the Search through Both option so that 1-2-3 searches both formulas and labels.

To begin the search, select Find Next. As you can see in the contents box of Figure 2-38A, 1-2-3 finds the first occurrence of @SUM in cell F2. If you now choose Replace, Edit Find replaces @SUM with @AVG, so that cell F2 contains @AVG(B2..D2). Figure 2-38B shows how Edit Find then moves you to the next occurrence of @SUM in cell E4. (You can tell that 1-2-3 changed the formula in cell F2 by comparing Figures 2-38A and B.)

Note: You can select Quit at any time to return to READY mode. The worksheet will contain any substitutions you have made to date. If you immediately press ALT+BACK-SPACE (Undo) after completing an Edit Find command, 1-2-3 for Windows undoes all replacements it may have made. The cell pointer isn't returned to its original position, however.

Choose Replace again, and 1-2-3 replaces @SUM with @AVG in cell E4 and moves on to the next occurrence in cell E5. (To move on to the next occurrence in cell E5 without replacing @SUM in cell E4 with @AVG, choose Find Next instead.) If you continue to choose Replace, 1-2-3 moves through all occurrences of @SUM in columns E and F, and replaces each one with @AVG. When 1-2-3 doesn't find another occurrence of @SUM, you'll see the "No more matching strings" error message. Press ESC or ENTER, or select OK to clear this message and return to the worksheet.

A

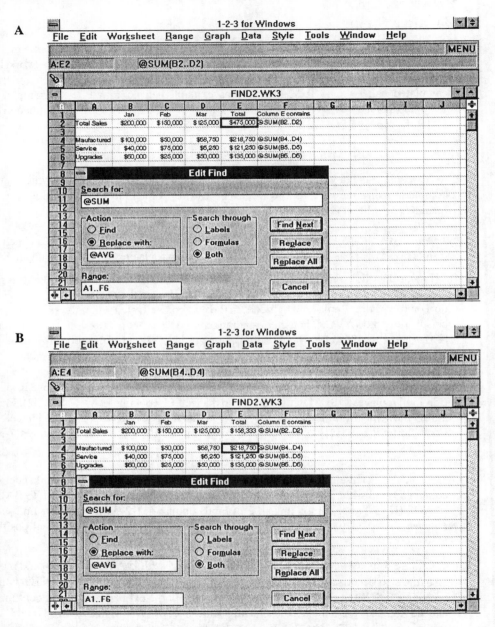

B

Figure 2-38 Replacing @SUM with @AVG in formulas and labels

C

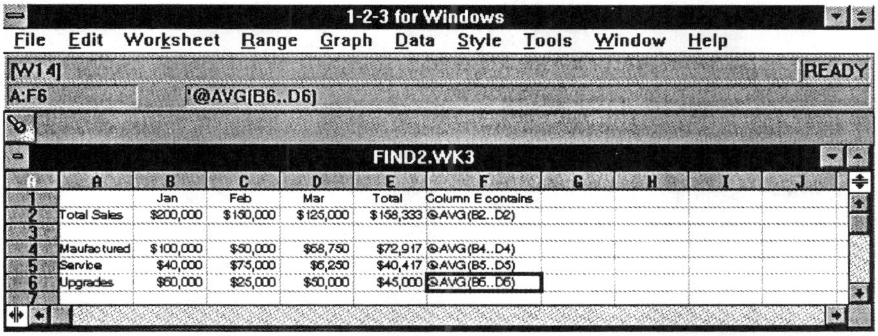

Figure 2-38 Replacing @SUM with @AVG in formulas and labels *(continued)*

The worksheet now looks like Figure 2-38C, where all the formulas in column E return average values, as explained by the descriptive labels in column F. Because 1-2-3 for Windows leaves the cell pointer in the last cell it found @SUM, you can see in the contents box that cell F6 now contains the label ' @AVG(B6..D6).

▼ *Tip:*   By selecting Replace All, 1-2-3 for Windows replaces all occurrences of the search string, @SUM, with the replace string, @AVG, without confirmation. It then returns you to the worksheet, where the cell pointer is located in cell F6. In effect, the Replace All option moves you from Figure 2-38A to Figure 2-38C all in one step.

3

Managing Windows

One of the most powerful features in 1-2-3 for Windows is its ability to handle multiple worksheet files simultaneously. In fact, in any given 1-2-3 for Windows session, you can open as many worksheet files as your computer's memory will allow (each in its own window), and quickly move among them viewing and editing data. This lets you do such things as compare one worksheet file with another, copy or move data between files, link files with formulas, and so on. In reality, though, a certain amount of complexity accompanies all this power and freedom. In fact, at times, effectively managing multiple windows presents a challenge in itself.

To further complicate matters, 1-2-3 lets you have multiple worksheets in each file. On the surface this seems like a power-user's dream—what with consolidation of worksheets through 3-D formulas, and so on—until you actually try it. Then it becomes apparent that you look at your worksheets through a relatively small viewing area—a worksheet window. At that point, topics such as navigating around the worksheet and finding ways to effectively display your data begin to take on a whole new meaning (especially if you're creating a large model). In fact, the more efficiently you can manage that small window in which your worksheets are displayed, the more efficient your 1-2-3 sessions will ultimately become.

This chapter shows you how to take advantage of 1-2-3's window-management tools by examining them in the order of increasing complexity. It begins by presenting techniques for controlling the display of a single worksheet window. It then discusses methods you can use to manage multiple-sheet windows, finally focusing on strategies you can use to manage several open worksheet windows at the same time. In the process you'll learn how to:

- Split a worksheet window so that you can view two different areas of the same worksheet at the same time.

- Freeze the rows and columns of a worksheet so you can keep them in view as you move around the worksheet.

- Change worksheet window display colors, screen display modes, the size of worksheet cells, and worksheet frame displays.

- Tile and stack windows so that it's easy to view multiple files at once and to move from one window to another, performing operations that are specific to whichever window you're in.

Many of the windowing techniques discussed in this chapter apply to 1-2-3's Graph, Transcript, and Help windows. The focus here, however, is on showing you the skills you'll need to manage worksheet windows and to navigate between windows to quickly find the data you need. For a discussion of graph windows, see Chapter 10; for transcript windows, see Chapter 15; and for a discussion of using 1-2-3's Help window, see Chapter 1.

MANAGING A SINGLE WINDOW

In much the same way that Windows provides a desktop on which you can display your applications, 1-2-3 provides a desktop on which you can display your worksheet files. What's more, just as Windows displays your applications in separate windows, 1-2-3 displays each of your worksheet files in a separate window. Finally, in the same way that an application's window is confined to the Windows desktop, a worksheet window is confined to the 1-2-3 desktop.

Worksheet windows also have the same properties as your application windows. You can move, maximize, minimize, restore, and close a worksheet window by using the same techniques as you would an application window. And, like your application windows, only a single worksheet window can be *active* at any one time. The active window is the one that contains the cell pointer.

Because worksheet windows are so similar to your application windows, managing a single worksheet window presents no particular challenge. Instead, the challenge comes when you attempt to manage what is displayed inside your worksheet windows. The sections that follow discuss this topic in detail.

Splitting a Worksheet Window

As your worksheets grow in size, it can become difficult to keep important data in view. One solution is to split the window either horizontally or vertically into two *panes*, and view different parts of the same worksheet in each pane. Another solution, if you have multiple worksheets in the same file, is to display those worksheets stacked one behind the other in perspective view.

Splitting Windows Horizontally

When you split a window horizontally, the worksheet is displayed in two panes, as shown in Figure 3-1. Splitting a window in this way lets you view and edit portions of the same worksheet that are a considerable number of rows apart. 1-2-3 lets you split a window horizontally using either your mouse or your keyboard. Because of its speed and simplicity, however, most users prefer the mouse.

To split a window horizontally with your mouse, begin by moving the mouse pointer to the box located just above the up arrow on the vertical scroll bar on the right side of the worksheet window. This box contains a rather unusual looking icon that is shaped like a vertical double arrow (‡).

As you move the mouse pointer into this box, the pointer's shape is transformed into an image that matches the icon inside. To split the window vertically, drag the icon down the vertical scroll bar until it reaches the bottom border of the row where you want the window split to occur. When you release the mouse button, 1-2-3 splits the window and displays another view of the same worksheet in a second pane below the original, as shown in Figure 3-1. You'll notice the bottom pane has its own vertical scroll bar that allows you to navigate up and down within that window by using your mouse.

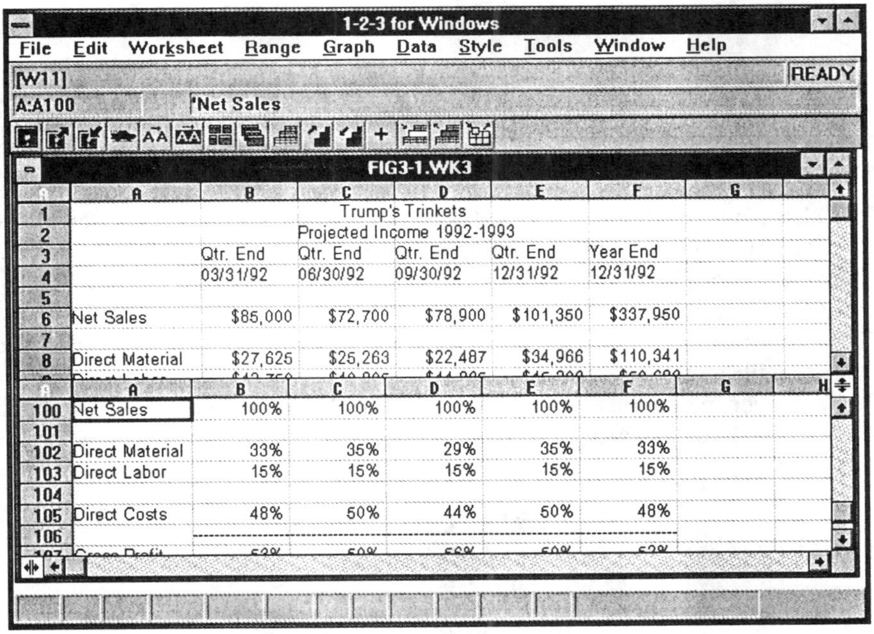

Figure 3-1 A window split horizontally

To move the cell pointer back and forth between the top and bottom panes, you can then press F6, the Pane key, or you can simply click on any cell in either pane to locate the cell pointer there. Once the cell pointer is located in the appropriate pane, you can then scroll to whichever area of the spreadsheet you want to use. You'll notice as you scroll from right to left that 1-2-3 always keeps the same columns in view in both panes.

For example, suppose you want to split the current worksheet window at row 9, as shown in Figure 3-1. To do this, drag the split icon to the bottom border of row 10—which leaves one row for the border frame. When you release your mouse button, 1-2-3 splits the screen and leaves the cursor in the current cell of the upper pane. Initially, the two panes show the same area of the worksheet. However, you can scroll either the top or bottom pane to another area of the worksheet. For example, in Figure 3-1, the range A1..F9 is displayed in the top pane and the range A100..F107 is displayed in the bottom pane. To set up this view yourself, click on any cell in the bottom window (or press F6), and then scroll the bottom pane down until the range A100..F107 is displayed.

The 1-2-3 Classic menu equivalent for the Window Split commands can be found in the /Worksheet Window menu.

To split the window horizontally using the keyboard, use the Window Split Horizontal command. Before selecting this command, first situate the cell pointer in the cell directly below where you want the horizontal split to occur, then select Window Split. 1-2-3 displays the dialog box in Figure 3-2. Turn on the Horizontal radio button, and select OK or press ENTER to complete the command. You can then use the Pane key (F6) to switch between panes and then use the pointer keys to move the top or bottom pane to an area of the worksheet you want to view.

Note: If you've mistakenly split the window in the wrong place, use the Window Split Clear command to clear the current split, then try again.

Although the previous example shows two different areas of the same worksheet, you can also display portions of different worksheets in the same file. For example, to shift the contents of the bottom pane in Figure 3-1 to display the same region (A100..F107) in worksheet B, place the cell pointer in the bottom pane and press CTRL+PGUP. 1-2-3 shifts the bottom pane to display the range A100..F107 in worksheet B, as shown in Figure 3-3 . In this way you can visually compare different portions of different worksheets in the same file.

When you first split a window horizontally, 1-2-3 synchronizes column scrolling between the two window panes. In other words, the same columns always appear in both

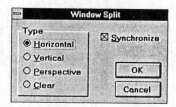

Figure 3-2 The Window Split dialog box

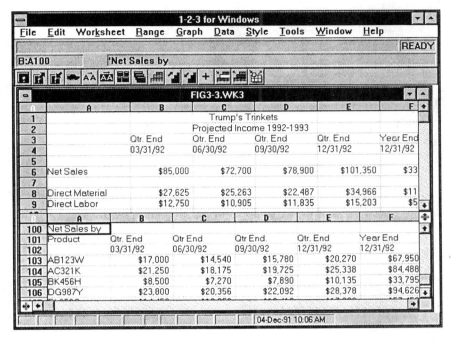

Figure 3-3 Portions of different worksheets displayed in horizontal window panes

the top and bottom panes, regardless of where you move the cell pointer. You can unsynchronize the scrolling, if you wish. See "Unsynchronizing Panes" later for more details.

Splitting Windows Vertically

1-2-3 for Windows also lets you split a worksheet window vertically into two panes using either the mouse or the keyboard. Figure 3-4 shows an example of what the two vertical panes might look like.

To split a window vertically with your mouse, begin by moving the mouse pointer to the small box located at the lower-left corner of the worksheet window (just to the left of the horizontal scroll bar.) As you approach this box with your mouse pointer, you'll notice the pointer's shape is transformed into a black horizontal double arrow icon (⬌) to match the one already in the box.

To split the current window vertically, drag the icon to the right along the horizontal scroll bar. As you drag, 1-2-3 displays a vertical bar marking the location where the split will occur. Continue dragging until the bar reaches the right border of the column where you want the vertical split to occur and release your mouse button. 1-2-3 splits the worksheet window at the column you specified.

Once the current window has been spit vertically, you can use the Pane key (F6) to move the cell pointer back and forth between the left and right panes or you can simply

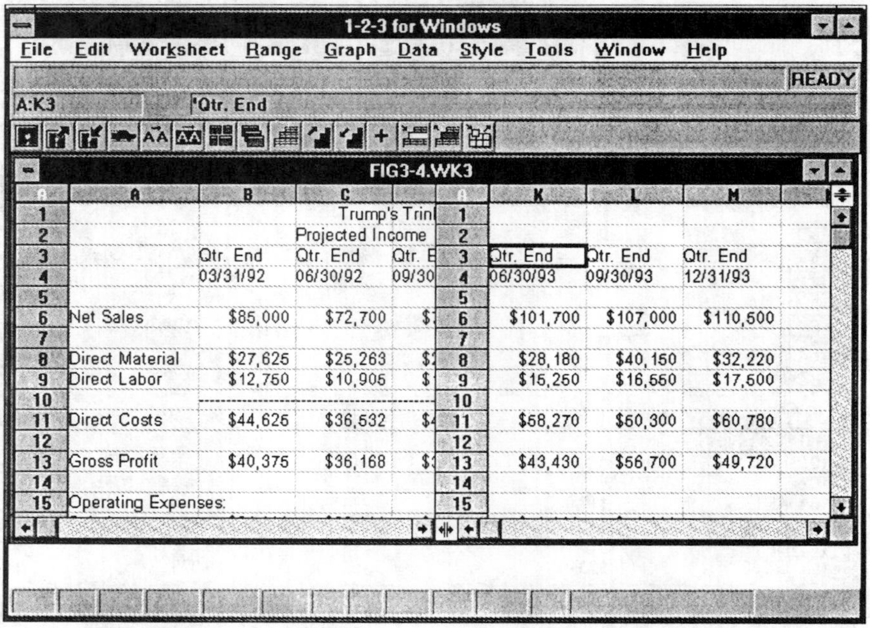

Figure 3-4 A window split vertically

click on any cell in either pane to locate the cell pointer there. Once the cell pointer is located in the appropriate pane, you can then scroll to whichever area of the spreadsheet you want to use.

You can also create a vertical split with your keyboard by using the Window Split Vertical command. Before selecting the command, you must first position your cell pointer in the column immediately to the right of where you want the split to occur. When you're ready, select the Window Split command. 1-2-3 displays the dialog box shown earlier in Figure 3-2. Turn on the Vertical radio button, and then select OK. 1-2-3 splits the current window vertically at the location of the cell pointer.

Note: There must be at least one column between the cell pointer and the left border of the worksheet window when you select the Window Split Vertical command. Otherwise, 1-2-3 will beep and ignore the command.

Although Figure 3-4 shows areas of the same worksheet displayed in two vertical panes, 1-2-3 also lets you display different worksheets in vertical panes. For example, suppose you want to have the right pane in Figure 3-4, which displays the range K1..M15 in worksheet A, display the same range in worksheet B. To do this, simply locate the cell pointer in the right pane and press CTRL+PGUP. 1-2-3 will shift the right pane to display the range K1..M15 in worksheet B. You can then scroll that pane within worksheet B to locate specific data.

Perspective View

Perspective view allows you to view equal portions of three consecutive worksheets at the same time. The worksheets appear stacked, one behind the other, with the current worksheet in front, as shown in Figure 3-5. Perspective view can be very helpful when you're pointing to three-dimensional ranges while entering either commands or formulas.

To create a display like the one in Figure 3-5, use the Window Split Perspective command. If there are at least three worksheets in the current file, 1-2-3 will display them in the stepped fashion shown in Figure 3-5. If there are fewer than three worksheets, 1-2-3 still displays a stepped view but leaves the areas that would have been occupied by the missing worksheets blank. (To insert blank worksheets into a file either before or after the current one, use the Worksheet Insert Sheet command discussed in Chapter 2.)

1-2-3 always displays consecutive worksheets in perspective view. The worksheet containing the cell pointer is used as the starting position for the Windows Split Perspective command. For example, imagine you have the cell pointer located in worksheet A of a four worksheet file. When you select Window Split Perspective, 1-2-3 displays worksheets A, B, and C in the current window. If you then press CTRL+PGUP three times, 1-2-3 will advance the cell pointer to worksheet D and display worksheets B, C, and D in the current window.

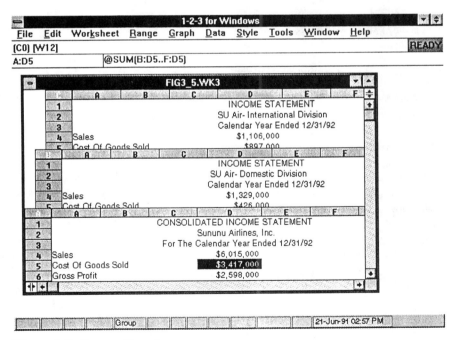

Figure 3-5 Perspective view

> ▼ *Tip:*   The easiest way to switch to perspective view is to click on the ▦ icon
> in the icon palette.

As you move among your worksheets in perspective view, you'll notice that 1-2-3 always keeps the same portion of each worksheet in view. Thus, the worksheets are said to be synchronized. However, you can unsynchronize the scrolling of worksheets in perspective view such that different portions of each worksheet are displayed. See the next section "Unsynchronizing Panes" for further details on this.

Note: While 1-2-3 is displaying a perspective view, you cannot use the Window Split Horizontal or Vertical commands. Conversely, you cannot use perspective view while either the Window Split Horizontal or Vertical command is in effect. In either case, you must clear the current Window setting before establishing a new one. See "Clearing Split Window Settings" later in this chapter for details on how to clear horizontal or vertical windows.

Unsynchronizing Panes

As mentioned, when you split a worksheet window, whether using your mouse or the Window Split commands, 1-2-3 synchronizes the scrolling of window panes as follows:

- Horizontal: The same columns always appear in both the top and bottom window panes.

- Vertical: The same rows always appear in the left and right panes.

- Perspective view: The same portions of each worksheet are always displayed.

You can, however, unsynchronize the scrolling of window panes, which allows you to view different columns in horizontal window panes, different rows in vertical panes, and different portions of each worksheet in perspective view.

To unsynchronize window scrolling, select the Window Split command. 1-2-3 displays the Window Split dialog box shown earlier in Figure 3-2. In the upper-right corner is a check box labeled *Synchronize.* By default this box always appears checked (turned on). To unsynchronize the scrolling of window panes, click on this check box to turn it off. From then on, the scrolling of window panes is confined to the pane containing the cell pointer. Panes without the cell pointer remain static on your screen. To resynchronize windows, turn the Synchronize check box back on.

Figure 3-6 shows an example of what you can do with horizontal window panes if you turn the Window Split Synchronize check box off. Notice that the columns displayed in the top and bottom window do not match. This was done by moving the cell pointer to the bottom pane and then beyond the right edge of the current window.

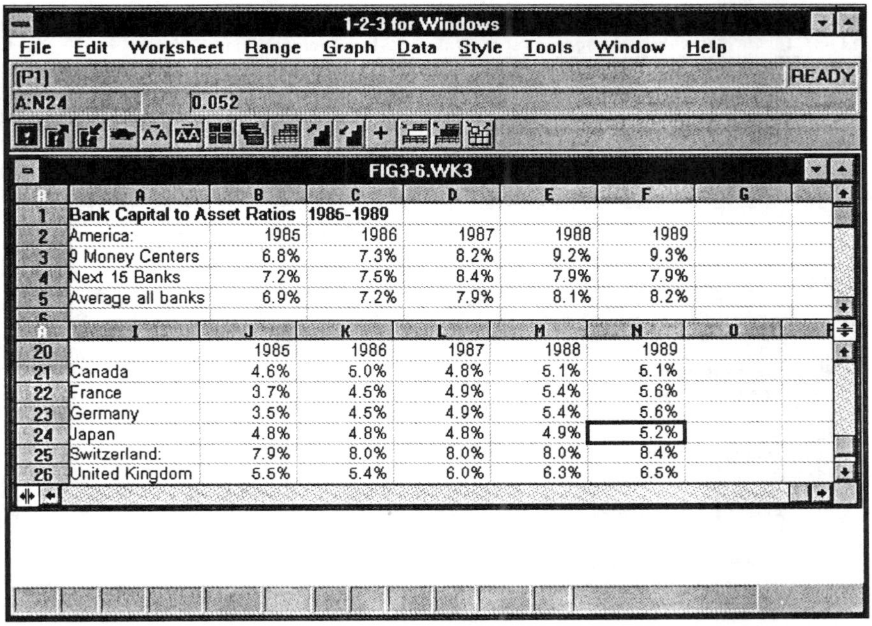

Figure 3-6 Turning off the Window Split Synchronize check box unsynchronizes window scrolling

Notice further in Figure 3-6 that only a single horizontal scroll bar appears in the display. When split windows are unsynchronized, the horizontal (or vertical) scroll bar only controls cell movement in the window pane that contains the cell pointer.

Clearing Split Window Settings

Clearing split window settings means returning a window to its default single-worksheet, single-pane display. One way to do this is by selecting the Window Split Clear command; this command clears any Window Split settings. Another way, in the case of vertically or horizontally split windows, is to use the mouse to drag the split icon (⬌ or ⬍) off the edge of the window.

▼ *Tip:*   In previous DOS versions of 1-2-3, you must clear one split window setting before you can make another. In 1-2-3 for Windows, however, any split window setting you make overrides the previous one, except in the case of perspective view.

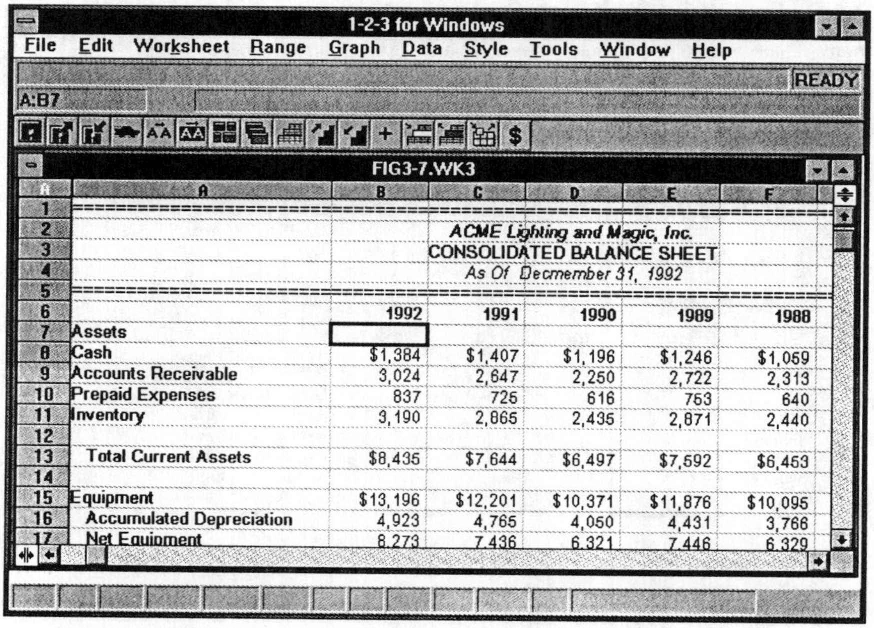

Figure 3-7 A sample worksheet with column and row titles

Displaying Worksheet Titles

Many worksheets have entries in the first few columns and along the top few rows that identify the contents of the worksheet. For example, Figure 3-7 shows an accounting worksheet where the name of each account appears in column A. Along the top of the worksheet, in row 5, the years corresponding to each account balance are shown. When you move the cell pointer beyond the edge of the worksheet window, however, some or all of these titles may disappear from view, making it difficult to understand what the numbers in the worksheet mean.

Fortunately 1-2-3 allows you to freeze selected rows and columns along the top and left edge of the worksheet window. The entries in these columns and rows will remain static and in view at all times, regardless of where you move the cell pointer in the current worksheet.

Freezing Rows

To freeze one or more rows so that they are always displayed along the top edge of the worksheet, begin by positioning the cell pointer one row below the rows you want to freeze. For example, to freeze rows 1 through 6 in Figure 3-7, locate the cell pointer in any cell in row 7. When you're ready, select the Worksheet Titles command. 1-2-3 displays the Worksheet Titles dialog box. Turn on the Horizontal radio button and then

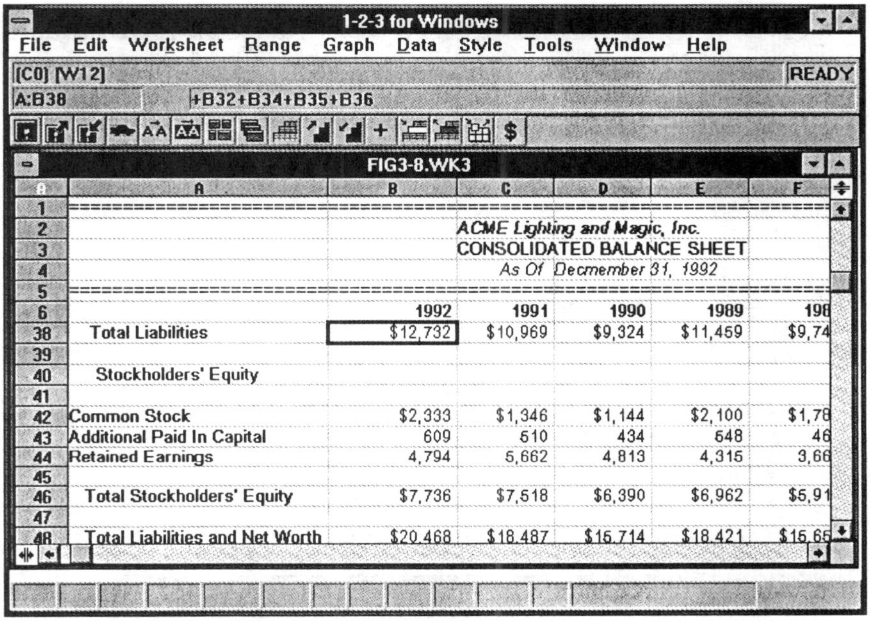

Figure 3-8 Worksheet Titles Horizontal freezes rows

select OK or press ENTER. 1-2-3 then returns you to the current worksheet. From then on, when you move the cell pointer below the bottom edge of the worksheet window, the contents of rows 1 through 6 will remain constantly in view, as shown in Figure 3-8.

Freezing Columns

To freeze one or more columns so that they are always displayed along the left edge of the current worksheet, position the cell pointer one column to the right of the last column you want to freeze. For example, to freeze column A in Figure 3-7, place the cell pointer in any cell in column B. Once the cell pointer is positioned, select the Worksheet Titles command, turn on the Vertical radio button, and then select OK. Now, when you move the cell pointer beyond the right edge of the worksheet window, the contents of column A will remain constantly in view.

Freezing Both Rows and Columns

You can also freeze both rows and columns by using the Worksheet Titles command. To do so, first position the cell pointer one row below and one column to the right of the rows and columns you want to freeze. For example, to freeze rows 1 through 6 and column A in Figure 3-7, position the cell pointer in cell B7. When you're ready, select

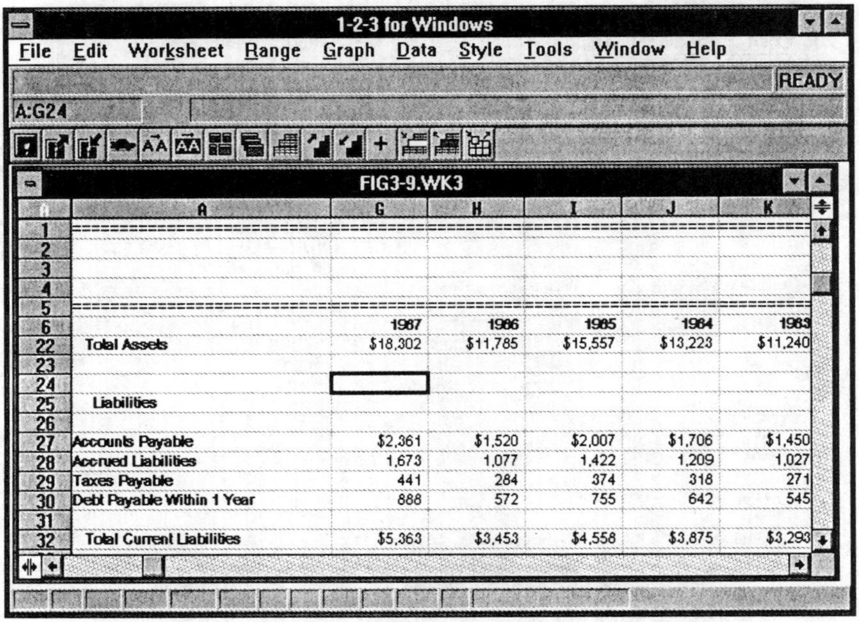

Figure 3-9   Worksheet Titles Both freezes both columns and rows

the Worksheet Titles command, select Both, and then select OK. From then on, the contents of rows 1 through 6 and column A will remain in view. For example, Figure 3-9 shows what happens when the cell pointer is moved beyond the edge of the current window.

Tips on Worksheet Titles

When you freeze columns and/or rows with Worksheet Titles, cell pointer movement is restricted to cells outside the title area. For example, in Figure 3-9 in which column A and rows 1 through 6 are frozen, pressing HOME moves the cell pointer to cell B7, not cell A1. What's more, although 1-2-3 will let you move the mouse pointer into column A and rows 1 through 6, you cannot move the cell pointer there—clicking the mouse button has no effect.

If you need to move the cell pointer into the title area you must use GOTO (F5) or the Range Goto command. In response to either of these, enter an address (or range name) within the title area and then select OK. 1-2-3 moves the cell pointer to the specified cell, even though it is within the title area.

When you move the cell pointer into a title area, 1-2-3 temporarily displays a double image of the rows and columns included in the title area. Do not be alarmed by this. Simply move the cell pointer within the title area to enter and edit data in the usual way. When you complete editing, press PGDN followed by PGUP or CTRL+→ followed by

CTRL+← to move the cell pointer beyond the edge of the worksheet window and then back again. 1-2-3 once again displays a single image of the title area, and cell pointer movement is restricted to cells outside of it.

Note: If you attempt to include hidden columns within the title area, 1-2-3 issues an error message.

MANAGING MULTIPLE WINDOWS

As mentioned, 1-2-3 lets you open as many worksheet windows as your computer's memory will support, each window containing a single- or multiple-worksheet file. In addition to your worksheet windows, 1-2-3 also lets you open one or more graph windows, each associated with a given worksheet file. Each new window you open is displayed on top of the previously active window, often leaving only the title bar of the previously active window in view. Thus, 1-2-3 stacks your windows one on top of the other, with the files you opened first toward the back of the stack and the files you opened more recently toward the front.

The more windows you open and work with, the more cluttered 1-2-3's desktop can become. For example, Figure 3-10 shows a view of multiple windows open on the 1-2-3 desktop. Notice that the windows vary in size and position, with one window often obscuring another.

Fortunately 1-2-3 provides an extensive set of tools for navigating between windows and for arranging them to better suit the way you work. The sections that follow discuss both of these topics in detail.

Note: To create new files on the 1-2-3 desktop, you use the File New command. To open existing files, you use File Open. Both of these commands are discussed at length in the next chapter—Chapter 4, "Managing Files."

Moving between Windows

Although you can have multiple windows open at the same time, only one of those windows can be the active window. The active window is the one you happen to be working in at the time. Most of the commands you select and data you enter apply only to the currently active window. To activate another window you must move to it. You can move to a window by using any of the following techniques:

- Click your mouse on any exposed part of a window. When you do, 1-2-3 makes that window active. If the window contains a worksheet, 1-2-3 moves the cell pointer to that window.

- Press NEXT WINDOW (CTRL+F6) or select Next from the window Control menu to move to the next open window. By using either of these methods, you can cycle through all open windows, including worksheet, graph, and transcript windows.

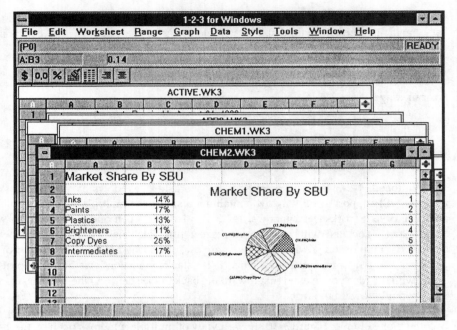

Figure 3-10 Multiple windows open in the work area

- Choose Window from 1-2-3's worksheet or graph menu. 1-2-3 displays a list of open windows. (The currently active window has a check mark next to its name.) Select the name of the window you wish to activate.

- Press GOTO (F5) or select the Range Go To command. In either case, 1-2-3 displays the Range Go To dialog box. Specify a cell address (or range name) in the currently active worksheet file, or another active file (enclose the file name in double-angle brackets followed by a cell address or range name), and then select OK. 1-2-3 then takes you to the range you've specified. See "Using GOTO (F5) to Move Between Windows" later for more details.

In addition, 1-2-3 provides other shortcut keys for moving between active files. For example, suppose you want to quickly jump to the first file you opened at the beginning of the current session. Rather than using 1-2-3's Window command, or NEXT WINDOW (CTRL+F6), you can simply press CTRL+END HOME. This key sequence takes you to the last highlighted cell in the first file you opened. You can just as quickly jump back to the most recent file you've opened by pressing CTRL+END END. All of 1-2-3's file navigation shortcut keys are summarized in Table 3-1.

- A window can still be active even though you've minimized it. For example, when you press NEXT WINDOW (CTRL+F6) to move to the next window, 1-2-3 will still activate the next window, even if it is an icon. Similarly, clicking on an icon serves

TABLE 3-1   File Navigation Keys

Key	Movement
CTRL+PGUP	When the cell pointer is in the last worksheet in a file, relocates the cell pointer to the cell you last highlighted in the next active file.
CTRL+PGDN	When the cell pointer is in the first worksheet of a file, moves the cell pointer to the cell you last highlighted in the previous active file.
CTRL+END HOME	Relocates the cell pointer in the last highlighted cell in the earliest file you opened (the first active file).
CTRL+END END	Repositions the cell pointer to the last highlighted cell in the last (most recently opened) active file.
CTRL+F6	Moves to the next open worksheet, graph, or transcript window.

to activate the window it represents. Therefore, you can apply commands to a window even though it has been minimized.

Note: The order in which the cell pointer moves between active files, depends on: (1) the order in which you open your files and (2) which file is current when you open a new or existing file. In early releases of 1-2-3 for Windows, the performance of the file-navigation keys tends to be somewhat inconsistent.

Using GOTO (F5) to Move Between Windows

As mentioned, the GOTO key (F5) lets you quickly jump between open worksheet files. The more you work with 1-2-3, the more you will find GOTO (F5) to be an invaluable part of your 1-2-3 command repertoire.

When you press GOTO (F5), 1-2-3 displays the dialog box in Figure 3-11, prompting you for a range address to go to. A list of the range names in the current file are displayed followed by the names of files that are currently open on the desktop enclosed in double-angle brackets (<< >>). To move to another active file, double-click on a bracketed filename from the list. 1-2-3 takes you to the last highlighted cell in the file you've selected. In addition to selecting a bracketed filename, you can also type any one of the following entries in the Range text box to specify a range address to jump to:

- A filename in double-angle brackets, such as <<SALES_Q1>>. 1-2-3 locates the cell pointer in the last cell you were in when you left the SALES_Q1 file. Note that to specify an "Untitled" window, you must specify <<>>.

- A filename followed by a cell address, such as <<SALES_Q1>>C:D25. This takes you to cell C:D25 in the SALES_Q1 file.

- A filename followed by a worksheet letter, such as <<SALES_Q1>>C:. This moves the cell pointer to the same location you were last at in worksheet C before you left the SALES_Q1 file.

- A filename in double-angle brackets, followed by a range name from that file, such as <<SALES_Q1>>WESTDIV. If you can't remember the range names in SALES_Q1, first double-click on <<SALES_Q1>> to move to the file. Next, press GoTo (F5) again to display a list of range names. You can then select the one you want.

Note: GOTO (F5) will have no effect when a graph window is the active window.

> ▼ *Tip:* Using GOTO (F5) is one of the best ways to jump between worksheet windows in a macro. In fact, it is the only way you can be sure that you are jumping to the correct window when there are more than two open worksheet windows. (See Chapter 14 for more on macros.)

Tiling and Cascading Windows

With multiple windows open, you are constantly faced with the challenge of arranging those windows on your screen so that you see their contents. 1-2-3 offers at least a partial solution to this problem by providing menu commands that allow you to cascade and tile windows.

With a cascaded window arrangement, each window is adjusted to the same size, and they appear stacked (one behind the other) with the title bar of each window exposed. The currently active window is placed at the front of the stack. That way, you can easily see the name of each open window and you can move quickly to a specific window simply by clicking on its title bar. To stack windows in this way, select the Window Cascade command. Figure 3-12 shows an example of cascaded windows.

With a tiled window arrangement, the windows appear side-by-side, much like the tiles on a tiled floor. 1-2-3 adjusts the size of each window as necessary so that a section of each is displayed. The currently active window is placed in the upper-left corner of 1-2-3's window. Tiling windows is helpful when you want to view the contents of two or more windows at the same time. To tile windows, select the Window Tile command. Figure 3-13 shows an example of tiled windows.

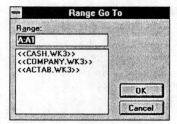

Figure 3-11 The Range Go To dialog box

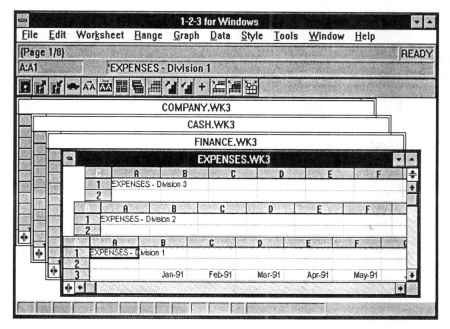

Figure 3-12 Cascaded windows

▼ *Tip:* When 1-2-3 tiles windows, it arranges them from left to right, in the
order they were last activated. If you don't like the order in which the
tiles appear, the easiest way to rearrange them is by simply clicking on
the windows in the reverse order of how you want them tiled. Then select the Window Tile command again. In this way, you can shuffle your
tiled windows to suit your needs.

Closing Windows

Each window that you open requires additional memory, making less memory available
for other uses. The more windows you have open, the more crowded and confusing
1-2-3's work area can become. To cut down on memory usage and to minimize confusion,
it's always a good idea to close windows you no longer need, thus removing them from
the work area. You can close a specific window or all the windows in the work area.

To close a specific window, you must make it active. Once active, you can close it in
any of the following ways:

- Double-click on the Control menu box for the worksheet window.
- Click once on the window Control menu box (or press ALT-Hyphen) to display the
  document window's Control menu, and then select Close from that menu.
- Press CTRL+F4.

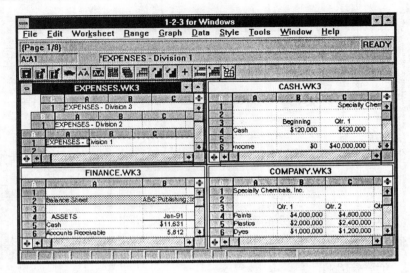

Figure 3-13 Tiled windows

If you haven't made any changes or additions to the worksheet since it was last saved, 1-2-3 for Windows immediately closes the current window. If you have made changes, but haven't yet saved them, 1-2-3 prompts you to decide whether you want to save the file before it is closed by displaying a dialog box with Yes, No, Cancel options. If you select Yes, 1-2-3 will save the file without any confirmation using the existing filename, and remove the window from 1-2-3's work area. If you select No, 1-2-3 will simply remove the window from the work area without saving your changes. Finally, if you select Cancel, 1-2-3 will abort the window closure.

When you close a window, 1-2-3 moves the cell pointer to the next open file, making it the current window. If only a single worksheet window is open, 1-2-3 will close that window and automatically open a new "Untitled" worksheet window so that you can start a new project with a clean slate.

WINDOW DISPLAY OPTIONS

1-2-3 lets you make various display option settings that affect the display of worksheet and graph windows. For example, you can change the color of the worksheet frame, cell background, grid lines, and so on. You can also change 1-2-3's default display mode from color to black and white or graphics to draft mode. You can even zoom the size of worksheet cells up or down to display more or less data on your screen.

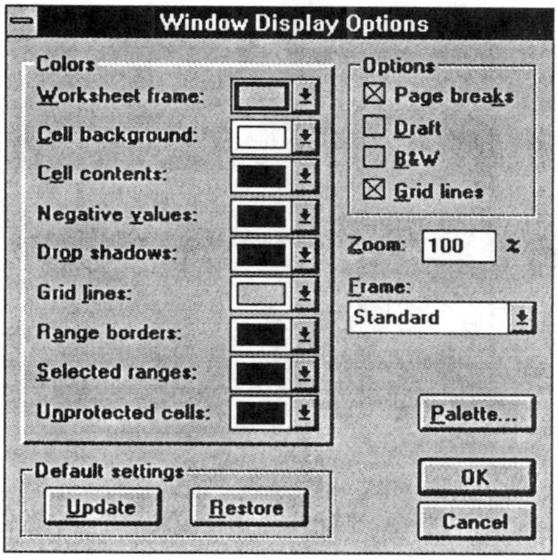

Figure 3-14 The Window Display Options dialog box

The 1-2-3 Classic equivalent for the Window Display Options command can be found by selecting SHIFT+COLON (:) to open the WYSIWYG extension menu, and then selecting Display.

To change 1-2-3's window display options, use the Window Display options command. When you select this command, 1-2-3 displays the dialog box in Figure 3-14, showing the current default display options for 1-2-3. The sections that follow discuss each component of this dialog box in detail. Once you've made the display settings you want, you have one of two choices. On the one hand, you can select OK to return to the current worksheet; 1-2-3 will use the settings you've made for the balance of the current session. On the other hand, you can select Update from the Window Display Options dialog box followed by OK. When you select the Update button, 1-2-3 writes the changes you've made to the 123.INI file. That way, your settings will be used in both the current and future 1-2-3 sessions.

Changing Colors

To change the colors of individual worksheet elements, use the Colors section of the Worksheet Display Options dialog box in Figure 3-4. This section contains a series of drop-down boxes that let you change the colors currently assigned to 1-2-3's worksheet elements, including the worksheet frame, cell background, cell contents, negative values, drop shadows, grid lines, range borders, selected ranges, and unprotected cells.

To change the color of a particular display element, select the drop-down list box associated with that element. 1-2-3 displays a small palette of eight standard colors for your selection; choose the one you want, then select OK to return to the worksheet. 1-2-3 will display the element you've selected in the color you've selected for all currently open worksheets as well as any worksheets you subsequently open.

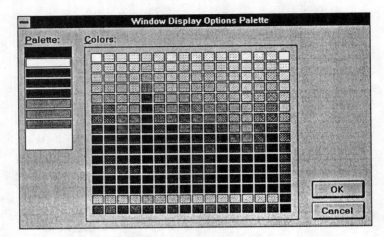

Figure 3-15   The Window Display Options Palette dialog box

Changing the Palette

1-2-3 also lets you assign custom colors to worksheet elements. This is a two step process. First, you must change the default color palette for the system. 1-2-3 uses a default palette of eight standard colors to display its screen elements. Once you've made the appropriate change to the default palette, you can then change the color of a particular worksheet element.

To change the colors assigned to the default palette, select the Palette button from the Window Display Options dialog box (Figure 3-14). 1-2-3 displays the Window Display Options Palette dialog box in Figure 3-15. The eight colors currently assigned to 1-2-3's default palette are displayed in a box labeled Palette in the upper-left corner of this dialog box. To change a particular color in the default palette, first select the color from this box, then select a color from the Colors palette to the right. You can do this by clicking on a color with your mouse or by pressing TAB to move to the Colors palette and then using the arrow keys. To confirm your selection, select OK or press ENTER. 1-2-3 will then return you to the Window Display Options dialog box (Figure 3-14).

When you change a color in the default palette, 1-2-3 automatically adjusts the color of all screen elements that use that color. For example, if you replace the color black— normally assigned to cell contents, negative values, drop shadows, and range borders— with bright green, 1-2-3 changes the color of these screen elements to reflect your selection. Thus, changing a single palette color may affect several screen elements.

Assigning Custom Colors

Once you've made the needed change(s) to 1-2-3's default color palette, you're ready to assign your new colors to specific worksheet screen elements. To do this, select the drop-down box corresponding to the screen element whose color you want to change from the Window Display Options dialog box (Figure 3-14). When you open the appropriate drop-down box, 1-2-3 shows you its newly revised default color palette. Select the color you want from the palette, then select OK to confirm the Window Display Options command. 1-2-3 then returns you to the current worksheet and implements your new color selection.

Other Display Options

Besides worksheet colors, 1-2-3 also lets you change other default display options by using the Options section of Window Display Options dialog box (Figure 13-14). A brief summary follows:

- Page breaks: Lets you hide or display page breaks. 1-2-3 inserts page breaks into the worksheet when you insert a page break manually with the Worksheet Page Break command. See Chapter 8, "Printing," for more details on setting page breaks.

- Draft: Changes the worksheet screen display from the default graphics mode, where screen display and printed output are virtually identical, to Draft mode. In Draft mode, 1-2-3 uses a monospace font and does not display borders or formatting on screen. Instead, 1-2-3 indicates the formatting of the current cell on the format line. Draft mode printing does, however, reflect all current formatting settings. Because the Draft mode display is limited to text only, without fonts or graphics, you may notice that 1-2-3 runs a little faster.

- B&W: Changes the screen display from color to black and white, and vice versa. The main purpose of the B&W option is to display your screen contents in shades of gray so you can get an idea of what your worksheet will look like when printed.

- Grid lines: Controls the display of grid lines in worksheet windows.

To change any one of these options, click on the appropriate check box, and then select OK. 1-2-3 returns you to the current worksheet and implements the settings you've made for all worksheets you have open as well as those you subsequently open.

Zooming the Worksheet Display

The Zoom option in the Window Display Options dialog box (Figure 3-14) lets you either shrink or expand the displayed size of worksheet cells. You can adjust the size from the default, 100%, to any percentage from 20% (cells appear 1/5 the normal size) to 400% (about four times the normal cell size). The size of contents of the cells is also adjusted accordingly. This handy option allows you to display either more or fewer worksheet cells in your worksheet windows.

To change the default cell display size, click on the Zoom text box, and enter a number between 20 and 400, then select OK. 1-2-3 redraws all active worksheet windows with the cell display size you've specified. This setting will also be used for any worksheet windows you subsequently open.

Changing the Frame Display

The Frame option in the Window Display Options dialog box (Figure 3-14) lets you change the display of the worksheet frame (column letters and row numbers). The associated drop-down list contains the following options:

- Standard: the default frame display setting of column letters and row numbers. With this setting, column widths and row heights are based on the default font currently in use by 1-2-3 (see Chapter 6, "Fonts and Styles," for more information on setting a default font for 1-2-3).

- Characters: column letters and row numbers are replaced with numbers ranging from 1 to 98 repeating. Each of these numbers represents the number of 10-point characters measured from the upper-left corner of the worksheet.

- Inches: column letters and row numbers are replaced by one-inch rulers emanating from the upper-left corner of the worksheet. This feature is handy for determining the approximate size of your printed output.

- Metric: column letters and row numbers are replaced by metric rulers emanating from the upper-left corner of the worksheet.

- Points/Picas: column letters and row numbers are replaced with picas in 10-point type emanating from the upper-left corner of the worksheet.

- None: removes the worksheet frame altogether.

Saving and Restoring Display Settings

When you select OK to confirm the Window Display Options command, 1-2-3 uses the settings you've made for all currently open worksheet windows. In addition, those same settings will be used for worksheet windows that you open during the remainder of the current session. However, the next time you start 1-2-3, it will revert to its old default settings.

You can make the current display option settings the default for future 1-2-3 sessions by selecting the Update button from the Window Display Options dialog box (Figure 3-14). When you select this button, 1-2-3 writes the current display-option settings to the 123W.INI file, thus recording the choices you've made for future 1-2-3 sessions.

You can also reset the display-option settings to match the previous default (either 1-2-3's original display-option settings or those for which you previously selected Update). To do this, select the Restore button from the Window Display Options dialog box (Figure 3-14). This restores the earlier default display-option settings for all open worksheet windows as well as for all those you subsequently open.

4

Managing Files

In early DOS Releases of 1-2-3, file management was pretty much limited to file maintenance and housekeeping chores. However, with the advent of 1-2-3 Release 3 and 3.1—the first releases of 1-2-3 to support 3-D worksheet files, multiple open files, and file linking—the scope of file management was broadened. For the first time, you could easily integrate information from different worksheets—through the use of 3-D ranges—and from different files—through the ability to link files with formulas.

The file management features in 1-2-3 for Windows are similar to those of 1-2-3 Release 3.1. In fact, if you're already familiar with 1-2-3 Release 3.1, you've got a jump on the situation in 1-2-3 for Windows. This chapter will serve to show you how to port your skills to the graphical environment of 1-2-3 for Windows. If you're *not* familiar with the file-management features in Release 3.1, don't worry about it; this chapter details the file-management features in 1-2-3 for Windows from the ground up.

The chapter begins by showing you how to manage and maintain a single 1-2-3 for Windows file, then goes on to show you how to manage multiple files. During the process, you'll learn a great deal about the File command, 1-2-3's primary file management tool. This command lets you create, save, and open worksheet files, as well as extract a portion of a worksheet file to another file on disk and to combine two or more worksheet files. The File command is available from both 1-2-3's worksheet and graph menu bars. This chapter approaches the File command from the standpoint of the worksheet menu, however, primarily because it offers the most comprehensive set of options. Figure 4-1 shows the worksheet window's File menu.

The chapter concludes by showing you how to link files through the use of formulas. As you'll see, you can create a formula in one file that references information in another file that is either open on the desktop or closed on disk. This feature lets you easily share information among worksheet files.

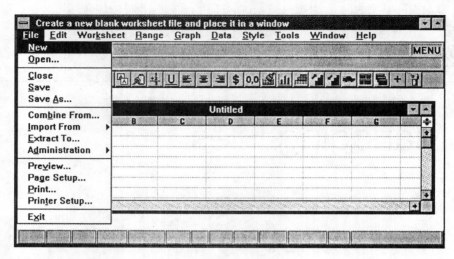

Figure 4-1 The File menu

Note: 1-2-3's file-management features are too broad to adequately cover in a single chapter. Therefore, certain aspects of file management are covered in other chapters. For example, 1-2-3 includes features for managing files across a network. These features are covered in Chapter 16, "Networking." In addition, 1-2-3 includes features that let you share data between 1-2-3 and other programs either through an ASCII file exchange, direct support of foreign file formats, conversion of foreign file formats, or through Dynamic Data Exchange. See Chapter 17, "Sharing Data," for more details on these topics.

FILE BASICS

Like any software program, 1-2-3 identifies the location of your data files by their respective filenames and paths (drive and directory names). However, by default, 1-2-3 always looks for and saves your data files in a specific directory known as the *default working directory*. Initially, 1-2-3's default working directory is C:\123W\WORK. This directory is created when you install 1-2-3 for Windows. You can check or modify the current default directory for 1-2-3 by using the Tools User Setup command (see "Changing Directories" later).

When you first start 1-2-3, a blank worksheet window is displayed in 1-2-3's work area. This window contains a worksheet file with a single worksheet. The title bar of this window bears the name "Untitled," indicating that the worksheet file contained therein does not yet have a name. At this point, you have two options.

One choice is to begin entering data into the Untitled worksheet, keeping in mind that the data you enter is only temporary (stored in your computer's RAM). To save the data you've just entered for future reference, you must save the file containing that data to disk (see "Saving Files" later). When you save a file, 1-2-3 gives you the opportunity to assign a name to it and store it in a directory of your choosing. If you do not specify an alternative directory during this operation, 1-2-3 will save the file in the current default working directory.

The second option is to ignore the Untitled window and open an existing file or create a new one. (See "Creating New Files" and "Opening Existing Files" later for details on how to perform either of these operations.) When you open an existing file or create a new one, 1-2-3 replaces the worksheet file in the Untitled window with either a new file or the existing file you've specified. If you open a new file, 1-2-3 assigns it a default file—for example, FILE0001.WK3—and displays that name in the worksheet window title bar. (See the next section "Creating New Files" for a description of how 1-2-3 assigns default file names.) You can accept this filename or provide one of your own when you later save the file to disk. If you open an existing file, 1-2-3 replaces the Untitled worksheet file with the file you've specified and displays the name of that file in the worksheet window title bar.

About Filenames

Later, under "Saving Files", you'll learn how to assign a filename to your 1-2-3 worksheet files and save them to disk. Before you are ready to do so, though, you should know a little about 1-2-3's file-naming conventions.

Basically, 1-2-3 conforms to the same file-naming conventions as its DOS host. Briefly, the following rules apply:

- You can use any combination of letters, numbers, and underscores (_) when naming files. However, the characters ", /, \, [,], :, |, >, <, +, =, ;, comma, *, ?, &, TAB, and period have special meanings either for DOS or 1-2-3 and should not be used in filenames. Further, DOS does not allow blank spaces in file names, despite the fact that 1-2-3 for Windows does.

- DOS filenames are limited to a total of eight characters in length.

- You can also follow the filename with an optional file extension that begins with a period (.) followed by up to three characters. In most cases, however, you won't need to provide a file extension; 1-2-3 does this for you automatically.

- If you do decide to assign your own file extension, you should avoid assigning file extensions that are associated with DOS file operations—for example, .BAS, .BAT, .COM, .EXE, or .SYS.

- You can use any combination of upper and lower case letters when naming files; DOS automatically converts all filenames to upper case.

Note: You can also specify a filename without an extension by adding a period (.) at the end of the filename.

Within the above guidelines, you can use just about any filename you'd like. It's always a good idea, though, to assign filenames that will help you identify the contents of the file later on. For example, the filenames TAX91FED.WK3 and TAX91ST.WK3 might help you remember that the first file contains information about 1991 federal taxes and the second file contains 1991 state tax information.

1-2-3's File Extensions

Although file extensions are optional, 1-2-3 uses them extensively to locate and list specific file types for different commands. For example, if you use the File Open command to open a worksheet file, 1-2-3 searches the current working directory for files with a .WK3 extension—the default file extension assigned to all worksheet files.

You can use the file extensions assigned by 1-2-3 as an indicator of the type of file you are dealing with. Here are some of the more common file extensions you'll encounter while using 1-2-3:

.AF3	1-2-3's font set files
.ALL	Allways add-in format file (Release 2.x)
.AL3	Named print-settings file
.BAK	Backup file you create for a .WK3 file created with File Save As or File Extract To commands
.CGM	Computer Graphics Metafile
.ENC	Encoded file created with the /Print Encoded command
.FM3	Formatting file saved for each worksheet file
.FMB	Backup file created for .FM3 formatting file
.FMT	WYSIWYG (Impress) style format file
.MAC	Macro file for a customized 1-2-3 SmartIcon
.PIC	1-2-3 graphics file (Release 2.x)
.WK3	Worksheet file, 1-2-3 for Windows and Releases 3 and 3.1
.WK1	Worksheet file, 1-2-3 Releases 2, 2.01, 2.2, and 2.3
.WKS	Worksheet file, 1-2-3 Release 1A
.WR1	Worksheet file, Lotus Symphony Version 1.1 and later
.PRN	ASCII file, all 1-2-3 Releases

You can also assign your own file extensions to 1-2-3's files, if you so desire. When 1-2-3 prompts you for a filename, simply enter the filename you want, press period, and type your special extension. If you use your own extensions, though, you may have trouble finding your files later. When 1-2-3 lists files for commands, it only lists those files whose extensions it recognizes. To list files with different extensions, you must make a special effort to specify the extensions in the File name text box associated with the command you're using. Often the extra steps associated with locating your files may outweigh the benefit you gain by using your own file extensions.

Note: 1-2-3 also lets you save your .WK3 files in a file format that is compatible with previous releases of 1-2-3 by assigning an appropriate extension when you save the file. For example, you can save a file in Release 2 format by simply assigning it a .WK1 extension. See Chapter 17, "Sharing Data," for more details on saving a file in Release 2 format.

CREATING NEW FILES

The 1-2-3 Classic equivalent for the File New command is /File New.

To create a new file, use the File New command. When you select this command, 1-2-3 will open a new single-worksheet file in its own window. When you create a new file, 1-2-3 automatically assigns it a default filename and displays that name in the worksheet window title bar. Default filenames take the form FILEXXXX.WK3, where XXXX is a sequential number. The first new file is assigned the name FILE0001.WK3, the second FILE0002.WK3, the third FILE0003.WK3, and so on. To assign the correct number, 1-2-3 checks the current default working directory for the existence of default file names and then assigns the next available one. You may accept this default filename or assign a more descriptive one of your own when you later save the file to disk.

▼ *Tip:* You can also customize your icon palette to include 1-2-3's File New SmartIcon ( ), which allows you to quickly create a new file. See Appendix A, "Customizing 1-2-3," for more details on customizing the SmartIcon palette.

SAVING FILES

1-2-3 offers three commands for saving worksheet files: File Save, File Save As, and File Save As Save All. The File Save As command is used either when you're saving a file for the first time or when you want to save an existing file under a new name. The File Save command, on the other hand, is used to replace an existing file on disk with the contents of the current file of the same name. Finally, selecting the File Save As command and then selecting the Save All button saves all modified worksheet files in a single operation. The following sections present these commands in more detail.

You can also password-protect your files when you save them. When you password-protect a file, 1-2-3 will not let anyone open the file without the correct password. In addition, 1-2-3 lets you protect certain settings in a file by "sealing" them with a password. Both these topics are also discussed in the sections that follow.

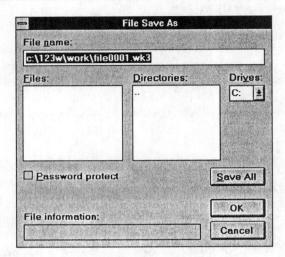

Figure 4-2   The File Save As dialog box

Saving a File for the First Time

The closest 1-2-3 Classic equivalent for the File Save As command is /File Save.

To save a new file for the first time, select the File Save As command. When you select this command, 1-2-3 will display the File Save As dialog box shown in Figure 4-2. In the File name text box, 1-2-3 displays the path to the current default working directory followed by the default filename assigned to the file. You can accept the default filename, edit it, or type in a name of your own. When you begin typing, 1-2-3 will clear the text box so that you can enter an appropriate path and filename. If you only want to edit the default path or filename, click on that part of the entry you wish to change, then edit the entry accordingly. When you've got the appropriate path and filename displayed in the File name text box, select OK to complete the File Save As command. 1-2-3 then saves the file to disk under the name you've specified.

When you save a worksheet file, 1-2-3 saves all data and formulas as well as all current worksheet settings. This includes range names, cell formats, fonts and styles, window display settings, and the location of the cell pointer.

▼ *Tip:*   You can save your .WK3 files in Release 2 (.WK1) format by using the File Save As command. When 1-2-3 prompts you for a filename, simply add a .WK1 file extension, and then select OK. Before using this feature, however, you should be aware of its limitations. For example, you cannot save a .WK3 file in .WK1 format if it contains multiple worksheets. There may be other problems as well. For a complete discussion of saving your 1-2-3 for Windows worksheet files in Release 2 format, see Chapter 17, "Sharing Data."

Saving an Existing File Under the Same Name

To save an existing file under the same name, use the File Save command. When you select this command, 1-2-3 will save the currently active file to disk, without requesting confirmation of any kind. Although this command is very convenient, it can also be very dangerous. You cannot undo this command—that is, the Edit Undo command or ALT+BACKSPACE key sequence has no effect.

You may also use 1-2-3 File Save SmartIcon (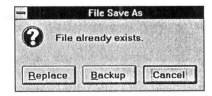) to quickly execute the File Save command. This icon has the same effect as selecting the File Save command from the worksheet menu bar.

Saving Under a Different Name

To save the current file under a different name or in a different directory, select the File Save As command. 1-2-3 displays the File Save As dialog box with the current path and name for the file in the File name text box. At this point, you can type a new name for the file or edit the existing one. Alternatively, you can select the path and name of another file you want to replace by using any combination of the Drive drop-down list box and the Files and Directories list boxes. Once you have specified an appropriate filename, select OK; 1-2-3 then saves the current worksheet file under the new name and leaves the old version of the file intact. If you select the name of an existing file, 1-2-3 will prompt you with the dialog box in Figure 4-3 containing Cancel, Replace, and Backup buttons.

As you might imagine, selecting Cancel halts the save operation and you are returned to the worksheet. If you select Replace, 1-2-3 will overwrite the file on disk with the new version of the file from memory. Finally, if you select Backup, 1-2-3 will rename the existing file on disk with a .BAK extension before saving the current worksheet file to disk under the existing filename.

Saving All Files

You can save all open files in a single operation by selecting the File Save As command and then choosing the Save All button. 1-2-3 will save all new and existing files that have been modified since you opened them. If an open file is not new or it has not been modified since you opened it, 1-2-3 will not resave the file.

Figure 4-3 1-2-3 prompts you before replacing an existing file

Although the Save All option can be very convenient, you should be aware of its quirks. For example, if any new, unsaved files are open on the desktop, 1-2-3 will save them in the current default working directory under their default file names. This may or may not be what you want. What's more, if one or more open files already exist on disk, 1-2-3 will prompt you with the Cancel, Replace, Backup dialog box in Figure 4-3 for each of them.

Saving Files with a Password

You can protect your files by saving them with a password. That way, unless someone knows the password, 1-2-3 will not allow the file to be opened. To save a file with a password, make sure the file you want to password protect is active and then select the File Save As command. 1-2-3 displays the File Save As dialog box shown previously in Figure 4-2. The name of the current file appears in the File name text box. To protect the file with a password, turn on the Password protect check box, then select OK to save the File. 1-2-3 then displays the File Save As Password dialog box shown in Figure 4-4. Type a password of no more that 15 characters in the Password text box. As you type, 1-2-3 displays asterisks (*). Press TAB to move to the Verify text box and type the password again exactly as you typed it the first time. To complete the command and save the file with a password, select OK. The next time you attempt to open the file, 1-2-3 will prompt you to supply the password.

You can use any combination of letters and numbers in a password. You can even use Compose sequences—ALT+F1 followed by an appropriate character code number—to create characters not available on your keyboard. Passwords are case sensitive, however, so be sure to remember the exact sequence of upper and lower case characters you used when defining the password. If you cannot replicate the same sequence of characters in the future, 1-2-3 will not allow you to open the file.

Note: 1-2-3 will not prompt you for a password when you select Save All from the File Save As dialog box.

Changing or Deleting a Password

To delete a password, make sure the file whose password you want to delete is current, then select the File Save As command. 1-2-3 displays the familiar File Save As dialog

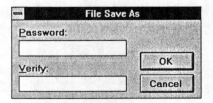

Figure 4-4 The File Save As Password dialog box

box with the Password protect checkbox turned on. To eliminate the current password, turn off the checkbox and select OK to save the file.

To change a password, you must first delete the old password. To do this, select the File Save As command and turn off the Password protect check box, then select OK to save the file. Finally, select the File Save As and follow the steps outlined in the previous section to assign a new password to the file.

Protecting Settings

1-2-3 also lets you "seal" certain settings in a file with a password. Once a file is sealed, certain commands appear grayed (unselectable). That way, another user cannot change those settings without the correct password.

Besides sealing worksheet settings with the File Administration Seal File command, you can also seal a file's reservation status on a network. (See Chapter 16).

To seal a file, first make it current, then select the File Administration Seal File command. 1-2-3 then displays the dialog in Figure 4-5. Select the File and network reservation status radio button and then select OK. 1-2-3 displays the File Administration Seal Password dialog box in Figure 4-6. Enter a password of up to 15 characters in the Password text box. As you type, 1-2-3 displays asterisks. When you're done, press TAB to move to the Verify box. Type the password again exactly as you typed it the first time, then select OK. 1-2-3 will then seal the file.

To unseal a file that has been sealed, you must first select File Administration Seal File and then select the Disable all restrictions radio button (Figure 4-5). When you select OK to confirm your selection, 1-2-3 prompts you to enter and verify the current password. If you do so successfully, 1-2-3 disables the seal. Otherwise, the seal remains in force.

As mentioned, when you seal a file, 1-2-3 disables certain commands that affect settings in the current file. A list of these follows:

- Graph: Name, Delete Name
- Range: Format, Protect, Unprotect
- Range Name: Create, Delete, Label Delete
- Style: Alignment
- Worksheet: Column Width, Hide, Unhide, or Global settings

Figure 4-5 The File Administration Seal dialog box

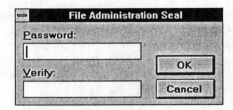

Figure 4-6 The File Administration Seal Password dialog box

Note: In addition to sealing the settings in a file, you can also protect certain areas of the worksheet from data entry. To do this, you use a combination of the Worksheet Global Settings Protection, Range Protect, and Range Unprotect commands (see Chapter 5).

OPENING EXISTING FILES

To open an existing file on disk, you can use either the File Open command from the 1-2-3 menu bar or the File Open SmartIcon ( ) from the icon palette. Whichever tool you use, 1-2-3 displays the File Open dialog box shown in Figure 4-7. In the File name text box, 1-2-3 displays the path to the current working directory, usually C:\123W\WORK, followed by the file descriptor ***.wk***. This causes 1-2-3 to display an alphabetical listing of all files in the current directory that have a file extension that begins with .WK in the Files list box below. This includes all .WK1 files (Release 2) and .WK3 files (Release 3 and 1-2-3 for Windows).

To select a file to open, double-click on its name in the Files list box. 1-2-3 opens the file you specified in its own window. That window then becomes the active window, and other open windows are shifted to the background. If the "Untitled" startup window is the only window open and it contains no data, the file you open will replace the "Untitled" startup file.

Although double-clicking on a filename in the Files list box is perhaps the easiest way of selecting a file to open, the following techniques are also available:

- Type the path and name of the file you want to open in the File name text box and then select OK or press ENTER.

- Use the arrow keys to highlight a name in the Files list and then select OK or press ENTER.

- Make the appropriate selections from the Drives and Directories boxes to see a list of files on a different drive or directory, then double-click on the name of the file you want to open.

You can also use wild cards in the File name text box to add or remove certain types of files from the Files list box. For example, if you want to see a list of worksheet files

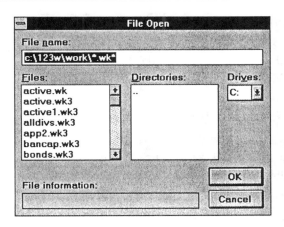

Figure 4-7   The File Open dialog box

that begin with the letter S, you might enter **S*.WK3** as a file descriptor in the File name text box. You could broaden the search to include all Lotus worksheet files, including those from previous releases of 1-2-3 and Symphony, by entering **S*.W??**. That way, all files whose filenames begin with letter S followed by a .WKS, .WK1, .WRK, .WR1, or .WK3 extension will be displayed.

▼ *Tip:*   When you highlight the name of a file in the File name list box, 1-2-3 shows the size of that file as well as the date and time it was last saved in the File information text box. Knowing the size of the file can be useful when you are loading multiple files and have limited memory available.

You can also use the File Open command to open files from previous releases of both 1-2-3 and Symphony inside 1-2-3 for Windows. This allows you to capitalize on work you've already done, rather than rebuilding your important worksheet files from scratch. However, there are a number of considerations you ought to be aware of when opening files from previous Releases in 1-2-3 for Windows. These are discussed at length in Chapter 17, "Sharing Data."

If you attempt to open a file stored on a shared network directory, you may get a Yes/No message box that reads "Unable to obtain reservation, Open Read Only?" This means that someone else is already using the file you are attempting to open, or that the directory that contains the file is read-only to you. If you select Yes, 1-2-3 opens the file, but it will be read-only. That is, you can view the file, but you cannot save it under the same name in the same directory. You can, however, save the file under a different name. For more details about using 1-2-3 on a network, see Chapter 16.

> ▼ *Tip:*   If you want to replace the current file with another from disk, use the
> 1-2-3 Classic /File Retrieve command. This saves you the extra step of
> having to close the old file.

Loading a File on Startup

You can have a specific worksheet loaded automatically when you start 1-2-3 for Windows. There are several ways you can go about doing this. The sections that follow
explain each method in detail.

From the DOS Prompt

You can use a special command line from the DOS prompt to start Windows, launch
1-2-3, and then load a specific file. This command line takes the form

```
WIN C:\123W\123W.EXE filename
```

where WIN starts windows, C:\123W\123.EXE initiates 1-2-3 for Windows' executable
file, and *filename* is the name of a 1-2-3 worksheet file you want to open. For example,
to load the file EXPENSE1.WK3 located in 1-2-3's default working directory,
\123W\WORK, you would use the following command line:

```
WIN C:\123W\123W.EXE EXPENSE1
```

On the other hand, if the file you want to open is located in another directory—for
example, \123W\INCSTAT—you'll need to precede the filename with the directory
name; for example

```
WIN C:\123W\123W.EXE C:\123W\INCSTAT\EXPENSE1
```

From File Manager

When you install 1-2-3, the install program automatically creates a file association in the
[Extensions] section of Windows' WIN.INI file. This means that you can double-click
on the name of a .WK3 file in a File Manager window to have Windows start 1-2-3 and
load that file automatically. See your *Windows User's Guide* for more about file associ-
ations.

▼ *Tip:*   You can also use the File Run command from Program Manager or File
Manager to autoload a worksheet file and 1-2-3 by association. For example, to launch 1-2-3 and have it automatically load CITRUS.WK3, select File Run, type **CITRUS.WK3,** and choose OK. Of course, if
CITRUS.WK3 is not located in 1-2-3's default working directory, you'll
need to include its path along with the filename.

From Program Manager

You can also create an icon in Program Manager that will start 1-2-3 and automatically
load a specific worksheet file. To do so, first open the group window where you'd like
the icon located. Next, select the File New command and turn on the Program Item radio
button. When you select OK, Windows will display a Program Item Properties dialog
box like the one in Figure 4-8. In the Description text box, enter whatever you want to
appear beneath the icon—the worksheet filename is a good choice. Then, in the Command
Line text box, enter the full path of 1-2-3's executable file (123.EXE) followed by the
name of the worksheet file you want the icon to load. For example, Figure 4-8 shows the
command you would use to load the EXPENSE.WK3 file located in C:\INC.

▼ *Tip:*   The quickest way to create an icon to automatically load a worksheet file
is to start with a copy of the original 1-2-3 for Windows icon. To create a
copy, press CTRL, then click on the 1-2-3 for Windows icon and drag.
As you start to move the mouse pointer, a copy of the original icon appears. After dragging the new icon where you want it, release the mouse
button. You can then change the new icon's description and command
line by using the File Properties command and modifying the contents of
the text boxes as shown in Figure 4.8.

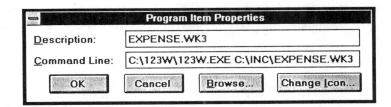

Figure 4-8 Windows' Program Item Properties dialog box

Using an AutoLoad Worksheet

1-2-3 also lets you designate a worksheet file as an autoload worksheet file by saving it with the name AUTO123.WK3. Normally, this file is saved in the current default working directory for 1-2-3 (typically C:\123W\WORK). That way, every time you start 1-2-3, it will search the current working directory for this file and load it automatically.

Although there are a myriad of potential applications for an autoload worksheet file, perhaps the most common application is in the macro arena. As you'll learn in Chapter 14, "Creating Macros," 1-2-3 lets you designate a macro as a *startup macro*. This macro runs automatically whenever you load the worksheet file that contains it. If you include such a macro in an autoload worksheet file, you can start 1-2-3 for Windows and have it come up with your macro in control. This allows you to create professional-looking applications that can be used by others who are not familiar with 1-2-3 for Windows.

CHANGING DIRECTORIES

The 1-2-3 Classic equivalent of Tools User Setup Worksheet directory is /File Dir.

1-2-3 normally uses C:\123W\WORK as its default working directory. This directory is referenced as the default for all file-related commands on the File menu. For example, when you select File Open or File Save As, 1-2-3 shows you the contents of the C:\123\WORK directory. As you grow with 1-2-3, you'll no doubt wish to reference other directories as the default so that you can better focus on a given set of files associated with a particular project.

1-2-3 lets you change its default working directory either temporarily—just for the current session—or permanently—for the current session and future sessions. To change the default directory for the current session, select the Tools User Setup command. When you select this command, 1-2-3 displays the dialog box in Figure 4-9. The name of the current default working directory appears in the Worksheet directory text box. You can,

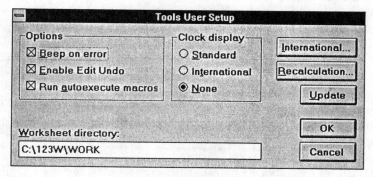

Figure 4-9 The Tools User Setup dialog box

of course, replace the contents of this box with another directory name of your choosing. To complete the Tools User Setup command, select OK. 1-2-3 will use the directory you've specified for the remainder of the current session. However, the next time you start 1-2-3, it will again use the old default working directory.

To change the default working directory permanently, select the Update button from the Tools User Setup dialog box (Figure 4-9). When you select this button, 1-2-3 updates the 123W.INI file with your new setting. (See Appendix A for more details on the 123.INI file). 1-2-3 gets its default settings from the 123.INI file each time you start the program.

CLOSING FILES

To close an active file, first make that file current, and then do one of the following:

- Select File Close from 1-2-3's menu bar.

- Double-click on the file's window Control menu box.

- Click on the window Control menu box (or press ALT+Hyphen) to display the Window Control menu, and select the Close option.

- Press CTRL+F4.

If you haven't yet saved the contents of the file, or you've made changes to the file since you opened it, 1-2-3 will prompt you to save the file before closing it by displaying a dialog box with Yes, No, and Cancel options. As you might expect, selecting Yes saves the changes and closes the file, returning you to the previously active file. If the file you closed is the only active file, 1-2-3 opens a new "Untitled" worksheet. Selecting No closes the file, without saving the changes to disk, and returns you to the previous file, if any. Finally, if you select Cancel, the close operation is aborted and you are returned to the file you attempted to close.

Closing All Files and Exiting 1-2-3

You can close all active files and end the current 1-2-3 session by selecting the File Exit command (or its shortcut ALT+F4). If you've made no changes to your active files before selecting this command, 1-2-3 returns you to Program Manager. Otherwise, 1-2-3 prompts you with a dialog box that asks you whether you want to save your changes before exiting, giving you the familiar Yes, No, and Cancel options. Selecting Yes saves all modified files to disk at once, ends the 1-2-3 session, and returns you to Program Manager. Selecting No ends the session, and returns you to Program Manager without saving any files to disk. Finally, selecting Cancel revokes the command and returns you to your 1-2-3 session.

ERASING FILES ON DISK

One of the more curious features of the new 1-2-3 for Windows menu bar is that it does not include a File Erase command. There are, however, a number of ways you can erase a worksheet file on disk:

- Activate Windows' File Manager, select the appropriate worksheet file, and press DEL.

- Select the 1-2-3 Classic /File Erase Worksheet command. When you do, 1-2-3 displays the dialog box in Figure 4-10. Specify the name of the file you want to erase and press ENTER.

- Choose the Classic menu's /System command to shell to DOS, use the DOS DEL command, and then type **exit** to return to 1-2-3.

Don't confuse the Classic menu's /File Erase, /Worksheet Erase, and /Worksheet Delete commands. Briefly, these commands perform the following functions:

- /File Erase: Erases a file on disk, but leaves the active version of the file in memory, if any.

- /Worksheet Erase: Removes all active files from memory, leaving you with the "Untitled" worksheet, but keeps the associated files on disk intact.

- /Worksheet Delete (Sheet or File): Removes the current worksheet or file from active memory, but does not delete the corresponding file on disk.

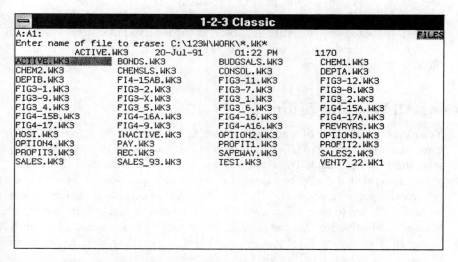

Figure 4-10 The /File Erase dialog box in the Classic window

EXTRACTING DATA TO FILES ON DISK

You can use the File Extract To command to extract a portion of an active worksheet file and save it to a file on disk. Extracting a portion of a file can be useful when you want to break down a large worksheet file into a number of smaller, more manageable worksheet files on disk. You may also want to extract part of a worksheet so you can work on it independently and explore different scenarios with a smaller data set.

File Extract To offers three extracting options: Formulas, Values, and

For more on the Text option, see Chapter 17, "Sharing Data." Text. The Formulas option copies a specified range of data to disk, including all numbers, labels, formulas, range names, cell formatting, and worksheet settings but does not copy any style settings. The Values option copies these same elements, but automatically converts any formulas to their current values in the destination file. The Text option saves the contents of the selected range to an ASCII text file, which can then be loaded into Notepad or any other program that reads ASCII files.

When you extract data to disk using the Formulas or Values option, 1-2-3 begins placing worksheet data in cell A:A1 of the destination file on disk. Any cell references in formulas extracted to the new file are automatically adjusted to reflect their new position in the worksheet relative to cell A:A1.

When you select the File Extract To command, 1-2-3 displays the dialog box in Figure 4-11. Ultimately, the File name text box will contain the name of the file on disk you want to extract data to. Initially 1-2-3 displays the drive and path of the default directory,

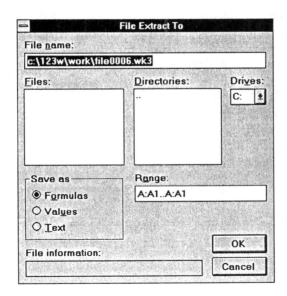

Figure 4-11 The File Extract To dialog box

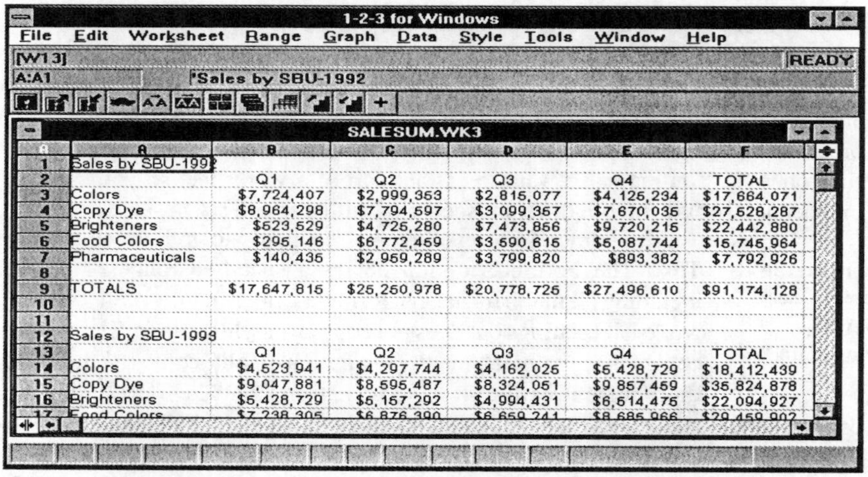

Figure 4-12 Extracting data from a sample worksheet file

followed by the name of the first available new worksheet file. For example, if the last worksheet file you allowed 1-2-3 to create was named FILE0002.WK3, the name that appears in the File name will be FILE0003.WK3. You can accept this filename, edit it, or type in one of your own. To choose the type of extract option you want to perform, you use the Save As group box below.

Perhaps the best way to clarify how to use the File Extract To command is by using an example. Figure 4-12 shows a sample worksheet that includes data on two years' sales by a strategic business unit for a small chemical company. To extract the range A:A12..A:F20 from this file to a file named SALES_93.WK3 on disk, begin by selecting the range. Next, choose the File Extract To command. In the File name text box, specify the filename **SALES_93.WK3**. (You'll notice that the Formulas option appears selected in the Save As group box by default.) When you select OK, 1-2-3 writes the data in the range A:A12..A:F20 to the file on disk. To see the results of your work, use the File Open command to open the SALES_93.WK1 file. When you open the file, you'll notice that the data which occupied the range A:A12..A:F20 in the original file is now displayed in the range A:A1..A:F9 of the new file, as shown in Figure 4-13.

Here are some things you'll need to know when using the File Extract To command:

- 1-2-3 automatically assigns a .WK3 extension to files you create with File Extract To.

- You can use the File Extract To command to extract data from any open worksheet file. This includes worksheet files from previous versions of 1-2-3, including 1-2-3 Releases 1A, 2, and 3 as well as Lotus Symphony.

- You can create a Release 2 (.WK1) file with the File Extract To command by simply specifying a .WK1 extension in the File name text box.

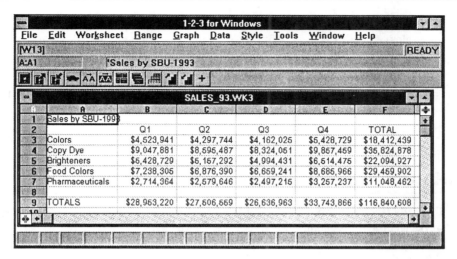

Figure 4-13 A new file created with File Extract To

- You cannot extract data from a file that has been sealed with the File Administration Seal File. You must first unseal the file with the File Administration Seal File Disable all restrictions command before using the File Extract To command.

- You cannot extract from a file stored on a shared network directory unless you have the file's reservation (see Chapter 16).

- If you use the Values option with the File Extract To command to extract formulas that refer to data located in files on disk, select File Administration Update Links to make sure the formulas are updated with the most recent data. Otherwise, the file you extract to may contain outdated information.

- If you extract a range containing a formula, make sure you also extract all data that is referenced by the formula. Otherwise, the formula will not produce the same results in the target file.

- If the data you're extracting contains formulas that refer to a named range, make sure you extract the named range as well. Otherwise, the formulas will evaluate to ERR in the extracted file.

- If you extract a formula that refers to data in another file, make sure you use an absolute reference in that formula. Otherwise, when the formula arrives in the new file, it may return the wrong result. 1-2-3 automatically adjusts cell references in all formulas to reflect their new position relative to cell A:A1 in the extracted file and the same is true of formulas that refer to data in other files. For example, suppose you have a formula in cell A:A10 of the original file that contains the formula +<<SALES.WK3>>A:A100 and you extract that formula to cell A:A1 in a new file. When the formula arrives in the new file, 1-2-3 will adjust it to +<<SALES.WK3>>A:A90.

- If the CALC indicator appears at the bottom of the screen, press CALC (F9) to recalculate the worksheet before you use the Values option with the File Extract To command.

- 1-2-3 doesn't create a format (.FM3) file for the new worksheet files you create with File Extract To. Therefore any formatting (fonts, styles, borders, and so on) applied to the data in the original file will be lost.

MANAGING MULTIPLE FILES

Typically, the commands you select from the worksheet menu bar apply only to the worksheet file that contains the cell pointer. However, as you'll soon see, 1-2-3 also lets you enter a command in one worksheet file and apply that command to a range in another open worksheet file.

1-2-3 also lets you use data from other files in the current worksheet file. The method you use to access this data depends on whether you want the current worksheet to reflect a particular point in time or to be updated continuously for changes in the supporting worksheets. For example, the File Combine From command lets you consolidate subsidiary worksheet files into a single master file. This command might be useful for producing periodic reports that reflect a "snapshot" of your data at a given moment.

1-2-3 also lets you link your worksheet files together with formulas. This process is known as *file linking* and the formulas themselves are referred to as *link formulas*. Link formulas have the same structure and content as any other formula, except that they contain a reference to a range in another worksheet file. And, whenever the data in the supporting worksheet file changes, the link formula in the current file is automatically updated for that change.

File linking is also significant in that it lets you break your work down into smaller, more manageable units. Rather than creating a large, complex model in a single worksheet file, you can create a series of smaller files and link them together. This also gives you the flexibility to create different reports and analyses from the same group of supporting worksheet files. In addition, because 1-2-3 lets you link to worksheet files on disk, you can create worksheet models that exceed the limits of your PC's RAM.

Specifying Ranges in Different Files for Commands

One feature you'll find useful when working with multiple files is the ability to specify a command or create a formula in one worksheet file and have it reference a range in another worksheet file. To specify a range in another worksheet file for a 1-2-3 command or formula, you must enclose the filename in double-angle brackets, << >>, followed by a range name or address from that worksheet file. If the file you want to reference is located in the current directory, you need only specify the filename. On the other hand,

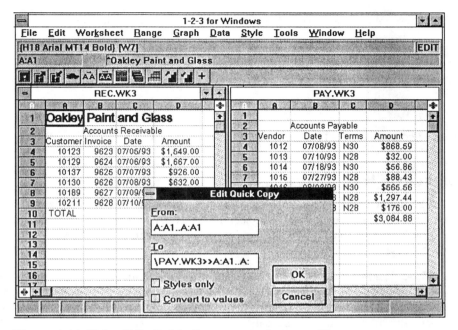

Figure 4-14 Using Edit Quick Copy to copy between files

if the file you want to reference is located in another directory, you must enclose both the path and filename in brackets.

You can specify a file and range specification for a command using any of the following techniques:

- Type in the file and range specification in the Range(s) text box during the command.

- Highlight a range from another file during a command.

- Press NAME (F3) during a command to select from a list of currently open files.

For example, Figure 4-14 shows how you can use the Edit Quick Copy command to copy data in the currently active worksheet file to another open worksheet file. The figure shows two files currently open in the work area: REC.WK3 and PAY.WK3. The active file is REC.WK3 (on the left side of Figure 4-14) and it contains the cell pointer. To copy the label "Oakley Paint and Glass" from cell A:A1 of REC.WK3 to the same cell in PAY.WK3, follow these steps:

1. With the cell pointer in cell A1 of REC.WK3, select the Edit Quick Copy command. 1-2-3 displays the dialog box in Figure 4-14 with the From range already set as A:A1..A:A1.

2. Press TAB to move to the To text box and then do one of the following:

    • Type **<<PAY.WK3>>A1**.

    • Click on any exposed portion of the worksheet in PAY.WK3 window, highlight cell A:A1, and click on the Confirm icon.

3. Select OK to complete the command.

1-2-3 copies the label from cell A:A1 of REC.WK3 to cell A:A1 of PAY.WK3.

Combining Files

1-2-3's File Combine From command lets you combine all or just a portion of another worksheet file with the current worksheet file. You might use this command, for example, to combine the financial statements of subsidiary companies into a yearly or monthly consolidated corporate statement.

Note: The File Combine From command is used to combine the contents of a file on disk with the current file. Therefore, the file you're combining from need not be open on the desktop. However, if you have opened the file you intend to combine from and made changes to it, make sure you save those changes to disk before using the File Combine From command.

The File Combine From command can be useful in cases where formula links may not be appropriate—for example, if you're combining large amounts of data from multiple sources. Here File Combine From may be preferable to setting up multiple link formulas.

The File Combine From command offers three types of combining operations:

• Copying information from another worksheet file on disk to the active worksheet file.

• Adding numbers from a worksheet file on disk to numbers in the active worksheet file.

• Subtracting numbers in a worksheet file on disk from numbers in the active worksheet file.

If you're adding or subtracting, it's important that the data from both the incoming file and the current file be organized and laid out identically.

The File Combine From command combines data from the worksheet file on disk with the current worksheet file starting at the location of the cell pointer. Therefore, positioning the cell pointer beforehand is critical to successfully executing the command. You should also make sure that sufficient space is available in the current file to accommodate all incoming data, otherwise, you might unintentionally overwrite valuable data. To minimize the effect of mistakes when using File Combine From, save the current worksheet file before you use this command. Also, remember that you can reverse the effects of this command with 1-2-3's Edit Undo (or ALT+BACKSPACE) command.

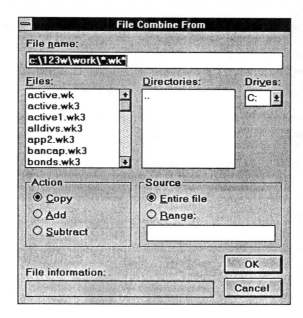

Figure 4-15 The File Combine From dialog box

File Combine From changes cell formats in the current file to reflect those of the incoming data, but it does not change column widths or styles in the current file. This means, for example, that you may have to widen column widths in the current worksheet to make the data more legible.

When you select the File Combine From command, 1-2-3 displays the dialog box in Figure 4-15. To begin, select the name of the source file whose contents you want to combine into the active worksheet. Then select an option button from the "Action" section of the dialog box to specify the type of combining operation you want. The combine options include:

- Copy: Copies all or part of the file on disk to the current file, starting at the location of the cell pointer. Any information in the active worksheet that is below and to the right of the cell pointer is replaced by the information from the disk file. Cells in the active worksheet file that are overlaid by blank cells from the file on disk are not affected. All relative, mixed, and absolute cell addresses in formulas copied from the file on disk are adjusted and now reference cells in the active worksheet file. See Chapter 7, "Cutting and Pasting Data," for a discussion of relative, mixed, and absolute cell references.

- Add: Adds the numbers and the results of numeric formulas from the file on disk to the corresponding cells in the active worksheet file. If a cell in the active file is blank, it takes on the value of the corresponding cell in the file on disk. If the cell in the active file contains a label or formula, the incoming entry is ignored.

- Subtract: Subtracts numbers and the results of numeric formulas in the file on disk from the corresponding cells in the active worksheet file. If a cell in the active worksheet is blank, and the corresponding cell in the file on disk contains a number or the result of a numeric formula, the incoming value is subtracted from zero. Cells in the active file containing labels or formulas are not affected.

Note: Because the Add and Subtract options have no effect on cells in the active worksheet file when they contain numeric formulas, this can lead to incorrect consolidation values. For this reason, you should only use these options when ranges in the active file contain values, not numeric formulas.

If you want to combine only part of a file on disk with the current worksheet file, rather than the entire file (the default), select the Range radio button. When you click on this button, 1-2-3 activates the text box below, where you can enter a range address or a range name from the file on disk. When you select OK to complete the File Combine From command, 1-2-3 combines the contents of the specified range in the file on disk with the file in the active window starting at the current location of the cell pointer.

A File Combine From Example

In this example, we'll create a consolidated balance sheet using the data from the two subsidiary worksheet files, DIV1.WK3 and DIV2.WK3, shown in Figure 4-16. When we're done, the two will be combined into a single worksheet file named AL-LDIVS.WK3.

Note: While the files in Figure 4-16 are shown as being open in memory for the purposes of this example, assume they are closed on disk instead.

You can begin consolidating the two files in Figure 4-16 into a separate file by combining the entries of one of the files, for example DIV1.WK3, into another worksheet file. To do this, use the File New command to create a new blank worksheet file and make sure that file is active (contains the cell pointer), then do the following:

1. Locate the cell pointer in the upper-left cell of where you want the incoming information to be combined, say cell A:A1.

2. Select the File Combine From command. 1-2-3 displays the File Combine From dialog box with the "Copy" and "Entire file" options selected by default.

3. Enter your source file, **DIV1.WK3**, in the File name text box.

4. Select OK to complete the File Combine From command. 1-2-3 copies the entire DIV1.WK3 file from disk into the current worksheet, starting in cell A:A1. Your screen should now look like Figure 4-17.

5. As a precaution, save the information in the current worksheet file under the name ALLDIVS.WK3 by using the File Save As command.

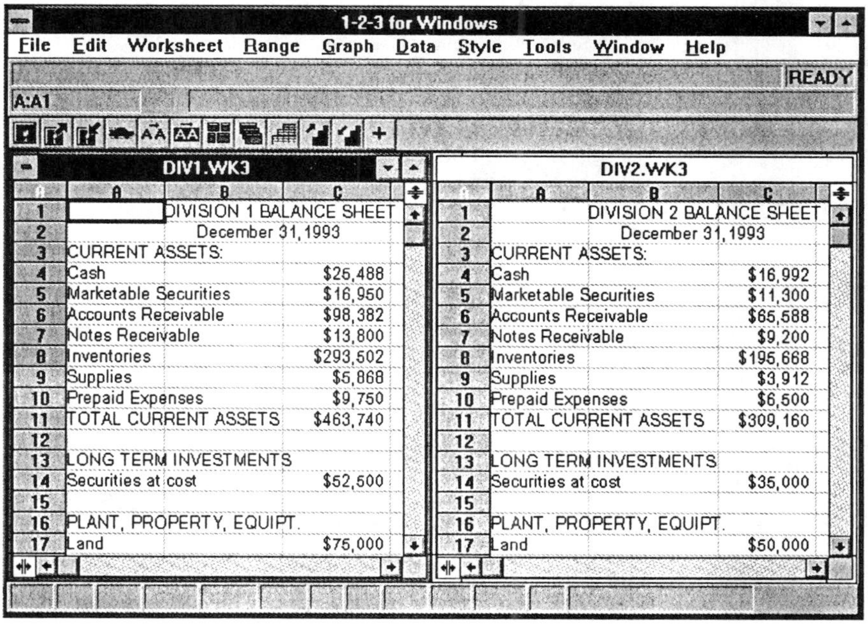

Figure 4-16 Two worksheets with matching structure

Next, we'll add the information for Division 2, DIV2.WK3, to the Division 1 information now in ALLDIVS.WK3. To do this:

1. Move the cell pointer to cell A:C4 of ALLDIVS.WK3. This ensures that the combining process will take place starting at that location.

2. Select the File Combine From command. 1-2-3 displays the File Combine From dialog box.

3. Specify the name of the file on disk whose values you want to add to those in the active file in the File name text box. To do this, simply select DIV2.WK3 from the Files list box or type its name and path.

4. Select the "Add" radio button from the "Action" section.

5. Select the "Range" radio button from the "Source" section.

6. In the text box below the Range radio button, specify A:C4..A:C41 as the range in your source file you want to add to your consolidated file.

7. Select OK. 1-2-3 adds the numbers in the range A:C4..A:C41 of DIV2.WK3 on disk to the values in the same range of the active file, ALLDIVS.WK3. Your screen should now look like Figure 4-18.

8. To reflect the fact you now have a consolidated statement, change the label in cell B1 to read "CONSOLIDATED BALANCE SHEET."

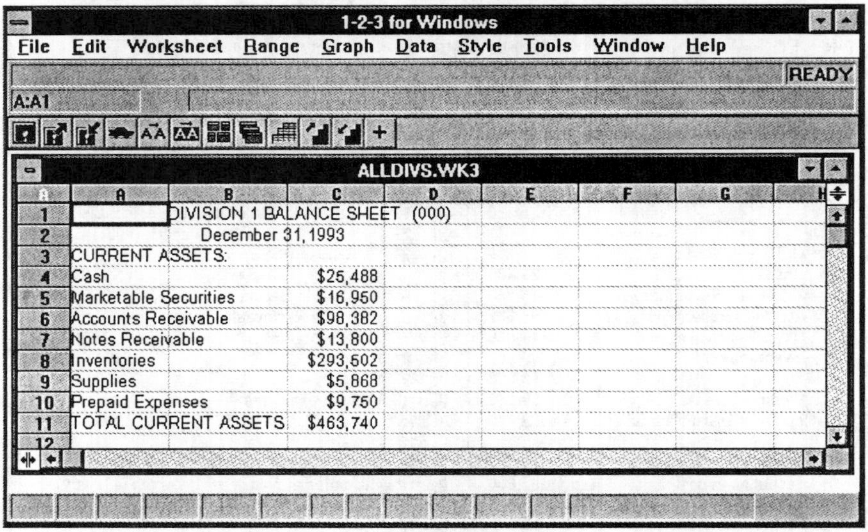

Figure 4-17 After the File Combine Copy command

The File Combine From Subtract command uses a similar procedure, but has the opposite effect of the Add option. It subtracts numbers and the results of numeric formulas in the worksheet file on disk from the corresponding cells in the current worksheet file. Like the Add option, Subtract does not disturb labels (or label formulas) in the current worksheet. The Subtract option can be useful in subtracting values from statements. For

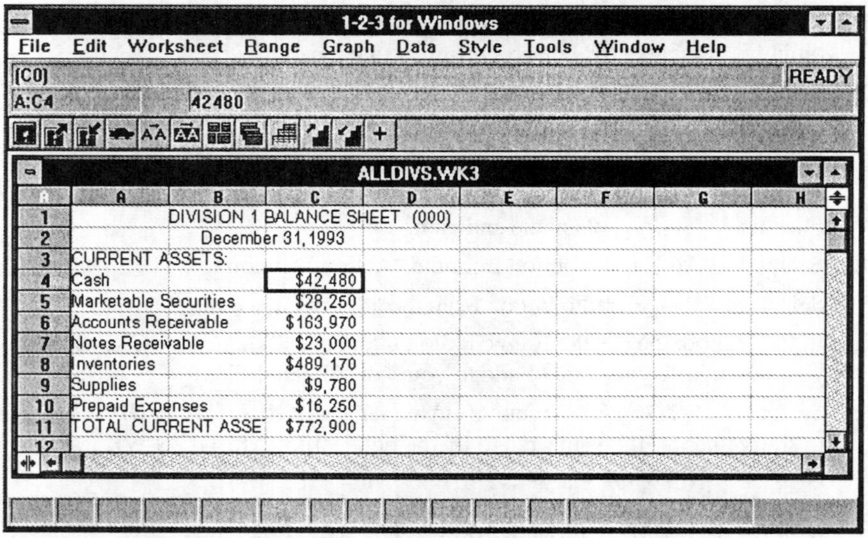

Figure 4-18 The resulting consolidated file

example, you might use this option to analyze what corporate statements might look like without the contribution of a certain subsidiary, or without certain key accounts. Or you could use the Subtract option to remove the accounts of a certain business segment from the statements to correct errors, and then reconsolidate the accounts with the File Combine From Add command.

Linking Files

1-2-3 lets you create formulas in the current file that refer to data in other files. When you create such a formula, 1-2-3 in effect forms a link between the two files. Thus, link formulas lets you perform calculations in the current worksheet file using the contents of cells or range names from other 1-2-3 worksheet files.

Link formulas can refer to data in other open files or to data in files on disk. The formula links you create are dynamic, meaning that when you change the data in the *source* file—the file referenced by the link—the data in the *destination* file—the file containing the link formula—is automatically updated for the change. Thus, 1-2-3 lets you set up a live transfer of data between files.

Note: While formula links are useful for linking 1-2-3 files with one another, Dynamic Data Exchange (DDE) is required for linking 1-2-3 files with files from Windows' other applications. For more information on DDE, see Chapter 17, "Sharing Data."

Linking Worksheet Files with Formulas

Earlier in this chapter you saw how 1-2-3 lets you specify a range from another file when issuing a command. You can use this same external file-referencing capability to create a link formula in the current file. To create a link formula in the current worksheet file, use an external file reference in place of an ordinary cell address. To create an external file reference, enclose the name of the file to be linked in double-angle brackets << >> and follow this with a range name or address from that file. For example, to link the single-cell range A:A100 in the file SALES.WK3 located in the current directory to the current file, you can use the following formula in any cell in the current file:

```
+<<SALES.WK3>>A:A100
```

1-2-3 copies the data from cell A:A100 of SALES.WK3 to the current cell in the current worksheet file.

If you are a 1-2-3 Release 2.x or 3.x user, you'll notice that the linking scheme in 1-2-3 is very similar to those releases. In Release 2.x, however, you are limited to single-cell linking, as shown in the previous example. That is, you can only reference the contents of a single cell in another file. In Release 3.x and 1-2-3 for Windows, you can reference multiple-cell ranges in other files. For example, you might use the following formula:

```
@SUM(<<SALES.WK3>>A:A1..A:A10)
```

to sum the values in the range A:A1..A:A10 of SALES.WK3.

When you link two active files, 1-2-3 updates the destination file automatically whenever the data in the source file changes. If you've set recalculation to manual you'll need to press CALC (F9) (or select the RECALC icon) to update the link instead.

1-2-3 updates your formula links whenever you load the worksheet file containing them into memory. This ensures that the current file is updated for any changes that may have occurred in linked files on disk. If you have a large number of formula links in the current file, however, 1-2-3 may take slightly longer to load the file than you expect.

If you're working on a network where the data in the source file may have changed since you opened the destination file, you should periodically use the File Administration Update Links command. This command lets you manually update your formula links for changes to linked files on disk so that you'll be sure you're using the most current data available.

 Tip: It is always a good idea to include a path in the file reference of a link formula. That way, 1-2-3 can always find the source file, even when you change the current directory. If 1-2-3 cannot find the file referenced in a link formula when you load a file into memory, it will display ERR in the cell containing the link formula.

Formula Links: An Example

Figure 4-19 shows how you might use a link formula to consolidate information from several worksheet files into the current file. In this example, three files are shown: HOST.WK3, DEPTA.WK3, and DEPTB.WK3. Cell A:B4 of HOST.WK3 (on the left side of the figure) contains the formula

```
+<<C:\123W\WORK\DEPTA.WK3>>A:B4..A:B4+<<C:\123W\WORK\DEPTB.WK3>>A:B4..A:B4
```

Thus, the contents of cell A:B4 in the DEPTA.WK3 and DEPTB.WK3 files are added together and the result is displayed in cell A:B4 of the HOST.WK3 file. You can enter this formula manually or by pointing. To construct the formula by pointing, perform the following steps:

1.   Move the cell pointer to cell A:B4 of the HOST.WK3 file and press **+**. This operator puts 1-2-3 into POINT mode.

2.   Click on cell A:B4 in DEPTA.WK3. 1-2-3 now displays

```
+<<C:\123W\WORK\DEPTA.WK3>>A:B4..A:B4
```

in the Edit Line.

3.   Press **+** again. 1-2-3 returns the cell pointer to the HOST.WK3 window and remains in POINT mode. 1-2-3 now displays

```
+<<C:\123W\WORK\DEPTA.WK3>>A:B4..A:B4+
```

in the Edit Line.

4.   Click on cell A:B4 of the DEPTB.WK3 window. 1-2-3 now shows

```
+<<C:\123W\WORK\DEPTA.WK3>>A:B4..A:B4+<<C:\123W\WORK\DEPTB.WK3>>A:B4..A:B4
```

in the Edit Line.

5.   Complete the formula by pressing ENTER.

▼ *Tip:*   You can also customize your icon palette to include 1-2-3's 　⊞　
SmartIcon, which you can use to preselect a cell reference to link to.

You can also use range names in place of range addresses in link formulas by either typing in the range name or by selecting it by pressing NAME (F3) to display a list of files, selecting one, and then typing the appropriate range name.

If a range name is unique among the files in memory, you can use a wild-card file reference, <<?>>, in your link formula followed by the range name. When you do this, 1-2-3 searches all the files currently open in the work area to find that range name. For example, if the range name JAN_LABOR is unique to all the files in memory, you can use the reference <<?>>JAN_LABOR in a formula to refer to that range.

When you use a wild-card file reference <<?>> followed by a range name in a link formula, the file containing that range name must be present in memory. Otherwise, 1-2-3 assumes the range name is undefined and returns ERR in the cell containing the formula.

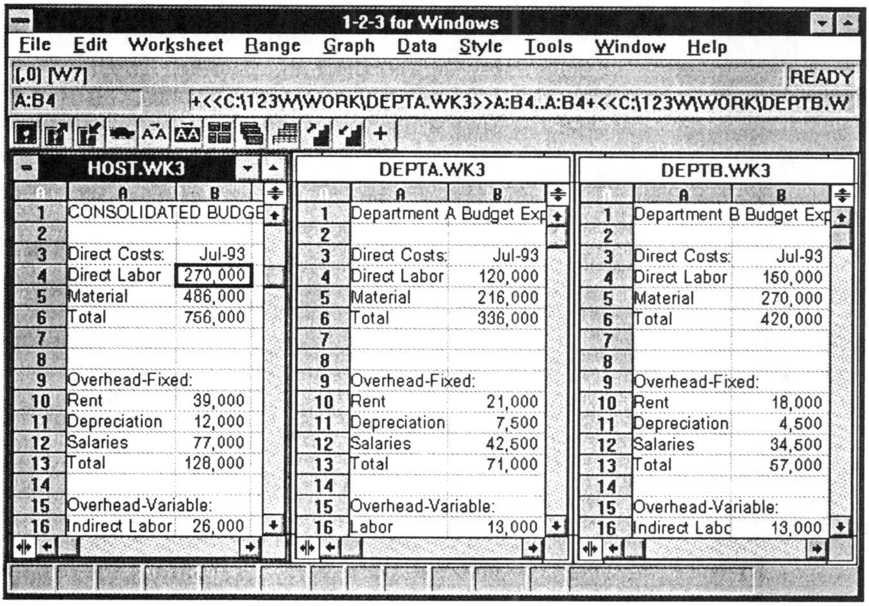

Figure 4-19 Linking Worksheet files with formulas; an example

In subsequent 1-2-3 sessions, when you load the file containing that formula into the work area, the file containing the range name must also be loaded, otherwise, 1-2-3 will not be able to find the range name and will return ERR in the cell.

You can also create forward references with link formulas. For example, imagine you have three open worksheet files: SHEET1.WK3, SHEET2.WK3, AND SHEET3.WK3. In cell A:A1 of SHEET2.WK3 you have the formula +<<SHEET3>>A:A1. In cell A:A1 of SHEET1.WK3, you have the formula +<<SHEET2>>A:A1. 1-2-3 uses the link formula in cell A:A1 of SHEET1.WK3 to get the value from call A:A1 of SHEET2.WK3, which gets its value from cell A:A1 of SHEET3.WK3. You can do the same thing using named ranges.

▼ *Tip:*   1-2-3 does not tell you if the current file contains formula links. However, you can easily check by using the File Administration Paste Table command and selecting the Linked files option. This command creates a table of filenames that are linked to the current worksheet file by formula. See Chapter 16, "Networking," for more details on this command.

5

Formatting Worksheets

Because formatting allows you to control how data appears—both on the screen and when printed—it can make data more distinctive and easier to read. For example, you can assign numeric formats, such as currency or percent, to an entire file or to specific ranges in a file. You might want to justify a series of long labels to fit into paragraph form.

Formatting also means working with columns, rows, and worksheets. For instance, you may want to increase or decrease column widths or row heights to accommodate data or simply to enhance the appearance of the worksheet. Or when you're preparing a worksheet for use by others, you may want to hide confidential information in columns or worksheets from view. You can even prevent data entry in a worksheet or limit it to certain cells.

Note: Formatting labels and assigning styles like fonts and borders are discussed in Chapter 6.

GLOBAL FORMAT SETTINGS

During installation, 1-2-3 for Windows preassigns *global format* settings—numeric format, label alignment, column width, row height, the display of zeros, and the font—that affect how data is displayed in every cell in a new worksheet. These are also known as the *default format* settings. Although you can't change these settings for all future 1-2-3 sessions, you can change them for a specific worksheet file.

You can use the Worksheet Global Settings command to change most of the global format settings any time a worksheet is active. When you select this command, you'll see a dialog box like the one shown in Figure 5-1. As you can see, by default 1-2-3 automatically displays zeros, aligns labels to the left, and sets the width of every column to 9. If you select Format on the right side of this dialog box, you'll see the Worksheet Global

A    B

Figure 5-1 The Worksheet Global Settings command

Settings Format dialog box shown in Figure 5-1B, indicating that the default numeric format is General.

It's important to realize that under normal circumstances, when you change the global format settings, only the *current* worksheet (worksheet A, for example) is assigned the new settings you specify. If you turn on the Worksheet Global Settings Group mode option, however, the global settings you assign to the current worksheet will be simultaneously applied to all the existing worksheets in the file. (Group mode is discussed in Chapter 1.) Any new data you enter will automatically use this new global setting, except in ranges where you have previously assigned nonglobal formats (see the next section).

Two other global format settings are the font and row height. 1-2-3 for Windows automatically uses the first font displayed in the Style Font dialog box, Arial MT 12-point, as its global default. This font also determines the height 1-2-3 for Windows assigns to each row in the worksheet. If you change the default font, 1-2-3 adjusts the default row height in the entire file. (See Chapter 6 for information on changing the default font for a worksheet file or even for all future 1-2-3 sessions, as well as the resulting effect on row height.)

Note: The default font also controls the column width unit of measurement. See "Working with Columns," later in this chapter.

Some global settings that affect the display of values—the currency symbol and its placement, whether negative values are enclosed in parentheses, as well as the International date and time formats—are controlled through the Tools User Setup International command discussed in Appendix A. Select Update in the Tools User Setup dialog box to make your International changes the default for all future 1-2-3 sessions.

RANGE FORMAT SETTINGS

You can also assign a nonglobal format to smaller areas of a worksheet. When you assign a format to a range, it *always* takes precedence over, or overrides, the existing global format setting. You can use the Range Format command to assign a numeric format to a range, Style Alignment to specify its label alignment (see Chapter 6), and the Worksheet Row Height and Column Width commands to change its row height and column widths. 1-2-3 for Windows doesn't let you override the Worksheet Global Settings Zero display setting in a range.

You can also use the Style Font command (see Chapter 6) to assign a font other than the default font to a range. In some instances, 1-2-3 will automatically adjust the row height in this range to conform to the font you specify. Other times you'll need to use the Worksheet Row Height command to set the row heights in a range yourself.

Note: If you insert a row or column within a formatted range, that row or column assumes the global format, not the format assigned to the range.

You'll want to use some discretion when formatting large ranges. 1-2-3 for Windows requires little or no extra RAM to store global default settings. But using Range Format to assign a worksheet a nonglobal numeric format takes up approximately 20K of RAM; using Style Font to assign a font other than the default font takes more than 160K of RAM. To conserve RAM, set formats that apply to the majority of a worksheet as global defaults, and assign other formats to small ranges as needed.

Selecting the Range to be Formatted

This chapter assumes that you know how to select ranges in 1-2-3 for Windows. Although this is discussed in detail in Chapter 2, the following should serve as a convenient reference guide. In addition, there are some shortcuts you'll want to keep in mind when selecting a range to be formatted.

The most efficient way to format a range is to preselect it before you choose a command. Because a preselected range remains selected after you complete the command, you can assign several different types of formatting without having to select the same range for each command. For instance, you might want to preselect the range A1..B2 using either of these methods:

- Outline A1..B2 using the mouse.
- Use the keyboard to move the cell pointer to A1, press F4 to anchor this cell, press ↓ then → to outline A1..B2, and then press ENTER to confirm.

Now you can use Range Format to assign a numeric format. Because A1..B2 remains selected, you can then choose the Worksheet Column Width command to assign a different column width.

If you want to use the keyboard to point to a range after you select a command, Range Format for example, remember to press F6 from the Range text box to return to the worksheet. Since the cell pointer is anchored in its current location, you may need to press ESC to unanchor it. When you move to the upper-left corner cell of the range you want to format, such as cell A1, remember that pressing . (period) will reanchor the cell pointer.

> ▼ **Tip:**   Before you enter data in a range, you can preassign any format except label alignment.

You'll also want to consider using Group mode (see Chapter 2) to simultaneously format the same range in all worksheets in a file. To put 1-2-3 for Windows into Group mode, turn on the Group mode option in the Worksheet Global Settings dialog box. Now when you preselect a range, or specify it after you choose a formatting command, you need only specify the range in one worksheet, A:A1..A:A20, for instance. Although the corresponding ranges in other worksheets won't appear selected, 1-2-3 for Windows will nevertheless apply any new formats you assign to A1..A20 in *each* worksheet in the file.

CHANGING THE APPEARANCE OF NUMBERS

The numeric format assigned to a cell determines how a number is displayed in that cell. In the default numeric format, General, there are no commas to separate thousands, and you have no control over the number of places displayed after the decimal. 1-2-3 for Windows offers a variety of other numeric formats (shown in Table 5-1) you can choose from to change the appearance of numbers.

Because of the limitations of the General format, you'll probably want to use the Worksheet Global Settings Format command to change the global numeric format for an entire worksheet. (Remember to use Group mode to change the numeric format for all worksheets in the file.) You'll also want to assign other numeric formats to specific ranges using the Range Format command. Both commands offer the same numeric formatting options.

Formatting Does Not Affect Cell Contents

1-2-3 for Windows applies a format setting to a cell, not to the contents of the cell. For example, the value 1000 entered in a cell assigned a Currency 2 places numeric format will be displayed as $1,000.00. The contents box, however, will still show that it is stored as 1000.

Note: 1-2-3 can store and calculate a value that includes up to 18 decimal places, even when the displayed value is rounded, truncated, or displayed in scientific notation.

Changing the Global Numeric Format

When a particular numeric format is appropriate for most of a worksheet, it should be made the global numeric format. For example, to make Currency 0 places the global default, select Worksheet Global Settings, then Format. Choose Currency from the Format list box and specify 0 places in the Decimal places text box. Select OK or press ENTER to confirm and return to the worksheet. When you assign a new global numeric

TABLE 5-1 Numeric Formatting Options

Cell format	Description	Indicator	Examples
Fixed	Displays a value with from 0 to 15 decimal places. Decimal value preceded by a leading zero. Negative value preceded by a – (minus sign).	(F2)	1000.00 0.10 -1000.00
Scientific	Exponential or scientific notation. Base from 0 to 15 decimal places is raised to a power of 10.	(S2)	1.00E+03 1.00E-01 -1.00E+01
Currency	Currency symbol precedes a value with from 0 to 15 decimal places. Commas separate thousands. Parentheses enclose a negative number.	(C2)	$1,000.00 ($1000.00) $.10
, Comma	Commas separate thousands, a negative value appears in parentheses, 0 to 15 decimal places. Decimal value is preceded by a leading 0.	(,2)	1,000.00 (1,000.00) 0.00
General	Displays a value as entered. A value too long to fit in a cell is rounded or displayed in scientific notation. Decimal value is preceded by a leading 0.	(G)	1000 -1000.1 1.0E+08 0.1
(+/-)	Horizontal bar format converts the integer portion of a positive or negative number to + or – symbols. A value between -1 and 1 is represented by a . (period).	(+)	+++ -------- .
Percent	Multiplies a value with 0 to 15 decimal places by 100. Adds a a trailing % symbol. A decimal value is preceded by a leading 0.	(P2)	10.00% -10.00% 0.00%
Text	Displays the formula entered instead of the value returned.	(T)	+A:D3-B:D3
Hidden	Hides the contents of a cell, although the cell entry remains visible in the contents box.	(H)	

(continued)

TABLE 5-1 Numeric Formatting Options *(continued)*

Cell format	Description	Indicator	Examples
Automatic	Formats a value as entered, including format symbols like $.	(A)	$1,000.00 12/21/91 .0000012
Label	Formats a label, number, formula, date, or time as a label. Displays an existing value in General format.	(L)	'1000.1 1000.1
Date	Five format options display a date-number as a date.		
(1: 31-Dec-90)		(D1)	21-Apr-98
(2: 31-Dec)		(D2)	21-Apr
(3: Dec-90)		(D3)	Apr-98
(4: Long Intl Date)		(D4)	04/21/98
(5: Short Intl Date)		(D5)	04/21
Time	Four format options display a time-number as a time.		
(6: 11:59:59)		(D6)	2:30:00 PM
(7: 11:59)		(D7)	2:30 PM
(8: Long Intl Time)		(D8)	14:30:00
(9: Short Intl Time)		(D9)	14:30
Reset	Returns a range to the Worksheet Global Settings Format setting.		

format to a worksheet any ranges you've previously formatted with Range Format won't be affected.

Remember, 1-2-3 for Windows assigns the new global numeric format, Currency 0 places for instance, only to the active worksheet, worksheet A perhaps. To assign it to other worksheets in the file, you'll have to reuse the Worksheet Global Settings Format command for each worksheet—or use Group mode (see Chapter 1) to simultaneously assign Currency 0 places as the default for all worksheets in the file.

When you change the global numeric format from General, you may need to make other formatting adjustments. For example, if you assign a Currency 2 places global numeric format, the column width has to accommodate the extra currency symbol, commas, and decimal place added to each value. In this format, only values smaller than or equal to $99,999.99 are displayed in the default column width of 9; anything larger is displayed as asterisks.

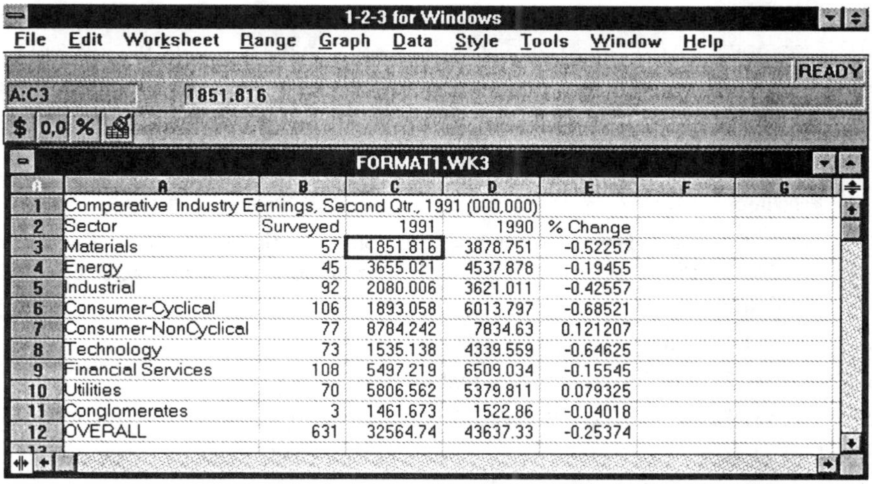

	A	B	C	D	E
1	Comparative Industry Earnings, Second Qtr., 1991 (000,000)				
2	Sector	Surveyed	1991	1990	% Change
3	Materials	57	1851.816	3878.751	-0.52257
4	Energy	45	3655.021	4537.878	-0.19455
5	Industrial	92	2080.006	3621.011	-0.42557
6	Consumer-Cyclical	106	1893.058	6013.797	-0.68521
7	Consumer-NonCyclical	77	8784.242	7834.63	0.121207
8	Technology	73	1535.138	4339.559	-0.64625
9	Financial Services	108	5497.219	6509.034	-0.15545
10	Utilities	70	5806.562	5379.811	0.079325
11	Conglomerates	3	1461.673	1522.86	-0.04018
12	OVERALL	631	32564.74	43637.33	-0.25374

Figure 5-2 Data using the default General numeric format

> ▼ ***Tip:*** The default font, Arial MT 12-point, displays larger values in the default column width of 9 than previous 1-2-3 releases. See "Working with Columns," later in this chapter.

One way to solve this problem is to increase the column width for the affected columns, or globally for all columns (see "Working with Columns," later). You can also try changing the font (see Chapter 6). Yet another solution is to decrease the number of decimal places displayed. For example, the default column width of 9 can handle values up to $9,999,999 in the Currency 0 format.

Note: The Worksheet Global Settings Format Parentheses option encloses both positive and negative numbers in parentheses using the global numeric format. For example, 220 is displayed as (220) while -220 is displayed as (-220). To change the way negative numbers are displayed, see "International Formats" in Appendix A.

Assigning a Format to a Range

Although the General global numeric format may work well to enter and calculate results, you may need currency signs or percent symbols to clarify the meaning of some types of data. Presenting data in different formats in adjacent ranges can also make the data easier to analyze.

Note: If you insert a row or column within a range assigned a nonglobal numeric format, 1-2-3 will assign that row or column the global numeric format.

For example, while the General numeric format is appropriate in column B of Figure 5-2, the amounts in Columns C and D are hard to distinguish, and the decimals in Column E don't line up with the decimal point. The solution is to assign different numeric formats using the Range Format command. For example, to specify a Currency 0 places format in the range C3..D12, follow these steps:

1. Preselect the range C3..D12.
2. Select the Range Format command and you'll see the dialog box shown in Figure 5-3. Notice that 1-2-3 for Windows displays the preselected range A:C3..A:D12 in the Range text box.
3. Choose Currency from the Format list box.
4. Specify 0 in the Decimal places text box.
5. Press ENTER or select OK to confirm your settings and return to the worksheet.
6. Press ESC to unselect the range, or choose another formatting command.

Figure 5-4 shows the results. As you can see in cell C3, the (C0) indicator displayed in the format line shows the format assigned. Note that this format choice creates a cleaner-looking worksheet that is easier to read. Figure 5-4 also shows E3..E12 after it has been formatted with Percent 0 places.

▼ *Tip:*   The ⊠ icon automatically assigns a Percent 2 places format to a pre-selected range, while the ⊙⊙ icon assigns a , Comma 0 places format.

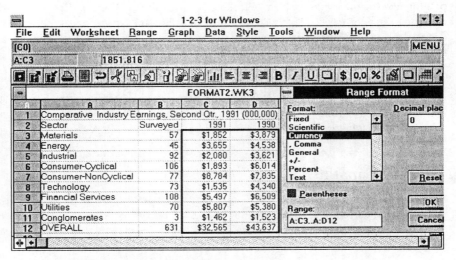

Figure 5-3 The Range Format dialog box

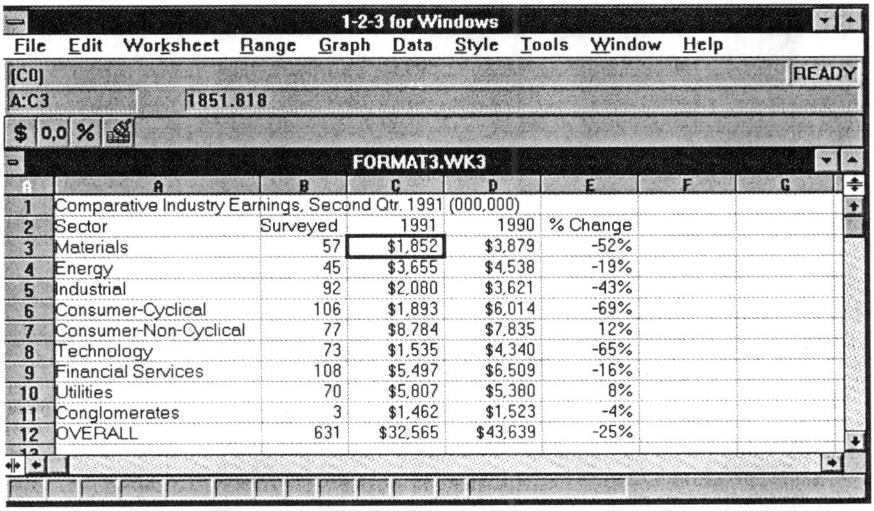

A	B	C	D	E
Comparative Industry Earnings, Second Qtr. 1991 (000,000)				
Sector	Surveyed	1991	1990	% Change
Materials	57	$1,852	$3,879	-52%
Energy	45	$3,655	$4,538	-19%
Industrial	92	$2,080	$3,621	-43%
Consumer-Cyclical	106	$1,893	$6,014	-69%
Consumer-Non-Cyclical	77	$8,784	$7,835	12%
Technology	73	$1,535	$4,340	-65%
Financial Services	108	$5,497	$6,509	-16%
Utilities	70	$5,807	$5,380	8%
Conglomerates	3	$1,462	$1,523	-4%
OVERALL	631	$32,565	$43,639	-25%

Figure 5-4 Assigning numeric formats in Columns C, D, and E

When you're assigning a Currency format to a range, you may want to consider the alternative shown in columns C and D of Figure 5-5. By assigning a Currency format only in the first and last entries in a column, and a , Comma format in all other cells, you can create a crisper-looking worksheet. The easiest way to do this is to first use Range Format and assign a Currency 0 places format to the range C3..D12. Then reuse Range Format and assign a , Comma 0 places format to the range C4..D11.

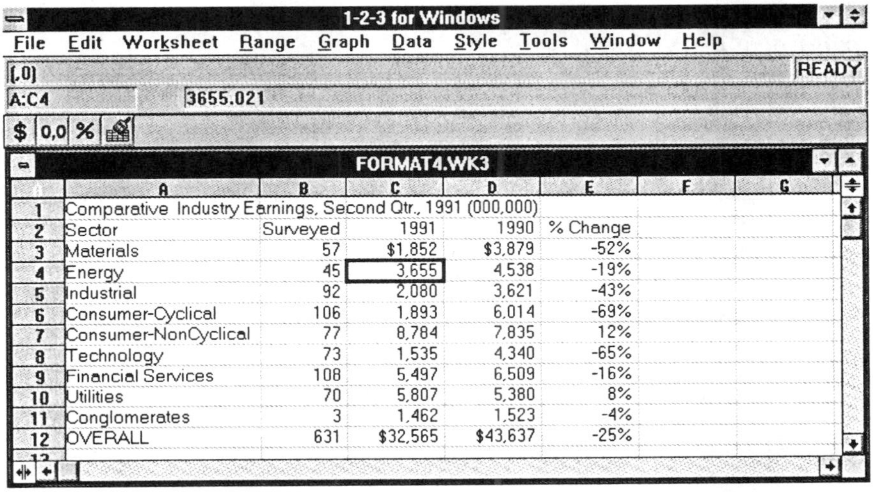

A	B	C	D	E
Comparative Industry Earnings, Second Qtr., 1991 (000,000)				
Sector	Surveyed	1991	1990	% Change
Materials	57	$1,852	$3,879	-52%
Energy	45	3,655	4,538	-19%
Industrial	92	2,080	3,621	-43%
Consumer-Cyclical	106	1,893	6,014	-69%
Consumer-NonCyclical	77	8,784	7,835	12%
Technology	73	1,535	4,340	-65%
Financial Services	108	5,497	6,509	-16%
Utilities	70	5,807	5,380	8%
Conglomerates	3	1,462	1,523	-4%
OVERALL	631	$32,565	$43,637	-25%

Figure 5-5 Reformatting a formatted range

> ▼ *Tip:*   Use the ⬛ icon to assign the format in the currently selected cell to
> other cells. For example, suppose in Figure 5-5 the cell pointer is located
> in cell C3, which has been assigned a Currency 0 places format. If you
> now select this icon, the mouse pointer turns into a paintbrush. Outline
> the range C4..C12, for instance, and all the cells in this range will be as-
> signed a Currency 0 places format.
>
> You'll get some unexpected results, however, if the cell pointer is
> located in a cell that still uses the global format. When you choose this
> icon, the cells you select will be assigned the global numeric format, ex-
> cept it will become a range format. In other words, if General is the
> global numeric format, each cell in the range you select will be assigned
> a General format as if you had used Range Format General.

Depending on the number of decimal places specified, 1-2-3 for Windows may round
the displayed value. This can create the appearance of an addition error when none was
made. For instance, if you add the values displayed in D3..D11 of Figure 5-5, you'll
discover that they total $43,639, not $43,637 as displayed. If you compare Figures 5-2
and 5-5, you'll see why this happened. Notice that column D in Figure 5-2 contains values
like 4537.878 in cell D4. Although 1-2-3 displays this value as 4538 when you assign a
Currency 0 places format, it still uses the stored value, 4537.878, when these values are
summed in cell D12. One way to handle this problem is to increase the number of decimal
places displayed. Or try using the @ROUND function covered in Chapter 9.

Note: For a range, the Range Format Parentheses option encloses both positive and
negative numbers in parentheses. For example, 50 is displayed as (50) while -50 is
displayed as (-50). To change the way negative numbers are displayed, see Appendix A.

Numeric Format Indicator

For a cell assigned a nonglobal numeric format, 1-2-3 for Windows displays a numeric
format indicator in the format line like the ones shown in Table 5-1. For instance, if you've
formatted a range for Currency 2 places, you'll see a (C2) indicator in the format line
whenever the cell pointer is located in any cell in this range. Similarly (,2) indicates ,
Comma 2 places; (P2) means Percent 2 places, and so forth. If a cell uses the global
numeric format, however, no format indicator is displayed.

Numeric Format Options

The following sections discuss each of 1-2-3 for Windows' numeric format options. As
you use these formats, remember that you can assign them to

- Different portions of a worksheet, such as a range, using the Range Format command.
- The current worksheet using the Worksheet Global Settings Format command, and to
  all existing worksheets in a file when the Worksheet Global Settings Group mode
  option is turned on.

While you're deciding what numeric format to use, keep in mind that the format you assign determines the size of a value that will fit in a cell. For example, you can display the value 123456789 in a Fixed 0 format (assuming the default Arial MT 12-point font and the default column width of 9). However, this same number will be displayed as 1.2E+08 in the General format, all else being the same. This is discussed further in "Working With Columns," later in this chapter.

General Format

General is the default numeric format 1-2-3 for Windows assigns to all the cells in a worksheet file. The General format displays values as you enter them, with these exceptions:

- Currency signs and commas are eliminated.

- Trailing decimals are eliminated. If you enter 10.00, it is displayed as 10, 1.50 as 1.5.

- Values less than 1 are displayed with a leading 0. For example, .1 appears as 0.1.

The General format doesn't allow you to control the number of places 1-2-3 for Windows displays after the decimal point, and no commas separate thousands. General only lets you display negative values preceded by a minus sign (-), so in many instances the global numeric default format, General, can make your worksheet look disorganized.

Values too large or too small to be displayed within the width of a cell are either rounded, displayed in scientific notation, or displayed as asterisks. Here are the rules that the General format follows:

- When the integer portion can fit into a cell, but the decimal portion can't, 1-2-3 rounds the entry to fit within the cell. For example, the value 12345678.1234567 is stored as entered, but will be displayed as 12345678. On the other hand, π (pi) is stored as 3.1415926535898, but is displayed as 3.141593 in a cell with a width of 9.

- When not even the integer portion can fit into a cell, 1-2-3 for Windows displays the integer portion in scientific notation. For instance, when the column width is 9, the value 120000000 (9 digits) is displayed as 1.2E+08. When this happens, you can display the full value by increasing the column width (see "Working with Columns") or changing the font (see Chapter 6).

- When the integer portion in scientific notation is too large to fit into a cell, 1-2-3 for Windows displays asterisks.

Fixed Format

The Fixed format is a clean-looking format that aligns values on the decimal point. You can specify from 0 to 15 decimal places. Decimal values are displayed with a leading zero, and negative values are displayed with a leading minus sign (-). You can see how the Fixed format looks in these examples:

Cell Entry	Format	Decimal Places	Display
100000.123	Fixed	0	100000
100000.123	Fixed	1	100000.1
100000.123	Fixed	2	100000.12
-100000.123	Fixed	2	-100000.12

Scientific Format

1-2-3's Scientific format is particularly useful for displaying a very large or very small number in a cell using exponential or scientific notation. In this format, a number is represented by its base (a value up to 15 decimal places) which is raised to the power of 10 as many times as is indicated by the exponent.

For example, 1,000,000 is represented by 1 raised to the power of 10 6 times: $1*10*10*10*10*10*10$ or $1*10^6$. In this case, 1 is the *base* and 6 is the *exponent*. In the Scientific 0 places format, this value is represented by 1E+06; in the Scientific 2 places format, it is displayed as 1.00E+06. Here are some other examples of the Scientific format:

Cell Entry	Format	Decimal Places	Display
10000	Scientific	2	1.00E+04
123123	Scientific	3	1.231E+05
–123	Scientific	3	-1.230E+02

Currency Format

The Currency format displays a currency symbol ($ by default) in front of values, separates thousands with commas, and lets you specify from 0 to 15 decimal places. Decimal values are displayed with a leading zero, while negative values are enclosed in parentheses. Here are some examples of how the Currency format displays values:

Cell Entry	Format	Decimal Places	Display
10000.123	Currency	2	$10,000.12
-100.125	Currency	2	-$100.13
1234567.89	Currency	0	$1,234,568

▼ *Tip:*   Use the [$] icon to assign a preselected range a Currency 2 places format.

You can use the Tools User Setup International command to specify a different currency symbol or have the currency symbol follow, instead of precede, a value. You can even specify that 1-2-3 for Windows leave a space between the currency symbol and the value; or you can precede negative values with a minus sign (-) instead of enclosing them in parentheses. (See Appendix A.)

The Currency format can create a column width problem because of the extra characters ($. and ,) it displays. When this happens, either increase the column width (see "Working with Columns"), change the font (see Chapter 6), or use a simpler numeric format like , Comma.

, *Comma Format*

The , Comma format distinguishes hundreds, thousands, millions, and so on, with commas. This format automatically adds a leading zero in front of decimal values, uses parentheses to surround negative numbers, and lets you specify from 0 to 15 decimal places. Here are some examples of the , Comma format:

Cell Entry	Format	Decimal Places	Display
123456.789	, Comma	2	123,456.79
-123.456	, Comma	2	(123.46)
-12345678.9	, Comma	0	(12,345,679)

You can use the Tools User Setup International command to specify a separator character other than , (comma) or to precede a negative value with a minus sign, rather than enclosing it with parentheses. (See Appendix A.)

▼ *Tip:*   You can use the [0.0] icon to assign a preselected range a , Comma 0 places format.

+/- *Horizontal Bar Format*

The Horizontal Bar format (+/-) portrays the integer portion of a positive number as a series of plus signs (+), the integer portion of a negative number as a series of minus signs (-), and a value between -1 and 1 as a . (period). For example, both 3 and 3.9 are displayed as +++, -3 as - - -, and -.45 as . (period). If the symbols exceed the column width, 1-2-3 for Windows displays asterisks instead.

To display large values in the +/- format, you'll first want to divide the values by a common denominator. For example, divide 10,000,000 and 5,000,000 by 1,000,000 so that the +- format displays symbols for 10 and 5.

Percent Format

The Percent format displays a number with 0 to 15 decimal places as a percentage. The number appears as if it were multiplied by 100 with a trailing percent (%) symbol and 0 to 15 decimal places. A negative number is preceded by a minus sign (-), while a decimal value includes a leading 0. Some examples of the Percent format are:

Cell Contains	Format	Decimal Places	Display
0.0001	Percent	2	0.01%
0.01	Percent	0	1%
1	Percent	0	100%
0.5	Percent	2	50.00%
-.666666	Percent	3	-66.667%

Notice that 0.01 is displayed as 1%, while 1 appears as 100%.

▼ *Tip:*   Use the ☒ icon to format a preselected range for Percent 2 places.

Date and Time Formats

Time formats in the 1-2-3 Classic menu are accessed through /Range Format Date.

Once a cell contains a date-number, time-number, or combined date/time number (see Chapter 2), you'll want to make it recognizable by using Range Format to assign one of the five date or four time formats shown in Figure 5-6. As you can see, the date December 25, 1993, which is represented by the date-number 34328, is displayed as 25-Dec-93 in the

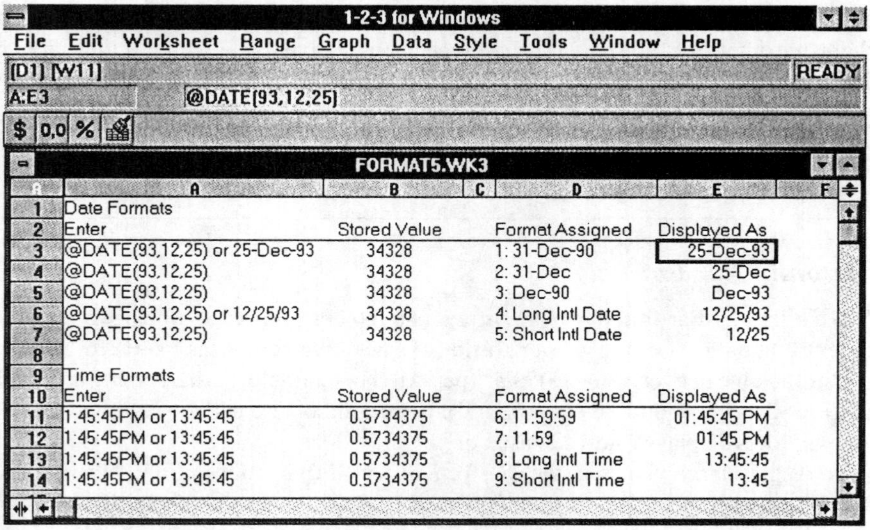

Figure 5-6 Date and time formats

D1 (1:31-Dec-90) format, 25-Dec in the D2 (2: 31-Dec) format, Dec-93 in the D3 (3: Dec-90) format, 12/25/93 in the D4 (4: Long Intl Date) format, and 12/25 in the D5 (5: Short Intl Date) format.

Similarly, the time 1:45:45 PM, which is represented by the time-number 0.5734375, is displayed as 01:45:45 PM in the D6 (6: 11:59:59) format, 1:45 PM in the D7 (7: 11:59) format, 13:45:45 in the D8 (8: Long Intl Time) format, and 13:45 in the D9 (9: Short Intl Time) format. Notice that the Long Intl Time and the Short Intl Time formats both use a military clock—1:00 PM, for example, is represented by 13:00.

You can use the Tools User Setup International command to change the Long and Short Intl Date formats, as well as the Long and Short Intl Time formats. You can also use this command to change the default character / (slash) that 1-2-3 for Windows uses to separate the month, date, and year in dates, and the default character : (colon) that 1-2-3 uses between hours, minutes, and seconds in times. (See Appendix A.)

▼ **Tip:**   You can use the Automatic format to enter a date or time in one of the date or time formats, and have 1-2-3 automatically assign this format to the cell. Enter June 10, 1995 as **95-6-10** in a cell formatted for Automatic, for example, and 1-2-3 will assign a D4 (4: Long Intl Date) format to that cell. See "Automatic Format," next.

On the other hand, by assigning a cell a Label format, you can enter a date or time using any of the Date or Time formats, and have it displayed as a *label*. If you enter **10-Jun-95** in a Label-formatted cell, for instance, 1-2-3 for Windows adds the default label prefix (usually ') and stores this date as the label '10-Jun-95. Because this date isn't a date-number you can't use it in calculations. (See "Label Format").

Automatic Format

The Automatic format uses the numeric, date, or time entry you make to assign a format. It's also handy to enter labels that begin with values, such as an address. Here are some examples:

Enter	Stored	Displayed	Format Assigned
1.50	1.5	1.50	F2 (Fixed 2 places)
1.5	1.5	1.5	F1 (Fixed 1 places)
2%	.02	2%	P0 (Percent 0 places)
15,000	15000	15,000	,0 (Comma 0 places)
$20.5	20.5	$20.5	C1 (Currency 1 places)
93-12-31	34334	93-12-31	D4 (4: Long Intl Date)
Dec 31,1993	'Dec 31,1993	Dec 31,1993	L (Label)
221 Sevilla	'221 Sevilla	221 Sevilla	L (Label)

You can use the Automatic format to enter a date or time in one of the acceptable date or time formats discussed above, and have 1-2-3 automatically assign that format to the cell. For example, note in the table above that if you enter **93-12-31** in a cell formatted for Automatic, 1-2-3 for Windows assigns a D4 (4: Long Intl Date) format. If you don't use an acceptable date or time format, 1-2-3 assumes you entered a label. Enter **Dec 31,1993**, for instance, and 1-2-3 assigns a label format to that cell.

Once 1-2-3 for Windows evaluates an entry and assigns a format to a cell, this format is retained even if you make an entry that uses another format in that cell. For example, suppose you enter 1.50 in cell A1, which is formatted for Automatic, so that 1-2-3 assigns a Fixed 2 places format. The numeric format indicator in the format line changes to (F2). If you then enter $200 in cell A1, 1-2-3 still uses the F2 format, and displays this value as 200.00. To get around this, use Range Format and specify another format, or select Reset to return cell A1 to the global numeric format.

Text Format

The Text format can be useful when you want to display a formula rather than the result returned. For example, suppose that cell A5 contains the formula @SUM(A1..D4), which returns 500. In addition, cell B5 contains the formula +A5. If you assign a Text format to cell A5, the formula @SUM(A1..D4) will be displayed. This formula only *looks* like a label; it can still be used in calculations. So in cell B5, the formula +A5 will still return 500.

The Text format displays an existing value using the General format. For example, imagine that cell A1 contains the value 1.5. When this cell is formatted for Currency 2 places, it is displayed as $1.50. If you now assign a Text format to this cell, however, it is displayed as 1.5.

Label Format

The Label format causes all entries—labels, numbers, formulas, dates, and times—to be formatted as labels. Use this format when you want to enter labels that begin with values, like zip codes, addresses, and social security numbers. The Label format is also useful for entering data in a database field that must be entered as a label (see Chapter 11).

Once you assign a Label format to a cell, 1-2-3 for Windows will automatically add the global label prefix, usually ' (apostrophe) for left alignment, before any entry. (To change the label prefix 1-2-3 uses, see "Global Format Settings".) Enter 08502 for example, and 1-2-3 stores it as the label '08502; enter the formula +A5*100, and 1-2-3 for Windows stores it as the label '+A5*100.

Note: When you assign a Label format to a cell already containing a value, 15.00 for example, 1-2-3 stores this value as 15, which uses the General format. Furthermore, although you'll see [L] in the format line indicating the cell is assigned a Label format, the existing value *won't* be preceded by a label prefix.

By assigning a cell a Label format, you can enter a date or time using any of the Date or Time formats and have it displayed as a label. (See "Date and Time Formats".) If cell A1 is assigned a Label format, for example, and you enter **31-Dec-93** in this cell, 1-2-3 for Windows adds the default label prefix (usually ') and stores this date as the label '31-Dec-93. Because this date isn't a date-number (see Chapter 2), you can't use it in calculations.

When a cell is assigned a Label format, removing the label prefix 1-2-3 inserts before the entry has no effect. Instead, you must reuse the Range Format command, and either select Reset or specify another format.

Hidden Format

The Hidden format can be useful when you're preparing or printing a worksheet for use by others and you wish to hide extraneous or confidential data. As its name implies, the Hidden format causes the contents of a cell to disappear from view. Because a hidden entry is still stored in a cell, however, it can be used in calculations.

For example, suppose you are preparing to print and distribute the employee list shown in Figure 5-7. The individual salary levels it contains are confidential and the personnel department has requested that this information be omitted. To conceal this data from view, use Range Format Hidden on the range E2..E13. As you can see in Figure 5-8, the individual salary levels are no longer displayed. If you locate the cell pointer in cell E4 of Figure 5-8 you can see that it still contains 68500. To redisplay the hidden information, just choose Range Format and select any option other than Hidden.

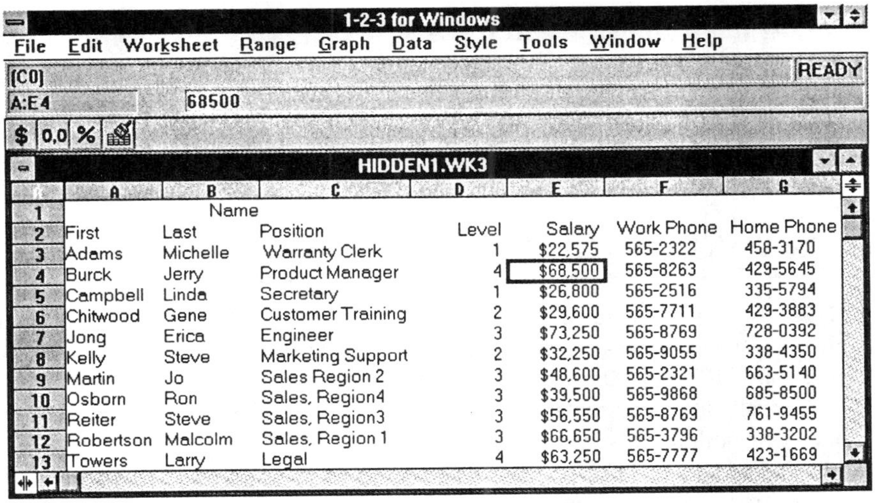

	A	B	C	D	E	F	G
1		Name					
2	First	Last	Position	Level	Salary	Work Phone	Home Phone
3	Adams	Michelle	Warranty Clerk	1	$22,575	565-2322	458-3170
4	Burck	Jerry	Product Manager	4	$68,500	565-8263	429-5645
5	Campbell	Linda	Secretary	1	$26,800	565-2516	335-5794
6	Chitwood	Gene	Customer Training	2	$29,600	565-7711	429-3883
7	Jong	Erica	Engineer	3	$73,250	565-8769	728-0392
8	Kelly	Steve	Marketing Support	2	$32,250	565-9055	338-4350
9	Martin	Jo	Sales Region 2	3	$48,600	565-2321	663-5140
10	Osborn	Ron	Sales, Region4	3	$39,500	565-9868	685-8500
11	Reiter	Steve	Sales, Region3	3	$56,550	565-8769	761-9455
12	Robertson	Malcolm	Sales, Region 1	3	$66,650	565-3796	338-3202
13	Towers	Larry	Legal	4	$63,250	565-7777	423-1669

Figure 5-7 A report containing confidential information

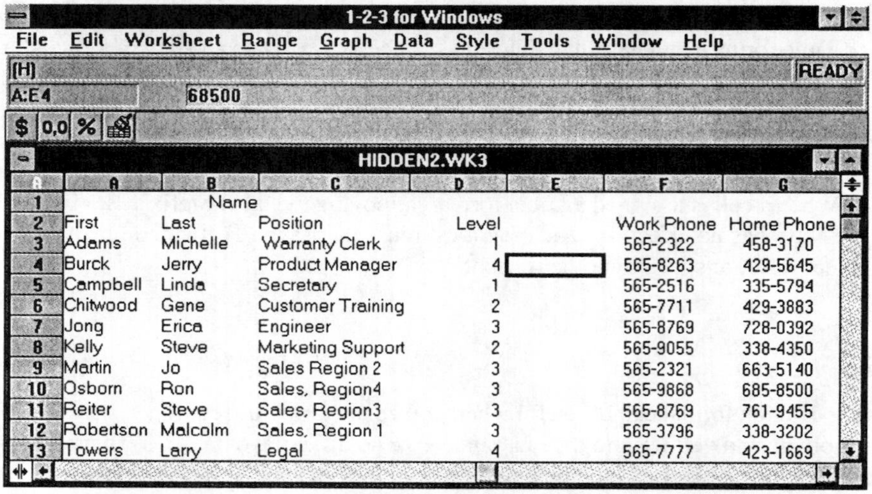

	A	B	C	D	E	F	G
1		Name					
2	First	Last	Position	Level		Work Phone	Home Phone
3	Adams	Michelle	Warranty Clerk	1		565-2322	458-3170
4	Burck	Jerry	Product Manager	4		565-8263	429-5645
5	Campbell	Linda	Secretary	1		565-2516	335-5794
6	Chitwood	Gene	Customer Training	2		565-7711	429-3883
7	Jong	Erica	Engineer	3		565-8769	728-0392
8	Kelly	Steve	Marketing Support	2		565-9055	338-4350
9	Martin	Jo	Sales Region 2	3		565-2321	663-5140
10	Osborn	Ron	Sales, Region4	3		565-9868	685-8500
11	Reiter	Steve	Sales, Region3	3		565-8769	761-9455
12	Robertson	Malcolm	Sales, Region 1	3		565-3796	338-3202
13	Towers	Larry	Legal	4		565-7777	423-1669

Figure 5-8 After hiding the contents of column E

▼ ***Tip:*** Sometimes hidden data is made more conspicuous by the blank space it leaves in a worksheet. Instead, you may want to hide a column entirely from view. Data in a hidden column isn't normally displayed in the contents box, although you can use it in calculations. See "Working with Columns," later in this chapter, for a complete discussion.

Resetting the Numeric Format

Use Range Format Reset to return a range of cells to the global numeric format. The range will revert to the Worksheet Global Settings Format setting currently assigned to the worksheet, General by default.

FORMATTING THE GLOBAL DISPLAY OF ZEROS

In 1-2-3 for Windows, you can change the display of cells that contain or evaluate to 0 (zero). You can suppress the display of zeros and have the cell appear blank, or you can elect to have 1-2-3 display a label of your own design. You can only change the format of 0's globally for the current worksheet or for all worksheets in a file by turning on Group mode. You can't, however, change the display of 0's in a range.

To change the display of zeros for the current worksheet, use the Worksheet Global Settings Zero display option (see Figure 5-1). You can choose from three options:

- **Display zeros,** the default, causes zeros to be displayed as 0's.
- **Leave zeros blank** causes 1-2-3 to suppress the display of zeros and have any cell containing a 0 appear blank.

- **Use label** allows you to enter a label in the text box, up to 512 characters, that will be displayed in place of a 0. 1-2-3 will display that label as right justified in cells that contain or evaluate to zero. For example, if you enter LOSS in the text box, 1-2-3 for Windows will right align LOSS in each cell containing or evaluating to 0. (The next time you choose Worksheet Global Settings, you'll see that 1-2-3 for Windows adds the " label prefix before this label in the text box.) You can control the alignment of the label you supply by preceding it with a label prefix such as ', ^, ", or \.

Caution: When you turn on the Leave zeros blank option, a cell previously displaying 0 appears blank. If you move the cell pointer to the cell you'll see in the contents box that the cell contains 0 or a formula that evaluates to 0. So there is a risk that you may accidentally assume the cell is blank and enter new data into it, or worse, erase its contents. To avoid this, you might want to consider protecting such cells from data entry altogether. See "Protecting Data" later in this chapter for more details.

WORKING WITH COLUMNS

By default, 1-2-3 for Windows assigns a column width of 9 to every column in a new worksheet. You'll sometimes need to increase column widths to fully display long labels that appear truncated, or large values displayed as asterisks. On the other hand, you'll need to decrease column widths to efficiently use worksheet space or to improve a worksheet's appearance.

1-2-3 for Windows makes it easy to adjust column widths by offering a variety of ways you can increase or decrease the column width of a single column, a range of columns, or every column in a worksheet. You can even hide columns from view.

The Column Width Character-Based Unit of Measurement

The character-based unit of measurement that 1-2-3 for Windows uses for column widths differs substantially from previous releases of 1-2-3. In earlier releases, each character represented one character of the fixed-width font displayed on the screen, so the default column width of 9 represented nine fixed-width characters of the screen font. Fonts are discussed in Chapter 6.

In 1-2-3 for Windows, this character-based unit of measurement varies depending on the default font assigned to a worksheet. To see this, look at Figure 5-9A, where the default font is Arial MT 12 point. Here, the default column width of 9 represents nine Arial MT 12-point characters. Because Arial MT 12 point is a proportionally spaced font (the width of each character differs), this column width actually represents the width of nine "average" numeric characters (usually a 5).

If you change the default font, the character-based column width settings conform to this new font. In Figure 5-9B, for instance, the default font has been changed to Arial MT 8 point. The default column width of 9 is unchanged, however, so in this case the column width of 9 represents nine Arial MT 8 point-characters. On the other hand, Figure 5-9C has been assigned Courier 10 point, a fixed-width font, as the default. Thus,

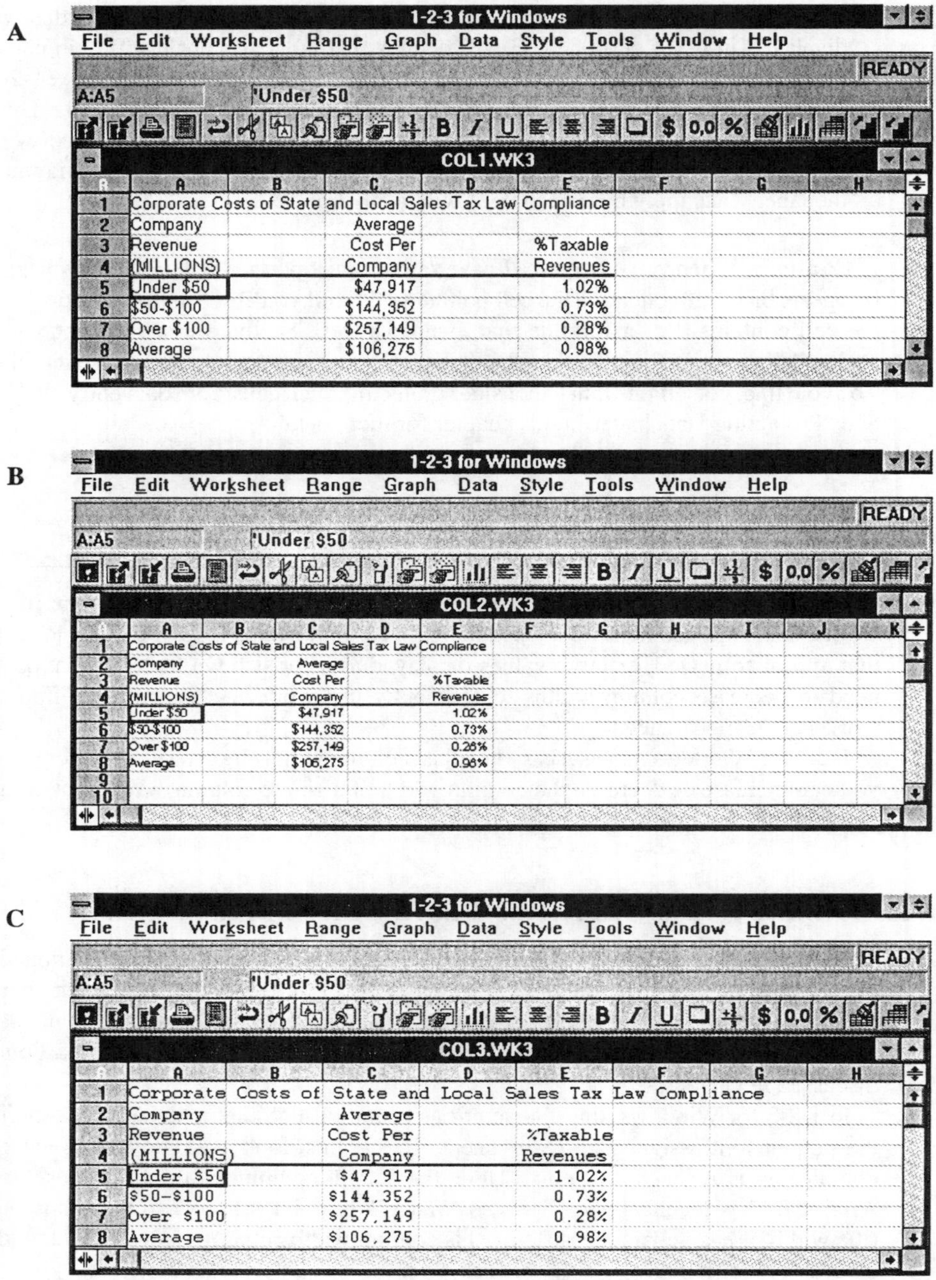

A

B

C

Figure 5-9 The column width character-based unit of measure

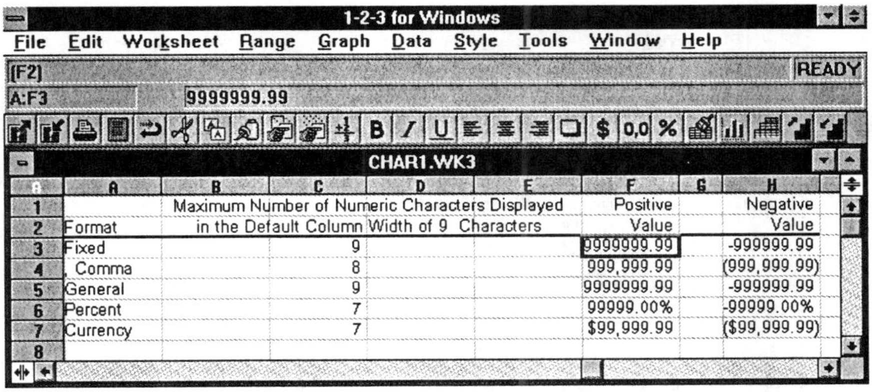

1-2-3 for Windows										
File	Edit	Worksheet	Range	Graph	Data	Style	Tools	Window	Help	

[F2] READY

A:F3   9999999.99

B / U $ 0,0 %

CHAR1.WK3

	A	B	C	D	E	F	G	H
1		Maximum Number of Numeric Characters Displayed				Positive		Negative
2	Format	in the Default Column Width of 9 Characters				Value		Value
3	Fixed		9			9999999.99		-999999.99
4	Comma		8			999,999.99		(999,999.99)
5	General		9			9999999.99		-999999.99
6	Percent		7			99999.00%		-99999.00%
7	Currency		7			$99,999.99		($99,999.99)
8								

Figure 5-10   Numeric formatting and column widths

the default column width of 9 represents nine Courier 10-point characters. You'll still have to adjust column widths yourself, however, to best display data assigned a font other than the default font.

Column Widths and Numeric Formatting

Another change you'll discover from previous releases of 1-2-3 is the increased number of characters that can fit within a given column width for each numeric format. As Figure 5-10 shows, the default column width of 9 and the default Arial MT 12 point font can accommodate nine numeric characters in the Fixed and General formats, eight numeric characters in the , Comma numeric format, and seven numeric characters in the Percent and Currency formats. In previous releases such as release 2.2, the addition of formatting characters, such as commas, reduced the number of characters that could be displayed. For example, in the default column width, $999.99 was the maximum value that could be displayed in the Currency 2 places format, 9,999.99 in the Comma 2 places format, and 99999.99 in the Fixed 2 places format.

Changing the Global Column Width

Many times you'll want to change the width of all columns in a worksheet. For instance, Figure 5-11A shows a model containing long labels that are truncated, and numbers assigned a Currency 0 places format that are displayed as asterisks because the default column width of 9 is too narrow. To set each column to a width of 12, select the Worksheet Global Settings command and specify 12 in the Column width text box. (You can specify a column width between 1 and 240.) Figure 5-11B shows how all cells in the current worksheet take on this new column width setting of 12 after you press ENTER or select OK.

A

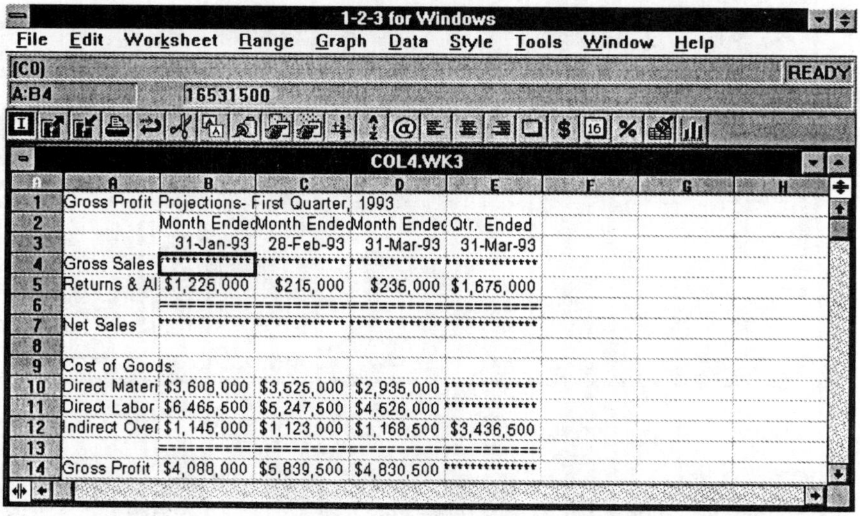

B

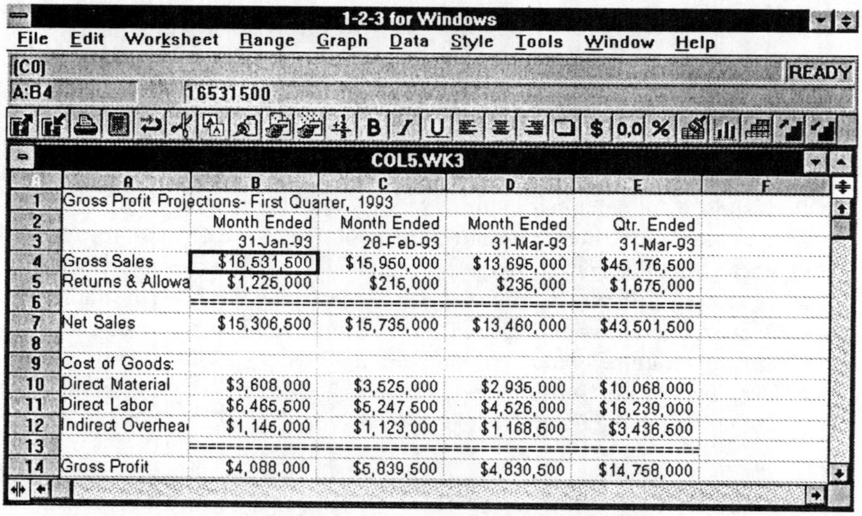

Figure 5-11 Specifying a new global column width of 12

Any global column width you assign doesn't affect those columns to which you have already assigned a nonglobal width using the Worksheet Column Width command (see the next section). So a nonglobal column width setting takes precedence over, and overrides, the global column width setting.

Normally, if you change the global column width, 1-2-3 for Windows only assigns it to the current worksheet. For example, the global column width of 12 in Figure 5-11B is only assigned to worksheet A. To specify a global column width for all existing worksheets in a file, remember to turn on Group mode in the Worksheet Global Settings dialog box.

Changing the Width of One Column

1-2-3 for Windows provides different methods that can be used to increase or decrease the width of a single column. You can use the Worksheet Column Width command, or adjust the column width manually using the mouse—and you can still use the 1-2-3 Classic command, /Worksheet Column.

For example, the global column width of 12 assigned in Figure 5-11B doesn't fully display the longest label, "Returns & Allowances" in cell A5. To increase the width of column A to accommodate this label, first position the cell pointer in any cell in column A—cell A5, for example. Next, choose the Worksheet Column Width command. As you can see in Figure 5-12, 1-2-3 automatically enters A:A5..A:A5 in the Range text box. Since the Set width to option is already selected, all you have to do is specify the number of characters you want the column width to be (from 1 to 240) in the text box. Let's try a column width of 17. When you select OK or press ENTER, you can see in Figure 5-12 that the label in cell A5 is now fully displayed. Because a nonglobal format is assigned, each cell in column A now displays the [W17] indicator in the format line, just like cell A5.

You can also employ a simple mouse technique to change the width of column A. In fact, you'll probably find this method more intuitive, because you can visually size a column width to display data. To do so in Figure 5-12, first move the mouse pointer to the worksheet border that contains column heading letter A, then move the pointer to the gridline between the column headings A and B. When you do so, the pointer becomes a two-headed horizontal arrow. To increase this column width, drag the mouse to the right. You'll notice as you move that the right edge of the column A becomes a solid black line. When the column reaches the desired width so that the label "Returns & Allowances" is completely displayed, release the mouse button. Once again, an indicator will be displayed in the format line showing the new width of this column.

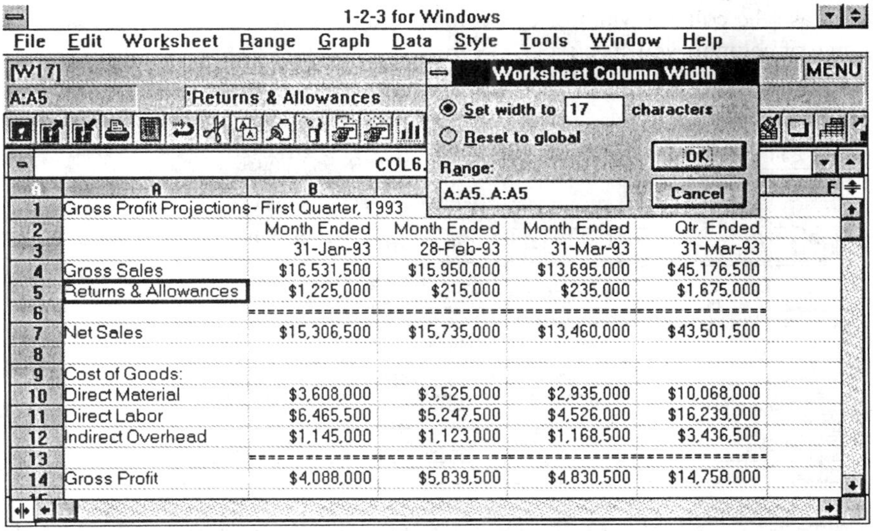

Figure 5-12 Assigning a nonglobal column width to column A

▼ *Tip:*   The 1-2-3 Classic /Worksheet Column command combines the features
of each of the methods discussed above. That's because this command
lets you use the arrow keys → and ← to visually increase or decrease the
column width in the worksheet.

Changing the Width of a Range of Columns

**The 1-2-3 Classic
equivalent is the
/Worksheet Col-
umn Column-
Range command.**

You can also use the Worksheet Column Width command to assign the
same column widths to a group of adjacent columns. For instance, suppose
you want to reduce the column width of columns B, C, D, and E in Figure
5-12 to 11 characters. One way to do this is to first preselect a range that
includes at least one cell in each column you want to change, for example
the range A:B4..A:E4 shown in Figure 5-13. When you choose the Worksheet Column
Width command, this range is automatically displayed in the Range text box. Since the
Set width to option is already selected, simply enter **11** in the text box. When you select
OK or press ENTER, Figure 5-13 shows how columns B, C, D, and E now use a column
width of 11. Because you assigned a nonglobal column width, each cell in these columns
displays [W11] in the format line, just like cell B4.

Note: To simultaneously change the width of the same column(s) in multiple worksheets, columns B through E in worksheets A, B, and C for instance, turn on Group mode
in the Worksheet Global Settings dialog box before you use the Worksheet Column Width
command.

You may also want to consider using the 1-2-3 Classic command, /Worksheet Column
Column-Range. This command allows you to use → and ← to visually increase or
decrease the column width of one column. This column width is then assigned to the
range of columns you specify.

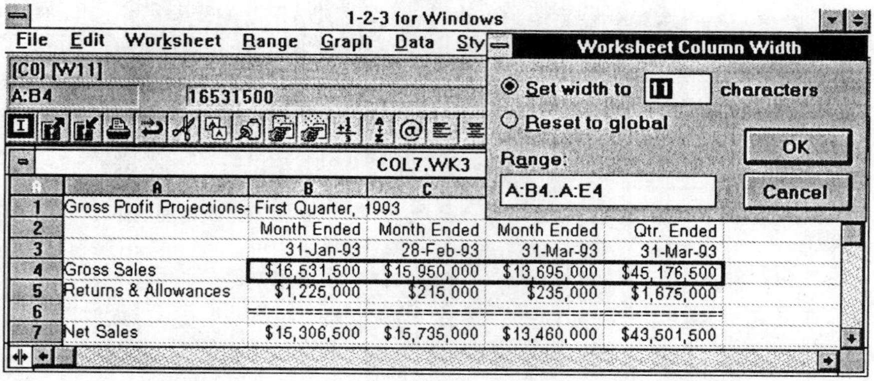

Figure 5-13 Assigning an 11-character column width to a range of columns

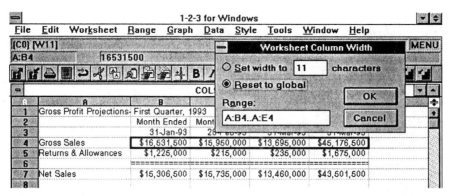

Figure 5-14 Resetting columns to the global column width

Resetting the Column Width

In some instances, you may want to restore the width of one or more columns to the default column width. For example, suppose in Figure 5-14 you want to restore columns B through E to the current global column width of 12. To do this, again preselect at least one cell in each column, such as A:B4..A:E4. Choose the Worksheet Column Width command, but this time turn on the Reset to global option. When you select OK or press ENTER, 1-2-3 for Windows returns these columns to the global column width. You can be certain of this because for any cell in these columns, the [W11] column width indicator previously shown in the format line is no longer displayed. You can now press ESC to unselect this range, or you can choose another formatting command.

HIDING COLUMNS AND WORKSHEETS

The Worksheet Hide command hides columns—or even entire worksheets—from view. (This is in contrast to 1-2-3 for Windows' Hidden format, which hides data from view, but not the column itself. See "Numeric Format Options".) The Worksheet Unhide command redisplays hidden columns or worksheets.

You'll want to hide columns or worksheets to exclude confidential or extraneous data. Or you might hide columns to make nonadjacent columns appear next to each other in a printed report.

> ▼ *Tip:*   To hide a row, see "Working with Rows," later in this chapter.

Hiding Columns

Column E of Figure 5-15 shows the same confidential salary information as Figure 5-7 does. To hide this salary data in column E, select any cell in this column, perhaps E1.

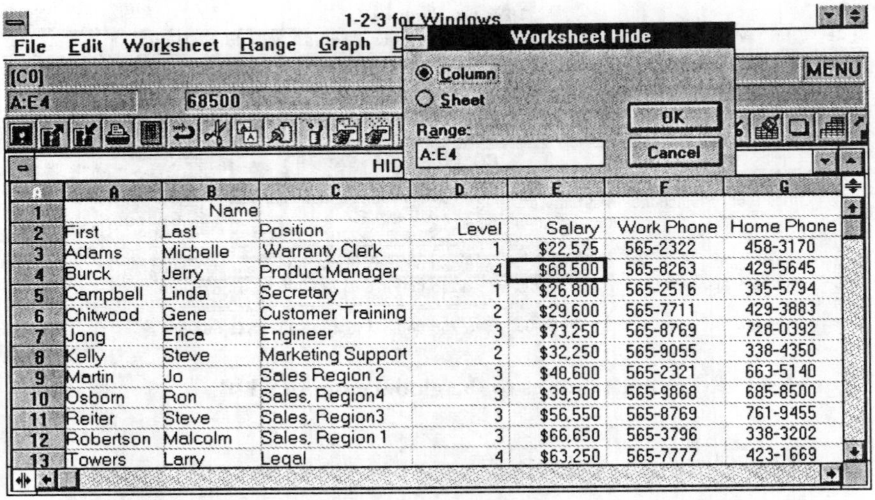

Figure 5-15   Hiding column E

Then choose the Worksheet Hide command. Because the Column option is already turned on by default and A:E4 is displayed in the Range text box, simply press ENTER or select OK to confirm.

Figure 5-16 shows the result. Note how columns D and F appear side by side. Column E is completely hidden: in fact, the column letter isn't displayed and you can't view the contents of column E in the contents box. You can still use the contents of hidden cells, however, in formulas and commands.

Note: All hidden columns are temporarily displayed and marked by an asterisk whenever you enter POINT mode to enter a formula. Hidden columns also reappear when you point to the worksheet from a dialog box, or when you select a 1-2-3 Classic command like /Move, which requires a cell address. Hidden columns aren't redisplayed, however, when you use GOTO (F5) or the Range Go To command.

You can also use the mouse to hide column E in Figure 5-15. To do this, move the mouse pointer to the gridline separating the column letters E and F so that the shape of the mouse pointer changes to a horizontal double arrow. Drag the mouse to the left (the gridline becomes a solid black line) until it converges with the gridline separating columns D and E. Column E will be hidden at this point, so just release the mouse button. In effect, you have just assigned a width of 1 character to column E.

> ▼ *Tip:*   If you compare Figures 5-16 and 5-8, you can see the difference between using the Worksheet Hide command and assigning a Hidden format using the Range Format command. Remember that column E in Figure 5-8 is still displayed when assigned a Hidden format, and that cell contents can be seen in the contents box.

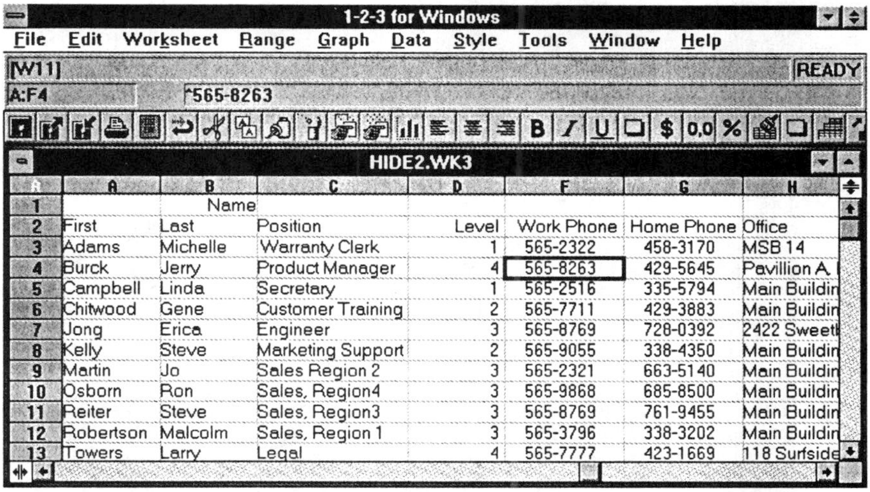

Figure 5-16 After hiding column E

Redisplaying Hidden Columns

To redisplay a hidden column like column E, you can use either of two methods. One way is to first preselect any cell in this hidden column by selecting cells in the columns to the right and left of column E. For example, Figure 5-17A shows how column E is redisplayed and marked by an asterisk when you move the cell pointer to cell D4, press F4, then press → twice to outline the range A:D4..A:F4 as shown in the contents box. (When you press ENTER to confirm column E is again hidden.)

Now you can choose the Worksheet Unhide command. As Figure 5-17B shows, A:D4..A:F4 is automatically included in the Range text box. Since Column is already turned on, simply press ENTER or select OK. As you can see in Figure 5-17C, column E reappears in the worksheet.

Note: You can also redisplay hidden column E by first choosing the Worksheet Unhide command, then entering any cell in column E, such as E4, in the Range text box—or press F6 to return to the worksheet. Because hidden column E will be redisplayed, you can then point to cell E4.

You can also use the mouse to redisplay hidden column E. First, move the mouse pointer to the gridline between column headings D and F. At this gridline, the mouse pointer will turn into a double horizontal arrow. Drag the mouse to the right (the gridline turns into a solid black line) until the gridline meets the right boundary of column F. When you release the mouse button, column E will reappear.

Note: Sometimes, using the mouse to redisplay hidden columns doesn't work. In the example above, for instance, you may end up increasing the width of column D rather than redisplaying hidden column E. When this happens, try again or use the Worksheet Unhide command instead.

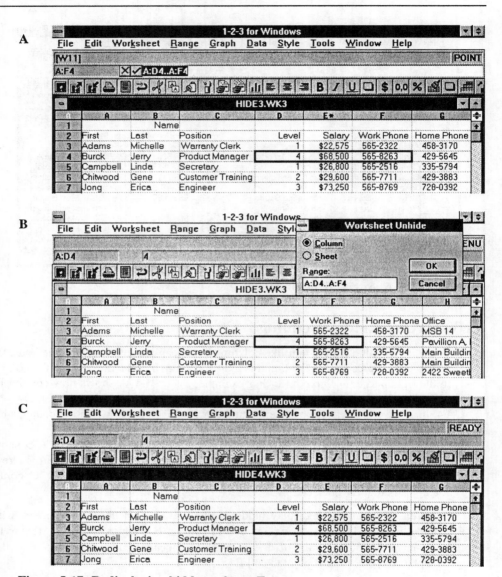

Figure 5-17 Redisplaying hidden column E

Hiding Worksheets

You can use the Worksheet Hide command to hide an entire worksheet, or all but one of the existing worksheets in a file. You can't, however, hide a worksheet when it's the only one in a file.

Note: Use the Worksheet Insert Sheet command to insert a blank worksheet (see Chapter 1). Remember that CTRL+PGUP and CTRL+PGDN will move you between worksheets.

For example, suppose you want to hide worksheet A in Figure 5-18A. (Although you can't see it, this file also contains a fourth worksheet, worksheet D.) Position the cell pointer in any cell in the worksheet, say cell A:A1. Next, choose the Worksheet Hide command. Since A:A1 is displayed in the Range text box, simply turn on the Sheet option. When you press ENTER or select OK, worksheet A disappears from view, as shown in Figure 5-18B. Worksheet B is now the first worksheet displayed, and the cell pointer is located in cell B:A1. Since worksheet A is hidden from view, worksheet D can now be seen.

As another example, suppose you want to simultaneously hide worksheets B and C in Figure 5-18A. The easiest way is to first preselect one cell in each of these worksheets, like the range B:A1..C:A1. When you select the Worksheet Hide command, B:A1..C:A1 will be displayed in the Range text box. Turn on the Sheet option, then press ENTER or

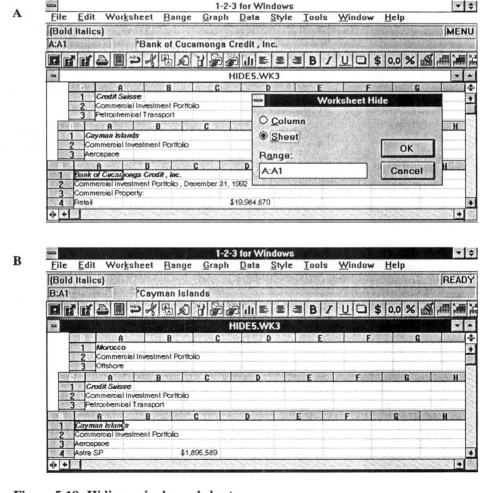

Figure 5-18 Hiding a single worksheet

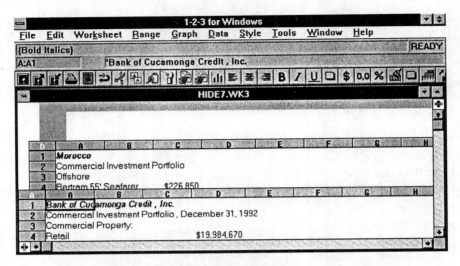

Figure 5-19   Hiding multiple worksheets in a file

select OK, and you'll get the result in Figure 5-19. 1-2-3 for Windows hides worksheets B and C so that worksheet D appears after worksheet A.

Note: Like hidden columns, hidden worksheets are temporarily displayed and marked by an asterisk next to the worksheet letter whenever you enter POINT mode to enter a formula; when you point to the worksheet from a dialog box; or when you select a 1-2-3 Classic command like /Move, which requires a cell address. Hidden worksheets aren't redisplayed when you use GOTO (F5) or the Range Go To command.

Redisplaying Hidden Worksheets

Redisplaying hidden worksheets is much like redisplaying hidden columns. For example, to redisplay hidden worksheets B and C in Figure 5-19, select Worksheet Unhide, then turn on the Sheet option. Next, in the Range text box, enter any 3-D range that includes at least one cell from each hidden worksheet, such as B:A1..C:A1. (You can also select cells in the worksheets before and after the hidden worksheet. For example, preselecting A:A1..D:A1 or pointing to this range from the Worksheet Unhide dialog box will also do the job.) When you press ENTER or select OK, worksheets B and C will reappear.

WORKING WITH ROWS

1-2-3 for Windows assigns a default height to each row in a worksheet. Since this height is determined by the default font, changing row heights is included in the discussion of fonts in Chapter 6. Here are the highlights, as well as a brief discussion of when you would want to change the height of a row yourself, and how to go about it.

The default font determines the default row height in 1-2-3 for Windows. For example, 1-2-3 assigns a height of 14 points to each row to accommodate the default font, Arial MT 12 point. (The point size of the row height is always slightly larger than the point size of the default font.) If you change the default font, 1-2-3 automatically adjusts the global row height to accommodate the new default font. When a larger font is assigned to cells in one or more rows, 1-2-3 for Windows automatically assigns a height to those rows to display the largest font.

The Worksheet Row Height command is not accessible through the 1-2-3 Classic menu. In some instances, you'll want to set the height of one or more rows yourself using the Worksheet Row Height command. You can specify a row height as small as 1 point (1/72 inch) or as large as 255 points (slightly more than 3 1/2 inches).

When would you want to change the row height yourself? Here are some typical situations:

- Setting the row height to 1 will hide a row.

- By slightly decreasing the row height, you can fit more rows within the same space but still display data. For example, decreasing the row height from 12 to 11 still displays data in a 10-point font, but it also lets you fit almost 10 percent more rows in the same space.

- Decreasing the height of a row that contains characters like ---- will make data appear more cohesive.

- Increasing the row height will display the contents of a cell that is partially obscured by a drop shadow. On the other hand, you may want to decrease the height of a row if only a drop shadow appears in that row. (To create a drop shadow, see Chapter 6.)

- Increasing the row height can better display objects like arrows created with Range Annotate (see Chapter 10).

For example, you'll want to increase the height of row 7 in Figure 5-20A so that the drop shadow no longer obscures the label "Acid Test." To do this, first select any cell in row 7, like cell A7, then choose the Worksheet Row Height command. Enter **20** in the Set height to text box. When you press ENTER or select OK, you can see the result in Figure 5-20B. You can tell that row 7 is assigned a nonglobal row height—whenever the cell pointer is located in a cell in this row, {H20} appears in the format line. Row 10 has also been assigned a height of 20 to fully display "Profit Margin on Sales."

 Tip: Turn on Group mode in the Worksheet Global Settings dialog box to simultaneously assign a row height to the same rows in all the worksheets in a file.

As with columns, you can also use the mouse to increase or decrease the height of a row. For example, you can use the mouse to increase the height of row 7 in Figure 5-20A. Begin by moving the mouse pointer to the gridline between the row headings 6 and 7 so

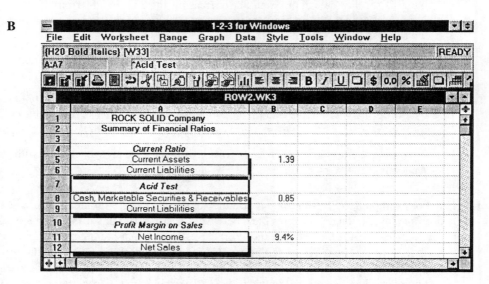

Figure 5-20 Increasing the height of rows 7 and 10

that the pointer turns into a vertical double arrow. Drag this gridline upward; when you reach the desired row height, release the mouse button.

You can also use the Worksheet Row Height command to restore a range to the current global row height setting. To reset rows 5 and 6, for example, preselect one cell in each row, like the range A5..A6. Choose Worksheet Row Height and turn on the Reset height option. When you press ENTER or select OK, 1-2-3 for Windows resets the height in these rows to 14 points, the row height for the default worksheet font, Arial MT 12 point.

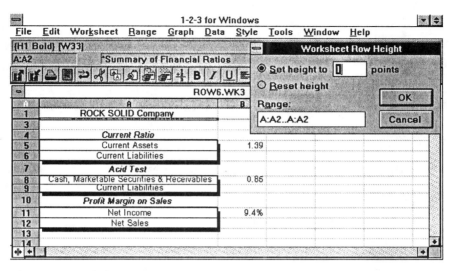

Figure 5-21   Hiding row 2

Hiding Rows

Imagine you want to evaluate how the worksheet in Figure 5-20 looks without the heading "Summary of Financial Ratios" in cell A2. By using the Worksheet Row Height command and specifying a height of 1, you'll get the result in Figure 5-21. Because row 2 is now hidden, you can evaluate the worksheet without this label. The advantage to this approach is that you didn't have to delete or move this data—by resetting the height of row 2, the label will reappear.

PROTECTING DATA

If you're preparing a worksheet for use by others that contains entries you don't want deleted, changed, or overwritten, you may want to turn on the Worksheet Global Settings Protection option. This protects a worksheet so that it essentially assumes a "read-only" status. If you like, you can then selectively turn protection off for certain parts of a worksheet to allow data entry in only these cells.

▼ *Tip:*   Turning on global protection in a worksheet containing macros is an excellent way to protect them. However, if the macros change the contents of any cells in the worksheet, make sure those cells are unprotected, or 1-2-3 for Windows will issue an error message when you run the macro. Macros are discussed in Chapters 14 and 15.

Turning Protection On and Off

Think of each cell in a worksheet as having an ON/OFF protection switch. When the protection switch for a cell is ON, you can't alter—move, delete, copy, or edit—the contents of a cell; when the protection switch is set to OFF, however, you can.

1-2-3's protection scheme requires that you protect all the cells in the worksheet first. Then, to allow data entry to selected cells, you turn protection off just for those cells.

To protect an entire worksheet, like worksheet A in Figure 5-22, position the cell pointer in any cell in this worksheet. Then choose the Worksheet Global Settings command and turn on the Protection option. When you select OK, 1-2-3 protects worksheet A. You can tell that global protection is on because each cell now displays a PR indicator in the format line.

▼ *Tip:* Turn on the Worksheet Global Settings Group mode option to automatically protect (or unprotect) the same areas in all existing worksheets in a file. For example, if both Group mode and Protection are on in the Worksheet Global Settings dialog box, all worksheets in the file will be protected. On the other hand, if Group mode is on, and you then use Range Unprotect for the range A1..B20 in worksheet A, 1-2-3 for Windows will unprotect this range in all existing worksheets in the file.

1-2-3 for Windows will issue an error message if you attempt to do anything like trying to select or edit a protected cell. You can, however, use commands that affect the way protected data is displayed. Thus, you can change the formatting and styles of protected cells using the Range Format, Worksheet Global Settings, Style, and Worksheet Display

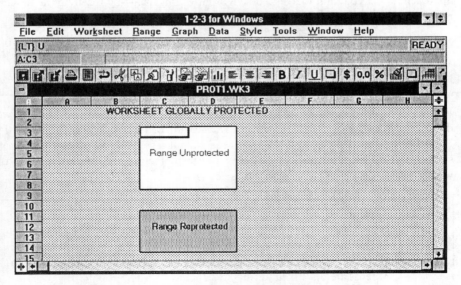

Figure 5-22 Disabling and reenabling worksheet protection

Options commands. (The exception is Range Justify.) You can also use commands like Worksheet Titles. When you use these commands you can't preselect a multicell range of protected cells—instead, point to protected cells from the Range text box after you choose a command.

Note: To disable global protection, simply reselect Worksheet Global Settings and turn Protection off.

In Figure 5-22, you can unprotect the range C3..D8 by choosing Range Unprotect and then specifying this range in the Range text box. This same procedure is also used to unprotect the range C11..D14.

Note: 1-2-3 for Windows won't let you preselect protected cells before you choose the Range Unprotect command. In fact, you can't even choose the Range Protect command when you've preselected a multicell range. You can, however, point to protected cells from the Range text box after you choose Range Unprotect.

By default, 1-2-3 displays the contents of unprotected cells in blue—the Window Display Options Unprotected cells default color selection. The contents of protected cells are usually displayed in black—the Window Display Options Cell contents default color. To change these settings, see Appendix A.

You can also use the Range Protect command to reprotect cells you have unprotected. If you select the range C11..D14 in Figure 5-22, for example, choose the Range Protect command, then select OK or press ENTER, 1-2-3 for Windows will reenable protection in this range. Each cell in the range will again display the PR indicator in the format line.

> ▼ *Tip:*   Because knowledgeable 1-2-3 users can turn off global protection, you may want to seal or password-protect a sensitive file instead. See Chapter 4.

JUSTIFYING A RANGE OF LONG LABELS

1-2-3 for Windows is by no means a word processor, but its Range Justify command does let you justify a series of long labels located in a single column to fit within a specified width. For example, you can rearrange a column of labels to fit into paragraph form, or to rejustify an edited paragraph. You'll probably find this command most useful when you include notes to financial information in your 1-2-3 for Windows worksheet.

> ▼ *Tip:*   Rather than use the Range Justify command to justify long labels, a better approach is to switch to a Windows word processor (or even Notepad) to create your text, then use the Clipboard to copy the text to your 1-2-3 worksheet. (If you use Notepad, be sure to turn on word wrap with the Edit Word Wrap command.)

Justifying a Multi-Row Range

The Range Justify command can only handle long labels in consecutive cells in the same column in a worksheet. To see this, let's justify the body of the memo that is arranged as a consecutive series of long labels in column A of Figure 5-23A. Choose the Range Justify command, and in the Range text box, enter or point to a range that:

- Includes all the text you want to justify. In Figure 5-23A, this would be the labels in the range A7..A11.

- Encompasses the width over which you want to justify the text. In Figure 5-23A, for instance, you would specify at least one cell in columns A, B, C, and D to limit the text in each justified line to the width of these columns.

That's why the range A:A7..A:D11 is specified in the Range text box.

Note: If you preselect a multi-row range before you choose Range Justify, 1-2-3 for Windows executes the command without displaying the dialog box or asking for confirmation.

Here are the rules 1-2-3 for Windows follows when it justifies the labels in this multi-row range:

- Range Justify will stop wrapping data if it encounters a blank cell or one containing a value or formula.

- The width of the cells in the range control the length of the justified labels as long as the total combined width of the columns specified is less than 512 characters. Because columns A through D are included in the justify range in Figure 5-23A, for example, and all are assigned a width of 9, 1-2-3 for Windows will place no more than 36 (9*4) characters on each line.

- Words aren't hyphenated—if a word can't fully fit in a row, 1-2-3 moves it to the next row.

- If the range you specify is too small to accommodate the text, 1-2-3 won't move text outside of this range.

- A 3-D range is treated as separate 2-D ranges; that is, 1-2-3 for Windows justifies the labels in each worksheet separately.

As you can see in Figure 5-23B, 1-2-3 for Windows fits as much text in cell A7 as will fit across the width of columns A through D. It then wraps the remaining text to cell A8, fits as much text as will fit across the widths of these columns again, wraps the remaining text to cell A9, and so on. In the process, it adds the protection status and label prefix from the first cell in the justification range, ' in this case, to each justified label.

However, the range specified in Figure 5-23A is too small for 1-2-3 to justify the text within it. (We've outlined the justify range in Figure 5-23B so that you can see this.)

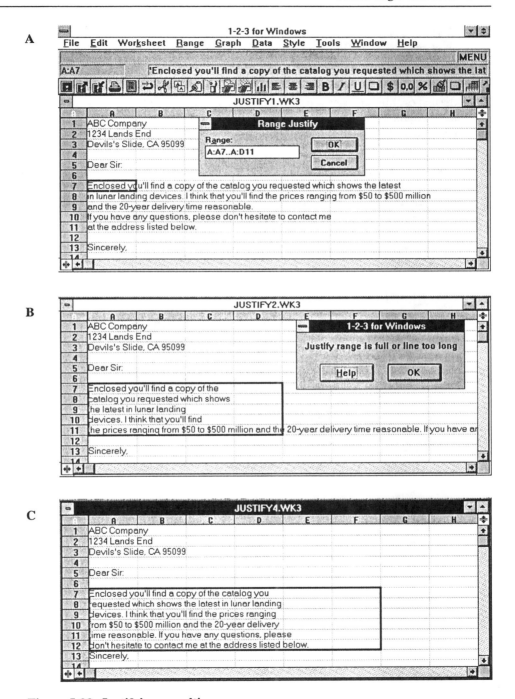

Figure 5-23 Justifying a multi-row range

When this happens, you'll see the "Justify range is full or line too long" error message shown in Figure 5-23B. Notice how 1-2-3 for Windows leaves the unjustified text in the last row—row 11. It doesn't wrap this text outside of the justify range.

Note: If you look at Figure 5-23B, you can see that 1-2-3 for Windows isn't justifying the text over the entire width of the justify range. That is, it isn't justifying any of the text past column C, even though column D is included in the range. In fact, 1-2-3 for Windows consistently seems not to use the last column in the range you specify in the Range Justify command.

When this happens, you can use the Range Justify command again on this text, but specify a larger range. Because of the problems 1-2-3 for Windows is having justifying text, you'll actually get better results if you immediately press ALT+BACKSPACE (Undo) to put the justified text back as it was, then reuse Range Justify and specify a larger range, like A7..F12. (We've outlined this justification range in Figure 5-23C.) Note that this range is one row and two columns larger than the first justification range used. As Figure 5-23C shows, this range is large enough for 1-2-3 to justify the text.

Justifying a Single Row of Text

The Range Justify command treats a single row of text a little differently than a multi-row range of text. For example, suppose you use the Range Justify command to justify the label in cell A2 of Figure 5-24A over the range A2..G2. Note that cell A3 contains a label.

Figure 5-24B shows the results. 1-2-3 for Windows not only commandeers additional rows if necessary, but also incorporates any existing text in these rows into the justification. Since 1-2-3 can't fit the label in cell A2 into the justification range A2..G2, it continues to justify this label in cell A3; because cell A3 already contains a label, 1-2-3 for Windows incorporates it into the justification. In fact, because it can't fully display the second sentence over the width of columns A through G in row 3, 1-2-3 continues to justify this text in cells A4 and A5.

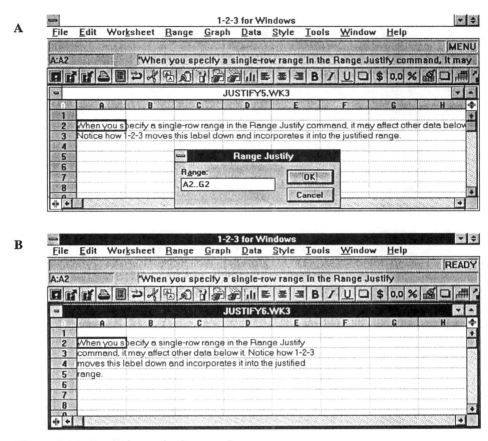

Figure 5-24 Justifying a single row of text

6

Fonts and Styles

The Style com-
mand is not acces-
sible through the
1-2-3 Classic
menu.

Traditionally, 1-2-3 has fallen short in providing presentation-quality features. In 1-2-3 for Windows, however, you can add a variety of finishing touches to a worksheet—fonts, shading, borders, colors, and label alignment—through the Style menu shown in Figure 6-1.

1-2-3 for Windows also allows you to use style enhancements efficiently. You can save a named combination of styles—font, shading, and borders, for example—then assign this named style to other portions of the worksheet. By using the File Import From Styles command, you can import the Style settings in one file to another file. In fact, by creating a worksheet entirely composed of styles, you can create a "template" file for future worksheets.

Figure 6-1 The Style menu

▼ *Tip:*   You'll find it's easiest to preselect a range before you select a Style command. You can even use Group mode to preselect the same range in multiple worksheets. Because a preselected range stays selected after you've completed a Style command, you can continue to assign Styles to this range. If you specify a range from a Style command's dialog box, remember that pressing F6 will move you back to the worksheet. Chapter 2 discusses how to specify ranges.

FONTS

In previous releases of 1-2-3, you were only able to access fonts external to 1-2-3. For example, you could access printer-specific fonts by inserting embedded setup strings in your worksheets. Another alternative was to use the ALLWAYS add-in to access your printer's fonts. In either case, you couldn't view these fonts on the screen. The WYSIWYG add-in in Releases 2.3 and 3.1 addressed this problem by letting you view fonts on the screen. However, font alternatives were still quite limited.

By contrast, 1-2-3 for Windows accesses fonts from multiple sources: your printer, Windows, and third-party font packages like Adobe Type Manager. You can even create your own custom fonts. Even more important, because fonts are displayed on the screen, you can take a hands-on, visual approach when working with fonts in 1-2-3 for Windows.

1-2-3 for Windows may be the first product that gives you easy access to fonts in a worksheet. If you've previously worked with Windows, however, you'll find that 1-2-3 for Windows accesses and handles fonts somewhat differently than other Windows programs.

Font Basics

A font is described by a typeface and point size. A *typeface* is the design of a printed character. Figure 6-2 shows typical typefaces you can access in 1-2-3 for Windows. As you'll see, 1-2-3 supports different fonts depending on the printer specified and the font packages installed in Windows.

The *point size* indicates the height of a printed character. One point is equal to approximately 1/72 of an inch; so a 12-point font means that the maximum height of a character is 12/72 or 1/6 of an inch. In 1-2-3 for Windows, you can usually assign a point size between 6 and 72.

For a particular typeface, you can also specify three different style *attributes*: bold, italics, and underline. You can even combine them, such as bold and underline. How 1-2-3 handles style attributes is discussed further in "Assigning Existing Fonts" and "How 1-2-3 for Windows Assigns Attributes," later.

Fixed-Width versus Proportionally Spaced Fonts

Font typefaces are categorized as fixed width or proportionally spaced. If a typeface is *fixed width*, each character takes up the same amount of space; that is, the width of each

Arial MT	Helv
TimesNewRomanPS	Bodini BoldCondensed
Tms Rmn	*BrushScript*
CG Times (WN)	DomCasual
Perpetua	
Univers (WN)	LetterGothic
`Courier`	NewsGothic
`LinePrinter`	Χουριερ (SYMBOL)

Figure 6-2   Typical typefaces accessible through 1-2-3 for Windows

character is constant. In Figure 6-2, the only fixed-width typefaces are Courier and LetterGothic. You can see this in Figure 6-3, where the five i's and m's in the Courier font are the same width. In fact, a fixed-width font is also described by its *pitch*, or characters per inch (cpi). For instance, 10 cpi means that 10 characters will fit in one inch.

In a *proportionally spaced* font, the width of each character differs. You can see this in the Arial MT font in Figure 6-3. The advantage of a proportionally spaced font is that more characters will fit on a line than when a fixed-width font is used. The disadvantage is that it is more difficult to determine the amount of data that will fit on a line.

Soft versus Printer-Specific Fonts

1-2-3 for Windows supports both soft (prebuilt) fonts and printer-specific (resident) fonts. *Soft fonts*, provided by Windows and font packages like Adobe Type Manager, are printed using software instructions. 1-2-3 for Windows also supports *printer-specific fonts*—internal character sets built into a printer or printer cartridge—for the HP LaserJet and PostScript families of printers. For example, CG Times (WN) and Univers (WN) in Figure 6-2 are printer-specific fonts 1-2-3 for Windows includes when a LaserJet III is the default printer. Printer-specific fonts are discussed further in Chapter 8.

Raster versus Vector Fonts

Windows screen fonts come in two varieties, raster and vector. Both types are stored in .FON files in your \WINDOWS\SYSTEM directory. With *raster* fonts, each individual character is displayed (and stored in its .FON file) as a bitmap pixel pattern. On the other hand, *vector* fonts are defined by strokes. Table 6-1 lists the default raster and vector Windows fonts.

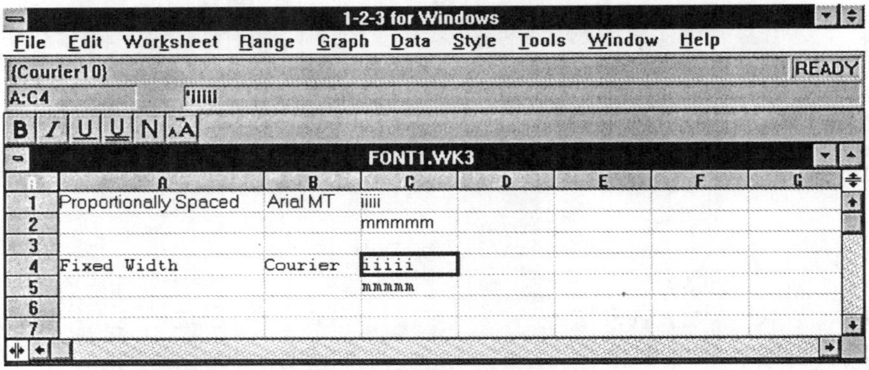

Figure 6-3 Fixed-width versus proportionally spaced fonts

Because raster fonts are defined as bitmaps, they are designed to be displayed using a specific aspect ratio (height to width) and a specific point size. That's why Windows provides only a discrete number of point sizes for a raster font. For example, if you select Fonts from the Windows Control Panel, you'll see that Courier is available only in 10, 12, and 15-point sizes. When you increase the point size of a raster font beyond that for which it was designed, Windows simply duplicates rows and columns of pixels to accommodate the new size. The end result is a stair-step effect, sometimes called "jaggies."

Note: In 1-2-3 for Windows, you can only access Windows' raster fonts.

Vector fonts are stroke-based—defined by line segments. Because this makes them more scalable than raster fonts, a vector font can be displayed in any size by increasing or decreasing the length of the strokes that define the character.

For high resolution video, there's really no difference in appearance between raster and vector fonts. At lower quality resolution, the appearance of a vector font is smoother-looking than a raster font. In either case, as the point size is increased, the appearance of a vector font becomes weaker than a raster font.

TABLE 6-1 Default Raster and Vector Windows Fonts

Windows 3.0 Raster Typefaces	*Windows 3.0 Vector Typefaces*
Helv	Roman
Tms Rmn	Modern
Courier	Script
Symbol	

Windows Fonts Available in 1-2-3 for Windows

If you've worked at all with 1-2-3 for Windows' fonts, you've probably noticed it doesn't recognize some of Windows' fonts. Although all of Windows screen fonts are usually available in most Windows applications, in 1-2-3 for Windows you can access only Windows' raster fonts. So Windows' vector fonts—Script, Modern, and Roman—are ignored. (See the previous section for a discussion of raster and vector fonts.)

Adobe Type Manager Fonts Available in 1-2-3 for Windows

In 1-2-3 for Windows, the Adobe Type Manager (ATM) provides additional raster fonts to supplement Windows default raster fonts (see "Customizing the Font Set," later and Appendix B.) Because you assign style attributes—italic, bold, and underline—using 1-2-3's Style Font command, any ATM fonts that already include these attributes aren't available in 1-2-3 for Windows. For instance, if you examine the Adobe Type Manager font list (see Appendix B), you'll see that it includes four different Courier fonts, of which three include style attributes: one is italicized, one is bolded, and another is bolded and italicized. So 1-2-3 only includes ATM's plain Courier font, and drops those with style attributes.

Default Spreadsheet Font and Default Font Set

By default, 1-2-3 for Windows provides the font set in Figure 6-4 whether the Adobe Type Manager is on or off. You can change this font set to include fonts provided by Windows and third-party font packages like the Adobe Type Manager, as well as printer-specific fonts.

1-2-3 automatically displays worksheet data using the first font in the Style Font set—Arial MT 12 point by default. The only way to specify a new default font is to change the first font in the Styles Font list. "Customizing the Font Set," later in this section, shows how to change the default font and customize the font set.

Note: Any headers and footers specified in the File Print command always use the default font. (See Chapter 8.)

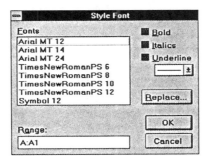

Figure 6-4 1-2-3's default font set

The default font also causes a radical departure from previous releases of 1-2-3 with respect to column widths. As you'll see, 1-2-3 for Windows adjusts the column width unit of measurement to conform to the default font. (See "Fonts and Column Widths" later in this chapter.)

 Tip: It's easy to tell if a cell is using the default font. 1-2-3 for Windows always includes information in the format line about a non-default font assigned to a cell. (You can see examples in the next section.) If no font information is displayed in the format line, then any data in the cell will be displayed in the default font—the first font in the Style Font list.

Assigning Existing Fonts

Although 1-2-3 for Windows automatically displays worksheet data using the default font, you can assign up to eight fonts in one worksheet. For instance, in Figure 6-5A the data is displayed in 1-2-3's default Arial MT 12-point font. Suppose you want to use the existing 10-point TimesNewRomanPS font, except for the title in row 1, which will be

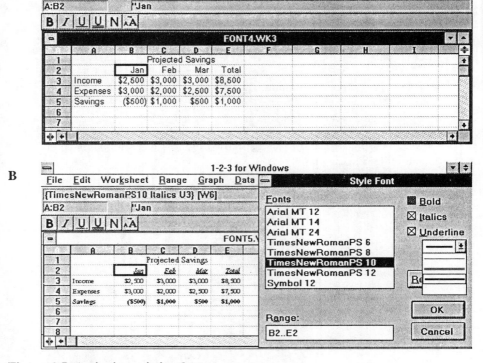

Figure 6-5   Assigning existing fonts

assigned the existing 12-point TimesNewRomanPS font; you also want to italicize and underline the column headings in row 2 and bold the savings data in row 5. You can assign these fonts to Figure 6-5 by following these steps:

1. Specify the 10-point TimesNewRomanPS font by first preselecting the range A2..E5. Next, select Style Font, and in the Fonts list box shown in Figure 6-5B, choose TimesNewRomanPS 10. Select OK to confirm. 1-2-3 for Windows immediately assigns TimesNewRomanPS 10 to this data.

> ▼ *Tip:* You can also use the ⬛ icon shown in Figure 6-5 to cycle through the existing font set and immediately see how data in a preselected range looks in each font. To customize your icon palette, see Appendix A.

2. Add Italics and Underline styles to the column headings in row 2 by preselecting B2..E2, then specify the Style Font settings shown in Figure 6-5B by first turning on the Italics option. Next, open the Underline drop-down box and choose the third option—a single, thick line style. Select OK to confirm.

Note: To create a continuous line across the bottom of row 2, see "Borders" later in this chapter.

> ▼ *Tip:* You can also use the icon palette to assign and delete style attributes without accessing the Style Font command. In the icon palette shown in Figure 6-5, ⬛B⬛ assigns a bold style to a preselected range, ⬛I⬛ an italic style, ⬛U⬛ a thin underline style, and ⬛U⬛ a double underline style. Likewise, to delete a Bold attribute assigned to a range, select ⬛B⬛ again. See Appendix A to customize your icon palette. See also "Deleting All Style Settings in a Range," later.

3. Assign a Bold style to row 5 by preselecting A5..E5 then choosing the ⬛B⬛ icon in the icon palette.

4. Assign a 12-point TimesNewRomanPS font to the title "Projected Savings" in cell C1 by selecting this cell, choosing Style Font, selecting TimesNewRomanPS 12 from the Fonts list box, and then OK.

Figure 6-5B shows the end result. By comparing the format lines in Figures 6-5A and B, you can see that 1-2-3 provides information about a nondefault font. In Figure 6-5A, no font information is included in the format line, but in Figure 6-5B, {TimesNewRomanPS10 Italics U3} explains that cell B3 is assigned an italicized, underlined (with option 3), 10-point TimesNewRomanPS font.

> ▼ *Tip:* The ⬛N⬛ icon shown in Figure 6-5 deletes all style attributes and returns a preselected range to the default font. To customize the icon palette, see Appendix A.

How 1-2-3 for Windows Assigns Attributes

As the previous example shows, 1-2-3 for Windows assigns attributes—italic, bold, and underline—to a cell. Attributes are *not* assigned to a font. One result is that you can assign attributes to a cell either before or after you assign a font. You can even assign attributes to empty cells.

When you assign a different font to a cell that has been assigned attributes, the new font is automatically displayed using these attributes. For example, cell B2 in Figure 6-5B is assigned a TimesNewRomanPS 10-point font, as well as two attributes: italics and a thick underline. If you now change the font to the default font, or to any other font, the label "Jan" will still use the italics and thick underline attributes.

 Tip:　1-2-3 for Windows provides icons that assign and delete style attributes in a preselected range. (See "Assigning Existing Fonts," earlier.)

Customizing the Font Set

You can also change the eight fonts available through the Style Font command by customizing your font set, either for a specific worksheet or for all future 1-2-3 for Windows sessions.

 Tip:　To create a named font set that is saved separately from a worksheet file, see "Creating a Named Font Set," in this section.

Accessing Other Fonts

While the Style Font command accesses the default font set shown in Figure 6-4, you can use the Style Font Replace option to access fonts from

- Windows, but only the raster fonts (see "Windows Fonts Available in 1-2-3 for Windows," earlier)

- Any font packages installed in Windows, like the Adobe Type Manager (see "Adobe Type Manager Fonts Available in 1-2-3 for Windows," earlier, and Appendix B of this book), Bitstream's Facelift, and Zsoft's SoftType.

- The printer specified either through the Windows Control Panel or 1-2-3's File Print Setup command (see Chapter 8).

For example, Figure 6-6A shows the font library you can access through the Style Font Replace option when the Adobe Type Manager has been installed in Windows and a LaserJet Series III printer has been specified. Even more typeface options are displayed as you scroll down this list.

A
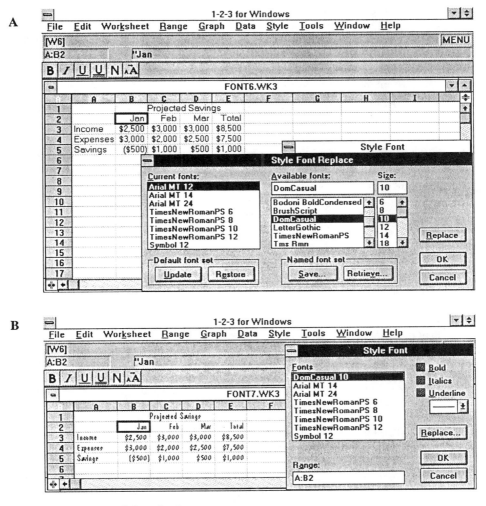

B

Figure 6-6 Customizing the font set

Note: When the Adobe Type Manager isn't turned on, you'll see a much more limited selection of typefaces and point sizes. Your options may be further limited or expanded depending on your default printer and printer cartridges.

The Style Font Replace option also allows you to specify a point size. Usually you can select from 6 through 72 points in the Size list box shown in Figure 6-6A. However, because the available point sizes are also a function of where the typeface comes from—Windows, a third-party font package, or a printer—you'll find that some typefaces, especially printer-specific fonts, provide a limited number of point sizes. For example, if you scroll down the Available fonts list and choose the LinePrinter typeface, you'll see in the Size list box that this printer-specific font is only available in 8 point.

Creating a New Font Set

When you customize your font set, you should follow these general guidelines:

- Specify the font you want to use for most of the worksheet as the default font—the first font in the Style Font set.

- Specify other fonts you want to assign to specific ranges as the second through eighth fonts.

To see this, let's return to the example in Figure 6-5. However, now imagine that you want all the data to be displayed in DomCasual 10 point. The easiest way to accomplish this is to make DomCasual 10 the default font.

First, select Style Font and then the Replace option to access the dialog box shown in Figure 6-6A. In the Current fonts list displayed on the left, select the font to be replaced, Arial MT 12 in this instance. Then choose the new typeface, DomCasual, from the Available fonts list. When you do so, 1-2-3 displays the available point sizes in the Size list box. Choose 10 point.

When you select OK, 1-2-3 for Windows returns you to the Style Font dialog box shown in Figure 6-6B, where DomCasual 10 is now listed as the first font (the default font) in the font set. (Choose Replace instead of OK to continue to change the font set.) The worksheet data is now displayed in this new default font because no font setting is included for cell B2 in the format line.

> ▼ **Tip:**   Use Style Color to change the color of a font in a specified range. See "Assigning Colors to a Range" later in this chapter.

When you create a custom font set, 1-2-3 for Windows normally saves it for just the current worksheet file. To save this new font set for all future sessions, select the Default font set Update option in the Style Font Replace dialog box. Update, however, doesn't affect previously saved worksheet files. (To restore 1-2-3's original font set, select Restore.) To create a font set saved separately from a worksheet file, see "Creating a Named Font Set," later.

Fonts and Column Widths

As you know, 1-2-3 measures the width of each column in characters. For example, the default column width of 9 represents the width of 9 characters. In previous releases of 1-2-3, each character represented one character of the fixed-width font displayed on the screen, so a column width of 9 was equivalent to nine fixed-width characters of the screen font.

In 1-2-3 for Windows, the default font you assign to a worksheet determines the character-based unit of measurement 1-2-3 uses for column widths. To see this, compare Figures 6-7A, B, and C. In Figure 6-7A, the default font—the first font in the Style Font

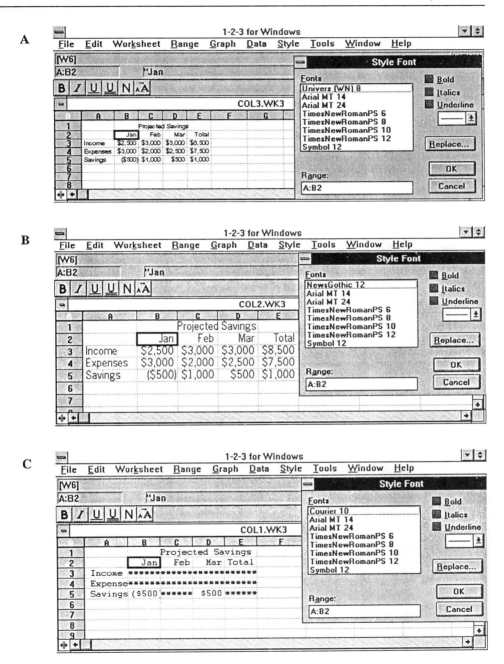

Figure 6-7 How the default font affects the character-based column width

dialog box—is Univers (WN) 8 point. The column width of 6 in cell B2 (look at the format line) represents 6 Univers characters.

> ▼ **Tip:** Because the width of each character in a proportionally spaced font differs, 1-2-3 for Windows bases each column width character on an "average" character—usually a 5. In effect, a column width of 9 represents the width of nine 5's when the default font is proportionally spaced.

If you change the default font, the character-based column width settings automatically conform to the new font. In Figure 6-7B, for instance, the default font is changed to NewsGothic 12 point, but the column widths are left unchanged. In this case, the column width of 6 represents six "average" NewsGothic 12-point characters. The result is that you don't have to adjust the column widths to conform to this new default font—1-2-3 for Windows does this for you.

There are two exceptions when you'll need to adjust column widths yourself. The first you can see in Figure 6-7C. When Courier, a fixed-width font, is the default font, 1-2-3 for Windows doesn't adjust the column widths correctly, and much of the data is replaced by asterisks. In this case, then, you'll have to increase the column widths to display this data. Interestingly, this problem doesn't seem to occur for all fixed-width fonts. If you make LetterGothic the default font, for instance, the column widths in Figure 6-7C are adjusted to display the data.

The second exception occurs when you assign data a font other than the default font. For example, imagine that in Figure 6-7B you assign Arial MT 24 point to the labels in column A. However, 1-2-3 for Windows won't change the column width unit of measurement because the default font is NewsGothic 12 point. You'll need to increase the width of column A to display these labels in Arial MT 24 point. You'll want to decrease the width of column A if you assign these labels a font smaller than the default font.

When you assign fonts to a worksheet, you'll also want to keep in mind the following:

- For the same point size, one typeface may take up more space—a larger column width—than another.

- Because larger point sizes require larger column widths, assigning a large point size to just one cell can affect the width of an entire column.

By comparing Figures 6-6A and B, for instance, you can see that for a 10-point size, the DomCasual typeface takes up less space than the Arial MT typeface. So even though the width of each column stays the same—the width of column B is 6 in both instances— six DomCasual characters take up less space than six Arial MT characters.

Fonts and Row Heights

The row height in 1-2-3 for Windows automatically accommodates the default font, Arial MT 12 point. If you change the point size of the default font, 1-2-3 adjusts all row heights in the worksheet to accommodate it. You can see how this works in Figure 6-8A. Here, TimesNewRomanPS 14 has been specified as the default font. So 1-2-3 for Windows adjusts the default row height to 17 points, to accommodate a 14-point font. (1-2-3 for Windows normally uses a slightly larger row height than the point size of the default font.)

> ▼ *Tip:*   You can see the default row height 1-2-3 for Windows uses by selecting the Worksheet Row Height command (see Chapter 5).

In most instances, 1-2-3 for Windows automatically adjusts a row height to best accommodate the point size of fonts. You can see this in Figure 6-8A. Because both TimesNewRomanPS 14-point and 24-point fonts are assigned to row 2, 1-2-3 automatically adjusts the height of the entire row to accommodate the largest point size. If cell B2 is then assigned a 10-point font, you can see in Figure 6-8B that 1-2-3 automatically reduces the height of row 2 to fit the largest font—in this case the default 14-point font.

A

B

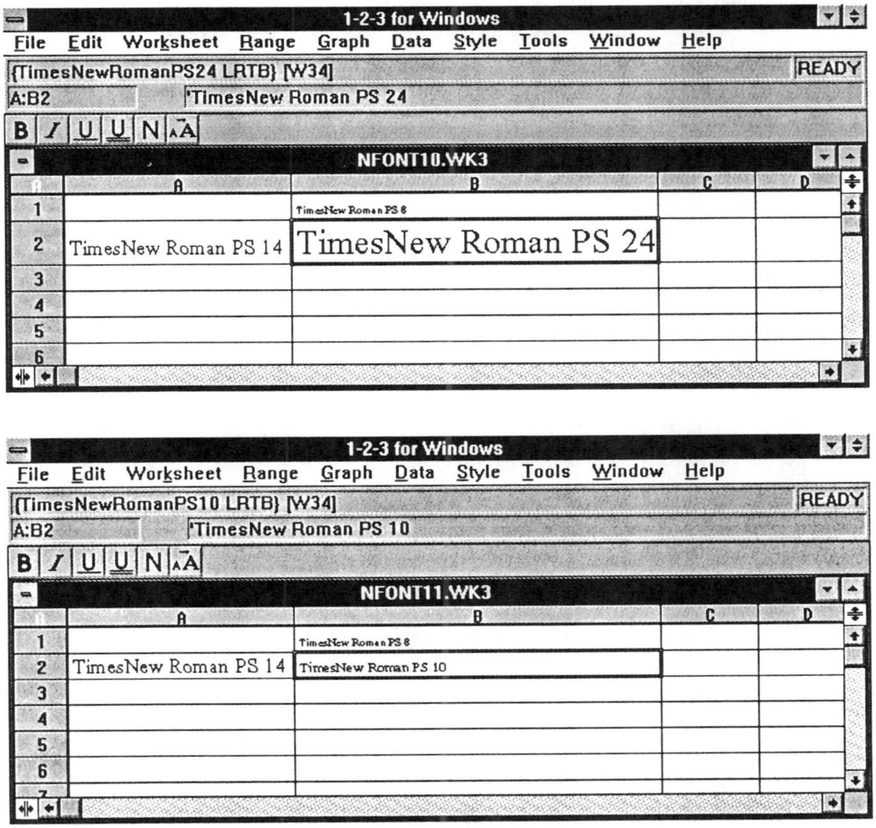

Figure 6-8 When 1-2-3 automatically adjusts row heights

Figure 6-8B also shows that in some cases 1-2-3 for Windows does not automatically adjust the row height. Because the TimesNewRomanPS 8-point font assigned to A2 is smaller than the default font, TimesNewRomanPS 14-point in this instance, the row height isn't adjusted. 1-2-3 would only decrease the row height if each cell in row 1 is assigned a point size smaller than the default font. You can change the row height yourself, however, using the Worksheet Row Height command (see Chapter 5).

Creating a Named Font Set

In 1-2-3 for Windows, you can create a named font set that is saved separately from a worksheet file. The advantage to this approach is that you can leave the current font set intact, yet save and retrieve another font set for special circumstances.

Note: To create your own font set, see the previous section, "Customizing the Font Set."

Figure 6-9 shows a customized font set (look at the Current fonts list box) that includes different Times Roman fonts. Times Roman 10 point, for example, is the default font. Once you've created this customized font set, you can save it in a separate file that is not part of the worksheet file. Choose Style Font Replace, and then select the Named font set Save option displayed in the dialog box. When you do so, 1-2-3 will display a Style Font Replace Save dialog box like the one in Figure 6-9.

Note: You can't save style attributes—italics, bold, and underline—in a named font set. You *can* save them using the Style Name command. See "Naming Style Settings" later in this chapter.

To save this font set, enter a name, **TMSRMN**, for example, in the File text box. You don't have to add an extension; 1-2-3 automatically includes .AF3. Additionally, by

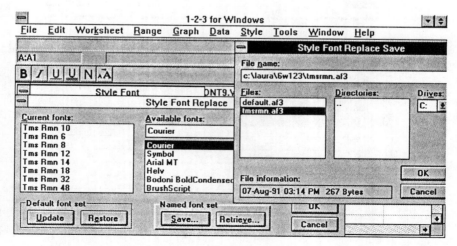

Figure 6-9 Saving a named font set

default 1-2-3 for Windows will save this file in the current directory, in this case C:\LAURA\6W123. If you'd like, you can use the Drive and Directories options to change this path. When you select OK, 1-2-3 for Windows saves this font set as the file TMSRMN.AF3 and returns you to the File Save Replace dialog box.

Of course, you can use the Named font set Retrieve option to retrieve an existing named font set. When you choose this option, 1-2-3 will display a similar dialog box. If you then select TMSRMN.AF3, 1-2-3 for Windows will replace the font set in the current file with the one shown in Figure 6-9. When you save the worksheet file, this font set is also saved with the file.

> ▼ *Tip:*   Before you specify a new default font set for all future 1-2-3 sessions, you can save 1-2-3's default font set by first using the Named font set Save option. In Figure 6-9, for example, 1-2-3's default font set has been saved in the file DEFAULT.AF3.

LABEL ALIGNMENT

The equivalent 1-2-3 Classic command for Style Alignment is /Range Label. It doesn't, however, include the Align over columns option.

As you know, by default labels are left-aligned in a worksheet. You can change the global label alignment using Worksheet Global Settings Align labels, or change the label alignment in a particular cell by preceding it with ", ', or ^. 1-2-3 for Windows also provides the Style Alignment command, which you can use to align a range of labels. You can even use this command to align a label over a range of cells.

Note: To justify text within a specified range, see Chapter 5.

Assigning a Label Alignment to a Range

Assigning a left, right, or centered label alignment to a range is really a simple matter. For example, to center the year labels in B2..D2 of Figure 6-10A, first preselect this range. Next, select Style Alignment, and in the dialog box shown in Figure 6-10B, choose Center. When you select OK, you'll get the result in Figure 6-10B. Remember that a label will always appear left-aligned if its width is the same as or greater than the column width. Additionally, Style Alignment has no effect on values in a range.

> ▼ *Tip:*   You can use the to left align, to right align, and to center align a preselected range of labels.

You can't use Style Alignment to preassign label alignments in blank cells. For instance, imagine you use Style Alignment to specify a right label alignment in the blank cells E2..F2 of Figure 6-10A. If you then enter a label in E1, 1-2-3 for Windows will

A

	1-2-3 for Windows									
File	Edit	Worksheet	Range	Graph	Data	Style	Tools	Window	Help	

{B} [W10]   READY

A:B2   '1993

ALIGN1.WK3

	A	B	C	D	E	F	G	H
1	PROJECTIONS: Best Case							
2		1993	1993	1994				
3	Sales	$10,000,000	$15,000,000	$20,000,000				
4	COGS	$3,000,000	$3,750,000	$5,000,000				
5	Gross Profit	$7,000,000	$11,250,000	$15,000,000				
6								

B

	1-2-3 for Windows									
File	Edit	Worksheet	Range	Graph	Data	Style	Tools	Window	Help	

{B} [W10]   MENU

A:B2   '1993

ALIGN2.WK3

Style Alignment

Align label
- ○ Left
- ◉ Center
- ○ Right

■ Align over columns

Range:
A:B2..A:D2

[OK]   [Cancel]

	A	B	C	D
1	PROJECTIONS: Best Case			
2		1993	1993	1994
3	Sales	$10,000,000	$15,000,000	$20,000,000
4	COGS	$3,000,000	$3,750,000	$5,000,000
5	Gross Profit	$7,000,000	$11,250,000	$15,000,000
6				

Figure 6-10 Aligning a range of labels

automatically use the worksheet's global left label alignment, not the Style Alignment setting. (Global format settings are discussed in Chapter 5.)

Note: To change a label alignment assigned to a range, reuse Style Alignment. See also "Deleting All Style Settings in a Range," later.

Aligning a Label Over a Range of Cells

In previous releases of 1-2-3, you aligned a title over more than one column by manually inserting blank spaces to make the label span multiple cells. In 1-2-3 for Windows, however, Style Alignment's Align over columns option automatically aligns a label within a single-row range—that is, across columns.

Note: Make sure that labels exist only in the leftmost column of the range you specify. Otherwise, the display of a leftmost label may be truncated if there are values or labels in the other columns of the range.

To see how this works, let's suppose that in Figure 6-11A you want to center the label "Projections: Best Case" in A1 over the data. In other words, you want to center this label within the range A1..D1. If you preselect this range, then specify the Style Alignment

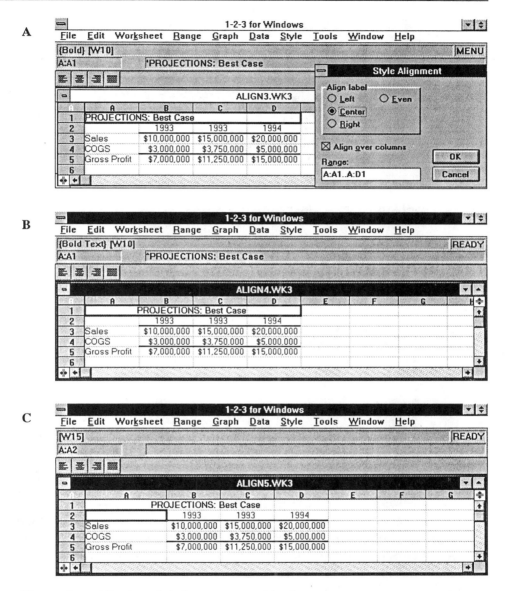

Figure 6-11   Aligning a label over a range of columns

settings shown—select Center and turn on Align over columns—you'll get the results in Figure 6-11B. As you can see, 1-2-3 for Windows centers this label within the four-cell range A1..D1.

Even if you subsequently change a column width in this range, 1-2-3 automatically adjusts the position of the label. When the width of column A is increased from 10 to 15

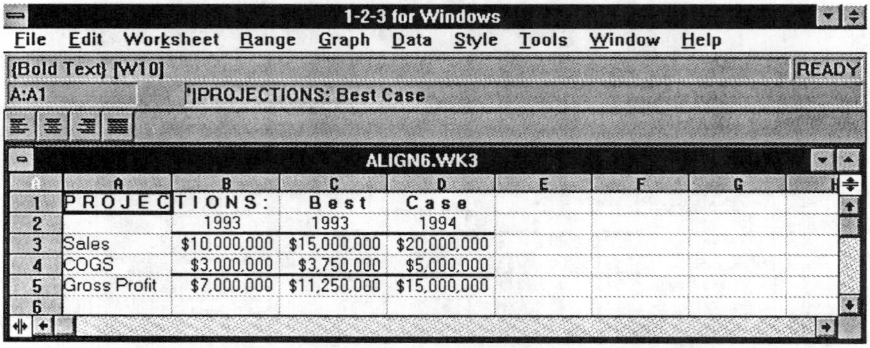

Figure 6-12   Aligning a label evenly over a row

in Figure 6-11C, for example, 1-2-3 for Windows automatically adjusts the positioning of the "Projections: Best Case" label so that it is still centered within A1..D1. 1-2-3 can do this because it assigns a {Text} setting (see the format line in Figure 6-11B) to each cell in the Style Alignment Align over columns range. But, to increase the range over which a label is aligned, you must reuse the Style Alignment command.

Note: To delete this {Text} style setting in a range, reuse Style Alignment, turn off the Align over columns option, and specify an Align label option. See also "Deleting All Style Settings in a Range," later. To edit a label that has been aligned over columns, you must press F2 to enter EDIT mode; double-clicking with the mouse brings up the Classic menu.

You've probably noticed in Figure 6-11, that when you turn on Align over columns 1-2-3 for Windows includes a fourth alignment option, Even. This option evenly spaces a label over the width of a column, as long as a label doesn't end with a . (period), ! (exclamation point), ? (question mark), or : (colon) (although a semicolon or a hyphen works).

For instance, Figure 6-12 shows the results when you start with Figure 6-11A, turn on Align over columns, and select Even for the range A1..D1. Note that the space 1-2-3 adds between each character is about the same width as one character. For instance, if the label "Projections: Best Case" is assigned a 14-point font, 1-2-3 for Windows will make the space between characters equal to approximately one character of that point size.

> ▼ *Tip:*   Use 🖾 shown in Figure 6-12 to evenly align a label over a preselected range. To customize the icon palette, see Appendix A.

CELL CONTENTS AND BACKGROUND COLORS

Within a range, you can use the Style Color command to change the color of cell contents, the cell background color, and to display negative numbers in red. These settings override the global colors for the worksheet set with Window Display Options—by default, white for the cell background and black for cell contents, including negative values.

Assigning Colors to a Range

Imagine you want to customize the colors in B6..D6 of Figure 6-13A, which currently uses the Window Display Options Colors default settings. To make this range stand out in relation to other data, let's try yellow for the cell background color, and a contrasting blue for the cell contents. Additionally, if a profit value is negative, let's display it in red.

Note: Depending on your printer's color capabilities, the colors displayed and printed may vary. But, even if you use a black and white printer, you may be able to distinguish some background colors by the pattern 1-2-3 for Windows assigns to it.

First, preselect the range B6..D6 and then choose the Style Color command. You'll see a dialog box like the one in Figure 6-13B, which already displays B6..D6 in the Range text box.

▼ *Tip:*   Use ⬚ (A with Blue Background/A with Red Background) repeatedly to cycle through the available Style Color Background colors in a pre-selected range, and ⬚ (Blue A/Red A) to cycle through the available Style Color Cell Contents options. You can see these icons in Figure 6-13. To customize your icon palette, see Appendix A.

Next, change the cell contents from black (the default) to blue by opening the Cell contents drop-down box and choosing the darker blue from among the eight different color choices. To change the cell background color for this range from white (the default), open the Background drop-down box and select yellow. Then, turn on the Negative values in red option. When you select OK, you'll get the results in Figure 6-13B. In the format line, {Dark-Blue/Yellow -} explains that D6 is assigned a yellow background and dark blue cell contents, except for negative numbers.

▼ *Tip:*   Use the Window Display Options Palette command (see Chapter 3) to change the colors or even the intensity of colors available through the Style Color command.

Clearing Colors Assigned to a Range

To change background or cell contents colors previously assigned to a range, you can use either the Style Color command or the icons shown in Figure 6-13. To turn off the display of negative values in red, however, you must reuse the Style Color command. For example, to display negative values in Figure 6-13 in the same color as positive values, again preselect B6..D6, choose Style Color, and then click twice to turn off the Negative

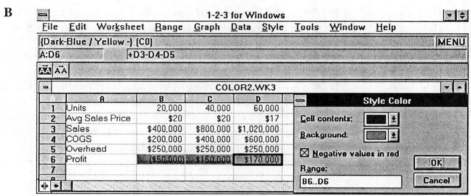

Figure 6-13 Assigning colors to a range

values in red option. (See also "Deleting All Style Settings in a Range," later in this chapter.)

▼ *Tip:* The first Style Color Cell contents color selection is always the default cell contents color for the worksheet, and the first Style Color Background color selection is always the default background color for the worksheet.

SHADING

By adding shading, you can contrast and emphasize worksheet data. As you'll see, however, you'll probably find shading most effective when it is used around a range you want to emphasize, rather than shading the range itself.

Assigning Shading to a Range

When you select the Style Shading command, you'll see these options shown in the dialog box in Figure 6-14:

- **Light** is a relatively light, dotted shading.
- **Dark** is a dark, dotted shading.
- **Solid** is a dark, solid shading.

> ▼ *Tip:*   You can also use 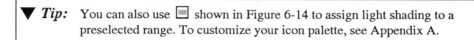 shown in Figure 6-14 to assign light shading to a preselected range. To customize your icon palette, see Appendix A.

Figure 6-14 shows the results each of these choices produces. For all three shading options, 1-2-3 for Windows always uses black, regardless of other color settings. Because black is also the default cell contents color, the color of cell contents, like the value 100 in column B, and the color of these shading options is the same. This can make it difficult to distinguish values and labels in a cell that includes shading. In fact, you can see in cell B5 that the Solid shading option normally obscures cell contents; to overcome this, the cell contents color in cell C5 has been changed to yellow.

Note: Depending on the resolution of your printer, the printed shading intensity may differ from what you see on your screen.

When shading overwhelms the display of data, any of the following techniques might help:

- Assign data a color that contrasts with the shading using the Style Color Cell contents option.
- Assign a complementary background color to the shaded range using the Style Color Background option.
- Shade the area around the range you want to emphasize, not the range itself.

Note: Style Color is discussed in "Cell Contents and Background Colors," above; the Window Display Options Cell Contents command is discussed in Chapter 3.

If you look ahead to Figure 6-19A, you'll see how the light shading around the Gopher Sightings data complements and emphasizes this range— shading the range itself would obscure the data. When you use shading in this way, you'll get the cleanest-looking effect if you remove worksheet grid lines (see Chapter 3).

Clearing Shading Assigned to a Range

You also must use the Style Shading command to change or delete shading when you don't want to affect data and other Style settings assigned to a range. For example, to delete the shading in A1..B1 of Figure 6-14, preselect this range, choose Style Shading,

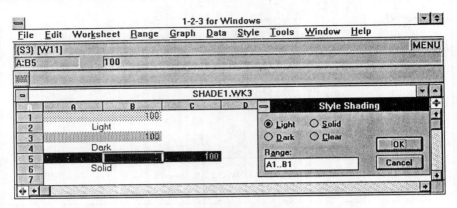

Figure 6-14 Different ways to shade in 1-2-3 for Windows

and then turn on the Clear option. When you select OK, 1-2-3 for Windows will delete just the shading in this range.

Note: See also "Deleting All Style Settings in a Range," later.

BORDERS

By adding borders—single lines, double lines, thick lines, or even shadows—you can create outlines, grids, underlines, and shadow boxes without adding extra columns or rows. In fact, once you begin adding borders to your worksheets, you'll probably find yourself becoming addicted to the way they highlight and enhance important data.

Adding Borders to a Range

When you select the Style Border command, you'll see these options shown in the dialog box in Figure 6-15:

Option	Result
All edges	Outline around each cell to create a grid
Top	Horizontal line across the top of each cell
Bottom	Horizontal line across the bottom of each cell
Left	Vertical line down the left of each cell
Right	Vertical line down the right of each cell
Outside	Outline around the outside of the range to create a border
Shadow box	Thick black line along the bottom and right

▼ *Tip:* ▣ shown in Figure 6-15 adds an outline around the edge of a preselected range using a thin line style; ▣ creates a shadow box with a
thin line style. To customize your icon palette, see Appendix A.

A

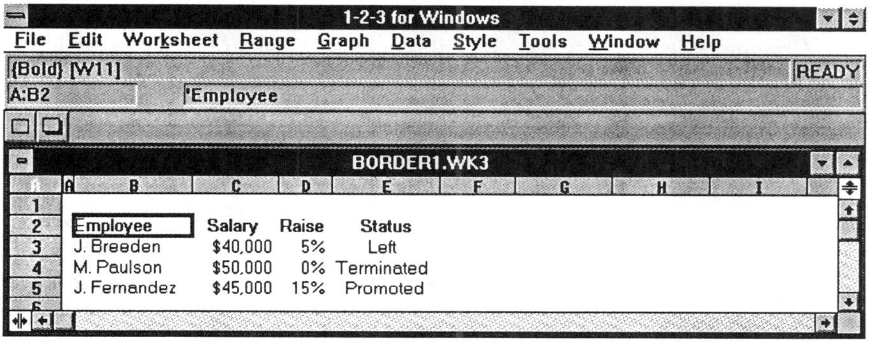

B

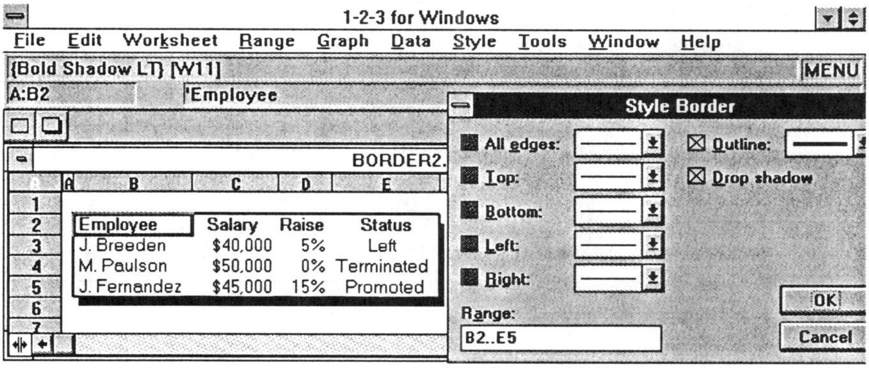

C

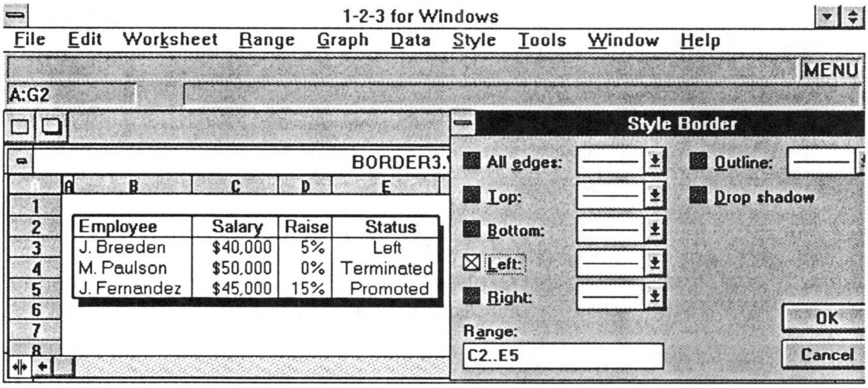

Figure 6-15 Creating borders and a shadow box

To create a shadow box with a thick line style around the employee data in Figure 6-15A, for example, preselect the range B2..E5, select Style Border, and specify the settings shown in Figure 6-15B—turn on the Outline option, choose a thick line style from its drop-down box, and turn on the Drop shadow option. When you select OK, 1-2-3 will draw the shadow box in Figure 6-15B.

By default, the shadow color is black, but you can change it using the Window Display Options Drop shadows command discussed in Chapter 3. The line color, also black by default, is controlled by the Window Display Options Range borders setting.

> ▼ *Tip:*   A drop shadow may obscure other worksheet data. Although 1-2-3 for Windows assigns a shadow to the bottom row of the specified range— row 5 in Figure 6-15B for example—it is displayed in row 6, the row directly below this range. If this makes data difficult to see, try increasing the height of row 6. Likewise, the shadow assigned to the rightmost column, column E, is displayed in column F; if data is obscured, try increasing the width of column F, or centering or right-aligning the data.

To add the thin vertical lines to the left of columns C, D, and E in Figure 6-15C, preselect the range C2..E5, select Style Border, then turn on the Left option, which uses a thin line style by default. Similarly, add the thin bottom line to row 2 by preselecting B2..E2, selecting Style Border, and turning on the Bottom option.

> ▼ *Tip:*   To underline just the data in a cell, not the entire cell, use the Style Font Underline option. See "Assigning Existing Fonts," earlier.

Clearing Borders

To remove border settings from a range, you also use the Style Border command. Since 1-2-3 for Windows attaches a border to the cell to which it is assigned, you can only remove the border from that cell. For example, if a vertical line has been created between cells A1 and A2 by assigning a right border to cell A1, you must remove this border from cell A1; trying to remove this border from cell B1 won't work. You can tell which borders are attached to a specific cell by looking at its settings displayed in the format line.

Note: See also "Manipulating Style Settings in a Range."

To delete the bottom border along row 2 of Figure 6-15C, for instance, preselect B2..E2, choose Style Border, click twice on the Bottom option to turn it off, and then choose OK. If you try to remove this border by preselecting B3..E3, then turning off the Style Border Top option, 1-2-3 for Windows won't remove it because it wasn't originally assigned to these cells.

To delete all the borders and the shadow in Figure 6-16A, first preselect the range B2..E5. This is the range 1-2-3 for Windows assigned the outline and shadow box to in

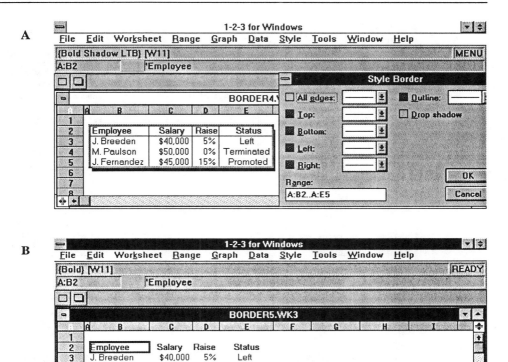

Figure 6-16 Removing an outline and shadow

Figure 6-15B. Then, specify the settings shown in the Style Border dialog box—turn off Drop shadow and All edges—to get the result in Figure 6-16B.

Note: When you insert a row or column in the middle of an outline, 1-2-3 for Windows automatically adds the outline to that row or column. But if you delete the top or bottom row or column in which an outline is displayed, that portion of the outline is deleted. Any shadow is automatically adjusted, however.

NAMING STYLE SETTINGS

The Style Name command allows you to name the Style settings (except label alignment) in a single cell, which you can then assign elsewhere in the worksheet. Unfortunately, you can't save Style settings in a multicell range under one name, although you can assign a named style to multiple cells in a range.

A
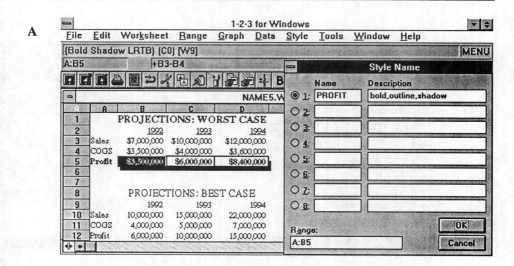

B
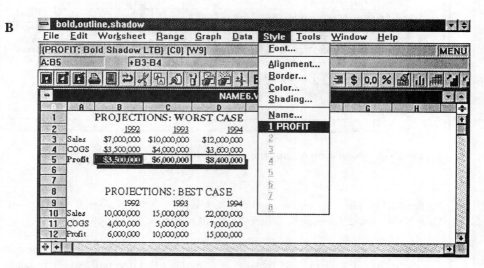

Figure 6-17 Assigning a name to Style settings

For example, to name the Style settings in cell B5 of Figure 6-17A—the bolded default
font, thick border outline, and shadow box—first select this cell. Then choose the Style
Name command to access the dialog box shown. In the Name 1 text box, enter a name,
such as PROFIT; if you'd like, also use the corresponding Description text box to enter
identifying information, like bold, outline, shadow. When you select OK, you can see in
the format line of Figure 6-17B that 1-2-3 for Windows assigns the name PROFIT to the
Style settings assigned to cell B5.

C

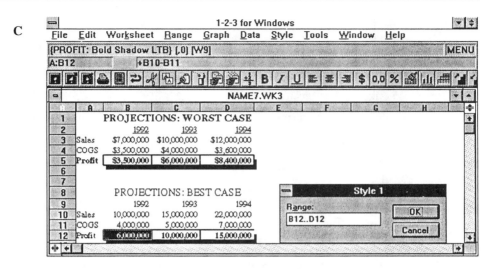

Figure 6-17 Assigning a name to Style settings *(continued)*

Note: If you specify a multicell range when you create a named style, 1-2-3 will use the Style settings assigned to the upper-left cell of this range. 1-2-3 for Windows then assigns this named style only to this upper-left cell.

You can now assign this named style to another area of the worksheet, such as B12..D12 of Figure 6-17B, by choosing Style Name 1 PROFIT. (Notice that 1-2-3 displays the PROFIT Description at the top of Figure 6-17B.) When you specify this range and select OK from the Style 1 dialog box in Figure 6-17C, you can see that 1-2-3 for Windows assigns the PROFIT styles to each cell in this range, although label alignment and numeric formatting aren't copied. If you preselect this range, 1-2-3 will automatically assign PROFIT settings without displaying the Style 1 dialog box.

Although 1-2-3 for Windows assigns a named style to the Style settings within a cell, the named style doesn't automatically take on any new Style settings that are later added to this cell. You can see this in Figure 6-18A. Here, a cyan background color has been assigned to cell B5 using the Style Color command. Note in the format line that 1-2-3 for Windows removes the named style PROFIT from cell B5. Although the range B12..D12 is still assigned the PROFIT named style, these cells aren't updated—they don't assume the cyan background color.

To update all cells previously assigned the PROFIT named style, you must first assign PROFIT to the new Style settings in cell B5. As Figure 6-18B shows, when you preselect cell B5, select Style Name again, and accept the PROFIT name and description by choosing OK, 1-2-3 for Windows updates PROFIT to include the new Style settings, and again displays PROFIT in the format line of cell B5. However, any cells previously assigned PROFIT, B12..D12, for example, still don't reflect the updated PROFIT Style settings. To accomplish this, you'll need to preselect B12..D12, select the Style command,

A

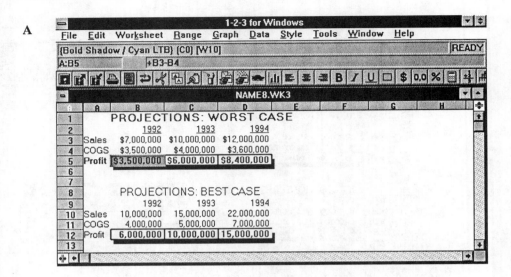

B

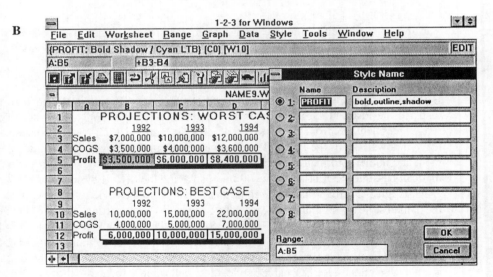

Figure 6-18   Changing the Style settings assigned to PROFIT

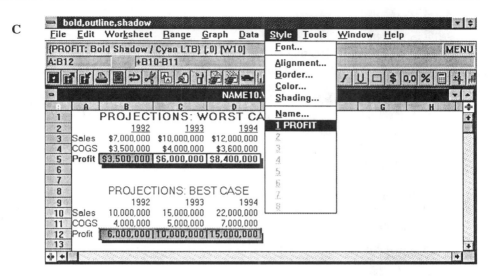

Figure 6-18 Changing the Style settings assigned to PROFIT *(continued)*

and then choose PROFIT. Only then, as in Figure 6-18C, does 1-2-3 for Windows assign the new PROFIT Style settings to this range.

Note: To copy, move, or delete only the Style settings in a range, see "Manipulating Style Settings in a Range" at the end of this chapter. To copy only the named styles in a file to another file, see the next section.

RETRIEVING STYLES FROM ANOTHER FILE

File Import From Styles is not accessible through the 1-2-3 Classic menu.

By using 1-2-3 for Windows' File From Import Styles command, you can import Style settings from a 1-2-3 .FM3 file, an Impress .FMT file, or an Allways .ALL file on disk to a worksheet file. Existing data, such as numbers, labels, and formulas, are unaffected. In fact, by creating a worksheet entirely composed of styles, you can, in effect, create a "template" file that can be accessed for future worksheets.

Note: 1-2-3 for Windows saves all Style settings assigned to a worksheet in a separate file. When you save the file GOPHERS1, for example, 1-2-3 saves the Style settings in GOPHERS1.FM3 and all else in GOPHERS1.WK3. See Chapter 4 for further discussion.

Suppose that in Figure 6-19A, you want to import the Style settings in the GOPHERS1 file to the UNTITLED file, which already contains information about rabbit sightings. To do this, begin by locating the cell pointer anywhere in the untitled file. Next, select the File Import Styles From command, and you'll see the dialog box shown in Figure 6-19B.

By examining the Files list box, you can see that 1-2-3 for Windows only displays the .FM3, .FMT, and .ALL files in the current directory, in this case C:\LAURA\6W123. (If you'd like, you can use the Drive and Directories options to change this path.) Specify GOPHERS1.FM3 (If you type the name, 1-2-3 will automatically include the FM3 extension for you). Then, choose one of these Import options:

- **All**: Copies all Style settings—except label alignment—as well as Range Numeric Format settings. This option also copies graphs and text graphs in the same way as the Graphics option.

- **Named Styles**: Copies only the Style Name settings (see "Naming Style Settings," above).

- **Fonts**: Copies only the Style Font font set, not fonts assigned to the worksheet.

- **Graphics**: Copies all text graphs created with Range Annotate, as well as their position in the worksheet. For a graph inserted in the worksheet using Graph Add View, however, this option copies only the position of the graph, not the graph and Graph settings. (See Chapter 10 for further discussion.)

If you leave All (the default) turned on and select OK, 1-2-3 for Windows copies all Style, Range Numeric Format, and graphics settings from GOPHERS1.FM3 to the same cells in the untitled file. The format line in Figure 6-19C, for instance, shows that cell C4 is now assigned a bolded, underlined, 10-point Tms Rmn font, top and bottom borders, and a drop-shadow style. The numeric and label formats, column widths, and row heights aren't copied, however. And notice that the values, labels, and formulas in the UNTITLED file are unaffected.

Note: Immediately pressing ALT+BACKSPACE (Undo) will reverse the effect of File Import From Styles.

Using a Template File of Styles

You'll also want to use the Files Import Styles command to copy a "template" .FM3 file of Styles settings to new files. For example, suppose you want to use the Styles settings in GOPHERS1 for all new worksheets. When a new file is opened, such as FILE0002.WK3 in Figure 6-20, select the File Import Styles command. In the dialog box displayed, choose GOPHERS1.FM3 from the list box and accept the default, All turned on. When you press ENTER or select OK, 1-2-3 for Windows copies the Styles settings to the active file, FILE0002. When you save FILE0002.WK3, 1-2-3 for Windows will save these Style settings in the file FILE0002.FM3.

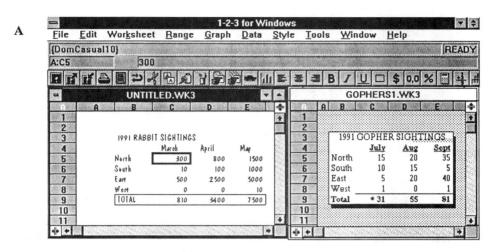

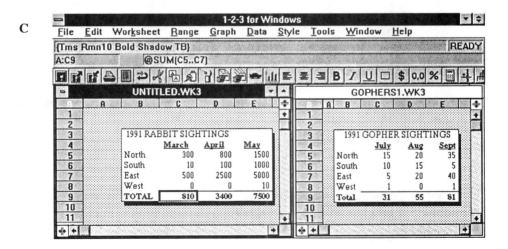

Figure 6-19 Importing Style settings

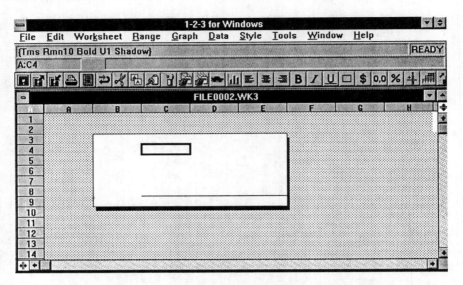

Figure 6-20   Importing Styles from a template .FM3 file to a new file

MANIPULATING STYLE SETTINGS IN A RANGE

Many times you'll want to manipulate—erase, move or copy—*only* the Style settings in a range. Although this is discussed in detail in Chapter 7, here are the highlights:

- To delete only the Style settings in a range, use the Edit Clear Special Style option.

- To delete cell contents but not the Style settings, use the 1-2-3 Classic /Range Erase command.

- To delete all the Style settings in a file, delete the .FM3 file (see Chapter 4).

- To copy only the Style settings in a range, use the Edit Quick Copy Styles only option.

- To copy everything but the Style settings, and, in the destination range, leave existing Style settings intact, use the 1-2-3 Classic /Copy command.

- To move only the Style settings in a range, use the Edit Move Cells Styles only option.

7

Cutting and Pasting Data

1-2-3 for Windows adds many new ways to cut and paste—to move, copy, and erase—most of which can be accessed through the Edit menu or the icon palette. 1-2-3 for Windows also provides the familiar /Copy, /Move, and /Range Erase commands accessed through the 1-2-3 Classic menu.

At first you may find the number of commands that perform one type of operation, like erasing data, confusing. As you'll see, some of these new cut and paste methods handle 1-2-3 for Windows features like Style settings and multiple worksheets, while others take advantage of the Clipboard. On the other hand, you'll find that in some instances the equivalent 1-2-3 Classic command is still the best way to go.

You'll also discover that some cut and paste methods produce the same result. For example, you can use Edit Clear, its shortcut DEL, /Range Erase, and even Edit Clear Special to erase only the contents of a range of cells. Then the "best" method is the one you feel most comfortable with.

And finally, the Range Transpose command is also covered in this chapter. Traditionally, this command has been used to transpose data in a 2-D range from a columnwise to a rowwise orientation, or vice versa. In 1-2-3 for Windows, as in Release 3, you can even transpose 2-D or 3-D ranges to multiple worksheets.

Note: Edit Undo is discussed in Chapter 1, Edit Find in Chapter 2, and Edit Paste Link and Edit Link Options in Chapter 4.

SELECTING A RANGE

This chapter assumes that you know how to select ranges in 1-2-3 for Windows. Although this is discussed in detail in Chapter 2, the following should serve as a convenient reference guide when you are cutting and pasting data.

For most cut and paste commands, including 1-2-3 Classic commands, you can select a range either before or after you choose the command. However, you must preselect a range before you select Edit Clear or one of the commands that uses the Clipboard—Edit Cut, Copy, and Paste. Similarly, you must preselect a range before you choose one of the icons that represent Edit Clear, Cut, Copy, or Paste.

For example, imagine you want to specify the 2-D range A1..B2 in the Edit Clear command, which erases all data, yet leaves formatting and Style settings intact. You can preselect this range by outlining A1..B2 using the mouse. Or, if you are using the keyboard, move the cell pointer to cell A1, press F4 to anchor this cell, press → then ↓ to outline A1..B2, and then press ENTER to confirm. When you select the Edit Clear command, A:A1..A:B2 will be displayed in the Range text box.

There are three ways to specify a range after choosing a command. Imagine that you choose Edit Clear. Then in the dialog box displayed, you press TAB to move to the Range text box. You can

- Type **A1..B2**.

- Use the mouse to point to A1..B2 in the worksheet. When you release the mouse button, 1-2-3 will return you to the dialog box, where A:A1..A:B2 will be displayed in the Range text box.

- Use the keyboard to point to A1..B2 in the worksheet. First, press F6 to return to the worksheet, where the cell pointer will be anchored in its location before you invoked Edit Clear. If you need to, press ESC to unanchor the cell pointer, and then move to cell A1. Press . (period) to anchor the cell pointer, press → then ↓ to outline A1..B2, then press ENTER to confirm. 1-2-3 will return you to the dialog box where A:A1..A:B2 will be displayed in the Range text box.

If you want to point to a 3-D range like A:A1..B:B2 you can only use the keyboard; the mouse won't work. To preselect this range move the cell pointer to cell A:A1, press F4 to anchor this cell, press → then ↓ to outline A:A1..A:B2. Press CTRL+PGUP so that A:A1..B:A2 is outlined, and then press ENTER to confirm.

ERASING

Once you've entered information in 1-2-3, you'll soemtimes need to delete some of it. 1-2-3 for Windows provides you with four different ways to erase information.

- Edit Clear (DEL)

- Edit Clear Special

- /Range Erase, the 1-2-3 Classic command

- Edit Cut

You'll want to use DEL (the shortcut for Edit Clear), or the 1-2-3 Classic command, /Range Erase, to delete data while leaving formatting and Style settings intact. On the other hand, you can use Edit Clear Special to control what is erased with cells. For example, you can erase cell contents, numeric formatting, Style settings, graphic elements, or any combination thereof. Edit Cut is the easiest way to delete everything in a range of cells. None of these commands will affect column width or row height settings.

Erasing Only Cell Contents

Suppose that—like every other business owner—you want to erase your overhead expenses, which are displayed in the range A4..C4 of Figure 7-1A. However, in this instance, you want to leave the formatting and Style settings intact.

You'll find that using DEL (the shortcut for Edit Clear) is the easiest way to accomplish this. For example, if you preselect the range A4..C4, then press DEL, you'll get the result in Figure 7-1B. 1-2-3 erases only the information in A4..C4, and leaves the formatting and Styles settings intact. If you look at the input line, you'll see that the P0 (Percent 0 places) formatting in cell C4 still remains. Likewise, the bold font, shadow, and borders are also retained.

> ▼ *Tip:*   The 🔲 icon is equivalent to DEL, Edit Clear, and /Range Erase.

The 1-2-3 Classic command, /Range Erase, also produces the same result. Be aware, however, that if you preselect a range like A4..C4 in Figure 7-1A, and then select /Range Erase, 1-2-3 doesn't ask for confirmation; it automatically deletes the contents of A4..C4.

> ▼ *Tip:*   If you erase information you need, you can restore the data by immediately pressing ALT+BACKSPACE (Undo), or selecting the 🔲 icon.

Note: 1-2-3 displays hidden information when you point to a range in the worksheet or select /Range Erase. Hidden information isn't redisplayed, however, when you type a range into the Edit Clear Special Range text box. On the other hand, you can't erase protected information. In fact, 1-2-3 won't even let you select Edit Clear or Edit Clear Special when protected cells are selected. (Chapter 5 discusses protecting and hiding data.)

Erasing Only Style Settings

You'll want to use Edit Clear Special to erase only the Style settings—font, colors, shading, and borders—in a range, and return them to the global default settings. (Notice that label alignment is not affected.) In Figure 7-2, for example, the Edit Clear Special

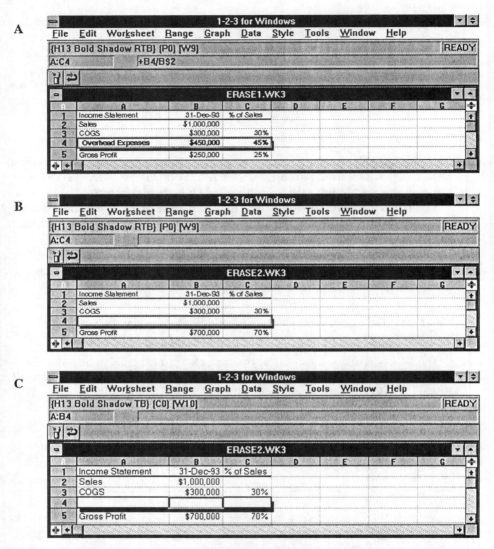

Figure 7-1 Erasing cell contents using DEL, Edit Clear, or /Range Erase

settings shown in the dialog box—Cell contents, Number, and Graph format turned off, Style turned on, and the Range A:A1..A:C5 specified—are used to erase only the Style settings in this range.

Figure 7-2B shows the results. The range A1..C5 still contains the data with its C0 (Currency 0), P0 (Percent 0), D1 (1: DD-MMM-YY), and centered label formats, but the bold font, shadow, and borders are gone. In general, 1-2-3 returns the font to the default Style Font setting, changes color settings to the Window Display Options defaults, and

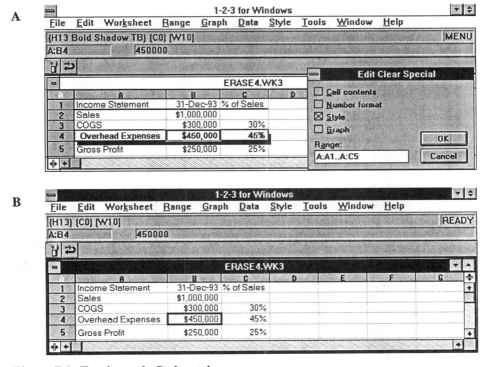

Figure 7-2   Erasing only Style settings

deletes any shading. You can see in the format line, however, that the [W10] column width and {H13} row height settings in cell B4 are unaffected.

Note: After an erase operation is completed or cancelled, the Edit Clear Special dialog box always reverts to its default settings—all options selected.

Erasing Only Numeric Formats

The Edit Clear Special option, Number format, erases only numeric formats set with the Range Format command, which revert to the Worksheet Global Settings Format default. In effect, the Number format option is equivalent to Range Format Reset (see Chapter 5).

For example, if you specify the Edit Clear Special settings shown in the dialog box in Figure 7-3A—Cell contents turned off so only Number format is on, and the Range A:B1..A:C5 selected—you'll get the results in Figure 7-3B.

If you examine Figures 7-3A and B, you'll see that only the numeric formats in the range A1..C5 have changed. For example, by comparing the format lines, you'll see that the D1 (1: DD-MMM-YY) format in cell B1 has been erased and the date value, 34334, has reverted to the global numeric format—General, in this case.

A

B

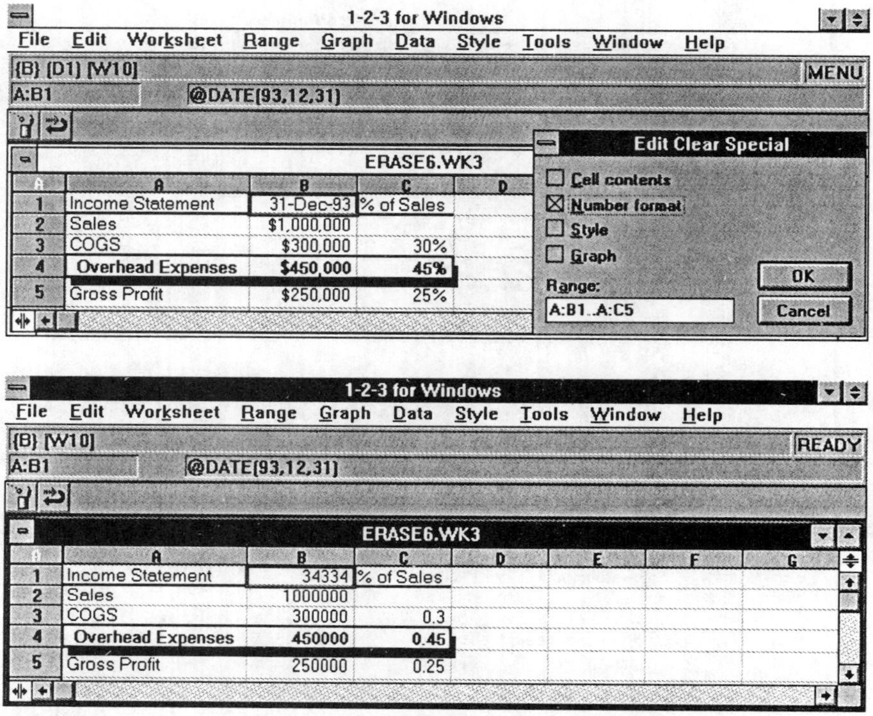

Figure 7-3 Erasing only Range Format settings

Erasing Cell Contents, Formatting and Style Settings

The easiest way to erase the contents, formatting, and Style settings of a cell or range is to preselect it, then choose Edit Cut. Edit Clear Special will also produce the same results when the Cell contents, Number format, and Style options are all turned on.

For instance, imagine that Figure 7-4 shows the well-deserved merit raises for your employees. To delete the three-dimensional range A:B1..B:D4, follow this procedure:

1. Preselect A:B1..B:D4 by positioning the cell pointer in A:A1, pressing F4 to anchor this cell, pressing END followed by →, then END followed by ↓ to select B1..D4 in worksheet A. Press CTRL+PGUP to also select this range in worksheet B. Press ENTER to confirm. (Remember, you can't use the mouse to select a 3-D range.)

2. Choose Edit Cut.

> ▼ *Tip:* The ⬚ icon is a shortcut for Edit Cut.

As you can see in Figure 7-4B, 1-2-3 for Windows deletes the cell contents in this range, as well as the formatting and Style settings, which revert to the worksheet global settings. Column width and row height settings are unaffected.

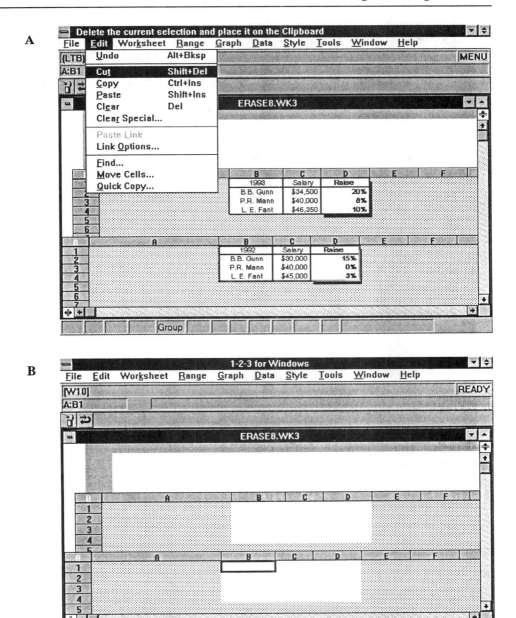

Figure 7-4 Erasing contents, formatting, and Style settings

Although Edit Cut deletes data from the worksheet, the data is actually moved to the Clipboard (see "Clipboard Basics," later). If you mistakenly delete data you need, using Edit Paste will restore the data in the worksheet, as long as you haven't cut or copied other data to the Clipboard.

▼ *Tip:*   To erase an entire worksheet and move other worksheets up to fill in the gap, use the Worksheet Delete Sheet command. Similarly, to erase an entire row or column from a worksheet and have other rows or columns move to fill the graph, use Worksheet Delete Row or Column. (See Chapter 1.)

Erasing Graphic Elements Inserted in a Worksheet

As you can see in Figure 7-3, Edit Clear Special includes a Graph option that erases any graphic elements inserted in a worksheet—a graph created using the Graph command, a text graph created using the Range Annotate command, or even an imported CGM file. This option, however, doesn't erase these graphic elements from memory or on disk.

For example, imagine you have previously used the Graph command to create a graph called GRAPH1 and inserted it into the range A1..A5. (See Chapter 10.) If you preselect this range, choose Edit Clear Special, turn on the Graph option, and select OK, 1-2-3 for Windows will delete this graph from the worksheet. Choose Graph View and you'll see that GRAPH1 is still intact.

▼ *Tip:*   Preselecting a graphic element inserted in a worksheet and then selecting Edit Cut or 🖺 produces the same result as the Edit Clear Special Graph option.

CLIPBOARD BASICS

1-2-3 for Windows lets you use the Clipboard to cut and paste data. The *Clipboard*, accessed through the Edit menu, is a special memory buffer that holds whatever was last cut (moved) or copied. Think of it as an invisible worksheet area used to store data. As long as Windows remains open, data remains in the Clipboard until you cut or copy new data to it—even if you leave 1-2-3.

If you look at Figure 7-5, you'll see that you can paste data from the Clipboard to another location in your worksheet file, to another worksheet file, and even to another Windows application, such as WordPerfect for Windows.

Copying and moving data using the Clipboard has distinct advantages. For example, you can

- Paste data to multiple locations.

- Perform other operations before you paste.

- Paste data to other Windows applications (see Chapter 17).

- Link worksheet files (see Chapter 4).

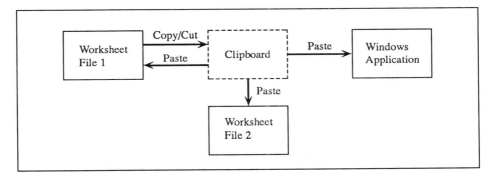

Figure 7-5 How the Clipboard works

MOVING

Moving data is one of the easiest operations to master in 1-2-3 for Windows. You can move information to another location, even to another open file, by using any of the following methods:

- Edit Move Cells
- Edit Cut and Edit Paste
- /Move, the 1-2-3 Classic command

Moving in 1-2-3 has become more powerful and more versatile. As you'll see, these move methods not only provide you with different ways to move data, they also produce different results when you move formulas.

Note: This section assumes that you know how to select ranges in 1-2-3 for Windows. "Selecting a Range," earlier in this chapter, provides a quick refresher course.

▼ *Tip:*   To move a column to a row, or a row to a column, see "Transposing Data" later in this chapter.

The Difference between Edit Move Cells, Edit Cut and Paste, and the 1-2-3 Classic /Move Command

When you use move data, here's what typically happens:

- Information in one location is moved to a new location. Any existing information in the new location is overwritten.
- The contents of the original location are blanked and return to the global worksheet, format, and Style settings.

The major difference between /Move, Edit Move Cells, and Edit Cut and Paste is how they affect formulas in a worksheet. When moving formulas then, you'll want to use different move methods depending on the result you want to achieve.

When you use either /Move or Edit Move Cells, 1-2-3 for Windows automatically adjusts cell references both inside and outside the moved range to reference the new location of moved cells. However, these move methods also produce problems usually associated with moving data—creating formulas that return ERR if referenced data is overwritten during a move, and changing the size of a formula range reference when a cell defining a formula range reference is moved. (See "How /Move and Edit Move Affect Cell References," later in this chapter.)

Moving data using the Clipboard through Edit Cut and Paste affects cell references differently than /Move or Edit Move Cells. (The Clipboard is explained in "Clipboard Basics," above.) A cell reference that refers to moved data isn't adjusted, while a moved cell reference is typically adjusted to account for its new location. One substantial benefit is that you can overcome the problems often associated with moving data. (See "How Edit Cut and Paste Affect Cell References," later in this chapter.)

You'll also find that Edit Cut and Edit Paste give you additional flexibility. Not only can you perform other operations before you move data from the Clipboard, but you can also paste data to multiple locations, or even move data to another Windows application.

▼ *Tip:*   Rather than moving large blocks of data, try using the Worksheet Insert Sheet command to insert a new worksheet in a file and move the other worksheets back to make room. Similarly, to insert a new column or row in a worksheet and move the other columns or rows to make room, use the Worksheet Insert Row or Column (see Chapter 1).

Moving Cell Contents, Formatting, and Style Settings

Edit Cut and Paste, Edit Move Cells, and /Move, the 1-2-3 Classic command, all move cell contents, formatting, and Style settings—fonts, label alignment, shading, colors, and borders. In Figure 7-6A for example, imagine that you want to move the 1992 and 1993 advertising analysis and its formatting in worksheets A and B to worksheets B and C. The following sections show how you can do this using Edit Move Cells, /Move, and Edit Cut and Paste.

Note: You can use /Move or Edit Move Cells—but not Edit Cut—to move information from a protected area of a file as long as the destination is unprotected; you can't, however, move information to a protected area. On the other hand, you can use all three methods to move hidden information. 1-2-3 automatically displays hidden data when you point to a worksheet or select /Move. Hidden data isn't redisplayed, however, when you type your To and From ranges into the Edit Move Cells text boxes. (Chapter 5 discusses protecting and hiding data.)

A
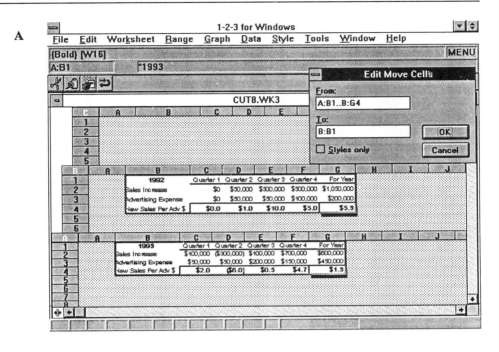

B
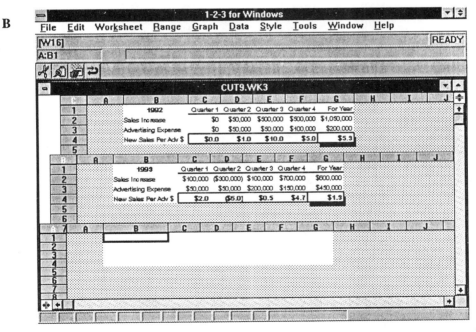

Figure 7-6 Moving cell contents, formatting, and Style settings using Edit Move Cells

Using Edit Move Cells

Although you can use Edit Move Cells to move cell contents, formats set with the Range command, and Style settings, you'll probably find it the least appealing of all methods of moving information. The dialog box seems constantly in the way, even though you can move it, and the way 1-2-3 for Windows zooms in and out when you point in the worksheet—especially using the mouse—can be very annoying.

In Figure 7-6, for example, you can move the 1992 and 1993 advertising analysis and formatting back one worksheet, by using this procedure:

1. Choose Edit Move Cells. You'll see the dialog box in Figure 7-6A.

2. Use the keyboard to specify the three-dimensional From range A:B1..B:G4. (Remember that you can't use the mouse to point to a 3-D range.)

> ▼ *Tip:* If you preselect the From range A:B1..B:G4 in Figure 7-6A, then select Edit Move Cells, A:B1..B:G4 will automatically be displayed in the To text box, and the cursor will be located in it.

3. Specify B:B1 as the upper-left cell of the destination range. (If you specify a larger To range, 1-2-3 ignores all but the upper-left cell.) Then select OK.

You can see the results in Figure 7-6B, where 1-2-3 moves the 1993 data and numeric formatting to worksheet B, beginning in cell B1, and the 1992 data and its formatting to worksheet C, also beginning in cell B1. The font, border, and shadow Style settings are also moved.

> ▼ *Tip:* You can perform a move operation without accessing the Edit Move Cells command. To do this in Figure 7-6, preselect the range A:B1..B:G4. From the icon palette, select . The cell pointer will turn into a hand. Select the upper-left corner of the destination, cell B:B1, and you'll get the same results as Figure 7-6B. You should be aware, however, that this icon seems to be somewhat temperamental—sometimes you need to perform this sequence twice before 1-2-3 for Windows actually performs the move.

Using /Move, the 1-2-3 Classic Command

If you're an experienced 1-2-3 user, you'll probably find yourself still using /Move, the 1-2-3 Classic command, to move data. However, you might like to use some of the new shortcuts available in 1-2-3 for Windows. Here are some things to keep in mind:

- You can point to your To and From ranges in the worksheet using the mouse.

- If you preselect a range before you select /Move, 1-2-3 assumes it's your From range and prompts you for a To range. If you preselect A:B1..B:G4 in Figure 7-6, for example, and then select /Move, you'll see the "Enter range to move TO:" prompt. Simply type **B:B1** and press ENTER to complete the command.

- You can perform a move operation without accessing the /Move command. For example, preselect the range A:B1..B:G4. Then select 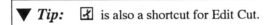 shown in Figure 7-6. Select the upper-left corner of the destination, cell B:B1, and you'll get the same results as in Figure 7-6B.

Using Edit Cut and Paste

You can also use Edit Cut and Edit Paste to move the data in Figure 7-6. In fact, you might find this the easiest way of all to move data. To do this:

Note: If you're moving formulas, be sure to read "How Edit Cut and Paste Affect Cell References," later in this section.

1. Preselect the 3-D range A:B1..B:G4 using the keyboard. Then choose Edit Cut or use its shortcut, SHIFT+DEL, to move this data, formatting, and Style settings to the Clipboard, just as in Figure 7-7A.

▼ *Tip:*   ⬜ is also a shortcut for Edit Cut.

---

2. Select only the upper-left cell of the destination, B:B1.

Note: If you specify a destination range *larger* than the data cut to the Clipboard, 1-2-3 for Windows will write over and blank the extra cells to which data is not moved. If you select a multicell range *smaller* than the range cut to the Clipboard, Edit Paste only pastes data to the selected cells. For example, if you select the two-cell range B:B1..B:B2 in Figure 7-7B, then select Edit Paste, 1-2-3 for Windows *only* pastes the data originally in cell A:B1, the label "1993", to cell B:B1, and the label "Sales Increase" originally in cell A:B2, to cell B:B2.

3. Choose Edit Paste or press SHIFT+INS, its shortcut, to paste the data from the Clipboard.

▼ *Tip:*   ⬜ is also a shortcut for Edit Paste.

You can see in Figure 7-7B that once again you get the same results. 1-2-3 moves the 1993 data and numeric formatting to worksheet B, and the 1992 data and its formatting to worksheet C. The font, border, and shadow Style settings are also moved. However, because the data still resides in the Clipboard, you can continue to paste it to other locations. (See the next section for an example.)

Note: Pressing ALT+BACKSPACE (Undo) or selecting ⬜ immediately after completing Edit Cut and Paste, Edit Move Cells, or a /Move command will restore the worksheet to its previous condition. Undo, however, won't restore the previous Clipboard data.

A

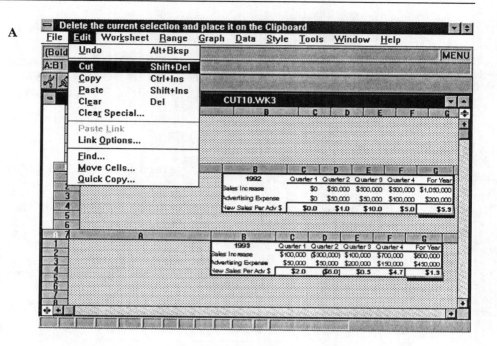

B

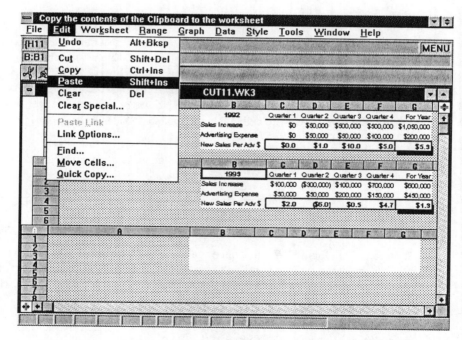

Figure 7-7 Moving cell contents, formatting, and Style settings using Edit Cut and Paste

Cutting and Pasting to Multiple Destinations

Because moved data still resides in the Clipboard after it is pasted, you can paste it again in yet another location. To see this, consider Figure 7-8A. Here, the range C1..E1 is preselected, then Edit Cut or its shortcut, SHIFT+DEL, is selected to move this data, formatting, and Style settings to the Clipboard. Then Edit Paste (SHIFT+INS) is used in cell D1 of Figure 7-8B to paste the date headings, including the date format and bottom border, from the Clipboard to D1..F1.

If you now select cell D6 and then press SHIFT+INS, you'll get the result shown in Figure 7-8C. Not only does the moved data reside in D1..F1, but it is also pasted to D6..F6. Furthermore, because it still resides in the Clipboard, you can continue to paste this data to other locations.

Moving Only Style Settings

You can also use Edit Move Cells to move only the Style settings in a range. For instance, suppose you specify the Edit Move Cells settings shown in the dialog box in Figure 7-9A—From as A1..C6, To as E1, and Styles only turned on. When you select OK, you'll get the result in Figure 7-9B. 1-2-3 for Windows moves the font, borders, and shadow Style settings, but not the label alignment, from A1..C6 to E1..G6. If you look at the format line in Figure 7-9B, you'll see that the bold style originally assigned to A1 has been moved to E1. However, the data and the numeric formatting in A1..C6 aren't moved.

Note: To copy only Style settings, use Edit Quick Copy's Styles only option discussed later in this chapter.

Moving Data to Another File

As in Release 3, you can move information between open files. In 1-2-3 for Windows, however, you have to use Edit Cut and Edit Paste. Release 2 users should find moving data between files using Edit Cut and Paste much simpler and less prone to error than the File Extract To command. If you move formulas between files, be sure to read "How 1-2-3 Adjusts Cell References Moved to Another File," later in this chapter.

Note: Edit Move Cells and /Move can't copy data between files.

For example, suppose in Figure 7-10 you want to move the Final test score information in A8..C13 of TEST1.WK3, to the file in the lefthand window, TEST2.WK3, beginning in A1. To do this, select the data to be moved, A8..C13 in TEST1.WK3, then move this data to the Clipboard by pressing SHIFT+DEL (Edit Cut). Next, select the upper-left cell of the destination, cell A1 of TEST2.WK3, then paste the data from the Clipboard by pressing SHIFT+INS (Edit Paste). As you can see in Figure 7-10B, 1-2-3 for Windows pastes all data, formatting, and Style settings to TEST2.WK3, beginning in cell A1. It doesn't, however, move row heights or column width settings.

Note: When you move data to another file, [icon] and [icon] can also be used as shortcuts for Edit Cut and Edit Paste.

A
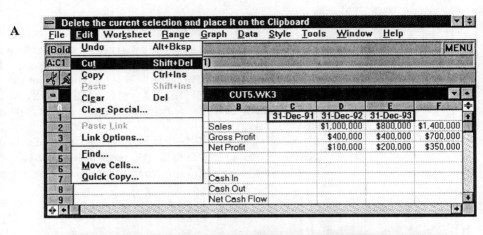

B

C
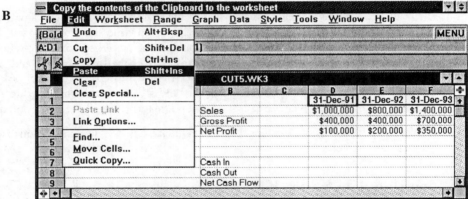

Figure 7-8 Using the Clipboard to move data

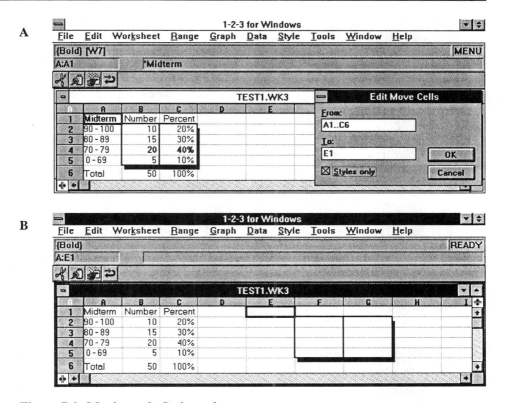

Figure 7-9 Moving only Style settings

How /Move and Edit Move Cells Affect Cell References

When you use Edit Move Cells or the /Move command, 1-2-3 for Windows automatically adjusts cell references affected by the move. You can see this in Figure 7-11, where sales of different products are related. For example, Cold Medicine sales in C2 are computed as +F2, or equal to Aspirin sales. Likewise, the formula in D2, +C2*.5, calculates Vitamin C sales as a function of Cold Medicine sales.

When you use /Move or Edit Move Cells to move the contents of C2 to E2, the results are shown in Figure 7-11B. 1-2-3 adjusts any affected formulas both inside and outside the moved range. For instance, the moved formula is adjusted to +F2 so that Cold Medicine sales are still a function of Aspirin sales. Similarly, the formula in D2 is adjusted to +E2*.5 so that Vitamin C sales still reference Cold Medicine sales.

Note: Edit Move Cells and /Move also adjust mixed and absolute references (discussed later in "Copying Formulas") in the same manner.

A
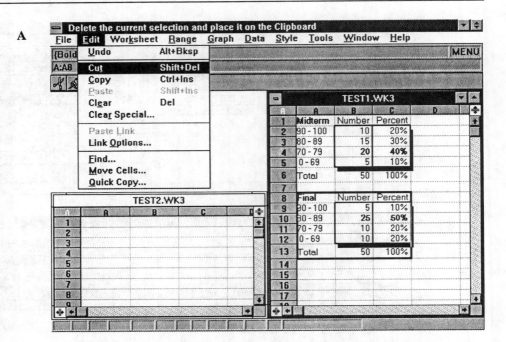

B
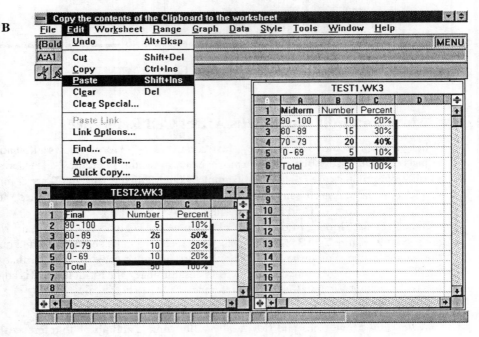

Figure 7-10 Moving data between files

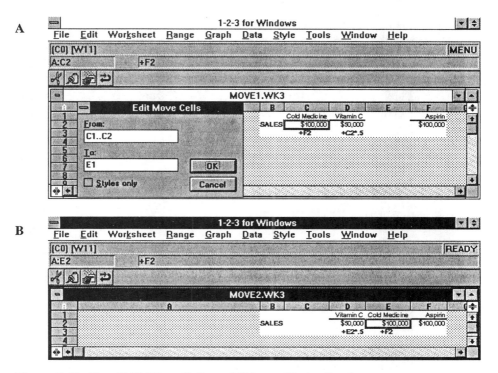

Figure 7-11 How Edit Move Cells and /Move affect cell references

How Edit Cut and Paste Affect Cell References

Edit Cut and Edit Paste affect cell references outside and inside the moved range differently than Edit Move Cells and /Move. You can see this in Figure 7-12A, which contains the same data as Figure 7-11A. However, Edit Cut and Paste are now used to move the Cold Medicine formula in C2 to E2.

By comparing Figures 7-12A and B, you'll see that the Vitamin C sales formula, +C2*.05, remains the same in D2. So Vitamin C sales are still calculated as +C2*0.5, but are now $0 since C2 is blanked after the move. Therefore, 1-2-3 for Windows *doesn't* adjust a formula outside the moved range to refer to the new location of moved data.

By examining Figures 7-12A and B, you'll also see that the moved Cold Medicine sales formula is adjusted from +F2, which refers to Aspirin sales, to +H2, which refers to a blank cell. So Edit Paste adjusts a moved cell reference to conform to its new location; because this formula moved two columns, 1-2-3 adjusts the column component by two columns. In effect, Edit Cut and Paste adjust a relative reference in the same way as if you copied it. (For a discussion of relative references, see "Copying Formulas," later.)

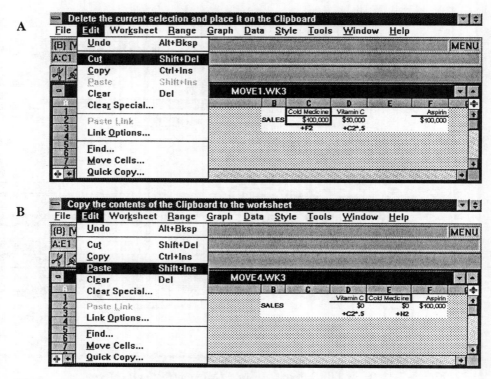

Figure 7-12 How Edit Cut and Paste affect cells references

▼ *Tip:*   By using an absolute reference (see "Copying Formulas"), you can force
a formula moved with Edit Cut and Paste to refer to the same information. In Figure 7-12, for instance, if you move the formula +$F$2 in C2
to E2, the result is still +$F$2—Cold Medicine sales are still a function
of Aspirin sales after the move. This only works if you move a formula
within the same worksheet file, however.

Common Move Problems Solved by Edit Cut and Paste

When you move data in a worksheet using either /Move or Edit Move Cells, you are
likely to cause yourself two problems. These are

- Writing over cells referenced in a formula, which causes the formula to return ERR.

- Moving the upper-left or lower-right cell that defines a formula range reference, which
can change the size of the range.

As you'll see, when you encounter these move problems, you'll want to consider using
Edit Cut and Paste instead of /Move or Edit Move.

Writing Over Cell References

As you know, when you move data, 1-2-3 for Windows writes over any existing information in the destination range. When you use /Move or Edit Move Cells you can cause a side effect—formulas referring to the erased data will return ERR—that you won't encounter when you use Edit Cut and Paste.

To see this, let's continue to build on the previous example. In Figure 7-13A, however, only Vitamin C sales are a function of other sales. That is, Vitamin C sales in D2 are a function of Kleenex sales, as reflected by the formula +E2*.5.

When you use /Move or Edit Move Cells to move the contents of C2 (Cold Medicine sales) to E2, you'll write over the $200,000 Kleenex sales. You can see the result in Figure 7-13B. Because the formula in D2 changes from +E2*.5 to +ERR*.5, Vitamin C sales now return ERR, so this formula doesn't refer to the $100,000 Cold Medicine sales moved to cell E2.

If you look at Figure 17-14, you'll see that you can overcome this problem by using Edit Cut and Edit Paste to move the Cold Medicine formula from C2 to E2. Because Edit Cut and Paste *don't* adjust cell references that originally referred to the moved data, you can see in Figure 17-14 that D2 still contains +E2*.5, so Vitamin C sales are now calculated as 50% of Cold Medicine sales.

You get the same problem—formulas evaluating to ERR—when you use /Move or Edit Move Cells to move the contents of a cell to another cell that defines the upper-left

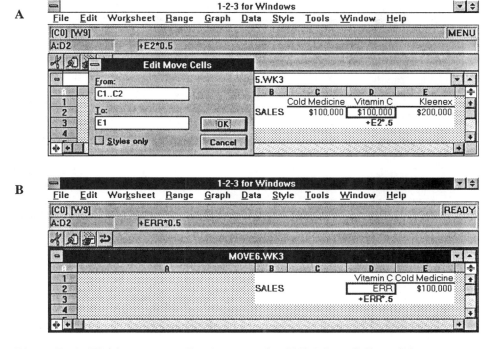

Figure 7-13 Writing over a cell reference using Edit Move Cells or /Move

Copy the contents of the Clipboard to the worksheet

File Edit Worksheet Range Graph Data Style Tools Window Help

MENU

Undo   Alt+Bksp

Cut   Shift+Del
Copy   Ctrl+Ins
Paste   Shift+Ins
Clear   Del
Clear Special...

Paste Link
Link Options...

Find...
Move Cells...
Quick Copy...

CUT2.WK3

	B	C	D	E
			Vitamin C	Cold Medicine
1				
2	SALES		$50,000	$100,000
3			+E2*.5	
4				
5				
6				

Figure 7-14 Writing over a cell reference using Edit Cut and Paste

or lower-right corner of a formula range reference. In 1-2-3 for Windows, the solution once again is to move the data via the Clipboard.

Consider Figure 7-15A, for example, where July Total expenses are calculated as @SUM(C2..C4) in cell C5, and Total Misc. expenses as @SUM(C4..E4) in cell F4. Imagine that you're not sure whether your actual vacation expenses in July were $1,500 or $2,000. Regretably, your credit card charges confirm $2,000.

If you use Edit Move Cells or /Move to move $2,000 from B1 to C4, Figure 7-15B shows the resulting side effect. Both C5 and F4 now contain @SUM(@ERR) because the information in C4 was overwritten during the move, and C4 defined a corner of the formula range references in these cells. On the other hand, if you use Edit Cut and Paste to move $2,000 from B1 to C4, you'll get the result shown in Figure 7-16. As you can see, the formulas in C5 and F4 referring to the overwritten data are unaffected and incorporate the moved information.

Moving a Cell within a Referenced Range

When you use Edit Move Cells or /Move to move data in cells used in a formula range reference, you can get some unwelcome results. A formula isn't affected if you move cells in the middle of its range reference. But move a cell that represents the upper-left or lower-right corner of the range reference, and you'll change the range in the formula references. You can end up with incorrect formulas and even circular references. However, you'll see that 1-2-3 for Windows provides a solution—Edit Cut and Edit Paste.

Building on the previous example, Figure 7-17 sums quarterly rent, food, and miscellaneous expenses in column F. The quarterly rent, for instance, is calculated in cell F2 as @SUM(C2..E2). On the other hand, total monthly expenditures are computed in row 5; cell C5 contains @SUM(C2..C4), for instance.

Everything works out fine in Figure 7-17B when you use Edit Move Cells, /Move, or Edit Cut and Paste to move the $300 August food expense in D3 to G6, because cell D3 represents the *middle* of formula range references. However, the values returned by the affected formulas change because D3 is now blank. So the Total Food expense in F4 is

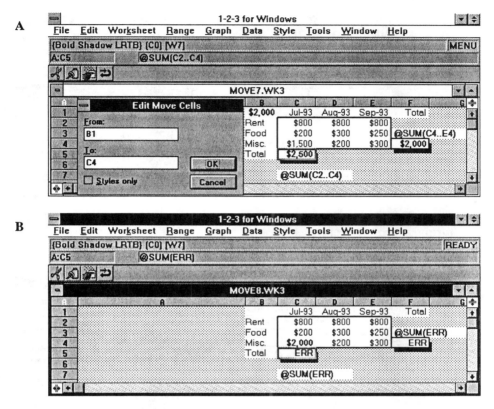

Figure 7-15 Using /Move or Edit Move Cells to move data to a cell that defines a formula range reference

still calculated as @SUM(C3..E3), but the formula now returns $450; likewise, the Total August expense in D5 is still computed as @SUM(D2..D4), but returns $1,000.

Things work out quite differently in Figure 7-18, when Edit Move Cells or /Move is used to move the $300 September Misc. expense in E4, which represents the lower-right corner of two formula range references, to G6. Although Total September expenses in E5 are originally calculated as @SUM(E2..E4), after the move 1-2-3 adjusts this formula to @SUM(E2..G6), which returns $15,000. In a similar manner Total Misc. expenses in F4, originally computed as @SUM(C4..E4), changes to @SUM(C4..G6) and returns $9,150. So in both cases, 1-2-3 for Windows adjusts the formula range reference to match the new location of the lower-left corner cell, which results in incorrect results and circular references.

Note: 1-2-3 also expands or contracts the size of a named range in the same manner.

Figure 7-19 shows the different result when you use Edit Cut and Paste to move the $300 September Misc. expense in E4 to G6. Because a formula outside of the moved

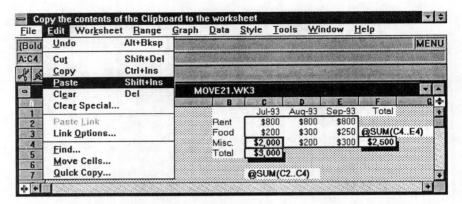

Figure 7-16 Using Edit Cut and Edit Paste to move data to a cell that defines a formula range reference

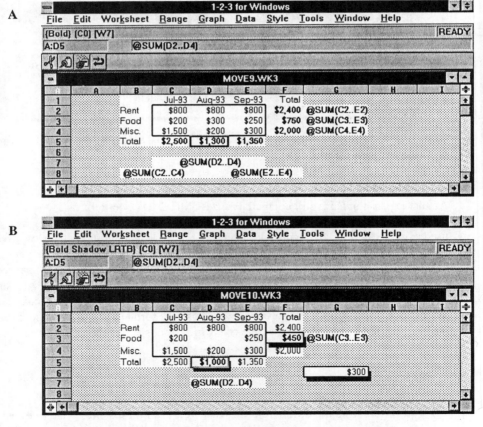

Figure 7-17 Moving data in the middle of a formula range reference

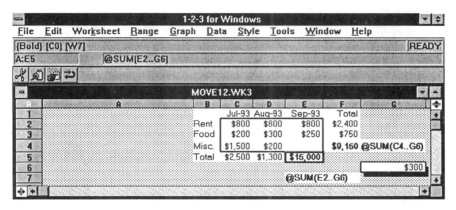

Figure 7-18 Using Edit Move Cells or /Move to move a cell reference that defines a formula range reference

range that originally referred to moved data *isn't* adjusted, the formula in E5, @SUM(E2..E4), and @SUM(C4..E4) in F4 are unaffected. The results, however, do change, because E4 is now blank.

How the Clipboard Affects Cell References Moved to Another File

When you use Edit Cut and Edit Paste to move data between files, 1-2-3 for Windows adjusts cell references as if you moved data within a file. For example, suppose in Figure 7-20 you use Edit Cut (SHIFT+DEL) to move the Oct, Nov, and Dec sales data in F1..H2 of SUMMER.WK3 to the Clipboard, and Edit Paste (SHIFT+INS) to move this data from the Clipboard to cell C1 of FALL.WK3. As you can see in Figure 7-20B, 1-2-3 moves this data to C1..E2 of FALL.WK3, including formatting and Style settings.

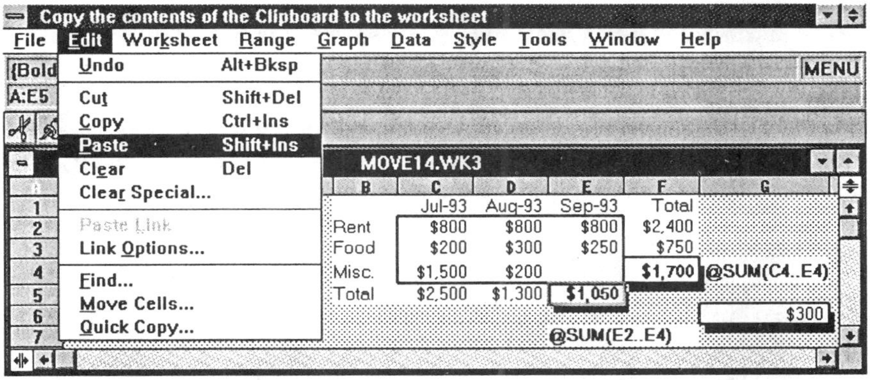

Figure 7-19 Using Edit Cut and Paste to move a cell reference that defines a formula range reference

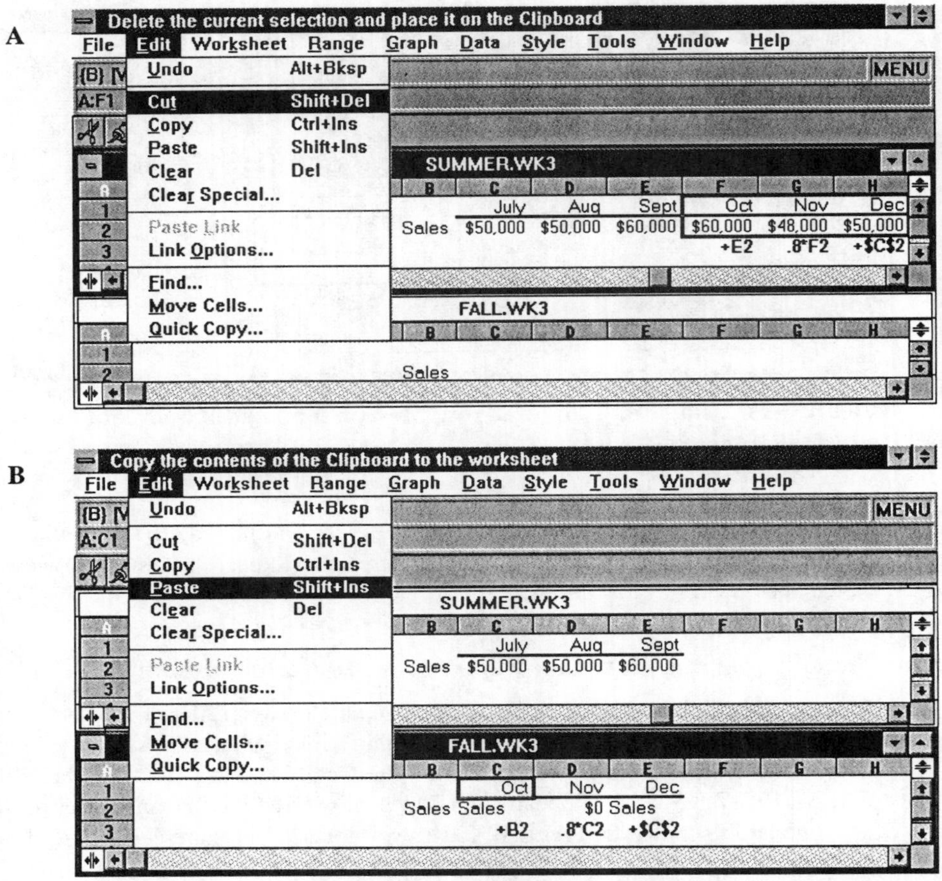

A

B

Figure 7-20 How Edit Cut and Paste affects cell references moved between files

By comparing Figures 7-20A and B, you'll see that the Oct sales formula +E2 origi-nally in cell F2 of SUMMER.WK3 becomes +B2 in cell C2 of FALL.WK3. So Edit Paste adjusts this reference to conform to its new location—because this formula moved three columns, 1-2-3 adjusts the column component of the formula cell reference by three. (In effect, Edit Cut and Paste adjust a moved relative reference as if you copied it—see "Copying Formulas," later in this chapter.) Before the move, the Oct sales formula references the Sept sales in cell E2 of SUMMER.WK3; after the move, it refers to the label "Sales" in cell B2 of FALL.WK3.

Similarly, the Nov sales formula .8*F2 in cell G2 of SUMMER.WK3 becomes .8*C2 in cell D3 of FALL.WK3. However, this formula still references Oct sales since the value for October has also moved to FALL.WK3.

On the other hand, 1-2-3 for Windows doesn't adjust the absolute reference +$C$2, which calculates Dec sales. Before the move this formula references July sales in cell C2 of SUMMER.WK3; after the move it refers to Oct sales in cell C2 of FALL.WK3.

Note to Release 3 Users: Using Edit Cut and Paste *doesn't* link files. In Release 3, however, moving data between files created file linking. For example, 1-2-3 would have linked the files in Figure 7-20 by adjusting the Oct sales formula +E2 to +<<SUM-MER.WK3>>E2, and the Dec sales formula +$C$2 to <<SUMMER.WK3>>$C$2 when they were moved to FALL.WK3. To link a file with 1-2-3 for Windows, see Chapter 4.

COPYING

1-2-3 for Windows provides three different ways to copy information:

- Edit Quick Copy
- Edit Copy and Edit Paste
- /Copy, the 1-2-3 Classic command

All these methods let you copy data from a source range to a destination range, even in a different worksheet file. (Copying between 1-2-3 and another Windows application is discussed in Chapter 17.)

Because copying is so versatile in 1-2-3 for Windows, it is presented here in two sections. This first section covers the basic mechanics of copying—for example, how to copy from one range to another. A second section addresses copying formulas, the implications of copying relative, absolute, and mixed cell addressing, as well as how to copy formulas as values.

Note: This section assumes you know how to select ranges in 1-2-3 for Windows. "Selecting a Range," earlier in this chapter, provides a quick refresher course.

The Difference Between Edit Copy and Paste, Edit Quick Copy, and the 1-2-3 Classic /Copy Command

When you copy data in 1-2-3 for Windows, here's what typically happens:

- The source location is left unchanged.
- Labels, values, formulas, and formatting set with the Range command are copied to the new location.
- Any existing information in the new location is overwritten.

However, each of the copy methods produce different results when it comes to Style settings—fonts, label alignment, borders, colors, and shading. Edit Copy and Paste copies all Style settings. Edit Quick Copy copies all Style settings; conversely, its Styles only option copies only Style settings, no data or formatting. The 1-2-3 Classic /Copy command copies all Style settings except borders. And if the destination already includes borders, /Copy doesn't write over them.

In most situations, you'll find Edit Copy and Edit Paste the easiest method to use. Since these commands use the Clipboard (see "Clipboard Basics," earlier), they also provide you with the flexibility to copy data to multiple locations, perform other operations before you paste, or even copy data to another Windows program.

By contrast, Edit Quick Copy is the least appealing of all. The dialog box constantly seems in the way (even though you can move it), and the way 1-2-3 zooms in and out when you point to the worksheet is rather irritating.

Note: You can use /Copy or Edit Quick Copy, but not Edit Copy, to copy information from a protected area of a file as long as the destination is unprotected; you can't, however, copy information to a protected area.

You can use all three methods to copy hidden information. 1-2-3 for Windows automatically displays hidden data when you point to a worksheet or select /Copy. Hidden data isn't redisplayed when you type your To and From ranges into the Edit Quick Copy text boxes. (Chapter 5 discusses protecting and hiding data.)

Copying a Single Cell to Another Cell

The most basic form of copying, from one cell to another cell, can be accomplished using Edit Copy and Edit Paste. For example, suppose in Figure 7-21A you want to copy the value in cell B1, $250.20, to cell D1. To do this:

1. Select the cell you want to copy from, B1. (Or position the cell pointer in B1.) Then choose Edit Copy or its shortcut, CTRL+INS, to copy the data to the Clipboard.

▼ *Tip:* The 🔳 icon is a shortcut for Edit Copy.

2. Select the destination, cell D1. Then copy the data from the Clipboard to this cell by using Edit Paste or SHIFT+INS, its shortcut.

▼ *Tip:* The 🔳 icon is a shortcut for Edit Paste.

As you can see in Figure 7-21B, 1-2-3 copies $250.20 from the Clipboard to D1, including the C2 (Currency, 2 places) format, bold font, shadow, and border settings. In addition, this data remains in the Clipboard until you cut or copy other data to it.

Copying a Single Cell to a Range

To copy the value $250.20, its numeric format, and Style settings from cell B1 of Figure 7-22 to *each* cell in a range, you can use either Edit Copy and Edit Paste or Edit Quick

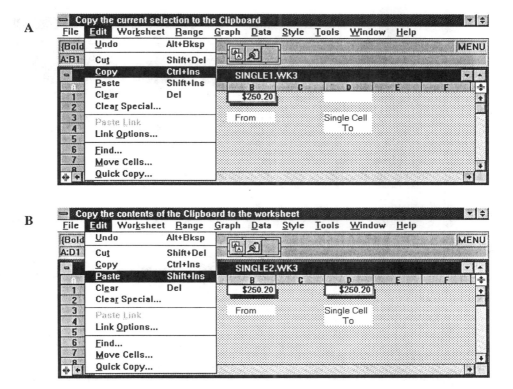

Figure 7-21 Copying a single cell to another cell

Copy. If you use the 1-2-3 Classic command, /Copy, it won't copy the borders and shadow.

To use Edit Copy and Edit Paste, select B1, then choose Edit Copy or press CTRL+INS to copy the data to the Clipboard. Next, select the range to which you want to copy the data, D1..E2, then copy the data from the Clipboard to this range by selecting Edit Paste or pressing SHIFT+INS. As you can see in Figure 7-22B, 1-2-3 copies $250.20 with its C2 format, bold font, and outline to each cell in D1..E2. Although 1-2-3 for Windows also copies the shadow to each cell, it's displayed around the entire range instead (see Chapter 6).

▼ *Tip:*   🖼   also copies data from the upper-left cell to each cell in a selected range. In Figure 7-23A, for example, try selecting the range B1..E4. Then select 🖼 . Figure 7-23B shows how 1-2-3 for Windows copies $250.20 with its C2 format, bold font, outline, and shadow from B1 to all cells in the range B1..E4.

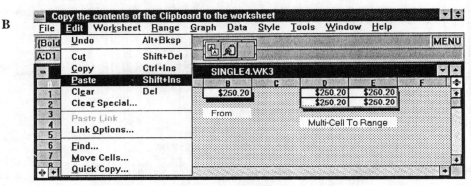

Figure 7-22 Copying a single cell to a multicell range

Copying a Single Cell to Noncontiguous Locations

Edit Copy and Edit Paste can also be used to copy the data in one cell to multiple, noncontiguous locations. For example, Figure 7-24 shows the results when the centered, bolded label in cell B1, "Year Ending," is copied first to the range D1..F1, and then to the range D5..F5.

To do this, first select B1, then copy this data to the Clipboard by choosing Edit Copy or pressing CTRL+INS. Next, select the range D1..F1 and then choose Edit Paste or press SHIFT+INS. 1-2-3 for Windows copies the data from the Clipboard to each cell in this range. When you select the range D5..F5 and press SHIFT+INS again, 1-2-3 also copies the data from the Clipboard to this range, just as in Figure 7-24. Because this data remains in the Clipboard, you can continue to use Edit Paste to copy it to other locations.

Copying a Two-Dimensional Range

In many instances, you'll want to copy a two-dimensional range to another location. Although you can use Edit Quick Copy, you'll probably prefer Edit Copy and Paste. You

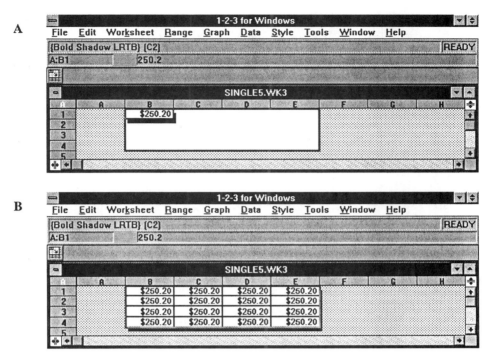

Figure 7-23 Copying data from the upper-left cell of a range

can also use the 1-2-3 Classic command, /Copy, if you don't need to copy any borders, or want to retain existing borders in the destination. (See "Copying Cell Contents, Formatting, and Styles except Borders," later in this chapter).

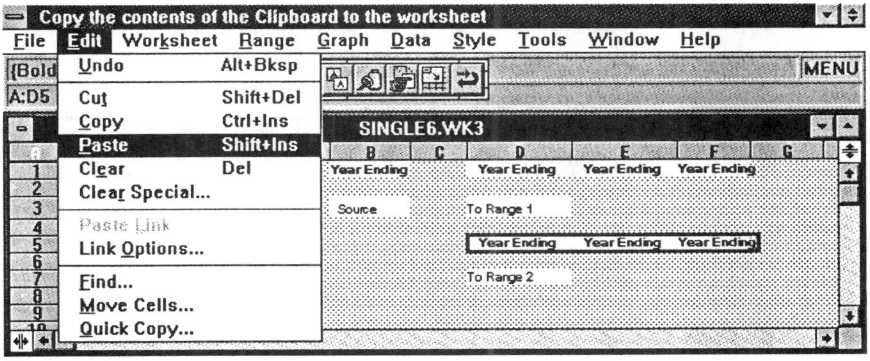

Figure 7-24 Copying a single cell to noncontiguous destinations

Suppose you want to copy the 2-D range in B1..C4 of Figure 7-25 to the range E1..F4. You can use Edit Quick Copy by following this procedure:

1. Select the Edit Quick Copy command. You'll see the dialog box shown in Figure 7-25A.

2. Specify the From range B1..C4.

▼ *Tip:* If you preselect the From range B1..C4 in Figure 7-25A and then select Edit Quick Copy, A:B1..A:C4 will automatically be displayed in the From text box, and the cursor will be located in the To text box.

3. Specify the upper-left cell of the destination in the To text box as E1. Then press ENTER or select OK to complete the command.

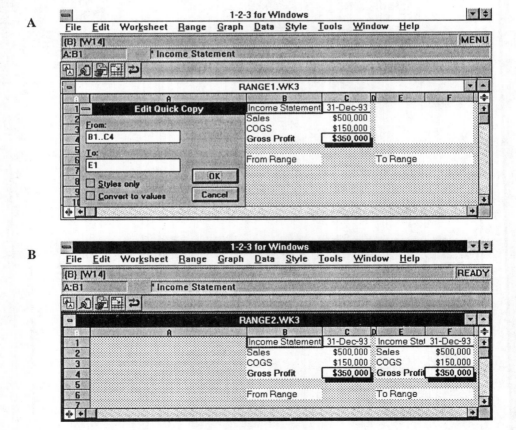

Figure 7-25 Copying a range

As you can see in Figure 7-25B, 1-2-3 for Windows copies the data from B1..C4 to the range E1..F4. 1-2-3 also copies the Date and Currency formatting, as well as the Style settings. Because the column width settings aren't copied, you'll have to widen column E yourself (see Chapter 5).

You'll also get the same result if you first copy the data to the Clipboard by selecting the range B1..C4 and pressing CTRL+INS (Edit Copy), then copy this data from the Clipboard to the destination by selecting the upper-left cell of the destination, E1. When you press SHIFT+INS (Edit Paste), 1-2-3 will copy the data beginning in cell E1, just as in Figure 7-25B.

Note: If you select a paste range *larger* than the data in the Clipboard, you'll blank out the extra cells to which data is not copied. If you select a multicell range *smaller* than the range cut to the Clipboard, Edit Paste only pastes data to the selected cells. For example, if you select the two-cell range E1..E2 in Figure 7-25B, then select Edit Paste, 1-2-3 for Windows *only* copies the label "Income Statement" with its bottom border to cell E1, and the label "Sales" to E2.

Note: Pressing ALT+BACKSPACE (Undo) or selecting the ⊇ icon immediately after completing a /Copy, Edit Quick Copy, or Edit Copy and Paste operation will restore the worksheet to its previous condition. Undo won't restore the previous Clipboard data, however.

Copying a 2-D Range to Multiple Worksheets

Either of two methods work well when you want to copy a range to back-to-back worksheets. For instance, imagine you want to copy the data in A1..B5 of worksheet A to the same position in worksheets B and C—that is, to the range B:A1..B:B5 and the range C:A1..C:B5. To do this, use Edit Quick Copy and specify From as A:A1..A:B5 and To as B:A1..C:A1, which includes the upper-left cell of each destination worksheet. The other alternative is to use Edit Copy to copy A:A1..B:B5 to the Clipboard, and then use Edit Paste once at B:A1, and again at C:A1.

Copying from a Single-Column or a Single-Row Range

When you copy a single column or a single row to a multicell destination, you can create multiple copies in the destination. For example, suppose you realize that the personnel in the North sales region shown in Figure 7-26A will remain unchanged in July and August. To copy this data, use Edit Quick Copy and specify the single-column From range, B2..B4, and the single-row To range C2..D2. (You need only specify the first cell in each column you want to copy to.) As you can see in Figure 7-26B, 1-2-3 for Windows copies the data in B2..B4 two times, to columns C and D, beginning in row 2 each time.

Note: To get the same results using Edit Copy and Paste, you must specify the entire destination C2..D4. If you select the single-row destination range C2..D2 before you use Edit Paste (SHIFT+INS), 1-2-3 copies only the value 1 to cells C2 and D2.

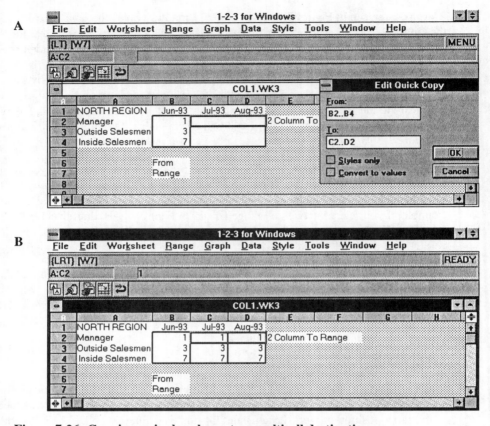

Figure 7-26   Copying a single column to a multicell destination

1-2-3 for Windows also evaluates a single-row To range in a similar manner. For instance, if you select Edit Quick Copy and specify the single-row From range A2..D2 in Figure 7-26B, and the single-column To range A8..A10, 1-2-3 will copy the information in row 2 three times: to rows 8, 9, and 10, all beginning in column A.

Note: To copy the values or labels in a column and transpose them to a row (or transpose a row to a column), see "Transposing Data" later in this chapter.

Copying Repetitively

In some cases you'll want to copy information—like headings—repeatedly in a worksheet. For example, suppose in Figure 7-27A you want to copy the form in A1..C3 down the length of the worksheet four times. Although you could use Edit Copy and then Edit Paste four times to accomplish this, using Edit Quick Copy is actually the most efficient way if you specify:

- The From range A1..C12, which includes both the data being copied and the range you want to copy to.
- The single-cell To destination within the From range, A4.

You can see the result in Figure 7-27B. 1-2-3 for Windows copies the labels in A1..C3 four more times, beginning in cell A4.

A

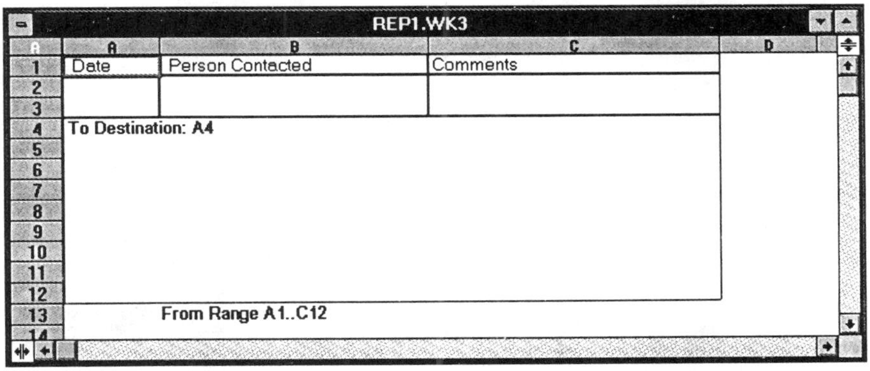

	A	B	C	D
1	Date	Person Contacted	Comments	
2				
3				
4	To Destination: A4			
5				
6				
7				
8				
9				
10				
11				
12				
13		From Range A1..C12		
14				

REP1.WK3

B

	A	B	C	D
1	Date	Person Contacted	Comments	
2				
3				
4	Date	Person Contacted	Comments	
5				
6				
7	Date	Person Contacted	Comments	
8				
9				
10	Date	Person Contacted	Comments	
11				
12				
13	Date	Person Contacted	Comments	
14				
15				
16				

REP2.WK3

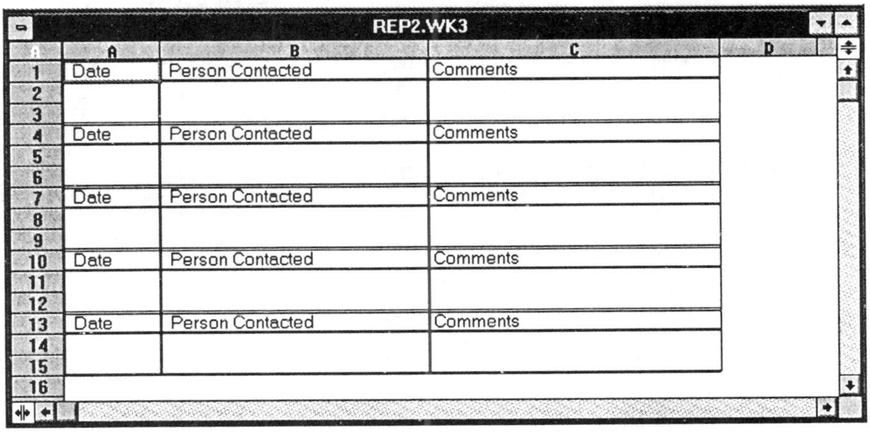

Figure 7-27 Copying repetitively

Copying a Three-Dimensional Range

You can copy information in a 3-D range (spanning more than one worksheet) using Edit Quick Copy, or Edit Copy and Paste. You can even use /Copy if you don't want to copy borders.

For example, Figure 7-28 shows what happens when you use Edit Quick Copy to copy the column headings in worksheets A, B, and C. To do this, first preselect the 3-D range by moving the cell pointer to A:A1, pressing F4 to anchor this cell, then pressing END then → to outline A:A1..A:D1. When you press CTRL+PGUP twice, 1-2-3 for Windows also outlines this range in worksheets B and C. Press ENTER to confirm. (Remember, you can't use the mouse to select a 3-D range.)

When you select Edit Quick Copy, the 3-D range A:A1..C:D1 is displayed in the From text box, just as in Figure 7-28A. Next, specify the single-cell destination A:E1. When you press ENTER or select OK, you can see in Figure 7-28B that 1-2-3 copies these headings to the range A:E1..C:H1. So even in three-dimensional space, 1-2-3 for Windows duplicates the size and shape of the From range in the destination.

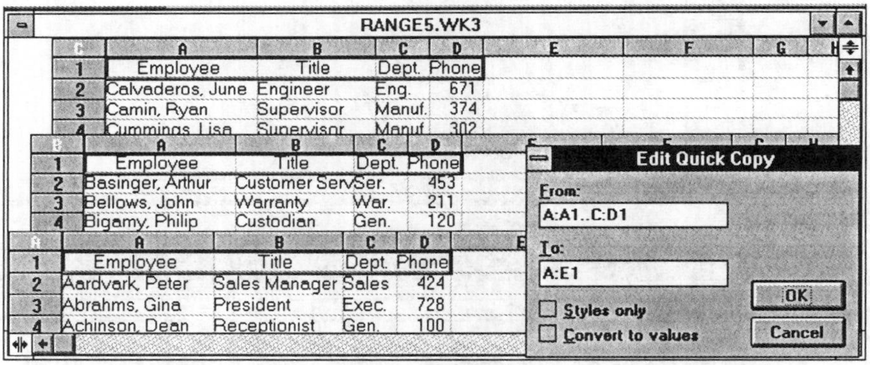

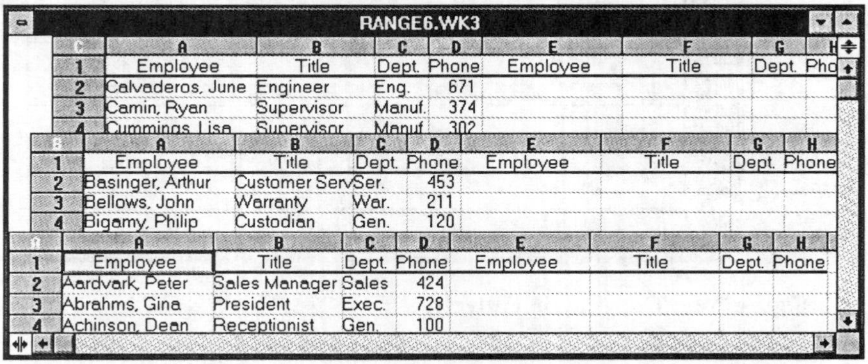

Figure 7-28 Copying a three-dimensional range

Copying Cell Contents, Formatting, and Styles Except Borders

You can use the 1-2-3 Classic command, /Copy, to copy the cell contents, formatting, and all Style settings except borders. You can even copy data and formatting to a range while retaining existing borders.

For example, consider Figure 7-29A. Suppose you use /Copy and specify the From range B2..D5, then specify cell E2 as the upper-left cell of the To range. You can see in Figure 7-29B that although 1-2-3 copies the data, formatting, and bold font to E2..G5, it doesn't copy the outlines and drop shadow.

Suppose you then reuse /Copy and again specify B2..D5 as the From range, but H2 as the single-cell To range. You can see in Figure 2-29C that 1-2-3 again copies the data, formatting, and bold font to H2..J5, but not the Style Border settings. In fact, 1-2-3 for Windows even retains the existing borders and drop shadow in the destination.

▼ *Tip:*   If you're an experienced 1-2-3 user, you may want to keep in mind these new /Copy shortcuts in 1-2-3 for Windows:

- You can point to your To and From ranges in the worksheet using the mouse.

- If you preselect a range before you select /Copy, 1-2-3 assumes it's your From range and only prompts you for a To range. If you preselect B2..D5 in Figure 7-29B, for example, and then select /Copy, you'll see the "Enter range to copy TO:" prompt. Simply type **E2** and press ENTER to complete the command.

- You can perform a copy operation without accessing the /Copy command. For example, preselect the range B2..D5. Then select 🖼 . Select the upper-left corner of the destination, cell E1, and you'll get the same results as Figure 7-29B.

Copying Only Style Settings

You can use Edit Quick Copy's Styles only option to copy just the Style settings in a range, except for label alignment. This option, however, doesn't copy column width, row height, or Range settings, such as numeric format or protection status. In effect, the Styles only option is equivalent to assigning named Style settings (see Chapter 6) to a cell or range.

You can see how the Styles only option works in Figure 7-30. The settings shown in the Edit Quick Copy dialog box—the From range B1..D5, the single-cell To, E1, and Styles only turned on—are used to copy the bold font, borders, and shadow Style settings to the range E1..G5. If you compare Figures 7-30A and B, you'll see that 1-2-3 for Windows doesn't copy the C0 (Currency, 0 places) numeric format, the right label alignment, and the [W7] column width. Note also that 1-2-3 doesn't overwrite the existing data in the destination, E1..G5.

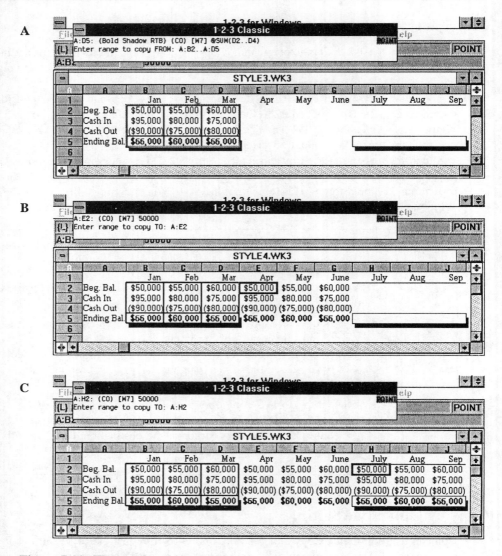

Figure 7-29 The results of /Copy

Copying between Files

As in Release 3, you can copy information between files in 1-2-3 for Windows. Although you can use Edit Quick Copy, you'll find Edit Copy and Paste the easiest method to use. (Similarly, you can use /Copy if you want to copy everything but Style Border settings.) If you are copying formulas, be sure to read "How Copying between Files Affects Cell References," later in this chapter.

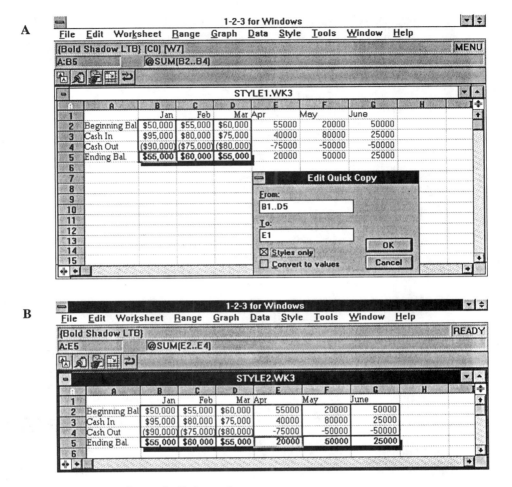

Figure 7-30 Copying only Style settings

▼ *Tip To Release 2 Users:*   Rather than using File Combine to copy between files, instead try using Edit Copy and Paste, or Edit Quick Copy, which are much simpler to use and less prone to error.

In Figure 7-31A, for example, you can copy the information in CASH1.WK3 to the same location in CASH2.WK3, the file in the right-hand window. To do this, select the data to be copied, A1..D5 in CASH1.WK3, then copy this data to the Clipboard by pressing CTRL+INS (Edit Copy). Next, select the upper-left cell of the destination, cell A1 of CASH2.WK3. (If you're using the keyboard, remember that CTRL+F6 [Next Window] will move the cell pointer to CASH2.WK3.) Then paste the data from the Clipboard by pressing SHIFT+INS (Edit Paste).

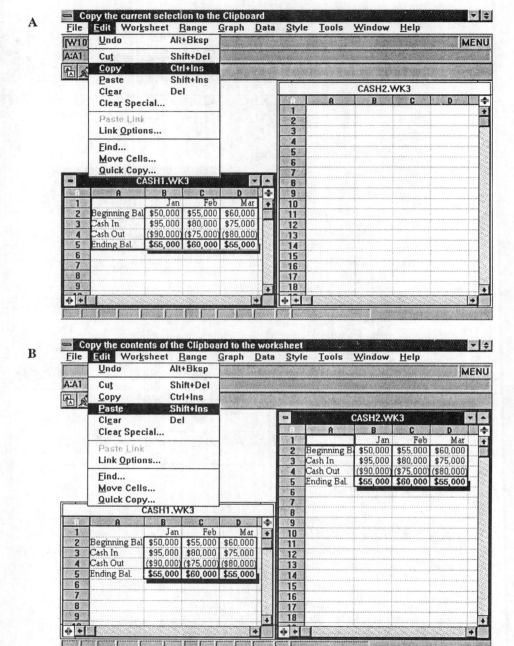

Figure 7-31 Copying between files

▼ *Tip:*   When you copy between files, you can also use the 🖻 and 🖹 icons as shortcuts for Edit Copy and Edit Paste.

As you can see in Figure 7-31B, copying information to another file produces the same results as copying data within a file. That is, all data, formatting, and Style settings in the From range in CASH1.WK3 are copied to CASH2.WK3. However, 1-2-3 doesn't copy column widths, row heights, global worksheet settings, and the like, so you'll need to adjust the width of column A in CASH2.WK3 yourself.

Note: If data is assigned a font other than the default font, then 1-2-3 for Windows copies the font setting between files. If the data to be copied is displayed in the default font, however, then the copied data takes on the default font of the destination file.

If you do decide to use Edit Quick Copy to copy the data in Figure 7-31, the easiest way to do this is to first preselect A1..D5 in CASH1.WK3. When you select Edit Quick Copy, A:A1..A:D5 will be displayed in the From text box, and the cursor will be located in the To text box. Since you can't use the keyboard to point to a range in another file from a dialog box, either type **<<CASH2>>A:A1**, or use the mouse to select A:A1 in CASH2.WK3. When you select OK, you'll get the results in Figure 7-31B.

COPYING FORMULAS

The ability to copy formulas is by far the most powerful copy feature in 1-2-3 for Windows. However, to maintain accuracy in a worksheet and yet efficiently copy data, you need an in-depth understanding of how 1-2-3 copies formulas.

Note: Within a file, Edit Quick Copy, Edit Copy and Paste, and /Copy all copy formulas in the same way.

As you know, a formula in 1-2-3 for Windows usually contains at least one cell reference, such as +B1. When you copy a formula to another location in a worksheet, or even another worksheet file, 1-2-3 automatically adjusts the cell references within a formula to account for the new location. However, 1-2-3 adjusts a cell reference differently, depending on whether the address is

- relative
- absolute
- mixed

Relative References

Although you may not be aware of it, most of the formulas you create in 1-2-3 use relative references. The formula 55+C1+@SUM(A1..A3), for example, contains relative references to C1, as well as to A1, A2, and A3 in the range A1..A3.

When you copy a formula containing a relative address, 1-2-3 for Windows automatically adjusts the cell address *relative* to the new location of the formula. To see how this works, look at cell B5 of Figure 7-32A, which contains relative references in the formula @SUM(B2..B4).

If you copy the formula in B5 across row 5 to the range C5..D5, you'll get the results shown in Figure 7-32B. Because this formula is copied across a row, 1-2-3 leaves the row component constant and only adjusts the column component. For example, because cell C5 lies one column to the right of cell B5, 1-2-3 adjusts the column component by 1 so that C5 contains the formula @SUM(C2..C4).

Figure 7-32 also contains the formula @SUM(B2..D2) in cell E2. If you copy it down column E to the range E3..E4, 1-2-3 adjusts the row component but not the column component. For example, if you look at the contents box of Figure 7-32C, you'll see that cell E4 contains the formula @SUM(B4..D4). Because cell E4 is two rows down from cell E2, 1-2-3 adjusts the row component of each relative reference by 2.

1-2-3 for Windows also adjusts the worksheet component when you copy a relative reference to another worksheet. In Figure 7-33, the formula in A:E2, @SUM(B2..D2), is copied to cell B:E2. As you can see in the contents box, the result is that cell B:E2 also contains @SUM(B2..D2). This formula references cells in worksheet B, however, not worksheet A, because 1-2-3 automatically adjusts the worksheet component. (Chapter 2 discusses when 1-2-3 includes the worksheet component in a cell address.)

Problems with Relative References

By using relative references, you can easily copy a formula to many other locations in a worksheet file, saving yourself substantial time and effort in the process. But you'll also create substantial errors if you use relative references incorrectly.

Most often, a relative reference causes an error when it is copied to a cell in a different column and row. For example, imagine you are going to fulfill your lifelong dream and open a sub shop called Hogan's Heros. In Figure 7-34A you want to create projections for the first six months. Because you predict that sales will increase 5% monthly, February's food sales of $6,300 are calculated as +C2*B5 in cell D2, or January's food sales of $6,000 times 1.05.

However, if you copy this formula to cells E2 and D3, Figure 7-34B shows that you get incorrect results. In cell E2, the formula +D2*C5 correctly references the $6,300 February sales in D2, but C5 incorrectly references the $10,000 Total Sales in January. On the other hand, the formula in cell D3, +C3*B6, correctly references the January Sales of $3,000 in C3, but incorrectly references blank cell B6.

1-2-3 for Windows' solution to this problem is *absolute* addressing. By using absolute addressing, you can maintain the B5 reference to the growth rate when the formula +C2*B5 is copied anywhere in a worksheet.

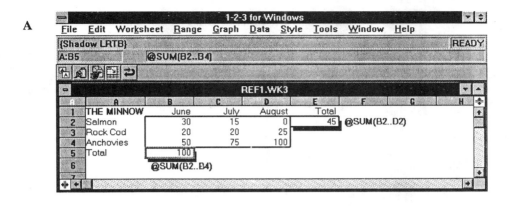

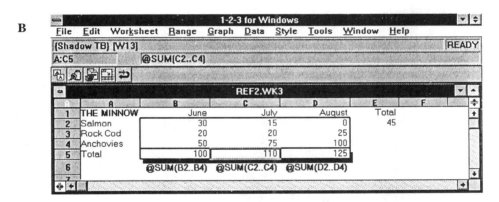

Figure 7-32   Copying a relative reference

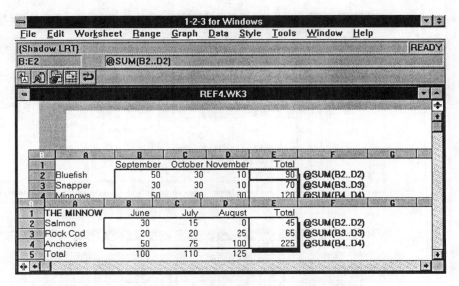

Figure 7-33   Copying a relative reference to another worksheet

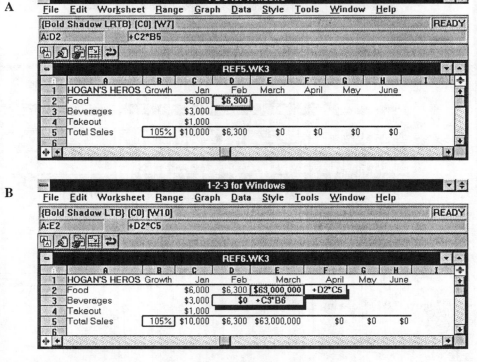

Figure 7-34   Incorrectly copying a relative reference

Absolute References

An *absolute reference*, which is the opposite of a relative reference, remains the same no matter where you copy it. You can create an absolute reference in either of two ways:

- By typing a dollar sign before each component of the cell reference (the worksheet, the column letter, and the row number), such as $A:$B$10 or $C:$AZ$105.

- By pressing ABS (F4) to have 1-2-3 enter the dollar signs for you automatically (see "Using ABS (F4)," later).

A true absolute reference, such as $A:$C$7, freezes the worksheet, column, and row component. But if you enter or copy $A:$C$7 anywhere in worksheet A, 1-2-3 converts it to the abbreviated cell address $C$7. The worksheet component is still frozen, however. When you copy it to another worksheet, worksheet C perhaps, 1-2-3 again displays it as $A:$C$7.

To see when to use an absolute address, let's return to Hogan's Heros sub shop. Figure 7-35A differs from Figure 7-34 because the formula in cell D2, +C2*$B$5, uses the absolute reference $B$5. (Remember, 1-2-3 drops the worksheet component when the location of the formula and the cell it addresses are in the same worksheet.) When you

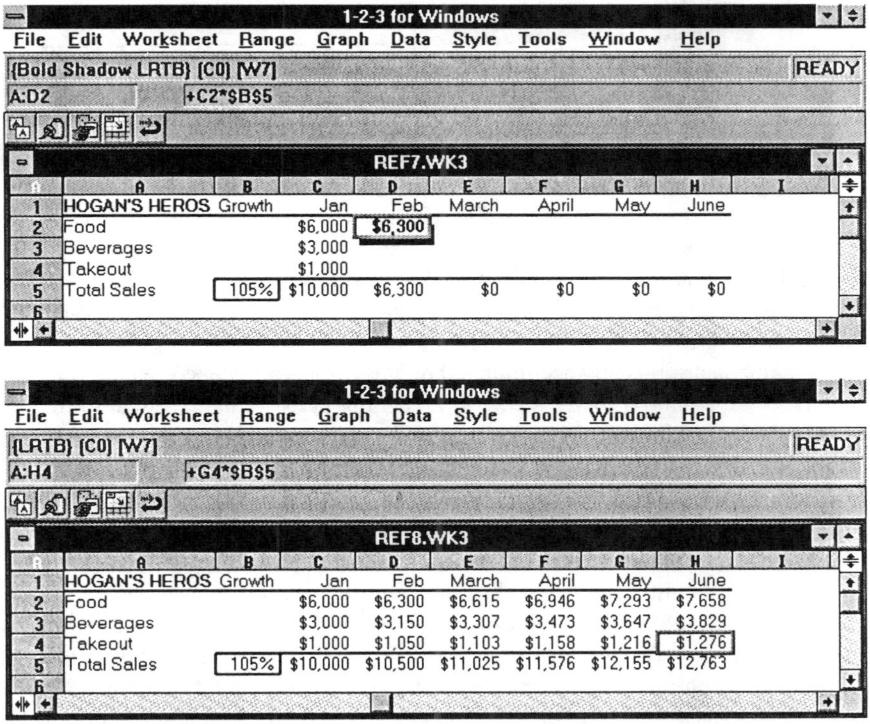

Figure 7-35 Copying an absolute reference

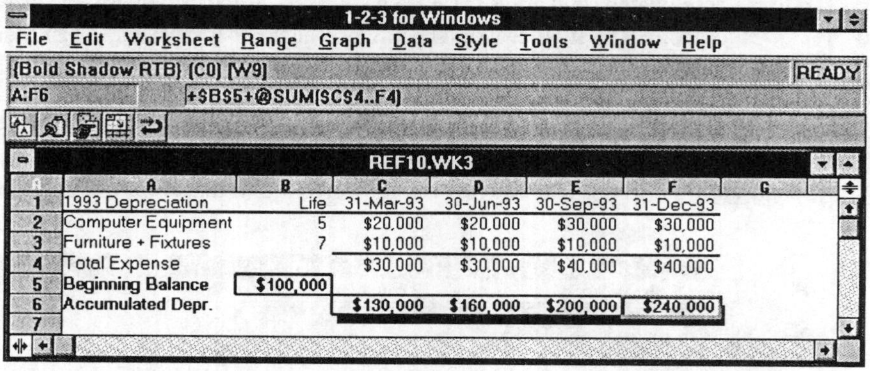

Figure 7-36 Creating a running totals

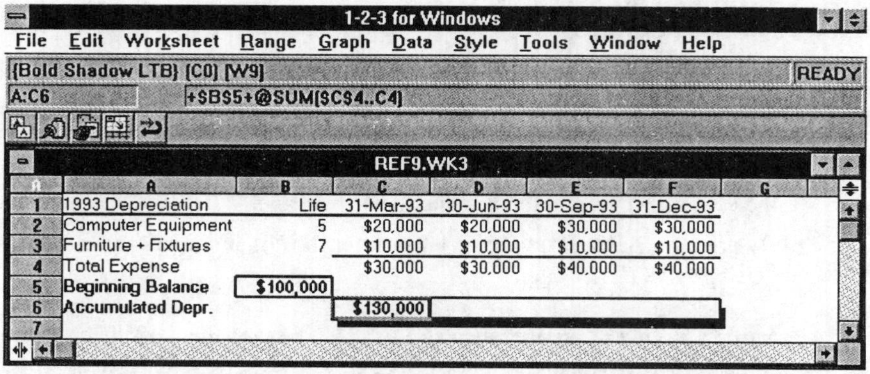

copy this formula to the range D2..H4, the absolute reference is copied to all cells in this range. For example, if you look at the contents box in Figure 7-35B, you'll see that cell H4 contains the formula +G4*$B$5. Therefore, the $1,275 June Takeout sales are computed as the $1,216 May Takeout sales times the 105% growth rate.

Absolute references are also used to create *running totals* for balance sheet items like retained earnings and accumulated depreciation, or even to create a running checkbook balance. Running totals is simply an ending period balance equal to the current period balance plus the accumulated balance for prior periods.

For example, to keep a running or year-to-date total of the accumulated depreciation in Figure 7-36A, first enter +$B$5+@SUM($C$4..C4) in cell C6. As you can see in the contents box, this formula uses the absolute address +$B$5 to freeze the accumulated depreciation beginning balance of $100,000. Additionally, the range reference, $C$4..C4, contains both an absolute and relative reference.

Figure 7-36B shows the results of copying this formula from C6 to the range D6..F6. For example, the contents box shows that cell F6 contains +$B$5+@SUM($C$4..F4). Although the absolute references $B$5 and $C$4 remain fixed, the relative range reference changes to F4. So the $240,000 ending accumulated depreciation in 1993 is calculated as the beginning $100,000 balance in cell B5 plus the total 1993 depreciation expense in the range C4..F4.

Mixed References

A *mixed reference*, as its name implies, includes both relative and absolute components in the same cell address. For example, the mixed reference A:A$1 keeps the row component fixed when you copy the reference to another cell but lets the worksheet and column components vary. On the other hand, +$A:$A1 freezes the worksheet and column components but lets the row component change.

Note: See "Using ABS (F4)," next, to create a mixed address.

Mixed cell references are a godsend when you create a financial model. For example, the model in Figure 7-37 calculates Hogan's Heros food, beverage, and takeout sales as a percentage of total projected sales. In cell C4, the formula +$B4*C$2 computes January Food sales. You can calculate the remaining sales by copying this formula to the range C4..H6. When you do so:

- The $B4 reference keeps column B fixed while allowing the row to vary—it always refers to $B4 in row 4, $B5 in row 5, and $B6 in row 6.

- The C$2 reference keeps row 2 fixed, but lets the column change. Therefore, it always refers to the corresponding sales value in row 2; for instance, the reference is always D$2 in column D.

For example, the contents box in Figure 7-37B shows that cell H6 contains +$B6*H$2. June Takeout sales, then, are calculated as 10% of the $12,763 Total Sales in June, or $1,276.

Using ABS (F4)

Rather than typing $ signs, you can use the ABS (F4) key to create absolute and mixed references while typing a reference (VALUE mode), pointing to a reference (POINT mode), or editing a formula (EDIT mode).

For example, imagine in cell B2 that you type + and then point to cell A1. 1-2-3 for Windows enters POINT mode, and displays +A:A1 in the contents box. If you press ABS (F4), 1-2-3 automatically converts it to +$A:$A$1. You can continue to press ABS (F4) repeatedly and cycle through these cell references:

Press ABS (F4)	Formula	Cell Address	Worksheet	Column	Row
Once	+$A:$A$1	Absolute	Fixed	Fixed	Fixed
Twice	+$A:A$1	Mixed	Fixed	Changes	Fixed
Three times	+$A:$A1	Mixed	Fixed	Fixed	Changes
Four times	+$A:A1	Mixed	Fixed	Changes	Changes
Five times	+A:$A$1	Mixed	Changes	Fixed	Fixed

(continued)

Press ABS (F4)	Formula	Cell Address	Worksheet	Column	Row
Six times	+A:A$1	Mixed	Changes	Changes	Fixed
Seven times	+A:$A1	Mixed	Changes	Fixed	Fixed
Eight times	+A:A1	Relative	Changes	Changes	Changes

To accept the address you choose, either press ENTER or click on the Confirm (✔) icon in the contents box.

You can also use ABS (F4) while in EDIT mode to change the cell references in an existing formula. For instance, in cell B2 you can press EDIT (F2) or click on the contents box to edit the existing formula +A1*A2. To change the address of A1, position the cursor anywhere on or near it, or press HOME and then → twice. If you then press ABS (F4) twice, for example, the formula will appear as +$A:A$1*A2. You can either accept this formula, or move to the A2 reference and use ABS (F4) to change its type of address.

With range references, ABS (F4) doesn't always work the way you want it to, because 1-2-3 for Windows always converts both cell addresses to the same type of

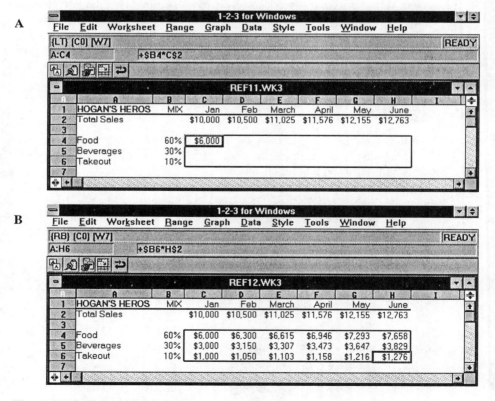

Figure 7-37   Using mixed references

reference. For example, pressing ABS (F4) once converts @SUM(A1..A3) to @SUM($A:$A$1..$A:$A$3); press ABS (F4) again and it becomes @SUM($A:A$1..$A:A$3). To use different types of references, like @SUM($A:$A$1..A:A3), you have to manually insert or delete the dollar signs.

ABS (F4) has an even bigger problem with range names. For instance, imagine the range name OLD is assigned to A:A3..A:A10, and you enter @SUM(OLD) in a cell. When you press ABS (F4), 1-2-3 shows @SUM($OLD) in the contents box, the equivalent of @SUM($A:$A$3..$A:$A$10). Press ABS (F4) a second time, and it appears as @SUM(OLD) again. Therefore, don't use range names unless an absolute or relative range reference will work.

How Copying Between Files Affects Cell References

Note: See also "Copying Between Files," earlier.

When you copy a formula from one file to another, 1-2-3 for Windows adjusts cell references to refer to the destination file. For instance, if you copy +$A:$B$1 from cell A1 of the open file SALES.WK3 to cell C1 of another open file, PROFIT.WK3, the resulting absolute reference +$A:$B$1 refers to A:B1 in the destination file (PROFIT.WK3), not SALES.WK3.

Copying relative and mixed cell references between files also produces cell references that refer to the destination file. However, the cell references are adjusted in the usual way to reflect the new location in the worksheet. For instance, imagine that cell A1 in SALES.WK3 contains the formula +B1, which you copy to cell C1 of PROFIT.WK3. The resulting formula, +D1, references cell D1 in PROFIT.WK3, not SALES.WK3.

How Copying Affects Cell References in Link Formulas

When you copy a formula that links worksheet files (see Chapters 4 and 17), the result you get depends on whether the formula contains an absolute or relative address as well as whether you use Edit Quick Copy, /Copy, or Edit Copy and Paste.

For example, suppose cell A1 of the active file TEENY contains the formula +<<BUDGET>>A:A1, linking the TEENY and BUDGET files. Now imagine you copy this link formula, which contains the relative reference A:A1, to cell A:B1 in the file TINY.

If you use /Copy or Edit Quick Copy, the result is <<BUDGET>>A:B1..A:B1. (1-2-3 for Windows always converts it to a range address.) Although this formula now links TINY and BUDGET, 1-2-3 adjusts the BUDGET cell reference relative to its new location in TINY. You'll get the same result when you copy +<<BUDGET>>SALES, when cell A:A1 of BUDGET is assigned the relative range name SALES. Because 1-2-3 first converts SALES to its relative cell reference A:A1, the result is again +<<BUDGET>>A:B1..A:B1.

Imagine you use /Copy or Edit Quick Copy to copy the link formula +<<BUDGET>>$A:$A$1, which contains an absolute address, from cell A:A1 of TEENY to any cell in TINY. You'll get <<BUDGET>>$A:$A$1..$A$1, which links

BUDGET and TINY. Similarly, when A:A1 of BUDGET is assigned the range name SALES, copying +<<BUDGET>>$SALES from TINY to any cell in TEENY produces +<<BUDGET>>$SALES.

By contrast, Edit Copy and Paste don't adjust a cell reference when you copy a link formula that contains either a relative or absolute cell address. Instead, the result is always as if you had copied an absolute address. Copy +<<BUDGET>>$A:$A$1..$A:$A$1 from cell A1 of TEENY to cell A:B1 of TINY, and the result is +<<BUDGET>>$A:$A1..AA1; copy +<<BUDGET>>A:A1..A:A1, and the result is +<<BUDGET>>A:A1..A:A1. You'll get similar results when cell A:A1 of BUDGET is assigned the range name SALES. Copy +<<BUDGET>>SALES from A:A1 of TEENY to cell A:B1 of TINY, and the result is +<<BUDGET>>SALES; copy +<<BUDGET>>$SALES, and you'll get +<<BUDGET>>$SALES.

Copying Formulas as Values

The 1-2-3 Classic equivalent is /Range Value. This command, however, doesn't copy Style Border settings.

You can use Edit Quick Copy to copy the values and labels returned by formulas, rather than the underlying formulas themselves. Because this allows you to take a "snapshot" of data at a particular moment, you'll find Edit Quick Copy useful in scenario generation, or to decrease memory consumption in a large file.

Many times when you build a financial model, you'll want to run multiple scenarios, then compare the results. By copying the results in one scenario as values and labels to another location, you can then run a second scenario.

For instance, imagine that you plan to open a manufacturing business. Figure 7-38 contains the first year's projections, which assumes $100,000 sales in the first quarter. The current scenario assumes that sales will aggressively grow by 100% each quarter—the assumption in B3—and that cost of goods sold (COGS) is 50% of the sales price—the assumption in B4. Quarterly overhead expenses of $500,000 are assumed for the first six months, decreasing to $300,000 thereafter.

Note: If recalculation is set to manual, be sure to press CALC (F9) before you use Edit Quick Copy, or you may not copy current values.

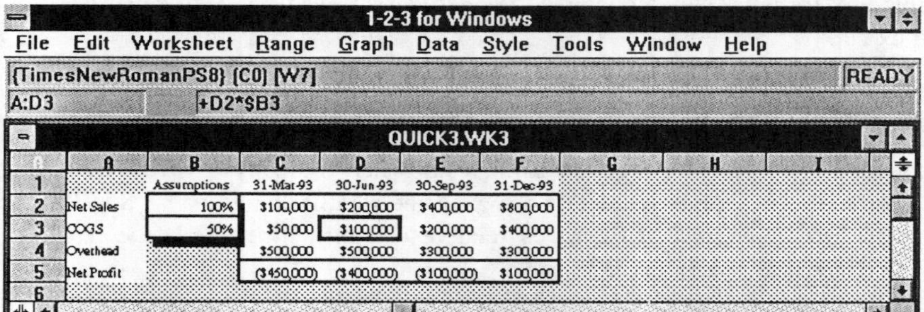

Figure 7-38   A worksheet containing formulas

To compare two scenarios, you first need to create worksheet B (see Chapter 1), then copy the results currently in worksheet A as labels and values to worksheet B. To do this, select Edit Quick Copy and specify the settings shown in the dialog box in Figure 7-39—the range you want to convert to values, A:A1..A:F5, in the From text box, and To as B:A1, the upper-left cell of the destination. Then turn on the Convert to values option before you select OK.

Figure 7-39 shows how 1-2-3 for Windows copies the resulting values and labels, beginning in cell B:A1. Although worksheets A and B appear identical, if you look at the contents box you'll see that worksheet B doesn't contain underlying formulas. You can also see that 1-2-3 for Windows copies the shading, but not the borders and drop shadow.

Note: Edit Undo (ALT+BACKSPACE) or the ⮌ icon will reverse the effects of Edit Quick Copy if used immediately after the command is completed.

Because the formulas in worksheet A are still intact, you can now run a second scenario by changing the quarterly sales growth in A:B2 to 85% and the COGS in A:B3 to 30% of sales. As you can see in Figure 7-40, you can now easily compare the "frozen" values in worksheet B to the dynamic ones in worksheet A.

▼ *Tip:*   To convert a formula in a single cell to its underlying value, select the cell, press EDIT (F2), CALC (F9), and then either press ENTER or click on the Confirm (✔) icon in the input line.

You can also use Edit Quick Copy to decrease memory consumption in a large file. Because literal values require less memory than formulas, memory consumption de-

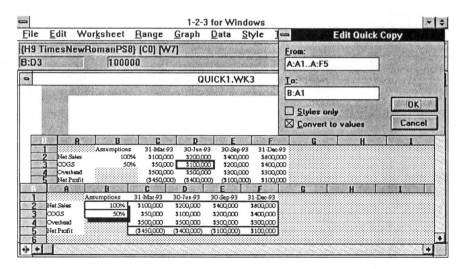

Figure 7-39 The results of copying formulas as values

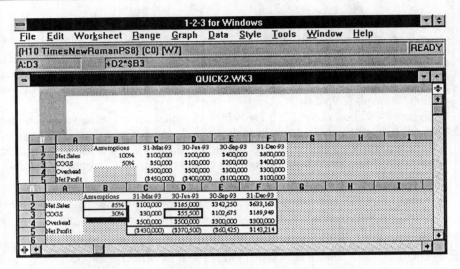

Figure 7-40 Comparing two scenarios

creases when you convert formulas to values in their current location. To do so, use Edit Quick Copy, specify the *same* To and From ranges, and turn on the Convert to values option.

TRANSPOSING VALUES AND LABELS

1-2-3 for Windows' Range Transpose command lets you *transpose*, or change the orientation—from rows to columns for example—of a range of values as you copy it to a new location. As in Release 3, you can transpose two- or three-dimensional ranges, even between two open files.

Like the Edit Quick Copy command's Convert to values option, Range Transpose *always* converts formulas to their underlying values in the new location. Range Transpose also copies formats set with the Range command to the new location, and all Style settings except borders.

Transposing a Two-Dimensional Range

In 1-2-3 for Windows, you can transpose a two-dimensional range from

- Rows to columns.
- Columns to two or more worksheets.
- Rows to two or more worksheets.

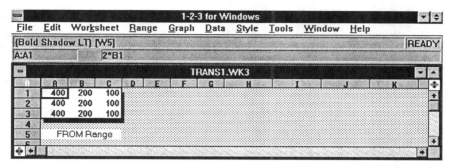

Figure 7-41 A 2-D range containing formulas and values

For example, in Figure 7-41 cell C1 contains the value 100, B1 the formula 2*C1, and as you can see in the contents box, cell A1 contains the formula 2*B1. Rows 2 and 3 contain similar formulas. Let's transpose this range A1..C3 using each of these orientations, and examine the results.

From Rows to Columns

Unless you tell it otherwise, 1-2-3 for Windows automatically transposes each row to a column. For instance, suppose you select Range Transpose, and in the dialog box shown in Figure 7-42, you specify the From range to be transposed as A1..C3, and the single cell To destination as E1. (Don't let the From and To ranges overlap, or you'll lose data.)

Caution: If recalculation is set to manual, be sure to press CALC (F9) so values are current before you transpose a range. Additionally, if the range to be transposed contains link formulas (see Chapter 4), use File Administration Update Links to update the linked values.

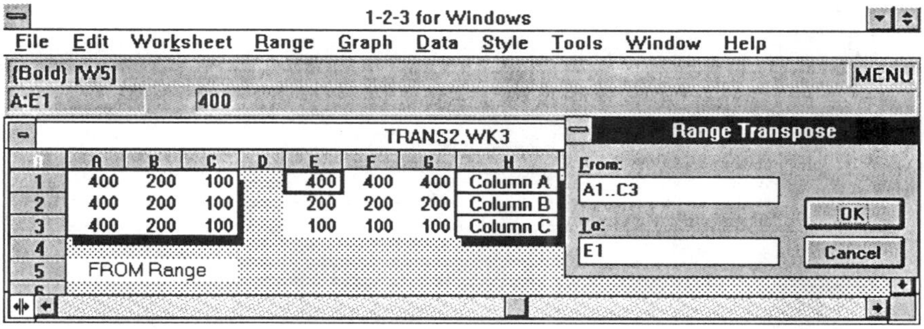

Figure 7-42 Transposing a 2-D range

When you select OK, 1-2-3 transposes the range A1..C3 to the range E1..G3. The first From column A1..A3 is transposed to the first row E1..G1, the second From column B1..B3 to the second row E2..G2, and the third From column C1..C3 to the third row E3..G3. The transposed range E1..G3 only contains values; the formulas themselves are not copied. You can see this by comparing the contents box in Figure 7-41, which shows that A1 contains the formula 2*B1, with the contents box in Figure 7-42, which shows that the corresponding data transposed in E1 is 400, the resulting value of this formula.

Note: Pressing ALT+BACKSPACE (Undo) or selecting the ⏎ icon immediately after a completed Range Transpose command will restore a worksheet to its previous condition.

From Columns to Worksheets

1-2-3 for Windows also lets you transpose each column in a 2-D range to a column in a separate worksheet. For example, Figure 7-43 shows the results when you specify A1..C3 as the From range, the 3-D To destination A:E1..C:E1, and turn on the Columns/Worksheet option in the second Range Transpose dialog box. (You must specify a 3-D To range, or 1-2-3 won't display the second dialog box.) As you can see, the first From column A1..A3 is transposed to column E in worksheet A, the second From column B1..B3 to column E in worksheet B, and the third From column, C1..C3, to column E in worksheet C.

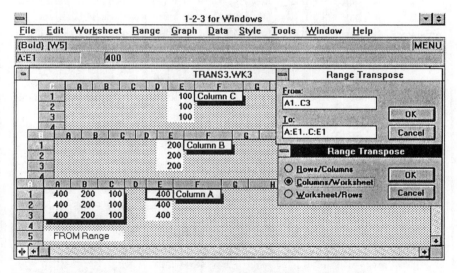

Figure 7-43 Transposing a 2-D range using Columns/Worksheet

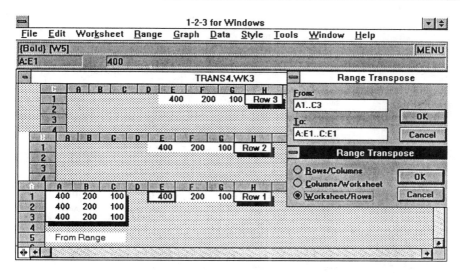

Figure 7-44 Transposing a 2-D range using Worksheet/Rows

From Rows to Worksheets

You can also transpose each row in a 2-D range to a row in a separate worksheet. For example, suppose you again select Range Transpose and specify A1..C3 in Figure 7-44 as the From range, the 3-D To destination A:E1..C:E1, but you turn on the Worksheet/Rows option. (You must specify a 3-D To range, or 1-2-3 won't display the second dialog box.) Figure 7-44 shows the results. In this case, 1-2-3 for Windows transposes the first From row A1..C1 to row 1 in worksheet A, beginning in E1, the second From row A2.C2 to row 1 in worksheet B, beginning in E1, and the third From row A3..C3 to row 1 of worksheet C, also beginning in E1.

Transposing a Three-Dimensional Range

You can also transpose a 3–D range to another 3–D range. You'll get varying results, however, depending on whether you choose a Rows/Columns, Columns/Worksheet, or a Worksheet/Rows orientation.

For example, suppose you use Range Transpose and specify the 3-D From range A:A1..C:C3 in Figure 7-45, and the single-cell To destination A:E1. (When you specify a 3-D From range, 1-2-3 will display the second dialog box even if you don't specify a 3-D To range.) Now let's select the different transpositions displayed in the second Range Transpose dialog box, and examine the results.

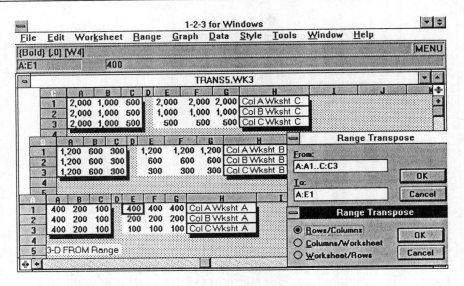

Figure 7-45 Transposing a 3-D range using Rows/Columns

From Rows to Columns

If you accept the Rows/Columns option (the default) you can see the results in Figure 7-45. Each worksheet in the 3-D From range is treated as a separate 2-D range—each column in worksheet A is transposed to a row in worksheet A, the first To worksheet, each column in worksheet B is transposed to a row in worksheet B, and so on.

From Columns to Worksheets

Figure 7-46 shows how this same 3-D range is transposed using the Columns/Worksheet option. The first column of each worksheet in the From range, column A, is transposed to a column in the first To worksheet, worksheet A. Likewise, the second column in each From worksheet, column B, is transposed to a column in the second worksheet, worksheet B, and column C in each From worksheet is transposed to a column in worksheet C.

From Rows to Worksheets

Finally, Figure 7-47 shows what happens when you turn on the Worksheet/Rows option. The first row in each worksheet in the From range, row 1, is transposed to a row in the first To worksheet, worksheet A, the second row in each From worksheet, row 2, is transposed to a row in a second worksheet, worksheet B, and so on.

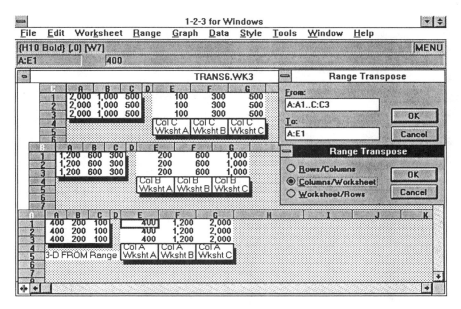

Figure 7-46 Transposing a 3-D range using Columns/Worksheet

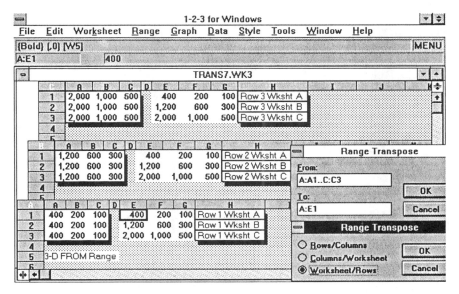

Figure 7-47 Transposing a 3-D range using Worksheet/Rows

8

Printing

With 1-2-3 for Windows, you can produce some spectacular-looking printed output. In fact, if you have a graphics printer, 1-2-3 provides an almost WYSIWYG (What You See Is What You Get) relationship between what is displayed on your screen and what comes out on your printer.

This chapter brings you up to date on all of 1-2-3's printing features. It begins with a basic overview of the printing process. It then goes on to show you how to take advantage of 1-2-3's page-layout features, including headers and footers, margin control, and much more. It also shows you how to use the Preview utility, which lets you see how your print job will look before it is actually printed. In addition, this chapter shows you how to save and name the current print settings so that you can use them in the future with just a few clicks of the mouse. Finally, the chapter concludes with a discussion of fonts and printing.

Note: This chapter assumes you have already installed a printer for use with Windows. It also assumes that you are familiar with managing the Windows printer driver for your particular make and model of printer. If these topics are foreign to you, you may want to take a moment to scan the pertinent chapters in the *Microsoft Windows User's Guide*. Having a good working knowledge of how to install and configure a printer for use with Windows will help you to get the most from this chapter.

PRINTING FUNDAMENTALS

The 1-2-3 Classic equivalent for the File Print command is a combination of the /Print Printer Range and /Print Printer Go commands.

Printing your data from 1-2-3 for Windows is a snap. For example, suppose you want to print the data in the range A:A1..A:G14 of Figure 8-1. To do this, simply select the File Print command. 1-2-3 displays the dialog box shown in Figure 8-2. In the Ranges(s) text box, specify the range name or address of the range you want to print (in this case, A:A1..A:G14). When you're ready, select OK. 1-2-3 begins sending the data in the range you've specified to the default printer currently in use by 1-2-3. That's all there is to it. (See "Printer Control" later for more on selecting a default printer for use with 1-2-3.)

Note: You can also access the File Print dialog box by selecting the Printer Smart Icon 🖨 from the 1-2-3 for Windows' icon bar.

To indicate that a print job is underway, 1-2-3 for Windows displays the dialog box in Figure 8-3. You'll notice this dialog box shows the destination for the current print job along with a Cancel push button. You can stop the printing process at any time by selecting this button. Of course, any data processed before you select Cancel will be sent on to your printer, but further progress on the current print job is halted.

Note: The Page Setup and Preview buttons in the File Print dialog box give you access to 1-2-3's page-layout features and the Preview utility. These are covered later in this chapter under "Page Layout Options" and "Using the Preview Utility," respectively.

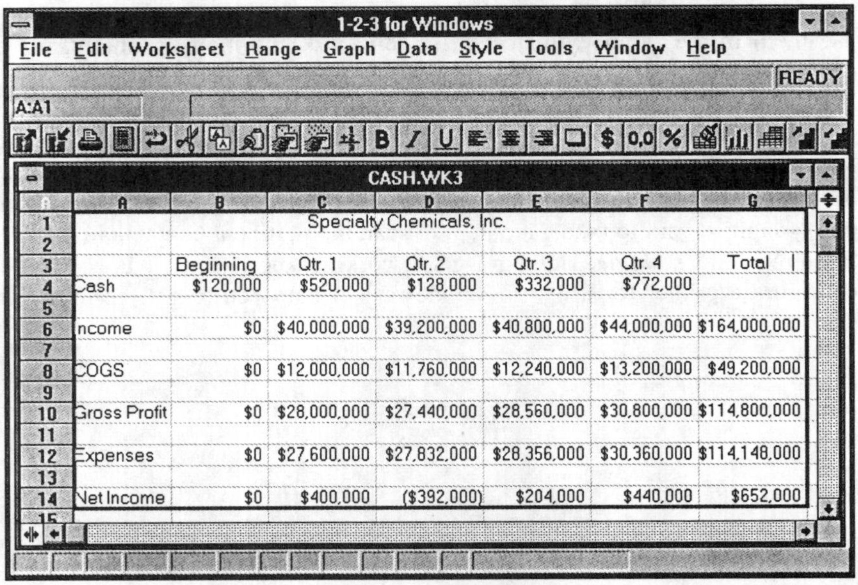

Figure 8-1 A sample worksheet range for printing

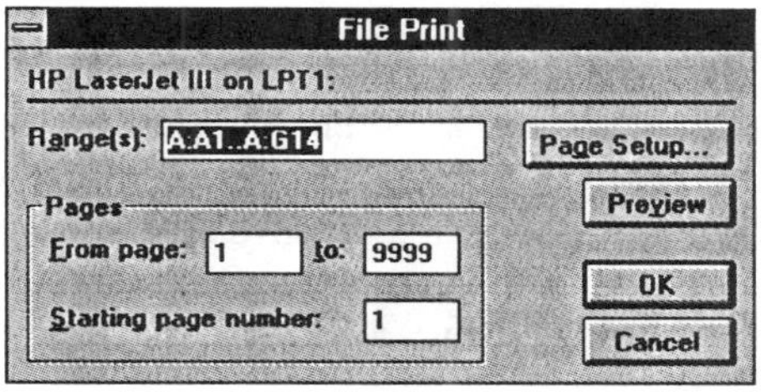

File Print

HP LaserJet III on LPT1:

Range(s): [A:A1..A:G14]   Page Setup...

Pages
From page: [1]   to: [9999]   Preview

Starting page number: [1]   OK

Cancel

Figure 8-2   The File Print dialog box

When you print from 1-2-3 for Windows, all activity is temporarily suspended until the print job is completed. If the current print range contains multiple fonts or graphics images, this process may take quite some time. However, by virtue of the Windows Print Manager, you can print several jobs—one right after the other—and keep wait time down to a minimum.

▼ *Tip:*   Printing to a parallel port—for example, LPT1—rather than a serial port can often speed up the printing process, especially if you're printing a complex image that involves multiple fonts and graphics images.

The example above demonstrates printing from 1-2-3 in its most basic form. As you'll soon see, you can do more with 1-2-3's printing features than simply send a range of data to your printer. For example, you can use 1-2-3's page-layout options to embellish your print job with headers and footers. Headers and footers let you print custom text, and possibly a date or page number, at the top or bottom of each page. You can also control the positioning of the printed output on the page either by modifying the current margins or by using 1-2-3's compression feature. You can even print in landscape mode (sideways) if your printer supports this feature.

Before jumping into page-layout options, though, the next four sections explain more about basic printing skills. For example, you'll learn about the following topics:

- Selecting a range to print
- Printing part of a report
- How 1-2-3 breaks up a large report into pages automatically
- Using the Preview utility
- Controlling where 1-2-3 breaks your printed pages

Figure 8-3   1-2-3 for Windows indicates a print job is underway

Tips on Selecting a Print Range

You can specify a range to print either before or after you select the File Print command. If you specify a range beforehand, 1-2-3 will display that range in the Ranges(s) box of the File Print dialog box (Figure 8-2). Conversely, when you select the File Print command, the Range(s) text box is activated automatically and shows the current location of the cell pointer. At this point, you can select a range to print with either the mouse or the keyboard.

You can also use a range name to specify a range to print, if you so desire. Simply type the range name that defines the range you want to print in the Range(s) text box. Or, while the Range(s) box is active, press NAME (F3) to select from a list of existing range names.

To indicate the current print range, 1-2-3 displays a dotted, gray line around it. In addition, once you specify a print range, 1-2-3 remembers that range for the balance of the current session or until you change it. In fact, 1-2-3 will show you that same range specification in the Range(s) box the next time you select the File Print command. And, if you save a file containing a defined print range, 1-2-3 will show you that same print range the next time you load the file.

You can also specify a collection of ranges in the Range(s) text box, separated by commas. When you do this, 1-2-3 sends each range from the collection to your printer in the order in which you selected or specified them. For example, you might specify a collection of ranges as follows:

```
A:A1..A:G14,PRINT1,A:A17..C:G34
```

where A:A1..A:G14 is a two-dimensional range in worksheet A, PRINT1 is a range name that defines a range somewhere in the current file, and A:A17..C:G34 is a three-dimensional range. (See "Printing a 3-D Range" later for more details on printing a 3-D range.)

Note: If your print range includes a long label—a label that is wider than the current column and overlaps into adjacent columns—make sure you include the entire label in your print-range specification. Otherwise, the label will be truncated (cut off) when printed.

Deciding Which Pages to Print

When you print a report that covers more than a single page, 1-2-3 breaks that report up into individual pages. (The next section gives you more details as to how this is done.) Each page in your printout is automatically assigned a sequential number from 1 to 9,999. As you'll soon see, 1-2-3 lets you begin and end printing on specific pages.

To specify which pages are to be printed, use the From page: and to: boxes in the Pages section of the File Print dialog box (Figure 8-2). By default, the From page: box contains 1 and to: box contains 9999, meaning the entire report will be printed. Suppose, however, you want to begin printing on page 2 and end printing on page 7. To do this, type **2** in the From page: box and **7** in the to: box. When you select OK to begin printing, only pages 2 through 7 of the current report will be printed.

Note: The Starting page number box in the Pages section of the File Print dialog box lets you define the page number that will be printed on the first page of a report. Essentially, this allows you to override 1-2-3's default page number assignment when printing. This option is useful when you have defined either headers or footers that contain page numbers. For example, you might want to start printing on page 7 but you want page number 1 to appear on that page. See "Headers and Footers" later for a description of how to create page numbers for a printed report.

Printing a Large Range

When you print a large range (a range that is wider or longer than a single page), 1-2-3 for Windows breaks that range up into individual pages. 1-2-3 for Windows determines the amount of data that will fit on each page by using a combination of the column widths and row heights in the print range as well as the current top, bottom, left, and right margin settings. The margin settings determine the amount of white space between the edges of the paper and your document.

Normally, 1-2-3 for Windows measures margins in inches. You can also specify millimeters, if you so desire. The default setting for the top, bottom, left, and right margins is 0.5 inch measured from the edge of the paper to the edge of your document. See "Controlling Margins" later in this chapter for information on how to change 1-2-3's margin settings.

1-2-3 for Windows prints the data in the print range in sets of columns, working from left to right. The number of columns that will fit across each page is determined by the width of the columns in the print range as well as the left and right margin settings. 1-2-3 will complete printing the data in the first set of columns before moving on to the next set of columns, and so on.

1-2-3 also uses the number of rows in the print range to determine where to end one page and start the next. The number of rows of data that will fit on each page is determined by a combination of the row heights in the print range as well as the top and bottom margin settings.

For example, Figure 8-4 shows a worksheet that encompasses the range A:A1..A:U96. Figure 8-5 shows that same worksheet printed with 1-2-3's default column-width, row-height, and margin settings. Notice that the upper-left portion of the worksheet is printed on page 1, the lower-left portion on page 2, the upper-right portion on page 3, and the lower-right portion on page 4. In this example, 1-2-3 for Windows prints the first 6 columns and 50 rows of the print range on page 1. It completes printing the data in the first six columns on page 2 before starting with the next set of columns in the print range, which are printed on pages 3 and 4.

▼ *Tip:*   When you define a print range that encompasses multiple pages, 1-2-3 will show you each page by surrounding its columns and rows with a dotted grey line. In addition, 1-2-3 will show you the page number associated with the current cell in the format line at the top of your screen—for example, Page 1/4—when the cell pointer is located in the cell that corresponds to the upper-left corner of a page.

Balance Sheet — ABC Software, Inc.

	Jan-91	Feb-91	Mar-91	Apr-91	May-91	Jun-91	Jul-91	Aug-91	Sep-91	Oct-91	Nov-91	Dec-91
ASSETS												
Cash	$10,956	$14,516	$16,665	$17,660	$21,764	$25,508	$30,340	$34,371	$35,922	$33,468	$23,363	$20,488
Accounts Receivable	5,437	5,437	5,437	5,437	5,437	5,662	5,662	5,662	5,662	5,662	5,662	5,662
Prepaid Expense	600	600	600	600	600	600	600	600	600	600	600	600
Development Costs	158,202	155,669	153,136	150,603	148,070	145,537	143,004	140,471	137,938	135,405	132,872	130,339
Inventory	19,883	19,883	19,883	19,883	19,883	19,711	19,711	19,830	19,883	19,883	19,883	19,883
Equipment	20,000	20,000	20,000	20,000	20,000	20,000	20,000	20,000	20,000	20,000	25,000	25,000
Accumulated Depreciation	13,174	13,225	13,276	13,327	13,378	13,429	13,480	13,531	13,582	13,633	13,684	13,735
Organizational Costs	429	423	417	411	405	399	393	387	381	375	369	363
Total Assets	215,506	216,528	216,138	214,593	216,158	217,416	219,709	221,321	220,386	215,392	207,748	202,334
LIABILITIES												
Accounts Payable	3,262	3,262	3,262	3,262	3,262	3,397	3,397	3,397	3,397	3,397	3,397	3,397
Accrued Expenses	4,257	4,363	4,257	4,257	4,257	4,257	4,257	4,363	4,562	4,562	4,562	4,562
Long Term Debt	35,000	35,000	35,000	35,000	35,000	35,000	35,000	35,000	35,000	35,000	35,000	35,000
OWNERS EQUITY												
Common Stock	145,000	145,000	145,000	145,000	145,000	145,000	145,000	145,000	145,000	145,000	145,000	145,000
Retained Earnings	27,987	28,902	28,618	27,073	28,639	29,762	32,055	33,560	32,426	27,432	19,789	14,375
Total Equity	172,987	173,902	173,618	172,073	173,639	174,762	177,055	178,560	177,426	172,432	164,789	159,375
Liab. & Net Worth	215,506	216,527	216,137	214,592	216,158	217,416	219,709	221,320	220,385	215,392	207,748	202,334

Income Statement

	Jan-91	Feb-91	Mar-91	Apr-91	May-91	Jun-91	Jul-91	Aug-91	Sep-91	Oct-91	Nov-91	Dec-91
Gross Sales	21,747	21,747	21,747	21,747	21,747	22,647	22,647	22,647	22,647	22,647	22,647	22,647
Cost of Goods Sold	3,118	3,118	3,118	3,118	3,118	3,290	3,290	3,171	3,118	3,118	3,118	3,118
Gross Margin	18,629	18,629	18,629	18,629	18,629	19,357	19,357	19,476	19,529	19,529	19,529	19,529
Operating Expenses	14,088	14,838	16,037	17,298	14,188	15,358	14,188	15,095	17,787	21,647	24,297	22,067
Amortization	2,533	2,533	2,533	2,533	2,533	2,533	2,533	2,533	2,533	2,533	2,533	2,533
Depreciation	51	51	51	51	51	51	51	51	51	51	51	51
Net Earnings	1,957	1,207	8	(1,253)	1,857	1,415	2,585	1,797	(842)	(4,702)	(7,352)	(5,122)
Interest Expense	(292)	(292)	(292)	(292)	(292)	(292)	(292)	(292)	(292)	(292)	(292)	(292)
Net Income (Loss)	1,665	915	(284)	(1,545)	1,565	1,123	2,293	1,505	(1,134)	(4,994)	(7,644)	(5,414)

Cash Flow

#		Jan-91	Feb-91	Mar-91	Apr-91	May-91	Jun-91	Jul-91	Aug-91	Sep-91	Oct-91	Nov-91	Dec-91
49	REVENUE												
50	Profit 1	3,670	3,670	3,670	3,670	3,670	3,670	3,670	3,670	3,670	3,670	3,670	3,670
51	Profit 2	3,910	3,910	3,910	3,910	3,910	3,910	3,910	3,910	3,910	3,910	3,910	3,910
52	Profit 3	2,917	2,917	2,917	2,917	2,917	2,917	2,917	2,917	2,917	2,917	2,917	2,917
53	Profit 4	1,550	1,550	1,550	1,550	1,550	1,550	1,550	1,550	1,550	1,550	1,550	1,550
54	Profit 5	4,230	4,230	4,230	4,230	4,230	4,230	4,230	4,230	4,230	4,230	4,230	4,230
55	Profit 6	5,470	5,470	5,470	5,470	5,470	6,370	6,370	6,370	6,370	6,370	6,370	6,370
57	Total	21,747	21,747	21,747	21,747	21,747	22,647	22,647	22,647	22,647	22,647	22,647	22,647
59	COGS												
60	Profit 1	551	551	551	551	551	551	551	551	551	551	551	551
61	Profit 2	587	587	587	587	587	587	587	587	587	587	587	587
62	Profit 3	438	438	438	438	438	438	438	438	438	438	438	438
63	Profit 4	233	233	233	233	233	233	233	233	233	233	233	233
64	Profit 5	635	635	635	635	635	635	635	635	635	635	635	635
65	Profit 6	676	676	676	676	676	848	848	729	676	676	676	676
67	Total	3,118	3,118	3,118	3,118	3,118	3,290	3,290	3,171	3,118	3,118	3,118	3,118
69	EXPENSES												
70	Insurance	0	0	500	760	0	0	0	0	0	0	0	0
71	Legal/Accounting	0	0	0	0	0	0	0	0	0	0	0	0
72	Inventory Purchases	3000	3000	3000	3000	3000	3000	3000	3000	3000	3000	3000	3000
73	Salaries	6,846	6,846	7,769	6,846	6,846	6,846	6,846	6,846	7,769	9,500	9,500	9,500
74	Payroll Tax	787	787	893	787	787	787	787	787	893	1,093	1,093	1,093
75	Supplies	50	150	50	150	50	150	50	150	50	150	50	150
76	Rent	900	900	900	1,000	1,000	1,000	1,000	1,000	1,000	1,000	1,000	1,000
77	Phone	200	200	200	200	200	200	200	200	200	200	200	200
78	Technical	0	150	0	150	0	150	0	150	0	150	0	150
79	Consulting	0	0	0	0	0	0	0	0	2,150	2,150	2,150	2,150
80	Travel	0	400	0	400	0	400	0	400	0	400	0	400
81	Advertising	1,300	1,300	1,300	1,300	1,300	1,300	1,300	1,300	1,300	1,300	1,300	1,300
82	S/T Debt	400	400	400	400	400	400	400	400	400	2,000	400	400
83	Misc	100	100	100	100	100	100	100	100	100	100	100	100
84	Mailing	75	75	75	75	75	75	75	75	75	75	75	75
85	Printing	50	150	50	150	50	150	50	150	50	150	50	150
86	Storage	110	110	110	110	110	110	110	110	110	110	110	110
87	Equipment	0	0	0	0	0	0	0	0	0	0	5,000	0
88	Benefits	170	170	590	170	170	590	170	170	590	170	170	590
89	Bank Charges	15	15	15	15	15	15	15	15	15	15	15	15
90	Utilities	85	85	85	85	85	85	85	85	85	85	85	85
91	Property Tax	0	0	0	0	0	0	0	157	0	0	0	0
92	Income Tax	0	0	0	1,600	0	0	0	0	0	0	0	1,600
94	Total	14,088	14,838	16,037	17,298	14,188	15,358	14,188	15,095	17,787	21,647	24,297	22,067
96	CASH FLOW	4,541	3,791	2,592	1,331	4,441	3,999	5,169	4,381	1,742	(2,118)	(4,768)	(2,538)

Figure 8-4 A large worksheet

Page 1

Balance Sheet — ABC Software, Inc.

	Jan-91	Feb-91	Mar-91	Apr-91	May-91
ASSETS					
Cash	$10,956	$14,516	$16,665	$17,660	$21,764
Accounts Receivable	5,437	5,437	5,437	5,437	5,437
Prepaid Expense	600	600	600	600	600
Development Costs	158,202	155,669	153,136	150,603	148,070
Inventory	19,883	19,883	19,883	19,883	19,883
Equipment	20,000	20,000	20,000	20,000	20,000
Accumulated Depreciation	13,174	13,225	13,276	13,327	13,378
Organizational Costs	429	423	417	411	405
Total Assets	215,506	216,528	216,138	214,593	216,158
LIABILITIES					
Accounts Payable	3,262	3,262	3,262	3,262	3,262
Accrued Expenses	4,257	4,363	4,257	4,257	4,257
Long Term Debt	35,000	35,000	35,000	35,000	35,000
OWNERS EQUITY					
Common Stock	145,000	145,000	145,000	145,000	145,000
Retained Earnings	27,987	28,902	28,618	27,073	28,639
Total Equity	172,987	173,902	173,618	172,073	173,639
Liab. & Net Worth	215,506	216,527	216,137	214,592	216,158

Income Statement

	Jan-91	Feb-91	Mar-91	Apr-91	May-91
Gross Sales	21,747	21,747	21,747	21,747	21,747
Cost of Goods Sold	3,118	3,118	3,118	3,118	3,118
Gross Margin	18,629	18,629	18,629	18,629	18,629
Operating Expenses	14,088	14,838	16,037	17,298	14,188
Amortization	2,533	2,533	2,533	2,533	2,533
Depreciation	51	51	51	51	51
Net Earnings	1,957	1,207	8	(1,253)	1,857
Interest Expense	(292)	(292)	(292)	(292)	(292)
Net Income (Loss)	1,665	915	(284)	(1,545)	1,565

Cash Flow

	Jan-91	Feb-91	Mar-91	Apr-91	May-91
REVENUE	3,670	3,670	3,670	3,670	3,670
Profit 1	3,670	3,670	3,670	3,670	3,670

Page 2

Balance Sheet

	Jun-91	Jul-91	Aug-91	Sep-91	Oct-91	Nov-91	Dec-91
Cash	$25,508	$30,340	$34,371	$35,922	$33,468	$23,363	$20,488
Accounts Receivable	5,662	5,662	5,662	5,662	5,662	5,662	5,662
Prepaid Expense	600	600	600	600	600	600	600
Development Costs	145,537	143,004	140,471	137,938	135,405	132,872	130,339
Inventory	19,711	19,711	19,830	19,883	19,883	19,883	19,883
Equipment	20,000	20,000	20,000	20,000	20,000	25,000	25,000
Accumulated Depreciation	13,429	13,480	13,531	13,582	13,633	13,684	13,735
Organizational Costs	399	393	387	381	375	369	363
Total Assets	217,416	219,709	221,321	220,386	215,392	207,748	202,334
Accounts Payable	3,397	3,397	3,397	3,397	3,397	3,397	3,397
Accrued Expenses	4,257	4,257	4,363	4,562	4,562	4,562	4,562
Long Term Debt	35,000	35,000	35,000	35,000	35,000	35,000	35,000
Common Stock	145,000	145,000	145,000	145,000	145,000	145,000	145,000
Retained Earnings	29,762	32,055	33,560	32,426	27,432	19,789	14,375
Total Equity	174,762	177,055	178,560	177,426	172,432	164,789	159,375
Liab. & Net Worth	217,416	219,709	221,320	220,385	215,392	207,748	202,334

Income Statement

	Jun-91	Jul-91	Aug-91	Sep-91	Oct-91	Nov-91	Dec-91
Gross Sales	22,647	22,647	22,647	22,647	22,647	22,647	22,647
Cost of Goods Sold	3,290	3,290	3,171	3,118	3,118	3,118	3,118
Gross Margin	19,357	19,357	19,476	19,529	19,529	19,529	19,529
Operating Expenses	15,358	14,188	15,095	17,787	21,647	24,297	22,067
Amortization	2,533	2,533	2,533	2,533	2,533	2,533	2,533
Depreciation	51	51	51	51	51	51	51
Net Earnings	1,415	2,585	1,797	(842)	(4,702)	(7,352)	(5,122)
Interest Expense	(292)	(292)	(292)	(292)	(292)	(292)	(292)
Net Income (Loss)	1,123	2,293	1,505	(1,134)	(4,994)	(7,644)	(5,414)

Cash Flow

	Jun-91	Jul-91	Aug-91	Sep-91	Oct-91	Nov-91	Dec-91
REVENUE	3,670	3,670	3,670	3,670	3,670	3,670	3,670
Profit 1	3,670	3,670	3,670	3,670	3,670	3,670	3,670

#	A	B	C	D	E	F	G	H	I	J	K	L	M
51	Profit 2	3,910	3,910	3,910	3,910	3,910	3,910	3,910	3,910	3,910	3,910	3,910	3,910
52	Profit 3	2,917	2,917	2,917	2,917	2,917	2,917	2,917	2,917	2,917	2,917	2,917	2,917
53	Profit 4	1,550	1,550	1,550	1,550	1,550	1,550	1,550	1,550	1,550	1,550	1,550	1,550
54	Profit 5	4,230	4,230	4,230	4,230	4,230	4,230	4,230	4,230	4,230	4,230	4,230	4,230
55	Profit 6	5,470	5,470	5,470	5,470	5,470	6,370	6,370	6,370	6,370	6,370	6,370	6,370
56													
57	Total	21,747	21,747	21,747	21,747	21,747	22,647	22,647	22,647	22,647	22,647	22,647	22,647
58													
59	COGS												
60	Profit 1	551	551	551	551	551	551	551	551	551	551	551	551
61	Profit 2	587	587	587	587	587	587	587	587	587	587	587	587
62	Profit 3	438	438	438	438	438	438	438	438	438	438	438	438
63	Profit 4	233	233	233	233	233	233	233	233	233	233	233	233
64	Profit 5	635	635	635	635	635	635	635	635	635	635	635	635
65	Profit 6	676	676	676	676	676	848	848	729	676	676	676	676
66													
67	Total	3,118	3,118	3,118	3,118	3,118	3,290	3,290	3,171	3,118	3,118	3,118	3,118
68													
69	EXPENSES	Jan-91	Feb-91	Mar-91	Apr-91	May-91	Jun-91	Jul-91	Aug-91	Sep-91	Oct-91	Nov-91	Dec-91
70	Insurance	0	0	0	760	0	0	0	0	0	0	0	0
71	Legal/Accounting	0	0	500	0	0	0	0	0	0	0	0	0
72	Inventory Purchases	3000	3000	3000	3000	3000	3000	3000	3000	3000	3000	3000	3000
73	Salaries	6,846	6,846	7,769	6,846	6,846	6,846	6,846	6,846	7,769	9,500	9,500	9,500
74	Payroll Tax	787	787	893	787	787	787	787	787	893	1,093	1,093	1,093
75	Supplies	50	150	50	150	50	150	50	150	50	150	50	150
76	Rent	900	900	900	1,000	1,000	1,000	1,000	1,000	1,000	1,000	1,000	1,000
77	Phone	200	200	200	200	200	200	200	200	200	200	200	200
78	Technical	0	150	0	150	0	150	0	150	0	150	0	150
79	Consulting	0	0	0	0	0	0	0	0	2,150	2,150	2,150	2,150
80	Travel	0	400	0	400	0	400	0	400	0	400	0	400
81	Advertising	1,300	1,300	1,300	1,300	1,300	1,300	1,300	1,300	1,300	1,300	1,300	1,300
82	S/T Debt	400	400	400	400	400	400	400	400	400	2,000	400	400
83	Misc	100	100	100	100	100	100	100	100	100	100	100	100
84	Mailing	75	75	75	75	75	75	75	75	75	75	75	75
85	Printing	50	150	50	150	50	150	50	150	50	150	50	150
86	Storage	110	110	110	110	110	110	110	110	110	110	110	110
87	Equipment	0	0	0	0	0	0	0	0	0	0	5,000	0
88	Benefits	170	170	590	170	170	590	170	170	590	170	170	590
89	Bank Charges	15	15	15	15	15	15	15	15	15	15	15	15
90	Utilities	85	85	85	85	85	85	85	85	85	85	85	85
91	Property Tax	0	0	0	0	0	0	0	157	0	0	0	0
92	Income Tax	0	0	0	1,600	0	0	0	0	0	0	0	1,600
93													
94	Total	14,088	14,838	16,037	17,298	14,188	15,358	14,188	15,095	17,787	21,647	24,297	22,067
95													
96	CASH FLOW	4,541	3,791	2,592	1,331	4,441	3,999	5,169	4,381	1,742	(2,118)	(4,768)	(2,538)

Page 3

Page 4

Figure 8-5 The same worksheet as in Figure 8-4, printed with 1-2-3's default settings

In addition to the column-widths, row-heights, and margin settings, there are other factors that determine the amount of data that will fit on each page. Among the most important of these is the size of the fonts you select for printing. As you may recall from Chapter 6, you can use the Style Font command to specify various type styles and sizes (fonts) for displaying and printing a given worksheet or range data. The larger the font you select, the less data will print on each page. See "Fonts and Printing" later in this chapter for more discussion on this topic.

Finally, even headers and footers have a bearing on the amount of data that will fit on each page. Headers and footers contain one or more lines of descriptive text that appear at the top and/or bottom of each printed page. For example, a typical header or footer might include the name of the report, your company name, and a page number. When you include a header or footer in a document, 1-2-3 for Windows allocates additional space between the top and bottom margins. For more about including headers and footers in your documents, see "Headers and Footers" later in this chapter.

Because of the numerous factors that influence the amount of data that can fit on a page, about the only way you can get an accurate picture of what data will be printed on which page is to use 1-2-3's Preview utility, discussed later in this chapter. The Preview utility lets you sequentially view the pages in the current print job before you print them.

 Tip: To further assist you in determining the amount of data that will fit on a page, 1-2-3 lets you change the display of the worksheet frame to replace column letters and row numbers with either characters in a 10-point font, inches, millimeters, or points/picas. That way, as long as you know the size of the paper on which you will be printing, you can closely estimate what data will go on which page. You can control the display of the worksheet border by using the Window Display Options command. This command is discussed briefly later under "Display Options that Affect or Enhance Printing" and in detail in Chapter 3, "Managing Windows."

Printing a 3-D Range

When you print a 3-D range, 1-2-3 prints each worksheet in the range, one right after the other, without blank lines or page breaks between them. In some cases, this may cause a confusing printout. For example, suppose you are working with a model similar to the one in Figure 8-6. (Only a small portion of the model actually appears in the figure.) This model includes three matching worksheets, one for each division of a small company, with data in the range A1..N30 (the first 13 columns and 30 rows) of each worksheet. All the data is formatted in a 10-point Ariel MT (Adobe Type Manager) font.

To print the entire 3-D model in Figure 8-6, select the File Print command, specify the range A:A1..C:N30, then select OK. 1-2-3 sends the contents of the range to your printer. Assuming you are using a LaserJet printer with 1-2-3's default margins, column widths, and row heights, the data is printed as follows:

- Page 1: The range A1..J30 of worksheet A and the range A1..J28 of worksheet B, with no blank line between them.

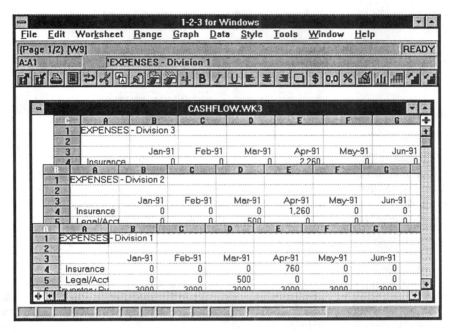

Figure 8-6 A sample 3-D worksheet model

- Page 2: The range A29..J30 of worksheet B and the range A1..J30 of worksheet C, with no blank line between them.

- Page 3: The range K1..N30 of worksheet A and the range K1..N28 of worksheet B, with no blank line between them.

- Page 4: The range K29..N30 of worksheet B and the range K1..N30 of worksheet C, with no blank line between them.

Obviously, making sense of this printout is difficult at best. Therefore, rather than printing a 3-D range in its entirety, you're usually better off printing the contents of each worksheet individually. Although this process involves more work, the output is more intelligible. If you have to print the same range frequently, you can compose a macro to do the job for you.

▼ *Tip:* You can use page breaks to have the contents of each worksheet in a 3-D range printed on a separate page. See "Controlling Page Breaks" later for more details on this.

Using the Preview Utility

You can use the Preview utility to view each of the pages in the current print job before you print them. This allows you to identify formatting and page-break problems before you print.

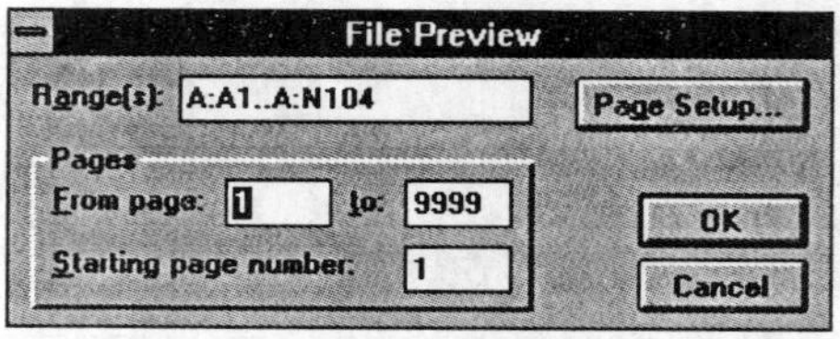

```
┌─────────────────────────────────────────────┐
│ ▭                    File Preview              │
├─────────────────────────────────────────────┤
│  Range(s):  [A:A1..A:N104          ]  [Page Setup...] │
│  ┌─ Pages ──────────────────────────┐         │
│  │  From page:  [1]    to:  [9999]   │  ┌──────┐│
│  │  Starting page number:   [1]      │  │  OK  ││
│  └──────────────────────────────────┘  └──────┘│
│                                         ┌──────┐│
│                                         │Cancel││
│                                         └──────┘│
└─────────────────────────────────────────────┘
```

Figure 8-7   The File Preview dialog box

To use the Preview utility, select the File Preview command. 1-2-3 displays the dialog box shown in Figure 8-7. You'll notice this dialog box is very similar to the File Print dialog box shown earlier in Figure 8-2, and you use it in the same way. Specify the range you want to preview in the Ranges(s) text box and then select OK. 1-2-3 displays the first page of the current print job in the Preview window, similar to Figure 8-8.

Note: You can also access the File Preview dialog box by selecting the Preview icon 🔲 from 1-2-3's icon palette.

To see the next page in the Preview window, press ENTER or PGDN. (Pressing ENTER or PGDN when the last page is displayed returns you to the current worksheet.) To see the previous page, press PGUP. To leave the Preview window and return to the current Worksheet at any time, press ESC.

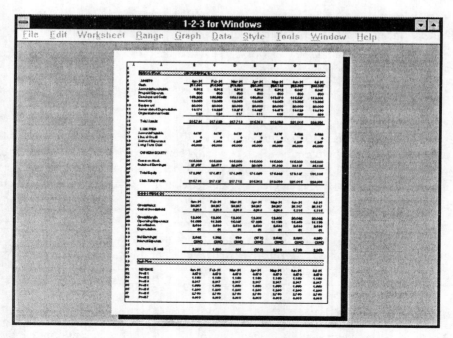

Figure 8-8   The Preview window shows the first page of a report

Note: You can also access the Preview window by selecting the Preview button from the File Print dialog box (Figure 8-2).

Controlling Page Breaks

You can control how 1-2-3 breaks up a range into printed pages by inserting page breaks into the print range. Page breaks simply tell 1-2-3 where to end one page and start the next. Unlike previous DOS versions of 1-2-3, however, 1-2-3 for Windows allows you to create both horizontal and vertical page breaks. Horizontal page breaks cause 1-2-3 to begin a new page starting at a specific row, and vertical page breaks begin a new page starting at a specific column.

To insert a page break into the worksheet, you use the Worksheet Page Break command. When you select this command, 1-2-3 displays the dialog box shown in Figure 8-9. This dialog box contains four radio buttons that let you select the type of page break you want or remove a page break. All types of page breaks are inserted at the location of the cell pointer. Horizontal page breaks are inserted along the top edge of the cell pointer, while vertical page breaks are inserted along the left edge of the cell pointer. Therefore, properly positioning the cell pointer beforehand is critical to getting the results you want from the Worksheet Page Break command.

Briefly, each of the radio buttons in the Worksheet Page Break dialog box perform the following functions:

- Horizontal: Inserts a horizontal page break into the worksheet, causing 1-2-3 to begin a new page when it encounters the current row in a print range. The row containing the page break will be the first line on the new page.

- Vertical: Inserts a vertical page break into the worksheet, causing 1-2-3 to begin a new page when it encounters the current column in a print range. The column containing the page break will be the leftmost column on the new page.

- Both: Inserts both a horizontal and a vertical page break at the location of the cell pointer. The cell containing the page break marks the upper-left corner of the new page.

- Clear: Removes a horizontal or vertical page break.

When you insert a page break into the worksheet, 1-2-3 marks the spot with a dotted grey line. In addition, (MPage) is displayed in the format line when you move the cell

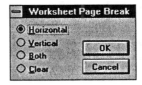

Figure 8-9 The Worksheet Page Break dialog box

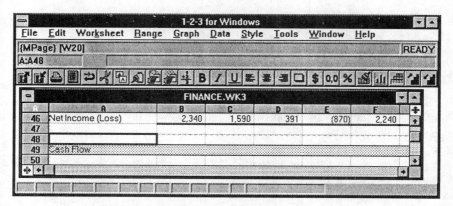

Figure 8-10   A sample horizontal page break

pointer into a row or column that contains a page break. For example, Figure 8-10 shows a horizontal page break in cell A:A48.

Page breaks apply to the entire row or column in which they reside. Thus, whenever, the row or column containing a page break is included in a print range, 1-2-3 will start a new page. For example, the horizontal page break in Figure 8-10 occurs in row 48. Therefore, whenever row 48 is included in a print range, 1-2-3 will begin a new page starting with that row.

If 1-2-3 is in GROUP mode, the Worksheet Page Break command applies to all the worksheets in the file.

As you might imagine, the row or column containing a horizontal or vertical page break must be included on the print range for the page break to take effect. For example, suppose you're working with the 3-D example shown earlier in Figure 8-6. As you may recall, the print range in that example is A:A1..C:N30, causing 1-2-3 to print the range A1..N30 of worksheets A, B, and C with no separation of any kind between them. If you were to place a horizontal page break in cell A:A31, for example, the page break is outside the print range and will have no effect. On the other hand, if you place a horizontal page break in cell A:A30 (within the print range), 1-2-3 will print worksheet A and then print worksheet B starting on a new page.

Note: The 1-2-3 Classic equivalent for the Worksheet Page Break command is / Worksheet Page. This command inserts a new row into the worksheet and inserts a page-break symbol, |::, at the location of the cell pointer. This type of page-break symbol yields a horizontal (row) page break only, and it must be located in the leftmost column of the print range. This type of page break will only be honored when you print with the / Print Printer command rather than with the File Print command.

PRINTING 1-2-3 FOR WINDOWS GRAPHS AND OTHER IMAGES

Up to now, printing from 1-2-3 for Windows has been discussed solely in the context of printing worksheet data. However, you can also use the techniques described above to print or preview your 1-2-3 for Windows graphs as well as other graphics images, including:

- Bitmaps: Windows bitmaps pasted from the Windows Clipboard
- .PIC Files: Lotus' proprietary graphics format
- .CGM files: Computer graphics metafiles

Of course, to print these graphics images, the current default printer for 1-2-3 must be a graphics printer.

To print your 1-2-3 for Windows graphs, you must display them in the worksheet. To do this, begin by creating the graph in a 1-2-3 graph window. (See Chapter 10 for more details on how to do this.) Figure 8-11, for example, shows a sample sales graph that is ready to add to the worksheet.

When you're ready, use the Window command from the Graph menu to return to the current worksheet, or click on the worksheet to make it active. Once the worksheet window is displayed, select the Graph Add to Sheet command from the worksheet menu. 1-2-3 displays the Graph Add to Sheet dialog box in Figure 8-12 showing the names of graphs associated with the current worksheet file.

Select the name of the graph you want to add from the list and specify a worksheet range in which it will be displayed in the Range box below. For example, suppose you want to add the graph named GRAPH2 to the worksheet and display it in the range

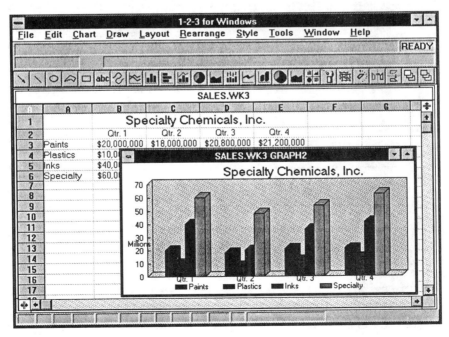

Figure 8-11 A sample graph displayed in a graph window

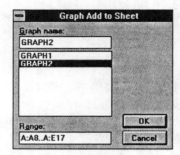

Figure 8-12 The Graph Add to Sheet dialog box

A:A8..A:E17. To do this, select GRAPH2 from the list box and specify A:A8..A:E17 (or its range name) in the Range text box, then select OK. 1-2-3 displays the graph you've selected in the range you've specified, as shown in Figure 8-13.

When you first add a graph to the worksheet, its aspect ratio (height to width) may be distorted, causing the graph to appear unsightly. To fix this, you'll need to change the size of the range in which the graph is displayed. To do this, you use the Graph Size command from the worksheet menu. When you select this command, 1-2-3 displays the Graph Size dialog box. This dialog box looks exactly like the Graph Add to Sheet dialog box in Figure 8-12. The graph names that appear in the list box are confined to those

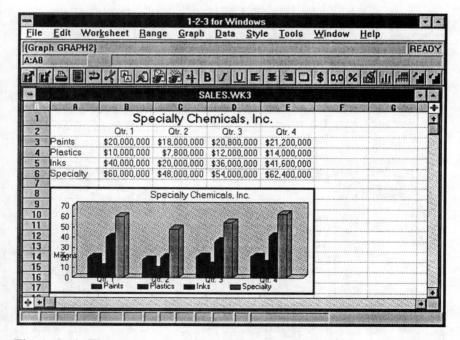

Figure 8-13 The sample graph displayed in the worksheet

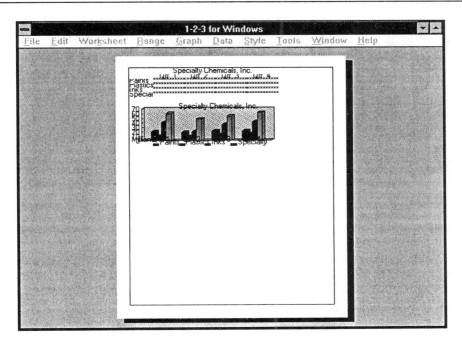

Figure 8-14 A graph and its supporting data in the Preview window

graphs displayed in the current worksheet. When you select a graph name from the list, 1-2-3 shows you the range currently occupied by that graph in the Range box below. To change the size of the selected graph, simply change the size of the range in the Range box. When you select OK to confirm the command, 1-2-3 adjusts the size of the graph to fit within the range you've specified.

Once your graph is displayed in the worksheet, you can print it just as you would any other data in your 1-2-3 worksheet. Simply select the File Print command, specify a worksheet range that includes the graph, and then select OK. 1-2-3 sends the graphics image to your printer. For example, Figure 8-14 shows a sample graph along with its supporting worksheet data displayed in the Preview window.

Printing bitmaps from within 1-2-3 is just as easy. To do this, first make sure an appropriate bitmap image is on the Clipboard. (You can do this by using the Edit Cut or Edit Copy command from within another Windows application. Or you can press PRINTSCREEN to capture the entire Windows screen or ALT+PRINTSCREEN to capture just the current window.) Once a bitmap image is on the Clipboard, select an appropriate size range for the image in your 1-2-3 worksheet, and then select the Edit Paste command from 1-2-3's menu. 1-2-3 pastes the bitmap in the range you've specified. You can now print the bitmap by using 1-2-3's File Print command.

As mentioned, you can also print a .PIC or .CGM file from within 1-2-3 for Windows. Before you can do this, you must import the file and display it in a worksheet by using the Graph Import command. This command, which is discussed in Chapter 10, lets you not only select a specific .PIC or .CGM file to import, but also to specify a range in which it will be displayed. Once the file is displayed in the worksheet, you can use the File Print command to print it.

1-2-3 FOR WINDOWS PAGE LAYOUT OPTIONS

1-2-3 for Windows offers a number of page-layout options that let you enhance your printed output. For example, you can specify headers and footers, which allow you to print custom text, page numbers, and dates at the top or bottom of each page. Another handy page-layout feature is the ability to print each page with column and row borders. For example, most worksheets have titles in the top row and leftmost column that identify the contents of the worksheet. By designating these as print borders, you can have the appropriate column and row titles printed on each page of your output.

1-2-3 also lets you control the placement and orientation of data on the printed page. For example, by changing the margins, you can specify where 1-2-3 both begins and ends printing on each page. You can also control whether 1-2-3 prints in portrait mode (the default) or landscape (sideways). In addition, 1-2-3 includes a compression feature that lets you scale the size of your printed output to fit more, or less, on a page.

1-2-3 lets you save the page-layout settings you select as the default for future 1-2-3 sessions. Or, if you desire, you can save the current page-layout settings to a file with a name of your choosing. Once the settings are saved, 1-2-3 allows you to easily recall those same settings by simply loading the file that contains them.

To specify page-layout options for the current print job, use the File Page Setup command. When you select this command, 1-2-3 displays the dialog box in Figure 8-15. (You can access this same dialog box by selecting the Page Setup button from either the File Print or File Preview dialog box.) The settings you create in this dialog box will remain in effect for the balance of your 1-2-3 session. The components of this dialog box are discussed in detail in the sections that follow.

Headers and Footers

Headers and footers are descriptive lines of text that appear at the top and/or bottom of each page. For example, a typical header or footer might include a page number, the name of the report, and possibly the date on which the report was printed. As you might imagine, the header appears at the top of each page and the footer at the bottom.

To specify a header for the current print job, you use the Header text box in the File Page Setup dialog box shown in Figure 8-15. To specify a footer, you use the Footer text box.

The conventions for specifying headers and footers are exactly the same. Therefore, the two will be discussed almost interchangeably throughout this section.

The maximum length of a header or footer is 512 characters. However, 1-2-3 will not print any part of a header or footer that extends beyond the right margin of the current page.

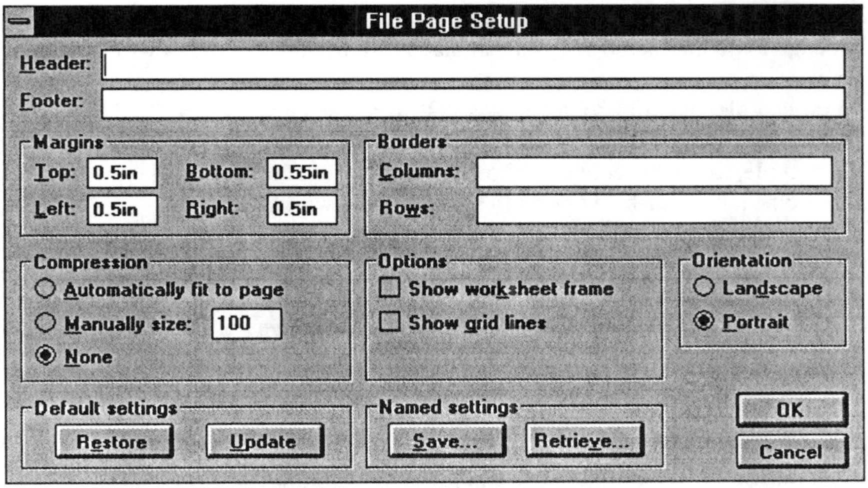

Printing 315

Figure 8-15 The File Page Layout dialog box

Note: 1-2-3 leaves two blank lines measured in the current print font between the header and the top line of printed data and between the footer and the bottom line of printed data.

You can include up to three entries in a header or footer. The first entry is left-aligned, the second is centered, and the third is right-aligned. Separate each of these entries with a split vertical bar (|). (On some computers this character may appear as a solid bar.) If a header or footer has only a single entry, that entry will appear left-aligned. However, if you precede that entry with a single split vertical bar, it will appear centered, and if you precede it with two split vertical bars, it will appear right-aligned.

To have sequential page numbers printed in a header or footer, you use the number sign (#). To print today's date, you use the @ sign. The default date format used is always Date 1 (DD-MMM-YY). You can precede either of these symbols with text to identify them—for example, **Page #** or **Printed @**.

You can combine the various alignment and symbol options in a header or footer to create the effect you want. For example, if you are printing a budget analysis report, you might use the following as a header or footer:

```
Printed @|Budget Analysis|Page #
```

This causes the text string "Printed" followed by today's date to be left-aligned. The string "Budget Analysis" is centered, and the string "Page" followed by the current page number is right-aligned, as in:

```
Printed 01/01/93        Budget Analysis        Page 1
```

You can also control the starting page number that 1-2-3 prints in a header or footer. To do this, you use the Starting page number box in the File Print dialog box. Normally, this box contains 1, meaning the first page number will be 1. However, if you want the first page to be numbered 10, you can place a 10 in this box. 1-2-3 will use the number you provide as the starting page number in your header or footer.

You can also use the contents of a cell in a header or footer. To do this, enter a \ (backslash) followed by a cell address or range name in the Header or Footer text box. For example, to use the contents of cell A100, type **\A100**. You must type the entry; you cannot type a backslash and point to the cell in the worksheet.

This method allows you to include a date other than the current system date in a header or footer. It also allows you to display a date in a different format. For example, imagine you have the function @DATE(92,1,10) in cell A:E1. Imagine further that you have formatted that cell as Date 4 (DD/MM/YY) using the Range Format command. To display this date in a header or footer, you would use the entry \A:E1 in the Header or Footer text box. When your report is printed, 1-2-3 for Windows displays the date 01/01/92 as a left-aligned label.

If you use the backslash method to specify the contents of a cell as header or footer text, it must be the only entry; you cannot specify additional text or a second backslash cell reference. However, you can precede the entry with one or two split vertical bars to control its alignment.

Note: If you use the backslash (\) cell address method of specifying header or footer text, 1-2-3 for Windows does not update the Header or Footer text boxes when you move the data in the referenced cell to another location. Therefore, your header or footer text is lost. For example, if you use Edit Move Cells, Edit Cut, Worksheet Insert, or Worksheet Delete to move the header or footer text, 1-2-3 for Windows continues to refer to the cell you referenced in the Header or Footer text box.

Controlling Margins

Margin settings determine the amount of white space between the edges of the paper and your document. 1-2-3 for Windows allows you to specify a setting for the top, bottom, left, and right margins.

1-2-3 measures margins in inches (or millimeters, if you prefer). The default setting for the top, bottom, left, and right margins is 0.5 inch. Margins are measured from the edge of the page to the edge of your document.

To change the margin settings, use the Margins section of the Page Setup dialog box (Figure 8-15). To change a specific margin, select the text box that corresponds to that margin and type a new value for the margin. For example, to change the left margin to 1.5 inches (meaning 1.5 inches from the left side of the paper), select Left and type the number 1.5 in the adjacent text box. You can specify a number with up to three places after the decimal.

You can also specify margins in millimeters (there are about 2.5 millimeters in an inch). To do this, type a value corresponding to the number of millimeters followed by **mm**—for example, 2.5 mm. You can also specify a margin value in centimeters using the **cm** suffix. 1-2-3 will convert this value to millimeters.

1-2-3 for Windows uses the margin settings you specify to position your output on the printed page. Margin settings also affect the amount of data that will fit on a page and, therefore, at what point 1-2-3 for Windows ends one page and begins the next one. See "Printing a Large Report," earlier in this chapter for a discussion of how 1-2-3 for Windows uses the current margin settings to break up a large print range into multiple pages.

Note: To see the impact that the current margin settings will have on your printed document, use the Preview utility discussed earlier in this chapter. This utility allows you to view each of your pages before printing them.

Using the Compression Feature

As one of its page-layout options, 1-2-3 for Windows includes a compression feature that you will find very useful. This feature allows you to proportionally compress a print job so that more data will fit on a page, or to expand it, so that less data will be printed on each page. You might liken this feature to using a photocopier that is capable of reducing and enlarging. The difference is that the margins for the print job are not affected.

To take advantage of the compression feature, use the Compression group box in the File Page Setup dialog box (Figure 8-15). This group box contains the following options:

- Automatically fit to page: Scales the current print job down by a factor of 7, with the goal of fitting everything in the current print range on a single page.

- Manually size: Lets you specify a percentage by which to proportionally compress or expand the data in the print range. The default setting here is 100, meaning 100% of original size.

- None: Turns off the compression feature (the default).

The Automatically fit to page option is surprisingly powerful. For example, Figure 8-16 shows the same worksheet depicted in Figure 8-4 after it has been printed with the Automatically fit to page option. As you may recall, this same worksheet required four pages when printed in a standard 12-point Ariel MT typeface. Yet, in Figure 8-16, it all appears on a single page.

In some cases, however, using the Automatically fit to page option is simply not appropriate. Because this option reduces your printed output by a factor of 7, the print may often be very small and hard to read. In these cases, you'll want more control over just how the print job is scaled up or down, and that's where the Manually size option can be of use.

The Manually size option lets you define a percentage by which to compress or expand the current print job. To compress the current print job, specify a value from 15 to 99 in the adjacent text box. For example, to compress the current print job to 66% of its original size, type 66. To expand the current print job, type a value from 101 to 1000 in the adjacent text box. For example, to expand a print job to 1.5 times its original size, type 150 on the adjacent text box.

	A	B	C	D	E	F	G	H	I	J	K	L	M
1													
2	Balance Sheet	ABC Software, Inc.											
3													
4	ASSETS	Jan-91	Feb-91	Mar-91	Apr-91	May-91	Jun-91	Jul-91	Aug-91	Sep-91	Oct-91	Nov-91	Dec-91
5	Cash	$10,956	$14,516	$16,665	$17,660	$21,764	$25,508	$30,340	$34,371	$35,922	$33,468	$23,363	$20,488
6	Accounts Receivable	5,437	5,437	5,437	5,437	5,437	5,662	5,662	5,662	5,662	5,662	5,662	5,662
7	Prepaid Expense	600	600	600	600	600	600	600	600	600	600	600	600
8	Development Costs	158,202	155,669	153,136	150,603	148,070	145,537	143,004	140,471	137,938	135,405	132,872	130,339
9	Inventory	19,883	19,883	19,883	19,883	19,883	19,711	19,711	19,830	19,883	19,883	19,883	19,883
10	Equipment	20,000	20,000	20,000	20,000	20,000	20,000	20,000	20,000	20,000	20,000	25,000	25,000
11	Accumulated Depreciation	13,174	13,225	13,276	13,327	13,378	13,429	13,480	13,531	13,582	13,633	13,684	13,735
12	Organizational Costs	429	423	417	411	405	399	393	387	381	375	369	363
13													
14	Total Assets	215,506	216,528	216,138	214,593	216,158	217,416	219,709	221,321	220,386	215,392	207,748	202,334
15													
16	LIABILITIES												
17	Accounts Payable	3,262	3,262	3,262	3,262	3,262	3,397	3,397	3,397	3,397	3,397	3,397	3,397
18	Accrued Expenses	4,257	4,363	4,257	4,257	4,257	4,257	4,257	4,363	4,562	4,562	4,562	4,562
19	Long Term Debt	35,000	35,000	35,000	35,000	35,000	35,000	35,000	35,000	35,000	35,000	35,000	35,000
20													
21	OWNERS EQUITY												
22													
23	Common Stock	145,000	145,000	145,000	145,000	145,000	145,000	145,000	145,000	145,000	145,000	145,000	145,000
24	Retained Earnings	27,987	28,902	28,618	27,073	28,639	29,762	32,055	33,560	32,426	27,432	19,789	14,375
25													
26	Total Equity	172,987	173,902	173,618	172,073	173,639	174,762	177,055	178,560	177,426	172,432	164,789	159,375
27													
28	Liab. & Net Worth	215,506	216,527	216,137	214,592	216,158	217,416	219,709	221,320	220,385	215,392	207,748	202,334
29													
30													
31	Income Statement												
32													
33		Jan-91	Feb-91	Mar-91	Apr-91	May-91	Jun-91	Jul-91	Aug-91	Sep-91	Oct-91	Nov-91	Dec-91
34	Gross Sales	21,747	21,747	21,747	21,747	21,747	22,647	22,647	22,647	22,647	22,647	22,647	22,647
35	Cost of Goods Sold	3,118	3,118	3,118	3,118	3,118	3,290	3,290	3,171	3,118	3,118	3,118	3,118
36													
37	Gross Margin	18,629	18,629	18,629	18,629	18,629	19,357	19,357	19,476	19,529	19,529	19,529	19,529
38	Operating Expenses	14,088	14,838	16,037	17,298	14,188	15,358	14,188	15,095	17,787	21,647	24,297	22,067
39	Amortization	2,533	2,533	2,533	2,533	2,533	2,533	2,533	2,533	2,533	2,533	2,533	2,533
40	Depreciation	51	51	51	51	51	51	51	51	51	51	51	51
41													
42	Net Earnings	1,957	1,207	8	(1,253)	1,857	1,415	2,585	1,797	(842)	(4,702)	(7,352)	(5,122)
43	Interest Expense	(292)	(292)	(292)	(292)	(292)	(292)	(292)	(292)	(292)	(292)	(292)	(292)
44													
45	Net Income (Loss)	1,665	915	(284)	(1,545)	1,565	1,123	2,293	1,505	(1,134)	(4,994)	(7,644)	(5,414)
46													
47	Cash Flow												
48													
49	REVENUE	Jan-91	Feb-91	Mar-91	Apr-91	May-91	Jun-91	Jul-91	Aug-91	Sep-91	Oct-91	Nov-91	Dec-91
50	Profit 1	3,670	3,670	3,670	3,670	3,670	3,670	3,670	3,670	3,670	3,670	3,670	3,670
51	Profit 2	3,910	3,910	3,910	3,910	3,910	3,910	3,910	3,910	3,910	3,910	3,910	3,910
52	Profit 3	2,917	2,917	2,917	2,917	2,917	2,917	2,917	2,917	2,917	2,917	2,917	2,917
53	Profit 4	1,550	1,550	1,550	1,550	1,550	1,550	1,550	1,550	1,550	1,550	1,550	1,550
54	Profit 5	4,230	4,230	4,230	4,230	4,230	4,230	4,230	4,230	4,230	4,230	4,230	4,230
55	Profit 6	5,470	5,470	5,470	5,470	5,470	6,370	6,370	6,370	6,370	6,370	6,370	6,370
56													
57	Total	21,747	21,747	21,747	21,747	21,747	22,647	22,647	22,647	22,647	22,647	22,647	22,647
58													
59	COGS												
60	Profit 1	551	551	551	551	551	551	551	551	551	551	551	551
61	Profit 2	587	587	587	587	587	587	587	587	587	587	587	587
62	Profit 3	438	438	438	438	438	438	438	438	438	438	438	438
63	Profit 4	233	233	233	233	233	233	233	233	233	233	233	233
64	Profit 5	635	635	635	635	635	635	635	635	635	635	635	635
65	Profit 6	676	676	676	676	676	848	848	729	676	676	676	676
66													
67	Total	3,118	3,118	3,118	3,118	3,118	3,290	3,290	3,171	3,118	3,118	3,118	3,118
68													
69	EXPENSES	Jan-91	Feb-91	Mar-91	Apr-91	May-91	Jun-91	Jul-91	Aug-91	Sep-91	Oct-91	Nov-91	Dec-91
70	Insurance	0	0	0	760	0	0	0	0	0	0	0	0
71	Legal/Accounting	0	0	500	0	0	0	0	0	0	0	0	0
72	Inventory Purchases	3000	3000	3000	3000	3000	3000	3000	3000	3000	3000	3000	3000
73	Salaries	6,846	6,846	7,769	6,846	6,846	6,846	6,846	6,846	7,769	9,500	9,500	9,500
74	Payroll Tax	787	787	893	787	787	787	787	787	893	1,093	1,093	1,093
75	Supplies	50	150	50	150	50	150	50	150	50	150	50	150
76	Rent	900	900	900	1,000	1,000	1,000	1,000	1,000	1,000	1,000	1,000	1,000
77	Phone	200	200	200	200	200	200	200	200	200	200	200	200
78	Technical	0	150	0	150	0	150	0	150	0	150	0	150
79	Consulting	0	0	0	0	0	0	0	0	2,150	2,150	2,150	2,150
80	Travel	0	400	0	400	0	400	0	400	0	400	0	400
81	Advertising	1,300	1,300	1,300	1,300	1,300	1,300	1,300	1,300	1,300	1,300	1,300	1,300
82	S/T Debt	400	400	400	400	400	400	400	400	400	2,000	400	400
83	Misc	100	100	100	100	100	100	100	100	100	100	100	100
84	Mailing	75	75	75	75	75	75	75	75	75	75	75	75
85	Printing	50	150	50	150	50	150	50	150	50	150	50	150
86	Storage	110	110	110	110	110	110	110	110	110	110	110	110
87	Equipment	0	0	0	0	0	0	0	0	0	0	5,000	0
88	Benefits	170	170	590	170	170	590	170	170	590	170	170	590
89	Bank Charges	15	15	15	15	15	15	15	15	15	15	15	15
90	Utilities	85	85	85	85	85	85	85	85	85	85	85	85
91	Property Tax	0	0	0	0	0	0	0	157	0	0	0	0
92	Income Tax	0	0	0	1,600	0	0	0	0	0	0	0	1,600
93													
94	Total	14,088	14,838	16,037	17,298	14,188	15,358	14,188	15,095	17,787	21,647	24,297	22,067
95													
96	CASH FLOW	4,541	3,791	2,592	1,331	4,441	3,999	5,169	4,381	1,742	(2,118)	(4,768)	(2,538)

Figure 8-16   A worksheet printed using Automatic compression

It's doubtful you'll get the precise results you want with the Manually size option on the first try. In fact, you'll probably have to try a few different percentage settings, and test them with the Preview utility—before you get the right percentage for the current print job.

When you compress or expand a print job, 1-2-3 looks to Windows for the closest installed font supported by your printer. If the exact size required is not available, Windows will substitute the closest one it has. Therefore, in some cases, what you see in the Preview window may not match what actually comes out on your printer. Furthermore, if you expand a print job beyond the size of your available fonts, Windows will be forced to substitute and scale up its closest available raster font. As a result, the characters in your output may appear with jagged edges.

Printing Column and Row Borders

Many worksheet models have labels in the top row and leftmost column that identify the contents of each column and row. However, when you select a range to print that is far removed from these labels, your column and row titles are lost. To solve this problem you can specify rows of data that will print along the top edge of each page. You can also specify columns of data that will print along the left edge of each page. That way, when the final output is printed, 1-2-3 for Windows will print the appropriate titles for each column and row, regardless of the print range you specify.

To specify rows and/or columns of data that will print along the top and/or left edges of each page, you use the Borders section in File Page Setup dialog box. (As you may recall, this dialog box was shown earlier in Figure 8-15.) For example, suppose you want to print the range highlighted in Figure 8-17 (A:D81..A:F93), but you want the dates in row 77 to appear at the top of the page and the labels in column A to appear along the left side of the page. That way, the finished printout will appear as shown in Figure 8-18.

To create this printout, select the range A:D81..A:F93 then select the File Print command. When the File Print dialog box is displayed, select the Page Setup button to access the File Page Setup dialog box. In the Borders section, specify a cell from column A in the Columns text box—for example, A:A78. This entry specifies that the appropriate cells from column A will be printed along the left edge of each page. In the Rows text box, specify any cell from row 77—for example, A:B77. That way, the appropriate contents of row 77 will be printed along the top edge of each page. When you're ready, select OK to return to the File Print dialog box, then select OK to begin printing. 1-2-3 prints your output with appropriate column and row borders, as shown in Figure 8-18.

You can specify more than one column or row for your column and row borders. If you decide to do this, make sure the columns and rows you specify are adjacent, otherwise, 1-2-3 will beep and ignore the setting.

Note: Make sure the print range you select does not overlap the columns and/or rows you've selected as border ranges. If there is an overlap, 1-2-3 for Windows will print your column and row borders twice.

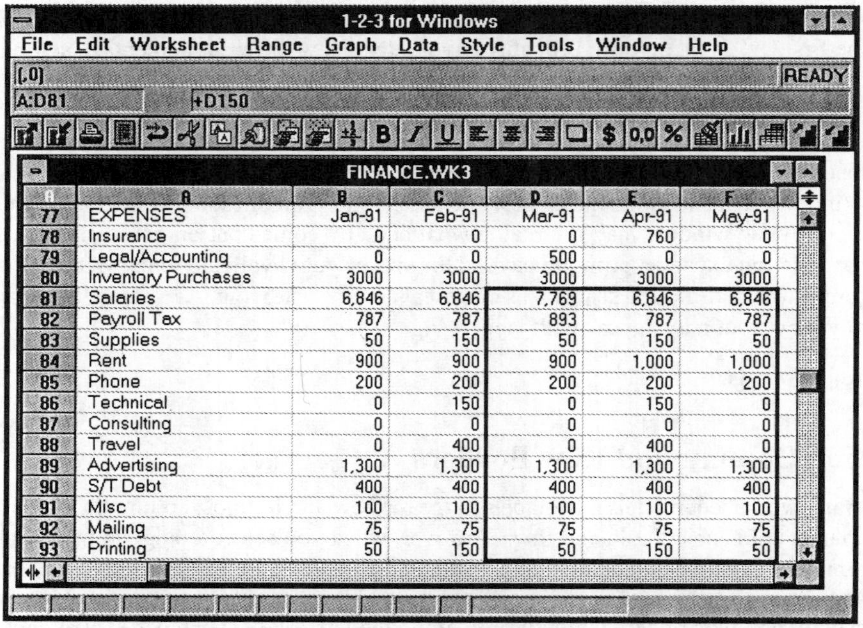

A	A	B	C	D	E	F
77	EXPENSES	Jan-91	Feb-91	Mar-91	Apr-91	May-91
78	Insurance	0	0	0	760	0
79	Legal/Accounting	0	0	500	0	0
80	Inventory Purchases	3000	3000	3000	3000	3000
81	Salaries	6,846	6,846	7,769	6,846	6,846
82	Payroll Tax	787	787	893	787	787
83	Supplies	50	150	50	150	50
84	Rent	900	900	900	1,000	1,000
85	Phone	200	200	200	200	200
86	Technical	0	150	0	150	0
87	Consulting	0	0	0	0	0
88	Travel	0	400	0	400	0
89	Advertising	1,300	1,300	1,300	1,300	1,300
90	S/T Debt	400	400	400	400	400
91	Misc	100	100	100	100	100
92	Mailing	75	75	75	75	75
93	Printing	50	150	50	150	50

Figure 8-17 A sample range highlighted for printing

A	A	D	E	F
77	EXPENSES	Mar-91	Apr-91	May-91
81	Salaries	7,769	6,846	6,846
82	Payroll Tax	893	787	787
83	Supplies	50	150	50
84	Rent	900	1,000	1,000
85	Phone	200	200	200
86	Technical	0	150	0
87	Consulting	0	0	0
88	Travel	0	400	0
89	Advertising	1,300	1,300	1,300
90	S/T Debt	400	400	400
91	Misc	100	100	100
92	Mailing	75	75	75
93	Printing	50	150	50

Figure 8-18 A sample range printed with column and row borders

Printing the Worksheet Frame and Grid Lines

1-2-3 for Windows also lets you print a range with the worksheet frame (column letters and row numbers) displayed. That way, you can identify the exact location of the printed data within the worksheet. In addition, 1-2-3 lets you print a range with grid lines, just as they appear in the worksheet. This can sometimes make a busy report appear more readable.

To create a printout with the worksheet frame displayed, turn on the Show worksheet frame in the Options section of the File Page Setup dialog box (Figure 8-15). This option was used to create the large printout shown earlier in Figure 8-4. As you may recall, that figure shows the column letters and row numbers for each cell in the printout.

To print the current job with grid lines displayed, turn on the Show grid lines check box in the File Page Setup dialog box (Figure 8-15). Be aware that your worksheet will take a little longer to print if grid lines are displayed.

Printing in Landscape (Sideways)

If your print range is rather wide (more than 10 columns) you might consider printing in landscape mode (sideways), provided that your printer supports this feature. In landscape mode, the paper appears to be flipped on its side, so that the 11-inch edge is at the top of the page. That way, although fewer rows will fit on each page, you can fit more columns across. The effect is often a more readable printout.

To print in landscape mode, select the Landscape radio button in the Orientation section of the File Page Setup dialog box (Figure 8-15). From then on, 1-2-3 will print in landscape mode. To return to printing in portrait orientation (the default) again, select the Portrait radio button.

If you want to see the effect that selecting the Landscape option will have on your printed output, you can use the Preview utility. To do this, highlight the range you want to print and then select the File Preview command, followed by OK. 1-2-3 will show you the Preview window in Landscape mode. For example, if you are printing on 8.5 × 11-inch paper, the 11-inch edge appears at the top of the Preview window.

Note: Selecting the Landscape option from 1-2-3's File Page Setup dialog box may affect your other Windows applications. When you select this option, the setting is passed directly on to the Windows printer driver supporting the printer that is currently in use by 1-2-3. If that printer happens to be the default printer for Windows, your other Windows applications will also print in landscape. Therefore, unless you want all your applications printing sideways, take a moment to select the Portrait button from the File Page Setup dialog box before you leave 1-2-3. For more on selecting different printers for use with 1-2-3 (as well as a default printer for Windows), see "Printer Control" later in this chapter.

Saving Your Settings as the Default

To save the setting you make in the File Page Setup box as the default for future sessions, select the Update command button. 1-2-3 saves the current settings for Header, Footer,

Margins, Borders, Options, and Orientation as the default page settings. That way, the current settings will be used not only for the remainder of the current session, but also for all future sessions, until you change them.

To restore the settings in the File Page Setup dialog box to their original defaults, select the Restore button. 1-2-3 will restore the current page-layout settings to the way they were when you first installed 1-2-3 for Windows.

Using Named Settings

1-2-3 for Windows allows you to save the current page-layout settings to a named file with an .AL3 extension. What's more, 1-2-3 lets you retrieve that same file at a later time, making the settings it contains current for the File Print command. Thus, you can create several different sets of named print settings, if you so desire, and quickly recall the particular set you need for use with the current worksheet file.

To create named settings, use the "Named settings" section of the File Page Setup dialog box (Figure 8-15). This section allows you not only to assign a name to the current print settings, but also to retrieve an existing set of named settings you've previously created.

To assign a name to the current print settings, select the Save button from the named settings section. 1-2-3 for Windows displays the dialog box in Figure 8-19 showing a list of .AL3 files in the current working directory. Type a filename of eight characters or less and press ENTER. 1-2-3 saves the current print settings to a file with the name you specified and an .AL3 extension. Alternatively, you can select the name of an existing .AL3 file from the list box, and then select OK. When you save to a filename that already exists, 1-2-3 will prompt you with a Cancel/Replace dialog box.

To activate an existing set of named settings, select the Retrieve button from the Named settings section. 1-2-3 for Windows displays the File Page Setup Named Retrieve box. This dialog box looks exactly like the Save dialog box in Figure 8-19. Either type the

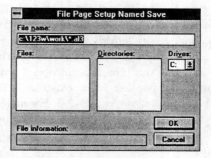

Figure 8-19 The File Page Setup Named Save dialog box

filename of the settings file you want to make active in the File name text box or select the name from the list box below. When you're ready, select OK. 1-2-3 for Windows replaces the current print settings with the named settings you've selected. If you have not as yet assigned a name to the current print settings, they will be lost.

Note: The 1-2-3 Classic equivalent for the File Page Setup Named command is /Print Printer Options Name. This command lets you create, make current, and delete named settings. However, those named settings are associated with the current worksheet file only; they are not saved in separate files. Therefore, the /Print Printer Options Name command has no effect on named settings files you create with the File Page Setup Named Save command.

PRINTER CONTROL

Unlike DOS, where each application is responsible for providing its own printer drivers, Windows allows you to install a single printer driver for use with multiple applications. (Printer drivers are software programs that tell Windows how to interact with a specific printer.)

Windows also provides facilities for managing printer drivers. For example, through the Windows Control Panel Printers dialog box you can install printers, switch from one installed printer driver to another, and activate specific features offered by a particular printer driver. For information on how to install a printer for use with Windows, consult your *Windows User's Guide.* Or, if you have a LaserJet Series III printer, see "Installing The HPPCL5A.DRV Driver" later in this chapter for an example of how to install the Hewlett Packard Series III driver that comes with 1-2-3 for Windows.

1-2-3 for Windows' File Printer Setup command gives you access to Windows' printer management facilities without your having to leave 1-2-3. The sections that follow show you how to use the File Printer Setup command to change from one installed printer to another. You'll also learn how to activate specific printing features offered by a given printer driver from within 1-2-3. The example printer driver used is the one provided with 1-2-3 for Windows that drives the Hewlett Packard LaserJet Series III printer.

Changing Printers

To select a printer for use with 1-2-3, use the File Printer Setup command. When you select this command, 1-2-3 for Windows displays the dialog box in Figure 8-20 showing a list of printers currently installed for Windows. The name of the printer currently in use is highlighted. To select a different printer, click on the name of that printer or highlight it, and select OK or press ENTER. 1-2-3 for Windows returns you to the worksheet and will now use the printer you specified both for printing and for creating encoded files. (See "Printing to a File" later for details on creating encoded files.)

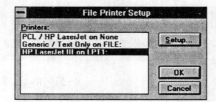

Figure 8-20   The File Printer Setup dialog box

The /Print com-
mand in the 1-2-3
Classic menu does
not offer an equiv-
alent for the File
Printer Setup
command. There-
fore, if you wish
to make another
printer current,
you must use the
File Printer Setup
command.

The printer you select with the File Printer Setup command becomes the default printer for 1-2-3. In fact, 1-2-3 writes your selection to the DefaultPrt= statement in the [PRINTER] section of the 123W.INI file. That way, the next time you start 1-2-3 for Windows, it will come up recognizing the printer you specified.

Note: For a printer to be listed in the File Printer Setup dialog box, you must first install a driver for that printer by using the Windows Control Panel. See the *Windows User's Guide* for details on installing a printer for use with Windows. Or, if you have an HP LaserJet III printer, see "Installing the HPPCL5A Driver" later in this chapter.

Specifying Printing Properties

Once you've installed a printer for Windows, you can use the File Printer Setup command to activate specific printing properties supported by that printer. For example, if your printer supports properties such as manual feed or number of copies control, you can modify those properties.

The File Printer Setup dialog box does not in itself allow you to control the printing properties of a particular printer. Instead, it simply gives you access to a driver-specific dialog box that controls the operation of an installed printer. To access a driver-specific dialog box, first select the name of the printer whose operation you want to control from the File Printer Setup dialog box (Figure 8-20), then select the Setup command button.

When you select the Setup command button, 1-2-3 shows you the driver-specific dialog box that corresponds to the specific printer you selected. Therefore, the content of the dialog box displayed varies depending on the printer you selected.

Figure 8-21, for example, shows a driver-specific dialog box that corresponds to the Hewlett Packard LaserJet III printer driver (HPPCL5A.DRV version 3.77) that ships with 1-2-3 for Windows. This printer driver allows you to configure numerous features for the LaserJet III, including the following:

- Paper Source: Allows you to choose a specific paper tray for the printer as well as specify manual feed.

- Paper Size: Lets you choose the size of the paper you will be printing on.

- Memory: Lets you specify the amount of memory available in the printer. This option is usually set when the printer is installed.

- Page Protection: Lets you specify that an entire page be sent to the printer as one large bitmap, rather than segments of information. Of course, you must have sufficient memory in the printer to use this feature. The default setting here is OFF.

- Orientation: Lets you choose from Portrait (the default) or Landscape (sideways) printing. You can also control this option by using 1-2-3's File Page Setup Orientation command.

- Graphics Resolution: Lets you choose from the different dpi (dots per inch) settings. The highest setting, 300 dpi, will produce the highest quality image, but it will require the most memory and take the longest to print.

- Cartridge: Lets you select up to two font cartridges you may have installed in slots in the printer.

- Grey Scale: Lets you choose the type of pattern you want for printing graphics images. About the only way to determine the setting that is best for you is to experiment and see which setting yields the best results.

- Number of Copies: Lets you specify the number of copies that will be printed when you print from a Windows application, like 1-2-3 for Windows.

Be aware that when you make a printer-settings change through the File Printer Setup command, Windows records that change as the default setting for the printer you've selected. In fact, if you leave 1-2-3 for Windows (or Windows itself) and restart it again, Windows will use those same settings to print your work. Unless you intend to use those settings permanently, make sure you use the File Printer Setup command a second time to change those settings back to the way they were.

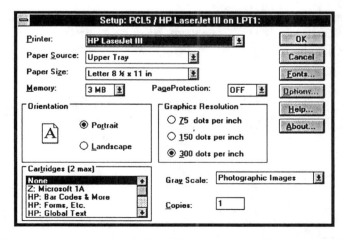

Figure 8-21 A sample printer-specific dialog box for the HP LaserJet III printer

Installing the HPPCL5A.DRV Driver

As you've probably noticed, 1-2-3 for Windows Release 1.0 comes with a Printer Driver disk. Actually, this disk contains only a single Windows printer driver, the HPPCL5A.DRV version 3.77 driver for the HP LaserJet III printer. If you are currently using an earlier version of this printer driver, Lotus recommends that you install the new driver for use with Windows. You'll find the version 3.77 driver offers significantly improved output quality versus the version 3.42 driver that ships with Windows.

Note: To determine the version of the HPPCL5A.DRV driver you are currently using, select the About button from the PCL/5 HP LaserJet III dialog box shown earlier in Figure 8-21.

To install the HPPCL5A.DRV driver, double-click on the Windows Control Panel icon in Program Manager's Main group window. A short time later, the Windows Control Panel will appear on your screen. Double-click on the Printers icon. Windows displays the Printers dialog box as shown in Figure 8-22.

Select the Add Printer button from the Printers dialog box. Windows expands the dialog box to show a list box of printers and an Install button. Scroll down through the list box and select the last option, Unlisted Printer, and then select the Install button. Windows prompts you to insert the disk with your new printer driver into drive A.

Insert the 1-2-3 for Windows Printer Driver disk into drive A and select OK. Windows copies the HPPCL5A.DRV driver to your \WINDOWS\SYSTEM directory. When this operation is complete, Windows displays **HP LaserJet III on None:,Inactive** in the Installed Printers list box.

Select the Configure button from the Printers dialog box. Windows displays the Printers - Configure dialog box. From the list box provided, select the port you want to use for the printer—for example, LPT1, and then select the Setup button. Windows takes you to the HP LaserJet III dialog box shown earlier in Figure 8-21. You can use this dialog box to configure various options for the HP LaserJet III printer. (These options are described briefly in the previous section.)

When you've finished configuring the HP LaserJet III driver, select OK twice to return to the Printers dialog box. Once there, select the Active radio button from the Status section. This activates the new Series III driver. If you want the HP LaserJet III printer

Figure 8-22 The Windows Control Panel Printers dialog box

to be the default printer for the system, double-click on its name in the Installed Printers list box.

If this is a first-time installation of the HP LaserJet III printer, you can select OK to return to Windows and begin using your new LaserJet III printer driver. Otherwise, you'll need to perform the procedures described in the next paragraph.

Before returning to Windows, make sure you remove any old listings for the HP LaserJet III printer in the Printers dialog box. To do this, simply select the old listing from the Installed Printers list box and then select the Configure Button. Windows displays the Printers - Configure dialog box. Select the Remove button, and then select OK to return to the Printers dialog box. Select OK again to close the Printers dialog box and return to Windows. Your new HP LaserJet III driver should now be ready for use with your Windows applications.

Note: Once the HPPLC5A version 3.77 driver has been installed, you can begin taking advantage of its internal Univers and CGTimes scalable outline fonts. In fact, ATM's Ariel and Helvetica fonts, as well as Windows' Helv raster font, will be mapped to Univers. What's more, ATM's TimesNewRomanPS, as well as Windows' TmsRmn, will be mapped to CGTimes.

DISPLAY OPTIONS THAT AFFECT OR ENHANCE PRINTING

Obviously, changes in fonts, column widths, cell formatting, and so on will directly affect the appearance of your printed output. There are a few other display options that may also affect your printed output. For example, if you format a range as hidden, or if you hide a column, row, or worksheet, 1-2-3 will not print the data in the hidden range. Or if you change the color of the cell background for a range of cells, 1-2-3 will attempt to replicate that color when you print the range. If you don't have a color printer, 1-2-3 substitutes a black and white pattern (shading) in place of the color.

In other cases a display option may not affect the appearance of your printed output, but may help you better determine what your printed output will look like. For example, 1-2-3 lets you change the appearance of the worksheet frame to show inches, millimeters, or picas. This may allow you to better determine what your printed output will look like before you print.

Hiding Data from Your Printer

As you learned in Chapter 5, you can use the Range Format Hidden command to hide a range of data. The hidden cells still contain data and formulas, but appear blank. Similarly, you can use the Worksheet Hide command to hide an entire column or worksheet. Finally, if you reduce the height of a row until it disappears from view, the row is, in effect, hidden. In each of these cases, when you select a print range that includes a hidden range, column, row, or worksheet, 1-2-3 will not print the data in the hidden range.

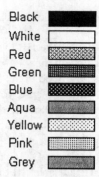

Figure 8-23   1-2-3 substitutes black and white patterns for colors when you print

You can use 1-2-3's ability to hide ranges to simplify your work. For example, suppose the range you want to print contains confidential data. Rather than reorganize the entire worksheet just to relocate this data outside the print range, you can hide the data. That way, when you print, the data is ignored. When you are finished printing, you can unhide the affected range, making it once again available for your personal viewing.

About Cell Background Colors

As you learned in Chapter 6, you can use the Style Colors command to change the background color for a range of cells. If you have a color printer, 1-2-3 will attempt to replicate the color you've selected when printing. If you have a black and white printer, 1-2-3 will substitute a black and white pattern in place of the cell-background color when printing. Figure 8-23 shows the patterns 1-2-3 substitutes in place of colors when printing on a black and white printer.

Display Options That Enhance Printing

As you learned in Chapter 3, you can use the Window Display Options command to change the default display of 1-2-3's worksheet and graph windows. A few of the options for this command can help you better determine what your printed output will look like.

Converting to a Black and White Display

When you print to a black and white printer, 1-2-3 must substitute black and white patterns in place of the colors on your screen. Usually, the effect is rather pleasing, but sometimes you don't quite get the results you'd like. To eliminate some of the guess work, you can convert 1-2-3's display to black and white. That way, you can get a pretty good idea of what your output will look like before you print.

To convert 1-2-3's display to black and white, you use the Window Display Options command and turn on the B&W check box. When you select OK to confirm this command, 1-2-3 converts the display of both graph and worksheet windows to black and white. Where graphs are concerned, 1-2-3 substitutes the appropriate patterns in place of the colors in the graph, causing it to appear very similar to what it will look like when printed. If you like what you see, you can paste the graph into the worksheet and print it. Otherwise, you can use the Chart Options Colors command to make a few color adjustments that will make the chart appear more pleasing.

Changing the Display of the Worksheet Frame

Another display option you may find helpful when printing is 1-2-3's ability to alter the display of the worksheet frame. For example, rather than the default display of column letters and row numbers, 1-2-3 lets you change the display of the worksheet frame to show inches, millimeters, or points/picas. That way, if you know the size of the paper you will be printing on, you can get a pretty good idea of the positioning of your data before you print.

To modify the Display of the worksheet frame, you use the Window Display Options Frame command. This command leads you to a drop-down list box that includes the following options.

- Standard: The usual column letters and row numbers.

- Characters: Displays characters (1 though 98 repeating) in 10-point type in place of the column letters and row numbers.

- Inches: Displays the worksheet frame as a ruler with one-inch increments. Figure 8-24 shows an example.

- Metric: Displays the worksheet frame as a ruler with one centimeter increments.

- Point/picas: Displays the worksheet frame as a ruler with points (1/72nd of an inch) along the top and picas (1/16th of an inch) on the left.

- None: Hides the worksheet frame.

As mentioned, Figure 8-24 is an example of what the worksheet frame looks like when it is displayed in inches. Although it is not an exact science—margins will have an impact—you can get a pretty close indication of where your data will be positioned on the page.

FONTS AND PRINTING

Chapter 6 of this book provides a lengthy discussion of how to apply fonts in 1-2-3 for Windows. Here we'll discuss how the font choices you make may affect your printed output.

Note: To print different fonts from within 1-2-3 for Windows, you must use a graphics printer.

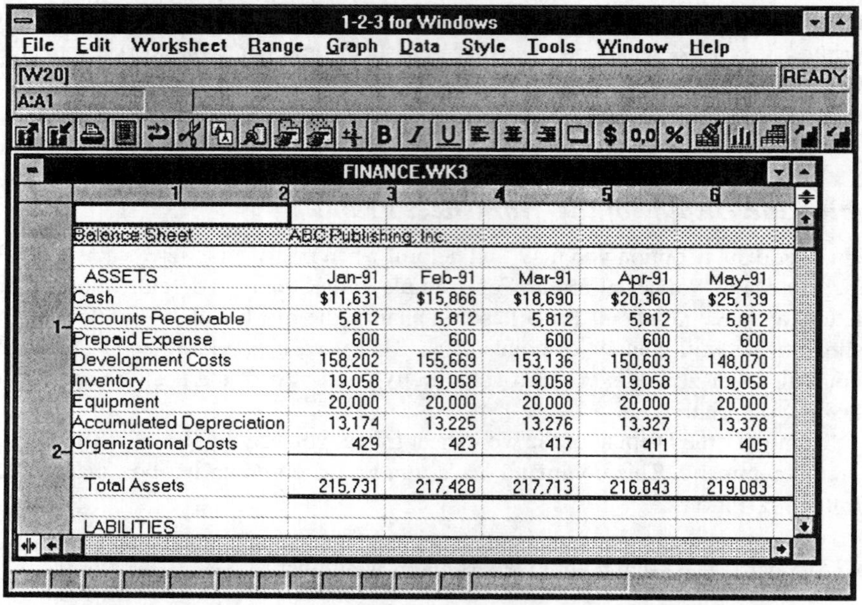

Figure 8-24 The worksheet frame displayed as a ruler with 1-inch increments

As you learned in Chapter 6, 1-2-3 automatically assigns a default font to the all the cells in a worksheet file. The default font is the first font listed when you select the Style Font command. Normally, this font is a Helvetica 12-point font, unless ATM is installed, in which case Ariel MT 12-point is used as the default font. You can change the default font for the worksheet file by using the Style Font Replace command and selecting a font of your choosing.

1-2-3 for Windows uses the current default font to determine the height and width of rows and columns in the worksheet. The default font is also used when printing headers and footers. Therefore, changing the default font can have a definite impact on your printed output.

Note: If a printer has not been installed for Windows, no font names will appear in the Available box when you select the Style Font Replace command. To have font names appear in this box, you must install a printer for Windows.

Changes in Column Widths and Row Heights

As mentioned, 1-2-3 for Windows prints your work in sets of columns. The number of columns of data that will fit on each page is determined by the width of the columns included in the print range. The wider the columns are, the fewer will fit on each page.

Similarly, the number of rows of data that will fit on each page is determined by the height of the rows included in the print range. As you know, 1-2-3 automatically adjusts the height of a row to accommodate the largest font in that row. The taller each row becomes, the fewer rows will print on each page.

Initially, 1-2-3 uses the default font to determine both the width and height of each column and row in the worksheet. The default width of each column is nine characters, and the width of those characters is measured using the default font for the worksheet. Normally, with the default 12-point Helvetica font, you can fit about 7 columns across on an 8.5 × 11-inch page when printing in portrait mode. The height of each row in the worksheet is determined by the default font. Normally, with the default 12-point Helvetica font, you print about six rows per vertical inch or approximately 50 lines per page.

If you change the default font for your worksheet file, 1-2-3 automatically adjusts the height and width of each cell in the worksheet to accommodate nine characters in the new font you've selected. Thus, increasing the size of the default font forces 1-2-3 to increase both the height and width of each row and column in the worksheet. As a result, fewer rows and columns will print on each page. To determine the effect that changing the default font will have on your printed output, your best bet is to use the Preview utility.

Note: Assigning a given font to an individual worksheet cell or range has no effect on the number of columns that will print on each page. 1-2-3 does not adjust the column width of a cell when you change its font. However, the number of rows on each page may be affected. 1-2-3 will increase the height of all cells in a given row to accommodate the largest font in that row.

Headers and Footers

1-2-3 prints both headers and footers using the current default font for the worksheet file. What's more, 1-2-3 leaves two blank lines measured in the current default font between the header and the top line of printed data and between the footer and the bottom line of printer data. Thus, if you change the default font for the worksheet file, both headers and footers, and the amount of space they occupy, will be affected.

Choosing Fixed versus Proportionally Spaced Fonts

As mentioned in Chapter 6, 1-2-3 gives you access to both fixed-pitch and proportionally spaced fonts. With a fixed-pitch font (for example, Courier), each character has the same width. The width of the characters in a proportionally spaced font (for example, Helvetica) may vary, lending a more pleasing appearance to the type.

The advantage to using a fixed-pitch font is that you can accurately predict the amount of data that will fit in each cell, provided the font assigned to the current cell matches the default font for the worksheet file. What you gain in predictability with a fixed-pitch font, you lose in style—frankly, fixed-pitch fonts just aren't that attractive.

On the other hand, although proportionally spaced fonts have a more pleasing appearance, it is often very difficult to predict the amount of data that will fit in each cell, and therefore on each line in your printout. This problem is further compounded when the font you've selected for a range of worksheet cells doesn't match the default font for the worksheet file.

Print Time and Memory Issues

Typical of most Windows applications, 1-2-3 for Windows does not produce its own fonts internally. Instead, it gets its fonts from the same place as every other Windows application—the Windows *font table*. Windows uses this table to maintain a running tally of fonts that are available to the system. These fonts are in turn made available to all Windows applications that ask for them.

The fonts provided to Windows can come from several sources. The source you choose may have an effect on the amount of time it takes to print your work from 1-2-3 for Windows. The choice you make may also have an impact on the amount of memory required by your printer to print the fonts you have selected. Briefly, the following sources of fonts are currently available:

- Windows' own raster (bitmap) and vector (stroke-based) soft fonts.

- Soft (disk-based) fonts that are installed on your hard disk and downloaded to the printer at print time.

- Font packages such as Adobe Type Manager or Bitstream's FaceLift, that produce fonts "on-the-fly." That is, your fonts are produced as needed for display purposes and again for downloading to your printer at print time.

- Printer-specific fonts. This includes fonts internal to the printer (burned into its memory or provided by a cartridge), as well as PostScript fonts.

The sections that follow discuss each of these font types in more detail. In general, though, when it comes to print time and required printer memory, you'll find that printing with either prebuilt bitmap soft fonts, or fonts that are resident to the printer (with the exception of PostScript fonts), will require less time and memory than printing with fonts from packages such as Adobe Type Manager (ATM).

Windows Fonts

As mentioned in Chapter 6, Windows 3.0 provides its own set of internal fonts. These come in two varieties, raster and vector. Both are stored in the .FON files in your \WINDOWS\SYSTEM directory.

Windows' raster fonts are bitmap fonts. That is, they are prebuilt (stored on disk) and downloaded to your printer at print time. Windows' raster fonts appear on your menu as Helv, TmsRmn, Courier, and Symbol. Because these fonts are prebuilt bitmap fonts, they tend to print rather quickly and require less memory from your printer. On the downside, because Windows' raster fonts are prebuilt bitmaps, they are designed to be displayed only at a specific aspect ratio (height to width). Therefore, they only come in a discrete number of point sizes (usually 8, 10, 12, 14, 18, and 24) for reasons of disk space. If you specify a point size outside this range, Windows will duplicate or remove rows or columns of pixels to approximate the size you've selected. As a result, the outline of the characters may take on a stairstep-like appearance, often referred to as the "jaggies."

Windows vector fonts are stroke-based fonts—that is, they are defined by line segments. This makes them almost infinitely scalable. The Windows vector fonts include Roman, Modern, and Script. Since Lotus has decided not to support the Windows vector fonts, however, you will not see these fonts listed when you select the Style Font Replace option.

Soft-Font Packages

A number of third-party soft-font packages on the market today allow you to create prebuilt soft fonts in discrete point sizes that are Windows compatible. Once installed, these packages provide matching fonts for both screen display and for downloading to your printer at print time. Each of these packages comes with its own install program that not only installs the fonts themselves on your hard disk, but also associates them with a particular printer driver. Often, the use of these fonts is limited to a specific type of printer—for example, an HP-compatible or a PostScript printer.

In most cases, selecting a prebuilt soft font for printing (particularly on an HP LaserJet) will reduce the amount of memory required to print some pages and may improve printing performance. On the downside, creating prebuilt soft fonts can often require a tremendous amount of disk space.

Examples of some packages that allow you to create downloadable soft fonts for HP LaserJet and PostScript-compatible printers are

- Adobe Font Foundry (included with all Adobe Type Library Packages): Lets you create downloadable bit-map fonts for HP LaserJets and compatibles. Once the soft fonts are created, you can configure them for use with ATM through the ATM control panel.

- Bitstream FaceLift: Bitstream FaceLift is somewhat like ATM—that is, it produces fonts "on the fly" for screen display and then builds and downloads the necessary fonts to your printer at print time. In addition, FaceLift lets you create downloadable bitmap fonts for HP LaserJet and compatibles as well as PostScript outline fonts for PostScript printers.

- SoftType from ZSoft: This package lets you create downloadable fonts for HP and compatible printers as well as PostScript printers. Unlike some other soft-font packages, SoftType lets you customize the appearance of the fonts before you create them. For example, you can change the weight or slant of a particular type style and you can add drop shadows, lending a 3-D appearance to the type.

On-the-Fly Font Packages

Another way of providing fonts to Windows is through on-the-fly font packages like Adobe Type Manager (ATM). Generally, these font packages end up building your fonts twice, once for screen display and again for downloading at print time. For this reason, using a product like ATM can take longer to print and require additional printer memory. However, for most Windows enthusiasts, longer print time and the investment in more printer memory is a small price to pay for the enhanced printer output.

Most of the on-the-fly packages print with scalable outline fonts. That is, the outline of the character is defined first and then filled in with dots. As a result, the printed characters appear more sharply defined (fewer "jaggies") and can be scaled up or down to suit your needs.

Adobe is not the only vendor to tap the on-the-fly market—Atech Software's Powerpack, Bitstream's FaceLift, MicroLogic's Morefonts, and ZenoGraphics Super-Print all provide non-Type 1 scalable outline fonts for printing with matching on-the-fly screen fonts for screen display. ATM, which uses PostScript Type 1 outline fonts, appears to be leading the pack at present. Perhaps this is due to its ease of use and a large library of PostScript Type 1 fonts from which to choose.

Caution: 1-2-3 for Windows has been optimized for use with ATM. In fact, Lotus recommends that you do not have another font package running while ATM and 1-2-3 for Windows are present. If you do, a conflict may result, possibly causing certain ATM fonts (or those from the other font package) to fail to appear in 1-2-3's Style Font Replace dialog boxes.

Printer-Specific Fonts

Another source of fonts available to Windows is printer-specific fonts. These fonts are either "burned" into the printer's memory or provided by a font cartridge that plugs into the body of the printer. Often, printer-specific fonts are only available in discrete point sizes. Windows gets information about which fonts and which point sizes are available by means of the currently active printer driver. For example, if the HP LaserJet printer driver is currently selected as the default printer for 1-2-3, you will see a LinePrinter font listed when you select 1-2-3's Style Font Replace command. This font comes in a single size (8-point) and is burned into the printer's memory.

Printer-specific font technology is changing, though. The HP LaserJet III printer, for example, now comes with two scalable-outline fonts (Universe and CGTimes); both are resident to the printer. Like ATM's outline fonts, these fonts have a crisp appearance and are almost infinitely scalable.

In general, you'll find that printing with printer-specific fonts is a great deal faster and requires less memory than printing with other types of fonts. Because printer-specific fonts are already resident to the printer, you don't lose time waiting for them to be downloaded from your PC. What's more, the character sets are prebuilt in the printer and don't require as much memory to print. To see which fonts are specific to your particular printer, you'll have to consult your printer manual.

PostScript Fonts

Another source of fonts available to Windows is PostScript fonts. PostScript fonts are a form of outline font used largely by PostScript printers. Most PostScript printers come with a standard set of 35 internal fonts. To scale and define these fonts, an internal PostScript language interpreter is also supplied with the printer. Based on incoming PostScript language code sent by the Windows PostScript printer driver, the interpreter defines the outline of each character in precise mathematical curves. Once the outline is defined, it is filled in with dots that are appropriate for the resolution of the printer. Although this technology results in spectacular output, it can often take a long time to print even a simple document.

If you are using a PostScript printer, 1-2-3 includes a unique feature you should know about. To print as efficiently as possible on PostScript printers, 1-2-3 bypasses portions of the Windows PostScript printer driver and uses its own internal drivers. This is necessary to ensure compatibility with PostScript output from 1-2-3 Release 3.1. In some cases, 1-2-3's internal drivers may make printing to your PostScript printer go a little faster than relying solely on the Windows PostScript driver.

Although using 1-2-3's internal drivers may reduce print time, there are limitations. For example, 1-2-3 limits the number of fonts that can be downloaded to a PostScript printer; the default limit is five fonts. On a more realistic level, the maximum number of downloadable fonts is limited by the size of the fonts you download and the available memory in your printer.

To enforce the maximum number of downloadable fonts, 1-2-3 relies upon the numpostfonts= statement in the [PRINTER] section of 123W.INI. The default value assigned to this statement is 5. You can, of course, increase this value if your printer has sufficient memory. Nevertheless, if the number of downloaded fonts exceeds this value, 1-2-3 defers printing to the Windows PostScript printer driver, which in turn must generate the code for the entire print job, possibly extending the amount of time it takes to print.

Through its internal drivers, 1-2-3 for Windows supports the 35 standard PostScript fonts. If your PostScript printer supports a different set of fonts, you may experience some discrepancies between what appears on your screen and what actually comes out on your printer. You can, however, disable 1-2-3's internal PostScript driver so that all printing operations are handled by the Windows PostScript driver. This should clear up any problems you may have.

To disable 1-2-3's internal PostScript driver, you'll have to edit the postscript= statement in the [PRINTER] section of the 123W.INI file. Simply add the word "system" (in all lowercase letters) to this statement—for example, postscript=system. That way, 1-2-3 will rely entirely on the Windows PostScript printer driver when printing.

Note: The / Print command on the 1-2-3 menu does not work with PostScript printers.

PRINTING TO A FILE

1-2-3 for Windows also allows you to send printed output to a file on disk. You can select from two different types of files, an ASCII text file or an encoded file. Encoded files contain the same information that would normally be sent to your printer. In addition to data, encoded files contain printer control codes, text formats, and graphics. What's more, encoded files can be printed from the DOS prompt, so you can print your output either at a later time or on another computer that does not have 1-2-3 for Windows installed.

ASCII files, on the other hand, contain only lines of data, each line ending with a carriage-return/line-feed character. ASCII files can be imported directly into many popular software programs or back into 1-2-3 for Windows with the File Import From Text command. Because ASCII files are a common way of sharing data between applications, printing to an ASCII file is discussed at length in Chapter 17, "Sharing Data." Printing to an encoded file is discussed here.

To print to an encoded file using the 1-2-3 Classic menu, use the /Print Encoded command.

To create an encoded file, use the File Print command. However, in preparation for printing to an encoded file, you must configure the appropriate Windows printer driver to print to an encoded file. This is done by using the Windows Control Panel.

To configure a printer driver to print to a file, open the Windows Control Panel by double-clicking on its icon, which is located in Program Manager's Main group window. Once the Control Panel is displayed, double-click on the Printers icon to access the Printers dialog box. From the Installed Printers list box, select the printer for which you want to create the encoded file and then select the Configure button. Windows displays the Printers - Configure dialog box. Select File from the list box provided and then select OK twice, once to close the Printers - Configure dialog box and again to close the Printers dialog box. The printer driver you selected should now be configured to print to an encoded file.

Once the printer driver has been configured to print to a file, make sure that printer is selected as the default printer for 1-2-3. You can do this by using 1-2-3's File Printer Setup command (see "Changing Printers" earlier). From then on, when you select the File Print command, 1-2-3 will display the dialog box in Figure 8-25, prompting you for the name of a file. Type the directory and name of your choice and press ENTER. 1-2-3 sends the current print job to an encoded file under the name you specified.

Note: As mentioned, when you create an encoded file, printer-specific control codes are sent to that file. Thus, the encoded file can only be printed on the same make and model of printer that is listed as the current printer in 1-2-3's File Printer Setup dialog box.

You can print an encoded file directly from the DOS system prompt by using the COPY command. To do this, follow the COPY command with the appropriate filename and printer port. For example, to print the encoded file MYFILE.ENC to the first parallel port, use the command COPY MYFILE.ENC/b LPT1. Notice the /b (binary file) switch here. This switch is simply a precaution to assure that the entire file will be copied based on its physical size. Without this switch, DOS will stop copying if it encounters an end-of-file

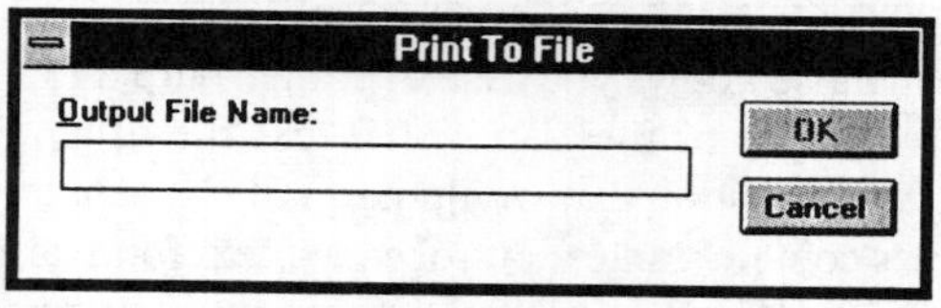

Figure 8-25   1-2-3 prompts you for the name of a file

marker (CTRL-Z). Although this character is normally located at the end of the file, it can be located almost anywhere in a file that contains 1-2-3 for Windows graphics.

PRINTING CELL FORMULAS

There is an option on the 1-2-3 Classic menu that lets you create a cell-contents listing for the current worksheet. (This option is not supported in the 1-2-3 for Windows menu.) A cell contents listing can be useful for documenting an important worksheet.

Normally, 1-2-3 for Windows will print your data as it appears on your screen but you can also create a listing that shows you the contents and formatting of each cell. A small excerpt of a cell-contents listing would appear similar to the following:

```
A:C1:  '          Specialty Chemicals, Inc.
A:B3:  ^Beginning
A:C3:  ^Qtr. 1
A:D3:  ^Qtr. 2
A:E3:  ^Qtr. 3
A:F3:  ^Qtr. 4
A:G3:  ^Total
A:A4:  'Cash
A:B4:  (C0) 120000
A:C4:  (C0) +B4+C14
A:D4:  (C0) +C4+D14
A:E4:  (C0) +D4+E14
A:F4:  (C0) +E4+F14
A:A6:  'Income
A:B6:  (C0) 0
A:C6:  (C0) 40000000
```

To create a cell contents listing, use the /Printer Printer Options Other Cell Formulas command in the 1-2-3 Classic menu. Once this command has been selected, 1-2-3 will print in the form of a cell-contents listing each time you use the /Print Printer command. To turn off the cell-contents listing option, select the /Print Printer Options Other As Displayed command.

Each line in a cell-contents listing may include four items: the cell address, the formatting for the cell, the width of the cell, and the contents of the cell, in that order. The listing is presented row by row, and only nonblank cells are listed. If the width or formatting for a cell matches the current global settings, no reference is made to the format or width of the cell. For example, the ninth entry in the listing above reads A:B4: (C0) 120000. This identifies cell A:B4, formatted as Currency with 0 displayed decimal places and containing the number 120000. No reference is made to the width of the cell, because the width of the column containing the cell matches the current global setting for the worksheet.

9

Functions

1-2-3 for Windows includes *functions*, which are powerful tools that perform specialized calculations. Functions are essentially abbreviated formulas that are used to efficiently and easily perform a specific task. For example, mathematical and statistical functions perform typical numeric calculations such as summing numbers. Other functions perform trigonometric, financial, date and time calculations, as well as logical analysis. 1-2-3 also includes string functions, which manipulate labels, and special functions, which let you determine the position of the cell pointer, return operating system information, indirectly reference cells, and more.

Since functions are valuable time-saving tools for every 1-2-3 user, this chapter serves both as a tool to learn how to use functions and as a convenient reference guide. And because functions are used in a wide range of disciplines, such as financial analysis, accounting, statistics, and trigonometry, this chapter also serves as a refresher course on these subjects.

If you're upgrading from Release 2 or 2.2, you'll find many new functions in 1-2-3 for Windows. Most of these functions were first introduced in Release 3.

In addition, some existing functions have been improved over earlier releases. For example, functions such as @SUM and @AVG now automatically adjust a range argument even if you delete a cell that begins or ends the range.

Note: See Chapter 11 for a discussion of database functions.

FUNCTION BASICS

1-2-3 for Windows' functions all use the following *syntax*, or structure:

```
@FUNCTION(argument1,argument2,...,argumentn)
```

You must follow this syntax otherwise 1-2-3 disallows the entry or evaluates a function as a label. *Always* enter the @ symbol before the function name (which tells 1-2-3 you are entering a function), and don't leave any space between the @ symbol and the function name. You may type in the name of the function using any combination of uppercase and lowercase letters. The maximum length of a function plus its arguments is 512 characters, which is the maximum length of a cell entry in 1-2-3.

Arguments provide the information on which a function acts. *Always* enclose arguments in parentheses, and don't leave any space between the ending parenthesis and an argument. (In 1-2-3 for Windows, a space between arguments, or between the beginning parenthesis and an argument, is ignored.) You must specify arguments while you are entering a function; 1-2-3 won't let you preselect an argument, such as a range.

▼ *Tip:*   In 1-2-3 for Windows, you can choose a function by "pointing-and-shooting". For example, if you select , or if you enter the @ symbol and then press F3 (NAME), 1-2-3 for Windows will display an @Function Index in the @Function Names dialog box. You can scroll down this function list and select the one you want, @SUM for instance. Press ENTER or select OK, and @SUM(will now appear in the contents box (note the beginning argument parenthesis). If you choose a function like @PI which doesn't use an argument, 1-2-3 won't include a beginning parenthesis.

Some functions require a single argument, such as @SQRT(A1), while others like @CHOOSE(3,A1,"Costs",55,B:P10,A5) use multiple arguments. Multiple arguments are separated by *argument separators*, by default a comma (,); but you can change it to a semicolon (;), the international argument separator, or a period (.).

▼ *Tip:*   Use the Tools User International Setup Style Punctuation option to change the argument separator. (See Appendix A for more details.)

Functions also use different types of arguments. For example, many functions use *value* arguments, which can be any of the following:

- Literal numbers
- Numeric formulas or functions that return values
- Locations: cell or range addresses containing values or formulas that return values (including another function)

For instance, the functions @SUM(A1..A3) and @SUM(COSTS), where the range name COSTS is assigned to the range A1..A3, would both return the sum of the values in cells A1, A2, and A3.

Similarly, functions that accept *string* arguments use literal strings (letters, numbers, and symbols enclosed in double quotation marks); string formulas or functions that return strings; and locations—cell or range addresses containing string formulas or literal strings. For example, the function @UPPER(*string*) converts all letters in a string to uppercase. If you enter a literal string directly into this function, such as @UPPER("Help!!"), you *must* enclose it in double quotes.

Other functions use both *value* and *string* arguments. The function, @REPEAT(*string,n*), for instance, duplicates the *string n* times in a cell.

1-2-3 for Windows has functions that use other types of arguments. For example, the @IF function requires a *condition* argument, or logical test, usually incorporating a logical operator such as = or >. Some special functions require an *attribute* argument. For example, @CELLPOINTER(*attribute*) returns a value or label describing a specific attribute of a cell, such as its color or format. Other functions, such as @PI and @ERR, don't use arguments.

Note: If your argument is a location in another 1-2-3 for Windows worksheet file, you'll create file linking. For example, if FIN1.WK3 and FIN2.WK3 are open, the value returned by @SUM(<<FIN2.WK3>>A1..G5) in the file FIN1.WK3 is automatically updated when the referenced information in FIN2.WK3 changes. (See Chapters 4 and 17.)

On-Line Help with Functions

For more about using 1-2-3 for Windows' Help system, see Chapter 1.

1-2-3 for Windows provides easy access to on-line help for functions. Simply press F1 (HELP), or select the Help @Functions command. If you then select @Function Index, you'll see a list of functions you can scroll down. Choose one, such as @AVG, and 1-2-3 for Windows displays the help screen in Figure 9-1 giving a description of this function, including its arguments.

You can also access Help while you are building a function. For instance, if you enter @ and then press F1 (HELP), 1-2-3 will display the @Function Index. If you type @AVG(, for instance, then press F1 (HELP), 1-2-3 for Windows goes directly to the help screen in Figure 9-1 describing @AVG.

GENERAL MATHEMATICAL FUNCTIONS

1-2-3 for Windows' mathematical functions, shown in Table 9-1, either manipulate or calculate values.

Note: If an argument *x* evaluates to a label, label prefix, or a blank cell, a general mathematical function will return 0 because 1-2-3 assigns these a value of 0.

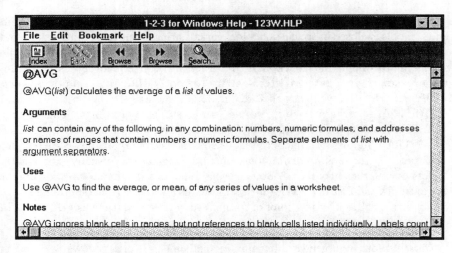

Figure 9-1 Using Help for the @AVG function

Absolute Value: @ABS

The @ABS function calculates the positive or absolute value of a number. The form of this function is

```
@ABS(x)
```

where *x* must evaluate to a value. @ABS is helpful in forcing the result of a formula or function to be positive—using *ABS(x)*—or negative—using *–ABS(x)*. For example, the function @ABS(-2.3) returns 2.3, while -@ABS(2.3) returns -2.3. You can also use -@SQRT(@ABS(*–x*)) to calculate the square root of a negative number.

TABLE 9-1 Mathematical Functions

Function	*Returns*
@ABS	Absolute (positive) value of a number
@SQRT	Square root of a positive number or 0
@ROUND	Rounded value of a number at a specified precision
@INT	Integer portion of a number
@MOD	Modulus (remainder) of a division operation
@RAND	Random value between 0 and 1

Calculating the Square Root: @SQRT

1-2-3's @SQRT function returns the square root of a non-negative value. The form of this function is

`@SQRT(x)`

where x must evaluate to 0 or any positive number. For instance, @SQRT(841) returns 29. Since @SQRT(-4) returns ERR, you must use -@SQRT(@ABS(-4)) to return -2, the square root of a negative value.

Using the @SQRT function is the same as raising a value to the 1/2 power using ^.5. For example, both @SQRT(9) and 9^.5 return the value 3.

Note: Use 1-2-3's ^ operator to raise a value to different powers. For instance, 2^3 cubes the value 2 and returns 8; 8^(1/3) takes the cube root of 8 and returns the value 2. However, 8^1/3 is evaluated as (8^1)/3 and returns the value 2.67 due to 1-2-3's order of precedence (see Chapter 2).

Rounding a Value: @ROUND

The @ROUND function rounds a value to a specified number of decimal places, or *precision*. The form of this function is

`@ROUND(x,places)`

where x and *places* must both evaluate to values. The x argument is the value that you want to round, while *places* specifies where to round this value. Enter the number of places to the right or left of the decimal point where you want rounding to occur, up to 100 places. Any digit less than 5 will be rounded down, while numbers equal to or greater than 5 will be rounded up.

When *places* is positive, @ROUND rounds to the *right* of the decimal place. For instance, @ROUND(456.789,2) returns 456.79; @ROUND(-456.789,2) evaluates to -456.79. When *places* is negative, the value is rounded to the *left* of the decimal point. @ROUND(456.789,-2) evaluates to 500, for example, and @ROUND(-456.789,-2) returns -500.

A formula that references a cell containing @ROUND uses the rounded value. See "The Difference Between @ROUND, @INT, and Range Format" in this section.

Returning an Integer: @INT

The @INT function returns only the integer portion of a value without rounding that value. The form of this function is

`@INT(x)`

where x must evaluate to a value. For example, @INT(456.79) returns the integer 456. Similarly, @INT(-456.79) returns the value -456.

A formula referencing a cell containing @INT uses the integer returned by this function. See "The Difference Between @ROUND, @INT, and Range Format," next.

> ▼ *Tip:*   Use @INT(@NOW) to obtain the date number of the current date. The current time, which is the decimal portion of the date value, is truncated.

The Difference Between @ROUND, @INT, and Range Format

1-2-3 for Windows offers three different options that affect how a value is displayed, and how another cell containing a formula referencing this cell displays and stores its value:

Function or Command	Current Cell	Cells Referencing Current Cell
@ROUND(x,*places*)	Rounds value up or down	Displays and stores rounded value only
@INT(x)	Returns integer portion of value	Displays and stores integer only
Range Format 0 places	Changes only displayed value	Displays and stores full precision

Let's examine the different results obtained using each of these methods. Imagine that you must project the labor cost associated with your company's increased sales. As shown in cell B5 of Figure 9-2, if 72,000 units are needed and each worker can produce 11,000 units per month, then 6.545 workers are necessary. If you could actually employ 6.545 people, the correct labor cost would be $130,909, as shown in cell D5.

The method used in row 6 also calculates this labor cost. Cell B6, which contains the formula +B5, is formatted for 0 decimal places, so 6.545 is rounded up and the value 7 is displayed. But this cell still *contains* the value 6.545. This results in a calculated labor cost of 6.545*$20,000, or $130,909. So a formula referencing a formatted cell uses the stored value, *not* the displayed value.

Now imagine that management decides that until an additional full-time employee is needed, other employees will work overtime to meet the production quota. To reflect this policy, @INT(B5) in cell B7 truncates, or loses the decimal portion of 6.55 and returns 6 employees. If the employees work overtime without pay, the formula in cell D7, +B7*C7, correctly calculates the projected labor cost as 6*20,000, or $120,000. So a formula referencing a cell containing @INT uses the integer returned.

Suppose the employees—not surprisingly—balk at this policy. To avoid a walkout, management decides that when an extra person is needed more than 50% of the time, another person will immediately be hired. In cell B8, @ROUND(B5,0) displays the correct number of employees, 7, and the projected labor cost is correctly calculated as

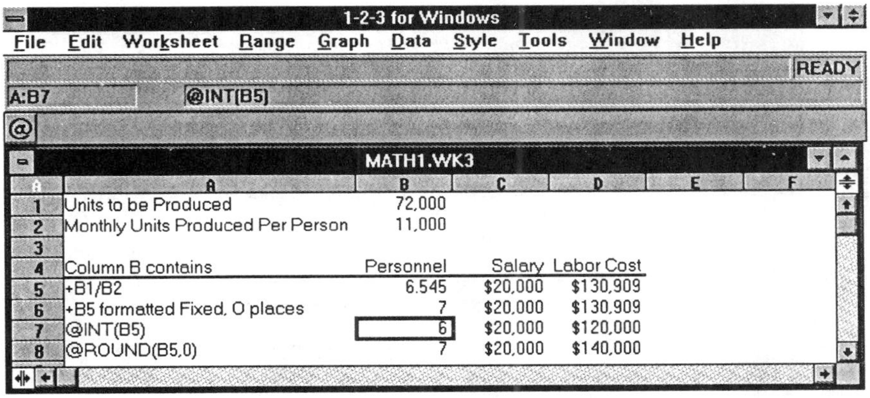

Figure 9-2   The difference between @ROUND, @INT and Range Format

7*20,000 or $140,000. So a formula referencing a cell containing @ROUND uses the rounded value.

Returning the Remainder: @MOD

Use the @MOD function to calculate the remainder, or *modulus* of a division operation. For instance, the modulus of 5/2 is 1; 2 goes into 5 two times and leaves 1 remaining, the modulus. The form of this function is

```
@MOD(numerator,denominator)
```

where *numerator* is the value to be divided, and *denominator* is the value you divide your *numerator* by. If the *denominator* is 0, @MOD returns ERR.

The sign of the numerator determines the sign of the value returned. For example, @MOD(-5,2) returns -1, but @MOD(5,-2) returns 1. Additionally, @MOD(2,5) returns the numerator value 2 when the numerator is smaller than the denominator.

> ▼ *Tip:*   Use @MOD to calculate the day of the week. See "Date and Time Arithmetic" in this chapter for an example.

Figure 9-3 shows a typical application of @MOD, calculating the number of unpalleted units left over each month. In cell B5, @MOD(B3,B4) calculates 30 remaining unpalleted units in April. Notice in cell E5, for the quarter ended June 30, 1992, @MOD(E3,E4) returns the modulus 0, since all of the units produced in that quarter fit on pallets.

Generating Random Values: @RAND

Use the @RAND function to generate random numbers in your worksheet. Since this function uses no arguments, simply enter @RAND in a cell. This function generates a

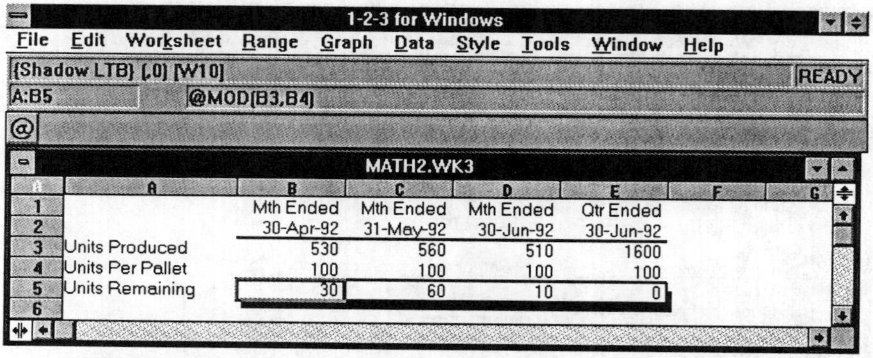

Figure 9-3 Using the @MOD function

random number from 0 to 1, up to 18 decimal places. To create a table of random numbers, use @RAND in each cell in your table.

Whenever your worksheet is manually or automatically recalculated, the random number returned by @RAND changes. So save random numbers as literal values using the Edit Quick Copy command discussed in Chapter 7.

You'll find @RAND useful to

- Generate random invoice numbers, check stub numbers, or orders in a *test of internal controls* (a test to verify the accuracy of internal accounting procedures).

- Generate random serial numbers to test for adherence to production specifications for quality control.

- Create a random integer between 10,000 and 99,999. Use @INT(@RAND*100000) to return an integer without rounding. Use @ROUND(@RAND*1000000,0) to round a value to 0 places.

STATISTICAL FUNCTIONS

1-2-3 for Windows includes the functions listed in Table 9-2 for statistical analysis. Some of these functions, such as @SUM and @AVG, are among the most commonly used 1-2-3 functions. If you are upgrading from Release 2, you will find @SUMPRODUCT, @STDS, and @VARS new.

Note: You can use three-dimensional ranges and references to other worksheet files as statistical function arguments. However, you must include a file reference, such as <<CASH.WK3>>, when you reference information that is located outside the current worksheet file.

TABLE 9-2 Statistical Functions

Function	Returns
@SUM	Sum of a list of values
@SUMPRODUCT	Sum of the products of equal-sized ranges of values
@COUNT	Number of nonblank cells in a list of values
@AVG	Average of nonblank cells in a list of values
@MIN	Minimum value in a list of values
@MAX	Maximum value in a list of values
@VAR	Population variance of a list of values
@STD	Population standard deviation of a list of values
@VARS	Sample variance of a list of values
@STDS	Sample standard deviation of a list of values

Summing Values: @SUM

@SUM is the most commonly used function in 1-2-3. This function adds a group of values. The form of this function is

```
@SUM(list)
```

where *list* consists of one or more items, each separated by an argument separator (usually a comma), and each item represents a single value or a group of values. For example, @SUM(5,C6,B1..B6) includes a valid *list* argument. The three items in this *list* represent eight values. Most often, *list* is a range such as @SUM(B1..B6).

Suppose you have created the worksheet SUM1 in Figure 9-4. You want to sum the values in column A, worksheet A, and record the result. Simply use @SUM(A1..A4) to return the value 1,000 shown in cell A:A5. This is equivalent to @SUM(A1,A2,A3,A4) or +A1+A2+A3+A4. You also get the same result if you sum across columns. For example, in cell A:E1 of the SUM1 file, @SUM(A1..D1) sums the values in row 1 and also returns 1,000.

Note To Release 2 Users: When you add or delete cells at the beginning or end of a range in a statistical function, 1-2-3 for Windows automatically adjusts the range coordinates. Suppose, in the example on the following page, you delete row 1. In the process, the beginning range reference A1 is deleted. In previous editions, @SUM(A1..A4) would become @SUM(ERR) and return ERR. In 1-2-3 for Windows, @SUM (A1..A4) becomes @SUM(A1..A3).

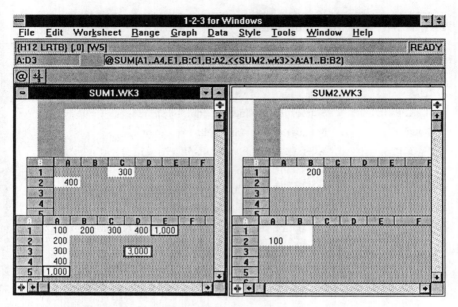

Figure 9-4 Using the @SUM function

In another instance, cell A:D3 in the file SUM1 (see Figure 9-4) contains the formula

```
@SUM(A1..A4,E1,B:C1,B:A2,<<SUM2.WK3>>A:A1..B:B2)
```

and returns the value 3,000. In SUM1, this *list* argument includes the two-dimensional range A:A1..A:A4, and the single-cell addresses A:E1, B:C1, and B:A2. This *list* also includes the three-dimensional range A:A1..B:B2 in the file SUM2.WK3. Note that you must include the file reference, <<SUM2.WK3>>, when you reference a range that is located outside the current worksheet file.

You'll get the same result—3,000—if you arrange these arguments separately and then combine them, as in:

```
@SUM(A1..A4)+E1+B:C1+B:A2+@SUM(<<SUM2.WK3>>A:A1..B:B2)
```

▼ *Tip:*   The ⊞ icon sums an adjacent single-row range or single-column range. In Figure 9-4 for example, if the cell pointer is located in cell A:E1 of SUM1.WK3 when you select this icon, @SUM(A1..D1) is entered in this cell. Likewise, if you choose this icon when the cell pointer is located in cell A:A5 of SUM1.WK3, 1-2-3 enters @SUM(A1..A4) in this cell.

Summing Products: @SUMPRODUCT

The @SUMPRODUCT function is a statistical function that saves worksheet space and memory. Use @SUMPRODUCT to return the resulting sum of a series of products (multiplication formulas). The form of this function is

@SUMPRODUCT(*list*)

where *list* must be composed of equal-sized, multiple-cell, parallel ranges, each separated by an argument separator (usually a comma). Otherwise, @SUMPRODUCT returns ERR. For example, @SUMPRODUCT(A1..A5,B1..F1) returns ERR because the range A1..A5 runs down a column, while B1..F1 runs across a row. @SUMPRODUCT(A1..B2,A3..D3) also returns ERR because, although these ranges are parallel and contain the same number of cells, they are not equally shaped. @SUMPRODUCT returns ERR if you use single-cell range references, such as @SUMPRODUCT(A1,A2,A3), but the correct result when you structure these single-cell arguments as if they were multiple-cell ranges, as in @SUMPRODUCT(A1..A1,B1..B1,C1..C1).

To see how efficient @SUMPRODUCT is, let's look at an example. Suppose Figure 9-5 represents your investment portfolio. To calculate the net sale proceeds after broker commissions, you could enter +B3*C3*D3 in cell E3, then copy this formula to cells E4 and E5. Then you could use @SUM(E3..E5) in cell E6 to arrive at the total. Or you can just use @SUMPRODUCT(B3..B5,C3..C5,D3..D5), as in cell F6, and arrive at the same result. Here, @SUMPRODUCT multiplies across rows, since each range is one column wide. For example, it first multiplies +B3*C3*D3, then +B4*C4*D4, and so on, then returns the total, $92,134.50.

If each range spans more than one column, @SUMPRODUCT multiplies by columns. That is, @SUMPRODUCT multiplies each cell in the first column of the first argument

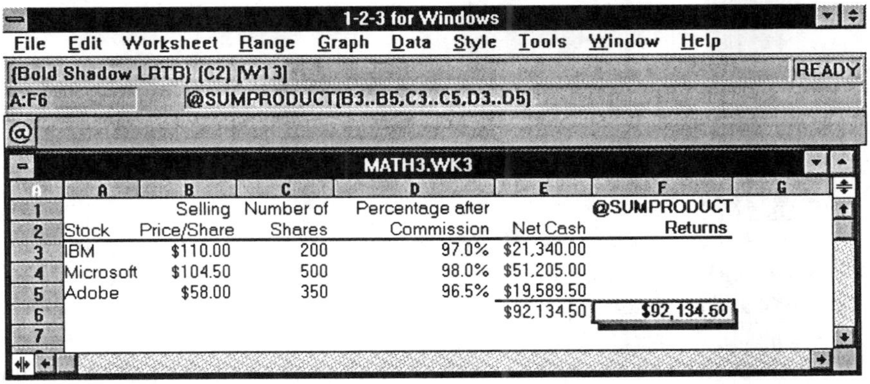

Figure 9-5 Using @SUMPRODUCT to multiply across rows

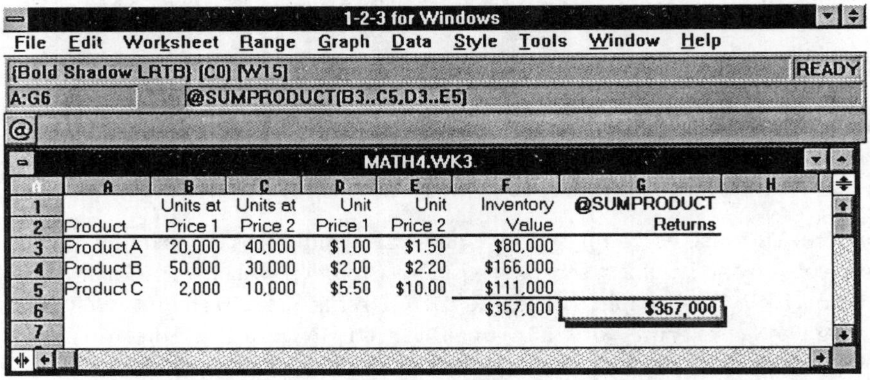

Figure 9-6 Using @SUMPRODUCT to multiply by columns

by the corresponding cell in the first column of the second argument, then multiplies each cell in the second column of the first argument by the corresponding cell in the second column of the second argument, and so on. You can see this in Figure 9-6, where the total inventory value of three products is calculated. In cell F3, you could use +B3*D3+C3*E3, copy this formula to cells F4 and F5, and then use @SUM(F3..F5) in cell F6 to arrive at the inventory value of $357,000. You could also use @SUMPRODUCT (B3..B5,D3..D5)+@SUMPRODUCT(C3..C5,E3..E5) to arrive at this total. Or, as in cell G6, you can just use @SUMPRODUCT(B3..C5,D3..E5) to arrive at the same result. Notice that @SUMPRODUCT in this case multiplies the value in the first cell in the first range, cell B3, by the value in the first cell in the second range, cell D3. It also multiplies the information in cell C3 by the value in cell E3. So you can use multi-column ranges in @SUMPRODUCT, as long as each range contains the same number of cells, is shaped the same, and the ranges are parallel to one another.

Finding the Number of Values in a Range: @COUNT

1-2-3 for Windows' @COUNT function counts the number of nonblank cells in an argument. The form of this function is

```
@COUNT(list)
```

where *list* consists of one or more items, each separated by an argument separator (usually a comma), and each item represents a single value or a group of values. Usually you'll use a range.

Understanding how @COUNT works will help you understand the @AVG function, which you'll use much more frequently. @COUNT returns the number of cells in *list* that are *not* blank. It counts (assigns a value of 1 to) a value, a label, a cell containing a value, a cell that evaluates to ERR or NA, a cell containing a label or label-prefix, or an undefined range name.

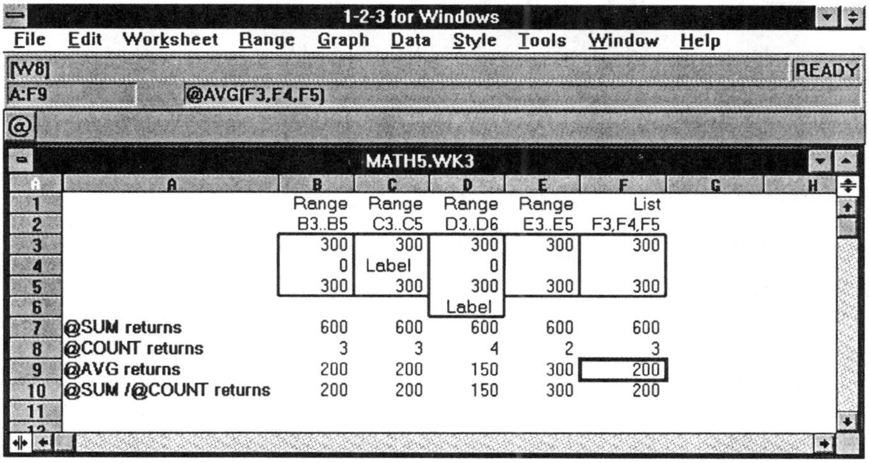

Figure 9-7 Using @COUNT and @AVG

It's easier to understand how @COUNT works by looking at an example. Suppose you want to analyze the values in Figure 9-7. @COUNT appears in row 8 of this figure and returns the following:

Cell	Function	Value	Reason
B8	@COUNT(B3..B5)	3	0 in cell B4 counted
C8	@COUNT(C3..C5)	3	label in cell C4 counted
D8	@COUNT(D3..D6)	4	label in cell D6 counted
E8	@COUNT(E3..E5)	2	blank cell E4 not counted
F8	@COUNT(F3,F4,F5)	3	blank cell F4 counted

▼ *Tip:* Use the Data Distribution command to create a frequency distribution table that counts the number of occurrences, by interval, in a range of values. See Chapter 12 for more details.

Problems with @COUNT

The @COUNT function *sometimes* counts blank cells. You can see this in Figure 9-7, when @COUNT(F3,F4,F5) returns 3 in cell F8, even though cell F4 is blank. This happens because @COUNT returns an incorrect result if a single-cell item in *list* is a blank cell. For example, if cell F4 is blank, @COUNT(F4) returns 1—and that's exactly what causes the incorrect result returned by @COUNT(F3,F4,F5) in cell F8. 1-2-3 evaluates it as @COUNT(F3)+@COUNT(F4)+ @COUNT(F5), and returns 3 instead of 2. You can see the solution to this problem in Column E—@COUNT ignores blank cell E4 when @COUNT(E3..E5) is used in cell E8, and returns the correct count of 2.

In addition, you'll get incorrect results when a cell containing a label is counted. In fact, that's what causes the result in cell D8 of Figure 9-7—@COUNT counts the label in cell D6 and returns 4.

Calculating an Average: @AVG

1-2-3's @AVG function calculates the average, or the *arithmetic mean* of a group of values. This is the sum of all values divided by the number of values. The form of this function is

```
@AVG(list)
```

where *list* consists of one or more items, each separated by an argument separator (usually a comma), and each item represents a single value or a group of values. Most often, *list* is a range such as @AVG(B1..B6). In Figure 9-7, the @AVG function appears in row 9 and returns the following:

Cell	Function	Value	Reason
B9	@AVG(B3..B5)	200	0 in cell B4 counted
C9	@AVG(C3..C5)	200	label in cell C4 counted
D9	@AVG(D3..D6)	150	cells D4 and D6 counted
E9	@AVG(E3..E5)	300	blank cell E4 not counted
F9	@AVG(F3,F4,F5)	200	blank cell F4 counted

Problems with @AVG

The @AVG function can return an incorrect average value when *list* includes any of the following:

- A label or label-prefix, a blank cell that contains spaces, or an undefined range name
- A blank cell that is a single-cell item

You can see this in Figure 9-7, where @AVG returns an incorrect average in cells F9 and D9.

To understand the inherent problems of the @AVG function, you should think of the way that @AVG(*list*) computes an average as @SUM(*list*)/@COUNT (*list*). (Notice that @SUM/@COUNT in row 10 of Figure 9-7 returns the same values as @AVG.) In the numerator, @SUM includes and assigns a 0 value to a label or label-prefix, a blank cell that contains spaces, or an undefined range name. In the denominator, @COUNT also includes them in its count, which increases the denominator value.

In *most* cases, @AVG (really @COUNT in the denominator) ignores blank cells. For instance, when cell E4 is blank, @AVG(E3..E5) correctly returns 300 in cell E9 of Figure 9-7.

@AVG will return an incorrect average value if a single-cell item in *list* is a blank cell. That's what causes the incorrect result returned by @AVG(F3,F4,F5) in cell F9. In the numerator, @SUM assigns a 0 value to the blank cell F4. Remember that @COUNT returns 1 when a single-cell argument is a blank cell. So @AVG(F3,F4,F5) incorrectly returns 600/3, or 200, because it is equivalent to SUM(F3..F5)/(@COUNT(F3) +@COUNT(F4)+ @COUNT(F5).

When a label is included in *list*, the @AVG function also returns an incorrect average that is lower than the correct average value. You can see this in column D of Figure 9-7; because @COUNT counts the label in cell D6, which @SUM evaluates as 0, @AVG(D3..D6) in cell D9 returns the incorrect result, 150 (600/4).

Returning Minimum and Maximum Values: @MIN and @MAX

The @MIN and @MAX functions return the minimum and maximum values in a group of values. The forms of these functions are

```
@MIN(list)
@MAX(list)
```

where *list* consists of one or more items, each separated by an argument separator (usually a comma), and each item represents a single value or a group of values. Usually you'll use a range.

Suppose you have created the worksheet in Figure 9-8 projecting net cash flow for the first six months in 1993. To find the minimum and maximum monthly cash balances for the first quarter in worksheet A, @MIN(A:B2..A:D2) is used to return the minimum monthly cash balance of -$100,000 while @MAX(A:B2..A:D2) returns the maximum monthly cash balance of -$20,000. Note that both functions ignore the blank cell A:C2.

Similarly, in worksheet B, @MIN(B:B2..B:D2) returns the correct monthly minimum cash balance, -$100,000. However, @MAX(B:B2..B:D2) returns an incorrect maximum monthly cash balance of $0 because it evaluates the label in cell B:C2, "Positive," as 0.

▼ *Tip:*   You can use @MAX and @MIN to calculate an average after discarding the smallest and largest values. For example, suppose you want to discard the smallest and largest values in a range, such as A1..A5, before you calculate the average value. To do so, you use @MIN(A1..A5) in cell B1, to return the smallest value, and @MAX(A1..A5) in cell B2 to return the largest value, then @SUM(A1..A5,-B1,-B2)/(@COUNT(A1..A5)-2) to return the correct average. Don't use @AVG(A1..A5,-B1,-B2), because it will include seven items instead of three in the calculation and return an incorrect average.

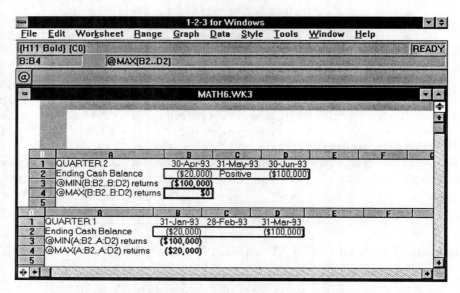

Figure 9-8 Using @MIN and @MAX

Advanced Statistical Functions: @VAR, @STD, @VARS, and @STDS

1-2-3 for Windows provides advanced statistical functions to evaluate both a population and a sample of that population. A population is the entire group of values you want to analyze—for example, the age of each individual in the United States, or the average number of errors in a 1-2-3 for Windows worksheet. You generally evaluate a sample of a population, however, when it is uneconomical or impossible to gather information about the entire population. When a sample includes 30 or more *random* selections from a population, statistical analysis has shown that it can provide an accurate indication of the characteristics of the population.

An important statistic when evaluating a population is the *mean* (average value). You can calculate the mean for either the entire population or a sample from that population using the @AVG function.

Two other indicators, the variance and the standard deviation, measure the reliability of a calculated mean value. The *variance* measures the amount of variation of all values from the mean (average), while the *standard deviation* calculates the degree of dispersion about the mean. 1-2-3 for Windows provides two advanced statistical functions, the *population variance* (@VAR) and the *population standard deviation* (@STD) for evaluating the reliability of a population mean. 1-2-3's *sample variance* (@VARS) and *sample standard deviation* (@STDS) are used to evaluate the reliability of a sample mean.

Population Statistics: @VAR and @STD

The *population variance* measures the amount of dispersion in an entire population by calculating the amount of variation of all values from the mean (average). The equation for the population variance is

$$\text{Population Variance} = \frac{\sum (i - avg)^2}{n} = \frac{\sum (i - @AVG(list))^2}{@COUNT(list)}$$

where *i* is the value of one item in the population and *n* is the number of values (items). You would manually calculate the variance by subtracting the average value of the population from each value, squaring each result, adding all these squared values, and finally dividing this total by *n*, the number of values in the population.

The variance indicates the reliability of the average value. If all values in the population are the same, each item then equals the average value, and the variance is 0. So the *lower* the variance, the less the individual values vary from the mean, and the more reliable the average value is.

The *standard deviation* is used more often than the variance because it returns a number that is easier to analyze. The standard deviation calculates the *degree* of dispersion within a population of values. That is, it calculates the degree to which all values in the population deviate from the mean value (average). The equation for the population standard deviation is

$$\text{Population Standard Deviation} = \sqrt{\text{Population Variance}}$$

Approximately 68% of the items in a normally distributed population fall within plus or minus one standard deviation of the mean (average). Approximately 95% fall within plus or minus two standard deviations of the mean. A low standard deviation indicates that all of the items in a population are closely clustered around the mean value.

1-2-3 for Windows' population variance and standard deviation functions are much easier to use than these mathematical formulas. The forms of these functions are

```
@VAR(list)
@STD(list)
```

where *list* consists of one or more items, each separated by an argument separator (usually a comma), and each item represents a single value or a group of values. Most often *list* is a range, such as @VAR(B1..B6).

Note: As shown in the mathematical equations above, you should think of the way that 1-2-3 calculates the variance and standard deviation as functions of @AVG and @COUNT. This means that *all* advanced statistical functions have the same problems as the @AVG and @COUNT functions. To ensure correct results, make sure that your *list* doesn't include any blank cells containing spaces, labels, label prefixes, and undefined range names. (See "Problems with @COUNT" and "Problems with @AVG" for more details.)

```
┌──────────────────────────────────────────────────────────────────────┐
│ ━                        1-2-3 for Windows                      ▼ ┃│
│ File   Edit   Worksheet   Range   Graph   Data   Style   Tools   Window   Help │
│ (F2)                                                              READY │
│ A:B5              @STD(D5..I9)                                          │
│ @                                                                      │
│ ┌────────────────────────────────────────────────────────────────┐   │
│ │ ━                          MATH7.WK3                        ▼ ▲ │   │
│ │      A            B          C     D  E  F  G  H  I  J  K    L ▲│   │
│ │ 1              Population   Sample                              ▲│   │
│ │ 2              Statistics   Statistics                          │   │
│ │ 3 Average        51.17       51.17                              │   │
│ │ 4 Variance      502.01      519.32  Age of People in Group      │   │
│ │ 5 Standard Deviation 22.41  22.79   32 65 19 105 26 74          │   │
│ │ 6 One Standard Deviation Range      68 42 59  61 70 24          │   │
│ │ 7  Minimum Range  28.76     28.38   92 37 31  29 60 30          │   │
│ │ 8  Maximum Range  73.57     73.96   21 24 36  46 47 69          │   │
│ │ 9                                   53 81 43  55 87 49          │   │
│ │ 10                                                             ▼│   │
│ └────────────────────────────────────────────────────────────────┘   │
└──────────────────────────────────────────────────────────────────────┘
```

Figure 9-9 Using advanced statistical functions

Suppose you have compiled and entered the ages of 30 randomly selected people in the range D5..I9 of Figure 9-9. First, let's assume that this group is the entire population. As shown in cell B3, @AVG(D5..I9) shows that, on average, the population is 51.17 years old. In cell B5, @STD(D5..I9) calculates that one population standard deviation is 22.41. Thus, approximately 68% of the population is between 28.76 and 73.57 years old. In cell B4, @VAR(D5..I9) shows that the population variance is 502.01, which is simply the population standard deviation squared, or $(22.41)^2$.

Sample Statistics: @VARS and @STDS

The *sample* variance calculates the amount of variation of all *sample* values from the *sample* mean value (average). The equation for the sample variance is

$$\text{Sample Variance} \quad = \quad \frac{\sum (s - avg)^2}{n - 1} = \text{Population Variance} \times \frac{n}{(n - 1)}$$

where s is the value of one item in the sample, n is the number of values (items), and the average is calculated for the sample.

As you can see in this formula, the sample variance is equal to the population variance multiplied by $[n/(n - 1)]$, or the *degrees of freedom*. This factor compensates for sample errors, and always creates a slightly larger sample variance than the population variance.

The sample standard deviation calculates the degree to which the values in the sample deviate from the sample mean (average). The sample standard deviation is calculated as

$$\text{Sample Standard Deviation} = \sqrt{\text{Sample Variance}}$$

1-2-3's forms of these functions are

```
@VARS(list)
@STDS(list)
```

where *list* consists of one or more items, each separated by an argument separator (usually a comma), and each item represents a single value or a group of values. Usually *list* is a range. If *list* includes any undefined range names, blank cells, blank cells containing spaces, labels, or label prefixes, you'll get incorrect results.

Building on the example in Figure 9-9, let's suppose that this group of values is just a random sample of the entire population you want to analyze. In cell C3, the mean age is still calculated using @AVG(D5..I9). However, in cell C5, the sample standard deviation @STDS(D5..I9) shows that one sample standard deviation is 22.79 years. Thus, if this group of values is only a sample, approximately 68% of the population is between 28.38 and 73.96 years of age. This span is larger than that calculated above for a population. Although in this case the average age of the population and the sample are the same, the sample mean is a *less* reliable number than the population mean. The sample variance, 519.32, returned in cell C4 using @VARS(D5..I9) is simply the sample standard deviation squared or $(22.79)^2$.

TRIGONOMETRIC AND LOGARITHMIC FUNCTIONS

1-2-3 for Windows includes the same trigonometric and logarithmic functions, shown in Table 9-3, as previous releases of 1-2-3. These functions are primarily used in engineering and other scientific applications.

Calculating Pi and Angle Conversions: @PI

Use the @PI function to calculate the value of π to 17 decimal places. π, defined as the ratio of the circumference of a circle to the diameter, is equal to 3.14159265358979324. Figure 9-10 shows the relationship between the 360 degrees of a circle and π (2π = 360 degrees).

Since this function takes no argument, simply enter @PI in a cell. Because 1-2-3 for Windows uses the entire 17-digit value regardless of the format you use, @PI will retain accuracy in your other calculations.

Note: Calculate the circumference, C, of a circle, as $C = @PI*D$, where D is the diameter, and the area, A, using $A = @PI*R^2$, where R is the radius.

Most of 1-2-3's trigonometric functions use arguments expressed in radians, so you'll need to use @PI to convert values expressed in degrees to radians before you use these functions. Or, with 1-2-3's inverse trigonometric functions, use @PI to convert values obtained in radians to degrees. Just use the following conversion formulas:

Conversion	*Conversion (Multiplication) Factor*
Degrees to radians	@PI/180
Radians to degrees	180/@PI

TABLE 9-3 Trigonometric and Logarithmic Mathematical Functions

Function	*Returns*
@PI	Constant value π 3.14159265358979324
@SIN	Sine of an angle β in radians
@COS	Cosine of an angle β in radians
@TAN	Tangent of an angle β in radians
@ASIN	Arcsine of the sine of an angle β
@ACOS	Arccosine of the cosine of an angle β
@ATAN	Arctangent of the tangent of an angle β
@TAN2	Arctangent of the tangent of x and y
@EXP	Value of the constant e raised to a power x
@LN	Natural logarithm of x in base e
@LOG	Base 10 logarithm of x

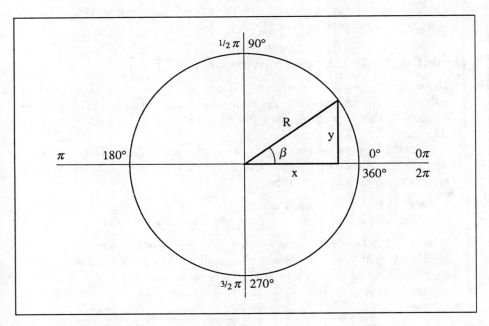

Figure 9-10 Trigonometric relationships

For example, to convert 180 degrees to radians use 180*(@PI/180), which returns 3.14159 radians (which is π); to convert 1.5 π (1.5*@PI radians) to degrees, use 1.5*@PI*(180/@PI), which returns 270 degrees.

Other Trigonometric Conversions: @SIN, @COS, and @TAN

The @SIN, @COS, and @TAN functions calculate the sine, cosine, and tangent of an angle. The forms of these functions are

```
@SIN(angle β in radians)
@COS(angle β in radians)
@TAN(angle β in radians)
```

where the *angle* β in radians must be a value expressed in *radians*. To convert an angle in degrees to radians, multiply it by the conversion factor @PI/180 before you use one of these functions.

Table 9-4 shows these trigonometric functions for the triangle in Figure 9-10. This table also includes other trigonometric relationships, such as the secant and tangent, that can be calculated using 1-2-3's trig functions.

Here's a typical example of how you would use Figure 9-10 and 1-2-3's trigonometric functions. Suppose you know that the angle β is 30 degrees, and that X is 7 feet. What is Y? Since the tangent of β equals Y/X, you can use @TAN to solve for Y. First convert β, 30 degrees, to radians using 30*@PI/180. Now use @TAN(30*@PI/180), which returns .57735. So Tan(β) = .57735 = $Y/7$, and solving for Y returns 4.0414 feet.

TABLE 9-4   Trigonometric Functions

Trig Function	*Mathematical Formula*	*1-2-3 Function*
Sine β	Y/R	@SIN(*angle β in radians*)
Cosine β	X/R	@COS(*angle β in radians*)
Tangent β	Y/X = Sine β/Cosine B	@TAN(*angle β in radians*)
Cotangent β	X/Y = 1/Tangent β	1/@TAN(*angle β in radians*
Secant β	R/X = 1/Cosine β	1/@COS(*angle β in radians*
Cosecant β	R/Y = 1/Sine β	1/@SIN(*angle β in radians*)

TABLE 9-5 Inverse Trigonometric Functions

Trig Function	1-2-3 Function	Argument Min	Max	Result Min	Max
Arcsine β	@ASIN(*sine* β)	-1	1	-π/2	π/2
Arccosine β	@ACOS(*cosine* β)	-1	1	0	π/2
Arctangent β	@ATAN(*tangent* β)	none	none	-π/2	π/2
Arctangent β	@ATAN2(*X, Y*)	none*	none*	-π	π

* If Y = 0, @ATAN2 = 0. If X = 0 and Y = 0, @ATAN2 returns ERR.

Inverse Trigonometric Functions: @ASIN, @ACOS, @ATAN, @ATAN2

The @ASIN, @ACOS, @ATAN, and @ATAN2 functions calculate an angle's size using the sine, cosine, and tangent as their arguments. These functions are the inverse functions of the @SIN, @COS, and @TAN functions. Table 9-5 provides an overview of these inverse functions, including their minimum and maximum acceptable arguments, as well as the range of results each function returns.

The @ASIN, @ACOS, and @ATAN functions all return a result in *radians*. For example, suppose for the triangle in Figure 9-10, X is 5 and R is 10. Cosine β is then 5/10 (X/R) or .5 radians. The arccosine of β, or the angle β, can be calculated as @ACOS(.5), which returns 1.0472 *radians*. Multiply this value by 180/@PI to convert it to 60 degrees. Actually, you can perform these steps all at once using @ACOS(5/10)*(180/@PI).

The @ATAN2 function calculates the arctangent, or angle size, as the tangent Y/X. These arguments represent the triangle sides in Figure 9-10. @ATAN2 returns an angle in *radians*. Note that @ATAN2(1,0) returns 0 but @ATAN2(0,0) returns ERR.

An Example

Suppose you fly your own plane and you want to build a runway in a cornfield. The maximum runway length can be 750 feet. Unfortunately, a 75-foot barn is located at the end of the field, which you want to clear by 50 feet. Under these conditions, your plane's maximum angle of climb is 15 degrees. Is this an acceptable runway for this plane? Using Figure 9-10, X is 750 and Y is 125 (barn and margin). Using @ATAN2(750,125) returns .165149 radians. Using .165149*180/@PI converts this value to 9.46 degrees. So you can build this runway and safely take off without hitting the proverbial wall of the barn.

Logarithmic Functions: @EXP, @LN, and @LOG

1-2-3 for Windows provides three logarithmic functions: @EXP, @LN, and @LOG, which are all closely related. The @EXP function computes the value of e^x, or the constant value e (approximately 2.718282) raised to the power of x. The form of this function is

    @EXP(x)

where x must evaluate to a number between -11,355 and 11,356. For example, @EXP(1) returns 2.7182818, while @EXP(@LN(1)) returns 1, since the natural log is the inverse of the exponential function. If x is between -227 and 230, 1-2-3 for Windows can display the results of @EXP. For values of x between -227 and -11,355, and between 230 and 11,356, however, 1-2-3 for Windows can store but not display the results.

The @LN function computes the natural logarithm of a value in *base e*. The mathematical equation of the natural logarithm is $e^z = x$, where $z = \ln(x)$. The form of this function is

    @LN(x)

where x must evaluate to a value greater than 0. For instance, @LN(5) returns 1.61, @LN(.0001) returns -9.21, but @LN(0) returns ERR. @LN(@EXP(1)) returns 1, since the natural log is the inverse of the exponential function.

> ▼ *Tip:* You can use @LN to determine a learning curve. For instance, imagine that you plot some x and y data points and they seem to represent an exponential curve of the general form $Y = Kx^n$ (a learning curve). You want to confirm that they do represent a learning curve, and if so, determine K and n. Use @LN to convert this exponential formula to a linear formula by taking the natural log of each side of the equation. This yields @LN(y)=@LN(K)+n@LN(x). Now, by performing a linear regression for your points @LN(y) and @LN(x), you can determine @LN(K), the y intercept, and n, the slope of the line. You can also use the exponential formula to determine new data points, since you have solved for K and n using @LN. See Chapter 12 for a discussion of linear regression.

The @LOG function computes the common logarithm using base 10. Mathematically, the base 10 log equals $10^z = x$, where $\log(x) = z$. The form of this function is

    @LOG(x)

where x must evaluate to a value greater than 0. For example, @LOG(5) returns .69897, @LOG(.05) returns -1.30103, but @LOG(0) returns ERR. @LOG(10) returns 1, since this function uses base 10.

LOGIC AND ERROR-TRAPPING FUNCTIONS

1-2-3 for Windows includes logic and error-trapping functions you can use to evaluate or test conditions. By using these functions, you can add decision-making to a spreadsheet, database, or macro.

Table 9-6 shows 1-2-3 for Windows' logical and error-trapping functions, including the new function @ISAM, as well as @ISRANGE, previously introduced in 1-2-3/G. Release 3 users will also find @ISAFF and @ISAPP new.

Conditional Tests: @IF

One of the most powerful tools in 1-2-3 for Windows is the @IF function. You can use @IF to create conditional or decision-making tests for almost any situation that has at least two possible outcomes. The form of this function is

```
@IF(condition,true-result,false-result)
```

where *condition* is the test that you want to evaluate. If the *condition* is true, @IF returns the *true-result*; if it is false, @IF returns the *false-result*.

The Condition Argument

Usually, the *condition* argument is a *conditional test*, which compares two items to each other using a *logical operator* such as = or >. Simple logical operators are listed in Table 9-7.

Logical operators create a *condition* that 1-2-3 evaluates as equal to either the value 1, if true, or the value 0, if false. For example, the conditional test 5>20 returns false (0) since 5 is not greater than 20, while B5="Noel" returns true (1) if cell B5 contains the string Noel and false (0) if it doesn't.

You can also use functions or formulas, +B5/40*45<0 and @SUM(A:B5..D:Z20)<>2000, for instance, as valid *condition* arguments. You can even reference information in other files. For example, in the file TEST1, B5=<<TEST2.WK3>>C4 is a valid conditional test.

True-Result and False-Result Arguments

If 1-2-3 evaluates a *condition* as true (value 1), it returns the *true-result* argument; if *condition* is false (value 0), the *false-result* is returned. In the function @IF(B2=20,20,"ERROR"), for instance, the *condition* B2 = 20 compares the value in cell B2 and the value 20. If they are equal, @IF returns 20, the *true-result*; otherwise, it returns ERROR, the *false-result*.

TABLE 9-6 Logic and Error-Trapping Functions

Function	*Returns*
@IF	True if condition is true, false otherwise
@TRUE	Value 1
@FALSE	Value 0
@ERR	Value ERR
@NA	Value NA
@ISERR	Value 1 if argument is the value ERR, 0 otherwise
@ISNA	Value 1 if argument is the value NA, 0 otherwise
@ISNUMBER	Value 1 if argument is a value or a blank cell, 0 otherwise
@ISSTRING	Value 1 if argument is a string, 0 otherwise
@ISRANGE	Value 1 if argument is a defined range name, 0 otherwise
@ISAPP	Value 1 if argument is a currently loaded add-in, 0 otherwise
@ISAM	Value 1 if argument is a currently defined add-in macro, 0 otherwise
@ISAFF	Value 1 if argument is a defined add-in function, 0 otherwise

Note: When you enter a literal string directly into the @IF function, be sure to enclose it in double quotes or @IF will return ERR.

Both the *true-result* and *false-result* can be a string, a value, or another condition. If you use another @IF function, it is known as *nesting* (see "Nesting @IF Functions" below).

TABLE 9-7 Simple Logical Operators

Operator	*Operation*
=	Equal to
<	Less than
>	Greater than
<=	Less than or equal to
>=	Greater than or equal to
< >	Not equal to

Using @IF to Evaluate Values

Imagine you must compute the printing cost of *1-2-3 for Windows*. For print runs of 10,000 books or less, the cost is $20 per book. For runs greater than 10,000, the cost decreases to $15 per book. To perform these calculations, you can create a spreadsheet like Figure 9-11. In cell C2, @IF(B2>10000,B2*15,B2*20) calculates the cost of the April 15, 1992 run. The *condition* compares the 10,001 print run in cell B2 to 10,000. Since it exceeds 10,000, @IF returns the *true-result* B2*15, or $150,015. In cell C3, however, @IF returns the *false-result*, B3*20, or $200,000, because the 10,000-unit run is *not* greater than 10,000.

Note: Remember that 1-2-3 evaluates a blank cell as equal to the value 0.

Using @IF to Evaluate Strings

You can also use @IF to evaluate strings. When you do so, 1-2-3 for Windows evaluates a string in the *condition* using these rules:

- Spelling differences matter. So do spacing differences, which includes extra leading or trailing spaces or spaces between words and letters.

- Capitalization differences and label prefixes don't matter.

> ▼ *Tip:*   To differentiate between upper and lower case, use @EXACT in @IF. For example, if cell A1 contains the label SALES, @IF(@EXACT(A1,"Sales"),1,0) returns the *false-result* 0. See "String Functions" in this chapter for more details.

To see how this works, let's look at the expense sheet in Figure 9-12. To categorize these expenses, @IF($B2=D$1,$C2,"") is entered in cell D2. (The mixed references

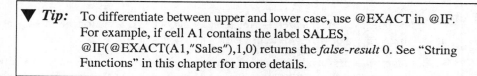

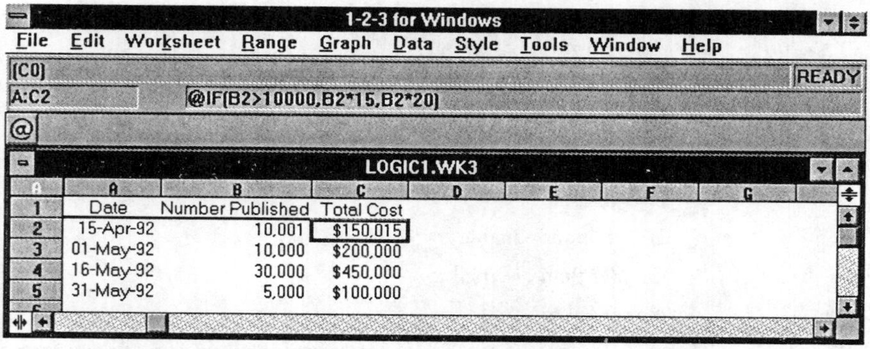

Figure 9-11   Using @IF with values

freeze the row reference in D1 and the column references in B2 and C2 for copying to E2..F2 and D3..F6.) Since @IF in cell D2 evaluates the uppercase string in cell B1, "RENT", and the proper case string in cell B2, "Rent", as equal, the *true-result* is returned—$800 from cell C2. @IF also evaluates the capitalized headings in row 1 as equal to the upper- and lower-case strings in cells B3 and B4. However, because "Rente" is incorrectly spelled, the *false-result*, a null string, is returned in cell D5. This also occurs in cell F6 because the label in B6, "   Phone", includes leading spaces.

Caution: 1-2-3 assigns a value of 0 to a string. This can create problems when it is tested against a blank cell, which 1-2-3 also evaluates as 0. For example, @IF("LABEL"=A2,1,0) returns the *true-result* 1 when cell A2 is blank, because 1-2-3 evaluates both LABEL and the blank cell A2 as 0.

Using @IF to Concatenate Strings and Blank Cells

To *concatenate*, or add together, a string and a blank cell, you must use the @IF function or 1-2-3 for Windows will return ERR. For example, suppose you want to concatenate the first, middle, and last names in the Figure 9-13 database. However, some people don't have a middle name—that's why cell B2 is blank.

In cell D2, @IF(B2 ="",A2&" "&C2,A2&" "&B2&" "&C2) tests cell B2. (Notice that *true-result* and *false-result* add a space between the concatenated strings.) Since cell B2 is blank, @IF returns the *true-result* Elisabeth Kleinmann by adding together only the first and last names. On the other hand, @IF returns the *false-result* Clayton Reid Sikes III by concatenating the first, middle, and last names.

Column F shows what happens when you use a concatenation formula without the @IF function. Because a middle name is included in row 3, things work out fine in cell F3—the formula +A3&" "&B3&" "&C3 successfully concatenates the strings and returns Clayton Reid Sikes III. But when no middle name is included in row 2, the formula +A2&" "&B2&" "&C2 in cell F2 returns ERR.

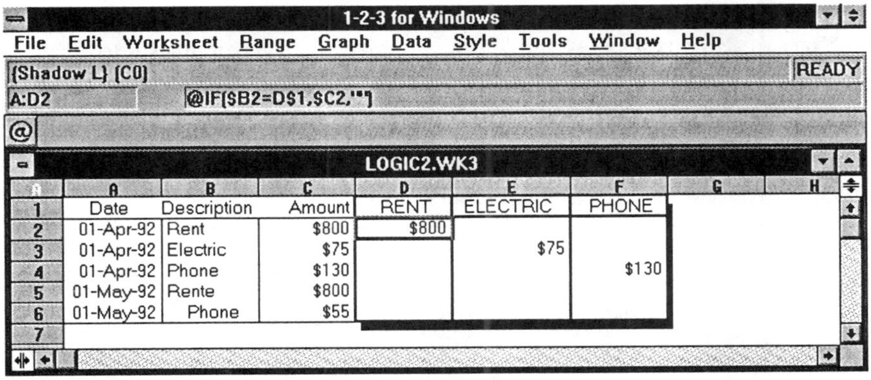

Figure 9-12 Using @IF with strings

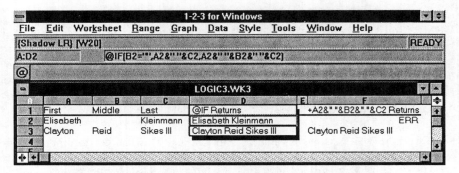

Figure 9-13 Using @IF to concatenate strings and blank cells

Compound Logical Operators

The compound logical operators, shown in Table 9-8, allow you to create complex tests by combining multiple conditions in one @IF function. For example, the #AND# operator in

```
@IF(B2>100#AND#B3>20#AND#B4>15,"MET GOALS","BELOW GOALS")
```

creates a three-condition test. @IF will return the *true-result* MET GOALS if B2>100 *and* B3>20 *and* B4>15, but if *any* of these conditions are false, the *false-result* BELOW GOALS will be returned.

The #OR# operator returns the *true-result* if any *condition* is true. So, @IF(B2>100#OR#B3>20#OR#B4>15,"MET GOALS","BELOW GOALS") returns the *true-result* MET GOALS if B2>100 *or* B3>20 *or* B4>15 is true. Only when none of these *conditions* are met is the *false-result* BELOW GOALS returned.

On the other hand, #NOT# negates the conditional test. In other words, #NOT# tells the @IF function to analyze the *opposite* of the *condition*. So @IF(#NOT#B2>100,"MET GOALS","BELOW GOALS") returns the *true-result* MET GOALS if B2 < 100, and returns the *false-result* BELOW GOALS otherwise.

You can also mix #AND# and #OR#, provided you use parentheses to create separate and distinct conditions that control the order of precedence. (Remember from Chapter 2

TABLE 9-8 Compound Logical Operators

Operator	*Operation*
#AND#	And
#OR#	Or
#NOT#	Not

that the compound logical operators all have the same precedence level.) For example, 1-2-3 for Windows correctly evaluates the conditions in

```
@IF((B2>100#AND#B3>20)#OR#(B2>100#AND#B4>15),"MET
GOALS","BELOW GOALS").
```

You can also use *nest* @IF functions to represent this logic.

Nesting @IF Functions

When you need to create a hierarchy in your logic, you should *nest* @IF functions—include another @IF function as the *true-result* and/or the *false-result*. In fact, by combining nested @IF functions and compound operators, you can create a function that not only performs very complex decision-making, but is easier to understand and debug.

Using nested @IF functions really helps when there are more than two solutions. For instance, suppose you are evaluating the projected financial results in Figure 9-14 against sales of 100, gross profit of 20, and net profit of 15. If only the 100 sales goal is met, MET SALES GOAL should be displayed. If no goals are reached, the result should be BELOW GOALS. However, if the sales goal is met and *either* the gross or net profit goal is achieved, then MET GOALS should be displayed. All of these conditions are handled in cell B6 by

```
@IF(B2>100,@IF(B3>20#OR#B4>15,"MET GOALS","MET SALES
GOAL"),"BELOW GOALS")
```

which evaluates the first @IF function as follows:

B2>100 Condition	*Result*
True	Evaluates *true-result* @IF(B3>20#OR#B4>15,"MET GOALS", "MET SALES GOALS")
False	Returns *false-result* BELOW GOALS

Because the 1992 sales value of 95 is less than 100, in cell B6 the *false result* of the first @IF function BELOW GOALS is returned. However, if the *condition* in the first @IF function is *true*, 1-2-3 for Windows then evaluates the second @IF function as follows:

B3>20 Condition	*B4>15 Condition*	*Result*
True	True or False	Returns *true-result* MET GOALS
True or False	True	Returns *true-result* MET GOALS
False	False	Returns *false-result* MET SALES GOAL

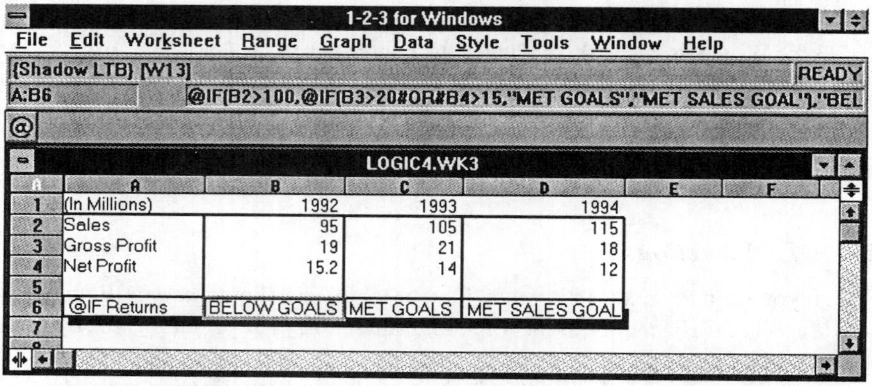

Figure 9-14 Nesting @IF functions

For example, because the 1993 sales of 105 exceeds 100, 1-2-3 evaluates the *true-result* of the first @IF function, which is the second @IF function. Although the gross profit of 21 exceeds the 20 goal, the 14 net profit doesn't exceed the goal of 15. Since only one of these conditions must be met, the *true-result* of the *second* @IF function, MET GOALS, is returned in cell C6.

On the other hand, in 1994 neither of the conditions in the second @IF function is met. Although sales of 105 exceed the 100 goal, neither the gross profit of 18 nor the net profit of 12 meet the conditions. So 1-2-3 evaluates the second @IF function as false and returns its *false-result*, MET SALES GOAL.

True and False Values: @TRUE and @FALSE

1-2-3's @TRUE function returns the *Boolean* true value 1. @FALSE returns the Boolean false value 0. Neither require an argument.

These functions are typically used as the *true-result* and *false-result* arguments in @IF or @CHOOSE (see "Lookup Functions" in this chapter), or in macros. For example, the function @IF(A6="Expenses",@TRUE,@FALSE) returns the value 1 if cell A6 contains the label Expenses, and the value 0 otherwise.

Indicating an ERR Value: @ERR

Sometimes you may actually want to place the value ERR (error) in a spreadsheet. The @ERR function, which requires no argument, returns the special *value* ERR, not the label ERR.

Combining @ERR with @IF is an easy way to create error-trapping logic. For example, suppose you are projecting personnel in cell D10 which, by corporate mandate, can't exceed 100 employees. The function @IF(D10<100,D10,@ERR) will return the projected personnel in cell D10 if it is under 100, and ERR otherwise.

Using @ERR, however, can create a ripple effect throughout a spreadsheet, because the value ERR takes precedence over all other values. For example, imagine cell A1 contains @ERR. If cell A2 contains the formula +A1, it will also return ERR. If cell A3 indirectly references cell A1 through the formula +A2, it too will return ERR. To stop this ripple effect, use @ISERR, which is discussed below.

Flagging an Unknown Value: @NA

1-2-3 for Windows' @NA function, which also requires no argument, returns the special *value* NA (not available). Enter @NA in a cell to flag missing information, or to easily determine which formulas in a spreadsheet depend on a particular value.

Any cells and formulas that directly or indirectly reference a cell containing @NA also return the value NA unless ERR overrides it. For instance, suppose that cell A1 contains @NA, and cell A2 contains +A1 which returns NA. However, cell A3 contains ERR, so +A2+A3 returns ERR, not NA, because ERR takes precedence over all other values.

Note: To stop the ripple effect of @NA, use @ISNA discussed next.

Testing for ERR and NA: @ISERR and @ISNA

Use the @ISERR and @ISNA functions to test for the special values ERR (error) and NA (not available). The forms of these functions are

```
@ISERR(x)
@ISNA(x)
```

where x, although usually an address, can be any value or string, or even a condition. These functions evaluate x and return the following:

Argument evaluates to	@ISERR returns	@ISNA returns
value ERR	1	0
value NA	0	1
other	0	0

Using @ISERR to Divide by Zero

One of the most common causes of ERR is a division by 0. If cell A1 contains the formula +100/A2 and cell A2 contains 0, for example, cell A1 will return the value ERR. If you use @IF(@ISERR(100/A2),0,100/A2) in cell A1, however, it returns 0 instead of ERR when cell A2 contains 0. Otherwise, it returns the result of +100/A2.

Blocking the Ripple Effect

You can use @ISERR to stop the ripple effect of ERR throughout a spreadsheet, and use @ISNA in a similar manner to stop the ripple effect of NA. To see this, let's return to the previous example, where cell A1 contains @ERR, cell A2 contains +A1 which returns ERR, and cell A3 indirectly references cell A1 through the formula +A2 and also returns ERR. In cell A2, @IF(@ISERR(A1),0,A1) will return 0 instead of ERR and +A1 otherwise, so ERR will no longer be returned in cells A2 or A3.

Testing the Contents of a Cell: @ISSTRING and @ISNUMBER

The @ISSTRING and @ISNUMBER functions test whether an argument is a string, a value, or a blank cell. The forms of these functions are

```
@ISSTRING(x)
@ISNUMBER(x)
```

where x, although usually an address, can be any value or string, or even a condition. These functions evaluate x and return the following:

Argument evaluates to	@ISSTRING returns	@ISNUMBER returns
Label, label prefix, or blank cell with spaces	1	0
Single value, including special values ERR or NA	0	1
Blank cell	0	1

The Boolean true value 1 is returned only when the @ISNUMBER argument evaluates to a value or a blank cell, or the @ISSTRING argument evaluates to a string. If x is a range address or name, both of these functions return the false value 0.

> ▼ *Tip:* You can also use @CELLPOINTER and @CELL to determine whether a cell contains a string. See "Special Functions" for more details.

You'll usually use @ISNUMBER or @ISSTRING to prevent the incorrect *type* of information from being entered into a formula or cell location, or to flag needed database information, such as missing zip codes. For example, look at Figure 9-15, where a database of city, state, and zip code are *concatenated* into one string. Zip codes have been entered as either strings or values, and some are even missing. In cell D2, the formula

```
@IF(@ISSTRING(C2)=1,+A2&", "&B2&""&C2,@IF(C2>0,+A2&", "&B2&"
"&@STRING(C2,0),"NEED ZIP CODE"))
```

concatenates the strings in cells A2, B2, and C2 if the zip code in cell C2 contains a string (@ISSTRING returns 1). If cell C2 contains a zip code entered as a value (C2>0), @STRING converts it to a string (see "String Functions" below) when the strings are joined. Otherwise, cell C2 must be blank (C2=0) and it returns the false result, the label

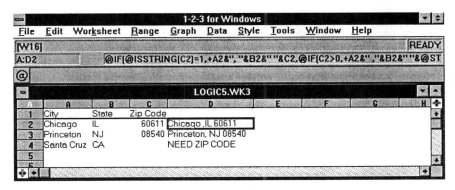

Figure 9-15 Using @ISSTRING to concatenate strings and values

NEED ZIP CODE. Note that the concatenation formulas add a space between each string, as well a comma (,) between the city and the state.

Testing for Range Names: @ISRANGE

The @ISRANGE function, first introduced in Release 3, tests for a defined range name. The form of this function is

```
@ISRANGE(x)
```

where x is the address or name of a range. If you enter x as a single cell address, @ISRANGE converts it to a range. For the name or address of a defined range, @ISRANGE returns 1. It returns 0 for the name or address of an undefined range.

@ISRANGE is often used with @IF to test for a named range before it is used in a formula or function. For instance,

```
@IF(@ISRANGE(COSTS)=1,@AVG(COSTS),"NOT A RANGE NAME")
```

computes the average value in the range COSTS, if COSTS is a defined range. Otherwise, it returns the label "NOT A RANGE NAME".

The @ISRANGE function is also commonly used with an {IF} macro command to test for the presence of a named range. For example, the following macro tests for the presence of the range named OUTPUT:

```
\P              {IF @ISRANGE(OUTPUT)}{ALT}fpOUTPUT~{QUIT}
                {BRANCH SETRANGE}
SETRANGE        {ALT}rncOUTPUT{TAB 2}A1..I110~
                {BRANCH \P}
```

If OUTPUT is a defined range name, @ISRANGE returns 1 and the macro executes the commands to print the range to the printer. If @ISRANGE returns 0, the range name is not defined and the macro skips to the next line where {BRANCH} causes the macro to branch to a routine, SETRANGE, that defines the output range.

Logic Functions for Add-ins: @ISAM, @ISAPP, and @ISAFF

1-2-3 for Windows includes three new functions—@ISAPP, @ISAM, and @ISAFF— that perform logical tests on your currently attached add-ins. The forms of these functions are

```
@ISAPP(name)
@ISAM(name)
@ISAFF(name)
```

where *name* must evaluate to a string.

@ISAPP tests whether an add-in application is attached. If *name* is an attached add-in, @ISAPP returns 1 (true) and 0 (false) otherwise.

@ISAM and @ISAFF test for the presence of macro commands and @functions within your attached add-ins. For example, @ISAM("FEDFUNDS") returns 1 if {FEDFUNDS} is a valid macro command that is defined within an add-in that is currently in memory. However, @ISAM("BRANCH") returns 0, because {BRANCH} is a built-in macro command.

Similarly, @ISAFF("CELSIUS") returns 1 if @CELSIUS is a defined add-in @function, and @ISAFF("DAVG") always returns 0, because @DAVG is a built-in @function.

LOOKUP FUNCTIONS

1-2-3 for Windows provides the functions in Table 9-9 that "look up" or retrieve a specific item from a list or table. Each item in a list or table can be a string or a value.

TABLE 9-9   Lookup Functions

Function	*Returns*
@CHOOSE	Specified item from a list
@INDEX	Specified item from an index table
@VLOOKUP	Specified item from a vertical lookup table
@HLOOKUP	Specified item from a horizontal lookup table

Selecting an Item from a List: @CHOOSE

The @CHOOSE function returns a specified item from a list. The form of this function is

@CHOOSE(*offset,list*)

where *list* is a group of items from which you want to choose. Enter each item directly into @CHOOSE, separating each by an argument separator (usually a comma). If you enter a literal string as an item in *list*, remember to enclose it in double quotes.

That's why @CHOOSE is usually used with a small *list*—if you specify *list* as a range, @CHOOSE returns ERR. To retrieve an item from a large group of items or from a range, use one of the other lookup functions discussed below.

The *offset* argument specifies the item in *list* to retrieve. Item 1 in *list* has an *offset* value of 0, the second item an *offset* value of 1, and the last item in a list of *n* items has an *offset* value of *n* - 1. For example, in @CHOOSE(2,5,B5,"Tom") the first item in *list*, the value 5, has an *offset* value of 0, while the last item in *list*, the label Tom, has an *offset* value of 2. If *offset* is negative or larger than *n* - 1, @CHOOSE returns ERR.

Note: If you retrieve an item in *list* that refers to a blank cell, @CHOOSE returns the value 0.

You can use @CHOOSE to calculate 1991 federal taxes for different taxable incomes. To do this, you might set up the worksheet in Figure 9-16, which contains a tax table for

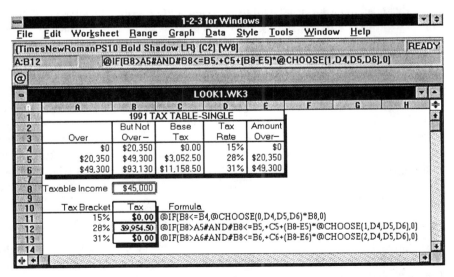

Figure 9-16 Using @CHOOSE to calculate the tax due for a single individual

single persons. The range D4..D6 contains the different federal tax rates. So @CHOOSE(0,D4,D5,D6) selects the lowest tax rate, 15%, because an *offset* value of 0 returns the first item in the *list*.

To calculate the actual tax for a specified taxable income, such as $45,000 in cell B8, use a series of @IF functions that include @CHOOSE in the *true-result*. (Each formula is listed to the right of B11..B13.) For example, in cell B12,

```
@IF(B8>A5#AND#B8<=B5,+C5+(B8-E5)*@CHOOSE(1,D4,D5,D6),0)
```

is used. The @IF *condition* evaluates the $45,000 taxable income in cell B8. Since it exceeds $20,350 in cell A5 (the bottom of the 28% bracket) *and* doesn't exceed $49,300 in cell B5 (the top of this bracket), the *true-result* is used—the base tax of $3,052.50 in cell C5 plus the tax on the remaining income in this bracket ($45,000 in cell B8 minus $20,350 in cell E5) times the appropriate tax rate. So @CHOOSE(1,D4,D5,D6) uses an *offset* value of 1 to select the second item in the *list*, 28%, and the tax due in cell B12 is calculated as $3,052.50+($45,000-$20,350)*.28 or $9,954.50.

Note that the *false-result* of this @IF function is 0. If taxable income is not within this 28% tax bracket, then 0 tax is returned, and the tax due is calculated by one of the other @IF functions.

Selecting an Item from an Index Table: @INDEX

The @INDEX function is a useful way to organize and retrieve data when a nonlinear relationship exists, as in tax tables or in accelerated depreciation tables. Actually, 1-2-3's lookup functions were originally developed for tax tables.

@INDEX selects a specified item from an *index table*. An index table is a continuous range, either 2-D or 3-D (spanning more than one worksheet), where each cell contains a string or value. The form of this function is

```
@INDEX(range,column-offset,row-offset,[worksheet-offset])
```

where *range* is an index table entered as a range address or name.

@INDEX selects an item from *range* using "offset coordinates." An item in a two-dimensional *range* is described by two offset coordinates: the *column-offset* and the *row-offset*. The *column-offset* specifies the column position of the item you want to retrieve. Column 1 is offset 0, while the last column in the index table has an offset of $n - 1$. Similarly, *row-offset* specifies the row position of the item in the index table you want to retrieve, where row 1 is offset 0. @INDEX returns ERR if you specify an *offset* that is negative or greater than $n - 1$ (for example, a *row-offset* of n).

Note: If an item selected in *range* is a blank cell, @INDEX returns the value 0.

An optional *worksheet-offset* is used for a three-dimensional *range* spanning multiple worksheets. The first worksheet is represented by a *worksheet-offset* of 0; the last worksheet in the index table is represented by a *worksheet-offset* of $n - 1$. If you don't include a *worksheet-offset*, @INDEX assumes that it's 0 and only returns items from the first worksheet in the index table.

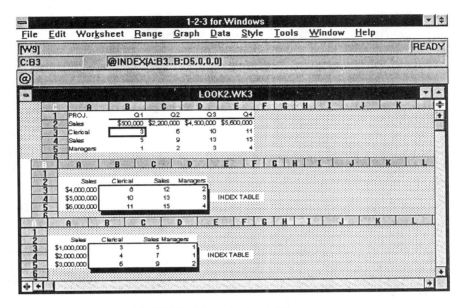

Figure 9-17 Using @INDEX with an index table

To see how @INDEX works, look at the three-dimensional index table in Figure 9-17. The *range* A:B3..B:D5, spanning two worksheets, lists the nonlinear relationship between sales and personnel. When sales are $500,000, @INDEX(A:B3..B:D5,0,0,0) in cell C:B3 uses the offset coordinates 0,0,0 to return 3 clerical employees from the first cell in the index table, A:B3. Similarly, when sales are $5,600,000, @INDEX(A:B3..B:D5,2,2,1) in cell C:E5 uses the offset coordinates 2,2,1 to retrieve 4 managers from column 3, row 3, worksheet 2 of the index table, or cell B:D5.

Selecting an Item from a Vertical Lookup Table: @VLOOKUP

The @VLOOKUP function selects and returns a specified item from a *vertical lookup table*. A vertical lookup table is a two-dimensional continuous range composed of at least two columns and two rows.

The leftmost column in a vertical lookup table is called the *index column*. All cells in this column *must* contain only values or only strings. The other columns can contain a mixture of strings and values.

The @VLOOKUP function searches the index column of the vertical lookup table to find the information (value or string) that you specify. Once that information is found, @VLOOKUP returns information from the same row in the vertical lookup table.

The form of this function is

```
@VLOOKUP(x,range,column-offset)
```

where *range* is the vertical lookup table entered as a range address or name, and *x* is what you want to search for in the index column.

Note: Although @VLOOKUP accepts a three-dimensional *range*, it only returns information from the first worksheet in *range*.

Column-offset specifies the column position of the item you want to retrieve in the vertical lookup table. The index column has a *column-offset* of 0, the second column, 1, and the last column has a *column offset* of *n* - 1. So, *column-offset* must be between 1 and *n* - 1. @VLOOKUP returns ERR when *column-offset* is greater than *n* - 1 or is negative. If you use a *column-offset* of 0, however, @VLOOKUP returns the value or string in the index column specified by *x*.

Using @VLOOKUP with Values

Let's examine how @VLOOKUP works when you use values in the index column. For example, suppose after a year's employment your company gives a year-end bonus that is a percentage of an employee's salary. This percentage varies, depending on the number of years of employment and whether the employee is considered management. In Figure 9-18, the vertical lookup table in the range A4..C9 properly expresses this relationship because the index column

- is the leftmost column.
- contains values in ascending order.
- contains no duplicate values.
- includes the lowest employment years, 0.
- includes *critical values*, values for which the corresponding values in columns B and C change.
- includes the highest value, 20 years, for which the highest values in columns B and C apply.

In cell G4, @VLOOKUP(E4,A4..B9,F4) begins at the top of the index column (cell A4) to search for *x*, 5, which it encounters in cell A6. It then uses the *column-offset* of 1 and moves across row 6 one column. Since it retrieves 4% from cell B6, an employee receives a 4% bonus for five years of employment.

Note: When @VLOOKUP encounters a value equal to or closest to but not greater than *x*, it ends its search of the index column. That's why you should never include duplicate values in the index column, and why the values in the index column must always be in ascending order.

In cell G5, @VLOOKUP(E5,A4..B9,F5) also returns a 4% bonus for seven years of employment. To do so, it searches for the value closest to but not greater than 7 in the index column, and uses the value 5 in cell A6. In cell G6, however, @VLOOKUP returns

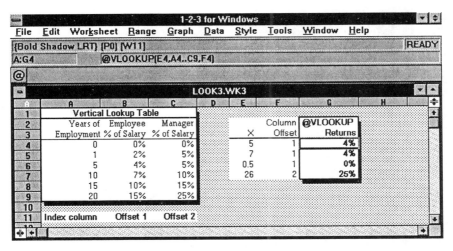

Figure 9-18 Using @VLOOKUP with values

that an employee with six month's employment receives no bonus. Without the value 0 in the index column, @VLOOKUP would have returned ERR.

Using similar logic in cell G7, @VLOOKUP evaluates 20 in cell A9 of the index column as the closest value not exceeding 26 (x). It then uses the *column-offset* of 2 to return a 25% bonus for a manager with 26 years of employment.

Using @VLOOKUP with Strings

When you use strings in the index column of a vertical lookup table, @VLOOKUP requires an *exact match* between one of these strings and the x argument. For @VLOOKUP to consider these strings equal, they *must* have the same capitalization, leading or trailing spaces, spacing between words, and spelling.

In Figure 9-19, for instance, the vertical lookup table in A3..C7 is composed of an index column listing the last names of employees and two other columns listing the corresponding city and state of birth. In cell G3, when x, Watson, and the label in cell A3 are an *exact* match, @VLOOKUP(E3,A3..C7,F3) uses the *column-offset* of 1 and returns the city of birth, Indianapolis, from cell B3. Similarly, when x, Zealer, is an exact match to the label in cell A7, @VLOOKUP uses the *column-offset* of 2 and returns California as the state of birth from cell C7. However, @VLOOKUP returns ERR when the capitalization of WATSON (x) doesn't match a label in the index column.

Selecting an Item from a Horizontal Lookup Table: @HLOOKUP

The @HLOOKUP function is similar to @VLOOKUP in all respects except that it selects and returns a specified item from a horizontal lookup table. A *horizontal lookup table* is also a two-dimensional range composed of at least two columns and two rows. But @HLOOKUP evaluates x against the information in the index row—the top row of the

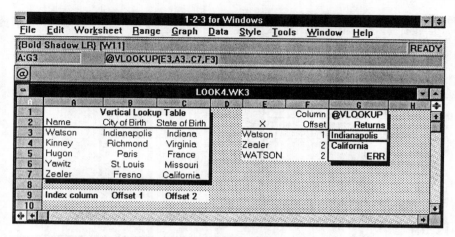

Figure 9-19 Using @VLOOKUP with strings

table. Starting with the leftmost cell, it evaluates each cell along the index row until it finds the first value that is closest to but not greater than x, or the first string that is an exact match for x. Based on the index row item it selects, @HLOOKUP then retrieves information from the same column, but in the row you specify.

The form of this function is

```
@HLOOKUP(x,range,row-offset)
```

where *range* is the two-dimensional horizontal lookup table entered as a range address or name, and x is the information you want to search for in the index row.

Note: Although @HLOOKUP accepts a three-dimensional *range*, it only returns information from the first worksheet.

The *row-offset* specifies the row position of the item you want to retrieve in a horizontal lookup table. The index row has a *row-offset* value of 0, the second row, 1, and the last row has a *row-offset* of $n - 1$. So *row-offset* must be between 1 and $n - 1$. @HLOOKUP returns ERR when *row-offset* is negative or greater than $n - 1$. If you use a *row-offset* of 0, @HLOOKUP returns the value or string in the index row specified by x.

Using @HLOOKUP with Values and Strings

Suppose in Figure 9-20 you want to access the data in the range B2..E4. The index row (row 2) includes the last names of employees. The other rows include the first name of these employees and the number of children for whom the company pays health insurance.

For example, for the employee Hugon, @HLOOKUP(A8,B2..E4,B8) in cell C8 starts in the leftmost cell in the index row, cell B2, then compares x in cell A8 to each cell in this row until it finds an *exact* match in cell D2. It then uses the *row-offset* value 1 and returns the first name, Sarah, from cell D3. Similarly, in cell C9, @HLOOKUP(A9,B2..E4,B9)

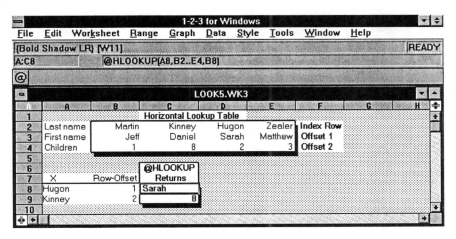

Figure 9-20 Using @HLOOKUP

uses a *row-offset* of 2 and returns the value 8, indicating that employee Kinney has eight children enrolled in the company's insurance program.

FINANCIAL FUNCTIONS

1-2-3 for Windows' financial functions help you analyze financial opportunities and alternatives using the time value of money. The premise is that cash in hand today is worth more than cash received in the future, where this extra value is any interest you can earn between today and a future date. To analyze financial opportunities, you must convert any future cash values to a present value through discounting. These future cash flows are discounted by a rate of return (interest rate) that compensates you for the risk of the investment.

1-2-3 for Windows' financial functions are powerful tools you can use in financial analysis. Because of their complexity, however, they can easily be misused. So make sure that you thoroughly understand the underlying assumptions of a financial function before you use it to model an investment scenario. For easy reference, the important assumptions have been listed for each financial function.

1-2-3 includes functions that analyze single investments, annuities, and unequal cash flows. Table 9-10 is a handy reference guide that lists these functions, as well as their arguments, assumptions, and the results returned.

The Interest or Discount Rate Argument

All of 1-2-3 for Windows' financial functions either use or solve for an *interest rate* or *discount rate*. The underlying assumptions of the *rate* are fundamental to understanding 1-2-3's financial functions.

Table 9-10 Financial Functions

1-2-3 Function	Calculates	Cash Flow Argument	Interest or Discount Rate AND Time Period	Payment Occurs in Period
@PV(p,i,n)	Present Value of an annuity	One annuity payment	Per period of annuity	Beginning
@PV(p,i,n)*(1+i)	Present Value of an annuity due	One annuity due payment	Per period of annuity due	Ending
@PMT(p,i,n)	Annuity payment per period	One annuity payment	Per period of annuity	Beginning
@PMT(p,i,n)(1+i)	Annuity due payment per period	One annuity due payment	Per period of annuity due	Ending
@FV(p,i,n)	Future Value of an annuity	One annuity payment	Per period of annuity	Beginning
@FV(p,i,n)*(1+i)	Future Value of an annuity due	One annuity due payment	Per period of annuity due	Ending
@TERM(p,i,FV)	Payment periods for annuity to reach FV	One annuity payment	Calculated as per period of annuity	Beginning
@TERM(p,i,FV/(1+i))	Payment periods for annuity due to reach FV	One annuity due payment	Calculated as per period of annuity due	Ending
@CTERM(i,FV,PV)	Payment periods for initial investment to reach FV	Initial investment, enter as positive	Per period of compounding period calculated	Ending
@RATE(FV,PV,n)	Compound return on initial investment	Initial investment, enter as positive	Per period of compounding period calculated	Ending
@NPV(i,cash flow range)	Net Present Value, no initial investment	Range of equal or unequal cash flows	Per period between flows	Ending
@NPV(i,cash flow range)-IO	Net Present Value, initial investment	Range of equal or unequal cash flows, excluding initial investment	Per period between flows	Ending, except initial investment on Day 1
@IRR(i guess, cash flow range)	Internal Rate of Return, initial investment	Range of equal or unequal cash flows, initial investment in first cell	Per period between flows, rate calculated	Ending, except initial investment on Day 1

Relevant Assumptions:

Cash Flow Argument	Interest or Discount Rate AND Time Period
All payments of interest reinvested at interest or discount rate until end of investment period	All periods must be equal
Rate is constant over investment period	Rate determines time period
	Period is largest interval that makes intervals equal

p = payment per period
i = interest rate per period in decimal or percentage form
n = number of payments
IO = initial investment

In any cash flow analysis, there are three distinct variables—the cash flow, the interest rate, and the number of periods (number of payments)—and one implicit variable, the time period between cash flows. The *interest rate* determines the *equal* time period between cash flows that a financial function uses in its calculation. Thus, if you use a yearly interest rate, 1-2-3 for Windows assumes that the time period between cash flows is one year. If you use a monthly interest rate, the time period between cash flows will be one month. Therefore, when you use one of the financial functions, remember:

- All time periods between cash flows must be equal.

- The *interest rate* must correspond to one time period.

- The *interest rate* determines the time period between cash flows.

- The *interest rate* is constant over the investment period.

- Interest is compounded at the end of each equal time period.

- Any cash received during the investment period is immediately reinvested at this *rate* until the end of the investment period.

- Express the *interest rate* in either decimal or percentage form.

> ▼ *Tip:*   A common convention is to use a monthly interest rate equal to the an-
> nual rate divided by 12.

Present Value of an Annuity and Annuity Due: @PV

1-2-3 for Windows' @PV function computes the *present value (PV)* of an *ordinary annuity* assuming equal payments at the *end* of equal time periods. In other words, @PV calculates the value today of a future stream of equal cash flows discounted at some fixed *discount* (interest) rate. This is expressed mathematically as

$$PV = \text{payment per period} * \frac{1 - (\,1 + \text{interest rate}\,)^{-n}}{\text{interest rate}}$$

where n is the number of payments made. The syntax of 1-2-3's Present Value function is

```
@PV(payment,interest rate,number of payments)
```

which assumes:

- *Payment* is the value of one of the annuity payments. All payments are equal and occur at the end of equal time periods.

- *Interest rate* is the rate for one time period and is constant over the investment period.

- *Number of payments* is the number of equal payments made.

- All payments (interest) received are immediately reinvested at your *interest rate* until the end of the investment period.

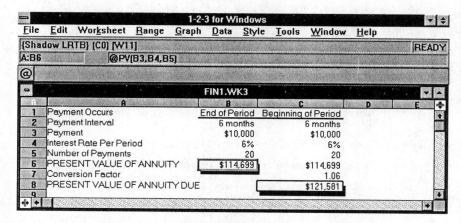

Figure 9-21 Calculating the PV of an annuity and an annuity due

Calculating the PV of an Annuity

Imagine that you need to evaluate two investment alternatives. The first option pays you $10,000 at the *end* of every six-month period for 10 years. You can invest these payments and earn 12% annually. What is the present value of this alternative? As you can see in Figure 9-21, using a $10,000 *payment*, a 6% semiannual *interest rate*, and 20 *number of payments*, @PV(B3,B4,B5) returns $114,699 in cell B6.

Note: For an annuity with unequal payments, use the @NPV function.

Calculating the Present Value of an Annuity Due

Your second financial alternative is to receive the same payments but at the *beginning* of each period: an *annuity due*. This is equivalent to moving all payments ahead one period. To do this, you must adjust the result of the @PV function using this conversion:

```
(1+interest rate)*@PV(payment,interest rate,number of
payments)
```

Returning to Figure 9-21, in cell C8 the formula +C6*C7 multiplies the result of the @PV function of an annuity by the conversion factor 1.06. So the PV of an annuity due is $121,581, while the PV of the same annuity is $114,699. Obviously, it would be best to have payments occur at the beginning of each period.

Payment Per Period for an Annuity and an Annuity Due: @PMT

The @PMT function calculates the fixed payment per period needed to repay a principal amount, given a fixed interest rate and a specified number of payments. Typically, @PMT is used to calculate a fixed-rate mortgage or loan payment. Since the amount borrowed is the present value, the *payment per period* can be expressed mathematically by rearranging the PV equation to

$$\text{Payment per period} = \text{pricipal amount} * \frac{\text{interest rate}}{1 - (\,1 + \text{interest rate}\,)^{-n}}$$

where *n* is the number of payments made. The syntax of 1-2-3's function is

```
@PMT(principal,interest rate,number of payments)
```

which assumes:

- *Principal* is the amount borrowed.

- *Interest rate* is the rate for *one* time period, which is constant over the repayment period—so for monthly payments, use the annual rate divided by 12.

- *Number of payments* is the number of equal time periods over which payments are made until the *principal* is repaid.

- All payments are equal and occur at the end of equal time periods. The payment amount applied to principal and interest varies for each period.

Calculating Fixed Payments at the End of Each Period

Suppose you are evaluating three 12% fixed-rate $150,000 mortgages for 20, 30, and 40 years, each requiring a payment at the end of every month. As shown in Figure 9-22, you can use @PMT to figure the different monthly payments. In cell B6, for instance, @PMT(B1,B2,B5) returns a monthly payment of $1,652 for the 20–year mortgage when a 1% monthly *rate* and 240 monthly *payments* are used. Likewise, @PMT(B1,B2,C5) calculates a $1,543 monthly payment for the 30–year mortgage, while @PMT(B1,B2,D5) returns a $1,513 monthly payment for the 40-year mortgage.

Calculating Fixed Payments at the Beginning of Each Period

You can also use @PMT to calculate the fixed payment per period when each payment is made at the beginning of each time period. This is equivalent to making all payments one period early, so one period of interest is not paid. To calculate this, just use the following conversion formula:

```
@PMT(principal interest rate,number of payments)/(1+interest rate)
```

Now imagine that you can also pay the different fixed-rate mortgages in Figure 9-22 at the beginning of the month. To calculate the new monthly payments, you still use the result of @PMT, but divide it by the conversion factor (1+*interest rate*), or 1.01. In cell B8, for example, +B6/B7 returns a revised payment of $1,635 for the 20-year mortgage.

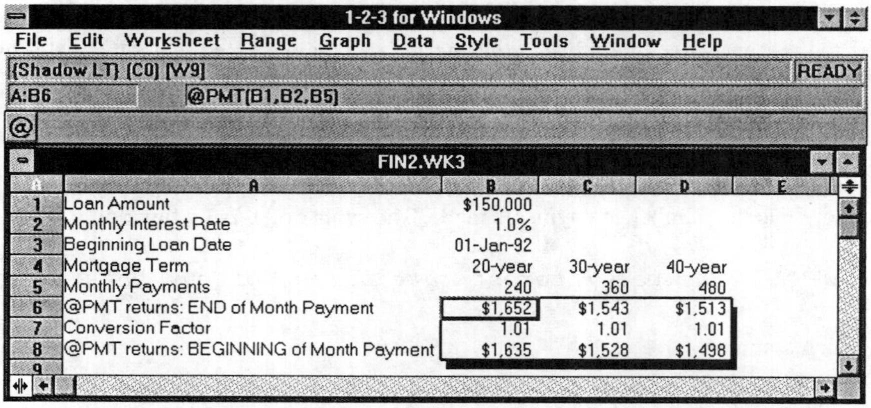

	A	B	C	D	E
1	Loan Amount	$150,000			
2	Monthly Interest Rate	1.0%			
3	Beginning Loan Date	01-Jan-92			
4	Mortgage Term	20-year	30-year	40-year	
5	Monthly Payments	240	360	480	
6	@PMT returns: END of Month Payment	$1,652	$1,543	$1,513	
7	Conversion Factor	1.01	1.01	1.01	
8	@PMT returns: BEGINNING of Month Payment	$1,635	$1,528	$1,498	

Figure 9-22 Using @PMT to evaluate loans paid at the beginning and ending of periods

As you might expect, payments are smaller if paid at the beginning rather than at the end of each month.

Using @PMT to Create an Amortization Table

Suppose you've decided on the $150,000, 30-year, 12% fixed-rate mortgage, which you incur on January 1, 1992. You can use the results of the @PMT function to create an amortization table and determine the principal balance at the end of the first year.

Note: You can also create an amortization schedule based on a 360-day year using 1-2-3 for Windows' @D360 function. See "Date and Time Arithmetic" in this chapter.

First, you need to calculate the monthly payment. As shown in Figure 9-23, @PMT(B2,B3,B4) in cell B5 of FIN3 returns a $1,543 monthly payment.

Now you can create an amortization table like the one in the file FIN4 in Figure 9-23. In column A, the payment dates have been entered using 1-2-3's @DATE function. The beginning balance in column B is simply the previous month's ending balance in column F. The $1,543 fixed monthly payment in column C is the @PMT result from cell B5 in FIN3. In column D, interest paid is calculated as the daily interest rate times the days in the month times the beginning principal balance. In cell D4, for instance, the interest paid in February, 1992 is +<<FIN3.WK3>>A:B$3*12/365*(A4–A3)*B4, or $1,430. The interest paid in the first month uses the beginning loan date, January 1, 1992 in cell B1 of FIN3, in the formula +<<FIN3.WK3>>A:B3*12/365*(A3–<<FIN3.WK3>>A:B1)*B3.

The principal paid in column E is simply the monthly payment in column C less the interest paid in column D. Finally, in column F, the ending balance is the beginning balance in column B less the principal paid in column E.

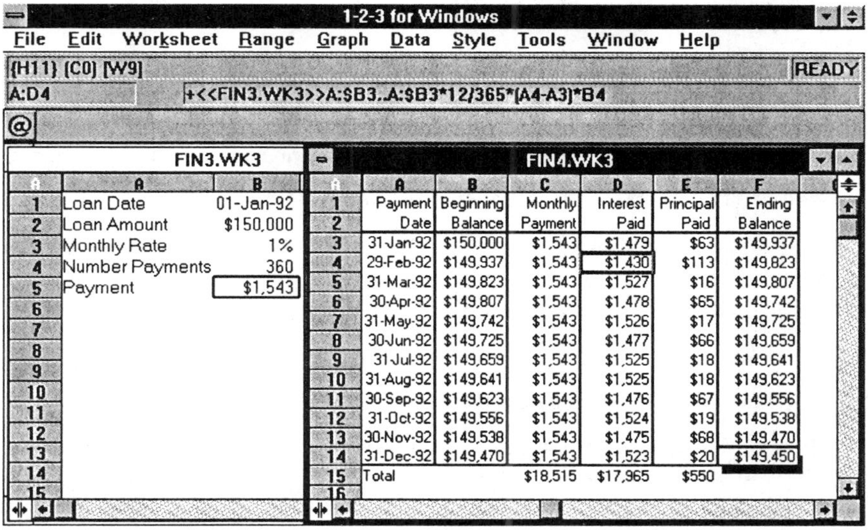

	A	B
1	Loan Date	01-Jan-92
2	Loan Amount	$150,000
3	Monthly Rate	1%
4	Number Payments	360
5	Payment	$1,543

	A	B	C	D	E	F
1	Payment	Beginning	Monthly	Interest	Principal	Ending
2	Date	Balance	Payment	Paid	Paid	Balance
3	31-Jan-92	$150,000	$1,543	$1,479	$63	$149,937
4	29-Feb-92	$149,937	$1,543	$1,430	$113	$149,823
5	31-Mar-92	$149,823	$1,543	$1,527	$16	$149,807
6	30-Apr-92	$149,807	$1,543	$1,478	$65	$149,742
7	31-May-92	$149,742	$1,543	$1,526	$17	$149,725
8	30-Jun-92	$149,725	$1,543	$1,477	$66	$149,659
9	31-Jul-92	$149,659	$1,543	$1,525	$18	$149,641
10	31-Aug-92	$149,641	$1,543	$1,525	$18	$149,623
11	30-Sep-92	$149,623	$1,543	$1,476	$67	$149,556
12	31-Oct-92	$149,556	$1,543	$1,524	$19	$149,538
13	30-Nov-92	$149,538	$1,543	$1,475	$68	$149,470
14	31-Dec-92	$149,470	$1,543	$1,523	$20	$149,450
15	Total		$18,515	$17,965	$550	

Figure 9-23 Creating a loan amortization table using @PMT

As you can see, in 1992 you would make payments totaling $18,515, of which $17,965 is interest and $550 is principal. So, on December 31, 1992, the principal balance is $149,450.

> ▼ ***Tip:*** For adjustable-rate mortgages, you can also use @PMT to figure the new fixed payment. Decrease the *number of payments* by those already made, use the new beginning balance from your amortization table as *principal*, and use the new monthly *interest rate*. In the example above, if the annual interest rate increases to 14% in year two, @PMT(149450,.14/12,(360-12)) returns $1,775 as the new payment.

Future Value of an Annuity and Annuity Due: @FV

The @FV function returns the future value (FV) of an ordinary annuity based on equal payments made at the end of equal time periods. Mathematically, the future value is computed as

$$FV = \text{payment per period} * \frac{(1 + \text{interest rate})^{-n} - 1}{\text{interest rate}}$$

where *n* is the number of payments that will be made. The syntax of 1-2-3's Future Value function is

```
@FV(payment,interest rate,number of payments)
```

which assumes:

- *Payment* is the value of one of the equal payments of the annuity that occurs at the end of equally spaced time periods.

- *Interest rate* is the rate for one time period and is constant over the investment period.

- *Number of payments* is the number of equal payments made.

- All payments (interest) received are immediately reinvested at *interest rate* until the end of the investment period.

- Future value is calculated on the date of the last payment.

Calculating the FV of an Annuity

Once again, imagine that you have two investment alternatives to evaluate. The first option is to automatically deposit $1,000 from each end-of-the month paycheck into a savings account that returns 10% annually. What will be the future value of these savings in one year? As shown in Figure 9-24, a $1,000 *payment*, a monthly *interest rate* of .10/12, which is displayed as .83% in cell B4, and 12 *number of payments* used in @FV(B3,B4,B5) return $12,566 in cell B6.

Calculating the FV of an Annuity Due

The second option is to save the same $1,000 monthly but at the beginning of each period, which would be the same as moving all payments ahead one period. To calculate the future value of this alternative, use this conversion formula:

```
(1+interest rate)*@FV(payment,interest rate,number of
payments)
```

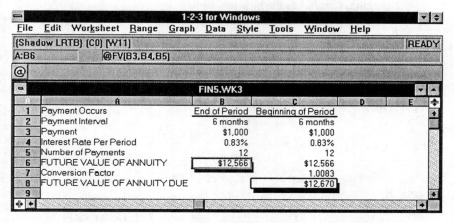

Figure 9-24 Calculating the FV of an annuity and an annuity due

Returning to Figure 9-24, you can now determine the FV of this option. In cell C8 the formula +C6*C7 multiplies the @FV result by the conversion factor 1.0083. The FV of the annuity due is $12,670, while the FV of the annuity is $12,566. Once again, the financial analysis advises payment at the beginning of each month.

Calculating the Term of an Annuity: @TERM

For an ordinary annuity that earns a fixed interest rate, @TERM calculates the number of time periods required to reach a specified future value. Mathematically, this can be expressed as

$$\text{Term} = \frac{\text{Ln} \,[\, 1 + (\, FV * \text{interest rate}\,)/\text{payment}\,]}{\text{Ln}\,(\, 1 + \text{interest rate}\,)}$$

where Ln is the natural log. The syntax for 1-2-3's function is

@TERM(*payment,interest rate,FV*)

which assumes:

- *Payment* is the value of one of the equal payments of the annuity, that occur at the end of equally spaced time periods.

- *Interest rate* is the rate for one time period and is constant over the investment period.

- Interest is compounded at the end of each period—monthly if payments are made monthly, yearly if payments are made yearly.

- All payments received are immediately reinvested at the *interest rate* until the day the future value is achieved.

- *FV* is the desired value in the future you want to achieve through this investment strategy.

@TERM returns a value that represents the number of compounding periods needed to reach the future value. This value is in the *same unit* as the time period used in the *interest rate* argument, which you may need to convert to years.

Calculating the Term for an Annuity

Imagine you want to amass $100,000 for your retirement. You plan to save $1,000 at the end of each month, on which you can earn a guaranteed 12% annual return. How long will it take you to reach your objective? In Figure 9-25, a $1,000 monthly *payment*, a 1% monthly *interest rate*, and a $100,000 *FV* used in @TERM(B2,B3,B4) calculates that it will take 69.66 time periods, or months, to reach this goal. In cell B9, 69.66 periods is divided by 12 to convert this term to 5.81 years.

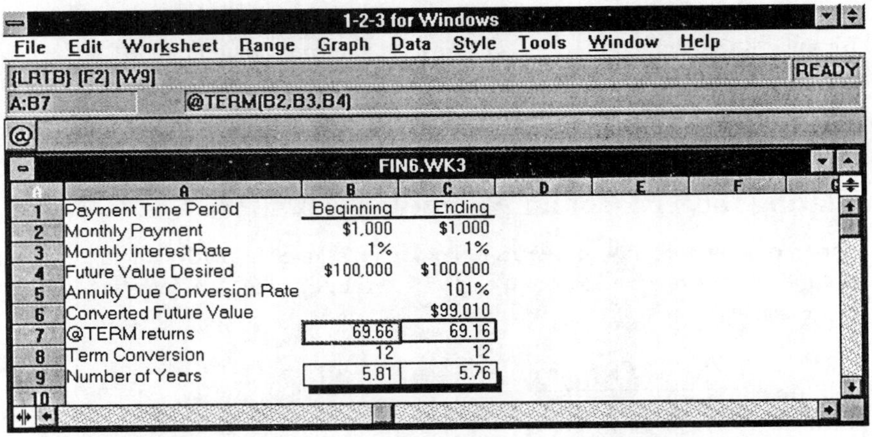

Figure 9-25 Using @TERM for an annuity and an annuity due

Calculating the Term for an Annuity Due

You can also use @TERM to calculate the number of periods required for an annuity due to reach a future value, when payments occur at the beginning of each period. This is equivalent to moving all payments ahead one period, so each payment in effect earns one more period of interest. Just use this conversion formula:

```
@TERM(payment,interest rate,FV/(1+interest rate))
```

Returning to Figure 9-25, if you save $1,000 at the beginning of each month, @TERM(C2,C3,C6) in cell C7 calculates that it will take 69.16 months, or 5.76 years to reach $100,000. Notice that the converted future value of $99,010 in cell C6 has been used.

Note: You can also calculate the payment per period needed to reach a future value using @TERM and 1-2-3 for Windows' Backsolver. See Chapter 13 for an example.

> ▼ *Tip:* You can use @TERM to calculate the number of payments needed to pay off a mortgage for a given monthly payment. The trick to using @TERM in this application is to use a *negative* monthly *payment* and a *positive* loan balance as the *future value*.
>
> Suppose you have a 12% fixed-rate mortgage with a $100,000 outstanding balance. In Figure 9-26, @TERM(A4,B1,B2) in cell B4 returns the current mortgage term, 480 months or 40 years, when you use a monthly *payment* of -$1,008 and a $100,000 *FV*. On the other hand, if you increase the monthly payment to -$1,100, @TERM(A5,B1,B2) in cell B5 calculates 241 monthly payments, or 20.1 years. Figure 9-26 also shows other calculated *terms* for increasing monthly mortgage payments.

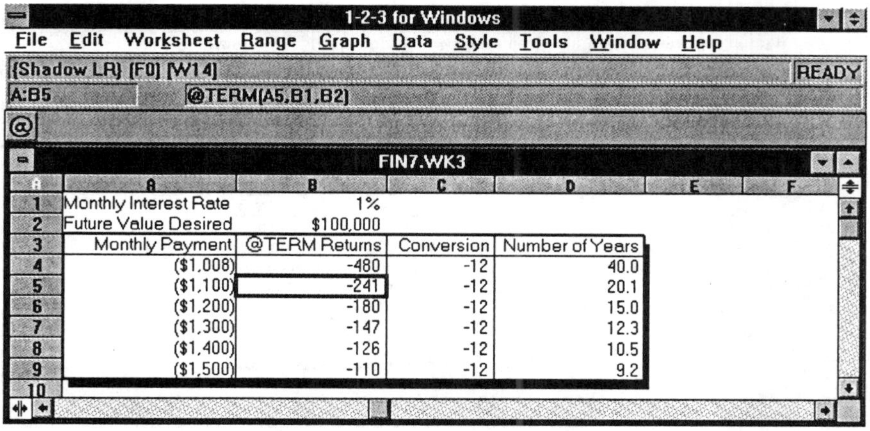

	A	B	C	D
1	Monthly Interest Rate	1%		
2	Future Value Desired	$100,000		
3	Monthly Payment	@TERM Returns	Conversion	Number of Years
4	($1,008)	-480	-12	40.0
5	($1,100)	-241	-12	20.1
6	($1,200)	-180	-12	15.0
7	($1,300)	-147	-12	12.3
8	($1,400)	-126	-12	10.5
9	($1,500)	-110	-12	9.2
10				

Figure 9-26 Using @TERM to calculate the number of remaining payments

Calculating the Term of an Investment: @CTERM

The @CTERM function computes the number of periods required for a *single investment* to reach a specified future value. This can be expressed mathematically as

Term of an investment = Ln(*FV*/*PV*)/Ln(1+interest rate)

where Ln is the natural logarithm. 1-2-3's function is

```
@CTERM(interest rate,FV,PV)
```

which assumes:

- *PV* is the initial and only investment made, that occurs on the first day of the investment period.
- *FV* is the desired value you want to achieve in the future.
- *PV* and *FV* are both entered using the same sign, even though one is a cash outflow and the other is a cash inflow.
- *Interest rate* is the rate for one time period over which interest is compounded. It is constant over the investment period. So if interest is compounded monthly, use a monthly *interest rate*.
- Interest is earned at the end of each equal time period and immediately reinvested at your *interest rate* until the day the future value is achieved.

The @CTERM function returns a value that represents the number of compounding periods needed to reach the *future value*. This value is in the *same unit* as the time period used in the *interest rate* argument, which you may want to convert to years.

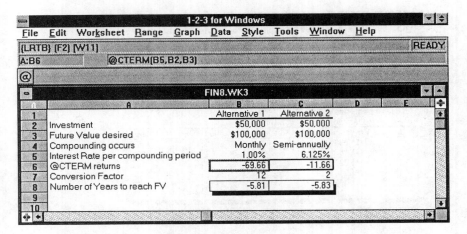

Figure 9-27 Using @CTERM to evaluate investments

Suppose you can invest $50,000 in an instrument that pays 12% annually, compounded monthly. You also might invest in another financial instrument that pays 12.25% annual interest, compounded semiannually. Which will reach $100,000 first?

In Figure 9-27, Alternative 1 is evaluated in column B. @CTERM(B5,B2,B3) shows that it takes 69.66 compounding periods to grow a $50,000 *PV* to a $100,000 *FV* when you earn a 1% monthly compounded *interest rate*. In cell B8, +B6/B7 divides 69.66 by 12 to convert these monthly periods to 5.81 years. In column C, @CTERM(C5,C2,C3) returns 11.66 compounding periods for Alternative 2 using a 6.125% semiannual *rate*. In cell C8, 11.66 is divided by 2 to convert these semiannual periods to 5.83 years. The conclusion then, is to invest in Alternative 1.

Note: As you can see in Figure 9-27, @CTERM returns a negative term when PV and FV are positive. If you enter either FV or PV as negative, however, @CTERM returns ERR.

Calculating the Interest Rate of an Investment: @RATE

The @RATE function calculates the *implied* periodic interest rate an initial investment earns to reach a specified future value. Mathematically, the compound implied rate is equal to

$$\text{Compound Interest Rate} = (FV/PV)^{1/n} - 1$$

where *n* is the number of time periods over which interest is compounded. The syntax of 1-2-3's function is

```
@RATE(FV,PV,number of compounding periods)
```

which assumes:

- *PV* is the initial and only investment made, which occurs on the first day of the investment period.
- *FV* is the value at the end of all compounding periods.
- *PV* and *FV* are both entered using the same sign, even though one is a cash outflow and the other is a cash inflow.
- *Number of compounding periods* is the number of equal periods for which interest is compounded. For example, if your investment returns a specified future value in 1.5 years, then the number of equal compounding periods is 3.
- Interest is earned at the end of each period and is immediately reinvested at the calculated @RATE value until the FV is achieved.

@RATE returns an *interest rate* for *one* period of compounding, which you may want to convert to an annual rate.

Note: To calculate the rate returned by an annuity or unequal cash flows, use @IRR discussed later.

The @RATE function is commonly used to calculate implied compound interest rates of zero-coupon bonds, compound rates of return on equity investments, and implied compound growth rates for sales, profits, and other financial indicators. For example, suppose you purchased 1,000 shares each of two stocks on January 1, 1990, for $10 a share. You sell Stock 1 for $40,000 on December 31, 1991 and Stock 2 on June 30, 1992 for $70,000. Which stock earned a greater annualized return?

As you can see in cell B8 of Figure 9-28, @RATE(B5,B3,B7) returns a 100% compounded return for Stock 1 using a $40,000 *FV*, a $10,000 *PV*, and 2 for the *number of compounding periods*. Since the compounding period is one year, this is the annualized return realized. In cell C8, @RATE(C5,C3,C7) computes a 47.58% compounded return per period for Stock 2—because this stock was held for 2.5 years, or 5 six-month periods, 5 is the correct *number of compounding periods*. Although Stock 2's annualized return is actually 95.15% (47.58% * 2 six-month periods), Stock 1 still yielded the highest annualized return.

Net Present Value: @NPV

The *Net Present Value* (NPV) is the value today of a stream of future cash flows discounted at some rate back to the first day of the investment period. Mathematically, NPV is equal to

$$NPV = \frac{\text{cash inflows} - \text{cash outflows}}{(1 + \text{discount rate})^{-n}} - \text{initial investment}$$

where *n* is the number of time periods over which the cash flows occur. The *discount rate* is the return you require, given the risk of the investment. The NPV mathematical

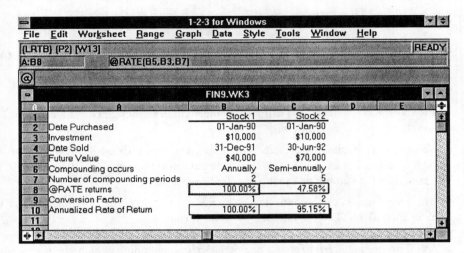

Figure 9-28 Using @RATE to find the implied rate of return of two investments

equation includes an initial investment on the first day of the investment period, and allows unequal cash flows, each occurring at the end of equal time periods. 1-2-3's syntax for this function is

```
@NPV(discount rate,cash flow range)
```

which assumes:

- Any initial investment is *not* included in *cash flow range*, but is subtracted from the result of @NPV.

- All cash flows occur at the end of each time period.

- All time periods between cash flows are equal.

- *Discount rate* is the rate in decimal or percentage form for one time period, which is constant over the investment period. If you use a yearly discount rate, 1-2-3 assumes that the time period between cash flows (each cell in *cash flow range*) is one year.

- All cash inflows are immediately reinvested at the *discount rate* until the end of the investment period.

The *cash flow range* is the stream of unequal or equal cash flows being evaluated. Enter each cash flow, except for any initial investment, in a separate cell in a two- or three-dimensional *continuous* range (even in another 1-2-3 for Windows' file)—cash inflows as positive, and cash outflows (investments) as negative. The first cell in this range represents the first cash flow at the end of the first period, *not* your initial investment. Include a cell for each equal time period, even if no cash flow occurs. (@NPV evaluates any blank cell or any cell containing a label as equal to a 0 cash flow for that period.) Each cell represents a payment date, all time periods between payments are equal, and cash flows occur only at the end of each time period.

Evaluating the Result of @NPV

The *discount rate* used in the @NPV function is the rate you require to compensate for the risk of an investment. A negative NPV indicates that the investment should not be made, a positive NPV indicates it should; but in a world of scarce funds, an investment that yields a positive NPV is usually evaluated and ranked against other positive Net Present Value projects.

An Example

Suppose you are asked to invest $200,000 in a company in two stages. The first $100,000 is needed on June 30, 1992 to finance a new product introduction, and the second $100,000 is needed on June 30, 1993 for the second phase of this product roll-out. In return, you will receive three payments of $100,000 every six months beginning on December 31, 1993, then $200,000 on June 30, 1995. You have analyzed the risk of this venture and decided that 18% is an appropriate annual discount rate. Should you make this investment?

To analyze this opportunity, you need to create a worksheet like Figure 9-29. The *cash flow range*, B4..G4, which excludes the initial investment, uses six-month time periods. Notice that in the period ending December 31, 1992 no cash flow occurs. Since each time period is six months, a six-month *discount rate* of 9% is appropriate. In cell B9, the NPV of the investment is calculated as the @NPV(B6,B4..G4) result of $248,139 in cell B7 less the initial $100,000 investment. Since $148,139 is positive, you should make the investment.

Note: As Figure 9-29 shows, you can use the @NPV function when cash flows occur in unequal time periods. In this case, some cash flows occur annually, while others occur every six months. The range B4..G4 uses a six-month time period, the *lowest common denominator* for all time periods. Any period when no cash flow occurs, such as in cell B4, is represented as a 0 cash flow. The correct @NPV *discount rate* is then the six-month rate to reflect the six-month time period between cash flows.

Internal Rate of Return: @IRR

1-2-3 for Windows' @IRR function calculates the *internal rate of return (IRR)* of an investment. The IRR is the discount rate for which the NPV mathematical equation is 0. That is, IRR is the discount rate when the present value of cash inflows equals the present value of cash outflows. IRR can be expressed mathematically as

$$0 = NPV = \frac{\text{cash inflows} - \text{cash outflows}}{(1 + IRR)^{-n}} - \text{initial investment}$$

where n is the number of equal time periods over which the cash flows occur.

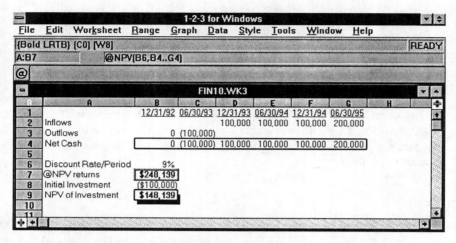

Figure 9-29 Using @NPV with unequal cash flows

Traditionally, you would calculate an IRR by trial and error, entering guesses into the NPV mathematical equation, then manually calculating the NPV until you find the IRR for which the NPV equals 0. 1-2-3's equivalent performs this iterative process for you:

```
@IRR(rate of return guess,cash flow range)
```

which assumes:

- An initial investment is included in the *cash flow range*.

- All cash flows, except the initial investment, occur at the end of each time period.

- All time periods between cash flows are equal, and each time period must be represented by a cell in *cash flow range*, even when no cash flow occurs.

- All cash inflows are immediately reinvested at the calculated *IRR* rate until the end of the investment period.

The *rate of return guess*, entered in decimal or percentage form, is the value the @IRR function uses to calculate the actual IRR. In most cases, you should use a value between 0 and 1.

The *cash flow range* is the stream of unequal or equal cash flows being evaluated. Enter these cash flows into a two- or three-dimensional *continuous* range, cash inflows as positive values, cash outflows (investments) as negative. The first cell represents the first day of the investment period, while all other cells represent the *ending* day of a time period, where all time periods are equal. Therefore, in the first cell, enter the initial investment as negative. In the second cell, enter the cash flow at the end of the first period,

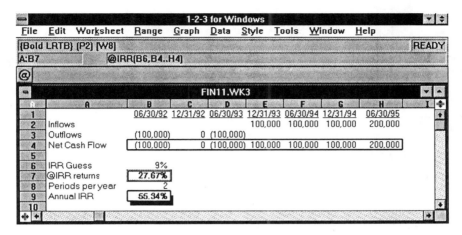

Figure 9-30   Calculating the IRR for a range of cash flows

then all other cash flows in this manner. Remember to include a cell for each time period, even if no cash flow occurs. @IRR will evaluate any blank cell or any cell containing a label as equal to a 0 cash flow for that period.

The @IRR function uses the *rate of return guess*, and, in 30 or fewer iterations, tries to calculate an IRR value to within .0000001. If successful, it returns the IRR value for one time period of your *cash flow range*, which you may need to convert to an annual rate; if unsuccessful, it returns ERR.

An Example

Suppose you are again evaluating the potential investment in Figure 9-29, but you want to calculate the IRR of this investment. Figure 9-30 shows how IRR is computed for these cash flows. The *cash flow range* B4..H4, which includes the initial investment, uses six-month time periods. Note that in the period ending December 31, 1992, no cash flow occurs. In cell B7, @IRR(B6,B4..H4) returns 27.67%. But since this IRR value is for one six-month time period, the annualized IRR for this investment is 55.34%.

Evaluating the Result of @IRR

The @IRR function returns a *rate of return* value. This value is usually compared to a "hurdle rate" or minimum return, to determine whether this investment should be made. Like the NPV discount rate, the required rate of return should be evaluated so that the risk of an investment is taken into account. In the example above, suppose you require an 18% annualized rate of return for an investment with this type of risk. Since this particular project has an IRR of 55.34%, you should certainly make the investment.

When @IRR Returns ERR

In previous releases, 1-2-3 returned an incorrect IRR value instead of ERR for many nonnormal cash flows.

The @IRR function returns an IRR value for a *normal* stream of cash flows: one or more time periods of net cash outflows, followed by a series of cash inflows. In 1-2-3 for Windows, however, @IRR returns ERR when the *cash flow range* is not normal or the *rate of return guess* is too far from the actual IRR value. A cash flow is considered *nonnormal* when it includes any of the following:

- A $0 initial investment.
- An investment near the end of the investment period, so the sign changes more than once.
- Relatively large outflows near the end of the investment period.
- IRR is less than 0% or greater than 100%.

Figure 9-31 shows a situation when @IRR returns ERR for different *rate of return guesses*. This nonnormal cash flow changes sign more than once and includes a large cash influx late in the investment period. In addition, the cash outflows exceed expected inflows during the time period analyzed, so the rate of return is obviously negative. Depending on the *rate of return guess* in row 5, the @IRR function in row 6 returns either ERR or -60.18%.

As you can see, @IRR returns ERR when the *rate of return guess* is too far from the actual IRR and 1-2-3 can't calculate it within 30 iterations. The obvious solution when this happens is to try a different *rate of return guess*.

You can check the value @IRR returns by using it in the @NPV function to see if it returns an NPV of $0. If you do so, remember not to include the initial investment in the @NPV *cash flow range* but instead add it to the result @NPV returns.

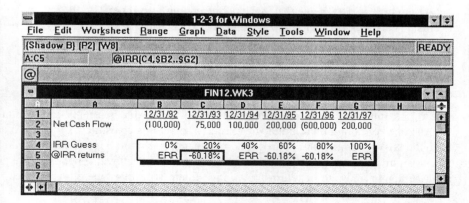

Figure 9-31 A situation when @IRR returns ERR for some *rate of return guesses*

Note: In a few instances, @IRR may return completely different IRR values (usually one is negative and one is positive) depending on the *rate of return guess* used. This only seems to happen if the cash flows are nonnormal to the extent that there actually are two different IRR values that make the NPV equation equal to 0.

DEPRECIATION FUNCTIONS

1-2-3 for Windows offers the four functions shown in Table 9-11 for calculating depreciation. If you are upgrading from Release 2, you'll notice a new depreciation function, @VDB, which allows you to calculate depreciation using different MACRS (Modified Accelerated Cost Recovery System) depreciation methods.

Using Partial-Year Conventions

In many cases you'll want to use a *partial-year convention* with 1-2-3 for Windows' depreciation functions. The most commonly used, the *half-year convention*, assumes that all new assets are placed in service on July 1. The first year depreciation expense is one-half of a full year's depreciation. An asset is then depreciated over one more year than its classification, where the remaining one-half year depreciation is expensed in the last year. For example, a five-year asset is depreciated over six years. This is an important concept to understand when you use 1-2-3 for Windows' depreciation functions to calculate tax depreciation.

Straight-Line Depreciation: @SLN

The @SLN function calculates straight-line depreciation. This method, which allocates an equal portion of the asset cost over each period, computes depreciation for each period as

Depreciation/Period = (Cost − Salvage Value)/Periods of Useful Life

TABLE 9-11 Depreciation Functions

Function	Calculates
@SLN	Straight-line depreciation
@SYD	Sum-of-the-years'-digits depreciation
@DDB	Double-declining-balance depreciation
@VDB	Variable-declining-balance depreciation, switching to tax straight-line

```
 ⊟                        1-2-3 for Windows                         ▼ ▲
   File   Edit   Worksheet   Range   Graph   Data   Style   Tools   Window   Help
  {Shadow TB} {C0}                                                          READY
  A:C6              @SLN($B1,$B2,$B3)*2
  @
 ⊟                            DEPR1.WK3                              ▼ ▲
          A               B          C         D         E       F    G  ▼ ▲
  1  Cost             $20,000                                            ▲
  2  Salvage Value     $2,500
  3  Life in Periods        6
  4
  5                       1992       1993      1994      1995
  6  Straight-Line Depreciation  $2,917    $5,833    $5,833    $2,917
  7
  8  Ending Asset Balance  $17,083   $11,250    $5,417    $2,500        ▼
 ⬦ ◄                                                                ►
```

Figure 9-32 Calculating straight-line depreciation with a half-year convention

The syntax of 1-2-3's function is

@SLN(*cost,salvage value,life*)

where *cost* is the total of the purchase price and installation costs, including freight in. *Salvage value* is the estimated asset value at the end of the depreciation period. *Life* is the total number of equal periods over which the asset is depreciated. If you use a half-year convention, *life* is the number of six-month periods. Using these arguments, @SLN calculates the depreciation expense for one *life* time period.

Note: Current tax laws allow switching to a *modified* straight-line depreciation when it yields a larger expense than the MACRS declining-balance method. Use @VDB, not @SLN, to correctly figure MACRS straight-line depreciation.

Using @SLN with the Half-Year Convention

Suppose you purchase and install an asset for $20,000 on June 30, 1992. It has a three-year life and an estimated $2,500 salvage value. To compute SL depreciation using a half-year convention, you need to create a worksheet similar to that in Figure 9-32 expensing depreciation over four years. Since only a half-year's depreciation is expensed in the first year, 1992, and in the last year, 1996, a $2,917 depreciation expense for these periods is calculated using @SLN($B1,$B2,$B3). (The mixed addressing keeps these arguments constant when this function is copied across row 6.) In 1993 and 1994, a full-year's depreciation is returned by @SLN($B1,$B2,$B3)*2. Notice that the fully depreciated asset balance in cell E9 equals the estimated salvage value.

Sum-of-the-Years'-Digits Depreciation: @SYD

The *Sum-of-the-years'-digits* method, which allocates a larger expense in the earlier years, calculates depreciation per period as

$$\text{SYD per period} = (\text{cost} - \text{salvage value}) * \frac{(n - p + 1)}{(n * (n + 1)/2)}$$

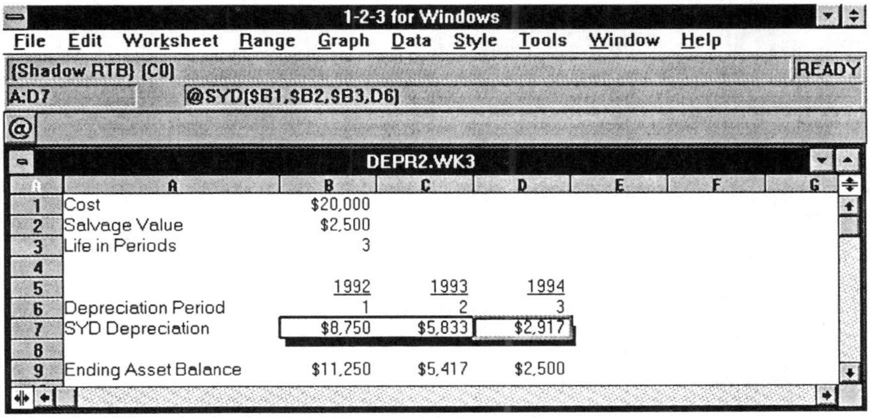

Figure 9-33 Calculating depreciation using @SYD

where *n* is the number of periods of useful life and *p* is the period for which depreciation is being calculated. The depreciation *rate* for each period is $(n - p + 1)/(n * n + 1)/2)$ or Remaining years of useful life/Sum of the years of useful life. For an asset with a two-year useful life, the numerator equals (2-1+1) or 2 in the first year of depreciation. The denominator is $2*(3/2)$ or 3 (1 + 2, the sum of the years' digits). So 2/3 of the asset value is depreciated in the first year.

1-2-3's syntax for this function is

```
@SYD(cost,salvage value,life,depreciation period)
```

where *cost* is the total of the purchase price and installation costs, including freight in. *Salvage value* is the estimated value at the end of the depreciation period. *Life* is the total number of equal periods over which an asset is depreciated. Remember, if you use a half-year convention, *life* is the number of six-month periods. @SYD calculates the depreciation expense for the time period specified by the *depreciation period* argument. If you use 6, for instance, @SYD returns the depreciation for period 6.

Returning to our previous example (a three-year $20,000 asset with a $2,500 salvage value), Figure 9-33 shows the calculations for SYD depreciation. For each depreciation period, you use a $20,000 *cost*, a $2,500 *salvage value* and a 3-year *life*. The only argument that varies is the *depreciation period* in row 6. In cell D7, @SYD($B1,$B2,$B3,D6) returns a $2,917 depreciation expense in year three. (Mixed addressing keeps the arguments fixed when copying across row 7.) As you can see in cell D9, the fully-depreciated asset balance equals the $2,500 salvage value.

Double-Declining-Balance Depreciation: @DDB

The DDB (double declining balance) is another method that allocates more depreciation in the early years of an asset's life. The DDB depreciation per period is calculated as

DDB per period = (2/useful life in periods) * remaining book value

In the DDB method, the depreciation rate (2/useful life in periods) remains constant. However, the *remaining book value varies* (original cost – accumulated depreciation), and decreases each period by the previous period's depreciation expense. Instead, the depreciation rate per period is constant at 66.67% of *adjusted* book value. The DDB formula never fully depreciates an asset, so a "plug" value is always used in the final depreciation period to write off the remaining depreciable portion not expensed.

▼ **Tip:**   For 200% declining-balance MACRS depreciation, use @VDB instead of @DDB to handle the half-year convention, $0 salvage value, and switch to straight-line depreciation.

1-2-3 for Windows' function is

`@DDB(cost,salvage value,life,depreciation period)`

where *cost* is the total of the purchase price and installation costs, including freight-in. *Salvage value* is the estimated value at the end of the depreciation period. *Life* is the total number of *equal periods* over which the asset is depreciated. Remember, for a half-year convention, *life* is the number of six-month periods.

@DDB calculates the depreciation expense for the time period specified by the *depreciation period* argument. If you use 2, for instance, @DDB calculates the depreciation for period 2.

Calculating DDB Depreciation Using the Half-Year Convention

Let's again return to the three-year asset purchased and installed for $20,000 on June 30, 1992, with a $2,500 salvage value. To calculate DDB depreciation using the half-year convention, you need to set up a spreadsheet similar to Figure 9-34.

For each period of depreciation, a $20,000 *cost* and a $2,500 *salvage value* are used. A *life* of 6 six-month periods properly handles the half-year convention. Only the *depreciation period* used with @DDB varies, as follows:

Year	Depreciation Period	@DDB Function
1992	1	@DDB(B1,B2,B3,1)
1993	2 and 3	@DDB(B1,B2,B3,2)+@DDB(B1,B2,B3,3)
1994	4 and 5	@DDB(B1,B2,B3,4)+@DDB(B1,B2,B3,5)
1995	6	@DDB(B1,B2,B3,6)

For example, the expense for *depreciation period*s 2 and 3 is summed in cell C6 to return $7,407 for 1993. Note that in cell E6, @DDB correctly computes the final period "plug" value of $134.

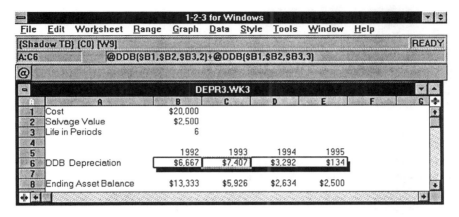

Figure 9-34 Using @DDB with the half-year convention

Caution: Many times, for a $0 salvage value, a salvage value less than 5% of *cost*, or for relatively small asset values, @DDB does *not* correctly calculate the "plug" value in the final year. To overcome this problem, use @VDB with a 200% declining balance.

Declining-Balance Depreciation: @VDB

The @DDB function, which uses the double-declining-balance method, is a specific case of 1-2-3's @VDB function. @VDB allows you to calculate MACRS depreciation for different asset classes by

- Specifying the *rate* of declining-balance depreciation.

- Switching to a MACRS straight-line method of depreciation when it exceeds MACRS declining-balance depreciation.

Note: MACRS is a relatively recent tax depreciation method. As a result, @VDB may not be appropriate for assets placed in service before MACRS went into effect.

A variable declining-balance depreciation expense is calculated each period as

VDB per period = (*rate*/useful life in periods) * remaining book value

where *rate* is some declining-balance depreciation rate. For example, a 150% declining-balance method uses a 1.5 depreciation *rate*. Any declining-balance rate remains constant while the *remaining book value varies* (original cost minus accumulated depreciation), decreasing each period by the previous period's depreciation expense. Because no VDB method ever fully depreciates an asset, a "plug" value is always used in the last period to expense the remaining depreciation.

1-2-3 for Windows' syntax for this function is

```
@VDB(cost,salvage value,life,start-period,end-period,
[depreciation rate],[SL-switch])
```

where *cost* is the total of the purchase price and installation costs, including freight-in. *Salvage value* is the estimated asset value at the end of the depreciation period.

Time Period Arguments

@VDB uses three arguments to specify the period for which depreciation is being calculated. *Life* is the total number of depreciation periods in *years*, even if the half-year convention is used.

For a specific depreciation period, *start-period* is the beginning of the depreciation period, while *end-period* is the end of this depreciation period. By looking ahead to Figure 9-35, you can see that, assuming a half-year convention, the *start-period* and *end-period* arguments for year 1 are 0 and .5 respectively, .5 and 1.5 for year 2, and so on.

Optional Arguments

The @VDB function has two optional arguments, the *depreciation rate* and the *SL-switch*. Use the *depreciation rate* to specify any declining-balance method you'd like by entering any value greater than 0. A 175% declining-balance method, for example, is represented by 1.75. If you don't include this argument, @VDB automatically uses a 200% declining balance. You must include a *depreciation rate* if you want to include an *SL-switch* argument.

SL-switch tells 1-2-3 for Windows whether to switch to MACRS straight-line depreciation once it exceeds MACRS declining-balance depreciation. *SL-switch* must be either 0 or 1. If *SL-switch* is 0, @VDB switches to straight-line when appropriate; if it is 1, @VDB only calculates the declining-balance method you specify. If you don't specify this argument, 1-2-3 for Windows uses 0 by default.

Using @VDB Without Switching to Straight-Line

Suppose you want to calculate the depreciation per year of a $20,000 asset with $0 salvage value. For current tax laws, this equipment is a five-year class asset that is depreciated using a 200% declining-balance method and the half-year convention. You don't want to switch to straight-line depreciation.

This depreciation is calculated in Figure 9-35 using a $20,000 *cost*, a $0 *salvage value*, a *life* of 5 years, a *depreciation-rate* of 2, a *SL-switch* of 1, and the appropriate *start-period* and *end-period* arguments in rows 4 and 5. In cell B10, the depreciation for the first year is calculated as $4,000 using the formula @VDB($B1,$B2,$B3,B4,B5,$B6,$B7). (The mixed addressing keeps all arguments fixed except *start-period* and *end-period* when copied across row 10.) In C10..G10, similar @VDB functions are used to calculate the depreciation in the remaining years. Note that @VDB correctly calculates the "plug" value in the final year of depreciation.

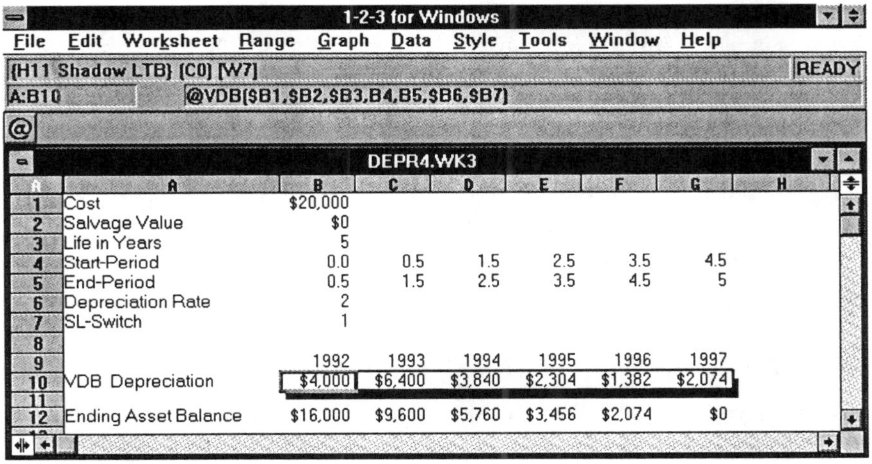

Figure 9-35 Using @VDB and a *SL-switch* of 1

MACRS Straight-Line Depreciation

At the time this book was written, current tax laws allowed you to switch to a straight-line method of depreciation for the first tax year that this method yields a larger expense than MACRS declining-balance expense. Table 9-12, taken from IRS publications, shows the applicable declining-balance rate for each class of property, and the first year that the straight-line method yields an equal or greater deduction.

MACRS straight-line depreciation uses a rate for each period equal to

$$\text{Straight-Line rate} = \frac{\text{Years of depreciation in period}}{\text{Years of life remaining at beginning of period}}$$

TABLE 9-12 Depreciation Periods when MACRS Straight-Line Is More Advantageous Than Declining Balance

Class	Declining-balance rate	Year when SL more advantageous
3	66.67%	3
5	40.00%	4
7	28.57%	5
10	20.00%	7
15	10.00%	7
20	7.50%	9

For example, for a five-year asset, the MACRS straight-line depreciation rate in the first year is 10% (.5/5), since a half-year convention is used. In the second year the rate is (1/4.5) or 22.22%, since only .5 year of depreciation has been expensed in the previous year. Each year this rate increases as the number of years remaining decreases.

MACRS and @VDB compute straight-line depreciation per period as the *Rate Per Period * Remaining Book Value*. The *remaining book value* (original cost minus accumulated depreciation) decreases each period by the previous period's expense. The remaining book value is the asset value after *either* the declining-balance rate *or* the straight-line rate is applied.

Using @VDB to Calculate MACRS Depreciation

Note: If you use @VDB to calculate tax depreciation, make sure you check your results against current tax publications.

Let's return to our example of a five-year, $20,000 asset. MACRS depreciation assumes a $0 salvage value, a half-year convention, and switching to straight-line in year four. In Figure 9-36 MACRS depreciation in year one is calculated as @VDB($B1,$B2,$B3,B4,B5,$B6,$B7), which is the same formula used in the previous example (Figure 9-35), except that *SL-switch* is 0. All other depreciation expenses in row 10 are calculated in a similar manner. By comparing Figures 9-35 and 9-36, you'll see that the straight-line expense is returned in years five and six, since it exceeds the DDB expense.

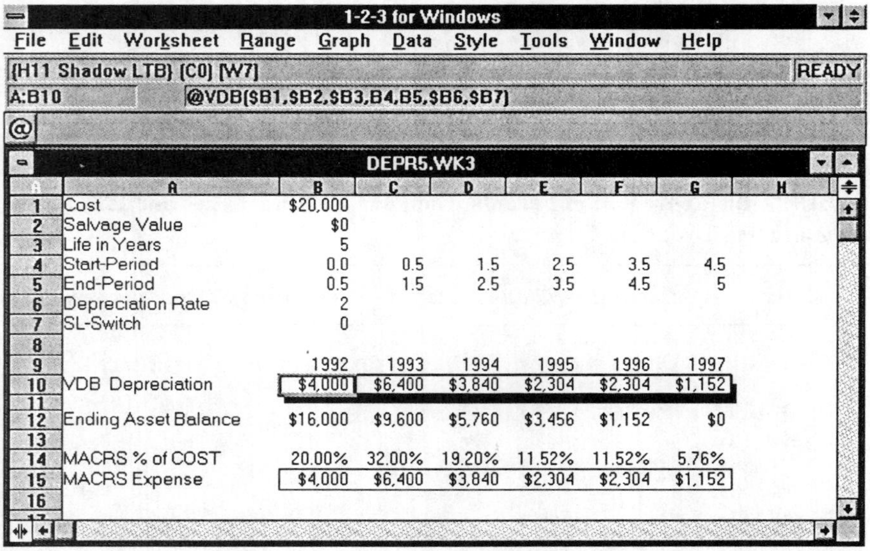

	A	B	C	D	E	F	G	H
1	Cost	$20,000						
2	Salvage Value	$0						
3	Life in Years	5						
4	Start-Period	0.0	0.5	1.5	2.5	3.5	4.5	
5	End-Period	0.5	1.5	2.5	3.5	4.5	5	
6	Depreciation Rate	2						
7	SL-Switch	0						
8								
9		1992	1993	1994	1995	1996	1997	
10	VDB Depreciation	$4,000	$6,400	$3,840	$2,304	$2,304	$1,152	
11								
12	Ending Asset Balance	$16,000	$9,600	$5,760	$3,456	$1,152	$0	
13								
14	MACRS % of COST	20.00%	32.00%	19.20%	11.52%	11.52%	5.76%	
15	MACRS Expense	$4,000	$6,400	$3,840	$2,304	$2,304	$1,152	
16								

Figure 9-36 Using @VDB to calculate MACRS depreciation

In row 15, the MACRS depreciation expense is computed as a check, using IRS 1990 MACRS rates for a five-year asset as a percentage of *cost*. Notice that these values are the same as those calculated by @VDB in row 10.

STRING FUNCTIONS

1-2-3 for Windows offers numerous functions that operate on strings, all listed in Table 9-13 and organized by functionality. Just some of the operations that you can perform with these functions are

- *Concatenating* (joining together) strings, or strings and values
- Editing strings and labels
- Converting values to strings and strings to values
- Testing for strings and values

Note: If you use a literal string in a string function, such as @UPPER("LITERAL"), remember to enclose it in double quotes. If you don't, 1-2-3 for Windows will disallow the entry.

String Information Functions

Two functions, @LENGTH and @FIND, return information about a particular string. In many cases, you will *nest* these functions within one of the Text Editing functions (see Table 9-13) to help you edit a *string*. They are also commonly used in macros to return information about cell contents.

Returning the Length of a String: @LENGTH

@LENGTH returns a *value* equal to the number of characters in a string. @LENGTH is usually used to determine the length of a string or substring within a string (see "Text Editing Functions" below) or in a macro to test entries for a specific length, such as zip codes. The form of this function is

```
@LENGTH(string)
```

@LENGTH counts all characters within *string*, including numbers, leading and trailing spaces, and spaces between words. For example, in cell B3 of Figure 9-37, @LENGTH(A3) returns the value 4, while in cell B4, @LENGTH(A4) returns 6. Since the string "Bora", in cells A3 and A4 appear the same, the string in cell A4 must then contain 2 trailing spaces.

Similarly, in cell B5, @LENGTH(A3&A4) returns 10, when the strings in cells A3 and A4 are concatenated without adding a space in between. But in cell B6, @LENGTH(A6) returns 11, when the formula +A3&" "&A4 in cell A6 concatenates these strings and adds a space in between them.

TABLE 9-13   String Functions

String Functions	Operation
Information	*Calculates*
@LENGTH	Number of characters in a string
@FIND	Starting position of a substring in a string
Text Editing	*Performs*
@LOWER	Converts all characters to lower case
@UPPER	Converts all characters to upper case
@PROPER	Converts first character in each word to upper case; all others to lower case
@TRIM	Deletes leading and trailing spaces, and extra spaces between words
@REPLACE	Replaces *n* characters in a string with a new string, or adds a new string to the start or end of a string
@LEFT	Extracts *n* characters starting from the left of a string
@RIGHT	Extracts *n* characters starting from the right of a string
@MID	Extracts *n* characters starting from the left of a string
@REPEAT	Repeats a string *n* times
Conversion	*Converts*
@STRING	Value to a string
@VALUE	String to a value
Test	*Tests*
@EXACT	Two strings for equality
@N	The first cell in a range for a value
@S	The first cell in a range for a string
Lotus Multibyte Character	*Performs*
@CHAR	Converts Lotus Multibyte Character code number to a character
@CODE	Converts a character to a Lotus Multibyte Character code number

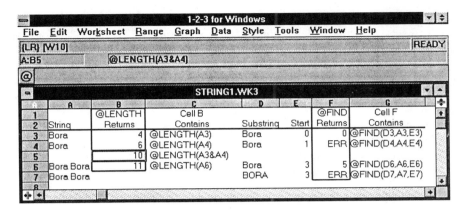

Figure 9-37 Using @LENGTH and @FIND

Returning the Starting Point of a Substring: @FIND

The @FIND function returns the position of the first occurrence of a substring within a string after a specified start-point. Typically, you'll use this function to

- Return offset locations (*start-point* arguments) of substrings for the @REPLACE, @MID, @LEFT, and @RIGHT functions.

- Return *number of character* arguments for the @REPLACE function.

- To locate a particular sequence of characters in a macro.

The form of this function is

@FIND(*substring,string,start-point*)

where *string* is the one you want to evaluate, and *substring* is the string you are searching for within *string*. *Substring* must be an *exact* match for @FIND to locate it within *string*. @FIND does *not* recognize different spelling, capitalization, accent marks, and spacing as an exact match. If it doesn't find an exact match for these reasons or for any other reason, @FIND returns ERR. If you use a literal string, remember to enclose it in double quotes.

Start-point specifies the point in *string* where you want @FIND to begin searching. Enter it as a value between 0 and *n* - 1, where *n* is the number of characters in *string*, including blank spaces. *Start-point* assumes an offset of 0. That is, the leftmost character in *string*, position 1, has a *start-point* of 0. So for a 0 *start-point*, @FIND begins searching at the first character. The last *string* character, *n*, has a *start-point* of *n* - 1. If *start-point* is negative or greater than *n* - 1, @FIND returns ERR.

The @FIND function returns a value, using an offset of 0, that represents the *first* occurrence of *substring* beginning at the *start-point*. In Figure 9-37, for instance, @FIND(D3,A3,E3) in cell F3 begins searching for the *substring* "Bora" using a *start-point* of 0. Since it finds an exact match in the first position of *string*, @FIND returns the offset value 0. In cell F4, however, @FIND(D4,A4,E4) returns ERR because a *start-point* of 1 says to start searching at the *o* in the *string* "Bora"; no match is found for the *substring* "Bora."

In cell F6, @FIND uses a *start-point* of 3 and so begins searching at the leftmost *a*. When it finds the second occurrence of "Bora", @FIND returns an offset value of 5. When the *substring* "BORA" in cell D7 is used, however, @FIND returns ERR, because the capitalization is not an exact match.

Text Editing Functions

1-2-3 for Windows provides nine functions that edit text in a worksheet, all of which are listed in Table 9-13 under Text Editing functions.

Changing Character Case: @LOWER, @UPPER, and @PROPER

1-2-3 for Windows' @LOWER, @UPPER, and @PROPER functions alter the *case* or capitalization of a string. Common applications of these functions include converting strings to one case or converting all labels in a database to one case before using Data Sort, since capitalization can affect how this command sorts labels.

The forms of these functions and the results they return are as follows:

Function	Converts string to
@LOWER(*string*)	Lowercase characters.
@UPPER(*string*)	Uppercase characters.
@PROPER(*string*)	Proper case: the first letter in *string*, and each letter after a space or nonalphabetic character, are changed to upper case; all other characters are converted to lower case.

As you can see in Figure 9-38, @UPPER, @LOWER, and @PROPER return different results for the same *string* argument in cell A2. In cell C2, @LOWER(A2) converts all letters to lower case, while in cell C3, @UPPER(A2) converts all letters to upper case. In cell C4, @PROPER(A2) converts to upper case:

- The leftmost character
- Each letter after a blank space
- Any letter after a nonalphabetic character (punctuation marks, values, and other characters such as + and $), even when no blank space separates them

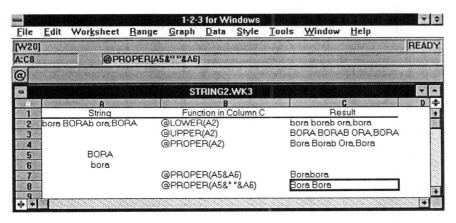

Figure 9-38 Using @LOWER, @UPPER, and @PROPER

@PROPER doesn't change capitalization correctly when there is incorrect spacing between words. In cell C4, for example, @PROPER(A2) doesn't capitalize the *b* in the third "bora"; instead, the second letter, *O*, is capitalized. The *B* in the fourth "Bora", however, is correctly capitalized, because it directly follows a comma.

When *string* is the result of concatenating two strings, the capitalization returned by @PROPER depends on the spacing between the concatenated strings. In cell C7, for instance, @PROPER(A5&A6) joins two strings without a space, so the *b* in cell A6 isn't capitalized. In cell C8, @PROPER(A5&" "&A6) adds one space between the two strings, so both *B*'s are capitalized.

Trimming Extra Blank Spaces in a String: @TRIM

The @TRIM function deletes, or trims, unnecessary blank spaces in a string. Common uses of this function include:

- Editing labels in a spreadsheet.
- Trimming extra spaces when concatenating strings.
- In a macro, controlling the number of spaces in data entry.
- In a database, trimming spaces that can affect how the Data Sort command sorts entries.

The form of this function is

```
@TRIM(string)
```

which deletes any leading spaces at the beginning of *string*, any trailing spaces at the end of *string*, and any consecutive blank spaces after a blank space within *string*. However, @TRIM always leaves one space between concatenated strings.

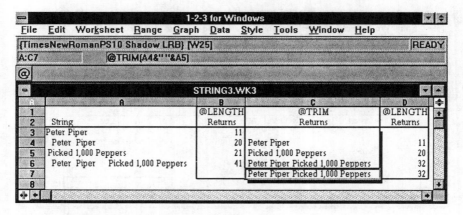

Figure 9-39 Using @TRIM

To see how @TRIM works, look at Figure 9-39. In cell B3, @LENGTH(A3) shows that the *string* "Peter Piper" in cell A3 is 11 characters long, including one blank space. However, in cell B4, @LENGTH(A4) shows that a similar-looking *string* is 20 characters long, which includes three leading spaces at the beginning of the *string*, two blank spaces between "Peter" and "Piper," and five trailing spaces. Now look at the result of @TRIM(A4) in cell C4. It trims all but one space and returns a string 11 characters long, just like the original "Peter Piper" in cell A3.

@TRIM always leaves one space between two concatenated strings. In Figure 9-39, for example, cell A6 contains the formula +A4&A5, which has a length of 41 (20 from cell A5, 21 from cell A6). In cell C6, @TRIM(A6) returns a string with a length of 32, deleting all leading, trailing, and extra spaces between words. Notice that 32 is one greater than the combined lengths of the trimmed strings in cells C3 and C4. This is the extra space @TRIM leaves between two concatenated strings. Likewise, @TRIM(A4&" "&A5) in cell C7 also returns a string with a length of 32; extra space is included in the concatenation formula.

Extracting a Substring from a String: @LEFT, @RIGHT, @MID

1-2-3 for Windows provides three functions, @LEFT, @RIGHT, and @MID, that return a specified portion of a string while leaving your original *string* intact. You'll usually use these functions to

- Copy only part of a label to another cell.

- Extract part of a label to use in a database or macro.

- Truncate entries so that they are consistent (such as converting Expenses and Expense to a consistent entry, Exp).

The form of these functions are

```
@LEFT(string,number of characters)
@RIGHT(string,number of characters)
@MID(string,start-point,number of characters)
```

These functions extract the specified *number of characters* (including blank spaces) from *string* using the following *start-points*:

Function	Start-Point
@LEFT	Leftmost edge of *string*
@RIGHT	Rightmost edge of *string*
@MID	*Start-point* argument you specify, beginning from the leftmost edge of *string*

The *start-point* for @MID must be between 0 and $n - 1$, where n is the number of characters in *string*, including blank spaces. The first character has a *start-point*, or offset value, of 0. The last character in *string*, n, has an offset of $n - 1$. If *start-point* is negative, @MID returns ERR; if it is greater than $n - 1$, @MID returns a null string (" ").

Number of characters can be between 1 and n, where n is the total length of *string*. If you use a value outside of this range, these functions return the following:

Number of Characters	@LEFT,@RIGHT, @MID Return
Negative	ERR
0	null string (" ")
Greater than $n-1$	@LEFT and @RIGHT return entire *string*, @MID returns the remaining portion of *string* after *start-point*.

Figure 9-40 shows the results each of these functions return for the *string* "Peter Piper" in column A. (Notice that its length is 11.) Here are the substrings of this *string* that the @LEFT and @RIGHT functions extract, given the same *number of characters* argument:

String	Number of Characters	@LEFT Returns	@RIGHT Returns
Peter Piper	1	Leftmost character "P"	Rightmost character "r"
Peter Piper	5	Five leftmost characters "Peter"	Five rightmost characters "Piper"
Peter Piper	12	Entire 11-character string "Peter Piper"	Entire 11-character string "Peter Piper"

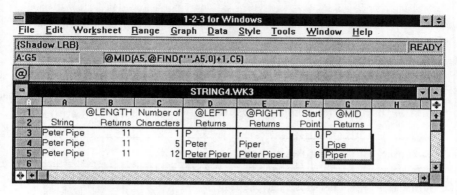

Figure 9-40 Using @LEFT, @RIGHT, and @MID

For example, @LEFT(A3,C3) in cell D3 begins extracting from the leftmost edge of *string* and returns the leftmost character "P" when *number of characters* is 1. Conversely, the same arguments in @RIGHT(A3,C3) in cell E3 causes @RIGHT to begin extracting from the rightmost edge of *string*, and return the rightmost character "r."

On the other hand, @MID begins extracting at the leftmost edge of *string*, beginning with the *start-point* you specify. When you use a *start-point* of 0, such as in @MID(A3,F3,C3) in cell G3, @MID is the same as @LEFT—it begins extracting at the first character (offset value of 0), and returns the leftmost character "P."

In cell G4, @MID uses a *start-point* of 5 and begins extracting at the sixth character, a blank space. It then uses the 5 *number of characters* argument and returns the substring "Pipe."

You can also use @FIND(*substring,string,start-point*) to determine @MID's *start-point*. Because you want to start extracting at the blank space, which is a unique character in *string*, @FIND(" ",A4,0) will return an offset value of 5. So @MID(A5,@FIND(" ",A4,0),C4) is used to return the substring "Pipe."

You can also use @FIND to determine a *start-point* that is not a unique character in *string*. For example, suppose you want to begin extracting at the "P" in "Piper." Although "P" is not unique in *string*, the blank space preceding it is, so you can use @FIND (" ",A5,0)+1 to return the *start-point* argument of 6. As you can see in cell G5, @MID(A5,@FIND(" ",A5,0)+1,C5) returns the correct string "Piper."

Replacing or Adding a String: @REPLACE

@REPLACE is a powerful text editing function. The form of this function is

```
@REPLACE(string,start-point,number of characters,
new-string)
```

which replaces the *number of characters* in a *string*, beginning at the *start-point*, with a *new-string*. Table 9-14 shows the results you obtain by using the @REPLACE function with different arguments.

TABLE 9-14   Results of @REPLACE

Start-Point	Number of Characters	@REPLACE
Less than 0	Any	Returns ERR.
0	0	Adds *new-string* in front of *string*.
	n	Replaces string with *new-string*.
	1 to *n* - 1	Replaces *number of characters* in *string* with *new-string*.
1 to *n* - 1	1 to *n* - 1	Replaces portion of *string* specified by *number of characters* argument, beginning with *start-point*.
n	Any	Adds *new-string* to end of *string*.
Larger than *n*	Any	Treats *start-point* as equal to *n*.

The *start-point* must be between 0 and *n*, where *n* is the number of characters in *string*, including any blank spaces. The leftmost character has a *start-point*, or offset value, of 0. The last character in *string*, *n*, has an offset of *n* - 1.

Number of characters specifies the total number of characters, including blank spaces, that you want replaced in *string*. This argument can be between 0 and *n*, the total length of *string*.

You can use @REPLACE to

- Add a new string at the beginning or end of an existing string.

- Replace an entire string with a new string.

- Replace a portion of a string with a new string.

To see this, look at Figure 9-41. Column A contains the *string* "Peter P.", while column B contains the length of these strings. For example, cell B4 contains @LENGTH(A4) and returns a length of 8. Column C contains *start-point* arguments, column D, *number of character* arguments, and column E, *new-string* arguments. Column F contains @REPLACE functions and displays the results returned. (Each of these functions is discussed in the following sections.) Finally, column G gives a description of the operation each @REPLACE function in column F performs.

Adding a New String at the Beginning or End of a String   In some cases, the @REPLACE function is equivalent to concatenating two strings—when you use it to add a *new-string* at the beginning or end of a *string*. In cell F3, @REPLACE uses both a *start-point* and *number of characters* of 0. So this function adds the *new-string* in front of the *string* to create "Mr. Peter P."

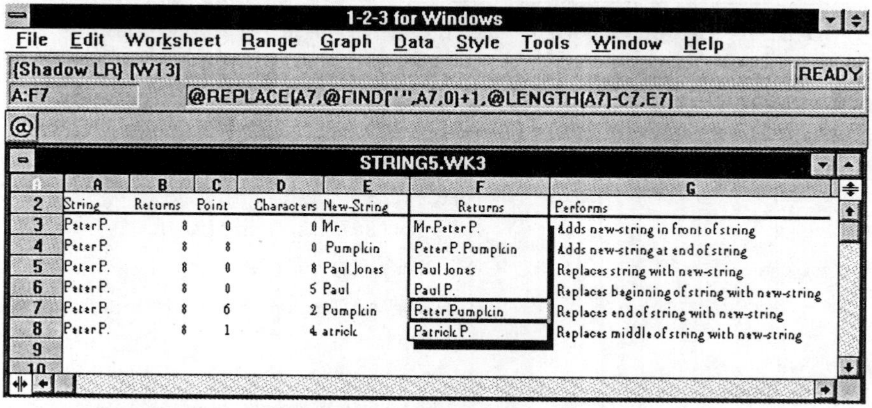

```
┌──────────────────────── 1-2-3 for Windows ──────────────────── ▾ ⬍ ┐
│ File  Edit  Worksheet  Range  Graph  Data  Style  Tools  Window  Help │
├──────────────────────────────────────────────────────────────────┤
│ {Shadow LR} [W13]                                          READY │
│ A:F7              @REPLACE[A7,@FIND[" ",A7,0]+1,@LENGTH[A7]-C7,E7]  │
│ @                                                                  │
├──────────────────────────────────────────────────────────────────┤
│ ⊟ ──────────────────── STRING5.WK3 ──────────────────── ▾ ▲ ┐     │
│     A       B       C       D          E         F         G    ⬍  │
│   2 String  Returns Point  Characters New-String  Returns   Performs │
│   3 PeterP.   8      0          0 Mr.     Mr.PeterP.  Adds new-string in front of string │
│   4 PeterP.   8      0          0 Pumpkin PeterP.Pumpkin Adds new-string at end of string │
│   5 PeterP.   8      0          8 PaulJones PaulJones Replaces string with new-string │
│   6 PeterP.   8      0          5 Paul    PaulP.    Replaces beginning of string with new-string │
│   7 PeterP.   8      6          2 Pumpkin PeterPumpkin Replaces end of string with new-string │
│   8 PeterP.   8      1          4 atrick  PatrickP. Replaces middle of string with new-string │
│   9                                                                │
│  10                                                                │
└──────────────────────────────────────────────────────────────────┘
```

Figure 9-41 Different applications of @REPLACE

On the other hand, the @REPLACE function in cell F4 uses a *start-point* of 8, but a *number of characters* argument of 0. Since the length of *string* is 8, the last character has an offset value of 7 ($n - 1$), so this *start-point* says to begin after the end of *string*. This function adds the *new-string* to the end of the existing *string* and returns "Peter P. Pumpkin." Notice that a blank space is included at the beginning of the *new-string* to separate the end of the *string* and the beginning of the *new-string*.

An easy way to add to the end of an existing string is to use @LENGTH as the *start-point*. So in this case, "Peter P. Pumpkin" is the result of @REPLACE-(A4,@LENGTH(A4),D4,E4).

Replacing an Entire String with a New String   It's also an easy matter to replace an entire string with a new string. In Figure 9-41 for instance, the @REPLACE function in cell F5 uses a *start-point* of 0 and a *number of characters* argument equal to the entire length of *string*, 8. The result is that the entire *string* is replaced with the *new-string* "Paul Jones." An easy way to do this is to use the use @LENGTH function as the *number of characters* argument, as in @REPLACE(A5,C5,@LENGTH(A5),E5).

Replacing a Portion of a String with a New-String   You can also use @REPLACE to replace a portion of a *string* with a *new-string*. Returning to Figure 9-41, the @RE-PLACE function in cell F6 uses a *start-point* of 0 to replace only the beginning portion of *string* with the *new-string*. To replace the first five characters, "Peter", or all the characters before the blank space (a unique character), @FIND(" ",A6,0) is used as the *number of characters* argument to return 5. So "Peter" is replaced by "Paul" to return the label "Paul P."

Similarly, only the end-portion of *string* is replaced in cell F7. In this case, both @FIND and @LENGTH are used in the @REPLACE function. The *start-point* @FIND(" ",A7,0)+1 returns an offset value of 6. To replace all characters beginning with the second "P" in *string*—which is not a unique character—the blank cell directly preceding this character, which is unique, is used in @FIND. To replace the remaining *string, number of characters* is simply @LENGTH(A7)-C7, where cell C7 contains the *start-point.* So @REPLACE(A7,@FIND(" ",A7,0)+1,@LENGTH(A7)-C7,E7) replaces the last two characters of *string* "P." with the *new-string* "Pumpkin."

Replacing a middle portion of a *string* can be a little tricky. For example, to replace "eter" with the *new-string* "atrick," you need to use a *start-point* of 1. This causes @REPLACE to begin replacing at the second character. Actually, @FIND("e",A8,0) will return this *start-point.* The *number of characters* argument representing the portion of *string* to be replaced, "eter," is calculated as 4 using @FIND("r",A8,0)+1-C8, where C8 is the *start-point.* Using these arguments, the @REPLACE function in cell F8 replaces the four characters after the first "P" with the *new-string* in cell E8, and returns the label "Patrick P."

▼ *Tip:* The @LENGTH and @FIND functions can make it considerably easier to calculate the *start-point* and *number of character* arguments in the @REPLACE function. To do this, use the following table as a convenient reference guide:

@REPLACE New-String	@REPLACE Start-Point	@REPLACE Number of Characters
Added:		
In front of *string*	0	0
At end of *string*	@LENGTH(*string*)	0
Replaces:		
Entire *string*	0	@LENGTH(*string*)
At start of *string*	0	@FIND("C",*string*,0)
At end of *string*	@FIND("C",*string*,0)	@LENGTH(*string*)-*start-point*
In middle of *string*	@FIND("C",*string*,0)	@FIND("E",*string*,0)+1-*start-point*

where "C" is a unique character in *string*, or the first occurrence of a nonunique character. "E" is the last character in the portion of *string* to be replaced, and must also be either a unique character in *string*, or the first occurrence of a nonunique character.

Creating Repeating Labels: @REPEAT

The @REPEAT function repeats a character pattern a specified number of times. You'll find this function useful when formatting worksheets and creating spreadsheet headings. The form of this function is

```
@REPEAT(string,n)
```

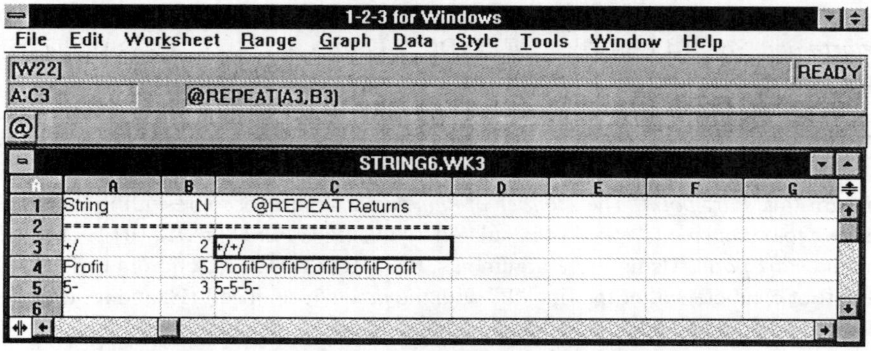

```
┌────────────────────────────────────────────────────────────────────────┐
│ ▄                         1-2-3 for Windows                      ▼│◆│    │
│  File   Edit  Worksheet  Range  Graph  Data  Style  Tools  Window  Help  │
│ ┌────────────────────────────────────────────────────────────┬──────┐   │
│ │[W22]                                                         │READY │   │
│ ├────────────┬───────────────────────────────────────────────┴──────┤   │
│ │A:C3        │       @REPEAT(A3,B3)                                   │   │
│ ├────────────┴───────────────────────────────────────────────────── │   │
│ │@                                                                    │   │
│ ├─────────────────────────────────────────────────────────────────── │   │
│ │ ▄                          STRING6.WK3                    ▼│▲        │   │
│ │┌───┬────────┬─────┬─────────────────────┬─────┬─────┬─────┬───┬─┐    │   │
│ ││   │   A    │  B  │         C           │  D  │  E  │  F  │ G │◆│    │   │
│ ││ 1 │String  │  N  │@REPEAT Returns      │     │     │     │   │▲│    │   │
│ ││ 2 │────────────────────────────────────────────────────────│ │    │   │
│ ││ 3 │+/      │  2  │+/+/                 │     │     │     │   │ │    │   │
│ ││ 4 │Profit  │  5  │ProfitProfitProfitProfitProfit   │     │   │ │    │   │
│ ││ 5 │5-      │  3  │5-5-5-               │     │     │     │   │ │    │   │
│ ││ 6 │        │     │                     │     │     │     │   │▼│    │   │
│ │└───┴────────┴─────┴─────────────────────┴─────┴─────┴─────┴───┴─┘    │   │
│ │◆│◆                                                            ◆│     │   │
│ └─────────────────────────────────────────────────────────────────────┘  │
└────────────────────────────────────────────────────────────────────────┘
```

Figure 9-42 Some results returned by @REPEAT

The @REPEAT function duplicates the *string n* times in a cell. *String* can be any printable character or combination of characters, including numbers and symbols. Make sure you enter it as a label. The *n* argument must be a value specifying the number of times that you want *string* to be repeated in a cell.

Figure 9-42 shows the labels' different @REPEAT functions return given the *string* arguments in column A and the *n* arguments in column B. In cell C3, @REPEAT(A3,B3) repeats the *string* "+ /" two times. Because two repeats of a two-character string are specified, the result is a label four characters long. Similarly, @REPEAT(A4,B4) displays the string "Profit" five times and @REPEAT(A5,B5) repeats the string "5-" three times.

Note that in Figure 9-42 the @REPEAT function repeats a *string n* times without regard to the width of column C. So @REPEAT differs from the repeating label prefix \ (backslash), which repeats a label the width of a cell. You can see this in Figure 9-42, where the entry \= in cell C2 repeats the label "=" for the entire column width of the cell.

Conversion Functions: @VALUE and @STRING

1-2-3 for Windows includes two conversion functions: @VALUE and @STRING. The @VALUE function converts strings into values, while @STRING converts values into strings.

Converting a Value to a String: @STRING

The @STRING function converts a value to a string or label. It is frequently used in database applications and sometimes used in worksheets to create headings and labels. The most powerful application of @STRING is in concatenating, or joining together, a value and a string into a single string.

The form of this function is

```
@STRING(value,number of places)
```

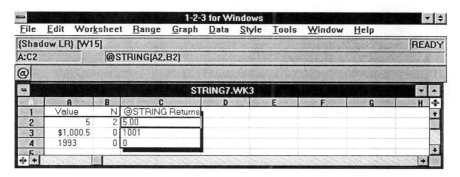

Figure 9-43 Using @STRING to convert values to labels

where the *value* argument is the number you want to convert to a label. 1-2-3 for Windows disregards any formatting of the value, such as commas or dollar signs. *Number of places* must be an integer between 0 and 15, which specifies the number of decimal places @STRING includes in the label it returns. If *number of places* is negative or greater than 15, @STRING returns ERR.

The @STRING function returns a label that is the *value* argument rounded to the *number of places* you specify, similar to the @ROUND function. If *value* is actually a label or a blank cell, @STRING returns the value 0, not a label.

Figure 9-43 shows the different results returned by @STRING for the *value* arguments in column A and the *number of places* arguments in column B. In cell C2, for example, @STRING(A2,B2) adds two decimal places and returns the *label* 5.00. Similarly, @STRING(A3,B3) rounds the *value* $1,000.5 to 0 places, disregards all formatting ($ sign, comma, and period), and returns the label 1001. Finally, @STRING returns the *value* 0 when cell A4 contains the centered label "1993."

Concatenating a Value and a Label

The most useful application of the @STRING function is to concatenate a value and a string into one label. For example, suppose in Figure 9-44 you want to combine the labels in column A with the values in column B to create one label in column C. In cell C2, +A2&" "&@STRING(B2,0) returns the label "Year Ended 1993." Likewise, in cell C3, +A3&" "&@STRING(B3,0) returns the label "Illinois 60611." Both of these functions add a space between the label and value and use a 0 *number of places* so that each value is displayed as an integer in the resulting label.

Converting a String to a Value: @VALUE

1-2-3 for Windows' @VALUE function converts strings to values. It is usually used to convert data from external sources, such as the Dow Jones News Retrieval Service, or CompuServe, that has been imported into a worksheet as text. (See Chapter 17 for more details.)

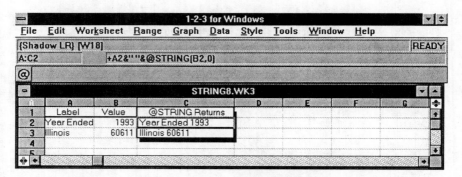

Figure 9-44 Using @STRING to concatenate a value and a label

The form of this function is

```
@VALUE(numeric string)
```

where *numeric string* must be a value expressed as a string. @VALUE can convert a *numeric string* containing a standard number (2.7), a number in scientific format (2E-1), a mixed number (3 1/3), a number using one of 1-2-3's standard formats ($20.5 or 2%), and any of these numbers that include leading or trailing spaces (2.7). Of course, you can also use the address of a cell containing any of these kinds of numbers. This function, however, returns ERR for a nonnumeric *string* argument.

▼ *Tip:* Use the Edit Quick Copy command to convert a range of labels to values. (See Chapter 7.) Use the Data Parse command to convert a range of numeric strings to values. (See Chapter 17.)

The @VALUE function *cannot* convert a *numeric string* when:

- The value and formatting are separated ($ 3.20).
- It includes nonnumeric characters (5 percent).
- It is composed of a formula or a function (@SUM(A3..A5)).

Figure 9-45 shows the results returned by @VALUE in row 2 for the *numeric string* arguments in row 1. The results are summarized as follows:

Numeric String	@VALUE	@VALUE Returns
100	Ignores two leading spaces	100
$100.00	Ignores $ sign and two decimal places	100

(continued)

Numeric String	@VALUE	@VALUE Returns
$ 100	Cannot evaluate $ sign separated from numeric label	ERR
99 4/5	Converts fraction to decimal	99.8
@SUM(A3..A7)	Cannot convert function	ERR
2*50	Cannot convert formula	ERR

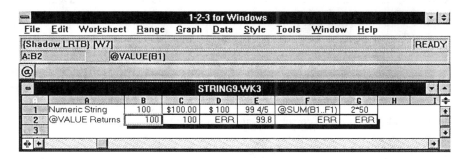

Figure 9-45 Using @VALUE

Test Functions: @EXACT, @N, and @S

1-2-3 for Windows provides three string functions that can be used to test worksheet entries—@EXACT, @N, and @S. Typically, these functions are used in database applications.

Testing Two Strings for Equality: @EXACT

The @EXACT function performs a conditional test to see if two strings are *exactly* equal. (For more information on conditional testing, see the @IF function in this chapter.) The form of this function is

```
@EXACT(string1,string2)
```

where *string1* and *string2* must each evaluate to a string. @EXACT evaluates these arguments as being equal if they have the same capitalization, accents, punctuation, spacing between words, leading and trailing spaces, and length. This function returns 1 (true) if the two strings are identical, and 0 (false) if they are not. If either *string1* or *string2* is a value or a blank cell, however, @EXACT returns ERR.

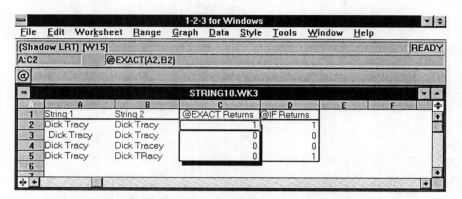

Figure 9-46   @EXACT versus @IF

The @EXACT function performs a more rigorous equality test than the conditional test performed by the @IF function. For this reason, @EXACT is commonly used to

- Test existing database entries during query operations.
- Test information as it is being entered into a database by a macro.
- Test a password for equality before running a macro.

Figure 9-46 compares the results returned by the @EXACT and the @IF functions for the same arguments in columns A and B. For example, @EXACT(A2,B2) in cell C2 and @IF(A2=B2,1,0) in cell D2 both evaluate *string1* and *string2* as equal and return the true value 1. Both of these functions return the false value 0 in row 3, when these arguments use different spacing (*string1* in cell A3 contains two leading spaces), and in row 4, when the arguments are spelled differently (*string2* in cell B4 contains an "e"). In row 5, @EXACT returns the false value 0 when *string1* and *string2* use different capitalization (the "R" is capitalized in *string2*), but @IF returns the true value 1 since it is not case sensitive.

> ▼ *Tip:*   Use @IF instead of @EXACT to evaluate null strings, blank cells, and cells containing spaces only. The @EXACT function returns ERR when either argument evaluates to a blank cell, a null string (" "), or a cell containing only spaces. For example, if cell A8 is a blank cell, and cell B8 is either a blank cell, a null string, or a cell containing only spaces, @EXACT(A8,B8) returns ERR, but @IF(A8=B8,1,0) evaluates all of these cell contents as equal and returns 1.

Testing Ranges for Values and Strings: @N and @S

1-2-3 for Windows provides two functions that test the first cell in a range for a value or string. The forms of these functions are

```
@N(range)
@S(range)
```

where the *range* argument can be a range name or address in the current worksheet file or another open file. If you enter a single cell address, 1-2-3 for Windows converts this argument to a range address.

These functions test only the upper leftmost cell in *range*. @N tests for a value, while @S tests for a string, and they return the following:

Upper Leftmost Cell in Range Contains	@N returns	@S returns
Value	Value in cell	Null String (" ")
String	0	String
Blank Cell	0	Null string (" ")

Note: The @ISNUMBER and @ISSTRING logical functions also test for strings and values in a cell. These functions return logical true and false results, rather than the cell contents. See "Logic and Error-Trapping Functions" earlier in this chapter.

Most often, @N and @S are used to test user input during data entry. For example, you can use the following statements in a macro to ensure that zip codes are entered as labels and not values:

```
{IF @S(B2)=""}{INDICATE "ENTER ZIP AS A LABEL"}
```

If cell B2 doesn't contain a label, the function @S(B2) returns a null string (" "), and the macro then displays the indicator ENTER ZIP AS A LABEL.

Lotus Multibyte Character Set Functions: @CHAR and @CODE

When you type a character in Windows, and in most Windows applications, it is stored using the ANSI (American National Standards Institute) character set. There are 256 characters in the ANSI set, numbered 0 to 255. Characters on your keyboard are represented by numeric values between 32 and 126. ANSI characters outside this range represent special characters, such as fractions and accented characters. (Appendix B in the *Windows User's Guide* includes a complete table of ANSI characters.)

Earlier releases of 1-2-3 use LICS (Lotus International Character Set).   Unlike most other Windows applications, 1-2-3 for Windows doesn't use the ANSI character set but instead uses Lotus's own proprietary character set, the Lotus Multibyte Character Set (LMBCS), designed to work with a variety of Lotus products including 1-2-3/G and Freelance. LMBCS is identical to ANSI for the characters on your keyboard in the range 32 to 126. Outside that range, however, LMBCS bears little resemblance to ANSI.

The LMBCS character set is divided into three distinct groups, as follows:

- Group 0—Characters numbered 32 to 255. These characters are the same as those found in the Code Page 850 character set, and include characters and symbols that are commonly found in the English language, as well as in 18 other European languages. (See the table at the back of the *1-2-3 for Windows User's Guide* for a complete list of LMBCS characters.)

- Group 1—Characters numbered 256 to 511. These characters include many of the same characters found in the Lotus International Character Set (LICS), the character set used in previous DOS versions of 1-2-3. Besides LICS characters, this group also includes many characters from the Code Page 437 character set, such as commonly used mathematical symbols.

- LMBCS characters 512 and above. Because most of these characters are neither displayable nor printable in 1-2-3, they are rarely used.

1-2-3 provides two functions that work with the Lotus Multibyte Character set: @CHAR and @CODE.

Displaying Lotus Multibyte Characters: @CHAR

The @CHAR function takes a Lotus Multibyte Character Set code number and returns the character that code number represents. The form of this function is

```
@CHAR(value)
```

where *value* must be a number between 0 and 4095, representing the value of a character in LMBCS. Otherwise, @CHAR returns ERR. For example, @CHAR(100) returns lowercase *d*, CHAR(171) returns 1/2, but @CHAR(4099) returns ERR because *value* is not a valid Lotus Multibyte Character. When *value* is not an integer, @CHAR uses only the integer portion without rounding the value.

Note: Some monitors cannot display and some printers cannot print all Lotus Multibyte Characters. When possible, 1-2-3 for Windows then uses a fallback presentation that resembles the desired character. If no character approximates the desired character, nothing will be displayed or printed.

Returning the Lotus Multibyte Character Code: @CODE

The @CODE function returns the opposite of @CHAR. This function converts a Lotus Multibyte Character Set character to its corresponding code number. The form of this function is

```
@CODE(character)
```

where *character* must be a Lotus Multibyte Character Set character entered as a *label*, even if the character is a number. Otherwise, @CODE returns ERR. For instance, @CODE("2") returns the number 50, indicating that 1-2-3 for Windows uses code number 50 for the character 2. If cell A1 contains the label "Perpendicular," @CODE(A1) only operates on the first character and returns 80, the code number for uppercase P.

DATE AND TIME ARITHMETIC

One of the most powerful features of 1-2-3 for Windows is its date and time functions. Date functions allow you to perform calculations using date-numbers, and time functions allow you to perform calculations using time-numbers. 1-2-3 for Windows also offers the @NOW function, which returns both the date and time.

You can use these functions to calculate a particular date or time and to compute the difference between dates or times. You'll also find them helpful in accounts receivable and payable aging, scheduling, calculating interest on loans, and creating loan amortization tables.

Date Functions

1-2-3 for Windows includes seven date functions shown in Table 9-15. Release 2 users will find that @D360 is new, and that @TODAY is back again.

Date Function Basics

Date functions either use or return a date-number. A *date-number* is an integer assigned by 1-2-3 for Windows to a particular date using a basic unit of 1 day (equal to the value 1) and an arbitrary starting point of January 1, 1900. So January 1, 1900 has a date-number of 1, January 2, 1900, a date-number of 2, and so on through 73050, or December 31, 2099.

Entering a Date: @DATE

The @DATE function is the most commonly used date function in 1-2-3. You'll usually use @DATE to create date headings or to enter a date that can be used in calculations. The form of this function is

```
@DATE(year,month,day)
```

where the *year*, *month*, and *day* arguments must evaluate to a number within these ranges:

Argument	Minimum Value	Maximum Value
year	0 (year 1900)	199 (year 2099)
month	1 (January)	12 (December)
day	1	last day in a particular month

@DATE uses only the integer portion of an argument. For example, if *month* evaluates to either 5 or 5.6, @DATE uses the integer 5.

@DATE automatically detects nonexisting dates. For example, 1-2-3 for Windows won't let you enter @DATE(99,11,31) since November only has 30 days, or @DATE(95,2,29) because 1995 isn't a leap year.

The @DATE function converts a date to a single date-number (see "Date Function Basics," above) such as:

Date	*@DATE Function*	*Date-number @DATE Returns*
January 1, 1900	@DATE(00,1,1)	1
April 17, 1995	@DATE(95,4,17)	34805
February 29, 1996	@DATE(96,2,29)	35124
December 31, 2001	@DATE(101,12,31)	37256

You can't easily interpret one of these results, however, unless you format it as a date using the Range Format command. (Formatting dates is discussed in Chapter 5.)

TABLE 9-15 Date Functions

Date Function	Performs
@DATE	Returns a date-number given a day, month, and year
@D360	Calculates the number of days between two date-numbers using a 360-day year
@DATEVALUE	Converts a date string to a date-number
@DAY	Returns the day of the month from a date-number
@MONTH	Returns the number of the month from a date-number
@YEAR	Returns the year from a date-number
@TODAY	Returns the date-number of the current date

▼ *Tip:* You can also enter a date directly into a cell if you enter it in the D1 (1: 31-Dec-90), D2 (2: 31-Dec), or D4 (4: Long Intl Date) date formats. For example, type **20-Nov-93** or **11/20/93** in a cell, and 1-2-3 automatically converts it to the date-number 34293. But if you type **20-Nov**, 1-2-3 for Windows assumes the current year from your system clock and during 1991 returns the date-number 33562 (20-Nov-1991). You still have to use Range Format, however, to display the date rather than the date-number. Another drawback is that you can't use this method to enter a date in a formula. Enter **20-Nov-93+50**, for instance, and 1-2-3 for Windows returns ERR.

Another alternative is to assign an Automatic Format to a cell before you enter a date; 1-2-3 for Windows will then automatically display a date in the format you entered it in. For instance, if a cell has been assigned an Automatic format, and you enter **20-Nov-93**, it is stored as the date-number 34293, but is displayed as 20-Nov-93.

▼ *Tip:* There are two ways you can easily enter dates as labels rather than date-numbers. You can't use the results in date calculations, however.

Select the ▣ icon to enter the name of each month across a row, beginning with January. 1-2-3 for Windows will enter the left-aligned label January in the selected cell, February in the cell to the right, and so on. The last label entered is December, even if you choose a range larger than 12 cells. This icon won't enter these labels down a column, even if you preselect such a range.

You can also enter a date as a label if you first assign a Label format to the cell (see Chapter 5). Then, when you enter the date in any of the five 1-2-3 date formats, it will be stored as a label. Enter **20-Nov-93**, for instance, and 1-2-3 for Windows stores and displays it as the label 20-Nov-93.

▼ *Tip:* You can determine the day of the week a date represents by using

`@CHOOSE(@MOD(@DATE(`*year,month,day*`),7),"Saturday, "Sunday","Monday",Tuesday",Wednesday",Thursday", Friday")`

Saturday is *always* used as the first item in *list* because date-number 1 (January 1, 1900) fell on a Sunday. So this *list* is designed such that Sunday, item 2, has an offset value of 1.

To find the day of the week June 6, 1956 fell on, for instance, use @DATE(56,6,6) in this formula. @MOD takes the date-number returned, 20612, divides it by 7, and returns the modulus 4. @CHOOSE then uses 4 as its *offset*, and returns the fifth item in *list*, Wednesday.

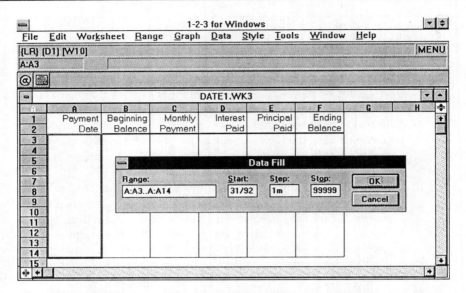

Figure 9-47   Using Data Fill to create a progressive series of date numbers

Using @DATE and the Data Fill Command To Create Payment Dates   An easy way to create a range of consecutive dates occurring on a specific day of the month is to use @DATE with the Data Fill command. For example, suppose you want to create a loan amortization table for the first year of a $150,000, 30-year, 12% fixed-rate mortgage incurred on January 1, 1992. Payments are made at the end of each month.

You can create sequential monthly payment dates beginning on January 31, 1992 by selecting the Data Fill command and specifying the Fill range **A3..A14**, and the Start as the first payment date **@DATE(92,1,31)** or **1/31/92**. (The next time you select Data Fill, this Start value will be shown as the date-number 33634). Then enter a Step of **1m** (the "m" tells 1-2-3 for Windows to step the dates by month) and a very large Stop, such as **999999**. Figure 9-47 shows these selections in the Data Fill dialog box. When you click on OK or press ENTER, 1-2-3 for Windows will create a progressive series of date-numbers, each on the last day of a month. To recognize these date-numbers, you need to format them using the Range Format 1: 31-Dec-90 command so they are displayed as in Figure 9-48.

▼ *Tip:*   To enter a sequential range of dates that increase or decrease by year, quarter, month, week, or day, use Data Fill, which is discussed in Chapter 12.

Adding and Subtracting Dates to Create a Loan Amortization Table   One of the most common uses of @DATE is adding and subtracting dates. When you add the results of two @DATE functions, the result is a new date-number equal to the sum of the two

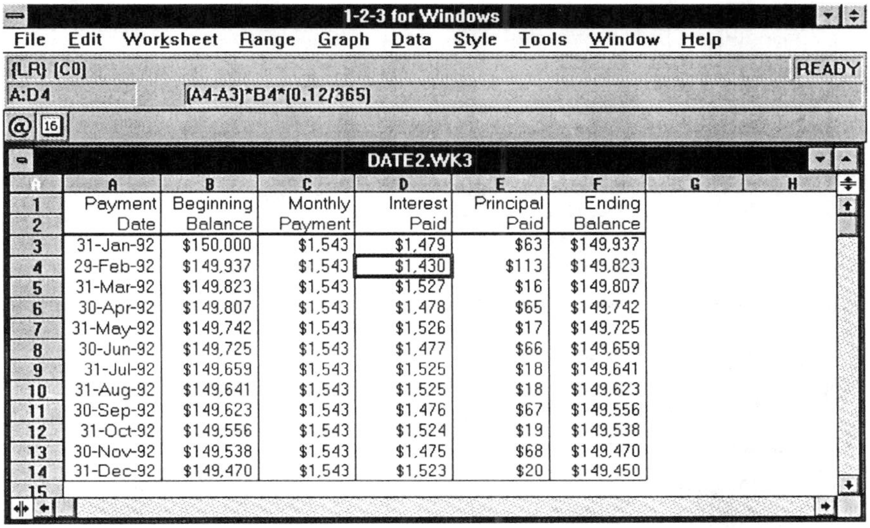

1-2-3 for Windows

File Edit Worksheet Range Graph Data Style Tools Window Help

{LR} {C0} READY

A:D4 (A4-A3)*B4*(0.12/365)

DATE2.WK3

	A	B	C	D	E	F
1	Payment	Beginning	Monthly	Interest	Principal	Ending
2	Date	Balance	Payment	Paid	Paid	Balance
3	31-Jan-92	$150,000	$1,543	$1,479	$63	$149,937
4	29-Feb-92	$149,937	$1,543	$1,430	$113	$149,823
5	31-Mar-92	$149,823	$1,543	$1,527	$16	$149,807
6	30-Apr-92	$149,807	$1,543	$1,478	$65	$149,742
7	31-May-92	$149,742	$1,543	$1,526	$17	$149,725
8	30-Jun-92	$149,725	$1,543	$1,477	$66	$149,659
9	31-Jul-92	$149,659	$1,543	$1,525	$18	$149,641
10	31-Aug-92	$149,641	$1,543	$1,525	$18	$149,623
11	30-Sep-92	$149,623	$1,543	$1,476	$67	$149,556
12	31-Oct-92	$149,556	$1,543	$1,524	$19	$149,538
13	30-Nov-92	$149,538	$1,543	$1,475	$68	$149,470
14	31-Dec-92	$149,470	$1,543	$1,523	$20	$149,450

Figure 9-48 Using @DATE to create a loan amortization table

date-numbers. Conversely, when you subtract the results of two @DATE functions, you get the number of days between these dates.

For example, by subtracting dates you can create the loan amortization table in Figure 9-48. In this table, the payment dates have been entered in column A using @DATE and the Data Fill command, as discussed earlier. The beginning balance in column B is simply the previous month's ending balance in column E. The monthly payment in column C, $1,543, is returned by @PMT(150000,.12/12,30*12). (See "Payment Per Period of an Annuity and Annuity Due: @PMT" earlier in this chapter.) In column D, interest paid is calculated as

days between payments * principal balance * daily interest rate

For example, in cell D4, the interest paid in February 1992 is (A4–A3)*B4*(.12/365), or $1,430. However, the January interest paid, $1,479, is computed as (A3–@DATE(92,1,1))*B3*(.12/365) because interest begins to accrue on January 1, 1992.

To complete this table, the principal paid in column E is calculated as the monthly payment in column C less the interest paid in column D, while the ending balance in column F is the beginning balance in column B less the principal paid in column E.

Calculating the Number of Days Between Two Dates Using a 360-day Year: @D360

The @D360 function, originally introduced in Release 3, calculates the number of days between two dates, assuming a 360-day year. Typical applications of the @D360 func-

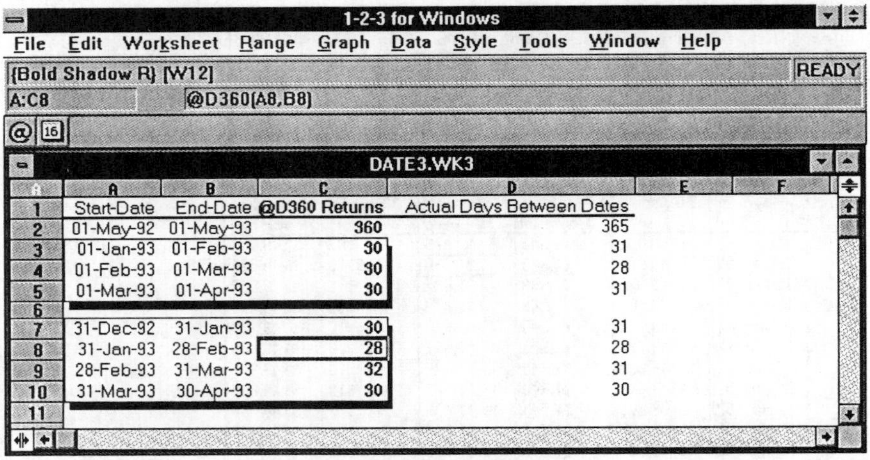

Figure 9-49   Using @D360 to calculate the number of days between dates

tion include calculating accounts receivable and payables aging as well as interest on loans and bonds using a 360-day year. The form of this function is

@D360(*start-date,end-date*)

where the *start-date* and *end-date* arguments must each evaluate to a *date-number* between 1 and 73050, representing dates between January 1, 1900 and December 31, 2099. (See "Date Function Basics," above.) Otherwise, @D360 will return ERR. @D360 then returns an integer representing the number of days between the *start-date* and *end-date*, assuming a 360–day year.

Unfortunately, the @D360 function returns different values, depending on the *start-date* or *end-date* used. You can see when this occurs in Figure 9-49. *Start-date* and *end-date* arguments in columns A and B have been entered using @DATE and formatted using Range Format 1: 31-Dec-90. Column C contains the @D360 function. For instance, @D360(A2,B2) in cell C2 calculates 360 days between the *start-date* May 1, 1992, and the *end-date* May 1, 1993. In column D, the actual difference between the dates in columns A and B is calculated. For example, +B2-A2 in cell C2 returns 365 days.

You can see in cells C3, C4, and C5 that @D360 returns 30 days when a *start-date* and an *end-date* both occur on the first day of a month. However, if you examine cells C7, C8, C9, and C10, you'll see that @D360 returns different results when a *start-date* or an *end-date* doesn't occur on the first day of a month. @D360 then assigns 28 days to February, and 32 days to March. (In leap years, @D360 assigns 29 days to February and 31 to March.)

Using @D360 to Create a Loan Amortization Table   You can use @D360 to create a loan amortization table when interest is computed using a 360-day year. To see this,

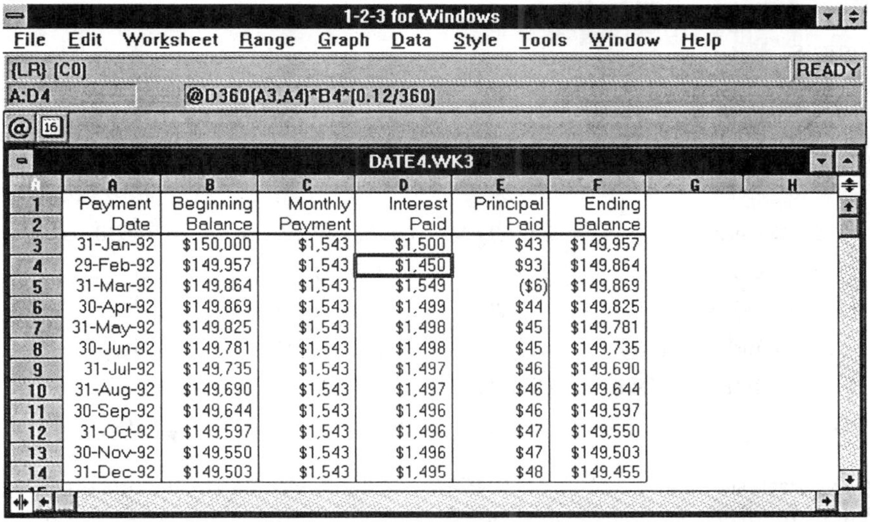

	A	B	C	D	E	F
1	Payment	Beginning	Monthly	Interest	Principal	Ending
2	Date	Balance	Payment	Paid	Paid	Balance
3	31-Jan-92	$150,000	$1,543	$1,500	$43	$149,957
4	29-Feb-92	$149,957	$1,543	$1,450	$93	$149,864
5	31-Mar-92	$149,864	$1,543	$1,549	($6)	$149,869
6	30-Apr-92	$149,869	$1,543	$1,499	$44	$149,825
7	31-May-92	$149,825	$1,543	$1,498	$45	$149,781
8	30-Jun-92	$149,781	$1,543	$1,498	$45	$149,735
9	31-Jul-92	$149,735	$1,543	$1,497	$46	$149,690
10	31-Aug-92	$149,690	$1,543	$1,497	$46	$149,644
11	30-Sep-92	$149,644	$1,543	$1,496	$46	$149,597
12	31-Oct-92	$149,597	$1,543	$1,496	$47	$149,550
13	30-Nov-92	$149,550	$1,543	$1,496	$47	$149,503
14	31-Dec-92	$149,503	$1,543	$1,495	$48	$149,455

Figure 9-50 Using @D360 in interest calculations

look at Figure 9-50, which is the same as Figure 9-48 in all respects (see "Using @DATE and the Data Fill Command to Create Payment Dates," above), except the interest paid in column D is calculated as

> days in the month of 360-day year*principal balance*daily interest rate of 360-day year

For example, in cell D4, the February interest of $1,450 is calculated as @D360(A3,A4)*B4*(.12/360). The $1,500 January interest, however, is computed as @D360(@DATE (91,12,31),A3)*B3*(.12/360). This formula uses @DATE(91,12,31), one day before the beginning loan date, to return 30 days. (The negative amortization in March occurs because @D360 uses 31 days for March in a leap year.)

Converting a Date String to a Date-number: @DATEVALUE

The @DATEVALUE function converts a date entered as a string to a date-number, which can then be used in calculations. You'll usually use this function to convert date-label worksheet headings and date labels imported from another file, such as a word processing file, to a date-number. The form of this function is

```
@DATEVALUE(string)
```

where *string* must be a date label between January 1, 1900 and December 31, 2099 in one of the five 1-2-3 date formats. Otherwise, @DATEVALUE will return ERR. If you enter *string* as a literal string, remember to enclose it in double quotes.

For example, @DATEVALUE returns the following date-values for each of the date formats:

Range Format	@DATEVALUE	@DATEVALUE Returns
1: 31-Dec-90 (D1)	@DATEVALUE("31-Oct-94")	34638
2: 31-Dec(D2)	@DATEVALUE("31-Oct")	33542
3: Dec-90(D3)	@DATEVALUE("Oct-94")	34608
4: Long Intl Date (D4)	@DATEVALUE("10/31/94")	34638
5: Short Intl Date (D5)	@DATEVALUE("10/31")	33542
None	@DATEVALUE("Oct 31,1994")	ERR

As you can see in this table, @DATEVALUE returns the corresponding date-number, 34638, for the D1 and D4 date formats. For the D2 and D5 formats, 1-2-3 uses the current year from your system clock, and @DATEVALUE returns 33542 (October 31, 1991). For the D3 format, however, @DATEVALUE assumes the first day of the month and returns 34608 (October 1, 1994). But for an unacceptable date format, such as "Oct 31,1994," @DATEVALUE returns ERR.

Returning the Day, Month, or Year from a Date-number: @DAY, @MONTH, and @YEAR

Three functions extract the day, month, or year from a date-number:

```
@DAY(date-number)
@MONTH(date-number)
@YEAR(date-number)
```

where *date-number* must evaluate to a number between 1 and 73050, representing dates between January 1, 1900 and December 31, 2099. (See "Date Function Basics" above.) Otherwise, 1-2-3 for Windows will return ERR.

▼ *Tip:* Use @YEAR+1900 to return the year of the date. For example, when cell A1 contains @DATE(98,7,22), @YEAR(A1)+1900 returns 1998.

@YEAR returns the year, @MONTH the month, and @DAY the day a *date-number* represents. These functions return values that are equivalent to the corresponding arguments in the @DATE function. For example, the date-number 33839 is returned by the function @DATE(92,8,23). So @YEAR(33839) returns the value 92. Note that the results returned by these functions are *not* date-numbers, but values.

▼ *Tip:* You can use @DAY, @MONTH, and @YEAR to calculate the number of days, months, and years between two dates. To calculate the time between August 15, 2005 and December 3, 1961 in Figure 9-51 for example, @DATE(105,8,15) in cells A2 and B2 returns the date-number 38579, or 15-Aug-2005. Similarly, @DATE(61,12,3) in cells A3 and B3 returns the date-number 22618, or 03–Dec-61. The difference, or number of days between these dates, 15,961, is used in @YEAR(B4), @MONTH(B4)-1 (you must *always* subtract 1 from the value @MONTH returns), and @DAY(B4) to calculate 43 years, 8 months, and 12 days between December 31, 1961 and August 15, 2005.

▼ *Tip:* You can use @MONTH with @CHOOSE to return the *name* of a month. For example, if cell A1 contains a date-number, the function

```
@CHOOSE(@MONTH(A1)-1,"January","February",
"March","April","May","June","July","August",
"September","October","November","December")
```

assigns an offset value of 0 to the label January, an offset value of 1 to February, and an offset value of 11 to December. However, because @MONTH returns a value of 1 for January and a value of 12 for December, @MONTH(A1)-1 is used as the *offset* argument in @CHOOSE. For the date-number 34486 (01-June-94), this formula returns the label June; for 2186 (25-Dec-05), it returns the label December.

Returning the Current Date: @TODAY

1-2-3 for Windows' @TODAY function, which requires no arguments, uses the system clock to return the current date as a date-number. So make sure your operating system time and date are correct. You'll want to use @TODAY to date a worksheet or in date calculations.

If you enter @TODAY in a date-formatted cell, it will return today's date, November 15, 1991, for instance. The result returned by @TODAY is updated every time your worksheet is manually or automatically recalculated. When you open this file the next day then, @TODAY will return November 16, 1991. To freeze the date returned by @TODAY, use the Edit Quick Copy command.

▼ *Tip:* If you select the 🔳 icon shown in Figure 9-52, 1-2-3 for Windows not only enters today's date as a date-number in the selected cell, but also formats the cell in the D4 (4: Long Intl Date) format.

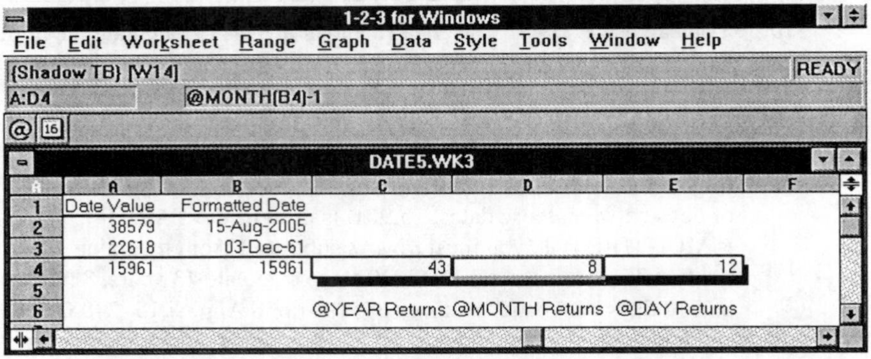

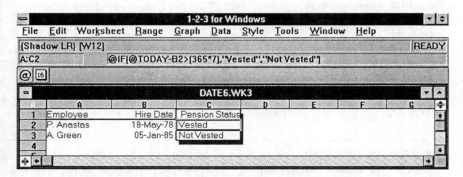

Figure 9-51 Using @DAY, @MONTH, and @YEAR

Figure 9-52 shows how @TODAY can be used in calculations. This worksheet uses @TODAY to *automatically* create an updated list of vested employees each time the file is opened. To do this, column A contains a list of employees, while Column B contains their hire dates entered using @DATE. Since vesting in this company's pension program occurs after seven years, cell B2 contains the formula:

```
@IF(@TODAY-B2>(365*7),"Vested","Not Vested")
```

This formula uses (@TODAY-B2) to calculate the number of days between the current date and an employee's hire date and then compares the result to (365*7), the number of days in seven years. When it is greater than seven years, as in cell C2, the *true-result* Vested is returned; otherwise the *false-result* Not Vested is returned, as in cell C3.

▼ *Tip:*   Use @NOW to return a date/time-number representing both the current date and time.

Figure 9-52 Using @TODAY with @IF

TABLE 9-16 Time Functions

Time Function	Performs
@TIME	Returns a time-number for a given hour, minute, and second
@TIMEVALUE	Converts a time string to a time-number
@HOUR	Returns the hour of day from a time-number
@MINUTE	Returns the minutes from a time-number
@SECOND	Returns the seconds from a time-number

Time Functions

1-2-3 for Windows includes five time functions shown in Table 9-16. All of these functions were available in previous releases of 1-2-3.

Time Function Basics

Time functions either use or return a time-number. A *time-number* is a decimal between 0 and 1, where one day or 24 hours equals 1.0. In other words, a time-number represents the amount of time that has elapsed since midnight. So noon, or 12 hours after midnight, is represented by the time-number .5.

1-2-3 for Windows' time values don't differentiate between days. Rather, time values are cyclical, starting over at each midnight. So the time-number .5 represents noon for each day.

You'll find the following values useful when using 1-2-3's time functions:

Time Unit	Decimal Value	Time Unit	Decimal Value
1 day	1.0	1 minute	0.000694444
1 hour	0.041666667	1 second	0.000011474

Entering a Time: @TIME

The @TIME function is helpful to create time headings and to enter a time that can be used in calculations. The form of this function is

```
@TIME(hours,minutes,seconds)
```

where the *hours*, *minutes*, and *seconds* arguments must evaluate to a value within these limits:

Argument	Minimum Value	Maximum Value
hours	0 (midnight)	23 (11 PM)
minutes	0	59
seconds	0	59

Note that *hours* is based on military time (6 PM, for example, is 18:00:00). If you use an argument outside of these ranges, 1-2-3 will return ERR. For example, @TIME(24,05,00), returns ERR because *hours*, 24, is outside of the acceptable range.

The @TIME function converts a time to a time-number, or a decimal between 0 and 1. (See "Time Function Basics" above.) For example, @TIME returns the following time-numbers:

Time	@TIME Function	Time-number @TIME Returns
12:15:00 AM	@TIME(0,15,0)	0.0104166667
12:00:01 PM	@TIME(12,00,01)	0.5000115474
11:59:59 PM	@TIME(23,59,59)	0.9999884259

As you can see, you can't easily interpret a time-number unless it is time-formatted using the Range Format command. (Formatting times is discussed in Chapter 5.)

▼ *Tip:* You can also enter a time directly into a cell using any of 1-2-3 for Windows' time formats. For example, if you type **11:30:00** or **11:30AM** in a cell, 1-2-3 automatically converts it to the time-number .470167. Type **23:30:00** or **11:30:00 PM**, and 1-2-3 for Windows converts it to the time-number .97917. You still have to use Range Format, however, to display the time rather than the time-number. Furthermore, you can't use this method to enter a time in a formula. Try to enter **2:02PM+20**, for instance, and 1-2-3 for Windows will disallow the entry.

Another alternative is to assign an Automatic format to a cell before you enter a time; 1-2-3 for Windows will then automatically display the time in the time format you entered it in. For instance, if a cell has been assigned an Automatic format, and you enter **11:30PM**, it is stored as the time-number .97917, but displayed as 11:30PM.

Yet a third alternative is to enter a time as a label by first assigning a Label format to a cell. However, like dates, the result is a label that can't be used in calculations. See Chapter 5.

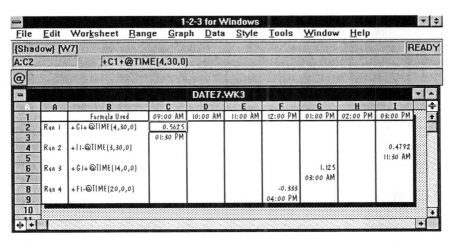

Figure 9-53 Adding and subtracting times

▼ *Tip:*   1-2-3 for Windows' Data Fill command is an easy way to create a range of sequential time-numbers that increase or decrease by hours, minutes, or seconds. For example, you can create a production schedule worksheet like Figure 9-53, where the headings in cells C1 through I1 are time-numbers that are used in calculations.

To create these headings, select Data Fill, and use the Fill range **C1..I1**, a Start of **@TIME(9,0,0)** or **9:00AM,** representing the first production hour, a Step of **1h** (the "h" tells 1-2-3 for Windows to step the times by hour) and a very large Stop such as **999999**. The result is a progressive series of time-numbers in this range, beginning at 9:00AM and increasing by one hour thereafter. To format these time-numbers, use the Range Format 7: 11:59 AM command.

Adding and Subtracting Times   To correctly add or subtract times, you must use the @TIME function. In Figure 9-53 for instance, the completion time of the 4.5-hour Run 1 begun at 9:00 AM is calculated in cell C2 using +C1+@TIME(4,30,0), which returns the time-number .5625, or 1:30 PM. If you don't use @TIME, and use the formula +C1+4.5 instead, you'll incorrectly get the time-number 4.875, or 9:00 PM.

To end the 3.5-hour Run 2 at 3:00 PM, the formula +I1-@TIME(3,30,0) in cell I4 returns the time-number .479167, which means you must begin at 11:30 AM. If you use the formula +H1-3.5 instead of @TIME, you'll incorrectly end up with the time-number –2.875, or 3:00 AM.

In cell G6, the formula +G1+@TIME(14,0,0) returns the time-number 1.125. This means that if you begin a 14-hour Run 3 at 1:00 PM, it will end at 3:00 AM. Since 1-2-3 for Windows' time values are cyclical, starting over each midnight, this is 3:00 AM the next day. Similarly, to finish a 20-hour Run 4 at noon, +F1-@TIME(20,0,0) in cell F8 returns the time-number –.33333 or 4:00 PM the previous day. Therefore, you must start Run 4 at 4:00 PM the day before it is to be finished.

Converting a String to a Time-number: @TIMEVALUE

You can use the @TIMEVALUE function to convert a time label (a time entered as a string) to a time-number, which can be used in calculations. This function is commonly used to convert time label worksheet headings and time labels imported from another file, such as a word processing file, to a time-number.

The form of this function is

```
@TIMEVALUE(string)
```

where *string* must be a time label in one of the four 1-2-3 time formats. @TIMEVALUE returns ERR if you use unacceptable time formats or time values outside of the acceptable ranges for @TIME function arguments (see "Converting Times to Time-numbers: @TIME" above). If you use a literal string, remember to enclose it in double quotes.

For example, @TIMEVALUE returns the following time-numbers for each of the time formats:

Range Format	@TIMEVALUE	@TIMEVALUE Returns
6: 11:59:59 AM (D6)	@TIMEVALUE("1:30:30 PM")	0.562847222
7: 11:59 AM (D7)	@TIMEVALUE("1:30 PM")	0.562500000
8: Long Intl Time (D8)	@TIMEVALUE("13:30:30")	0.562847222
9: Short Intl Time (D9)	@TIMEVALUE("13:30")	0.562500000
	@TIMEVALUE("26:30")	ERR

In this table, @TIMEVALUE returns the time-number .562847222 for the D6 and D8 time formats. For the D7 and D9 time formats, 1-2-3 for Windows assumes 0 seconds and returns a time-number of .5625. However, @TIMEVALUE("26:30:30") returns ERR because 26 is an unacceptable *hours* argument in the @TIME function.

Returning the Hours, Minutes, or Seconds from a Time-Number: @HOUR, @MINUTE, and @SECOND

1-2-3 for Windows includes three functions you can use to extract the hour, minute, or second from a time-number:

```
@HOUR(time-number)
@MINUTE(time-number)
@SECOND(time-number)
```

where *time-number* must evaluate to a decimal value between 0 and 1, representing times between 12:00 midnight and 11:59:59 PM (see "Time Function Basics," above). Otherwise, these functions will return ERR.

@HOUR returns the hour of the day, @MINUTE the minutes, and @SECOND the seconds a *time-number* represents. These functions return values that are equivalent to the corresponding arguments in the @TIME function. For example, suppose the function @TIME(23,5,0), which returns the time-number .96180556, is in cell A1. @HOUR(A1) then returns the value 23, and @MINUTE(A1) returns 5. Notice that the results returned by these functions are *not* time-numbers, but values.

Since time-numbers are cyclical, starting over again from 0 at each midnight, 1-2-3 evaluates the time-number 1.5 as .5, or 12 noon, @HOUR will return 12 in this instance.

Combined Dates and Times

Combined date and time values use the same concepts as 1-2-3 for Windows' date and time functions. A combined date/time-number is a single value, with the integer portion representing a date-number and the decimal portion representing a time-number on that date. (See "Date Function Basics" and "Time Function Basics" above for more details.) For instance, the formula @DATE(95,4,12)+@TIME(14,2,0) returns 34801.5847, which represents 2:02 PM on April 12, 1995.

You can't format one cell to display both the date and time represented by 34801.5847. Instead, this value must exist in two cells, one date formatted to display 12-Apr-95, for example, and the other time formatted to display 2:02 PM.

Calculating with Combined Dates and Times

Suppose you only travel by train, like John Madden. Imagine you need to be in Los Angeles on October 1, 1992 at 3:00 PM. A train trip from New York takes three days and seven hours, assuming no delays. To find the latest you can leave, specify your arrival time as @DATE(92,10,1)+@TIME(15,0,0) and your travel time as (3+@TIME(7,0,0)). So the formula

```
@DATE(92,10,1)+@TIME(15,0,0)-(3+@TIME(7,0,0))
```

returns the date/time value 33875.333. Date format this value to display 28-Sep-92; time format it to see 8:00 AM. The last train you can take and arrive on time must leave no later than 8:00 AM on September 28, 1992.

Returning the Current Date and Time: @NOW

The @NOW function, which requires no arguments, uses your system clock to return a combined date/time-number that represents the current date and time. The integer portion of the value returned is a date-number representing the current date, while the decimal portion is a time-number representing the current time. (So be sure Windows' time and date are correct.)

For example, suppose the operating system date is set to May 30, 1991 and the time is set to 5:35 AM. If you enter @NOW in a cell, it returns the value 33388.23278. Every time this worksheet is manually or automatically recalculated, however, this value is automatically updated using your system clock. If you want to freeze the value @NOW returns, use the Edit Quick Copy command.

Note: You can also use @TODAY to return the current date.

Remember that you can't format one cell to display both the current time and date. To get around this, enter @NOW in two cells. Date format one cell, and 1-2-3 for Windows uses the integer portion, 33388, as a date-number and returns 30-May-91. Time format the other cell, and 1-2-3 uses the decimal portion, .2278, as a time-number, and displays 5:35AM.

SPECIAL FUNCTIONS

1-2-3 for Windows has several functions listed in Table 9-17 that don't fit into the other categories. Release 2 users will find @COORD, @SHEETS, and @INFO new.

Note: The @SOLVER function is discussed in Chapter 13.

Counting the Number of Columns, Rows, or Worksheets in a Range: @COLS, @ROWS, and @SHEETS

1-2-3 for Windows includes three functions that return the number of columns, rows, and worksheets in a range. The forms of these functions are

```
@COLS(range)
@ROWS(range)
@SHEETS(range)
```

where *range* must be a two- or three-dimensional range entered as a range name or address.

@COLS and @ROWS return the same number of columns or rows for a two-dimensional and a three-dimensional range. For example, both @COLS(A1) and @COLS(A:A1..B:A1) return 1, since 1-2-3 for Windows evaluates column A in worksheets A and B as a single column. On the other hand, @SHEETS(A1) returns 1, while @SHEETS(A:A1..B:A1) returns 2, since @SHEETS counts the number of worksheets.

You'll usually use these functions to determine the number of columns, rows, and worksheets in a named range. Another common application is to use them in macros, when other tasks performed are based on the number of columns, rows, or worksheets in a range. For example, @SHEETS might be used in a macro to determine the number of sequential worksheets.

TABLE 9-17 Special Functions

Function	Returns
@COLS	Number of columns in a range
@ROWS	Number of rows in a range
@SHEETS	Number of worksheets in a range
@COORD	Absolute, mixed, or relative cell address
@@	Value or string referenced by another cell
@CELL	Attribute of upper-left cell in a range
@CELLPOINTER	Attribute of current cell
@INFO	Operating system information for one of eight query arguments

Creating an Address from Offset Coordinates: @COORD

The @COORD function uses the numeric coordinates of a cell location in a worksheet file, then returns the corresponding cell address using the type of cell referencing you specify—absolute, relative, or mixed. The form of this function is

```
@COORD(worksheet,column,row,absolute)
```

where *worksheet*, *column*, and *row* are a cell's numeric coordinates within the following ranges:

Argument	Range of Acceptable Values
Worksheet	1 to 256
Column	1 to 256
Row	1 to 8,192

As you may recognize, these ranges correspond to the minimum and maximum number of worksheets, columns, and rows that are possible in a worksheet file. For an argument outside these ranges, @COORD returns ERR.

The *absolute* argument conveys the type of mixed, relative, or absolute addressing you want the cell address to be. For example, for the *worksheet*, *column*, and *row* arguments of 1,1,1 and the *absolute* values below, @COORD returns the following type of address:

Absolute Argument	@COORD Returns	Cell Address	Worksheet	Column	Row
1	$A:$A$1	Absolute	Fixed	Fixed	Fixed
2	$A:A$1	Mixed	Fixed	Changes	Fixed
3	$A:$A1	Mixed	Fixed	Fixed	Changes
4	$A:A1	Mixed	Fixed	Changes	Changes
5	A:$A$1	Mixed	Changes	Fixed	Fixed
6	A:A$1	Mixed	Changes	Changes	Fixed
7	A:$A1	Mixed	Changes	Fixed	Fixed
8	A:A1	Relative	Changes	Changes	Changes

Note that these *absolute* values correspond to the number of times you press ABS (F4) to create the same mixed, absolute, or relative cell address (see "Copying Formulas" in Chapter 7 for further discussion).

In cell E3 of Figure 9-54, for instance, @COORD (A3,B3,C3,D3) uses the worksheet coordinates (1,1,1) and the *absolute* argument 8 to return the relative cell address A:A1. It does *not* return the contents of cell A:A1. In cell E4, @COORD uses the worksheet coordinates (5,20,300) and the *absolute* argument 8 to return the relative cell address E:T300. For these same coordinates, @COORD returns the absolute cell address $E:$T$300 when *absolute* is 1, and the mixed cell address $E:T300 when *absolute* is 4.

> ▼ *Tip:* Use @COORD with the @@ function to return the *contents* of the cell address returned by @COORD. In Figure 9-54, for example, @@(@COORD(1,1,1,8)) would return the label "Worksheet" in cell A1.

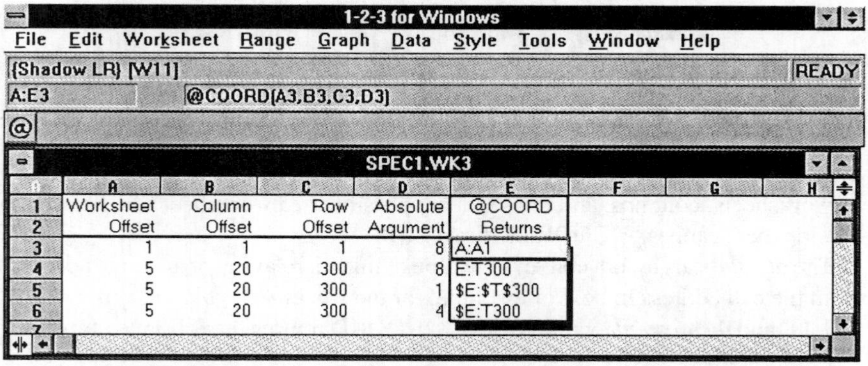

Figure 9-54 Using @COORD

Indirectly Referencing Cells: @@

You can use 1-2-3 for Windows' @@ function to indirectly reference a cell through another cell. The form of this function is

```
@@(location)
```

where *location* must be the address or name of a single cell expressed as a string. The @@ function returns ERR if *location* is a multiple-cell range.

The following scenarios show how @@ works:

	Scenario 1			*Scenario 2*	
Cell	*Contents*	*Displays*	*Cell*	*Contents*	*Displays*
A1	25	25	A1	25	25
B1	+A1	25	B1	'A1	A1
C1	@@(B1)	ERR	C1	@@(B1)	25

Since cell B1 contains the formula +A1 in Scenario 1, the function @@(B1) in cell C1 returns ERR. In Scenario 2, the @@ *location* argument evaluates to a single cell address expressed as a string, A1. Thus, the @@ function returns the contents of the cell referenced by the label 'A1, or 25.

You can use the @@ function to build powerful conditional formulas. For example, imagine @IF(A1="","B1","C1") is in cell B10, and cell C10 contains @@(B10). If cell A1 is empty (or has a 0 value), this @IF function returns the label "B1", and @@(B10) returns the contents of cell B1. If cell A1 is *not* empty, @IF returns the label "C1" and @@(B10) returns the contents of C1.

Determining an Attribute of a Cell: @CELL and @CELLPOINTER

1-2-3 for Windows has two functions that return information about an attribute of a cell. The @CELLPOINTER function returns a value or label that describes an attribute of the current cellpointer location. The @CELL function returns a value or label that describes an attribute of the upper-left cell of a range. The forms of these functions are

```
@CELLPOINTER(attribute)
@CELL(attribute,range)
```

where @CELL's *range* can be either a range name or address. The *attribute* must be one of those listed in Table 9-18. Remember to enclose an *attribute* in double quotes if you enter it directly into @CELL or @CELLPOINTER.

Note: Some of the results returned by @CELL and @CELLPOINTER are not automatically updated until the worksheet is recalculated.

TABLE 9-18 Attribute Arguments for @CELL and @CELLPOINTER

Attribute	Status
"address"	2-D absolute address of cell, such as $A$1
"color"	Color status of a negative value in cell: 1 if in color, 0 otherwise
"col"	Cell column number, 1 to 256
"contents"	Contents of cell, such as 2*B5
"coord"	3-D absolute address of cell, such as $A:$A$1
"filename"	Cell filename, including path, such as C:\123W\WORK\FILE0001.WK3
"format"	Cell format: C0 to C15 for Currency, F0 to F15 for Fixed, G for General, a label, and a blank cell, P0 to P15 for Percent, S0 to S15 for Scientific, ,0 to ,15 for Comma, + for +/- format, D1 to D9 for Date/Time, T for Text, H for Hidden, L for Label, A for Automatic,—if a Color is assigned for negative numbers, 0 for Parentheses
"parentheses"	Parentheses format: 1 if formatted with parentheses, 0 otherwise
"prefix"	Label prefix: ^ for centered, ' for left-aligned, " for right-aligned, \ for repeating label, | for nonprinting label, blank for blank cell or value
"protect"	Cell protection status: 1 if protected, 0 otherwise
"row"	Cell row number, 1 to 8192
"sheet"	Cell worksheet number, 1 to 256
"type"	Type of data in cell: b for blank, l for label, v for value or formula
"width"	Column width of cell

Figure 9-55 shows examples of the results @CELL and @CELLPOINTER return for the *attribute* arguments in column A. Only the range A1..C1 has been formatted using the Range command; all other cells are globally formatted.

The @CELL function evaluates cell A1, the upper-left cell in the range A1..C1, regardless of the cellpointer location. For example, in cell B4, @CELL(A4,A1..C1) returns the center label prefix ^ for the *attribute* "prefix". Additionally, @CELL returns the 3-D absolute address $A:$A$1 for "coord" and 1 for "col", "row", and "sheet" since cell A:A1 has the worksheet coordinates of (1,1,1).

In column C, @CELLPOINTER also returns results for these *attribute* arguments, but for the cellpointer location, cell B4. Because nothing is returned for the "prefix" attribute, you know that this cell hasn't been assigned a nonglobal label prefix. @CELLPOINTER also returns the 3-D absolute address $A:$B$4 for "coord," 2 for "col", 4 for "row", and 1 for "sheet" since cell B4 has the worksheet coordinates of (2,4,1).

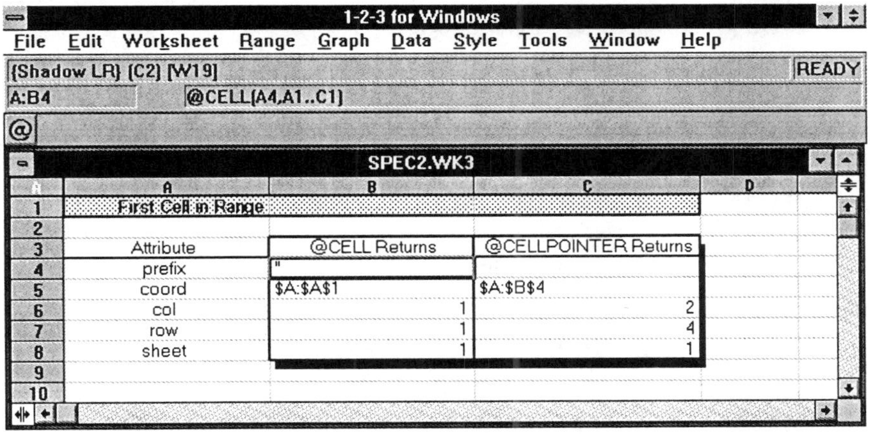

Figure 9-55 Using @CELL and @CELLPOINTER

@CELLPOINTER returns different results depending on the cell pointer location. If you locate the cell pointer in cell A1, for instance, @CELLPOINTER will return information for that cell—the same results @CELL returns in Figure 9-55. You have to press F9 (RECALC), however, to view the updated information, because 1-2-3 doesn't automatically recalculate the worksheet.

Typically, @CELL is used in a macro to check the attributes of a cell location before a certain type of entry is allowed. @CELLPOINTER is also commonly used in macros as well as in @IF functions to check the contents of the current cell pointer location. For example, the following macro checks the contents of the current cell pointer location. If the cell is empty, this macro branches to the routine named FILL_IT. Otherwise, it branches to the routine named FORMAT_IT.

```
{IF @CELLPOINTER("contents")=""}{BRANCH FILL_IT}
{BRANCH FORMAT_IT}
```

Returning Operating System Information: @INFO

The @INFO function returns specified information about the operating system. The form of this function is

```
@INFO(attribute)
```

where the *attribute* argument must be one of the attributes listed in Table 9-19. Three new attributes have been added to return information about DataLens, and "mode" has been enhanced from previous versions. If you enter an *attribute* directly into @INFO, remember to enclose it in double quotes.

TABLE 9-19 Attribute Arguments for @INFO

Attribute	@INFO Returns
"dbdrivemessage"	Most recent DataLens message
"dbreturncode"	Most recent error code returned by the DataLens driver
"dbrecordcount"	Number of records modified, extracted, or inserted in the worksheet or an external database during the last query
"directory"	Current path, including the drive letter
"system"	Name of operating system
"osversion"	Current operating system version
"release"	Major release number, upgrade level, and version number of 1-2-3
"numfile"	Current number of open files
"memavail"	Amount of available memory
"totmem"	Total memory (both available and in use)
"origin"	Address of the upper lefthand cell in the window that contains the cell pointer
"osreturncode"	Value returned by the most recent system command or {SYSTEM} macro command
"recalc"	The strings "automatic" or "manual" describing the current recalculation mode
"mode"	Current mode: 0-WAIT, 1-READY, 2-LABEL, 3-MENU, 4-VALUE, 5-POINT, 6-EDIT, 7-ERROR, 8-FIND, 9-FILES, 10-HELP, 11-STAT, 13-NAMES, 99-all other modes

Most often @INFO is used in a macro to

- Provide 1-2-3 for Windows status information to the user, such as a warning that memory is low.
- Act on 1-2-3 for Windows status information, such as determining the current path and using it to save a file, or closing open windows if memory is low.

For example, the following statements in a macro use @INFO to determine if available memory is less than 50K. If it is, the macro displays a MEMORY LOW indicator.

```
{IF @INFO("memavail")<50*1024}{INDICATE "MEMORY LOW"}
```

10

Graphs

One of the most notable features of 1-2-3 for Windows is its improved graphics capability. For example, you can now choose from an array of different graph types: area and 3D area, bar and 3D bar, high-low-close-open (HLCO), line and 3D line, pie and 3D pie, and XY. You can even combine a bar graph with a line or area graph to create a mixed graph. In 1-2-3 for Windows, you'll also find that many of these graph types offer even more choices. For example, you can choose from three 3D bar graph options: the default, 3D unstacked, and 3D stacked.

1-2-3 for Windows also provides a variety of ways you can enhance a graph. For example, you can change fonts, colors, patterns, and background colors. You can add descriptive labels, legends, and annotation—such as notes, lines, and arrows. In fact, 1-2-3 for Windows even offers freehand drawing and the ability to load and use clip art.

In many ways, 1-2-3 for Windows' graphics capabilities rival that of Freelance Plus, a leading presentation graphics program from Lotus. In fact, with the intuitive way that 1-2-3 uses the menus and icons in the Windows graphical user interface (GUI), you'll find that creating visually appealing graphs is easier and faster than ever before.

For the most part, this chapter covers topics in the order that you are likely to use them. First, you'll learn how to create a basic graph, and how to save it for later sessions. You'll then learn all the different ways you can enhance a graph—for example, by changing the graph type, or by adding legends, titles, and annotation.

Note: To print a graph, see Chapter 8.

ELEMENTS OF A GRAPH

When you create a graph with 1-2-3 for Windows, it appears within a graph window, as shown in Figure 10-1. The *title* and *subtitle* at the top of the graph explain what data is

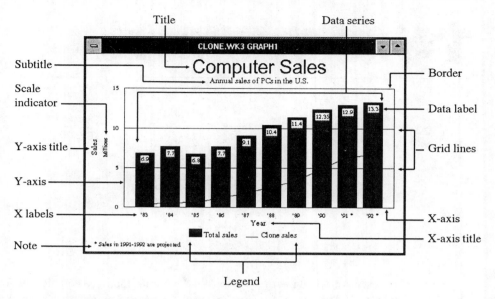

Figure 10-1 Elements of a graph

graphed. Figure 10-1 is, for example, a graph of computer sales, featuring annual sales of PCs in the United States.

The bulk of the information for a graph appears within the graph *borders*, the rectangular area surrounding the bars in Figure 10-1. The left border is the *y-axis*, and the bottom border is the *x-axis*. The lower-left corner of the plot frame, where the x- and y-axes meet, is the *origin*. All graphs, except pie graphs, have x- and y-axes.

When you select values to appear in a graph, they are represented as a data series. A *data series* is simply the graphic representation of a *data range* or set of worksheet values. There are two data series in Figure 10-1. The first data series depicts total PC sales as bars, and the second data series depicts clone sales as a line. Depending on the graph type you choose, each data series can also be represented by an area, a group of pie slices, or a group of symbols.

The y-axis always contains a numeric scale that 1-2-3 automatically assigns based on the values you are graphing. *Y-axis labels* appear to the left of the y-axis and describe its scale. The *scale indicator* describes the unit of measure used on the y-axis. In Figure 10-1, for example, the scale is in millions. And finally, the *y-axis title*, "Sales" in Figure 10-1, further describes the y-axis scale.

In most graphs, the x-axis is not a numeric scale. Rather, it conveys descriptive information about each data series. In Figure 10-1, for example, the *x-axis labels* convey the time period the graph is concerned with, '83–'92. The x-axis can also represent expense items, salespeople, regions, and the like. In Figure 10-1, the *x-axis title*, "Year," further describes the x-axis labels.

In an XY graph, the x-axis *does* represent a second numeric scale. When the x-axis is used in this way, 1-2-3 automatically creates x-axis labels based on the graphed data.

Other elements of a graph are designed to provide easier interpretation of the graphed information. In Figure 10-1 for instance, *data labels* are used to convey the actual value each bar represents. A *legend*, composed of labels and their corresponding patterns, serves as a key to the data series being graphed. You can even add *annotation* like lines, arrows, and text boxes (see "Annotating a Graph").

CREATING A GRAPH: AN EXAMPLE

Previous versions of 1-2-3 offered many different ways to start building a graph. In 1-2-3 for Windows, however, there is only one basic way. Suppose you want to create a graph that compares the yearly sales of PCs versus "clones" using the data in the worksheet file in Figure 10-2. Although it's clear from the numbers that clone sales have increased over the years, the relationship of clone sales to overall PC sales is hard to discern. Creating a graph of the data will make any trends more apparent.

Before you create a graph in 1-2-3 for Windows, it helps to plan its layout. By default, 1-2-3 uses a line graph type when you first create a graph, and each data series is represented by a line. For example, total sales in column B will appear as one line and clone sales in column C will appear as another. In addition, the year abbreviations in column A will be used as x-axis labels.

The text at the top of the worksheet will explain the graphed information. For example, you can use the label in cell A1, "Computer Sales," as the title for the graph. Next, the label "Annual sales of PCs in the U.S." in cell B1 can be used as the subtitle. You'll want to use the column headings "Total sales" and "Clone sales" in the graph's legend. Finally, you'll need to supply some additional text for the axis labels—for example, "Sales" for the y-axis label and "Year" for the x-axis label.

After you've decided on the graph's layout, you can use the worksheet window's Graph New command to create the graph. From that point on, the graph appears within its own

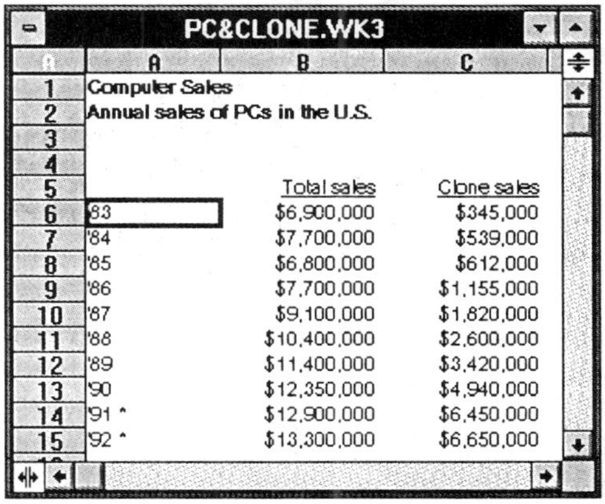

	A	B	C
1	Computer Sales		
2	Annual sales of PCs in the U.S.		
3			
4			
5		Total sales	Clone sales
6	'83	$6,900,000	$345,000
7	'84	$7,700,000	$539,000
8	'85	$6,800,000	$612,000
9	'86	$7,700,000	$1,155,000
10	'87	$9,100,000	$1,820,000
11	'88	$10,400,000	$2,600,000
12	'89	$11,400,000	$3,420,000
13	'90	$12,350,000	$4,940,000
14	'91 *	$12,900,000	$6,450,000
15	'92 *	$13,300,000	$6,650,000

PC&CLONE.WK3

Figure 10-2 Sample data to be graphed

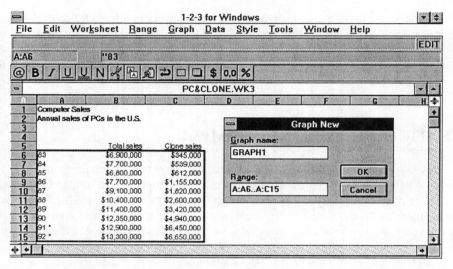

Figure 10-3   The Graph New dialog box

graph window, and you'll need to use that window's menu commands to enhance the graph. Here are the steps:

1.   Select the range to graph by outlining A6..C15.

2.   Choose the Graph New command. 1-2-3 displays the dialog box in Figure 10-3, suggesting GRAPH1 as the name for the graph. Select OK to accept the name, and 1-2-3 presents the unadorned graph shown in Figure 10-4.

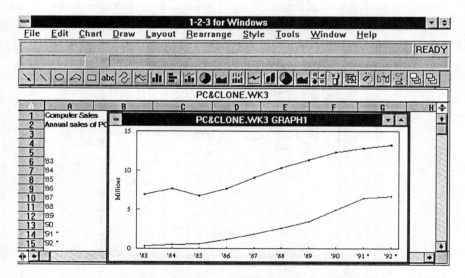

Figure 10-4   A line graph with two data series

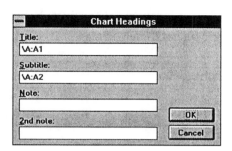

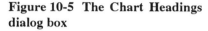

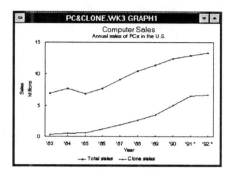

Figure 10-5 The Chart Headings dialog box

Figure 10-6 The example graph after adding titles and a legend

3. To add titles to the graph, choose the Chart Headings command. After entering the text shown in Figure 10-5, select OK. Note that you can instruct 1-2-3 to apply a label from a cell—for example, typing \A1 tells 1-2-3 to use the label "Computer Sales" in cell A1.

4. To add an x-axis title to the graph, select the Chart Axis X Options command, type **Year** in the Axis title box, and select OK twice.

5. For the y-axis title, use Chart Axis Y Options, type **Sales** in the Axis title box, and select OK twice.

6. Add a legend to the graph by choosing the Chart Legend command. Type **\B5** for the A range and **\C5** for the B range and select OK.

As you can see in Figure 10-6, the completed graph displays the data reasonably effectively. Nevertheless, the graph still lacks punch. At this point, you may want to use the Chart Type command to experiment with different graph types. For example, you'll find that changing from a standard line graph to a 3D-line graph communicates the information more effectively (see "Graph Types" for more details).

INTERACTION BETWEEN CLASSIC AND GRAPH MENUS

If you're an experienced 1-2-3 user, you'll be interested to know that you can change almost any graph setting using 1-2-3 Classic's /Graph command. For the new setting to take effect, however, you'll need to manage the interaction between the Classic and graph window menus as follows:

- To have the /Graph menu take on the settings for the current graph, use the /Graph Name Use command and choose the appropriate graph name—for example, GRAPH1—from the list. (Without this step, the /Graph menu settings will appear blank.)

- From this point on, any changes you make to the /Graph settings will appear only when you select /Graph View (or press F10). They will not appear when you switch back to the graph window.

- To have your new settings reflected in the graph window, use /Graph Name Create and save the new settings on top of the old.

If you follow these simple guidelines, you should have no trouble using the /Graph command to create and modify graphs.

CLOSING OR MINIMIZING A GRAPH WINDOW

Because a graph is assigned its own window separate from the worksheet file it resides in, you can minimize it just like any other window. For instance, you can minimize GRAPH1 in Figure 10-6 and then make changes in the worksheet file or even create another graph. If you make changes to worksheet data that affect this graph, GRAPH1 will incorporate these changes when you restore it.

When you finish working in a graph window, you can close it the same way you would a Worksheet window—either press CTRL+F4 or double-click on the Window control icon. When you return to the worksheet the graph will still be intact. In fact, if you select the Graph View command, you'll see the graph name in the list. For example, Figure 10-7 shows that GRAPH1 still exists. If you select this name from the list and choose OK, the GRAPH1 window will reappear.

SAVING AND REDISPLAYING A GRAPH

Because 1-2-3 for Windows forces you to name each graph you create, graph settings are maintained in a somewhat different manner than in previous releases. When you save a worksheet file, 1-2-3 for Windows automatically saves *all* graphs you created in the worksheet file.

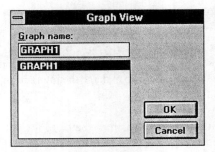

Figure 10-7 The Graph View dialog box

After reloading a file, you can redisplay a graph, such as GRAPH1, by selecting the Graph View command and choosing GRAPH1 from the list box. 1-2-3 for Windows will once again display GRAPH1 in a graph window, just as in Figure 10-6.

> ▼ *Tip:*   To simultaneously view multiple graphs from the same worksheet file, GRAPH1 and MARKET SHARE for instance, first use Graph View to open one of these graphs, GRAPH1 perhaps. Next, press CTRL+F6 to move back to the worksheet. Select Graph View a second time, but now open MARKET SHARE. Both GRAPH1 and MARKET SHARE will then be open, each in a separate window. Of course, you may want to re-size and move these windows, so you can see both of them in their entirety.

SPECIFYING DATA TO BE GRAPHED

The nucleus of any graph is the data it displays. You tell 1-2-3 which data to use by assigning data ranges. In 1-2-3 for Windows, you can usually plot up to six different data ranges in one graph, designated A through F. Some graph types, however, limit the number of data ranges you can use; others plot specific data ranges in special ways. These special cases are discussed in the next section, "Graph Types."

As a companion to the data ranges, 1-2-3 for Windows requires an X data range. It uses the labels from this range as x-axis labels. In Figure 10-6, for example, the labels '83 through '92 appear as x-axis labels because the range A6..A15 in Figure 10-3 was designated as the X data range.

Note: Even when the X data range includes values, 1-2-3 evaluates them as labels. The exception is an XY graph (see "Graph Types").

You can assign data ranges in two ways. The first method is to have 1-2-3 assign them. This happens automatically when you preselect a range to graph within a worksheet window and select Graph New. For example, Figure 10-8 shows how 1-2-3 assigns data to data ranges when you select the range A6..C15 in Figure 10-3.

Note that the first column of the preselected range, A6..A15, is assigned to the X data range; the second column, B6..B15, is assigned to the A data range; and the third column, C6..C15, is assigned to the B data range. In fact, 1-2-3 for Windows always assigns a preselected range in columnwise fashion.

> ▼ *Tip:*   You can use the Chart Ranges command to assign data ranges by row.

The second way to assign data ranges is to assign them yourself using the graph window's Chart Ranges command. The best time to use this method is when you need to modify 1-2-3's automatic assignments. For example, Figure 10-8 shows the dialog box that appears when you select Chart Ranges from the GRAPH1 window created previously.

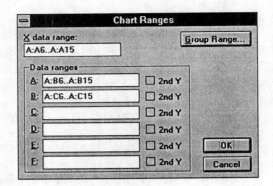

Figure 10-8 The Chart Ranges dialog box

Suppose you add the mouse sales data shown in Figure 10-9 to the PC&CLONE worksheet. Follow the steps to add this data as another data series to the GRAPH1 graph:

1. With the GRAPH1 window active, select the Chart Ranges command.
2. Move to the C range text box and specify the range D6..D15. Select OK to confirm.
3. Add a legend label for this data range by choosing the Chart Legend command and entering \D5 in the B text box. Press OK to confirm and return to the graph.

As shown in Figure 10-10, 1-2-3 adds the C data series to the graph. The third legend label identifies it as Mouse sales.

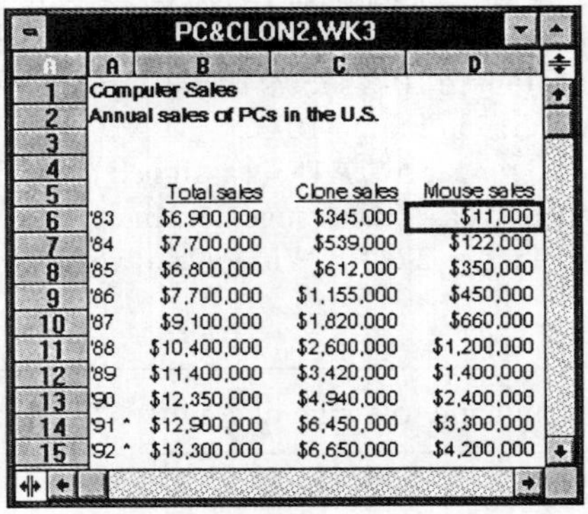

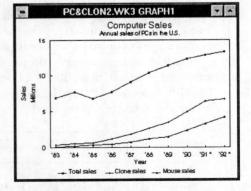

Figure 10-9 The sample worksheet with additional data in D6..D15

Figure 10-10 After manually adding a data series using Chart Ranges

When assigning data ranges manually using Chart Ranges, you'll want to keep in mind the following:

- Although the easiest way to enter information for a particular data range is to place it in a single column or row, 1-2-3 will accept a multicolumn, multirow range.

- All entries in the A through F data ranges are treated as values. A label is assigned a value of 0 and graphed accordingly. If you leave a cell blank within a data range, 1-2-3 omits the data point from the graph.

- To remove one or more data ranges from a graph, use the Chart Clear command.

- To temporarily suppress a series from being graphed but not remove its series settings, use the Chart Options Lines command and turn off the Connectors, Symbols, and Area fill boxes for the data series.

- You can use 1-2-3 for Windows' file linking capability to access data ranges from different files. The easiest way to do this is to open all the files and then point to the appropriate data ranges from within the Chart Ranges dialog box. 1-2-3 will automatically enter the appropriate file linking syntax, including the proper directory, filename, and range address. (See Chapter 4 for more on file linking.)

Choosing a Group Range

When you preselect a range to graph within a worksheet and then select Graph New, you are actually specifying a group range. A *group range* encompasses all the data ranges (including the X data range) that you want to graph. As you may have already discovered, all the data ranges must be in adjacent columns, with one data range per column.

As mentioned, when Graph New is used to create a graph, 1-2-3 always evaluates the preselected range in a columnwise fashion and assigns the first column to the X data range, the second column to the A data range, the third column to the B data range, and so on. This is fine if your data happens to have a columnwise orientation, but if your data has a rowwise orientation you'll want to use the Chart Ranges Group Range command to control how 1-2-3 interprets the group range. Figure 10-11 shows the dialog box that appears when you select this command.

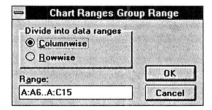

Figure 10-11 The Chart Ranges Group Range dialog box

To specify rowwise interpretation, turn on the Rowwise option and then specify the range. When you select OK, 1-2-3 will use the first row for the X data range, the second row for the A data range, the third row for the B data range, and so on.

Note: You can't use Chart Ranges Group Range for an XY graph.

GRAPH TYPES

By default, 1-2-3 for Windows creates a line graph. You can however, use the Chart Type command to choose from 11 different graph types: Line, Area, Bar, Pie, XY, HLCO, Mixed, 3D Line, 3D Area, 3D Bar, and 3D Pie. 1-2-3 for Windows also provides additional choices for particular graph types. Choose Bar in the Chart Type dialog box, for example, and you'll see two options: bar (the default) and stacked bar. Select 3D Bar, and you're offered three more: 3D bar (the default), 3D unstacked bar, and 3D stacked bar. Once you've created a graph, you'll want to experiment with the numerous graph types and graph type options 1-2-3 for Windows offers to see which one displays your data most effectively.

▼ *Tip:* Selecting the icon displays the Chart Type dialog box. To customize the graph icon palette, see Appendix A.

Line Graphs

A line graph—the default graph type in 1-2-3 for Windows—is often used to emphasize differences between related data, such as sales of different product lines. A line graph is also a good way to demonstrate one or more trends over time, such as the increase in the prime rate and the decrease in mortgage rates.

In 1-2-3 for Windows you can create two types of line graphs: the default, which assigns a line to each data range, and a stacked line graph, where each line represents the cumulative total of the data ranges graphed.

Default Line

By default, 1-2-3 for Windows creates a line graph using the first option shown in Figure 10-12. Each data range is plotted as a separate line. On a particular line, each value in the data range is represented by a marker.

▼ *Tip:* The icon assigns the default Line option.

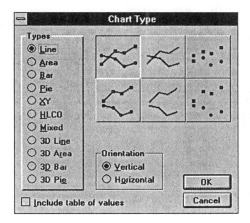

Figure 10-12 The line graph options

For example, the spreadsheet in Figure 10-13 contains monthly fleet damage for three sales offices: Monterey, San Jose, and Santa Cruz. One way to compare this information is by using the settings in Table 10-1 to create the line graph in Figure 10-14, where the losses for each office are represented by a separate line.

Because the line style is the same, marker styles differentiate the data. Each line is also assigned a different color. Although you can't change the line or marker styles, you can customize the line colors. Then a legend can be used to explain what each line represents. (See "Adding a Legend," later.) 1-2-3 for Windows uses the line color and the marker style to tie each legend label to the corresponding line.

You can also change the way the data ranges are displayed in a line graph. One alternative is to use the line graph type options shown in Figure 10-12. Choose the second option in the first line, for instance, to remove all markers, so that just lines will be displayed. By contrast, the third option displays only the data points (values) as markers without connecting lines. If you want to present each data range in a different way—one

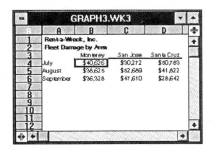

Figure 10-13 Data used in the line graphs in Figures 10-14, 10-15, 10-17, and 10-18

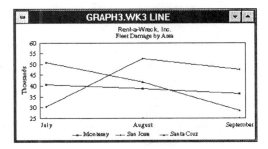

Figure 10-14 A line graph of the data in Figure 10-13

TABLE 10-1 Chart settings used to create the line graphs in Figures 10-14, 10-15, 10-17, and 10-18

Chart Command	Setting	Setting	Setting	Setting
Type	Line	Stacked Line	3D Line	3D Stacked Line
Ranges				
X	A4..A6	A4..A6	A4..A6	A4..A6
A	B4..B6	B4..B6	B4..B6	B4..B6
B	C4..C6	C4..C6	C4..C6	C4..C6
C	D4..D6	D4..D6	D4..D6	D4..D6
Headings				
Title	\A1	\A1	\A1	\A1
Subtitle	\A2	Cumulative Fleet Damage	\A2	Cumulative Fleet Damage
Legend				
A	\B3	Monterey	\B3	Monterey
B	\C3	Monterey & San Jose	\C3	Monterey & San Jose
C	\D3	Monterey, San Jose & Santa Cruz	\D3	Monterey, San Jose & Santa Cruz
Options Hatches				
A			Heavy (###)	Heavy (###)
B			Right diagonal (///)	Right diagonal (///)
C			Solid	Solid

data range as only markers, another as a line with markers, for example—you'll have to customize the graph (see "Assigning Different Styles to Different Lines").

Note: The y-axis values 1-2-3 for Windows automatically assigns to a line graph can sometimes make the graph visually misleading. You can see the potential problem in Figure 10-14, where 1-2-3 assigns the origin a beginning y-axis value of 25 as just a little smaller than the smallest data point in the graph. From a visual standpoint, this can magnify the difference between data ranges. You can solve this problem, however, by customizing the y-axis. See "Customizing Axes," later.

Stacked Line

1-2-3 for Windows offers a new line graph option, *stacked line* (the first option in the second line of the dialog box shown in Figure 10-12). In a stacked line graph, each line represents the cumulative total of the graphed data ranges. For example, the first line represents values in the A data range, the second line represents the combined values of the A and B data ranges, and so on.

▼ *Tip:*   An area graph (discussed later) usually presents cumulative data more effectively than a stacked line graph.

Figure 10-15, for instance, shows the data in Figure 10-13 plotted as a stacked line graph using the settings shown in Table 10-1. The bottom line represents the Monterey losses assigned to the A data range. The middle line represents the total of the A and B data ranges—the combined Monterey and San Jose losses. For example, the first marker on this line represents $70,898, the sum of the July losses for Monterey and San Jose in cells B4 and C4. And finally, the top line, as indicated by the third legend label, represents the total losses at all three offices—the total of the A, B, and C, data ranges. Notice that we've changed the legend labels and graph subtitle to convey this.

For a stacked line graph, 1-2-3 for Windows provides the same options as for the default line graph. The second graph option for a stacked line graph (the second option in the second line of Figure 10-12) displays each data range as a line without markers. Because the third option graphs only the data points (values) as markers, it usually isn't a good choice for a stacked line graph. You can also change how each data range is displayed (see "Assigning Different Styles to Different Lines").

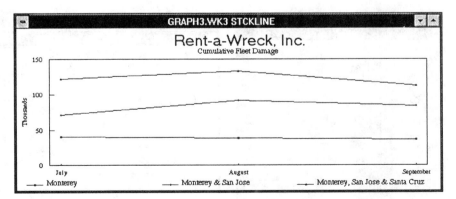

Figure 10-15 A stacked line graph of the data in Figure 10-13

3D Line

1-2-3 for Windows provides yet another line graph choice, the 3D line. As you can see in Figure 10-16, two options are offered. The default depicts each data range as a 3D ribbon. So this option treats data ranges just like the 2D default line graph, but adds a three-dimensional effect. The second option graphs data ranges just like a 2D stacked line graph, but adds a three-dimensional effect. To see this, let's continue to graph the Rent-a-Wreck data shown in Figure 10-13, using the 3D line options and the other Chart settings in Table 10-1, and then compare the results.

Default 3D Line

As Figure 10-17 shows, the default 3D line option plots each data range as a separate line. Due to the three-dimensional effect, each line looks like a ribbon. Notice that the data ranges are displayed from front to back along the z-axis. The A data range (Monterey) is plotted first at the front of the graph, then the B data range (San Jose) behind the A data range, and finally the C data range (Santa Cruz) at the back.

▼ *Tip:*   The 🖼 icon assigns the default 3D Line option.

By default, 1-2-3 for Windows differentiates each data range in a 3D line graph by the color assigned to each ribbon. In this case, however, we've used the Chart Options Hatches command to assign fill patterns to differentiate them—a heavy crosshatch (###) to Monterey, a right diagonal hatch (///) to San Jose, and a solid pattern to Santa Cruz.

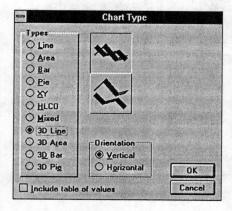

Figure 10-16   The 3D Line graph options

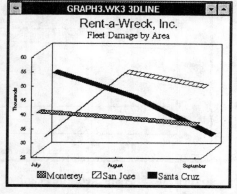

Figure 10-17   A 3D unstacked line graph of the data in Figure 10-13

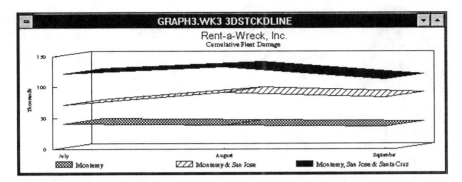

Figure 10-18 A 3D stacked line graph of the data in Figure 10-13

3D Stacked Line

The 3D stacked line graph shown in Figure 10-18 is essentially the same graph as the 2D stacked line graph in Figure 10-15, except that a three-dimensional effect has been added. The bottom ribbon represents the Monterey data in the A data range, the middle ribbon represents the total of the A and B data ranges—the Monterey and San Jose data—and the top ribbon represents the total of the A, B, and C data ranges—the Monterey, San Jose, and Santa Cruz data.

Because 2D and 3D stacked line graphs portray data in the same way, the same graph titles and legend labels as in Figure 10-15 are used. Because 1-2-3 for Windows displays each line in 3D stacked and unstacked graphs as ribbons, the same fill patterns as in Figure 10-17 are assigned to differentiate the graphed data.

▼ *Tip:*   In most cases, a 3D stacked area graph, discussed next, portrays data more effectively than a 3D stacked line graph.

Area Graphs

An area graph plots the values in each data range as a line, and then fills in the area below the line. The data ranges are then stacked on top of one another. You'll find that an area graph emphasizes the contribution each component makes to the total over time.

▼ *Tip:*   The ☐ icon assigns an Area graph type.

Consider the sales data for the three stores of The Unlimited retail chain shown in Figure 10-19. An area graph is a good way to demonstrate the contribution each of these stores makes to total sales. For a cyclical industry like retail, an area graph also emphasizes the relationship between sales and the time of year. Figure 10-20 shows an area graph of the sales data in columns B, C, and D using the Chart settings shown in Table 10-2.

	A	B	C	D	E	F	G
	The Unlimited						
2		Store 1 Sales	Store 2 Sales	Store 3 Sales	Mall Traffic	Avg Sales	
3	Jun	$80,000	$110,000	$30,000	90,000	$73,333	
4	Jul	$50,000	$90,000	$30,000	80,000	$56,667	
5	Aug	$120,000	$130,000	$80,000	150,000	$110,000	
6	Sep	$130,000	$200,000	$100,000	175,000	$143,333	
7	Oct	$130,000	$170,000	$300,000	160,000	$200,000	
8	Nov	$200,000	$300,000	$400,000	250,000	$300,000	
9	Dec	$300,000	$400,000	$500,000	400,000	$400,000	
10	Jan	$150,000	$180,000	$250,000	200,000	$193,333	
11	Feb	$100,000	$160,000	$150,000	150,000	$136,667	
12	Mar	$80,000	$100,000	$50,000	125,000	$76,667	
13	Apr	$90,000	$120,000	$50,000	125,000	$86,667	
14	May	$70,000	$80,000	$40,000	100,000	$63,333	

GRAPH4.WK3

Figure 10-19   The data graphed in Figures 10-20, 10-22, and 10-23

In Figure 10-20, 1-2-3 for Windows first graphs the A data range, Store 1 Sales, at the bottom of the graph. It then stacks the area for the B data range, Store 2 Sales, on top of the A data range area, and the area for the C data range, Store 3 Sales, on top of the B data range area. So at each x-axis label, the topmost line represents the total sales for that period. In December, for example, the peak of the graph represents total sales of $1.2 million—the sum of $300,000 Store 1 sales, $400,000 Store 2 sales, and $500,000 Store 3 sales.

The filled area below each line represents the amount a particular data range contributes to the total. By default, 1-2-3 for Windows differentiates a data range by assigning a different color to its graphed area. In this case, we've differentiated each data range by

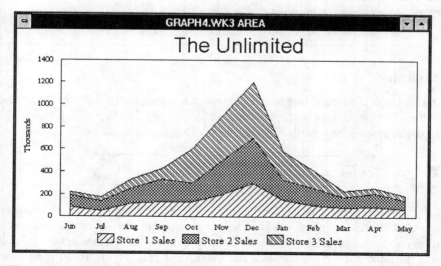

Figure 10-20   An area graph of the data in Figure 10-19

TABLE 10-2 Chart settings for the area graphs in Figures 10-20, 10-22, and 10-23

Chart Command	Setting	Chart Command	Setting
Type	Area, 3D Unstacked Area or	Headings	
	3D Stacked Area	Title	\A1
Ranges		Legend	
X	A3..A14	A	\B2
A	B3..B14	B	\C2
B	C3..C14	C	\D2
C	D3..D14		
Options Hatches			
A	Right diagonal (/ / /)		
B	Heavy (###)		
C	Left double diagonal (\\ \\)		

assigning contrasting hatches (see "Assigning Hatch Patterns," later). And a legend is added to explain what each hatch pattern represents (see "Adding a Legend").

▼ *Tip:*   See "Adding a Horizontal Orientation," later, to view the area graph in Figure 10-20 with a horizontal orientation.

3D Area Graph

1-2-3 for Windows offers the two 3D area options shown in the dialog box in Figure 10-21. The first option, the default, creates a 3D unstacked area graph—that is, each data range is graphed separately. The second option stacks data ranges just like a 2D area graph, but adds a three-dimensional effect. To see the different results these 3D options produce, let's continue to graph The Unlimited data shown in Figure 10-19 using the Chart settings in Table 10-2.

Default 3D Area

The default 3D area graph (the first option in the dialog box in Figure 10-21) plots the data ranges separately in 3D space. In effect, the data ranges are "unstacked." You'll find that a 3D unstacked area graph emphasizes the relative difference between each component (data range), rather than the contribution each component makes to the total.

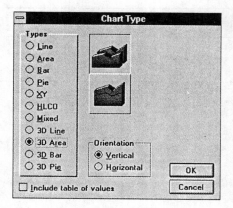

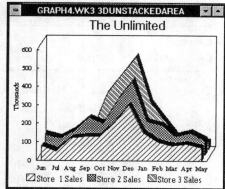

Figure 10-21 The 3D Area graph options

Figure 10-22 A 3D unstacked area graph of the data in Figure 10-19

▼ *Tip:* The 🔲 icon assigns the default 3D Area option.

Figure 10-22 is a 3D unstacked area graph of The Unlimited sales data in Figure 10-19 created with the Chart settings in Table 10-2. As you can see, the data ranges are plotted from front to back along the z-axis. The A data range, Store 1 Sales, is plotted in front, the B data range, Store 2 Sales, is graphed next directly behind the A data range, and so on.

If you examine Figure 10-22 closely, you'll realize that a 3D unstacked area graph works best when there is a distinct difference between each data range. It's also important that you specify the data range with the smallest values as the A data range, the data range with the next smallest values as the B data range, and so on. Otherwise, data may be hidden from view.

Like other area graphs, 1-2-3 for Windows automatically assigns a different color to each data range to differentiate them. In Figure 10-22, we've assigned hatches to each data range and added a legend to tie each hatch pattern to the graphed data. If you want, you can assign a different color and hatch pattern to each value in a data range. See "Assigning Colors" and "Assigning Hatch Patterns" to add these enhancements.

3D Stacked Area

The second 3D area graph option (see the dialog box shown in Figure 10-21) produces the same result as a 2D area graph—the data ranges are stacked on top of each other—but with an added three-dimensional effect. By comparing the 3D area graph in Figure 10-23 with the 2D area graph in Figure 10-20, you can see the effect this option produces. Both are graphs of The Unlimited sales data in Figure 10-19, and are created using the Chart settings in Table 10-2.

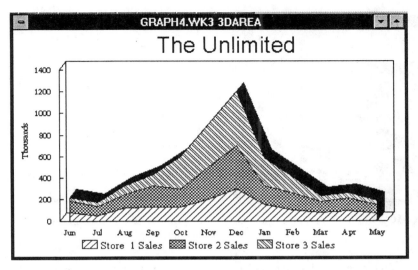

Figure 10-23   A 3D stacked area graph of the data in Figure 10-19

XY Graphs

An XY graph is often used to analyze trends or predict the frequency of an event. For example, you can use an XY graph to plot the relationship between the number of sales calls made and the number of orders received, or the number of ice cream cones sold and the outside temperature.

Although at first glance an XY graph may resemble a line graph, they are substantially different. In an XY graph, 1-2-3 for Windows plots a data point using both *x* and *y* values. For this reason, an XY graph is different from all the other graph types in 1-2-3 for Windows.

You can create two types of XY graphs in 1-2-3 for Windows. The default XY displays each data range as a separate line. In the second alternative, stacked XY, each line represents the cumulative total of the data ranges graphed.

Default XY

In an XY graph, 1-2-3 for Windows assumes that the X data range contains *x* values, and that all other data ranges contain corresponding *y* values. That is, the first value in the A data range corresponds to the first value in the X data range; the first value in the B data range also corresponds to the first value in the X data range. In this case, 1-2-3 for Windows would graph two lines, with the first line representing the *x* values in the X data range and the corresponding *y* values in the A data range. The second line would represent the *x* values in the X data range and the corresponding *y* values in the B data range.

To see when an XY graph is an appropriate choice, let's return to the sales data of The Unlimited retail chain in Figure 10-19. Suppose that you now want to illustrate the

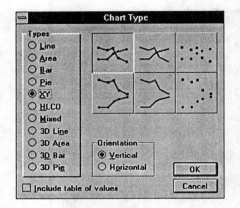

Figure 10-24 The XY graph options

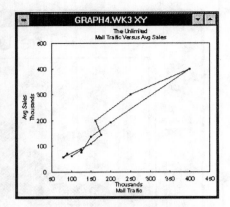

Figure 10-25 An XY graph of the data in Figure 10-19

relationship between mall traffic and average sales shown in columns E and F. You can use the default (first) XY option shown in the dialog box in Figure 10-24 and the Chart settings in Table 10-3 to create the XY graph shown in Figure 10-25.

Figure 10-25 shows that you need to take into consideration how 1-2-3 graphs each data range in an XY graph. Here, it plots the first value in the X data range, 90,000 in cell E3 of Figure 10-19, and then the corresponding value in the A data range, 73,333 in cell F3, to create the first data point. Next, it uses the second X data range value, 80,000 in cell E4, and the second value in the A data range, 56,667 in cell F4, to create the second data point. 1-2-3 for Windows continues this process for all values in the X range. What's important here is that 1-2-3 plots the *x* values sequentially according to their position in the X data range, *not* in ascending order, lowest *x* value first and highest *x* value last. As a result, the line connecting xy points "backtracks".

TABLE 10-3 Chart settings used to create the XY graphs in Figures 10-25 and 10-27

Chart Command	Setting	Chart Command	Setting
Type	XY	*Axis*	
Ranges		Y Options Axis title	\F2
X	E3..E14	X Options Axis title	\E2
A	F3..F14		
Headings			
Title	\A1		
Subtitle	Mall Traffic Versus Avg Sales		

GRAPH5.WK3

A	B	C	D	E	F
The Unlimited					
	Store 1 Sales	Store 2 Sales	Store 3 Sales	Mall Traffic	Avg Sales
Jul	$50,000	$90,000	$30,000	80,000	$56,667
Jun	$80,000	$110,000	$30,000	90,000	$73,333
May	$70,000	$80,000	$40,000	100,000	$63,333
Mar	$80,000	$100,000	$50,000	125,000	$76,667
Apr	$90,000	$120,000	$50,000	125,000	$86,667
Aug	$120,000	$130,000	$80,000	150,000	$110,000
Feb	$100,000	$160,000	$150,000	150,000	$136,667
Oct	$130,000	$170,000	$300,000	160,000	$200,000
Sep	$130,000	$200,000	$100,000	175,000	$143,333
Jan	$150,000	$180,000	$250,000	200,000	$193,333
Nov	$200,000	$300,000	$400,000	250,000	$300,000
Dec	$300,000	$400,000	$500,000	400,000	$400,000

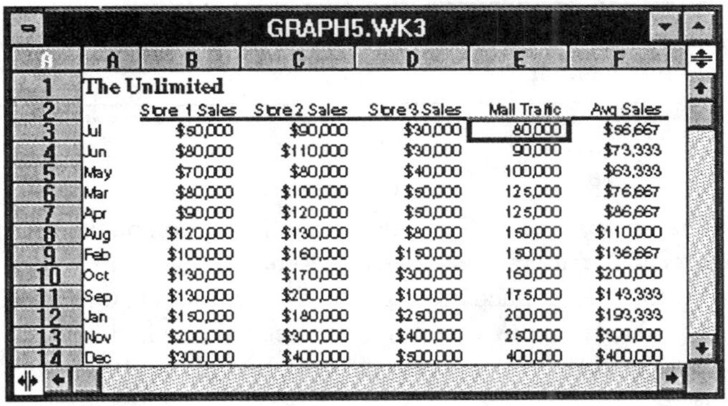

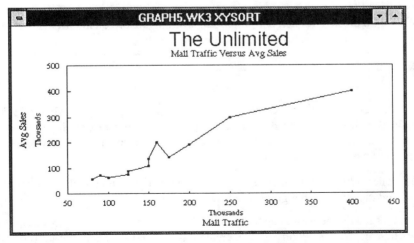

Figure 10-26 Sorting the data for an XY graph

You can overcome this problem by first sorting the data so the values in the X data range are in ascending order. In Figure 10-26, the data has been sorted using the Data Sort command and specifying the *x* values (Mall Traffic) in column E as the primary sort key and an ascending sort order (see Chapter 11). You can see the result in Figure 10-27. This XY graph emphasizes the strong relationship between mall traffic volume and average sales.

You can also change the way each data range is displayed in an XY graph. One alternative is to use the XY graph options shown in Figure 10-24. Choose the second option in the first line to remove all markers—just lines are displayed. The third option creates a "scatter diagram," where only the markers representing the data points (values) are displayed. You'll have to customize the graph, however, to display each data range a different way—for example, one data range as only markers, and another as a line with markers (see "Assigning Different Styles to Different Lines").

Figure 10-27 An XY graph of the sorted data in Figure 10-26

> ▼ **Tip:**   The 🖼 icon assigns the first XY option—with both lines and markers—and creates an XY graph.

Stacked XY

1-2-3 for Windows offers a new, stacked XY option—the first option on the second line in Figure 10-24. In a stacked XY graph, each line represents the cumulative total of the data ranges. For example, the first graphed line represents the *x* values in the X data range and the corresponding *y* values in the A data range; the second graphed line represents the *x* values in the X data range and the sum of the corresponding *y* values in the A and B data ranges; and so on.

The second option in the second line of the dialog box in Figure 10-24 is a stacked XY graph with all markers removed—just lines are displayed. By contrast, the third option creates a scatter diagram where only the markers representing the data points (values) are shown. To display each line differently in an XY graph, see "Assigning Different Styles to Different Lines."

Bar Graphs

A bar graph is frequently used to compare values at a specific point in time, such as the 1992 net profit generated by three different companies. A bar graph is also an effective way to emphasize how data changes over time, such as the 1992, 1993, and 1994 net profit of one or more companies.

In 1-2-3 for Windows, you can create the two types of bar graphs shown in Figure 10-28. The default—unstacked bar—displays each value in a data range as a separate bar. The second option creates a stacked bar graph, where the corresponding values from each data range are stacked one on top of another.

> ▼ **Tip:**   To create a rotated bar graph, see "Adding a Horizontal Orientation," later in this section. Another alternative is to use the 🖼 icon.

Default Bar

By default, 1-2-3 for Windows creates a bar graph using the first option shown in Figure 10-28. Each positive value in a data range is represented as a bar extending upward from the x-axis, and each negative value is represented as a bar extending below the x-axis. The height of each bar is determined by its *y* value.

Note: The width of the bars in a bar graph will vary, depending on the number of bars graphed and the width of the graph window.

Consider the sales generated by four Scotts Valley Office Supply employees in Figure 10-29. The bar graph in Figure 10-30, created using the Chart settings in Table 10-4, emphasizes the difference in performance during July, August, and September.

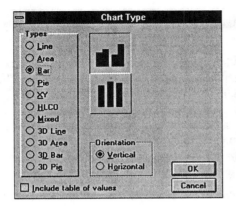

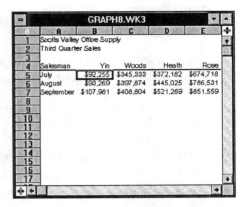

Figure 10-28 The Bar graph options

Figure 10-29 Data used in the bar graphs in Figures 10-30 and 10-31, and in the 3D bar graphs in Figures 10-33, 10-34, and 10-35

TABLE 10-4 Chart settings for the bar graphs in Figures 10-30, 10-31, and 10-33 through 10-35

Chart Command	Setting	Chart Command	Setting
Type	Bar, Stacked Bar	Headings	
	3D Bar, 3D Stacked Bar or	Title	\A1
	3D Unstacked Bar	Subtitle	\A2
Ranges		Legend	
X	A5..A7	A	\B4
A	B5..B7	B	\C4
B	C5..C7	C	\D4
C	D5..D7	D	\E4
D	E5..E7		
Options Hatches			
A	Left diagonal (\ \ \)		
B	Solid		
C	Light (xxx)		
D	Right double diagonal (// // //)		

> ▼ *Tip:*   The ▥ icon assigns the default Bar option.

Note in Figure 10-30 how 1-2-3 for Windows groups bars at each of the x-axis labels. Above the July x-axis label, for instance, the leftmost bar represents the first value in the A data range—Yin's sales of $92,255 in cell B5 of Figure 10-29. The second bar represents the first value in the B data range—Wood's sales of $345,333 in cell C5. Likewise, the third bar represents the first value in the C data range, and the fourth bar represents the first value in the D data range. Because the height of a bar corresponds to its value on the y-axis, the difference in sales generated is obvious. 1-2-3 for Windows repeats this process for all values in the data ranges.

Note: In a bar graph, 1-2-3 for Windows graphs a 0 value, a blank cell, and a cell containing a label in the same way. For example, imagine that you enter 0 in cell C6 of Figure 10-29, Woods' sales in August. Remember that this cell is part of the B data range. In Figure 10-30, 1-2-3 for Windows would graph this 0 value as a blank space where the second July bar is currently located.

By default, 1-2-3 for Windows uses the same solid color to visually tie the bars representing a particular data range, but assigns a different color to each data range. (If you want, you can assign a different color or hatch to each value in a data range.) In Figure 10-30, however, we've differentiated each data range by assigning contrasting hatches, and added a legend to explain what each hatch pattern represents. You may also want to add data labels to convey the value each bar represents. Later in this chapter you'll learn how to add these custom touches.

Stacked Bar

1-2-3 for Windows also provides a stacked bar graph—the second option shown in Figure 10-28. In a stacked bar graph, the corresponding values from each data range are stacked on top of each other. You can see this effect in Figure 10-31, which shows a stacked bar graph of the sales data in Figure 10-29 created using the Chart settings in Table 10-4. Although this stacked bar graph contrasts the difference in monthly sales each employee generates, it emphasizes the difference between total monthly sales.

Here, 1-2-3 for Windows stacks the July values—the first value in each data range—in one bar. The first value in the A data range, Yin's sales of $92,255 in cell B5 of Figure 10-29, is graphed at the bottom of this bar. The first value in the B data range, Wood's sales of $345,333, is then stacked on top of this segment. The first value in the C data range, Heath's sales of $372,182, is added next. Finally, the first value in the D data range, Rose's sales of $674,718, is plotted at the top of this bar. 1-2-3 for Windows then repeats this stacking process for all values in the data ranges.

Note: The width of the bars in a stacked bar graph vary, depending on the number of bars graphed and the width of the graph window.

1-2-3 for Windows automatically uses the same solid color for the portion of each bar representing a particular data range and each data range is assigned a contrasting color.

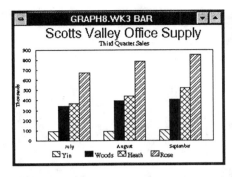 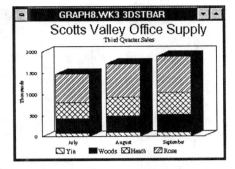

Figure 10-30 A bar graph of the data in Figure 10-29

Figure 10-31 A stacked bar graph of the data in Figure 10-29

In Figure 10-32, however, contrasting hatch patterns are used to differentiate each data range, and a legend is added to tie each hatch to the graphed data (see "Assigning Hatch Patterns" and "Adding a Legend," later).

> ▼ *Tip:* In Figure 10-31, the relatively small values in the A data range are especially hard to distinguish because that data range is graphed at the bottom of each bar. Sometimes, making relatively small data the topmost data series helps improve a graph's readability. In this case, you would assign the range B5..B7 in Figure 10-29 as the D data range.

3D Bar Graphs

1-2-3 for Windows offers the three types of 3D bar graphs shown in Figure 10-32. The first option, the default, creates a 3D bar graph that is simply a 2D bar graph with a three-dimensional effect. The second option also creates a bar graph, but in 3D space—that is, each data range is graphed separately along the z-axis. The third option produces a 2D stacked bar graph but adds a three-dimensional effect. To see the effect each of these 3D bar options produces, let's continue to graph the sales generated by the Scotts Valley Office Supply employees shown in Figure 10-29 using the Chart settings in Table 10-4.

Note: In 3D bar graphs, just as in 2D bar graphs, 1-2-3 for Windows uses the same solid color to visually tie the bars or the portions of stacked bars representing a particular data range. Each data range is assigned a different color. In the following sections, we've distinguished each data range by assigning contrasting hatches, then we've added a legend to explain what each hatch pattern represents. If you'd like, you can even assign a different color or hatch to each value in a data range. You can also add data labels to convey the value each bar represents. Later in this chapter you'll see how to add these custom touches.

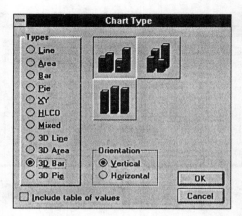

Figure 10-32 The 3D Bar graph options

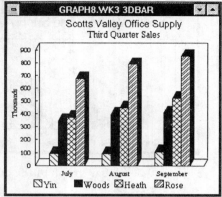

Figure 10-33 A 3D bar graph of the data in Figure 10-29

Default 3D Bar

As Figure 10-33 shows, the default 3D bar option creates a 2D bar graph, but adds a three-dimensional effect to each bar. If you compare Figures 10-30 and 10-33, you'll see that in all other respects this graph type is the same as a 2D bar graph.

▼ *Tip:*   The 📊 icon assigns the default 3D Bar option.

3D Unstacked Bar

Like a 2D bar graph, the second 3D bar graph option (see the dialog box shown in Figure 10-32) plots each value in a data range as a bar. However, each data range is graphed separately in 3D space. Note in Figure 10-34 how the relative difference between each data range is emphasized.

In Figure 10-34, 1-2-3 for Windows graphs the data ranges from front to back along the z-axis—the A data range in front, then the B data range, next the C data range, and finally the D data range at the back of the graph. So remember to specify the data range with the smallest values as the A data range, and the data range with the largest vales as the last data range. Otherwise, data may be hidden from view. Because of this graphing technique, you'll also find that a 3D unstacked bar graph is most effective when there is a distinct difference between each data range.

3D Stacked Bar

As you can see in Figure 10-35, a 3D stacked bar graph is functionally equivalent to a 2D stacked bar graph. The only difference is the three-dimensional effect added to each bar.

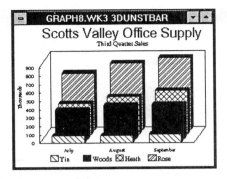

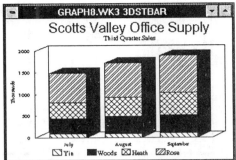

Figure 10-34 A 3D unstacked bar graph of the data in Figure 10-29

Figure 10-35 A 3D stacked bar graph of the data in Figure 10-29

If you examine Figure 10-35, you'll notice that the three-dimensional effect downplays the relatively small values in the A data range. Although changing to a 2D stacked bar graph helps somewhat, a better alternative is to make relatively small data the topmost data series graphed. In this case, you would specify the range B5..B7 in Figure 10-29 as the D data range.

Pie Charts

You'll find that a pie chart is an effective way to portray the proportion that related values contribute to the total. For example, you can use a pie chart to demonstrate the market share each competitor holds in an industry, or to show how each tax dollar gets spent.

A pie chart works well to convey the percentages of students earning each different grade on the Calculus 101 Final shown in Figure 10-36. A pie chart of this data is shown in Figure 10-37, which is created using the settings in Table 10-5.

▼ *Tip:* The ⊙ icon assigns a Pie graph type.

When creating a pie chart, 1-2-3 for Windows calculates the total value of the pie by summing the values in the A data range. However, 1-2-3 for Windows only graphs the positive values; any negative numbers, labels, or blank cells are ignored. 1-2-3 then assigns each value the portion of the total pie it represents.

Note: For a pie chart, 1-2-3 for Windows ignores data ranges D through F. On the other hand, data ranges B and C are reserved for customizing a pie chart (see "Enhancing Pie Charts," later).

1-2-3 for Windows begins graphing a pie chart at the 3 o'clock position, and then adds slices in a counterclockwise direction. In Figure 10-37, for example, 1-2-3 graphs the first value in the A data range, 5 from cell B2 of Figure 10-36, as the first slice. To the

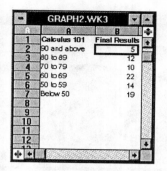

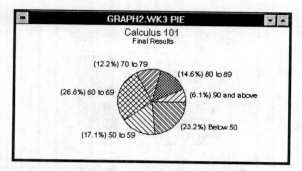

Figure 10-36 Data graphed in the pie charts in Figures 10-37 and 10-38

Figure 10-37 Pie chart of the data in Figure 10-36

left of this slice, it then plots the second value, 12, and so on. To change the order of the graphed slices, you'll have to change the order of the data in the worksheet.

1-2-3 for Windows uses the labels in the X data range as the corresponding labels for each graphed slice. For example, the first label in the X data range, "90 and above" in cell A2 of Figure 10-36, becomes the label for the first slice—the first value in the A data range. In addition, 1-2-3 automatically adds the percentage of the total a slice represents at the beginning of each label. (To suppress these percentages, see "Enhancing Pie Charts.") So 5, or 6.1% of the students scored 90 or above.

When you plot more than 10 values in a pie chart, you'll often find that the data labels look crowded, or aren't clearly displayed. You'll run into a similar problem when small slices are graphed next to each other. When this happens, try changing the order of the data being graphed. For example, placing a relatively large value between two smaller values may help. Another solution is to group several small values together. A third solution might be to change the font assigned to the labels (see "Adding Text").

TABLE 10-5 Graph settings used with the data in Figures 10-36 to create the pie charts in Figures 10-37 and 10-38

Chart Command	Setting	Chart Command	Setting
Type	Pie, 3D Pie	*Headings*	
Ranges		Title	\A1
X	A2..A7	Subtitle	\A2
A	B2..B7		

By default, 1-2-3 for Windows assigns each slice a different solid color. In Figure 10-37, however, hatches are used to differentiate each slice. "Enhancing Pie Charts" explains how you can change colors, assign hatches, and explode or even hide slices.

Note: Although a pie chart may not appear round when you view it on the screen, it usually looks round when printed.

3D Pie Graphs

As Figure 10-38 shows, a 3D pie chart is functionally equivalent to a 2D pie chart. The only difference is the 3D effect, which portrays each value as a wedge instead of a slice.

▼ *Tip:*   The 🔘 icon assigns a 3D Pie graph type.

High-Low-Close-Open (HLCO) Graphs

1-2-3 for Windows offers a high-low-close-open (HLCO) graph, primarily used to graph stock market data. You'll also want to consider using an HLCO graph, however, to graph any data that contains high, low, and average values, such as daily or monthly temperatures.

An HLCO graph is appropriate for the data in Figure 10-39—the price and volume information for Coast Optical stock during 10 trading days in October. Table 10-6 contains the settings used to create the HLCO graph in Figure 10-40.

▼ *Tip:*   The ▦ icon assigns an HLCO graph type.

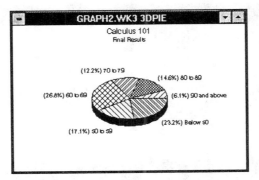

Figure 10-38 3D pie chart of the data in Figure 10-36

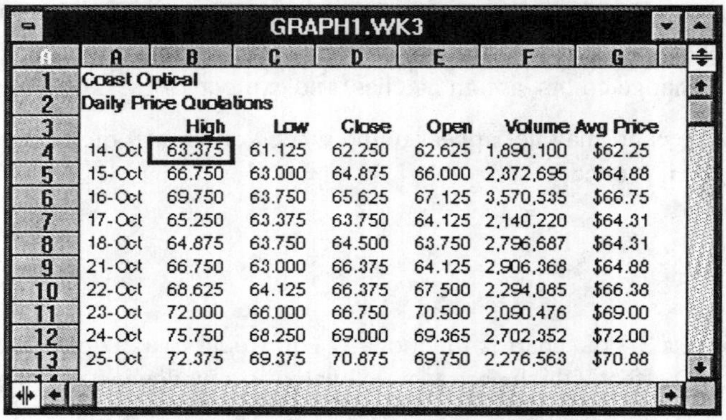

GRAPH1.WK3

	A	B	C	D	E	F	G
1	Coast Optical						
2	Daily Price Quotations						
3		High	Low	Close	Open	Volume	Avg Price
4	14-Oct	63.375	61.125	62.250	62.625	1,890,100	$62.25
5	15-Oct	66.750	63.000	64.875	66.000	2,372,695	$64.88
6	16-Oct	69.750	63.750	65.625	67.125	3,570,535	$66.75
7	17-Oct	65.250	63.375	63.750	64.125	2,140,220	$64.31
8	18-Oct	64.875	63.750	64.500	63.750	2,796,687	$64.31
9	21-Oct	66.750	63.000	66.375	64.125	2,906,368	$64.88
10	22-Oct	68.625	64.125	66.375	67.500	2,294,085	$66.38
11	23-Oct	72.000	66.000	66.750	70.500	2,090,476	$69.00
12	24-Oct	75.750	68.250	69.000	69.365	2,702,352	$72.00
13	25-Oct	72.375	69.375	70.875	69.750	2,276,563	$70.88

Figure 10-39 Stock market data graphed in Figure 10-40

Because this graph type is usually used to track stock market data, 1-2-3 graphs each data range in an HLCO graph a specific way. Here are the rules 1-2-3 follows:

Data Range	1-2-3 Assumes Data Range Includes	Each Value Appears As
A	High values	The top of a vertical line
B	Low values	The bottom of a vertical line
C	Closing values	Right tick mark on a vertical line
D	Opening values	Left tick mark on a vertical line
E	Daily volume	Bar plotted against a 2nd y-axis
F	Average values	Part of a line

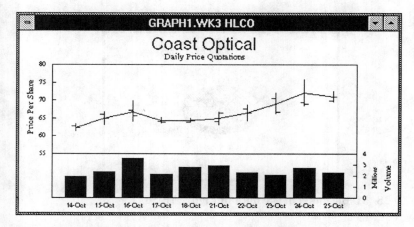

Figure 10-40 An HLCO graph of the data in Figure 10-39

TABLE 10-6 Chart settings used for the HLCO graph in Figure 10-40

Chart Command	Setting	Chart Command	Setting
Type	HLCO	*Headings*	
Ranges		Title	\A1
X	A4..A13	Subtitle	\A2
A	B4..B13	*Axis*	
B	C4..C13	Y Options Axis title	Price Per Share
C	D4..D13	2nd Y Options Axis title	Volume
D	E4..E13		
E	F4..F13		
F	G4..G13		

In Figure 10-40, for example, 1-2-3 for Windows uses the first high value from the A data range, 63.375 in cell B4 of Figure 10-39, and 61.125 in cell C4, the corresponding low value from the B data range, to create the leftmost vertical line between these two values. The closing value from the C data range, 62.250 in cell D4, is represented by the right tick mark extending from this line. Similarly, the opening value from the D data range, 62.625 in cell E5, is represented by the left tick mark.

If you compare the values in Figure 10-39, you'll see that the Daily Volume values in F4..F13, assigned to the E data range, are substantially larger than the other values. 1-2-3 for Windows expects this for the E data range in an HLCO graph. When you include an E data range, 1-2-3 for Windows essentially splits the graph into two graphs. As Figure 10-40 shows, the E data range is graphed as a bar chart against a second y-axis below the first portion of the HLCO graph. For example, the first value in the E data range, 1,890,100 in cell F4, is represented by the leftmost bar graphed against the second y-axis.

In this example, the F data range contains average daily selling prices. So it's appropriate that this data is represented by a line in the HLCO portion of the graph, and is plotted against the primary y-axis.

Note: The way 1-2-3 for Windows positions the second y-axis is unique to an HLCO graph. Although you can't change this placement, you can customize the second y-axis, just as you can customize the primary y-axis. See "Customizing Axes," later.

Note: For 1-2-3 to create a HLCO graph, you must include an E data range, or just the F data range, or both the A and B data ranges. Once you've met one of these minimum requirements, however, you're free to customize an HLCO graph as you wish. For example, you can graph just the A, B, and C data ranges, or only the D and E data ranges. But if you find yourself not using the A and B data ranges, you're probably better off using a line, bar, or mixed graph rather than an HLCO graph.

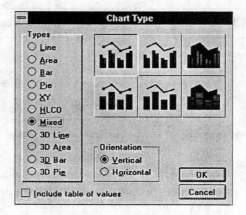

Figure 10-41   The Mixed graph options

Mixed Graphs

A mixed graph, useful to contrast related data, combines two graph types. In an improvement from earlier releases, 1-2-3 for Windows provides six different mixed graph options, shown in Figure 10-41. From left to right, here are the mixed graphs these options create:

- bar and line (with markers)
- bar and line (without markers)
- bar and area
- stacked bar and line (with markers)
- stacked bar and line (without markers)
- stacked bar and area

▼ *Tip:*   The 📊 icon assigns the first Mixed option—bar and line with markers.

Depending on the option you choose, 1-2-3 for Windows graphs each data range this way:

Data Range	Graphed As
A, B, and C	Bars
D, E, and F	Lines or Areas

For the Pacific Tile per-share earnings and dividend data shown in Figure 10-42, a good choice is the default mixed graph—bar and line (with markers). You can see the

GRAPH6.WK3

	A	B	C
1	Pacific Tile		
2	Earnings and Dividends Per Share		
3			
4	Quarter Ending	Earnings	Dividends
5	Mar-92	($5.70)	$0.00
6	Jun-92	($3.00)	$0.50
7	Sep-92	$3.00	$1.00
8	Dec-92	$5.00	$2.00
9	Mar-93	$12.00	$3.00
10	Jun-93	$15.00	$6.00
11	Sep-93	($5.00)	$2.00
12	Dec-93	$4.00	$2.00
13			

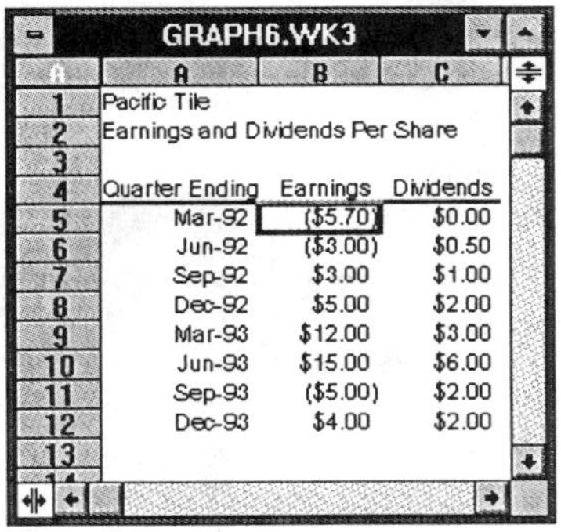

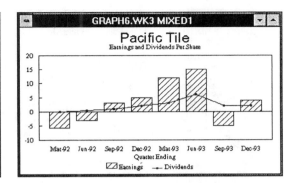

Figure 10-42 Data graphed in Figure 10-43

Figure 10-43 A mixed bar and line graph of the data in Figure 10-42

result in Figure 10-43, which is created using the settings in Table 10-7. Here, 1-2-3 for Windows graphs the Earnings data in the A data range as bars, and the Dividends data in the D data range as a line. Note how the relationship between earnings and dividends is emphasized by this graph type.

> ▼ ***Tip:*** In a mixed bar and line graph, choose bar hatch patterns that don't obscure the line(s).

You'll want to use a different mixed graph type to effectively graph the data in Figure 10-44. In this instance, the sales for the three regions (shown in columns B, C, and D) contribute only a portion of the Total Corporate sales (shown in column E). For example,

TABLE 10-7 Chart settings used for the mixed graph in Figure 10-43

Chart Command	*Setting*	*Chart Command*	*Setting*
Type	Mixed Line and Bar	*Headings*	
Ranges		Title	\A1
X	A5..A12	Subtitle	\A2
A	B5..B12	*Legend*	
D	C5..C12	A	\B4
Axis		D	\C4
X Options Axis title	Quarter Ending		
Options Hatches			
A	Left diagonal (\\\\\\)		

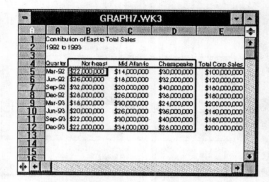

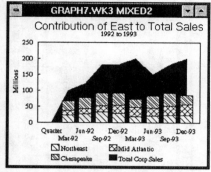

Figure 10-44 Data graphed in Figure 10-45

Figure 10-45 A mixed stacked bar and area graph of the data in Figure 10-44

if you add the March '92 data in row 5, you'll see that the total is considerably less than the corresponding Total Corporate sales of $100,000,000 in cell E5.

In this instance, a stacked bar and area mixed graph (option 6 in Figure 10-41) is a good choice. Using the Chart settings in Table 10-8 then produces the graph shown in

TABLE 10-8 Chart settings for the mixed graph in Figure 10-45

Chart Command	Setting	Chart Command	Setting
Type	Mixed Stacked Bar and Area	Headings	
Ranges		Title	\A1
X	A5..A12	Subtitle	\A2
A	B5..B12	Legend	
B	C5..C12	A	\B4
C	D5..D12	B	\C4
D	E5..E12	C	\D4
Options Hatches		D	\E4
A	Left diagonal (\ \ \)		
B	Light (xxx)		
C	Left double diagonal (\\ \\ \\)		
Axis			
X Options Axis title	Quarter Ending		

Figure 10-45. Notice how the area portion of the graph acts as a backdrop for the stacked bars and emphasizes the portion of total corporate sales these regions generate.

▼ *Tip:*   Consider adding a second y-axis to a mixed graph when the graphed data varies wildly in magnitude. For example, imagine that you create a mixed line and bar graph when the values assigned to data ranges A through C vary from 0 to 100. You won't be able to discern this graphed data if the values assigned to data ranges D through F vary from 1,000 to 10,000. The solution is to graph data ranges A through C against the y-axis, and graph data ranges D through F against a second y-axis. See "Customizing Axes," later.

Adding a Horizontal Orientation

By default, 1-2-3 for Windows assigns all graph types a *vertical orientation*—the x-axis runs horizontally along the bottom of the graph, and the y-axis runs vertically along the left side of the graph. The Horizontal option in the Chart Types dialog box, however, changes this orientation by 90 degrees for all graph types except Pie and 3D Pie. That is, in a *horizontal orientation*, the x-axis runs vertically along the left side of the graph, and the y-axis runs horizontally along the top of the graph.

Whenever you choose Horizontal, 1-2-3 for Windows automatically changes the options for the currently displayed graph type to reflect this new orientation. For example, notice how in Figure 10-46 the Bar options are turned sideways when Horizontal orientation is selected.

▼ *Tip:*   Usually, a horizontal orientation works best with 2D graphs; the three-dimensional (shadow) effect can make a 3D graph with a horizontal orientation look busy.

When would you want to use a horizontal orientation? One situation is when 1-2-3 for Windows can't fully display, or poorly displays, x-axis labels in a vertically oriented graph. For example, for the data in Figure 10-47 and the Chart settings in Table 10-9, Figure 10-48 shows the graph created by the default Bar option but with a Horizontal orientation. Note how the long x-axis labels are easily displayed.

▼ *Tip:*   The horizontally oriented bar graph shown in Figure 10-46 is commonly known as a rotated bar graph. You can also use the icon to produce this effect.

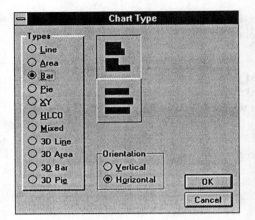

Figure 10-46 The Bar options when Horizontal orientation is chosen

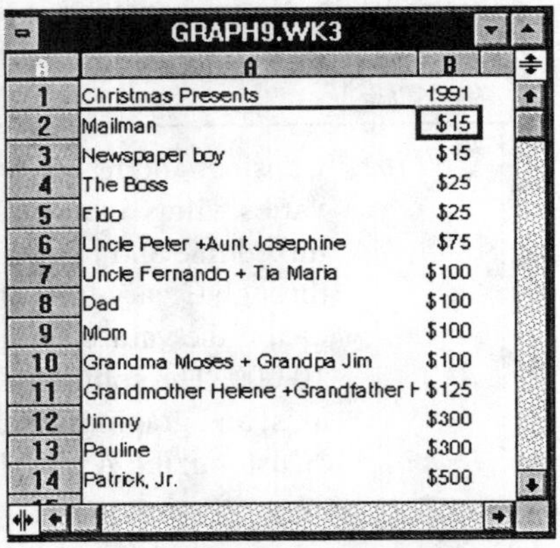

Figure 10-47 Data for the horizontal bar graph in Figure 10-48

▼ *Tip:*   You can emphasize the message conveyed by a rotated bar graph by graphing the data in ascending order, just as in Figure 10-48. This graduated effect is accomplished by sorting the values in the range A2..B14 of Figure 10-47 using the Data Sort command, and specifying an ascending sort order and column B (the values in the A data range) as the primary sort key. Chapter 11 discusses the Data Sort command.

Figure 10-49 shows another situation when a horizontal orientation is a good choice. Notice how the horizontal orientation in this area graph emphasizes the difference in sales generated by each store. Compare this to Figure 10-20, which is the same area graph but with a vertical orientation.

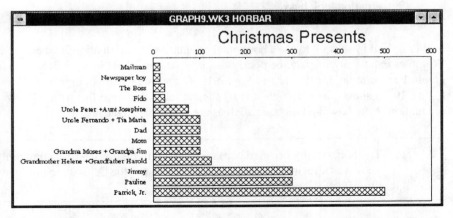

Figure 10-48 A horizontal, or rotated bar graph of the data in Figure 10-47

TABLE 10-9 Chart settings for the bar graph in Figure 10-48

Chart Command	Setting	Chart Command	Setting
Type	Bar	*Headings*	
Orientation	Horizontal	Title	\A1
Ranges		*Options Hatches*	
X	A2..A14	A	Light (xxx)
A	B2..B14		

▼ *Tip:* A new feature in 1-2-3 for Windows, the Rearrange command, offers many different ways you can change the orientation of a graph. For example, you can rotate a graph by 90 degrees in a clockwise direction, or rotate a graph about its x-axis, its y-axis, or its center point. You can even flip a graph upside down or backwards. See "Repositioning the Overall Graph" for more details.

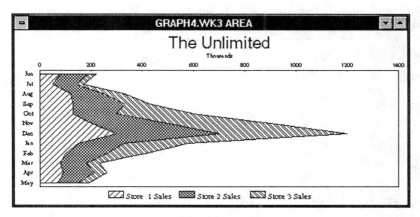

Figure 10-49 An area graph with a horizontal orientation

ADDING TEXT

1-2-3 for Windows, like previous releases of 1-2-3, lets you add explanatory titles to a graph. You can add two graph titles at the top of a graph (called the title and subtitle), an x-axis title, a y-axis title, and, if needed, a second y-axis title. 1-2-3 for Windows also lets you add two notes to the bottom left corner of a graph.

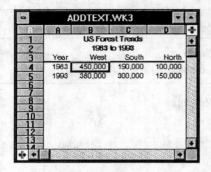

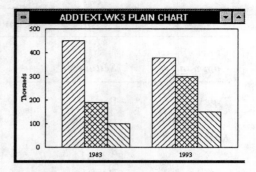

Figure 10-50 Data for the graphs in Figures 10-51 and 10-52

Figure 10-51 A bar graph of the data in Figure 10-50

To see the difference explanatory text can make to a graph, compare Figures 10-51 and 10-52. Both are created using the data in Figure 10-50 and the settings in Table 10-10. Here are the settings used to add the text in Figure 10-52:

TABLE 10-10 Chart settings for the graph in Figure 10-51

Chart Command	Setting	Chart Command	Setting
Type	Bar	Options Hatches	
Ranges		A	Right diagonal (///)
X	A4..A5	B	Light (xxx)
A	B4..B5	C	Left diagonal (\\\)
B	C4..C5		
C	D4..D5		
Headings			
Title	\A1		
Subtitle	\A2		
Note	West includes production from Alaska		
2nd note	South includes production from Puerto Rico		
Axis			
X Options Axis title	\A3		
Y Options Axis title	Growing Volume		

You can see many of these settings in the Chart Headings dialog box shown in Figure 10-53, and in the Chart Axis Y Options dialog box shown in Figure 10-54.

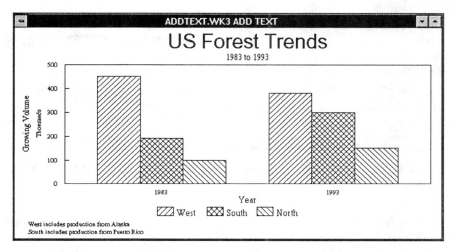

Figure 10-52 Adding explanatory text to the bar graph in Figure 10-51

▼ *Tip:* 1-2-3 for Windows provides two ways you can enter graph text. In a text box, you can enter the label itself, or you can enter a backlash (\) followed by the cell address referencing a label in the worksheet. Enter \A:A1, for instance, and 1-2-3 will use the label in cell A:A1.

Unlike previous releases, 1-2-3 for Windows treats such a cell address as a relative address (see Chapter 7). So even if you move the label to another cell, or delete columns and rows in the worksheet, 1-2-3 for Windows adjusts the cell reference in the text box. The exception is when you move data via the Clipboard using Edit Cut and Paste—then, the cell reference isn't adjusted. (Cutting and pasting data is discussed in Chapter 7.)

Even if text in a cell has been assigned Style settings such as label alignment, borders, and fonts, you can still use it as graph text without changing it. In Figure 10-50, for example, the bolded labels "US Forest Trends" in cell A1 and "1983 to 1993" in cell A2 have been centered over columns A through D using the Style Alignment command (see Chapter 6). Note that 1-2-3 for Windows disregards this formatting when this text is used as the graph titles in Figure 10-52.

In Figure 10-52, the title "US Forest Trends" and the subtitle "1983 to 1993" convey summary information about the graph. Notice that 1-2-3 for Windows displays the title in a single line centered over the graph. Likewise, the subtitle is also centered and limited to a single line.

In Figure 10-52, the x-axis title "Year" conveys what the x-axis labels "1983" and "1993" represent. An x-axis title, limited to one line, is usually centered below the x-axis.

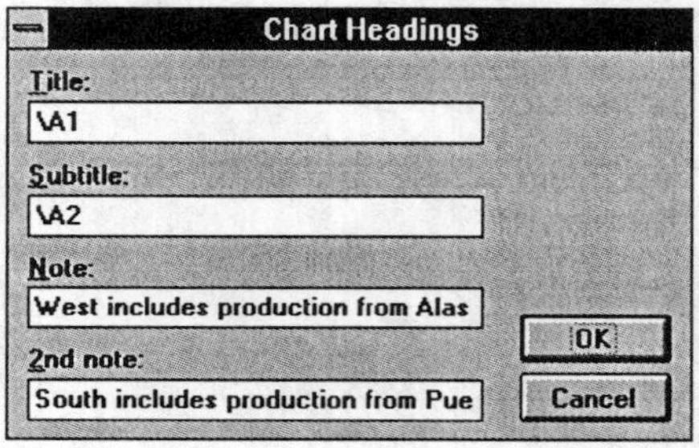

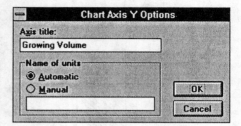

Figure 10-53 The Chart Headings dialog box

Figure 10-54 The Chart Axis Y Options dialog box

However, when a table of values is included, the x-axis title is moved to act as a title for the first row of the table (see "Adding a Table of Values," later in this chapter).

Likewise, the y-axis title, "Growing Volume," conveys what is plotted along the y-axis. Running parallel with and to the left of the y-axis, the centered y-axis title is also limited to one line.

Note: If you look at Figure 10-52, you'll notice that the "Thousands" label along the y-axis hasn't been specified as part of the y-axis title. 1-2-3 for Windows automatically adds this scaling multiplier, which you can suppress or change (see "Customizing Axes," later).

Notes—new in 1-2-3 for Windows—are a handy way to explain some aspect of a graph in greater detail. In Figure 10-52, for example, the note "West includes production from Alaska" clarifies that Alaskan production is included in the West data, not in the North data, just as the second note, "South includes production from Puerto Rico" conveys that Puerto Rican production isn't left out, but is included in the South data.

Notes are always left-aligned in the bottom left corner of the graph, the first note immediately above the second note. You can't change this positioning. Each note is limited to a single line.

▼ *Tip:*   One way to set off a text in a graph, like a note, is to draw a box around it. See "Annotating a Graph," later in this chapter.

How 1-2-3 for Windows Handles Long Graph Text

The size of the graph window and the length of text both affect how 1-2-3 for Windows displays graph text. For example, if 1-2-3 for Windows can't fit a title on one line, it will first shrink the point size the text is displayed in; if this doesn't work, 1-2-3 will truncate the label from right to left. However, the change 1-2-3 makes to the point size isn't reflected in the Chart Options Fonts dialog box. Therefore, keep each line of graph text brief—usually shorter than 30 characters—if you want to use a specific font and point size (see "Changing Text Fonts," later). Increasing the size of a graph window also helps.

Deleting Graph Text

Deleting text added to a graph is a simple matter. For example, to delete the Subtitle shown in Figure 10-52, select Chart Headings. In the dialog box shown in Figure 10-53, move to the Subtitle text box, and then press DEL. You can also delete all Chart Headings settings simultaneously, along with other graph enhancements, using the Chart Clear Chart Settings option. See "Resetting Graph Settings," later.

ADDING A LEGEND

Depending on the graph type you choose, colors, hatches, and/or marker styles differentiate each data range graphed. You'll need to add a *legend*, however, to tie each color, hatch pattern, and/or marker style to a descriptive label you specify.

> ▼ *Tip:*   If your worksheet includes descriptive headings for the data range values—the headings in B3..D3 of Figure 10-50, for instance—you can usually use them as legend labels.

In Figure 10-51 for example, you can't tell what the three different hatch patterns represent. Compare this to Figure 10-52, where the legend labels "West," "South," and "North," taken from cells B3, C3, and D3 of Figure 10-50, explain each hatch pattern. One way to create this legend is to select the Chart Legend command and specify the settings shown in Figure 10-55.

When you create a legend, here are the rules 1-2-3 for Windows follows:

- The legend is always displayed at the bottom of a graph. Unlike previous versions of 1-2-3, you can't change this position.

- A legend key is displayed only for the data ranges currently graphed. For example, Figure 10-52 includes legend keys for the data ranges graphed—A, B, and C. If you delete the Chart Ranges A setting, but don't delete the corresponding legend setting, the legend will contain keys only for the B and C data ranges.

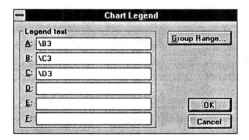

Figure 10-55 The Chart Legend dialog box

- A legend is automatically updated whenever you change settings assigned to data ranges, such as colors or hatches.

- When you include a table of values in a graph, the legend keys are displayed in a columnwise fashion and act as descriptive labels for each row of values (see "Adding a Table of Values," later).

- Usually, 1-2-3 displays a legend on one line. How a legend is displayed, however, is actually a function of the size of the graph window and the size of the legend. When the legend doesn't fit on one line, 1-2-3 uses a three-point approach: first, it splits the legend into two lines, then it shrinks the font; and finally it truncates the legend from right to left (see "Changing Text Fonts," later).

1-2-3 for Windows offers different ways to customize a legend. You can change the font (see "Changing Text Fonts") or the text color (see "Changing Text Colors") of the legend labels, for example. Or you can add a box around the entire legend as a finishing touch (see "Annotating a Graph").

Adding a Legend as a Group

Instead of assigning a Chart Legend setting for each data range, you can assign all legend settings simultaneously. The labels you use, however, must be located sequentially in contiguous cells. In Figure 10-50, for example, the labels used for the legend in B3..D3 meet this criteria because "West" is appropriate as the legend label for the A data range, "South" for the B data range, and "North" for the C data range.

To assign these legend labels all at once, select the range of labels B3..D3 in the worksheet window and then switch to the graph window. From the graph window's menu, select the Chart Legend Group Range option. 1-2-3 then uses this range to assign the Chart Legend settings shown in Figure 10-55.

CHANGING TEXT COLORS

By default, 1-2-3 for Windows displays all graph text in black. You can, however, use the Chart Options Colors command and customize the color of text. In the Chart Options Colors dialog box, the Chart title option controls the color of the graph title. The Subtitle, axis titles, legend option controls the color of the graph subtitle, legend labels, the x-axis title, the y-axis title, and, if applicable, the second y-axis title. You can use the third option, Labels, notes, name of units, to control the color of notes, interior data labels, values in a table of values, the labels along the x-axis, y-axis, and second y-axis, as well as the labels describing each slice in a pie chart.

For all three options, 1-2-3 for Windows provides a drop-down box containing eight different colors from which you can choose. You can change this color palette using the Windows Display Options Palette command accessible through the worksheet (see Chapter 3).

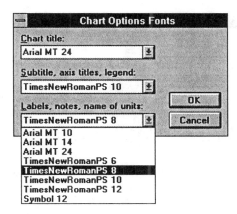

Figure 10-56 The Chart Options Fonts dialog box showing the default fonts and default font set

CHANGING TEXT FONTS

If you've created any graphs in 1-2-3 for Windows, you've probably noticed that graph text is displayed in different fonts. In fact, even when you specify graph text by referencing a cell in the worksheet, 1-2-3 for Windows disregards any font settings in this cell when the label is displayed in the graph. That's because 1-2-3 uses the default fonts shown in Figure 10-56. Here's how 1-2-3 for Windows assigns these default fonts to graph text:

Chart Options Fonts	Default Font	Graph Text
Chart title	Arial MT 24	Graph title
Subtitle, axis titles, legend	Arial MT 10	Graph subtitle, legend labels, and x-, y- and 2nd y-axes titles
Labels, notes, name of units	TimesNewRomanPS 8	X-, y-, and 2nd y-axis labels, interior data labels, notes, and values in a table of values

Many times you'll want to change these fonts. For example, a large title may distract attention from the graph, or the labels along the x- and y-axes may be too small. You can see the difference fonts can make in a graph by comparing Figure 10-52, which uses the default fonts, to Figure 10-57. The graph title in Figure 10-57 is assigned Bodoni BoldCondensed 24 point to make it more distinctive. All other text is assigned TimesNewRomanPS 12 point to render it more readable.

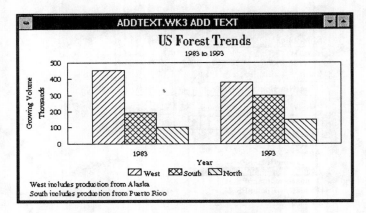

Figure 10-57 Adding custom graph text fonts

Changing the Font Set

The font set (composed of eight fonts) in the Chart Options Fonts dialog box is the same font set the worksheet currently uses. This is always true; you can't create one font set for the worksheet and another font set for the graphs attached to that worksheet. For example, Figure 10-56 shows 1-2-3's default font set. You can change this font set, however, using the Style Font command (see Chapter 6).

How 1-2-3 for Windows Handles Fonts in Long Labels

As explained earlier, the length of text affects how 1-2-3 for Windows displays graph text. When 1-2-3 can't fit a label, such as a note, on one line, it maintains the assigned typeface but shrinks the point size. (1-2-3 for Windows first splits a legend into two lines before it starts shrinking the point size.)

Note: The size of the graph window also affects the point size a label is displayed in.

The change 1-2-3 makes to the point size isn't reflected in the Chart Options Fonts dialog box. If you decrease the length of a label sufficiently, however, 1-2-3 for Windows will again use the specified point size. Therefore, keep graph text brief if you want 1-2-3 to use the font you specify.

▼ *Tip:*   When you use large point sizes, 1-2-3 uses an order of precedence to display text in a graph. In this precedence scheme, notes are given the least weight. For example, imagine that you assign a 24-point font to all the options in the Chart Options Fonts dialog box. If 1-2-3 can't display all the graph text in 24 point, it will shrink the point size of notes so that the other graph text can be displayed in 24 point. On the other hand, imagine that you now assign a 10-point font for the first two options in the Chart Options Fonts dialog box. Because there is no longer a space problem, 1-2-3 will now display notes in 24 point.

ADDING A TABLE OF VALUES

You can make a graph more informative by adding a table of values, a new feature in 1-2-3 for Windows. A *table of values* not only shows the values graphed at each x-axis label, but it also ties each legend key to the corresponding graphed values. You can create a table of values for any graph type except pie, 3D pie, and HLCO.

To create a table of values, you simply turn on the Add Table of Values option in the Chart Types dialog box. As you can see in Figure 10-58, 1-2-3 left-aligns a table of values, then positions it below the x-axis. Note that a table of values is composed of

- An x-axis title in the upper-left corner, which acts as a descriptive heading for the x-axis labels

- X-axis labels, which act as the column headings

- Legend keys, which act as the row headings

- Data values for each data range graphed

Obviously, if you haven't added an x-axis title, a legend, or x-axis labels to a graph, they won't be included in the table of values. On the other hand, when you include a table of values, 1-2-3 for Windows moves the x-axis title and the legend from their normal positions in a graph.

In a table of values, the data points from each data range are displayed in columns directly below the corresponding x-axis label. In Figure 10-58, for example, "1983" is the first label in the X data range. So directly below this x-axis label, 450,000 represents the first value in the A data range, 190,000 represents the first value in the B data range, and 100,000 represents the first value in the C data range.

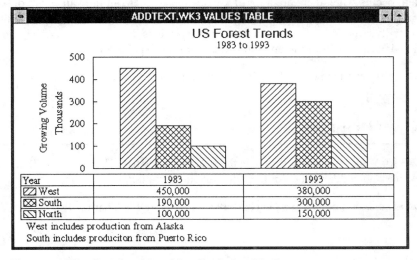

Figure 10-58 Graph with table of values added

Each legend key at the left of a table explains the values in each row. For example, the first legend key explains that this row contains the West values.

In a table of values, 1-2-3 for Windows uses the numeric format assigned to each value in the worksheet. However, here are the Chart commands that control the text font and color displayed in a table of values:

Chart command	*Controls in a Table of Values*
Options Fonts	
Subtitle, axis titles, legend label, notes, name of units	Legend labels, x-axis title, x-axis labels, values in the table
Options Colors	
Subtitle, axis titles, legend label, notes, name of units	Legend labels, x-axis title, x-axis labels, values in the table

Be aware that these Chart commands also affect other text in a graph. See "Changing Text Colors" and "Changing Text Fonts," earlier.

When you include a table of values, try to keep the legend labels short. Although 1-2-3 allows long legend labels to overflow into the first column of values, when these labels try to overflow into the next column, 1-2-3 begins shrinking this text; when this doesn't work, it begins truncating the legend labels from right to left. (See also "Changing Text Fonts.")

What's more, when you include a table of values in any type of line or area graph, the values in the leftmost column (under the first x-axis label) appear left-aligned rather than centered; the values in the rightmost column (under the last x-axis label) appear right-aligned. This usually causes the values to be obscured by the vertical gridlines. A similar problem occurs when there are a lot of x-axis labels—then, all the values are obscured by gridlines. You can sometimes solve this problem by assigning the legend a point size substantially larger than that assigned to the x-axis labels. For example, try assigning the legend labels a 14-point font, and the x-axis labels an 8-point font.

Note: You can't suppress the grid lines in a table of values.

ASSIGNING COLORS

In 1-2-3 for Windows, you can change the color assigned to each data range. In fact, you can even assign a different color to each value in a data range.

Note: To assign colors to a pie chart, see "Enhancing Pie Charts."

Assigning a Color to a Data Range

In any type of bar, line, or area graph, 1-2-3 for Windows automatically uses these colors to differentiate each data range:

Data Range	Color	Data Range	Color
A	Red	D	Yellow
B	Green	E	Purple
C	Dark blue	F	Light blue

Changing the color assigned to a data range is simple. For example, imagine that you have created a bar graph of the data in columns A through D of Figure 10-59 by using the Chart Ranges command to specify X as A4..A8, A as B4..B8, B as C4..C8, and C as D4..D8. 1-2-3 would display all A data range bars in red, the B data range bars in green, and the C data range bars in dark blue. (You can see a bar graph of this data in Figure 10-63.)

To assign purple to the A data range, select the Chart Options Colors command. From the drop-down box displayed when you select A, choose purple. When you select OK, 1-2-3 returns you to the graph, where the bars representing the A data range are now displayed in purple. (If you've assigned a hatch pattern to this data range, it will now be displayed in purple.) What's more, 1-2-3 for Windows updates the A data range legend key to show this new color.

Note: The last selection, H, in the Chart Options Colors drop-down box, hides a data range. Any data labels or legend labels assigned to that data range, however, aren't suppressed.

> ▼ *Tip:* You can change the default color selections using the Windows Display Options Palette command accessible through the worksheet (see Chapter 3).

Assigning a Different Color to Each Value in a Data Range

For a particular data range, you can also display each graphed value in a different color. For example, imagine you want to assign different colors to each value in the B data range: the Bond values in B4..B8 of Figure 10-59. To do this, you must first set up a colors range in your worksheet like the one shown in cells F4..F8. Make sure that the colors range is the same size as the B data range, because 1-2-3 assumes that each cell corresponds to a value in the B data range. If you want to assign colors to each value in another data range, the C data range for instance, you must set up another colors range for it.

In a colors range, you assign a color to each value using these codes:

Code	Color	Code	Color	Code	Color
1	Black	6	Purple	11	Dark green
2	Red	7	Aqua	12	Dark brown
3	Green	8	Pink	13	Olive
4	Blue	9	White	14	Dark pink
5	Yellow	10	Maroon		

You may have noticed that codes 1 through 8 correspond to the color sequence in the Chart Options Colors drop-down box. For codes 9 through 14, however, you may get shades different from those listed above, depending on your monitor, video card, and display drivers.

Note that the colors range in Figure 10-59 will assign a different color to each value in the B data range. For instance, the third value in the colors range, 5 in cell F6, will assign yellow to the third value in the B data range, 12 in cell C6.

Note: When you don't specify a color code for a particular value—that is, you leave the corresponding cell in the colors range blank—1-2-3 indiscriminately uses one of the colors from the Chart Options Colors drop-down box.

Once you've created a colors range, you must specify this range using the Chart Options Advanced Styles command. As shown in the dialog box in Figure 10-60, the range F4..F8 is entered in the leftmost text box for the B data range. When you select OK, 1-2-3 assigns these colors settings to the B data range and updates the corresponding legend key to show the color assigned to the first value in this data range.

Whenever you assign a colors range to a data range using the Chart Options Advanced Styles command, 1-2-3 deletes the Chart Options Colors setting for that data range. If you then use Chart Options Colors and assign a color to that data range, 1-2-3 for Windows deletes the Chart Options Advanced Styles colors range setting. On the other hand, if you delete the Chart Options Advanced Styles setting, 1-2-3 for Windows assigns the data range its default color—for example, green for the B data range.

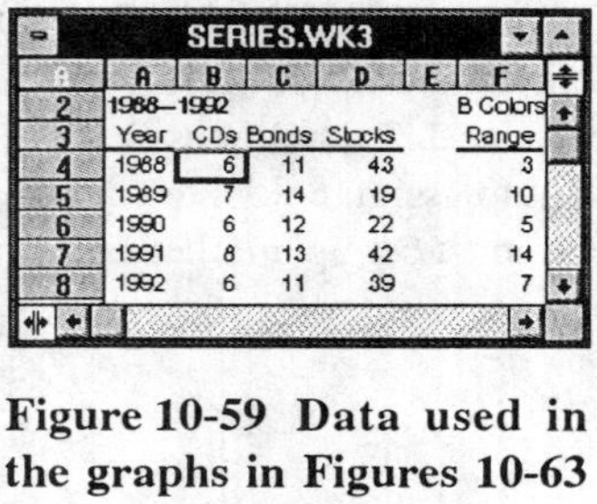

Figure 10-59 Data used in the graphs in Figures 10-63 and 10-65

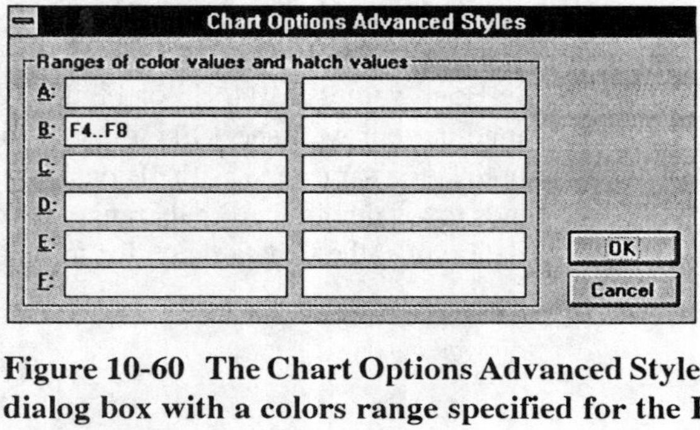

Figure 10-60 The Chart Options Advanced Styles dialog box with a colors range specified for the B data range

ASSIGNING HATCH PATTERNS

Hatch patterns, like colors, can be used to differentiate data ranges in a graph. So, like colors, 1-2-3 for Windows lets you assign a hatch pattern to each data range, or even to each value in a data range. (To assign hatch patterns to a pie chart, see "Enhancing Pie Charts.")

Assigning a Hatch Pattern to a Data Range

In 1-2-3 for Windows, you'll want to consider using hatch patterns to distinguish data ranges in all types of bar and area graphs, mixed graphs, and even 3D line graphs. In fact, you'll need to use hatch patterns to differentiate data ranges when you print a graph in black and white.

For example, let's graph the financial data in Figure 10-61 as a bar graph using the Chart settings in Table 10-11. To assign the hatch patterns listed in this table, select the Chart Options Hatches command. Select A, and you'll see a drop-down box like the one displayed in Figure 10-62. Choose the fifth pattern, light crosshatch (xxx). Use the same procedure to assign a left diagonal (\ \ \) pattern to B, and a solid pattern to C.

You can see the contrasting effect these hatch patterns produce in Figure 10-63. (Although you can't see it in this graph, 1-2-3 for Windows displays a hatch pattern in the color assigned to that data range.) Also notice how 1-2-3 includes hatch patterns in the legend.

Assigning a Different Hatch Pattern to Each Value in a Data Range

You can assign hatch patterns to each value in a data range by employing a technique very similar to the one used to assign colors to each value in a data range. That is, in the worksheet, you enter hatch codes in a hatches range, in which each cell corresponds to a value (cell) in a data range. Then use the Chart Options Advanced Styles command and assign this range in the rightmost range text box for that data range.

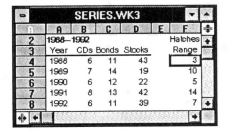

Figure 10-61 Data graphed in Figures 10-63 and 10-65

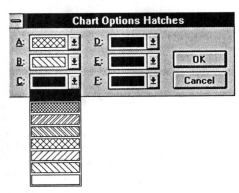

Figure 10-62 The Chart Options Hatches dialog box

TABLE 10-11   Chart settings used to create the graphs in Figures 10-63 and 10-65

Chart Command	Setting	Chart Command	Setting
Type	Bar	*Headings*	
		Title	\A1
Ranges		Subtitle	\A2
X	A4..A8	*Legend*	
A	B4..B8	A	\B3
B	C4..C8	B	\C3
C	D4..D8	C	\D3
Data Labels		*Axis*	
A	B4..B8	X Options Axis title	\A3
B	C4..C8	Y Options Axis title	Asset Value
C	D4..D8		
Options Hatches			
A	Light (xxx)		
B	Left diagonal (\ \ \)		
C	Solid		

For example, suppose in Figure 10-63 you want to display all the bars at each x-axis label in the same hatch pattern. In other words, you want to assign all the bars clustered at the 1988 x-axis one hatch pattern, all the bars at the 1989 x-axis label another hatch pattern, and so on. Therefore, in this particular situation, you'll use the same hatches range for all the data ranges graphed. You can then use colors to distinguish each data range.

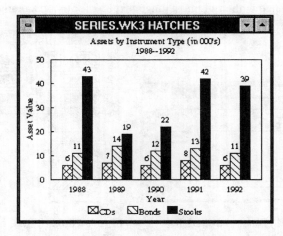

Figure 10-63   A bar graph with hatch patterns and interior data labels

When you create the hatches range in F4..F8 shown in Figure 10-61, 1-2-3 for Windows evaluates the hatch codes this way:

Code	Hatch	Code	Hatch
1	Solid	9	Dense crosshatch
2	Heavy crosshatch (###)	10	Heavy dots
3	Right double diagonal (// //)	11	Solid
4	Left double diagonal (\\ \\)	12	Dense crosshatch
5	Light crosshatch (xxx)	13	Tight crosshatch
6	Right diagonal (/ / /)	14	Light dots
7	Left diagonal (\ \ \)		
8	Empty		

As you've probably noticed, hatch codes 1 through 8 correspond to the hatch sequence in the Chart Options Hatches drop-down box. The hatch codes 9 through 14, however, may seem to display different hatch patterns on your monitor than those listed above. You'll find that for EGA monitors, and even VGA monitors at standard resolutions, some of the hatch patterns appear solid for certain colors. For example, when you assign the color red and use hatch code 9, the result is a heavy red crosshatch. Assign a yellow color, however, and the result may appear solid yellow.

▼ *Tip:*   When you assign a data range a solid hatch pattern and a black color, the hatch codes 9 through 14 represent different shades of gray. Code 9 produces the lightest shade of gray; code 14 produces the darkest.

As Figure 10-64 shows, the hatches range F4..F8 is then specified in the Chart Options Advanced Styles rightmost A, B, and C text boxes. You can see the graphed result in Figure 10-65.

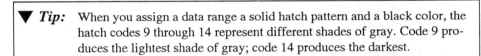

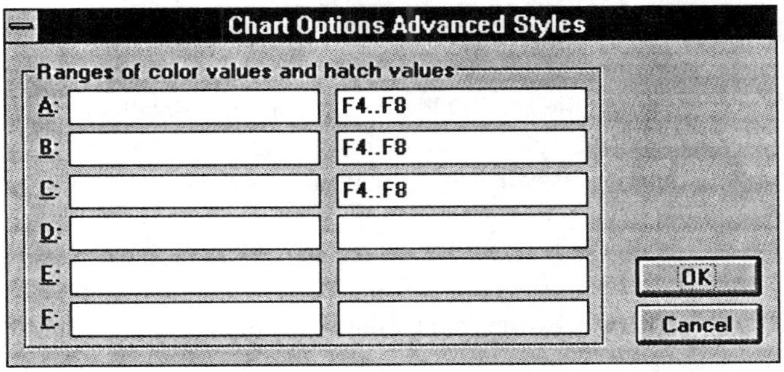

Figure 10-64   The Chart Options Advanced Styles dialog box with the same hatches range assigned to the A, B, and C data ranges

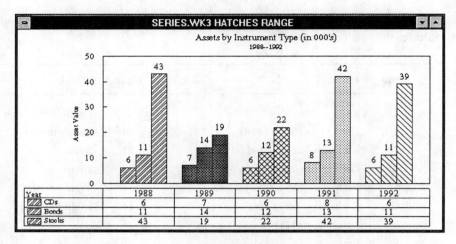

Figure 10-65   Assigning the same hatch patterns to each data range

Now, all the bars clustered at the 1988 x-axis label are displayed in a right double-diagonal (// //) pattern, those at the 1989 x-axis label are displayed in a light crosshatch (xxx) pattern, and so on. Unless you specify otherwise, the colors of each hatch pattern differentiate the data series. Because each legend key shows the same hatch pattern—the hatch pattern assigned to the first value in each data range—a table of values has been added to avoid confusion.

When you assign a hatches range to a data range using the Chart Options Advanced Styles command, 1-2-3 deletes the Chart Options Hatches setting for that data range. If you then use Chart Options Hatches and assign a hatch pattern to that data range, 1-2-3 for Windows deletes the Chart Options Advanced Styles hatches range setting. On the other hand, if you delete the Chart Options Advances Styles hatches range setting yourself, 1-2-3 for Windows assigns each data range its default hatch pattern—solid in all cases.

ADDING INTERIOR DATA LABELS

Many times a graph won't distinctly convey the actual values graphed. The solution for all graph types except Pie and 3D Pie is to add interior data labels. An *interior data label* identifies a particular graphed value—for instance, a bar in a bar graph, or a marker in a line graph. In fact, it's easy in 1-2-3 for Windows to label each or only some values in a data range.

You can see the difference interior data labels make in Figure 10-65. Although it's obvious that each bar represents a different asset value, the interior data labels at the top of each bar clearly convey the exact value a bar represents.

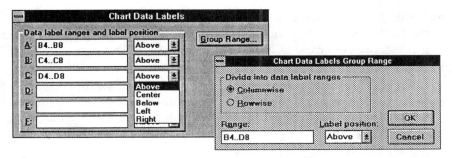

Figure 10-66 Using the values graphed as data labels

Labeling Each Value in a Data Range

Many times you'll want to display a data label for each graphed value, as in Figure 10-65. In this case, you can use the data range values in the worksheet as your interior data labels. All you have to do is choose the Chart Data Labels command and specify the settings shown in Figure 10-66, which reference the data range values in Figure 10-61.

Note: In a data labels range, a data label can be a value, a label, or a formula returning a value or label. In fact, 1-2-3 for Windows incorporates the numeric format of a value into the data label. Like other graph text, however, Style settings such as label alignment, borders, and fonts are ignored. To assign a font to data labels, see "Changing Text Fonts"; to assign a text color, see "Changing Text Colors."

> ▼ *Tip:*   If data labels appear too close to one another, try increasing the x-axis scale to spread the graphed data out. See "Customizing Axes," later.

Changing the Position of Data Labels

By default, 1-2-3 for Windows places data labels above the bars in bar graphs, and above the data points in other graph types. You can however, use the drop-down box shown in Figure 10-66 to assign a different placement to each data range.

When you specify a data label position, you should keep in mind the following:

- In a bar or 3D bar graph, data labels are always placed above the bars. The exception is when you choose a Bottom placement—then, data labels are positioned immediately below the top of each bar.

- In a stacked bar or 3D stacked bar graph, data labels are always placed inside the section of the bar the data label corresponds to.

- Use the Below position for an area or 3D area graph. An Above placement positions the data labels for a particular data range in the area representing the next data range graphed. Labels assigned a Center, Left, or Right placement are obscured by the lines delineating each area.
- If you specify an Above position and let 1-2-3 create the y-axis scale, a data label assigned to the largest value graphed usually won't be displayed. You can overcome this problem by customizing the y-axis and increasing the y-axis scale. See "Customizing Axes," later.

Assigning Interior Data Labels as a Group

You can have 1-2-3 assign all your interior data labels for you by using the Chart Data Labels Group Range option. The interior data labels must be grouped in contiguous cells in the worksheet, and must be in the same sequence as the Chart Data Labels dialog box. For example, the range B4..D8 in Figure 10-61 meets these criteria because the interior data labels for the A data range are in B4..B8, those for the B data range are in C4..C8, and those for the C data range are in D4..D8.

To assign these interior data labels all at once, select the Chart Data Labels Group Range option. In the dialog box shown in Figure 10-66, specify B4..D8 in the Range text box. Since the data labels used for each data range are in columns in Figure 10-61, the Columnwise option is correct. Likewise, accept the Above position, although you can use the drop-down box to specify a different position. When you select OK, 1-2-3 uses this range to assign the settings shown in the Chart Data Labels dialog box.

Labeling Some Values in a Data Range

Sometimes you'll want to label just some of the values graphed. For example, note the interior data labels in Figure 10-67, which is a line graph of the Michigan Machine Tools export data in Figure 10-68 created using the Chart settings in Table 10-12. Here, interior data labels are used to communicate significant events in 1986, 1988, and 1990.

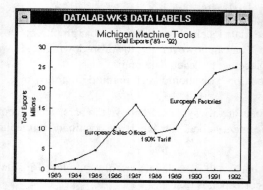

Figure 10-67 Labeling just some of the values in a data range

	A	B	C	D
1	Michigan Machine Tools			
2	Total Exports ('83 – '92)			
3	Year	Total Exports		Data Label Range
4	1983	900,000		
5	1984	2,500,000		
6	1985	4,800,000		
7	1986	10,500,000		European Sales Offices
8	1987	16,000,000		
9	1988	9,000,000		150% Tariff
10	1989	10,200,000		
11	1990	18,500,000		European Factories
12	1991	23,800,000		
13	1992	25,400,000		
14				

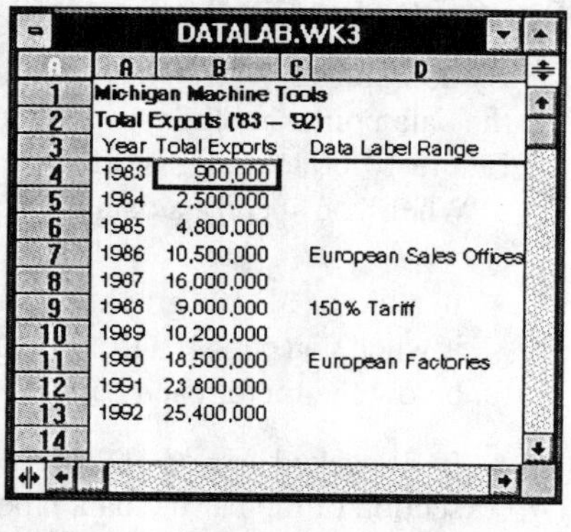

Figure 10-68 Data used to create the line graph in Figure 10-67

TABLE 10-12 Chart settings for the line graph in Figure 10-67

Chart Command	Settings	Chart Command	Settings
Type	Line	*Headings*	
Ranges		Title	\A1
X	A4..A13	Subtitle	\A2
A	B4..B13	*Axis*	
Data Labels		Y Options Axis title	\B3
A	D4..D13		
Position	Below		

To label just the 1986, 1988, and 1990 values, you need to create a data labels range in your worksheet like the one in D4..D13 of Figure 10-68. Note that this data labels range is the same size as the A data range—1-2-3 assumes that each cell in this data labels range corresponds to a value in the A data range. Furthermore, the data labels range contains labels only for the cells corresponding to the 1986, 1988, and 1989 values in the A data range.

Note: You need to create a separate data labels range for each data range you want to partially label.

Once you create a data labels range, you specify it in the usual way using the Chart Data Labels dialog box. In this case D4..D13 is specified as the Chart Labels A setting. A Bottom position is used to place the data labels below the data points (markers).

> ▼ *Tip:* You can use a trick to position interior data labels differently for the same data range. First, assign the same data range twice, as the A and B data ranges, perhaps. Next, use Chart Options Colors to hide the B data range in the graph by specifying the last selection in the drop-down box, H. Now you can create two separate data label ranges in your worksheet, one for the graphed A data range and another for the hidden B data range. When you specify these data labels ranges in the Chart Data Labels dialog box, you can specify a different placement for each.

ASSIGNING DIFFERENT STYLES TO DIFFERENT LINES

As you know, 1-2-3 for Windows automatically displays each data range in a line or XY graph as a line with markers (except 3D line graphs). Each data range graphed as a line in a HLCO or mixed graph is also displayed in the same manner. Because the line style

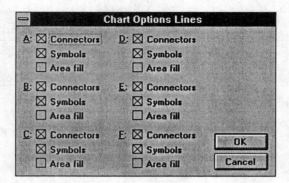

Figure 10-69 The Chart Options Lines dialog box

for all data ranges is the same, each data range is differentiated by its marker style and line color. Only the line color can be changed.

You can, however, display each data range a different way—one as markers only, another as just a line, perhaps—using the Chart Options Lines command. As the dialog box in Figure 10-69 shows, each data range in a line or XY graph is displayed as a line because Connectors is selected, and each data point is represented by a marker because Symbols is selected. So to display a data range as markers only, turn off its Connectors setting; to display a data range as just a line, turn off its Symbols setting. Naturally, turning off both Connectors and Symbols hides a particular data range in the graph.

Note: To display each data range as a line without markers, or as markers without lines (a scatter diagram), use the options 1-2-3 provides in the Chart Ranges dialog box when you choose a Line or XY graph type.

 Tip: Because line and area graphs are very similar, the Area fill option controls whether 1-2-3 for Windows fills in the area below each line in an area graph. So to suppress a data range from being graphed in an area graph, turn off its Connectors and Area fill options.

CUSTOMIZING AXES

All 1-2-3 for Windows graph types, except Pie, include an x-axis and a y-axis. All 3D graphs, except 3D Pie, also include a z-axis. Graphed values are plotted against the y-axis, which 1-2-3 automatically scales to include the lowest and highest values graphed. On the other hand, the x-axis normally isn't a numeric scale. Instead, the x-axis labels convey descriptive information about the data graphed. Likewise, the z-axis in 3D graphs provides a three-dimensional effect; values aren't plotted against it.

Because of the different function each axis performs, you'll usually customize only the y-axis. For example, you can change the y-axis scale, and even specify a logarithmic or percentage scale. You can also change how the y-axis looks by suppressing or changing the scaling multiplier, or changing the numeric format, font, and color of y-axis labels. If you'd like, you can even graph some of the data ranges against a second y-axis, which can also be customized.

Because the x-axis normally displays descriptive values, 1-2-3 for Windows only lets you change which x-axis labels are displayed. When you create an XY graph, however, you can customize the x-axis in the same way you customize the y-axis, with two exceptions. You can't add a second x-axis, and you can't specify a percentage scale.

Note: Adding a title to an axis is discussed in "Adding Text," earlier. To change the font of axis labels and titles, see "Changing Text Fonts"; to change the text color, see "Changing Text Colors."

Customizing the Y-Axis

By examining the graph in Figure 10-67, you can see how 1-2-3 automatically creates a y-axis scale. First, it determines a range that includes all of the values graphed. Then it adds an additional amount at the top and bottom of this range. For example, you can see in column B of Figure 10-68 that the graphed values range from 900,000 to 25,400,000. However, in Figure 10-67 the y-axis scale ranges from 0 to 30 million. Based on this automatic scale, 1-2-3 adds tick marks at evenly spaced increments, then labels these tick marks with y-axis labels.

Note: Because 1-2-3 begins a y-axis scale just a little below the smallest value graphed, many times the first y-axis value is greater than 0. You can solve this problem by creating your own y-axis scale.

In Figure 10-67, 1-2-3 for Windows divided all values in the y-axis scale by 1,000,000, and added a Millions scaling multiplier. (1-2-3 for Windows automatically does this when the values graphed are in the thousands or greater.)

If you like the y-axis scale 1-2-3 for Windows creates, you may just want to customize the appearance of the y-axis. In other instances, you may want to create your own y-axis scale.

Customizing 1-2-3's Y-Axis Scale

Many times you'll want to use the y-axis scale that 1-2-3 generates for a graph, but add custom features to it. For example, let's suppose that in Figure 10-67 you want to display the full value represented by each y-axis tick mark—5,000,000, 10,000,000, and so on.

To do this, you'll need to use the Chart Axis Y command and, as shown in Figure 10-70, specify these settings:

Chart Axis Y Command	Setting	Chart Axis Y Command	Setting
Scale axis	Automatic	Format	Currency
Axis units	Manual	Decimal places	0
Exponent	0	Options Name of units	Manual
Type of scale	Standard		US Dollars

Turning on Axis units Manual tells 1-2-3 to use the setting in the Exponent text box shown in Figure 10-70. 1-2-3 evaluates the Exponent setting of 0 as 10^0. Because 10^0 equals 1, this setting tells 1-2-3 to display the entire value at each y-axis tick mark. (You can specify any base 10 exponent between -95 and 95.)

Unless you specify otherwise, the Exponent setting is reflected in the y-axis scaling multiplier. For example, if you specify an Exponent of 4, 1-2-3 displays the scaling multiplier "Times 1E+04." (The exceptions are when you specify an Exponent of 3 or 6—then, 1-2-3 displays "Thousands" or "Millions.") Chart Axis Y Options Name of units Manual, however, overrides 1-2-3, and allows you to specify your own scaling multiplier or descriptive label, such as "US Dollars." If you wish, turning on Manual and leaving the text box blank suppresses a scaling multiplier altogether.

Note: Adding a y-axis title is discussed in "Adding Text," earlier.

Chart Axis Y Format controls the numeric format, General by default, of the y-axis labels. You can use the dialog box shown in Figure 10-70 to specify any of 1-2-3's numeric formats, such as a Currency 0 places.

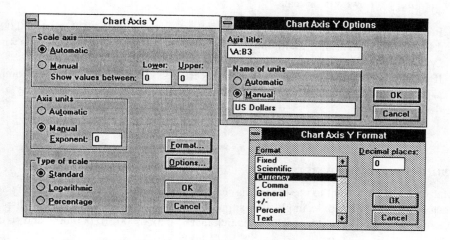

Figure 10-70 The Chart Axis Y and Options dialog boxes

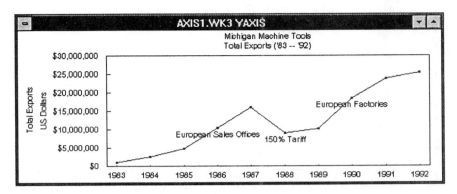

Figure 10-71 Customizing 1-2-3's y-axis scale

You can see the result these settings produce in Figure 10-71. Each y-axis tick mark is labeled with a fully displayed value in a Currency format—the second tick mark, for example is labeled "$5,000,000." And notice how the y-axis scaling multiplier has been replaced by the label "US Dollars."

Creating Your Own Y-Axis Scale

Many times you'll want to create your own y-axis scale rather than use the one 1-2-3 automatically creates. To see how to do this, let's create a new y-axis scale for the line graph in Figure 10-71 by specifying these Chart Axis Y settings:

Chart Axis Y Command	Setting	Chart Axis Y Command	Setting
Scale axis	Manual	Format	Currency
Lower	5,000,000	Decimal places	0
Upper	26,000,000	Options Name of units	Manual
Axis units	Manual		US Dollars
Exponent	0		

Scale axis Manual overrides 1-2-3's automatic scaling. When Manual is selected, you can see in Figure 10-72 that 1-2-3 for Windows uses the Low and High values 5,000,000 and 26,000,000, to create the y-axis scale. However, notice that 1-2-3 automatically creates a scale composed of evenly spaced 5,000,000 increments that encompass the high and low values. So because 26,000,000 isn't a multiple of 5,000,000, 1-2-3 uses 30,000,000 as the highest value. 1-2-3 controls the increment between each y-axis value; you can't change this.

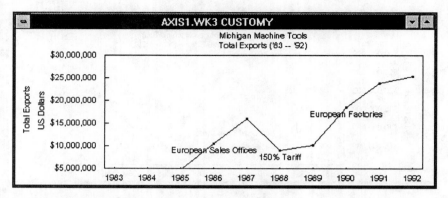

Figure 10-72   Creating a y-axis scale

Note: The Axis units, Option Name of units, and Format settings are discussed in "Customizing 1-2-3's Y-Axis Scale," above.

When you create your own y-axis scale, 1-2-3 for Windows doesn't graph any data range values that fall outside of this scale. In Figure 10-72, for example, the 1983 and 1984 values—900,000 and 2,500,000 in cells B3 and B4 of Figure 10-68—aren't graphed because they are less than the 5,000,000 Low value specified.

Creating a Logarithmic Scale

Like Release 3, 1-2-3 for Windows lets you create a logarithmic or log scale. As you may already know, in a log scale, each y-axis value is 10 times larger than the previous one. A log scale is a good choice when you are graphing values that vary wildly in magnitude, and especially when you want to emphasize the linear relationship between such different values. A log scale is also commonly used to graph data like population growth, which increases or decreases geometrically.

For example, the data in Figure 10-68 is a good candidate for a log scale because, in general, exports are growing in a linear fashion. Notice how this trend becomes apparent when a logarithmic y-axis scale is used in Figure 10-73. This y-axis scale is created with the following settings:

Chart Axis Y Command	*Setting*	*Chart Axis Y Command*	*Setting*
Scale axis	Automatic	Format	Currency
Type of scale	Logarithmic	Decimal places	0
Axis units	Manual	Options Name of units	Manual
Exponent	0		US Dollars

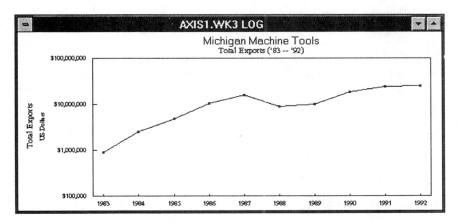

Figure 10-73 Using a logarithmic y-axis scale

Note that when you create a log scale, it's usually best to let 1-2-3 automatically create the scale for you by specifying Scale axis Automatic. On the other hand, you'll probably want to specify your own numeric format and scaling multiplier. (The Axis units, Options name of units, and Format settings in the above table are discussed in "Customizing 1-2-3's Y-Axis Scale," above.)

Creating a Percentage Scale

1-2-3 for Windows provides a new scale type, percentage. The easiest way to see how a percentage scale works is through an example. For instance, the bar graph in Figure 10-74 portrays the percentage of total revenues that COGS (Cost of Goods Sold), G+A expense, Marketing expense, and Profit represents in 1989, 1990, and 1991. It is created using the data shown in Figure 10-75 and the Chart settings in Table 10-13. Notice that for this

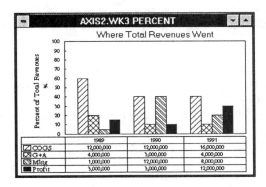

Figure 10-74 Using a percentage y-axis scale

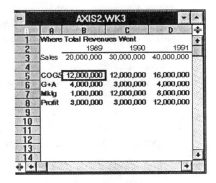

Figure 10-75 The data graphed in Figure 10-74

TABLE 10-13 The Chart settings used to create the graph in Figure 10-74

Chart Command	Setting	Chart Command	Setting
Type	Bar	*Headings*	
Table of values	On	Title	\A1
Ranges		*Legend*	
X	B2..D2	A	\A5
A	B5..D5	B	\A6
B	B6..D6	C	\A7
C	B7..D7	D	\A8
D	B8..D8	*Options Hatches*	
Axis Y		A	Right diagonal (/ /)
Scale	Automatic	B	Light (xxx)
Axis units	Automatic	C	Left double diagonal
Type of scale	Percentage		(\\ \\)
Options		D	Solid
Name of units	Manual		
	%		
Axis title	Percent of Total Revenues		

data, 1-2-3 automatically creates a y-axis scale from 0 to 100%. If you'd like, you can tell 1-2-3 the percentage scale to use (see "Creating Your Own Y-Axis Scale," earlier).

When you specify a percentage scale, 1-2-3 automatically calculates the total value at each *x-axis label*, then assigns each value its percentage of that total. For example, the table of values in Figure 10-74 shows that the bars at the first x-axis label, 1989, represent the first values in the A, B, C, and D data ranges. 1-2-3 calculates the total of these values—20,000,000—then plots each value as the percentage it represents.

Note: If a data range includes a negative value when you specify a percentage scale, 1-2-3 for Windows still calculates the percentage of all the positive values at that axis label as if the negative value is positive. For example, imagine that the 1989 net profit value in Figure 10-74 is -3,000,000 rather than 3,000,000. 1-2-3 would represent this value as a bar extending below the x-axis, but would calculate all the other 1989 values as a percentage of 20,000,000 not 14,000,000.

Adding a Second Y-Axis

Sometimes when you graph related data, a single y-axis creates an ineffective graph because the values are substantially different in size. The data in Figure 10-76, for

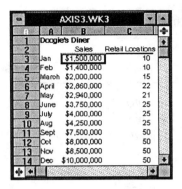

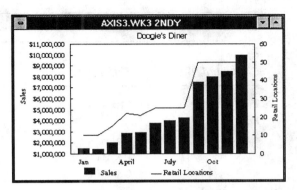

Figure 10-76 Related data with different orders of magnitude graphed in Figure 10-77

Figure 10-77 Graphing the data in Figure 10-76 by adding a second y-axis

example, is just such a situation. Here, the number of Retail Locations vary from 10 to 50, while Sales vary from $1.5 to $10 million. If you plot this data against the same y-axis, the Retail Locations would be indistinguishable.

The solution is to add a second y-axis. Then you can plot one set of values, such as Sales, against the primary y-axis, and the second set of values, Retail Locations, against the second y-axis. You can see the result in Figure 10-77, which is created using the Chart settings in Table 10-14.

When you specify a second y-axis, you must use the Chart Ranges dialog box and specify what data ranges you want plotted against that axis. Here, the D data range, represented as a line, is plotted against the second y-axis. Otherwise, you specify and customize a second y-axis the same way you do a primary y-axis. In this case, we've let 1-2-3 create the second y-axis scale shown in Figure 10-77.

Note: If you specify a percentage scale for the y-axis, 1-2-3 automatically applies this scale to the second y-axis.

Customizing the X-Axis

In all cases except XY graphs, x-axis labels are used to convey descriptive information about the graphed data. So the only thing 1-2-3 lets you control is when x-axis labels are displayed.

For example, compare the labels in column A of Figure 10-76 and the x-axis labels displayed in Figure 10-77. You can see in Table 10-14 that the entire range of labels, A3..A14, is specified as the X range. The Display label every 3 ticks setting shown in Figure 10-78 tells 1-2-3 to display every third label in the X range.

You can also change the font and text color of x-axis labels. See "Changing Text Fonts" and "Changing Text Colors," earlier for more details.

TABLE 10-14 The Chart settings used to create the graph in Figure 10-77

Chart Command	Setting	Chart Command	Setting
Type	Mixed	*Headings*	
Ranges		Title	\A1
X	A3..A14	*Legend*	
A	B3..B14	A	\B2
D	C3..C14	D	\C2
2nd Y	On	*Axis 2nd Y*	
Axis Y		Scale	Automatic
Scale	Automatic	Axis units	Automatic
Axis units	Manual	Type of scale	Standard
Exponent	0	Options	
Type of scale	Standard	Axis title	\C2
Options		Name of units	Automatic
Axis title	\B2	*Axis X Options*	
Name of units	Automatic	Display label every	3
Format	Currency		
Decimal places	0		

Note: Although the Chart Axis X dialog boxes are very similar to the Chart Axis Y dialog boxes, most of the settings are inactive unless an XY graph type is chosen.

In an XY graph, however, you can use the Chart Axis X command to customize the x-axis, just as you can the y-axis. The two exceptions are that you can't add a second x-axis or specify a percentage scale. See "Customizing 1-2-3's Y-Axis Scale" and "Creating Your Own Y-Axis Scale."

ENHANCING PIE CHARTS

As in previous releases of 1-2-3, you can enhance the appearance of a pie chart by changing the colors assigned to each slice, assigning hatches, and exploding pie slices. And, as in Release 3, 1-2-3 for Windows also provides more color selections, as well as the ability to hide slices and suppress the display of percent labels. You'll find, however, that in some cases the method you use to add these enhancements differs from previous releases.

As an example, let's suppose that a study of productivity in your division produces the results shown in Figure 10-79. Although a pie chart would effectively convey this data,

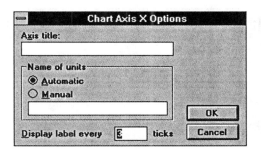

Figure 10-78 Specifying which x-axis labels are displayed

the enhanced pie chart in Figure 10-80, created using the settings in Table 10-15, emphasizes the message of this graph. Suppressing the percentages of all slices except for the Productive slice, for example, focuses attention on this information. Likewise, exploding the Productive slice focuses on this data. By contrast, hiding the Lunch and Breaks slices conveys that these categories shouldn't be considered unproductive time. And adding hatch patterns and changing the label font add visual impact.

Slice Labels

As you know, 1-2-3 for Windows automatically adds the percentage each slice represents to the end of its corresponding label. You can, however, suppress some or all of these percentages to focus attention on one or more slices of the pie. You can also change the font and text color assigned to these labels.

For example, here's how you can suppress the percent labels for all the pie slices in Figure 10-80, except for the one labeled "Productive." First, in your worksheet, you'll need to create a percent labels range the same size as the A data range, just like the one in Figure 10-79. 1-2-3 for Windows evaluates this data range in a special way. It assumes that each cell corresponds to a particular slice in the pie—the first cell to the first slice,

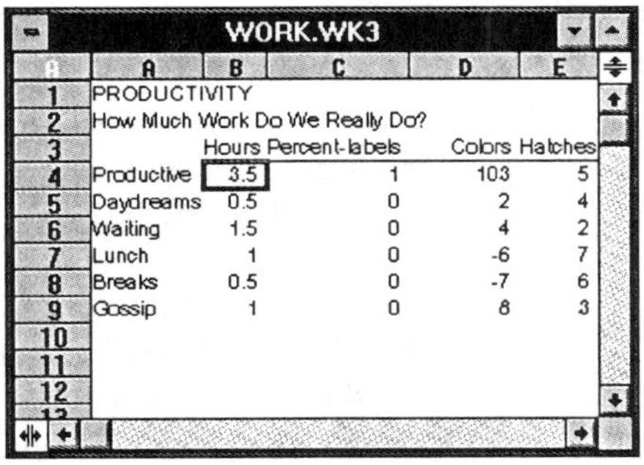

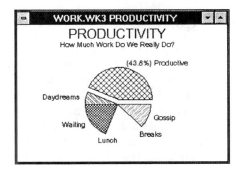

Figure 10-79 Data graphed in the pie chart in Figure 10-80

Figure 10-80 Pie chart of the data in Figure 10-79

TABLE 10-15   Chart settings used to create the pie chart in Figure 10-80

Chart Command	*Setting*	*Chart Command*	*Setting*
Type	Pie	*Heading*	
Ranges		Title	\A1
X	A4..A9	Subtitle	\A2
A	B4..B9	*Options Advanced Styles*	
C	C4..C9	A: color values	D4..D9
		A: hatch values	E4..E9

the second cell to the second slice, and so on. A 0 value tells 1-2-3 for Windows to suppress the percent label; a value of 1, on the other hand, displays the percent label.

Next, you'll need to tell 1-2-3 to use C4..C9 as a percent labels range. For a pie chart, 1-2-3 for Windows always evaluates the C data range as a percent labels range. So, in the Chart Ranges dialog box, simply specify C4..C9 in the C text box.

Many times, you'll want to change the appearance of the labels describing each pie slice. You can change the default font, TimesNewRomanPS 8, using the Chart Options Fonts Labels, notes, name of units option. In the enhanced pie chart shown in Figure 10-80, for example, the labels are assigned Ariel MT 14 point. On the other hand, the Chart Options Colors Labels, notes, name of units option controls the text color of these labels. Although the default is black, you can choose from seven other colors displayed in a drop-down box. Be aware, however, that these settings also control the font and color of any notes you've added to a pie chart.

Note: To change the fonts available through the Chart Options Fonts command, see "Changing Text Fonts," earlier in this chapter. To change the color selections available through the Chart Options Colors command, see "Changing Text Colors," earlier.

Slice Colors

When you specify a pie or 3D pie graph type in 1-2-3 for Windows, each slice is assigned a color. The first slice is assigned red, the default color assigned to the A data range in the Chart Options Colors dialog box; the second slice is assigned green, the default color assigned to the B data range; and so on.

You're in for a surprise, however, the first time you try to change the color of a slice. The minute you use the Chart Options Colors dialog box and change the color setting for *any* of the data ranges, 1-2-3 for Windows displays every slice in red—the default color assigned to the A data range. What's more, once this occurs, you can't use the Chart

Options Colors command to reverse this effect. Thereafter, each pie slice takes on the Chart Options Colors A data range color setting.

1-2-3 for Windows does provide an alternative way you can assign different colors to pie slices. First, you must set up a colors range in your worksheet like the one shown in Figure 10-79. Make sure that the colors range is the same size as the A data range; 1-2-3 assumes that each cell corresponds to a value in the A data range.

You can assign a color to a slice using these codes:

Code	Color	Code	Color	Code	Color
1	Black	6	Purple	11	Dark green
2	Red	7	Aqua	12	Dark brown
3	Green	8	Pink	13	Olive
4	Blue	9	White	14	Dark pink
5	Yellow	10	Maroon		

Notice that color codes 1 through 8 correspond to the color sequence in the Chart Options Colors drop-down box. The codes 9 through 14, on the other hand, may display different shades on your monitor than those listed above. For instance, code 10 may represent a reddish-brown color rather than maroon.

Once you understand this code concept, it's easy to assign colors to a pie chart. Notice that the color codes used in Figure 10-79 assign a different color to each slice. (The effects produced by adding 100 to a color code, or including a negative sign, are discussed in "Exploding and Hiding Slices," later.)

1-2-3 for Windows provides two ways to assign a colors range. For a pie chart, 1-2-3 always evaluates the B data range as a colors range. So one alternative is to specify D4..D9 in the Chart Ranges B text box. The second method is to specify D4..D9 in the leftmost text box for the A data range in the Chart Options Advanced Styles dialog box.

 Tip: Assigning the same color to multiple slices can visually tie related slices. For example, instead of hiding the Lunch and Break slices in Figure 10-80, assigning the same color to these slices would communicate their similarity.

Slice Hatch Patterns

You assign hatch patterns to each slice of a pie chart by employing a technique very similar to the way you assign colors. That is, in the worksheet, you enter hatch codes in a hatches range. Then you use the Chart Options Advanced Styles command and assign this range in the rightmost A text box.

1-2-3 for Windows evaluates values in a hatches range this way:

Code	Hatch	Code	Hatch
1	Solid	8	Empty
2	Heavy crosshatch (###)	9	Dense crosshatch
3	Right double diagonal (// //)	10	Heavy dots
4	Left double diagonal (\\ \\)	11	Solid
5	Light crosshatch (xxx)	12	Dense crosshatch
6	Right diagonal (/ / /)	13	Tight crosshatch
7	Left diagonal (\ \ \)	14	Light dots

As you've probably noticed, hatch codes 1 through 8 correspond to the hatch sequence in the Chart Options Hatches drop-down box. The hatch codes 9 through 14, however, may display different hatch patterns on your monitor than those listed above. You'll also find that at lower resolutions some of the hatch patterns appear solid for certain colors. For example, when a slice is assigned a black color, hatch code 9 produces a heavy black crosshatch. But assign that slice a green color, and the result may appear to be a solid green slice.

Note: 1-2-3 for Windows always displays a hatch pattern in the color assigned to the slice.

Exploding and Hiding Slices

You can call attention to important data by exploding a pie slice—pulling it away from the pie. On the other hand, you may want to consider hiding a pie slice that isn't relevant to the message a graph is conveying.

In 1-2-3 for Windows, you use the colors range to hide and explode slices. This means that whenever you want to explode or hide slices, you must also use the colors range to assign a color to each slice. The value 100, when added to the color code, explodes a slice; adding a negative sign to a color code hides a slice. ("Slice Colors," earlier, discusses how to create and assign a colors range for a pie chart.)

Note: In a colors range, the value 0 hides a slice; so the value 100 explodes yet hides a slice.

The Productive slice in Figure 10-80 is a good candidate for exploding because it's the most important slice in this pie. Because this slice represents the first value in the A data range, the 100 portion of 103—the first color code in Figure 10-79—explodes this slice.

Hiding deemphasizes a pie slice by removing it from view. Because its corresponding label is still displayed, however, a hidden slice is still "part" of the pie. In Figure 10-80, for example, the focus of the graph is the amount of productive and unproductive time in a workday. So hiding the Lunch and Breaks slices conveys that these categories shouldn't be considered unproductive time. Because these are the fourth and fifth slices in the A data range, adding a negative sign in front of the fourth and fifth color codes in Figure 10-79 hides these slices.

Note: To prevent the label assigned to a hidden slice from being displayed, you must delete that label in the worksheet.

CUSTOMIZING THE OVERALL GRAPH

1-2-3 for Windows offers a variety of ways you can give a graph a more polished overall look. For example, you can emphasize data by adding grid lines or by changing background colors. You can even resize and reposition a graph to help focus the reader's attention.

Adding Grid Lines

Although the primary purpose of a graph is to portray relationships between numbers, many times it's hard to determine the value each data point represents. Grid lines make it easier to compare the data points to the corresponding values along an axis.

Because a 1-2-3 for Windows graph doesn't normally include grid lines, you'll have to add them yourself. You can add y-axis grid lines that extend from each y-axis tickmark horizontally across a graph, and x-axis grid lines that extend vertically from each x-axis tickmark. You can also create a second set of y-axis grid lines extending horizontally from each tickmark on a second y-axis.

The graph in Figure 10-81 depicts a typical situation when the addition of both x-axis (vertical) and y-axis (horizontal) grid lines will make it easier to determine the value that each data point represents. To add these grid lines, select the Chart Borders/Grids command, then in the dialog box (shown in Figure 10-82), turn on the X-axis and Y-axis Grid lines options. When you select OK, 1-2-3 for Windows returns you to the graph shown in Figure 10-83, which includes grid lines extending from the tickmarks on each axis.

As Figure 10-83 shows, adding grid lines for all axes can sometimes result in a cluttered graph, so you may want to consider adding grid lines for only one axis. In a bar graph, for example, y-axis grid lines help you determine the corresponding y-value for each data point. In this case, x-axis grid lines would be superfluous.

To eliminate grid lines, use the Chart Borders/Grid command, and then turn off the appropriate Grid lines option(s).

▼ *Tip:*   Grid lines created with the Chart Borders/Grids command always appear as thin black lines. If you want a different look for the grid lines in your graph you can create your own lines with the Draw Line command. Lines created with this command can be thick, thin, dotted, or dashed. You can also change the color of these lines. See "Line" and "Changing the Appearance of Graph Lines," later, for more information.

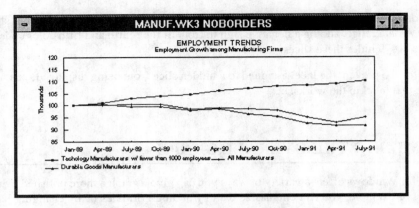

Figure 10-81 A graph without grid lines

Changing the Graph Borders

By default, 1-2-3 for Windows encloses a graph within a *graph border*—a thin line surrounding the plot frame. You can see the default border in Figure 10-83. The bottom and left sides of the graph border are comprised of the x- and y-axes of the graph. Therefore, the x- and y-axis labels are outside of the graph border. The top of the graph border extends horizontally from the topmost y-axis tickmark; the right side extends vertically from the rightmost x-axis tickmark.

Use the Chart Borders/Grid command to indicate which of the four sides of the graph border you want displayed. For example, to turn off all graph borders, as illustrated in Figure 10-84, select Chart Borders/Grids and turn off the Top, Bottom, Left, and Right Borders options. When you select OK, 1-2-3 for WIndows displays the graph with no borders.

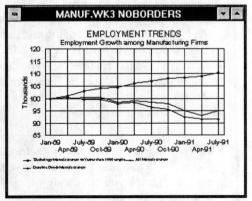

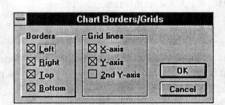

Figure 10-82 The Chart Bor-ders/ Grids dialog box

Figure 10-83 Clarifying a graph with grid lines

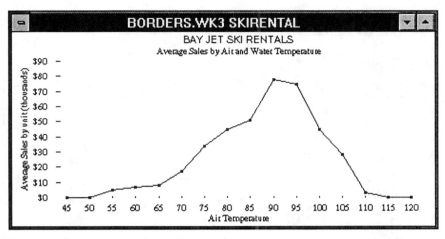

Figure 10-84 A graph with no borders

When you customize the graph border, you may want to consider the following:

- When you've included horizontal grid lines in a graph, such as in Figure 10-83, it seems that 1-2-3 for Windows doesn't remove the top border when you turn off the Chart Borders/Grids Top option. Actually, you're seeing the topmost grid line in its place. Turn off the y-axis grid lines, and the border disappears.

- Because 1-2-3 uses the bottom and left graph borders to help create an illusion of depth in three-dimensional bar, line, and area graphs, turning off these portions of the border may lessen the three-dimensional effect.

Note: Since pie charts have no x- or y-axis, and consequently no plot frame, 1-2-3 for Windows does not create a border for these graph types. Therefore, the Chart Borders/Grids border settings don't affect pie charts.

Creating a Graph Frame

1-2-3 for Windows' graphs can actually display an additional border, or frame, around the entire graph area. In Figure 10-85, for example, a frame surrounds the entire graph. By default, this frame is not visible because the frame occupies the same area as the graph window frame, and the line color of the frame is the same as the background color of the graph.

You can make the graph frame visible by following these steps:

1. Select the graph by clicking anywhere along the inside edge of the graph window frame. Or choose Edit Select Chart as shown in Figure 10-86. When the graph is selected, you can see that handles appear on each side of the frame.

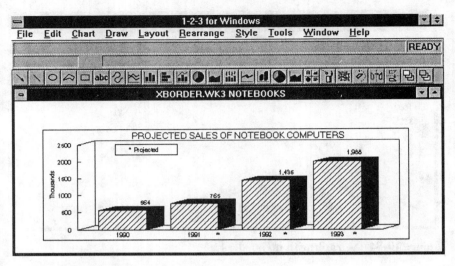

Figure 10-85   A graph frame

Note: Selecting a graph is also discussed in "Selecting Graph Objects" later in this chapter.

2.   Use the Style Color Line command to select a line color other than the graph's background color, red perhaps.

3.   Use the Rearrange Adjust Size command to reduce the size of the graph so that the frame can be seen inside the window (see Figure 10-86).

See "Changing Colors" for more on the Style Color command and "Changing the Graph Size" for more on the Rearrange Adjust Size command.

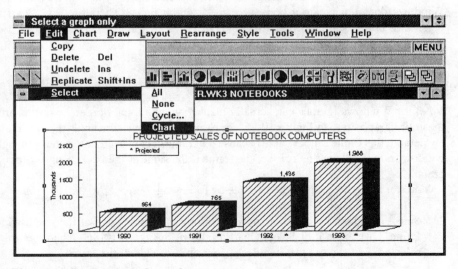

Figure 10-86   A selected graph

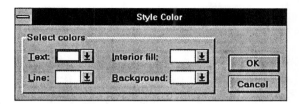

Figure 10-87 The Style Color dialog box

Background and Interior Fill Colors

Changing the background color of a graph can further emphasize your graphed data. The background color controls the area outside of the plot frame, which contains the x- and y-axis values, graph titles, and legends. The interior fill color controls the area inside the axes containing the data ranges.

To change the background and interior fill colors of a graph, use the following steps:

1. Begin by selecting the graph. The easiest way to do this is to click anywhere along the inside edge of the graph window frame. (Or choose Edit Select Chart.) The graph is selected when handles appear along each side of the frame.

2. Use the Style Color command to display the dialog box shown in Figure 10-87.

3. Choose Background and select the color that will appear outside the plot frame.

4. Choose Interior Fill and select the color that will appear inside the graph's plot frame.

When you select OK, 1-2-3 for Windows displays the graph in these new colors.

Note: Because Pie charts have no x- and y-axes, these graphs have no plot frame or interior fill area. Consequently, the color of the area surrounding a pie chart is determined by the Style Color Background setting. The Style Color Interior Fill command has no effect on a pie chart.

CHANGING THE GRAPH DISPLAY

The graph window's Window commands allow you to change the size of the graph display. Each command and its effect on the graph display is listed below:

Window Command	*Result*
Enlarge	Enlarges the contents of the graph window.
Reduce	Reduces the contents of the graph window if enlarged.
Full	Displays the graph at normal size.
Zoom	Enlarges a selected area of a graph to fill the entire window.

As this list suggests, the Graph Window commands let you easily adjust the graph display to suit your working style.

Enlarging and Reducing the Contents of the Graph Window

To enlarge the contents of a graph window, use the Window Enlarge command or press the + key. 1-2-3 for Windows then magnifies the graph within the window. Because the graph is now too large to see as a whole, 1-2-3 adds scroll bars to the window so you can bring outlying areas of the graph into view. If you want your graph larger still, you can continue to use the Window Enlarge command or press the + key until the display is the right size.

To reduce an enlarged graph display, select the Window Reduce command or press the - key. Window Reduce decreases the size of the graph display in the same increments it was increased.

> ▼ *Tip:* The 🔍 and 🔍 icons provide quick alternatives for enlarging and reducing graphs.

> ▼ *Tip:* You can't reduce a graph that hasn't been enlarged with the Window Enlarge command. To make a graph smaller than its normal size, you must use the Rearrange Adjust Size command. (See "Changing the Graph Size," later in this chapter.)

To return an enlarged graph display to its normal size, use the Window Full command, or press the * key. 1-2-3 then displays the entire contents of the graph window.

Zooming in on a Portion of a Graph

The Window Zoom command lets you magnify, or zoom in on, a section of a graph, filling the entire graph window with the selected area. This command differs from the Window Enlarge command by allowing you to specify the area you want enlarged, as opposed to the entire graph.

For example, to zoom in on a specific area of the graph in Figure 10-88A, select Window Zoom or press the @ key. Next, move the mouse pointer to the upper-left corner of the area you want enlarged. As you drag the mouse to indicate the area you want to see, it is enclosed in a rectangle, just as in Figure 10-88A. When you release the mouse button, you can see in Figure 10-88B that the selected area fills the entire window. Because all the graph window commands work in Zoom mode, you can reposition the arrow or the text Aug-91.

To display the entire graph again, use the Window Full command, or press the * key.

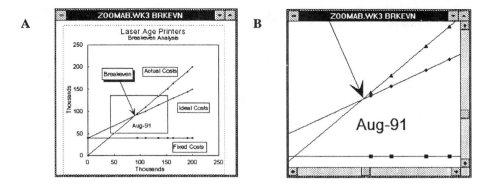

Figure 10-88 Zooming in on a portion of a graph

▼ *Tip:* You can also select the area you want to zoom in on, then select the 🔍 icon. Use the 🔍 icon to reduce the zoom level.

Changing the Graph Size

When you create a new graph, it fills the entire graph window. You can, however, adjust the size of the graph inside the window by using the Rearrange Adjust Size command. You'll want to use this command to downsize a graph before you attempt to rotate or reposition it, for example. Downsizing a graph also allows you to bring the graph frame into view (see "Creating a Graph Frame," earlier in this chapter).

For example, to change the size of the graph in Figure 10-89A, select it by clicking on the graph frame or by using the Edit Select Chart command. Next, choose the Rearrange Adjust Size command. A dotted line, called a *bounding box*, appears around the frame of the graph. Use the mouse to adjust the bounding box to the size you want, such as in Figure 10-89A. You can see the result in Figure 10-89B—1-2-3 resizes the graph to fit within the bounding box.

To return the graph size to its default size, use the Rearrange Clear command.

▼ *Tip:* You can't make a graph larger than the graph window with the Rearrange Adjust Size command. To magnify the graph display, use the Window Enlarge or Window Zoom commands instead.

Repositioning a Graph

When you change the size of a graph using the Rearrange Adjust Size command, the graph is no longer centered in the graph window. It's easy to reposition the graph within

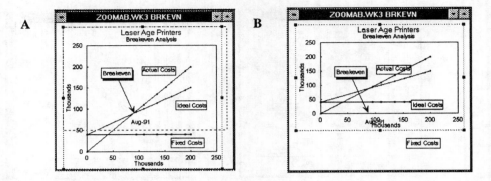

Figure 10-89   Resizing a graph

the graph window, however. To begin with, select the graph by clicking on the graph frame or using the Edit Select Chart command. Point to a spot on the graph frame and hold down the mouse button while you drag the graph to its new position. When you have the graph where you want it, release the mouse button.

RESETTING GRAPH SETTINGS

The Chart Clear command allows you to reset some or all of your graph settings using the dialog box shown in Figure 10-90. Each of the Chart Clear options and its effect on a graph is listed in the table below:

Chart Clear Option	*Clears*
Entire chart	All Chart settings, but not Style settings or annotation created with the Draw command
Chart settings	All Chart settings except Chart Ranges
All (X,A–F)	Chart Ranges and Data Labels settings
Individual data ranges	Chart Ranges and Data Labels settings for the selected data ranges

Suppose that you have created the line graph shown in Figure 10-89, and you want to reset the existing data ranges. You don't want to lose your other settings, however, such as headings, legends, and data-range colors. To reset just the data-ranges without losing the other settings, select Chart Clear and turn on the All (X, A–F) option in the dialog

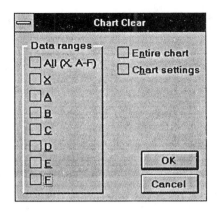

Figure 10-90 The Chart Clear dialog box

box. When you select OK, 1-2-3 clears only the data ranges. Your other settings are unaffected.

However, any graph objects created with the Draw command, such as the arrow and text boxes in Figure 10-89, aren't cleared by the Chart Clear command. To delete annotation, see "Deleting Graph Objects."

 Tip: A quick method of resetting an entire graph is to select the graph by clicking anywhere on the frame or using the Edit Select Chart command and then pressing the DEL key.

ANNOTATING A GRAPH

One new feature of 1-2-3 for Windows that is bound to delight most users is its graph annotation. The Draw commands available in the graph window allow you to add annotations to your graphs in the form of text, lines, arrows, boxes, ellipses, polygons, and even freehand drawings. Annotations can help emphasize important data. For example, you can see the effect of adding annotations by comparing Figures 10-81 and 10-91.

Annotations that you create with the Draw command, or with the first seven icons shown in Figure 10-92, are referred to as *objects*. You can manipulate these objects by copying or moving them, or by changing their attributes—such as size, color, or font. As you'll soon see, each object can be manipulated as a single entity or as part of a group of objects. Figure 10-92 shows some examples of the different graph objects you can create in 1-2-3 for Windows.

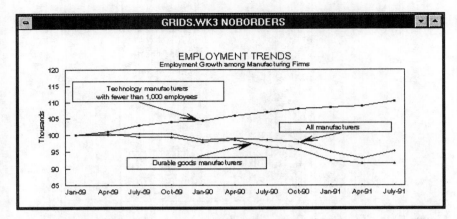

Figure 10-91   Adding annotation to Figure 10-81

Note: A graph is also treated as an object, and, to a certain extent, can be manipulated. For example, you can change the size, position, and background colors of a graph, just as you can annotation objects. The components of a graph—such as titles, data ranges, and legends—are considered part of the graph, however, and can't be manipulated as separate objects.

Text

As you know, 1-2-3 for Windows allows you to add text to a graph in the form of titles, subtitles, legends, and interior data labels. Nevertheless, it controls the positioning of these text enhancements, and sometimes leaves you wishing you had more control of them yourself.

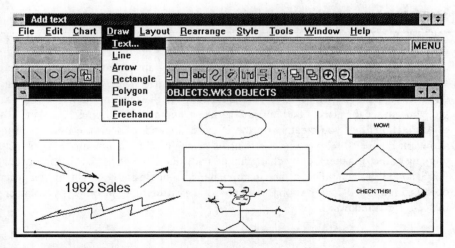

Figure 10-92   Examples of graph objects

Fortunately, 1-2-3 for Windows lets you add text notations to a graph using the graph window's Draw Text command. Each text notation can contain up to 512 characters. For example, here are the steps for adding the bottommost text in Figure 10-91:

1. Select Draw Text or the ⓐⓑⓒ icon, and 1-2-3 displays a dialog box where you can enter the text notation.

2. Type the text **Durable goods manufacturers** in the New text box. If you want 1-2-3 to use the text from a worksheet cell, type \ (backslash) and specify the cell that contains the text—for example, \B1.

3. Select OK, and the cursor changes to a crosshair.

4. Using the mouse or the pointer-movement keys, move the cursor to where you want to locate the text.

5. Click or press ENTER to add this text to the graph.

6. Because this text is selected (handles appear around it), click elsewhere in the graph to unselect it.

Note: To add the box around this text shown in Figure 10-91, see "Rectangle," later. To add the arrow connecting this text to the graphed line, see "Arrow."

If you want to move the text, simply select it and drag it to the new location. If you later decide to change the text, simply select it and press EDIT (F2). 1-2-3 displays the original text for you to modify. Then, when you select OK, 1-2-3 replaces the existing text with the new text.

Line

Using the Draw Line command, or the ◻ icon, you can add a single straight line, or a series of connected line segments, to a graph window. Here are the steps:

1. Select Draw Line, and the mouse cursor changes to a crosshair.

2. Move the mouse cursor to where you want to begin drawing the line.

3. Drag the mouse in the direction you want the line to go in and release the mouse button. (If you prefer the keyboard, use the pointer-movement keys to move to where you want to start the line and then press SPACEBAR; use the pointer-movement keys again to move in the direction you want the line to go in and press SPACEBAR again when you arrive at the point where you want the line to end.)

4. (Optional) If you want to draw another line segment, drag the mouse in the direction you want the line segment to go in and release the mouse again (or press SPACEBAR). Repeat this step until you've drawn all the line segments you want.

5. To end line drawing, double-click the mouse or press ENTER.

After adding the line (or line segments) to the graph window, 1-2-3 displays them as a selected object (a handle appears on the line).

Here are some pointers that should help make drawing lines easier:

- While drawing a line, you can erase a previously drawn line segment by clicking the right mouse button or pressing ESC.

- If you want to align a line segment at the nearest 45-degree increment as you draw it, press SHIFT as you drag the mouse or use the pointer-movement keys.

- To move a line, simply select it and drag it.

- You can smooth connected line segments into curves by using the Style Lines command (see "Changing the Appearance of Graph Lines," later).

Arrow

To draw an arrow—a line segment, or series of connected line segments, with an arrowhead on the end—use the Draw Arrow command or click on . In fact, after selecting the Draw Arrow command, the steps for drawing an arrow are the same as for drawing a line. The only difference is in the result—1-2-3 adds an arrowhead to the end of the line when you double-click or press ENTER to complete drawing the arrow.

> ▼ *Tip:* You can add or delete arrowheads, or smooth connected line segments into curves, using the Style Lines command (see "Changing the Appearance of Lines").

Rectangle

The Draw Rectangle command is handy for drawing a box around graph text or a graph legend. It is also handy for creating a drop shadow effect (see "Restacking and Protecting Objects" for more information).

For example, here's how to add a rectangle around the text "Durable goods manufacturers" in Figure 10-91:

1. Move the mouse cursor slightly above and to the left of the "D."

2. Select Draw Rectangle or the ▣ icon, and the cursor changes to a crosshair.

3. Drag the mouse to stretch the rectangle's bounding box until it encompasses this text. Release the mouse button to complete the rectangle. (If you prefer to use the keyboard, press SPACEBAR to anchor the first corner of the rectangle's bounding box, and then use the pointer-movement keys to stretch the box until it reaches the size and shape you want. Press ENTER to complete drawing the rectangle.)

4. Because this rectangle is selected—handles appear around it—click elsewhere in the graph to unselect it.

Here are some pointers to help you when drawing rectangles:

- To draw a square, press SHIFT as you drag the mouse.

- To move a rectangle, select and then drag it.

- You can smooth the corners of a rectangle into curves by using the Styles Lines command (see "Changing the Appearance of Graph Lines").

Ellipse

To draw an ellipse like the one in Figure 10-92, use the Draw Ellipse command or select the ⊡ icon. Otherwise, the steps for drawing an ellipse are identical to those for drawing a rectangle.

Polygon

Drawing a polygon—a multi-sided object—is similar to drawing multiple connected line segments. For example, here's how to create the triangle in Figure 10-92:

1. Choose Draw Polygon or select the ⬠ icon. The mouse cursor changes to a cross-hair.

2. Move the mouse to where you want to begin drawing. Drag the pointer to the end of the first side.

3. To create the second side, *move* the mouse cursor (don't drag it) and click at the end of this side. 1-2-3 draws a line between the two points.

4. To create the last side and close the triangle, double-click the mouse or press ENTER. Because handles indicate that the triangle is selected, click elsewhere in the graph to unselect it.

Here are some additional pointers for drawing a polygon:

- You can also create a polygon by dragging the mouse to the end of a side, releasing the mouse button to establish the end point, then dragging the mouse to draw the second side, releasing the mouse button, and so on.

- To erase the last drawn line segment in a polygon, click the right mouse button or press ESC.

- To move a polygon within the graph window, select it and drag it to the new location.

- To smooth the corners of the polygon into curves, use the Style Lines command (see "Changing the Appearance of Graph Lines" later).

Freehand Drawing

If you have the skill to create a freehand drawing, 1-2-3 has a tool for you—the Draw Freehand command. For example, here are the steps for creating the stick figure at the bottom of Figure 10-92:

1. Select Draw Freehand or select the ✐ icon, and the mouse cursor becomes a crosshair.

2. Move to where you want to begin drawing—for example, to the top of the line representing the stick figure's body.

3. Drag the mouse to draw the line. As soon as you start dragging, the mouse cursor changes to a pencil. Release the mouse (or press ENTER) when you've completed the object.

Because each part of the stick figure is a separate object, you'll need to repeat this procedure for the head, eyes, mouth, and so on.

SELECTING GRAPH OBJECTS

Before you can copy, delete, or change the attributes of an object, you must first select it. To select an object, use the mouse or the graph window's Edit Select commands. When an object is selected, like the rectangle in Figure 10-93A, 1-2-3 places square handles on the perimeter of the object.

Note: The graph window's Edit, Layout, Rearrange, and Style commands all require that you select an object.

Selecting with the Mouse

To select an object or graph with the mouse, place the mouse cursor on the perimeter of the object or graph and click.

If you want to select several objects as a group, the simplest way is to place the mouse cursor at one corner of the area containing the group of objects, and then hold down the mouse button as you drag the bounding box to include all the objects. When you release

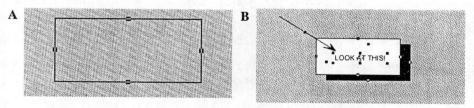

Figure 10-93 Selecting objects

the mouse button, each object in the group will have handles. Figure 10-93B shows a group of selected objects.

A second method of selecting a group of objects with the mouse is to hold down the SHIFT key while you click on the perimeter of each object in the group. Handles are added to each object as you go.

Note: When you select a graph, any Draw objects that have been added to the graph are not selected. To include Draw objects and a graph in a group, hold down the SHIFT key while you click on the graph frame, then on each object.

To unselect an object with the mouse, place the mouse cursor on the perimeter of the object and click. The handles disappear, indicating that the object is no longer selected.

To unselect a single object in a group of selected objects, such as the text "LOOK AT THIS!" in Figure 10-93B, place the mouse cursor on it, hold down the SHIFT key, and click the mouse. The handles disappear from this text, but remain on all other objects in the group.

Selecting with the Keyboard

To select an object with the keyboard, use the Edit Select commands described below:

Edit Select Command	*Action*
All	Selects all objects in a graph window except the graph itself.
None	Unselects all objects in the graph window, including a selected graph.
Cycle	Cycles through and selects each object in the graph window, starting with the item that was created first.
Chart	Selects a graph in the graph window.

MOVING GRAPH OBJECTS

1-2-3 makes it easy to move an object anywhere in the graph window using the mouse—simply click on the object to select it, and then drag it to the new location.

▼ *Tip:* To move an entire graph without preselecting it, locate the mouse cursor near the perimeter of the graph before dragging.

To move a group of objects like those in Figure 10-93B, first preselect them. Then, position the pointer within this group. When you begin to drag the mouse, 1-2-3 displays a bounding box that encompasses all the selected items and moves the items within the box in tandem.

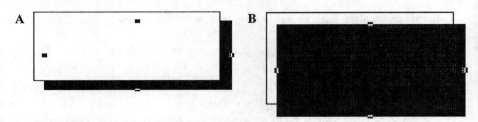

Figure 10-94 Using Layout Send Forward to bring an object to the front

Restacking and Protecting Objects

Occasionally, you'll want to stack objects in a graph window to achieve a desired graphical effect. For example, placing a dark rectangle behind a light one, as in Figure 10-94A, produces a drop shadow.

To make stacked objects easier to work with in a graph window, use these Layout commands:

Layout Command	Action
Send Forward	Brings a selected object to the front of a stack of objects.
Fall Back	Places a selected object at the back of a stack of objects.
Lock	Locks a selected object, preventing changes to it; selection handles change from squares to diamonds.
Unlock	Unlocks a selected object that has been previously locked with Layout Lock; handles revert to squares.

For example, Figures 10-94A and B show what happens when you select the black rectangle that serves as a drop shadow and then choose Layout Send Forward to bring the rectangle to the front.

▼ *Tip:*   The 🔲 and 🔲 icons let you bring an object forward and send it back within a stack of objects.

Adjusting the Orientation and Size of Objects

The graph window's Rearrange commands let you adjust the orientation and size of graph objects. In general, you'll find these commands work better with Draw objects than with an entire graph. Here's a summary of the commands:

Rearrange Command	Action
Flip	Flips an object or the entire graph horizontally or vertically.
Quarter-Turn	Rotates an object or the entire graph in 90-degree increments.
Skew	Slants an object or the entire graph at a chosen angle.
Turn	Rotates an object or the entire graph around its center at any angle.
Adjust Size	Changes the size of an object or the entire graph.
Clear	Returns an object or the entire graph to its original state, canceling the effect of all the Rearrange commands.

COPYING GRAPH OBJECTS

It's easy to create a duplicate of a graph object, or a group of graph objects, using the Edit Replicate command. For example, to copy the rectangle in Figure 10-95A, first select it. Then use the Edit Replicate command, or its shortcut, SHIFT+INS. As you can see in Figure 10-95B, 1-2-3 creates a duplicate of the rectangle, and places it in front of the original. The new rectangle is the object now selected.

DELETING GRAPH OBJECTS

To delete a graph object, or a group of graph objects, such as the rectangles in Figure 10-95B, first select them as a group. Then use the Edit Delete command, or its shortcut, DEL.

▼ *Tip:*   The 🔲 icon provides another quick way to delete an object.

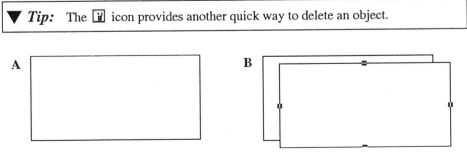

Figure 10-95 Copying a graph object

> **Tip:**   If you change your mind after pressing DEL to delete a graph object, you can recover the object by immediately pressing INS.

CHANGING THE APPEARANCE OF GRAPH OBJECTS

Like graphs, 1-2-3 lets you easily change the look of a graph object by modifying its interior fill color using the Style Color command. You can also use the Style command to change the fonts assigned to a text object or the line styles assigned to a line, arrow, rectangle, or polygon.

Changing Fonts

After adding text to a graph using the Draw Text command, you may want to change the font that 1-2-3 uses, Arial MT 10 point by default. After selecting the text, use the Style Font command to assign a new font from the list of installed fonts. To customize the font set, see "Changing Text Fonts," earlier.

> **Tip:**   Use the Style Font command to change the size of *all* the text within a graph. For example, by selecting the Style Font command and entering **150** in the Magnify all fonts text box, you increase all the text in the graph to 150% of its current size.

Changing Colors

The graph window's Style Color command lets you change the color of a selected graph object. Figure 10-96 shows the Style Color dialog box, and the following list summarizes its options and their effects:

Style Color Option	*Item affected*
Text	Text added to the graph with the Draw Text command. Select "H" to hide the selected text.
Line	The selected line or arrow, or the outline of a selected rectangle, polygon, ellipse, or freehand drawing. Select "H" to hide the chosen lines.
Interior fill	The inside of a selected object.
Background	The background color of the entire graph.

Note: See "Customizing the Overall Graph" earlier for a discussion of how to use the Style Color command to change the colors of the graph frame, the area inside the frame, and the graph's background.

Figure 10-96 The Style Color dialog box

Changing the Appearance of Lines

The Style Lines command controls the appearance of lines or arrows, and the outlines of rectangles, polygons, ellipses, or freehand drawings. Here's a summary of the different Style Lines command options you can see in Figure 10-97:

Option	Effect
Line	Changes the style (full, dashed, or dotted) and width of lines or outlines. The default is thin solid.
Smoothing	Smooths the corners of rectangles, polygons, freehand drawings, and connected line segments by replacing jagged corners with curves. The default is None—no smoothing.
Add arrowheads	Changes the placement of arrowheads. The default is End of line.

For example, Figures 10-98A and B show the effect on a rectangle when you change the Smoothing to Medium and use the Line Width option to specify a wider line.

Changing the Alignment of Text

The graph window's Style Alignment command lets you left-align, center, or right-align text that you've added to a graph using the Draw Text command. The position of the

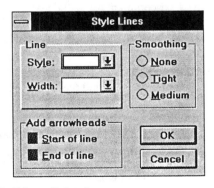

Figure 10-97 The Style Lines dialog box

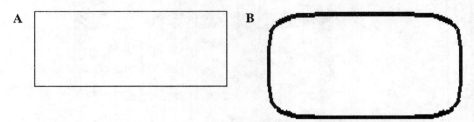

Figure 10-98   The effect of changing the Smoothing and Line Width options

crosshair that appears within the text when you select a text object indicates the current alignment setting. For example, if the crosshair appears at the right of the text object, you know that the text is right-aligned. By default, text is left-aligned.

ANNOTATING A WORKSHEET RANGE

By using the worksheet window's Range Annotate command, you can annotate a range in the current worksheet. When you select this command, 1-2-3 creates an empty graph window and associates it with the currently selected range. Within that graph window, you can then use the Draw commands to place lines, arrows, text, freehand drawings, or any other graphics objects you want. Although cumbersome, this method does allow a fair amount of creativity when annotating a range.

For example, suppose you want to attach a text annotation to cell C1 in the current worksheet. Here are the steps:

1.   Highlight the range you want to annotate—in this case, cell C1.

2.   Select Range Annotate. 1-2-3 displays a small blank graph window and associates it with cell C1. (You can tell that 1-2-3 has created an association because it displays {Graph <Blank>.1}, or a similar setting, in the format line when you locate the cell pointer on cell C1.)

3.   Choose the Draw Text command, type the text you want to use for the annotation, and select OK.

1-2-3 places the text in the graph window. In addition, it displays the contents of the graph window in the worksheet cell.

Here are some pointers for creating and managing annotations:

• To remove an annotation from the screen, close the graph window in the usual manner—for example, double-click on its window control icon.

• To reveal an annotation, highlight the appropriate range and double-click on it.

• Because you are working in a graph window when you create an annotation, you can use any of the graph window commands except the Chart commands to create an annotation.

- To delete an annotation from a worksheet cell, use the Edit Clear Special command with the Graph option turned on. To delete the annotation from the worksheet file, see "Deleting a Graph Name."

CUSTOMIZING THE GRAPH WINDOWS' SMARTICONS

As you know, 1-2-3 for Windows has a complete set of SmartIcons specially tailored for the graph window. To customize the graph window's icon palette, you use the Tools SmartIcons Customize command. (See Appendix A for a complete discussion of this topic.)

RENAMING AN EXISTING GRAPH

After creating a graph in 1-2-3 for Windows, you may decide that you want to give it a new name. The easiest way to rename a graph in 1-2-3 for Windows is to use the Classic menu. For example, here are the steps for renaming a graph named GRAPH1 to WORSTCASE:

1. Select the /Graph Name Use command and choose the graph that you want to rename from the list—in this case, GRAPH1. 1-2-3 displays a full-screen view of the graph.
2. Press ENTER (or any other key) to return to the /Graph menu.
3. Select Name Create and type the new name you want to assign the graph—in this case, WORSTCASE. When you press ENTER, 1-2-3 adds the new name to the list of graph names and returns you to the /Graph menu.
4. To delete the old name, select Name Delete and choose GRAPH1 from the list.
5. Select Quit to return to READY mode.

Caution: Any annotation objects created with the Draw command are lost when you use this method to rename a graph. If your graph includes annotation, see "Copying a Graph" later for a description of how to copy it using the Clipboard.

DELETING A GRAPH NAME

To delete a graph in 1-2-3 for Windows, use the Graph Name Delete command from the worksheet menu. When you select this command, 1-2-3 displays a dialog box like the one in Figure 10-99. If you then select a name from the list—for example, GRAPH1—followed by OK, 1-2-3 removes the chosen name and all its associated settings from the list of available graph names. (Use Delete in place of OK to continue to delete graph names.)

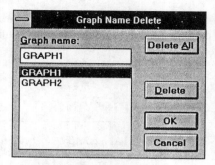

Figure 10-99 The Graph Name Delete dialog box

> ▼ *Tip:*   To delete all the graph names in the current worksheet file, use the Delete All button in the Graph Name Delete dialog box.

CREATE A TABLE OF GRAPH NAMES

Sometimes it's helpful to see a list of all the graph names you've created for a given worksheet file, along with their associated graph types and titles. To create such a list in 1-2-3 for Windows and place it in a worksheet, use the Graph Name Paste Table command. When you select this command, 1-2-3 requests a location for the table. After you provide a cell address representing the upper-left corner of the table and select OK, 1-2-3 creates a three-column table like the one in Figure 10-100.

Figure 10-100 Results of the Graph Name Paste Table command

COPYING A GRAPH

In previous releases of 1-2-3, copying a graph from one worksheet file to another wasn't easy. In fact, the most expedient way was to write down the graph settings on paper and then reenter them in the new file from scratch.

In contrast, the Windows Clipboard makes it relatively simple to copy graphs between worksheet files in 1-2-3 for Windows. For example, suppose you want to copy the graph named BESTCASE from one worksheet file to another. Here are the steps:

1. Make the BESTCASE graph window current and select the Edit Copy command. 1-2-3 copies the entire graph to the Clipboard.

2. Switch to the worksheet you want to copy the graph to and specify a range where you'd like the graph to temporarily reside.

3. Choose Edit Paste. 1-2-3 copies the graph to the current worksheet and inserts it in the chosen range. In the process, it assigns the next available graph name—for example, GRAPH1—to the newly pasted graph.

4. (Optional) If you don't want the graph to appear within the worksheet, select Edit Cut to remove it. The graph settings will remain within the file, however.

5. Specify new data ranges for the graph by displaying the graph in a graph window (use Graph View) and using the Chart Ranges command (see "Specifying Data to be Graphed" earlier).

> ▼ *Tip:*   Although you can also use the Clipboard to copy a graph within the same worksheet file, an easier method is to use the procedure outlined in "Renaming an Existing Graph" earlier, but omit step 4.

> ▼ *Tip:*   Another way to share Graph settings between worksheet files is to use the File Import From Styles command and turn on the Graphics option. Be aware that this command reads *all* the graph settings from the .FM3 file you select and imports them into the current file.

INSERTING GRAPHS INTO A WORKSHEET

1-2-3 for Windows makes it easy to insert a graph into a worksheet. Although it may not be immediately clear why you would want to do this, there are several reasons. The first, and most obvious, is that you *must* insert a graph into a worksheet before you can print it. Once the graph has been inserted, you can use the File Print command to print it along with the rest of your 1-2-3 data. (Printing graphs is discussed at length in Chapter 8.) What's more, when a graph is adjacent to its supporting values, you can include both in the same print range and print both on the same page, creating a strong visual impact.

A second reason for inserting a graph into the worksheet is strictly a visual one. When you insert a graph into a worksheet, 1-2-3 continues to update it dynamically for changes to its underlying worksheet values. In fact, if the graph and its supporting data are positioned alongside one another, you can change the supporting numbers and watch as the graph is updated.

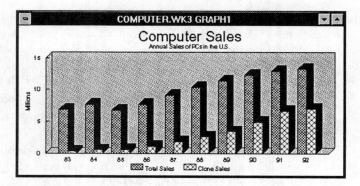

Figure 10-101 A sample graph

Lotus claims that 1-2-3 places no limit on the number of graphs you can insert into a worksheet. This claim is bolstered by the fact that each additional graph you insert consumes very little additional memory. In fact, we've found that inserting as many as 20 graphs has a negligible effect on memory.

Inserting a Graph: An Example

Suppose you've just created the graph in Figure 10-101, GRAPH1, which is displayed in a graph window. Here's how to insert it into the current worksheet:

1. Switch back to the worksheet window, and select the Graph Add to Sheet command. 1-2-3 displays the dialog box in Figure 10-102 listing the names of the available graphs in the current worksheet file.

2. Select the name of the graph you want to insert from the list, in this case GRAPH1.

3. In the Range text box, specify the range you want the graph to occupy—for example, A:D2..A:H14—and select OK.

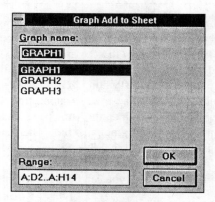

Figure 10-102 The Graph Add to Sheet dialog box

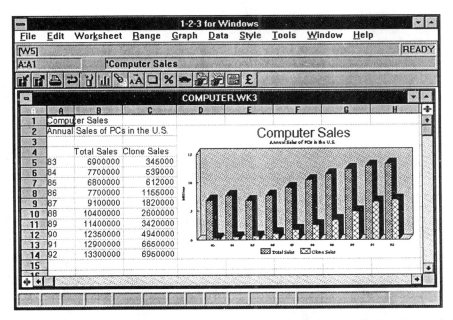

Figure 10-103 The sample graph from Figure 10-101 inserted into the worksheet alongside its supporting data

You can see in Figure 10-103 how 1-2-3 adds the graph to the worksheet and displays it in the range you've chosen. What's more, the name of the graph, GRAPH 1, appears in the format line whenever you move the cell pointer into the range it occupies.

When you insert a graph into a worksheet range, 1-2-3 lays the graph on top of the range you specify. Any data already in the range isn't affected, and lies underneath the inserted graph. (You can see this by looking ahead to Figure 10-106.)

Note: You'll change the size of an inserted graph, if you change the size of the range the graph is assigned to. This can happen when you adjust the column width or row height, or delete or insert columns or rows.

Changing the Display Size

After inserting a graph into the worksheet, you may notice that its aspect ratio (height to width) is unbalanced, causing the graph to appear unsightly. Fortunately, you can easily change the size of the inserted graph to improve its appearance.

For example, to change the size of the inserted graph in Figure 10-103, GRAPH1, select the Graph Size command from the worksheet menu. 1-2-3 displays the dialog box in Figure 10-104. Select GRAPH1 from the list box. (When you highlight GRAPH1 in the list box, 1-2-3 displays the range it currently occupies, A:D2..A:H14, in the Range text box.) To change the size of GRAPH1 in the worksheet, simply modify its current

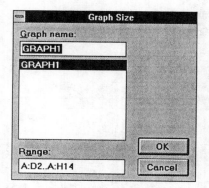

Figure 10-104 The Graph Size dialog box

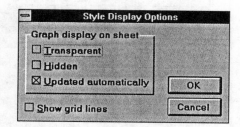

Figure 10-105   The Style Display Options dialog box

range assignment in the Range text box. For example, to increase the size of this graph, specify the range D2..I20. When you select OK, 1-2-3 adjusts the size and location of GRAPH1 to occupy this range.

Changing Display Options

1-2-3 for Windows lets you change the appearance of an inserted graph. For example, you can make an inserted graph transparent—that is, allow the worksheet data beneath the graph to show through. You can also hide an inserted graph from view or control its update mode—whether the graph is automatically updated whenever its underlying worksheet values change.

To change the display options for an inserted graph, use Graph View to view it in a graph window. Then select the graph window's Style Display Options command to access the dialog box shown in Figure 10-105.

By default, an inserted graph such as the one in Figure 10-103, obscures any data in the range in which it has been inserted. Turning on the Transparent option, however, causes the opaque background for an inserted graph to disappear and any data in the range beneath the graph to show through. (Remember, an inserted graph lies on top of the range you specify; the data underneath the graph isn't affected.) Figure 10-106 shows the graph in Figure 10-103 when Transparent is turned on. Notice that both the worksheet grid lines and the date entry in cell A:F5 show through.

The Hidden option simply turns off the display of an inserted graph. When used by itself, the inserted graph, such as GRAPH1 in Figure 10-104, ceases to appear in the worksheet. However, the opaque background for the graph continues to mask the range it occupies. (Even when an inserted graph is hidden from view, you can still print it by specifying its range in the File Print command.) To make the graph disappear completely from view, you turn on both the Hidden and Transparency options.

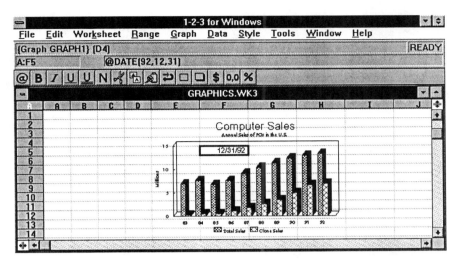

Figure 10-106 Using the Transparent display option

The Updated automatically option, which is on by default, updates an inserted graph whenever the worksheet is recalculated. This means that 1-2-3 must redraw the inserted graph each time the worksheet is recalculated. This can cause excessive screen repainting and slow down the operation of 1-2-3, especially if you have a large number of graphs inserted in a worksheet. Turn off this option to disable the automatic update feature.

Note: You can still update inserted graphs when automatic update has been disabled using the graph window's Graph Refresh command.

Oddly enough, the Show grid lines option has no effect on the display of inserted graphs. In fact, turning this option on merely displays a rendering of worksheet grid lines in the current graph window. Although this option lets you preview the effect of using the Transparent option just discussed, it serves no other purpose we know of. In all probability, you should have very little, if any, occasion to use it.

IMPORTING CGM AND PIC FILES

Because 1-2-3 lets you display CGM and PIC files in the worksheet, you can import and display graphs created with these previous versions of 1-2-3 in your 1-2-3 for Windows worksheet. CGM (Computer Graphics Metafile) is a common file format used for clip art. Freelance Plus, a presentation graphics program from Lotus, includes an extensive library of CGM clip-art files. PIC, on the other hand, is the proprietary file format used in 1-2-3 Releases 2.x and 3.x to store graphs created with those releases. You can import

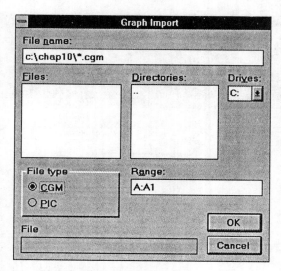

Figure 10-107 The Graph Import dialog box

and display graphs created with these previous versions of 1-2-3 in your 1-2-3 for Windows worksheet.

To import CGM or PIC files into the current worksheet, use the Graph Import command from the worksheet menu. You'll see the dialog box in Figure 10-107, which resembles 1-2-3's File Open dialog box with these two exceptions:

- The File type section lets you choose from either CGM (the default) or PIC. When you select one of these options, 1-2-3 changes the file descriptor in the File name box above to either *.cgm or *.pic, causing the appropriate files to appear in the list box below. You can then select the file you want to import from the list.

- The Range text box lets you define the range in the worksheet in which the CGM or PIC file will be displayed. You can specify a range from any worksheet in the current file.

After setting these options and selecting OK, 1-2-3 reads the file you've selected into memory and displays it in the specified range. Wherever the cell pointer is located in this range, Graph: followed by the path and name of the file is displayed in the format line at the top of your screen. For example, Figure 10-108 shows the results of importing a PIC file created with 1-2-3 Release 2.3 into the range A:A1..A:E13.

Note: If the aspect ratio of the imported CGM or PIC file appears distorted, use the Graph Size command to correct the problem (see "Changing the Display Size," earlier).

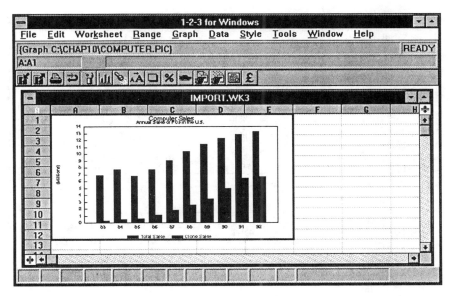

Figure 10-108 A .PIC file displayed in the worksheet

▼ *Tip:* You can also display bitmaps from the Windows Clipboard in your 1-2-3 worksheet. To do this, select an appropriately sized range in the worksheet and then select the Edit Copy command from the worksheet. 1-2-3 copies the bitmap in the Clipboard and fits it within the range you've specified. If the aspect ratio of the bitmap appears distorted, use the Graph Size command to correct the problem.

SHARING GRAPHS THROUGH THE CLIPBOARD

You can share your 1-2-3 for Windows graphs with other Windows applications by using the Clipboard. For example, suppose you want to display one of your graphs in Windows Paintbrush, such as GRAPH1 in Figure 10-101. To do this, use the Graph View command to open GRAPH1 in its own graph window. Next, select the Edit Copy command, and 1-2-3 for Windows will copy a bitmap image of GRAPH1 to the Clipboard. To paste the image from the Clipboard to Paintbrush, open Paintbrush, and select the Edit Paste command. Windows pastes the bitmap image of GRAPH1 into Paintbrush's work area, as shown in Figure 10-109. You can now work with the image from within Paintbrush.

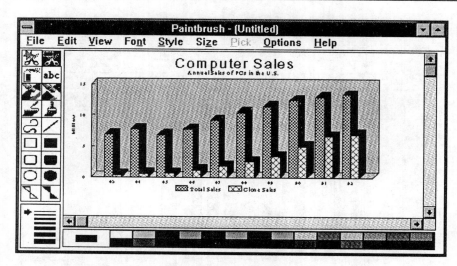

Figure 10-109 A 1-2-3 graph pasted into Paintbrush

When you use Edit Copy and Edit Paste to transfer a bitmap image of a 1-2-3 graph to another Windows application, the image is static. It is no longer linked to 1-2-3 for Windows in any way. If you have another Windows application that supports Dynamic Data Exchange (DDE), however, you may be able to create a link between that application and a 1-2-3 for Windows graph. That way, the graph will be displayed in the application's work area, but will still be linked to 1-2-3. When you change the numbers on which the graph is based from within 1-2-3, the graph in other application will be automatically updated. (For a complete discussion of how to use DDE, see Chapter 17.)

11

Database Management

Traditionally, database management has been one of the weakest areas in 1-2-3. Over the years, however, Lotus has gradually improved this area to make it more powerful. For example, you can now use 1-2-3 to manage a database table that is located either within a 1-2-3 worksheet or within a file created by another software program, such as Paradox or dBASE IV. Database files located outside 1-2-3 are referred to as *external* database tables.

To access information contained in external database tables from within 1-2-3 for Windows, Lotus has developed a system of drivers (software programs) called Datalens drivers. 1-2-3 for Windows comes with three such drivers, each supporting a different database management program—dBASE IV, Paradox, or SQL Server. The dBASE IV and Paradox drivers allow 1-2-3 to access information only in database tables created by either dBASE IV or Paradox, respectively; the host database management program is not involved. The SQL Server driver, on the other hand, is capable of interacting directly with the SQL Server engine itself. Therefore the capabilities of this driver exceed those of the Paradox and dBASE IV drivers. You'll find a detailed discussion of how to work with data in external database tables toward the end of this chapter under "Querying External Database Tables."

The equivalent for the Data command on the 1-2-3 Classic menu is /Data.
To manage a database table that is either internal or external to 1-2-3, you use the Data command. This command lets you search for and manipulate information in a database table and arrange its information in a more meaningful way. The following is a preview of the Data commands that will be discussed in this chapter:

- Data Sort: Sorts columns of data in worksheets in a specified order.

- Data Query: Locates and manipulates data in 1-2-3 database tables or in external database tables.

543

- Data Connect to External: Connects an external database table to 1-2-3 so that information can be exchanged between that table and your worksheet.

- Data External Options: Lets you create external tables, see what fields are included in an external table, send commands to an external database table, and disconnect from an external table.

DATABASE BASICS

A database provides a structured environment for the storage and retrieval of information. In 1-2-3, a database is a collection of one or more database tables. Each contains related information organized into columns and rows. Figure 11-1 shows a small section taken from an employee database table. This table will be used throughout this chapter to demonstrate 1-2-3's database management capabilities, and will be referred to simply as the EMPBASE table.

Each row in a database table constitutes a *record*. A record contains all the necessary information about a particular item in the database table. For example, in Figure 11-1 the first record in the database is located in the range A:A2..A:F2. It describes employee number 1239, named Suzanne Piper, hired 02/01/92, earning $30,000, and working in the Accounting department.

Each column in a database table constitutes a *field*. A field contains a specific type of information for each record. For example, in Figure 11-1, the first field is located in column A; it contains employee identification numbers for each record. The second field, located in column B, contains the first name of each employee, and so on. Each field in a database table must contain a single data type—either all labels, all numbers, all date values, and so on.

At the top of each field is a *field name*. The field name is a label that identifies the contents of each field. For example, the name of the first field in the database table in Figure 11-1 is ID. The second field is named FIRSTNAME, the third LASTNAME, and so on. 1-2-3 uses these field names when searching for information in a database table. The following rules apply to field names:

- Field names must be located at the top of the column of data to which they correspond. Further, there can be no blank cells between the field names and the first record in the database table.

- Field names must be labels. You cannot use a number or formula as a field name, unless you precede it with a label prefix (', ", or ^).

- Field names in a database table must be unique. If two field names are the same, 1-2-3 will not know which field name to use when searching the database and will issue an error message.

Each database table must be confined to a single worksheet. Therefore, the size of a database table is limited by the size of your worksheet. As you know, each worksheet

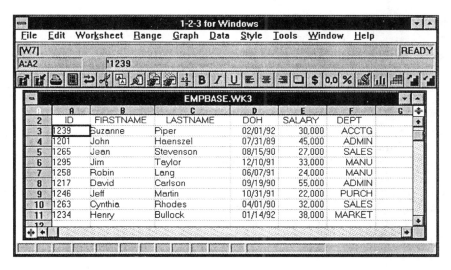

Figure 11-1 A sample database

can have 8,192 rows and 256 columns. Therefore, the maximum number of records you can have in a database table is 8,191 (8,192 less one row for the field names), and the maximum number of fields you can have in the table is 256. More often, though, the size of a 1-2-3 database table is limited by the memory available in your computer, rather than by the size of a 1-2-3 worksheet.

CREATING A DATABASE TABLE

This section shows you how to set up a 1-2-3 database table. It begins with a brief overview of database design considerations. It then shows you how to enter records in a database table, format its appearance, and edit selected records.

Designing a Database

Each database table you create should be geared to a specific purpose; that is, a particular report or function. Before creating a database table, consider how you will actually use the information in the table.

For example, consider the case of an employee database. Most likely, you will need information for paychecks, mailings, benefits, and so on. Rather than try to fulfill all these requirements with one huge database, it is to your advantage to break up the information into smaller database tables, each geared to a specific purpose. Because 1-2-3 is a relational database management system, you can relate the tables to one another and simultaneously search all of them for the information you need. For example, you might have one database table containing strictly payroll data, another containing addresses, and another benefits information. That way, each database table is a smaller, more manageable unit, and you will not be forced to view unrelated information when paging through the records in the table.

As you design your database, consider including a field in each table that uniquely identifies each record. In database parlance, this is referred to as a *key* field. For example, building on the employee database example, you can give each employee a unique number. That way, if two employees have the same name, you will still be able to accurately locate the record for a particular employee.

You can also use a key field to match records across two or more database tables. Imagine once again that you have an employee database composed of three tables, one for payroll, one for addresses, and one for benefits, each located in a separate worksheet. Imagine further that each table has a key field containing a unique number that identifies each employee's record in that table. Using this key field, you can, in effect, join all three tables together and search all three at the same time to locate information about a given employee.

If you elect to use one large database table instead of a series of smaller ones, you can group the fields you use most frequently at the beginning of the table. Grouping related information in adjacent fields will cut down on your having to scroll to the right or left when viewing the database.

Choosing a Location for the Database

You can locate a database table just about anywhere you'd like. In Figure 11-1, the first cell (upper-left corner) of the database table begins in cell A:A1, but it could just as easily begin in cell A:F100. You can also have several database tables in the same worksheet or individual database tables located in different worksheets in the same file. You can even locate different tables associated with the same database in different worksheet files; it's up to you.

If you create a database composed of multiple tables, the worksheet files containing those tables must be open in order to search them simultaneously. See "Querying Multiple Database Tables" later for details on how to query multiple database tables at the same time.

Entering Data

To enter data in a database table, begin by locating the cell pointer in the upper-left corner of where you want the table to begin. In the first row of the table, type in the field names in adjacent cells. For example, the field names in Figure 11-1 appear in the range A:A1..A:F1. To add the first record to the table, move the cell pointer to the first cell in the first row immediately below the row of field names (Cell A:A2 in Figure 11-1) and start typing the data for the record. To do this, simply type the information for each field in a row of adjacent cells, moving from left to right. When you complete the first record, move on to the second one, and so on, until you complete entering the initial set of records.

You can enter virtually anything you like in a database field, including numbers, text, @functions, or formulas. For example, to enter a date you might use the @DATE function. Or, to calculate the contents of a given field in a record, you might use a formula that refers to other cells in that same record or to cells outside the database table.

> ▼ **Tip:** You can also add records to an existing database table by using the Data Query Modify Insert command. This command allows you to copy records from a selected range and append them to the end of a database table. See "Adding Records" later in this chapter under "Using the Data Query Commands" for more details on this. You can also use the {FORM} and {APPENDBELOW} macro commands to create a custom form for entering data records and appending those records to a database table. See Chapter 15, "The Macro Programming Language," for more on these macro commands.

Caution: Placing formulas or @functions in a field of a database table may cause problems. Later under "Modifying Records" you'll learn how to use the Data Query Modify command to copy records to an output range, modify them, and then copy them back to their original locations. When 1-2-3 copies formulas to the output range for this command, it copies the current values of those formulas, not the formulas themselves. Therefore, when the records are copied back to their original locations in the database table, your formulas will be replaced with values. In addition, you may experience problems when sorting a database table that contains formulas. See "The Effect of Sorting on Formulas" later in this chapter under "Sorting a Database" for additional details.

Formatting the Database

Once you've entered the initial set of records for a database table, you may want to format it. The database in Figure 11-1 has been formatted in the following way:

- The Style Alignment Center command was used to center the field names in the range A:A1..A:F1.
- The Worksheet Column Width command was used to set the width of column A to seven characters, column B to 12 characters, and column C to 12 characters.
- The Range Format Date 4 command was used to display the date values in column D in Long Intl Date format.
- The Range Format , (Comma) 0 command was used to display the values in column E in Comma format with 0 places displayed after the decimal.
- The Style Alignment Right command was used to right-align the labels in column F.

Editing Records

You edit the cells in a 1-2-3 database table in the same way you edit the cells in any other area of the worksheet. For example, to edit the contents of a given cell, move the cell pointer to that cell and press EDIT (F2) to place its contents in the Edit Line. Then, edit the entry as necessary. When you're ready, press ENTER to confirm your changes.

To insert a record into the middle of a database, use the Worksheet Insert Row command to create a blank row where you want the new record to appear. Complete the job by typing in the information for each field in the new record.

Note: As an alternative to using the Worksheet Insert Row command to insert a record into a database, you can add the record to the end of the database and use the Data Sort command to sort it into position. See "Sorting a Database" in the next section for more details.

To delete records from a database table, you can use the Worksheet Delete Row command. To do this, move the cell pointer to the row that contains the record you want to delete. Then select the Worksheet Delete Row command and press ENTER. 1-2-3 deletes the row you've selected. The records located below this row are shifted upward to close up the space.

Note: Instead of using Worksheet Delete Row to delete a database record, you can use the Data Query Delete command (see "Deleting Records" later). The advantage to using the Data Query Delete command is that you can delete one or more records from the database table without removing entire rows, possibly wreaking havoc elsewhere in the worksheet. Data Query Delete also lets you delete records that meet specific criteria. Thus, instead of paging through the database looking for the records you want to delete, you can let 1-2-3 do the work.

To add a new field to the database, you can use the Worksheet Insert Column command. To do this, locate the cell pointer one column to the right of where you'd like the new field inserted. Then, select the Worksheet Insert Column command and press ENTER. 1-2-3 inserts a new column to the left of the cell pointer. To finish the job, enter a new field name in the cell that is adjacent to the other field names in the database. Beneath that field name, enter the new data for each record in the database table.

SORTING A DATABASE

The equivalent for the Data Sort command on the 1-2-3 Classic menu is /Data Sort.

You can sort the records in a database table by using the Data Sort command. This command allows you to rearrange records in a database table based on the contents of one or more of its fields. For instance, you might want to sort the records in the EMPBASE table shown earlier in Figure 11-1 by last name. That way, you can easily scan records in the table and quickly find the record for a particular employee.

Data Sort Basics

When you select the Data Sort command, 1-2-3 displays the dialog box in Figure 11-2. This dialog box allows you to select the range of database records you want to sort as

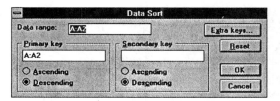

Figure 11-2 The Data Sort dialog box

well as one or more fields on which you want to sort those records. It also allows you to specify the order of the sort; you can choose from either descending or ascending.

Note: Although this section discusses the Data Sort command in the context of sorting records in a database table, you can also use the Data Sort command to sort adjacent columns of data in any 1-2-3 worksheet.

Use the "Data range" text box at the top of the Data Sort dialog box to specify the range of records you want to sort. You can specify a range that includes all the records in a database table, or just some of them. When you specify a range to sort, make sure that it does *not* include the field names at the top of the database table. Otherwise, when the sort is completed those field names may end up in the body of the database, thereby obscuring its structure. For example, to sort all the records in the EMPBASE table shown earlier in Figure 11-1, you would specify the range A:A2..A:F10 (or its range name).

You can select the range of records you want to sort either before or during the Data Sort command. If you select the range before, the Data range text box displays this range when you select the Data Sort command.

Note: When selecting a sort range, make sure you select all the fields that are included in each record you want to sort. Otherwise, when you later sort the database, 1-2-3 will only sort those fields included in the sort range, leaving the remaining fields unsorted. The result is a mismatching of fields from record to record. If this happens, select Edit Undo (or press ALT-BACKSPACE) immediately to have 1-2-3 reverse the Data Sort command. Provided the undo feature is not disabled, 1-2-3 will restore the database table to its previous order.

Once you've selected a range to sort, you're ready to select one or more fields on which you want to sort the database table. 1-2-3 allows you to select up to 255 fields on which to sort a database table. To select the fields on which to sort the database, you have the following options:

- Primary key: Specifies the field that receives the first order of precedence in the sort. In the text box provided, enter a single cell address or range name from the column that contains the field you want to use as the primary sort field.

- Secondary key: Specifies the field that receives the second order of precedence in the sort. In the text box provided, enter a single cell address or range name from the column that contains the field you want to use as the secondary sort field.

- Extra keys: Gives you access to a dialog box that lets you specify up to 253 additional sort fields beyond the primary and secondary sort fields. See "Sorting on More than Two Fields" later for more details.

You can also choose an ascending or descending sort order for each key field. For the primary and secondary key fields, you use the Ascending and Descending radio buttons in the appropriate section of the Data Sort dialog box (Figure 11-2). If you choose Descending (the default), the contents of the key field and the corresponding records in the database will be sorted from highest to lowest (Z to A and 9 to 0). On the other hand, if you choose ascending, the records in the database will be sorted from lowest to highest (A to Z and 0 through 9). You can also specify an ascending or descending sort for each extra key field (see "Sorting on More Than Two Fields" later).

To perform the sort, just select the OK button from the Data Sort dialog box. 1-2-3 will sort the contents of the sort range according to the settings you made in the Data Sort dialog box.

Sorting on a Single Field

This section shows how to sort the EMPBASE table shown in Figure 11-1 in ascending order using a single field. The field used to perform the sort will be the LASTNAME field (column C of Figure 11-1), which contains the last names of employees included in the EMPBASE table. When the sort is completed, the records in the EMPBASE table will be arranged in order by last name, as shown in Figure 11-3.

To sort the records in the EMPBASE table by last name, begin by selecting the Data Sort command. 1-2-3 displays the Data Sort dialog box. In the Data range text box, specify

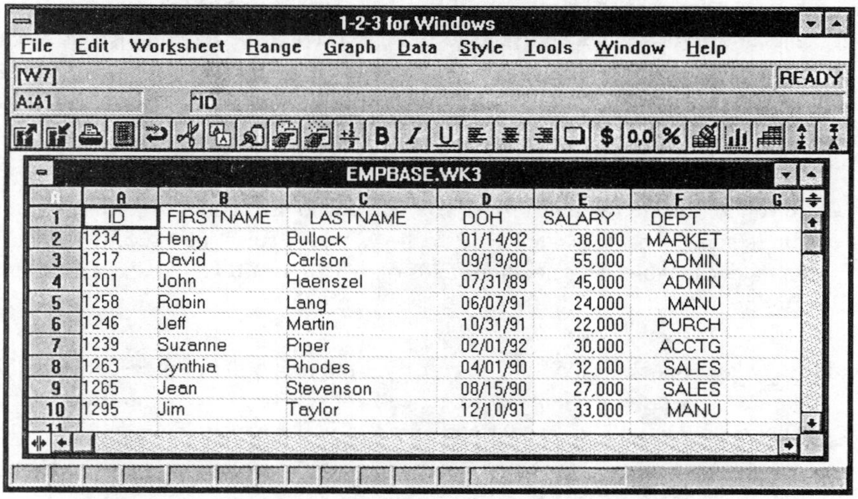

A	B	C	D	E	F
ID	FIRSTNAME	LASTNAME	DOH	SALARY	DEPT
1234	Henry	Bullock	01/14/92	38,000	MARKET
1217	David	Carlson	09/19/90	55,000	ADMIN
1201	John	Haenszel	07/31/89	45,000	ADMIN
1258	Robin	Lang	06/07/91	24,000	MANU
1246	Jeff	Martin	10/31/91	22,000	PURCH
1239	Suzanne	Piper	02/01/92	30,000	ACCTG
1263	Cynthia	Rhodes	04/01/90	32,000	SALES
1265	Jean	Stevenson	08/15/90	27,000	SALES
1295	Jim	Taylor	12/10/91	33,000	MANU

Figure 11-3 The EMPBASE table sorted by last name

the range A:A2..A:F10 (or its range name). Notice that this range includes all the records in the EMPBASE table, but not its field names.

To select a primary sort field, click on the Primary key text box or press TAB to move to it. In that box, specify a single-cell range (or range name) from column C (the LASTNAME field) of the EMPBASE table.

To specify an ascending order for the sort, click on the Ascending button in the Primary key section of the Data Sort dialog box. Alternatively, you can press ALT+A to select this button.

To complete the Data Sort command, select the OK button. 1-2-3 sorts the records in the EMPBASE table based on the contents of the last name field. The records now appear in ascending order by last name, as shown in Figure 11-3.

Note: 1-2-3 for Windows offers two Smart Icons, ⬆ and ⬇ , that allow you to quickly sort a database on a single field in either ascending or descending order using the current column as the primary key.

The Effect of Sorting on Formulas

Sorting records whose fields contain formulas or @functions may cause those formulas or @functions to return invalid results. In fact, if you anticipate sorting a database that contains formulas or @functions, keep the following two rules of thumb in mind:

- If the formula refers to data in the same record, use a relative reference.

- If the formula refers to data located outside the database, use an absolute reference.

When you sort a database table, 1-2-3 rearranges its records based on the contents of one or more of its fields. Thus, your formulas may be moved to new cell locations. Accordingly, 1-2-3 adjusts the cell references for those formulas to reflect their new locations relative to cell A1.

If the formula refers to data in the same record, the referenced data will move along with the record, and your formula will continue to return a valid result. If the formula refers to cells *outside* the database table, it may no longer refer to the appropriate range of cells. To solve this problem, use an absolute reference in the formula. That way, you can rest assured that the formula will always reference the correct range and return a valid result. (For more on absolute references, see Chapter 7.)

Sorting on Two Fields

In this section, you'll sort the EMPBASE table in ascending order by department and then by last name within each department. To do this, you'll select both a primary and a secondary sort field for the Data Sort command. The primary field will be the DEPT field (column F of Figure 11-3) and the secondary field will be LASTNAME (column C of Figure 11-3). When the sort is completed, your screen should look like Figure 11-4.

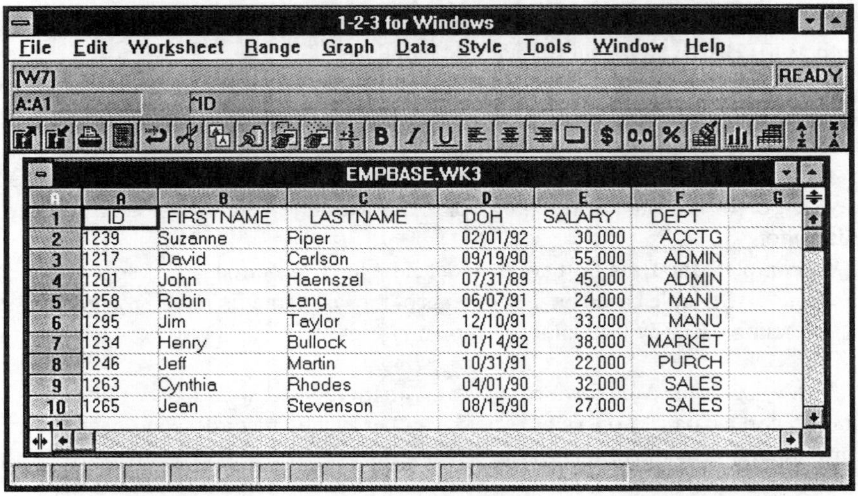

Figure 11-4   The EMPBASE table sorted by department and last names

In preparation for the Data Sort command, select the range A:A2..A:F10. When you're ready, select the Data Sort command. 1-2-3 displays the Data Sort dialog box with the range A:A2..A:F10 already displayed in the Data range text box.

To specify a primary sort field, press TAB to move to the Primary key text box, if it is not already highlighted, and specify the address or range name of any cell in the DEPT field (column F of Figure 11-3). To specify an ascending sort order for this field, select the Ascending button.

To specify a secondary sort field, activate the Secondary key text box and specify the address or range name of a single cell from the LASTNAME field (column C of Figure 11-3). Next, specify an ascending sort order for this field as well by selecting the Ascending button immediately below.

To perform the sort, select OK from the Data Sort dialog box. 1-2-3 sorts the EMPBASE table by department and by last name within those departments. Your screen should now look like Figure 11-4.

Sorting on More Than Two Fields

As mentioned, 1-2-3 allows you to specify up to 255 fields on which to sort a database. To specify additional fields beyond the primary and secondary fields, you use the Extra keys button in the Data Sort dialog box.

The following example illustrates how to use the Extra option button to sort the EMPBASE table in Figure 11-4 in ascending order using three fields. It will be sorted first by department, then by date of hire within each department, and finally by salary. When the sort is complete, the EMPBASE table will appear as in Figure 11-5.

In this example, the DEPT field (column F of Figure 11-4) will be the primary sort field. The DOH field (column D) will be the secondary sort field, and the SALARY field

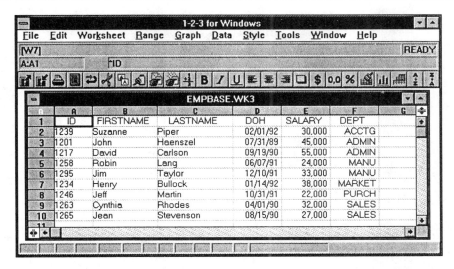

Figure 11-5 The EMPBASE table sorted by department, date of hire, and salary

(column E) will be the third sort field. To set up this configuration, perform the following steps:

1. Before issuing the Data Sort command, select the range A:A2..A:F10. When you're ready, select the Data Sort command. 1-2-3 displays the Data Sort dialog box with this sort range already displayed in the Data range text box.

2. Activate the Primary key text box and specify the address or range name of any cell from the DEPT field (column F) of the EMPBASE table—for example A:F2. Specify an ascending order for this field by selecting the Ascending button immediately below.

3. Activate the Secondary key text box and specify the address or range name of any cell in the DOH (Date of Hire) field (column D) of the EMPBASE table—for example A:D2. Specify an ascending order for this field by selecting the Ascending option button below.

4. Select the Extra keys button. 1-2-3 displays the dialog box in Figure 11-6.

5. Activate the Key range text box and specify a single-cell address or range name from the SALARY field (column E) of the EMPBASE table—for example, A:E2. Specify an ascending sort order for this field as well by selecting the Ascending radio button.

6. Select the Accept button to confirm your selection and add it to the list of extra sort keys. 1-2-3 adds the listing **1 A:E2 A** to the list box. The 1 indicates this is the first extra sort field, A:E2 is the address of the cell you selected, and the final A stands for ascending order.

7. Select OK to return to the Data Sort dialog box.

8. To perform the sort, select OK. 1-2-3 sorts the EMPBASE table as shown in Figure 11-5.

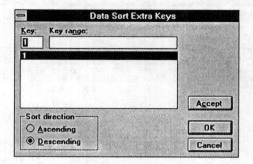

Figure 11-6 The Data Sort Extra Keys dialog box

In the preceding example, the Data Sort Extra Keys dialog box was used to specify a single extra sort field. As mentioned, you can specify up to 253 extra sort fields. To do this, specify a range in the Key range text box, specify a sort order (Ascending or Descending), and then select the Accept button to add it to the list box of extra sort keys. 1-2-3 keeps track of each new extra sort key you add and numbers them accordingly. The number assigned determines the field's order of precedence when the sort is performed.

You can also remove extra sort keys, although the procedure for doing so is somewhat unwieldy. To remove an extra sort key, you must assign that key to a range already in use by another extra-sort key; 1-2-3 will ignore the duplication when you perform the sort. For example, suppose you have three extra sort keys and you want to remove the third one. To do this, select the Extra keys button from the Data Sort dialog box to display the Data Sort Extra Keys dialog box. Next, type the number of the sort key you want to remove in the Key text box. 1-2-3 displays the range assigned to that key in the Key range text box. Modify this range to match that of another extra-sort key, then select Accept to confirm the change. Finally, select OK to return to the Data Sort dialog box.

Editing Sort Ranges

As you've probably noticed, 1-2-3 remembers the ranges you've set for the Data Sort command. In fact, 1-2-3 shows you those same ranges each time you enter the command. However, you can easily change the current range settings for the Data Sort command. To change the range specification in the Data range text box, simply click on the box, or press TAB to activate it, and specify a new range address or name.

To change a primary or secondary sort field specification, select either the Primary or Secondary key text boxes and specify a new range address or range name. You can also choose from the Ascending or Descending radio buttons to change the order of the sort for either field.

To change an extra sort field, select the Extra keys button from the Data Sort dialog box. 1-2-3 displays the Data Sort Extra Keys dialog box (Figure 11-6). Select the listing that corresponds to the extra field that you want to change. 1-2-3 updates the Key range text box accordingly. Specify the new range you want to use for the current sort key in the Key range text box and then select either Ascending or Descending from the Sort direction group box. Finally, select the Accept button to update the list of extra keys for the change.

To reset all ranges for the Data Sort command, select the Reset button from the Data Sort dialog box. 1-2-3 deletes all data range and sort field settings from the Data Sort dialog box.

Undoing a Bad Sort

Even the most careful user will occasionally perform a bad sort, so it's always a good idea to save the current worksheet file before using the Data Sort command.

You can, of course, reverse the effects of the Data Sort command by selecting Edit Undo (or by pressing ALT+BACKSPACE) immediately afterward. This causes 1-2-3 to read the undo history buffer and restore the worksheet to the way it was before the Data Sort command. In some cases, though, 1-2-3 may not have access to sufficient memory to restore the worksheet.

When you execute a command that 1-2-3 can undo, it records changes to the affected portion of the worksheet in an undo history buffer. If during the command, 1-2-3 does not have access to sufficient memory to record all changes, it deletes the contents of the history buffer in order to complete the command. Therefore, if you are performing a very large sort, 1-2-3 may not be able to undo it. (When this happens, 1-2-3 will issue an error message informing you that the current command cannot be undone.) In addition, many users prefer to disable undo because of the extra memory this releases for ordinary 1-2-3 operations.

Because you cannot always depend on undo, you may want to use another method of protecting your data from the Data Sort command. This involves creating an original record field before sorting the database table. An original record field is simply a column of sequential numbers, one for each record in the table. To create this field, you can use the Data Fill command (see Chapter 12) to fill an adjacent column with sequential values. When you later sort the database table, make sure this original record field is included in your sort range. Then, should something go awry, you can easily restore the database to its former order by sorting the database again using the original record field as your primary-key field.

Choosing a New Sort Sequence

You can change the collating sequence used by 1-2-3 to sort your data. In fact, 1-2-3 offers three different sort sequences from which you can choose: Numbers First (the default), Numbers Last, and ASCII.

The Numbers First sequence is the default sort order for 1-2-3. Assuming you sort in an ascending sort order, the Numbers First sequence sorts your data in the following order:

1. Blank cells.
2. Labels beginning with numbers from lowest to highest.
3. Labels beginning with letters from A to Z. Capitalization is ignored.

556 LeBlonds' 1-2-3 for Windows Handbook

4. Labels beginning with pure nonalphanumeric symbols sorted in Lotus Multibyte Character Set (LMBCS) order.

5. Numbers.

The Numbers Last sort sequence is similar to Numbers First. However, labels composed of all letters are sorted before labels containing numbers. In particular, the Numbers Last sequence sorts your data in the following way:

1. Blank cells.

2. Labels beginning with letters from A to Z. Capitalization is ignored.

3. Labels beginning with numbers from lowest to highest.

4. Labels beginning with pure nonalphanumeric symbols sorted in Lotus Multibyte Character Set (LMBCS) order.

5. Numbers.

The ASCII sort sequence sorts your data on the basis of each character's ASCII value, which means that uppercase letters will be sorted before lowercase letters. The ASCII sequence sorts data in the following order:

1. Blank cells.

2. All labels, using their ASCII values. Capitalization is honored.

3. Numbers.

To change the current collating sequence, you must use 1-2-3's Install program. To do this, quit 1-2-3 and start Install by using its icon located in your Lotus Applications window. When you double-click on this icon, Install opens a window with three different icons, one of which is labeled Choose international options. When you double-click on this icon, Install displays a dialog box containing an extensive list of collating sequences supported by 1-2-3 for Windows. In addition to the US ASCII, US Numbers Last, and Us Numbers First options, you'll find similar options for International, Nordic, Portuguese, Swedish, Group 2, and Group 3. Select the sort option you want from this list. To save the setting for future 1-2-3 sessions, select OK. The next time you start 1-2-3, it will use the collating sequence you've specified.

QUERYING A DATABASE

The 1-2-3 Classic equivalent for the Data Query command is /Data Query.

To query a database table, you use the Data Query command. This command allows you to perform the following operations with a database table:

- Locate records that meet specific criteria (Data Query Find).

- Copy all records that meet specific criteria to a new location (Data Query Extract).

- Copy only unique records that meet specific criteria to a new location (Data Query Unique).

- Delete records that meet specific criteria (Data Query Delete).

- Modify records that meet specific criteria (Data Query Modify).

- Append records to a database table (Data Query Modify Insert).

Data Query Basics

When you select the Data Query command, 1-2-3 displays the dialog box in Figure 11-7. At the left of this dialog box are three text boxes labeled Input range, Criteria range, and Output range. These text boxes allow you to specify the input, criteria, and output ranges used by the Data Query command. The buttons to the right allow you to specify the type of data query operation you want to perform.

The input range is the range address or range name that contains the database table you want to search. The criteria range is the range address or range name that contains the selection criteria that will be used to locate records in the database table. All Data Query commands require both an input range and a criteria range specification. The output range, on the other hand, is a range address or range name location to which records from the database table will be copied. Specifying an output range is only necessary when you use the Extract button to extract (copy) records from the database table. The records extracted are chosen based on the selection criteria in the criteria range.

Since this all might seem a bit confusing, the sections that follow will discuss the use of the input, criteria, and output ranges in greater detail. In addition, a short example follows that shows you how to extract records that meet specific criteria.

Input Range

As mentioned, the input range is a range name or address that defines the database table you want to search. This range includes the records you want to search as well as the *field names* at the top of the database table. As you'll soon see, 1-2-3 uses these field names to locate specific records in the database table. For example, to specify the EMPBASE table in Figure 11-8 as an input range for the Data Query command, you would use the

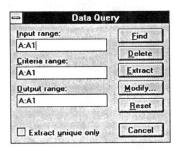

Figure 11-7 The Data Query dialog box

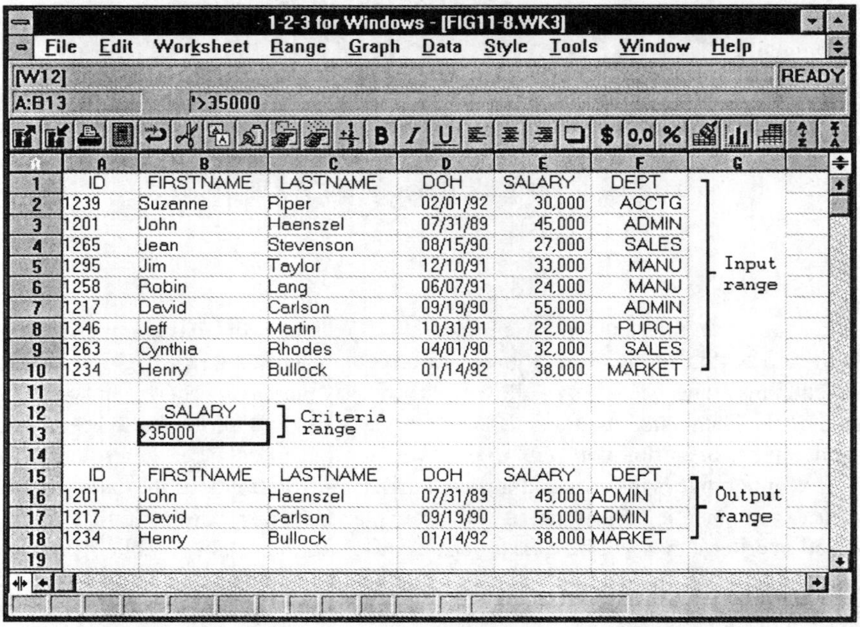

Figure 11-8 Extracting records from the EMPBASE table

input range specification A:A1..A:F10, or its corresponding range name, in the Input range text box of the Data Query dialog box.

The input range can be located in a worksheet in the current file, another open file, or in a file on disk. To specify an input range in another open file or in a file on disk, use a file reference enclosed in double angle brackets << >> followed by a range address or a range name from that file. For example, to use the range A:A1..A:H100 from a file named SALES.WK3 located in a directory called MARKET as an input range, specify the following in the Input text box:

```
<<C:\MARKET\SALES.WK3>>A:A1..A:H100
```

You can also specify multiple input ranges for the Data Query command. That way, 1-2-3 will search multiple database tables at the same time to find the information you want. To specify multiple input ranges in the Input text box, include the range address or range name of each table separated by commas, for example A:A1..A:F10,B:A1..B:F10. For more on using multiple input ranges with the Data Query command, see "Querying Multiple Database Tables" later in this chapter.

You can also use an external database table as an input range for the Data Query command. External database tables are created by software programs other than 1-2-3, such as dBASE IV or Paradox. To do this, you must first connect to the external table and assign it a 1-2-3 range name by using the Data External command. This command lets you activate a specific Datalens driver that allows 1-2-3 to access the external table.

For more on using external database tables, see "Querying External Database Tables" later in this chapter.

Criteria Range

The criteria range is a range address or range name that contains the selection criteria that will be used to locate records in the input range (database table). You must enter your selection criteria in the worksheet before you select the Data Query command. Once the criteria range is prepared, you may select the Data Query command and specify the criteria range address or name in the Criteria range text box.

The criteria range can be located in any open worksheet file and must contain at least two vertically adjacent cells. However, as you'll soon see, the criteria range can be multiple columns wide and multiple rows deep. In the top row of the criteria range are field names that match those in the input range. In one or more rows immediately beneath these field names are labels, values, or formulas that define search conditions for each field name.

In Figure 11-8, the contents of the criteria range used to search the EMPBASE table appear in the range A:B12..A:B13 as follows:

```
SALARY
'>35000
```

This tells 1-2-3 to search the SALARY field of the EMPBASE table to find all those records with a value greater than $35,000 in the SALARY field.

The selection criteria just shown are relatively simple. You can, of course, specify more complex criteria for selecting records from a 1-2-3 database table. An entire section, "Defining Criteria," devoted solely to the topic appears later in this chapter.

Caution: If you leave the criteria range blank, 1-2-3 automatically selects all the records in the input range when you execute a Data Query command. For example, if the criteria range contains only field names with nothing beneath them, 1-2-3 will select all records in the input range. You can, however, leave blank rows in the criteria range. If at least one row contains a valid search argument, 1-2-3 will honor that search argument and ignore any blank rows. On the other hand, if there are no valid search arguments and you leave a row blank, all the records in the input range will be selected.

Output Range

Defining an output range is necessary only when you want to extract (copy) selected records from the input range (database table) to another location in the worksheet. The output range simply defines the location to which those records are copied. Like the input and criteria ranges, you must prepare the output range before selecting the Data Query command. Once the output range is prepared, you can select the Data Query command and specify its location in the Output range text box.

The top row of the output range contains one or more field names that correspond to those in the input range. (A sample output range appears in the range A:A15..A:F15 of

Figure 11-8.) When data is copied from the input range, it appears in the rows immediately below this first row of field names.

The order of field names in the first row of the output range determines the order in which information is copied from the input range. You can place the field names in the output range in any order you want.

You don't have to use all the field names from the input range; you can use as many or as few as you need. When 1-2-3 copies data from the input range, it will do so only for those fields that are included in the output range.

At a minimum, the output range specification must consist of a row of field names. This is referred to as a single-row output range. You can, however, specify a multiple-row output range, if you so desire. A multiple-row output range includes the first row of field names as well as additional rows underneath.

You should specify a single-row output range when you're not sure how many records will meet your search criteria. That way, 1-2-3 will copy all the records it finds to the output range, regardless of how many there are. During the process, 1-2-3 will erase the contents of all cells beneath the first row of field names and the bottom of the worksheet. Therefore, if you specify a single-row output range, make sure you do not have any important data located beneath the first row of field names and the bottom of the worksheet.

Specifying a multiple-row output range lets you control the size of the output range. With a multiple-row output range, 1-2-3 only uses the number of rows you specified when data was copied from the input range. Data beneath the output range, however, are not affected. If 1-2-3 finds more records in the input range than there are rows in the output range, it displays an error message. This is 1-2-3's way of informing you that you need to expand the size of the output range to accommodate all the records it found.

Note: You cannot specify the same range as both an input and an output range.

Extracting Records: An Example

The following example shows you how to use the Data Query command to copy selected records from the EMPBASE table to an output range. Only those records with a value greater than $35,000 in the SALARY field of the EMPBASE table will be copied. When the data query is completed, your screen should look like Figure 11-8. To execute this data query, perform the following steps:

1. Make sure the EMPBASE table shown in Figure 11-8 is present on your screen.

2. Move the cell pointer to cell A:E1 (the cell containing the SALARY field name) and select the Edit Quick Copy command. 1-2-3 displays the Edit Quick Copy dialog box with A:E1..A:E1 on the From text box. Press TAB to move to the To text box, type **A:B12**, and press ENTER to complete the command. 1-2-3 copies the label SALARY from cell A:E1 to A:B12.

3. Press HOME to move the cell pointer to cell A:A1, press F4 to anchor it, and highlight the range A:A1..A:F1. Next, select the Edit Quick Copy command again. 1-2-3 displays the Copy dialog box with A:A1..A:F1 in the From text box. Press TAB to move to the To text box, type **A:A15**, and press ENTER to complete the command. 1-2-3 copies the field names in row 1 to row 15.

4. Move the cell pointer to cell A:B13 (beneath the SALARY field name) and enter the label **'>35000**.

5. Select the Data Query command. 1-2-3 displays the Data Query dialog box (Figure 11-7).

6. In the Input range text box, specify the range A:A1..A:F10. Notice that this range includes all the records in the EMPBASE table as well as its field names.

7. In the Criteria range text box, specify the range A:B12..A:B13. Notice that this range includes both the field name SALARY as well as the search argument '>35000. Thus, 1-2-3 will search for records with a value greater than $35,000 in the SALARY field of the EMPBASE table.

8. In the Output range text box, specify the range A:A15..A:F15. Notice that this single-row output range includes all the field names from the EMPBASE table, and that they appear in the same order. Therefore, all the fields from the appropriate records will be copied and the order of the fields will be the same as the EMPBASE table.

9. Select the Extract button located on the right side of the Data Query dialog box. 1-2-3 copies those records in the input range that meet the criteria in the criteria range to the output range. Your screen should look like Figure 11-8.

10. Select the Cancel button to leave the Data Query dialog box and return to the current worksheet.

1-2-3 remembers the ranges you've set for the Data Query command, and will show those same ranges in the Data Query dialog box the next time you enter the command. To change an individual input, criteria, or output range specification, select the appropriate text box and specify a new range address or range name. You can also cancel all Data Query ranges by selecting the Reset button from the Data Query dialog box.

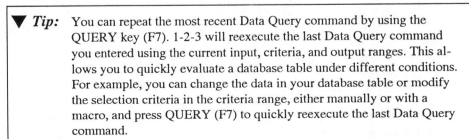

▼ *Tip:*   You can repeat the most recent Data Query command by using the QUERY key (F7). 1-2-3 will reexecute the last Data Query command you entered using the current input, criteria, and output ranges. This allows you to quickly evaluate a database table under different conditions. For example, you can change the data in your database table or modify the selection criteria in the criteria range, either manually or with a macro, and press QUERY (F7) to quickly reexecute the last Data Query command.

Defining Criteria

This section discusses the various types of selection criteria that you can define in the criteria range. As mentioned, 1-2-3 uses the selection criteria you specify in the criteria range to select records for the Data Query commands. You must prepare the criteria range in advance and then use the Data Query Criteria command to point to the range that contains those criteria.

At a minimum, each criteria you specify must be composed of two elements—a field name from the input range and a search argument. A field name appears in the first row of the criteria range and determines which field in the input range (database table) will be searched. The search argument, on the other hand, appears beneath the field name to which it corresponds and states a condition that must be met for a record to be selected. When you execute a Data Query command, 1-2-3 scans the fields in the input range referenced by the field names in the criteria range. Only those records that meet the search argument beneath these field names are selected.

You can have up to 32 field names in the first row of the criteria range. That way, you can designate criteria based on values from multiple fields in a database table at the same time. When you use multiple field names, however, you must locate each of them in adjacent cells in a single row. See "Defining Multiple Criteria" later for more details.

You can use various types of search arguments in the criteria range. For example, you can specify labels or values that exactly match an entry in a given field. If 1-2-3 finds that label or value, it selects the record that contains it. You can also use comparison formulas as search arguments in the criteria range. Comparison formulas are useful for selecting groups of records. For example, you can create a formula that causes 1-2-3 to select a record only when the value in a given field exceeds 35,000. The sections that follow show you how to create each of these search argument types.

Note: This section and the next, "Defining Multiple Criteria," are quite lengthy. If at any time you feel you are getting the hang of how to create selection criteria and want to try it out, feel free to jump forward to "Using the Data Query Commands."

Using Label Criteria

Figure 11-9 shows an example of how you might use label criteria to search a database table. In this case, the criteria range is A:B12..A:B13. A single field, DEPT, appears in the first row of this criteria range. Note that this field name matches the DEPT field name in the EMPBASE table. The DEPT field contains the name of the department in which each employee works. In the second row of the criteria range, A:B13, the label ADMIN appears. When this data query is performed, 1-2-3 will search the DEPT field in the EMPBASE table and select those records that contain the label ADMIN in the DEPT field.

The results of using this criteria with the Data Query Extract command are shown beneath the output range A:A15..A:F15. Notice that only two records have been selected, indicating that there are two records in the EMPBASE table that contain the label ADMIN in the DEPT field.

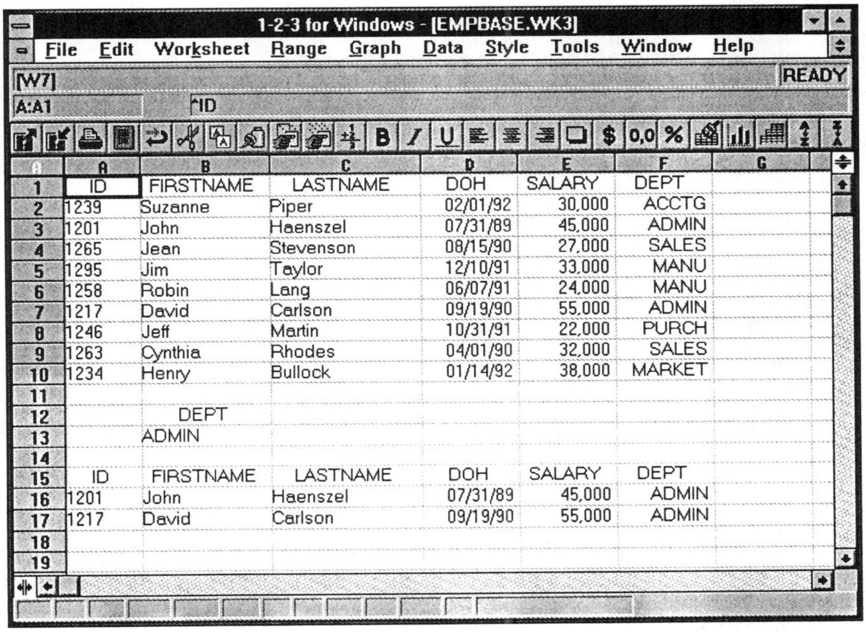

	A	B	C	D	E	F	G
1	ID	FIRSTNAME	LASTNAME	DOH	SALARY	DEPT	
2	1239	Suzanne	Piper	02/01/92	30,000	ACCTG	
3	1201	John	Haenszel	07/31/89	45,000	ADMIN	
4	1265	Jean	Stevenson	08/15/90	27,000	SALES	
5	1295	Jim	Taylor	12/10/91	33,000	MANU	
6	1258	Robin	Lang	06/07/91	24,000	MANU	
7	1217	David	Carlson	09/19/90	55,000	ADMIN	
8	1246	Jeff	Martin	10/31/91	22,000	PURCH	
9	1263	Cynthia	Rhodes	04/01/90	32,000	SALES	
10	1234	Henry	Bullock	01/14/92	38,000	MARKET	
11							
12		DEPT					
13		ADMIN					
14							
15	ID	FIRSTNAME	LASTNAME	DOH	SALARY	DEPT	
16	1201	John	Haenszel	07/31/89	45,000	ADMIN	
17	1217	David	Carlson	09/19/90	55,000	ADMIN	
18							
19							

Figure 11-9 Using a label to query a database table

To perform this data query, begin by setting up the criteria and output ranges as you see them in Figure 11-9. When you're ready, select the Data Query command. 1-2-3 displays the Data Query dialog box. In the Input range text box, specify the range A:A1..A:F10, which includes all the records in the EMPBASE table and its field names. In the Criteria text box, specify the range A:B12..A:B13, which includes the DEPT field name as well as the search argument ADMIN. In the Output text box, specify the range A:A15..A:F15, which includes the row of field names in row 15. Finally, select the Extract button. 1-2-3 copies the selected records from the EMPBASE table to the output range. To return to the worksheet, select the Cancel button.

Normally, 1-2-3 is not case sensitive when searching database fields for labels. For instance, in the previous example, the label search argument ADMIN will locate records with ADMIN, Admin, or admin in the DEPT field. If case sensitivity in label searches is important to you, there are two things you can do. First, you can use the @EXACT function in your criteria range search argument. To find records with the label Admin, but not ADMIN or admin, in the previous example, you can use the formula @EXACT(+F2, "Admin"). See Chapter 6, "Functions," for more details on the @EXACT function.

Alternatively, you can select the ASCII sort sequence. To do this, you must use 1-2-3's Install program (see "Choosing a New Sort Sequence" earlier). With this sort sequence, 1-2-3 interprets labels on the basis of each letter's ASCII value. Because each uppercase letter has a different ASCII value than its lowercase counterpart, 1-2-3 honors capitalization when scanning labels.

Using Wild Cards

You can use wild-card characters in place of letters in label search arguments. Wild-card characters serve as place holders for one or more letters in a label and serve to represent any letter. 1-2-3 offers the following wild-card characters:

?   Takes the place of any single letter.

*   Takes the place of all letters to the end of a label.

Imagine that you'd like to search the EMPBASE table for Jean Stevenson's record, but you can't remember whether the last name is spelled Stevenson or Stevensen. To find this record, you can use the label search argument Stevens?n beneath the field name LASTNAME. When this data query is executed, 1-2-3 will select records with either Stevenson or Stevensen in the LASTNAME field.

Figure 11-10 shows an example of how you might use the * wild-card character in a label search argument in the criteria range. Once again, the criteria range is A:B12..A:B13. In the top row of this range is the label DEPT, representing the DEPT field in the EMPBASE table. Beneath this field name, the label **a*** appears. When this data query is processed, 1-2-3 selects all records whose labels in the DEPT field begin with the letter a or A. The results of this data query are shown in the output range A:A15..A:F18.

As with DOS, you cannot use the * wild-card character to represent any group of letters. For example, you cannot use the search argument b*ger to find the labels Berger or Burger. Unfortunately, once 1-2-3 encounters the * wild-card character, it ignores all other characters to the end of the label.

Negating Labels

You can also precede a label search argument with a ~ (tilde) to exclude records with that label from being selected. For example, imagine you want to select all records from the EMPBASE table except those with Bullock in the LASTNAME field. To do this, you can specify the following criteria:

```
LASTNAME
~Bullock
```

You can also combine this negation symbol with a wild-card character. For example, to select all records from the EMPBASE table except those that begin with the letter B in the LASTNAME field, you can specify the following criteria:

```
LASTNAME
~b*
```

Value Criteria

1-2-3 also allows you to use values as search arguments to select records from database table. For example, Figure 11-11 shows a data query that uses a value as a search argument

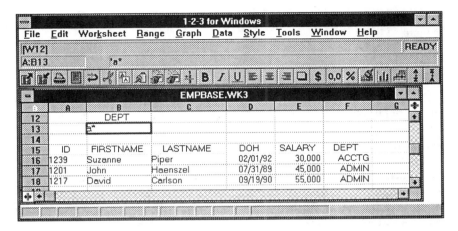

Figure 11-10 Using wild cards to query a database table

in the Criteria range. In that figure, the criteria range is A:B12..A:B13. In the top row of this criteria range the label SALARY appears, representing the SALARY field, which contains the annual salary earned by each employee in the EMPBASE table. In the second row of the criteria range, cell A:B13, the value 32000 appears. When this data query is processed, 1-2-3 will select only those records with 32,000 in the SALARY field.

The results of using these criteria with the Data Query Extract command are shown in the output range A:A15..A:F16 of Figure 11-11. Notice that only a single record has been selected, indicating that only one record in the EMPBASE table has the value 32,000 in the SALARY field.

You can also use date or time values to search for records. For example, using the EMPBASE table again, imagine you want to locate the records of all employees hired

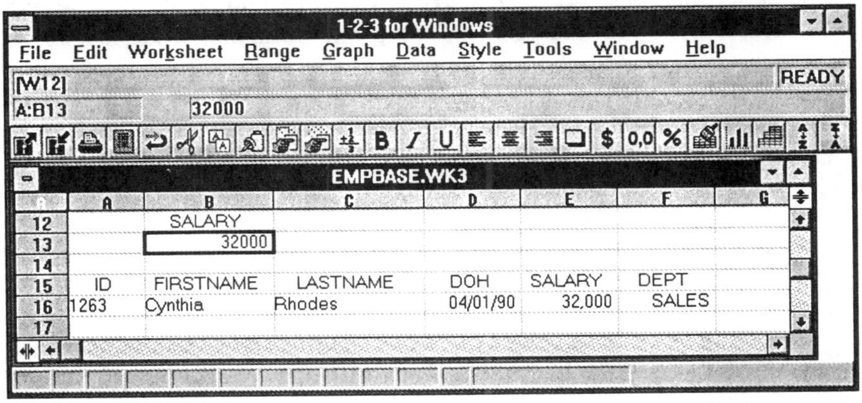

Figure 11-11 Using a value to query a database table

on 02/01/92. To do this, enter the following criteria in the criteria range A:B12..A:B13 of Figure 11-11:

```
DOH
@DATE(92,2,1)
```

The DOH field name refers to the DOH (Date of Hire) field in the EMPBASE table. The @DATE(92,2,1) function beneath this field name causes 1-2-3 to calculate the date value for 02/01/90, which is 33635. However, if you attempt to use a Data Query command at this point, 1-2-3 will issue an error message. To perform the data query, you must first transform the @DATE function to its current value. You can do this with the Edit Quick Copy command (/Range Value in the Classic menu). Simply highlight the cell containing the @DATE function and select Edit Quick Copy. 1-2-3 displays the Edit Quick copy dialog box. Select the Convert to values check box and then select OK. You can now perform the data query.

Comparison Formulas

You can also use comparison formulas in the criteria range. Comparison formulas allow you to select records when the value in a given field falls within a certain range. For example, using the EMPBASE table, you might want to select the records of those employees whose salaries exceed $35,000.

Comparison formulas contain three basic components as follows:

- A reference to the first data cell in a field of the input range

- An operator

- A value for comparison

Figure 11-12 shows the comparison formula +E2>35000 beneath the field name SALARY in the criteria range A:B12..A:B13. Breaking this formula down, the +E2 is a reference to the first data cell in the SALARY field of the EMPBASE table (A:A1..A:F10). The > symbol is a logical operator meaning greater than. Finally, the 35000 is the value used for comparison. When 1-2-3 processes this data query, it reviews each value in the SALARY field of the EMPBASE table. Those records with values in excess of $35,000 in this field are selected.

The results of the data query in Figure 11-12 are shown in the output range A:A15..A:F18. Notice that three records have been selected, indicating that three employees included in the EMPBASE table earn in excess of $35,000.

The greater than (>) logical operator shown in the previous example is only one of the available operators that you can use in a comparison formula. Table 11-1 shows a complete list of the logical operators you can use in a comparison formula.

The comparison formula in cell A:B13 of Figure 11-12 has been formatted with the Range Format Text command so that you can see it. Normally, when you enter a comparison formula, 1-2-3 displays a 0 or 1 in the cell. That's because comparison formulas perform a logical test that is either true (1) or false (0). For example, when you

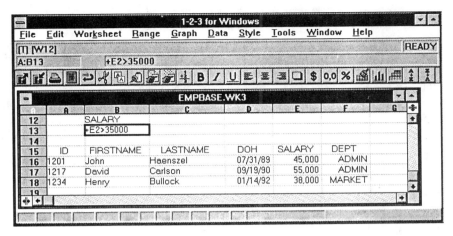

Figure 11-12 Using a comparison formula to search a database table

first enter the formula +E2>35000 in cell A:B13 of Figure 11-12, 1-2-3 displays 0, because the contents of cell A:E2 (30,000) when compared to the value 35,000 returns false.

Because comparison formulas include a reference to the first data cell of a field in the input range, you can locate them under any field name in the criteria range. Imagine in Figure 11-12 that there are several field names in the first row of the criteria range (row 12). You can locate the formula +E2>35000 under any field name and 1-2-3 will still process the data query correctly.

You can also leave out the input-range reference in a comparison formula. For example, instead of using the formula +E2>35000 in cell A:B13 of Figure 11-12, you can enter the label '>35000. This label search argument must appear under the field name to which it corresponds, in this case SALARY. Otherwise, you may not get the results you expect.

You can also use a label as a comparison value in a comparison formula. However, make sure you enclose the label in quotation marks. Otherwise, 1-2-3 will issue an error message. For example, imagine you'd like to extract the records of employees in the

TABLE 11-1 1-2-3's Logical Operators

Operator	Meaning	Operator	Meaning
=	Equals	>=	Greater than or equal to
< >	Not equal	#NOT#	Logical NOT
<	Less than	#OR#	Logical OR
>	Greater than	#AND#	Logical AND
<=	Less than or equal to		

EMPBASE table whose last names are between L and Z. To do this, you can use the formula +C2> "K*" in cell A:B13 of Figure 11-12. The +C2 in this formula references the LASTNAME field in the EMPBASE table. Once again, the logical operator > is used to specify a greater than test. Finally, the letter K appears followed by the * wild-card character. When this data query is processed, 1-2-3 will select the records of those employees whose last names start with a letter that comes after the letter K.

If you do not use an input-range reference in a comparison formula, you do not have to enclose labels in quotes. For example, building on the example in the previous paragraph, you can use the following criteria in the range A:B12..A:B13 of Figure 11-12:

```
LASTNAME
'>K*
```

In this case, the LASTNAME field name refers to the LASTNAME field in the input range (EMPBASE table). When 1-2-3 encounters an operator as the first character in the label '>K* below, it automatically substitutes the input-range reference for you.

> ▼ *Tip:*   Name the first data cell in each field. Use the Range Name Label Create Down command to name the first data cell in each field of the input range (database table) by using the field names in the first row. In that way, you can substitute range names in place of cell addresses in your comparison formulas, making them appear more intelligible. For example, instead of the formula +E2>35000 in cell A:B13 of Figure 11-12, you can use the formula +SALARY>35000.

Defining Multiple Criteria

The data query examples thus far in this chapter all use a single criterion to select records from a database table, but 1-2-3 also allows you to define multiple criteria to select records. For example, using the EMPBASE table, imagine you'd like to select the records of those employees who were hired after 01/01/91 and who make more than $30,000. That is, for a record to be selected, both the first *and* second conditions must be true. Or imagine you'd like to see the records of those employees who work either in Sales or in Manufacturing. In this case, either one *or* the other condition must be true for the record to be selected.

As mentioned, you can include more than one field name in the first row of the criteria range with a search argument beneath each one.

The "AND" Query

When search arguments appear in the same row of the criteria range, there is an implied "AND" relationship between them. That is, the conditions defined by all the search arguments in that row must be met for a record to be selected from the input range.

Figure 11-13 shows two field names in the criteria range with a search argument beneath each one. The first field name, DOH, appears in cell A:B12. Beneath this field

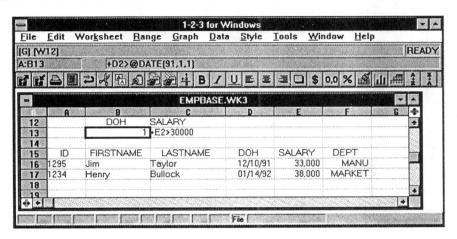

Figure 11-13 Multiple search arguments in the same row

name, the comparison formula +D2>@DATE(91,1,1) instructs 1-2-3 to select records with a date value after 01/01/91 in the DOH (Date of Hire) field of the EMPBASE table. The second field name, SALARY, appears in cell A:C12 of Figure 11-13. Beneath this field name, the comparison formula +E2>30000 instructs 1-2-3 to select all records with a value greater than $30,000 in the SALARY field. Since both search arguments appear in the same row of the criteria range, both must be met for a record to be selected from the EMPBASE table.

To process this data query, begin by setting up the criteria and output ranges as they appear in Figure 11-13. When you're ready, select the Data Query command. 1-2-3 displays the Data Query dialog box. In the Input range text box, specify the range A:A1..A:F10 which includes the EMPBASE table. In the Criteria text box, specify the range A:B12..A:C13, which includes both field names and their search arguments. In the Output range text box, specify the single-row output range A:A15..A:F15, which includes the field names in row 15. Finally, select the Extract button. 1-2-3 extracts those records from the EMPBASE table with a date value after 01/01/91 in the DOH field and a value greater than $30,000 in the SALARY field.

The "OR" Query

You can also have more than one row of search arguments in the criteria range. When search arguments appear in different rows of the criteria range, there is an implied "OR" relationship between them. That is, 1-2-3 selects records when either one *or* the other condition is true.

For example, Figure 11-14 shows a single field name in the criteria range A:B12..A:B14 with two search arguments in different rows immediately beneath it. The field name, DEPT, appears in cell A:B12. Beneath this field name, the label SALES appears in cell A:B13 and the label MANU appears in cell A:B14. When this data query

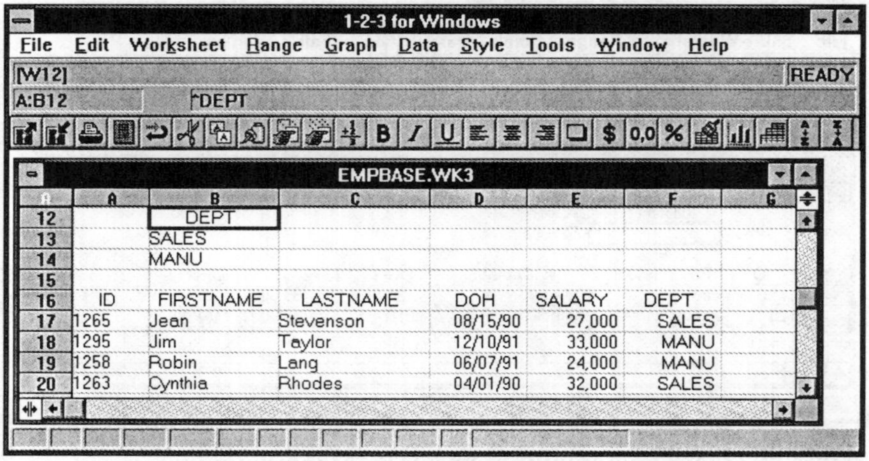

Figure 11-14 Multiple search arguments in different rows

is processed, 1-2-3 will select those records from the EMPBASE table with either the label SALES or the label MANU in the DEPT field.

The results of using these selection criteria with the Data Query Extract command data are shown in the range A:A16..A:F20 of Figure 11-14. Notice that only those records from the EMPBASE table with SALES or MANU in the DEPT field have been selected.

Combining "AND" and "OR" Queries

You can also combine "AND" and "OR" relationships in the criteria range. For example, Figure 11-15 shows three field names in the criteria range A:A12..A:C14 with multiple search arguments located in the two rows beneath each field name. The field names in the top row of the criteria range are DOH, SALARY, and DEPT. Beneath the DOH and SALARY field names, the same search arguments appear in both rows. However, in the two rows beneath the DEPT field name, the search arguments differ. 1-2-3 will select records from the EMPBASE table, either when all the arguments in the first row are true or when all the arguments in the second row are true.

The criteria range in Figure 11-15 breaks down as follows. Beneath the DOH field name (cell A:B14), the argument +D2>@DATE(91,1,1) appears in rows 13 and 14. This causes 1-2-3 to select records when the DOH field in the EMPBASE table contains a date value after 01/01/91. Beneath the SALARY field name (cell A:B12), the argument '>30000 appears in rows 13 and 14, causing 1-2-3 to select records with a value greater than $30,000 in the SALARY field of the EMPBASE table. Finally, different labels appear in rows 13 and 14 beneath the DEPT field name (cell A:C12). Row 13 contains the label SALES and row 14 contains the label MANU. When this data query is processed, 1-2-3 will select records with either the label SALES or the label MANU in the DEPT field. For a record to be selected from the EMPBASE table, however, it must also contain a value greater than $30,000 in the SALARY field and a date value after 01/01/91 in the

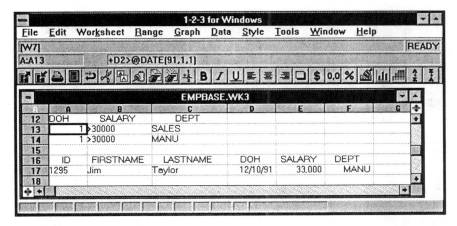

Figure 11-15 Combining "AND" and "OR" queries

DOH field. As you can see, only one record in the EMPBASE table meets this stringent criteria.

The #AND#, #OR#, and #NOT# Logical Operators

You can also use the #AND#, #OR#, and #NOT# logical operators to combine search arguments in the criteria range. When you use the #AND# operator to combine two search arguments, both arguments must be met for a record to be selected. When you use the #OR# logical operator to combine search arguments, 1-2-3 will select a record when either one or the other argument is met. Finally, the #NOT# operator allows you to exclude a search argument. That is, all records will be selected except those that meet the search argument.

Figure 11-16 illustrates how you might use the #AND# operator in the criteria range to query the EMPBASE table. The criteria range in Figure 11-16 is A:B12..A:B13. In the first row of this range, the field name DOH appears, which corresponds to the DOH (Date of Hire) field in the EMPBASE table. In the second row of this range, the following search argument appears:

```
+D2>=@DATE(91,1,1)#AND#D2<=@DATE(91,12,31)
```

The first half of the search argument, before the #AND# operator, selects all records from the EMPBASE table with a date value greater than or equal to 01/01/91. The second part of this search argument, after the #AND# operator, selects all records with a date value in the DOH field that is less than or equal to 12/31/91. The #AND# operator in effect joins the two conditions, and both must be met before a record is selected. Therefore, when this data query is processed, 1-2-3 will select the records of those employees hired between 01/01/91 and 12/31/91. The results of this data query are shown in the output range A:A15..A:F18 of Figure 11-16.

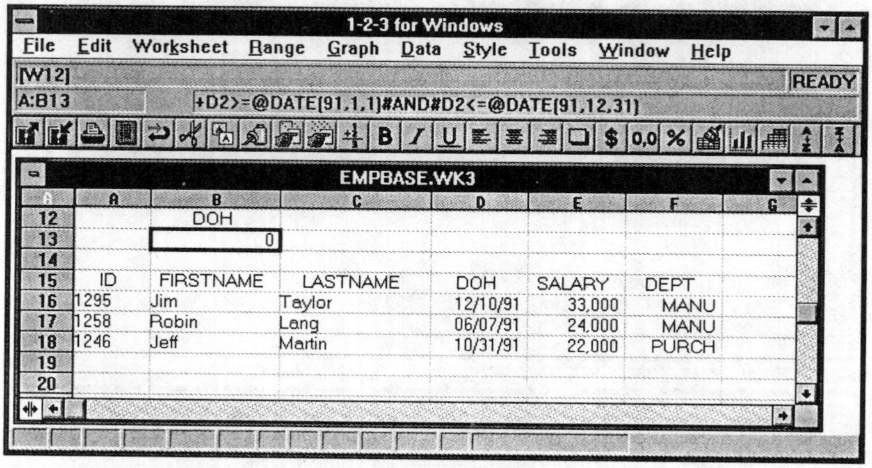

Figure 11-16 Using the #AND# logical operator

Figure 11-17 shows an example of how you might use the #OR# operator in the criteria range to query the EMPBASE table. The criteria range in this figure is A:B12..A:B13. The first row of this range contains the field name DEPT, corresponding to the DEPT field (column F) in the EMPBASE table. Beneath this field name appears the search argument +F2="SALES"#OR#F2="MANU". The first half of this search argument, before the #OR# operator, selects all records with the label SALES in the DEPT field. The second half, after the #OR# argument, selects all records with the label MANU in

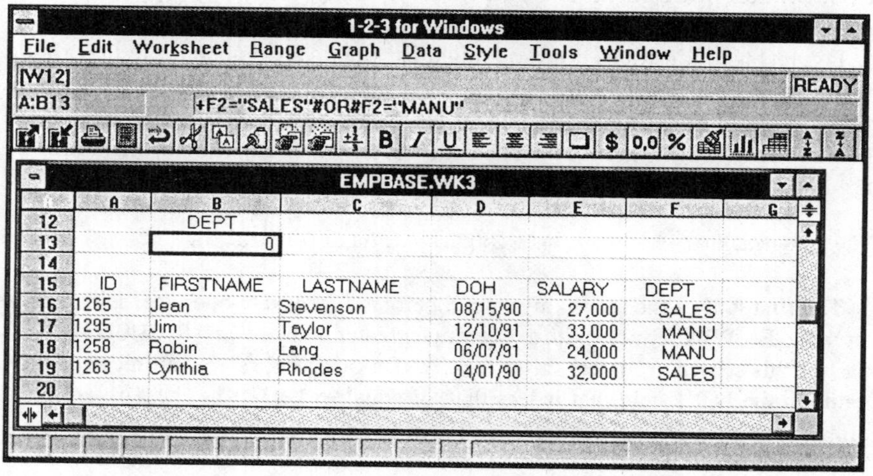

Figure 11-17 Using the "OR" logical operator

the DEPT field. In this case, the #OR# operator joins the two conditions so that a record will be selected when either one of the conditions is true. The results of this data query are shown in the output range A:A15..A:F19 of Figure 11-17.

The #NOT# logical operator allows you to select all records except those that meet a specific condition. For example, imagine you want to select all records from the EMPBASE table except those with the label MANU in the DEPT field. To do this, you can use the search argument #NOT#F2="MANU" in the cell A:B13 of the criteria range (A:B12..A:B13) of Figure 11-17. When this data query is processed, 1-2-3 will select all the records in the EMPBASE table except those with the label MANU in the DEPT field.

Using the Data Query Commands

In the preceding sections of this chapter, the Data Query Extract command was used to demonstrate how you can copy selected records from a database table to an output range. However, the Data Query Extract command is but one of the Data Query commands offered by 1-2-3. In addition, you can use the following Data Query commands to manage database tables:

- Data Query Find: Finds selected records in the input range that match the criteria in the criteria range.

- Data Query Extract (Extract unique only): Copies only unique records from the input range to the output range.

- Data Query Delete: Deletes selected records in the input range that match the criteria in the criteria range.

- Data Query Modify: Allows you to copy selected records to an output range, modify them, and then put them back where they came from. This command also allows you to append records from an output range to the end of a database table.

Each of these commands is covered in more detail in the sections that follow.

Finding Records

To search for specific records, you can use the Data Query Find command. This command allows you to locate records in the input range (database table) that match the criteria in the criteria range. When a matching record is found, 1-2-3 highlights that record. The Data Query Find command is useful when you want to find and edit specific records, or when you want to test the criteria in the criteria range prior to deleting or extracting records.

The Data Query Find command requires that you specify an input range and a criteria range. Since it is only used to locate specific records, an output range specification is not required.

Figure 11-18 shows an example of a record from the EMPBASE table that has been located and highlighted by using the Data Query Find command. Notice that all the fields

		1-2-3 for Windows						
File	Edit	Worksheet	Range	Graph	Data	Style	Tools	Window	Help

[W7]   FIND
A:A4   '1265

| | B | I | U | | | | | $ | 0,0 | % | | | | | |

	EMPBASE.WK3							
	A	B	C	D	E	F	G	
1	ID	FIRSTNAME	LASTNAME	DOH	SALARY	DEPT		
2	1239	Suzanne	Piper	02/01/92	30,000	ACCTG		
3	1201	John	Haenszel	07/31/89	45,000	ADMIN		
4	1265	Jean	Stevenson	08/15/90	27,000	SALES		
5	1295	Jim	Taylor	12/10/91	33,000	MANU		
6	1258	Robin	Lang	06/07/91	24,000	MANU		
7	1217	David	Carlson	09/19/90	55,000	ADMIN		
8	1246	Jeff	Martin	10/31/91	22,000	PURCH		
9	1263	Cynthia	Rhodes	04/01/90	32,000	SALES		
10	1234	Henry	Bullock	01/14/92	38,000	MARKET		
11								
12		DEPT						
13		SALES						

Figure 11-18 Using Data Query Find to locate specific records

in the record are highlighted. The input range specification for this data query is A:A1..A:F10, which includes all the records from the EMPBASE table and its field names. The criteria range is A:B12..A:B13, which includes the field name DEPT with the label SALES beneath it. Thus, when this data query is executed, 1-2-3 will locate all records in the EMPBASE table that have the label SALES in the DEPT field.

To execute the data query in Figure 11-18, select the Data Query command. 1-2-3 displays the Data Query dialog box. Use the Input range and Criteria range text boxes to specify the input and criteria ranges described in the previous paragraph. As mentioned, an output range is not required. Finally, select the Find button. 1-2-3 locates and highlights the first record in the EMPBASE table that has the label SALES in the DEPT field. In addition, a FIND indicator is displayed in the title bar of the worksheet window. Your screen should look similar to Figure 11-18.

If no matching records are found during the Data Query Find command, 1-2-3 beeps and returns you to the Data Query dialog box. Once a record has been successfully located, you can perform any of the following:

- Press → or ← to move among the fields in a highlighted record. The contents of the Edit Line will change to indicate which cell contains the cell pointer.

- Press EDIT (F2) to edit the contents of the current field in the current record. To confirm your changes, and continue with Data Query Find, press ENTER or click on the confirm (✔) button in the Edit Line. To cancel the edit and continue using Data Query Find, press ESC or click on the Cancel (X) button in the Edit Line.

- Press ↓ to see the next record in the input range that meets the criteria in the criteria range. Press ↑ to see the previous record.

- Press HOME to move to the first record in the input range that matches your selection criteria. Press END to move to the last record.

- Press ENTER, ESC, or QUERY (F7) to return to the Data Query dialog box.

Extracting Only Unique Records

To extract only unique records from a database table, use the Data Query Extract command and select the Extract unique only check box. This command lets you eliminate duplicates when extracting records from a database table. For example, imagine you are working with a customer mailing-list database table. Imagine further that the names and addresses of some customers are listed twice. To create a new database table that includes a single record for each customer, you can extract a single copy of each unique record to an output range.

Like the Data Query Extract command, the Data Query Extract's Extract unique only command requires that you specify an input range, a criteria range, and an output range.

The uniqueness of records is determined by the field names that are included in the output range for this command. That is, two records are only considered to be duplicates when both records have the same contents in each field included in the output range.

For example, the only field in the EMPBASE table in which information is repeated is the DEPT field. Otherwise, the information in the remaining fields varies from record to record. Therefore, there are no duplicate records in the EMPBASE table. However, Figure 11-19 shows what happens when you use DEPT as the only field in the output range with the Data Query Unique command. Note that only a single copy of each department name is copied to the output range. This is because the contents of the DEPT field alone were used as the basis for determining if there were duplicate records in the EMPBASE table.

To perform the data query in Figure 11-19, start by setting up the criteria and output ranges as they appear in Figure 11-19. For example, to set up the criteria range, enter the field name DEPT in cell A:B12, leaving cell A:B13 blank. 1-2-3 will then automatically select all the records in the input range. For the output range, enter the field name DEPT in cell A:B15. To execute the data query, select the Data Query command to display the Data Query dialog box. In the Input range text box, specify the range A:A1..A:F10, which includes the EMPBASE table. In the Criteria range text box, specify the range A:B12..A:B13. In the Output range text box, specify the range A:B15. Next, select the Extract unique only check box. Finally, select the Extract button. 1-2-3 searches the DEPT field of the EMPBASE table and extracts only the unique department names from each record in the table.

When you use the Extract Unique only option to copy unique records to an output range, 1-2-3 sorts those records in ascending order. For example, notice in the output range (A:B15..A:B22) of Figure 11-19, 1-2-3 displays the department names in alpha-

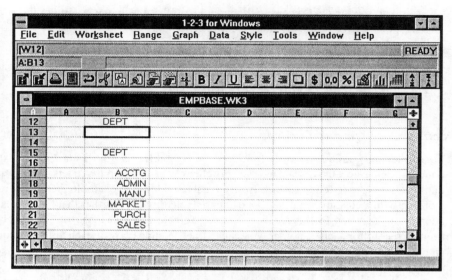

Figure 11-19 Extracting unique records from a database table

order. If you copy more than one field in each record to the output range, 1-2-3 uses the first field included in the output range to sort the records.

Deleting Records

To delete records that meet specific criteria, use the Data Query Delete command. When you execute this command, 1-2-3 deletes the records in the input range that match the criteria in the criteria range. The input range is then compressed to close up the space previously occupied by the deleted records. Because no records are extracted by Data Query Delete, you need only specify an input and criteria range for this command.

   Caution: It's always a good idea to use the Data Query Find command prior to Data Query Delete to make sure your criteria correctly selects the records you want to delete. Otherwise, you may lose important data. If you do accidentally delete records with Data Query Delete, select Edit Undo immediately (or press ALT-BACKSPACE) to reclaim the lost data.

   Suppose that an employee has left the company and you want to delete his or her record from the EMPBASE table. To do this, you might set up the data query shown in Figure 11-20. In the criteria range (A:B12..A:B13) of Figure 11-20 a single field name, ID, appears with the number 1234 beneath it. The ID field name corresponds to the ID (employee identification number) field in the EMPBASE table. The number beneath this field name belongs to Henry Bullock (row 10) in the EMPBASE table.

   To delete this record, select the Data Query command to display the Data Query dialog box. In the Input text box, specify the range A:A1..A:F10, which includes the EMPBASE table. In the Criteria text box, specify the range A:B12..A:B13. Then, select the Delete button. 1-2-3 displays a message box (also shown in Figure 11-20), asking you whether to "Delete matching records." If you select Delete, 1-2-3 deletes the record for Henry Bullock from the EMPBASE table and closes up the space previously occupied by the record. The size of the input range for the Data Query command is now reduced to A:A1..A:F9. On the other hand, if you select Cancel, 1-2-3 returns you to the Data Query dialog box.

Modifying Records

To modify records that meet specific criteria, use the Data Query Modify command. When you select this command, 1-2-3 displays the dialog box in Figure 11-21. The Extract button in this dialog allows you to copy records that meet specific criteria to an output range. When you extract records with this option, 1-2-3 remembers where it got the records. Once the records are copied to the output range, you can edit the contents of fields in those records as you like. After editing is complete, you can use the Replace button to put those records back in their original positions in the input range.

Because the Data Query Modify command extracts records from a database table, you'll need to specify an input, criteria, and output range for the command.

Imagine that an employee included in the EMPBASE table has been moved to a new department and been given a raise, and you want to modify the record for that employee. To do this, begin by setting up the criteria and output ranges, as shown in Figure 11-22. In that figure the criteria range is A:B12..A:B13. In that range, the field name ID appears in cell A:B12 with the label 1234 beneath it. When this data query is processed, 1-2-3 will search the ID field (column A) of the EMPBASE table to find the record with 1234

Figure 11-20 Deleting records from a database table

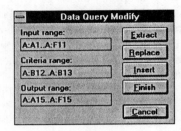

Figure 11-21 The Data Query Modify dialog box

in that field. The record selected will be that of Henry Bullock (row 10) of the EMPBASE table. Finally, the output range in Figure 11-22 is A:A15..A:F15 and includes all the field names from the EMPBASE table.

To modify one or more records, select the Data Query command. 1-2-3 displays the Data Query dialog box. In the Input range text box, specify the range A:A1..A:F10. In the Criteria range text box, specify the range, A:A12..A:A13. In the Output range text box, specify the range A:A15..A:F16. When you're ready, select the Modify button. 1-2-3 displays the Data Query Modify dialog box (Figure 11-21).

Select the Extract button from the Data Query Modify dialog box. 1-2-3 copies those records in the input range that meet the criteria in the criteria range to the output range. In this case, only a single record is copied. You are then returned to the Data Query dialog

	A	B	C	D	E	F	G
1	ID	FIRSTNAME	LASTNAME	DOH	SALARY	DEPT	
2	1239	Suzanne	Piper	02/01/92	30,000	ACCTG	
3	1201	John	Haenszel	07/31/89	45,000	ADMIN	
4	1265	Jean	Stevenson	08/15/90	27,000	SALES	
5	1295	Jim	Taylor	12/10/91	33,000	MANU	
6	1258	Robin	Lang	06/07/91	24,000	MANU	
7	1217	David	Carlson	09/19/90	55,000	ADMIN	
8	1246	Jeff	Martin	10/31/91	22,000	PURCH	
9	1263	Cynthia	Rhodes	04/01/90	32,000	SALES	
10	1234	Henry	Bullock	01/14/92	38,000	MARKET	
11							
12		ID					
13		1234					
14							
15	ID	FIRSTNAME	LASTNAME	DOH	SALARY	DEPT	
16	1234	Henry	Bullock	01/14/92	38,000	MARKET	

Figure 11-22 Modifying records in a database table

box. To edit that record, select the Cancel button. 1-2-3 returns you to the worksheet. You can now modify the record in output range as you like.

To return the modified record in the output range to the input range (database table), select the Data Query command. 1-2-3 displays the Data Query dialog box. Select the Modify button to display the Data Query Modify dialog box. This time, select the Replace button. 1-2-3 copies the record currently in the output range back to its original location in the input range.

The Finish button in the Data Query Modify dialog box lets you cancel the most recent Data Query Modify Extract operation. For example, suppose after selecting the Extract option from the Data Query Modify dialog box, you decide not to replace the records in the input range with the Replace option. In this case, select Finish. After selecting this button, 1-2-3 will not let you use the Replace option for those records currently in the output range.

Caution: When 1-2-3 copies formulas to the output range for the Data Query Modify command, it copies the current values of those formulas, not the formulas themselves. Therefore, when the records are copied back to their original locations in the database table with the Replace option, your formulas will be replaced with values.

Adding Records

You can use the Data Query Modify Insert command to append records to the end of a database table. This command copies records from an output range and adds them to the end of the input range. The input range is then expanded to accommodate the additional records. For this command, you need only specify an input range and an output range. A criteria range is not necessary.

Imagine you want to add a record to the end of the EMPBASE table. To do this, first set up your output range—that is, place the field names from the input range in a row of consecutive cells in the worksheet. Next, type in the appropriate data beneath each field name. To add those records to the EMPBASE table, begin by selecting the Data Query command. 1-2-3 displays the Data Query dialog box. In the Input range text box, specify the range A:A1..A:F10, which includes the EMPBASE table and its field names. In the Output text box, specify the range that contains the row of field names in the output range as well as the new records you want to append. When you are ready, select the Modify button. 1-2-3 displays the Data Query Modify dialog box. Select the Insert button. 1-2-3 appends the records in the output range to the end of the input range and expands the input range specification accordingly.

Caution: Be careful not to locate the output or criteria ranges for the Data Query Modify Insert command below the input range. When 1-2-3 copies records from the output range to the input range, it erases the contents of as many cells below the input range as is necessary to accommodate the new records added to the database table.

Creating Computed Columns in the Output Range

Computed columns allow you to perform calculations in the output range using information extracted from a database table. To create computed columns in the output range,

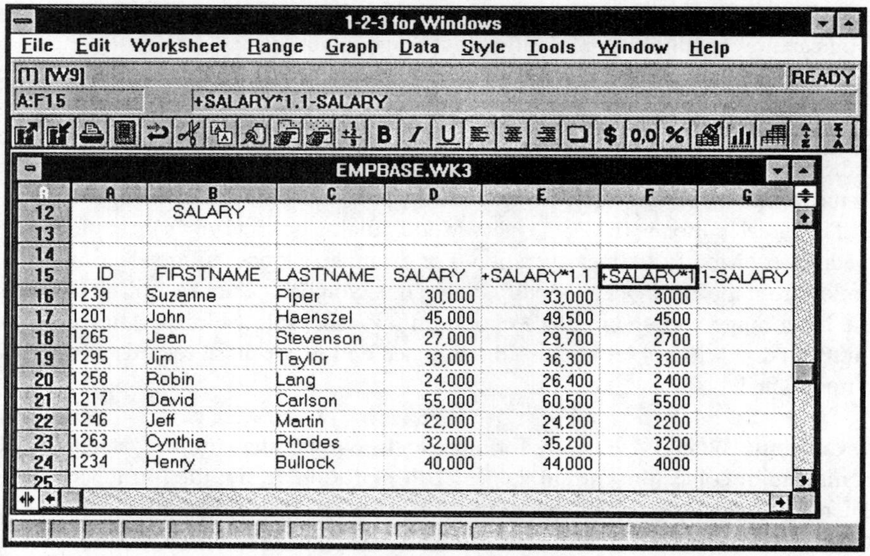

Figure 11-23 Creating computed columns in the output range

use formulas in the first row of the output range instead of field names. For example, suppose you want to evaluate the impact of giving every employee in the EMPBASE table a 10% raise next year. To do this, you can use formulas in the output range, as shown in Figure 11-23.

The output range in Figure 11-23, which starts in row 15, was generated by using the Data Query Extract command with the criteria in the range A:B12..A:B13. (This criteria selects all the records from the EMPBASE table.) The first four cells of this output range (A:A15..A:D15) contain field names from the EMPBASE table. However, cells A:E15 and A:F15 contain formulas that create computed data in the output range. For example, cell A:D15 contains the formula +SALARY*1.1. The output in the column beneath this formula is computed by multiplying the data from the SALARY field of the EMPBASE table by 1.1 for those records that have been selected. Additionally, cell A:E15 contains the formula +SALARY*1.1-SALARY. The output beneath this formula is computed by multiplying the data in the SALARY field by 1.1 and then subtracting the contents of the SALARY field for those records that have been selected.

Note: The cells containing the formulas in the range A:E15..A:F15 of Figure 11-23 have been formatted with the Range Format Text command, so that you can see them. Otherwise, 1-2-3 displays ERR in the cell when you enter these formulas.

This example shows a single field name used in computed column formula. However, you can also use more than one field name reference in a computed column formula. For example, if you are working with a sales database table that includes fields for unit price, units sold, and sales tax, you can create a computed column that multiplies units sold by unit price and adds the sales tax.

Aggregate Columns in the Output Range

You can use selected @functions in place of field names in the output range to create aggregate columns. Aggregate columns are used to compute values for a group of related records. For example, if you want to calculate the total and average salaries paid to each department included in the EMPBASE table you can set up the data query shown in Figure 11-24.

Note: The output in Figure 11-24 was generated by using the Data Query Extract command with the criterion shown in the range A:B12..A:B13. This criterion has the effect of selecting all records from the EMPBASE table.

The output range in Figure 11-24 starts in row 15. The aggregate columns in this output range are columns C and D. The data in these aggregate columns are computed by using the formulas that appear in cells A:C15 and A:D15. These cells have been formatted with Range Format Text; otherwise the formulas in these cells would display as ERR.

The values computed by these aggregate column formulas are based on the field names that appear in the top row of the output range. As you can see in Figure 11-24, only the DEPT field name appears in cell A:B15. This field name has the effect of grouping the selected records based on the contents of the DEPT field of the EMPBASE table. As you know, the DEPT field of the EMPBASE table contains the name of the department in which each employee works.

The values in the aggregate columns are computed as follows. Cell A:C15 contains the formula @SUM(SALARY). This formula totals the values in the SALARY field of the EMPBASE table for each group of selected records. Cell A:D15, on the other hand, contains the formula @AVG(SALARY), which calculates an average of the SALARY field for each group of selected records. As mentioned, the grouping of the records selected is determined by the DEPT field name that appears in cell A:B15.

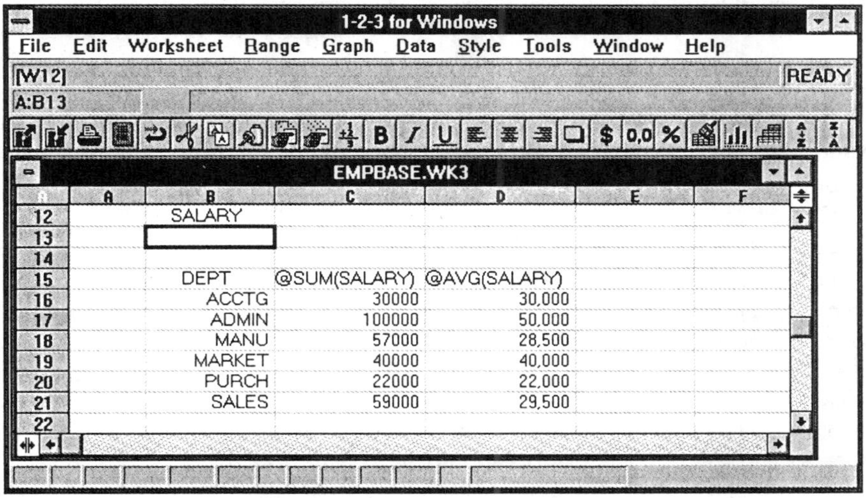

Figure 11-24 Creating aggregate columns in the output range

1-2-3 allows you to use the following @functions to create aggregate columns in the output range:

- @AVG   Takes an average for a group of values.
- @SUM   Sums a group of values.
- @COUNT   Provides a count of the number of values in a group.
- @MIN   Returns the smallest value in a group.
- @MAX   Returns the highest value in a group.

For more about these @functions, see Chapter 6, "Functions."

Querying Multiple Database Tables

1-2-3 also allows you to query multiple database tables at the same time. Before you can query multiple tables, however, you must first join the tables by using the contents of a key field that is common to all the tables. Then you must specify the range addresses or names of the tables as multiple input ranges for the Data Query command. In this fashion, 1-2-3 allows you to set up a semi-relational database system in which you can search for related records in two or more database tables at the same time.

Earlier in this chapter, it was recommended that when you design a database table, you include a key field. A key field allows you to uniquely identify each record in a database table. For example, in the EMPBASE table used throughout this chapter, the key field is the ID field. This field contains a unique number for each employee in the EMPBASE table. This number can be used to match records in the EMPBASE table to records in other tables.

For example, Figure 11-25 shows a companion table, ADDRESS (worksheet C), to the EMPBASE table (now in worksheet B). As you might imagine, the ADDRESS table contains the addresses of employees listed in the EMPBASE table. The ADDRESS database table has a key field, also named ID (column A), that corresponds to the ID field in the EMPBASE table (column A). Both fields use the same unique number to identify the record that belongs to each employee. Thus, the ID field can be used to match the record for an employee in the EMPBASE table to his or her associated record in the ADDRESS table.

To join two tables, a special formula, called a *join formula*, must be created in the criteria range. Join formulas allow you to match a record in one table to an associated record in another table. This is done by equating the contents of a key field in one table to the contents of a key field in another table. The two fields must contain the same type of data (label or value) and should contain the same information. For example, you might create a join formula that equates the contents of the ID fields in the EMPBASE and ADDRESS tables shown in Figure 11-25. See the next section entitled "Joining Tables" for more on how to create join formulas in the criteria range.

As mentioned, to query two database tables at the same time, you must specify the range addresses or names of each table as multiple input ranges for the Data Query

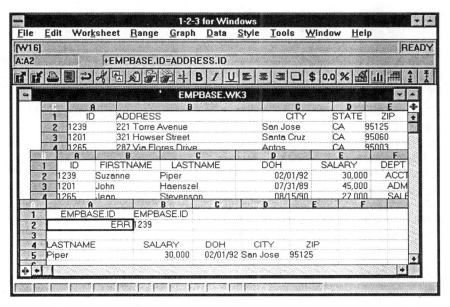

Figure 11-25 Querying multiple database tables

command. To do this, select the Data Query command to display the Data Query dialog box. In the Input range text box, specify the range addresses or range names of the tables you want to search, separated by commas.

Note: You cannot specify multiple input ranges for the Data Query Delete or the Data Query Modify commands.

Joining Tables

To query two related tables at the same time, you must, in effect, join the database tables. To do this, you must create a join formula in the criteria range. Join formulas equate the contents of a field in one table to a field in another table. That way, you can match a record in one table to an associated record in another table. Join formulas take the following form:

```
+field1=field2
```

where *field1* is a field name from the first table and *field2* is a field name from the second table.

If the field name you want to use is the same in both tables, you must use the Range Name Create command to assign each table a range name. That range name is then used in the join formula to identify the field for that table. In this case, the join formula takes the following form:

```
+range1.field1=range2.field2
```

where *range1* is the range name for the first table and *range2* is the range name for the second table. Notice that a period (.) is used to separate the table name and the field name.

Note: If you've used the Tools User Setup International Punctuation command to specify the period as the argument separator in macros and @Functions, make sure you use the comma (,) to separate table and field names in join formulas.

For example, suppose you want to link the EMPBASE and ADDRESS tables shown in worksheets B and C of Figure 11-25 on the ID field. To do this, use the Range Name Create command to assign the name EMPBASE to the range B:A1..B:F10 in worksheet B. Then use the same command to assign the name ADDRESS to the range C:A1..A:F10 in worksheet C.

Now that the two tables have been named, you're ready to create the criteria-range that will, in effect, join the two tables. To do this, begin by entering the field names at the top of the criteria range as shown in the range A:A1..A:B2 of Figure 11-25. For example, you'll note that in cell A:A1 the label EMPBASE.ID appears, referring to the ID field in the EMPBASE table. Below this, in Cell A:A2, enter the following join formula:

```
+EMPBASE.ID=ADDRESS.ID
```

When you enter this formula, 1-2-3 displays ERR in the cell, as shown in Figure 11-25. This has no bearing on the success or failure of your data query. If the ERR bothers you, use the Range Format Text command to format the display of the formula as text.

In the previous example, the key fields in both tables have the same name. Therefore, it is necessary to use a range name to correctly identify the table to which the field belongs. However, if the two field names are unique, the use of range names is not required. For example, to join two tables using the unique field names PART_NO and STOCK_NO, you can use the following formula:

```
+PART_NO=STOCK_NO
```

The same basic naming principles apply when setting up your criteria and output ranges for a multiple-table query. That is, if the field names are unique to both tables, you do not need to precede the field name with a range name. If the *same* field name occurs in both tables, you must precede it with a range name. For example, the field ID appears in both the EMPBASE and ADDRESS tables. To refer to the ID field in the EMPBASE table, you would use the field name EMPBASE.ID. Conversely, to refer to the ID field in the ADDRESS table, you would use the field name ADDRESS.ID. If you do not use this convention, you may get the error message "Ambiguous field reference in query" when you eventually execute the data query.

If two database tables from different files have the same range name, you can differentiate them by using their filenames enclosed in double-angle brackets followed by their respective range names. For example, suppose you've assigned the range name EMPBASE to tables in DIV1.WK3 and DIV2.WK3. Assume for the moment that both tables have a field named ID. To refer to the ID field in the EMPBASE table in the DIV1.WK3 file, you would use the following:

```
<<DIV1.WK3>>EMPBASE.ID
```

To join more than two tables for a data query, you must use two join formulas. You can locate these formulas in vertically adjacent cells in the criteria range. Alternatively, you can create a compound join formula by using the #AND# operator between two or more join formulas; for example:

```
+range1.field1=range2.field2#AND#range2,field2=range3.field3
```

Querying Multiple Tables: An Example

This section shows you how to set up the data query in Figure 11-25. Throughout this section, it is assumed that the EMPBASE table is located in worksheet B and the ADDRESS table is located in worksheet C of the active file.

The EMPBASE and ADDRESS tables have matching field names. Therefore, to be able to freely use these field names in your data query, you must assign a range name to both tables. You can do this by using the Range Name Create command to assign the name EMPBASE to the range B:A1..B:F10 and the name ADDRESS to the range C:A1..C:G10.

The next step is to set up your criteria range. In this example, the criteria range appears in worksheet A in the range A:A1..A:B2. In cell A:A1 of this range, the field name EMPBASE.ID is shown. The same field name appears in cell A:B1. In both cases, this field name refers to the ID field in the EMPBASE table. The EMPBASE range name is necessary here because both the EMPBASE and ADDRESS tables contain an ID field name, and 1-2-3 requires that you specify one or the other.

Beneath the field name in cell A:A1, the join formula

```
+EMPBASE.ID=ADDRESS.ID
```

appears in cell A:A2. This formula equates the ID field in the EMPBASE table to the ID field in the ADDRESS table. Finally, in cell A:B2, the label '1239 appears. When this data query is processed, 1-2-3 will equate the ID field in the EMPBASE and ADDRESS tables and locate the record in each table that has the employee number 1239 in the ID field.

Once the criteria range is set up, you're ready to set up an output range. For example, in Figure 11-25, the output range begins in row 4 of worksheet A. Note that the first three field names, LASTNAME, SALARY, and DOH, come from the EMPBASE table, and the last two field names, CITY and ZIP, come from the ADDRESS table. Because all these field names are unique to their respective tables, you do not need to precede them with range names.

To execute the data query, select the Data Query command to display the Data Query dialog box. In the Input text box, type the range names of the two tables with a comma between them, for example, **EMPBASE,ADDRESS**. Alternatively, press NAME (F3) to display the range names in the current file, and select the range names from that list. In the Criteria text box, specify the range A:A1..A:B2. In the Output text box, specify the range A:A4..A:E4. Finally, select the Extract button. 1-2-3 locates the record with the number 1239 in the ID field of both the EMPBASE and ADDRESS tables. It then refers to the field names included in the output range to determine which fields to copy from which record to the output range. As you can see, data in the output range belongs to employee Piper (EMPBASE table), earning $30,000 (EMPBASE table), hired 2/01/92 (EMPBASE table), living in San Jose (ADDRESS table), zip code 95125 (ADDRESS table).

USING THE DATABASE @FUNCTIONS

1-2-3 offers a number of @functions that are useful for analyzing information contained in database tables. Like all 1-2-3 @functions, the database @functions take specific input arguments and return a particular result based on those arguments. The database @functions are covered here, rather than in Chapter 9, "Functions," because of their close relationship to database management.

Syntax and Usage

All the database @functions begin with the symbol @ followed by the letter D, for example @DSUM. The syntax for all the database @functions, except @DQUERY, is as follows:

@Dfunction(*input*, *field*, *criteria*)

Each component of this syntax has the following meaning:

- @Dfunction: The name of the @function you want to use. You can choose from @DAVG, @DCOUNT, @DGET, @DMAX, @DMIN, @DSUM, @DSTD, @DSTDS, @DVAR, or @DVARS. You can either type in this name or you can type @ and then press NAME (F3). 1-2-3 displays the @Functions dialog box. Select the name of the @function you want, for example @DSUM, and press ENTER. 1-2-3 adds the function name to the @ in the Control Line and displays @DSUM(. You can then add the remaining arguments for the database @function.

- *input*: The range name or address of the database table you want to query. This input range argument performs exactly the same function as the input range for the Data Query command. You can specify a single input range or multiple input ranges separated by commas.

- *field*: The field in the input range you want to search. This argument can be an *offset value*, an actual field name enclosed in quotes, or a reference to a cell that contains one of these. To use an offset value, specify the number of the field you want to search. The first field in the database table is automatically assigned the value 0, the second field is 1, the third field 2, and so on. To use a field name, enclose the name of the field you want to search in quotes. For example, to specify a field named SALARY in the input range, type "**SALARY**". If you specify either multiple input ranges for the database @function, or the input range is an external database table, you must use a field name enclosed in quotes rather than an offset value.

- *criteria*: The range that contains the criteria that will be used to select records from the input range. Use exactly the same conventions to specify criteria for the database @functions as you do for the Data Query command. See "Defining Criteria" earlier in this chapter for more details on how to define selection criteria.

Figure 11-26 shows an example of a database @function in cell A:F13 that reads @DAVG(A1..F10,"SALARY",B14..B15). (This same function is shown as text starting in cell A:C13.) The @DAVG function computes an average of the values in a field of the input range, for those records selected from the database table. The input range argument in this case is A1..F10, which includes the EMPBASE table and its field names. The field argument "SALARY" refers to the SALARY field in the EMPBASE table. The equivalent offset value in this case would be 4, because the SALARY field is the fifth field in the EMPBASE table. Finally, the criteria range argument is B12..B13. This range includes the field name SALARY with the label >30000 beneath it, therefore, only records that contain a value in excess of $30,000 in the SALARY field of the EMPBASE table are selected for use with the database @function.

One nice feature of the database @functions is that they are recalculated whenever the data to which they refer changes. Therefore, you can change the selection criteria in the criteria range and watch as the database @function is updated.

You can also use the database @functions to query external database tables. See "Querying External Database Tables" later in this chapter for more on how to work with external database tables.

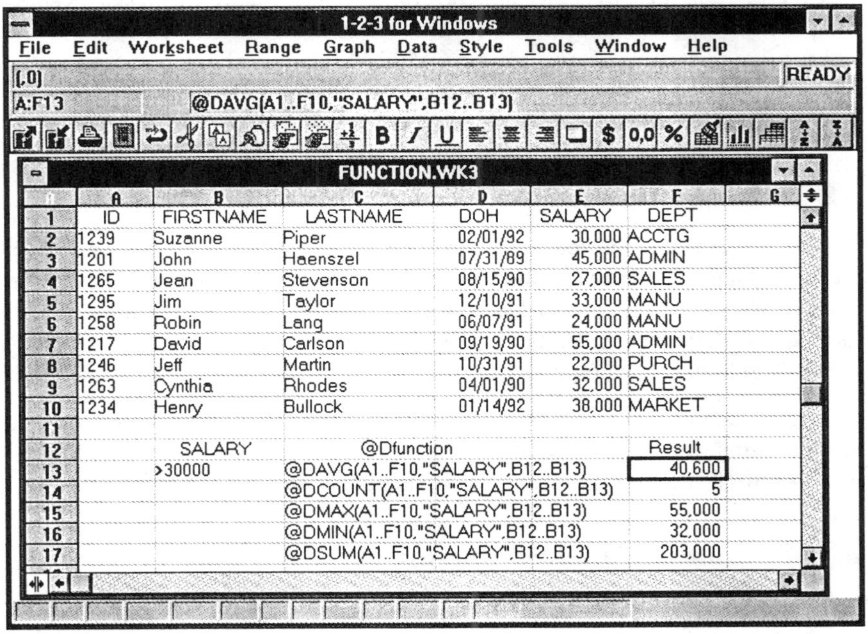

Figure 11-26 Examples of database @functions

You can also specify multiple input ranges for the database @functions. When 1-2-3 reads the arguments for database @functions, it does so from right to left. The first argument encountered is the criteria range, the second is interpreted as the field argument, and any remaining arguments are input ranges.

When you specify multiple input ranges for a database @function, you must use a join formula in the criteria range to join the two tables on a common field. You must also use a field name reference in the database @function, or a reference to a cell that contains a field name instead of an offset value. See "Querying Multiple Database Tables" earlier in this chapter for more details on how to set up a data query that uses multiple input ranges.

> ▼ *Tip:*   Although 1-2-3 tolerates only a single *field* argument in a database @function that contains multiple input ranges, you can make that *field* argument a reference to a cell that contains a field name. When you change the field name in that cell, either manually or with a macro, 1-2-3 stuffs the new field name into the database @function. Thus, by modifying a single cell, you can quickly search a different field in a different table without having to directly edit the database @function.

The @DAVG Function

The @DAVG function takes an average of the values in a field of the input range for those records that meet the criteria in the criteria range. Figure 11-26 shows an example of the @DAVG function in cell A:F13. This function adds the contents of the SALARY field for five records selected from the EMPBASE table using the criteria in the range A:B12..A:B13. That sum is then divided by the number of records selected to compute the average salary for those records.

The @DCOUNT Function

The @DCOUNT function counts the nonblank cells in a field of the input range for those records that meet the criteria in the criteria range. Figure 11-26 shows an example of the @DCOUNT function in cell A:F14. Notice that this cell contains the number 5, indicating that five records in the EMPBASE table meet the criteria in the range B:12..B:13 of Figure 11-26. Therefore, five employees in the EMPBASE table earn in excess of $30,000.

Note: Keep in mind that @DCOUNT only counts nonblank cells (cells that are not empty). Therefore, if one or more cells in the field referenced by the *field* argument for the @DCOUNT function are blank, you may not get an accurate count.

The @DMAX and @DMIN Functions

The @DMAX function returns the highest value in a field of the input range for those records that meet the criteria in the criteria range. The @DMIN function returns the lowest value. An example of the @DMAX function appears in cell A:F15 of Figure 11-26. It returns the value 55000. An example of the @DMIN function appears in cell A:F16 of Figure 11-26; it returns the value 32000. Thus, of the five records that meet the criteria in the range B12..B13 of Figure 11-26, the highest value in the SALARY field is $55,000 and the lowest is $32,000.

The @DSUM Function

The @DSUM function adds the values in a field of the input range for those records that meet the criteria in the criteria range. This particular function is among the most frequently used of the database @functions. An example of the @DSUM function appears in cell A:F17 of Figure 11-26. Notice that this function returns a value of 203,000. Thus, the sum of the values in the SALARY field for the five records selected from the EMPBASE table is $203,000.

The @DGET Function

The @DGET function gets a single value or label from a field of the input range for the record that meets the criteria in the criteria range. Figure 11-27 shows an example of this function in cell A:B15. As you can see in the Control Line of Figure 11-27, the input argument for this @function is A1..F10, which includes the EMPBASE table and its field names. The field argument is "SALARY", which refers to the SALARY field in the EMPBASE table. The criteria range argument is B12..B13. This range includes the field name LASTNAME with the label Piper beneath it. Thus, only the record with Piper in the LASTNAME field will be selected.

The @DGET function is useful only when you want to get a single value or label from a database table. In fact, if more than one record meets the criteria in the criteria range, the @DGET function returns ERR. Therefore, you should only use this function when you want to get a single unique value or label from a database table.

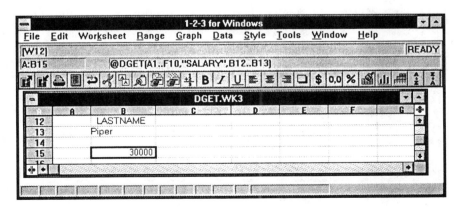

Figure 11-27 Using the @DGET function

The @DQUERY Function

The @DQUERY function is used exclusively to query external database tables. This function gives you access to a product-specific function or command in an external database and returns the result of that function to a 1-2-3 criteria range. See "Using @DQUERY" later in the chapter under "Querying External Database Tables" for more information on this @function.

The @DSTD and @DVAR Functions

The @DSTD function calculates the standard deviation for a population of values taken from a field of a database table. The standard deviation is a measure of the degree to which a series of values varies from the mean (average). The closer the value of the standard deviation is to zero, the more reliable is the mean value. For example, Figure 11-28 shows an example of the @DSTD function in cell A:F13. (The same formula is also shown as a label starting in cell A:C13, making it easier to read and understand.)

The values used by the @DSTD function come from a field of the input range for those records that meet the criteria in the criteria range. For example, the formula in cell A:F13 of Figure 11-28 reads @DSTD(A1..F10,"SALARY",B12..B13). Thus, the *input* range for this function is A:A1..A:F10, which includes the EMPBASE table and its field names. The *field* argument is "SALARY", which refers to the SALARY field (column E) in the EMPBASE table. Finally, the *criteria* range argument is B12..B13. This range contains

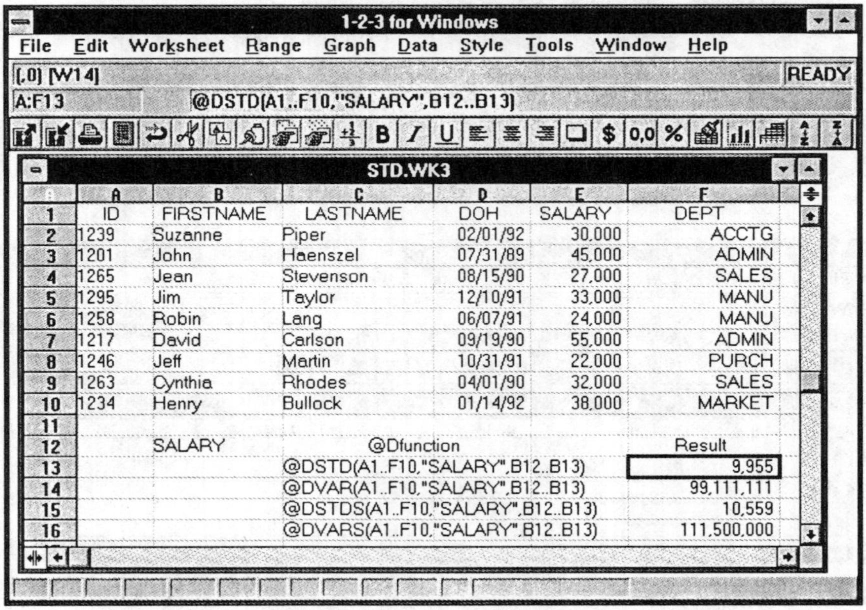

	A	B	C	D	E	F
1	ID	FIRSTNAME	LASTNAME	DOH	SALARY	DEPT
2	1239	Suzanne	Piper	02/01/92	30,000	ACCTG
3	1201	John	Haenszel	07/31/89	45,000	ADMIN
4	1265	Jean	Stevenson	08/15/90	27,000	SALES
5	1295	Jim	Taylor	12/10/91	33,000	MANU
6	1258	Robin	Lang	06/07/91	24,000	MANU
7	1217	David	Carlson	09/19/90	55,000	ADMIN
8	1246	Jeff	Martin	10/31/91	22,000	PURCH
9	1263	Cynthia	Rhodes	04/01/90	32,000	SALES
10	1234	Henry	Bullock	01/14/92	38,000	MARKET
11						
12		SALARY	@Dfunction			Result
13			@DSTD(A1..F10,"SALARY",B12..B13)			9,955
14			@DVAR(A1..F10,"SALARY",B12..B13)			99,111,111
15			@DSTDS(A1..F10,"SALARY",B12..B13)			10,559
16			@DVARS(A1..F10,"SALARY",B12..B13)			111,500,000

Figure 11-28 Calculating standard deviation and variance

a single field name, SALARY, with nothing beneath it, so 1-2-3 will select all the records from the input range.

The value for the @DSTD function in cell A:F13 is 9955. This means that, as a general rule of thumb, the salaries in the EMPBASE table will fall within $9,955 of the mean (one standard deviation) 68% of the time, and 95% of the time salaries will fall within two standard deviations or $19,910 of the mean. To determine the mean, you can use the @DAVG function with the same *input*, *field*, and *criteria* arguments.

The @DSTD function uses the population method of calculating the standard deviation for a list (population) of values. This method assumes that the values selected from the database table represent the entire population instead of a sample. If the values do not represent the entire population, this method may not be reliable due to possible errors in collecting the data. The population method is most reliable when the population is somewhat large. In fact, when the population is less than 30 values, the result of the @DSTD function may be called into question. In these cases, the @DSTDS function covered in the next section is a better choice.

Note: The standard deviation is the square root of the variance from the mean for all selected values.

The @DVAR function is used to calculate the population variance for a series of values. The variance is a calculation of the average squared deviation from the mean and is the square of the standard deviation. Variance is the traditional method for measuring the variability of a data set.

The values used by @DVAR are taken from a specific field of a database table. For a value to be selected for use, it must meet the criteria in the criteria range. Figure 11-28 shows an example of the @DVAR function in cell A:F14. The value calculated is 99,111,111. Notice that this function uses the same *input*, *field*, and *criteria* arguments as the @DSTD function in cell A:F13. Therefore, this variance is related to the standard deviation calculation in that cell. In fact, if you take the square root of 99,111,111, you get 9,955.

Once again, the @DVAR function uses the population method for calculating the variance for a list (population) of values. This method assumes that the values selected from the database table represent the entire population, instead of only a sample. If the values do not represent the entire population, this method may not be reliable, due to possible errors in collecting the data. As mentioned, the population method is most reliable when the population is large. When the population is less than 30 values, the result of the @DVAR function may be questionable. In these cases, try using the @DVARS function covered in the next section.

The @DSTDS and @DVARS Functions

You can use the @DSTDS function to calculate the sample standard deviation for a list of values taken from a specific field of a database table. For a value to be selected for use, it must meet the criteria in the criteria range. Figure 11-28 shows an example of the @DSTDS function in cell A:F15.

The @DSTDS function is similar to the @DSTD function. However, it uses the sample method, as opposed to the population method, to calculate the standard deviation. The sample method is more reliable when the values in a list represent only a sample of the available values, instead of the entire population, or when the number of values is small (less than 30). In general, the sample method results in a standard deviation that is slightly larger than the population method. This tends to compensate for any errors in the sampling process. For example, as you can see in Figure 11-28, the value calculated with @DSTDS (A:F15) is slightly higher than the value calculated with @DSTD (A:F13) for the same set of data.

The @DVARS function calculates the sample variance for a series of values in a field of a database table. For a value to be selected for use, it must meet the criteria in the criteria range. Figure 11-28 shows an example of the @DSTDS function in cell A:F16.

The @DVARS function works the same way as the @DVAR function. However, it uses the sample method instead of the population method to calculate the variance. Once again, the sample method results in a variance that is slightly larger than the population method. This tends to compensate for any errors in the sampling process. For example, as you can see in Figure 11-28, the value calculated with @DVARS (A:F16), is slightly higher than the value calculated with @DVAR (A:F14) for the same set of data.

QUERYING EXTERNAL DATABASE TABLES

As we have mentioned, to work with data in external tables, you use the Data Connect to External and Data External Options commands. External database tables are tables created by software products other than 1-2-3—for example, dBASE IV or Paradox. The Data External command allows you not only to access information in external tables from within 1-2-3, but also to add records to external tables and to create new external tables.

To use an existing external database table, or to create a new one, 1-2-3 must have access to a special driver called a Datalens driver. Datalens drivers tell 1-2-3 how to interact with a specific type of database table.

There are two types of Datalens drivers, those that interact directly with the Database Management System (DBMS) software, and those that interact only with database tables created by the DBMS. At present, there are very few Datalens drivers that interact directly with the DBMS. Nevertheless, Lotus has been encouraging independent software developers (ISDs) to develop such drivers, so you may be able to get a Datalens driver for your particular database product directly from the company that manufactures and distributes it. When you get the Datalens driver, it should come with instructions on how to install it and use it with 1-2-3.

To give you an idea of how Datalens drivers work, Lotus has included three sample drivers with 1-2-3. These drivers support dBASE IV, Paradox, and SQL Server. The dBASE IV driver supports the table formats of both dBASE IV and dBASE III PLus, and the Paradox driver supports the table formats of Paradox 3.0 and 3.5. Both of these drivers interact directly with database tables created by the DBMS, rather than the DBMS itself.

The SQL Server driver, on the other hand, is capable of interacting directly with the DBMS. This driver will be discussed only briefly here.

The dBASE IV Datalens driver is copied to your 1-2-3 program directory automatically when you install the program. In addition to this sample driver, a sample dBASE IV table, EMPLOYEE.DBF, is also provided. This table is copied to your C:\123W\SAMPLE directory when you elect to install 1-2-3's sample files. The dBASE IV driver and the EMPLOYEE.DBF table will be used in the sections that follow to show you how to work with data in external database tables.

As we have mentioned, to work with data in external tables, you use the Data Connect to External and Data External Options commands. The Data Connect to External command allows you to connect to an external database table and assign it a 1-2-3 range name. Once the external table has been connected, you can refer to it by using its range name in 1-2-3 commands and formulas. The Data External Options command, on the other hand, offers the following options:

- Paste Fields: Creates a list of fields in an external table in your worksheet.

- Send Command: Sends a command to a database table in its own product-specific command format.

- Create Table: Creates an external table by using either an existing 1-2-3 table or a table definition as a model.

- Disconnect: Disconnects an external table that has been connected with Data Connect to External.

Connecting to an External Table

The 1-2-3 Classic equivalent for Data Connect to External is /Data External Use. Before you can use information in an external database table, you must connect that table to 1-2-3. To do this, use the Data Connect to External command. Once a particular table is connected to 1-2-3, you can use the Data Query commands or the database @functions to access information in that table. When you select the Data Connect to External command, 1-2-3 displays the dialog box in Figure 11-29.

Note: For the Data Connect to External command to work, 1-2-3 must be able to find the files that make up the Datalens driver you intend to access. These Datalens files are normally located in your 1-2-3 program directory. Therefore, make sure you include the path to your 1-2-3 program directory in the PATH statement in your AUTOEXEC.BAT file.

At the top of the dialog box in Figure 11-29 is a text box initially entitled "Connect to driver." Ultimately this text box will contain a *table name* that describes the table you want to connect to 1-2-3. You can use the list box below to build a table name, or you can type the table name in the Connect to driver text box. A table name consists of three elements: a Datalens driver name, a database name (the disk location where the database resides), and the name of the table you want to use. A single space must appear between

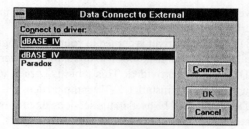

Figure 11-29 Connecting to an external database table

each element. For example, to specify the EMPLOYEE.DBF table associated with the dBASE IV driver, type the following table name in the Connect to drivers text box:

```
DBASE_IV C:\123W\SAMPLE EMPLOYEE
```

To connect the EMPLOYEE table to 1-2-3, select the Connect button. 1-2-3 prompts you for a range name for the table. It does this by changing the title of the Connect to driver text box to "Enter range name for table" and displays a default range name that matches the filename for the table, in this case EMPLOYEE. You refer to the table in commands and formulas by using this range name.

To confirm the default range name, select the Connect button again. To complete the Data External Use command, select the OK button. The EMPLOYEE table is now connected to 1-2-3 and you can refer to it by using the EMPLOYEE range name.

If you don't want to use the default range name for an external table, you can provide one of your own. To do this, simply type the range name when prompted by 1-2-3. (The range name cannot match an existing range name.) Select the Connect button or press ENTER to confirm the range name and then complete the Data Connect to External command by selecting the OK button. 1-2-3 connects the table you selected and assigns it the range name you've specified.

As mentioned, rather than typing the table name in the Connect to driver text box, you can select the components that make up the table name from the list box below. Before you try this, make sure the directory containing the database table is current. If it is not, take a moment to use the Tools User Setup Worksheet directory command to make that directory current for 1-2-3.

When you select the Data Connect to External command, 1-2-3 displays the names of available Datalens drivers. The first item in the list, DBASE_IV, appears in the Connect to driver text box. To confirm this name, press ENTER, double-click on it in the list box below, or select the Connect button. 1-2-3 changes the name of the Connect to driver box to "Connect to database," and displays (**Show Drivers**) in the list box below followed by the directories and names of external databases, for example C:\123W. Double-click on the name of the database (its directory, that is) in the list box, highlight it and press ENTER, or select the Connect button. 1-2-3 adds the selected database name to the Connect to driver text box.

Once the driver and database names are selected, 1-2-3 will change the name of the Connect to database text box to "Connect to table" and displays a list of available tables.

Double-click on the table name you want, highlight it and press ENTER, or select the Connect button. 1-2-3 adds the name of the table to the table name above and changes the name of the Connection to table text box to "Enter range name for table." At this point 1-2-3 displays a default range name that matches the filename for the table. You can confirm this range name, and complete the Data Connect to External command, by selecting the Connect button followed by the OK button.

Note: As mentioned, to use the list box method to define a table name, the directory that contains the Datalens driver must be the current directory. You can have 1-2-3 list the names of associated tables in different directories by modifying your LOTUS.BCF file. See "Modifying the LOTUS.BCF File" later in this chapter for details on how to do this.

You use the range name assigned to an external table to refer to it in commands and formulas. You can also connect to the same table several times and assign it a different range name each time. Thus, you can refer to the same table by using different range names (aliases). If a table is already connected, 1-2-3 displays ???? as its default range name. To assign the table a new range name, change ???? to a unique range name of your choosing.

Caution: When you connect to an external table with Data Connect to External, 1-2-3 only establishes that connection for the current worksheet file—when you remove the current worksheet file from memory, your connection is lost.

Listing Fields in External Tables

The 1-2-3 Classic Equivalent for Data External Options Paste Fields is /Data External List Fields. /Data External List also includes a Tables option that lets you create a list of tables associated with a database to which you are connected.

The Data External Options Paste Fields command lets you create a list of fields in an external table in your worksheet. You can use this command before querying an external table, so you'll know exactly what fields that table contains. Before you use this command to create a list of fields for an external table, that table must already be connected to 1-2-3. To connect an external table to 1-2-3, use the Data Connect to External command, as described in the previous section.

When you select the Data External Options Paste Fields command, 1-2-3 displays the dialog box in Figure 11-30, which lists the range names of tables that are currently connected to 1-2-3. The first item in the list appears in the Connected Tables text box. Select the name of the table whose fields you want to list or specify its name in the Connected Tables text box. To specify a location for the table, use the Ranges text box below.

In this box, specify a cell address or range name of the cell that marks the upper-left corner of where you want the table to begin. When you're ready, select OK. 1-2-3 writes a six-column listing into the worksheet, starting at the location you specified. The number of rows in the table is determined by the number of fields in the external table. For example, Figure 11-31 shows a field listing for the EMPLOYEE.DBF table starting in cell A:A1; it has six rows, one for each field in the database table.

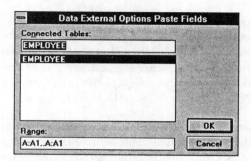

Figure 11-30 The Data External Options Paste Fields dialog box

Each column of the fields listing in Figure 11-31 gives you information about the content and structure of the fields in the EMPLOYEE.DBF file. The contents of each of these columns and what they mean will be discussed in more detail in the next section. Collectively the fields listing in Figure 11-31 represents a *table definition* for the EMPLOYEE.DBF file. You can use this table definition as a reference when you copy records from the EMPLOYEE table into a 1-2-3 worksheet. You can also use it as a model for creating a new 1-2-3 database table or an external database table.

About 1-2-3's Table Definitions

1-2-3's table definitions describe the structure of a database. For example, the table definition for the EMPLOYEE.DBF file in Figure 11-31 describes the fields in that table. 1-2-3 uses a standard table definition format for all Datalens drivers.

Each row in a table definition describes a different field in an external table. Therefore, the number of rows in the table is determined by the number of fields in the table.

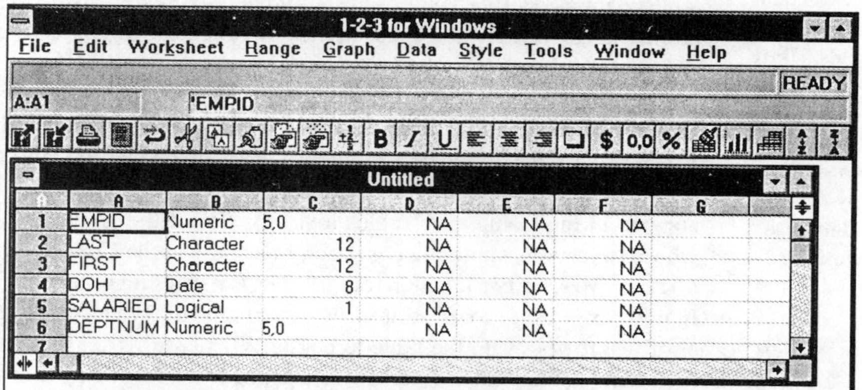

Figure 11-31 A sample table definition

Each table definition you create contains six columns; each column describes an attribute for a specific database table field. Some Datalens drivers use all six columns. However, many drivers—for example, the Paradox and dBASE IV drivers—only need some of the fields in the table definition to adequately describe a database field.

The following is a description of each of the columns shown in the table definition in Figure 11-31.

Column 1:   Field name. The first column in a table definition shows the name of the field. For example, the first field (column A) in the table definition in Figure 11-31 is EMPID. The length and format of field names are often restricted by the Datalens driver you are using.

Column 2:   Data type. The second column (column B, Figure 11-31) describes the type of data in the field. This is analogous to 1-2-3's classifications of data as labels or values. The data types available may vary from one Datalens driver to the next, depending on the database product supported by that driver.

Column 3:   Field width. The third column (column C) of the table definition in Figure 11-31 contains the overall character width for each field. If the data type of the field is numeric, this column may also show the number of decimal places.

Column 4:   Column labels. The fourth column in a table definition is used to provide an alternate name for a field. The column is not needed by dBASE IV or Paradox. Therefore, 1-2-3 displays NA in this field.

Column 5:   Field description. The fifth column in a table definition contains a brief description for a field. The column is not used by dBASE IV. Therefore, 1-2-3 displays NA in this field. This field is, however, used by the Paradox driver. An example of a Paradox table definition appears later in this chapter under "How the Paradox Driver Treats Index Files."

Column 6:   Field creation string. The sixth column in a table definition provides a field creation string. This field is not required by the Paradox driver. This column can be used with the dBASE IV driver to define Float fields.

About the dBASE IV Datalens Driver

The dBASE IV Datalens driver can be used to manage database tables that are created with dBASE IV or dBASE III PLUS. You may also use the dBASE IV driver to manage data in database tables whose file format is compatible with dBASE IV. You cannot use the dBASE IV driver with dBASE II files.

The dBASE IV driver is only intended for use with database (.DBF) files. You cannot use it to modify other types of dBASE files—for example, form files (.FRM), label files

(.LBL), or memo files (.DBT). You can, however, update index files (.NDX or .MDX) associated with a particular database table. To do this, you must use Data External Options Send Command to send a command string to the database table that activates a specific index (.NDX or .MDX) file. See "Sending Commands to a DataLens Driver" later for more details on the Data External Options Send command.

The dBASE IV driver, known as the SAMPLE driver in previous versions of 1-2-3, has been improved substantially for 1-2-3. You can now use this driver to:

- Create a new dBASE IV .DBF database file by using the Data External Options Create Table command.

- Append records to the end of an existing dBASE database table by using Data Query Modify Insert, Data Query Extract, and Data Query Unique. The records you want to append can be located in either a 1-2-3 worksheet or in another dBASE database table.

- Copy records from a dBASE database table into a 1-2-3 worksheet by using the Data Query Extract or Data Query Unique commands.

- Delete records in a dBASE database table using Data Query Delete.

- Modify existing records in a dBASE database table by using Data Query Modify Extract and Data Query Modify Replace.

- Delete an existing dBASE database table using the /Data External Delete command from the 1-2-3 Classic menu.

- Send commands to a dBASE table by using Data External Options Send Command.

- Use the database @functions to analyze information in a dBASE table.

How the dBASE IV Driver Treats Index Files

Index files are commonly used in dBASE IV to address the records in a database table in a certain order. For example, you might want to address the records in a mailing list database table in zip-code order when printing mailing labels.

Index files are always associated with a particular database table, but they exist independently of that table. Nevertheless, to address the records in a given table in the order specified by an index file, the index file must be opened. If you modify the records in a database table or append new records, the associated index file must be open in order to be updated for the changes.

dBASE IV supports two types of index files, single index files (.NDX) and multiple index files (.MDX). Single index (.NDX) files contain only a single index (list of pointers) to a particular field in a database table. To activate this type of index, you need only open the index file. Multiple index files (.MDX), on the other hand, can contain as many as 47 different indexes, each of which addresses the records in a database table in a different order. Each of these indexes is referred to as a *tag*. The .MDX file associated with a particular database table is automatically opened when you open the database file. To make a particular index active you must activate its tag.

You can make a particular index active from within 1-2-3 by using the command Data External Options Send Command. This command lets you pass a command string to the database table in its own command format. To activate a single index (.NDX) file, the command string will take the form:

SET INDEX TO [*Index-filename*] TABLE [*Table-name*]

where *Index-filename* is the .NDX file you want to open and *Table-name* is the name of the database table you want to use with the index. You do not need to specify file extensions or paths in either of these arguments.

To activate a specific tag in a multiple index file, your command string will take the following form:

SET ORDER TO [*tag-name*] TABLE [*Table-name*]

where *tag-name* is the name of the index tag you want to make active and *Table-name* is the name of the table you are using.

The dBASE IV driver only supports one open index or tag per database table. Therefore, before you can activate a new index or tag, you must close the old one. You can do this with a command line that takes the following form:

CLOSE INDEX TABLE [*Table-name*]

where *Table-name* is the name of the table you are currently using. Once again, you do not need to specify either a path or extension in *Table-name*.

Note: If you modify the information in a dBASE table from within 1-2-3 without activating the appropriate index beforehand, the index will become outdated. Therefore, be sure you use the dBASE REINDEX command the next time you use the table from within dBASE.

Commands and Files Supported by the dBASE IV Driver

The dBASE IV driver only allows you to work with database files (.DBF) and index files (.NDX or .MDX). You cannot work with any other type of dBASE file. And, although you can delete a given database (.DBF) table from with 1-2-3, you cannot delete any other type of dBASE file.

As mentioned, the dBASE IV driver does not interact with the dBASE DBMS engine, only with a particular table. Therefore, the only commands supported by the dBASE IV driver are those that open and close index files. You cannot execute any other dBASE commands from within 1-2-3.

About dBASE IV Tables

The dBASE IV driver supports the field naming conventions and most of the data types supported by dBASE IV. However, there are certain restrictions you should know about, some of which are imposed by the dBASE IV driver and others by 1-2-3.

The dBASE IV driver fully supports the field naming conventions of dBASE IV. That is, a field name can only be a maximum of 10 characters in length, including underscores, and must begin with a letter. dBASE IV supports a maximum of 128 total fields per table, with a total of 4000 characters in each record.

The dBASE IV driver supports the following data types from dBASE IV:

- Character: Character fields contain text strings. The contents of these fields appear as labels in 1-2-3. The maximum width of a character field in dBASE IV is 254 characters.

- Numeric: Numeric fields contain type *n* numbers. The *n* means that these numbers are not subject to rounding errors and are useful in business and financial applications where totals must balance. The maximum width of a numeric field in dBASE IV is 19 characters, including the decimal. You can specify the number of places to appear after the decimal by using the third (Field width) column of the 1-2-3 table definition (Figure 11-31). To do this, provide a number that represents the number of places in front of the decimal followed by a comma and the number of places to appear after the decimal. For example, the entry 6,2 will result in a nine-character width with six places in front of the decimal and two after.

- Float: A Float field is also a numeric field that contains type *f* numbers. (This data type is not supported by dBASE III PLUS.) Unlike type *n* numbers, the position of the decimal is allowed to "float." And, although these types of numbers are subject to rounding errors, they are more accurate, which can be useful for scientific and engineering applications. When you use Data External Options Paste Fields to create a table definition in 1-2-3, column 3 (Field width) shows the width of Float fields, but not the number of places after the decimal. To specify the number of places after the decimal, use column 6 (Field creation string). In this column, place the label DEC=*xx*, where *xx* is a number from 0 to 15, specifying the number of places after the decimal. The number you provide must be at least 2 less than the field width value in column 3.

  If you do not provide a DEC=*xx* value in column 6, and the width in column 3 is 2 or less, the dBASE IV driver defaults to 0 decimal places. Or, if the width value in column 3 is 3 through 17, the number of decimal places will be two less than the width. For example, if the width in column 3 is 16, there will be 14 decimal places. The dBASE IV driver supports Float fields up to 17 characters wide with 15 decimal places. If you provide a value outside this range, 1-2-3 will issue an error message.

- Date: Date fields contain dates. The contents of these fields are translated into date values and given a Date 4 format when brought into a 1-2-3 worksheet. Date fields are always eight characters wide in dBASE IV. Therefore, if you create an external table with a date field from within 1-2-3, it will automatically have an eight-character width.

- Logical: Logical fields are a single character wide and contain a "true" (T, t, Y, or y) or "false" (F, f, N, or n) value. In 1-2-3, true values are assigned the number 1 and false values are assigned the number 0. Logical fields are useful in situations where there are only two possibilities, for example SALARY=TRUE and HOURLY=FALSE. When you create a dBASE table with a logical field, that field is automatically assigned a width of one character.

- Memo: The dBASE IV driver does not support dBASE IV memo fields. Memo fields reference a file with a .DBT extension that contains variable amounts of text for individual database records. When you copy records from a dBASE table that contains memo fields into the worksheet, the worksheet column that will ultimately contain the memo field is left blank. Additionally, you cannot create a dBASE IV table that contains a memo field from within 1-2-3. You can, however, append records to a table that already contains a memo field, but the new records are given blank memo fields.

About the Paradox Driver

The Paradox Datalens driver has much the same capability as the dBASE IV driver. For example, the Paradox driver allows you to:

- Create a new Paradox .DB database file by using the Data External Options Create Table command.

- Append records to the end of an existing Paradox database table by using Data Query Modify Insert, Data Query Extract, and Data Query Unique.

- Copy records from a Paradox table into a 1-2-3 worksheet by using the Data Query Extract or Data Query Unique commands.

- Delete records in a Paradox table by using Data Query Delete.

- Modify existing records in a Paradox table by using Data Query Modify Extract and Data Query Modify Replace.

- Delete an existing Paradox table using the /Data External Delete command from the 1-2-3 Classic menu.

- Send a command to a Paradox table from within 1-2-3 by using Data External Options Send Command.

- Use the database @functions from within 1-2-3 to analyze information in a Paradox table.

Files Supported by the Paradox Driver

The Paradox driver is intended only for use with Paradox database (.DB) files and their associated primary index (.PX) files. You cannot use the Paradox driver to modify or update any other type of Paradox file. When you delete a Paradox table from within 1-2-3, its associated primary index (.PX) file is also deleted. Other files associated with the table—like secondary index files, script files, report files, and so on—are not affected.

Commands Supported

As we have mentioned, you can send a command to an external database table from within 1-2-3 by using Data External Options Send Command. However, because the Paradox driver does not interact directly with the Paradox DBMS engine, the types of commands you can send are limited. In fact, only those commands that encrypt and decrypt a table or change the current password are supported.

The term *encrypt* refers to scrambling the information in a table. The information in the table is not damaged; it is simply made unreadable to unauthorized users. On the other hand, the term *decrypt* means unscrambling the information in a table to make it readable again. To encrypt a particular table, you can use Data External Options Send Command to send a command string to the table that takes the following form:

```
ENCRYPT=filename, [password]
```

where *filename* is the name of the database table you want to encrypt and *password* is an optional password the next user must supply to decrypt the table. If you do not supply a *password* argument, the Paradox driver will use the current password.

Conversely, you can decrypt a table by using Data External Options Send Command to send the table a command string that takes the following form:

```
DECRYPT=filename, [password]
```

where *filename* is the name of the database table you want to decrypt and *password* is the password you assigned when you encrypted the table. If you do not supply a *password* argument, the Paradox driver will use the current password.

Finally, you can change the current password by using Data External Options Send Command to send a command string that takes the following form:

```
PASSWORD=password
```

where *password* is the new password you want to use.

For additional information on how to use the Data External Options Send command, see "Sending Commands to a DataLens Driver" later in this chapter.

How the Paradox Driver Treats Index Files

When you change the information in a Paradox table from within 1-2-3, the Paradox driver automatically updates the primary index (.PX) file for that table, provided one exists. If you create a Paradox table from within 1-2-3, you can also create a primary index for that table as part of the operation, if you so desire. You cannot, however, create a new table with a secondary index. Although you can access and modify information in tables with secondary indexes from within 1-2-3, those secondary indexes will not be

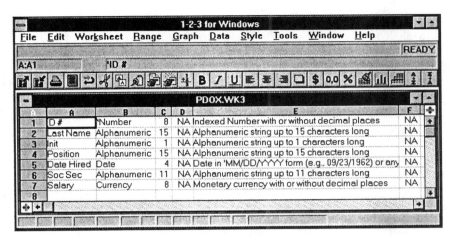

Figure 11-32 A sample Paradox table definition

updated. (These indexes will be updated the next time you use the table from within Paradox.)

You can create a new external table from within 1-2-3 by using the Data External Options Create Table command. This command lets you create a new Paradox table by using a custom table definition as a model. A sample Paradox table definition appears in Figure 11-32. This table definition was created by using the Data External Options Paste Fields command to list the fields for an existing Paradox table called EMPLOYEE.DB. (You'll find this file located in your C:\123W\SAMPLE directory.)

To create a new Paradox table with a primary index, you must place an asterisk (*) in front of the data type for appropriate field names in the table definition that will be used to create the new external table. For example, if the field on which you want to index the table is Alphanumeric, you would use the designation *Alphanumeric in column 2 (column B) of the table definition in Figure 11-32. All indexed fields must be listed first in the table definition in their respective order of precedence, before any nonindexed fields.

Note: The Paradox driver will not allow you to modify the primary fields of indexed records from within 1-2-3 by using the Data Query Modify Extract and Replace commands. In addition, the Paradox driver will not let you add records to an external table with the Data Query Modify Insert command when the contents of fields in the records you are adding are identical to the indexed fields of existing records, since it assumes these are duplicate records. This is a serious shortcoming of the Paradox driver.

About Paradox Tables

From within 1-2-3, you can create new Paradox tables as well as modify and analyze the data they contain. When you work with these tables, you'll find it helpful to know about the field specifications and data types in a Paradox table. Perhaps the best way to do this is to take you on a brief tour of the Paradox table definition in Figure 11-32.

Each field in a Paradox table is identified by a field name. For example, the first column in the table definition in Figure 11-32 shows the field names for the EMPLOYEE.DB table. Field names can be up to 25 characters in length, and you can have up to 255 fields in a Paradox table.

The second column in the table definition in Figure 11-32 shows the data type for each field. Paradox supports the following data types:

- Alphanumeric: These fields contain character strings made up of letters, numbers, and symbols. Their width can be from 1 to 255 characters. When the contents of these fields are brought into a 1-2-3 worksheet, they appear as labels.

- Number: These fields contain numeric data. The default width for these fields is eight characters, but they can contain numbers with up to 15 significant digits including decimal places. Values with more than 15 significant digits are rounded and stored in scientific notation.

- Currency: The same as Number, except for the default display format. For purposes of display, all numbers are rounded to two decimal places, include thousands separators, and negative values are displayed in parentheses.

- Short: These fields contain integer numbers that range from –32,676 through 32,676. These fields are sometimes used by advanced Paradox users or programmers because they require less disk storage space than Number fields.

- Date: These fields contain dates between January 1, 100 and December 31, 9999. When these dates are brought into a 1-2-3 worksheet, they are converted to date values and are formatted as Date 4 (Long International).

Note: The Paradox driver does not support 1-2-3's time numbers. If you add a record containing a date/time number to a Paradox table from within 1-2-3, the time portion of the number will be truncated.

The third column (column C) of the Paradox table definition in Figure 11-32 shows the width of each field. However, the Paradox driver ignores the field-width setting for all data types except Alphanumeric. When designing a table definition that will be used to create a new Paradox table, you must supply a value in the field-width column.

Normally, the fourth, fifth, and sixth columns in the table definition in Figure 11-32 are not used by the Paradox driver. Therefore, although you must include them to conform to 1-2-3 table definition format, they will usually contain NA. However, when you use the Data External Options Paste Fields command to create a table definition for a Paradox table in the worksheet, the Paradox driver will show data for column 5 (Field description).

Choosing a Default Sort Order

The Paradox driver also supports different Paradox sort orders for indexing, including ASCII (the default), Intl (International), SwedFin (Swedish and Finnish), and NorDan (Norwegian and Danish). The Paradox driver maintains the index for a given table using the sort order that was in force when the table was created. To choose a specific type of index sort order for a given table, you must do so by defining a table creation string when you create the table.

To create a new table, use the Data External Options Create Table command. This command results in a dialog box that lets you name and create a new external database table. This dialog box also contains a text box named "Table creation string" that lets you define a creation string for the new database. You can use any of the following entries in this box to define a default sort order for a new Paradox table:

Creation String	Sort Order
SORT ASCII	ASCII
SORT INTL	International
SORT NORDAN	Norwegian and Danish
SORT SWEDFIN	Swedish and Finnish

For additional information on the Data External Options Create Table command, see Creating a New External Table" later in the chapter.

Copying Records from an External Table

Once you have connected an external table to 1-2-3, you can use the Data Query commands, as well as the database @functions, to query that table. In this section we'll take you through an example that shows you how to go about using the Data Query Extract command to copy records from the EMPLOYEE external table into the worksheet, as shown in Figure 11-33. (As you may recall, the EMPLOYEE table is a sample dBASE IV database that comes with 1-2-3.)

As the following procedure illustrates, using the Data Query Extract command to query an external database table is very similar to using the command to query a 1-2-3 database table. During this procedure, you'll define an input, output, and criteria range in the usual way. However, instead of defining an input range that points to a range in a 1-2-3 worksheet, you'll substitute the range name you've assigned to an external table.

To recreate the data query in Figure 11-33 yourself, perform the following steps:

1. Starting with a fresh worksheet, use the techniques described earlier in this chapter under "Connecting to an External Table" to connect the EMPLOYEE.DBF sample file to 1-2-3 and assign it the default range name of EMPLOYEE.

2. With the cell pointer in cell A:A1, use the Data External Options Paste Fields command to create a table definition for the EMPLOYEE table. The use of this command is described earlier in this chapter under "Listing Fields in External

Tables." As you may recall, this command allows you to create a list of fields in an external table in your worksheet, as shown in the range A:A1..A:F6 of Figure 11-33.

3. Select the Range Transpose command. 1-2-3 displays the Range Transpose dialog box. In the From text box, specify the range A:A1..A:A6. In the To text box, specify A:A11, then select OK. 1-2-3 copies the field names from the first column of the table definition and transposes them to row 11. These field names will form the top row of your output range.

4. Select the Edit Quick Copy command. In the From text box, specify cell A:A1. In the To text box, specify cell A:A8, then select OK. 1-2-3 copies the EMPID field name from the first row of the table definition to cell A:A8. This field name forms the top row of your criteria range.

5. Select the Data Query command. 1-2-3 displays the Data Query dialog box.

6. In the Input range text box, type **EMPLOYEE** (the range name of the external table). Alternatively, you can press NAME (F3) and select the EMPLOYEE range name.

7. In the Criteria text box, specify the range A:A8..A:A9. This includes the EMPID field name and the blank cell beneath it. As you may recall, if you leave the row below the field names in the criteria range blank, 1-2-3 will select all the records in the input range.

8. In the Output range text box, specify the single-row output range A:A11..A:F11. This includes the field names in row 11.

9. Select the Extract button. 1-2-3 copies the records from the EMPLOYEE external table into the worksheet. Your screen should look similar to Figure 11-33.

10. Select the Cancel button from the Data Query dialog box to return to the worksheet in READY mode.

 Tip: You can also query multiple external tables at the same time. To do this you must use a join formula in the criteria range to relate the two external tables to one another. You can then specify the range names of the two external tables as multiple input ranges for the Data Query command. See "Querying Multiple Database Tables" earlier in this chapter for more details on how to query multiple database tables.

Appending Records to an External Table

You can also append records to an existing external table. The records you append can be located in a 1-2-3 worksheet or in another external table. To append records to an external table, you can use either the Data Query Extract or Data Query Modify Insert commands.

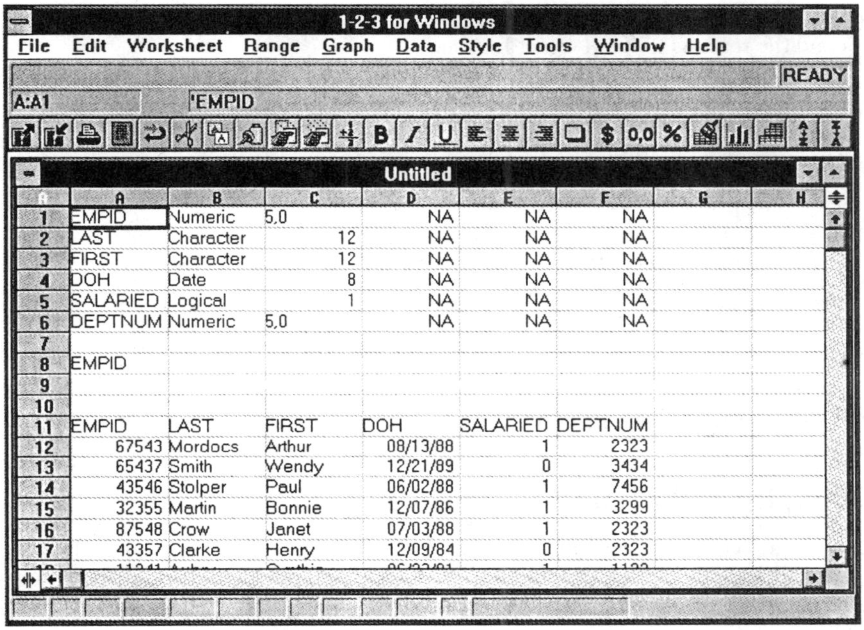

Figure 11-33 Copying records from an external table to the worksheet

Note: To append records to an external table, the data types within the fields of those records must match the data types of the fields in the external table; otherwise, 1-2-3 will issue an error message when you attempt to append the records. The width of the fields in the records you're appending should be less than or equal to the width of fields in the external table. If the field widths for the records you're appending are too wide, the contents of some entries may be truncated.

Imagine you'd like to append some records currently located in your worksheet to the end of the EMPLOYEE external table. To do this, select the Data Query command. 1-2-3 displays the Data Query dialog box. In the Input text box, specify the worksheet range that contains the records you want to append. In the Criteria text box, specify the range in the worksheet that contains criteria that will select the records you want to append. Finally, in the Output text box, specify the range name for the external table, in this case EMPLOYEE. When you're ready, select the Extract button. 1-2-3 appends the records from the input range in the worksheet to the end of the EMPLOYEE table.

You can also append records from one external table to another with Data Query Extract. To do this, specify in the Input range text box the range name of the external table that you want to append the records from. In the Criteria text box, specify the range that contains the criteria that will be used to select records from the input range (database table). In the Output text box, specify the range name of the external table you want to append the records to, then select Extract.

For the Data Query Modify Insert command, you swap the input and output ranges when appending records. That is, if you're appending records from the worksheet, your input range is the range name for the external table and your output range contains the records in the worksheet that you want to append. A criteria range is not required. If you're appending records from another table, your input range is the table you want to append to and your output range is the table you want to append from. Once again, the criteria range is not used. In both cases, since the criteria range is not used, all the records from the output range are appended to the input range.

Caution: If you press QUERY (F7) to repeat a Data Query Extract or Data Query Modify Insert command that references an external table, 1-2-3 appends all the records in the input or output range to the external table.

Modifying Records in an External Table

You can also use the Data Query Modify Extract and Replace commands to modify the records in an external table. For example, imagine you want to modify the record of Arthur Mordocs in the EMPLOYEE external table. To do this, set up your criteria and output ranges as shown in Figure 11-34. Notice that the value 67543 (Arthur's employee identification number) appears in cell A:A9 beneath the EMPID label in cell A:A8, so only Arthur's record will be selected when the data query is processed.

To modify Arthur's record, select the Data Query command. 1-2-3 displays the Data Query dialog box. In the Input range text box, enter the range name assigned to the

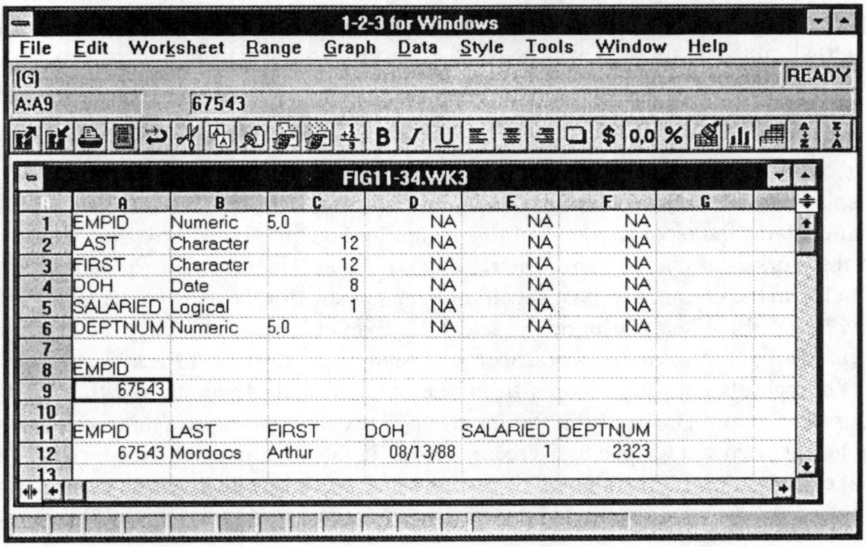

Figure 11-34 Modifying records in an external table

EMPLOYEE table (EMPLOYEE). In the Criteria range box, specify the range A:A8..A:A9. In the Output range box, specify the range A:A11..A:F11. When you're ready, select the Modify button. 1-2-3 displays the Data Query Modify dialog box. Select the Extract button. 1-2-3 then copies the record of Arthur Mordocs to the worksheet and returns you to the Data Query dialog box. Select Cancel to return to the worksheet.

Now that Arthur's record has been copied to the worksheet, you can modify it any way you'd like. To record the changes you've made in the EMPLOYEE table, select Data Query. 1-2-3 displays the Data Query dialog box with the appropriate input, criteria, and output ranges already displayed. Select Modify to have 1-2-3 display the Data Query Modify dialog box, then select Replace. 1-2-3 then updates Arthur Mordoc's record in the EMPLOYEE table to reflect the changes you've made. Select Cancel to return to the worksheet.

Deleting Records in an External Table

You can use the Data Query Delete command to delete selected records from an external table. For example, imagine you want to delete the record for Arthur Mordocs from the EMPLOYEE table. To do this, you can use the selection criteria shown in the criteria range A:A8..A:A9 of Figure 11-34. Once this criteria range is properly set up, select the Data Query command. In the Input range text box, specify the range name of the EMPLOYEE table (EMPLOYEE). In the Criteria range box, specify the range A:A8..A:A9, then select the Delete button, and 1-2-3 will delete the record of Arthur Mordocs from the EMPLOYEE table.

Note: When you use Data Query Delete to delete a record from a dBASE IV table, the DBASE IV driver only marks that record for deletion. To delete the record permanently, you must return to dBASE IV, open the database table, and use the PACK command.

Using Database @Functions with External Tables

You can also use the database @functions to analyze information in an external table. To do this, the external table must already be connected to 1-2-3 with the Data Connect to External command.

Querying an external table with the database @functions is very similar to querying a 1-2-3 table. However, as an *input* range argument for the database @function, you must use the 1-2-3 range name for the external table. For the *field* argument, you must use a field name from the external table enclosed in quotation marks (" "), as opposed to an offset value. For the *criteria* range argument, specify a range in the worksheet that contains the appropriate field names and search arguments to select the records you want to use in the external table.

For example, suppose you want to determine the total number of salaried employees in the EMPLOYEE external table. To do this, you might use the @DSUM function as follows:

```
@DSUM(EMPLOYEE,"SALARIED",CRITERIA)
```

In this case, EMPLOYEE is the range name assigned to the EMPLOYEE table. The *field* reference "SALARIED" refers to the SALARIED logical field in the EMPLOYEE table. Finally, CRITERIA is a range name that refers to a 1-2-3 worksheet range containing selection criteria that will select all the records in the EMPLOYEE table.

For more on how to use the database @functions, see "Using the Database @Functions" earlier in this chapter.

Note: When you use a database @function to query an external table, the database @function is recalculated each time the worksheet is changed. If the external table is large, this may slow down the operation of 1-2-3. To deal with this problem, you can use the Tools User Setup Recalculation command to specify a manual recalculation mode and thus control how often the worksheet will be recalculated.

Using @DQUERY

The @DQUERY function allows you to access a product-specific function in an external database program. The result of that function can then be used in a 1-2-3 criteria range to select records from an external table associated with the database. The syntax for the @DQUERY function is

```
@DQUERY(function[,extension-arguments])
```

where *function* is the name of the external database function you want to use enclosed in quotations marks and *extension-arguments* is a list of one or more arguments for the function separated by commas.

Note: The @DQUERY function is not supported by the dBASE IV or Paradox driver.

You can only use @DQUERY in a 1-2-3 criteria range to select records from a specific external table. Additionally, the @DQUERY function does not support multiple input ranges.

Imagine you are working with an external database program that supports the function SOUNDSLIKE(*character string*). This function returns the contents of a field in the record that is closest to *character string*. You will need to use this function in a 1-2-3 criteria range to search a character field called LASTNAME in an external table. To do this, you might use the following formula in a 1-2-3 criteria range:

```
+LASTNAME=@DQUERY(SOUNDSLIKE("Adams")
```

Creating a New External Table

The 1-2-3 Classic equivalent for Data Query Options Create Table is /Data External Create.

To create a new external table, use the Data External Options Create Table command. This command allows you to create a new table by using either another database table as a model or by using a table definition. When you select the Data External Options Create Table command, 1-2-3 displays the dialog box in Figure 11-35.

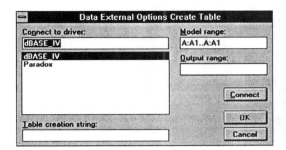

Figure 11-35 The Data External Options Create Table dialog box

When you create a new table with Data External Create, the new table is empty (has no records). However, once the new table is created, you can add records to that table by using either the Data Query Extract or Data Query Modify Insert commands.

Using an Existing Table as a Model

Imagine you want to create a new external table by using the EMPBASE table in Figure 11-36 as a model. To do this, perform the following steps:

1. Select the Data External Options Create Table command. 1-2-3 displays the dialog box in Figure 11-35.

2. In the Connect to driver text box, specify a name for the new table preceded by appropriate driver and database name. For example, to create a new table called NEW, type **DBASE IV C:\123W NEW** and press ENTER. Another method is to double-click on the dBASE_IV driver name in the list box. 1-2-3 lists the names of databases (C:\123W) in the current directory. Double-click on C:\123W in the Connection list box. Then, type **NEW** and select the Connect button.

3. After you specify a name for the new table, 1-2-3 prompts you for a range name for the table. It does this by displaying the default range name NEW. You can accept this range name by pressing ENTER or you can edit the name and press ENTER. 1-2-3 moves the cursor to the Table creation string text box.

4. Press TAB to bypass Table creation string text box and move to the Model range text box. Although some drivers support or require the use of table creation strings, the dBASE IV driver does not.

5. In the Model range text box, specify the range address or range name that includes the first row of field names in the EMPBASE table and the first record (A:A1..A:F2). Press TAB to move to the Output range text box. The output range in this case is the range in which 1-2-3 will create a table definition that will be used to create the new table.

6. In the Output range text box, specify a single-cell range in a blank area of the worksheet. Make sure there is plenty of room below and to the right of this cell. 1-2-3

will write a six-column table definition into the worksheet starting at this location; everything in the path of that table will be overwritten. The table definition will contain one row for each field in the database table.

7. Select OK. 1-2-3 creates a six-column table definition that starts in the cell you specified in the Output range text box. The table definition created matches that of the existing table you specified in the Model range text box. 1-2-3 then uses this table definition to create the new external table under the name you specified.

When you create a new table, that table is empty (contains no records). However, that table is connected to 1-2-3, and you can refer to it by using the 1-2-3 range name you assigned during the Data External Options Create Table command. Thus, you can use the Data Query Extract, Data Query Unique, or the Data Query Modify Insert command to add new records to the table. For more on how to append records to an external table, see "Appending Records to an External Table" earlier in this chapter.

You can also use another external table as a model for creating a new external table. To do this you must connect the model table to 1-2-3 and assign it a range name before using the Data External Options Create Table command. Once the table has been connected, follow the same steps outlined in the previous example. In step 5, specify the range name of the external table in the Model range text box.

Using a Table Definition

You can also create a new table by using a table definition. As you may recall, you can use the Data External Options Paste Fields command to create a table definition for an

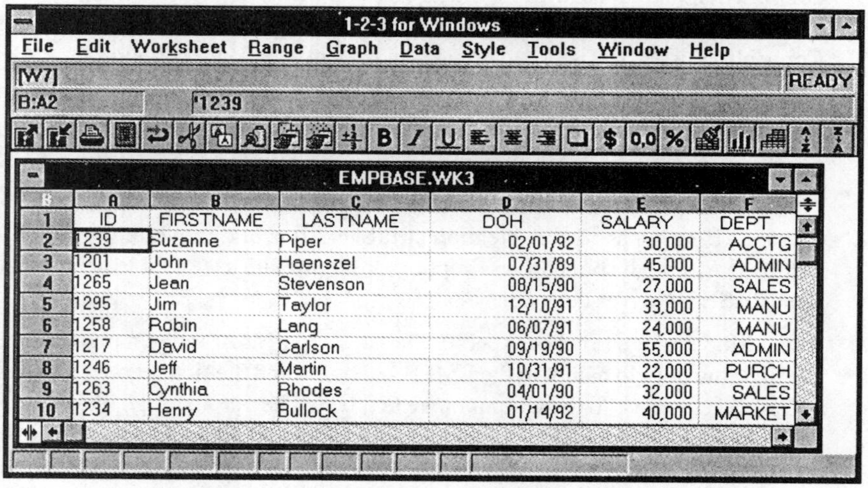

Figure 11-36 Using the EMPBASE table as a model for creating a new external table.

existing table. You can then modify that table definition to suit your needs. You may also type the table definition into the worksheet manually. For more about table definitions, see "About 1-2-3's Table Definitions" earlier in this chapter.

To create a new table by using a table definition, you must use the 1-2-3 Classic menu. To do this, perform the following steps:

1. Choose /Data External Create Name. 1-2-3 prompts you for a name for the new table.

2. Enter a full table name for the new table. As you may recall a full table name includes three parts: a Datalens driver name, database directory name, and a table name. For example, to create a new dBASE IV table named NEW, type **DBASE_IV C:\123W NEW** and press ENTER. 1-2-3 prompts you for a range name for the table.

3. Type a new range name of 15 characters or less for the table and press ENTER. 1-2-3 prompts you for a table creation string.

4. Press ENTER to bypass the creation of a table creation string.

5. Select Definition Use-definition and specify the range that contains your modified table definition. Press ENTER to confirm your selection.

6. Select Go. 1-2-3 creates the new table.

Deleting an External Table

To delete an external table, use the /Data External Delete command from the 1-2-3 Classic menu. When you select this command, 1-2-3 prompts you for the name of a table to delete and displays the names of Datalens drivers. Select the name of the driver that is associated with the table you want to delete. 1-2-3 prompts you for the name of a database directory and displays the current directory. Modify this entry, if necessary, to reference your C:\123W program directory and press ENTER. 1-2-3 prompts you for a table to delete and displays the names of tables to which it has access. Select the table name of your choice and press ENTER. 1-2-3 deletes the table you've specified.

Sending Commands to a DataLens Driver

The 1-2-3 Classic equivalent for Data External Options Send command is /Data External Other Command.

You can use Data External Options Send Command to pass a command string to an external database table. Before using this command, make sure you have connected the external database table to 1-2-3 by using the Data Connect to External command.

As mentioned, both the dBASE IV and Paradox drivers do not interact directly with the DBMS engine, only with database tables. Therefore, the command set for both the dBASE IV and Paradox drivers is very limited. See "About the dBASE IV Driver" and "About the Paradox Driver" earlier in this chapter for more details on this.

When you select Data External Options Send Command, 1-2-3 displays the dialog box in Figure 11-37. In the Connect to driver text box specify the name of the database table that is already connected to 1-2-3. Precede the table name with the appropriate Datalens

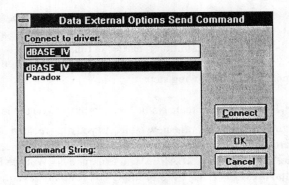

Figure 11-37 The Data External Options Send Command dialog box

driver name and directory. For example, to send a command to the EMPLOYEE table, type **DBASE_IV C:\123W\SAMPLE EMPLOYEE.** In the Command string text box type the command you want to send to the database table using the appropriate syntax for its host database management program. You can use commands that interact with the database table but that do not require any specific output. (See "How the dBASE IV Driver Treats Index Files" earlier in this chapter for a list of supported commands.) For example, to activate a particular multiple index tag for the EMPLOYEE.DBF database, you might use a command syntax similar to the following:

```
SET ORDER TO [tag-name] TABLE [table-name]
```

where *tag-name* is the name of the tag you want to make active and *table-name* is the name of the EMPLOYEE table. To send the command, select the OK button.

Specifying a Different Character Set

If your company does business in foreign countries, you may come across an external table that uses a character set that is different from 1-2-3's. To use this data within 1-2-3, you may have to change the character set for the Datalens driver that is associated with that table.

To specify a different character set for a Datalens driver, you must use the /Data External Other Translation command from the 1-2-3 Classic menu. In preparation for this command, use the Data Connect to External command to connect to an appropriate database table. When you are ready, select /Data External Other Translation. 1-2-3 displays the names of Datalens drivers. Choose the Datalens driver you want. 1-2-3 prompts you for the name of a database and displays the path to the current directory. Change this, if necessary, to your 1-2-3 program directory and press ENTER. 1-2-3 then displays the names of available character sets for the Datalens driver you've selected. Choose the name of the character set you need.

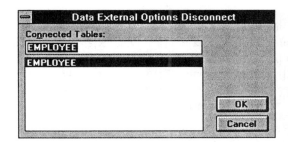

Figure 11-38 The Data External Options Disconnect dialog box

Disconnecting an External Table

The 1-2-3 Classic equivalent for the Data External Options Disconnect command is /Data External Reset.

To disconnect from an external table, use the Data External Options Disconnect command. When you select this command, 1-2-3 displays the dialog box in Figure 11-38. The range names of tables that are currently connected to 1-2-3 appear in the list box. Select the range name of the table you want to disconnect and select OK. 1-2-3 will then disconnect the table you selected.

It is always a good idea to disconnect an external table after you are finished using it. However, be aware that disconnecting an external table may have the following effects:

- Database @functions that refer to the table display ERR. However, when you reconnect to the table with Data Connect to External, those @functions will once again calculate correctly.

- Data Query commands that refer to the external table result in an error message. Once again, you can solve this problem by reconnecting the appropriate external table with Data Connect to External.

- If the disconnected table is the last table associated with a database, 1-2-3 will disconnect the database. If that database is the last database associated with a particular Datalens driver, 1-2-3 will also disconnect the driver.

Updating External Table References in a Multiuser Environment

The /Data External Other Refresh command in the 1-2-3 Classic menu allows you to specify a time interval in seconds to update external-table references in the worksheet. Database @functions are recalculated and the most recent Data Query command is reexecuted. This command is useful when you're working in multiuser environment where the external database you happen to be querying is updated frequently. That way, you can be sure you are using the most recent information.

When you select the /Data External Other Refresh command, 1-2-3 displays a menu with three options, Automatic, Manual, and Interval. To have the worksheet updated automatically, select Automatic. Then select Interval and specify the number of seconds you want between updates. Select Manual (the default) to turn off automatic update. To return to the worksheet, select the OK button.

Modifying the LOTUS.BCF File

The LOTUS.BCF file instructs 1-2-3 which directories to list when you select a Data External command. By default, 1-2-3 only searches the current directory when you select a Data External command. To have 1-2-3 search for tables in other directories, you must include the path to those directories in your LOTUS.BCF file.

The LOTUS.BCF file is an ASCII file that is automatically copied onto your 1-2-3 program directory when you install 1-2-3.

You can modify the contents of this file by using any editor that reads and saves files in ASCII format, like Notepad.

Initially, the LOTUS.BCF file contains the following two listings:

```
1.  DN="dBASE_IV" DL="L1WDBASE"
    DD="Datalens Driver for dBASE IV Tables, Release 1.0";

2.  DN="Paradox" DL="PARALENW"
    DD="DataLens Driver for Paradox Tables, Release 2.0"
    AC=UI,PW;
```

Although it may not seem like it, each of these listings is a single statement. The first applies to the dBASE IV driver and the second applies to the Paradox driver. We'll examine the dBASE IV statement first. It is composed of three elements, DN, DL, and DD. Each of these elements has the following meaning:

- DN: Shows the name of the Datalens driver as it appears on your screen when you select a Data External command. The driver name must appear in quotation marks. In this case, 1-2-3 will display DBASE_IV for Data External commands.

- DL: Informs 1-2-3 of the filename of a particular Datalens driver. In this case, 1-2-3 will look for a filename that begins with L1WDBASE when you select the dBASE IV driver. This file must reside in the 1-2-3 program directory.

- DD: Shows a description for the Datalens driver. This element of the statement is optional.

The Paradox driver statement includes the same three elements—DN, DL, and DD—and they perform the same functions. However, the Paradox driver also supports two additional elements as follows:

1.   AC=UI,PW: Allows you to control access to the Paradox driver. AC=UI causes 1-2-3 to prompt for a user ID when the driver is accessed. This ID identifies who is using the driver when another user is denied access. If the user does not provide an ID when prompted, the default ID, Paralens, is used. If you include the PW parameter, as in AC=UI,PW, the user will also be prompted for a password.

2.   DC=*"path"*: Defines the path to the PARADOX.NET file. This element is only useful when users will be sharing files on a network. For example DC="C:\PDOXNET" defines the \PDOXNET directory on drive C as the location of the PARADOX.NET file. If PARADOX.NET doesn't exist in this location, the driver will create it. To give users access to shared files on a network without using PARADOX.NET, use the DC="NOSHARE" statement.

Each statement you include in the LOTUS.BCF file *must* end with a semicolon (;). As you can see from the above listings, the statement can take up more than one line.

Normally, when you connect to a Datalens driver, 1-2-3 shows only the current directory when searching for databases. To have 1-2-3 list additional directories for Data External commands, you must add a special statement for each directory. These statements must begin with DB. In addition, you must include a DN statement that references the dBASE IV or Paradox driver. The words dBASE_IV or Paradox must be typed exactly as they appear in the first DN statements in the file. You can also include an optional DD statement to describe the directory. Each new statement will take the following form:

```
DB="path" DN="driver-name" DD="description";
```

For example, imagine you have a directory, C:\DBASE, that contains your dBASE database files. To have 1-2-3 list this directory when you select a Data External command, you can add the following statement to your LOTUS.BCF file:

```
DB="C:\DBASE" DN="dBASE_IV" DD="dBASE files";
```

The Paradox driver requires essentially the same syntax. You can also add two more optional parameters, AC=UI,PW and/or DC=*"path"*. (These parameters are explained above.) For example, you might use the following statement:

```
DB="C:\PARADOX\SAMPLE" DN="Paradox" DD="sample files"
AC=UI,PW;
```

12

Advanced Data Analysis

Hidden in the Data menu are a number of commands—Data Fill, Frequency, Regression, Matrix, and What-if Table—that let you perform sophisticated data analysis. Although these commands can be used to evaluate a database, their real power becomes apparent when you use them to perform statistical analysis, sensitivity analysis, or even matrix manipulation on other types of data.

For example, you can use two of these Data commands to perform statistical analysis: Data Regression analyzes trends or relationships through linear regression, and Data Frequency counts the number of times data falls within specified intervals. Data What-if Table performs what-if or sensitivity analysis by evaluating the effect of changing one, two, or three variables in a formula. And Data Matrix manipulates matrices and returns the unique solution to a set of constraints. Data Fill, always hard to categorize, creates a range of sequential, equally spaced values such as numbers, dates, times, or percentages.

To effectively use these Data commands, you'll need to have an understanding of the underlying math. So this section serves as a quick refresher course, and even shows you how to evaluate the results you get.

FILLING A RANGE WITH VALUES

The Data Fill command is an easy way to fill a range with sequential, equally spaced values. You'll find yourself using it to enter sequential numbers, dates, times, and even percentages.

Creating Evenly Spaced Values

Imagine that you want to enter the payment numbers 1 through 12 in column A, just as in Figure 12-1. Simply choose Data Fill, and the dialog box in Figure 12-1 appears. (You can also preselect a range before you invoke Data Fill.) In this case, specify the Range A2..A13. You can specify a range that is one column or row, or even a 3-D range.

Next, enter a Start—the first value you want to appear in Range—of 1. (Use TAB to move between the text boxes.) Then enter a Step—the increment between each value—of 1. Finally, specify a Stop—the highest value to appear in Range—of 12. A Start, Step, or Stop can be entered as a number, a function, or even a formula referencing information in a worksheet. However, because a formula is converted to its resulting value, you'll have to reenter it in Data Fill whenever its result changes.

> ▼ *Tip:* Use a very high Stop, like 99999, rather than a calculated one. This causes 1-2-3 for Windows to stop entering values when all cells in the Range are filled, rather than when the Stop value is reached. Or use a very low Stop, like -99999, for sequentially decreasing values.

When you select OK, 1-2-3 for Windows fills the range A2..A13. It enters the Start, 1, in cell A2, then adds the Step, 1, to it and enters the second value, 2, in cell A3. 1-2-3 for Windows continues this process until *either* the Range is filled, *or* it reaches the Stop value.

Only if you use a single row Range does Data Fill enter values in a rowwise fashion. If you specify a multirow Range, Data Fill fills each cell in the first column, then each cell in the second column, and so on. Similarly, if you use a 3-D Range, the first worksheet is filled by column, then the second worksheet is filled by column, and so on.

> ▼ *Tip:* Once you've used the Data Fill command, selecting 🖳 will create a filled range using the current Data Fill settings, except beginning in the current location of the cell pointer. For example, if the cell pointer is located in cell D2 of Figure 12-1 when you select this icon, 1-2-3 for Windows will create the same filled range you can see in column A, beginning in cell D2.

You can also enter sequential values in descending order, like the Payments Left in Figure 12-1. Enter the Range B2..B13, the highest value as the Start, 240, a negative Step of -1, and a Stop much lower than the Start, -99999.

Note: 1-2-3 for Windows remembers the Data Fill settings you specify and saves them with the file.

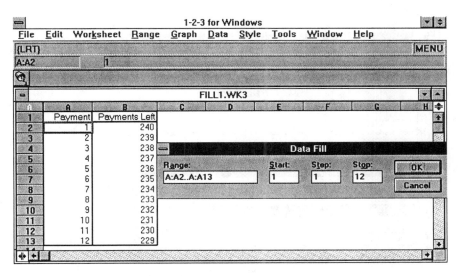

Figure 12-1 Using Data Fill to enter evenly spaced values

Creating Evenly Spaced Dates and Times

Data Fill also creates sequential dates spaced by days, weeks, months, quarters, or years, as well as sequential times spaced by seconds, minutes, or hours. For example, you can use this command to enter the dates in Figure 12-2, which are incremented by month. To do so, begin by selecting Data Fill, and specifying the Range A2..G2.

You'll probably want to enter the Start using the D1 or D4 date format. So you can enter 31-Dec-93 (the D1 or 1: 31-Dec-90 date format) or 12/31/93 (the D4 or 4: Long Intl Date format). If you use the D2 format (2: 31-Dec), 1-2-3 for Windows assumes the current year. On the other hand, if you use the D3 format (3: Dec-90), 1-2-3 supplies the missing day as 1, the first day of the month. When you use the D5 format (5: Short Intl Date), however, 1-2-3 doesn't supply the missing year; the resulting dates are for the year 1900. You can also enter the Start as @DATE(93,12,31).

Note: For more about entering dates and times, see "Date and Time Arithmetic" in Chapter 9. To format dates and times, see Chapter 5.

1-2-3 for Windows includes special Step notations for dates shown in Table 12-1. For example, if your Start is the 15th day of a given month, and you use a Step of 1m, 1-2-3 will automatically step dates so they occur on the 15th of each month. By entering a Step of 1m in our example, 1-2-3 for Windows returns dates on the last day of each month, because the Start, 12/31/93, represents the last day of January.

You can also enter the Stop as a date, or just enter a very high Stop like 99999. You can see these settings in Figure 12-2. When you choose OK, 1-2-3 for Windows enters

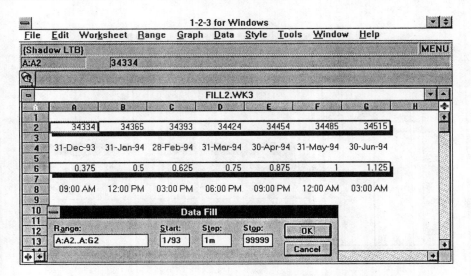

Figure 12-2 Using Data Fill to enter evenly spaced dates and times

the date-numbers shown in row 2. When you format them to look like row 4 using Range Format 1: 31-Dec-90, you can see that each date represents the last day of a month.

A similar approach is used to enter the times shown in Figure 12-2. which increase sequentially by 3 hours. Select Data Fill and specify the Range A6..G6, then enter the Start using one of 1-2-3 for Windows' four time formats. You can enter this Start as 9:00:00AM (6: 11:59:59 AM), 9:00 AM (7: 11:59 AM), 9:00:00 (8: Long Intl Time), or 9:00 (9: Short Intl Time). When you use the D7 or D9 format, 1-2-3 assumes the missing seconds are 0. When you use the D8 or D9 International time formats, 1-2-3 for Windows assumes a military clock; for instance, 8:00 PM is entered as 20:00. Another acceptable way to enter this Start is @TIME(9,00,00).

Note: When you enter a date or time, it appears as a date-number or time-number the next time you use Data Fill.

TABLE 12-1 The Data Fill Step Options

Date Step	Data Fill Increment	Time Step	Data Fill Increment
d	Day	s	Second
w	Week	min	Minute
m	Month	h	Hour
q	Quarter		
y	Year		

1-2-3 for Windows also provides special Step notations for times shown in Table 12-1. In this case, enter the Step 3h to space the times by 3 hours, then enter the Stop as a time, or use a very high Stop like 99999. When you select OK, 1-2-3 enters the time-numbers in row 6 of Figure 12-2. To format these time-numbers to look like row 8, use Range Format 7: 11:59 AM.

FREQUENCY DISTRIBUTION ANALYSIS

A *frequency distribution* records the number of times or the *frequency* that data occurs within a limited number of categories or *intervals*. For instance, a table categorizing the number of test scores below 69.99, and from 70 to 79.99, 80 to 89.99, and 90 to 100 is a frequency distribution. Instead of manually counting each occurrence and then categorizing the data, you can use 1-2-3's Data Distribution command to perform these operations for you.

For example, imagine that you are introducing a new, exciting line of... toasters! Suppose that, to give yourself a competitive advantage, you are considering a warranty program offering free repair for a specified period of time. Accelerated life testing has been performed on 15 of these nifty toasters, replicating the typical wear and tear for a family of 10. By categorizing this data in a frequency distribution table, you can determine a warranty period that won't be prohibitively expensive.

To do this, you must first enter the data you want tabulated, called the *Values range*, either as a column, row, or range. Actually, the Values range can even be in multiple files, open or on disk. For instance, the number of repair-free years for these 15 toasters has been entered in the range B3..B17 of Figure 12-3.

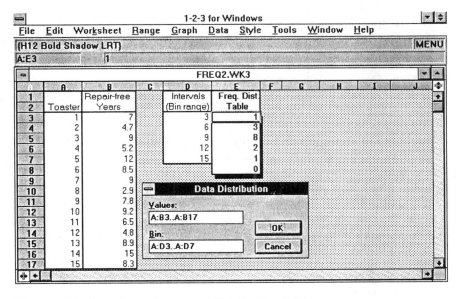

Figure 12-3 Creating a frequency distribution table

Caution: You'll get incorrect frequency counts if any cells in the Values range contain NA, which 1-2-3 for Windows assigns to the lowest interval, and ERR, which it assigns to the highest interval. Blank cells and labels are ignored.

The next step is to establish frequency intervals using these guidelines:

- Intervals should not overlap. Correct intervals, for instance, might be 0 to 3, 3.01 to 6, 6.01 to 9, and so on.

- The combined range of all intervals should encompass all values in the Values range.

- Intervals should usually be the same size or *span*, yet small enough so that the midpoint of an interval is representative of the values that fall into the category. Most often, 6 to 20 intervals work best.

- Enter a frequency interval as a value or formula (*not* a label) representing its upper limit. For the interval 3.01 to 6, for instance, you'd enter 6.

- Enter frequency intervals in *ascending* order in adjacent cells in a single *column*. Blank cells will corrupt the count.

Returning to the current example, 3-year intervals might return worthwhile data. These frequency intervals, called the *Bin range*, are entered in *ascending* order in adjacent cells in a *column*. (Otherwise, 1-2-3 for Windows returns an incorrect frequency distribution.) Notice that only the highest value in each interval is entered in the range D3..D7. 1-2-3 will evaluate the first interval as equal to or less than 3, the second interval as between 3.01 and 6.0, and so on.

▼ *Tip:*   To enter equally-spaced intervals in the Bin range, use Data Fill discussed earlier in this chapter.

To actually create the frequency distribution, select the Data Distribution command. You'll see a Data Distribution dialog box like the one in Figure 12-3. Specify the Values range B3..B17 and the Bin range D3..D7. Select OK, and 1-2-3 for Windows creates a frequency distribution table in the column directly to the right of the Bin range. (Since any data contained in these cells will be overwritten, make sure they're empty.)

As you can see in Figure 12-3, one sample value is less than or equal to 3. Similarly, three values are greater than 3.01 but less than or equal to 6.0. Note that 1-2-3 for Windows *always* adds an additional count, in this case 0 in cell E8, that represents sample values above the highest Bin value, 15.

You can use the information in this table to make a decision. If you institute a 3-year warranty program, for instance, you would most likely repair, at no charge, 6.7% (1/15) of the toasters sold. On the other hand, you may want to change the frequency intervals to return more precise information.

Note: When you update data, 1-2-3 for Windows doesn't update the frequency distribution table unless you reuse Data Distribution.

Using Standard Deviation Ranges as Frequency Intervals

In the current example, if the sample is normally distributed, you can use the frequency distribution output in a statistical analysis to judge the most cost-effective warranty period. A *normally distributed sample* looks like a bell-shaped curve. Approximately 68.3% of the values fall within ±1 Std Dev (standard deviation), 95.4% within ±2 Std Dev, and 99.7% within ±3 Std Dev. (See Chapter 9 for a discussion of the standard deviation.)

By using standard deviation ranges as frequency intervals, you can use the frequency distribution output to count the number of occurrences within these ranges. To create the intervals shown in Figure 12-4, the 7.92 sample mean (average) is calculated in cell D16 using @AVG(B3..B17), and the 3.02 sample standard deviation is computed in cell D17 using @STDS(B3..B17). (See "Statistical Functions" in Chapter 9 for a discussion of these functions.) So the first interval in Figure 12-4, -1.1, is entered as +D16-3*D17 or Mean-3*Std Dev in cell D3. 1-2-3 will evaluate the first interval as equal to or less than -1.1 (Mean-3*Std Dev), the second interval as between -1.11 and 1.9 (Mean-2*Std Dev), and so on.

To create this frequency distribution, select Data Distribution and specify the Values range B3..B17, the Bin range D3..D9, then choose OK. As you can see, three of the sample values are greater than 1.9 (Mean-2*Std Dev) but less than or equal to 4.9 (Mean-1*Std Dev). Likewise, four values are greater than 4.91 but less than or equal to 7.9 (Mean). No values are greater than the highest Bin value, 17.0 (Mean+3 Std Dev).

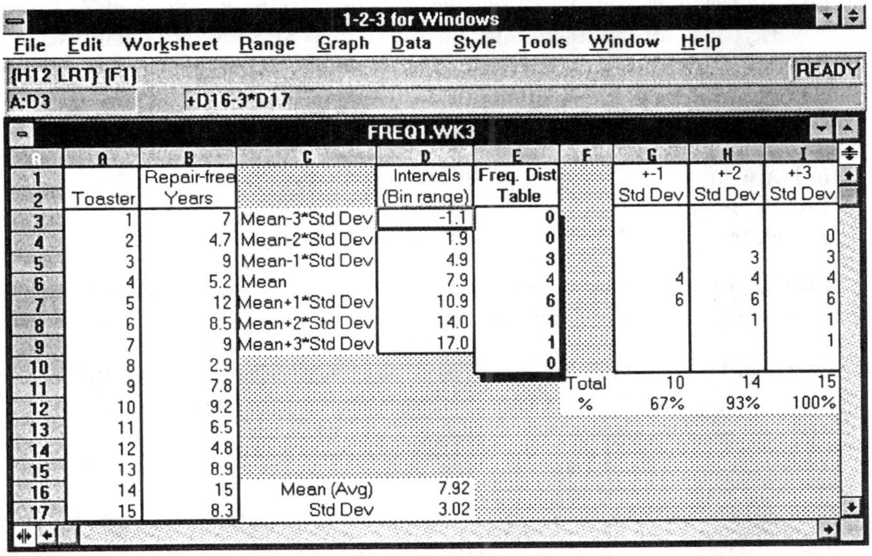

	A	B	C	D	E	F	G	H	I
1		Repair-free		Intervals	Freq. Dist		+-1	+-2	+-3
2	Toaster	Years		(Bin range)	Table		Std Dev	Std Dev	Std Dev
3	1	7	Mean-3*Std Dev	-1.1	0				
4	2	4.7	Mean-2*Std Dev	1.9	0				0
5	3	9	Mean-1*Std Dev	4.9	3			3	3
6	4	5.2	Mean	7.9	4		4	4	4
7	5	12	Mean+1*Std Dev	10.9	6		6	6	6
8	6	8.5	Mean+2*Std Dev	14.0	1			1	1
9	7	9	Mean+3*Std Dev	17.0	1				1
10	8	2.9			0				
11	9	7.8				Total	10	14	15
12	10	9.2				%	67%	93%	100%
13	11	6.5							
14	12	4.8							
15	13	8.9							
16	14	15	Mean (Avg)	7.92					
17	15	8.3	Std Dev	3.02					

Figure 12-4 Using Standard Deviation ranges as frequency intervals

In columns G, H, and I, these counts have also been used to verify that the sample is normally distributed. Approximately 67% of the values are within ±1 Std Dev, 93% within ±2 Std Dev, and 100% within ±3 Std Dev. In column G, for example, 10 sample values fall within ±1 Std Dev (the count for the 4.9 [Mean] interval and the count for the 7.9 [Mean+1*Std Dev] interval).

Now you can make your decision. For instance, you can see that no toasters required service within the first two intervals, or 1.9 years. So you can be like the Maytag repair man if you institute a warranty policy that covers repairs in the first two years. By contrast, a warranty program covering the first five years will burn you, because you will most likely repair at no charge 20% (3/15) of the toasters you sell.

MANIPULATING MATRICES

You'll want to use the Data Multiply and Invert commands, which manipulate matrices, to find a unique solution to a set of simultaneous linear equations or to efficiently calculate values that would normally require long multiplication formulas.

Finding a Unique Solution

Matrices are commonly used to find the unique solution that makes a system of simultaneous equations true. For example, imagine that you're trying to find the production levels of three products that best utilize your company's resources.

Each unit of Product X uses $1.50 of in-house labor, Product Y, $3.50, but Product Z doesn't use any. The total payroll at maximum capacity is $2 million. Additionally, Product X uses $.50 per unit of outside, unskilled labor, and Product Z, $4 per unit. However, your union contract limits outside labor to $1.5 million. Finally, each unit of Product X requires $2 of material, Product Y, $7, and Product Z, $6. A $5 million material constraint is caused by credit limitations. Using this data, you can create these simultaneous linear equations:

In-house labor: $1.5x + 3.5y + 0z = 2,000,000$
Outside labor: $0.5x + 0y + 4.0z = 1,500,000$
Material: $2.0x + 7.0y + 6.0z = 5,000,000$

A *matrix,* or rectangular table of values, is simply a shortcut to express simultaneous linear equations. These equations are represented in matrix form as

Matrix of Coefficients			**X**	Variables	=	Matrix of Constants
1.5	3.5	0	X	x	=	2,000,000
0.5	0	4.0		y		1,500,000
2.0	7.0	6.0		z		5,000,000

If a unique solution does exist, you can calculate it by first using the Data Matrix Invert command to return the inverse matrix of the Matrix of Coefficients, then multiplying this inverse matrix by the Matrix of Constants using Data Matrix Multiply.

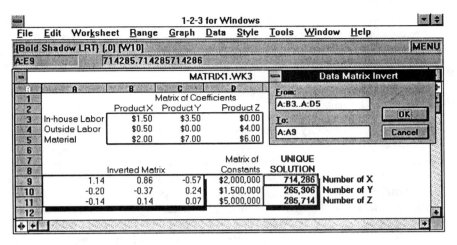

Figure 12-5 Inverting and multiplying matrices

Inverting a 2-D Matrix

The *inverse* of a matrix is another matrix which, when multiplied by the matrix itself, results in an *identity* matrix—a matrix composed of 0's and 1's whose determinant is 1. (See a linear algebra text for further discussion.) If a Matrix of Coefficients can be inverted, then there is only one unique solution. On the other hand, if it can't be inverted, there is either no solution or an infinite number of solutions to the simultaneous linear equations.

A matrix has an inverse if it is square (an equal number of columns and rows), its determinant is *not* equal to 0, and the columns are linearly independent. In addition, a matrix can't have any inconsistencies or redundancies. An *inconsistency* results from equations with conflicting results; for example, $x + y = 700$ and $x + y = 1200$ are inconsistent. A *redundancy* occurs when one equation, like $3x + 3y = 600$, is a just a multiple of a second equation, $x + y = 200$ for instance.

To invert the 3 x 3 (3 rows by 3 columns) Matrix of Coefficients in the example, you would begin by entering it in the range B3..D5 in Figure 12-5. Next, use the Data Matrix Invert command, and in its dialog box, specify B3..D5 in the From text box. In the To text box, enter cell A9, which represents the upper-left corner of the output range. When you select OK, 1-2-3 for Windows will try to invert this matrix.

If you don't specify a square matrix, 1-2-3 for Windows will display the error message "Not a square matrix." However, if the matrix is not invertible, you'll see "Cannot invert matrix."

▼ *Tip:*   If a matrix can't be inverted because multiple solutions exist, use 1-2-3 for Windows' Solver to return the optimal solution. (See Chapter 13.)

As you can see in Figure 12-5, 1-2-3 successfully inverts this Matrix of Coefficients and returns its inverse, beginning in cell A9. So, a unique solution does exist for these simultaneous linear equations, and it can be found by multiplying this matrix by the Matrix of Constants.

Multiplying 2-D Matrices

The Data Matrix Multiply command uses matrix multiplication rules to multiply the values in two matrices and return the resulting matrix. You'll successfully multiply matrices, however, only when the number of columns in the first matrix equals the number of rows in the second matrix. (Otherwise, 1-2-3 displays the error message "Matrices incompatible for multiplication.") The resulting matrix contains the same number of rows as the first matrix and the same number of columns as the second matrix. 1-2-3 can multiply two matrices each as large as 80 x 80.

To see how this works, look at Figure 12-5. The 3 x 3 inverted matrix and the 3 x 1 Matrix of Constants are multiplied using the Data Matrix Multiply command. In the Data Matrix Multiply dialog box, A9..C11 is specified as the First matrix, D9..D11 as the Second matrix, and cell E9 as the upper-left cell of the Output matrix. When you select OK, 1-2-3 multiplies these matrices. It then displays the new matrix, composed of one column and three rows, beginning in cell E9. For example, 1-2-3 multiplies 1.14 in cell A9 by 2,000,000 in cell D9, 0.86 in B9 by 1,500,000 in D10, and -0.57 in C9 by 5,000,000 in D11, then totals the results to return the first value, 714,286.

The resulting matrix contains the *only* values that make the simultaneous equations true. So an *x* of 714,286, a *y* of 265,306, and a *z* of 285,714 make up the unique solution.

Note: When you update data, you must reuse Data Matrix to update your results. However, 1-2-3 remembers the Data Matrix settings you specify, and even saves them with the file.

Inverting and Multiplying 3-D Matrices

1-2-3 multiplies and inverts 3-D matrices (spanning more than one worksheet) by treating a 3-D matrix as a group of individual 2-D matrices. For example, suppose you use Data Matrix Invert to invert the 3-D matrix A:A1..B:C3. 1-2-3 for Windows treats this matrix as two *separate* 2-D matrices, A:A1..A:C3 and B:A1..B:C3. So to be inverted, both must follow 2-D matrix rules; each must be square, for example. 1-2-3 then returns the inverse (if the matrices are invertible) for A:A1..A:C3 in one worksheet, and a separate inverted matrix for B:A1..B:C3 in a second worksheet.

Note: If you specify a 3-D Output range, rather than just the upper-left cell, it must contain the same number of worksheets as the matrix being inverted or the matrices being multiplied.

When you multiply a 3-D matrix, you must multiply it by another 3-D matrix containing the same number of worksheets. However, because 1-2-3 for Windows treats both of the 3-D matrices as a group of 2-D matrices, each 2-D portion must also follow 2-D matrix

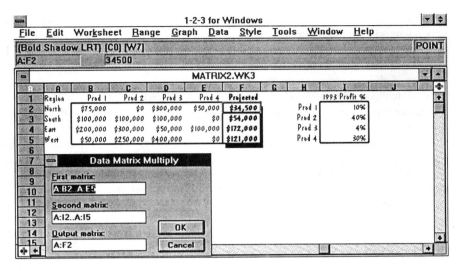

Figure 12-6 Using Data Matrix Multiply to calculate values

rules. For example, suppose you use Data Matrix Multiply to multiply the 3-D matrix A:A1..B:C3 by another 3-D matrix, C:C1..D:C3. 1-2-3 multiplies the 2-D matrix in worksheet A, A:A1..A:C3, by the 2-D matrix in worksheet C, C:A1..C:C3, and returns the resulting matrix in a worksheet. Similarly, it multiplies B:A1..B:C3 by D:A1..D:C3 and returns a separate matrix in a second worksheet.

Calculating Values Efficiently

The Data Matrix Multiply command also can be used to calculate values that normally require long multiplication formulas. For example, Figure 12-6 contains historical product sales by sales region in the range B2..E5 and the projected 1993 gross profit percentage by product in cells I2..I5.

To calculate the total gross profit each region is expected to contribute, use Data Matrix Multiply and specify the First matrix as B2..E5, the Second matrix as I2..I5, and cell F2 as the upper-left cell of the Output matrix. You can see these settings in the dialog box in Figure 12-6. 1-2-3 for Windows multiplies these matrices and returns the results in a new matrix beginning in cell F2. For instance, the North's 1993 expected profit contribution is $34,500.

REGRESSION ANALYSIS

Regression analysis allows you to analyze trends in data by examining relationships between variables. For instance, you might examine whether a consistent relationship exists between sales and advertising costs, or whether the number of tax evaders is dependent on tax rates.

Regression analysis is used in both a descriptive and predictive way. For example, by using historical data to determine if a mathematical relationship exists between the number of childbearing women and the number of babies born, you are using regression analysis to describe newborns as a function of childbearing women. On the other hand, if you use this mathematical relationship to predict the number of newborns next year, then you're using regression analysis as a predictive tool.

Using 1-2-3's Data Regression command is an efficient way to avoid the tremendous number-crunching typically required to perform a regression analysis. This section serves as a quick refresher course on regression analysis, discusses how to perform and evaluate a regression analysis in 1-2-3 for Windows, and even shows how to graph regression results effectively.

Regression Basics

The objective of any regression analysis is to determine if a *dependent* y variable whose value you are trying to predict can be described as a function of one or more *independent* x variables in a *linear* relationship. If a variable y, such as interest rates, is dependent on one x variable, the federal deficit perhaps, then you perform simple linear regression. *Simple linear regression* determines the "best" line through a series of data points to create a linear formula that expresses y as a function of x.

In regression analysis, it's usually uneconomical, impractical, or impossible to evaluate an entire population of data, such as daily interest rates. Instead, you'll usually use only a population sample like monthly or quarterly values. A simple linear regression for a sample is expressed mathematically as

$$\bar{y} = C + bx$$

where $\bar{y}$ is the sample mean (average) value of the dependent variable you want to predict. C is the y-intercept, or where this line crosses the y-axis, b is the *slope* (defined as the "rise over run," or y/x) of the regression line , and x is the independent variable. This formula is modified to create a *simple linear regression model*, expressed for a sample as

$$\bar{y} = C + bx + e$$

where C and b are called *regression coefficients*. The additional term e, known as the *residual*, represents the sample regression error caused by the difference between the y data points and the mean value $\bar{y}$.

When you use the Data Regression command to perform a regression analysis, 1-2-3 for Windows uses the *least-squares method* to calculate the regression coefficients C and b. It does so by minimizing the sum of the squared deviations, or the sum of the squared errors e^2, where e is the vertical deviation of a data point from the regression line. By looking at the sample linear regression model, you can see that when y equals $\bar{y}$ (mean), and x equals $\bar{x}$ (mean), then the error e equals 0 (assuming the y-intercept C is 0).

The least-squares method assumes the errors in a population, estimated by the sample error term e, are independent of x and of each other, are normally distributed, and have a mean value of 0 and a constant, finite variance.

Multiple linear regression also returns a linear formula describing the "best" line through a series of data points. However, one dependent y variable, such as interest rates, is expressed as a function of multiple independent x variables—the size of the federal deficit, the number of bank failures, and the money supply, for instance. The *multiple linear regression model* is expressed mathematically as

$$\bar{y} = C + B_1x_1 + B_2x_2 \ldots + B_n x_n + e$$

which is the simple linear regression model expanded to include multiple independent x variables and their corresponding B coefficients.

 Tip: If y is expressed by a nonlinear relationship, you may be able to perform a linear regression if you first manipulate the data. For example, you can use logarithms to convert an exponential relationship to a linear one.

Error Analysis Basics

The accuracy of any regression analysis depends on:

- whether a straight line approximation of the data—a linear relationship between y and the independent x variable(s)—is reasonable.

- the amount of error not explained by the regression line.

Error analysis in any linear regression, then, concentrates on the reliability of a regression line, which can be analyzed by the amount of unexplained error or *deviation*. The total deviation in a regression model is defined as

SST	=	SSE	+	SSR
(Total Deviation)		(Unexplained Deviation)		(Deviation explained by Regression Line)

Therefore, the higher the proportion of unexplained deviation (SSE) to the total deviation (SST), the less reliable the regression equation is.

Regression Output Table

When you use the Data Regression command to perform a regression analysis, 1-2-3 for Windows produces a table of data you can use to create a regression line equation and to analyze the reliability of this linear relationship. This table includes the following:

Constant (C) is the y-intercept—the point at which the regression line crosses the y-axis. If you specify Y-intercept Set to zero, however, it will be 0.

Number of Observations is the number of x values included in the X-range.

Degrees of Freedom is computed, if the *y*-intercept is forced to 0, as the number of observations in the X-range less the number of independent *x* variables. If 1-2-3 calculates the *y*-intercept, then it is this value less 1. If 1-2-3 for Windows calculates the degrees of freedom as less than 0, however, it won't perform a regression, and you'll see the message "Too few observations for number of variables."

X Coefficients is calculated for each independent *x* variable included in the X-range. If it is positive, an X Coefficient represents the amount the dependent *y* variable increases when *x* increases 1 unit; a negative X Coefficient represents the amount *y* decreases when *x* increases 1 unit.

Standard Error of the Y Estimate, also known as S_e, is a measure of the goodness of fit of the regression line to the data points. Mathematically, S_e is the standard deviation (a measurement of variability) of the *y* values about the regression line, expressed as

$$S_e = \sqrt{\text{SSE/No. of degrees of freedom}}$$

S_e can give a good estimate of the magnitude of potential error when you use a regression equation to predict a *y* value. Approximately 68.3% of the sample data falls within $\pm 1 S_e$, 95.4% within $\pm 2 S_e$, and 99.7% within $\pm 3 S_e$.

Note: For a discussion of SSE, SSR, and SST, see "Error Analysis Basics," above.

Standard Error of the X Coefficient(s), known as S_b, indicates the amount each independent *x* variable influences *y*. S_b measures the amount of the regression model error caused by *x*, even after accounting for all other independent *x* variables. It is expressed as

$$S_b = \sqrt{S_e\,[\,1/(\,x_i - x^2\,)\,]}$$

Typically, S_b is used in the *t-test*, $t = x/S_b$, where the higher the *t*-value, the more influential *x* is in determining *y*. If S_b is less than 50% of *x*, then *t* is greater than 2, and a statistically significant relationship exists between *x* and *y*.

R Squared, known as R^2, measures the strength of the linear relationship, or the goodness of fit of the regression line to the data. Because R^2 equals SSE/SST, it indicates the proportion of the total variation explained by the regression line. If the regression line is a perfect fit to the data, SSE equals 0 and R^2 equals 1; if R^2 is .7, then 70% of the variation in the *y* values to the regression line is explained by *x*. However, if 1-2-3 for Windows returns a negative R^2, then you specified Y-intercept Set to zero when you should have used Y-intercept Compute. For multiple regression models with the same *y* variable and the same number of independent *x* variables, the highest R^2 indicates the best fit.

Simple Linear Regression: An Example

Suppose you make $50,000 per year and can't seem to save any money. To see if this is universally true, you randomly canvas 15 of your nearest and dearest friends about their gross income and the amount they saved in 1992. To see if a consistent relationship exists

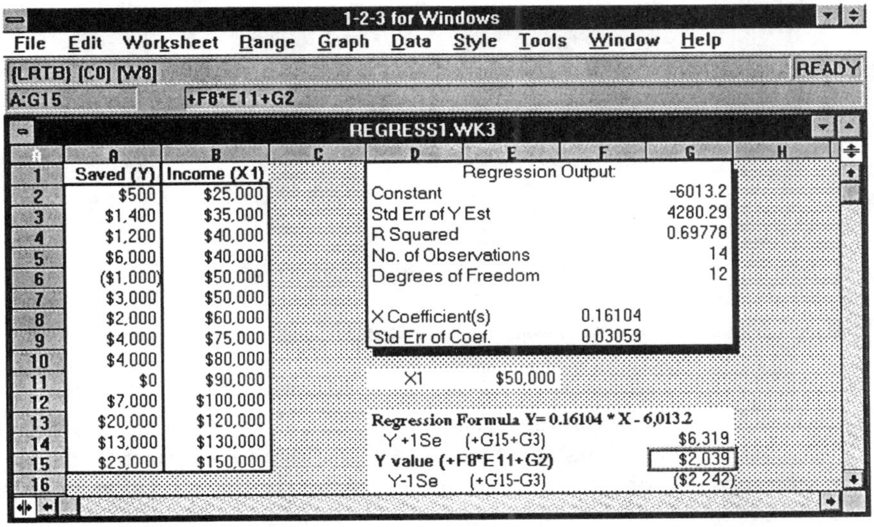

Figure 12-7 Performing a simple linear regression

between these two variables, you'll need to perform a simple linear regression using the Data Regression command.

In this case, income is the independent x variable used to predict the dependent y variable, the amount saved. As you can see in Figure 12-7, each x and its corresponding y value have been entered in adjacent columns A and B. (If you enter data points in rowwise fashion, or use unequal X- and Y-ranges, 1-2-3 for Windows will display the error message "Invalid Y range" when you try to perform the regression.)

To actually perform the linear regression, select the Data Regression command, and then specify the X-range B2..B15 and the Y-range A2..A15. Since you want to compute the Y-intercept, the default, Compute, is correct. Specify the upper-left cell of the Output range as D1. You can see these settings in Figure 12-8.

Note: Don't use Y-intercept Set to zero unless the dependent y variable equals 0 when the independent x variable(s) are 0.

When you select OK, 1-2-3 for Windows performs the regression analysis. Beginning in cell D1, it builds the 4-column, 9-row Regression Output table shown in Figure 12-7. The information in this table can be used to determine the linear relationship between savings and gross income, to analyze the strength and relative reliability of this relationship, and even to predict the amount saved for a given income.

The linear regression equation, developed using the Constant value -6013.2 and the X Coefficient 0.16104, is

$$y = .16104x - 6013.2$$

But, you may ask, how reliable is this equation, or in other words, how well does this equation fit the data? You can get a pretty good idea by examining R^2, the Std Error of the X Coefficient, and the Std Error of the Y Estimate.

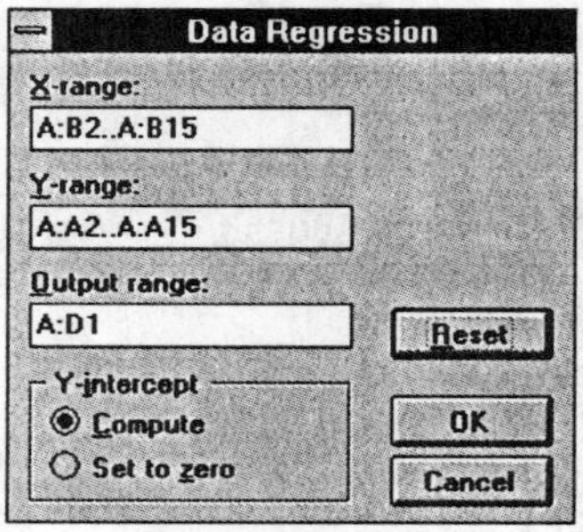

Figure 12-8 The Data Regression dialog box

Because R^2 is .69778, you know that 69.8% of the amount a person saves is explained by his gross income. Because the Standard Error of the X coefficient (S_b), 0.03059, is approximately 19% of the X Coefficient, .16104, a very strong relationship exists between the amount saved and gross income. You can conclude, then, that this linear regression equation is a moderately good "fit" to the data points, and it's reasonable to use it to predict the amount that would be saved for a given income.

In Figure 12-7, for example, the regression formula +F8*E11+G2, establishes that for the $50,000 gross income in cell E11, a person would normally save $2,039 in a year. However, because the Standard Error of the Y Estimate, S_e , is 4280.29, there's actually a 68.3% chance that such a person would go into debt for as much as -$2,242 ($y - 1S_e$) or save up to $6,319 ($y + 1S_e$). Because this is a relatively large range, you'd probably want to see if there is a second independent x variable you can use in a multiple linear regression to better predict the amount saved. But first, let's graph the results of this simple linear regression.

Note: When you update regression data, 1-2-3 doesn't update the regression results unless you reuse Data Regression. However, 1-2-3 remembers your Data Regression settings, and even saves them with the file.

Graphing Data Points and the Regression Line

Once you have performed a regression analysis, you can graph both the data points and the linear regression line on the same graph by using the Data Sort command, the regression equation, and the Graph command.

Note: See Chapter 11 for more about Data Sort, and Chapter 10 for more about the Graph command.

For example, to simultaneously graph the data points and regression line of Figure 12-7, you first need to sort the independent x values in ascending order. To do this, use the Data Sort command and specify the Data range A2..C15, the Primary Key as B2 (income x), and the Ascending option. Select OK, and you'll get the results shown in Figure 12-9.

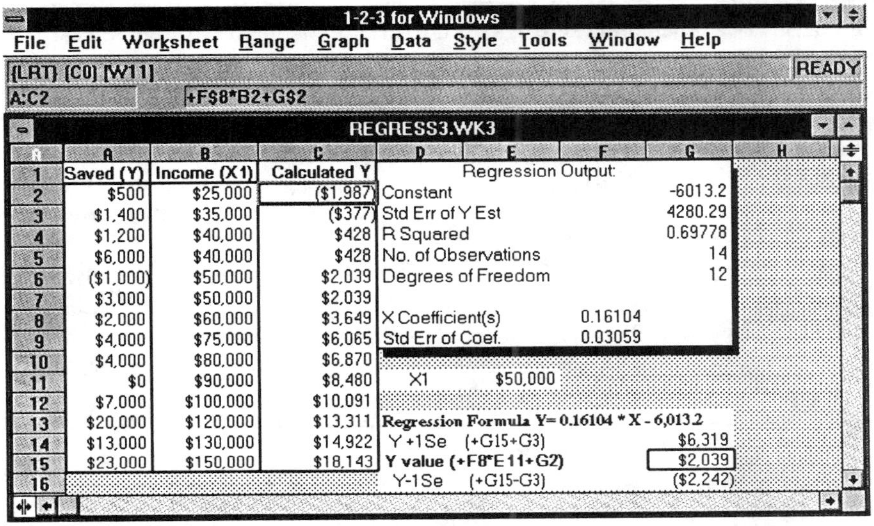

	A	B	C	D	E	F	G
1	Saved (Y)	Income (X1)	Calculated Y	Regression Output:			
2	$500	$25,000	($1,987)	Constant			-6013.2
3	$1,400	$35,000	($377)	Std Err of Y Est			4280.29
4	$1,200	$40,000	$428	R Squared			0.69778
5	$6,000	$40,000	$428	No. of Observations			14
6	($1,000)	$50,000	$2,039	Degrees of Freedom			12
7	$3,000	$50,000	$2,039				
8	$2,000	$60,000	$3,649	X Coefficient(s)		0.16104	
9	$4,000	$75,000	$6,065	Std Err of Coef.		0.03059	
10	$4,000	$80,000	$6,870				
11	$0	$90,000	$8,480	X1	$50,000		
12	$7,000	$100,000	$10,091				
13	$20,000	$120,000	$13,311	Regression Formula Y= 0.16104 * X - 6,013.2			
14	$13,000	$130,000	$14,922	Y+1Se (+G15+G3)			$6,319
15	$23,000	$150,000	$18,143	Y value (+F8*E11+G2)			$2,039
16				Y-1Se (+G15-G3)			($2,242)

Figure 12-9 Preparing regression data for graphing

Next, for each *x* value, use the regression equation to compute a corresponding "Calculated Y" value in column C, then use these values to graph the regression line. For example, in Figure 12-9, the formula +F$8*B2+G$2 is entered in cell C2, then copied to the range C3..C16 (the mixed addressing keeps the appropriate cell references fixed).

Now you can graph this data. Select the Graph New command, then accept the graph name 1-2-3 for Windows suggests or enter one of your own. From the Graph menu, use the Chart commands to specify the settings shown in Table 12-2.

Note in Table 12-2 (see page 636) that the *x* values in B2..B15 are specified as the X data range, the *y* values in A2..A15 as the A data range, and the calculated *y* values in C2..C15 as the B data range. To display just the regression line through the calculated *y* values, only Connectors is turned on in the Chart Options Lines dialog box for the B range. Likewise, to display the actual *y* values as data points, only Symbols is turned on for the A range. As you can see in Figure 12-10, the resulting graph displays the regression line as well as the actual *x* and *y* data points.

Multiple Linear Regression: An Example

In 1-2-3 for Windows, multiple linear regression relates a dependent *y* variable to as many as 75 independent *x* variables in a single linear equation. To see this, let's return to the previous example. Suppose you belatedly realize that the amount a person saves may also be dependent on what he or she spends. For instance, many people may choose to spend their money on vacations instead of saving it. If you look at Figure 12-11, you'll see that a second independent *x* variable—the amount spent on trips—has been added in column C. (When you perform multiple linear regression, you must always enter independent *x* variables in adjacent columns.)

TABLE 12-2   The Chart settings used to create the graph in Figure 12-10

Command	Setting	Chart Command	Setting
Ranges		Axis	
X	B2..B15	X Options Axis title	Yearly Income
A	A2..A15	Y Options Axis title	Amount Saved
B	C2..C15	Options Lines	
Type	XY	A	Symbols
Headings		B	Connectors
Title	Simple Linear	Options Fonts	
	Regression Analysis	Chart title	Arial MT 14
Subtitle	Y=0.16104X - 6013.2		

To perform this multiple linear regression, select Data Regression, and specify the
X-range as B2..C15, which includes both x variables. Continue to use the Y-range
A2..A15, cell D1 as the upper-left cell in the Output range, and Y-intercept Compute,
then select OK. 1-2-3 builds the 4-column, 9-row Regression Output table shown in
Figure 12-11, which includes an X Coefficient and a Standard Error of the X Coefficient
for each independent x variable. Using this data, the regression equation is

$$y = 0.20363 * x_1 - 1.0388 * x_2 - 6573.5$$

Note: For multiple linear regression, 1-2-3 for Windows builds an output table two
columns wider than the number of columns in the X-Range.

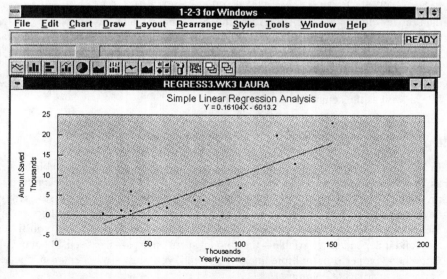

Figure 12-10   Graphing the regression line and the data points

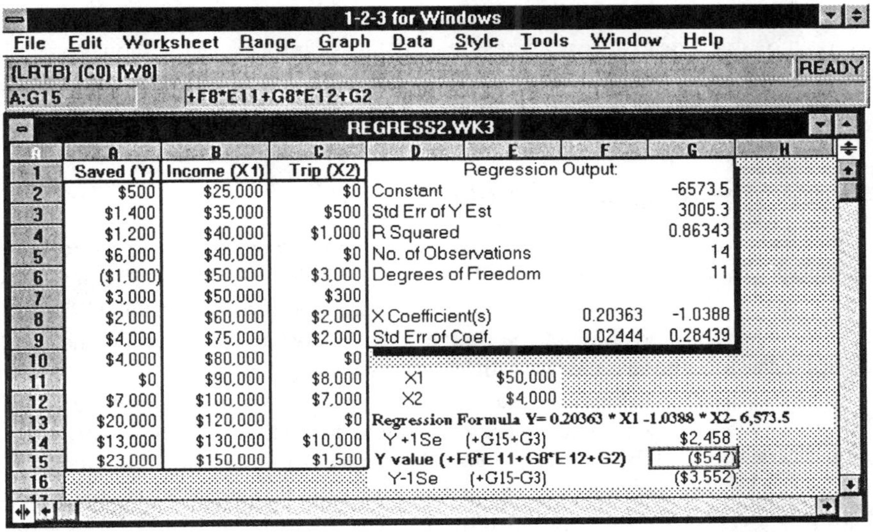

Figure 12-11 Performing a multiple linear regression

Because R^2 is .86343, you know that approximately 86% of the amount saved by a person is explained by his or her gross income and the amount he or she spends on vacations. In addition, the strength of each x variable offers additional insights. For x_1, S_b (the Standard Error of the X coefficient) is .02444, or approximately 12% of the X_1 Coefficient 0.20363. On the other hand, S_b for X_2 is .028439, or approximately 27% of the X_2 Coefficient -1.0388. So there is a very strong relationship between the amount saved and gross income, and a strong *inverse* relationship between the amount saved and the amount spent on vacations.

Using the regression formula, +F8*E11+G8*E12+G2 in cell G15, establishes that for $50,000 in gross income, a person would be expected to go $547 into debt. Actually, there is a 68.3% chance such a person would go in debt for as much as -$3,552 (y – $1S_e$) or save up to $2,458 (y + $1S_e$). By comparing Figures 12-7 and 12-11, you'll see that the multiple regression creates a better fit than the simple linear regression. Thus, gross income and the amount spent on vacations more accurately explain the amount a person saves. Feeling much better, you decide to start planning a trip to Rio.

DATA TABLE WHAT-IF ANALYSIS

The equivalent 1-2-3 Classic command is /Data Table.

The Data What-if Table command performs repetitive what-if calculations. You can create a *one-way data table* that analyzes the effect of changing one variable in one or more formulas. On the other hand, a *two-way data table* shows the effect of changing two variables in one formula, and a *three-way data table*, the effect of altering three variables.

A data table is a good way to store related information, so you'll want to use data tables as lookup tables, or to access and evaluate database information without corrupting the database. They're even an efficient way to generate a block of values rather than using formulas and Edit Quick Copy or Edit Copy and Paste.

Creating a One-Way Data Table

A one-way data table presents the effect of changing a single variable in one or more formulas while all else is held constant. For example, imagine you've just moved to California. To buy a house comparable to the one you just sold in the Midwest, you'd have to take out a $1,000,000 mortgage. Absolutely amazed, you decide to at least compute the monthly payment for different mortgage terms.

Figure 12-12 shows the resulting one-way data table when the mortgage term varies. Before you can use Data What-if Table 1-Way to create this table, however, you need to set up the framework by entering input values, a test formula, and an input cell.

Input values are the values you want 1-2-3 for Windows to substitute in a formula. In Figure 12-12, they are the mortgage terms being compared. Input values *always* represent the leftmost column of a one-way data table. For example, the input values 240, 360, and 480 in the one-column range B3..B5 represent monthly mortgage terms entered as either numbers or formulas.

The Data What-if Table 1-Way command uses an *input cell* to enter **The 1-2-3 Classic** each input value into a formula. This cell must either be the upper-left cell **equivalent is** of the table—cell B2 in Figure 12-12 for example—or be located out- **/Data Table 1.** side the data table—like cell A7. As you'll see, 1-2-3 for Windows will substitute each input value into the input cell, which causes each value to be used in the test formula.

A *test formula* establishes the relationship you want to analyze. For example, since the input values in Figure 12-12 are mortgage terms, and you want to compare the resulting mortgage payments, you need to use a formula that uses a mortgage term to return a mortgage payment. The @PMT(*principal,interest,number of payments*) function conveniently fits the bill. (See "Financial Functions" in Chapter 9 for a discussion of @PMT.)

For 1-2-3 for Windows to enter the mortgage term values in the @PMT function, you must use input cell A7 as the *number of payments* argument. In addition, the test formula must be placed one column over and one row up from the first input value. So in cell C2, the formula @PMT(C7,C8,A7) is entered, where C7 contains the $1,000,000 principal amount, and cell C8, the monthly interest rate, .12/12, or 1%. 1-2-3 for Windows returns ERR for this function because the *number of payments* argument references the blank input cell A7.

Now you're ready to calculate the one-way data table. Select the Data What-if Table 1-Way command, and you'll see the dialog box shown in Figure 12-12. Specify the Table range B2..C5, which includes the input values and test formula, and the Input cell A7.

When you select OK, 1-2-3 for Windows routes the input values through the input cell and into the test formula. For example, 1-2-3 enters the first term, 240, in input cell A7. The @PMT function then uses this value as its *number of payments* argument and returns $11,011 in cell C3. Moving down column C, 1-2-3 reiterates this process for each input

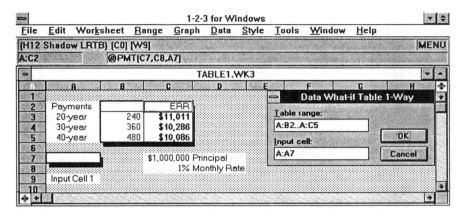

Figure 12-12   A one-way data table

value. As this table bleakly shows, you'd have to pay $11,011 each month to meet a $1 million, 20-year mortgage, but only $10,085 when the term increases to 40 years.

> ▼ *Tip:*   When you change input values or the test formula, the data table isn't up-
> dated. However, 1-2-3 for Windows remembers the latest Data What-if
> Table settings, so just press TABLE (F8) to update your results.

You can also use Data What-if Table 1-Way to calculate the results of multiple test formulas all using the same input values. For example, in cell D2 you could enter @PMT(1000000,.1/12,A7) to calculate the monthly payment at a 10% annual rate. You'd have to specify the Table range B2..D5, however. Then 1-2-3 for Windows would also enter the input values into this function, and return the results in column D.

Creating a Two-Way Data Table

As its name implies, a two-way data table shows the effect of changing two variables in a formula while all else is held constant. For instance, building on the previous example, Figure 12-13 contains a two-way data table showing the resulting monthly payments when both the term and interest rate of a $1,000,000 mortgage are varied.

The framework of a two-way data table varies slightly from that of a one-way data table. First, a two-way data table requires two sets of input values. One range of input values is still entered as the leftmost column of the table; the mortgage terms are still entered in B3..B5 in Figure 12-13. However, the second range of input values for the monthly interest rate define the top row of the table, and is entered in the range C2..F2.

Second, a two-way data table requires an input cell for each variable. So A7 remains Input cell 1 for the number of payments, while B7 is designated Input cell 2 for the interest rate values.

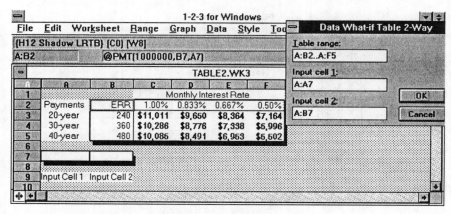

Figure 12-13 A two-way data table

Finally, the test formula must reference both input cells. Additionally, it must be placed in the upper-left cell of the table. In cell B2, the formula @PMT(1000000,B7,A7) references input cell B7 as the *interest rate* argument and input cell A7 as the *number of payments* argument. 1-2-3 returns ERR for this function because both of these arguments reference blank cells.

The 1-2-3 Classic equivalent is /Data Table 2.

Now Data What-if Table 2-Way can be invoked to create this two-way data table. In the dialog box shown in Figure 12-13, the Table range B2..F5 is specified to include the input values and test formula, as is A7 as Input cell 1, and B7 as Input cell 2.

When you press ENTER or select OK, 1-2-3 for Windows enters 240, the first number of payments, into input cell A7, and 1%, the first interest rate, into input cell B7. The @PMT function then uses these values as its *number of payments* and *interest rate* arguments and returns $11,011 in cell C3. Moving down column C, 1-2-3 reiterates this process for each *number of payments* value and continues down columns D, E, and F, using the interest rate from the corresponding column in row 2. For example, 1-2-3 for Windows computes the last value in the table, $5,502, by substituting the 480 term into input cell A7 and the 0.5% rate into input cell B7—so, if interest rates ever fall to 6% per year again, you'd have the honor of paying $5,502 per month for a $1,000,000, 40-year mortgage.

Creating a Three-Way Data Table

A three-way data table analyzes the effect of changing three variables in a formula. To see how to create one, let's continue to build on the current example. Previously, both the interest rate and mortgage term were varied for a $1,000,000 mortgage; now let's assume that you've decided to evaluate smaller mortgages. In this case, the principal becomes the third variable.

Three input cells are needed, one for each variable. In Figure 12-14, Input cell 1, A7, is still used for the input values in the leftmost column—the mortgage terms, and Input

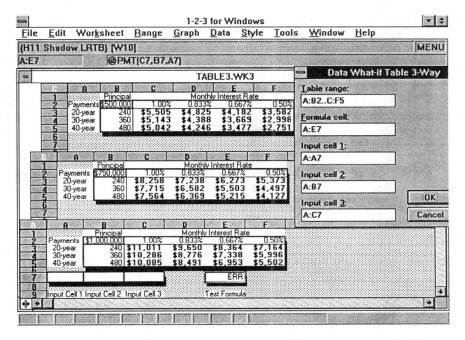

Figure 12-14 A three-way data table

cell 2, B7, for the input values along the top of the table—the interest rates. Input cell 3, C7 in worksheet A, is assigned to the third variable, the principal values.

In order to incorporate more than one input value for the third variable—the principal amount in this instance—a three-way data table is usually three-dimensional. Each input value for the third variable is then entered in the upper-left cell of the table in each worksheet. In Figure 12-14, cell B2 in worksheet A contains the $1,000,000 principal input value, cell B2 in worksheet B, $750,000, and cell B2 in worksheet C, $500,000.

When you want to evaluate the results of these principal input values for the same input values of the other two variables—the mortgage term and the interest rate—you'll want to create a three-way data table that looks like Figure 12-14. Here, the *same* mortgage term and interest rate input values are used in each worksheet. In all three worksheets, column B contains the same mortgage terms and row 2 contains the same interest rates.

Since the third input value displaces the test formula from the upper-left corner, the test formula is placed outside the three-way table. So @PMT(C7,B7,A7) is entered in cell A:E7, called the *formula cell*. Remember, cell C7 represents the input cell for the principal, B7 the input cell for the interest rate, and A7 the input cell for the term.

The 1-2-3 Classic equivalent is /Data Table 3. Once you've created this framework, it's easy to create the three-way data table. Select Data What-if Table 3-Way, and in the dialog box shown in Figure 12-14, specify the three-dimensional Table range A:B2..C:F5. Then specify the Formula cell as A:E7, Input cell 1 as A:A7, Input cell as A:B7, and Input cell 3 as A:C7. When you select OK, 1-2-3 fills in the three-dimensional data table shown in Figure 12-14.

In the first worksheet, 1-2-3 for Windows returns the same values as in the two-way table in Figure 12-13. In each case, it enters the corresponding mortgage term from column B into input cell A7, and the corresponding interest rate from row 2 in input cell B7. However, in input cell C7, it always enters the $1,000,000 principal value. 1-2-3 then repeats this process, except next it uses the mortgage terms, interest rates, and the $750,000 principal value from worksheet B, and finally those from worksheet C. By looking at cell C:C5, you can see that for a $500,000, 40-year mortgage at 12% annually, you only need to pay $5,042 a month. At this rate, the Midwest looks better and better.

Note: The 1-2-3 Classic menu includes the /Data Table Labeled command, which allows you to assess a virtually unlimited number of variables in an unlimited number of formulas. However, because this command is used so rarely (due to its complexity), Lotus has not included it in the 1-2-3 for Windows' main menu.

Using Data Tables to Evaluate a Database

One of the most powerful applications of the Data What-if Table command is in evaluating databases. By using a database function in a data table, you can access, manipulate, and evaluate database information without corrupting the database.

Using a Database Function in a One-Way Data Table

When you use a database function in a one-way data table, the test formulas, input values, and input cell need to be adjusted to accommodate database applications. For example, imagine you belong to a charitable organization that conducts an auction every year. The database in Figure 12-15 represents items donated by some of the members. To compute the number of donations in each TYPE category, as well as the average donation per category, you can use a one-way data table to search the database and return this information.

In this one-way data table, the input labels in the leftmost column A13..A17 represent the categories in the TYPE field. These categories will then be input into two test formulas that are database functions. (See Chapter 11 for a complete discussion of database functions.)

In cell B12, for instance, @DCOUNT(A1..E10,2,A19..A20) will determine the number of donations for each category in the TYPE field. Notice that when you use a database function in a data table, the database A1..E10 becomes the *input* argument, and the field you want to evaluate, TYPE, is represented by the *offset* argument 2. (You could also use the literal string "TYPE".) The *criteria* argument A19..A20 contains the name of the field you want to search, TYPE, as well as a blank input cell located directly below this name. Although @DAVG(A1..E10,3,A19..A20) in cell C12 also uses these *input* and *criteria* arguments, the *offset* of 3 will return the average donation from the AMOUNT field for each category in the TYPE field.

You can now fill in the data table in Figure 12-15 by using Data What-if Table 1-Way to specify the Table range A12..C17 and Input cell A20. For example, 1-2-3 for Windows

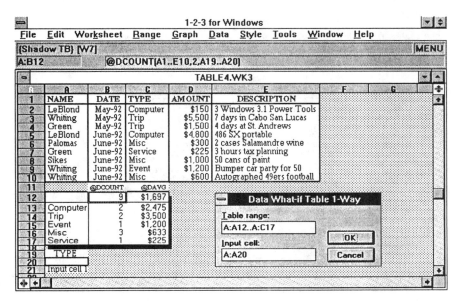

Figure 12-15 A one-way table for a database

enters the first input label, Computer, into A20, so @DCOUNT searches the TYPE field for Computer and returns two occurrences in cell B13. In cell C17, however, @DAVG searches the TYPE field, but uses an *offset* of 3 to return an average Service donation of $225 from the AMOUNT field.

Using a Database Function in a Two-Way Table

Imagine you'd like to query this database for each label in the TYPE field, and determine from the AMOUNT field the number of donations between 0 and $3,000 and between $3,001 and $6,000. You can do this by creating a two-way data table like the one in Figure 12-16.

Like other two-way data tables, the one in Figure 12-16 contains input labels in the leftmost column and input values along the topmost row. Column A still contains the input labels from the TYPE field. However, row 12 now contains input values representing the second search criteria—the $3,000 and $6,000 upper limits to be evaluated in the AMOUNT field.

The @DCOUNT(A1..E10,3,A19..B20) function, located in the table's upper-left cell, A12, still uses the database range A1..E10 as the *input* argument. By using an *offset* of 3, it will evaluate information in the AMOUNT field. @DCOUNT also uses the *criteria* argument A19..B20, which includes two field names, each with a corresponding input cell directly below it. The range A19..A20 will evaluate the TYPE labels, while B19..B20 will evaluate the upper limits in the AMOUNT field.

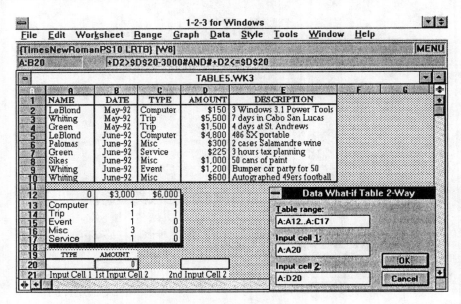

Figure 12-16 A two-way data table for a database

Caution: You must place the input cells in adjacent columns. If you place them sequentially in one column, 1-2-3 for Windows will return incorrect results in the data table.

Let's step back and analyze this situation. As it currently stands, when $3,000 is substituted into cell B20, @DCOUNT will only count the occurrences of $3,000 in the AMOUNT field. To return the count for the range $0 to $3000, and for the range $3,001 to $6,000, you have to add yet another input cell for the AMOUNT field. In Figure 12-16, cell D20—2nd Input Cell 2—performs this function. If you then enter in cell B20 (Input cell 2)

```
+D2>$D$20-3000#AND#+D2<=$D$20
```

this criteria will make @DCOUNT evaluate the range 0 to 3000 when D20 contains 3000, and the range 3,001 to 6,000 when D20 contains 6000. For these criteria to work, the second input cell for the AMOUNT field must be entered as the absolute address $D$20.

You can now specify the Data What-if Table 2-Way settings shown in Figure 12-16. Although you use the Table range A12..C17 and Input cell 1 A20, you *must* specify Input cell 2 as D20, the second input cell for the AMOUNT field. That way, 1-2-3 for Windows creates the table by first entering the input label, Computer, into cell A20 and the input value $3,000 into D20. Since cell B20 contains +D2>$D$20-3000#AND#+D2<=$D$20, @DCOUNT evaluates the range 0 to 3,000 and returns 1 Computer donation in cell B13. Likewise, @DCOUNT returns 0 Service donations between $3,001 and $6,000 in cell C17.

Using a Database Function in a Three-Way Table

Naturally, you can also create a three-way data table that queries three different database fields. To see this, let's return to the database A1..E10 in Figure 12-16. However, let's use @DSUM to determine the amount in each TYPE category that a specific person donated in May and June of 1992.

You can see the framework of this data table in Figure 12-17. Although column A still contains the input labels from the TYPE field, row 12 now contains the input labels May-92 and June-92 representing the categories in the DATE field.

Like other three-way data tables, the third variable is entered in the upper-left cell of the table. For example, to evaluate the donations made by different people, A:A12 contains the name LeBlond, B:A12, Whiting, and C:A12, Green. However, the *same* TYPE and DATE labels are used in worksheets A, B, and C.

As you can see, Input cell 1, A20, is still positioned directly below the field it will search, TYPE. Although B20 remains Input cell 2, it will now search the DATE field. Input cell 3, C20, is added to evaluate the NAME field in cell C19.

The test formula, @DSUM(A1..E10,3,A19..C20), is placed outside the table in the Formula cell A:E20. Once again, the *input* is the database range A1..E10 and the *offset* is 3 (the literal string "AMOUNT" also works) because the AMOUNT field is being analyzed.

By using the Data What-if Table 3-Way and the settings in Figure 12-17, you can create this three-way table. In worksheet A, @DSUM uses the corresponding TYPE label from column A, the corresponding DATE label from row 12, and the NAME LeBlond from A12 to calculate that LeBlond donated only Computer equipment—$150 in May and $4,800 in June. Using the input values in worksheet B, @DSUM shows that Whiting donated a $5,500 Trip in May, as well as a $1,200 Event and $6,000 Miscellaneous in June; using the input values in worksheet C, Green donated a $1,500 Trip in May and $225 in Services in June.

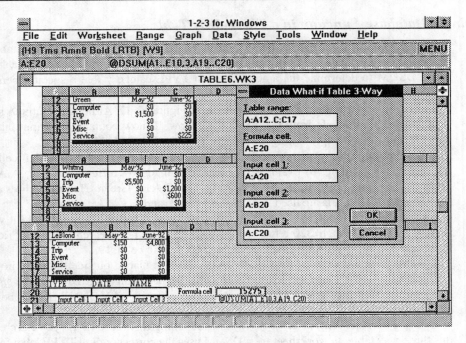

Figure 12-17 A three-way table for a database

13

Advanced Sensitivity Analysis

1-2-3 for Windows includes two advanced tools for what-if analysis: Backsolver and Solver. The Backsolver is appropriate when you already have a particular goal in mind and want to see what it will take to reach that goal. You'll want to use the Solver, however, to perform truly sophisticated sensitivity analysis when there isn't necessarily one "right" answer. You can specify multiple variables, include nonlinear relationships, and even impose constraints to reflect real-life limitations. Not only does Solver find as many different answers as it can, but it also identifies which one it considers the best or optimal solution.

THE BACKSOLVER

The Tools Backsolver command performs goal seeking for a specific objective, such as a net profit value, by *backsolving* (solving backwards) a formula which calculates net profit. To do this, the Backsolver computes the value of another variable in this formula, sales perhaps, that causes the formula to return this net profit target value.

Defining the Problem

Imagine you are 25 years old and want to retire at 45 with a $1,000,000 nest egg. Assuming a guaranteed 12% annual return, you'd like to calculate the amount you must put aside every month to make this happen.

Note: Backsolver only works with functions that return a value. See Chapter 9 for a discussion of @TERM and other functions.

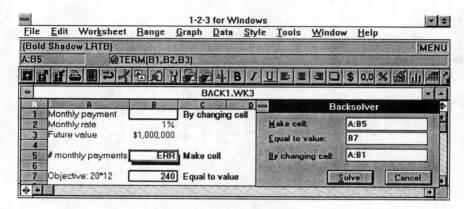

Figure 13-1 Setting up a problem to be solved by Tools Backsolver

Since the function @TERM(*payment,rate,FV*) returns the number of equal payments necessary to achieve an *FV* (future value), given a fixed *payment* amount and a fixed interest *rate*, you can use it with Tools Backsolver to backsolve for the monthly payment. Figure 13-1 shows how @TERM is used in this capacity.

The function @TERM(B1,B2,B3) in cell B5 references the 1% (.12/12) monthly interest *rate* in B2 and the $1,000,000 *FV* in B3. The blank cell B1 is designated as the *payment* argument. (The fact that it is empty causes @TERM to return ERR.) Backsolver will compute the monthly *payment* that causes this @TERM function to return the objective—240 (20 years*12) monthly payments.

Now, you can specify this problem in the Backsolver format shown in Figure 13-1. The *Make cell* is the location of the formula that calculates your objective as a function of another variable. In this case, the Make cell, B5, contains @TERM(B1,B2,B3), which calculates the number of monthly payments as a function of the fixed monthly payment.

The *Equal to value* is the objective you want to reach. In Figure 13-1, this is the number-of-payments target in B7, 240 months (20 years*12). Although you can specify the Equal to value as a number, a formula, or a cell reference, 1-2-3 for Windows always converts it to and uses the resulting value. In Figure 13-1 for instance, 1-2-3 automatically converts an Equal to value entered as B7 or 20*12 to 240. (You can see this the next time you access the dialog box.) If your target changes, remember to reenter the Equal to value in the Tools Backsolver dialog box.

The variable Backsolver can change to reach your desired objective is the *By changing cell*. In Figure 13-1, for example, the Monthly payment variable in B1 is designated the By changing cell. Although the cell you specify can be blank or contain a value, Backsolver won't solve the problem if it contains a formula or label. A blank cell, like cell B1, is a good idea because Backsolver will write over any information in the By changing cell.

Results Returned by Backsolver

Once you've specified the Backsolver settings shown in the dialog box in Figure 13-1, choose the Solve option to activate Backsolver. (If you return to the worksheet before

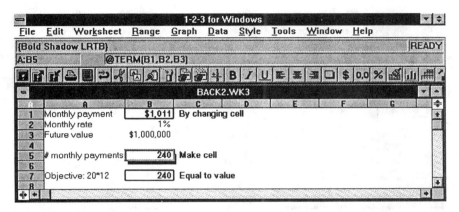

Figure 13-2   Backsolver's answer

you select Solve, you'll lose the Backsolver settings you specified.) Figure 13-2 shows Backsolver's results.

Backsolver solves this problem by calculating the By changing cell value that forces the Make cell formula to return the Equal to value. So it calculates the monthly payment value in B1 that forces the @TERM function in B5 to return 240. As you can see in Figure 13-2, Backsolver enters $1,011, the Monthly payment value it calculates, into B1, the By changing cell. As a result, the @TERM function in B5 returns 240, the Equal to value.

Note: If the By changing cell contains a formula or a label, or if the Make cell doesn't contain a formula, you'll see the error message "Invalid cell or range address."

Backsolver Limitations

Although Backsolver can be useful in some situations, you'll find that its application is limited. The Backsolver's inherent weakness stems from its inability to handle more than one variable. The Solver, however, can handle multiple variables.

In earlier releases, Backsolver had trouble solving a problem when the Make cell formula didn't directly reference the By changing cell. In 1-2-3 for Windows, Backsolver seems to be able to handle multiple layers of dependencies, although you'll still probably want to use the Solver for sophisticated models.

THE SOLVER

The Solver is 1-2-3 for Windows' most sophisticated sensitivity analysis tool. You can use it to solve both linear and nonlinear what-if problems that involve multiple variables and that may have multiple solutions. Solver finds as many different answers as it can, and also identifies which one it considers the best or optimal solution.

You can also use the Solver to generate reports about the problem being analyzed. The Answer table and How solved reports, for instance, provide comprehensive information

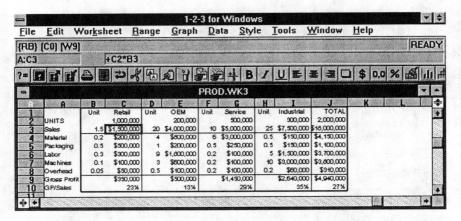

Figure 13-3 A gross profit model

about the problem and the results Solver returns. Others, like the Cells used and Inconsistent constraints reports, can help you in error analysis.

Defining the Problem

Imagine that cash has become the limiting factor for your growing company. You'd like to use the Solver to calculate a product mix that maximizes gross profit, given the current cash crunch. You can then structure sales incentives to reflect this optimal product mix.

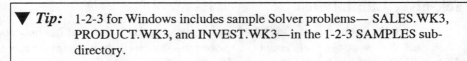

▼ *Tip:*   1-2-3 for Windows includes sample Solver problems— SALES.WK3, PRODUCT.WK3, and INVEST.WK3—in the 1-2-3 SAMPLES subdirectory.

Figure 13-3 shows the relevant information in a gross profit model for the four products manufactured and sold through different channels: Retail, OEM, Service, and Industrial. For example, gross profit for the product sold through retail channels is calculated in column C using the per-unit data in column B. Only Units of 1,000,000 is entered as a value in C2; all else is computed as a function of Units. In cell C3, for instance, the formula +B3*C2 calculates Sales of $1,500,000 as the 1.5 per-unit sales price times 1,000,000 units.

To use the Solver, you must define this problem using

- Adjustable cells, which specify the variables Solver is allowed to change.

- An Optimal cell (optional), which tells Solver the variable you want to optimize.

- Constraints, which limit the number of possible solutions.

Adjustable Cells

Any model you want to analyze must include variables that can be changed. In Solver, each variable is designated as an *adjustable cell*. When Solver solves the problem, each answer it returns will include a value for each adjustable cell.

> ▼ *Tip:*   Specify the variable you want to optimize as the optimal cell, discussed next.

In Figure 13-3, the number of units of each product drive the gross profit model; all other values depend on them. So the Units for each product in C2, E2, G2, and I2 are designated as adjustable cells in Figure 13-4. (Adjustable cells don't have to be adjacent to one another and can even be located in another open file.) Cell J2 isn't designated an adjustable cell because Total Units is only a result of the other Units values; it isn't important in relation to the problem being solved.

A variable designated as an adjustable cell *must* contain a value. The OEM Units in E2 of Figure 13-4, for example, is entered as 200000. If an adjustable cell contains a formula that references other information, Solver assumes that the resulting value is fixed and can't be changed. When you must use a formula that refers to other information, it shouldn't be specified as an adjustable cell. Rather, designate the data it depends on as an adjustable cell.

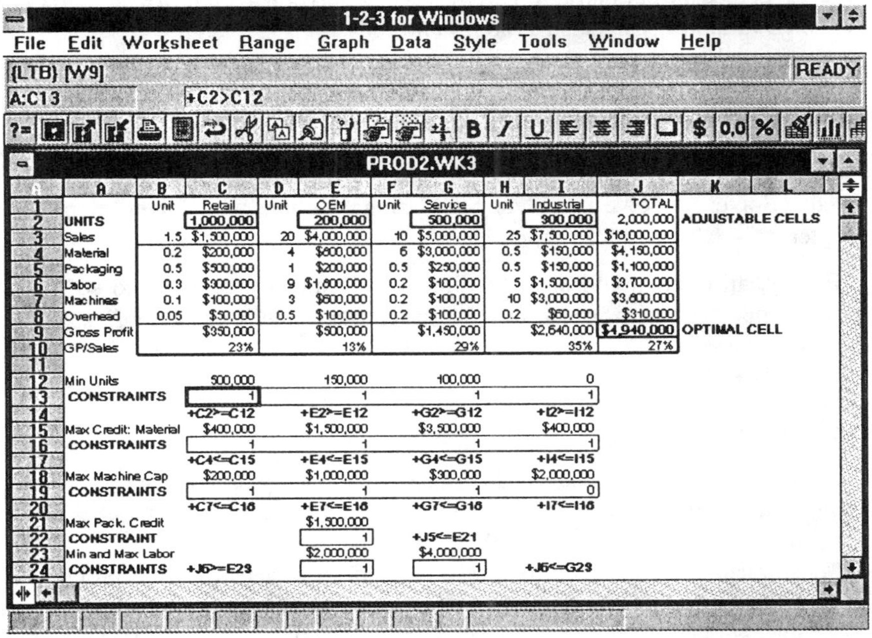

Figure 13-4 Setting up the problem in the Tools Solver format

Limits or constraints *must* be imposed on adjustable cells so that infinite solutions don't exist and Solver can solve the problem (see "Constraints" in this section). Moreover, a large number of variables (adjustable cells) increases the

- Number of possible solutions.
- Time it takes for Solver to solve the problem.
- Chance that there is insufficient memory available for 1-2-3 for Windows to solve the problem.

Imposing stringent constraints on adjustable cells can minimize these problems.

Optimal Cell

Because many solutions can exist for a problem, 1-2-3 for Windows lets you optimize one variable, designated the *optimal cell*, over the other variables, designated as adjustable cells. That is, Solver calculates the best answer for the optimal cell, given the other variables in the problem.

Note: Specifying an optimal cell further limits the number of possible answers for a particular problem.

Because the objective is to optimize gross profit in Figure 13-4, Total Gross Profit in J9 is designated the optimal cell. This means that Solver will optimize this variable before the Units variables designated as adjustable cells.

An optimal cell *must* directly or indirectly reference at least one adjustable cell. In Figure 13-4, for example, Total Gross Profit is calculated as +J3-@SUM(J4..J8), which indirectly depends on the Units for each product.

Note: Only some functions are compatible with Solver, and even these can affect whether Solver can solve a problem. See "Using Functions with Solver" at the end of this chapter.

Finally, an optimal cell *must* be directly or indirectly constrained so that infinite solutions don't exist and Solver can solve the problem. See "Constraints," next, for further details.

Constraints

Constraints are logical formulas that directly or indirectly limit the variables designated as adjustable and optimal cells. Consequently, constraints limit the number of solutions to a problem and allow Solver to solve a problem.

Constraints also allow you to specify realistic parameters for the problem you are modeling. Constraining production to maximum plant capacity, for example, limits the possible solutions to a real-world level. Constraints also provide a more significant set of answers, as well as decrease the time it takes Solver to solve a problem.

> ▼ **Tip:** When Solver can't find a solution to a problem, or returns unrealistic answers, try making your constraints more stringent.

Each constraint must be a logical formula using one of these operators: >, <, =, >=, or <=. Solver doesn't support < > (not equal) or the complex logical operators #AND#, #NOT#, and #OR# (instead, use multiple constraints). Initially, your constraints will evaluate to either 1 (true) or 0 (false). As you'll see, if Solver can make all the constraints simultaneously true (equal to 1), then it will return an answer to the problem. If Solver can't find an answer—at least one constraint isn't satisfied and returns 0 (false)—then Solver will return an attempt or will need a guess.

In Figure 13-4, for instance, most of the constraints represent *upper bounds* that restrict growth: credit limitations imposed by material and packaging suppliers, maximum machine capacity, as well as maximum labor capacity. Since these factors limit maximum values, the <= logical operator is used. For example, production of the product sold through retail channels is limited by the $400,000 credit limitation imposed by material suppliers. This is represented in C16 by the +C4<=C15 constraint. (This logical formula returns the true result 1 because the $200,000 material value in C4 is currently less than $400,000 in C15.)

Because one supplier provides all packaging materials, only one constraint is needed to limit packaging purchases of each product. In cell E22, +J5<=E21 limits total packaging material to less than or equal to $1,500,000, the credit limit imposed by the supplier.

Conversely, units produced for each product are constrained by minimum production levels in row 13, or *lower bounds*. The logical formula +C2>=C12 in C13, for instance, specifies that at least 500,000 units of the product sold through retail channels must be manufactured. This minimum represents the units required to meet current year-long contracts.

> ▼ **Tip:** Include lower-bound constraints to prohibit Solver from returning negative values for a variable (adjustable cell). That's why the constraint +I2>=0 in I13 of Figure 13-4 is included—to exclude a negative value for Industrial units.

Labor costs in Figure 13-4 are *fully bounded*. A current union contract guaranteeing a minimum number of jobs, translating into $2,000,000 in labor costs, is represented by the lower bound +J6>=E23 in cell E24. Plant capacity, on the other hand, limits the number of workers that can be employed and total labor costs to $4,000,000. This maximum capacity is represented by the upper-bound constraint +J6<=G23 in cell G24.

For Solver to solve a problem, constraints must also limit the number of solutions so that infinite solutions don't exist. The Min Units constraints in Figure 13-4 are lower bounds and only limit the minimum number of Units. Because gross profit is being maximized, however, only upper bounds will sufficiently limit the number of possible solutions. In this case, these are the constraints that indirectly limit the upside of Units and Total Gross Profit—Max Machine Capacity; Max Credit: Material; Max Pack Credit;

and Max Labor. (Notice that Constraint cells don't have to be adjacent to one another and can even be located in another open file.)

▼ **Tip:**   A How solved report will show you which constraints are limiting the optimal answer, and can also help you determine if you included incorrect or unrealistic constraints. (See "Generating Reports," later in this chapter.)

Therefore, when you are trying to *maximize* a variable in a model, such as gross profit, you must include sufficient *upper* bounds so that the adjustable and optimum cells are directly or indirectly limited. Otherwise, Solver won't be able to solve the problem. If you are attempting to *minimize* a variable, then you must limit the adjustable and optimal cells sufficiently through *lower* bounds.

▼ **Tip:**   It's essential that you use the correct logical operator in a constraint. If you use <= instead of >=, for example, Solver will return answers for a different problem than the one you are analyzing. When you're not sure which inequality constraint to use, follow these general rules:

- Use <= to create upper bounds if you're solving for the maximum optimum value.

- Use >= to create lower bounds if you're solving for the minimum optimum value.

When in doubt, be sure to check some of the answers Solver returns to see if they make sense for the problem being analyzed.

Activating Solver

Once you've defined a problem in a format compatible with the Solver, it's a simple matter to activate Solver and try to solve the problem. To optimize gross profit in Figure 13-4 for instance, follow this procedure:

1.   Select the Tools Solver command. You'll see the Solver Definition dialog box shown in Figure 13-5A, which displays the current path and filename of the active file. (If this is the wrong file, choose Cancel to return to the active file, make the correct file active, then choose Tools Solver again.)

2.   Specify the Adjustable cells as any combination of range addresses, range names, and cell addresses, each separated by a comma. The maximum entry is 512 characters. In this case, specify C2,E2,G2,I2. You could also enter C2..I2 because D2, F2, and H2 are blank.

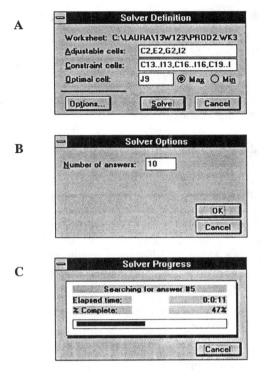

Figure 13-5 The Solver Definition, Options, and Progress dialog boxes

Note: Solver ignores an adjustable cell that is protected, blank, or contains a label. The exception is when you specify a single-cell address or range name for a blank cell, and formulas in your model refer to it. Solver then assumes it's an adjustable cell. Remember too, that when an adjustable cell contains a formula, Solver assumes the resulting value is fixed and can't be changed.

3. Specify C13..I13,C16..I16,C19..I19,E22,E24,G24 as the Constraint cells. Remember to separate each range address, range name, and cell address by an argument separator (a comma), and that the maximum entry is 512 characters. Any Constraint cells that don't contain logical formulas will be ignored by Solver.

4. Specify the Optimal cell J9. (If you don't include an optimal cell, Solver will only provide sample answers, not a best or optimal answer.)

5. If an Optimal cell has been specified, choose to minimize or maximize it. Because the objective is to maximize gross profit in this problem, accept Max, the default.

Note: If an Optimal cell isn't specified, Max and Min have no effect, and only your constraints determine how Solver looks for an answer.

6. Specify the maximum number of answers Solver will return by choosing Options to access the Solver Options dialog box shown in Figure 13-5B, then enter a value

between 1 and 999. In this case, press OK to accept the default of 10 and return to the Solver Definition dialog box.

7.   Choose Solve to start Solver analyzing the problem and searching for possible answers.

Caution: If you return to the worksheet before you select Solve, you'll lose the Tools Solver Definition settings you specified.

When Solver Won't Try to Solve a Problem

Before Solver tries to solve a problem, it estimates the problem's complexity by evaluating the number of variables in the adjustable and optimum cells, the number of constraints, and the complexity of the model (the number of cells containing formulas that are directly or indirectly used by the adjustable, optimal, and constraint cells). When the combined total of these cells exceed 1,000, Solver usually won't be able to solve the problem because more RAM or hard disk space is required than is available on most PCs. Solver also has trouble solving a problem that includes functions other than @SUM and @AVG (see "Using Functions with Solver" later).

Note: When Solver tries to solve a problem, it first uses all available RAM to store answers, and then tries to store the rest as temporary files on disk.

If Solver decides not to solve the problem, it will issue an error message. Some of those messages that you may see are:

- "Can't find optimal answer—optimal cell is unbounded" when constraints are insufficient to limit the problem or no constraints are specified.

- "No valid adjustable cells were specified" when none of the adjustable cells contain values.

- "Invalid cell or range address" when no constraints are specified.

- "No valid constraint cells were specified" when none of the constraint cells contain logical formulas.

- "Solver out of memory" or "Not enough memory available" when there is insufficient memory for Solver to solve the problem.

In some cases, Solver may begin to solve the problem before it displays one of these messages, and may return some representative attempts for the problem.

Results Returned by Solver

If Solver thinks it can solve a problem, it tries to do so using two different techniques. Solver first attempts to solve the problem symbolically (algebraically). If this technique doesn't work, Solver then tries to solve the problem numerically. In other words, it uses a time-consuming trial and error process of substituting values into the adjustable cells until they gradually converge on an answer that meets the specified constraints. Typically, Solver must resort to the numeric method for a complex problem containing many adjustable cells and constraints, when the problem is nonlinear, or when functions other than @SUM or AVG are included in the model.

While Solver tries to solve a problem, it conveys information about its progress. In the Solver Progress dialog box shown in Figure 13-5C, for example, "Searching for answer #5" is displayed, as well as the elapsed time Solver has been solving and the percentage of completion.

Note: You can't perform other tasks while Solver is solving. If you want to cancel the solving process, press CTRL+BREAK or choose Cancel in the Progress dialog box. Solver will stop solving, but retains the answers it found up to then. ("Closing Solver" discusses when Solver discards attempts.) To resume solving, select Solve in the Solver Answer dialog box.

Just because Solver has tried to solve a problem doesn't mean it can actually do so. If it can solve the problem, Solver will return a set of answers. If Solver can't solve the problem, you'll get attempts instead, and in certain situations, diagnostic messages.

When Solver Returns Answers

If Solver solves the problem, it uses the Solver Answer dialog box to convey the number of answers found (up to the number of answers you specified). You can see in Figure 13-6 that Solver found 10 different answers for the gross profit model analyzed.

In addition, Solver automatically displays the first answer in the worksheet by entering the corresponding value in each adjustable cell. In Figure 13-6, Solver enters 1,688,492 in C2, 264,087 in E2, 583,333 in G2, and 200,000 in I2. Because the optimal cell J9 indirectly depends on the adjustable cells through the formula +J3-@SUM(J4..J8), the optimal total Gross Profit of $4,702,857 is also displayed.

Solver evaluates the first answer as one of the following:

- The optimal answer if Solver mathematically maximized or minimized the optimal cell (as you specified).

- The best answer if Solver isn't sure it found the mathematical optimum for the optimal cell. You'll typically get a "best answer" if functions other than @SUM or @AVG are included in the problem, or if your constraints aren't stringent enough for Solver to determine an optimal answer.

- A sample answer that meets the constraints when an optimal cell isn't specified.

In Figure 13-6, Solver conveys that answer #1 is the optimal answer. Because an optimal cell was included in this example, the second answer is the one 1-2-3 for Windows perceives as the second best answer, the third is the next best, and so on. By contrast, sample answers aren't always graded in this way.

By examining the optimal answer in Figure 13-6, you can see that Solver mathematically optimized total gross profit, given the constraints. These constraints limited Solver's

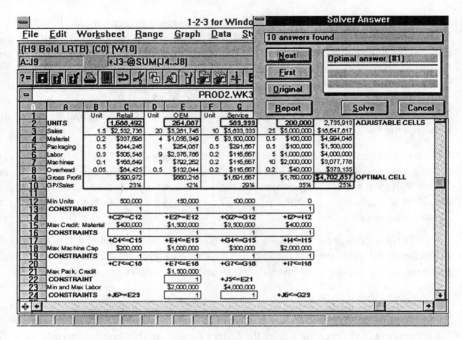

Figure 13-6 The optimal answer returned by Solver

ability to optimize total gross profit—otherwise, only industrial products would be sold and manufactured, because at 35% it has the highest gross profit return of all the product lines.

 Tip: To review all answers together, create an Answer table report. To see which constraints are limiting the optimal answer, create a How solved report. See "Generating Reports," later.

You can use the Next option in the Solver Answer dialog box to display each answer, one at a time, in the worksheet. Select Next once, for instance, and the second answer will be displayed. Keep pressing Next to cycle through the other answers. To display the optimal answer at any time, select the First option. To display the original values in the worksheet, select Original. To save the answers returned by Solver, see "Closing Solver," later.

Caution: Solver may return answers even if your model is incorrectly set up. To see this, imagine in Figure 13-6 that Total Gross Profit is incorrectly calculated as +J3-@SUM(J4..J7); Overhead in J8 is left out of the equation. Solver will certainly return a set of answers, but for a different problem than the one you think you are solving.

If a problem has a best or optimal answer, you can get Solver to return more answers (if they exist). If Solver returns a best answer, you can select Solve again to calculate more answers. For example, imagine that Figure 13-6 showed a best answer and you select Solve again. Solver will calculate 10 more answers, and display that it found 20 answers—the 10 previous and the 10 additional ones. If Solver returns an optimal answer, you can get more answers by first increasing the number of answers in the Solver Definition Options dialog box, then selecting Solve again.

When Solver Returns Attempts

When Solver can't find an answer to a problem, it returns representative attempts. By definition, an attempt makes at least one constraint false (0). Along with its attempts, Solver will also display an "Inconsistent" message to remind you that not all constraints are satisfied.

In rare instances, an attempt instead of an answer will signal that there is no solution to a problem given the constraints specified. Most times, Solver will return an attempt when the problem has been incorrectly modeled and an incorrect constraint or two conflicting constraints are preventing Solver from finding an answer.

In Figure 13-7 for example, the maximum credit extended by suppliers for Retail units in cell C15 has been decreased to 50,000. (You can see this by comparing the Max Credit material constraint in cell C16 to Figure 13-6.) Because the model is inconsistent, Solver only makes one attempt before it stops solving. By reviewing Figure 13-7, you'll see that the inconsistency arises because the Max Credit: Material constraint in C16 limits Retail units to 250,000 units (50,000/.2 material per unit), while the Min Units constraint in C13 specifies at least 500,000 Retail units.

Figure 13-7 also shows that Solver enters into the adjustable cells the values found during its attempt. This enables you to see which constraints are false (i.e., indicated by a 0)—Min Units for Retail in C13, and total Max Labor in G24.

Sometimes an Inconsistent constraints report (see "Generating Reports") can help you correct the inconsistency. Figure 13-8, for example, shows such a report in a cell format. Note that the first report displayed is for C13, the first false constraint. Solver even shows that it can return an answer if you change this constraint to +C2>C12+-250000. (Unfortunately, negative units don't make any sense for this problem.) By pressing Next, you can cycle through this information for all false (0) constraints. Press Next in Figure 13-8, and Solver would also provide similar data for the other false constraint in G24.

It's very important to realize that the Inconsistent constraints report hasn't identified the real culprit—the constraint in C16. That's because for the attempt Solver displays, this constraint is true (1). So just because Solver conveys that a constraint is false doesn't necessarily mean that it's the cause of the inconsistency. In fact, the unrealistic constraint Solver suggests for C13 is a good indication that something else is wrong in this problem. For this reason, make sure you evaluate a constraint deemed inconsistent in relation to other constraints in the problem. And before you make Solver's suggested change to a constraint, make sure that it is reasonable for the problem being solved. To reuse Solver after you modify a problem, see "Modifying a Problem," later.

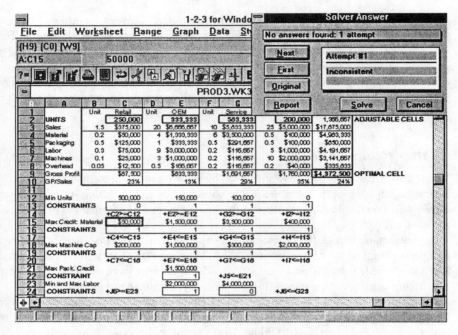

Figure 13-7   The result when constraints are inconsistent

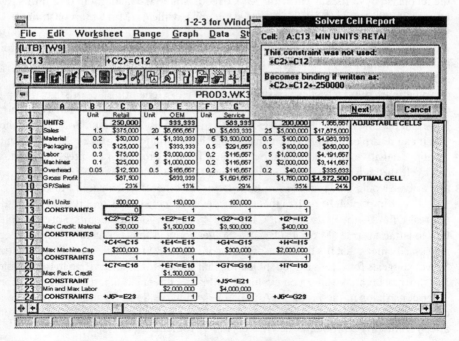

Figure 13-8   An Inconsistent report for a false constraint

> ▼ *Tip:*   Sometimes the Binding constraints in a How Solved table report will
> help you determine if any constraints are incorrect.

When Solver Needs a Guess

As you know, Solver switches from algebraic to numeric (trial and error) calculations to try to solve a complex problem that is nonlinear, includes many adjustable cells and constraints, or uses functions other than @SUM or @AVG. The number of attempts Solver makes depends on whether the problem is correctly modeled and on the number of constraints.

In some instances, Solver determines that it needs more information about the adjustable cells and abandons its effort. For example, after trying for 16 minutes to calculate an answer for a model that includes numerous adjustable cells and @IRR functions, Solver gave up. The Solver Answer dialog box in Figure 13-9A conveys that although 22 attempts were made, no answer was found that met all the constraints, and guesses are required to continue.

To provide a guess, select the Guess option (displayed only when Solver displays the "Guesses required" message) to access the Solver Guess dialog box shown in Figure 13-9B. As you can see, Solver indicates the first adjustable cell a guess is needed for (A:B3 in this case), the initial (original) value in this cell ($400,000), and the last value Solver used for this variable, before it gave up ($179).

When you enter a guess in the New guess text box, the closer it is to the value that results in an answer, the easier it will be for Solver to find a solution to the problem. Because Solver enters the last values it calculated for the adjustable cells into the worksheet, you'll want to examine your problem to determine an educated guess. (You should also examine your constraints, especially the false ones, to see if they are reasonable.) Creating a How solved report (see "Generating Reports") may also help you to determine a realistic guess.

Make sure that you select the Next option to see if Solver needs guesses for any other adjustable cells. After you enter all the guesses that Solver needs, choose the Solve option to reactivate Solver. If successful, Solver will discard any previous attempts and display answers in the Solver Answer dialog box. If Solver still can't solve the problem, you'll see updated attempt information and another request for guesses.

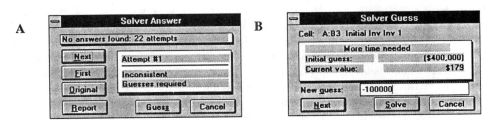

Figure 13-9 Specifying a guess

When Solver Identifies a Roundoff Error

Solver sometimes displays a "Roundoff error" or "Minor roundoff" message in the Solver Answer dialog box. When Solver returns an answer yet displays this message, Solver has actually found a valid answer. However, rounding differences between Solver and the data in the worksheet cause a constraint to be false (0).

When you get a "Roundoff error" message for attempts, however, Solver hasn't found a valid answer. For instance, one constraint may be "truly" false (which results in an attempt rather than an answer), while another may be false due to a roundoff error.

A roundoff error occurs when one or more constraints evaluate to false (0) when rounded to five or more decimal places. A minor roundoff error means that one or more constraints evaluate to false (0) when rounded to 16 decimal places. Solver's Inconsistent constraints and How solved reports may help you determine which constraints are affected (see "Generating Reports," later).

Roundoff error can also occur if columnwise or rowwise recalculation is being used instead of natural recalculation. (Use Tools User Setup Recalculation to remedy this, then run Solver again.) A second cause of this error message is when Solver can't change the values in protected cells that refer to adjustable cells.

Yet another cause is when nonlinear relationships are used in a problem, such as square roots, exponentiation, or nonlinear functions (see "Using Functions with Solver"). For the square root of an odd-numbered value, 9 for instance, both 3 and -3 are correct answers. Because the @SQRT function only calculates the square root of a nonnegative number, it will return ERR when Solver enters -3 in the worksheet. You can get around this problem by adding a constraint that excludes the offending value.

Closing Solver

After you leave the Solver and return to the worksheet, any answers or attempts are discarded when

- The worksheet is recalculated.

- You change a cell that directly or indirectly relates to the adjustable, optimal, or constraint cells.

- You close the file.

Only the answer or attempt displayed in the worksheet is retained. (To save more, see "Saving More Than One Answer or Attempt," next.)

If you want to retain the original values displayed in the worksheet, select Original in the Save Answer dialog box before you leave the Solver. To display the optimal answer, select First. Select Cancel to leave the Solver Answer dialog box, then Cancel again to leave the Solver Definition dialog box and return to the worksheet. At this point, all the answers or attempts are still intact. If you immediately choose Tools Solver again, the Solver Answer dialog box will still contain the same results as before.

When you make changes that cause the worksheet to be recalculated, Solver discards the results it previously found, although the Solver Definition settings are retained. This also happens when you change a cell that directly or indirectly relates to the adjustable, optimal, or constraint cells, even if the worksheet isn't recalculated. Similarly, Solver also discards its results when you close the file; the next time the file is opened, only the Solver Definition settings are still intact. To retrieve the answers, you have to reuse Solver to solve the problem again.

Note: Using Undo immediately after you close the Solver will also change which answer is displayed in the worksheet. For example, if you displayed the first three answers before you closed Solver, pressing ALT+BACKSPACE three times (once for each answer you displayed) will restore the worksheet to its original values.

Saving More Than One Answer or Attempt

To save one answer or attempt, see "Closing Solver."

One way to save more than one answer or attempt is to save each one to a separate file. For instance, imagine you want to save both the original values shown in Figure 13-4 and the optimal values displayed in Figure 13-6.

First use the Solver Answer dialog box and display the optimal (first) answer in the worksheet. Next, select Cancel twice to return to the worksheet, then save the file as PROD1.WK3, for instance. Make sure you don't do anything that makes 1-2-3 for Windows recalculate the worksheet. If you immediately select Tools Solver, the answers are still intact in the Solver Answer dialog box. Select Original to display these values in the worksheet, close the Solver again, then save this worksheet under another filename, like PROD2.WK3.

You can also create an Answer table report (see "Generating Reports") to save all the answers Solver returns. Because the answers in this report are saved as values in a separate file, you can then use file linking (see Chapter 4) to refer to them in your model.

Modifying a Problem

After you examine the answers or attempts Solver returns, you may want to modify the problem. To do this from the Solver Answer dialog box, select Cancel twice to close the Solver and return to the worksheet. Solver discards its answers or attempts the first time the worksheet is recalculated or you change a cell that directly or indirectly relates to the adjustable, optimal, or constraint cells, even if the worksheet isn't recalculated.

Note: When you move data specified in the Tools Solver Definition dialog box, 1-2-3 for Windows automatically adjusts the cell references for you.

To solve this modified problem, reselect Tools Solver. Because the settings you previously specified in the Solver Definition dialog box are still retained, you may only need to make minor adjustments to them. When you select Solve, Solver will attempt to solve this modified problem and return new answers.

> ▼ *Tip:*   If you don't need to change the Solver Definition settings, use the 🔳 icon to start Solver solving the modified problem.

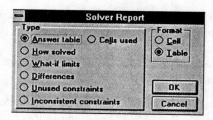

Figure 13-10 The Solver Report dialog box

Generating Reports

After Solver attempts to solve a problem, you can use the Report option in the Solver Answer dialog box to generate the seven different reports shown in Figure 13-10. Some of these reports, like the Answer table report, provide detailed information about answers or attempts. You'll find that most of these reports—What-if limits, How solved, Differences, and Unused constraints—provide sensitivity analysis data. Yet others—the Cells used, Inconsistent constraints, and How solved reports—act as diagnostic reports that may help you determine where inconsistencies occur or whether the problem is correctly modeled.

For most report types, you can also choose either a table or a cell format. You'll find the table format, discussed below, most useful when you want to save or access Solver information about a problem. On the other hand, because the cell format displays data for only one cell at a time, you'll find this report format helpful in troubleshooting.

Table Format Basics

A *table* report summarizes information about a problem in a separate worksheet file. That's why you'll find this report format especially helpful when you want to save information about a current set of answers or attempts.

For example, to create the Answer table report in Figure 13-11 for the model in Figure 13-6, first select Report from the Solver Answer dialog box. In the Solver Report dialog box, choose OK to accept the defaults—Answer table and Table format. 1-2-3 for Windows automatically creates this report in a separate worksheet file called AN-SWER01.WK3. (You can change this filename when you save the report.)

A table report shows the report type, the name of the worksheet file that contains the problem solved, as well as the date and time the problem was solved. So, Figure 13-11 is an Answer table report created on July 30, 1991 for the problem in PROD2.WK3.

Each cell listed in a table report, like the optimal cell A:J9 listed in D7 of Figure 13-11, is also described by its range name if one exists. Otherwise, Solver will use the column and row headings closest to the cell, TOTAL Gross Profit in this case.

Because the information in a table report are values and labels, you can edit, print, or graph this data. Figure 13-12 for instance, is an area graph of data from Figure 13-11. You can even use file linking (see Chapter 4) to reference these values in the file that contains your problem.

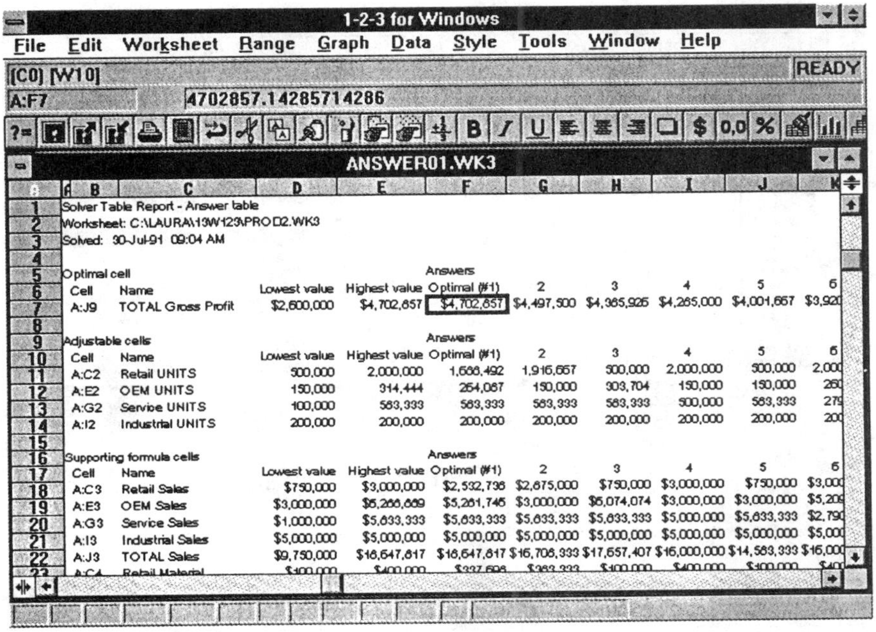

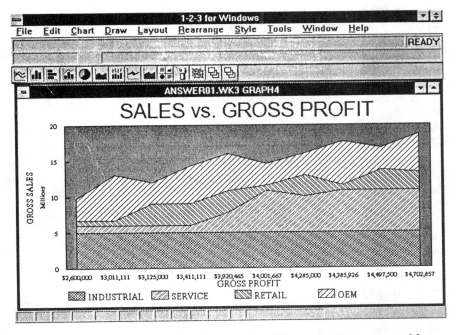

Figure 13-11   An Answer table report

Figure 13-12   An area graph of data from the Figure 13-11 Answer table report

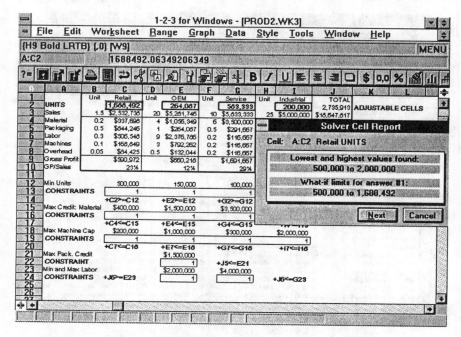

Figure 13-13   A What-if limits cell report

Cell Format Basics

You'll probably find a cell format most useful as a diagnostic tool. Although a cell format displays the same information as a table format, it is only displayed for one cell at a time.

Note: You can't generate an Answer table or How solved cell report.

You can see this in Figure 13-13, where a What-if limits cell report is shown. (A What-if limits report provides information about the adjustable cells.) The first cell for which information is displayed, the Retail Units adjustable cell C2, is highlighted in the worksheet.

You can use Next to cycle through the cells examined in the report. For example, because a What-if limits report contains information about adjustable cells, selecting Next will display information about OEM Units in E2, the second adjustable cell. Choose Cancel to return to the Solver Report dialog box.

One disadvantage of the cell format is that you can't save the information in it. In fact, you lose the data in a cell report whenever Solver discards its answers or attempts. To save report data, you'll have to create a table report.

Answer Table Report

An Answer table report is an excellent way to retain the answers or attempts Solver returns. You can then use file linking (see Chapter 4) in the file that contains your problem to reference the answers in this report.

Note: "Table Format Basics" above, discusses table reports. You can't generate an Answer table cell report, however.

Figure 13-11 shows an Answer table report created for the answers Solver returned in Figure 13-6. For the optimal and adjustable cells, this report shows the values for each answer or attempt Solver returned. For example, the $4,702,857 optimal Total Gross Profit answer (answer #1) in F7 results from the adjustable cell values shown in column F—1,688,492 Retail Units, 264,087 OEM Units, 583,333 Service Units, and 200,000 Industrial Units.

If you continue to scroll across an Answer table report, you can see that it also includes the optimal and adjustable cell values for each answer or attempt Solver generated. For example, you can see the values for answers #2 through #5 on the right of Figure 13-11. Continue to scroll to the right, and you'd see answers #6 through #10.

Summary data for this answer set is displayed in columns D and E. For instance, $2,600,000 in D7 is the lowest Total Gross Profit in this answer set, while $4,702,857 in E7 is the highest Total Gross Profit Solver returned.

Note: You can also edit, print, or graph the data in an Answer table report. Figure 13-12, for example, is an area graph of data in Figure 13-11.

For each answer or attempt, the Supporting formula cells section shows the corresponding values for other cells Solver used to solve the problem (*excluding* constraint cells). In other words, Solver used the values contained in the cells listed in this section to calculate a value either in the optimal cell or a constraint cell.

What-if Limits Report

You can only create a What-if limits report when Solver finds answers to a problem. This report tells you the range of values you can use in an adjustable cell and still satisfy all the constraints, assuming that all other adjustable cell values remain fixed. In effect, a What-if limits report provides you with a sensitivity analysis for each adjustable cell.

Note: Report formats are discussed in "Table Format Basics" and "Cell Format Basics," above.

A What-if limits report only shows the data for the answer currently displayed in the worksheet. Figure 13-14 is a What-if limits table report for the optimal answer (answer #1) displayed in Figure 13-6.

In F9 and G9, the What-if limits for C2, the Retail Units adjustable cell, tells you how much you can change this value and still satisfy all the constraints, assuming that the other adjustable cell answers aren't changed. If Retail Units are decreased to 500,000, for instance, all the constraints still remain true (1) as long as the answers in the other adjustable cells aren't changed. If you enter 500,000 in cell C2 of Figure 13-6, however, you'll find that total gross profit decreases to $4,286,885. This happens because Solver previously determined that 1,688,492 Retail Units created the optimal gross profit value.

The What-if limits report also provides the lowest and highest values Solver found for all answers. For example, Figure 13-14 shows that for all 10 answers, 500,000 in cell D9 is the lowest, and 2,000,000 in cell E9 is the highest value Solver used for Retail Units.

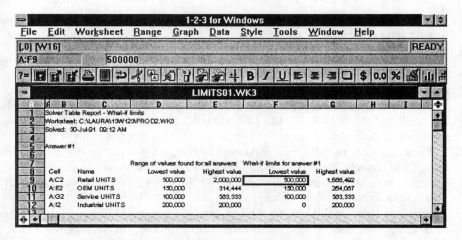

Figure 13-14 A What-if limits table report

You can also create a What-if limits cell report that displays the same information on a cell-by-cell basis. Figure 13-10 for instance, shows the What-if limits data for cell C2, the first adjustable cell. Selecting Next will move you to the next adjustable cell, E2, and the What-if limits data for it will be displayed.

Note: In some instances, the range of values for adjustable cells in a What-if limits report are only approximations, not the absolute highest and lowest values.

Differences Report

A Differences report is one way that you can examine the sensitivity of a model. This report type compares the relevant cells in one answer (or attempt) to the corresponding values generated by another answer, then reports the cells (except for constraints) that differ by an amount you specify.

Note: Report formats are discussed in "Table Format Basics" and "Cell Format Basics," above.

For example, to create a Differences table report for the problem in Figure 13-6, choose the Differences and Table options from the Solver Report dialog box. In the Differences dialog box shown in Figure 13-15, specify the answers you want to compare, for example answer 1, the optimal answer, and answer 2, the next best answer. Then, specify the minimum difference you want to examine—500,000 in this case. When you select OK, Solver creates the Differences table report shown in Figure 13-16, which reports all cells where the values differ by 500,000.

Note: Specify a difference that is meaningful. If you use a difference of 10,000 in this example, for instance, the Differences report would include almost every cell in the model.

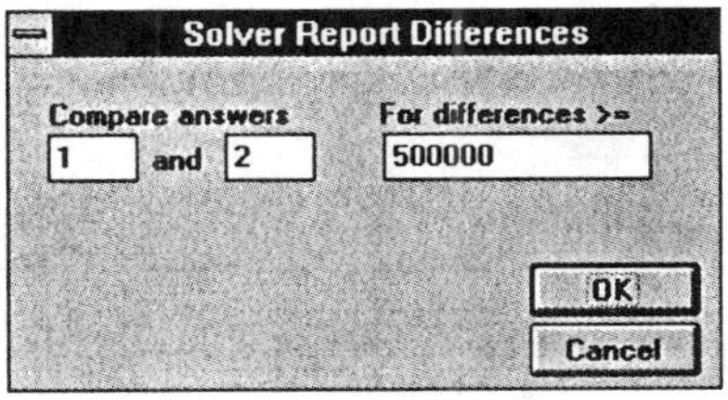

Figure 13-15 Specifying the minimum Differences value

Figure 13-16 shows that only four cells differ by more than 500,000 in answer 1, the optimal answer, and answer 2, the next best answer. In fact, the Total Sales difference of $1,939,484 is largely explained by the OEM Sales difference of $2,281,746. Likewise, the Total Labor difference of $958,333 is mostly due to the OEM Labor difference of $1,026,786. Therefore, you can conclude from this report that OEM Sales and Labor are the two major differences between answers 1 and 2.

You can also display the same information on a cell-by-cell basis by creating a Differences cell report like the one in Figure 13-17. As you can see, Solver first shows the Differences data for OEM Sales in cell E3, the first cell Solver identified in the Differences table report. Select Next to move to Total Sales in cell J3, the second cell identified in the table report, and display the Differences data for it.

Unused Constraints Report

The name "Unused constraints report" is a bit of a misnomer. Actually, this report shows the *nonbinding* constraints—in other words, the constraints that aren't causing Solver to limit the answer currently displayed in the worksheet. This report *doesn't* report constraints Solver didn't use at all.

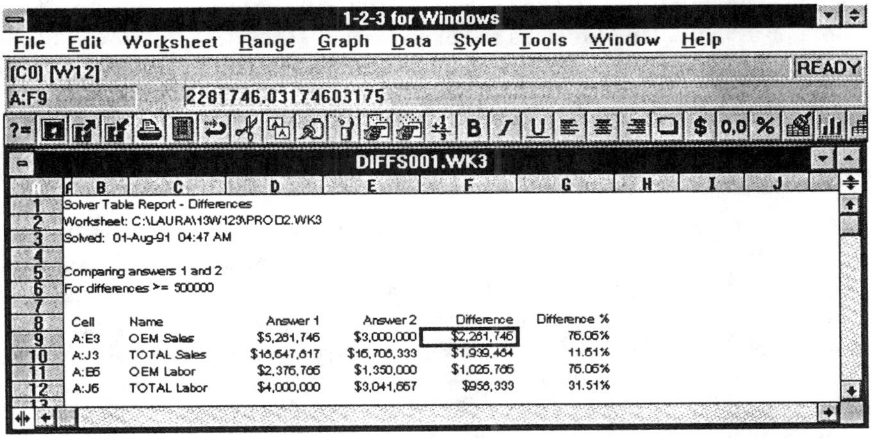

Figure 13-16 A Differences table report

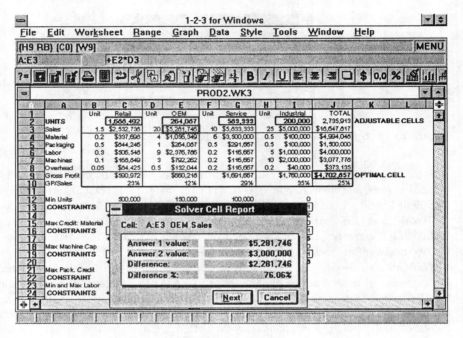

Figure 13-17   A Differences cell report

You'll find that an Unused constraints report can help you determine which constraints you can change, yet not affect the answer Solver returned. In fact, this report displays how much you can change each nonbinding constraint before Solver has to change its answer. An Unused constraint report can also help you determine any superfluous constraints that aren't really important to a problem.

The Unused constraints table report in Figure 13-18 shows which constraints aren't limiting or binding the $4,702,857 optimal Total Gross Profit answer displayed in Figure 13-6. For instance, the Min Units Retail constraint, +C2>=C12, is a lower bound constraint specifying at least 500,000 Retail units. However, it isn't limiting the $4,702,857 optimal gross profit.

Note: Report formats are discussed in "Table Format Basics" and "Cell Format Basics," above.

This report also shows how a constraint must change before it begins limiting total Gross Profit. For example, because Solver calculated that the optimal Retail units are 1,688,495, you can use the suggestion in E8 and change the Min Units Retail constraint so that Retail units must be at least 1,688,495 (500,000+1,188,492) units. Doing this won't affect the optimal gross profit answer. (Before you make Solver's suggested change to a constraint, make sure that it is reasonable for the problem being solved.) If you increase this Min Units Retail constraint to a level greater than this, Solver will return a gross profit answer lower than $4,702,857.

The Unused constraints cell report in Figure 13-19 displays the same information, but on a cell-by-cell basis, beginning with the first nonbinding constraint, Min Units Retail,

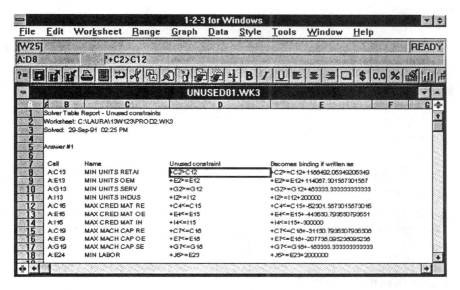

Figure 13-18   An Unused constraints table report

in cell C13. Choose Next once to see this data for the second nonbinding constraint, Min Units OEM in cell E13; continue to press Next to cycle through the nonbinding constraint cells listed in Figure 13-18.

> ▼ *Tip:*   The Binding constraints section in a How solved table report shows which constraints are binding and limiting the answer Solver returned. This report also lists the Unused constraints.

How Solved Report

You'll probably find a How solved report the most useful report for both sensitivity and error analysis. For the answer or attempt currently displayed in the worksheet, a How Solved report contains:

- A Binding constraints section listing the constraints that are limiting the answer or attempt.

- An Unused Constraints section listing the same information as an Unused constraints report—the amount each nonbinding constraint can change before it begins to limit the optimal answer. (See "Unused Constraints Report," above.)

- For an attempt, an Inconsistent Constraints section listing the same information as an Inconsistent constraints report—which constraints are false (0) and how to make these inconsistent constraints true so Solver can return an answer. (See "Unused Constraints Report," next.)

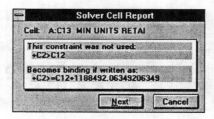

Figure 13-19 An Unused constraints cell report

Note: "Table Format Basics" discusses table format reports. You can't, however, generate a How solved cell report.

For example, look at the How solved table report in Figure 13-20, which has been generated for the optimal answer displayed in Figure 13-6. In cell E12, you can see that Solver returned an optimal Gross profit of $4,702,857.

Note: The constraint data in Figure 13-20 was moved and some blank lines were deleted from the report.

The Binding constraints are limiting this optimal answer. As you can see, the Max Cred Mat: Service constraint in cell G16 and the Max Pack Credit constraint in cell E22—the credit limits imposed by the Service product material supplier and the packaging material supplier—are limiting the optimal amount of products that can be manufactured, and are consequently limiting gross profit. So, to increase gross profit in this

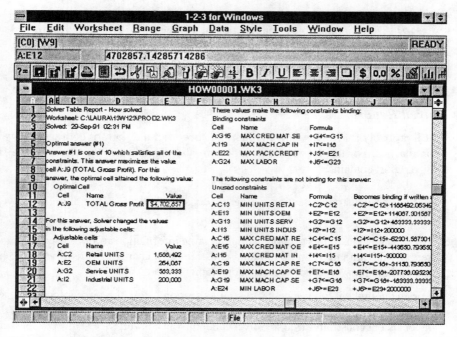

Figure 13-20 A How solved table report

problem, the credit limits set by these suppliers must be increased, or additional suppliers need to be found.

Similarly, the Max Mach Cap: Industrial and Max Labor constraints in cells I19 and G24, respectively, are also limiting gross profit. Thus, adding additional machinery to manufacture Industrial products will increase total gross profit. Finding ways to increase the work force (limited by plant size) or to make the work force more efficient will also increase total gross profit above $4,702,857.

For an attempt, a How solved report will also include the same information as an Inconsistent constraints report. However, many times the Binding constraints section rather than the Inconsistent constraints section will help you determine which constraints are really causing the problem. For example, sometimes an incorrect constraint that Solver identifies as binding can be causing Solver to return false (0) for other, realistic constraints. (For such a situation, see "When Solver Returns Attempts," earlier.)

Inconsistent Constraints Report

When Solver returns an attempt with inconsistencies, as it did in Figure 13-7, you can create an Inconsistent constraints table report, like the one in Figure 13-21, to report which constraints are false (0). This report also includes a way to make these inconsistent constraints true so Solver can return an answer.

The Inconsistent constraints cell report in Figure 13-22 displays the same information but on a cell-by-cell basis, beginning with the first false constraint, Min Units Retail in cell C13. Choose Next to see this data for the second false constraint, Max Labor in cell G24.

Note: Report formats are discussed in "Table Format Basics" and "Cell Format Basics," above.

Sometimes, but not always, an Inconsistent constraints report can help you correctly determine which constraints are causing Solver to return attempts instead of answers. To see why an Inconsistent constraints report and the solutions it suggests can be misleading, see "When Solver Returns Attempts" earlier in this chapter.

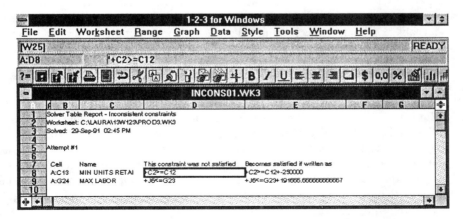

Figure 13-21 An Inconsistent constraints table report

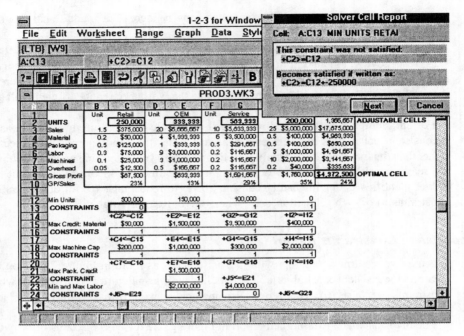

Figure 13-22 An Inconsistent constraints cell report

 Tip: The Binding constraints section in a How solved table report may help you determine if constraints are incorrect. This report also lists the Inconsistent constraints.

Cells Used Report

A Cells used report is best utilized when you need to check that you correctly specified a problem in the Solver Definition dialog box. A Cells used report simply identifies the adjustable, optimal, and constraint cells that Solver is using to return its answers or attempts.

Note: Report formats are discussed in "Table Format Basics" and "Cell Format Basics," above.

Figure 13-23 is a Cell used table report listing the optimal, adjustable, and constraint cells specified in the Solver Definition dialog box in Figure 13-5A. You'll probably want to use a cell format, however, so that you can physically check the optimal, adjustable, and constraint cells you specified. For example, the Cells used cell report in Figure 13-24 conveys that the outlined cell, C2, was specified as an adjustable cell.   Repeatedly pressing Next moves the cell pointer to each of the adjustable, constraint, and optimal cells currently specified.

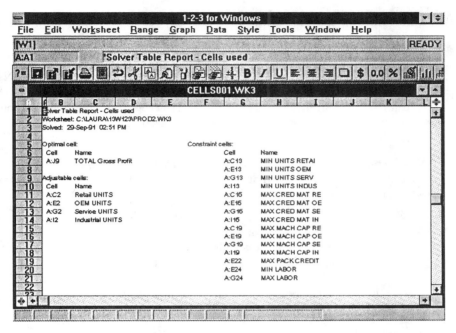

Figure 13-23 A Cells used table report

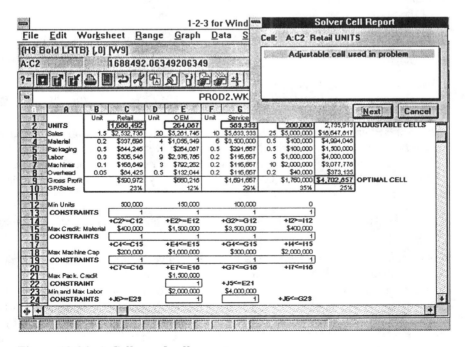

Figure 13-24 A Cells used cell report

Using Functions with the Solver

In general, only specific functions can be used with Solver. For example, because Solver discards its answers or attempts whenever the worksheet is recalculated, you can't use functions that cause a recalculation. This means that @@, @CELL, @CELLPOINTER, @INFO, @ISNAME, @ISRANGE, @NOW, @RAND, @TODAY, and database functions can't be used with Solver. Nor will Solver accept date and time functions, or functions that act on string arguments. Table 13-1 lists the functions for which Solver is capable of solving problems.

Note: You can use a function not included in Table 13-1 as long as it doesn't cause the worksheet to be recalculated and it isn't directly or indirectly used to compute a constraint or optimal cell.

See also "Results Returned by Solver," earlier. When a function other than @SUM or @AVG is included in a problem, Solver tries to find answers numerically (by trial and error). Even when you use one of the acceptable functions shown in Table 13-1, Solver may still have difficulty solving a problem using trial and error when

- The results returned by functions are added or multiplied.

- Large ranges are used as the argument for @VLOOKUP, @HLOOKUP, or one of the Statistical @functions.

- @MOD, @ROUND, @INT, @IF (especially when you nest @IF functions), or one of the Lookup functions are included in the problem.

- Functions like @SQRT, @EXP, and many of the Financial or Statistical functions are used, which make the problem nonlinear.

In Figure 13-9 for instance, Solver couldn't find an answer and required a guess when the results of multiple IRR functions were summed in a problem. (See "When Solver Needs a Guess," earlier.)

Even if Solver can find answers for a problem containing a function, it may only be able to find a "best" answer instead of an optimal answer. This usually happens when a function's arguments directly or indirectly depend on one or more adjustable cells, or when a constraint (logical formula) directly or indirectly refers to the cell containing an @function.

Note: Best and optimal answers are discussed in "When the Solver Returns Answers," earlier.

For example, you can see in Figure 13-25 that Solver returns a "best" answer rather than an optimal answer. If you examine this worksheet, you'll see that this is almost the same problem that Solver returned an optimal answer for in Figure 13-6. In Figure 13-25, however, the model now includes a price break for Retail material costs when total purchased material exceeds that for 1,500,000 units. This is expressed in cell C4 by the formula @IF(C2<=1500000,C2*B4,C2*.15). In this case, a best instead of an optimal answer is returned because this @IF function directly refers to adjustable cell C2.

TABLE 13-1   Functions Supported by Solver

General Mathematical			Lookup		
@ABS	@SQRT	@MOD	@CHOOSE	@INDEX	@VLOOKUP
@INT	@ROUND		@HLOOKUP		
Trigonometric			**Financial**		
@PI	@EXP	@LN	@PV	@FV	@PMT
@LOG	@COS	@SIN	@NPV	@IRR	@RATE
@TAN	@ACOS	@ASIN	@TERM	@CTERM	@SLN
@ATAN	@ATAN2		@SYD	@DDB	@VDB
Statistical			**Logic and Error Trapping**		
@SUM	@AVG	@COUNT	@IF	@TRUE	@FALSE
@MAX	@MIN	@STD	@ISNUMBER		
@STDS	@VAR	@VARS	**Special functions**		
@SUMPRODUCT			@COLS	@ROWS	@SHEETS

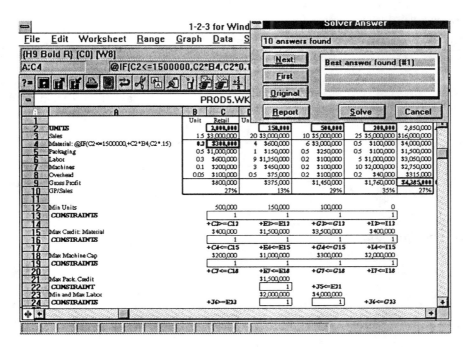

Figure 13-25   Getting a "best" answer when an @IF function refers to an adjustable cell

Returning Information about Solver: @SOLVER

The @SOLVER function returns information about the Solver. The form of this function is

```
@SOLVER(query-string)
```

where *query-string* must be one of the eight queries listed in Table 13-2. Remember to enclose a *query-string* in double quotation marks if you enter it directly into the @SOLVER function.

For a given *query-string* in Table 13-2, @SOLVER returns one of the values listed under @SOLVER Returns in the table. As you can see, there are several possible results for each *query-string*, depending on the Solver's ability to solve the problem.

In 1-2-3 for Windows, @SOLVER is *not* recalculated when the worksheet is automatically recalculated. To update @SOLVER, you must press F9 (RECALC).

The @SOLVER function is used primarily in macros that check the information returned by Solver. The example that follows shows you how you can use the value returned by the @SOLVER function to control the flow of a macro.

TABLE 13-2   The @SOLVER Query-String Arguments

Query-string Argument	Question asked by query-string	@SOLVER Returns	Meaning
"consistent"	All constraints satisfied by current answer	1	True
		2	At least one constraint is not satisfied and returns 0 (false)
		ERR	Solver not active or no answer found
"done"	Solver done?	1	Finished
		2	Still in process
		3	Solver active, but has not yet started
		ERR	Solver inactive
"moreanswers"	Can Solver find more answers?	1	All answers found
		2	More answers may exist
		ERR	Solver not active
"needguess"	Are guesses needed for Solver to find an answer?	1	No guesses needed
		2	Guesses needed
		ERR	Solver inactive, or no answer in worksheet

(continued)

TABLE 13-2   The @SOLVER Query-String Arguments *(continued)*

Query-string Argument	Question asked by query-string	@SOLVER Returns	Meaning
"numanswers"	Number of answers or attempts Solver found?	Number	Number of answers or attempts found
		ERR	Solver inactive or has not yet solved the problem
"optimal"	Status of optimal answer?	1	Optimal answer
		2	Best answer found
		3	Problem unbounded
		4	No answer found, or no optimization requested
		ERR	Solver inactive
"progress"	Progress made by Solver?	Number	Percent of solving completed
		ERR	Solver inactive, or has not begun solving
"result"	Solver's result?	1	Solver found at least 1 answer
		2	No answers found, but representative attempts are available
		ERR	Solver inactive, or has not yet solved the problem

An Example

Figure 13-26 shows a macro that checks the status of the Solver. Then, depending on the results Solver returns, one of two reports is generated. The macro is composed of a calling routine, \A, and the subroutines CHECKIT, ANSWER, and HOWSOLVED.

In the first line of \A, the PROD2.WK3 file (Figure 13-4), which contains a previously defined problem and corresponding Solver Definition settings, is opened. In the next line, the Tools Solver Solve command starts Solver solving the problem, then the CHECKIT subroutine is called.

In the first line of the CHECKIT subroutine, 1-2-3 waits three seconds before moving to the second line. Here, if Solver hasn't finished solving the problem ({IF @SOLVER("done")<>1}), a loop occurs; 1-2-3 for Windows waits three more seconds then checks Solver's status again. A continuous loop is executed until Solver stops solving the problem and returns either answers or attempts.

When Solver has finished solving the problem and the Solver Answer dialog box is displayed, {IF @SOLVER("consistent")=1} in the third line evaluates the results Solver returned. If this IF command is true, then Solver returned an answer and the ANSWER

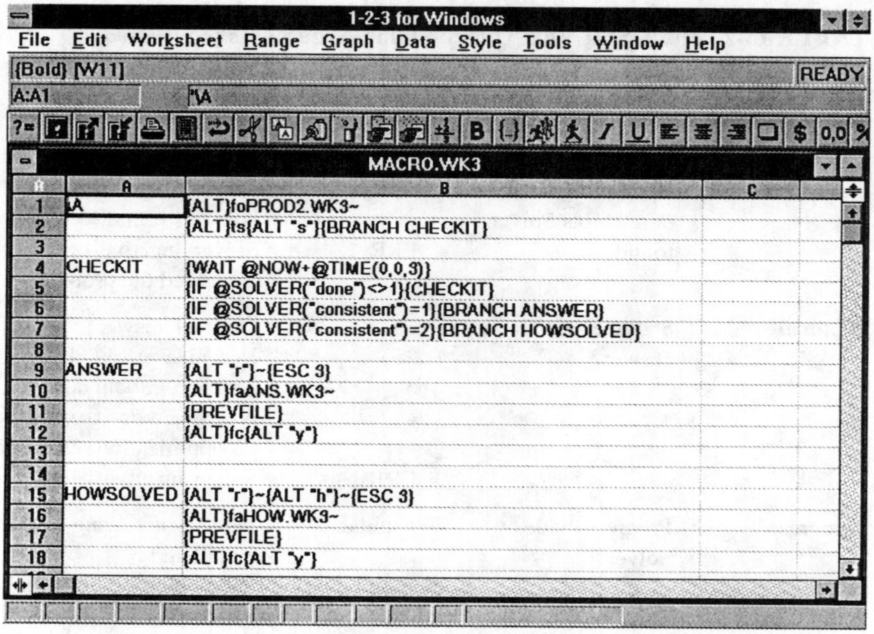

Figure 13-26 Using @SOLVER in a macro

subroutine is called. On the other hand, when {IF @SOLVER("consistent")=2} is true, then Solver found an attempt, and the HOWSOLVED subroutine is called.

If Solver returned answers, an Answer table report will save all the answers Solver generated. So {ALT "r"}~{ESC 3} in the ANSWER subroutine selects the Report option from the Solver Answer dialog box, and then accepts the Answer report and Table format settings in the Solver Report dialog box. After Solver creates this report, ESC is pressed three times to close the Solver. Because the file containing the answer table report is the active file, {ALT}faANS.WK3~ saves this report under the name ANS.WK3. Then {PREVFILE} makes PROD2.WK3 active, and {ALT}fc{ALT "y"} closes and saves this file which now displays the first answer Solver returned. This makes the Answer table report file active once again.

If Solver returned attempts, a How solved table report can help in diagnosing problems. So the HOWSOLVED subroutine acts almost the same as the ANSWER subroutine, except {ALT "h"} in the first line specifies How solved in the Solver Report dialog box. Then this report is saved under the name HOW.WK3.

14

Creating Macros

Macros allow you to store commands and keystrokes and have 1-2-3 for Windows play them back automatically. In its most basic form, a macro is a series of labels entered in consecutive cells in a column of a worksheet. The characters in each label mimic keystrokes entered from the keyboard that provide instructions to 1-2-3, telling it to move the cell pointer, make a cell entry, or select a command. Once these labels are entered, you can assign a name to the first cell of the macro—for example, \A. To run the macro, simply press CTRL+A. 1-2-3 sequentially executes the instructions you've specified, just as if you had typed them from the keyboard. In this context, macros can be used to perform repetitive tasks. For example, you might create a macro that prints a series of different reports for a given worksheet file.

Macros can also be more than an alternative to entering commands and keystrokes from your keyboard. 1-2-3's macro facility includes a comprehensive macro programming language with a rich assortment of commands. In many ways, this language has the power of a higher level language like BASIC or Pascal, but works entirely within 1-2-3. For example, the language has commands for getting user input, controlling the order in which macro instructions are executed, specifying the size and position of the worksheet and graph windows, and more. By using these commands, you can create custom applications that perform sophisticated data management tasks. For instance, you might create an application that lets a user enter data in a custom form and then add that data to a 1-2-3 database. The entire process can take place under the control of your macro.

This chapter gives you the basics you'll need to create simple macros. You'll learn how to enter a macro in the worksheet and run it and also how to use 1-2-3's Transcript window to automate the creation of simple macros. Programming with macros, however, is deferred to the next chapter.

Through the 1-2-3 Classic menu, 1-2-3 for Windows maintains keystroke compatibility with prior releases of 1-2-3. Therefore, all the macros you've created for prior releases should work without modification in 1-2-3 for Windows.

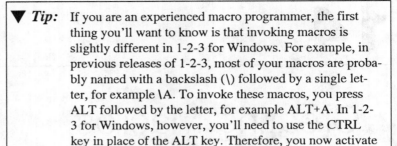

▼ *Tip:* If you are an experienced macro programmer, the first thing you'll want to know is that invoking macros is slightly different in 1-2-3 for Windows. For example, in previous releases of 1-2-3, most of your macros are probably named with a backslash (\) followed by a single letter, for example \A. To invoke these macros, you press ALT followed by the letter, for example ALT+A. In 1-2-3 for Windows, however, you'll need to use the CTRL key in place of the ALT key. Therefore, you now activate that same macro by pressing CTRL+A.

CREATING A MACRO: AN EXAMPLE

The easiest way to understand what a macro is and how it works, is to create a simple macro and then run it. For example, Figure 14-1 shows a macro that enters the labels Quarter 1, Quarter 2, Quarter 3, and Quarter 4 across a row of cells. You might use this macro or one like it to save yourself time in entering labels that you use frequently.

To create the macro, you must first enter the labels that contain the macro's instructions. Once the labels are entered, you must give the macro a name. Once named, the macro is ready to run.

Entering the Macro

The first step for creating a macro is to choose its location. Actually, you can place macros anywhere you'd like in the worksheet, but it's wise to locate them in an out-of-the-way area (see "Choosing a Macro Location" for more details). Once you've chosen a spot, you're ready to begin entering the macro. In the example that follows, the macro will be entered beginning in cell A:B1.

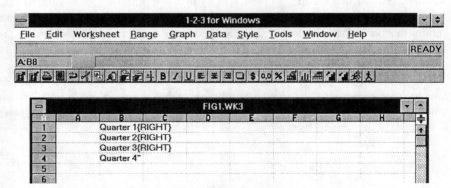

Figure 14-1 A macro that enters labels in a row of cells

To enter the macro, move the cell pointer to cell A:B1 and place the following labels in the worksheet. Do not be concerned about what these labels actually do; this will be discussed later. Enter the labels just as you would any other label in 1-2-3 (making sure, of course, that you enter them exactly as they appear here). Figure 14-1 shows what your screen should look like when you've finished.

Cell	Entry
A:B1	Quarter 1{RIGHT}
A:B2	Quarter 2{RIGHT}
A:B3	Quarter 3{RIGHT}
A:B4	Quarter 4~

Naming the Macro

Once you've entered the labels for the macro, you're ready to give the macro a name. To name a macro, you use the Range Name Create command to assign a range name to the first cell of the macro. You can then use that name to invoke the macro.

The range name you assign depends on how you want to invoke the macro (see "Naming Macros" later). For now, assume you want to invoke the macro by pressing a CTRL+*letter* sequence, for example CTRL+Q. To use this method, you must assign a range name that begins with a backslash (\) followed by the single letter that will be used to invoke the macro—in this case, \Q.

To name the macro, move the cell pointer to cell A:B1 and select the Range Name Create command. When 1-2-3 displays the Range Name Create dialog box, type \Q in the "Range name" text box and select OK. The macro now has a name and is ready to run.

Invoking the Macro

This particular macro writes labels into the worksheet, starting at the location of the cell pointer. Therefore, before you invoke the macro be sure to move the cell pointer to cell A:B7, away from the macro itself. If you leave the cell pointer in its current position, it will overwrite the first cell of your new macro.

To invoke the macro, press CTRL+Q. 1-2-3 then begins searching the current worksheet file for the \Q range. When it finds that range, it starts executing the macro, beginning at the location of the cell pointer. In this case, 1-2-3 places the quarters for the year (Quarter 1, Quarter 2, and so on) in a row of four adjacent cells (A:B7..A:E7), as shown in Figure 14-2. If 1-2-3 cannot find the \Q range when you press CTRL+Q, it simply beeps and does nothing.

How the Macro Works

The macro in Figure 14-2 works like this. When you press CTRL+Q and 1-2-3 locates the \Q range in the current file, it begins executing the macro instructions in the first cell

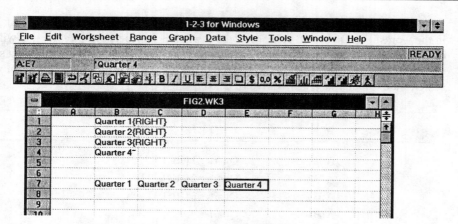

Figure 14-2 After running the quarter label macro

of that range (cell A:B1 in this case). Starting with the label in that cell, 1-2-3 begins interpreting the characters in the label, one at a time. Each character is acted on as if you entered it from the keyboard. For example, when 1-2-3 encounters the *Q* in Quarter 1, it acts as though you typed that character. The same is true for the *u, a, r,* and the rest of the characters in Quarter 1.

When 1-2-3 encounters a left curly brace ({) in a label, it knows that a special macro keystroke instruction is about to follow. (A left curly brace can also mean the start of a programming command, such as {IF} or {FOR}.) In this case, when 1-2-3 encounters {RIGHT} in the label in cell A:B1 of Figure 14-2, it acts as though you pressed the → key; the cell pointer is moved one cell to the right. This also has the effect of completing the entry Quarter 1. If you started the macro in cell A:B7, the label Quarter 1 now appears in that cell and the cell pointer moves to cell A:C7.

When 1-2-3 reaches the end of a label in a macro, it automatically moves down one cell and begins interpreting and executing the characters in the next label. For example, in the case of the macro in Figure 14-2, 1-2-3 moves to cell A:B2, which contains a label similar to cell A:B1. 1-2-3 executes the instructions in this label in the same way. That is, it enters the string Quarter 2 in cell A:C7 and moves the cell pointer one cell to the right. This same process is repeated for the label in cell A:B3. You'll notice that the label in cell A:B4 ends with a ~ (tilde) instead of {RIGHT}. In macros, the tilde is the equivalent of the ENTER key. Therefore, 1-2-3 places the label Quarter 4 in the current cell (A:E7) and leaves the cell pointer in that location.

After completing the last line of the macro, 1-2-3 moves down one cell to look for further macro instructions, but instead finds a blank cell. When 1-2-3 encounters a blank cell, it automatically terminates macro execution and returns to READY mode.

Note: Because the macro in Figure 14-1 duplicates a series of keystrokes, you can create it quickly and easily by using the Transcript window. See "Using the Transcript Window" later for more on how to do this.

MACRO BASICS

If you followed along in the previous part of this chapter, you just created your first simple macro and now have a sense of how macros work. To get the most out of your macros, though, you'll need to learn some more basic macro skills. For example, you'll need a thorough understanding of macro syntax and macro keystroke instructions. You'll also need to know more about naming, running, and documenting macros. These fundamentals are discussed in the sections that follow.

Syntax

In their simplest form, macros are made up of instructions that exactly replicate 1-2-3 keystrokes. The sections that follow show you the various types of keystroke instructions you can use in a macro.

Keystroke Instructions

Macro keystroke instructions represent keys on your keyboard. They cause 1-2-3 to respond as though you had actually pressed the keys themselves. There are two types of macro keystroke instructions:

- Single-character keys: Letters that represent characters on your keyboard such as r, f, c, or 2.
- Keynames: Names within curly braces ({ }) that represent cell pointer movement keys, function keys, and other special keys—for example {UP}, {DOWN}, {GOTO}, {NAME}, and {ALT}.

Single-character keys represent keys in the typewriter portion of your keyboard. You can string these keys together to have 1-2-3 perform commands. For example, imagine you want to create a macro that formats a single cell in Currency 2 format using the 1-2-3 Classic menu. To do this, type ' (a label prefix) to make the entry a label. Then type / (slash), which activates the Classic menu. Follow this with r to select the Range command, f to select the Format option, c to select the Currency format, and 2 to select the number of decimal places. As in the previous example, the ~ (tilde) symbol represents the ENTER key. This character should appear twice, once to confirm the number of decimal places and again to complete the Range Format Currency 2 command. When you enter this macro in the worksheet, it will appear in a single cell as follows:

```
'/rfc2~~
```

Note: See "Using Menu Commands in Macros" later for additional examples of macros that use menu commands.

The rest of the keys on your keyboard are represented by macro keynames enclosed in curly braces ({ }). For example, in the sample macro at the beginning of this chapter,

{RIGHT} was used to move the cell pointer one cell to the right. Other keynames are available for 1-2-3's arrow keys, function keys, certain editing keys, and other keys. Table 14-1 shows a list of the macro keynames available in 1-2-3.

For example, imagine you want to create a macro that sums a column of cells above the location of the cell pointer. To do this, you might use the @SUM function in the following macro:

```
'@SUM({END}{UP}{ANCHOR}{END}{UP})~
```

The first part of the macro, @SUM(, begins forming the function in the current cell. The first set of keynames, {END}{UP}, replicates the END UP key sequence, which places 1-2-3 in POINT mode and moves the cell pointer to the first filled cell above the location of the cell pointer. The {ANCHOR} command anchors the cell pointer for the @SUM function, causing 1-2-3 to begin highlighting a range. The {END}{UP} sequence appears a second time, causing the cell pointer to jump upward to the last filled cell in a range of consecutively filled cells. The closing parenthesis ")" finishes the @SUM function, and the tilde (the equivalent of ENTER) enters the finished @SUM function in the current cell.

Note: You cannot replicate mouse pointer actions in macros, only keyboard actions.

Selecting Keynames with NAME (F3)

If you prefer selecting macro keynames and macro commands from a list rather than typing them out, 1-2-3 for Windows offers a convenient feature for doing so. If you type a left curly brace and then press NAME (F3), 1-2-3 displays a list box of macro keynames and macro programming commands, as shown in Figure 14-3. To select a keyname or command, simply double-click on it and 1-2-3 will add the keyname or command to the edit line. Using this feature can help you avoid one of the most common macro errors, the misspelling of keynames or commands.

Keys That Do Not Have Macro Keynames

Certain keys on your keyboard do not have macro equivalents—therefore, you cannot use these keystrokes in a macro. A list of these keys follows:

SHIFT
CAPS LOCK
NUM LOCK
SCROLL LOCK
PRINT SCREEN
UNDO (ALT+BACKSPACE)
COMPOSE (ALT+F1)
STEP (ALT+F2)
RUN (ALT+F3)
NEXT WINDOW (CTRL+F6)
CLOSE WINDOW (ALT+F4)

TABLE 14-1 1-2-3's Macro Keynames

Category	1-2-3 Key	Macro Keyname
Pointer movement	→	{RIGHT} or {R}
	←	{LEFT} or {L}
	↑	{UP} or {U}
	↓	{DOWN} or {D}
	CTRL+→ or TAB	{TAB} or {BIGRIGHT}
	CTRL+← or SHIFT+TAB	{BACKTAB} or {BIGLEFT}
	HOME	{HOME}
	END	{END}
	PGUP	{PGUP}
	PGDN	{PGDN}
	CTRL+PGUP	{NEXTSHEET} or {NS}
	CTRL+PGDN	{PREVSHEET} or {PS}
	CTRL+HOME	{FIRSTCELL} or {FC}
	CTRL+END	{FILE}
	CTRL+END CTRL+PGUP	{NEXTFILE}, {NF}, or {FILE}{NS}
	CTRL+END CTRL+PGDN	{PREVFILE}, {PF}, or {FILE}{PS}
	CTRL+END END	{LASTFILE}, {LF}, or {FILE}{END}
	CTRL+END HOME	{FIRSTFILE}, {FF}, or {FILE}{HOME}
	END CTRL+HOME	{LASTCELL} or {LC}
Function Keys	F1 (HELP)	{HELP}
	F2 (EDIT)	{EDIT}
	F3 (NAME)	{NAME}
	F4 (ABS)	{ABS}
	F5 (GOTO)	{GOTO}
	F6 (PANE)	{WINDOW}
	F7 (QUERY)	{QUERY}
	F8 (TABLE)	{TABLE}
	F9 (CALC)	{CALC}
	F10 (MENU)	{ALT}, {MENUBAR}, or {MB}

(continued)

TABLE 14-1   1-2-3's Macro Keynames *(continued)*

Category	1-2-3 Key	Macro Keyname
	ALT+F6 (ZOOM)	{ZOOM}
	ALT+F7 (APP1)	{APP1}
	ALT+F8 (APP2)	{APP2}
	ALT+F9 (APP3)	{APP3}
Other Keys	/ (slash) or < (less than)	{MENU}
	INS	{INSERT} or {INS}
	DEL	{DEL}
	BACKSPACE	{BACKSPACE} or {BS}
	CTRL	{CTRL}
	F4 (in READY mode)	{ANCHOR}
	ESC	{ESCAPE} OR {ESC}
	ENTER	~
	ALT	{ALT}, {MENUBAR}, or {MB}
	CTRL+BREAK	{BREAK}
	~ (tilde)	{~}
	{ (open brace)	{{}
	} (close brace)	{}}

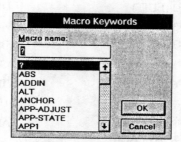

Figure 14-3   Typing { and pressing NAME (F3)

Keystroke Abbreviations

In Table 14-1, you'll note that 1-2-3 offers some alternative forms for certain keynames. For example, the macro keyname for the → key is {RIGHT} or {R}. Experienced macro programmers appreciate this, because it reduces the number of keystrokes required to write a macro. In addition, the Transcript window uses the abbreviated form when recording your keystrokes (see "Using the Transcript Window" later).

Abbreviating Duplicate Keystrokes

Often you will want to repeat a keystroke command in a macro. For example, the following commands move the cell pointer down three cells:

```
{DOWN} {DOWN} {DOWN}
```

You can express these duplicate keystrokes as

```
{DOWN 3}
```

Here the keyname is followed by a space and then by a value indicating the number of times you want the command repeated (the *repetition factor*).

You can also use a range name or cell address to express a repetition factor. For example, if cell A4 contains the number 6, the command {R +A4} will move the cell pointer right six columns. Likewise, if the cell named SHEETS contains the number 2, the command {PREVSHEET SHEETS} will move the cell pointer two worksheets forward.

Capitalization

1-2-3 for Windows accepts macro commands in any combination of upper- and lowercase letters. For example, {alt}RFC{TAB}2{alt "R"}range1~ will work every bit the same as {ALT}rfc{TAB}2{ALT R}RANGE1~. To make your macros more readable, here are a few standard conventions you might want to consider:

- Use uppercase for macro instructions in braces, for example {HOME}.

- Range names should also be capitalized, for example SALES.

- Keystrokes should be in lowercase, for example rfc.

Although these conventions are by no means mandatory, they will make your macros easier to read, both for you and for others. They will also make debugging your macros easier, because you'll be able to tell at a glance the difference between macro instructions, range names, and other keystrokes.

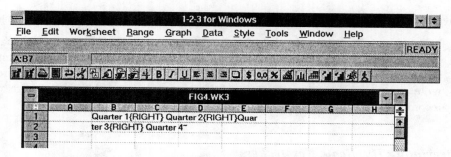

Figure 14-4 The example rewritten to span two lines

Breaking Up Macro Instructions

You can place as many macro instructions in a cell as you'd like, provided, of course, that the total number of characters does not exceed 512 (the maximum length of a label in 1-2-3). For example, Figure 14-4 shows the same macro as in Figure 14-2 rewritten to span only two lines. When you execute this macro, it has the same effect as the one in the earlier figure.

Notice that the entry Quarter 3 in Figure 14-4 is split onto two lines. This will not have any adverse effect on the macro, since 1-2-3 processes these keystrokes one at a time. You *cannot*, however, split up macro instructions that are enclosed in curly braces. These must appear all on one line. Otherwise, 1-2-3 will not be able to recognize the instruction and will issue an error message.

In general, you can split up your macro any way you'd like. You will sacrifice readability, though, if you jam multiple macro instructions onto a single line. For example, it is much easier to read the macro in Figure 14-2 than the macro in Figure 14-4.

Label Prefixes

All macros are text even if, when run, they enter numeric data into cells. Therefore, all macro instruction labels must begin with a label prefix ('). 1-2-3 ignores the first label prefix, however, when processing macro instructions. It uses the second character following the label prefix to determine the type of entry that will be placed in the cell.

For example, in the macro in Figure 14-2, the first macro instruction label in cell A:B1 reads 'Quarter 1{RIGHT}. When 1-2-3 processes this label, the first character it encounters after the label prefix is the letter Q. Because this entry starts with a letter, 1-2-3 determines that the entry in the current cell will be a label, just as if you were typing the entry from the keyboard. Accordingly, 1-2-3 provides the default label prefix (usually ') for the entry.

Imagine you want to modify the macro in Figure 14-2, so that the labels Quarter 1, Quarter 2, and so on appear centered when placed in each cell. To do this, you can provide an additional label prefix, for example, '^Quarter 1. That way, the macro will appear as shown in A:B1..A:B4 of Figure 14-5. When you run this macro, 1-2-3 ignores the first label prefix in each cell, but not the second, and centers the labels created by the macro. The output for the macro will then appear as shown in A:B7..A:E7.

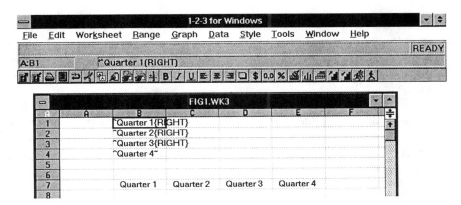

Figure 14-5 Adding label prefixes to a macro

On the other hand, suppose that instead of placing the labels Quarter 1, Quarter 2, and so on, you want to use the numeric label entries 3/92, 6/92, 9/92, and 12/92. To have these entries placed in the worksheet as labels, you must provide a second label prefix, for example ' '6/92. When 1-2-3 processes the entry, it will ignore the first label prefix but not the second, and will place the entry in the current cell as a label. (Without the second label prefix, 1-2-3 would enter the numeric formula 6/92 in the cell and immediately calculate the result, 0.065217.)

Imagine now that you want 1-2-3 to make a numeric entry from within a macro. To do this, place only a single label prefix (') in front of the entry when building the macro. For example, to place the numbers 1990, 1991, 1992, and 1993 in separate cells in the worksheet, you would use the labels '1990, '1991, '1992, and '1993. When you run the macro, 1-2-3 will ignore the first label prefix and encounter the number *1*. At that point, 1-2-3 determines that each entry is a value, just as if you were typing the entry from the keyboard.

Choosing a Macro Location

Because macros are stored in the worksheet as labels, you can easily edit them, just as you would any other labels. You can also move or copy them to new positions in the current worksheet or in another worksheet. If your macros are located in the same worksheet as the data ranges they affect, you can easily damage them with a careless command. For example, the following commands are notorious for damaging macros:

- Worksheet Insert Row: You might insert a row into the middle of a macro, causing it to end prematurely.

- Worksheet Delete Row: You might delete an important instruction from a macro, causing an error; or the deleted row might cause two macros to become joined, so that one executes immediately after the other.

- Worksheet Delete Column: You might delete the column containing the macro.

- Range Erase: You might erase the macro.

- /File Retrieve (from the 1-2-3 Classic menu): If you replace the file in the active window without first using File Save to save the worksheet containing the macro, you lose the macro and the worksheet. (File Open, on the other hand, will not damage a macro in any way.)

Virtually all these problems can be solved with a simple Edit Undo (ALT+BACK-SPACE). To use Edit Undo in a timely manner, though, you must be aware that there is a problem. Often, damaged macros are not discovered until long after it's too late to do anything about them.

Here are some techniques you can use to avoid damaging your macros:

- Do not locate macros in the same worksheet as the data ranges they affect. For example, if your macros will be performing their magic in worksheet A, locate them in worksheet B. (To create another worksheet in a file, use Worksheet Insert Sheet.) 1-2-3 will still be able to find your macros and run them as though they were located in the current worksheet.

- If you have macros that you intend to run regularly in various worksheet files, consider placing them in a macro library. A macro library is a worksheet file composed entirely of macros. As long as that worksheet file is open, you can run its macros from any active worksheet file. The macros will perform as though they were located in the current worksheet file. See the later sections "Starting Macros" and "Using a Macro Library" for more details.

- If you must place a macro in the same worksheet as the data ranges it affects, consider placing it well below and to the right of the active area of the worksheet. This location provides the most safety from the potentially damaging commands shown earlier. As added insurance, you may want to turn on the Worksheet Global Settings Protection check box to enable global protection for the worksheet. You can then use the Range Unprotect command to unprotect those data ranges that are either used by the macro or by you.

Naming Macros

The traditional way to name a macro in 1-2-3 is to assign it a range name that consists of a backslash followed by a single letter, for example \Q. (As you know, the \Q name serves as shorthand for CTRL+Q, which is the actual key sequence you use to start the macro.) The advantage of this kind of name is that you can easily launch the macro. A disadvantage is that you are limited to 26 macro names per worksheet file (\A—\Z), plus the additional name \0 for an autoexecute macro (see the later section "Autoexecute Macros").

However, you can also assign a conventional range name to the first cell of a macro, giving you a virtually unlimited number of macro names in a worksheet file. If you assign a conventional range name to a macro, you must use the RUN (ALT+F3) key or the Tools

Macro Run command to activate it (see "Starting a Macro with RUN (ALT+F3) or Tools Macro Run").

For example, to assign the range name QUARTER to a macro, move the cell pointer to the first cell of the macro and select Range Name Create. When 1-2-3 displays the Range Name Create dialog box, type **quarter** in the "Range name" text box and choose OK.

Here are some things to keep in mind when assigning conventional range names to macros:

- Range names can be up to 15 characters, and you can use any combination of letters or numbers. However, avoid using spaces, commas, semicolons, and periods.

- Take care not to use range names that are the same as cell addresses, @functions, macro programming commands, or macro keynames.

- Consider using a special character at the beginning of macro names, for example \ or !, to distinguish them from other range names. That way, 1-2-3 will list your macro names as a group when you select RUN (ALT+F3) or Tools Macro Run to activate a macro.

Using the Range Name Label Create Right Command

The easiest way to name a macro is to place its name in the cell immediately to the left of the macro's first cell and then use the Range Name Label Create Right command. By placing the name in the worksheet in this way, you have a direct reminder of the macro's name.

For example, imagine you want to use this technique to assign the name \Q to the macro in Figure 14-5. To do this, place the label '\Q in cell A:A1, as shown in Figure 14-6. (Do not forget the label prefix, or 1-2-3 will repeat the letter Q across cell A:A1.) Now, leaving the cell pointer in cell A:A1, select the Range Name Label Create command. When 1-2-3

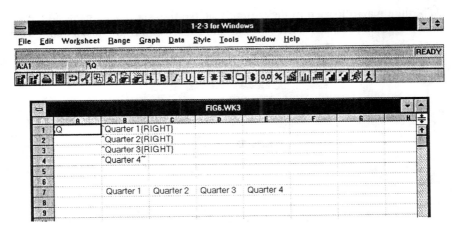

Figure 14-6 Naming a macro with Range Name Label Create Right

displays the Range Name Label Create dialog box, turn on the Right radio button and select OK. 1-2-3 uses the label in cell A:A1 to name the cell immediately to the right, in this case, the cell is A:B1, the first cell of the macro. You can now run the macro by pressing CTRL+Q.

Starting Macros

1-2-3 for Windows offers two different methods for starting your macros. The method you choose depends on the range name you assigned to the macro.

Starting a Macro with CTRL

If you named your macro using a backslash (\) followed by a single letter, for example \Q, you can run that macro by holding down the CTRL key and pressing the letter following the backslash. For example, CTRL+Q starts the macro named \Q.

Starting a Macro with RUN (ALT+F3) or Tools Macro Run

Whether you assign a backslash range name or a conventional range name to a macro, you can start that macro with RUN (ALT+F3) or the Tools Macro Run command. Whichever method you choose, 1-2-3 displays the dialog box in Figure 14-7. In the list box, 1-2-3 displays all the range names from the current file, along with the names of other open worksheet files; the filenames appear in double-angle brackets << >> at the end of the list.

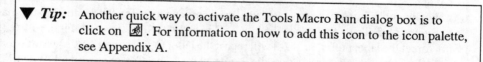

▼ **Tip:**   Another quick way to activate the Tools Macro Run dialog box is to click on [icon]. For information on how to add this icon to the icon palette, see Appendix A.

To run a macro located in the currently active file, specify its name in the "Range name" text box. (You can either type the name or select it from the list box.) When you select OK, 1-2-3 will start the macro.

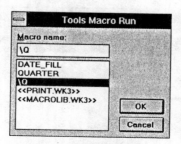

Figure 14-7   The Tools Macro Run dialog box

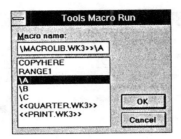

Figure 14-8 Starting a macro located in another file

To run a macro that is located in another open worksheet file but have it act on the current file, select the name of that file from the list box. For example, imagine you want to run one of the macros in the MACROLIB.WK3 file that appears in the list box in Figure 14-7. To do this, select <<MACROLIB.WK3>> from the list box. 1-2-3 then displays the range names from MACROLIB.WK3 in the list box, as shown in Figure 14-8. When you select a macro name, 1-2-3 runs the macro located in the MACROLIB.WK3 file, but its effects take place in the currently active file. For more on sharing macros across worksheet files, see "Using a Macro Library File" later.

You can also use RUN (ALT+F3) or Tools Macro Run to "test fly" a macro that does not as yet have a range name. To do this, simply press RUN, and when 1-2-3 displays the Tools Macro Run dialog box, press PANE (F6). 1-2-3 immediately shrinks the dialog box, displays the current cell pointer location in the edit line, and enters POINT mode. You can then use the arrow keys or the mouse to move the cell pointer to the first cell of macro instructions you want to execute and press ENTER. 1-2-3 then returns you to the Tools Macro Run dialog box. Select OK, and 1-2-3 starts executing the macro.

The Effect of Macros on the Cell Pointer

When 1-2-3 for Windows runs a macro, it reads through the macro's labels one instruction at a time. When it finishes the instructions in the first label, it moves to the label in the cell below and starts executing its instructions. However, the location of the cell pointer does not change. In fact, the location of the cell pointer is not affected by 1-2-3's current position in a macro. The cell pointer will only move if your macro instructions tell it to do so.

Documenting Macros

As a macro grows in size and complexity, it can become difficult to remember exactly what each line does, especially if you put the macro aside for a while. To help deal with this problem, it is wise to document your macros. That way, when it comes time to revise a macro, you can quickly determine what each line in the macro does.

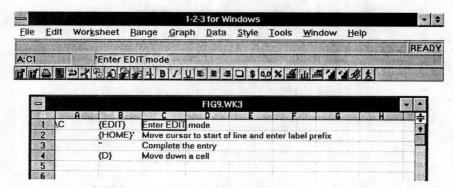

Figure 14-9 A documented macro

Here are the two things you can do to document a macro in 1-2-3:

- Place the name of the macro in the worksheet immediately to the left of its starting cell. (Figure 14-9 shows an example of this.) In addition, if you name another cell in the macro, place the name in the cell immediately to the left of the named cell.

- Place descriptive comments (labels) to the right of each macro label.

Figure 14-9 shows an example of a documented macro. The macro's name, \C, appears in cell A1. The labels that make up the macro appear in column B, and the descriptive comments for each line appear in column C.

Stopping a Macro

Suppose you are executing a macro and decide that you want to interrupt it. To stop a macro, you can press CTRL+BREAK. When you do, 1-2-3 immediately stops executing the macro and displays an error message. Select OK to clear the message and return to the worksheet in READY mode.

Note: To prevent a user from stopping your macro with CTRL+BREAK, use {BREAKOFF} (see Chapter 15).

Saving Macros

Once you've finished creating a macro, you can save it by using the File Save command to save the worksheet file that contains it. To use that macro again in another session, you must use the File Open command to open the worksheet file containing the macro.

Using Menu Commands in Macros

Thus far, most of the macro examples in this chapter have used simple keystroke instructions to enter data in the worksheet and move the cell pointer. However, you can also access 1-2-3's menu commands from a macro. This section will show you how and provide some examples with which you can experiment.

The Amazing {ALT} Command

In previous versions of 1-2-3, the / (slash) command was used to access the menu in a macro. In 1-2-3 for Windows, however, the / command accesses the Classic menu. To access the GUI menu bar in a 1-2-3 macro, you must use {ALT}, {MENUBAR}, or {MB}. For example, {ALT}r activates the menu bar and selects the Range popup menu, as does {MB}r.

The {ALT} command has another feature that makes it more flexible than {MENUBAR} or {MB}. By using an argument enclosed in quotation marks with {ALT}, you can choose a menu option directly. For example, when executed from READY mode, the command {ALT "r"} activates the Range menu, as does {ALT r}.

You can also use a range name or cell address as an argument for {ALT}. For example, if cell B5 contains the label 'G, the command {ALT +B5} activates the Graph menu. As another example, if cell D7 is named STOCK and contains the label 'D, {ALT STOCK} actives the Data menu.

▼ **Tip:** Besides using {ALT} to access menu options, you can also use it to access dialog box options. For example, if the Range Format dialog box is active, {ALT "R"} selects the Reset option. In fact, {ALT} provides the only way to select a dialog box option directly. (The only other choice is to use {TAB}.)

As you work with {ALT}, you'll find that is has a few peculiarities when it comes to menu navigation. For example, the commands {ALT}r{ALT}f bring up the File menu, but {ALT}rf brings up the Range Format dialog box.

A Command Macro Example

Suppose you are creating a model that requires numerous dates to be displayed in the worksheet. As you know, the @DATE function is handy for entering dates. When you place this function in a cell, 1-2-3 displays a date number. To have that number displayed as a recognizable date, you must use the Range Format command and, for example, specify 3 (Dec-90) as the date format. To automate the formatting of dates, you might create the macro in Figure 14-10.

The \D macro activates 1-2-3's main menu, displays the Range Format dialog box, and chooses 3: Dec-90 as the cell format ({ALT}rf3). At that point, the "Range" text box is activated ({ALT "a"}), and the macro returns to the worksheet with the current range setting displayed in the edit line ({WINDOW}), as shown in Figure 14-11. The macro then pauses for you to specify a range ({?}~). After you highlight a range and press ENTER, the Range Format dialog box reappears. The OK button is then selected (~), and 1-2-3 formats the range you selected in 3: Dec-90 format.

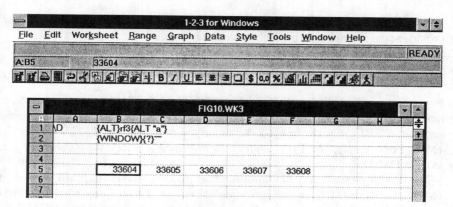

Figure 14-10 A Range Format 3 macro

Another Command Macro Example

Figure 14-12 shows an example of a print preview macro in the range A:AB1..A:AB5. This macro selects the Print Preview command and then pauses for you to specify a range. After you highlight a range and press ENTER, the macro accesses the Page Setup dialog box where it enters a header that will appear at the top of each page. The macro then selects OK to return to the Print Preview dialog box and OK again to have 1-2-3 display your printed output on the screen.

Here's a detailed description of the function of each line in the macro:

- **{ALT}fv:** This line activates 1-2-3's menu bar and then selects the File Preview command.

- **{WINDOW}{?}~:** Because the "Range" option is automatically selected when the File Preview dialog appears, the macro picks up from that point. Here the {WINDOW} command causes the dialog box to temporarily disappear and have 1-2-3 show the

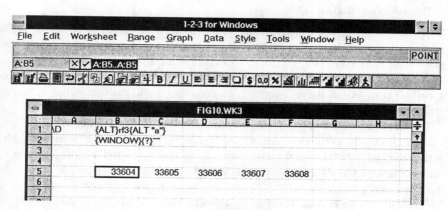

Figure 14-11 Running the macro in Figure 14-10

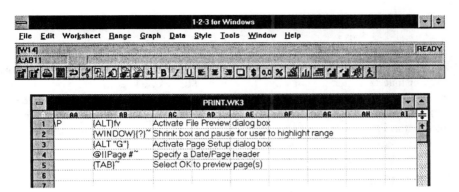

Figure 14-12 A sample print macro

current "Range" setting in the edit line. The {?} command (discussed in the next chapter) pauses macro execution temporarily and awaits input from the user. This allows you to select a range to preview using either the keyboard or the mouse. However, you must press ENTER to complete your selection. When you do, the ~ (tilde) confirms your choice, and 1-2-3 enters the new setting in the "Range" text box.

- **{ALT "G"}**: This line selects the Page Setup button.

- **@||Page #~**: When the Page Setup dialog box appears, the "Header" option is automatically selected. Next, the text @||Page #~ is entered in the header text box. (This causes the current date to be left-aligned and the current page number to be right-aligned at the top of each page.) The ~ (tilde) selects the OK button to return to the File Preview dialog box.

- **{TAB}~**: When the Page Preview dialog box reappears, {TAB} highlights the OK button and ~ (tilde) selects it.

Selecting Commands by Using Their First Letters

When you create macros that use menu commands, make sure your instructions select those commands by using their first letters, rather than arrow-key equivalents such as {RIGHT} or {LEFT}. For example, {ALT}rf3~ is preferable to {ALT}{RIGHT 3}~~{DOWN 14}~. Although both are functionally equivalent, {ALT}rf3~ is easier to read, understand, and debug. What's more, if your 1-2-3 macros depend on the precise position of commands in a menu, you are bound to run into compatibility problems later on if Lotus should happen to add any options to the menu, something they have been known to do in the past.

Using Range Names Instead of Cell Addresses

Imagine you have the instructions {ALT}fpA:A1..A:F20~ in a macro. These instructions select the File Print command, specify the print range A:A1..A:F20, and initiate the printing process. Now, imagine that you use Edit Cut and Edit Paste to move the data in the range A:A1..A:F20 to another location in the worksheet. Your macro is now outdated because 1-2-3 does not make the connection between the movement of the data and the addresses in your macro.

To guard against your macro being tied to particular cell addresses, use range names in your macros instead. That way, if the data in the worksheet moves, your macros will remain up to date. For example, suppose you assign the name PRINT1 to the range A:A1..A:F20 and use that range name in your macro. If you later move the range, 1-2-3 moves the PRINT1 range name along with it, and your macro is no worse off for the change.

Undoing a Macro

Suppose you run a macro and then decide that you don't like what just happened to your worksheet. You can undo the effects of the macro by selecting the Edit Undo command (or its shortcut, ALT+BACKSPACE).

When you select Edit Undo after a macro, 1-2-3 for Windows undoes the entire macro. If you press ALT+BACKSPACE during a pause in a macro, 1-2-3 will undo the effects of the macro up to that point.

Note: If you want to access the undo feature in a macro, use {ALT}eu. The sequence {ALT}{BS} will not work.

AUTOEXECUTE MACROS

An *autoexecute macro* is one that starts automatically when you open the worksheet file that contains it. To create an autoexecute macro, simply name the macro \0 (backslash zero) and save the worksheet file. The next time you load the worksheet file using File Open, 1-2-3 will automatically execute the macro.

Autoexecute macros are especially useful when you want to create a custom application for use by others. For example, you might create an autoexecute macro that presents a specially designed menu in the 1-2-3 Classic window. When an option from that menu is selected, the macro branches to a subroutine that helps the user perform a certain task. For more about creating custom menus and branching with macros, see Chapter 15.

Autoexecute macros may also be useful in worksheet files that you use often. For example, imagine that whenever a particular worksheet file is loaded, you want to open a companion macro library file. To do this, you might set up the autoexecute macro in Figure 14-13. The first line of the macro in cell A:B1 selects the File Open command. When the File Open dialog box appears, the name of the macro library file (in this case, MACROS.WK3) is entered in the "File name" text box. Next, the ~ (tilde) selects the OK button to complete the File Open command. The macro library file is then opened in a separate window, which by default becomes the active window.

To reactivate the original window—the window containing the autoexecute macro— the {PREVFILE} command appears in the second line of the macro (cell A:B2). This

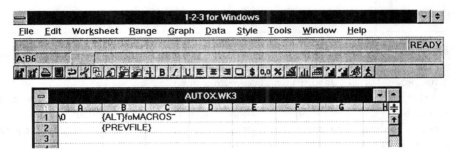

Figure 14-13   A sample autoexecute macro

keystroke command activates the previously active file. By reactivating the file containing the original autoexecute macro, you can then continue your work in that file.

If you install 1-2-3 for Windows using all the standard settings, it will always run autoexecute macros when you load the files that contain them. On occasion, you may not want autoexecute macros to run automatically. For example, consider the case whereby you want to load a file and edit its autoexecute macro. In this case, you can use the Tools User Setup command and turn off the Run autoexecute macros check box. (If you want to update this setting for future sessions, select the Update button.)

▼ *Tip:*   If you want to run an autoexecute macro again after you have already retrieved its file, use RUN (ALT+F3). Another alternative is to assign an additional name to the macro—for example, \a—and activate it using that name.

If a macro in the currently active file uses the Classic menu's /File Retrieve command to replace the currently active file, the macro ends when the new file is opened.

If a macro uses the File Open command to open another worksheet file that contains an autoexecute macro, the autoexecute macro in the newly opened file takes over. Although control will eventually return to the original macro once the autoexecute macro has finished running, the original macro will now operate on the newly opened worksheet file. To have the macro operate in the original window again, you must immediately follow the File Open command with the {PREVFILE} command to reactivate the original window.

▼ *Tip:*   If you want to have a file automatically load when you start 1-2-3 for Windows, name that file AUTO123.WK3; this is the worksheet file that 1-2-3 automatically loads (if present) on startup (see Chapter 4 for more). By placing an autoexecute macro within AUTO123.WK3, you can have the macro automatically execute on startup.

DEBUGGING A MACRO

Even the most experienced macro programmers make errors in their macros. Often an error is not immediately apparent, and you must debug the macro to find it. *Debugging* is the process of locating errors and correcting them.

1-2-3 offers two facilities for helping to debug your macros: Step and Trace. You access these facilities through the Tools Macro Debug command. As you use these facilities to debug your macros, it may help you in your search for errors to know what some of the more common macro errors are.

Note: 1-2-3 for Windows often displays an error message when an error occurs in a macro. This message includes the label instruction that was being executed when the error occurred along with its location (cell address).

Often macro errors are quite simple. For example, you may have misspelled a macro programming command or keyname. Or you may have omitted a ~ (tilde)—for example, you used

    {ALT}eqRANGE1{TAB}RANGE2

instead of

    {ALT}eqRANGE1{TAB}RANGE2~

You can easily correct this kind of problem by editing the label as you would any other label in 1-2-3. Here are some other common macro errors:

- You did not use {TAB} or {ALT} to move to the appropriate item in a dialog box before entering text (see "The Amazing ALT Key" earlier).

- You may have used parentheses to enclose a command or keyname instead of curly braces, or you may have omitted a curly brace.

- If your macro uses range names, you may have used a range name that is undefined. Or you may have assigned a range name that matches a macro keyname or command, for example {CLOSE} or {BREAK}.

- You may have forgotten a command menu letter or used the wrong letter.

- You may have omitted a space between a macro keyword, or a macro keyname, and its argument. For example, instead of {DOWN 3}, you used {DOWN3}.

Using STEP Mode

STEP mode allows you to run a macro one instruction at a time. This handy debugging tool also lets you watch a macro as it is executing, up to the point where an error actually occurs.

Note: To indicate that STEP mode is on, 1-2-3 for Windows displays a STEP mode indicator.

Figure 14-14 The Tools Macro Debug dialog box

To turn STEP mode on, select the Tools Macro Debug command. When 1-2-3 displays the dialog box shown in Figure 14-14, turn on the "Single step" check box and select OK. You can also turn on STEP mode by pressing STEP (ALT+F2). [To turn STEP mode off, turn off the "Single step" check box or press STEP (ALT+F2) a second time.]

> ▼ *Tip:* You can also turn STEP mode on and off by clicking on 🔲 . To add this icon to the icon palette, see Appendix A.

When STEP mode is on, 1-2-3 will execute your macros one instruction at a time. To move from one instruction to the next, press any key.

Note: You can turn on TRACE mode from the Tools Macro Debug dialog box at the same time that you turn on STEP mode. TRACE mode opens a window that displays the macro line that is about to be executed (see the next section).

For example, imagine you are having trouble with the macro in Figure 14-15. This macro uses the Data Fill command to fill a row of 12 consecutive cells with date numbers ranging from January 15, 1992 to December 15, 1992. It then uses the Range Format 3 (Dec-90) command to format the date values. Although it's hard to tell from the figure, this macro has an error in it. The first line of the macro (cell A:B1) reads {ALT}df{BS}.{R 11}~. The second to last character in the line is a closing parenthesis instead of the right curly brace that it should be.

To debug the macro in Figure 14-15, turn on STEP mode and start the macro (press CTRL+F). To execute the first command ({ALT}), press any key. 1-2-3 activates the main menu. When you press another key, the Data Fill command is executed. The Data

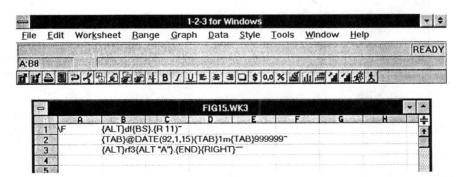

Figure 14-15 A macro with an error in the first line

Fill dialog box is then displayed with the "Ranges" text box activated. Pressing yet another key executes the {BS} command. (If a fill range already exists, this command serves to unanchor the cell pointer and return it to the current cell). Everything looks good so far; you know that the macro instructions up through {ALT}df{BS}. are working just fine. When you press another key, however, and 1-2-3 hits {R 11), an error message is displayed indicating a syntax error. At this point, you can see that a parenthesis exists where a curly brace belongs.

When you find an error with STEP mode, you do not need to turn STEP mode off to correct the problem. Instead, press CTRL+BREAK to terminate the macro. Then make your correction and start the macro again.

Note: When you write a new macro, it's wise to run through it in STEP mode at least once. This simple procedure may help you flag errors that wouldn't otherwise be apparent.

Using TRACE Mode

When you activate TRACE mode, 1-2-3 for Windows displays the Macro Trace window, as shown in Figure 14-16. If you then start a macro, the Trace window shows the command line that is about to be executed and its location in the worksheet.

To activate TRACE mode, select the Tools Macro Debug command. When 1-2-3 displays the dialog box in Figure 14-14, turn on the Trace check box and select OK. If

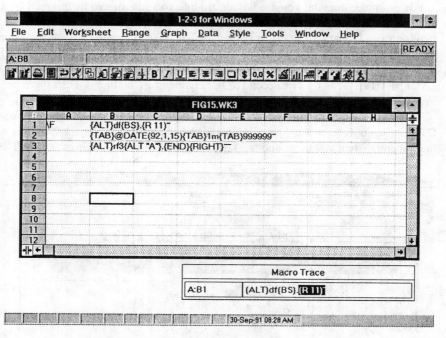

Figure 14-16 The Trace window highlights an error

you start a macro at this point, 1-2-3 will show each line in the Trace window as it executes. (To turn TRACE mode off, select Tools Macro Debug and turn off the Trace check box.)

The Trace window is divided into two sections. The left side of the window shows the cell address of the macro command line that is currently executing. The right side shows the command line itself. If an error occurs while the command line is executing, 1-2-3 highlights the errant instruction. For example, in Figure 14-16 the instruction {R 11)~ is highlighted. At a glance you can see that a closed parenthesis exists where a right curly brace belongs.

Tips on Debugging

You may find the following tips to be useful when debugging your macros:

- Use STEP mode and TRACE mode at the same time when debugging a macro. Otherwise, the commands in the Trace window may flash by so fast that you can't see what is going on.

- You can turn STEP mode off while a macro is executing. To do this, however, the macro must be pausing for user input. Some examples of commands that pause a macro for user input are {?}, {GETLABEL}, {MENUBRANCH}, and {MENUCALL}. See Chapter 15 for more on these commands.

- You can press STEP (ALT+F2) to turn STEP mode off while a macro is executing. When you press a key, 1-2-3 will execute the rest of the macro at normal speed.

- You can use RUN (ALT+F3) to start a macro at a specific line. Press RUN, move the cell pointer to the cell where you want macro execution to begin, and press ENTER. 1-2-3 will begin executing the macro, starting at the cell you specified.

- You can also put "break points" in your macros to test specific sections of code. To create a break point, place a blank cell at the point where you want the macro to stop; then start the macro. 1-2-3 will execute the macro up to the point where the blank cell occurs. To test the next section of the macro, select RUN (ALT+F3). When 1-2-3 displays the Tools Macro Run dialog box, press PANE (F6) to enter POINT mode and then move the cell pointer to the first cell in the next section of the macro. When you're ready, press ENTER. 1-2-3 executes the next section of the macro.

USING A MACRO LIBRARY FILE

Suppose you have a series of macros that you use regularly, but that are scattered throughout various worksheet files. Using those macros involves either loading the appropriate worksheet file and executing the macros with RUN (ALT+F3), or copying the macros to the file you happen to be using at the time.

As an alternative to storing your commonly used macros in different worksheet files, you can consolidate them into a *macro library* file. A macro library file is no different from any other worksheet file, except that it typically contains only macros. The primary advantages of using a macro library file are the disk space you save by storing your macros in a single location and the time you save by not having to search your worksheet files for the right macro. What's more, when you run a macro from another file in 1-2-3, it executes as though it were located in the current file.

Storing Macros in a Macro Library

To store macros in a macro library file, begin by using File New to create a new worksheet file. You can then consolidate your commonly used macros from various sources, including other worksheet files or the Transcript window, into the new file. To do this, simply use Edit Copy (or Cut) and Edit Paste to copy the macros to the new file. Make sure, however, to leave a blank cell between each of the macros in the worksheet file. Otherwise, you may get unexpected results.

Note: After copying macros into a macro library file, be sure to use Range Name Create or Range Name Label Create Right to assign range names to those macros.

After placing your macros in the new macro library file, you can give the file any name you like. For example, Figure 14-17 shows a sample macro library file named MACROS.WK3.

Running Macros in a Macro Library

Before you can run a macro in a macro library file, it must be open. You should also move the cell pointer to the appropriate location in the file that you want the macro to affect.

To run a macro from a macro library that will execute in another file, select Tools Macro Run or press RUN (ALT+F3). When 1-2-3 for Windows displays the Tools Macro Run dialog box, select the name of the macro library file from the list box to see the range names in that file. Next, select the name that matches the macro you want to run. When you select OK, 1-2-3 starts executing the macro.

▼ *Tip:*   You can also run a macro from a macro library directly, provided there isn't any key conflict with the active file.

When 1-2-3 executes a macro in a macro library file, its instructions are treated as though they were located in the current file. That is, cell addresses and range names not preceded by a file reference refer to the current file (the file the macro is acting on). If an instruction uses a branch or subroutine location, however, 1-2-3 will search for that location in the macro library file. Suppose a macro in your macro library file contains the command {BRANCH TOTALS}. If you run this macro in the file YEAREND, 1-2-3 will search for the range name TOTALS in the macro library file, not in the file YEAREND. If 1-2-3 cannot find the range name in the macro library file, an error message will result. (See Chapter 15 for more on branching and subroutines.)

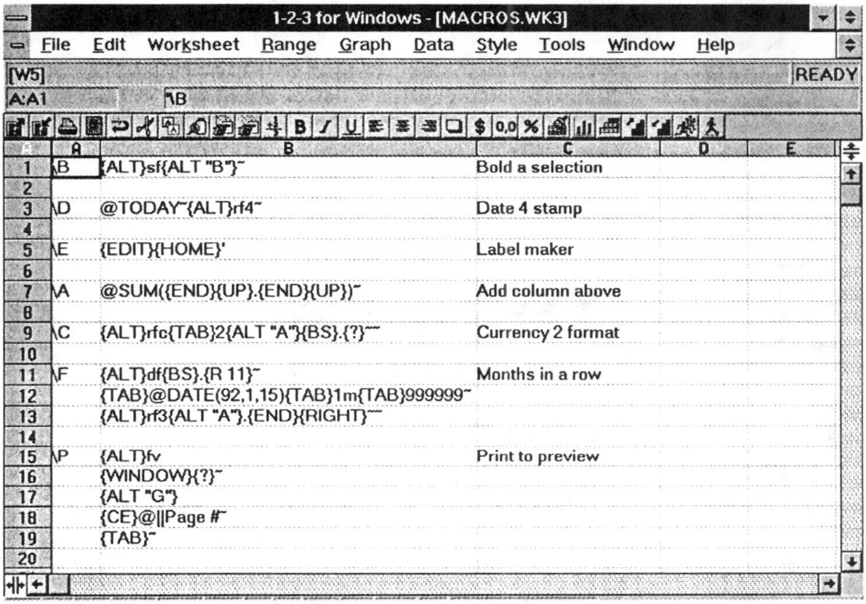

Figure 14-17   A sample macro library

Organizing a Macro Library

Like any 1-2-3 worksheet file, a macro library file can contain up to 256 worksheets. You can use these separate worksheets to help organize your macro library—you might put your general-purpose macros in worksheet A, your database macros in worksheet B, your graph macros in worksheet C, and so on. This will help you maintain an orderly macro library and quickly find a given macro when needed.

USING THE TRANSCRIPT WINDOW

The Transcript window captures every keystroke you make in 1-2-3 for Windows. These keystrokes are then translated into 1-2-3 macro commands. At any time, you can open the Transcript window and look at your previous keystrokes. If you'd like, you can then copy those keystrokes to the worksheet for use as a macro. You can also have the Transcript window "play back" selected keystrokes, a useful feature for performing repetitive worksheet operations. If changes are required, you can edit the keystrokes in the Transcript window before copying them to the worksheet.

Note: The Transcript window also captures mouse actions and translates them into their equivalent keystrokes.

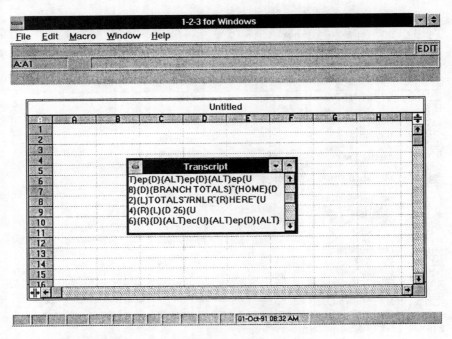

Figure 14-18 The Transcript window

Like a graph or worksheet window, the Transcript window has its own menu. To access the Transcript window, you use the Tools Macro Show Transcript command. 1-2-3 then displays the window and menu shown in Figure 14-18 when the Transcript window is active.

How 1-2-3 Stores Keystrokes

1-2-3 captures all your keystrokes, whether or not the Transcript window is displayed. However, the Transcript window only holds about 512 bytes (or characters). When the Transcript window is full, 1-2-3 will drop off the oldest characters one at a time in order to accommodate the newest ones.

Keystroke Translation

The Transcript window translates every keystroke you make into a macro instruction. For example, the File Print command becomes {ALT}fp; when you press DEL, 1-2-3 records {DEL}; and when recording function keys, 1-2-3 uses the names of those keys—for example, F3 is captured as {NAME}.

To make the best use of the Transcript window's limited size, 1-2-3 abbreviates keystroke instructions whenever it can. For example, instead of recording ↓ as {DOWN},

1-2-3 records it as {D}. What's more, if you press ↓ three times, 1-2-3 records this as {D 3}, instead of {D}{D}{D}.

Note: In Version 1.0, 1-2-3 for Windows does not always record your keystrokes reliably. It's wise to check them in the Transcript window before attempting to use them in a macro.

How the Transcript Window Works: An Example

This section takes you through an example of how you might use the Transcript window to create a simple macro and copy it to the worksheet. Ultimately, the macro will select the Style Font command and specify a 10-point Courier font for the current worksheet.

Note: The following example assumes that you are using the standard fonts that accompany the Adobe Type Manager shipped with 1-2-3 for Windows. If you are using a different set of fonts, you may need to modify the procedure slightly.

Clearing the Buffer

Before you create a macro with the Transcript window, it's always a good idea to clear the Transcript window of its contents and start with a clean slate. If you haven't already done so, select the Tools Macro Show Transcript command to display the Transcript window; if you've been using 1-2-3 for Windows for a while, the window should appear full of characters. To activate the Transcript window, click your mouse on its title bar or press CTRL+F6 to move to it. Next, select the Edit Clear All command from the Transcript window menu. 1-2-3 deletes the keystrokes from the window without copying them to the Clipboard. To return to the worksheet window, press CTRL+F6 again.

Note: When you return to the worksheet, the Transcript window drops into the background, but remains open.

Capturing the Keystrokes

Once you've returned to the worksheet, you are ready to start recording the keystrokes that will make up your macro. To begin, press ALT to activate 1-2-3's menu bar. Then type **sf**, for Style Font. When 1-2-3 displays the Style Font dialog box, press ALT+R to select Replace. With the Style Font Replace dialog box appearing on the screen, press ↓ once to select Arial MT 12 in the "Current fonts" list. (This is the font you will replace in the current font set. 1-2-3 will then use the new font, Courier 10, whenever you enter new data in the worksheet.) Next, press TAB twice to move to the "Available fonts" list and then use ↑ to select Courier in the list. Having selected the replacement font, press ALT+Z to move to the Size box. Once there, type **10**. To accept the new setting and leave the Style Font Replace dialog box, press ENTER. When 1-2-3 returns to the Style Font dialog box, press TAB to move to the OK button and then press ENTER to select it.

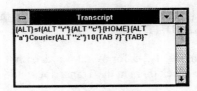

Figure 14-19 Captured keystrokes in the Transcript window

If you followed along in the previous paragraph, the Transcript window should contain the commands shown in Figure 14-19. To see if this happened, activate the Transcript window by clicking on its title bar or pressing CTRL+F6.

Editing Keystrokes

Editing keystrokes in the Transcript window is like editing text in Notepad or Windows Write. In fact, if you want to use the Transcript window to create macros, you'll find that editing is an integral part of the process.

For example, if you followed along in the previous section and you're using version 1.0, 1-2-3 has recorded a superfluous keystroke that you'll need to remove before playing back the keystrokes or creating a macro. Instead of "{HOME}" in the second line of the Transcript window, the section reads "{HOME}~" (the superfluous tilde needs to be removed). To remove the tilde, you must first make the Transcript window the active window. Next, drag the mouse to highlight the ~ and press DEL. 1-2-3 deletes the character and closes up the space it occupied. If you inadvertently delete too many characters, simply move the cursor to the spot where a missing letter should be and type a new letter.

Note: Undo is not available in the Transcript window.

If you have many characters to delete, use Edit Clear from the Transcript window's menu bar (or its shortcut DEL). In preparation for this command, first highlight the characters you want to delete. When you select Edit Clear, the characters you've highlighted are permanently deleted from the Transcript window.

Playing Back the Keystrokes

Once you have the appropriate keystrokes displayed in the Transcript window, you can test those keystrokes by "playing" them back, which allows you to watch as the keystrokes are performed a second time to verify their accuracy.

To play back keystrokes, highlight the keystrokes you want in the Transcript window by clicking and dragging the mouse, or hold down the SHIFT key and use the arrow keys to expand the highlight. Next, select the Macro Run command from the Transcript window menu. 1-2-3 deactivates the Transcript window and plays back the keystrokes you selected in the previously active worksheet window.

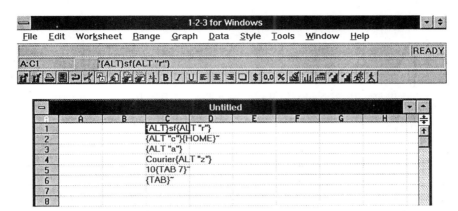

Figure 14-20 Keystrokes copied to the worksheet

When the playback is completed, you can reactivate the Transcript window and make any required changes. You'll notice when you return to the Transcript window that no additional characters have been added as the result of playing back the keystrokes. If the existing keystrokes have the desired effect, you can copy them to the worksheet for use as a macro. Otherwise, you can edit the keystrokes and play them back again.

Copying the Keystrokes to the Worksheet

To copy the keystrokes in the Transcript window to the worksheet, you use the Clipboard. Start by highlighting the characters you want. Next, select Edit Copy from the Transcript window's menu bar. 1-2-3 copies the characters you selected to the Clipboard.

To paste the characters from the Clipboard to the worksheet, first activate the worksheet by clicking on its title bar or pressing CTRL+F6. Next, move the cell pointer to where you want the new macro instructions to begin and select Edit Paste. 1-2-3 pastes the characters from the Clipboard to the worksheet, starting at the location of the cell pointer. The characters are pasted as labels in a column of consecutive cells. For example, Figure 14-20 shows what happens when you select the Edit Paste command with the cell pointer in cell A:B1.

Naming and Running the Macro

Once the keystroke instructions have been copied from the Transcript window to the worksheet as labels, you can then name the new macro and run it just as you would any other macro in 1-2-3 for Windows. For example, to name the macro in Figure 14-20, move the cell pointer to cell A:B1 and type \A. Next, leaving the cell pointer in cell A:B1, use the Range Name Label Create Right command to name the first cell of the macro (cell A:C1). To run the macro, press CTRL+A.

Tips on Using the Transcript Window

Here are some tips you may find useful when using the Transcript window to record macros:

- You can copy characters from the worksheet to the Transcript window. To do this, use Edit Copy while in the worksheet and Edit Paste in the Transcript window.

- To have the Transcript window minimized to an icon when keystrokes are played back, select the Macro Minimize on Run command from the Transcript window menu.

- To debug the keystrokes in the Transcript window before copying them to the worksheet, select the Macro Debug command from the Transcript window menu. When you select this command, 1-2-3 displays the same dialog box that appears when you select the Tools Macro Debug command from a worksheet window's menu bar. See "Debugging a Macro" earlier for more details.

- You can stop the Transcript window from recording keystrokes. To do this, select the Macro Pause Recording command from Transcript window's menu. To start recording keystrokes again, select Macro Pause Recording a second time.

- If you want to call another existing macro from within a macro you're currently recording, type the range name for that macro between curly braces, for example {MYMACRO}, in the Transcript window.

15

The Macro Programming Language

In the previous chapter, you learned how to create simple 1-2-3 for Windows macros. For the most part, the commands used in those macros were representations of keystrokes. Although macros of this kind can be quite useful, they can take you only so far in automating your work.

In this chapter, you will learn how to use 1-2-3 for Windows' more advanced macro commands, those used for programming 1-2-3. With these commands you can perform any of the following:

- Get user input.
- Manipulate data in cells.
- Stop and suspend macro execution.
- Perform conditional processing.
- Branch.
- Call subroutines.
- Trap errors.
- Work with data entry forms.
- Create custom menus.
- Change the effect of CTRL+BREAK.
- Sound tones.
- Control areas of the screen.
- Size and move application windows.

- Control recalculation.
- Access DOS.
- Launch Windows applications.
- Control the Clipboard.
- Control Dynamic Data Exchange (DDE) links.
- Control external database transactions.
- Read and write ASCII files.

Table 15-1 shows 1-2-3 for Windows' macro programming commands organized according to these categories.

TABLE 15-1 Macro Programming Commands

Getting User Input

Command	Description
{?}	Suspends a macro for input until you press ENTER.
{GET *location*}	Suspends macro execution until a key is pressed; stores the key press in *location* as a label.
{GETLABEL *prompt,location*}	Displays *prompt* in a 1-2-3 Classic prompt box, waits for input, and stores the input as a string in *location*.
{GETNUMBER *prompt,location*}	Displays *prompt* in a 1-2-3 Classic prompt box, waits for input, and stores the input as a number in *location*.
{LOOK *location*}	Stores the first keystroke you make while a macro is executing as a label in *location*.

Manipulating Data in Cells

Command	Description
{BLANK *location*}	Erases the contents of *location*.
{CONTENTS *target-location, source-location, [width], [cell-format]*}	Copies *source-location* to *target-location* as a label.
{LET *location,entry*}	Places *entry* (a value or string) in *location*.
{PUT *location, column-offset, row-offset,entry*}	Places a number or label in *location*.

(continued)

TABLE 15-1 Macro Programming Commands *(continued)*

Stopping and Suspending Macros

Command	Description
{QUIT}	Ends macro processing.
{WAIT *time-number*}	Suspends macro execution until the specified time number has elapsed.

Conditional Processing

Command	Description
{FOR *counter,start-number, stop-number,step-number, subroutine*}	Performs *subroutine* while *start-number* + *counter* is less than *stop-number*; each pass increases *counter* by *step-number*.
{FORBREAK}	Ends the current {FOR} loop.
{IF *condition*}	Evaluates whether *condition* is true or false. If true, executes the next command on the same line. If false, skips to the next line.

Branching

Command	Description
{BRANCH *location*}	Transfers macro control to *location*.
{DISPATCH *location*}	Performs an indirect branch to the cell whose name or address is in *location*.

Subroutines

Command	Description
{*subroutine* [argument1], [argument2],..., [argumentn]}	Performs a subroutine call, optionally passing arguments to it.
{DEFINE *location1, location2,...,locationn*}	Specifies cells that will be used to store arguments to be passed to a subroutine.
{RESTART}	Clears the subroutine stack; 1-2-3 then acts as though the next instruction is the beginning of a new macro.
{RETURN}	Used in subroutines to return macro control to the next macro instruction following the {*subroutine*} call.

(continued)

TABLE 15-1 Macro Programming Commands *(continued)*

Error Trapping

Command	Description
{ONERROR branch-location, [message-location]}	Branches to the macro instructions at *branch-location* when an error occurs.

Working with Data Entry Forms

Command	Description
{APPENDBELOW target-location, source-location}	Copies the data in *source-location* to the bottom of *target-location*.
{APPENDRIGHT target-location, source-location}	Copies the data in *source-location* to the right of *target-location*.
{FORM input-location, [call-table], [include-list], [exclude-list]}	Suspends macro execution, allowing you to enter input in *input-location*.
{FORMBREAK}	Terminates a {FORM} command.

Creating Custom Menus

Command	Description
{MENUBRANCH location}	Creates a custom menu with the items in *location*, waits for you to select an item from the menu, and branches to the instructions for that item.
{MENUCALL location}	Creates a custom menu with the items in *location*, waits for you to select an item from the menu, and performs a subroutine call to the instructions at *location*.

Changing the Effect of CTRL+BREAK

Command	Description
{BREAK}	Same as pressing CTRL+BREAK in a menu or a dialog box.
{BREAKOFF}	Disables {BREAK} and CTRL+BREAK during a macro.
{BREAKON}	Reinstates the use of {BREAK} and CTRL+BREAK during a macro.

(continued)

TABLE 15-1 Macro Programming Commands *(continued)*

Sounding Tones

Command	Description
{BEEP [tone-number]}	Sounds a tone.

Controlling Parts of the Screen

Command	Description
{FRAMEOFF}	Turns off the display of the worksheet frame.
{FRAMEON}	Turns the display of the worksheet frame back on.
{GRAPHOFF}	Cancels a {GRAPHON} command.
{GRAPHON [named-graph], [nodisplay]}	Displays the current graph or a named graph.
{INDICATE string}	Changes the mode indicator to *string*.
{PANELOFF}	Prevents 1-2-3 from updating the control panel and status line.
{PANELON}	Reinstates updating of the control panel and status line.
{WINDOWSOFF}	Prevents redrawing of 1-2-3's work area.
{WINDOWSON}	Reinstates redrawing of 1-2-3's work area.

Controlling Application Windows

Command	Description
{APP-ADJUST x,y,width,height}	Positions 1-2-3's window *x* pixels to the right and *y* pixels below the top left corner of the screen; sizes 1-2-3's window to *width* by *height* pixels.
{APP-STATE state}	Maximizes, minimizes, or restores 1-2-3's window.
{WINDOW-ADJUST x,y,width,height}	Positions the active worksheet or graph window *x* pixels to the right and *y* pixels below the top left corner of 1-2-3's work area; sizes the window to *width* by *height* pixels.
{WINDOW-SELECT windowname}	Makes the worksheet or graph window specified as *windowname* the active window.
{WINDOW-STATE state}	Maximizes, minimizes, or restores the active window in the 1-2-3 for Windows work area.

(continued)

TABLE 15-1 Macro Programming Commands *(continued)*

Controlling Recalculation

Command	Description
{RECALC location, [condition],[iterations]}	Recalculates the values in *location* in row-by-row fashion using the specified number of iterations.
{RECALCCOL location, [condition],[iterations]}	Recalculates the values in *location* in column-by-column fashion using the specified number of iterations or until *condition* is met.

Accessing DOS

Command	Description
{SYSTEM command}	Executes the specified DOS command from within a macro.

Launching Windows Applications

Command	Description
{LAUNCH command, [window]}	Starts a Windows application.

Controlling the Clipboard

Command	Description
EDIT-CLEAR [selection], [property]}	Deletes data (and its formatting) from the worksheet without copying it to the Clipboard.
{EDIT-COPY [selection], [format]}	Copies data (and its formatting) from the worksheet to the Clipboard.
{EDIT-COPY-GRAPH}	Copies the contents of the active graph window to the Clipboard.
{EDIT-CUT [selection], [format]}	Cuts data (and its formatting) from the worksheet to the Clipboard.
{EDIT-PASTE [selection], [format]}	Pastes data (and its formatting) from the Clipboard to the worksheet.
{EDIT-PASTE-LINK [range]}	Creates a DDE link between the active worksheet file and the file named in the Clipboard.

(continued)

TABLE 15-1 Macro Programming Commands *(continued)*

Controlling DDE Links

Command	Description
{DDE-ADVISE branch-location, item-name, [format]}	Lets you specify a location to branch to when data in the server application changes.
{DDE-CLOSE}	Ends the current conversation with a Windows application.
{DDE-EXECUTE execute-string}	Lets you send a command to an application.
{DDE-OPEN app-name, topic-name, [location]}	Starts a DDE conversation with a Windows application (the server) and, optionally, enters in *location* the unique decimal number Windows assigns to the conversation.
{DDE-POKE range, item-name, [format]}	Sends a range of data to the server application.
{DDE-REQUEST range, item-name, [format]}	Requests data from the server application.
{DDE-UNADVISE item-name, [format]}	Ends a {DDE-ADVISE} command.
{DDE-USE conversation-number}	Makes *conversation-number* the current conversation.
{LINK-ASSIGN link-name, range, [property1], [property2], [property3]}	Lets you specify the range you want to link to in the current worksheet.
{LINK-CREATE link-name, app-name, topic-name, item-name, [format], [mode], [branch-location]}	Creates a DDE link between the current worksheet file and another Windows application.
{LINK-DELETE link-name}	Cancels a link, but leaves the data obtained through the link unchanged.
{LINK-DEACTIVATE link-name}	Deactivates a link, but leaves the link in place.
{LINK-REMOVE link-name}	Detaches the current destination range from a DDE link, but does not delete the data in the range.
{LINK-TABLE location}	Places a table of DDE link information in the current worksheet.
{LINK-UPDATE link-name}	Updates a DDE link.

(continued)

TABLE 15-1 Macro Programming Commands *(continued)*

Controlling External Database Transactions

Command	Description
{COMMIT}	Commits all pending database transactions.
{ROLLBACK}	Cancels all pending external database transactions.

Reading and Writing ASCII Files

Command	Description
{CLOSE}	Closes an open ASCII text file.
{FILESIZE *location*}	Enters the size (in bytes) of the open ASCII text file in *location*.
{GETPOS *location*}	Determines the offset of the file pointer within the open text file and stores it in *location*.
{OPEN *file-name, access-type*}	Opens an ASCII file for processing.
{READ *byte-count, location*}	Reads the open ASCII file beginning at the current file pointer location, copies *byte-count* to *location*, and advances the file pointer by *byte-count*.
{READLN *location*}	Reads the open ASCII file beginning at the current file pointer location and places the remainder of the current line in *location*.
{SETPOS *offset-number*}	Positions the file pointer in the open ASCII file to *offset-number* byte positions from the start of the file.
{WRITE *string*}	Writes *string* to the open ASCII text file, beginning at the current file pointer location.
{WRITELN *string*}	Writes *string* followed by carriage return/linefeed to the open ASCII text file, beginning at the current file pointer location.

With the exception of additional commands for controlling the placement of its windows, Clipboard, DDE, and external databases, 1-2-3 for Windows' macro programming commands are the same as those for 1-2-3 Release 3.1.

Each of these categories is discussed in detail in this chapter. You'll find a section on using formulas in macro commands and on creating your own self-modifying macros near the end of the chapter.

MACRO COMMAND SYNTAX

In the previous chapter, you learned several rules of macro command syntax. For example, you learned that every macro instruction must appear within curly braces, such as {DOWN}, and that you cannot split a macro instruction on to more than one line.

The same basic rules apply to all of 1-2-3 for Windows' macro programming commands. However, macro programming commands that accept arguments, as is the case with most of 1-2-3's programming commands, have some additional syntax rules that are illustrated in Figure 15-1.

The first part of a macro instruction is the *keyword*, which names the action the macro instruction is to perform. The keyword is preceded by a left curly brace ({) and followed by a space.

Arguments provide the information necessary to execute the macro command and are separated by commas. (You can also use semicolons to separate arguments.) Arguments can be numbers, strings, cell addresses, range references, range names, or conditions (the result of logical formulas). The last argument is always followed by a right curly brace (}).

Some arguments are optional, in which case they appear in brackets ([ ]), for example, {BEEP [*tone-number*]}. This means that you can use {BEEP} without an argument.

When arguments appear in italics without brackets, you *must* include them in the argument list. For example, {GETLABEL *prompt,location*} means that you must provide a *prompt* and a *location* argument.

Occasionally, you may want to omit one optional argument but include another that follows in the argument list. For example, the general format of the {CONTENTS} command is {CONTENTS *target-location,source-location,[width],[cell-format]*}. If you want to omit the *[width]* argument, you would use this syntax: {CONTENTS *target-location,source-location,,cell-format*}.

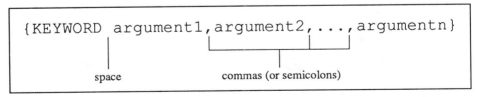

Figure 15-1 Macro command syntax

GETTING USER INPUT

1-2-3 for Windows has several commands for getting user input—{?}, {GET}, {GETLABEL}, {GETNUMBER}, and {LOOK}. You can use these commands to pause a macro and request numbers and labels, menu selections, responses to prompts, button selections, and the like.

The {?} Command

As you learned in the previous chapter, the {?} command lets you pause a macro until the user presses ENTER. While the macro is suspended, the user can type any number of keystrokes. These keystrokes might move the cell or menu pointer, complete part of a command, or enter data in a worksheet.

Note: While the {?} command is in effect, 1-2-3 will accept only keyboard input.

For example, the \N macro in Figure 15-2 shows how you might use the {?} command to solicit a response from the user. This macro places a table of active files in the current worksheet starting at the cell location you provide. The macro begins by issuing the File Administration Paste Table command. Then, after accessing the Ranges option, the {?} command pauses the macro for you to enter a starting location for the table. When you press ENTER, 1-2-3 interprets the key as an instruction to continue the macro. Therefore, you must include a ~ (tilde) following the {?} command to choose the OK button and leave the dialog box. (Without the tilde, the dialog box will remain on the screen.)

Note: There is one problem with the {?} command that is new to 1-2-3 for Windows. Suppose that before pressing ENTER, you press ESC, causing 1-2-3 to leave a dialog box. The {?} command remains in effect and may cause some problems farther down in your macro. In addition, if the {?} command is the last command in the macro, a CMD indicator remains, signifying that the macro has not actually ended but is pausing for input. If you try to run another macro, 1-2-3 will ignore your request; before you can invoke another macro, you must press ENTER until the CMD indicator is cleared.

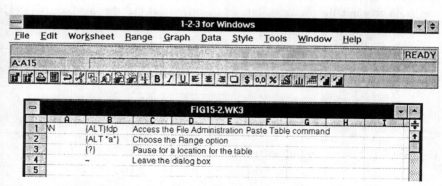

Figure 15-2 The {?} command

Keep in mind that you can use the {?} command to pause a macro at almost any point to get a response. For example, suppose you want to create a macro that jumps to a cell after pausing for you to provide a cell address or range name. Here is some sample code that you might use:

```
{GOTO} {?} ~
```

This macro presses GOTO (F5), which, as you know, causes 1-2-3 to display the Range Go To dialog box. You can then select a range name from the list, or enter a range name or cell address in the Range text box. When you press ENTER, 1-2-3 moves the cell pointer to the upper-left cell in the range. As with the previous example, a ~ (tilde) follows the {?} command because without it, you would have to press ENTER twice. (Note that if you enter POINT mode, you will have to press ENTER a second time or the Go To dialog box remains on the screen.)

The {GET} Command

The {GET} command pauses a macro until you press a key. The syntax of the command is

```
{GET location}
```

When you press a key, 1-2-3 stores your keystroke in *location* as a label. For example, if you press *y*, 1-2-3 stores it as 'y. When you press any of the keys in Table 14-1 of Chapter 14, however, 1-2-3 stores it in macro-instruction format. For example, if you press END, 1-2-3 stores it as '{END}.

You can specify a cell address or a range name for *location*. If you specify a range, 1-2-3 stores your keystroke in the upper-left cell of the range.

The {GET} command is used most frequently to get a single-letter response. For example, the first line of the macro in Figure 15-3 displays the prompt "Choose F(ile) or P(rinter):" in the Edit line, prompting you to type either **F** or **P**. The {GET KEYPRESS} command in the second line then pauses the macro and waits for you to press a key; it then records the key you press in the range KEYPRESS (cell B8). The next line in the macro, {ESC}, erases the prompt from the Edit line. The {IF} statement in the next line then tests the label in the KEYPRESS range. If it is equal to 'f or 'F (you pressed *f* or *F*), the macro executes the {BRANCH TO_FILE} command, which causes the macro to branch to the cell named TO_FILE (cell B10). As you can see, the instructions beginning in that cell issue the File Extract To command, choose the Text option followed by the File name option, pause the macro for you to enter a filename, then select OK.

If you pressed a key other than *f* or *F*, the macro executes the second {IF} command in cell B5, which tests whether the label in KEYPRESS is equal to 'p or 'P (you pressed *p* or *P*). If it is equal to either one, the macro executes the {BRANCH TO_PRINTER} command, which causes the macro to branch to TO_PRINTER (cell B15). The code in this cell issues the File Print command. However, if you pressed a key other than *f*, *F*, *p*, or *P*, the macro beeps, branches back to \P (the start of the macro, cell B1), and executes the macro again.

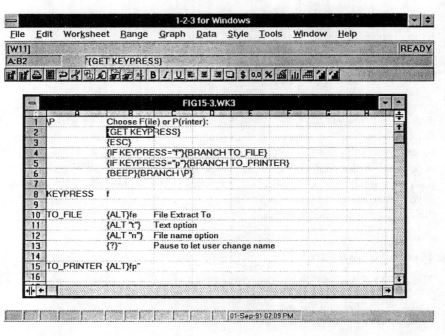

Figure 15-3   The {GET} command

Note: In certain instances, you may want the user to respond to a prompt with an END key sequence, such as END →, END CTRL+PGUP, END CTRL+PGDN, and the like. When this is the case, you should use two {GET} commands together—for example, {GET KEY1}{GET KEY2}. The first {GET} command stores the END keystroke, and the second one stores the keystroke that follows (for example, {R} for →).

The {GETLABEL} Command

The {GETLABEL} command displays a prompt in the 1-2-3 Classic window and lets you get string input. The syntax of the command is

```
{GETLABEL prompt,location}
```

The first argument, *prompt*, is any text string enclosed in quotation marks that is used as a prompt. You can also use a range name or the address of a cell that contains the prompt string.

Once you type a response and press ENTER, 1-2-3 stores your response in *location* as a left-aligned label. If you press ENTER before typing anything, 1-2-3 stores the default label prefix (usually ') in *location*. Like the other commands in this section, you can supply a range name or cell address for *location*. If you specify a multicell range, 1-2-3 will store your response in the upper-left cell of the range.

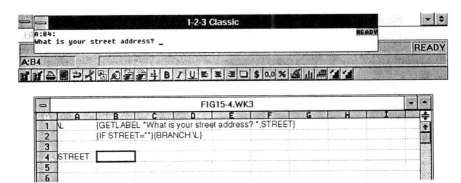

Figure 15-4 The {GETLABEL} command

Figure 15-4 shows a macro that uses the {GETLABEL} command to get a street address and the dialog box that the macro produces. (The macro code begins in cell B1.) As you can see, the {GETLABEL} command in the first line of the macro places the prompt "What is your street address?   " in a 1-2-3 Classic window. After you type a street address and press ENTER, 1-2-3 stores your response in the range STREET (cell B4) as a label. The {IF} command in cell B2 then tests the label in STREET to see if it is equal to null (""), meaning that you pressed ENTER without typing anything. If it is equal to null, control transfers to the start of the macro so that you can try entering the street address again.

By using {GETLABEL} in this way, you can get not only standard text strings, but also alphanumeric strings that begin with numbers (such as "1234 Newport Ave.") without any concern that 1-2-3 may reject them.

The {GETNUMBER} Command

The {GETNUMBER} command is similar to {GETLABEL} except that you use it to get numeric input. The syntax of the command is

```
{GETNUMBER prompt,location}
```

See {GETLABEL} for an explanation of the arguments.

The response you enter to a {GETNUMBER} command can be a number, a numeric formula (for example, @PI*3^2), or a reference to a cell containing a number or numeric formula. If you press ENTER before typing a response, 1-2-3 places ERR in *location*. In addition, if you enter a string, a string formula, or a reference to a string, 1-2-3 also enters ERR in *location*.

Figure 15-5 shows the 1-2-3 Classic window produced by the {GETNUMBER} command in cell B1. As you can see, the {GETNUMBER} command displays the prompt "What is the invoice amount?" in the window. After you type a number and press ENTER, 1-2-3 stores your response in the range INV_AMT (cell B4) as a number. For example, if you type **129.95** as a response, 1-2-3 places that value in cell B4. Similarly, if cell D10

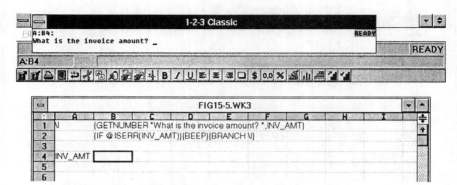

Figure 15-5 The {GETNUMBER} command

contains the number 129.95, and you type **D10** in response to the dialog box, 1-2-3 also records 129.95 (the value in cell D10) in cell B4.

After you type a response, the {IF} command in cell B2 then tests the value in INV_AMT to see if it is equal to ERR, meaning you either typed a label in response to the prompt or pressed ENTER immediately without typing a response. If the cell contains ERR, the macro beeps and control transfers to the start of the macro (cell B1) to have you enter an invoice amount again. (However, the macro does not beep if Beep on error is disabled.)

The {LOOK} Command

The {LOOK} command checks the contents of the typeahead buffer for keystrokes and places the first keystroke in the buffer in a cell. The syntax of the command is

```
{LOOK location}
```

where *location* is the address or name of a cell in which you want to store a representation of the keystroke. If the typeahead buffer contains no keystrokes, 1-2-3 stores the default label prefix (usually ') in *location*. If you specify a multicell range for *location*, 1-2-3 stores the keystroke in the upper-left cell of the range.

The *typeahead buffer* is a section of memory where 1-2-3 stores the keystrokes you type during the noninteractive part of a macro—that is, when the macro is not pausing for user input. 1-2-3 then uses the keystrokes in the buffer in the next interactive macro command (for example, the next {?}, {GET}, {GETLABEL}, or {MENUCALL} command).

One of the most common uses for the {LOOK} command is to break out of an infinite loop. For example, Figure 15-6 shows a macro that uses the {LOOK} command to look in the typeahead buffer and place the first keystroke in the buffer in the cell named FIRST_KEY (cell B4). The {IF} command then checks the contents of FIRST_KEY to see if it contains an entry. If the cell contains the default label prefix, which is the equivalent of an empty or null string (""), the macro branches back to the top to execute

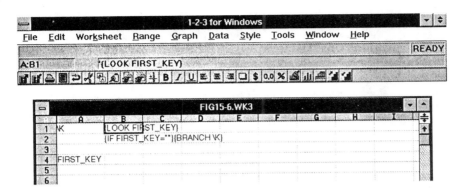

Figure 15-6 The {LOOK} command

the {LOOK} command again. The macro continues in an infinite loop until you press a key.

MANIPULATING DATA IN CELLS

1-2-3 for Windows has four commands that let you manipulate data in cells—{BLANK}, {CONTENTS}, {LET}, and {PUT}. With these commands you can perform operations similar to the Edit Clear Special, Edit Paste, and Edit Quick Copy commands. However, they are much quicker and in many ways more powerful.

The {BLANK} Command

The {BLANK} command lets you erase a cell (or range of cells) while retaining the cell formatting and style settings. In other words, the effects of the {BLANK} command are similar to the Edit Clear command without accessing the menu. The syntax of the command is

```
{BLANK location}
```

where *location* is a cell or range.

For example, the command {BLANK B:D3..B:D5} erases the contents of cells B:D3, B:D4, and B:D5. Likewise, {BLANK ENTRY_FORM} erases the contents of the cells in the range named ENTRY_FORM.

The {CONTENTS} Command

The {CONTENTS} command copies a value or label in one cell to another cell as a label. The label that 1-2-3 for Windows creates in the target cell resembles the contents of the original cell as they appear on the screen, including any cell formatting. This command

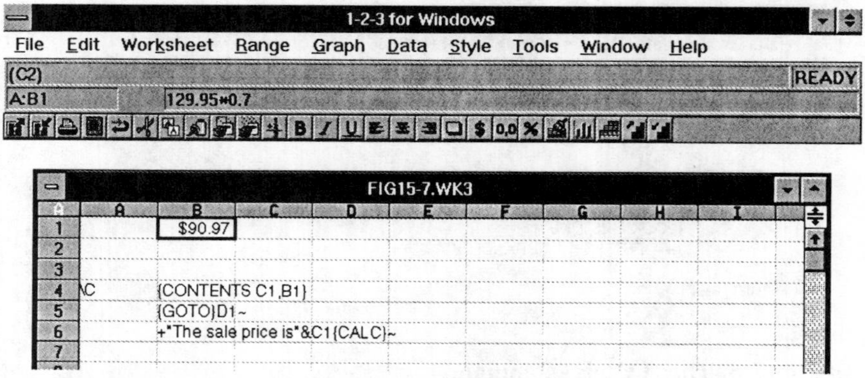

Figure 15-7　The {CONTENTS} command

is most often used when a worksheet contains a value that you would like to express as a label so that you can include it in a string formula. The syntax of the command is

```
{CONTENTS target-location,source-location,
    [width],[cell-format]}
```

where both *source-location* and *target-location* can be a cell or a range. If you specify a range, 1-2-3 uses only the upper-left cell in the range.

For example, suppose you have the worksheet shown in Figure 15-7, which contains the formula 129.95*0.7 in cell B1, formatted for Currency, two decimal places. The macro, which begins in cell B4, contains a {CONTENTS} command that takes the contents of cell B1 as they are displayed and copies them to cell C1. Next, the {GOTO} command in cell B5 moves the cell pointer to cell D1. The final line of the macro contains the label

```
'+"The sale price is"&C1{CALC}~
```

This macro code places the string formula **+"The sale price is"&C1** in cell D1, presses the CALC key to convert the string formula to an actual string, and enters the string in the cell. Figure 15-8 shows how your screen appears after running the macro.

As you view the results, note that in the Edit line cell C1 contains the label '　**$90.97**. This is a nine-character label that replicates the contents of cell B1 as they are displayed on the screen, including two blank spaces preceding the dollar sign ($) and one following the 7.

Suppose you want to limit the number of blank spaces that precede the dollar sign in the label. To do so, you can use the optional *width* argument, which lets you control the width of the label that the {CONTENTS} command produces. For example, by placing the statement {CONTENTS C1,B1,8} in the first cell of the macro, 1-2-3 displays the eight-character label ' $90.97 in cell C1 and, thus, the label 'The sale price is $90.97 in cell D1 when you run the macro. Notice that there is only one space preceding the $, whereas in Figure 15-8 there are two spaces.

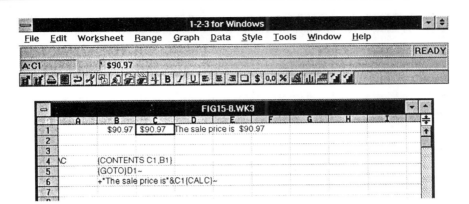

Figure 15-8 Results of the {CONTENTS} command

By including the optional *cell-format* argument as the last argument in the {CON-TENTS} command, you can have 1-2-3 format the label's contents to look like a numeric cell entry in the specified format. The *cell-format* argument must be one of the code numbers from Table 15-2 (see Chapter 5 for an explanation of the available cell formats).

Continuing with the previous example, suppose you want the label the {CONTENTS} command produces to appear in Currency format with 0 decimal places (code 32). You could use the statement {CONTENTS C1,B1,5,32} in the first line of the macro. 1-2-3 then displays the five-character label ' $91 in cell C1 and the label 'The sale price is $91 in cell D1 when you run the macro.

The {LET} Command

Use the {LET} command when you want a macro to enter a value or label into a cell but you do not want to disturb the current cell-pointer location. The syntax of the command is

    {LET location,entry}

where *location* can be either a cell or a range. As with the other commands in this section, if you specify a range, 1-2-3 for Windows will use the upper-left cell of the range.

The *entry* argument can be a number, literal string, formula, or reference to a cell that contains any of these. Note that if you use a formula for *entry*, 1-2-3 will evaluate the formula and place the result in *location*—you cannot use {LET} to enter a formula in *location*.

Note: {LET} does not force recalculation. If you want 1-2-3 to recalculate, place a ~ (tilde) after the {LET} command.

For example, suppose you want to create a macro that calculates net salaries after subtracting withholding. You could use the simple macro in Figure 15-9 to accomplish this. When you execute this macro, the {LET} command stores the result of the formula SALARY-(FED+STATE+LOCAL+FICA) in the range NET SALARY (cell B8). A ~

TABLE 15-2 Cell Formats for Use with the {CONTENTS} Command

Code number	Resulting Cell Format
0 to 15	Fixed, 0 to 15 decimal places
16 to 31	Scientific, 0 to 15 decimal places
32 to 47	Currency, 0 to 15 decimal places
48 to 63	Percent, 0 to 15 decimal places
64 to 79	Comma, 0 to 15 decimal places
112	+/-
113	General
114	1 (31-Dec-90)
115	2 (31-Dec)
116	3 (Dec-90)
117	Text
118	Hidden
119	6 (11:59:59 AM)
120	7 (11:59 AM)
121	4 (Long Intl Date)
122	5 (Short Intl Date)
123	8 (Long Intl Time)
124	9 (Short Intl Time)
127	Worksheet's global cell format (set with Worksheet Global Settings Format)

(tilde) is included at the end of the {LET} statement to have 1-2-3 recalculate the worksheet.

The :string and :value Suffixes

You can use a :string or :value suffix (or their abbreviations :s and :v) to control how 1-2-3 for Windows treats the {LET} command's *entry* argument. If you place a :string suffix following the *entry* argument, 1-2-3 treats the argument as a literal string and enters it in the worksheet as is. If you place a :value suffix following the *entry* argument, however, 1-2-3 evaluates the argument first before entering it in the worksheet.

For example, if cell B1 contains the value 2 and cell B2 contains the value 4, when 1-2-3 executes the command {LET B3,B1+B2:v}~, it places the value 6 in cell B3. When 1-2-3 executes the command {LET B3,B1+B2:s}~, it places the label 'B1+B2 in cell B3. See "The {DEFINE} Command" for more on these suffixes.

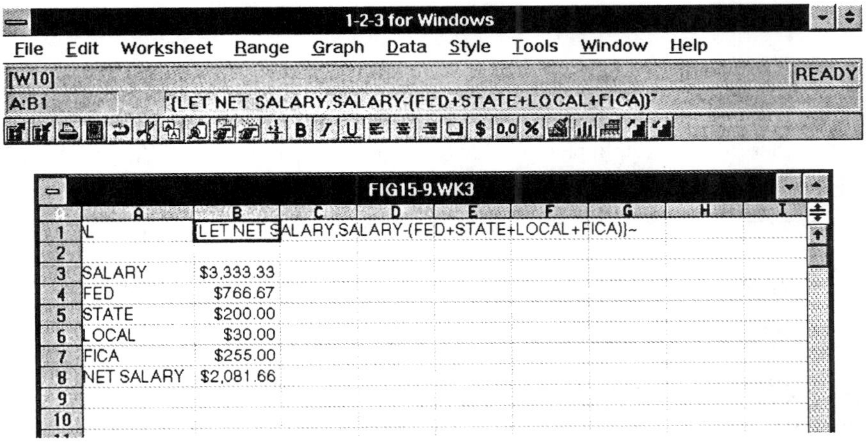

Figure 15-9 The {LET} command

The {PUT} Command

The {PUT} command is similar to the {LET} command in that it enters a value or label into a cell. {PUT} is different from {LET}, in that it enters the value or label into a range based on row and column offsets. The syntax of the command is

```
{PUT location,column-offset,row-offset,entry}
```

{PUT} enters a number or label in a cell within *location*, which can be a 2-D range of any size.

The *column-offset* and *row-offset* arguments are handled similarly to the offsets you use for the @VLOOKUP and @HLOOKUP functions (see Chapter 9). The first column of the range is offset 0, the second column is offset 1, and so on. The same numbering applies to rows. For example, if the cell you wish to address is in the fourth column and fifth row of *location*, the *column-offset* and *row-offset* arguments are 3 and 4.

Note: You must make sure that your *column-offset* and *row-offset* arguments do not reference a cell outside *location*. If they do, your macro will be interrupted with an error.

The *entry* argument can be a number, a literal string, a formula, or a reference to a cell that contains any of these. Note that if *entry* is a formula, 1-2-3 places the current value of the formula in *location*, not the formula itself.

Note: If *entry* is a string formula that begins with double quotes, be sure to include a + (plus) sign at the start of the string formula. Without it, 1-2-3 will probably have trouble evaluating the formula and will therefore place ERR in *location*.

For example, suppose you have assigned the name TAX_TABLE to the range A1..C4. The command

```
{PUT TAX_TABLE,1,2,.3}
```

places the value .3 in cell B3.

Or, suppose cell C1 contains the value 40 and C2 contains the value 20. The command

```
{PUT TAX_TABLE,0,3,C1*C2}
```

places the current value of the formula, 800, in cell A4.

Another instance might be if you have assigned the name MARITAL_STATUS to cell H2, and you have placed the label 'Married in that cell. The command

```
{PUT TAX_TABLE,2,3,+MARITAL_STATUS&"filing separately"}
```

places the current value of the string formula, 'Married filing separately, in cell C4.

STOPPING AND SUSPENDING MACROS

In the previous chapter, you learned that a macro ends when it encounters a blank cell. You can also end a macro by using the {QUIT} command. If you want to stop a macro temporarily, 1-2-3 for Windows offers the {WAIT} command. You can use this command to suspend a macro until a specified time.

The {QUIT} Command

The {QUIT} command terminates a macro immediately. You can use {QUIT} anywhere within a macro, either in the main macro routine or in a subroutine. If 1-2-3 for Windows encounters {QUIT} in a subroutine, it terminates not only the subroutine but also the macro that called the subroutine.

{QUIT} is often used in combination with {IF} to end a macro when a certain value is reached, as in the following:

```
{IF ACCOUNTS<=1000}{BRANCH CONSOLIDATE}
{QUIT}
```

In this example, if the value in the cell named ACCOUNTS is less than or equal to 1000, the macro branches to the routine named CONSOLIDATE. When the value is greater than 1000 the macro terminates.

The {WAIT} Command

The {WAIT} command suspends a macro until a specified time. The syntax of the command is

```
{WAIT time-number}
```

where *time-number* represents a future point in time and can be a number, a numeric formula, or a reference to a cell that contains one of these. Note that *time-number* must be expressed as a valid 1-2-3 date and time serial number (see Chapter 1 for an explanation of 1-2-3 for Windows' special date and time numbering system).

When {WAIT} suspends a macro, 1-2-3 pauses until the time defined by *time-number* has passed. 1-2-3 then proceeds with the commands following {WAIT}.

To interrupt a {WAIT} command, press CTRL+BREAK (all other keystrokes are ignored). 1-2-3 immediately stops the macro and issues an error message. Be aware that if a {BREAKOFF} command is in effect (which disables CTRL+BREAK), there is no way to stop the macro during the {WAIT} command. You can, of course, switch to another application while the macro is running and wait out the {WAIT} command. Barring this, the only way to stop the {WAIT} command is to quit Windows.

In the example below, 1-2-3 waits for five seconds, then beeps to alert you that the waiting period has elapsed.

```
{WAIT @NOW+@TIME(0,0,5)}
{BEEP}
```

CONDITIONAL PROCESSING

1-2-3 for Windows has three macro commands for performing conditional processing— {IF}, {FOR}, and {FORBREAK}. These commands let your macros make decisions and perform repetitive loops.

The {IF} Command

The {IF} command allows your macro to make a decision when there are two alternative outcomes. The syntax of the command is

```
{IF condition}
```

where *condition* is a logical expression—an expression that compares two values or strings using a logical operator (such as = or < —see Chapter 1) and returns a true (1) or false (0) result. If *condition* results in any value other than 0, 1-2-3 evaluates it as true, and the macro continues executing commands in the same cell immediately following the {IF}. If *condition* results in 0, 1-2-3 interprets it as false, and the macro continues executing commands in the cell immediately below the {IF}; all instructions in the same cell as the {IF} are ignored. Besides 0, other values that 1-2-3 interprets as false are logical false, a blank cell, text, ERR, and NA. Although *condition* is usually a logical expression, you can actually use any formula, number, literal string, or cell reference.

For example, suppose you want a macro to branch to different routines based on the result of a logical formula. The following {IF} command tests the value of a cell named ONORDER. If its value is greater than or equal to 500, the macro branches to the CUMULATIVE routine. If the value is less than 500, the macro branches to the GETNEXT routine.

```
{IF ONORDER>=500}{BRANCH CUMULATIVE}
{BRANCH GETNEXT}
```

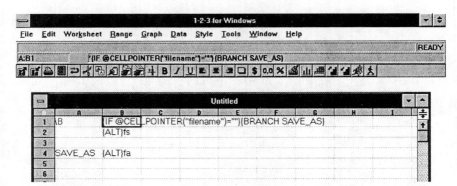

Figure 15-10 The {IF} command

Suppose you want to create a macro that saves the active file in either of two ways based on its current name. If the name is "Untitled"—that is, you haven't yet assigned a name to the file—you want the macro to issue the File Save As command and prompt you for a filename. On the other hand, if you have already assigned a name to the file, you want to issue the File Save command and save the file without any interruption. Figure 15-10 shows a macro that accomplishes this task.

In this example, the {IF} command branches based on the value of the following logical expression:

```
@CELLPOINTER("filename")=""
```

Here the function @CELLPOINTER("filename") returns the filename, including the path, of the current cell. If you haven't yet assigned a filename, the function returns an empty string (" "), and the logical expression evaluates to true. In this case, the macro executes the {BRANCH} instruction immediately following the {IF}, which causes the macro to branch to the cell named SAVE_AS (cell B4). The instructions in SAVE_AS issue the File Save As command.

Now suppose you have previously assigned a name to the file—for example, "C:\123W\WORK\BLUESKY.WK3." In this case, the logical formula evaluates to false. The macro then executes the instructions in the cell below the {IF}. These instructions issue the File Save command, and replace the file on disk with the current file.

The {FOR} Command

The {FOR} command lets you build *iterative* (repetitive) loops in a macro. The syntax of the command is

```
{FOR counter,start-number,stop-number,
    step-number,subroutine}
```

where the arguments are defined as follows:

- *counter* is a cell in the worksheet where 1-2-3 for Windows initially places the value in *start-number*. Each time the {FOR} command completes a loop, *counter* is updated.

- *start-number* is the number to which *counter* is initially set when the command begins.

- *stop-number* tells 1-2-3 when to stop the looping process. When *counter* exceeds *stop-number*, 1-2-3 knows to stop.

- *step-number* defines the increment by which *counter* is increased following a pass through the for-next loop.

- *subroutine* is an address or range reference that specifies the starting location of the for-next loop—the set of commands you want 1-2-3 to perform repeatedly.

Note: Once *subroutine* starts, the commands within it cannot modify the *start-number*, *stop-number*, or *step-number* arguments.

Suppose you want to create a macro that builds a sum-of-the-years'-digits depreciation table. Figure 15-11 shows such a macro. The macro begins by moving the cell pointer to TABLE (cell E11). It then prompts you for the purchase price of the asset and stores your response in HOWMUCH (cell B11). Next, the macro prompts you for the salvage value and places your response in WHATSLEFT (cell B12). It then prompts you for the useful life in years and saves the value in YRS (cell B13). The macro then executes the {FOR} command in cell B5. This command sets up the *counter* argument as COUNT (cell B14), the *start-number* argument as 1, the *stop-number* argument as a reference to the YRS range (cell B13), the *step-number* argument as 1, and the *subroutine* argument as a reference to the cell named DO_YEAR (cell B7).

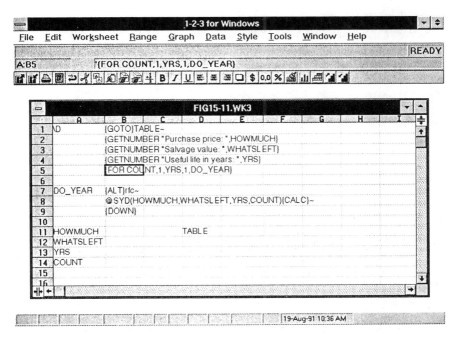

Figure 15-11 The {FOR} command

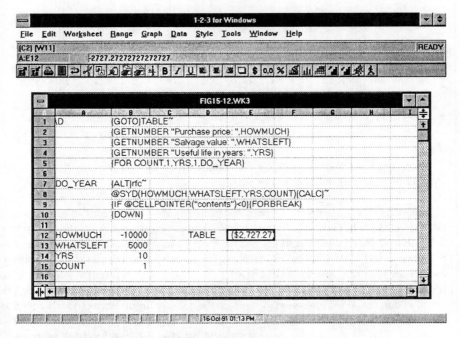

Figure 15-12 The {FORBREAK} command

Here's a sample of the table that the macro produces when you choose a purchase price of $10,000, a salvage value of $1,000, and a useful life of 10 years:

E11: $1,636.36
E12: $1,472.73
E13: $1,309.09
E14: $1,145.45
E15: $981.82
E16: $818.18
E17: $654.55
E18: $490.91
E19: $327.27
E20: $163.64

The {FORBREAK} Command

If you want to stop a {FOR} command before it is completed, you can use the {FORBREAK} command. This command terminates a for-next loop, even though the stop value has not been reached. When a macro encounters a {FORBREAK} command, it returns to the calling macro and executes the instruction in the cell below the one containing the {FOR} command.

Note: You should only place a {FORBREAK} command in the subroutine being called by a {FOR} command. Using it anywhere else will result in a macro error.

Suppose you want to modify the macro in Figure 15-11 so that it stops executing if the @SYD function returns a negative number—which occurs, for example, if you enter a negative number for the cost. You can insert a {FORBREAK} command in the macro as in Figure 15-12.

BRANCHING

As you know, 1-2-3 for Windows executes macro commands one after the other, moving from one cell of commands to the next until it encounters a blank cell or a {QUIT} command. You can, however, redirect the flow of macro control to a new cell location by branching. 1-2-3 offers two commands for branching—{BRANCH} and {DIS-PATCH}.

The {BRANCH} Command

{BRANCH} transfers macro control to a different location and does not return. The syntax of the command is

```
{BRANCH location}
```

where *location* is the cell that contains the commands you want the macro to execute next. You can specify a cell address, a range reference, or a range name for *location*.

{BRANCH} is usually combined with {IF}, to perform "if-then-else" processing, as in this sequence:

```
{IF CASH>0}{BRANCH SPEND_IT}
{BRANCH BROKE}
```

In this case, 1-2-3 tests the value in the cell named CASH. If the value is greater than 0, 1-2-3 executes the {BRANCH} command following the {IF}, which transfers macro control to the cell named SPEND_IT. If the value in CASH is less than or equal to zero, however, 1-2-3 executes the {BRANCH} command in the cell below the {IF}, which transfers control to the cell named BROKE.

Suppose you have created a worksheet file that contains two income statements, one for 1990 (stored in B:A1..B:H10) and the other for 1991 (stored in C:A1..C:H10). You now want to create a macro that will prompt you for which statement to print, and then print the appropriate statement based on your response. Figure 15-13 shows such a macro.

In this example, the {GETNUMBER} command at the start of the macro displays a 1-2-3 Classic window with the prompt "Print 1990 or 1991 results (90 or 91)?". When you enter a response, 1-2-3 stores it in YEAR (cell B7). Next, the macro executes the first {IF} command, which tests the number in YEAR and, if it is equal to 90, transfers control to the cell named PRINT_90 (cell B9). Otherwise, the macro executes the second

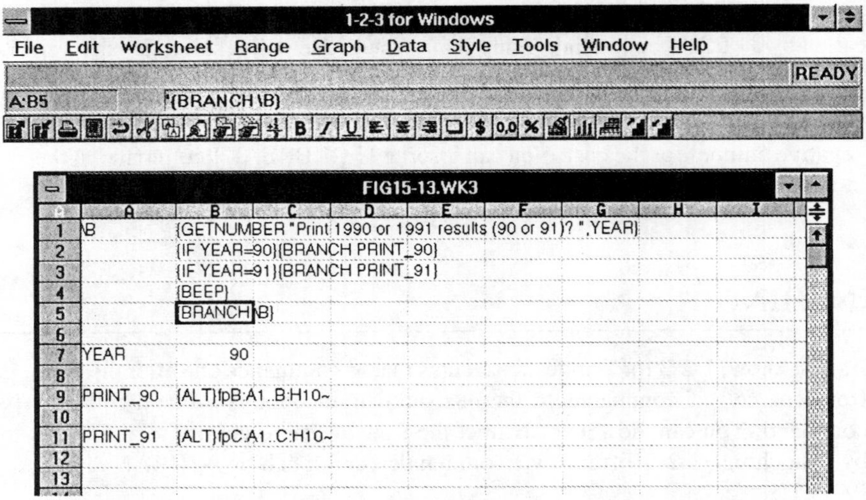

Figure 15-13 The {BRANCH} command

{IF}, which transfers control to the cell named PRINT_91 (cell B11) if the number in YEAR is equal to 91.

If you fail to enter either 90 or 91 in response to the {GETNUMBER} prompt, the macro beeps and then branches back to the start so that you can try again. (See Figure 15-3 for another example of the {BRANCH} command.)

Note: Do not confuse {BRANCH} with {GOTO}. {GOTO} moves the cell pointer, but {BRANCH} does not. {BRANCH} transfers macro control to a new location.

The {DISPATCH} Command

The {DISPATCH} command is similar to the {BRANCH} command, except that you use it for *indirect branching*, where you use the contents of one cell to point to another cell. The syntax of the command is

```
{DISPATCH location}
```

where *location* is a single cell containing the address or name of another cell.

The {DISPATCH} command causes 1-2-3 for Windows to transfer control to the cell whose name or address appears in *location*. For example, suppose the cell named DEST contains the label 'PRINT_90. If 1-2-3 encounters the command {DISPATCH DEST} in a macro, it does not branch to DEST but looks in DEST and uses its contents as the location to branch to, which in this case means that it branches to the cell named PRINT_90.

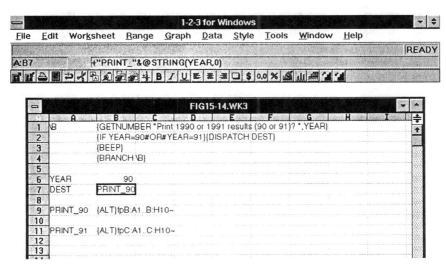

Figure 15-14   The {DISPATCH} command

Figure 15-14 shows how you might modify the macro in Figure 15-13 to use the {DISPATCH} command. After the {GETNUMBER} command stores 90 or 91 in YEAR (cell B6), the formula in DEST (cell B7) evaluates to either PRINT_90 or PRINT_91. Therefore, when 1-2-3 encounters the {DISPATCH} command, it performs an indirect branch to the contents of DEST. That is, 1-2-3 looks in DEST then branches to the routine whose name resides there, either PRINT_90 or PRINT_91.

SUBROUTINES

Although the {BRANCH} and {DISPATCH} commands let you change the flow of control to another macro, they do not return to the original macro. You can, of course, place another {BRANCH} or {DISPATCH} command at the end of the called macro to return control back to the original calling macro, but you will run into difficulty when you want to reuse the called routine more than once. You will find that you must modify the {BRANCH} or {DISPATCH} command at the end of the called routine in order to return control back to different points in the original calling macro.

To get around this problem, you can have the macro call a subroutine. When a macro calls a subroutine, 1-2-3 for Windows transfers control to the first cell of the subroutine. Then, when it completes processing the commands in the subroutine, it returns control back to the calling macro.

The simplest way to call a subroutine is

```
{subroutine}
```

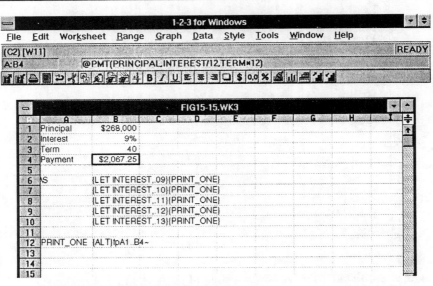

Figure 15-15 The {*subroutine*} command

where *subroutine* is the range name (or address) for the subroutine's starting cell. The range name can actually refer to the entire subroutine, in which case 1-2-3 begins executing commands in the first cell of the range. But you will be better off having the range name refer to the starting cell, in case you add or delete cells in the subroutine.

For example, the subroutine call {PRINT_IT} tells 1-2-3 to execute the commands starting in the cell named PRINT_IT. Similarly, the subroutine call {ZA1} tells 1-2-3 to execute the commands starting in cell ZA1.

When a macro calls a subroutine, 1-2-3 begins at the first cell in the subroutine and executes the commands in the usual way, moving from one command to the next in sequential fashion. When 1-2-3 encounters a blank cell or a {RETURN} command, it returns control back to the calling macro to the instruction following the {*subroutine*} command.

Subroutines are most useful when you want to reuse a block of code repeatedly. For example, suppose you have created the simple model at the top of Figure 15-15 to calculate the payment on a mortgage. You now want to create a macro to print the results of the model several times in a row, each time using a different interest rate.

The macro in Figure 15-15 uses a subroutine to print the payment model repeatedly. The macro begins with a {LET} command to place the value of .09 in the cell named INTEREST (B2). The next command, {PRINT_ONE}, makes a call to the PRINT_ONE subroutine, which transfers control to the cell named PRINT_ONE (cell B12) and begins executing the instructions in that cell. The instructions there issue the File Print command to print the range A1..B4. When 1-2-3 encounters the blank cell in B13, it transfers control back to the command following the subroutine call, in this case, to the {LET} command in cell B7.

> ▼ *Tip:*   Consider placing your most commonly used subroutines in a macro library so that you can call them from within any macro (see Chapter 14).

The {RETURN} Command

When 1-2-3 for Windows encounters a blank cell at the end of a subroutine, it transfers control back to the calling routine and executes the next command following the {*subroutine*} command. The {RETURN} command has the same effect as a blank cell.

The {RETURN} command is most often used when a subroutine includes conditional processing. For example, suppose you want to modify the macro in Figure 15-15 so that it prompts you each time before printing the simple payment model at the top of the worksheet. Figure 15-16 shows how you might do this. In this case, the subroutine executes the {GETLABEL} command, which, for the first pass through the subroutine, displays a dialog box with the prompt "Print for 0.09? (Y/N)" and stores your response in the cell named INPUT (B16). In the second line of the subroutine, the {IF} command tests the label in INPUT. If it is equal to "N," 1-2-3 executes the {RETURN} command, which transfers control back to the main routine to the instruction following the {PRINT_ONE} subroutine call. Otherwise, the macro executes the printing instructions in cell B14 before passing control back to the main routine.

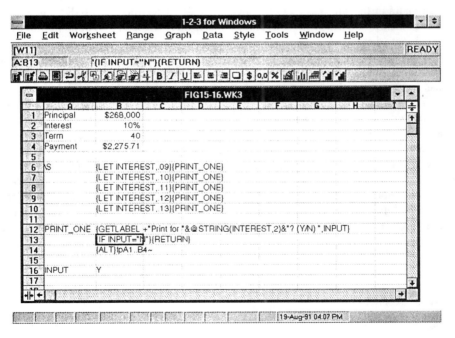

Figure 15-16 The {RETURN} command

Passing Arguments to Subroutines

Thus far, all the subroutine calls you have seen have been of the simple form {*subroutine*}. When you pass arguments to a subroutine, however, the syntax is

```
{subroutine [argument1],[argument2],...,[argumentN]}
```

The advantage of using arguments is that you can create more generic, multi-purpose routines and then have them act on a particular set of information. Arguments can be numbers, labels, formulas, or cell references. When you pass arguments, you must include a {DEFINE} macro command in the subroutine you are calling.

The {DEFINE} Command

The {DEFINE} command stores the arguments that are used in a subroutine. The syntax of the command is

```
{DEFINE location1,location2,...,locationn}
```

where each *location* argument specifies the storage location—a cell or range reference—for each argument used in a {*subroutine*} command.

When you pass arguments to a subroutine, the {DEFINE} command is usually the first command in the subroutine, but you can actually place the {DEFINE} command anywhere within the subroutine, provided it appears before the commands that use the arguments that are passed.

The purpose of the {DEFINE} command is to store arguments so that a subroutine can use them. Before 1-2-3 for Windows can do this, it must know what type of data you are passing (values or labels), so that it can store the data properly.

To tell 1-2-3 the type of data you are passing, you can include a suffix after each *location* argument in a {DEFINE} command. The choices are *:string* (or :s) for string and *:value* (or :v) for value. Omitting the suffix is equivalent to using a :string suffix. A :string suffix (or no suffix) causes 1-2-3 to store the argument as a label even if the argument looks like a number, formula, cell address, or range reference.

A :value suffix causes 1-2-3 to evaluate the argument before storing it. Of course, if the argument is a literal number, 1-2-3 stores it as is. If the argument is a formula, however, 1-2-3 evaluates it, then stores the result as either a number (in the case of a numeric formula) or a label (in the case of a string formula). Finally, if the argument is a cell address or range name, 1-2-3 looks in the referenced cell and stores its contents as a label or number.

An Example

Figure 15-17 shows a macro that positions the cell pointer to OUT (cell B15), then makes a subroutine call that passes four arguments. The {DEFINE} command at the beginning of the PUT_ROW subroutine stores the label Buy in the cell named FIRST (B10), the number 100 in SECOND (cell B11), the label "shares" in THIRD (cell B12), and the result of the formula @TODAY+1 in FOURTH (cell B13). The {LET} commands then

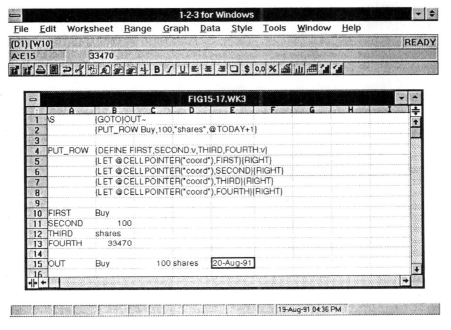

Figure 15-17 The {DEFINE} command

enter the contents of these ranges in four consecutive cells—B15, C15, D15, and E15—as shown in the figure.

Note that 1-2-3 for Windows treats label arguments in the same way whether or not you enclose them in quotes. For example, in Figure 15-17, the first argument (Buy) is not enclosed in quotes while the third argument ("shares") is.

Another Example

Suppose you are creating a macro that prompts users for numeric input several times in a row using the {GETNUMBER} command. To make sure users do not enter invalid numbers in response to {GETNUMBER}, you decide to write some error-checking code. Rather than create new code for each {GETNUMBER} command, you decide to write a subroutine that you can reuse as many times as you need.

Figure 15-18 shows an error-checking subroutine named GET_NO, which begins in cell B5. When you call GET_NO, you pass it three arguments—the first part of the prompt for a {GETNUMBER} command (the rest of the prompt is derived later), the lowest value you will accept in response to the {GETNUMBER} command, and the highest value you will accept.

When you execute the \O macro in cell B1, the first call to GET_NO passes the string "Enter order point" as the first part of the prompt, 100 as the lowest acceptable value, and 500 as the highest acceptable value. The {DEFINE SAY, LO:v, HI:v} command then stores the passed arguments. Because the first argument of the {DEFINE} command, SAY, has no suffix, 1-2-3 for Windows stores the data as a label in the SAY range (cell

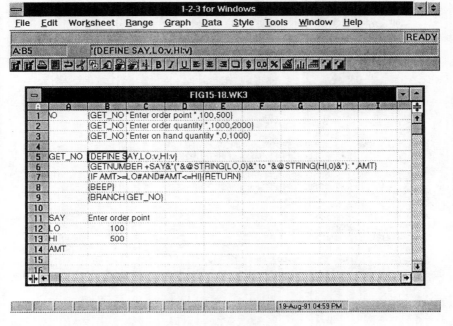

Figure 15-18 An error-checking subroutine

B11). For the LO and HI arguments, the :v suffix causes 1-2-3 to store the passed data as values in the ranges LO and HI (cells B12 and B13).

After 1-2-3 stores the passed data, it executes the {GETNUMBER} command in cell B6. Figure 15-19 shows the 1-2-3 Classic prompt that the command produces. The prompt is created with the following string formula:

```
+SAY&"("&@STRING(LO,0)&" to "&@STRING(HI,0)&"): "
```

After you enter a response to the prompt, 1-2-3 stores it in AMT (cell B14). The {IF} command in cell B7 then tests the value in AMT. If it is greater than or equal to the lowest acceptable value and less than or equal to the highest acceptable value, the macro executes the {RETURN} command to return control back to the calling routine. If your response is not within the acceptable bounds, 1-2-3 beeps, transfers control back to cell B5, and executes the subroutine again.

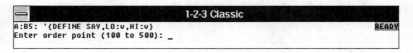

Figure 15-19 The prompt produced by the first {GETNUMBER} command in Figure 15-18

Note: Do not use the {BRANCH} command to leave a subroutine. If you do, 1-2-3 for Windows may not be able to return to the calling routine. As Figure 15-19 shows, however, you can use the {BRANCH} command to branch to different points within a subroutine.

The {RESTART} Command

When 1-2-3 for Windows encounters a *{subroutine}* command in a subroutine, it immediately starts executing the new subroutine. Then, when the second subroutine ends, 1-2-3 retraces its steps back to the first subroutine to the instruction following the initial subroutine call. When the first subroutine ends, 1-2-3 then returns control to the calling macro. When one subroutine calls another, it is known as *nesting* subroutines or creating a *subroutine stack*.

If you do not want 1-2-3 to retrace its steps back to previous subroutines, you can use the {RESTART} command. This command clears the subroutine stack. In other words, it causes the macro to end when the current subroutine ends. (Of course, if the current subroutine transfers control to another location, a new subroutine stack is built and the macro does not end.)

For example, suppose you have created the macro in Figure 15-20 for entering orders. The main routine, MAIN, first asks whether you want to add another record to the order entry database. If you type *Y* or *y*, the macro calls the GET_CUST# subroutine, which

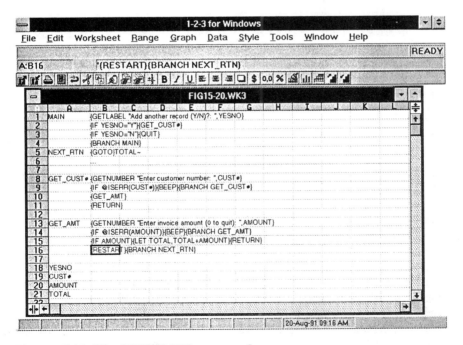

Figure 15-20 The {RESTART} command

begins in cell B8. This subroutine then prompts you for a customer number. If you enter an invalid customer number, such as a string, the macro beeps and branches back to the start of the subroutine to prompt you again. If your response is a number, the macro calls the GET_AMT subroutine that begins in cell B13. This subroutine prompts you for the invoice amount. If the invoice amount you enter is a number other than zero, the macro adds the amount to the total for the day and then returns to the GET_CUST# subroutine. If the invoice amount you enter is zero, meaning you wish to quit, the macro executes the {RESTART} command to clear the subroutine stack and then branches back to the main routine to execute additional commands.

Note that if you do not include the {RESTART} command to clear the subroutine stack, but instead let the macro branch to the main routine anyway, you get some unexpected results the next time 1-2-3 for Windows completes a subroutine and attempts to retrace its steps through the subroutine stack. You can see this effect by removing the {RESTART} command from B16 and replacing the ellipses (...) in cell B6 with a {RETURN} command. When you execute the modified macro and enter **0** for the invoice amount (0 to quit), 1-2-3 retraces its steps back through the subroutine stack and eventually reenters the loop in the main routine.

Note: You can use the {RESTART} command within a *call-table* to cancel a {FORM} command. See "Working with Data Entry Forms" later for an example.

ERROR TRAPPING: THE {ONERROR} COMMAND

When an error occurs during a macro, 1-2-3 for Windows normally displays an error message box and then terminates the macro. By using the {ONERROR} command, you can provide your own error handling and keep the macro running.

The {ONERROR} command lets you trap errors and branch to recovery routines during a macro. The syntax of the command is

```
{ONERROR branch-location, [message-location]}
```

where *branch-location* is a cell address or range name to which the macro can branch when a 1-2-3 error occurs. By including the optional *message-location* argument—a cell address or range name—you can gain access to the error message that 1-2-3 normally displays in the error message dialog box; 1-2-3 records the error message as a label in the specified location.

In the example in Figure 15-21, the macro begins with an {ONERROR} command that tells 1-2-3 to branch to the range TROUBLE_SAVING (cell B7) if a 1-2-3 error should occur, and to store the error message in ERROR_MSG (cell B10). Next, the {GETLABEL} command prompts you for a filename, and then saves the name in FILENAME (cell B4) as a label. The macro then tries to save the current file using the supplied name. If you should enter an invalid drive as part of the path, for example, the macro places an error message in ERROR_MSG (cell B10) and then branches to the error-handling routine that begins in TROUBLE_SAVING (cell B7). This routine causes 1-2-3 to beep (assuming that beep hasn't been disabled) and branch back to the start of the \F macro.

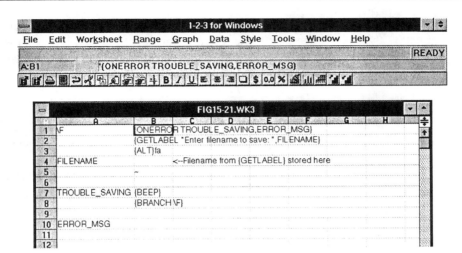

Figure 15-21 The {ONERROR} command

Note: When 1-2-3 encounters an {ONERROR} command, it does not immediately branch to *branch-location*. Instead, it waits until an error occurs before branching.

Although the macro in Figure 15-21 shows only one {ONERROR} command, you can actually place multiple {ONERROR} commands within a macro. In fact, you should place them at any point where there is a possibility of a 1-2-3 for Windows error. If you use multiple {ONERROR} commands within a macro, you should have each one branch to a different routine. Note that an {ONERROR} command remains in effect only while the macro is running, and only until an error occurs.

Here are some things to keep in mind as you use {ONERROR}:

- {ONERROR} does not trap macro syntax errors. When 1-2-3 encounters a syntax error, it displays an error message dialog box and terminates the macro.

- When you press CTRL+BREAK to stop a macro, 1-2-3 issues an error and branches to the *branch-location* specified by the last {ONERROR} command. To prevent this from happening, you can use the {BREAKOFF} command to disable CTRL+BREAK.

- {ONERROR} clears the subroutine stack. Therefore be sure to place a {BRANCH} command at the end of your error routine to transfer control back to some part of the regular program. Otherwise, you may leave the user in limbo.

WORKING WITH DATA ENTRY FORMS

Like Release 3.1, 1-2-3 for Windows has four commands for working with data-entry forms—{FORM}, {FORMBREAK}, {APPENDBELOW}, and {APPENDRIGHT}. Similar to the 1-2-3 Classic /Range Input command, the {FORM} command lets you limit data entry to a specified data range. {FORM} gives you much greater control over user entries than the /Range Input. After entering data in a form, you can then use the {APPENDBELOW} and {APPENDRIGHT} commands to copy the data to the bottom or right of a database and automatically extend the database range in the process.

The {FORM} Command

The {FORM} command suspends macro execution and allows you to enter input in a specified range. {FORM} is similar to /Range Input, but offers additional options, such as the ability to assign special action keys and to allow (or disallow) certain keys during input. The syntax of this command is

```
{FORM input-location, [call-table], [include-list],
    [exclude-list]}
```

where *input-location* is the range that you have set up for user input, as in the data-entry form that appears in Figure 15-22. Like the /Range Input command, the *input-location* argument must include cells that have been unprotected using the Range Unprotect command. For example, in Figure 15-22, the *input-location* is a range named DATA_AREA that occupies cells A:A1..A:F18, and the range A:C3..A:C9 consists of unprotected cells. During the {FORM} command, you can input data only in the

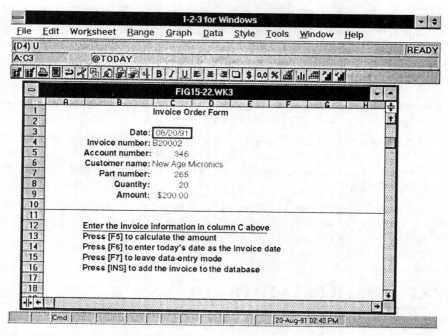

Figure 15-22 The {FORM} command

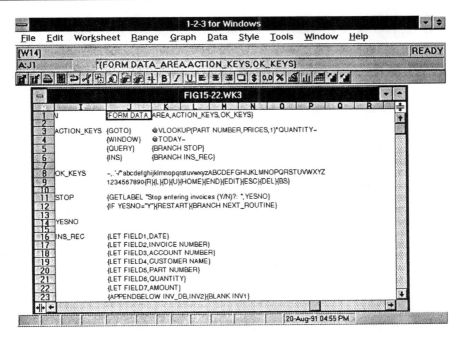

Figure 15-23 The {FORM} command and its associated options

unprotected cells in *input-location*, and pointer movement is restricted to those cells. The *input-location* can be any size you want, and can even be a 3-D range.

The optional *call-table* argument is a two-column range that includes a list of keys in the first column and macro commands (or formulas) that you assign each key in the second column. During the {FORM} command, these keys perform the commands you assign them, and revert to their original actions when the {FORM} command ends. (1-2-3 performs the commands assigned to each key as a subroutine.) You can assign actions to *any* keyboard key, including any typewriter keys and any macro keynames. (For a list of macro keynames, see Table 14-1 in Chapter 14.)

A sample *call-table* appears in Figure 15-23 in the ACTION_ KEYS range, A:J3..A:K6. (Table 15-3 shows all the ranges used in the example macro.) Notice that the *call-table* assigns macro instructions or formulas to the macro keynames {GOTO}, {WINDOW}, {QUERY}, and {INS} (F5, F6, F7, and INS).

You end the {FORM} command by pressing ESC or ENTER. When you press either key, here is what happens:

- 1-2-3 for Windows continues the macro by executing the next command following {FORM}.

- The cell pointer remains where it was when you pressed ENTER or ESC.

- All the keys in the *call-table* resume their default 1-2-3 actions.

TABLE 15-3 Range Names for the {FORM} Command Example

Range Name	Address
\I	A:J1
ACCOUNT NUMBER	A:C5
ACTION_KEYS	A:J3..A:K6
AMOUNT	A:C9
CUSTOMER NAME	A:C6
DATA_AREA	A:A1..A:F18
DATE	A:C3
FIELD1	C:A2
FIELD2	C:B2
FIELD3	C:C2
FIELD4	C:D2
FIELD5	C:E2
FIELD6	C:F2
FIELD7	C:G2
INS_REC	A:J16
INV1	A:C3..A:C9
INV2	C:A2..C:G2
INVOICE NUMBER	A:C4
INV_DB	C:A7..C:G13
OK_KEYS	A:J8..A:J9
PART NUMBER	A:C7
PRICES	B:A3..B:B15
QUANTITY	A:C8
STOP	A:J11
YESNO	A:J14

Note: You can locate a *call-table* anywhere within your worksheet file, or even in another worksheet file. If you select another worksheet file as the location for your *call-table*, be sure to use the full address (filename, worksheet letter, and range name or address) for the *call-table* argument.

The optional *include-list* argument is a range containing allowable keystrokes. Any keys omitted from this list are ignored during the {FORM} command. Like the *call-table* range, the *include-list* range can include any keyboard key. In Figure 15-23, the *include-*

list argument is OK_KEYS, the range name assigned to A:J8..A:J9. Note that because the {FORM} command is case sensitive, the range includes a full set of lowercase and uppercase letters, so when you place a letter key in the *call-table* or *exclude-list*, make sure to include both lower and upper case, for example, a and A.

Note: If you use an *include-list*, be sure to include ~ (tilde) and {ESC} in your list or you will not be able to use ENTER or ESC to exit the {FORM} command.

The optional *exclude-list* argument is a range containing a list of keystrokes to ignore during user input. Any keys omitted from this list are allowed during the {FORM} command. This argument, like the other optional arguments, can include any keyboard key. Here's a typical *exclude-list*:

```
BAD_KEYS    {HELP}{ZOOM}
```

This *exclude-list* prevents you from using the HELP (F1) and ZOOM (ALT+F6) keys during the {FORM} command.

Note: If you use an *include-list* and you want to be able to use the SPACEBAR when entering data in your form, make sure to include a blank space in the list of allowable keys. In fact, the label in cell A:J9 of Figure 15-23 includes a blank space following {BS}, although you cannot see it.

Note: 1-2-3 for Windows accepts only one list argument. Therefore, contrary to what you see in the example, if you specify an *include-list*, you should not specify an *exclude-list*, and vice versa. In fact, if you specify both an *include-list* and an *exclude-list*, 1-2-3 will use only the *include-list*.

If you wish to include an optional argument in the {FORM} command but omit preceding optional arguments, make sure you include an argument separator (usually a comma) for each missing argument. For example, here is the sample syntax for the {FORM} command in Figure 15-23 when you want to use an *exclude-list* named BAD_KEYS but omit the *include-list*:

```
{FORM DATA_AREA,ACTION_KEYS,,BAD_KEYS}
```

If you do not include any optional arguments for the {FORM} command, you can press any typewriter or pointer-movement key, as well as any of the following keys:

Key	*Condition*
ENTER	—
ESC	—
F1 (HELP)	—
F2 (EDIT)	—

(continued)

Key	Condition
F3 (NAME)	While typing or editing a formula
F4 (ABS)	While typing or editing a formula
F9 (CALC)	If the entry is a value
HOME	—
END	—
BACKSPACE	While typing or editing an entry
CTRL+PGUP	If *input-location* is a 3-D range
CTRL+PGDN	If *input-location* is a 3-D range

How the Example Macro Works

Here's how the {FORM} command in Figure 15-23 works. The *input-location* is DATA_AREA, A:A1..A:F18. The unprotected range within DATA_AREA, cells A:C3..A:C9, is assigned the name INV1. As Figure 15-22 shows, rows 12 through 16 provide information about special keys you can use during data entry.

When 1-2-3 for Windows encounters the {FORM} command, it moves the cell pointer to the first unprotected cell in DATA_AREA, which in this case is cell A:C3. From this point on, you can only move the cell pointer within the INV1 range. You can press any key included in the OK_KEYS range, A:J8..A:J9.

In addition, you can use any key in the *call-table* to assist in the data-entry process. These keys are assigned in the ACTION_KEYS range, A:J3..A:K6. Here are the descriptions of the actions assigned to the key names:

- {GOTO}   This key is intended for entering the invoice amount in cell C:C9. When you press F5, the macro performs a vertical lookup on a prices table (the range PRICES, B:A3..B:B15, in Figure 15-24), given the part number (the number you entered in cell A:C7). The macro then multiplies the price by the quantity in cell A:C8 (QUANTITY), places the result in the current cell, and returns to the {FORM} command.

- {WINDOW}   This key is intended for entering the date in cell A:C3. When you press F6, the macro inserts @TODAY in the current cell and returns to the {FORM} command.

- {QUERY}   When you press F7, the macro branches to STOP (cell A:J11) and displays a 1-2-3 Classic prompt asking whether you want to stop entering invoices. If you type *Y* or *y* and press ENTER, the macro executes the {RESTART} command to clear the subroutine stack, then branches to NEXT_ROUTINE (a routine not shown in the example). If you type any other key, the macro returns to the {FORM} command.

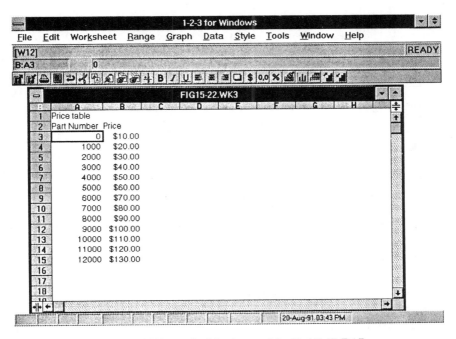

Figure 15-24 The PRICES vertical lookup table, B:A3..B:B15

- {INS}   When you press INS, the macro branches to the INS_REC routine. The purpose of this routine is to add a record to the end of the invoice database, INV_DB. The series of {LET} commands moves the data in the vertical range INV1 (A:C3..A:C9) to the horizontal range INV2 (C:A2..C:G2), one cell at a time beginning with DATE (A:C3). (The INV2 range is shown in Figure 15-25.) The final line of the routine uses the {APPENDBELOW} command to add a record to the end of the invoice database, INV_DB, automatically expanding the range in the process (see the next section for more on {APPENDBELOW}). The macro then blanks the input area, INV1, and returns to the {FORM} command.

Notes on the {FORM} Command

Here are some things to keep in mind when you use the {FORM} command in a macro:

- Despite the fact that the previous example uses an *include-list*, you are more likely to use an *exclude-list* than an *include-list*. The simple reason is that the list of keystrokes you want to disallow is usually far shorter than the list you want to accept. For example, suppose ABS (F4) and NAME (F5) are the only keys you want to disallow during data entry for the {FORM} command. You might enter the following EXCLUDE_KEYS range in place of the OK_KEYS range in Figure 15-23:

```
EXCLUDE_KEYS      {ABS} {NAME}
```

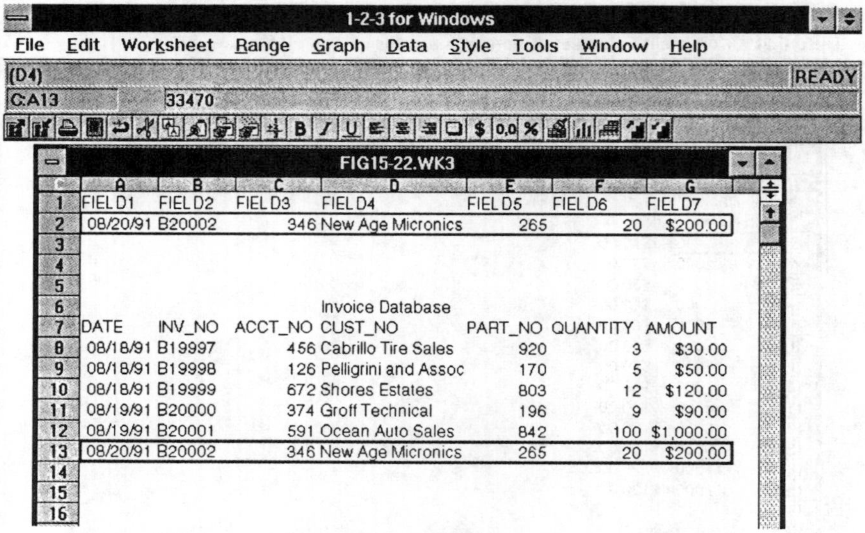

Figure 15-25 Results of the {APPENDBELOW} command

You would then use the following command in place of the existing {FORM} command in cell A:J1:

```
{FORM DATA_AREA,ACTION_KEYS,,EXCLUDE_KEYS}
```

- You cannot use any menu commands while the {FORM} command is in effect. This means, for example, that you cannot use the {MENU}, /, or {ALT} command in a *call-table* to access the 1-2-3 for Windows or Classic menus, even if you put these keys in the optional *include-list*. Therefore, you cannot use menu commands (for example, {ALT}rt for Range Transpose) in the second column of a *call-table*.

- Besides ESC and ENTER, another way to leave the {FORM} command is by pressing CTRL+BREAK. Thus, you cannot place the {BREAK} command in the *exclude-list*. If you do, 1-2-3 will simply ignore it and allow CTRL+BREAK anyway. Should you want to disallow CTRL+BREAK, place a {BREAKOFF} command before the {FORM} command.

The {FORMBREAK} Command

As the previous example shows, one way to exit from a {FORM} command is to place a {RESTART} command within a *call-table* subroutine. This command clears the subroutine stack, causing the macro to end when the subroutine ends.

Another way to exit from a {FORM} command is with {FORMBREAK}. After executing a {FORMBREAK}, 1-2-3 for Windows continues macro execution at the instruction immediately following the {FORM} command.

When using {FORMBREAK}, you should be careful to place it only in a *call-table* subroutine (or a subroutine to which you have transferred control using {BRANCH} or {DISPATCH}). Using it anywhere else will cause your macro to terminate with an error.

Suppose you wanted to modify the previous example so that when you press QUERY (F7) to signal that you want to stop entering invoices, the macro picks up execution following the {FORM} command. To do so, you would modify the contents of cell J12 in Figure 15-23 from

```
{IF YESNO= "Y"}{RESTART}{BRANCH NEXT_ROUTINE}
```

to

```
{IF YESNO="Y"}{FORMBREAK}
```

The {APPENDBELOW} and {APPENDRIGHT} Commands

The {APPENDBELOW} and {APPENDRIGHT} commands let you copy data from one range (the source range) to the bottom or right of another range (the target range), automatically extending the address of the target range to include the appended data. The syntax of these commands is

```
{APPENDBELOW target-location,source-location}
{APPENDRIGHT target-location,source-location}
```

where *source-location* and *target-location* are both range names. The range name definition for *target-location* expands to include the appended data.

By combining the {APPENDBELOW} or {APPENDRIGHT} command with the {FORM} command, you can take data from a data-entry form and copy it to a database. For example, an earlier section shows how to use {APPENDBELOW} with the data-entry form in Figure 15-23. Here's another way to use {APPENDBELOW} with the same form. The following code appends the data you enter in the form to the bottom of the invoice database:

```
{FORM DATA_AREA}
{ALT}rtINV1~INV2~{APPENDBELOW INV_DB,INV2}
```

When 1-2-3 for Windows encounters these commands, the {FORM} command pauses the macro, allowing you to enter invoice information in the unprotected range named INV1 (A:C3..A:C9) in the entry form named DATA_AREA (A:A1..A:F18). The macro then uses the Range Transpose command to transpose the data from its vertical orientation in the INV1 range to a horizontal orientation in the INV2 range (C:A2..C:G2). Next, the macro appends the data in INV2 to the invoice database table, INV_DB, and expands INV_DB to include the new record (from C:A7..C:G12 to C:A7..C:G13), as shown in Figure 15-25.

{APPENDBELOW} and {APPENDRIGHT} cannot execute if either of the following conditions exist:

- When the number of rows (for {APPENDBELOW}) or the number of columns (for {APPENDRIGHT}) in the *source-location* is greater than the number of rows or columns available below or to the right of the *target-location*.

- When appending data would overwrite data below or to the right of the *target-location*.

One disadvantage of the {APPENDBELOW} and {APPENDRIGHT} commands is that they are incapable of changing the orientation of your data when they copy it to a database. This is not a problem if your data-entry form and database have the same orientation (for example, they are both oriented horizontally). But suppose they are oriented differently. For example, suppose you have the vertical input range INV1 (A:C3..A:C9 in Figure 15-22), and you want to use the {APPENDBELOW} command to copy the data in INV1 to the bottom of the INV_DB database (C:A7..C:G12 in Figure 15-25) in a horizontal format. If you use the following commands:

```
{FORM DATA_AREA}
{APPENDBELOW INV_DB,INV1}
```

1-2-3 copies the data in INV1 to the end of the INV_DB database, all in the first column. It does not transpose the data to match INV_DB's horizontal format.

To get around this problem, you need to transpose the data to an intermediate range whose orientation matches your database. You can then use {APPENDBELOW} or {APPENDRIGHT} without any difficulty. Consider using Range Transpose (or a series of {LET} commands) to transpose the data to the proper orientation.

CREATING CUSTOM MENUS

If you have worked with a previous release of 1-2-3, you know that one of the most appealing features of its macro facility was the ability to create your own custom menus. These menus worked just like 1-2-3's command menu, complete with command highlight and capsule descriptions.

In bringing 1-2-3's macro facility to Windows, you might expect that Lotus would give you the ability to create custom Windows menus. Unfortunately, this is not the case. While you can create your own menus in 1-2-3 for Windows, they are drawn using the less aesthetic 1-2-3 Classic menu system. In addition, you must use the keyboard to select from macro menus—the mouse won't work. Nevertheless, macro menus are still quite useful, and allow you to build powerful macro-driven applications.

{MENUBRANCH} and {MENUCALL} are the commands you use to create custom menus. These commands are variations of the {BRANCH} and {subroutine} commands, allowing you to branch to macro instructions or call them as subroutines.

Whether you use {MENUCALL} or {MENUBRANCH} to create a menu depends on what you want to happen after an item in the menu is chosen and the commands associated with it are executed. If you want your macro to return to the original calling routine and execute the commands following the command that creates the menu, you use the {MENUCALL} command. If you do *not* want your macro to return to the original calling routine, use {MENUBRANCH}.

The next two sections, which describe {MENUBRANCH} and {MENUCALL} in detail, are followed by an example that will show you how to construct a custom menu. Some general rules for creating custom menus follow the example.

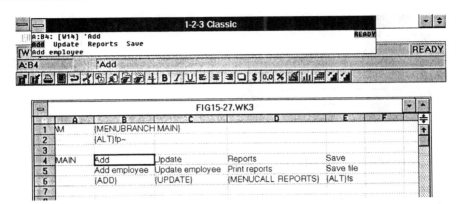

Figure 15-26 The {MENUBRANCH} command

The {MENUBRANCH} Command

The {MENUBRANCH} command creates a custom menu in a 1-2-3 Classic window, waits for you to select an item, and branches to the macro commands associated with that item. It does not return to the calling routine. The syntax of the command is

```
{MENUBRANCH location}
```

where *location* refers to the upper-left cell in the range that contains the menu items, descriptions, and associated commands.

For example, Figure 15-26 shows a {MENUBRANCH} command in cell B1 and the menu the command creates. The *location* argument for the {MENUBRANCH} command is MAIN, the name assigned to cell B4. Notice that this cell contains the label 'Add, which is used to produce the first menu item.

If you select Add from the menu, the macro executes the {ADD} command, which makes a call to the ADD subroutine (not shown in the figure). When the ADD subroutine is completed, the macro ends because B7 is blank; control never returns to the main routine that contains the {MENUBRANCH} command.

If you press ESC, the {MENUBRANCH} command is aborted and control returns to the instruction immediately following the {MENUBRANCH} command in the original calling routine. For example, if you press ESC while the menu in Figure 15-26 is active, the macro executes the printing instructions {ALT}fp~ in cell B2.

The {MENUCALL} Command

{MENUCALL} differs from {MENUBRANCH} in that it performs a subroutine call to the instructions associated with a menu item. When the subroutine has completed, control returns to the command following the {MENUCALL}. The syntax for {MENUCALL} is identical to that of {MENUBRANCH}.

```
{MENUCALL location}
```

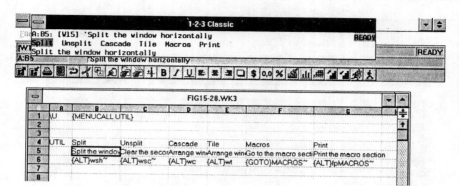

Figure 15-27 A sample utility menu

{MENUCALL} displays the menu referenced by *location*, and waits for you to select an item. Once the instructions associated with the selected item are completed, macro control returns to the instruction immediately following the {MENUCALL} command in the calling routine, and the macro continues execution from that point.

For example, suppose you replace the {MENUBRANCH} command in cell B1 of Figure 15-26 with a {MENUCALL} command, and execute the macro. If you select Add, the macro executes the ADD subroutine, then returns to the command following {MENUCALL}. Therefore, the macro always executes the printing instructions in cell B2, regardless of the menu item you select (even if you press ESC).

A Sample Menu

Each item in the sample menu in Figure 15-27 performs a simple 1-2-3 for Windows function, such as splitting a window horizontally, stacking or tiling windows, and printing the macro range. Perform the following steps to create this macro menu:

1. Starting with a fresh spreadsheet, move to cell A1 and enter the label '\U. Then use Range Name Label Create Right to assign the name to cell B1. In B1 enter **{MENUCALL UTIL}**.

2. Enter the label **UTIL** in cell A4. Next, use the Range Name Label Create Right command to assign the name UTIL to cell B4.

3. With the cell pointer in cell B4, enter the following menu items and descriptions, each in its own separate cell. Use Figure 15-27 as a guide.

Item	Description
Split	Split the window horizontally
Unsplit	Clear the second window pane

(continued)

Item	Description
Stack	Arrange windows in a stack
Tile	Arrange windows in tiles
Macros	Go to the macro section
Print	Print the macro section

4. Enter the macro instructions associated with each menu item in the third row of the menu range (row 6), as shown in Figure 15-27.

Now you are ready to try your macro menu. Since you have named the macro \U, press CTRL+U and the menu will appear as in Figure 15-27, waiting for you to select an item.

Rules for Creating a Custom Menu

Here are some other guidelines for entering menu items when you are building a custom menu:

- You can include up to eight items in your menu.

- You can enter items as labels, numbers, or string formulas.

- The longest menu item that 1-2-3 for Windows will display is 79 characters. Nevertheless, you should strive to keep your menu items relatively short and plan to use command descriptions to further explain each item as it is selected.

- Begin each menu item with a different letter or number. This lets you select from your menu by pressing the first character of the item. Suppose, for example, that you use Split and Stack as two items in your menu. If you press S when this menu is displayed, 1-2-3 selects the first item that starts with the character *S*, in this case, Split. You can still select Stack, however, by highlighting it and pressing ENTER.

- As you enter your menu items in the spreadsheet, do not be concerned if they look as though they overlap one another. As long as you place each item in a separate cell, 1-2-3 will have no trouble interpreting them.

CHANGING THE EFFECT OF CTRL+BREAK: {BREAKOFF} AND {BREAKON}

As you know, you can stop a macro at any time by pressing CTRL+BREAK. Suppose you are developing a model and are concerned that if a user presses CTRL+BREAK, it might adversely affect your macro, or the user might see some sensitive data or not know how to navigate in 1-2-3 outside of the macro. To prevent this from happening, you can place a {BREAKOFF} command at the beginning of a critical operation in your macro to disable CTRL+BREAK, and then use the {BREAKON} command to reenable CTRL+BREAK once the commands have executed. The syntax of these commands is

```
{BREAKOFF}
{BREAKON}
```

Because {BREAKOFF} disables CTRL+BREAK while a macro is running, you should include it only after you have thoroughly tested your macro. Otherwise, if an error occurs that causes the macro to go into an infinite loop, you will not be able to stop the macro or quit 1-2-3 for Windows.

▼ *Tip:* When {BREAKOFF} is in effect and a macro is stuck in an infinite loop, you can still switch away from 1-2-3 for Windows and save your work in other applications. Press CTRL+ESC to activate the Task List. You can then highlight another application in the list and select Switch To. After saving your work, you can leave Windows by switching to Program Manager and closing it in the usual fashion.

{BREAKON} undoes a {BREAKOFF} command, restoring the use of CTRL+BREAK in a macro. If you do not include a {BREAKON} command in your macro, 1-2-3 automatically restores the use of CTRL+BREAK when the macro ends.

In the following excerpt from a macro, {BREAKOFF} disables CTRL+BREAK prior to running the ACCTSREC subroutine. The macro then uses {BREAKON} to restore CTRL+BREAK following the completion of the subroutine.

```
{BREAKOFF}
{ACCTSREC}
{BREAKON}
```

The {BREAK} Command

The {BREAK} command produces the same effect as pressing CTRL+BREAK while you are in the middle of a 1-2-3 for Windows operation, such as when you are responding to a 1-2-3 command—it returns you to READY mode. Of course, if 1-2-3 is already in READY mode when the macro encounters a {BREAK} command, the command has no effect. Note that {BREAK} does not stop a macro, nor does it have any connection with the {BREAKOFF} and {BREAKON} commands.

For example, suppose you have the macro in Figure 15-28 that issues the File Save As command and then uses a {GETLABEL} command to pause the macro and request a filename. When you type a name and press ENTER, the {GETLABEL} command stores your response in FILENAME (cell B15). The macro then uses the contents of this range in the File Save As command's File name text box. However, if you do *not* type a filename but immediately press ENTER in response to the {GETLABEL} command, the macro executes the {BREAK} command following the {IF}. This command cancels the File

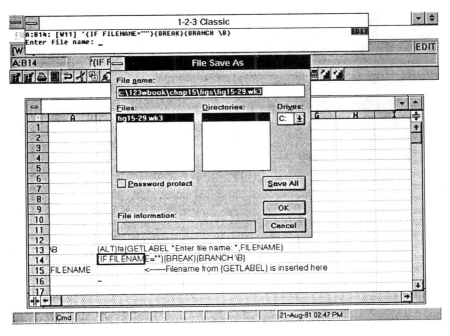

Figure 15-28 The {BREAK} command

Save As command and returns 1-2-3 to READY mode. The macro then branches back to the top and executes again.

▼ *Tip:* By placing {BREAK} at the beginning of a macro, you can ensure that the macro will run even if the user is entering data or is in the middle of a 1-2-3 for Windows command. Because {BREAK} always returns 1-2-3 to READY mode, you can be certain that the macro commands that follow will begin executing in the correct context.

SOUNDING TONES: THE {BEEP} COMMAND

The {BEEP} command sounds your computer's speaker. It is a carryover from previous releases and issues a short beep. {BEEP} is most often used to attract the user's attention—for example, to alert a user that an error has occurred or a process is complete. The syntax of the command is

```
{BEEP [tone-number]}
```

In previous releases of 1-2-3, the optional *tone-number* argument would control the tone of the bell. The four available tones corresponded to the numbers 1 to 4. In 1-2-3 for

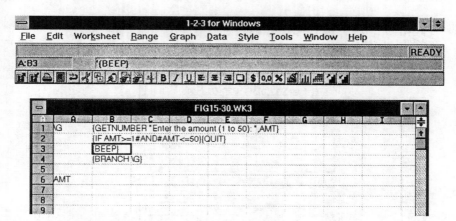

Figure 15-29 The {BEEP} command

Windows, however, the *tone-number* argument has no effect on the tone of the speaker. In other words, {BEEP}, {BEEP 2}, and {BEEP 4} all yield the same tone.

Note: If you have turned off your computer's sound using Tools User Setup or the Windows Control Panel, {BEEP} has no effect.

One of the most useful applications of {BEEP} is to signal an error. For example, the macro in Figure 15-29 prompts you for a number between 1 and 50. If you enter a number within the acceptable bounds, the macro quits; otherwise, it sounds the bell and then branches back to the top of the macro to have you try again.

CONTROLLING THE SCREEN

1-2-3 for Windows offers several commands for controlling the appearance of the screen during a macro. You can use these commands to change the mode indicator, turn off control panel updating, and freeze the window display.

The {INDICATE} Command

The {INDICATE} command lets you replace the mode indicator with a given string. The syntax of the command is

```
{INDICATE [string]}
```

where *string* can be a label, cell reference, or string formula. The maximum length of *string* is approximately 88 characters (depending on the size of your System font). If *string* is too long, it is truncated. The mode indicator box expands and contracts to fit the length of the string.

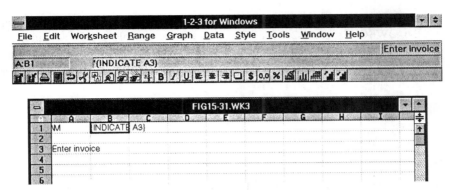

Figure 15-30 The {INDICATE} command

For example, suppose cell A3 contains the label 'Enter invoice. The command {INDICATE A3} sets the mode indicator to Enter invoice, as shown in Figure 15-30. Another instance might be {INDICATE SWITCH_MODE} using the contents of the SWITCH_MODE range as the *string* argument.

If you include a null (empty) string as the *string* argument, as in {INDICATE ""}, the mode indicator disappears.

Unlike other macro commands for controlling the screen, the effect of {INDICATE} remains after your macro has ended. For example, if your macro issues the command {INDICATE "Daily balance"} and then does not reset the mode indicator, the indicator continues to display Daily balance after the macro has finished. To reset the mode indicator, execute a macro that contains {INDICATE} without a *string* argument.

The {WINDOWSOFF} and {WINDOWSON} Commands

In previous versions, whenever 1-2-3 executed a macro, it would redraw the screen repeatedly as it processed commands, creating a kind of flashing effect. In 1-2-3 for Windows, the screen is not updated as frequently and flashing is less of a problem. The flashing can be eliminated altogether by using the {WINDOWSOFF} command, which prevents 1-2-3 for Windows from updating its work area. The {WINDOWSOFF} command remains in effect until the macro encounters a {WINDOWSON} command, or the macro ends. The syntax of these commands is

```
{WINDOWSOFF}
{WINDOWSON}
```

The {WINDOWSOFF} command affects only the noninteractive parts of a macro. In other words, if the user needs to see a dialog box or message box in order to respond to the macro (for example, the dialog box that appears when you select the Range Format command), 1-2-3 displays the box despite the {WINDOWSOFF} command.

In the following excerpt from a macro, the {WINDOWSOFF} command suppresses updating of the screen. Next, a data query operation extracts data to an output range, sorts the data in that range in ascending order using the first field as the primary key, and then print-previews the output range. Finally, the {WINDOWSON} command cancels the {WINDOWSOFF}, and 1-2-3 for Windows resumes normal worksheet display.

```
{WINDOWSOFF}
{ALT}dq{ALT "e"}{ESC}
{GOTO}OUTPUT~{DOWN}
{ALT}ds{BS}.{END}{RIGHT}{END}{DOWN}~{ALT "a"}~
{ALT}fv{BS}.{END}{RIGHT}{END}{DOWN}~~
{WINDOWSON}
```

If you remove the {WINDOWSOFF} command from this macro, you'll notice that 1-2-3 updates the screen intermittently as the macro runs, slowing down the macro's execution, as well as creating a distracting "light show" for anyone watching.

The {PANELOFF} and {PANELON} Commands

{PANELOFF} freezes the control panel (the first four lines of the 1-2-3 window) and the status line (the last line of the window) during macro execution. These areas of the screen are restored to their normal state when the macro encounters a {PANELON} command, or the macro ends. The syntax of these commands is

```
{PANELOFF}
{PANELON}
```

Note: In previous releases of 1-2-3, if you wanted to clear the control panel before freezing it, you could include the optional *clear* argument with the {PANELOFF} command, as in {PANELOFF clear}. Although the clear argument is documented in 1-2-3 for Windows, it has no effect—you cannot clear the control panel before freezing it.

For example, the following excerpt from a macro places the 12 months of the year in consecutive cells beginning at the location of the cell pointer. If you omit the {PANELOFF} command from this macro, you can see the control panel flash as 1-2-3 enters the months in the cells.

```
{PANELOFF}
Jan{R}Feb{R}Mar{R}Apr{R}May{R}Jun{R}
Jul{R}Aug{R}Sep{R}Oct{R}Nov{R}Dec~{L 11}
{PANELON}
```

▼ *Tip:*   You can use {PANELOFF} and {WINDOWSOFF} together to prevent 1-2-3 from updating any part of the screen during a macro's operation.

The {FRAMEOFF} and {FRAMEON} Commands

In previous releases of 1-2-3, the {BORDERSOFF} and {BORDERSON} commands work identically to the {FRAMEOFF} and {FRAMEON} commands. These commands are not available in 1-2-3 for Windows. The {FRAMEOFF} and {FRAMEON} commands are provided instead.

The {FRAMEOFF} command turns off the display of 1-2-3 for Windows' worksheet frame (column letters and row numbers). The frame remains turned off until the macro encounters a {FRAMEON} command or the macro ends. The syntax of these commands is

```
{FRAMEOFF}
{FRAMEON}
```

Note: These commands do not work in 1-2-3 for Windows Versions 1.0 or 1.0a.

For example, the following excerpt from a macro shows how you can eliminate the worksheet frame before displaying a data-entry form. This helps to focus the user's attention on the data-entry area:

```
{FRAMEOFF}
{FORM DATA_AREA,ACTION_KEYS,OK_KEYS}
{FRAMEON}
```

The {GRAPHON} and {GRAPHOFF} Commands

{GRAPHON} makes a graph current and displays it full-screen. {GRAPHOFF} removes a graph displayed with the {GRAPHON} command. The syntax of these commands is

```
{GRAPHON [named-graph],[nodisplay]}
{GRAPHOFF}
```

When 1-2-3 for Windows encounters a {GRAPHON} command with no arguments, it displays the current graph.

Note: When you use the {GRAPHON} command to display a graph, that graph remains in view until a {GRAPHOFF}, {?}, {GETNUMBER}, {GETLABEL}, {MENUBRANCH}, {MENUCALL}, or {INDICATE} command is encountered or the macro ends.

The optional *named-graph* argument lets you display a named graph. The name you use must be the one you assigned to the graph settings using the Graph New command (see Chapter 10, "Graphs," for more on Graph New).

If you use the optional nodisplay argument, *named-graph* is made the current graph but is not displayed. For example, the command {GRAPHON SALES91,nodisplay} makes the graph SALES91 the current graph but does not display it full-screen. 1-2-3 uses the SALES91 settings the next time it draws a graph.

The {GRAPHON} command lets you create a graph slide show that displays one graph after another at intervals you choose. For example, the following macro displays a series of three graphs (BARSALES, 3DBARSALES, and LINESALES), each for three seconds, until you press a key. When you press a key, the macro ends. If you do not press a key, the macro branches back to the top and executes again.

```
\G          {GRAPHON BARSALES}
            {WAIT @NOW+@TIME(0,0,3)}
            {GRAPHON 3DBARSALES}
            {WAIT @NOW+@TIME(0,0,3)}
            {GRAPHON LINESALES}
            {WAIT @NOW+@TIME(0,0,3)}
            {LOOK KEYMASHED}
            {IF KEYMASHED=""}{BRANCH \G}
            {GET KEYMASHED}
```

CONTROLLING WINDOWS

1-2-3 for Windows has two new macro commands for controlling the size and position of its main window—{APP-ADJUST} and {APP-STATE}. It also has three new commands for controlling worksheet and graph windows within the main 1-2-3 window—{WINDOW-ADJUST}, {WINDOW-STATE}, and {WINDOW-SELECT}. Using these commands, you can perform any sizing and positioning operation on a 1-2-3 window that you would normally perform in READY mode using the mouse or the keyboard. For example, you can resize the main 1-2-3 window on the Windows desktop or activate a particular worksheet window within 1-2-3's work area.

The {APP-ADJUST} Command

The {APP-ADJUST} command lets you size and position 1-2-3's window on the desktop. The syntax of the command is

```
{APP-ADJUST x,y,width,height}
```

where *x* and *y* specify the horizontal and vertical positions in pixels of the upper-left corner of the window; both are measured from the top left corner of the screen, point (0,0). The *width* and *height* arguments control the window's size, also in pixels.

For example, the following command sets the 1-2-3 window 100 pixels to the right and 50 pixels down from the top left corner of the screen. In addition, the width of the window is set to 500 pixels and the height to 400 pixels.

```
{APP-ADJUST 100,50,500,400}
```

Note: As you use 1-2-3 for Windows' commands to control the size of windows, be aware that they are device dependent. For example, suppose you have an EGA system, and you write a macro to the size of the 1-2-3 window on the screen. When you run that macro on a VGA system, the size of the 1-2-3 window will appear much smaller because there are more pixels per square inch on a VGA.

The {APP-STATE} Command

The {APP-STATE} command lets you maximize, minimize, or restore 1-2-3's window on the desktop. The syntax of the command is

```
{APP-STATE state}
```

where *state* is one of the following labels enclosed in quotation marks:

Argument	Action
Maximize	Maximizes 1-2-3's window.
Minimize	Minimizes 1-2-3's window.
Restore	Restores 1-2-3's window.

For example, the following macro minimizes 1-2-3's window, pauses for 5 seconds, and then restores the window to its original size:

```
{APP-STATE "minimize"}
{WAIT @NOW+@TIME(0,0,5)}
{APP-STATE "restore"}
```

The {WINDOW-ADJUST} Command

The {WINDOW-ADJUST} command lets you size and position the active window within the 1-2-3 work area. The syntax of the command is

```
{WINDOW-ADJUST x,y,width,height}
```

where *x* and *y* control the horizontal and vertical positions, in pixels, of the upper-left corner of the window; both are measured from the top left corner of 1-2-3's work area, point (0,0). The *width* and *height* arguments control the window's size, also in pixels.

For example, the following command places the upper-left corner of the active window 100 pixels to the right and 10 pixels down from the top left corner of the 1-2-3 work area. In addition, it sets the window to 500 pixels by 300 pixels.

```
{WINDOW-ADJUST 100,10,500,300}
```

▼ *Tip:*   In addition to worksheet and graph windows, you can use {WINDOW-ADJUST} to control the size and position of the transcript window.

The {WINDOW-STATE} Command

The {WINDOW-STATE} command lets you maximize, minimize, or restore the active window in the 1-2-3 for Windows work area. The syntax of the command is

```
{WINDOW-STATE state}
```

where *state* is one of the following labels enclosed in quotation marks:

Argument	Action
Maximize	Maximizes the window.
Minimize	Minimizes the window.
Restore	Restores the window.

For example, the following macro minimizes the active worksheet window before graphing the data in the range surrounding the cell pointer:

```
\G          {WINDOW-STATE "minimize"}
            {ALT}gn{ALT "a"}
            {BS}.{END}{R}{END}{D}~~
```

Note: Due to a quirk in 1-2-3 for Windows, this macro will not work if a graph window is already open or you have more than one worksheet file open. If you want to reproduce this example, make sure you try it with only a single active worksheet file.

The {WINDOW-SELECT} Command

The {WINDOW-SELECT} command makes the worksheet or graph window you specify the active window. The syntax of the command is

```
{WINDOW-SELECT windowname}
```

where *windowname* is the name of an open window in the 1-2-3 work area.

For example, the following macro activates the worksheet window containing SALES91.WK3 and print-previews the range TWELVE from that file:

```
\S          {WINDOW-SELECT SALES91.WK3}
            {ALT}fvTWELVE~
```

Once you activate a window, the menu associated with that window becomes active. For example, when you access a graph window, the graph menu becomes the active menu. In the following macro the graph window named YEAR_END.WK3 LINE is activated and the graph type is set to bar:

```
\G          {WINDOW-SELECT YEAR_END.WK3 LINE}
            {ALT}ct{ALT "b"}~
```

Note: You can use the {GRAPHON} command to display a graph full-screen. {GRAPHON} does not activate the graph's window, however.

CONTROLLING RECALCULATION: {RECALC} AND {RECALCCOL}

Suppose you have a macro that is located in a very large worksheet file with many complex formulas and dependencies. Rather than have the entire file recalculate when you change the contents of a cell, you can specify manual recalculation (using the Tools User Setup Recalculation Manual command) and then have your macro recalculate only specific areas of the worksheet as needed.

The {RECALC} and {RECALCCOL} commands allow you to specify a range within the worksheet file to be recalculated. {RECALC} recalculates the specified range row-by-row, and {RECALCCOL} recalculates it column-by-column. Both commands use the same syntax and accept the same arguments, as follows:

```
{RECALC location, [condition], [iterations]}
{RECALCCOL location, [condition], [iterations]}
```

where *location* refers to a range address or named range in your worksheet file that you want to recalculate.

The optional *condition* argument is usually a logical expression or a reference to a cell that contains a logical expression. You can also use a number, formula, string, or cell reference for *condition*. Whichever you use, 1-2-3 evaluates *condition* as true as long as it does not equal 0. When *condition* equals 0, 1-2-3 will evaluate it as false. Blank cells, strings, ERR, and NA equal 0 when used with *condition*.

Note: When *condition* references a cell that contains a formula that must be recalculated for each iteration of a {RECALC} or {RECALCCOL} command, be sure to place the formula within *location*.

The optional iterations argument is the number of recalculations that you want to take place. The iterations argument can be a number, a formula that evaluates to a number, or a reference to a cell with a number or formula. This argument overrides the Tools User Setup Recalculation Iterations setting.

Quite often you will use the *condition* and *iterations* arguments together. In this case, the *iterations* argument specifies the maximum number of recalculations that you want to take place. The recalculations occur until either the *condition* argument is met or the number of iterations expires.

For example, the following command recalculates the cells in the range PROJECT in a column-by-column fashion until the value in the cell named INVEST is greater than or equal to 20,000 or the number of recalculations equals 10.

```
{RECALCCOL PROJECT,INVEST>=20000,10}
```

With either {RECALC} or {RECALCCOL}, only cells within *location* are recalculated. If the formulas within that range refer to cells located outside the range, those cells are not updated.

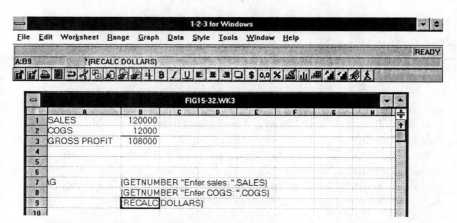

Figure 15-31 The {RECALC} command

Because {RECALC} recalculates location in a row-by-row fashion, you should use it to recalculate formulas that are below and to the left of the cells on which those formulas depend. On the other hand, {RECALCCOL} recalculates *location* in a column-by-column fashion, so you should use it to recalculate formulas that are located above and to the right of the cells on which those formulas depend. If neither of these conditions are met, you will need to use the {CALC} command to recalculate your entire worksheet file.

In actual practice, because of 1-2-3 for Windows' minimal and background recalculation, there are very few cases where you will need to use {RECALC} or {RECALCCOL} to recalculate a range independently of the rest of the worksheet file. In fact, you are likely to find a need for these commands only when you have a large model with many complex formulas and dependencies, and the worksheets in the model are set for manual recalculation.

The macro in Figure 15-31 shows an example of how you might use the {RECALC} command. This macro begins by using the {GETNUMBER} command to prompt you for sales and cost of goods sold (COGS). The {RECALC} command then tells 1-2-3 to recalculate the DOLLARS range (B1..B3).

In this example, you could easily have used the {CALC} command in place of {RECALC} to recalculate the entire worksheet. If you imagine this worksheet as part of a much larger model with many worksheets and dependent formulas, though, you can see that {RECALC} is preferable because you do not have to wait for the rest of the file to be recalculated before using the results of the gross profit formula.

ACCESSING DOS: {SYSTEM}

The {SYSTEM} command lets you execute a DOS command from within a macro. The syntax of the command is

```
{SYSTEM command}
```

where *command* is a DOS command or batch file enclosed in double quotation marks.

For example, the command {SYSTEM "FORMAT A:"} exits 1-2-3 for Windows temporarily, opens a DOS session either full-screen or in a window, and executes the FORMAT A: command to format the disk in drive A. When the FORMAT command is completed, 1-2-3 reappears on the screen.

One of the problems with {SYSTEM} is that, contrary to what the documentation says, 1-2-3 does not pause until the specified DOS command has completed before continuing on with the macro instructions that follow. For example, if you run this macro

```
\s          {SYSTEM "DIR"}
            {BEEP}
```

you'll notice that 1-2-3 beeps long before the DIR command has displayed all your files and directories.

In fact, it is because of this behavior that Lotus states in the 1-2-3 for Windows READ.ME file that {SYSTEM} is provided primarily to maintain compatibility with previous versions of 1-2-3, and that you should avoid using it when other Windows applications are running. Our experience shows that, despite these warnings, you can successfully use {SYSTEM} provided it's one of the last commands in your macro.

Here are some additional tips for making the most of the {SYSTEM} command:

- If you want your macro to display a full-screen DOS session and allow you to work in DOS interactively, place {SYSTEM COMMAND} in your macro. (If you have used a previous release of 1-2-3, {SYSTEM COMMAND} is the equivalent of using the /System command.) You can then return to Windows at any time by typing **EXIT** and pressing ENTER.

- If you are writing a macro whose instructions will vary depending on the version of DOS the user is running, you can use @INFO("osversion") to determine the operating system version. For example, if you are using DOS 5.0, @INFO("osversion") returns the label 'DOS Version 5.0 (see Chapter 9, "Functions," for more information on this function).

- When specifying an argument for {SYSTEM}, you do not have to enclose it in double quotation marks unless it contains a space. For example, {SYSTEM DIR} and {SYSTEM "COPY TEMP.PRN A:\"} are valid commands, but {SYSTEM COPY TEMP.PRN A:\} is not.

LAUNCHING WINDOWS APPLICATIONS: THE {LAUNCH} COMMAND

The {LAUNCH} command lets you start a Windows application from a macro. The syntax of the command is

```
{LAUNCH command, [window]}
```

where *command* is the command string that starts the Windows application, including the path and any command-line arguments.

> ▼ *Tip:*   If the application is in the \WINDOWS directory, the
> \WINDOWS\SYSTEM directory, or a directory in your path, you
> don't need to include any path information in *command*.

The optional *window* argument lets you control the initial state of the application and
is an integer from 0 to 9. The default value is 2. Table 15-4 shows the values you can
assign to *window* and their effects on the application you want to start. Be aware, however,
that few Windows applications support all of these *window* values.

For example, to start Notepad and have it automatically load the READ.ME file in
C:\123W, you would use the following command:

```
{LAUNCH "NOTEPAD C:\123W\READ.ME"}
```

When 1-2-3 executes this command, Notepad is started but is left minimized; 1-2-3
remains the active application.

If you want Notepad to be displayed full-size and made the active application, you
would use

```
{LAUNCH "NOTEPAD C:\123W\READ.ME",1}
```

TABLE 15-4 Window Argument Values for the {LAUNCH} Command

Argument	Action
0	Hides the application window and activates another window.
1	Activates the application and displays its window.
2	Activates the application and minimizes it.
3	Activates the application and maximizes it.
4	Displays the application's window in its most recently assigned size and position. 1-2-3 remains the active application.
5	Activates the application and lets Windows assign its current size and position.
6	Minimizes the application and activates the top-level window in the Task List (usually 1-2-3).
7	Minimizes the application's window. 1-2-3 remains the active application. (This is the default when you do not include a window argument.)
8	Displays the application in its current state. 1-2-3 remains the active application.
9	Activates and displays the application. If the window is minimized or maximized, restores it to its original size and position.

> ▼ **Tip:** You can also use {LAUNCH} to start DOS applications. When it is used in this way, it is identical to the {SYSTEM} command.

CONTROLLING THE CLIPBOARD

1-2-3 for Windows has several new commands for controlling the Clipboard. These commands offer similar capabilities to the Edit menu options, but are easier to use from within macros.

The {EDIT-CLEAR} Command

The {EDIT-CLEAR} command performs the same function as choosing Edit Clear Special from 1-2-3's menu. It lets you delete data and/or its formatting from the worksheet without copying it to the Clipboard. The syntax of this command is

```
{EDIT-CLEAR [selection],[property]}
```

where the optional *selection* argument is the range of data you want to delete; if you do not include a *selection* argument, 1-2-3 deletes the current selection.

The optional *property* argument is a string (enclosed in quotes) that lets you control what elements are deleted from the chosen range. The available choices are shown in Table 15-5. If you do not include a *property* argument, all the elements are cleared from the range.

Note: Because {EDIT-CLEAR} does not remove the contents of a range to the Clipboard, you cannot paste them back to the worksheet.

TABLE 15-5 Property Arguments for the {EDIT-CLEAR} and {LINK-ASSIGN} Commands

Argument	Action
contents	Deletes only cell contents; cell formatting is left intact.
formats	Deletes cell formatting from the selected range; cell formatting reverts to the current default (Worksheet Global Settings Format) setting.
styles	Deletes all style settings from the selected range. (Label alignment—left, center, and right—is not affected.) Returns the font and color settings to their defaults.
graphs	Deletes a graph from the selected range. Neither the graph name nor its data are affected, however.

If you want to remove the contents of the range CONSULT, as well as eliminate all cell formatting and style settings, you would use the following two {EDIT-CLEAR} commands:

```
{EDIT-CLEAR CONSULT,"formats"}
{EDIT-CLEAR CONSULT,"styles}
```

Note: {BLANK} is similar to {EDIT-CLEAR}, except that it erases only the contents of a range; it does not affect cell formatting or styles.

The {EDIT-COPY} Command

The {EDIT-COPY} command is the equivalent of choosing Edit Copy from 1-2-3's menu. It copies data, along with formatting and style settings, from the worksheet to the Clipboard. The syntax of the command is

```
{EDIT-COPY [selection],[format]}
```

where the optional *selection* argument is the range of data you want to copy; if you do not include a *selection* argument, 1-2-3 copies the current selection. In the case of a graph, {EDIT-COPY} affects the currently selected item (the item with handles around it). Of course, once data is copied to the Clipboard, you can paste it several times.

The optional *format* argument is a string (enclosed in quotes) that lets you explicitly control the Clipboard format. Table 15-6 shows the available choices. If you do not specify a *format* argument, 1-2-3 usually copies the data to the Clipboard in a variety of formats so that the application pasting the data can choose the one it wants. Otherwise, the format you choose affects the ability of 1-2-3 or another application to retain the original formatting information.

The following macro copies the data from the INV1 range to the Clipboard. It then pastes the data from the Clipboard to the INVOUT range, complete with the data's original formatting.

```
\C     {EDIT-COPY INV1}
       {EDIT-PASTE INVOUT}
```

If you change the first command to read {EDIT-COPY INV1,"text"}, 1-2-3 will copy only text to the Clipboard, and the cells in INVOUT will take on the default formatting when the data is pasted to them.

The {EDIT-COPY-GRAPH} Command

The {EDIT-COPY-GRAPH} command copies the contents of the active graph window to the Clipboard. The syntax of the command is

```
{EDIT-COPY-GRAPH}
```

Note: {EDIT-COPY-GRAPH} works only when a graph window is the active window. If you use this command when a worksheet window is active, 1-2-3 for Windows displays an error.

TABLE 15-6 Clipboard Formats for the {EDIT-COPY} Command

String	*Effect*
text	Copies an ANSI character string to the Clipboard.
bitmap	Copies a "device dependent" (Windows 2-compatible) bitmap to the Clipboard.
dib	Copies a "device-independent" (Windows 3-compatible) bitmap to the Clipboard.
metafilepict	Copies a "metafile picture" to the Clipboard.
lotus123graph	Copies a 1-2-3 for Windows graph to the Clipboard. This is a private (Lotus-specific) Clipboard format.
wk1	Copies the selection to the Clipboard in .WK1-compatible file format (a private Clipboard format).
wk3	Copies the selection to the Clipboard in .WK3-compatible file format (a private Clipboard format).

The following macro makes the PAYROLL 1991 graph window the active window and then copies its contents to the Clipboard:

```
\G    {WINDOW-SELECT"PAYROLL 1991"}
      {EDIT-COPY-GRAPH}
```

> ▼ *Tip:* Because 1-2-3 for Windows copies a graph to the Clipboard in a variety of different formats, you can easily paste a 1-2-3 graph into other Windows applications.

The {EDIT-CUT} Command

The {EDIT-CUT} command is the macro equivalent of 1-2-3's Edit Cut menu command. It lets you cut data (and its formatting) from the worksheet to the Clipboard. The syntax of the command is

```
{EDIT-CUT [selection],[format]}
```

(See the "The {EDIT-COPY} Command" earlier in this chapter for an explanation of the arguments.)

For example, the following macro cuts the data (and formatting) from cell E10 and then pastes it to cell F10.

```
{EDIT-CUT E10}
{EDIT-PASTE F10}
```

The {EDIT-PASTE} Command

Similar to 1-2-3's Edit Paste menu command, the {EDIT-PASTE} macro command copies data (and its formatting) from the Clipboard to the worksheet. The syntax of the command is

```
{EDIT-PASTE [selection],[format]}
```

where the optional *selection* argument lets you specify the range into which you want to paste the Clipboard contents. If you do not include the *selection* argument, 1-2-3 will paste the Clipboard contents into the current selection.

The optional *format* argument is a string (enclosed in quotes) that lets you designate the Clipboard format—for example, text or bitmap. (See Table 15-6 for a list of Clipboard formats.) If you omit the *format* argument, 1-2-3 will paste the Clipboard contents using its own private Clipboard format (Lotus123Private).

For example, the following macro copies the contents of the MILES91 range and pastes them into the MILES92 and MILES93 ranges.

```
{EDIT-CUT MILES91}
{EDIT-PASTE MILES92}
{EDIT-PASTE MILES93}
```

The {EDIT-PASTE-LINK} Command

{EDIT-PASTE-LINK} performs the same function as choosing Edit Paste Link from 1-2-3's menu. That is, it lets you create a DDE link between the active worksheet file and the file named in the Clipboard. The syntax of the command is

```
{EDIT-PASTE-LINK [range]}
```

where the optional *range* argument lets you specify the range into which you want to paste the Clipboard contents. If you do not include the *range* argument, 1-2-3 will paste the Clipboard contents into the current selection.

When you create a DDE link with {EDIT-PASTE-LINK}, 1-2-3 for Windows is the client, and the application whose contents you have copied to the Clipboard acts as the server. (See the next section for more on the relationship between applications in a DDE session.)

For example, suppose you are working with Word for Windows, and you want to copy some text from a Word document into your current 1-2-3 for Windows spreadsheet. In addition, you decide to create a DDE link so that whenever the contents of the document change, the text in the spreadsheet is automatically updated to reflect the change.

To establish this DDE link, start by activating Word for Windows and highlighting the text you want to link. Next, use Word's Edit Copy command to copy the text to the Clipboard. At this point, the Clipboard contains all the information 1-2-3 needs to create the DDE link. Then place the following command in a macro:

```
{EDIT-PASTE-LINK TEXT_IN}
```

Now, when you run the macro containing this command, 1-2-3 will copy the data from the Clipboard and place it in the TEXT_IN range. It also creates an automatic link between the Word document and the 1-2-3 spreadsheet so that when the text in the Word document changes, the contents of the TEXT_IN range is updated automatically.

CONTROLLING DDE LINKS

1-2-3 for Windows has two classes of commands for controlling DDE links through macros: high-level link commands and conversation-level link commands. The *high-level link commands* are the macro equivalent of 1-2-3's Edit Link Options commands. These commands let you easily create, manage, and even remove a DDE link, but they do not let you control the "nitty-gritty" details of a DDE session. For that kind of control, you must use the *conversation-level link commands*. With this class of commands, you can send and receive messages between 1-2-3 and other Windows applications—in effect, carrying on a conversation between applications from within a macro.

Note: This section assumes that you are familiar with DDE and that you are acquainted with such terms as client, server, application name, topic name, and item name. If these terms are new to you or you just want to brush up on your DDE vocabulary, see Chapter 17.

High-Level DDE Link Commands

As we have mentioned, 1-2-3 for Windows' high-level DDE link commands perform the same functions as the Edit Link Options commands. Use these commands when a server application does not let you create a DDE link using Edit Copy and Edit Paste Link, or when you want to modify link options.

The {LINK-CREATE} Command

Because some server applications do not let you create a DDE link using Edit Copy and Edit Paste Link, 1-2-3 for Windows offers the Edit Link Options Create command. This command lets you create a link between the current worksheet file and another Windows application without using the Clipboard. In this scenario, 1-2-3 for Windows is the client and the other Windows application is the server.

> ▼ *Tip:* If the application you want to use as the DDE server supports Edit Copy, it's much easier to use {EDIT-PASTE-LINK} rather than {LINK-CREATE} to create a DDE link. See "The {EDIT-PASTE-LINK} Command" earlier.

The macro-equivalent of Edit Link Options Create is {LINK-CREATE}. The syntax of this command is

```
{LINK-CREATE link-name,app-name,topic-name,item-name,
   [format],[mode],[branch-location]}
```

where

- *link-name* is a string argument identifying the name of the link. When specifying *link-name*, follow the same rules as for range names—for example, use 15 characters or less and avoid names that resemble cell addresses, @functions, or macro command names. You should not start *link-name* with ! (exclamation point); nor should you include spaces, commas, semicolons, periods, or any of the following characters:

  ```
  +  *  -  /  &  >  <  @  #  {  ?
  ```

- *app-name* is a string argument identifying the name of a Windows application that will act as the server—for example, "winword" for Word for Windows.

- *topic-name* is the name of the file or document to link to. In most cases, it's important to include the full path of the file—for example "C:\123WBOOK\CHAP15\NEWS.DOC".

- *item-name* defines the specific location of the information in *topic-name*.

▼ *Tip:*   Each server application has its own way of assigning item names. For example, Word for Windows Version 2.0 assigns "DDE_LINK1" to the first item name, "DDE_LINK2" to the second, "DDE_LINK3" to the third, and so on. On the other hand, 1-2-3 for Windows uses range coordinates for each item name—for example, "A:A1..A:D5."

The easiest way to determine the item name that an application automatically assigns is to highlight a block of data in the application (a paragraph in Word for Windows, for example) and use Edit Copy to copy it to the Clipboard. Next, activate 1-2-3 for Windows and use the Edit Link Options Create command. In the Item name text box, 1-2-3 displays the item name that the server application automatically assigns. This is the string that you should use for the *item-name* argument in the {LINK-CREATE} command.

- *format* is an optional string argument that lets you designate the Clipboard format—for example, text or bitmap. (See Table 15-6 for a list of Clipboard formats.) If you omit the *format* argument, 1-2-3 uses the text format.

- *mode* is an optional string argument that specifies when the link is updated. It can be either of the following:

Argument	Action
automatic	Updates data in the destination range each time the source is updated (the default).
manual	Updates data in the destination range only when you use {LINK-UPDATE}.

Note: The server application may not support automatic updating of DDE links. If not, the link must be updated manually. See "The {LINK-UPDATE} Command" later.

- *branch-location* is an optional range or cell reference that identifies where the macro will branch when the link is updated.

If the {LINK-CREATE} command executes successfully, control shifts to the next cell in the macro; any instructions that occur after {LINK-CREATE} are ignored. If {LINK-CREATE} is *not* successful, the macro continues in the same cell as {LINK-CREATE}.

Figure 15-32 shows how you can use the {LINK-CREATE} and {LINK-ASSIGN} commands to create a DDE link. In this example, text from a Word for Windows document (C:\123WBOOK\CHAP15\NEWS.DOC) is linked to the current 1-2-3 for Windows spreadsheet. Here the {LINK-CREATE} command uses a link name of "testlink", an application name of "winword", a topic name of "C:\123WBOOK\CHAP15\NEWS.DOC", and an item name of "DDE_LINK." In addition, the {LINK-ASSIGN} command specifies a destination range of TEXT_IN (A1..A7) for the incoming text.

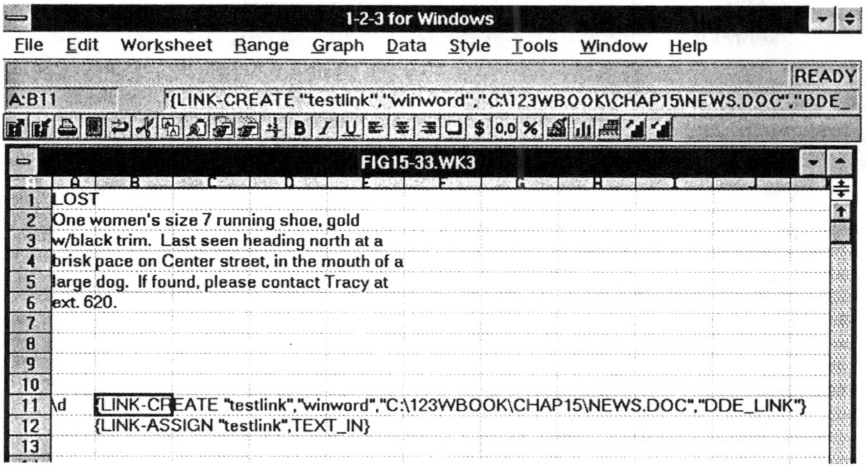

Figure 15-32 The {LINK-CREATE} command

Note: If you want to reproduce this example, be sure to use the Edit Copy command to copy a block of text from the Word for Windows document to the Clipboard. If you omit this step, 1-2-3 will display the message "Bad DDE link name {LINK-CREATE}" when you run the macro. If this message continues to appear, use the Edit Link Options Create command to verify the link name.

The {LINK-ASSIGN} Command

The {LINK-ASSIGN} command lets you specify a *destination range*— the range you want to link to in the current worksheet. The syntax of the command is

```
{LINK-ASSIGN link-name,range,[property1],
    [property2],[property3]}
```

where

- *link-name* is a string argument specifying the name of the link. It must be the same name used in the {LINK-CREATE} command.
- *range* is a cell or range reference that identifies the destination.

   Note: If *range* is not big enough to hold the incoming data, 1-2-3 shows only that data that will fit into the destination range. If the incoming data is a graph, it resizes the graph to fit within the destination range.

- The optional *property1*, *property2*, and *property3* arguments are string arguments that let you control what elements are deleted from the chosen range before every update. The available choices are shown in Table 15-5. If you do not include a *property* argument, all the elements will be cleared from the range.

   See the previous section for an example of {LINK-ASSIGN}.

> ▼ *Tip:*   You can use the Edit Link Options command to check the status of a
> DDE link.

The {LINK-UPDATE} Command

The {LINK-UPDATE} command updates a DDE link. The syntax of the command is

```
{LINK-UPDATE link-name}
```

where *link-name* is a string argument specifying the name of the link. It must be the same name used in the {LINK-CREATE} command.

Note: If a link has been deactivated with {LINK-DEACTIVATE}, the {LINK-AC-TIVATE} command activates the link and then updates it.

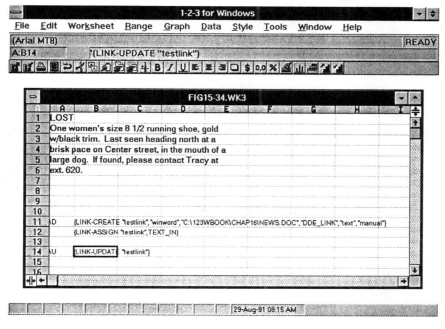

Figure 15-33 The {LINK-UPDATE} command

{LINK-UPDATE} is used primarily to update manual links. For example, the \D macro in Figure 15-33 uses the {LINK-CREATE} command to create a manual link. (This is a variation of the macro in Figure 15-32.) The \U macro is then used to update the link periodically. The {LINK-UPDATE} command in the macro copies current information from the server to the destination range (TEXT-IN).

The {LINK-DELETE} Command

{LINK-DELETE} cancels a link but leaves the data obtained through the link unchanged. The syntax of this command is

```
{LINK-DELETE link-name}
```

where *link-name* is a string argument specifying the name of the link. It must be the same name used in the {LINK-CREATE} command.

For example, to delete the link created in Figure 15-33, you would use the following command:

```
{LINK-DELETE "testlink"}
```

When 1-2-3 executes this command, it detaches the destination range from the link but does not delete the data in that range.

The {LINK-DEACTIVATE} Command

The {LINK-DEACTIVATE} command deactivates a link, but leaves the link in place. The syntax of the command is

```
{LINK-DEACTIVATE link-name}
```

where *link-name* is a string argument specifying the name of the link. It must be the same name used in the {LINK-CREATE} command.

After you deactivate a link, 1-2-3 does not update values in the destination range assigned to the link.

Note: Be aware that when you use {LINK-DEACTIVATE}, it deactivates all the links in the same conversation. In other words, besides the link specified in *link-name*, all other links that share the same application name and topic name will also be deactivated. Therefore, if you want to deactivate a single link, set its update mode to manual.

To reactivate a link, use {LINK-UPDATE}.

The {LINK-REMOVE} Command

{LINK-REMOVE} detaches the current destination range from a DDE link, but does not delete the data in the range. The syntax of the command is

```
{LINK-REMOVE link-name}
```

where *link-name* is a string argument specifying the name of the link. It must be the same name used in the {LINK-CREATE} command.

Note: {LINK-REMOVE} does not delete links. Use {LINK-DELETE} to delete links.

Suppose you have used the following commands to create a link named LINK99 and to assign the destination range B10..B20 to the link:

```
{LINK-CREATE "link99","winword","C:\NEWS.DOC","DDE_LINK"}
{LINK-ASSIGN B10..B20}
```

To detach the range from the link, you would use this command:

```
{LINK-REMOVE "link99"}
```

If you then use the Edit Link Options command to check the status of this link, you'll see that the link is still active but that it has no range assigned to it.

The {LINK-TABLE} Command

The {LINK-TABLE} command places a table of DDE link information in the current worksheet. The syntax of the command is

```
{LINK-TABLE location}
```

where *location* is the first cell of the range where the table is to be placed.

Note: 1-2-3 for Windows overwrites any existing data when it creates the table.

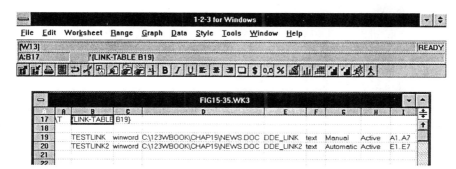

Figure 15-34 The results of the {LINK-TABLE} command

Figure 15-34 shows a sample table created with the {LINK-TABLE} command. Notice that for each link, the table includes the link name, application, topic, item, format, update mode, link status, and destination range.

Conversation-Level DDE Link Commands

When you want the maximum control over a DDE link, you use 1-2-3 for Windows conversation-level macro commands. These commands let you get as close to directly controlling the Windows messaging system as any commands in 1-2-3.

This section begins with an explanation of each of 1-2-3's conversation-level commands (you'll probably want to skim this section the first time through). Next, the three types of DDE conversations—cold link, hot link, and warm link—are described. At the end of this section are two examples that show how to carry out DDE conversations with macros.

As you read this section, keep in mind that 1-2-3 is the client and the other Windows application it is interacting with is the server.

The {DDE-OPEN} Command

{DDE-OPEN} starts a conversation with another Windows application and, optionally, enters the unique integer Windows assigns to the conversation in a specified location. The syntax of this command is

```
{DDE-OPEN app-name,topic-name,[location]}
```

where

- *app-name* is a string argument identifying the name of an open Windows application that supports DDE.

- *topic-name* is a string argument specifying the name of the application file to link to.

- *location* is an optional argument that specifies a cell address or range reference. This is where 1-2-3 enters the unique integer that Windows assigns to the conversation. If you use a range reference, 1-2-3 places the number in the first cell of the range.

Before you can use {DDE-OPEN} to start a DDE conversation with another Windows application, that application must already be active. You can start an application either from Program Manager or with 1-2-3's {LAUNCH} command.

As you know, it is possible to carry on more than one DDE conversation at a time, in which case you may need to use more than one {DDE-OPEN} command in your macro. When using more than one {DDE-OPEN} in a macro, be sure to use the optional *location* argument. Then, to make a particular conversation current, use {DDE-USE *conversation-number*} and specify the appropriate *location* as the *conversation-number* argument.

If a conversation is successfully initiated, macro control transfers to the cell below the {DDE-OPEN} command; all instructions following {DDE-OPEN} in the same cell are ignored. If a conversation could not be initiated, the next command in the same cell as {DDE-OPEN} is executed.

The {DDE-REQUEST} Command

The {DDE-REQUEST} command requests data from the server application. The syntax of the command is

```
{DDE-REQUEST range,item-name,[format]}
```

where

- *range* is a cell or range reference that identifies where 1-2-3 is to place the incoming data.

- *item-name* is a string argument identifying the item in the application file whose data you want.

- *format* is an optional string argument designating the Clipboard format—for example, text or bitmap. (See Table 15-6 for a list of Clipboard formats.) If you omit *format*, 1-2-3 uses the text Clipboard format.

Note: {DDE-REQUEST} will fail if a conversation is not already open.

If the data is successfully transferred, macro control will transfer to the cell below the {DDE-REQUEST} command; all instructions following {DDE-REQUEST} in the same cell will be ignored. If the data could not be transferred—for example, you specified an incorrect *item-name*—the next command in the same cell as {DDE-REQUEST} will be executed.

The {DDE-POKE} Command

{DDE-POKE} sends a range of data to the server application. The syntax of the command is

```
{DDE-POKE range,item-name,[format]}
```

where

- *range* is a cell or range reference identifying the data you want to send to the server application.

- *item-name* is a string argument identifying the item in the application file to which you want the data sent.

- *format* is an optional string argument designating the Clipboard format—for example, text or bitmap. (See Table 15-6 for a list of Clipboard formats.) If you omit *format*, 1-2-3 will use the text Clipboard format.

Some applications that can act as servers do not support {DDE-POKE}. Most major applications do support this function, however.

The {DDE-EXECUTE} Command

{DDE-EXECUTE} lets you send a command to an application. The syntax of the command is

```
{DDE-EXECUTE execute-string}
```

where *execute-string* is a string argument that represents any command from the application, usually in that application's command (or macro) language. For example, to send a command to Word for Windows, you must use WordBASIC.

If *execute-string* is successfully transferred to the server, macro control shifts to the cell below the {DDE-EXECUTE} command; all instructions following {DDE-EXECUTE} in the same cell are ignored. If the command could not be transferred—for example, the server was busy—the next command in the same cell as {DDE-EXECUTE} is executed.

The {DDE-ADVISE} Command

The {DDE-ADVISE} command lets you specify a location to branch to when data in the server application changes. The syntax of this command is

```
{DDE-ADVISE branch-location,item-name,[format]}
```

where

- *branch-location* is a cell or range reference identifying the macro instructions (usually a subroutine) to which you want to branch.

- *item-name* is a string argument identifying the item in the server application's file whose change will initiate the branch to *branch-location*.

- *format* is an optional string argument designating the Clipboard format—for example, text or bitmap. (See Table 15-6 for a list of Clipboard formats.) If you omit *format*, 1-2-3 will use the text Clipboard format.

Like the {ONERROR} command, {DDE-ADVISE} does not branch immediately. Instead, the branch only takes place when the data specified by *item-name* changes in the server application.

The {DDE-ADVISE} command remains in effect until 1-2-3 encounters a {DDE-UNADVISE} command or the macro ends.

If {DDE-ADVISE} was successfully processed, macro control will shift to the cell below the {DDE-ADVISE} command; all instructions following {DDE-ADVISE} in the same cell are ignored. If the command could not be transferred—for example, the server was busy—the next command in the same cell as {DDE-ADVISE} will be executed.

The {DDE-UNADVISE} Command

The {DDE-UNADVISE} command ends a {DDE-ADVISE} command. The syntax of the command is

```
{DDE-UNADVISE item-name, [format]}
```

where

- *item-name* is a string argument identifying the item in the server application's file whose change would initiate the branch set up by the {DDE-ADVISE} command.

- *format* is an optional string argument designating the Clipboard format—for example, text or bitmap. (See Table 15-6 for a list of Clipboard formats.) If you omit *format*, 1-2-3 will use the text Clipboard format.

Note: The *format* argument is only needed for {DDE-ADVISE} when the original {DDE-ADVISE} command used a *format* argument.

The {DDE-USE} Command

The {DDE-USE} command makes the specified conversation number the current conversation. The syntax of the command is

```
{DDE-USE conversation-number}
```

where *conversation-number* is the unique integer Windows has previously assigned to the conversation. Most often, *conversation-number* refers to the same cell as the {DDE-OPEN} command's *location* argument—this is where 1-2-3 enters the unique integer in the spreadsheet. {DDE-USE} is only used on the rare occasion when you are carrying on more than one DDE conversation in a macro.

The {DDE-CLOSE} Command

The {DDE-CLOSE} command ends the current conversation with a Windows application. The syntax of the command is

```
{DDE-CLOSE}
```

This command is typically used to end the current conversation before your macro completes its work.

Types of Conversations

As discussed in Chapter 17, there are three types of DDE conversations: cold link, hot link, and warm link. The following sections describe how to use 1-2-3's macro commands to set up each type of link and how information flows between 1-2-3 and the server application.

The Cold Link

To carry out a cold link conversation in your macro, start it with a {DDE-OPEN} command. This command causes 1-2-3 (the client) to broadcast the application and topic it needs. A server application that can respond to the topic sends an acknowledgement back to 1-2-3, and the conversation begins.

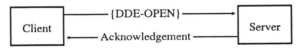

Your macro must then request the data item that it wants using the {DDE-REQUEST} command. If the server can provide the data item, it will do so.

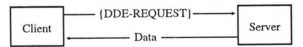

After receiving the data item, your macro terminates the conversation with the {DDE-CLOSE} command. The server application sends back a message of acknowledgement.

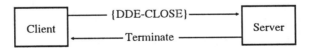

The Hot Link

A cold link is fine if you want to retrieve the data from the server only one time. This type of link will not do, however, when you want the data in the spreadsheet to always reflect the very latest data from the server. For that type of link, the data in the spreadsheet must be updated whenever the data in the server changes. The hot link provides this kind of support.

Actually, a hot link is the easiest of all to implement in a macro. Again, your macro must begin with a {DDE-OPEN} command.

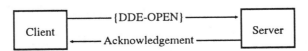

The only other command needed to establish the link is {EDIT-PASTE-LINK}. As you learned previously, {EDIT-PASTE-LINK} copies data from the Clipboard to the active worksheet file. In the process, a DDE link is created between the active worksheet file and the file named in the Clipboard.

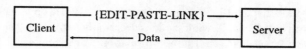

Now, whenever the relevant data item in the server changes, the worksheet file is automatically updated for the change.

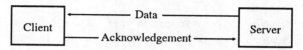

The Warm Link

In terms of 1-2-3 macro commands, the warm link more closely resembles the cold link than the hot link. It begins in the typical fashion.

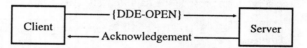

Your macro then indicates the data item it requires using the {DDE-ADVISE} command.

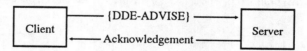

At this point, it's the server application's job to notify 1-2-3 whenever the data item changes.

When that notification comes, macro control transfers to the *branch-location* (usually a subroutine) specified by {DDE-ADVISE}. Here your macro must request the data item using the {DDE-REQUEST} command.

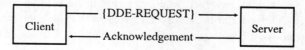

If you no longer want 1-2-3 to be advised of changes in the data item, you can use a {DDE-UNADVISE} command.

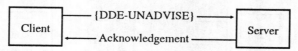

You can also end the conversation with the server at any time with {DDE-CLOSE}.

▼ *Tip:*   These links are not mutually exclusive. For example, a hot link can incorporate a {DDE-ADVISE} command to have macro control branch to a certain location when the data item changes.

An Example

One of the most frequent mistakes in spreadsheets is the misspelling of column headings and other descriptive labels. If 1-2-3 for Windows had a spelling checker, this could easily be avoided.

Although a spelling checker is not part of 1-2-3 for Windows, you can use DDE to "borrow" one from another Windows application. For example, Figure 15-35 shows a macro that uses Word for Windows' Version 2.0 spelling checker to check the contents of the current worksheet cell. When the cell contains a misspelling, a dialog box like the one in Figure 15-36 appears.

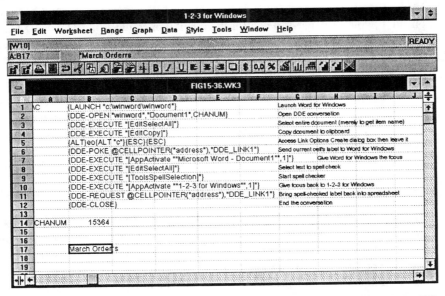

Figure 15-35 A macro that spell checks the current cell using Word for Windows spell checker

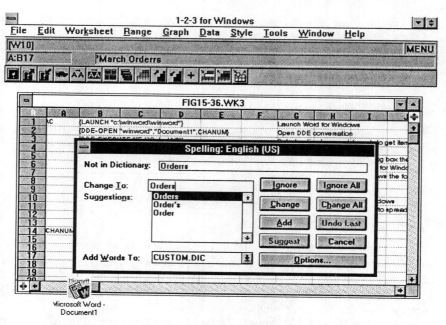

Microsoft Word -
Document1

Figure 15-36 Word's spell-checker dialog box

The model for this macro is the cold-link model shown earlier. As you can see, there are many other instructions threaded between the cold link's standard set. In fact, whenever you use 1-2-3's conversation-level commands to interact with another Windows application, you often need to control the other application using {DDE-EXECUTE} commands. What's more, if you want to do anything significant with that application, you typically have to use its own native macro language. For example, when controlling Word for Windows, you must use WordBASIC commands.

▼ *Tip:*   The WordBASIC command language is covered in a summary fashion in the TECHREF.DOC file that comes with Word for Windows. This file is an abridged version of a book entitled *Microsoft Word for Windows Technical Reference*, published by Microsoft Press (ISBN 1-55615-2906).

Another important point to note is that the WordBASIC instructions are enclosed in square brackets. If you omit the brackets, Word will treat the instructions as plain text and inserts them into the current document. You'll also need to use square brackets whenever you pass macro commands to other Windows applications (for example, Microsoft Excel), or even when passing macro instructions back to 1-2-3 for Windows.

The main strategy of this example macro is to launch Word for Windows and then use DDE to copy the current cell's contents to it. Next, Word's spelling checker is used to check the entire document, which in this case only includes the copied cell contents. When the spell checking is complete, the cell contents are copied back to 1-2-3 for Windows, and the conversation ends.

Here are some pointers that should help you decipher the macro instructions in Figure 15-35:

- Due to a quirk in 1-2-3 for Windows, the macro must access the Edit Link Options Create command before 1-2-3 will activate the link. That's the purpose of the fifth line in the macro. Without this line, the macro does not work consistently.

- Word for Windows automatically assigns the name "DDE_LINK1" to the first data item.

- 1-2-3 for Windows requires that the *execute-string* for {DDE-EXECUTE} be enclosed in double quotes. In this example, Word's AppActive command, which takes the form AppActivate *"window_title_text",immediate*, also requires double quotes. For Word to receive text enclosed in quotes, you must use two sets of double quotes, as in

```
{DDE-EXECUTE "[AppActivate ""Microsoft Word - Document1"", 1]"}
```

CONTROLLING EXTERNAL DATABASE TRANSACTIONS

1-2-3 for Windows has two commands for controlling external database transactions: {COMMIT} and {ROLLBACK}. These commands work only with the SQL Server DataLens driver and are the equivalent of SQL's classic COMMIT and ROLLBACK commands. That is, the {COMMIT} command commits all pending database transactions, and {ROLLBACK} cancels them. Because these commands are not used by the vast majority of 1-2-3 for Windows users, we will not discuss them further.

READING AND WRITING ASCII FILES

As you know, you can use File Import From to read ASCII files from disk into the current worksheet file and File Extract To to write a range from the current worksheet file to an ASCII file on disk. These commands are often used to read and write large chunks of data to and from disk.

Suppose you want to work with smaller segments of an ASCII file. For example, consider the case where you want to read specific lines from an ASCII file rather than the entire file. Alternatively, suppose you want to append information to the end of an existing file, without overwriting the rest of the file.

1-2-3 for Windows has several little-used though powerful commands for working with ASCII files—{OPEN}, {CLOSE}, {WRITE}, {WRITELN}, {READ}, {READLN}, {SETPOS}, {GETPOS}, and {FILESIZE}. The {OPEN} command allows you to open or create an ASCII file. Once the file is open, you can use {WRITE} or {WRITELN} to write information from your 1-2-3 worksheet file to the ASCII file. Conversely, you can use {READ} or {READLN} to read information from the ASCII text file into your worksheet file. Once you've finished working with the ASCII file, you can use {CLOSE} to close it.

To read or write information starting at a specific position in an ASCII file, you can use {SETPOS}. This command allows you to set the position of the file pointer within an ASCII text file before reading from or writing to that file. The {GETPOS} and {FILESIZE} commands complement {SETPOS}. {GETPOS} allows you to determine the current position of the file pointer, and the {FILESIZE} command allows you to determine the number of bytes (size) in the file.

The sections that follow explain the use of each of these commands in more detail. Two examples are then shown. The first shows you how to write data to an ASCII text file, and the second shows you how to read specific data from that file.

Opening a File

Before you can manipulate any data in an ASCII file, you must first open the file with {OPEN}. You can use this command to open either an existing ASCII file or to create an entirely new ASCII file. The syntax of the {OPEN} command is

```
{OPEN filename,access-type}
```

where filename is the name of the ASCII file, including its path and extension, that you want to open or create. You can provide a filename, or you can use a range address or range name that contains the full filename. If the file is located outside the current directory, be sure to include path information, for example, "C:\ACCOUNTS\CLIENTS.PRN".

The *access-type* argument is a letter that represents one of four modes for accessing a file. The access mode you use depends on what you want to do with the file. 1-2-3 offers the following four access modes for the {OPEN} command:

- W (write): Creates a new file using the name you specify and places the file pointer at the beginning of that file. If a file with the same name already exists, 1-2-3 will overwrite it and all of the file contents will be lost. With this option you can both write to and read from the file that is created.

- M (modify): Opens an existing file and positions the file pointer at the beginning of the file. With this option you can both read from and write to the opened file. Unlike the W (write) option, the M (modify) option can only be used to open an existing ASCII file, not to create a new one.

- R (read): Opens an existing ASCII file and places the file pointer at the beginning of that file. The file is read-only.

- A (append): Opens an existing ASCII file and places the file pointer at the end of the file. The file is write-only. Use this option when you want to add information to the end of an existing ASCII file.

Only one ASCII file can be open at a time. If 1-2-3 detects an open ASCII file when the {OPEN} command is encountered, it will close the first text file before opening the second one.

If 1-2-3 is successful in opening the specified text file, it then passes macro control to the next cell of the macro. If the {OPEN} command fails to open the file, 1-2-3 will process the instructions in the same cell as the {OPEN} command.

Closing a File

Once you open an ASCII file, it remains open until you close it in one of three ways. The first way is to use the {CLOSE} command to explicitly close the file. The second way is to include a second {OPEN} command in your macro. As mentioned, if an ASCII file is already open when 1-2-3 encounters an {OPEN) command, it will close the first file before opening the second. The third method of closing a file is to use File Exit to leave 1-2-3 for Windows. If an ASCII file is open, 1-2-3 will close it automatically before shutting down.

Because only one ASCII file can be open at a time, {CLOSE} requires no arguments. Nevertheless, using an argument with {CLOSE} does not produce an error message. In fact, you may find that using a filename argument with {CLOSE} is helpful for documenting your macros. For example, {CLOSE"CLIENTS.PRN"} has the same effect as {CLOSE} (both simply close the currently open ASCII text file), but the former is more descriptive.

1-2-3 for Windows will not execute any instructions that follow the {CLOSE} command in the same cell. Therefore, always use the {CLOSE} command on its own separate line.

In general, it's a good practice to explicitly close text files when you are finished using them. If you do not close a file, it will be closed for you automatically when you leave 1-2-3.

Writing to a File

When you open an ASCII text file with either the W (write), M (modify), or A (append) option, you can write information from your worksheet file directly to that file. 1-2-3 for Windows offers two commands that you can use to write to a file—{WRITE} and {WRITELN}.

The {WRITE} Command

The {WRITE} command allows you to begin writing to the currently open ASCII file starting at the location of the file pointer. The syntax of the command is

```
{WRITE string}
```

where *string* is a literal string, a string formula, or a reference to a cell that contains a label or string formula. You cannot use numbers or formulas that evaluate to numbers. After 1-2-3 finishes writing to the file, the file pointer is advanced one character beyond the last character written.

Note: {WRITE} only works if a text file is opened with the W (write), A (append), or M (modify) option of the {OPEN} command. The R (Read) option does not allow write access.

 Tip: To use {WRITE} or {WRITELN} to write a number (or the results of a numeric formula) to a text file, you can use the @STRING function to convert the number to a string. Here's a typical command:

```
{WRITE @STRING(SALES,2)}
```

1-2-3 evaluates the @STRING function, then writes the results to the open ASCII file.

When one {WRITE} command follows another, the second command picks up where the first one left off. For example, to write the character string NonprofitCorporation to an open text file, you can use the following macro:

```
{WRITE "Nonprofit"}
{WRITE "Corporation"}
```

The {WRITELN} Command

{WRITELN} performs the same function as {WRITE}, with one exception. It automatically adds a carriage return/line feed to the end of each line of text. Otherwise, the syntax and usage for the command is identical.

Reading from a File

1-2-3 for Windows offers two commands for reading from an ASCII text file, {READ} and {READLN}. Both commands allow you to read a string of up to 512 characters and store it in a cell of your choosing as a left-aligned label. To read from a file with either command, you must open the file with either the W (write), M (modify), or R (read) option.

The {READ} Command

The {READ} command allows you to copy a specified number of characters from an open ASCII text file to a 1-2-3 worksheet cell. The read operation begins at the current location of the file pointer. The syntax of the command is

```
{READ count,location}
```

where *count* represents the number of characters you want to read and *location* is the cell in which you want the characters stored. 1-2-3 starts reading at the current file-pointer position. When the {READ} command is completed, the file pointer is advanced one character beyond the last character read.

The *count* argument must be a number between 0 and 512. You can also use a formula, function, or a reference to a cell that contains one of these. The *location* argument can be either a cell address or a range name. If you use a range name that contains multiple cells, only the upper-left corner cell is used.

The {READ} command is most useful when you are reading from an ASCII file with entries of equal length. If the length of each line varies, you may want to use {READLN} instead.

The {READLN} Command

{READLN} is similar to {READ}, except that instead of reading a specified number of characters from an ASCII file, {READLN} reads characters until a carriage return/line feed combination is encountered. The syntax of the command is

```
{READLN location}
```

where *location* is a cell or range reference identifying where the characters are to be copied. The file pointer is then advanced to the beginning of the next line in the file. If 512 characters are read before a carriage return/line feed is encountered, however, the read operation will be cut off.

The {READLN} command can be of enormous benefit when the lines of text in an ASCII file are of variable length. Unlike the {READ} command, which requires that you provide a specific number of characters to be read, the {READLN} command allows you to use the end of the current line as the determining factor in reading characters from an ASCII file.

Moving the File Pointer

When you use the W (write), M (modify), or R (read) option with the {OPEN} command to open an ASCII file, the file pointer will automatically be positioned at the beginning of the newly opened file. On the other hand, when you use the A (append) option with {OPEN}, the file pointer is positioned at the end of the file. After reading data from or writing data to an ASCII file, the file pointer is positioned one character beyond where you finished reading or writing.

To read data from or write data to a location in the middle of an ASCII file, you must reposition the file pointer at that location. To do this, use the {SETPOS} command. To augment this command, 1-2-3 offers {GETPOS} and {FILESIZE}. {GETPOS} tells you the current position of the file pointer, and {FILESIZE} tells you the overall size of the ASCII file in bytes.

The {SETPOS} Command

The {SETPOS} command lets you position the file pointer in preparation for reading or writing to an ASCII file. The syntax of the command is

```
{SETPOS offset-number}
```

where *offset-number* is the offset within the file. (The first character in the file is located at offset 0, the second at offset 1, the third at offset 2, and so on.) The *offset-number* argument can be a number, a numeric formula, a function, or a reference to a cell that contains one of these. If you specify an offset that exceeds the offset of the last byte in the file, 1-2-3 will position the file pointer one character beyond the last character in the file. Once {SETPOS} is successfully executed, 1-2-3 passes control to the next line of the macro. Instructions following {SETPOS} in the same cell are not executed.

As you might imagine, you must use {OPEN} to open an ASCII text file before you use {SETPOS} to position within it. If the text file is not open, 1-2-3 will ignore the {SETPOS} command and continue to process the next instruction in the same cell as {SETPOS}.

The {GETPOS} Command

Use the {GETPOS} command to determine the current position of the file pointer in an open ASCII text file. The syntax of the command is

```
{GETPOS location}
```

where *location* is a cell address or range name. To this cell address or range name, 1-2-3 copies a number that represents the position of the file pointer within the currently open file, where 0 is the first position (character) in the file, 1 is the second position, 2 is the third position, and so on.

The {FILESIZE} Command

The {FILESIZE} command returns the total number of bytes in the currently open ASCII file. The syntax of the command is

```
{FILESIZE location)
```

where *location* is a range address or range name in the worksheet file in which the total byte count of the currently open ASCII will be stored.

Command Processing

If 1-2-3 is successful in executing an {OPEN}, {WRITE}, {WRITELN}, {READ}, {READLN}, {SETPOS}, {GETPOS}, or {FILESIZE} command, it will pass control to the next cell of the macro. If the command is *not* successful, 1-2-3 will process the instructions in the same cell that follows the command.

Examples

Figure 15-37 shows a simple macro that writes long labels in the range A1..A4 to the PAYROLL.PRN text file. Each label in the range is 29 characters long (a factor that will only become important when you later read from the PAYROLL.PRN file) and is assigned a Courier font for easy measurement.

The macro begins in cell B6 by positioning the cell pointer to cell A:A1. Next, the command

```
{OPEN "PAYROLL.PRN",w}{BRANCH OPEN_ERR}
```

opens the PAYROLL.PRN text file using the W (write) option. Therefore, each time the macro is used, the PAYROLL.PRN file is overwritten. The {BRANCH OPEN_ERR} command is also included for error handling, just in case the {OPEN} command is not successful in opening the file.

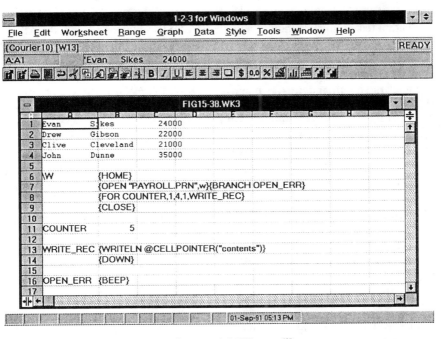

Figure 15-37 A macro that writes an ASCII text file

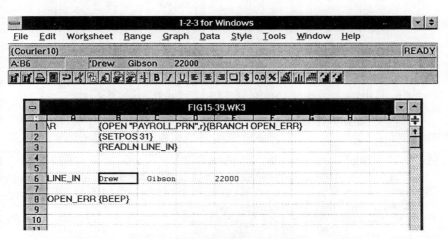

Figure 15-38 Using {SETPOS} to write to an ASCII file

Next, the {FOR} command in cell B8 executes the WRITE_REC subroutine four times. WRITE_REC starts in cell B13 and uses {WRITELN} to write data from the worksheet file to the open ASCII file. The *string* argument for {WRITELN} is @CELLPOINTER("contents"), which causes 1-2-3 to write the contents of the current cell to the open ASCII file. The next command in the subroutine, {DOWN}, moves the cell pointer down one cell each time the subroutine is executed. Finally, after the subroutine has executed four times, control returns to the cell following the {FOR} command, cell B9, in the calling program. There, the {CLOSE} command closes the ASCII file.

The next example, shown in Figure 15-38, reads data from the PAYROLL.PRN file created in the previous example. This macro includes the {SETPOS} command, which lets you position the file pointer in an ASCII text file before reading or writing data.

The first command in the macro {OPEN "PAYROLL.PRN", r} opens PAYROLL.PRN as read-only. In the next line, {SETPOS 31} sets the file pointer to character 32 in the PAYROLL.PRN file. (Recall from earlier that the first character in a file is at offset 0, the second at offset 1, and so on. Thus, an *offset-number* argument of 31 for {SETPOS} actually means character 32 in the file.) Also, note that in Figure 15-38 the length of each record written to PAYROLL.PRN is 31 characters (29 characters for each label plus a carriage return followed by a linefeed). Therefore, you can control the current line position within the file by using {SETPOS} to specify the file pointer position in 31-character increments. By specifying an offset value of 31, the file pointer is moved to the beginning of the second line in the PAYROLL.PRN file.

Once the PAYROLL.PRN file is opened, and the file pointer properly positioned, the {READLN} command reads data from the PAYROLL.PRN file and stores the data in LINE_IN (cell B6). As you can see, the label

```
'Drew       Gibson         22000
```

resides in the cell already. This label has been read from the second line of the PAYROLL.PRN file and copied to the worksheet.

USING FORMULAS IN MACRO COMMANDS

As in most recent releases of 1-2-3, Lotus has increased the power of 1-2-3 for Windows' macro language by allowing you to use @functions and formulas as arguments in macro commands. For example, rather than using a range address or range name as the *location* argument for the {BLANK} command, such as {BLANK A:C10}, you can include an @function, as follows:

```
{BLANK @CELLPOINTER("coord")}
```

The formula @CELLPOINTER("coord") returns the full address (worksheet letter, column letter, and row number) of the current cell, and provides the *location* argument needed for the {BLANK} command.

You can also substitute other types of formulas for string and numeric arguments, as long as each formula evaluates to the proper data type needed by the command. For example, suppose you want to prompt the user for his or her name using the {GETLABEL} command. You then want to incorporate the name, converted to proper case, in the prompt for a second {GETLABEL} command. You might use the following commands:

```
{GETLABEL "Please enter your name:",A4}
{GETLABEL +"Hello, "&@PROPER(A4)&". Please enter your SS#: ",A5}
```

If the user types the name BURT in response to the first {GETLABEL} prompt, the second prompt for the social security number looks like Figure 15-39.

As the first line of the macro shows, the {GETLABEL} command requires a string for its prompt argument. The prompt argument you've supplied in the second {GETLABEL} command is a formula that evaluates to a string.

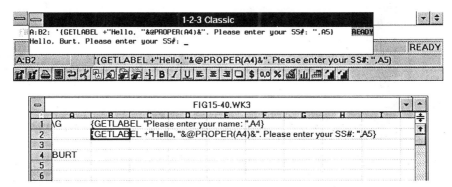

Figure 15-39   Using a formula to build the prompt for the {GETLABEL} command

SELF-MODIFYING MACROS

As you become more expert in programming macros, you will find yourself searching for ways to make your macros more flexible—that is, to have them work under a variety of circumstances. One of the most popular ways to increase the flexibility of macros is to make them self-modifying.

A *self-modifying macro* is one whose instructions change as certain conditions in the work area or in a worksheet file change. For example, suppose you want to create a macro that determines the number of open worksheet files, and if that number is 1, maximizes the current window within the work area. If the number of files is 2 or greater, you will want the macro to tile the windows on the desktop. You can place the following formula in a cell in your macro:

```
@IF(@INFO("numfile")>1,"{ALT}wt","{WINDOW-STATE ""maximize""}")
```

@INFO("numfile") returns the current number of open files. If that number is greater than 1, the formula evaluates to

```
{ALT}wt
```

causing the macro to issue the Window Tile command. If the current number of open files is less than or equal to 1, however, the formula evaluates to

```
{WINDOW-STATE "maximize"}
```

which maximizes the current window.

Or, for instance, suppose you want to create a macro that updates a summary section of a worksheet by copying the values from a column of monthly sales. Rather than tell 1-2-3 which month to update, you would prefer to let your macro select which month, based on the current date. You can use the following string formula in your macro:

```
+"{ALT}eqMONTH"&@STRING(@MONTH(@TODAY),0)&"{TAB}SUMMARY~"
```

@MONTH(TODAY) determines the number of the current month from the current date and inserts it into the macro, combining it with the other macro instructions. For example, if the current month is March, the resulting macro commands will look like this:

```
{ALT}eqMONTH3{TAB}SUMMARY~
```

These instructions cause the macro to copy the sales data from the range named MONTH3 to the summary section.

16

Networking

The Standard (single-user) Edition of 1-2-3 for Windows is not directly networkable. That is, you cannot share a single copy of the product among multiple users on a network. However, the Standard Edition of 1-2-3 for Windows does include commands and features that allow you to run it from a workstation and effectively manage data files that are stored in shared directories on the network. A built-in file reservation and file-locking system virtually eliminates the possibility of two users overwriting each other's data. Further, 1-2-3 for Windows's File Administration command provides facilities that allow you to protect, manage, and get information about 1-2-3 for Windows data files that are stored on shared network directories.

To share a single copy of 1-2-3 for Windows across a network, you must purchase the Server Edition of 1-2-3 for Windows. In addition, you must purchase the appropriate number of Node Editions (licenses) required to adequately service the users on your network. The Server and Node Editions of 1-2-3 for Windows are discussed only briefly in this chapter.

FILE-SHARING FUNDAMENTALS

One of the main concerns users have when operating in a network environment is file security. In an environment where two or more users have access to the same data files, there must be a mechanism that prevents those users from destroying each other's work. For example, imagine that you load a worksheet file into 1-2-3 for Windows and begin adding data to that file. At the same time, another user opens that same file and begins making changes. At this point, both users are working at cross purposes. If you save your copy of the file first, your changes will be overwritten when the other user saves his or her copy of the file.

Some of the responsibility for file sharing falls on your network software and your network administrator. Most network software packages allow your network administrator to assign special file-access privileges to specified directories and/or users on the network. For example, a given directory may have read/write/create privileges. That is, you can read an existing file from this directory and write the changes you make back to the original file, and you can also create new files in the directory. Some directories may not have all of these privileges. For example, a directory might be read-only. That is, you can view the files it contains but you cannot change them or add new ones. In addition, not all users may have access to full privileges. For example, selected users may have read-only access to a given directory—that is, they can view the contents of the files in the directory, but they are denied write and create privileges.

Some of the responsibility for file sharing also falls on your applications software. In a read/write/create/deny-none environment where multiple users have full access privileges to shared files, your applications software must have a way of protecting the integrity of existing files. That is, you don't want two users working on the same file at the same time and overwriting each other's work. Instead, you want only one user at a time to have access to a given file. However, as soon as that user is finished with that file, it must be immediately available to other users. Many network applications do offer such a protection system, but it can be somewhat difficult to understand and use.

HOW 1-2-3 FOR WINDOWS HANDLES FILE SHARING

Unlike some network applications, 1-2-3 for Windows's file-sharing system is relatively straightforward. A built-in reservation system allows only one user at a time to make changes to a given worksheet file. Generally speaking, when you load a worksheet file into memory, you get the *reservation* for that file. This reservation is your guarantee that you can make changes to the file and save it under the same name.

Until you release the reservation, other users cannot make changes to the file and save it under the same name. They can load the file, view it, and even print its contents, but they cannot modify it and save it under the same name. When you release the reservation for the file, however, other users can immediately load that file and get its reservation. They can then add their changes to yours.

AN EXAMPLE NETWORK SESSION

Unless you specify otherwise, you get the reservation for a file automatically when you load the file into memory—unless, of course, someone else is already using the file. For example, suppose you use the File Open command to load a worksheet file from a shared network directory and that no one else is using that file. Under these circumstances, the file is opened on 1-2-3's desktop, and you have the reservation for that file. This means that you can modify the file and save it to disk under the same name.

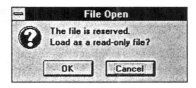

Figure 16-1 1-2-3 prompts you to load a file as read-only when its reservation is not available

Now suppose someone else on the network—say Norm from Marketing—tries to open that same file while you are using it. When Norm attempts to open the file, 1-2-3 for Windows displays the message box in Figure 16-1 on his screen, indicating someone else already has the reservation for the file. Norm's only options at this point are to select OK or Cancel. If Norm selects OK, 1-2-3 allows him to load the file without a reservation as a read-only file. That is, he can look at the file and change its contents, but he cannot save it under the same name. On the other hand, if Norm selects the Cancel button, 1-2-3 will cancel the file-load operation and return to READY mode.

Suppose that Norm elects to open the file anyway, as read-only. To indicate that the file is read-only to Norm, 1-2-3 for Windows displays an RO indicator in the status line at the bottom of 1-2-3's window, as shown in Figure 16-2.

If Norm attempts to use the File Save command to save the file under the same name, the error message box in Figure 16-3 will appear on his screen. His only option is to select

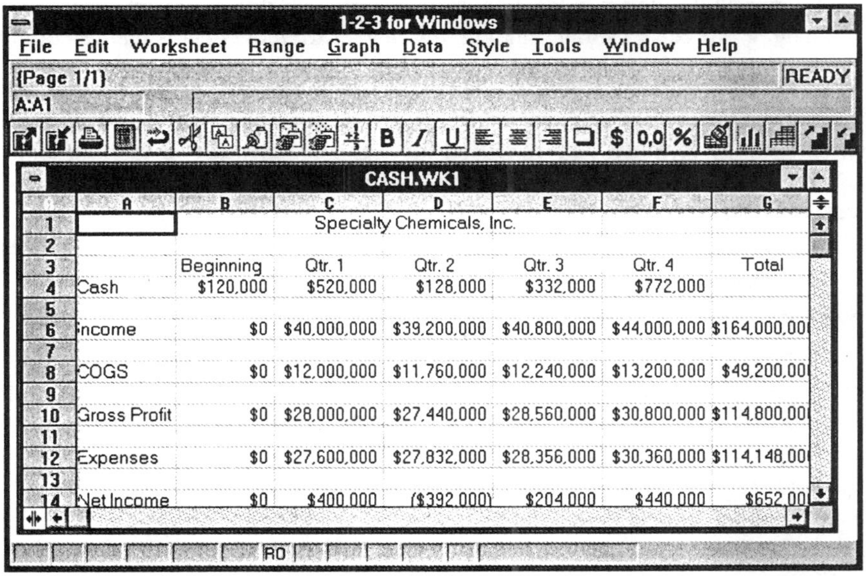

	1-2-3 for Windows								

File   Edit   Worksheet   Range   Graph   Data   Style   Tools   Window   Help

{Page 1/1}   READY

A:A1

		CASH.WK1					
	A	B	C	D	E	F	G
1			Specialty Chemicals, Inc.				
2							
3		Beginning	Qtr. 1	Qtr. 2	Qtr. 3	Qtr. 4	Total
4	Cash	$120,000	$520,000	$128,000	$332,000	$772,000	
5							
6	Income	$0	$40,000,000	$39,200,000	$40,800,000	$44,000,000	$164,000,00
7							
8	COGS	$0	$12,000,000	$11,760,000	$12,240,000	$13,200,000	$49,200,00
9							
10	Gross Profit	$0	$28,000,000	$27,440,000	$28,560,000	$30,800,000	$114,800,00
11							
12	Expenses	$0	$27,600,000	$27,832,000	$28,356,000	$30,360,000	$114,148,00
13							
14	Net Income	$0	$400,000	($392,000)	$204,000	$440,000	$652,00

RO

Figure 16-2 1-2-3 displays an RO (read-only) indicator in the status line indicating a file is read-only

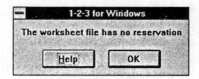

Figure 16-3   1-2-3 won't let you save a file under the same name if you don't have its reservation

the OK button from this message box to return to the current worksheet file in READY mode.

Now suppose you are finished viewing the file. Without saving your changes, you select the File Close command to remove the file from your desktop. This operation in effect clears the original file from your computer's memory. When you clear a file from memory, the reservation for that file is automatically released. Norm can now load that file into his computer's memory and automatically get the reservation for it. Because he has the reservation for the file, the RO indicator is not displayed in the status line at the bottom of his screen. Norm can now make his changes to the file and save it under the same name.

The foregoing is but one of many possible file-sharing scenarios that might be encountered on a network. It should give you a feel for how 1-2-3's file-reservation scheme works in its default state. You can, however, change the default—that is, you can change the reservation setting. Instead of a user getting the reservation for a file automatically, you can force him or her to explicitly get the reservation for a file each time the file is used. To do this, you use the File Administration Network Reserve command. See "Managing File Reservations" later in this chapter for more details on this command.

Note: The File Administration command also allows you to protect selected settings in a file and to get information about files that are either open in memory or linked to the current file by formula. You may find these two features useful both on and off the network. See "File Security" and "Getting Information about Files" later in this chapter for more information on these two topics.

SHARING 1-2-3'S DATA FILES

If you are planning to use 1-2-3 for Windows on a network, it may help you to know a little about the Lotus network strategy for 1-2-3 for Windows. Like Releases 2.x and 3.x, 1-2-3 for Windows comes in three different editions: Standard Edition, Server Edition, and Node Edition. The role of each of these editions is as follows:

- The Standard Edition of 1-2-3 for Windows is a single-user version, and is the edition that most users own. You cannot share this product across multiple workstations. However, the file-reservation and file-locking features discussed in this chapter are built into the product. Therefore, you can run it from a workstation and successfully share worksheet files stored in network directories. Thus, the Standard Edition is a single-user, single-license product for standalone use.

- The Server Edition is the true "network" edition of 1-2-3 for Windows. This edition allows multiple users to share the same copy of 1-2-3 for Windows. Once again, the file-reservation and file-locking system is built into the product, allowing you to safely share worksheet files in common network directories. The Server edition comes with the 1-2-3 for Windows program disks, the appropriate documentation, and a *single-* user license for the network administrator. You must purchase a sufficient number of Node Editions (licenses) to cover the number of users you estimate will be concurrently using 1-2-3 for Windows at any given time.

- The Node Edition is essentially a license to add another 1-2-3 for Windows user to the network. The Node Edition comes with documentation only. In general, you should purchase a Node edition for each potential 1-2-3 for Windows user on your system. However, the key here is concurrent usage. For example, imagine you have 12 people on the network who could potentially use 1-2-3 for Windows. However, you estimate that 99% of the time only 10 of those users will be using 1-2-3 for Windows concurrently. Therefore, you should purchase only 10 Node Editions. If all 10 are in use, the eleventh person will be denied the use of 1-2-3 for Windows—just hope that eleventh user will not be your boss trying out the network for the first time.

MANAGING FILE RESERVATIONS

As demonstrated above, 1-2-3's built-in file-protection system prevents you from opening a file unless you have its reservation. Normally, 1-2-3 gives you the reservation for a file automatically when you open it, provided, of course that no one else on the network is currently using that file. Having the file's reservation is your guarantee that you, and only you, can save that file under the same name in the same directory. If someone else attempts to open the file while you are using it, 1-2-3 only allows them to open the file as read-only, meaning they can view the file, but they can't save it in the same directory under the same name.

Rather than relying on 1-2-3 for Windows's automatic file-reservation system, you can also control file reservations manually. To do this, use the File Administration Network Reserve command. This command allows you to get the reservation for a file that is currently read-only to you. It also allows you to release the reservation for a file so that someone else can use it. In addition, this command lets you specify a reservation setting for the current worksheet file. You can choose from automatic or manual. If the setting is automatic (the default), the user gets the reservation for a file automatically whenever it is opened on the desktop, provided, of course, that no one else is using the file. On the other hand, if the setting is manual, the user is forced to manually request the reservation each time the file is opened.

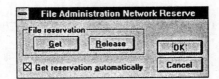

Figure 16-4 The File Administration Network Reserve dialog box

Getting and Releasing Reservations

When you select the File Administration Network Reserve command, 1-2-3 displays the dialog box in Figure 16-4. This dialog box contains two buttons, Get and Release. As you might imagine, the Get button is used to get the reservation for a file you currently have open as read-only. On the other hand, the Release button is used to release the reservation for a file so that someone else can use it.

When you select the Get button, 1-2-3 attempts to get the reservation for the current file (the file containing the cell pointer). Provided no one else is currently using the file or has saved the file since you opened it, 1-2-3 will give you its reservation. If someone has saved the file since you opened it, you must close your version of the file and load the new one.

For example, imagine that you use the File Open command to open a worksheet file that is currently in use by another workstation. The RO (read-only) indicator is now displayed on the status line at the bottom of 1-2-3's window. However, without saving the file, the current user releases the reservation for the file, thereby making it available to you. At that point, you can select the File Administration Network Reserve Get command and get the reservation for the file. 1-2-3 removes the RO indicator from the status line, indicating that you now have the reservation for the file. You can now make changes to the file and save it under the same name.

To release the reservation for a file, select the Release button from the File Administration Reserve dialog box. This releases the reservation for the file and causes the RO (read-only) indicator to appear in the status line at the bottom of 1-2-3's window. Use this option when you want to view a file but do not want to modify it and save the changes. That way, the reservation remains available for other users who *do* want to modify and save the file.

It bears mentioning again that you cannot get the reservation for a file if someone else has saved the file since you opened it. For example, imagine that you open a file and then use the File Administration Network Reserve Release command to release its reservation. Shortly thereafter, someone else loads the same file into memory, getting the reservation automatically. That user then modifies the file and saves it to disk. In the meantime, you discover a problem in the file and you decide to modify it and save the changes.

To get back the reservation for the file, you use the File Administration Network Reserve Get command. However, instead of giving you the reservation for the file, 1-2-3 displays the message box in Figure 16-5. (1-2-3 has detected that the file on disk has changed and will not allow you to get its reservation and possibly save your changes on

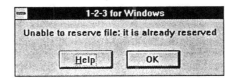

Figure 16-5 1-2-3 fails in its attempt to get the reservation for a file

top of those already made.) When you select OK to clear the error message, you are returned to the worksheet, and the RO indicator remains on your screen. If you still want to save your changes, you can do one of two things. First, you can save your copy of the file under a different filename. Or, you can clear your copy of the file from memory (File Close) and load the modified copy of the file from disk. You can then make your changes and save them under the same filename.

Changing the Reservation Setting

To change the reservation setting for the current file, you use the "Get reservation automatically" check box in the File Administration Network Reserve dialog box (Figure 16-4). By default, this box appears checked, meaning a user will automatically get the reservation for the current file upon opening it (provided the reservation is available). However, if you clear this check box, all network users—including you—will be forced to use the File Administration Network Reserve Get command to manually gain access to the file's reservation before it can be saved to disk under the same name.

To have 1-2-3 record the reservation setting you've made, select OK to close the File Administration Network Reserve dialog box and return to the worksheet. To save your new setting along with the rest of the settings for the current worksheet file, simply save the file to disk with the File Save command.

FILE SECURITY

The File Administration Seal File command allows you to protect (seal) a worksheet file from changes to selected settings. It also allows you to protect the current reservation setting for the file. The settings you protect are sealed with a password. To disable the seal, a user must know the password.

When you select the File Administration Seal File command, 1-2-3 for Windows displays the dialog box in Figure 16-6. As you can see, this dialog box contains three option buttons. The first option button, File and network reservation status, seals certain settings for the file as well as its current reservation status (automatic versus manual). The second button, Reservation status only, seals only the current reservation status for the file. Finally, the Disable all restrictions button lets you disable the seal for the file.

If you select either File and network reservation status or Reservation status only, 1-2-3 displays the dialog box in Figure 16-7 prompting you for a password that will be used to

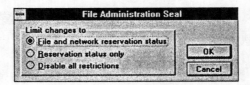

Figure 16-6   The File Administration Seal File dialog box

seal the file. At this point you can type the password of your choice. (As you type, 1-2-3 for Windows displays asterisks in place of the characters.) To verify the password, press TAB to move the Verify box and type the password again, exactly as you did the first time. To confirm the password, select OK. 1-2-3 seals the file with the password you specified.

Note: Passwords can be 15 characters in length and are case sensitive. Therefore, make sure you remember the exact sequence of upper and lower case letters you used. Otherwise, you will not be able to disable the seal for a file.

You can disable the seal for the current worksheet file by selecting the Disable all restrictions radio button from the File Administration Seal File dialog box. When you select OK to confirm this setting, 1-2-3 will prompt you for the password currently assigned to the file. Type the exact password you used to seal the file and select OK. 1-2-3 unseals the file.

Note: You can change the password for a sealed file if you'd like. To do so, first use the Disable all restrictions option to disable the seal for the file, then select the File Administration Seal File command again. Select from either File and network reservation status or Reservation status only and then select OK. When 1-2-3 prompts you for a password, type and verify the new password of your choice.

When you seal a file with the File and network reservation status option, the following commands are disabled—that is, 1-2-3 displays a "File is sealed" message when you select one of these commands:

- File Administration Network Reserve Get reservation automatically
- Graph Name Delete
- Graph New
- Range [Format, Protect, Unprotect]
- Range Name [Create, Delete, Label, Create]
- Style Alignment
- Worksheet [Column Width, Hide, Unhide]
- Worksheet Global Settings

Figure 16-7 1-2-3 prompts you for a password with which to seal the file

Note: You cannot seal a file and then save it in 1-2-3 Release 2 (.WK1) format. If you try, 1-2-3 for Windows will issue an error message when you attempt to save the file.

The File Administration Seal File command only seals settings for the current file. To protect the data in the file as well, you can use the Worksheet Global Protection Enable command. This command protects the worksheet from changes to existing data. To unprotect selected ranges for data entry, you can use the Range Unprotect command. Both these commands are discussed in Chapter 5.

In addition to protecting the data in the worksheet, you can save the file that contains that worksheet with a password. Unless a user knows the password, 1-2-3 for Windows will not allow him or her to open the file. (See Chapter 4 for details on how to save a file with a password.)

GETTING INFORMATION ABOUT FILES

The File Administration Paste Table command allows you to create a table of information about files that are either open on the desktop or linked by formula to the current file. The table this command creates is written to the current worksheet file. This command can be useful in either a single-user or a network environment. When you select the File Administration Paste Table command, 1-2-3 displays the dialog box in Figure 16-8.

Caution: The File Administration Paste Table command creates a table of information in the current worksheet file starting at the location you specify. All the cells in the path of the table are overwritten with the new data. The table includes as many columns and rows as are required to generate the specific type of table you request. If you accidentally overwrite important data with this command, you can select Edit Undo, or press ALT+BACKSPACE, to reclaim the lost information.

The File Administration Paste Table dialog box (Figure 16-8) contains two option buttons: Active files and Linked files. As you might imagine, the Active files option lets you create a table of files that are currently open on 1-2-3's desktop. The Linked files option lets you create a table showing the files linked to the current file by formula (both open on the desktop and closed on disk). To specify a location for the table, use the Range

File Administration Paste Table
Active files
Linked files
Range:
A:A1..A:A1
OK
Cancel

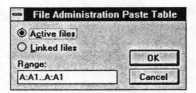

Figure 16-8 The File Administration Paste Table dialog box

text box to specify the range address or the range name of the cell marking the upper-left corner of where you want the table to begin. To create the table, select OK. 1-2-3 creates the table at the location you specified. The sections that follow describe each type of table in detail.

The Active Files Option

As mentioned, the Active files button creates a table of information about worksheet files that are currently open on 1-2-3's desktop. The table created is seven columns wide and contains one row for each open file, plus one blank row. Each of the seven columns in the table contains a different item of information about the file, as follows: filename, date last saved, time last saved, size in bytes, number of worksheets containing data, modification status, and reservation status. Figure 16-9 shows an example table of information about open worksheet files.

Note that 1-2-3 displays either 1 or 0 in the modification status column (column F) and reservation status column (column G) of the table in Figure 16-9. If a 1 is displayed in the modification status column, it means the file has been modified since it was opened. Otherwise 1-2-3 for Windows displays a 0 in this column. If a 1 is displayed in the reservation status column, it means you currently have the reservation for that file. If you do not have the reservation, 1-2-3 for Windows will display 0 in this column.

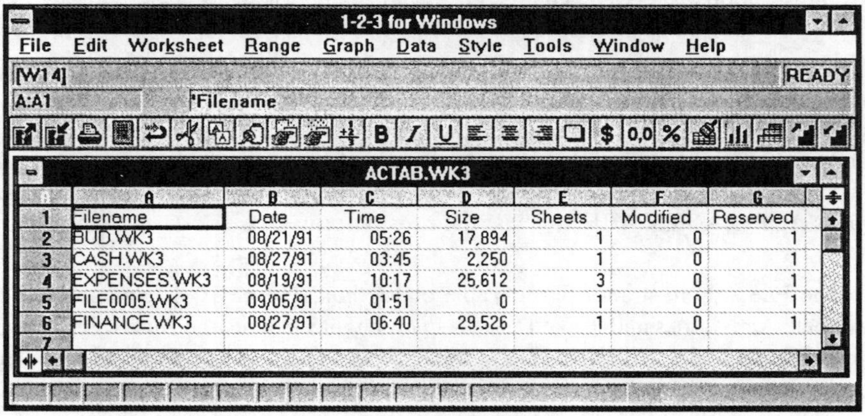

1-2-3 for Windows
File Edit Worksheet Range Graph Data Style Tools Window Help
[W14]
READY
A:A1
'Filename
ACTAB.WK3
A B C D E F G
1 Filename Date Time Size Sheets Modified Reserved
2 BUD.WK3 08/21/91 05:26 17,894 1 0 1
3 CASH.WK3 08/27/91 03:45 2,250 1 0 1
4 EXPENSES.WK3 08/19/91 10:17 25,612 3 0 1
5 FILE0005.WK3 09/05/91 01:51 0 1 0 1
6 FINANCE.WK3 08/27/91 06:40 29,526 1 0 1
7

Figure 16-9 A sample "active files" table

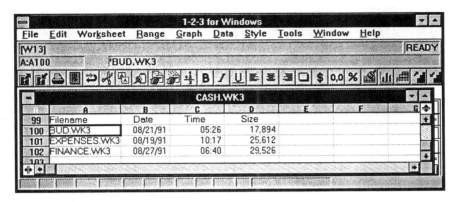

Figure 16-10 A sample "linked files" table

Figure 16-9 is slightly misleading, however. First of all, the titles in the range A:A1..A:G1 do not appear when you generate the table; these were added later. In addition, the dates and times in columns B and C do not appear as date and time values when you create the table. To make these values appear as dates and/or times, you must use the Range Format Date/Time command. Finally, the filenames in column A of the table were not displayed completely when the table was originally created. It was necessary to widen column A to fully display these labels. You'll find that similar format changes are necessary to display the information in most tables created with the File Administration Paste Table command.

The Linked Files Option

The Linked files option allows you to create a table of information about other files that are linked by formula to the current file. Formula links allow you to use information from other files in the current file (see Chapter 2). Before using this option, make sure the file containing the formula links is active. When you create the table, 1-2-3 for Windows lists the following information for each link in the current file in adjacent columns: source filename, date last saved, time last saved, and size in bytes of the file on disk. Figure 16-10 shows an example of a Linked files table.

Note: For the File Administration Paste Table Linked files command to work properly, the files linked to the current file must be open on the desktop. Otherwise, only the filename column will be properly filled in; the date, time, and size columns will all contain N/A.

UPDATING FORMULA LINKS TO OTHER FILES

When you open a file containing formula links, those links are automatically updated for any changes to files on disk to which the links refer. However, once the file is open, formula links are not updated for changes to files on disk. To update the links while the file is open, you must use the File Administration Update Links command. When you select this command, 1-2-3 for Windows recalculates the formulas in the current file that refer to other open worksheet files as well as to worksheet files on disk.

Updating your links can be especially important in a network environment where other users can make changes to source files without your knowledge. Using the File Administration Update Links command periodically is your assurance that you are using the most up-to-date information.

Note: Any DDE links you've created with the Edit Paste Link command must be updated with the Edit Link Options Update command discussed in Chapter 17.

17

Sharing Data

This chapter explores the topic of sharing data between 1-2-3 for Windows and other applications from several angles. It begins by showing you how to use an ASCII text file as a means to exchange data between 1-2-3 and other applications. It then explores commands on the 1-2-3 for Windows menu that let you save and load worksheet files from other Lotus spreadsheet products, including previous releases of 1-2-3. This chapter also explores the Translate utility, a program that lets you translate 1-2-3's worksheet files into formats that are usable by other software programs—for example, dBASE III PLUS. Finally, this chapter shows you how to share data between 1-2-3 and other Windows applications through the use of Dynamic Data Exchange (DDE).

USING ASCII TEXT FILES

ASCII (American Standard Code for Information Interchange) files are often viewed as the lowest common denominator among IBM-PC and compatible software programs. Therefore, many software programs save and read files in ASCII text format, allowing you to easily share data between them. As you'll soon see, 1-2-3 has this capability as well.

In addition to reading and writing ASCII text files, 1-2-3 lets you parse the numbers and words from the lines in an ASCII text file into individual cells in your 1-2-3 worksheet. That way, you can use the data just as you would any other data in 1-2-3.

Importing ASCII Text

To import the contents of an ASCII text file into the worksheet, use the File Import From command. You can use this command to read the lines from an ASCII file into the worksheet as a column of long labels, or you can have the words and numbers from each line of the ASCII file stored in separate cells as labels and values.

The 1-2-3 Classic equivalent for the File Import From command is /File Import.

When you select the File Import command, 1-2-3 displays a menu with three options—Text, Numbers, and Styles. The Styles option is used to retrieve 1-2-3's style sheets (.FM3 files) and is covered in Chapter 6, "Fonts and Other Styles." The Text and Numbers options apply to importing ASCII files and are covered here.

The Text option is used to import the contents of a standard ASCII text file into a worksheet as long labels. The lines of text from the ASCII file are stored as labels in a column of consecutive cells, one label per cell. The Numbers option imports either text strings and numbers or just numbers, leaving the text strings behind. However, instead of storing the incoming data as labels in a column of cells, the text strings and/or numbers are parsed into individual cells, a row of cells for each line in the ASCII file. For 1-2-3 to know how to appropriately split up each line of ASCII text file into individual cells, each line of the file must be properly *delimited*.

Figure 17-1 shows an example of a standard ASCII text file. Figure 17-2 shows a delimited ASCII text file. Note that the text strings and numbers in each line of the ASCII file in Figure 17-2 are separated by commas, and that the text strings are enclosed in quotation marks. The commas tell 1-2-3 where to end one entry and start the next—that is, how to split up the line into individual cells. The quotation marks indicate to 1-2-3 that a particular entry is to be imported and stored as a label.

Caution: When you use the File Import From command to import the contents of an ASCII file into the worksheet, 1-2-3 begins writing the data into the worksheet starting at the location of the cell pointer and working downward. Any cells in the path of the incoming data will be overwritten. Therefore, make sure you have plenty of room below and to the right of the cell pointer before using File Import From. If you do accidentally delete some important data, press ALT-BACKSPACE or select Edit Undo, to undo the File Import From command.

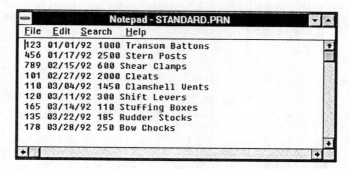

Figure 17-1 A standard ASCII file

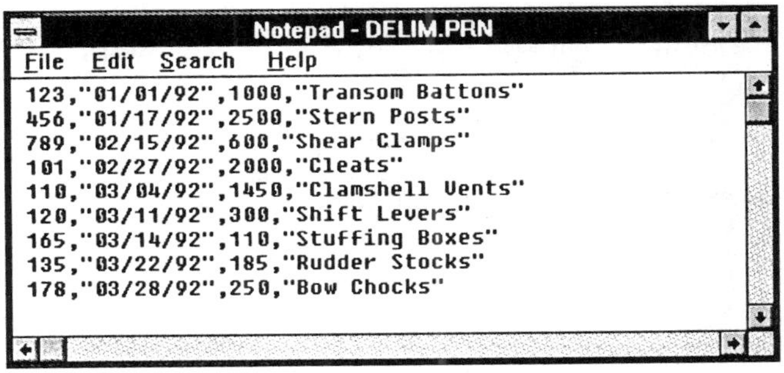

Figure 17-2 A delimited ASCII file

The Text Option

To import a standard (nondelimited) ASCII file into the worksheet, use the Text option. This option imports the contents of an ASCII text file into the worksheet as labels, starting at the location of the cell pointer. The lines of text from the ASCII file are stored as long labels in a column of cells, one label per cell. In preparation for using the Text option, position the cell pointer in the first cell where you want the listing to begin.

Note: Each line of the ASCII text file must end with a carriage return/line feed and may not exceed 512 characters. Lines longer than 512 characters will be truncated.

When the Text option is selected, 1-2-3 displays the dialog box in Figure 17-3. In the File name text box, 1-2-3 displays the drive and path to the current working directory followed by the wild-card file descriptor *.PRN, causing 1-2-3 to list all the .PRN files in the current directory. You can change this extension—to .TXT, for example—to see a list of different kinds of files. You can also use the Directories and Drives boxes in the usual way to choose from files in a different directory or another drive. When the file you

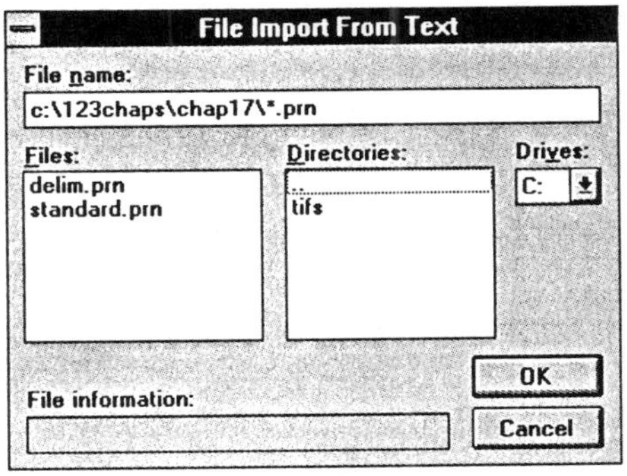

Figure 17-3 The File Import From Text dialog box

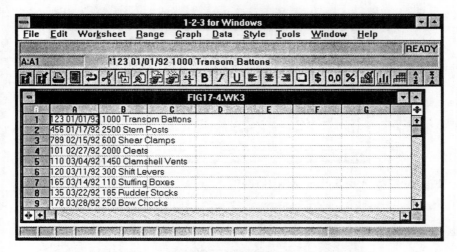

Figure 17-4 A standard ASCII file imported into the worksheet

want is displayed in the Files list box, select it and then select OK. 1-2-3 then imports the ASCII file into the worksheet, starting at the location of the cell pointer.

As we have discussed, the lines of text from the ASCII file are stored as long labels in a column of cells, one label per cell. (If there is a blank line in the ASCII text file, 1-2-3 will leave a blank cell in the column.) For example, Figure 17-4 shows the standard ASCII text file shown earlier in Figure 17-1 after it has been imported into the worksheet with File Import From Text. As you can see, each row in the worksheet contains a long label.

Note: If 1-2-3 encounters a CTRL-Z (end of file marker) anywhere in an ASCII file, it will stop importing data at that point, even though the end of the file may not have been reached.

The Numbers Option

The File Import Numbers command allows you to import just the numbers from a standard or delimited ASCII file or both text and numbers from a delimited ASCII file. Either way, 1-2-3 places each incoming data item in a separate cell, with one row of cells for each line in the ASCII file. Before you're ready to use the File Import Numbers command, you'll need to know a little about how to use delimiter characters in ASCII files.

As you may recall, in Figure 17-2 the text strings and numbers in each line of the ASCII file are separated by commas and the text strings are enclosed in quotation marks. When you import this type of file with the File Import Numbers command, the commas tell 1-2-3 where to end one entry and start the next—that is, how to split up the line into individual cells. The quotation marks indicate to 1-2-3 that a particular entry is to be imported and stored as a label.

In addition to using commas as delimiter symbols, you can use the semicolon (;), a colon (:), or a space. To indicate a text string, you must enclose it in double quotation

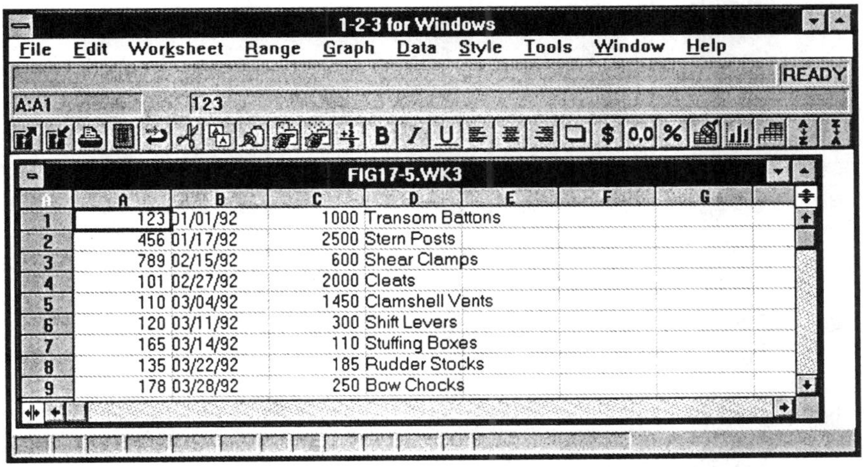

Figure 17-5 Using the Numbers option to import a delimited ASCII file

marks (""). If text strings of any length, including a single letter or a set of letters, are not enclosed in quotation marks, 1-2-3 treats them as delimiters and does not import them.

Note: If the ASCII file you are importing includes numbers with commas as a thousands separator, take them out—otherwise, 1-2-3 will split the number wherever a comma occurs. You do not need to worry about decimal separators as 1-2-3 honors the default decimal separator—usually the period (.) —when importing numbers.

When you select File Import From Numbers, 1-2-3 will display a dialog very similar to that of the Text option shown in Figure 17-3. In fact, the structure of this dialog box is exactly the same and you use its components in exactly the same way.

For example, suppose you want to import the delimited ASCII file shown earlier in Figure 17-2 into the current worksheet. In this case, the text strings are enclosed in quotation marks so they will be imported along with the numbers. (If they were not enclosed in quotation marks, they would act as delimiters and be left behind.) To import the file in Figure 17-2, place the cell pointer where you want the incoming data to begin in the current worksheet and select File Import From Numbers. 1-2-3 displays the File Import From Numbers dialog box. Specify the name of the ASCII file you want to import in the File name text box or select it from the list box below. To complete the command, select the OK command button. 1-2-3 then imports the ASCII file into the current worksheet starting at the location of the cell pointer. For example, Figure 17-5 shows what happens when the ASCII file shown earlier in Figure 17-2 is imported into the worksheet starting in cell A:A1.

Parsing Labels into Cells

You can use the Data Parse command to parse the words and numbers contained in long labels into individual cells. This command is often used after the File Import From Text

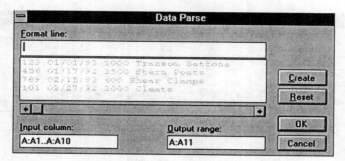

Figure 17-6   The Data Parse dialog box

command has been used to import the contents of an ASCII text file into the worksheet. After parsing, the words and numbers that make up the long labels are stored in individual cells as labels and values. That way, you can use the data in formulas and commands just as you would any other data in your 1-2-3 worksheet.

When you select the Data Parse command, 1-2-3 displays the dialog box in Figure 17-6. Briefly, the components of this dialog box perform the following functions:

- Format Line: Displays a format line containing special symbols that tell 1-2-3 how to break up the words and numbers in the long labels into individual cells. This format line is created by 1-2-3 when you select the Create button. The box below the Format line box shows the effect that the current format line will have on your data.

- Create: Creates a format line and displays it in the Format line text box.

- Input column: Defines the range of labels you want to parse.

- Output range: A single-cell range that marks the upper-left corner of the location where you want the parsed data copied to.

- OK: Copies the parsed data from the input column to the output range.

- Reset: Clears the range settings in the Input column and Output range text boxes.

Format Lines Basics

Before attempting to parse long labels into individual cells, you'll need to understand some format line basics. Format lines contain special symbols that tell 1-2-3 how to break up the words and numbers in long labels into individual cells. 1-2-3 creates this format line automatically as part of the Data Parse procedure. There are seven basic categories of format symbols:

L	Label
V	Value
D	Date
T	Time

S   Skip item

*   Blank space

>   Continuation character

When 1-2-3 encounters what is perceived to be a label, value, date, or time, it places one of the first four symbols in the format line. After that symbol, 1-2-3 uses continuation characters, >, for as long as the label, value, date, or time lasts. When 1-2-3 encounters a blank space, it assumes that the word or number to the left and to the right belong in separate cells. Blank spaces are symbolized by an asterisk (*). For example, imagine you have the label "By 12/31/92 sales will total $10,000,000" in the worksheet. 1-2-3 will create the following format line for this label:

```
L>*D>>>>>>>*L>>>>*L>>>*L>>>>*V>>>>>>>>>>
By 12/31/92 sales will total $10,000,000
```

If you want 1-2-3 to skip a particular entry when parsing a long label, you can use the S symbol. This symbol causes 1-2-3 to ignore the word or number beneath it. Because 1-2-3 assumes that all words and numbers in a long label are to be parsed, it does not automatically insert an S symbol when you create a format line. Instead, you must manually insert the S symbol, and any continuation characters required, by editing the format line.

When you use the Data Parse command to create a format line, 1-2-3 creates a "best-guess" format line. That is, the format line may not produce the results you want. To solve this problem, you must edit the format line. The example that follows shows you how to do just that.

Parsing Long Labels: An Example

In this section the Data Parse command will be used to parse the long labels in column A of Figure 17-7 into individual cells, as shown in Figure 17-8. During the example, each component of the Data Parse dialog box will be used.

In this example, it will be necessary to edit the format line created by 1-2-3. As we have mentioned, when 1-2-3 encounters a blank space in a long label it assumes you want the entries to the left and right of the space placed in separate cells. However, most of the long labels in Figure 17-7 contain two-word descriptions that should appear in a single cell. In the example that follows, a space symbol (*) and a label symbol (L) will be removed from the format line created by 1-2-3, and replaced with two continuation characters (>>).

In preparation for the Data Parse command, locate the cell pointer on the cell that contains the first label in the input column (cell A:A1 in Figure 17-7). When you're ready, perform the following steps:

1. Select Data Parse. 1-2-3 displays the dialog box in Figure 17-6.

2. Select the Create button. 1-2-3 analyzes the label in cell A:A1 and creates a best-guess format line in the Format line text box.

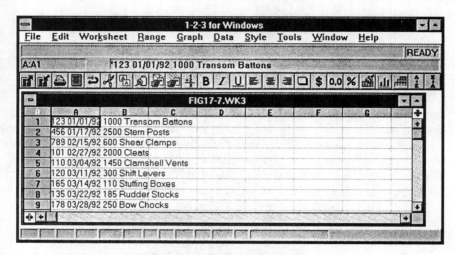

Figure 17-7 Long labels displayed in the worksheet

3. Activate the Format line text box and move the cursor to the last asterisk (*) in the new format line. Press DEL twice to remove both the asterisk (*) and the label symbol (L) that follows it. Type >> (greater than) twice to replace these characters with continuation characters.

4. Activate the Input column text box, specify the range A:A1..A:A9, which includes the long labels in column A of Figure 17-7.

5. In the Output range text box, specify a single-cell range that marks the upper-left corner of the location where you want the parsed data copied to (cell A:A12 in Figure 17-8).

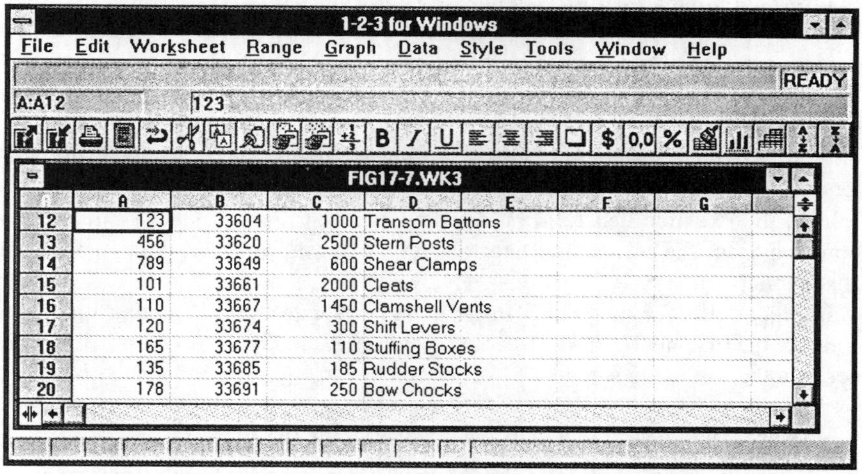

Figure 17-8 The long labels from Figure 17-7 after parsing with Data Parse

6. Select OK. 1-2-3 then inserts a new row into the worksheet and places the format line in the Format line text box into cell A:A1. All labels beneath the new format line are pushed downward to accommodate the new row. 1-2-3 then copies the long labels now in the range A:A2..A:A10 to the output range and parses the data into individual cells. Your screen should now look like Figure 17-8.

Tips on Data Parse

When 1-2-3 creates a format line, it does so by using the first long label in the input-column range as a model. If this label is not representative of the other labels in the column, 1-2-3 may not parse the data for all the labels correctly. You may then have to edit the format line and parse the data several times before you get the precise configuration you want.

Format lines are essentially nonprinting labels. When 1-2-3 creates a format line, it is preceded by a split vertical bar (|) label prefix. This prefix causes the format line to be displayed, but not printed. Therefore, you can create your own format lines directly from the keyboard, provided you use the split vertical bar to begin them. In some cases, you may prefer this method to avoid having a new row inserted into the worksheet by the Data Parse command.

In some instances you may want to use more than one format line. For example, imagine you are working with a column of labels that is 100 cells deep (A:A1..A:A100). The first 50 labels are somewhat uniform and can be properly parsed with a single format line. The format of the second set of 50 labels is noticeably different from the first 50. In this case, you can use the Data Parse command twice, once for the first 50 labels and again for the second 50.

Note: In the preceding example, the long labels in the input-column range appear in consecutive cells. However, if the input-column range contains a blank row, 1-2-3 will ignore that row when copying the parsed data to the output range.

Printing to an ASCII File

As noted earlier, many popular business applications—including 1-2-3 for Windows—can both read and write files in ASCII format. For this reason, ASCII files are commonly used as a medium for transferring data from one application to another (especially outside of Windows).

The 1-2-3 Classic equivalent for the File Extract To Text command is /Print File.

To create an ASCII text file from within 1-2-3 for Windows, you can use the File Extract To command. When you select this command, 1-2-3 displays the dialog box in Figure 17-9.

To print to an ASCII file, specify the range you want to print in the Ranges text box. Next, select the Text radio button. (1-2-3 changes the file descriptor in the File name text box from *.wk3 to *.prn.) Finally, specify a name for the ASCII file in the File name text box. (Although, 1-2-3 suggests an extension of .PRN here, you can use any extension you'd like—for example, .TXT.) When you're ready, select OK. 1-2-3 will then write the contents of the currently selected

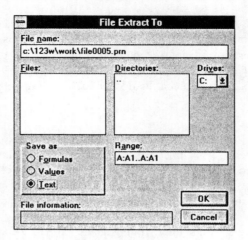

Figure 17-9 The File Extract To dialog box

range to an ASCII file under the name you've specified. Each row of cells (including blank rows) in the currently selected worksheet range ends up as a single line in the ASCII file. Each line in the ASCII file ends with a hard return.

Unlike previous DOS Releases of 1-2-3, 1-2-3 for Windows creates its ASCII files without top, bottom, left, or right margins. In most cases, margins tend to cause problems when the file is eventually imported into another software program. In prior releases, it was necessary to remove all margins before creating the ASCII file. With 1-2-3 for Windows, however, you don't have to make that special effort.

1-2-3 for Windows uses the current column-width settings in determining the spacing of data that is written to the ASCII file. For example, suppose all the columns in the current worksheet are set to their default width of nine characters and you write the following range to an ASCII file:

	A	B	C
1	Product	Quantity	Cost
2			
3	Widgets	123	$123,123
4	Didgets	1123	$32,132

The ASCII file ends up with the following spacing:

Product	Quantity	Cost
Widgets	123	$123,123
Didgets	1123	$32,132

You'll notice that the label "Product" in the first line of this ASCII file is seven characters long. However, because of the column-width setting of nine in 1-2-3, this label is followed by two spaces before the next label, "Quantity", begins.

If you are printing a range that contains long labels to an ASCII file, 1-2-3 will usually print those long labels in their entirety. However, if the long label is cut off in the worksheet file (there is an entry in the cell immediately to the right), the long label will also be cut off in the ASCII file. Its length will be limited to the width of the column in which it begins.

▼ **Tip:**   You can also print to an ASCII file from within 1-2-3 for Windows by installing the Generic / Text Only printer driver through the Windows Control Panel. To do this, perform the following steps:

1. Double-click on the Printers icon from the Control Panel. Windows displays the Printers dialog box.

2. Choose the Add Printer Button.

3. Double-click on "Generic / Text Only" (the first item in the List of Printers list box).

4. Insert Windows Disk 5 in response to the prompt and select OK. Windows copies the TTY.DRV driver to the WINDOWS\SYSTEM directory and adds "Generic / Text Only on None, Inactive" to the Installed Printers list.

5. Select the Configure button. Windows displays the Printers - Configure dialog box.

6. Choose FILE from the list followed by OK to return to the Printers dialog box.

7. Turn on the Active radio button in the Printers dialog box and then select OK to leave the dialog box.

Once the Generic / Text Only driver has been properly installed, you can use 1-2-3's File Printer Setup command to make that driver active. You can then use 1-2-3's File Print command to print to an ASCII file. When you select OK to confirm this command and begin printing, Windows will prompt you for the name of an ASCII file in which to store the output.

USING FILES FROM OTHER PRODUCTS

Lotus has gone out of its way to ensure backward compatibility between 1-2-3 for Windows and the various versions of its other DOS spreadsheet products—1-2-3 and Symphony. However, all is not smooth sailing. In many cases you can use 1-2-3 for Windows File Open or /File Retrieve command to open a file from a previous release of 1-2-3 or Symphony inside 1-2-3. However, the file may be read-only. That is, you can't save the file in its original format. (In these cases, you must use the Translate Utility covered in the next section.) There are a number of additional considerations you'll need to know about when opening and saving files from other Lotus products from within 1-2-3 for Windows. These are covered in the sections that follow.

Another welcome surprise to many 1-2-3 users is the ability to open both spreadsheet and macro files from Microsoft Excel inside 1-2-3. That way, if one of your associates is using Excel, you can share data with one another directly.

Briefly, you can use 1-2-3's File Open or /File Retrieve to load the following types of files directly into 1-2-3 for Windows:

Type	Description
.WKS	1-2-3 Release 1A
.WK1	1-2-3 Release 2.X
.WK3	1-2-3 Release 3
.WRK	Symphony Release 1.0
.WR1	Symphony Release 1.1
.XLS	Microsoft Excel Release 2.0, 2.1, and 3.0
.XLM	Microsoft Excel 2.0, 2.1, and 3.0

The sections that follow discuss each of these file formats in more detail.

Using Release 1A Files in 1-2-3 for Windows

You can use the File Open or /File Retrieve command to open .WKS worksheet files from 1-2-3 Release 1A inside 1-2-3 for Windows. However, these files will be opened as read-only. You can't save your change to the original file. Instead, these files are converted to 1-2-3 for Windows' .WK3 format when you open them. (The original file on disk, however, is not affected.) If you decide in the future that you need to use these files in Release 1A again, you must convert them to the appropriate format by using the Translate utility discussed later in this chapter.

Using Release 2 Files in 1-2-3 for Windows

You can use File Open or /File Retrieve to open 1-2-3 Release 2.X (.WK1) files in 1-2-3 for Windows. This includes .WK1 files from 1-2-3 Releases 2.0, 2.01, 2.2, and 2.3. What's more, you can save 1-2-3 for Windows worksheet files in a format usable by these same products by simply selecting the File Save As command and specifying a .WK1 extension.

When you load a Release 2.X (.WK1) file into 1-2-3, that file is translated into a (.WK3) format that is usable by 1-2-3 for Windows. 1-2-3 for Windows continues to display the .WK1 file extension in the worksheet window title bar, however. Conversely, when you save a 1-2-3 file in 1-2-3 Release 2.X format, 1-2-3 must translate the file to a (.WK1) format. All this translating to and from different file formats can be a time-consuming process. Therefore, unless you intend to use the file in Release 2 again, you're better off saving it in 1-2-3 for Windows' .WK3 format.

1-2-3 for Windows supports the formatting of both Allways (.ALL files) and Impress (.FMT files.). Allways is an add-in that ships with 1-2-3 Release 2.2. It allows you to switch the 1-2-3 display to graphics mode and perform spreadsheet publishing from within 1-2-3. You cannot, however, modify the worksheet while Allways is active. Impress, an add-in that ships with 1-2-3 Release 2.3, allows the 1-2-3 screen to be displayed in WYSIWYG (what you see is what you get) graphics mode and supports spreadsheet publishing as well. Unlike Allways, you can change the contents of the worksheet while Impress is active.

If you have used either Allways or Impress to format the data in a Release 2.X worksheet file, the formats you've specified (most of them, anyway) will be accurately displayed when you load the file into 1-2-3 for Windows. 1-2-3 for Windows pulls this off by reading either the .ALL (Allways) or .FMT (Impress) formatting file when you load its associated .WK1 file. If both a .FMT file and an .ALL file with the same name exist in the current directory, 1-2-3 for Windows will read the .FMT file first.

When you modify and save a 1-2-3 Release 2.2 (.WK1) file from within 1-2-3 for Windows, a new .FMT (Impress) file is created that contains the current formatting for the file. This means you can load the .WK1 file into 1-2-3 Release 2.3 and your formatting changes will be reflected, provided the .FMT file is present. However, your formatting changes will not be reflected when you load the same file into 1-2-3 Release 2.2. 1-2-3 for Windows does not update or support .ALL (Allways) files. See "Using 1-2-3 for Windows Files in 1-2-3 Releases 2 and 3" later for additional considerations regarding saving files in Release 2 format.

Using Release 3 Files in 1-2-3 for Windows

Both 1-2-3 for Windows and 1-2-3 Release 3.1 share the same worksheet file format and extension, .WK3. What's more, both share the same format and extension for their formatting files, .FM3 so you can use 1-2-3 for Windows' File Open or /File Retrieve to load a 1-2-3 Release 3.1 worksheet file directly into 1-2-3 for Windows—the file will retain its original format and extension. What's more, the .FM3 file that is associated with that worksheet file will be loaded automatically.

Using Release 2 and 3 Files in 1-2-3 for Windows

Here are some other issues you'll need to be aware of when working with 1-2-3 Release 2 and 3 files in 1-2-3 for Windows:

- 1-2-3 Release 2 uses the LICS character set (Lotus International Character Set) whereas 1-2-3 for Windows uses the Lotus Multibyte Character set (LMBCS), so when you open a Release 2 file in 1-2-3 for Windows, some strange characters may appear on your screen. To solve this problem, use 1-2-3's Tools User Setup command and select International. This command results in a dialog box that contains a group box entitled File translation. In that section, there is a drop-down list box titled 1-2-3 Release 2. From this box, you can select either LICS or ASCII, depending on the character set you want 1-2-3 for Windows to use when reading and saving files in 1-2-3 Release 2 format. After making a selection from this box, try loading the Release 2 file again.

- 1-2-3 for Windows does not support single-cell range names in Release 2 files. If a formula in the .WK1 file contains such a range name, 1-2-3 for Windows will display it as cell address, rather than a range name. However, the next time you load the file into 1-2-3 Release 2, the range name will again be displayed.

- If a 1-2-3 Release 2 or 3 file contains an @function provided by an add-in, 1-2-3 for Windows will display NA in the cell containing that function. Any formulas referring to this cell will return ERR. However, the next time you load the file into 1-2-3 Release 2 or 3, the @function will once again be correctly displayed.

- If a 1-2-3 Release 2 or 3 file contains settings for the /Print command, you must use the /Print command from the 1-2-3 Classic menu to take advantage of those settings.

Using 1-2-3 for Windows Files in 1-2-3 Releases 2 and 3

1-2-3 for Windows includes features that previous releases of 1-2-3 do not. Therefore, these features, and possibly some data associated with them, will be lost when you save a 1-2-3 (.WK3) file as a Release 2 or Release 3 file.

Release 3 supports multiple worksheet files, but Release 2 does not. Therefore, if you save a 1-2-3 file in Release 2 (.WK1) format, make sure all the data is stored in one worksheet. If it is not, use the File New command to create a new worksheet file. Next, use the Edit Quick Copy command to copy all the data from the old multiple-worksheet file into the new single-worksheet file. If formulas in the original .WK3 file refer to other worksheets, use the Edit Quick Copy command again to convert these formulas to their current values. (Also, be aware that Edit Quick Copy will not copy range names. You'll have to recreate these in the .WK1 file with the Range Name Create command.) Finally, use the File Save As command to save the single-worksheet file to disk with a .WK1 extension. That file should now be usable in 1-2-3 Release 2. For details on how to use the Edit Quick Copy command, see Chapter 7, "Cutting and Pasting Data."

Here are some other things you'll need to know about when saving files for use in 1-2-3 Releases 2 and 3:

- You cannot save a 1-2-3 for Windows (.WK3) file to 1-2-3 Release 2 (.WK1) format when it has been sealed with 1-2-3 for Windows' File Admin Seal command.

- When you save a .WK3 file to .WK1 (Release 2) format, any 1-2-3 for Windows-specific features are lost entirely. 1-2-3 informs you of the potential loss of data when you save the file.

- When you save a 1-2-3 for Windows file in Release 3 (.WK3) format, graph settings and named print settings are saved. However, if you save a .WK3 file in .WK1 (Release 2) format, named print settings are not saved.

- The maximum length of a label in Release 2 (.WK1) is 240 characters. However, as you know, the maximum length of a label in 1-2-3 for Windows is 512 characters. If you save a .WK3 file with labels in excess of 240 characters to Release 2 (.WK1) format, those labels are truncated at 240 characters.

- Release 2 does not support formulas in excess of 240 characters. If you save a 1-2-3 for Windows file containing such formulas to a Release 2 (.WK1) file, the formulas are saved intact. However, the formulas will not function in the Release 2 file unless you edit them down to 240 characters.

- If you save a 1-2-3 for Windows file to Release 2 format (.WK1), and the file contains formula references to other files, 1-2-3 converts the references to labels in the .WK1 file.

- 1-2-3 Release 2 does not support undefined range names. Therefore, if you save a 1-2-3 for Windows file containing undefined range names to Release 2 (.WK1) format, Release 2 displays ERR in place of those range names.

- If you save a 1-2-3 for Windows file that contains ANSI characters to Release 2 (.WK1), the ANSI characters will be converted to LICS characters.

- 1-2-3 for Windows contains a number of new @functions that are not included in 1-2-3 Releases 2 or 3. These @functions are stored as @? in the Release 2 or 3 file followed by any arguments they may have. The cells containing these @functions display NA.

- 1-2-3 Release 2 does not support range name notes or formula annotations. These will be lost.

Using Lotus Symphony Files in 1-2-3 for Windows

You can use 1-2-3 for Windows' /File Retrieve or File Open commands to load Lotus Symphony .WRK (Release 1.0) and .WR1 (Release 1.1) files. 1-2-3 for Windows immediately renames these files with a .WK3 extension and converts them to 1-2-3's file format. (The original file on disk remains unaffected.) You cannot save Lotus Symphony files in their original file formats. You can only save them as 1-2-3 for Windows (.WK3) or 1-2-3 Release 2 files (.WK1).

If you need to use a .WRK or .WR1 file in Symphony again after using it in 1-2-3 for Windows, save it as a .WK1 file. Lotus Symphony is capable of loading .WK1 files. Keep in mind, however, that some of the features you may have added to the file in 1-2-3 for Windows may be lost in Symphony.

Microsoft Excel

As mentioned, you can use 1-2-3 for Windows' /File Retrieve or File Open command to open Microsoft Excel Release 2.X and 3.0 spreadsheet (.XLS) and macro (.XLM) files.

Immediately upon loading, 1-2-3 for Windows converts these files to its own .WK3 format. To reflect this, 1-2-3 immediately renames these files with the same name and a .WK3 extension. The original Excel files on disk, however, are not affected.

Note: 1-2-3 for Windows version 1.0 will not allow you to load Microsoft Excel Release 3.X spreadsheet (.XLS) and macro (.XLM) files. 1-2-3 for Windows version 1.0a, however, will.

Macro Compatibility

Through its 1-2-3 Classic menu, 1-2-3 for Windows allows you to run the macros you've created in previous Releases of 1-2-3. In fact, you'll find you can run most of your macros without modification.

The 1-2-3 Classic menu is modeled after the 1-2-3 Release 3.1 menu. Although virtually all the menu options from Release 3.1 have been included in 1-2-3 Classic, not all of them work. The ones that don't work are obsolete and have been disabled. To indicate which commands are obsolete, 1-2-3 for Windows displays the message "Obsolete menu option—has no effect in 1-2-3 for Windows" when you select the command. Nevertheless, if your macro includes one of these commands, you'll have to update it for use with 1-2-3 for Windows.

When 1-2-3 for Windows encounters an obsolete command in a macro, it does not always issue an error message. In some cases, it simply ignores the command. This makes it very hard to spot problem areas in your more complex macros. About the only way to deal with this problem is to know which commands are obsolete and remove or replace them.

You should also check your macros from previous releases for commands that simply do not exist in 1-2-3 for Windows. For example, 1-2-3 Release 2.2 includes the command /Addin. This command is not available in 1-2-3 Release 3.1 or 1-2-3 for Windows. Therefore, if one of your Release 2.2 macros includes this command, the macro will have to be edited before you use it in 1-2-3 for Windows.

Running 1-2-3 Release 2 Macros in 1-2-3 for Windows

You can run your 1-2-3 Release 2 macros inside 1-2-3 for Windows by simply loading the .WK1 file containing them and then running the macro. However, rather than using the ALT key to run the macro, you'll have to press CTRL followed by the appropriate letter (or use 1-2-3 for Windows' Tools Macro Run command). If your 1-2-3 Release 2.2 macros are contained in a macro library supported by the Macro Library Manager add-in, you must transfer those macros to a .WK1 worksheet file before you can use them in 1-2-3 for Windows. To do this, use the Macro Library Manager's Load command to copy the macros from the macro library to the worksheet. Then save the worksheet under the name of your choice. You are now ready to load the file into 1-2-3 for Windows and run the macros it contains.

You can also use your 1-2-3 Release 2 macros in a .WK3 file. To do this, simply load the 1-2-3 Release 2 file containing the macro into 1-2-3 for Windows. Next use the File Open command to open the .WK3 file of your choice. Then use the Edit Quick Copy command to copy the macro from the .WK1 file to the .WK3 file. Finally, use the Range Name Create command to assign a new range name to the macro and then run the macro in the usual way.

Modifying Release 2 Macros

Another problem you may encounter when porting your Release 2 keystroke macros to 1-2-3 for Windows is that those macros are not written for a multiple-worksheet environment. Specifically, if your keystroke macros use abbreviated cell addresses (A2, B4, and so on), you may have to modify those addresses to include full-cell addresses (A:A2, A:B4, and so on) or range names. Otherwise, you may not get the results you expect.

In 1-2-3 for Windows, the operation of a macro containing abbreviated cell addresses depends on the location of the cell pointer. For example, suppose you have a simple keystroke macro like /cA2..A10~G25~, which includes abbreviated cell addresses. If the cell pointer is located in worksheet A when you run this macro, its actions will be executed in worksheet A. If the cell pointer is in worksheet B, the macro's actions will be executed in worksheet B, and so on. If you want to control where the macro is executed each time, you must "hard code" your cell references in one of the following ways:

- Modify the abbreviated cell address to include a worksheet letter—for example A:C100. That way, the macro will always reference cell C100 in worksheet A of the current file.

- Upgrade the abbreviated cell address to include both a worksheet filename and a worksheet letter—for example <<C:\FINANCE\BUDGET.WK3>>A:C100. That way, the reference in your macro is hardwired to cell C100 of worksheet A in the BUDGET.WK3 file in your C:\BUDGET directory.

- Replace the abbreviated cell reference with a range name.

You should also be careful when using abbreviated cell addresses with advanced macro commands. As a general rule, if an advanced macro command has an abbreviated cell reference as one of its arguments—for example, {GETLABEL "What is your first name", A2}—1-2-3 for Windows will interpret that address as being in the same worksheet and file as the macro itself.

USING THE TRANSLATE UTILITY

The Translate utility lets you convert your 1-2-3 for Windows files to a format that is directly readable by other spreadsheet and database management programs. In addition, the Translate utility lets you convert files from other software programs to 1-2-3 for Windows' file format. Thus, Translate lets you share data between 1-2-3 for Windows and other software programs without the bother of having to perform a cumbersome ASCII-text transfer.

The Translate utility is actually a DOS program. In fact, Lotus has essentially packaged the Translate utility for 1-2-3 Release 3.1 with 1-2-3. Therefore, if you already know how to use the Translate utility from 1-2-3 Release 3.1, you've got a jump on the situation in 1-2-3 for Windows.

Before you attempt to use the Translate Utility, make sure it has been installed in your 1-2-3 program directory. (It is not installed there by default.) To install Translate, run the 1-2-3 for Windows install program and select "Install with options," rather than the default installation procedure. During the "Install with options" procedure, you can elect to install the Translate utility. The Translate utility files are then copied to your 1-2-3 program directory, and a Translate (apples to oranges) icon is installed in your Lotus Applications group window.

The Translate utility is composed of a dozen or so files stored in your 1-2-3 program directory. You can see a list of these files by shelling to DOS (double-clicking on the DOS icon in Program Manager's Main group window), making your 1-2-3 program directory current, and typing **DIR TRAN*.***. This command should produce a list of 18 or so files. The Translate utility's main executable file, TRANS.EXE, should be among the files in the list.

Starting Translate

Because the Translate utility is a DOS application, you can run it either from within Windows or from the DOS prompt. To run Translate from within Windows, simply double-click on the Translate (apples to oranges) icon located in the Lotus Applications group window. A short time later the Translate Utility screen will appear, as shown in Figure 17-10.

You can also use either of the following methods to run Translate from within Windows:

- Select File Run from either Program Manager's or File Manager's menu, type **TRANS.EXE**, and press ENTER. If your 1-2-3 directory is not included in your path, be sure to precede this filename with the appropriate directory designation.

- From within File Manager, open a directory window that shows the files in your 1-2-3 directory and double-click on TRANS.EXE.

To run Translate from the DOS prompt, simple type **TRANS** and press ENTER. (If your 1-2-3 program directory is not included in your path, make sure you make that directory current before typing TRANS.) As you know, you can access the DOS prompt from within Windows by double-clicking on the DOS icon in Program Manager's Main group window. Or, from within 1-2-3, you can access DOS by selecting /System.

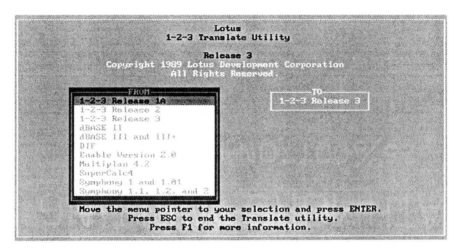

Figure 17-10   The Translate utility's opening screen

 Tip: The Translate utility (apples and oranges) icon is contained in a separate
file, TRANS.ICO, that is located in your 1-2-3 program directory. Therefore, you can "borrow" this icon for use with your other DOS and Windows applications. See your Windows documentation for information on
setting up Program Manager icons.

Translation Support

When you start the Translate utility, the screen in Figure 17-10 is displayed. The left-hand
side of this screen shows a list of source products whose files can be translated into 1-2-3
for Windows' file format. Frankly, the list is rather short. In fact, other than previous
releases of 1-2-3 and Lotus Symphony, the list is limited to the following products:

Source Program	*Extension*
dBASE II, III, and III Plus	.DBF
Products that use .DIF files, such as VisiCalc	.DIF
MultiPlan Release 4.2	.SLK
Enable 2.0	.SSF
SuperCalc4	.CAL

1-2-3 for Windows can read files from previous releases of 1-2-3 and Symphony, as
well as Excel 2.X, with no problem. However, 1-2-3 for Windows converts the file to its

own format (.WK3) when it is read into memory. What's more, when you save the file, 1-2-3 for Windows will save it as a .WK3 file. To use these files with their original source products, you will have to use the Translate utility to translate them. (This applies to 1-2-3 and Symphony only; Translate does not include an option for translating to Excel's file format.)

On the other hand, 1-2-3 for Windows can save files in Release 2 format directly, provided the files do not contain multiple worksheets or features that are specific to 1-2-3 for Windows. Therefore, you do not need to use the Translate utility to create a Release 2 file from 1-2-3 for Windows. If the file contains either multiple worksheets or features that are specific to 1-2-3 for Windows, you must save that file to disk as a 1-2-3 for Windows file and use the Translate utility to translate it to Release 2 format. When you translate a 1-2-3 for Windows file with multiple worksheets to Release 2 format, each worksheet becomes a separate Release 2 file (see "Running the Translate Utility").

To display a list of target products whose file formats Translate can create, move the highlight in Figure 17-10 down to 1-2-3 Release 3. The Translate screen then appears as shown in Figure 17-11. The right-hand side of the Translate screen shows a list of target products whose file formats Translate can create from a 1-2-3 for Windows file. The list includes the following:

Target Program	Extension
dBASE II, III, and III Plus	.DBF
1-2-3 Release 1A	.WKS
1-2-3 Releases 2, 2.01, 2.2, and 2.3	.WK1
Enable 2.0	.SSF
MultiPlan Release 4.2	.SLK
Products that use .DIF files such as VisiCalc	.DIF
SuperCalc4	.CAL
Symphony Release 1.0 and 1.01	.WRK
Symphony Release 1.1, 1.2, and 2	.WR1

Running the Translate Utility

This section describes how to use the Translate utility to translate a file from one format to another. It assumes you have the Translate Utility up and running as shown in Figure 17-10. Briefly, the steps for translating a file are as follows:

1. Move the highlight to the source product whose file you want to translate from and press ENTER. For example, if you want to translate a 1-2-3 for Windows file, highlight 1-2-3 Release 3 and press ENTER. Translate displays the available target products whose formats you can translate to. Your screen should look like Figure 17-11.

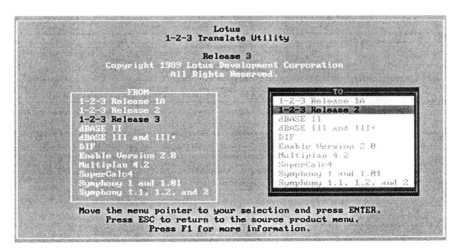

Figure 17-11 Translate shows the names of products whose file formats it can create

2. Highlight a target product and press ENTER. When you select a target product, Translate may display several message screens that provide you with information about the translation you're about to make. Press ENTER to move from one help screen to the next or ESC to proceed with the translation. Translate displays a screen that lists the source-product files in the current directory, similar to Figure 17-12.

3. Highlight the name of the file you want to translate and press ENTER. Release 3 displays a default target filename. This filename matches the source filename with the default extension of the target product. (To select from files in a different directory, edit the Source file path and press ENTER.)

   To select more than one file to translate, mark each file by highlighting it and pressing SPACEBAR. After you've selected your files, press ENTER. If you select more that one file to translate, the default target file name is replaced by an asterisk (*) followed by the appropriate extension—for example *.DBF.

4. To confirm the default target filename, press ENTER. To change the target filename and path, simply edit it and press ENTER. If you selected more than one file to translate, you cannot alter the default target filename.

5. Translate then shows different prompts depending on the source and target file types you've selected. These are described briefly in the next section, "Dealing with Product-Specific Features." After working your way through these prompts, Translate asks you to specify whether you want to proceed with translation.

6. Select Yes to proceed with translation, No to return to the list of source files, or Quit to return to the Translate menu without translating the currently selected file.

7. Press ESC to leave Translate. Translate displays the prompt "Do you want to end Translate?" and a Yes/No menu. Select Yes to end Translate or No to return to the main Translate menu.

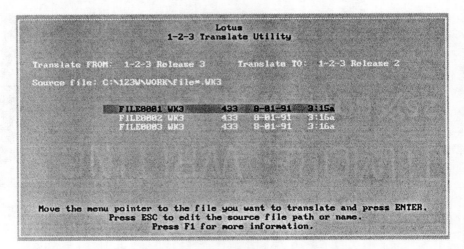

Figure 17-12 Translate shows the names of source files in the current directory

Note: You cannot translate 1-2-3 for Windows files that have been saved with a password or sealed using File Admin Seal nor can you translate a file that has been created with File Extract. To translate such a file, first open it in 1-2-3 for Windows and use the File Save As command to save it to disk, then use the Translate utility to translate the file.

Dealing with Product-Specific Features

As mentioned in step 5 of the procedure in the previous section, Translate may display prompts that are specific to the source and target products you have selected. This section outlines some of the prompts you may encounter.

If you're translating a 1-2-3 for Windows file to Release 2 format, and that file contains either multiple worksheets or features that are specific to 1-2-3 for Windows, Translate will prompt you to select from All Worksheets or One Worksheet. If you select All Worksheets, Translate converts all the worksheets in a multiple-worksheet file into Release 2 files, with one worksheet per file. To name each Release 2 file, Translate takes the seventh and eighth characters of the original filename and replaces them with the original worksheet letter. For example, if the name of the original file is SALESYTD, and it has three worksheets, Translate creates the files SALESY0A.WK1, SALESY0B.WK1, and SALESY0C.WK1. If the filename has fewer than eight characters, such as SALES, Translate adds the original worksheet letter to the end of the filename.

If you select One Worksheet, Translate prompts you to specify the letter of a specific worksheet to translate and displays the default of A (meaning worksheet A). To confirm this, press ENTER. To specify another worksheet letter, type its letter and press ENTER.

After dealing with the multiple-worksheet issue, Translate prompts you to select how features that are specific to 1-2-3 for Windows will be dealt with in the new Release 2 file. To do this, it displays a menu that prompts you to choose from either Labels or Add-ins. If you select Labels, all @functions specific to 1-2-3 for Windows, and formulas that reference data in other worksheets and files, will appear as labels in the translated file. If you select Add-ins, Translate creates the new file using the same conventions as if you had used 1-2-3 for Windows' File Save As command to create the file. These conventions are described above under "Using 1-2-3 for Windows Files in 1-2-3 Releases 2 and 3."

If you're translating to a .DIF (VisiCalc) file format, Translate prompts you to specify a row versus a column orientation. If you are translating multiple files to this format, all of them will be translated with the same orientation.

If you're translating to dBASE II, dBASE III, or dBASE III PLUS format, Translate will prompt you to specify whether you want to translate the entire file or a specific named range. If you select named range, Translate will prompt you for a range name. Type an appropriate range name at the prompt. Only data from that range will be translated to the new file. If you are translating multiple files, however, all of them must have the range name you specify.

Translating at the Operating System Prompt

You can also enter Translate commands directly at the operating system prompt. In fact, Translate offers six different executable files that allow you to specify a translation source and target file as well as provide specific instructions regarding the translation.

Because you can enter Translate commands at the operating system level, you can use them in batch files to automate the translations you perform often. Furthermore, because 1-2-3's Translate commands support the use of standard wild card characters (? or *), you can use them to translate a group of files with similar names or matching extensions. 1-2-3 for Windows offers the following Translate commands:

- TRANDB2: Translates 1-2-3 for Windows files to and from dBASE II's file format.

- TRANDB3: Translates 1-2-3 for Windows files to and from dBASE III and III PLUS file format.

- TRANDIF: Translates 1-2-3 for Windows files to and from a .DIF file format. This file format can be read by products that read and write .DIF compatible files, such as VisiCalc.

- TRANENA2: Translates 1-2-3 for Windows files to and from Enable 2.0 file format.

- TRANUP4: Translates 1-2-3 for Windows files to and from SuperCalc4 file format.

- TRANSYLK: Translates .SLK-compatible files to 1-2-3 for Windows file format only. The .SLK file format is used by MultiPlan 4.2.

- TRANWKS: Translates Release 3 files to and from 1-2-3 Release 1A, 2, 2.01 as well as Symphony Release 1, 1.01, 1.1, 1.2, and 2.

Each of these commands relies on the extension of a file in determining its file format. Therefore, you must use the default extensions of both the source and target product with these commands. If the source file does not have the default extension of its host program, you must rename the file to include the appropriate extension before translating it.

Entering a Command from the Operating System

When entering Translate commands at the DOS prompt, you must use the following format:

Command Source-file Target-file Flags

- *Command*: One of the Translate commands such as TRANDIF or TRANDB3.

- *Source-file*: The name of the file you want to translate from, such as BUDGET.WK3.

- *Target-file*: The name of the new file that you want to translate to, for example ACCT1.WK1.

- *Flags*: One or more instructions that are specific to the file format you're translating. In some cases, flags are optional. A list of available flags follows:

  -a: Translates @functions that are specific to 1-2-3 for Windows to the new file as add-in @functions, and link formulas as @@. Use this flag when you are translating to file formats compatible with either prior releases of 1-2-3 or Symphony. If you do not use this flag, new @functions and link formulas will be translated as labels.

  -lx: Used to translate a multiple worksheet file. X is the letter of the worksheet to be translated.

  -o: Overwrites an existing file with the same name.

  -r: Translates files to .DIF format with a rowwise, as opposed to a columnwise, orientation. (Columnwise is the default). Use this flag with TRANDIF.

  -r*name*: Translates a named range, as opposed to the entire file, when you're translating from 1-2-3 for Windows to dBASE file formats. Use this flag with TRANDB2 or TRANDB3.

Some Examples

The following command line translates a 1-2-3 for Windows file called SCHED.WK3 to a Multiplan (.SLK) file format and uses the -O flag to overwrite an existing file called SCHED.SLK.

```
TRANSYLK SCHED.WK3 SCHED.SLK -O
```

This next command line translates only worksheet A of a 1-2-3 for Windows file to a Release 2 file with a new name.

```
TRANWKS DATA.WK3 SALES.WK1 -LA
```

The following command line translates all the .DIF files in the current directory to a 1-2-3 for Windows-compatible file format and changes the columnwise orientation of the data to a rowwise orientation.

```
TRANDIF *.DIF *.WK3 -R
```

This next command translates a dBASE III PLUS file to 1-2-3 for Windows format.

```
TRANDB3 SALARY.DBF SALARY.WK3
```

DYNAMIC DATA EXCHANGE (DDE)

Dynamic Data Exchange (DDE) allows Windows applications to communicate with one another by means of Windows' messaging system. Two Windows applications can, in effect, carry on a "conversation" by passing messages back and forth to each other. Usually, the topic of the conversation is the exchange of information. The application requesting the information is known as the "client" and the application providing that information is known as the "server."

When information (text or a graphics image) is transferred from the server to the client, it is displayed in the client's work area. In addition, a link to the original source of the information is formed. That way, whenever the data in the server application changes, the client application is automatically updated for the change.

It is always the client application that starts a DDE conversation. The client does this by broadcasting a message to all currently running Windows applications requesting the specific type of information that it needs. The server application responds to this message by indicating that it can provide the requested information, and the conversation begins.

An application that supports DDE can be both a client and a server. That is, it can request data from one application while, at the same time, providing data to another. This requires two entirely separate DDE conversations, however.

When a client requests information from a server, it must define the type of information it wants. It does this by providing the following three things: an application name, a data topic, and a data item. For purposes of DDE, each application has its own unique *application name*. For example, the application name of Microsoft Excel is Excel, the application name of Microsoft Word for Windows is Winword, and the application name of 1-2-3 for Windows is (you guessed it) 123W.

The *data topic* is usually the name of a document file for the server application. For example, if 1-2-3 is acting as the server, the data topic would be the name of a worksheet file. Finally, the *data item* defines the specific location of the information in the data topic. For example, in 1-2-3, this might be a named block of worksheet cells.

There are three types of DDE links: hot, warm, and cold. Not all applications support all three types of links, however. With a hot link, the client application is always notified whenever the linked data item in the server application changes. This form of DDE link is truly dynamic and is perhaps the most common. A warm link, on the other hand, is updated only when the client requests it. Finally, with a cold link, the data is transferred from server to client once and is not updated. This type of link is useful when all you need is a "snapshot" as of the current point in time. As you'll soon see, 1-2-3 allows you to create both hot and warm links to other Windows applications. It also allows you to "deactivate" a DDE link, thereby making it a cold link.

In order to form a DDE link between two applications both must be open on the Windows desktop. As you'll soon see, DDE conversations are often initiated with the help of the Windows Clipboard; that is, the Clipboard is used as a means to communicate source information—application name, data topic, and data item—from server to client. In addition, the server application must provide information to the client in a format that the client can read. Once again, the Clipboard is often used as a means to communicate to the client the different formats that are available from the server.

In case this all seems a bit confusing, the sections that follow will take you through several sample DDE sessions. During the process, you'll learn about not only how 1-2-3 for Windows goes about forming hot and cold DDE links with other applications, but also how the Clipboard plays a role in helping to set up a DDE link.

1-2-3 for Windows and DDE

In 1-2-3, DDE is implemented through two different commands, Edit Paste Link and Edit Link Options. The Edit Paste Link command lets you create a DDE link to another Windows application in a 1-2-3 worksheet file. You can choose a specific location—range address or named range—where the DDE link is created.

The Edit Link Options command, is primarily used to edit an existing DDE Link and control how it is updated. The Edit Link Options command offers the following options:

- Create: Lets you create a DDE link to an inactive application (an application that is not currently open on the Windows desktop). Although this option has little to do with editing existing links, it is grouped under the Edit Link Options command.

- Edit: Lets you edit an existing DDE link. For example, you can change the application name, data topic, and data item for the link. You can also change its worksheet location and its method of update, Automatic (hot) versus Manual (warm).

- Update: Lets you update existing DDE links whose method of update is Manual (warm).

- Deactivate: Lets you deactivate an existing DDE link—that is, turn it off temporarily, making the link cold. You can reactivate a deactivated link by using the Update option.

- Delete: Lets you delete an existing DDE link.

Each of these options is explained in more detail in the sections that follow.

When you create a DDE link in a 1-2-3 worksheet file, it becomes part of that file. Therefore, when you save the worksheet file, your DDE link is saved along with it.

Note: The Edit Paste Link and Edit Link Options commands are only part of 1-2-3's DDE story. In fact, through its macro language, 1-2-3 for Windows not only lets you request information from other Windows applications that support DDE, but also lets you pass information and commands to those applications. See Chapter 15, "The Macro Programming Language," for more on using macros to control DDE.

Using Edit Paste Link

The Edit Paste Link command is common to many Windows applications that support DDE. Although the name of this command may vary from one application to the next, its function is essentially the same; it allows you to create a DDE link to another Windows application. The data item requested by the command is then displayed in a location of your choosing in the work area of the current application. The application initiating the Edit Paste Link command becomes the client and the application referenced by the command becomes the server.

Perhaps the best way to illustrate how to use 1-2-3's Edit Paste Link command is in the context of an example. The example we'll use will be to link a 1-2-3 for Windows worksheet to a Microsoft Word for Windows document file. The information from the Word document file will then be displayed in the 1-2-3 worksheet. The DDE link that is formed will be hot. Therefore, whenever the data in the Word document changes, the data in the 1-2-3 worksheet will be automatically updated for that change.

To form this DDE link, you begin by opening Word for Windows and creating some information. Just about anything will do. For example, Figure 17-13 shows a sample tax table that has been created in Word for Windows. Once the chart has been created, use your mouse to select the entire table and then select Word's Edit Copy command to copy the table to the Clipboard. When you copy the table to the Clipboard, its source information—its application name, data topic, and data item—is copied along with it.

Note: The Clipboard has relatively little to do with DDE. However, it is often used as a means of relaying the source information for a data item—its application name, topic name, and data item—from one application to another.

Once the table has been copied to the Clipboard, you're ready to link that table to a 1-2-3 worksheet. To do this, start 1-2-3 for Windows and highlight the range where you want the Word for Windows table to be displayed. Make sure you highlight a range that

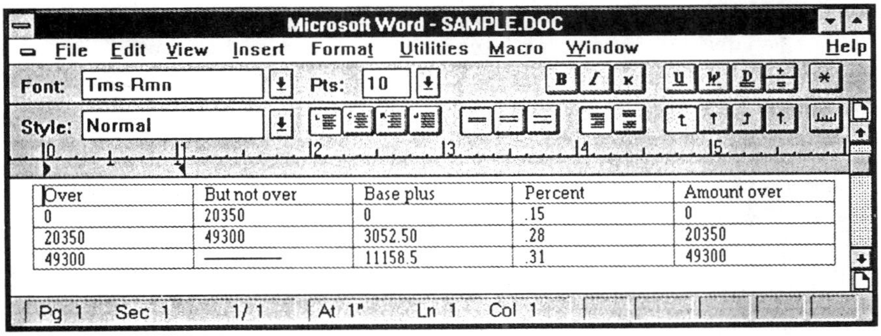

Over	But not over	Base plus	Percent	Amount over
0	20350	0	.15	0
20350	49300	3052.50	.28	20350
49300	———	11158.5	.31	49300

Figure 17-13 A sample table displayed in Word for Windows

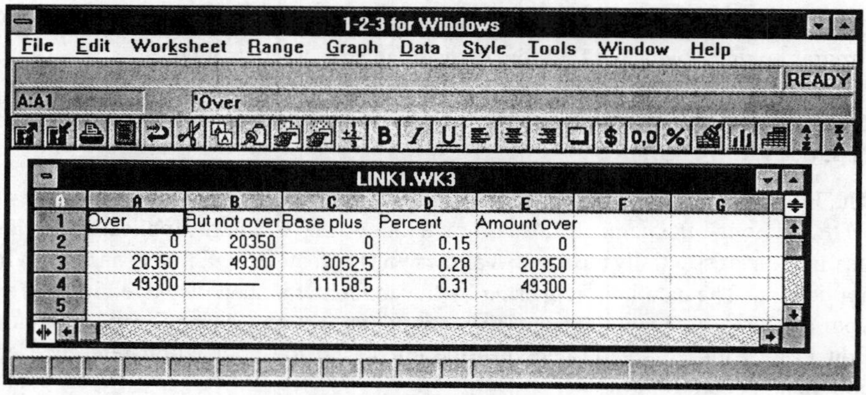

Figure 17-14 Information from Word for Windows that has been linked to 1-2-3 for Windows by DDE

is large enough to accommodate the entire table. Otherwise, 1-2-3 will only display part of the information you're attempting to link. The extent of the link formed will be limited to the amount of information that will fit within the range you've specified.

For example, the table in Figure 17-13 is five columns wide and four rows deep. Therefore, if you want the table to begin in cell A:A1, you would highlight the range A:A1..A:E4. When you're ready, select the Edit Paste Link command. 1-2-3 reads the source information on the Clipboard and pastes the Word table starting at the upper-left corner of the range you've specified. Your screen should appear similar to Figure 17-14.

If you take a close look at the data in the range A:A1..A:E4 of Figure 17-14, you'll notice that character strings from the Word document that begin with a letter are linked to the worksheet as labels, and character strings that begin with a number are linked as values. Therefore, the numbers in the table in Figure 17-14 can be used in calculations.

Note: If the Edit Paste Link command appears grayed (nonselectable), it means the source information on the Clipboard is not acceptable to 1-2-3. This can happen for one of several reasons. On the one hand, there may be nothing on the Clipboard. You can check this by using the Clipboard viewer application. Another possibility is that the server application does not support DDE. Finally, although this is rare, the server application may not be capable of providing information in a format that is usable by 1-2-3 for Windows. See "Editing an Existing Link" later in this chapter for additional information on this topic.

To test this DDE link, switch back to Word for Windows and change one or more of the numbers in the table. When you switch back to 1-2-3 for Windows, the table displayed in the 1-2-3 worksheet has been updated for the change.

Note: If you delete columns or rows in 1-2-3 that contain a DDE link, 1-2-3 does not delete the link. Instead, the link remains, but is no longer associated with a specific worksheet range. To reassign the link to a new worksheet range, you can use the Edit Link Options command. See "Editing an Existing Link" later for more details on this.

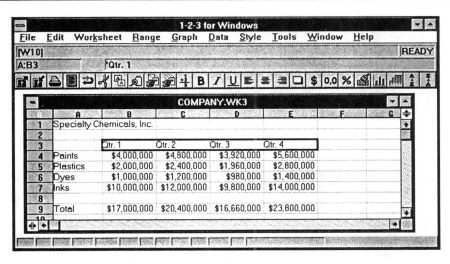

Figure 17-15 A sample table of data in 1-2-3

Using Information from 1-2-3 in Other Applications

You can use information from 1-2-3 for Windows in other Windows applications that support DDE. For example, suppose you want to link a table of numbers created in 1-2-3 for Windows to a Word for Windows document. To do this, first create the table in 1-2-3. Figure 17-15 shows an example table in the range A:A1..A:E9.

Once the table has been created, highlight it and select 1-2-3's Edit Copy command to copy it to the Windows Clipboard. When the table is copied to the Clipboard, its source information—application name, data-topic name, and data item—is copied along with it.

Next, start Word for Windows and open the document file of your choice. Once the document file is displayed, position the cursor where you want the table of numbers from 1-2-3 for Windows to be displayed (linked). When you're ready, select Edit Paste Link from Word's menu. Word displays the dialog box in Figure 17-16. At the bottom of this dialog box, Word shows the path and name of the 1-2-3 file. To create a hot link, turn on the Auto Update check box. (Otherwise, a cold link will be created.) To complete the command, select OK. Word pastes a field reference into the current document similar to the following:

```
{DDEAUTO 123W C:\\123W\\WORK\\COMPANY.WK3.A:A1..A:E9\*Mergeformat}
```

Figure 17-16 Word for Windows prompts you whether to create a hot link

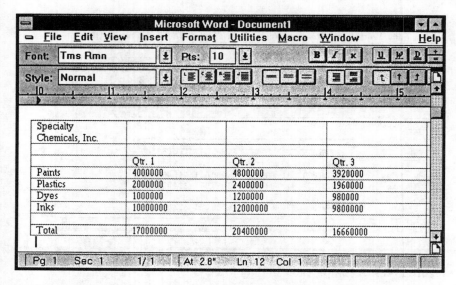

Figure 17-17   1-2-3 for Windows data linked to Word for Windows by DDE

Notice the application name, 123W, the data topic C:\123W\WORK\COM-PANY.WK3, and the data item, A:A1..A:E9, are included in this field code. To display the actual table itself, select the View Field Codes command from Word's menu. Word displays the 1-2-3 for Windows table as shown in Figure 17-17. To test the link, switch back to 1-2-3 and change one of the numbers in the table, then switch back to Word for Windows. When you return to Word, the table has been updated for the change.

Note: A common application of DDE is to display a graph created in Microsoft Excel in a Word for Windows document. However, you cannot display a graph created in 1-2-3 in a Word for Windows document. This is because Lotus has decided to use a proprietary format when placing its graphics information on the Windows Clipboard. See "Editing an Existing Link" later for more on what formats 1-2-3 for Windows places on the Clipboard.

The example just described shows how you might go about setting up a DDE link in Word for Windows. However, another Windows application may have an entirely different set of commands and procedures for creating a DDE link. For information on how to implement DDE in your particular application (as well as whether the application supports DDE in the first place), you'll have to check the manual that came with the application.

Using Edit Link Options

As mentioned, 1-2-3 lets you edit the properties of a DDE link using the Edit Link Options command. You can also use this command to create new links to inactive (unopened) applications, if you so desire.

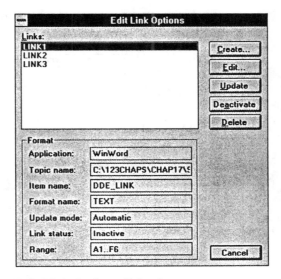

Figure 17-18 The Edit Link Options dialog box

When you select the Edit Link Options command, 1-2-3 displays the dialog box in Figure 17-18. The list box at the top of this dialog box shows the names of DDE links that presently exist in the current file. The first DDE link is assigned the name LINK1, the second LINK2, and so on. When you select one of these names, 1-2-3 displays the properties for the link in the information boxes below. The buttons to the right let you edit the properties for the link in various ways. For example, you can edit the link to reference an entirely different application, if you so desire. Or you can change its update mode from hot—updated automatically—to warm—updated only on request. The sections that follow explain the use of each of these buttons in detail.

Linking to an Inactive Application

Unlike most applications that support DDE, 1-2-3 lets you create a DDE link to an inactive application (an application that is not currently open on the Windows desktop). To do this, select the Create button from Edit Link Options dialog box. 1-2-3 displays the dialog box in Figure 17-19.

In the Link name text box, 1-2-3 displays the default name it has assigned to the link. The first new link in a worksheet file is assigned the name LINK1, the second LINK2, and so on. You can accept this default name or type in one of your own. If you do decide to type in a link name of your own, however, there are certain restrictions that apply. See "Defining Link Names" later for more details on this.

In the Application drop-down list box, 1-2-3 displays the names of applications that are currently open on the Windows desktop. You can select the name of an open application, or you can type the name of an inactive application on disk. You must use its special DDE application name—for example, Excel or Winword. If the application

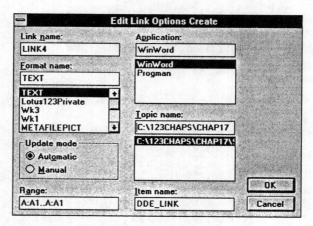

Figure 17-19   The Edit Link Options Create dialog box

supports DDE, you should be able to find its application name in the documentation that
came with the software. If you can't find it there, open the application and check for its
name here in the Application text box.

In the Topic name box, type the path and name of the application file you want to link
to. If there is currently information on the Windows Clipboard about a file that is presently
open in an application that supports DDE, 1-2-3 will display the name of that file in this
text box. Therefore, there may be an entry in this box that you have to replace.

In the Item name text box, type the name of the data item you want to link to in the
source application file. For example, if you are linking to another spreadsheet application,
such as Microsoft Excel, you would type the name that corresponds to a named block of
spreadsheet cells. Once again, if there is currently information on the Windows Clipboard
about a data topic in a particular file that is presently open in an application that supports
DDE, 1-2-3 will display the name of that data topic in this text box. Therefore, you may
need to replace the entry that is already in this box.

Note: In some cases, you may not know the name of the data item. Take the case of
Word for Windows, for example. Word does not have columns, rows, or range names to
define locations of specific blocks of data within its document files. In these cases, the
server application must provide the data item name. For example, when you copy a block
of data from a Word document to the Windows Clipboard, Word also copies a data item
name for that block. The first block of data is assigned the item name DDE_LINK, the
second DDE_LINK1, and so on. In these cases, you'll have to open the server application
and copy the appropriate information to the Windows Clipboard, before attempting to
create the link in 1-2-3. That way, when you select 1-2-3's Edit Link Options Create
command, the appropriate data item name will already be displayed in the Item name
text box.

From the Format name drop-down box, select an appropriate format for the transferred
data. This box contains the names of file data formats that 1-2-3 is capable of reading. In

most cases, 1-2-3 will suggest an appropriate format by displaying it in the Format name text box. 1-2-3 makes this suggestion by checking the Clipboard for a list of available formats from the server application. If nothing is on the Clipboard or an acceptable format is not available, 1-2-3 will suggest TEXT (meaning ASCII text). Most Windows applications are capable of providing this format when acting as the server in a DDE conversation. Nevertheless, if you don't specify an alternative format, 1-2-3 will transfer the data using an ASCII text format. (See "Editing an Existing Link" later for more details on specifying a different data format.)

From the Update mode group box, select from either Automatic or Manual. If you select Automatic (the default), 1-2-3 will create a hot link; that is the link will be updated automatically whenever the linked data in the source file is changed. If you select Manual, 1-2-3 will create a warm link. You can update this type of link by selecting the Update button from the Edit Link Options dialog box.

In the Range text box, specify the address or range name that defines the location where you want the link to be created. Make sure you specify a range that is large enough to accommodate the incoming data. Otherwise, 1-2-3 will truncate incoming text or clip (and possibly resize) an incoming graphics image.

To create the link, select OK. 1-2-3 will create the link in the location you specified in the Range box. If the source of the link is an inactive application and data file on disk, 1-2-3 will attempt to open that application and load the appropriate file prior to creating the link. If this operation fails, 1-2-3 will issue an error message and the link will not be created.

After creating your new DDE link, 1-2-3 returns you to the Edit Link Options dialog box. At this point, you can create another link or select Cancel to return to the current worksheet.

Defining Link Names As mentioned above, rather than using 1-2-3's default link names, you can define your own for the Edit Link Options Create command. If you decide to define your own link names, however, be aware that the following restrictions apply:

- Link names are limited to no more than 15 characters.

- Do not start a link name with ! (exclamation point), and do not include spaces, commas, semicolons, periods, or any of the following characters: +, *, -, /, &, >, <, @, #, {, ?.

- Do not use names that look like cell addresses, such as A12.

- Do not begin link names with numbers, such as 12JAN.

- Avoid @function names, key names, or macro command keywords as link names.

Editing an Existing Link

1-2-3 lets you edit the properties for existing links. To do this, first select the Edit Link Options command to display the dialog box shown earlier in Figure 17-18. The list box at the top of this dialog box shows the names of DDE links that exist in the current file. To edit the properties for a particular link, first select its name from the list box. When

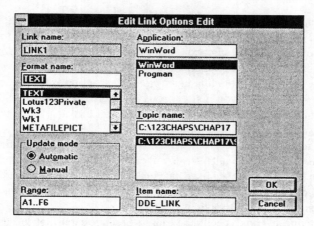

Figure 17-20 The Edit Link Options Edit dialog box

you select a link name, 1-2-3 displays the properties for that link in the information boxes below. To edit one or more of these properties, select the Edit button. 1-2-3 displays the dialog box in Figure 17-20.

You'll notice that the Edit Link Options Edit dialog box in Figure 17-20 matches the dialog box for the Edit Link Options Create command (Figure 17-19) in virtually every detail. What's more, you use its various components in precisely the same way, but there are a few details that bear further discussion.

You'll notice in Figure 17-20 that the Link name box appears grayed (nonselectable). This means you cannot change the name assigned to the link. You can, however, change just about everything else. You can change the contents of the Application, Topic name, and Item name boxes to reference a different data item in an entirely different application if you so desire.

You can also change the data format shown in the Format name text box. This controls the format in which data is transferred from the Windows Clipboard to your 1-2-3 worksheet when forming a DDE link. If you do not select a specific data format from this box, 1-2-3 will transfer the data in Text (ASCII) format. In reality, though, 1-2-3 cannot always control which data format is used when transferring information from the Windows Clipboard. Instead, this is determined by the source application.

When you use Edit Copy to copy information from a Windows application to the Clipboard, that information may be sent to the Clipboard in more than one format. In fact, the developer of the application can choose one of several predefined formats or develop a proprietary format. To see what formats are currently on the Clipboard for a data item, simply open the Clipboard viewer (double-click on the icon labeled Clipboard in Program Manager's group window) and select the Display option. Clipboard displays a list of data formats that are available.

Figure 17-21, for example, shows a list of formats provided by 1-2-3 when you copy a range of underlying numbers for a graph to the Clipboard. As you can see, multiple data formats are copied to the Clipboard, many of which are proprietary to Lotus. This may

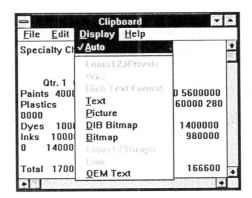

Figure 17-21 Data formats placed on the Windows Clipboard by 1-2-3 for Windows

explain why you have difficulty linking to 1-2-3 for Windows data objects—for example, graphs—from your other Windows applications. (A format option that appears grayed is still available, but it cannot be displayed in the Clipboard viewer window.) In most cases, however, you'll find that at least one of 1-2-3's data formats can be read by your particular application.

You can also change the update mode for the currently selected DDE link. To do this, use the Automatic and Manual buttons in the Update Mode group box. If you select Automatic (the default), 1-2-3 will update this link automatically whenever the linked data in the source file is changed. If you select Manual, 1-2-3 will update this link only on request; that is, only when you select the Update button from the Edit Link Options dialog box.

You can also change the location of the currently selected DDE link by modifying the range address or name shown in the Range text box. You must, however, specify a range that is within the current worksheet file. You cannot use a file reference—for example, <<SALES>>A:A1..A:E4—to move the link to a different worksheet file.

To record the changes you made, select OK. 1-2-3 implements your changes and returns you to the Edit Link Options dialog box. At this point, you can either edit another link or select Cancel to return to the current worksheet.

Deactivating a Link

You can also deactivate a link. When you deactivate a link, it is not deleted, only temporarily disabled. That way, 1-2-3 will not attempt to update the link when the linked data item in the source application is changed. This, in effect, makes the link a cold link.

To deactivate a DDE link, select Edit Link Options to display the Edit Link Options dialog box. From the list box provided, select the name of the link you'd like to deactivate, then select the Deactivate button. 1-2-3 deactivates the link. This change is reflected in the Link status information box below, which records the link as inactive. To return to the current worksheet, select the Cancel button.

As mentioned, when you deactivate a link, it is not deleted, only disabled temporarily. You can reactivate the link at any time by selecting it from the Edit Link Options dialog box and then selecting the Update button.

Updating Links Manually

If you selected a Manual update mode for one of your DDE links, that link is warm—that is, it will be updated only when you request it. To request an update for a warm link, select Edit Link Options to display the Edit Link Options dialog box. Next, select the link you want to update from the list box. Finally, select the Update button. 1-2-3 then updates the link you've selected.

You can also use the Update button to reactivate a DDE link that has been deactivated (temporarily disabled) with the Edit Link Options Deactivate command. To do this, select the name of the inactive link from the Edit Link Options dialog box and then select the Update button. 1-2-3 reactivates the link you've selected and updates it for any changes.

Caution: To update an existing link to another application, that application must be open on the Windows desktop. In fact, if the source application and data file referenced by the link are not open, selecting Update from the Edit Link Options dialog box will have no effect.

Deleting a DDE Link

1-2-3 also lets you delete an existing DDE link. To delete a DDE link, select Edit Link Options to display the Edit Link Options dialog box. From the list box provided, select the name of the link you wish to delete, then select the Delete push button. 1-2-3 then deletes the DDE link you've selected.

Appendix A

Customizing 1-2-3 for Windows

More than any previous version of 1-2-3, 1-2-3 for Windows lets you customize its operation to suit the way you work. This appendix focuses on the two most significant ways in which you can customize the program: changing 1-2-3's SmartIcons and changing your user setup and international settings.

CHANGING 1-2-3 FOR WINDOWS' SMARTICON PALETTE

1-2-3's SmartIcons provide a comprehensive set of over 100 predefined and customizable shortcuts for common worksheet and graph operations. 1-2-3 offers two icon palettes— one for worksheets and one for graphs—and you use and customize the two palettes in the same way.

> ▼ *Tip:* If you forget what an icon does, simply point to it in the icon palette of a worksheet or graph window, and press the right mouse button. When you do, 1-2-3 displays a description of the icon's operation at the top of your screen to jog your memory.

1-2-3 also gives you two types of SmartIcons: Standard and Custom. *Standard SmartIcons* provide single-step execution of many worksheet and graph operations, such as adding ranges of data, copying, moving, or printing data in a worksheet; or creating and enhancing a graph in the graph window. 1-2-3's Standard worksheet and graph SmartIcons are listed in Tables A-1 and A-2.

Custom SmartIcons, on the other hand, have macros attached to them. 1-2-3 provides some samples that you can use as is, or you can edit their underlying macros to perform actions more to your liking. 1-2-3 even lets you design your own Custom SmartIcons.

TABLE A-1   1-2-3 for Windows Standard Worksheet SmartIcons

Brings up the File New dialog box.

Same as selecting File Open.

Same as selecting File Save; immediately saves the current file to disk.

Same as selecting File Print.

Same as File Preview.

Same as Edit Undo; undoes the previous command or action.

Same as Edit Cut; cuts selected range of data to the Windows Clipboard.

Same as Edit Copy; copies the selected range of data to the Windows Clipboard.

Same as Edit Paste; automatically pastes the selected range of data to the Windows Clipboard.

Permanently deletes selected range of data without placing it on the Clipboard.

Copies the selected range of data to the current worksheet location you specify.

Immediately moves the selected range of data to the worksheet location you specify.

Same as Edit Find; used to search and/or replace labels and formulas in the worksheet.

Same as F5, or the Range Go To command; use to move the cell pointer to the range you specify.

Same as selecting Graph New, and pressing Enter; creates a default line graph from data in a preselected range.

Same as Style Alignment Left; aligns text in the selected range to the left of each cell.

Same as Style Alignment Center; center aligns text in the selected range in the center of each cell.

Same as Style Alignment Right; aligns text in the selected range to the right of each cell.

Same as Style Alignment Even; stretches text contained in the selected range so it's evenly displayed across each cell.

Converts the contents of the cells in the selected range to boldface type in the current font.

Converts all characters in the selected range to italic typeface in their current font.

Underlines the contents of the specified range.

(continued)

TABLE A-1 1-2-3 for Windows Standard Worksheet SmartIcons *(continued)*

⎡U⎤	Double underlines characters in the specified range.
⎡N⎤	Restores the contents of the specified range to a normal typeface in the current font.
⎡⋏A⎤	Displays the contents of cells in the selected range in 1-2-3's next font size (as listed in the Style Font Fonts list box).
⎡AA⎤	Assigns the next available 1-2-3 screen color to the contents of cells in the selected range.
⎡AA⎤	Assigns the next available 1-2-3 screen color to the cell background in the specified range.
⎡□⎤	Surrounds the selected range with a box.
⎡◱⎤	Surrounds the selected range with a box and adds a drop shadow.
⎡▦⎤	Adds shading to the cells in the selected range.
⎡$⎤	Formats the contents in the specified range for Currency 2 places.
⎡0,0⎤	Formats the contents in the specified range for Comma 0 places.
⎡%⎤	Formats the contents in the specified range for Percent 2 places.
⎡⊞⎤	Displays the current system date in the selected cell in Long International date format.
⎡⊞⎤	Recalculates the formulas in active files.
⎡⊞⎤	Sums the adjacent range (either column or row).
⎡↕⎤	Sorts the range surrounding the cell pointer in ascending order.
⎡↕⎤	Sorts the range surrounding the cell pointer in descending order.
⎡▣⎤	Fills the selected range with sequential integers beginning with 0.
⎡▦⎤	Repeats the contents of the current cell in all the cells of the range specified.
⎡▦⎤	Tiles all open windows.
⎡▣⎤	Cascades all open windows.
⎡▦⎤	Toggles the current worksheet between normal and perspective view.
⎡▦⎤	Moves the cell pointer to the next active worksheet.
⎡▦⎤	Moves the cell pointer to the previous worksheet.
⎡◤⎤	Moves the cell pointer Home (to cell A1).
⎡▣⎤	Same as END HOME; moves the cell pointer to the last cell entry in the current worksheet.

(continued)

TABLE A-1 1-2-3 for Windows Standard Worksheet SmartIcons *(continued)*

⊞   Same as END ↑; moves the cell pointer to the cell above the topmost cell in the column range.

⊞   Same as END ↓.

⊟   Same as END →.

⊟   Same as END ←.

@   Lets you choose from a comprehensive list of 1-2-3 for Windows' @functions.

[·]   Lets you choose from a list of macro commands, keywords, and symbols.

▨   Same as Tools Macro Run; prompts you to select a macro to run.

▨   Turns macro STEP and TRACE modes on and off.

[+]   Inserts a "+" (plus) at the start of the edit line.

▦   Inserts rows at the current location of the cell pointer equal to the number of selected rows.

▦   Inserts columns at the current location of the cell pointer equal to the number of highlighted columns.

▦   Deletes the currently highlighted rows.

▦   Deletes the selected columns.

▨   Inserts a blank worksheet after the current one.

▨   Deletes the selected worksheets in a multiple-sheet file.

▨   Use to select a range to which to apply the styles and formats in the current cell.

[?=]   Starts 1-2-3 for Windows' Solver.

▨   Same as selecting Tools SmartIcon Customize.

1-2-3 for Windows' configurable palette lets you change its position and customize its contents. In fact, you can move the palette, hide it, resize it, and add or remove icons at any time during the session, and your changes will be saved for future sessions.

Positioning the Icon Palette

To change the position of the icon palette in either a worksheet or a graph window, select the Tools SmartIcons command. When you do, 1-2-3 displays the dialog box in Figure A-1. The Top option is the default setting. It places the SmartIcon palette at the top of the work area. To move the palette to the left, right, or bottom of the work area, select

TABLE A-2 1-2-3's Standard SmartIcons Available in a Graph Window

Icon	Equivalent Command	Icon	Equivalent Command
◻	Draw Arrow	▯	Edit Delete
◻	Draw Line	▦	Edit Replicate
◻	Draw Ellipse	◻	Rearrange Turn
◻	Draw Polygon	◻	Rearrange Flip Vertical
◻	Draw Rectangle	◻	Rearrange Flip Horizontal
abc	Draw Text	◻	Layout Send Forward
◻	Draw Freehand	◻	Layout Fall Back
◻	Chart Type Line graph	◻	Chart Type XY
◻	Chart Type Bar Vertical	◻	Edit Copy
◻	Chart Type Bar Horizontal	◻	Rearrange Quarter-Turn
◻	Chart Type Mixed	◻	Window Enlarge
◻	Chart Type Pie	◻	Window Reduce
◻	Chart Type Area	◻	Window Zoom
◻	Chart Type 3D Area	◻	Window Tile
◻	Chart Type HLCO	◻	Window Cascade
◻	Chart Type 3D Line	◻	Chart Type
◻	Chart Type 3D Bar	◻	Tools SmartIcons Customize
◻	Chart Type 3D Pie		

the appropriate radio button. Whichever option you choose, a maximum of 26 icons will appear within the palette. Conversely, by selecting Floating, you can obtain a moveable, resizable palette, capable of displaying up to 135 SmartIcons. You can also select the Hide palette option to temporarily remove the SmartIcon palette from view.

Adding and Removing SmartIcons

Figure A-2 shows the worksheet icon palette that appears when you first install the program. To add or remove SmartIcons from the palette, begin by selecting Tools SmartIcons Customize. When you do, you'll see a dialog box like the one shown in Figure A-3.

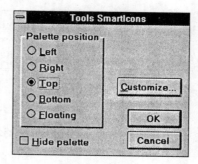

Figure A-1 The Tools SmartIcons dialog box

Note: When you select Tools SmartIcons Customize in a graph window, you'll get the dialog box shown in Figure A-4.

Adding a SmartIcon to the Icon Palette

To add a SmartIcon to the palette, first select the spot in the Current palette list box where you want the icon to appear by clicking on the icon currently there. (If you don't specify a position, 1-2-3 automatically adds the icon to the end of the palette.) Next, move to the Standard icons list box, and select the icon you want to add.

You have two options for selecting an icon from the Standard icons list: You can double-click on it, or you can click on it once and select the Add button. Either way, 1-2-3 moves a copy of it to the Current palette list box.

When you have the palette the way you want it, select OK twice to return to READY mode. The new palette you've created for the current worksheet (or graph) becomes the default palette from that point on.

> ▼ *Tip:*   When you click on any of the icons in the Tools SmartIcons Customize dialog box, 1-2-3 displays a brief explanation of the icon's operation in the Description text box below.

The procedure for adding Custom icons is the same as that for Standard icons. Before you add a Custom icon, though, you should make sure you're familiar with what it does. To check one out, highlight it in the Custom icons list and select the Assign macro... button (see Figure A-3). 1-2-3 displays a dialog box like the one shown in Figure A-5. If you like what you see in the Macro text box, select Cancel to return to Tools SmartIcons Customize, and add the Custom icon to the palette.

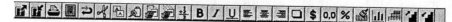

Figure A-2 The initial worksheet SmartIcon bar

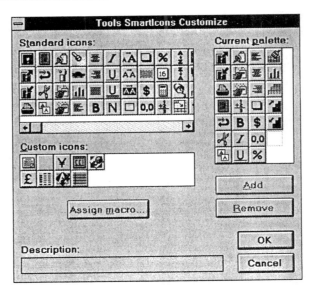

Figure A-3 Tools SmartIcons Customize (worksheet window)

Removing a SmartIcon from the Icon Bar

Deleting an icon from the icon bar is just as easy as adding one. From the Tools SmartIcons Customize dialog box, simply move to the Current palette list box, and remove the SmartIcon by either double-clicking on it, or clicking on it once and selecting the Remove button. Select OK twice to return to READY mode.

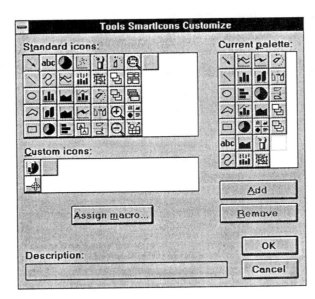

Figure A-4 Tools SmartIcons Customize (graph window)

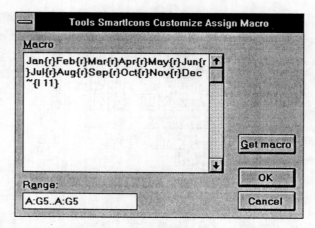

Figure A-5   The Tools SmartIcons Customize Attach Macro dialog box

Assigning a Macro to a SmartIcon

Once you've created, debugged, and saved a macro in a worksheet, it's easy to assign it to one of the existing Custom SmartIcons. For example, you might want to create a simple macro like the one in Figure A-6 that cycles through the available palette display positions on the screen. A SmartIcon like this makes it easy to relocate the icon bar should it get in the way of important data in a worksheet or graph window.

Note: If you have confidence in your macro programming ability, or are entering a simple macro, you can enter the macro code directly in the Macro text box.

To assign a macro to a custom worksheet SmartIcon:

1.   Highlight the entire macro that you want to assign within the worksheet.

2.   Select Tools SmartIcons Customize.

3.   Click on the icon you want to customize in the Custom icons list box (for example, the blank Custom SmartIcon).

4.   Select the Assign macro... button.

5.   Select the Get macro button. Your macro will be displayed in the Macro text box.

6.   Select OK, and 1-2-3 returns you to the Tools SmartIcons Customize dialog box.

You can now add the SmartIcon to the Current worksheet palette using the procedure outlined earlier.

Note: The maximum capacity of the Macro text box is 512 characters. To use longer macros with Custom icons, you should make the macro instructions in the Macro text box branch to a larger macro subroutine in the worksheet.

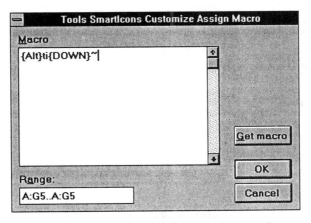

Figure A-6 A sample macro that relocates the SmartIcon palette

Creating Your Own Custom SmartIcons

One of the most appealing features of 1-2-3's Custom SmartIcons is that, in addition to controlling what task each icon performs, you can create your own SmartIcon images. Each Custom icon consists of two parts: a Windows 3 bitmap (.BMP) file that contains the icon image, and a text file that contains a macro (saved with a .MAC extension). By assigning the same filename to the bitmap and macro files—for example, BLUE-SKY.BMP and BLUESKY.MAC—and placing them in the same directory, 1-2-3 will use them together.

1-2-3 stores Custom worksheet SmartIcons in the \123W\SHEETICO directory, while Custom Graph SmartIcons are stored in \123W\GRAPHICO. To add a new Custom SmartIcon, therefore, simply copy the corresponding bitmap and macro files into the appropriate worksheet or graph subdirectory. Of course, to add the same Custom SmartIcon to both icon palettes, just copy the corresponding bitmap and macro files into both subdirectories.

To create a new SmartIcon image, you can use any program or utility capable of producing a Windows 3 compatible .BMP file. Probably the most convenient of these is Windows' own Paintbrush program. However, if you follow Lotus' advice and try to open the blank icon button frame, SAMPLE.BMP (in \123W\SHEETICO for worksheets, or \123W\GRAPHICO for graphs) in Paintbrush, you'll quickly discover that the image appears in its original size—too small for you to work with effectively.

What Lotus doesn't tell you is that 1-2-3 for Windows will automatically scale the bitmap image you create to fit the size of a SmartIcon button. Therefore, you can use a larger frame in Paintbrush. To create a 1″ x 1″ frame, for example, select Options Image Attributes. In the resulting dialog box, select Inches, type **1** for both Width and Height, and select OK. (Also, make sure you've selected a visible color for the frame, preferably black.) To create an image using the new settings, select File New. You can then use Paintbrush's tools and color palette selections to draw any image you'd like.

Since you're using a larger frame, you must also create an image that is large and bold enough to still be visible when 1-2-3 shrinks it to SmartIcon size. Figure A-7A shows an "I" image created with a series of boxes and the text tool using 60 point Courier bold. Believe it or not, it's just striking enough to be distinguishable when 1-2-3 shrinks it to SmartIcon size.

When you've finished drawing your image, save it using Paintbrush's File Save As command. (Windows automatically selects the 16 Color bitmap option for you.) When entering the path and filename for a worksheet SmartIcon, use the syntax `C:\123W\SHEETICO\filename.bmp;` and for a graph SmartIcon, use `C:\123W\GRAPHICO\filename.bmp.` (Figure A-7A, for example, was saved as

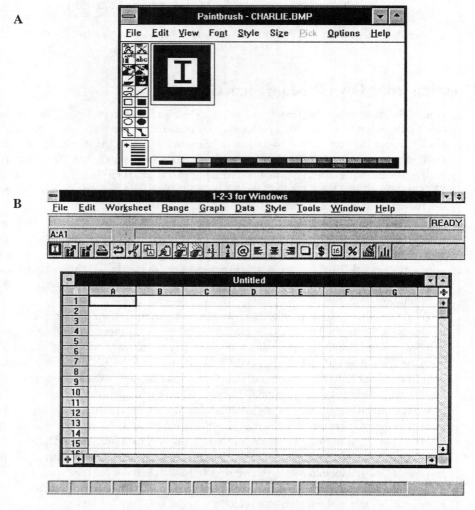

Figure A-7 Creating a SmartIcon image in Windows' Paintbrush and how it appears when you add it to the icon palette

C:\123W\SHEETICO\CHARLIE.BMP.) Then, when you return to 1-2-3 and select Tools SmartIcons Customize, you'll see your new icon displayed in the Custom icons list box. You can then attach a macro to the icon and add it to the current palette, as shown in Figure A-7B.

In "Attaching SmartIcons to Macros," you saw how you can use Tools SmartIcons Customize Attach Macro to create a macro for a Custom SmartIcon. Another valid approach is to create an ASCII text file containing a macro, save it with a .MAC extension, and then copy it to either the worksheet (\123W\SHEETICO) or graph (\123W\GRAPHICO) directory, or both. As mentioned, be sure to use the same root filename for the macro file and related icon bitmap file. For example, if the bitmap file you want to use is CHARLIE.BMP, name its companion macro file CHARLIE.MAC.

> ▼ *Tip:*   You can permanently remove custom SmartIcons by deleting their associated icon bitmap and macro files in either the \SHEETICO or \GRAPHICO subdirectory.

Viewing Macro Strings with Resource Workshop

As you know, you can change the macros assigned to Custom icons. The same is not true of Standard icons. With the help of Borland's Resource Workshop, however, you can view the actual macros attached to Standard SmartIcons. Specifically, Resource Workshop lets you decompile 1-2-3's .DLL (Dynamic Link Library) files and view the actual macro strings that Lotus uses. Among other things, you'll discover some interesting, as yet undocumented, macro commands that are new in 1-2-3 for Windows.

The strings you're looking for are located in the L1WENV.DLL file. After opening this file in the Resource Workshop, scroll down to the STRINGTABLE section and find items 9201 to 9328. Strings 9201 through 9268 contain the macros attached to Standard worksheet SmartIcons, while 9300 through 9328 contain the graph icon assignments. For example, Figure A-8 shows strings 9201–9215, the macros assigned to the first 15 Standard worksheet SmartIcons.

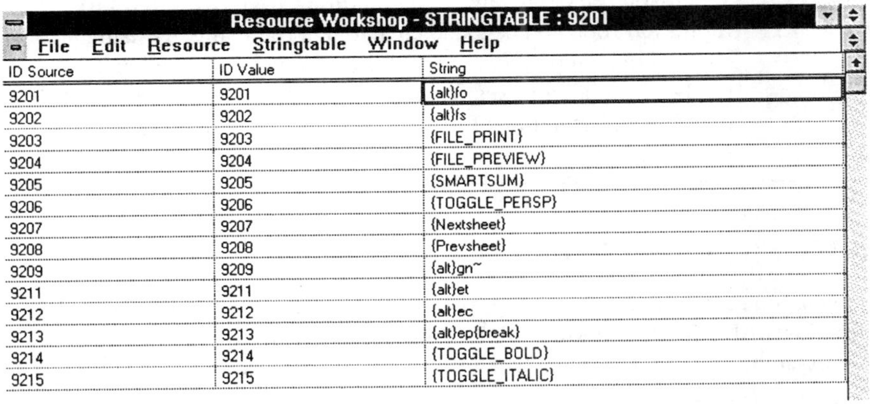 Resource Workshop - STRINGTABLE : 9201		
File Edit Resource Stringtable Window Help		
ID Source	ID Value	String
9201	9201	{alt}fo
9202	9202	{alt}fs
9203	9203	{FILE_PRINT}
9204	9204	{FILE_PREVIEW}
9205	9205	{SMARTSUM}
9206	9206	{TOGGLE_PERSP}
9207	9207	{Nextsheet}
9208	9208	{Prevsheet}
9209	9209	{alt}gn~
9211	9211	{alt}et
9212	9212	{alt}ec
9213	9213	{alt}ep{break}
9214	9214	{TOGGLE_BOLD}
9215	9215	{TOGGLE_ITALIC}

Figure A-8 Resource strings 9201 to 9215

TABLE A-3   Undocumented Macro Commands in 1-2-3 for Windows

{FILE_PRINT}	{FILE_PREVIEW}
{SMARTSUM}	{TOGGLE_PERSP}
{TOGGLE_BOLD}	{TOGGLE_ITALIC}
{TOGGLE_SINGLE}	{SORT_ASCENDING}
{SORT_DESCENDING}	{TOGGLE_SHADOW}
{TOGGLE_DOUBLE}	{TOGGLE_OUTLINE}
{TOGGLE_SHADE}	{PAINT_FORMAT}
{COPY_TO}	{MOVE_TO}

As you view this figure, you'll notice some unusual macro commands. For example, {SMARTSUM} sums an adjacent range of data. You'll find that this command works equally well in your own macros. Table A-3 provides a complete list of the undocumented macro commands that the Resource Workshop reveals.

CHANGING YOUR USER SETUP SETTINGS: TOOLS USER SETUP

1-2-3 for Windows offers a host of global customizing options available through the Tools User Setup command. If you change a Tools User setting (and select OK), the change will remain in effect for the rest of the current session. To make the new setting the default for future sessions, remember to select the Update option first before selecting OK to complete the command.

 Tip: When you select Update, 1-2-3 modifies your 123W.INI program configuration file. You can also change this file manually using an ASCII editor like Notepad. For example, you can change the background color for 1-2-3's dialog boxes from gray to white, modify the "great_looking_dialogs" statement from "great_looking_dialogs=2" to "great_looking_dialogs=0."

Tools User Setup Options

When you select Tools User Setup, you'll see the dialog box in Figure A-9. When you first install 1-2-3 for Windows, all the items in the Options group box are turned on. To eliminate the beep that sounds when you make an error, for example, turn off Beep on

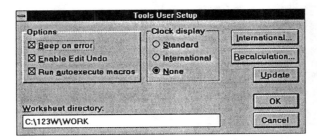

Figure A-9 The Tools User Setup dialog box

error option and select OK; the beep will remain turned off only for the current session. To turn the beep off for future sessions, select the Update button before leaving the dialog box.

By selecting the International option, you can change these options:

Option	Effect
Style	Lets you change the appearance of decimal points, thousands separators, argument separators, and negative numbers.
Currency	Changes the currency symbol and its position.
Format	Sets the International Date and Time formats.
File translation	Sets the way 1-2-3 reads and saves characters in Release 2 (.WK1) files, and sets the character translation table that 1-2-3 uses when importing and creating text files.

Appendix B

Adobe Type Manager

This appendix describes how to install and use Adobe Type Manager (ATM) with 1-2-3 for Windows. By necessity, some of the material presented here is a rehash of the rather sparse ATM manual that comes with 1-2-3. However, in many cases, you'll find this appendix picks up where the manual leaves off.

Adobe Type Manager (ATM) is a Windows-compatible font package that ships with 1-2-3 for Windows. ATM provides on-the-fly generation of fonts for screen display and matching fonts for printing. To gain a better understanding of how ATM works and its importance to Windows, it is helpful to know a little about fonts in Windows.

ABOUT WINDOWS FONTS

Windows 3.0 supports two types of fonts, Graphics Device Interface (GDI) fonts, often called "screen fonts," and device-based fonts, often called "printer fonts." The GDI (screen) fonts are provided by Windows and are stored on .FON files in your \WINDOWS\ SYSTEM directory. Generally, these fonts are used for screen display—thus the name "screen" fonts. However, they can also be used for printing on certain types of graphics printers—for example, dot-matrix, inkjet, and laser printers.

The Windows GDI fonts come in two varieties, raster and vector. The raster fonts (Helv, Tms Rmn, Courier, and Symbol) are defined by bitmaps that exist, prebuilt, on disk in a discrete number of point sizes (usually 8, 10, 12, 14, and 24). They are designed to be displayed and printed only in a specific aspect ratio (height to width). If you increase the point size of a raster font beyond that for which it was designed, Windows simply duplicates columns and rows of pixels to accommodate you. The result is the much talked-about stepped effect known as the "jaggies."

Windows vector fonts include Roman, Modern, and Script. These fonts are stroke-based—that is, they are defined by line segments rather than a bitmap pixel pattern. This makes vector fonts more scalable than raster fonts. As you increase their size, Windows simply extends the length of the lines that define each character. The problem, though, is that each character is defined by the same number of line segments, regardless of its size. Therefore, in larger point sizes, vector fonts tend to appear somewhat anemic.

Device-based, or printer, fonts, on the other hand, are provided by a hardware device—for example, your printer. Printer supplied fonts—sometimes called resident fonts—are either burned into the printer's memory chip or supplied by a cartridge that plugs into a slot on the printer. Windows recognizes these resident fonts by virtue of your installing a Windows printer driver for the printer through the Windows Control Panel.

One of the advantages of using device-based fonts is the sheer variety of available choices. On the downside, Windows cannot hope to provide a matching GDI (screen) font for every available device-based (printer) font. Therefore, when you specify a device-based font that is not available in the GDI set, Windows substitutes the closest available GDI font for screen display. For this reason, there is often a marked disparity between what is displayed on your screen and what is printed.

Another source of fonts to Windows are fonts provided by software programs, often called soft fonts. These fonts are installed on your hard disk, usually in the form of bitmaps. They are then downloaded to your printer at print time. Soft fonts are usually associated with a specific Windows printer driver—for example, the PCL/HP LaserJet driver—and are thus limited to use with that driver. In most cases, the packages that provide soft fonts for printing also provide matching fonts for screen display, which tends to solve the problem of your printed output matching what appears on your screen. On the downside, a separate soft font file must be generated for each size of a given type face. As result, soft fonts tend to require a tremendous amount of disk space to store them.

ADOBE TYPE MANAGER AND WINDOWS

Adobe Type Manager and packages like it help to fill the sizable font void left by Windows. On the one hand, instead of using bitmaps or line segments to display and print its fonts, ATM relies on PostScript scalable outline technology. With this technology, the outline of each character is scaled and defined first. Once the outline of the character is defined, it is filled in with pixels, in the case of your screen, or dots, in the case of your printer. As a result, PostScript fonts are almost infinitely scalable, and you don't get the same degree of "jaggies" associated with a raster font.

For example, Figure B-1 shows two lines of text displayed in 48-point type. Both lines are displayed as they would appear on your screen (about 72 dots per inch). The top line of text is displayed using the Windows Helv raster font with an italic attribute. Notice the jagged edges. The bottom line of text is displayed in ATM's Helvetica-italic Post-

Helv

Helvetica

Figure B-1 A Windows raster font versus an ATM outline

Script outline font. Notice the smoother edges and improved appearance of the characters. You'll get roughly the same results when these two lines are printed.

Another breakthrough for ATM is that it provides a matching screen font for each of its printer fonts. This means that the fonts displayed on your screen will match your printed output. To pull this off, ATM builds your fonts twice, once for screen display and again for printing.

To display your fonts on screen, ATM creates them as you type (on the fly) and stores them in a temporary cache in your computer's memory. That way, when you move from one part of the document to another, ATM can quickly refresh your screen. What's more, ATM lets you control the size of the cache. You can increase its size to improve ATM's performance, or decrease it to provide more memory to your other applications. See "Managing the Font Cache" later in this appendix for details on how to change the size of the font cache.

Another advantage of using ATM is its efficient use of disk space. Instead of generating a bitmap font file for each point size of a given typeface, ATM lets you generate different sizes of the same typeface from a single outline font file.

Once installed, ATM is automatically loaded each time you start Windows. That way, the fonts provided by ATM are available to all your Windows applications. You can turn ATM off if you'd like, however. See "Turning ATM off" later in this chapter for details on how to do this.

ATM comes with an impressive number of fonts from which you can choose. What's more, you can purchase additional fonts and install them for use with ATM. See "What You Get" later for a list of fonts that come with ATM, and "Adding and Removing Fonts" for more details on installing additional fonts for use with ATM.

WHAT YOU'LL NEED

ATM will run on just about any IBM PC, AT, PS/2, or 100% compatible computer with a 286, 386, or 486 processor. Of course, you'll also need a copy of Windows 3.x installed on the machine before you attempt to install ATM. In addition, your computer must be able to run Windows in standard or 386 enhanced mode. ATM will not run under Windows' real mode.

You also need some free hard-disk space. In fact, to install all the fonts that come with ATM, you'll need about 1.1 MB.

ATM supports most of the graphics printers supported by Windows, including:

- Hewlett Packard LaserJet Printers
- IBM Laser Printers and LaserPrinter E
- PostScript Printers
- IBM Proprinter, Epson, and other dot-matrix printers
- High resolution PostScript imaging devices. However, ATM does not affect the output of these devices.

ATM uses and supports only PostScript Type 1 fonts. This type of font is available in packages you purchase from the Adobe Type Library and in Type 1 font packages from Linotype, Agfa-Compugraphic, Varityper, Monotype, Autologic, and The Font Company.

INSTALLING ADOBE TYPE MANAGER

When you finish installing 1-2-3 for Windows, you are asked whether you also want to install ATM. If you select Yes, you are prompted to insert the ATM Program Disk into the same floppy drive used to install 1-2-3. At that point, the ATM install program takes over, taking you through a complete ATM install session.

If you elect not to install ATM after installing 1-2-3, you can always do so later. To install ATM independently of 1-2-3, make sure Windows is running and insert the ATM Program Disk into drive A. From Program Manager's menu, select the File Run command. Windows displays the Run dialog box. Type **a:\install** and Press ENTER. A short time later the dialog box in Figure B-2 will appear on your screen.

The two text boxes at the bottom of Figure B-2 define the directories to which the install program will copy ATM's PostScript outline and metric font files. The install program recommends C:\PSFONTS for the PostScript outline (.PFB) files and C:\PSFONTS\PFB for the metric (.PFM) font files. You can, of course, change these directories. If you change the directory for the PostScript outline files, the install program will automatically recommend a subdirectory of that same directory, named \PFM, for the metric font files. You can accept this directory name or type in one of your own. (If the directory you specify does not already exist, the install program will create it.)

To proceed with installation, select the Install button or press ENTER. The install program displays a status box indicating the progress of the install process. Once all of ATM's program and font files have been copied to your hard disk, the install program displays the dialog box in Figure B-3, asking you whether you also want to install the PCL (HP LaserJet) compatible bitmap fonts. You are also prompted to specify a directory in which those fonts will be installed. The default directory recommended is C:\PCLFONTS. You can accept this directory or specify a different one.

Figure B-2   The ATM Installer

Installing the PCL bitmap fonts may help to improve the performance of your HP LaserJet, especially if your printer has 512K or less of memory (HP LaserJet and HP LaserJet Series II without added memory). However, only two of ATM's typefaces will actually be installed, Arial MT and TimesNewRomanPS in 10- and 12-point sizes. The cost in disk space is about 102K (not bad). What's more, these fonts will automatically be associated with the currently installed HP LaserJet printer driver as "Temporary" fonts. This means that they will be downloaded to the printer only at print time. You can change the status of these fonts to "Permanent"—downloaded to your printer automatically when you start Windows. To do this, you must use the Font Installer option accessed by the Fonts button in the PCL/HP LaserJet printer driver dialog box.

If you elect to install the PCL bitmap fonts, select the Install button from the dialog box in Figure B-3. Otherwise, select the Skip button. If you select Install, ATM's install program will create the PCL bitmap fonts in the directory you specified. Ultimately, selecting either button will eventually lead you to the dialog box in Figure B-4, indicating that ATM has been successfully installed.

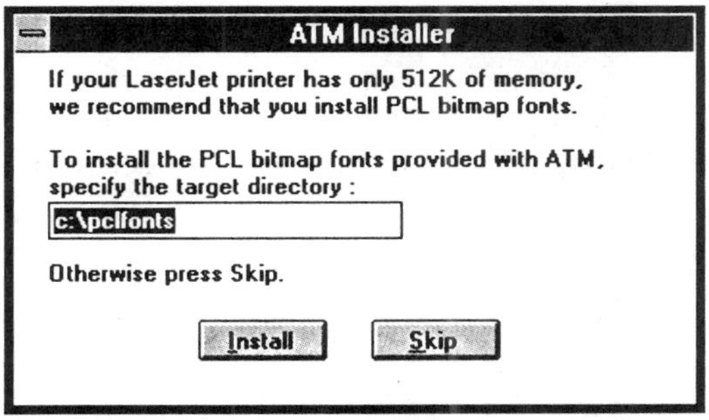

Figure B-3   ATM prompts you whether to install HP compatible soft fonts

Figure B-4   ATM's install program tells you when installation is complete

Before ATM is actually ready for use, you must leave and restart Windows. Otherwise, Windows will not recognize ATM. (The following section explains why.) To confirm the presence of ATM, a small ATM icon will appear temporarily at the lower left corner of the screen when you start Windows.

What Just Happened?

In addition to installing the ATM program files, ATM's install program modifies the [boot] section of the Windows SYSTEM.INI file. As you know, Windows gets its default system and driver information from this file each time you start the program. That way, ATM is started automatically whenever you start Windows. Specifically, the statement

```
system.drv=system.drv
```

is replaced with

```
system.drv=atmsys.drv
atm.system.drv=system.drv
```

As these statements suggest, ATM gains access to the same information that is available to the Windows system driver. ATM needs this information to be able to display and print its fonts in Windows. Processing these statements in SYSTEM.INI is one of the main reasons you must quit and restart Windows after installing ATM.

In addition to modifying your SYSTEM.INI file, ATM's install program copies the following files to your hard disk:

- ATMCNTRL.EXE: Supports the ATM control panel discussed later under "Using Adobe Type Manager." This file is copied to your \WINDOWS program directory.

- ATM.INI: An ASCII configuration file that provides the default settings for ATM. This file is copied to your \WINDOWS program directory and can be edited with Notepad. See "Exploring the ATM.INI File" for details on the contents of this file.

- ATMSYS.DRV: The ATM system hardware driver. This file is copied to your \WIN-DOWS\SYSTEM directory.

- ATM.DLL: The ATM dynamic link library. This file is also copied to your \WIN-DOWS\SYSTEM directory.

- .PFB files: These files define ATM's PostScript outline fonts. Normally, these files are copied to C:\PSFONTS.

- .PFM files: The matching font metric for ATM's PostScript outline fonts. The information in these files is needed by your Windows applications when using ATM's PostScript outline fonts. Normally, these files are copied to C:\PSFONTS\PFM.

In addition to copying the necessary files, the ATM install program places an icon for ATM in Program Manager's Main Group window. This icon gives you access to the ATM Control Panel, which allows you to configure the operation of ATM.

What You Get

ATM comes with a dozen different fonts—some examples are shown in Figure B-5. These fonts will appear in the menus for your Windows applications, along with the Windows GDI fonts and any printer-resident fonts associated with the default printer driver currently in use by Windows.

You may notice some overlap between ATM's PostScript outline fonts and the Windows GDI screen fonts Helv, Tms Rmn, and Courier in your application menus. In fact, ATM's Arial MT and Helvetica fonts are very close to Windows' Helv. In addition, ATM's Times and TimesNewRomanPS are very close to Windows' Tms Rmn. Finally, ATM's Courier is almost a dead match for Windows' Courier. There is a reason for these similarities.

Arial MT
BondiniBoldCondensed
BrushScript
Courier
DomCasual
Helvetica
LetterGothic
NewsGothic
Perpetua
Σψμβολ
Times
TimesNewRomanPS×

Figure B-5 Samples of ATM's fonts

ATM will often substitute a Windows raster font for screen display in place of one of its outline fonts when the characters get below a certain point size, usually 9 points. In these smaller sizes, Windows' raster fonts tend to appear fairly presentable to the human eye. In fact, only when you get into the larger point sizes—10 points and above—do you really need ATM's outline technology. In this way, ATM optimizes its own performance by substituting Windows raster fonts, rather than building an outline font.

Note: Substitution of fonts is controlled by the [Synonyms] section of ATM.INI. See "Exploring the ATM.INI File" later for more details on this.

USING ADOBE TYPE MANAGER

This section shows you how to configure ATM to suit your particular needs. For example, you'll learn how to add and remove fonts, manage the size of the font cache, and turn ATM off when you need to. In addition, you'll learn how ATM works with both HP LaserJet and PostScript printers.

Opening the ATM Control Panel

As mentioned, the ATM install program creates an icon for the ATM Control Panel in Program Manager's Main group window. When you double-click on this icon, the ATM Control Panel appears on your screen, as shown in Figure B-6. The sections that follow discuss each component of this Control Panel in detail.

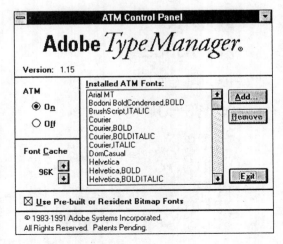

Figure B-6 The ATM Control Panel

Turning ATM Off

You can turn off ATM whenever you'd like to by selecting the Off radio button from the ATM Control Panel. To confirm your selection, select the Exit button to return to Windows. When you select Exit, ATM displays a message box informing you that you must quit and restart Windows in order for your changes to take effect.

When you select the Off radio button, ATM changes the ATM=On statement in the [Settings] section of the ATM.INI file to ATM=Off. Quitting and restarting Windows simply gives ATM a chance to read the ATM.INI file and disable itself. You'll notice when you restart Windows that the ATM icon appears temporarily in the lower-left corner of the Windows desktop in the usual way. However, it will be crossed out with a yellow X, indicating ATM is disabled.

Managing the Font Cache

As mentioned earlier, ATM uses a cache (a portion of available system memory) to store your fonts for screen display. That way, when you move from one part of a document to another, ATM can quickly refresh your screen, rather than forcing you to wait while your fonts are rebuilt.

The default size for the font cache is 96K. You can adjust the size of the cache from 64K to 8192K by using the Font Cache section of the ATM Control Panel (see Figure B-6). Clicking on the up or down arrows in this section increases or decreases the size of the font cache in 32K increments.

You should only change the size of the font cache if you need to. For example, if your applications appear sluggish when you scroll up or down or select fonts, you probably need to increase the size of the font cache. On the other hand, if you frequently get an out-of-memory error message when starting a new application, you may need to decrease the size of the font cache to make more memory available to your applications.

Adding and Removing Fonts

As mentioned, ATM allows you to install additional fonts besides those that come with the program. ATM supports only PostScript Type 1 fonts, however. You can purchase a wide variety of PostScript Type 1 fonts in packages from the Adobe Type Library, Linotype, Agfa-Compugraphic, Varityper, Monotype, Autologic, and The Font Company. The Adobe Type Library, for example, consists of over 1,000 typefaces in 200 different packages, each package containing from 1 to 12 different typefaces.

ATM also allows you to remove fonts. For example, if you have installed a font that you simply don't use that much, ATM lets you remove it from the list of installed fonts. Once the font has been removed from ATM's installed list, you can delete the necessary files from your hard disk.

Adding Fonts   To install additional fonts for ATM, select the Add button from the ATM Control Panel (Figure B-6). A short time later, ATM displays the Add ATM Fonts dialog box in Figure B-7.

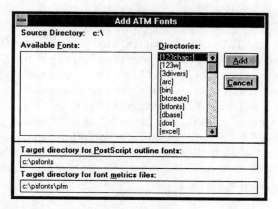

Figure B-7 Adding additional fonts for ATM

The dialog box in Figure B-7 lets you specify the disk or directory containing the fonts you want to install. It also lets you define the directory in which those fonts will be installed for use with ATM. The names of available fonts in the current directory are listed in the Available Fonts list box. Of course, you can view a different list of available fonts on another drive or directory by using the Directories list box.

The location in which the fonts (.PFB and .PFM files) will be installed is indicated by the two text boxes at the bottom of Figure B-7. The text box labeled "Target directory for PostScript outline fonts" defines the location where the outline (.PFB) files will be installed, and the box labeled "Target directory for font metric files" defines the location where the font metric (.PFM) files will be installed. ATM recommends its usual default directories (C:\PSFONTS and C:\PSFONTS\PFM) which you can change, if you'd like.

In most cases, you'll probably end up inserting the disk containing the fonts you want to add in drive A and selecting a: from the Directories list. ATM will then show you a list of fonts available on that disk in the Available Fonts list box. Depending on the vendor whose fonts you are adding, Adobe recommends the following:

- If you're adding Revision 3 Adobe Type Library fonts (narrow cardboard package), insert the disk labeled Font. Or, if you're adding Revision 2, 3.5-inch disk Adobe Type Library fonts (large cardboard package), insert the disk labeled Printer Font.

- If you're adding Revision 2, 5.25-inch disk Adobe Type Library fonts (large cardboard package), insert the disk labeled Windows.

- If you're adding Revision 1 Adobe Type Library fonts (plastic package), insert the disk labeled Program.

- If you're adding non-Adobe PostScript Type 1 fonts, insert the disk containing the font metric (.PFM) files.

When the fonts you want to add are displayed in the Available Fonts list box, select the name of each font you want to add by clicking on it with your mouse. (Make sure you select the appropriate style attributes for each typeface as well. For example, if you are installing a Garamond typeface, select Garamond, Garamond.BOLD, Garamond.ITALIC, and Garamond.BOLDITALIC.) When you're ready, select the Add button. ATM begins copying the fonts you've selected to your hard disk.

At this point, ATM may or may not prompt you to insert additional font disks. If additional disks are not required, you will be returned to the ATM Control Panel, and the fonts you've installed will appear listed there. You can then select Exit to return to Windows. To begin using your new fonts, quit and then restart Windows.

ATM may prompt you for additional disks. In fact, depending on the manufacturer of the fonts you're installing, you may be asked to insert additional disks containing outline (.PFB) files. If this happens to you, you may have to do one of the following:

- If you're installing non-Adobe fonts, Revision 1 Adobe fonts, or Revision 2, 5.25-inch disk Adobe Fonts, insert the Printer Font disk and select the appropriate directory from the Directories list box.

- If you're installing another Adobe Type Library package, insert any supplemental disks and select the appropriate drive from the Directories list box.

Once the needed files have been copied, you will be returned to the ATM Control Panel, and the fonts you've installed will be listed there. You can then select Exit to return to Windows. To begin using your new fonts, quit and then restart Windows.

Removing Fonts   As we have discussed, you can also remove installed fonts, if you'd like. To do this, open the ATM Control Panel in the usual way. Select the name of each font you want to remove from the list of installed fonts, then select the Remove button.

When you select the Remove button, ATM displays the dialog box in Figure B-8. Select Yes to remove the font whose name appears in the dialog box. This same dialog box will be displayed for each font you've selected to remove, unless you turn on the "No confirmation to remove fonts" check box.

Using Prebuilt and Resident Bitmap Fonts

If you elected to create soft fonts when you installed ATM, those fonts will be used automatically in place of ATM's matching outline fonts. In addition, ATM will automatically recognize and use any printer-resident fonts (fonts burned into your printer's memory chip or supplied by a cartridge) when you specify them in a document.

Occasionally, though, you may prefer not to use either prebuilt soft fonts or printer-resident fonts and rely solely on ATM's outline fonts. For example, some applications—like Ventura for Windows—support autokerning (trimming of excessive space between specific letter pairs). For these applications, ATM's fonts will be kerned, but the prebuilt soft fonts or printer-resident fonts will not. In other cases, the pre-built or printer-resident font may not match the quality or appearance of a matching font provided by ATM. Finally, if you change the resolution for the printer by changing the settings in your

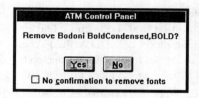

Figure B-8   ATM prompts you before removing an installed font

Windows printer driver, ATM's fonts will be printed at the new resolution, but the prebuilt soft fonts or printer resident fonts may not.

To disable the use of prebuilt soft fonts or printer-resident fonts, turn off the Use Pre-built or Resident Bitmap Fonts check box in the ATM Control Panel (see Figure B-6), then select Exit to return to Windows. From that point forward, ATM will use only its own outline fonts for printing. (You do not need to leave and restart Windows for this setting to take effect.)

ATM and HP LaserJet Printers

You can often improve printing performance on your HP LaserJet printer by using either prebuilt soft fonts or printer-resident bitmap fonts. Your output may not be as crisp as that generated by ATM's PostScript outlines, but what you lose in clarity you often gain in shorter print cycles and a reduced burden on your printer's memory.

ATM will use its own prebuilt soft fonts in place of its outline fonts automatically, provided a matching size and typeface are available. Furthermore, ATM will use printer-resident fonts when you specify them in a document.

Unfortunately, ATM allows you to create only a limited variety of prebuilt soft fonts when you install the program. However, if you purchase an additional font package from the Adobe Type Library, you'll also receive a utility called the Adobe Type Foundry. This utility allows you to generate an HP LaserJet compatible prebuilt soft font for each of the fonts included in the package.

 Tip: You can substantially improve printing performance on your HP LaserJet by printing to a parallel port rather than a serial port. (Both the HP LaserJet Series II and Series III printers, for example, offer both a parallel- and serial-port interface.) If you are currently using a serial-port to print your work, consider changing to a parallel port. See your HP LaserJet manual as well as the Windows *Users Guide* for details on how to specify a parallel port for your printer.

ATM and PostScript Printers

As you might imagine, ATM fully supports PostScript printers. In fact, ATM gives you access to the 35 standard typefaces supplied with most PostScript printers. However,

ATM does not supply these typefaces, either for screen display or for printing. Instead, ATM relies entirely on the Windows PostScript printer driver to supply the standard set of 35 PostScript typefaces. Those typefaces currently installed for ATM over and above the standard PostScript set are simply added to the list of typefaces in your application menus.

You may get the error message "ATM fonts and PostScript fonts don't match on XXXX," where XXXX is the name of a typeface—for example Helvetica—when you start an application. When this happens, only PostScript printer fonts will appear in your application menus, and ATM's fonts will not. This occurs when the number of fonts installed for ATM in the ATM.INI file exceeds the number of installed fonts in the [PostScript] Printers section of the WIN.INI file. This can happen when you've installed the PostScript printer driver after installing ATM. You can solve this problem in several ways. The way that is right for you depends on your system. Generally, you might try one of the following:

- Use the Windows Control Panel to open the Printers dialog box and select the Post-Script Printer listing from Installed Printers list box. Then, select Configure to display the Printers-Configure dialog box. From there, select Setup to display the PostScript Printer driver dialog box. Finally, select OK three times to return to Windows.

- Use the Windows Control Panel Printers dialog box to make sure the PostScript Printer driver is the default printer for Windows. Then, open the ATM Control Panel and select the Add button. ATM displays the Add ATM Font dialog box. Make sure your C:\PSFONTS\PFM directory is current and select the names of all the fonts in the Available Fonts list box. You can do this by clicking and dragging downward. Select Add to add the fonts. ATM returns you to the ATM control panel. Select Exit to return to Windows, then quit and restart Windows.

- If neither of the above ideas works, you'll probably have to add the needed fonts to the [PostScript] section of WIN.INI manually. To do this open the WIN.INI file in Notepad and page down to the [PostScript] Section. When you get there, you'll see something similar to the following:

```
[PostScript,FILE]
feed1=1
feed15=1
softfonts=7
softfont1=c:\psfonts\pfm\_a_____.pfm
softfont2=c:\psfonts\pfm\bdbc____.pfm
softfont3=c:\psfonts\pfm\bs_____.pfm
softfont4=c:\psfonts\pfm\dc_____.pfm
softfont5=c:\psfonts\pfm\lg_____.pfm
softfont6=c:\psfonts\pfm\ng_____.pfm
softfont7=c:\psfonts\pfm\ptrg____.pfm
```

- To add the necessary ATM soft fonts, you'll need to increase the value for the softfonts= statement and then add entries for the ATM font files you are missing. For example, if you need to add the Helvetica typeface, you would modify the [PostScript] section as follows:

```
[PostScript,FILE]
feed1=1
feed15=1
softfonts=11
softfont1=c:\psfonts\pfm\_a_____.pfm
softfont2=c:\psfonts\pfm\bdbc_____.pfm
softfont3=c:\psfonts\pfm\bs_____.pfm
softfont4=c:\psfonts\pfm\dc_____.pfm
softfont5=c:\psfonts\pfm\lg_____.pfm
softfont6=c:\psfonts\pfm\ng_____.pfm
softfont7=c:\psfonts\pfm\ptrg_____.pfm
softfont8=c:\psfonts\pfm\HV_____.pfm
softfont9=c:\psfonts\pfm\HVB_____.pfm
softfont10=c:\psfonts\pfm\HVBO____.pfm
softfont11=c:\psfonts\pfm\HVO_____.pfm
```

- If you're still getting errors and your ATM fonts don't appear in your application menus, you may need to change the entries in the [Aliases] section of the ATM.INI files discussed in the next section.

Exploring the ATM.INI File

As noted earlier, ATM gets its default settings from the ATM.INI file. This file is automatically copied to your \WINDOWS program directory when you install ATM. Because the ATM.INI is an ASCII file, you can edit the file with any word processor capable of reading and writing ASCII files—for example, Notepad.

ATM reads the settings in the ATM.INI file and configures itself accordingly each time you start Windows, thus starting ATM. In many cases, when you make a change to one of ATM's settings through the ATM Control Panel, the new setting is written to the ATM.INI file. For this reason, you must quit and restart Windows (thus restarting ATM), thereby giving ATM a chance to read the ATM.INI file.

The ATM.INI file has six sections, each marked by a header—[Fonts], [Setup], [Settings], [Mono], [Aliases], and [Synonyms]. As you might imagine, each section serves a specific purpose in configuring the operation of ATM. What follows is a general discussion of those sections that are immediately pertinent to the operation of ATM.

The [Fonts] section lists each of the fonts currently installed for ATM. Each line in this section lists the name of a particular font as it will appear in your application menus, followed by the disk location of both the .PFB (PostScript outline file) and the .PFM (metric font file) associated with the font.

The [Setup] section of ATM.INI file contains two statements (PFM_Dir= and PFB_Dir=) that provide the names of ATM's default font directories. These directory names appear in the Add ATM Fonts dialog box (Figure B-7) that appears when you select Add from the ATM Control Panel. The default settings for these two statements are as follows:

```
[Setup]
PFM_Dir=c:\psfonts\pfm
PFB_Dir=c:\psfonts
```

The [Settings] section of ATM.INI provides most of the general parameters for ATM's operation. When you first install ATM, the [Settings] section looks like this:

```
[Settings]
FontCache=96
ATM=On
BitmapFonts=On
SynonymPSBegin=9
QLCDir=c:\psfonts
ScanBufSize=16
```

The FontCache= statement defines the size of the ATM's on-the-fly font cache. As you might imagine, this statement is updated when you change the size of the font cache through the ATM Control Panel.

The ATM=On statement corresponds to the On and Off radio buttons in the ATM Control Panel, which turn ATM either on or off. The default value for this statement is On. Specifying a value of Off will turn ATM off the next time you start Windows.

The BitmapFonts= statement corresponds to the setting for the Use Pre-built or Resident Bitmap Fonts check box in the ATM Control Panel. If this check box is turned on (checked), the value assigned to this statement is On. Otherwise a value of Off is assigned.

The SynonymPSBegin= statement defines the point size below which ATM will substitute a matching Windows raster font in place of one of its outline fonts (for screen display only). This allows ATM to optimize its own performance by using a Windows raster font, rather than building one of its outline fonts. This statement works in conjunction with the [Synonyms] section of ATM.INI covered later. The default value assigned to this statement is 9, meaning that below 9 points, ATM will substitute a matching Windows raster font. For example, if you format some text using ATM's Helvetica 8-Point, the Windows raster font Helv will be displayed instead.

The QLCDir= statement defines the directory that contains the ATMFONTS.QLC file. ATM uses this file to check for working fonts each time the program is started, allowing ATM to start more quickly. The default value for this statement is usually QLCDir=c:\psfonts.

The Aliases section of ATM.INI lets you substitute an ATM font in place of a Windows raster font. This allows you to use ATM's fonts in existing documents you've created before installing ATM. For example, the default settings for the [Aliases] section are as follows:

```
[Aliases]
Helv=Arial MT
Tms Rmn=TimesNewRomanPS
Courier=Courier
```

The first statement, Helv=Arial MT, equates ATM's Arial MT font to the Windows Helv raster font. Thus, for those documents formatted with Windows Helv, ATM will substitute its Arial MT.

As mentioned, the [Synonyms] section of the ATM.INI file works in conjunction with the SynonymPSBegin= statement in the [Settings] section (discussed previously). ATM will substitute a font specified as a synonym when the point size is larger than the value assigned to the SynonymPSBegin= statement, which is usually 9 points. For example, the default values for the statements in the [Synonyms] section are as follows:

```
[Synonyms]
Helv=Arial MT
Tms Rmn=TimesNewRomanPS
Courier=Courier
```

The first statement, Helv=Arial MT, specifies that ATM's Arial MT font will be substituted in place of Windows Helv raster font when the point size is larger than 9 points. Correspondingly, when the point size is below 9 points, Windows Helv font will be used.

REMOVING ADOBE TYPE MANAGER

This section shows you how to remove ATM from your system, should the need arise. To remove ATM, start by modifying your SYSTEM.INI file. (You can do this with Notepad.) As you may recall, ATM places the following lines in the [boot] section of SYSTEM.INI:

```
system.drv=atmsys.drv
atm.system.drv=system.drv
```

(These lines may appear slightly different if you are running an HP Vectra.) Move the cursor until it comes to rest on the first letter after the = (equal) sign in the first system.drv= statement. Then, hold down the DEL key until the two statements become one, as follows:

```
system.drv=system.drv
```

In addition to modifying your SYSTEM.INI file, you'll need to delete the following files from your hard disk:

• ATMCNTRL.EXE: Located in your \WINDOWS program directory.

• ATM.INI: Located in your \WINDOWS program directory.

- ATMSYS.DRV: Located in your \WINDOWS\SYSTEM directory.

- ATM.DLL: Located in your \WINDOWS\SYSTEM directory.

- .PFB files: The files defining ATM's PostScript outline fonts. Normally, these files are located in C:\PSFONTS.

- .PFM files: The font metric file for ATM's outline fonts. Normally, these files are located in C:\PSFONTS\PFM.

Lastly, you'll need to delete the ATM icon from Program Manager's Main group window. To do this, simply select the icon by clicking on it and then press DEL. Windows will display a message box asking you to confirm the deletion. Select OK.

Index

Abbreviated cell addressing
    jumping to specific cells and, 44
    of multiple worksheets, 29
Abbreviated cell references, in
    formulas, 69–71
Abbreviations for macro keynames, 689
About 1-2-3 dialog box, 86
@ABS function, 342
ABS key, creating absolute and mixed
    cell references with, 285–287
Absolute cell references, 73–74
    copying formulas and, 279, 283–284
    function to determine, 439–440
    using ABS key to create, 285–287
Absolute values, 342
Accelerator keys, 9–10
    in menus, 23
    tables of, 10, 11–12
Accessing menus, 22–23
Accessing type fonts in other packages,
    214–215
@ACOS function, 360
Active area of a worksheet, 21
Active files, 810–811
Active windows, 116, 127–128
Add-in applications, testing for, 372
Adding data in a disk file to the active
    worksheet file, 158–163
Adding fonts (ATM), 871–873
Adding new fields to databases, 548
Adding records to databases, 579
Adding records to external database
    tables, 606–608
Addition, 68
    functions for, 347–350, 589
Adjustable cells, for Solver, 650,
    651–652, 654–655
Adobe Type Manager (ATM), 863–879
    fonts, 211, 332, 333–334, 863–879

    installing, 866–870
    removing, 878–879
    using, 870–878
    Windows and, 863–866
Aggregate columns, 581–582
Alignment of labels, 57–60
    changing for an entire worksheet, 60
ALT+BACKSPACE key. *See* Undo
    feature
{ALT} command, accessing menu
    options from macros with,
    697–698
.AL3 files, 322
American National Standards Institute
    (ANSI) characters, 421–422
Amortization tables, functions to
    create, 384–385, 426–427,
    428–429
Ampersand (&) character,
    concatenating strings with, 67, 74
Anchor cells, 90
#AND# operator, 366–367
    in multiple criteria, 571–573
"AND" queries, 568–569, 570–571
Angles, 359–360
Annotating graphs, 447, 521–526,
    532–533
    with arrows, 524
    with ellipses, 525
    by freehand, 526
    with lines, 523–524
    with polygons, 525
    with rectangles, 524–525
    with text, 522–523
Annuities and annuities due, functions
    to calculate, 381–388
Answers from Solver, 657–659
    saving, 663

Answer table reports from Solver,
    666–667
Apostrophe (') character, Label format
    and, 182–183
{APP-ADJUST} command, 766
{APPENDBELOW} command,
    747–748, 754, 755–756
Appending records to databases, 579
Appending records to external database
    tables, 606–608
{APPENDRIGHT} command,
    747–748, 755–756
{APP-STATE} command, 766, 767
Arccosine, 360
Arcsine, 360
Arctangent, 360
Area graphs, 459–463
    default 3D, 461–462
    3D stacked, 462–463
Arguments
    in macros, 721
    passing to subroutines, 742–745
Argument separators, 340
Arguments of functions, 339–341
Arial MT 12-point font
    column widths and, 185–187
    default row heights for, 197
    as global default font, 168, 211
    numerical display and, 173
    numeric formatting and, 187
Arithmetic mean, 352, 354
Arrowheads in graphs, 531
Arrow keys
    moving cell pointer with, 16–17
    setting column widths with,
    189–191
Arrows, as graph objects, 524
Arrows in menus, 23
Ascending sort, 550